Putting Islam to Work

Comparative Studies on Muslim Societies

General Editor, Barbara D. Metcalf

1. *Islam and the Political Economy of Meaning*, edited by William R. Roff
2. *Libyan Politics: Tribe and Revolution*, by John Davis
3. *Prophecy Continuous: Aspects of Aḥmadī Religious Thought and Its Medieval Background*, by Yohanan Friedmann
4. *Sharī'at and Ambiguity in South Asian Islam*, edited by Katherine P. Ewing
5. *Islam, Politics, and Social Movements*, edited by Edmund Burke, III, and Ira M. Lapidus
6. *Roots of North Indian Shī'ism in Iran and Iraq: Religion and State in Awadh, 1722–1859*, by J. R. I. Cole
7. *Empire and Islam: Punjab and the Making of Pakistan*, by David Gilmartin
8. *Islam and the Russian Empire: Reform and Revolution in Central Asia*, by Hélène Carrère d'Encausse
9. *Muslim Travellers: Pilgrimage, Migration, and the Religious Imagination*, edited by Dale F. Eickelman and James Piscatori
10. *The Dervish Lodge: Architecture, Art, and Sufism in Ottoman Turkey*, edited by Raymond Lifchez
11. *The Seed and the Soil: Gender and Cosmology in Turkish Village Society*, by Carol Delaney
12. *Displaying the Orient: Architecture of Islam at Nineteenth-Century World's Fairs*, by Zeynep Çelik
13. *Arab Voices: The Human Rights Debate in the Middle East*, by Kevin Dwyer
14. *Disorienting Encounters: Travels of a Moroccan Scholar in France in 1845–1846, The Voyage of Muḥammad aṣ-Ṣaffār*, translated and edited by Susan Gilson Miller
15. *Beyond the Stream: Islam and Society in a West African Town*, by Robert Launay
16. *The Calligraphic State: Textual Domination and History in a Muslim Society*, by Brinkley Messick
17. *The Rise of Islam and the Bengal Frontier, 1204–1760*, by Richard Eaton
18. *Rebel and Saint: Muslim Notables, Populist Protest, Colonial Encounters (Algeria and Tunisia, 1800–1904)*, by Julia A. Clancy-Smith

19. *The Vanguard of the Islamic Revolution: The Jama'at-i Islami of Pakistan*, by Seyyed Vali Reza Nasr
20. *The Prophet's Pulpit: Islamic Preaching in Contemporary Egypt*, by Patrick D. Gaffney
21. *Heroes of the Age: Moral Faultlines on the Afghan Frontier*, by David B. Edwards
22. *Making Muslim Space in North America and Europe*, edited by Barbara D. Metcalf
23. *Nationalism and the Genealogical Imagination: Oral History and Textual Authority in Tribal Jordan*, by Andrew Shryock
24. *Between Marriage and the Market: Intimate Politics and Survival in Cairo*, by Homa Hoodfar
25. *Putting Islam to Work: Education, Politics, and Religious Transformation in Egypt*, by Gregory Starrett

Putting Islam to Work

Education, Politics, and Religious Transformation in Egypt

Gregory Starrett

UNIVERSITY OF CALIFORNIA PRESS
Berkeley / Los Angeles / London

University of California Press
Berkeley and Los Angeles, California

University of California Press, Ltd.
London, England

Library of Congress Cataloging-in-Publication Data

Starrett, Gregory, 1961–.
Putting Islam to work: education, politics, and religious
transformation in Egypt / Gregory Starrett.
p. cm. — (Comparative studies on Muslim societies; 25)
Includes bibliographical references (p.) and index.
ISBN 0-520-20926-5 (cloth: alk. paper).—ISBN 0-520-20927-3 (pbk.: alk. paper)
1. Islam—Egypt. I. Title. II. Series.
BP64.E3S73 1998
306.6′0962—dc21
96-50454

Manufactured in the United States of America

9 8 7 6 5 4 3 2 1

The paper used in this publication meets the minimum requirements
of American National Standard for Information Sciences—
Permanence of Paper for Printed Library Materials, ANSI Z39.48-
1984.

For my parents

Contents

PART IV

Preface

In the chapter on "character" in his classic *Manners and Customs of the Modern Egyptians*, first published in 1836, Edward Lane included a note on "religious pride" as one of "the leading features of [Egyptian] character." "I am credibly informed," he wrote, "that children in Egypt are often taught, at school, a regular set of curses to denounce upon the persons and property of Christians, Jews, and all other unbelievers in the religion of Mohammad."[1] Noting that these curses were recited daily in some of Cairo's government schools (but not those held in mosques), he quoted from an Arabic transcription given to him by his friend Richard Burton:

O God, destroy the infidels and polytheists, thine enemies, the enemies of the religion. O God, make their children orphans, and defile their abodes, and cause their feet to slip, and give them and their families and their households and their women and their children and their relations by marriage and their brothers and their friends and their possessions and their race and their wealth and their lands as booty to the Muslims.[2]

Lane went to some trouble to deny that these maledictions represented a universal Egyptian sentiment toward Europeans. He implied instead that the Turkish overlords of the country bore responsibility for the reproduction of this traditional curse within the officially sanctioned arena of the school, which, as part of the governmental framework of the country, might be one of the factors that "altered, in a remarkable degree," the innate characteristics of the Egyptians, "gradually lessen[ing] their mental energy," and dulling the ready apprehension, wit, and memory that Egyptians possessed when young.[3]

A generation later in a radically altered political climate, another Englishman, Noel Temple Moore, wrote to Lord Dufferin, the British ambassador to the Sublime Porte in Constantinople and Her Majesty's Envoy Extraordinary to Egypt, with his observations on the public mood. The 1882 British bombardment of Alexandria had ended barely five months before, and the popular leader Colonel Ahmad 'Urabi had been convicted for his leadership of a rebellion against the European powers who were assuming control over his country. 'Urabi's death sentence had just been commuted to permanent exile, and Moore, asserting that the native population seemed grateful for this restraint of British policy, illustrated popular sentiment by writing that "A rhymed couplet is, I am informed, being sung by the children in the streets of Cairo, of which this is a translation:—'Oh, our Lord, Oh, Holy One/ Grant success to the English.' "[4]

Whether or not either one of these contradictory reports was an accurate reflection of Egyptian character or opinion—Moore himself was unsure of the extent to which "a public opinion may be said to exist in an Oriental country"[5] —they do show that the content of children's minds has long interested ethnographers, officials, and visitors to Egypt. Perhaps this is because the outlook of children is thought to provide the clearest possible insight into a society's fundamental worldview, stripped of adult accretions of interest and calculation. In a way, this book is another attempt to approach the contents of the child's mind, but it does so from the opposite direction. Rather than asking first and foremost what children know or believe as a clue to some basic cultural knowledge, I have focused largely on what it is that adults want and expect children to know and believe; or, to add another complication, what adults want each other to think that children should know and believe.

The relevance of these questions for Americans is acute, as debates rage in our own country over the goal and content of schooling in a changing global economy, the importance of prayer and values education in public schools, and other issues. But the significance of this research reaches beyond school-based issues as well. It touches on historical changes in the nature of religion, on the relationship of Islam specifically to state bureaucracies and political interest groups, and the role of communications media in the construction of national identities and public spaces. It is not, strictly speaking, a school ethnography, and those who read it with the expectation of one will be disappointed. Instead of focusing attention on activities and interactions within a particular school or sample of schools, I have chosen instead to explore the way that education, and religious education in particular, has been used by Egyptians (and Europeans) as a way to talk about and to address fundamental political issues, and how formal schooling is related to a range of other cultural institutions.

In examining this question, I have used several kinds of information: historical, ethnographic, and textual. I have spent fifteen months in Egypt, mostly in Cairo, first in June and July of 1987, studying at the Center for Arabic Study Abroad; again from October through September, 1988–89, and most recently during July 1993. During the middle period of fieldwork I interviewed and observed Egyptian teachers and students in two schools; talked with civil servants, writers, journalists, and intellectuals representing many political perspectives; routinely monitored the Egyptian press and television; and scouted street stalls and bookstores in all parts of the city, collecting a substantial library of books, pamphlets, periodicals, and other materials on the subject of Islam—particularly children's books, works on Islamic education, Islam and medicine, and Islam and the family.

Interviews were conducted both in Arabic and in English. In all cases I took notes during the interview or immediately afterward, using these to reconstruct as nearly as possible the details of the conversation. Aside from isolated words and short phrases, I usually remembered and recorded the Arabic interviews in English. Most of the people with whom I spoke did not relish the thought of speaking into a tape recorder (I realized later that most of the journalists I interviewed had spent time in jail as political prisoners, and feared the thought of having their opinions paired with their voices). In only one case did I even try to tape-record an interview; it turned out to be one of the least satisfactory ones I did. Except for the names of government officials and those drawn from published accounts, all names of individuals have been changed, and other details of their lives have been altered slightly.

Most of the period between January and July 1990 was spent doing historical research at the library and archives of the Hoover Institution, taking advantage of the James Heyworth-Dunne collections; and at the Jonsson Government Documents Library at Stanford University, reading the reports and correspondence concerning Egypt that are contained in the Sessional Papers of the British House of Commons (referred to in citations as the *Parliamentary Papers* [*Parl. Pap.*]), from the late 1870s until 1922. I had not originally planned to make so much of the historical background of religious education in Egypt; I had merely wanted to find a basic summary of the development of the school system. Several such summaries already exist, but as I looked through the material in the parliamentary records, I began to realize what a rich source of information they were, and what a different light they shed on the subject than did most of the secondary sources that had used these documents previously. The result is that fully a third of the present work deals with the historical development of religious education in the Egyptian public schools. Although my summary covers, in part, the broad historical outline of previous work, it is largely different in emphasis and detail, and offers substantially new interpretations of the subject. It also constitutes an important part of the intellectual framework on which the rest of the book is based.

My preference has been to quote frequently and extensively from printed sources and from my interviews. In addition to providing the reader with some of the data on which discussion of the issues is based, I think this simply makes the work more interesting to read. When quoting interviews, I cite the date and the page from my fieldnotes on which the quotation appears.

A Note on Transliteration

Transliterating Arabic words into English is made difficult both by the differences in orthography and phonology between the two languages, and because "Modern Standard" Arabic differs from Egyptian dialect. There are five pairs of consonants that pose a special problem, because although their Arabic forms are quite different, their pronunciation differs by only a slight raising or lowering of the tongue, or a difference in aspiration. I have chosen, despite the problems this causes, to use a simple transliteration that represents these with identical letters in English. I have retained double consonants, but not double (long) vowels, and have elided the final *ta marbuta* (word-final *h*) in words with the feminine ending, and word-final glottal stops. The symbol ʾ represents the glottal stop, which is to be distinguished from the symbol ʿ, representing the consonant *ʿayn*, a voiced pharyngeal fricative. Commonly recognized words and proper nouns, including place names, are transliterated in their most recognized form; for example, *Cairo* rather than *al-qaahirah*, and *Sayyida Zeinab* rather than the more consistent *Sayyida Zaynab*. Formal Arabic is transliterated as it is written (without, for example, the assimilation of the *l* of the definite article to certain consonants). Since Egyptian Arabic is not usually written, I have transliterated Egyptian words as they sound, rather than as they might be written in Arabic.

Unless otherwise noted, quotations from the Qur'an are from the translation by A. Yusuf 'Ali, and other translations from Arabic and French are my own.

Acknowledgments

This book is based on doctoral research conducted at Stanford University. It has taken far too long to produce, and too many people have been too patient with me, for which they all deserve my deepest thanks. I want to thank Clifford Barnett, Joel Beinin, Joseph Greenberg, and Bernard Siegel, who agreed, probably against their better judgment, to be responsible for me, giving me their unfailing and generous support despite chronic confusion about what in the world I thought I was doing; the late Lawrence Berman for providing me with the intellectual tools to think comparatively about Islam; Dale Eickelman for providing invaluable advice, encouragement, and much-needed collegial support for a decade now. In Egypt, I benefited from the extraordinarily generous help of Drs. Wadi' and Yvonne Haddad, each of whom taught me more than I thought there was to know. Many others have carefully read, considered, and thoughtfully criticized the work in its various incarnations, including Michael Chamberlain, Denis Sullivan, Barbara Metcalf, Patricia Horvatich, Roslyn Mickelson, Adeeb Khalid, Dan Bradburd, Patrick Gaffney, John Bowen, and Steven Caton. I am grateful to all of them for helping improve the manuscript immeasurably, but apologize for not being able to meet all of the challenges they posed. The good stuff is largely theirs; the mediocre is entirely mine. Thanks also to Lynne Withey, Mark Chambers, and Juliane Brand at University of California Press, for shepherding the work through the editing and publication processes.

The institutions that aided me, financially and otherwise, are Stanford University and its Center for Research in International Studies, the Social Science Research Council's Committee for the Comparative Study of Muslim Societies, the Binational Fulbright Commission in Egypt, the Center for Arabic Study Abroad, the Mrs. Giles Whiting Foundation, the University of North Carolina at Charlotte, and the National Endowment for the Humanities Summer Seminar for College Teachers program. The marvelous staff at the Hoover Institution library at Stanford University, and at the Dartmouth College Library, made a number of difficult tasks much easier. I want to thank the Egyptian government for sponsoring my Fulbright research, and all of the people who spoke with me, particularly the teachers and staff at the Nasr Language School, and Samia ʿAbd al-Rahman and Layla al-Shamsi, who provided extraordinary models of devotion to Islam.

Finally, I will always be indebted to the many friends who supported me before, during, and after the research for this book. In Egypt, Paul and Arzetta Losensky, Regina Soos, and Jennifer Thayer; in the United States, Laura Leach-Palm, Maidie Golan, Eric Ramirez, and especially Barbara Bocek and Anna Laura Jones, who deserve all praise. Finally, for my parents, my lovely daughter Katherine Grace, and for my wife, Martha Louise Catt, who has supported, fed, and put up with me and without me for these many, many years, I am everlastingly grateful.

PART I

There are no secular states. All states are religious.

Nawal Saʿdawi, at a meeting of the
Middle East Studies Association
of North America, 1993.

CHAPTER I

Creating an Object

Elementary education is one of the pillars of national security.
Husayn Kamal Baha' al-Din, Egyptian
minister of education, 1993[1]

An Alexandria Quartet

In the early morning hours of Tuesday, 29 August 1989, agents of the Egyptian Bureau for National Security Investigation stormed four apartments in Alexandria, breaking down the doors to arrest twenty young men and take into custody eighty boys between the ages of four and ten. The men, among whom were two university and two law students, a private school teacher, a student of *da'wa* (Islamic outreach) at al-Azhar University, and an employee of the Helwan Fertilizer Company, were accused of "enticing the children with religious slogans and planting extremist ideas in their minds in preparation for transforming them into an extremist religious group."[2] After initial interrogations the arrestees were driven to bureau headquarters in their respective governorates to be questioned further and then remanded to the national security prosecutor, and the children were ordered by then Interior Minister Zaki Badr to be returned to their parents.

On 31 August the story was front-page news in the government press: *al-Akhbar* headlined the story, "Arrest of an Extremist Religious Organization Aimed at Luring in Children under the Guise of Religion." *Al-Jumhuriyya* ran a photograph of six of the accused, standing with eighteen of the boys sitting on the floor before them. Six of the boys had their heads bowed and faces covered in shame, and the headline read, "Arrest of an Organization for Training Children in Extremism at Summer Camps in Alexandria." The next day *al-Akhbar* ran another photograph showing Colonel Muhammad Rashid, chief of the Bureau, returning two of the boys to their father and "warning him not to neglect his sons at this age."[3]

The incident had begun the previous week when children and parents in a number of governorates, particularly Minufiyya, Alexandria, and Giza, began to hear about free four-day trips being organized for children to see the sights of Alexandria starting on Saturday, 26 August. Parents outside Alexandria were approached in mosques and asked to contribute nominal subscription fees (of ten Egyptian pounds; about $4) for the trip. One boy from Alexandria itself heard about the opportunity from some boys he met at the beach; another from neighbor children he met near his local mosque; a third was invited by the principal of his elementary school. Some of the local children went along not knowing the duration of the trip, and began to worry when, at the end of the day, they were not returned home, but taken to one of the apartments instead.

After the arrests the children reported that during their stay in the Alexandria apartments they were awakened before the dawn prayer each day to learn lessons, then taken to the beach for a couple of hours before returning to one of the flats. There they would be fed, and the rest of the day would be divided between lessons, prayers, and sightseeing trips, including an excursion to the historic fort of Qaytbay. The lessons they learned included the principles of brotherhood and obedience, as well as more specific advice. One eleven-year-old boy reported to *al-Akhbar* that "the organizers of the trip accompanied him and the children to a number of mosques where they gave lectures to them along with other people, and they told them that watching television was forbidden [*haram*] and that men's socks have to reach to the knee, and he adds that he heard a lot of talk that he didn't understand."[4]

The tone of the newspaper articles was strident, *al-Ahram* reporting that the "extremist organization" intended "to establish a new generation bearing their beliefs" and that children who disagreed with the daily lessons were deprived of food; *al-Jumhuriyya*, on the other hand wrote that the organizers of the trip showered the children with food "in order to win them over, offering them [all] kinds of sweets and beverages." The latter paper claimed that the frequent prayer sessions were "all aimed at implanting blind obedience in their psyches, and they slipped the extremist ideas inside of them until within a few short hours of their being given their instructions, the child victims (*al-atfal al-dahaya*) would carry them out with obedience." It pointed to leaders of an unnamed organization behind the accused, who allegedly put the young men up to the task of enticing the children's participation.[5]

Reaction to the arrests by Egypt's major Islamic opposition party was swift. Shortly afterward, Ma'mun al-Hudaybi, Mustafa al-Wardani, and Dr. 'Asam al-'Uryan, three leaders of the Muslim Brotherhood, issued a statement accusing the security forces of brutality during the arrests and calling on President Mubarak to step in and halt the irresponsible persecution of the detainees. The Brotherhood regularly organized recreational trips for the nation's children, the report said, removing them from the suffocation and heat of inner cities to the healthful climate of the seashore, where they learn Islamic *adab* (manners, etiquette, comportment, culture). Furthermore, parents had consented to the trips and "clearly expressed their hopes that this activity would protect their children from the diseases of society, such as [drug] addiction and moral corruption." It accused the government press of merely reprinting a report distributed by the Ministry of the Interior the day after the arrests, and asked where in the entire episode was there any manifestation of extremism: "The trip to the sea, or visiting the sights in Alexandria? The diligence of prayer, or the continence of tongue and comportment? Or that these children constitute a danger to public security through their trip?"[6]

The arrests and subsequent publicity were intended to make a dramatic and frightening statement to Egyptians about the danger of parents entrusting their children to unregulated organizations and individuals, and to underscore the government's self-assumed role of protecting the spiritual and physical well-being of the nation's children. The dual weapons of state power—the deployment of force and the deployment of information—worked in tandem to frame the incident as a threat both to the family and to the government. Groups claiming independent authority to interpret Islamic scriptures and transmit Islamic culture undermine one of the basic foundations of the state's moral legitimacy: its protection of the Islamic heritage, including the responsibility to provide children and youths with trustworthy religious guidance. Islam, the official religion of the Egyptian state, is a matter of vital government interest.

These twin issues of religious legitimacy and political authority are at the heart of a dilemma faced today by Muslim states throughout the world. As international political credibility comes more and more to be measured by the extension of public services and the trappings of electoral democracy, the tensions between mass sentiment and incumbent power structures become acute, as the government of Algeria learned in early 1992 when it was dissolved by its own military in the face of a threatened electoral victory by the Islamic Salvation Front. Egypt could very well be next in line to experience a political and military crisis on the same order. An unusually gloomy prognosis of this sort recently found its way into the policy-oriented *Middle East Journal*, penned by a U.S. government official who would only be identified with the frightening byline "Cassandra."[7] In the academic world, too, senior scholars are beginning to say publicly "that the future of the Muslim world lies with the Islamic political alternative."[8]

Our tendency in the face of such drama is to perceive a civilizational crisis arising from a fundamental conflict between democracy and theocracy, or between tradition and modernity. But such an analysis, specious in the case of Algiers, is useless even superficially in the case of Alexandria. For it is precisely Egypt's integration into the modern — or postmodern — world system of economy, politics, and culture that has secured for Islam an integral part in the governance of the nation. In Egypt as elsewhere in the Muslim world, the connections between religion and national security descend deep into the infrastructure of the modern state. The consequences of this fact for the limits of public policy choices and for the production and manipulation of religious culture are to be our central concern.

In a narrow sense, this book is about one aspect of Egyptian religious culture as it has developed since just before the turn of the century: the use of a modern public school system to teach children about Islam and introduce them to the official public persona of God. In documenting the role of the contemporary school in teaching Islam, I hope to show how the expansion and transfer of religious socialization from private to newly created public sector institutions over the last century has led to a comprehensive revision of the way Egyptians treat Islam as a religious tradition, and consequently of Islam's role in Egyptian society. In the light of this revision, I will argue that the increasing hegemony of religious discourse in Egyptian public life since the 1970s is a straightforward result of the country's institutional transformation rather than — as is usually argued — an accidental by-product of its current economic and political difficulties. As part of this institutional transformation, programs of mass public instruction conceived in the nineteenth century as cost-efficient means of social control have instead helped generate the intellectual, political, and social challenges posed by the country's broad-based "Islamist" movement, the most significant political opposition to the current Egyptian government.

The Anthropology of Islam

These institutional transformations have implications far broader than the sociology of religious knowledge or political conflict in Egypt. The present study occupies a space where three distinct bodies of literature converge. Its conclusions reflect back into those literatures — that on the anthropology of Islam, that on cultural and social reproduction, and that on the intellectual history of the social sciences — in different directions. First, I hope to contribute to current discussions of the role of Islam as an organizing force in Muslim societies. Talal Asad, voicing his discontent with anthropological approaches that either essentialize or disintegrate "Islam" as an object of study, has held that scholars should treat Islam "neither [as] a distinctive social structure nor a heterogeneous collection of beliefs, artifacts, customs, and morals," but as a tradition.[9] If anthropological studies of Islam are to avoid the pitfalls of treating religious phenomena either as wholly dependent (and therefore politically trivial) or entirely independent (and therefore incomprehensible) variables in the social life of Muslim nations, we need to recognize Islam as a discursive tradition that links past, present, and future in a variety of ways.[10] Seen in this light, the focus of study should be "the interplay between . . . everyday practices and discourses and the religious texts they invoke, the histories of which they are a part, and the political enterprises of which they partake."[11]

Introducing this sense of the term *tradition* to anthropological discussion does more than merely translate the Arabic term *al-turath*, which is used by Muslims to designate the complex heritage they have inherited from the past and are bound to pass on to the future. It points not to a body of literature, but to culturally and historically specific systems of interactions between people, texts, and institutions. Asad points out that social distributions of "correct" knowledge mirror distributions of power. Regardless of how a Muslim society is organized, the definition of what is and is not "Islamic" is likely not to be about how closely society mirrors a known textual blueprint, but about how and by whom specific texts are used to underwrite specific practices and general notions of authority. Orthodoxy "is not a mere body of opinion but a distinctive relationship—a relationship of power. Wherever Muslims have the power to regulate, uphold, require or adjust *correct* practices, and to condemn, exclude, undermine, or replace *incorrect* ones, there is the domain of orthodoxy"[12]

Phrased in a different manner, its ear attuned specifically to the deep, pervading vibrations of power, this is basically the dialectic Clifford Geertz began to articulate a quarter-century ago in *Islam Observed*, between the content of religions and their careers, a dialectic that is currently becoming the focus of increasingly sophisticated anthropological analyses of the human mediation between images and institutions. From Morocco to Indonesia, anthropologists have documented the disputes that arise between Muslims who stand in different relationships to institutions of power and of formal socialization. Framed by recent anthropological research on religious education and politics in countries from Morocco to Oman and Iran, and on textual practices in Yemen, Indonesia, and the Philippines, this book seeks to advance our understanding of religious traditions in complex societies.[13] By focusing explicitly on state-supported mass education, one of the institutions that most powerfully shapes the interplay between written tradition and daily practice, the present research outlines some of the mechanisms by which Islam's universal message is consciously and strategically articulated to local social, political, and economic structures.

Similar social and political projects are underway across the Muslim world. Like Turkey, Pakistan, Malaysia, and Indonesia,[14] the Egyptian government has brought Islamic institutions increasingly under its control over the last century, a process that has accelerated during the last twenty years. All three of its twentieth-century constitutions have declared Islam Egypt's official religion, granting the state both the right and the duty to co-opt Islamic discourse for itself, a practice made particularly expedient in the face of mass movements like the Muslim Brotherhood, which has been a political force in the country since 1928, as well as the more recent Islamist guerrilla movements of the seventies, eighties, and nineties.

But just as wild plants have to undergo systematic genetic alterations to make them useful as cultivated foods, so "Islam" has to be altered to make it useful as a political instrument. Two interrelated processes have been operating throughout the Muslim world thus to domesticate the tradition of Islam. First, there is the process of "objectification," the growing consciousness on the part of Muslims that Islam is a coherent system of practices and beliefs, rather than merely an unexamined and unexaminable way of life. This is a pervasive process throughout the Muslim world. In Oman, a rural schoolteacher observes that "People here do not know Islam; they pray and sacrifice, but they do not know why."[15] "Knowing" Islam means being able to articulate the religion as a defined set of beliefs such as those set down in textbook presentations.

> At its most basic, the style of intellectual technology introduced by modern schooling constitutes a significant break with the earlier emphasis upon the written word, mediated by an oral tradition and oriented toward a mastery of accepted religious texts acquired through study under religious scholars recognized by the wider community. At least in formal terms, a curriculum of specifically delineated subjects and prescribed texts is taught by a changing array of teachers, and competence is measured by examination. . . . An unintended consequence of making Islam a part of the curriculum is to make it a subject which must be "explained" and "understood."[16]

Since mass education has been available in Oman only since the 1970s, this change in the perception of Islam is striking, and matches changes that have been occurring in Egypt since the nineteenth century. In both countries official educational programs aimed at the general public purposely ignore differences among various sects and schools of legal interpretation in Islam, portraying the faith synoptically. A new plan for teaching religion in Egyptian universities, for example, stresses the application of dogma to life and to social conditions, "avoiding the legal school [*madhhab*] differences in the study of doctrine and Islamic law [*shari'a*]."[17] As Brinkley Messick has shown with respect to Yemen, the codification of Islamic law for application in Western-style court systems induces a comparable series of changes in the way that politicians, scholars, jurists, and citizens relate to different sorts of sacred and derivative texts. The result is monovocal, reified "Islamic Law" that lacks the flexibility characteristic of older styles of jurisprudence.[18]

The second process through which the Islamic tradition is passing operates on several levels, and serves to make the newly synoptic and systematized "Islam" practically useful. I call this process *functionalization*. In general, functionalization refers to processes of translation in which intellectual objects from one discourse come to serve the strategic or utilitarian ends of another discourse. This translation not only places intellectual objects in new fields of significance, but radically shifts the meaning of their initial context. In the Egyptian case, a whole series of existing religious discourses have been reified, systematized in novel fashion, and set to work fulfilling the strategic and utilitarian ends of the modern and secular discourse of public policy. Traditions, customs, beliefs, institutions, and values that originally possessed their own evaluative criteria and their own rules of operation and mobilization become consciously subsumed by modern-educated elites to the evaluative criteria of social and political utility. On an institutional level, independent local religious study circles are brought under the control of central or district government bureaucracies to act as tools of mass socialization. On a logistical level, formal religious studies curricula are fashioned by educators, and formal testing patrols the borders of class mobility. On a philosophical level, ancient rituals and beliefs as well as the facts of history are reinterpreted to underscore political legitimacy, or are brought to bear on social concerns like public health, economic productivity, and crime. In all of these processes, existing discursive logics are altered and control is shifted to a central authority or entrusted to groups other than those who traditionally set the terms of religious discourse.

The functionalization of religion — putting it consciously to work for various types of social and political projects — appears to stand opposed to the modernization paradigm in which religion is viewed alternately as benignly irrational and as actively obstructionist. The ideals of Soviet-style state atheism and the American separation of church and state — as internally complex and unstable as both rhetorical complexes have been — are merely different expressions of the same philosophy of progress, the Comtean journey from Religion through Metaphysics to Science. But many Muslim states have followed a different course to modernity, insisting explicitly that progress requires a centrally administered emphasis upon moral as well as economic development.

Cultural Production and Social Reproduction

What significance do these processes have for understanding broader anthropological questions? In writing about Islamic higher education in Morocco, Dale Eickelman has remarked that "the study of education can be to complex societies what the study of religion has been to societies variously characterized by anthropologists as 'simple,' 'cold' or 'elementary,' "particularly insofar as this study can reveal some of the "culturally valued cognitive style[s]" implicit in these cultures.[19] But neither "cold" ritual nor "hot" education is merely a window onto thought and ideas. Summarizing one of Emile Durkheim's lesser-known works on education, Eickelman wrote that

> changes in ideas of knowledge in complex societies and the means by which such ideas are transmitted result from continual struggles among competing groups within society, each of which seeks domination or influence. . . . Thus the forms of knowledge shaped and conveyed in educational systems . . . must be considered in relation to the social distribution of power.[20]

Explorations of the institutional intersections between knowledge and power have long motivated European social theory, from Marx's discussion of "ruling ideas" to Althusser on the ideological state apparatus, Gramsci on hegemony, Foucault on disciplinary formation, and Raymond Williams on the politics of culture. With respect to formal education, it is undoubtedly true that different interests are served—and created—by particular curricula and by different definitions and technologies of useful knowledge. But class-based models are inadequate to deal fully with the political and ideological implications of modern educational systems, because these systems continuously erase and redraw the boundaries between social groups and disrupt the association between them and the "ideas about knowledge" they seek to promote.[21] New modes of thought emerging from nascent classes and social institutions not only express new modes of consciousness, but contribute in turn to the formation of new structures of interest and conflict, perpetuating the struggles that gave them birth and subverting subsequent attempts unilaterally to control the course of debate. One of the central conclusions of this book is that elites can profit from the manipulation of power/knowledge only insofar as they create competitors possessing the tools of opposition. (Such problems are increasingly familiar, for example, to the U.S. military, whose development of computer and communications systems—intended to create strategic superiority over its superpower rivals—now puts it at risk from bright teenagers with home computers and Internet connections.) Educational systems thus have a direct political role in creating the intellectual and institutional technologies that generate distinctly new social groups, not just an indirect role diagnostic of a standing distribution of power. In Egypt, religious education is only one of the school-related issues around which political conflict has crystallized. But unlike debates over the institution of literacy programs, vocational training, or examination reform, controversies surrounding religious instruction have the unique power—as we saw in Alexandria—to provoke the activity of the state's security apparatus.

So if our starting point—the anthropology of Islam—is perhaps tangential to the main body of contemporary anthropological concerns, studying the role of educational institutions in cultural production and social reproduction is near the center. With the ever-growing oeuvre of Pierre Bourdieu, and the diffusion of Paul Willis's 1977 *Learning to Labour* outside the relatively small circle of educational sociology, questions of cultural production and social reproduction have moved toward the forefront of anthropological theory. Willis's study of the reproduction of class stratification among British working-class youth has been built on by many others, most recently Douglas Foley in *Learning Capitalist Culture*, an analysis of the reproduction of ethnicity and class in south Texas, and Dorothy Holland and Margaret Eisenhart in *Educated in Romance*, a devastating portrait of the reproduction of gender inequality among U.S. university women. Each of these works demonstrates that, contrary to top-down models of the imposition of unequal social relations, educational institutions are one of many social sites within which specific populations actively reproduce their own subordinate status. Status negotiations within and between peer groups, conscious and unconscious strategies of resistance to institutional authority, and the realistic perception of often limited employment opportunities after leaving school life, together channel the creative interactions of students themselves toward the reproduction of standing relations of power.

The trinity of ethnicity, class, and gender inequalities has consumed nearly all the attention of critical theorists of education. Systematic critical treatments of the reproduction of religious traditions are conspicuously absent.[22] This is partly, of course, because of the immediate and overriding gravity of ethnic, class, and gender inequalities in the U.S. and Western Europe, where most educational sociologists have worked. But it is also because the sense in which there is an intriguing "inequality" at stake in religious socialization—one that cannot entirely be subsumed under the rubric of socioeconomic class or gender—is less immediately clear.[23] Despite our growing interest in how they are invented and transformed,[24] anthropologists still tend to treat "traditions" (religious or otherwise) as bounded capsules of observed behavior and recorded belief, rather than as segments of larger-scale social relationships that are constantly in the process of being created, renewed and dissolved. But — to refine Asad's use of the word *tradition* — it is those unequal relationships of authority and compliance that are constructed around and through specific discourses that constitute the social core of religious traditions. How these relations are transformed in the process of their reproduction, and the ways they interact with other dimensions of social inequality are important questions. But relations of orthodoxy are a peculiar kind of property relation — a relation between people with regard to texts and intellectual technologies — that are potentially more fluid than other sorts of class relations. One interesting feature of the Alexandria police raids is precisely that they were *not* held against striking workers, marching peasants, or armed terrorists, but against individuals quietly and privately using the social and intellectual technologies of the modern state to create an alternative to it. Their other interesting feature is that the majority of individuals caught up in the raids themselves were children, actors we hardly ever consider politically significant. So it is precisely the *processes* of creating relationships of orthodoxy that are at stake here, rather than the finished product.

To understand these processes without assuming a simple mechanical reproduction of class relations, we need to address the cultural significance of the choices people make in creating their own social worlds. According to Paul Willis,

> We might think of this process of reproduction [of the social group, its relation to other classes and the productive process] as having two basic "moments". In the first place, outside structures and basic class relationships are taken in as symbolic and conceptual relations at the specifically cultural level. . . . Structural determinations act, not by direct mechanical effect, but by mediation through the cultural level where their own relationships become subject to forms of exposure and explanation. In the second "moment" of the process, structures which have now become sources of meaning, definition and identity provide the framework and basis for decisions and choices in life . . . which taken systematically and in the aggregate over large numbers actually helps to reproduce the main structures and functions of society.[25]

Granting some autonomy to the realm of culture, through which larger structural determinants have to pass in order to reproduce themselves, he points out nevertheless that this model, by "ignoring important forms and forces such as the state, ideology, and various institutions," is an oversimplification.[26]

In order to recomplicate the picture, I would like to take a step back — at the risk of losing some of the fine resolution — to reincorporate the state, ideology, and social institutions into this model of reproduction. Doing so points us in two directions somewhat different from that taken by Willis and others, who question how and why subordinate populations aid in the reproduction of their own inequality. First, as outlined in the discussion of objectification and functionalization in the last section, we can ask what changes have occurred in the cultural level itself as it has mediated the creation and reproduction of social relationships. How has cultural production changed over the last century to accomodate new technologies as well as new economic and political forces?

And second, we can reverse the question of subordination, and ask why the political and educational strategies chosen by Egypt's ruling elites over the last century have resulted in the diminution rather than the augmentation of their ability to control the public discourse on Islam. How have socialization practices established explicitly in order to provide every citizen with a uniform appreciation for the state's legitimate religious authority resulted instead in the fragmentation of that authority and the proliferation of groups challenging the moral judgment and legitimacy of official religious institutions? Why, as we saw in Alexandria, is the state forced to resort to physical violence to retain its monopoly on religious socialization?

These are the issues we will be concerned with: changes in the cultural mediation of Islamic knowledge, and the problematic results of implementing mass education as a mechanism of social control. If it seems odd to us that the powerless act in ways that reinforce their subordination (even as they seek to resist it), it should seem equally odd that the powerful act in ways that diminish their dominance (even as they seek to increase it). Willis stresses "that there are deep disjunctions and desperate tensions within social and cultural reproduction. Social agents are not passive bearers of ideology, but active appropriators who reproduce existing structures only through struggle, contestation, and partial penetration of those structures."[27] In his own case study, he finds that the working-class student's choice of manual labor as a means of making a living is experienced not as a surrender to social subordination, but as "an assertion of . . . freedom and of a specific kind of power in the world";[28] it "is felt, subjectively, as a profound process of learning: it is the organisation of the self in relation to the future."[29]

This structuring of experience and perception operates on the social and cultural elites who frame policy and produce school curricula and educational materials, as well as on the working classes and students who are their targets. The concept of hegemony, it is too often forgotten, refers to structures of thought, feeling, and practice that are as commonsensical to cultural elites as they are to subordinates.[30] Egypt's incorporation into the modern European imperial system was one of the experiential sources of a new hegemony that relied on the modern school for its force.[31] As we will see in chapters 2 and 3, European political and cultural domination during the latter half of the nineteenth century presented both British and Egyptian elites with ambiguous and often contradictory conceptual models of social structure, change, and hierarchy. The deep tensions within the imperial project resulted, on the cultural level, in conflicting experiences of cultural process that were rationalized as being a choice between the twin dichotomies of "religious" versus "secular" government, and "traditional" versus "modern" society. Choosing the secular and modern meant, among other things, embracing the notion that mass schooling would provide an inexpensive mechanism of centralized and nearly total control over the inner lives of Egyptians. The choice to provide the nation with schooling was experienced by elites and the nascent middle classes as a drive toward national emancipation that would take place through a new means of reinforcing their own position. That this project has resulted instead in new modes of political opposition, a renewed public attachment to religious values, and finally the forced resort to the tactics of the police state indicate that the culturally mediated choice between tradition and modernity rested on false premises.

History and Typology

The dichotomies of religion/secularism and tradition/modernity are cultural concepts derived initially from social philosophy and its offspring, the professionalized social sciences. Johannes Fabian has argued, in his celebrated essay on "How Anthropology Makes Its Object,"[32] that the discipline of anthropology (and Western science in general) systematically distorts its relationship to the cultures it studies by constructing cultural typologies — hot and cold, primitive and modern, developed and developing, peasant and industrial, rural and urban — that present cultural differences as differences of *time*. Historical sequence, in becoming the basis of a system of analytical categories, retains its chronological connotations, so that the "traditional" and the "modern" seem separated not only by spatial but by temporal distance. And in the process of implicitly denying the "coevalness" of anthropology and its "Other," such typologies also deny the close relationships of influence, domination, and, in fact, the mutual constitution of contemporaneous societies. "When modern anthropology began to construct its Other," Fabian writes, "in terms of topoi implying distance, difference, and opposition, its intent was above all . . . to construct ordered Space and time — a cosmos — for Western society to inhabit, rather than 'understanding other cultures,' its ostensible vocation."[33]

While he omits them from his own enumeration of false typological opposites, Fabian might well have mentioned *religious* and *secular*, a pair of terms that runs through the scholarly literature on Egypt from the very beginning of the modern European presence there. When a correspondent for Public Television's *McNeil-Lehrer News Hour* reported, shortly after the World Trade Center bombings in 1993, that Islamic radicals were attacking the government of Husni Mubarak because he was "trying to drive Egypt further down the secular road"; or when newspapers in the U.S. claim that radical Islamic movements are threatening to topple "Egypt's secular government," they are not only engaging in a complex strategy of distancing (the secular West versus the religious East; the (necessarily) secular allied government versus the (fanatically) religious internal threat). They are also — as we will see throughout this book — constructing an astounding fiction: that Egypt's government is a secular one. Although this fiction is useful for purposes of political convenience and Western self-definition, it makes understanding of the current political tensions in Egypt impossible.

Just as typology is always part of a larger narrative that explains its form and origin, so theories of education are always derived not merely from theories of human psychology, but from theories of history. As I will argue in the conclusion, the ideas indigenous and foreign elites hold concerning Islam and education in modern society have been central elements in contemporary public policy formation, and the state's halting and ineffective strategies for counteracting its Islamic political opposition are built partially upon a central flaw in its conception of the social effects of the school. During the 1950s and 1960s intellectuals both in the West and in the Middle East were confident that "in the contemporary Arab world Islam has simply been bypassed . . . the relaxing of Islam's grip on Arab society in the nineteenth and early twentieth centuries. . . . resulted in an inner collapse and a withering away of its position and effective power in social and political life."[34] With respect to education, this confidence was founded upon the political marginalization of the traditional religious hierarchy, which "by the end of the First World War . . . had not only lost its position as the defender and interpreter of the Law in society, but also its function as the upholder and transmitter of Islamic learning and tradition. . . . "[35] Even the phenomenal growth of the Muslim Brotherhood in the 1930s and 1940s served as the exception that proved the rule of modernization in Egyptian society:

> The tremendous appeal which the movement exercised served to show the extent to which Islam could still move the masses of the people. But it came too late to stem the tide of secularism, and its fate was sealed with the triumph of Abdul Nasser's secular revolution. The Muslim Brothers may well be the last serious effort of traditional Islam to regain its position in Arab society.[36]

This passage encapsulates two fallacies of modernization theory that have found their way into more recent attempts to account for the rise of Islamism — or, the term I prefer, the Islamic Trend — in Egypt. First, there is the false assumption that movements like the Muslim Brothers or the radical Jihad and al-Gamaʿa al-Islamiyya groups represent "traditional Islam" reasserting itself. And second, there is the false assumption that, in the case of Egypt as in the case of historical development generally, secularism will replace religion in a global and irreversible evolutionary process. On such an assumption, scholarly concern with religious education in the public school would be a misplaced effort, since the role of the nation was assumed to have eclipsed that of God as the focal point of public veneration.[37]

Consequently, the richest evocations of religious education in the contemporary Muslim world confine their attention to the socialization of religious elites,[38] and their implications cannot fruitfully be extended to popular education. There has been a good deal of research on the traditional Qurʾanic school (*kuttab*), particularly in Morocco,[39] and some very recent work on education in postrevolutionary Iran.[40] But aside from important historical work on Czarist Central Asia[41] and a single content analysis of religious textbooks used during the Nasser period,[42] scholars have remained relatively silent about the interaction of religion and mass instruction. As preparation for our entry into the case study, let us remind ourselves again why this is important. As intellectual technologies and political institutions from the West have penetrated the Islamic world, they have helped to create new ways of conceiving of, practicing, and passing on the Islamic tradition. This sort of outcome is a common feature of colonial and postcolonial life. In East Africa, the system of "customary law" itself was a creation of British colonialism.[43] In eighteenth- and nineteenth-century India, the British Asiatic society "initiated the integration of the vast collection of myths, beliefs, rituals, and laws into a coherent religion, and shaped an amorphous heritage into the faith now known as Hinduism,"[44] and in Morocco, French understandings of tribalism became the de facto basis for tribal organization, making "[the French] view of Moroccan society a significant component of social reality."[45] In the same way, contemporary Islam in Egypt is as much the result of the European-style school as it is of "traditional" texts and intellectual institutions. In this as in so much else—and in a sense even more direct than Fabian's critique of categories—western scholarship has quite literally made the object it now purports to study.

The rest of the book falls into three parts. The next two chapters show how educational goals and philosophies invented in Europe to quell the social unrest of the Industrial Revolution were transplanted at an increasing pace into Egypt by the British after 1882. In appropriating the indigenous Qur'anic schools as the basis for a cheap system of mass instruction, the imperial administration altered the aims and methods of religious teaching to resemble those of Christian Britain. With the subsequent professionalization of teachers and the declining role of the traditional religious elite in formal socialization, religious instruction gained by the 1930s its current function as an explicit tool for social planning.

Chapters 4, 5, and 6 describe the content and context of Islamic education in contemporary Egyptian primary and secondary schools. This will not take the form of a traditional school ethnography, but will instead focus on the way schooling is viewed by different populations as an Islamizing influence in conjunction with other social institutions. Based on interviews, classroom observation, and analysis of religious studies textbooks, it will explore the way that school-based religious education is thought to fulfill national goals, including the attempt of the national government to counteract the appeal of *al-tatarruf*, religious "extremism" among the country's youth. I will argue that, far from counteracting the appeal of private-sector religious forces like the Muslim Brotherhood and the smaller Islamic splinter groups that call for revolt against the state, the religious studies curriculum in schools (and other programs for children and youth) both lays the government open to radical criticism and increases the hunger for religious resources that cannot be met solely by the public sector.

The resulting political challenge to the ruling party has evoked a range of responses ably summarized by the interior minister, who is in charge of domestic security. In a July 1993 speech to the official national union of journalists, he explained that "the newspapers defend democracy and the police work to secure that democracy . . . and because of this the relationship between the police and the newspapers is strong and profound."[46] This dual strategy combining cultural and police operations informs chapters 7 and 8, which examine the complex ways in which the Islamic Trend has penetrated the public space created by the school, the media, and the market. On the one hand, a violent fringe of religious terrorists is used as a foil for representations of popular virtue and the masses' rejection of underground Islamist organizations. On the other hand, institutions as varied as the media themselves and the court system are turned to the service of the Islamist political opposition as civil society is penetrated by the discourses of religion. As the government simultaneously increases its investment in Islamic symbols and represses competing groups that deploy them as well, clear alternatives disappear, and the country is moved ever closer to political crisis. In the end, I bring together these tangled historical, textual, and ethnographic threads to show why educational idioms have become part of the language in which political conflict is expressed. Public discourse on the origin of the Islamic Trend is coming more and more to resemble the debates that took place during the British Occupation concerning the pernicious effects of educating the new Egyptian elites. I will argue that flawed applications of social and educational theory — by both Egyptian policymakers and Western scholars — have contributed to the consistent misunderstanding of contemporary political developments, dooming the state to weaken its own position in every attempt it makes to enhance it.

PART II

"Fact, fact, fact!" said the [government officer]. And "Fact, fact, fact!" repeated Thomas Gradgrind.

"You are to be in all things regulated and governed," said the gentleman, "by fact. We hope to have, before long, a board of fact, composed of commissioners of fact, who will force the people to be a people of fact, and of nothing but fact. You must discard the word fancy altogether . You have nothing to do with it. You are not to have, in any object of use or ornament, what would be a contradiction in fact. You don't walk upon flowers in fact; you cannot be allowed to walk upon flowers in carpets. You don't find that foreign birds and butterflies come and perch upon your crockery; you cannot be permitted to paint foreign birds and butterflies upon your crockery. You never meet with quadrupeds going up and down walls; you must not have quadrupeds represented upon walls. You must see," said the gentleman, "for all these purposes, combinations and modifications (in primary colours) of mathematical figures which are susceptible of proof and demonstration. This is the new discovery. This is fact. This is taste."

Charles Dickens, *Hard Times*, 1854

CHAPTER 2

Education and the Management of Populations

No fallacy is more transparent or more monstrous than that which assumes that knowledge, or whatever training is got in schools, is a natural want, certain to assert itself like the want of food, or clothing, or shelter, and to create a demand. The fact is the very reverse of this assumption. . . . All statesmen who have wished to civilize and instruct a nation have to create this appetite.

Sir James Kay-Shuttleworth, ca. 1870[1]

Colonising Egypt, in the broad sense of the penetration of a new principle of order and technique of power, was never merely a question of introducing a new physical discipline or a new material order. In the first place, disciplinary powers were themselves to work by constructing their object as something twofold. They were to operate in terms of a distinction between the physical body that could be counted, policed, supervised and made industrious, and an inner mental space within which the corresponding habits of obedience and industry were to be instilled.

Timothy Mitchell, *Colonising Egypt*, 1988[2]

Schooling and the Colonial Project

Timothy Mitchell, in his fascinating book *Colonising Egypt*, has described schooling in nineteenth-century Egypt as the basis of "the new politics of the modern state,"[3] which took hold, after an extended infancy, in the late 1860s during the reign of Khedive Isma'il. Even before formal European control was established over the country in 1876, Egyptian intellectuals educated abroad began to imagine schooling as a means of producing model citizens and a model society. "The power of working upon the individual offered by modern schooling," Mitchell writes, "was to be the hallmark and method of politics itself," a politics "modelled on the process of schooling,"[4] which would utilize the school's "precise methods of inspection, coordination and control" to "change the tastes and habits of an entire people . . . and by a new means of education make him or her into a modern political subject — frugal, innocent, and, above all, busy."[5] Inspired by Foucault's reading of disciplinary formation in Europe, Mitchell portrays the sea change in Egyptian politics as a process of

> replacing a power concentrated in personal command, and always liable to diminish, with powers that were systematically and uniformly diffused. The diffusion of control required mechanisms that were measured rather than excessive and continuous rather than sporadic, working by invigilation and the management of space.[6]

In a sense the present chapter can be read as a documentary supplement to Mitchell's description of the establishment of European-style schools in Egypt, focusing much more specifically on their use as arenas of religious instruction, and concentrating on the detailed strategies of imperial administrators. But at the same time, I will argue that we need to go considerably beyond Mitchell's reading of Egyptian history in order to understand the unique dynamic of the school. While the school may be a mechanism of diffuse and invisible power, it is also — as we saw in chapter 1 — an engine of tension and contradiction. As sociologists of education have shown us, students are neither the passive pawns of educational organization and ideology, nor are educators their absolute masters. The belief held by cultural elites that "modern" education is the most effective machine of social pacification has acted to stunt their own recognition of its ambiguous and unpredictable influence.

Exoticizing the Classroom

During the last quarter of the nineteenth century, Europeans were still debating the appropriateness of state-sponsored education, although opposition was quickly fading. In 1876 Herbert Spencer, whom the Egyptian religious reformer Muhammad ʿAbduh described as "the chief of the philosophers on social questions,"[7] complained in his *Principles of Sociology* that the growing power of the state over the individual was contrary to the natural order of social evolution, a regression to an earlier form of political organization. Belittling government by "public analyzers" and "the tacit assumption that State-authority over citizens has no assignable limits," Spencer contradicted the reigning progressivism of his day, which held that national interests could and did excuse public trespass across the natural boundaries of the family. Such interference disrupted the division between the "law of the family," by which resources are bestowed upon helpless individuals without reservation, and the "law of society," by which resources are distributed proportional to individual effort. When this happens, he warned, society "fails to hold its own in the struggle against other societies, which allow play to the natural law that prosperity shall vary as efficiency."[8]

> Legislation has of late further relaxed family bonds by relieving parents from the care of their children's minds, and replacing education under parental direction by education under governmental direction; and where the appointed authorities have found it needful partially to clothe neglected children before they could be taught, and even to whip children by police agency for not going to school, they have still further substituted national responsibility for the responsibility of parents. The recognition of the individual, rather than the family, as the social unit, has indeed now gone so far that by many the paternal duty of the state is assumed as self-evident.[9]

Spencer's discomfort with the practice of state paternalism in education led him to compose substantial essays on the subject both at the beginning and at the end of his career.[10] The tenacity of his beliefs went unrewarded, however, and he was forced to admit that, in this conviction as in others, "it became a usual experience with me to stand in a minority—often a small minority, approaching sometimes a minority of one."[11]

This bristling rejection of state-led educational reform in late nineteenth-century Great Britain illuminates the school from an unusual angle, exoticizing practices we have long since come to perceive as normal. For despite the patriotic mythology surrounding the development of popular schooling in Europe and the United States, the rapid expansion of popular education during the mid-nineteenth century was motivated not as much by a humanistic longing to open children's minds to the glories of culture, civilization, and personal growth as by the desire of political elites to manage the outlook and behavior of the working classes through promoting and institutionalizing programs of mass socialization.[12] Fears of social disruption by the lower classes — through crime, vice, and popular rebellion — motivated the creation of prophylactic measures like popular schooling that would, in theory, produce disciplined, competent workers with little incentive to disturb the status quo. The advent of European control over Egypt during the last quarter of the nineteenth century transported these same fears and responses in a long southeastward arc across the Mediterranean and down through the Red Sea, completing finally the strategic geographical circuit between Great Britain and India.

In examining the political needs and cultural assumptions underlying the importation to Egypt of European-style mass schooling, we can view the consequent transformation of the individual Egyptian into a social unit over which the state wished to assume parental responsibility, the development Spencer so despised. This ideological change answered the colonial administration's need to justify its extension of influence across barriers of class and family, to reinforce the former and weaken the latter, and it took place in part through the appropriation of indigenous Qur'anic schools for public use. This is where we can see how the process of functionalization, first aimed at the physical institutions in which formal religious socialization occurred, began to transform people's ideas about the subject matter itself.

Furnishing Children for the Schools

In 1801, after the British had routed Napoleon Bonaparte's three-year army of occupation from Egypt, the Ottoman sultan Selim III sought to reestablish control of his territory by dispatching troops led by Albanian-born Muhammad ʿAli, to the province. But within a few years Muhammad ʿAli had consolidated power on his own behalf and established a dynasty that lasted nominally until Egypt's 1952 Revolution. It was his effort to consolidate control over Egypt and gain military parity with Europe that motivated the initial importation of the European-style school to Egypt.

Military parity with Europe — which comprised every feature of modern armies up to and including the indispensable regimental brass band — required industrial parity, which in turn presupposed technological parity, which finally demanded a system by which people could be recruited and trained in those techniques and manufactures that would sustain a new type of armed forces. By the 1820s, Muhammad ʿAli had already begun to use Egypt's rural *kuttab*s (pl. *katatib*; small local institutions for the memorization of the Qurʾan) as the recruiting grounds for his newly established preparatory and technical schools. Needing students with basic reading and writing skills, he requisitioned provincial commissioners for healthy and literate boys between the ages of ten and twenty to study at these new military facilities.[13] One of the unexpected consequences of this system of recruitment was that enrollment in kuttabs plummeted. Parents refused to send their children to study at local kuttabs, which, by making them literate, would now subject them to impression into distant technical schools that were little more than auxiliary branches of the military. "The antipathy that the Egyptian feels against military conscription," wrote a future Egyptian minister of education, "extends to scholarly conscription."[14]

Because of this, by 1833 the deterioration of the kuttabs was so advanced that the government was forced to establish several new state-run primary schools in the provinces of Girga and Asyut, and to extend control over a number of existing kuttabs to increase the number of boys eligible for recruitment. Students in these new schools received uniforms, rations, supplies, and stipends, and though the content and method of instruction were similar to indigenous *madrasa*s (pl. *madaris*; institutions for more advanced study of classical Islamic texts), the students—drawn from poor families attracted by the financial support of their children—were subject to strict military discipline.[15]

The literate culture of both the kuttab and the madrasa depended on oral instruction and only secondarily on the use of writing, either the child's copying on slates or the more advanced scholar's perusal of manuscript copies of important works.[16] The first *printed* book used in Egypt's government schools was the *Alfiyya* of Ibn Malik (with a commentary by Ibn ʿAqil), an eighth-century Muslim legal text distributed by Muhammad ʿAli to the new provincial schools in December of 1834.[17] Unlike neighboring kuttabs in which children attended irregularly at the pleasure of their elders and masters, Muhammad ʿAli's newly systematized primary schools were rigidly scheduled for up to nine hours a day. By 1835 an ideal syllabus for the primary school at Cairo outlined a three-year program of study that resembled that of the mosque-university al-Azhar in miniature, stressing Qurʾan memorization and the use of classical theological texts for memory training and penmanship practice.[18]

By the following decade some interest was shown in using more contemporary works, and the government's agent in London sent to Egypt books of stories, geographies, and arithmetic texts suitable for children. Though some of these works were translated and used in schools, the authorities failed to distribute notebooks in which the children could write, leaving them with the old slates which they had used to copy passages from their Islamic texts.[19]

With support from an expatriate community of French St. Simonist utopians, Muhammad ʿAli developed further plans for expanding the system of government primary schools through the late 1830s, planning to scatter fifty throughout the country (four in Cairo, one in Alexandria, and the rest in the provinces), which together would enroll some five thousand students. The three- to four-year primary program, covering Arabic, arithmetic and religious studies, would feed students to the two four-year preparatory schools in Cairo and Alexandria, which would in turn send pupils to the higher technical institutes. The preparatory curriculum covered geometry, algebra, history, geography, drawing, calligraphy, Arabic, Persian, and Turkish; together these two schools could accommodate two thousand pupils.[20] Muhammad ʿAli's schools, like his factories, were not only intended to supply military needs, but were supplied with students by the same system of conscription. The British diplomat John Bowring described in 1840 how the district shaykhs of Cairo "are charged with the collection of the *Ferdeh*–with furnishing children for the schools, and workpeople for the fabrics."[21]

During the first four months of 1837 alone, nearly fifty new primary schools were opened, each staffed by principals and teachers recruited from the ranks of the mosque-university of al-Azhar. But the political considerations that had prompted the explosive expansion of schools soon changed. In mid-July 1841, Muhammad ʿAli was forced by joint Ottoman and European pressure to end a long-running military incursion into the Ottoman province of Syria, and reduced his army from over a quarter-million troops to fewer than a tenth that number. Without the army's need for the same level of technical support the new school system collapsed. Even before the disengagement treaty had been signed, sixteen of the new primary schools closed. More than two dozen were shut down the following October, and five in November, leaving, according to James Heyworth-Dunne, only three government-sponsored primary schools left in the country, and plans afoot to cut the educational budget by a further 50 percent.[22] It was not until 1863, with the accession of Muhammad ʿAli's son Ismaʿil, that royal interest in education began to rebound, but even then the foundation of significant national education projects proved nearly impossible for financial and logistical reasons. Efforts in 1868, 1871, and 1880 to extend modern primary schools widely into the provinces and to integrate the rural kuttabs into a national system of schools failed to produce much result.[23] The five thousand or so local kuttabs that were estimated to exist in 1878 remained the country's only formal source of entrée into the literate tradition.[24] The number of kuttab students represented between 2 and 4 percent of children between the ages of five and fifteen in Egypt's approximately nine million population at that time.

Along with the remaining technical schools, there were also schools run by the indigenous Christian and Jewish communities, and by the many foreign communities in Egypt, although most students still attended indigenous religious schools, both elementary (the kuttab) and advanced (the mosque schools of al-Azhar in Cairo, al-Ahmadi in Tanta, and Ibrahim Pasha in Alexandria). Given Europe's accelerating interest in educational extension, reform, and centralization during the course of the century, the maintenance of such a complex and unregulated conglomeration of schools usually struck members of the foreign community as a hindrance to national progress, but inevitable given the "innate defects" of oriental character. M. Octave Sachot, for example, an officer of the Académie Française, visited Egypt in the late 1860s to report on the status of education there, and to make recommendations to Victor Duruy, the French minister of education. Commenting on Muhammad 'Ali's effort to look toward "the social organization of the West, and in particular that of France" for his inspiration, Sachot wrote,

> The task is arduous, for each people has its innate qualities and defects, the results of ancient and often inaccessible causes which cannot be modified overnight by the importation of foreign institutions. And in the same way that in architecture it is much easier to construct an assemblage of parts upon a bare terrain, than it is to graft a new style onto an existing monument, so it is with civilization: it is perhaps much easier to operate on the terrain of complete barbarism, than on a soil encumbered by a social state it has propped up for a long time, and upon the immutable doctrines of a religion hostile to the introduction of any new idea or custom.[25]

Lacking barren ground in which to set the foundations of a new civilization, the task before Egypt's foreign and domestic reformers was to build on the irregular foundations already in place. Meanwhile, a few model institutions like the Tawfiqiyya, Khidiwiyya, and Ra's al-Tin secondary schools opened during Isma'il's reign, and Victoria College in Alexandria (largely for the use of local elites and foreigners) would illustrate the advantages of European education.[26]

Education and British Colonial Policy, 1882–1922

The metaphoric spirit of the age, as evoked by the inventions of science, intercourse with European countries, and other invigorating influences have already done something to inspire the [peasant] with the rudiments of self-respect, and a dim conception of hitherto unimagined possibilities.

Lord Dufferin, 1883[27]

Fourteen years after Sachot's visit, and bound by the same notion of the civilizing mission, the British administration of Egypt set out to reshape and systematize existing educational institutions, using as models both its Indian experience and the lessons of rural popular education at home.[28] British attitudes toward education were conditioned by their belief that Egyptian society could be bettered (and the country's debt to European creditors liquidated) only through a carefully managed set of reforms aimed at increasing the country's agricultural productivity. Consequently their greatest fear was of a misdirection of effort toward a rapid industrial development that might divert resources from agriculture, threatening both the interests of the powerful local landowning class, and the supply of cotton to British textile mills.[29] Concern for the potential loss of the rural labor force was articulated as early as 1840 by Bowring, and in 1905 Lord Cromer, the British consul general, warned that "any education, technical or general, which tended to leave the fields untilled, or to lessen the fitness or disposition of the people for agricultural employment, would be a national evil."[30]

Philosophically, the relationship between colonial economic and educational policy was based on Britain's Indian experience, which the historian and politician Thomas Babington Macaulay had articulated in his famous speech to the House of Commons in July of 1833, outlining for his colleagues "the most selfish view of the case":

It is scarcely possible to calculate the benefits which we might derive from the diffusion of European civilisation among the vast population of the East.

It would be . . . far better for us that the people of India were well governed and independent of us, than ill governed and subject to us; that they were ruled by their own kings, but wearing our broadcloth, and working with our cutlery, than that they were performing their salams to English Collectors and English magistrates, but were too ignorant to value, or too poor to buy, English manufactures. To trade with civilised men is infinitely more profitable than to govern savages. That would, indeed, be a doting wisdom, which, in order that India might remain a dependency, would make it a useless and costly dependency, which would keep a hundred millions of men from being our customers in order that they might continue to be our slaves.[31]

In Egypt, educational effort was therefore to be split along class and geographical axes, reinforcing the barriers between country and city and maintaining an appropriate class hierarchy. The course of instruction in elementary schools or kuttabs — usually the only schools available outside the provincial capitals — did not allow successful students to continue on to European-language education in preparatory and technical schools, or to obtain the certificates that would allow them employment in the civil service. Instead the village schools were, from 1898, allowed to compete for financial support by a competitive system of grants-in-aid from the Ministry of Public Instruction, which entailed bringing themselves under that ministry's inspection. One of the criteria for eligibility was that all instruction be in Arabic. But since instruction in higher schools was at least partially in French or English until 1908,[32] this meant an automatic bar to social mobility for the poorest section of the population, who could not afford school fees in the higher primary schools. After this date, a ceiling placed on the potential salary of individuals without secondary certificates meant that, unless a family possessed sufficient resources to see their child through both paid primary and secondary education, even beginning the process would be pointless.

The British-controlled government articulated specific educational goals having to do with the staffing of the local civil service, the spread of basic literacy in the countryside, and later, the creation of a thrifty peasantry and an artisan class skilled in European manufactures.[33] They and their domestic allies pursued these objectives with different degrees of official energy and different degrees of success. But alongside these restricted official aims were the goals of affirming colonial authority and creating a new social order in Egypt. These latter ambitions, broad practical components of the colonial enterprise articulated as long-term cultural goals rather than as school policy, were: (1) the creation of a new moral consciousness in the population; (2) the maintenance of public order; (3) the Europeanization of the class structure; and (4) The Europeanization of the family, glossed as the liberation of Egyptian women. Examining each of these goals in turn, we can see how intellectual and political trends in Europe influenced the development of educational theory and practice in Egypt.

Moral Order: The Primitive Conception of the Teacher

In both Egypt and England, the development of rural education in the nineteenth century took place largely through the subvention of religion-based popular schools, and the tension between supporting a school's teaching of secular subjects (arithmetic, for instance) and consequent support of its religious programs, proved at times to be a political irritant. Just two decades prior to the Occupation of Egypt, the Revised Code of 1862 set a new course for the elementary schools of Great Britain, making the efficient teaching of reading, writing, and arithmetic, rather than doctrinal matters, the acknowledged center of the curriculum and the subjects qualifying a school for government grants-in-aid.[34] Prior to this legislation, and the 1870 code following it that made elementary schooling compulsory in England, the purpose of elementary education for the masses had been — according to its proponents — to overcome the ruinous moral influences of the home environment.[35]

The kuttab and the British elementary school of the early nineteenth century both arose from the need for communally sanctioned religious instruction, the need to reproduce a sacred tradition of writing as well as the skills of reading and writing themselves. For its part, Victorian anthropological theory recognized that the social roles of priest and teacher could be traced to a common ancestor, for since the most precious knowledge is that which cannot be gathered through everyday experience, specialists in esoteric wisdom — those who know the ways of supernatural beings — are called upon to help others regulate their conduct in ways pleasing to the gods. "The primitive conception of the teacher," wrote Spencer, "is the conception of one who gives instruction in sacred matters."[36]

In 1839 the British home secretary wrote that the "four principal objects" of elementary schooling should be "religious instruction, general instruction, moral training, and habits of industry."[37] Consider the following passages, the first from a Lancasterian teacher's manual of 1816, and the second from a speech delivered by the Evangelical Reverend Daniel Wilson three years later in support of a charity school in the center of England's silk-weaving region:

> The cultivation of the mind bestowed in these elementary schools, opens and expands the faculties of the children, gives them clear notions of the moral and social duties, prepares them for the reception of religious instruction, forms them to habits of virtue, and habituates them to subordination and control.[38]

> In every country, but especially in this free state, the mass of your Poor, like the base of the cone, if it be unsteady and insecure, will quickly endanger every superincumbent part. Religious education, then, is the spring of public tranquility. It not only cherishes the interior principle of conscience; but by infusing the higher sentiments of penitence and faith and gratitude and the love of God, communicates the elements of a cheerful and uniform subjection to all lawful authority.[39]

In the first case instruction as such is granted a social benefit through the symbiotic adjustment of the individual to society. Habituation to subordination and control develops simultaneously with the expansion of the child's faculties; in fact, these amount to one and the same thing. In the second case a metaphor combining schoolbook geometry and classical political economy is completed by the elegant stabilizing influence of religious instruction, which has the power and precision of a mathematical function. This emphasis was of long standing. In schools sponsored by churches and benevolent societies, teaching methodologies in the early 1800s did not differ substantially from those used centuries before: reading and writing (penmanship) were means for acquiring moral betterment through the Scriptures.[40] With this as a background, the halting development of secular instruction in Great Britain is not surprising. Each new bill brought before Parliament for the extension of fiscal support for education encountered critics on all sides, but particularly from clergy who feared that government schemes for subvention of private schools would favor one denomination — or bald secularism — over their own. Even attempts to avoid the appearance of favoritism encountered harsh opposition. The creation of board schools supported by local taxation set off a furious public debate about the substance of religious education for the masses, as the new schools restricted religious instruction to "mere" Bible-reading without sectarian content.

See-sawing Backwards and Forwards the Whole Time

In Egypt, Europeans perceived their Christian moral code and its cultural axioms pitted against the entrenched interests of an indigenous religious establishment they portrayed in their writing as both venal and reactionary.

> At this moment there is no real justice in this country. What passes under that name is a mockery. . . . In ancient days the Cadi, an essentially religious functionary, took cognizance of all disputes and gave judgement according to his own lights, without reference to any procedure; though he occasionally invoked such a text from the Koran, or such a phrase from a commentator as appeared most applicable to the matter in hand. His real inspiration, however, was too often drawn from the money bags of one, or perhaps both parties to the case.[41]

The perceived venality of the *'ulama* (religious scholars)was just one manifestation of the pervading corruption of Egyptian officialdom. The mark distinguishing the "shaykh class" from other traditional elites was its possession of the qualities of "fanaticism and bigotry." So powerful an effect did these qualities exercise, and so pervasive their influence on the population at large, that they formed a convenient hook on which to hang criticisms of the slow pace of Egyptian reforms and the occasional outbreaks of political or religious excitement. "The Egyptian," recalled Alfred Milner, the former under secretary for finance in Egypt, " . . . is not by nature in the least fanatical. But he has been brought up in fanatical traditions, and he is greatly under the influence of religious teachers, who are fanatics by profession."[42] To extirpate this imputed fanaticism and bigotry from the country therefore became essential, and reformers searched for their source like explorers seeking the headwaters of the Nile, finding it finally in the method and content of instruction in indigenous schools. Change these, and the conservatism of the Egyptian, as well as his incapacity for logical thought, would be replaced by those mental qualities necessary to national progress.[43]

Foreign visitors to kuttabs were struck by two things that distinguished them from the schools they knew at home: the single subject of instruction and the arrangements for its communication. (Some other features of the indigenous schools differed hardly at all from rural institutions in Britain.)[44] James Augustus St. John, writing of his 1832–33 journey in Egypt, gave a concise description of the "fanatic" Shaykh Ibrahim's kuttab in Alexandria:

> In the appearance of the Medressy there was nothing remarkable, except that, instead of being seated on forms ranged regularly in the centre of the apartment, the boys were all squatted cross-legged upon a mat, with the pedagogue in the midst of them. In Egypt, Nubia, and, I believe, generally in Mohammedan countries, boys are taught to write upon a smooth thin tablet painted white, about the size of an ordinary ciphering-slate, with a handle at one end. From this the characters are easily effaced by washing. While studying, or rather learning to repeat, their lessons, each boy declaims his portion of the Koran aloud at the same time, rocking his body to and fro, in order, according to their theory, to assist the memory; and as every one seems desirous of drowning the voices of his companions, the din produced by so many shrill discordant notes reminds one of the "labourers of Babel."[45]

The lack of furniture and the children's occasional involvement in economic pursuits (e.g., plaiting straw mats for the teacher's use, or for sale) during their lessons tended to upset foreign visitors, in whose mind education was a specialized task requiring its own set of equipment, trained professionals, and the full, uninterrupted attention of all parties.[46] Observers criticized the shabby appearance of kuttabs and, interpreting their physical organization as the result mainly of poverty, appealed for their provision with symbols of modern learning such as textbooks and blackboards. The European obsession with the physical setting and scheduling of formal socialization extended to discussions of Islamic higher education as well, where some descriptions of the system lapse into self-parody. Here is Amir Boktor, for example, an Armenian professor of education at the American University in Cairo, describing the traditional organization of instruction at al-Azhar:

> Suffice it to say that it has remained as primitive as it was ten centuries ago. Imagine a group of student Sheikhs numbering from 11 to 15 thousand squatting on mats of the Azhar Mosque in small classes, each class listening

to an old teacher Sheikh, sitting on a wooden form, with legs crossed in oriental fashion, swinging his head left and right, as he lectures on the controversial dogmas of religion and Arabic rhetoric. . . . Picture also hundreds of individual students scattered all over the place, noisily reciting their studies, with the inevitable constant swinging of the head, their shoes placed beside them. Some students attend the very early morning lectures soon after the morning prayers from 3:30 a.m. Others attend the evening lectures after the evening prayers. In other words, it is sort of a Platoon system starting from 3:30 a.m. and ending at 9:30 p.m., but with no blackboards, seats, equipment, swimming pool, or cafeteria.[47]

For Boktor (citing an 1872 Swiss evaluation of Egyptian schools as his authority), al-Azhar's lack of swimming pool and cafeteria discredited it as an educational institution just as the lack of "forms ranged regularly in the centre of the apartment" had discredited the kuttab. But the rocking behavior of student and teacher in the kuttab was more remarkable still, drawing comments from nearly all travelers. Bowring's description of a school in Qena told his readers that "the mode of instruction is the same as is adopted throughout the Ottoman empire. While the lesson is giving [*sic*], the master's head is in a state of perpetual vibration backwards and forwards, in which he is imitated by all the children."[48] In Alexandria, Nightingale wrote of the children "learning the Koran (see-sawing backwards and forwards the whole time)";[49] in al- Mahalla al-Kubra, Worsfold said that education "consisted, so far as the children were concerned, in the recital of passages from the Kuran, accompanied by a more or less energetic swaying of their bodies from the hips backwards and forwards."[50] Sachot emphasized the movement's lasting influence on students and its identification with social class: "This sort of invariable sing-song, produced in a loud voice and accompanied by a rocking back and forth of the body, soon develops into a tic preserved in adulthood by most natives of the lower classes."[51] And Milner, with characteristic venom, turned the practice into a reverse metaphor for the learning process itself:

. . . to sit on the ground swinging your body backwards and forwards, and continually repeating, in a monotonous chant, a quantity of matter which you are taught to regard with religious reverence, but never taught to understand, is, if anything, an anti-educational process. If the object of true education be intellectual gymnastic, if it be to exercise and render supple the joints of the mind, then this system is its very opposite, for it tends to stiffen them. It is not calculated to enlighten, but to obfuscate.[52]

Milner's polemic highlights two important features of the Victorian perception of the kuttab: that it violated reasonable standards of religious and moral instruction ("repeating . . . a quantity of matter which you are taught to regard with religious reverence, but never taught to understand"); and that it violated reasonable standards of instruction in general ("If the object of true education . . . be to exercise and render supple the joints of the mind, then this system is its very opposite"). The kuttab's exotic setting and the constant, disconcerting physical motion of its tenants marked it as something sensual and primitive. This perception found its intellectual charter in contemporary anthropological theory, which held that, while higher religions (like philosophy itself) were systems of pure thought, primitive religions had significant physical and sensual components. Durkheim, for example, while admitting that all religions were true after their own fashion, nevertheless held that some could be rated superior to others "in the sense that they call into play higher mental functions, that they are richer in ideas and sentiments, [and] that they contain more concepts with fewer sensations and images."[53] And Oxford's R. R. Marett claimed even more plainly that "savage religion is something not so much thought out as danced out; . . . in other words, it develops under conditions, psychological and social, which favour emotional and motor processes, whereas ideation remains relatively in abeyance."[54] On this classification, not only the physical rocking during lessons, but the ritual prostrations during Muslim worship itself, appeared as backward as the unreasoning dance of the savage or the mystical abandon "of dervishes during certain religious festivals."[55] The civilized individual could accord such an undertaking no more respect than the serious adult could accord to children's play. Along with the reliance on memorization of an obscure text, the sensuality of study disqualified the indigenous system of learning as rational.[56]

Kuttab learning resulted ideally in the student's literal incorporation of the text of the Qur'an, and accordingly the practice of its inculcation "was ordered around the meaning and the power of words."[57] Significantly, kuttab practice was primarily oral. The skills of reading and writing were always secondary to the acquisition of the skill of exactly reproducing the recited word of God. Through daily exposure to and repetition of sacred verse, a young boy could within the space of a few years gain the ability to repeat the text by himself (a skill often lost and then sometimes refreshed once he left the kuttab). Students who showed a talent for learning and continued to study at teaching mosques (madrasas) like al-Azhar would later be taught the meaning of the text they had memorized in the kuttab, along with the sciences of grammar and interpretation, which had historically resulted in particular readings. Throughout the Muslim world madrasa study was based on the memorization of a set corpus, but the particular texts as well as the style of learning and the attitude toward scholarly authority differed from one place to another. While Iranian madrasas, for example, featured lively talmudic-style interchanges between scholar and teacher, questioning of the corpus was actively discouraged in Morocco. A young man who had studied with a particular shaykh, and who acquired the ability to recite the texts and commentaries on which the latter was an authority, could earn a written declaration of competence to transmit those same texts to others. Creating and maintaining this genealogy of recitation, memorization, and transmission is what ensured the authority of "texts in the world of the Text," the divine word of God.[58]

For the British, on the other hand, religious instruction meant the inculcation not of recited truth, but of behavioral guidelines, whether of a straightforwardly religious character or popular wisdom cloaked with post-hoc scriptural or patriotic authority.[59] Even after doctrinal formulations were shut out of the curriculum of publicly funded schools, to the chagrin of the clergy,[60] Bible reading was retained, forming part of "the rapid growth of an unsectarian religion, in which the moral element reigns supreme, and in which, if the dogmatic element is not wholly suppressed, it is at least regarded as doubtful, subordinate, and unimportant."[61] Early in the century, Joseph Lancaster's popular school movement had brought literacy to hundreds of thousands of children as preparation for moral instruction. Lancaster, a Quaker, commented on the role of Scripture in the school by saying that

> there is no important head under which the Scriptures can be arranged, but it is likely to point the mind to some virtue, to prevent some practical error, or arm it against some vice. . . . I do not approve of boys being required to learn whole chapters, or long portions of Scripture by rote, unless united with emulation; and then they should be concise, and connected with some subject that has been recently, or is intended to be introduced particularly to their notice.[62]

True moral instruction lay in the study and understanding of "lessons" drawn from Scripture. The text itself, aside from refining literary taste, was secondary to the conveyance of such lessons, and in any case the text had to be understood in order to be useful. Some Europeans hoped to encourage such "moral" study in the kuttab, replacing the memorization of text with the formulation and inculcation of abstract ethical guidelines. In this way "the Koran might be made, like the Bible, a means of imparting moral truth combined with instructive history. This is not done, the poor little children's nascent powers are warped and stunted, and the results appear when their higher education is attempted."[63]

With a population so ethically stunted, moral enlightenment could hardly be expected in Egyptian institutes of higher study, either. Bowring commented upon "the most worthless character" of such teaching as it stood in Egypt in the 1830s, long before the doctrinal element in English Christianity had come to be "regarded as doubtful, subordinate, and unimportant."

> It turns principally upon the religious observances required by the Koran, and degenerates into extreme frivolity. Rarely is any lesson of morality given, and the passages of the Koran, which teach the cultivation of the virtues, are much less introduced and commented on than those which bear upon the ceremonials of the Mussulman faith. Inquiries as to the quantity of adulteration, which makes water improper for ablution — into the grammatical turn of the language of prayer— into the cases in which the obligations to fast may be modified — into the gestures in adoration most acceptable to Allah — into the comparative sanctity of different localities, and similar points — are the controversies which are deemed of the highest importance, and the settlement of which is supposed to confer a paramount reputation upon the Ulema.[64]

The differences Europeans saw between their own "moral" approach to religion and the merely "ritual" concern of Egyptians formed an important part both of European self-definition and of their strategic intervention in Egyptian religious socialization. Half a century after Bowring, Milner denounced such education as "a blight upon the religious and intellectual life of the country," in which the "ideals . . . permeating the whole body . . . are narrow and perverted," and the "ignorant population looks up with superstitious reverence . . . [to] the men most remarkable for the vehemence of their bigotry and of their immersion in antiquated formulae and barren traditions."[65] But what, in a practical sense, would a new manner of moral education accomplish in Egypt? The answer lies on the long road from the rolling English countryside to the urban factory, the world of Adam Smith and the classical doctrines of political economy that popularized the notion that education was an ideal tool for crowd control.

Public Order: The Best Way of Keeping These People Quiet

Early in 1847, the House of Commons was preparing to request a grant from the Crown of one hundred thousand pounds for the support of public instruction, and Macaulay, whom we heard earlier outlining the purpose of education in India, defended the measure against its conservative detractors, delivering a passionate speech supporting popular education. Citing *The Wealth of Nations*, Macaulay called education for the poor one of the most urgent concerns of the commonwealth, for "just as the magistrate ought to interfere for the purpose of preventing the leprosy from spreading among the people, he ought to interfere for the purpose of stopping the progress of the moral distempers which are inseparable from ignorance."[66]

"The most dreadful disorders," he quoted Smith, would follow from the inflammation of religious animosities among the uninstructed masses, as they had in the "No Popery" riots of 1780, which had seen urban prisons emptied, Parliament besieged, dozens of fires set in London, and a shocking loss of life.[67] The cause of the incident, "a calamity which . . . ranks with the great plague and the great fire . . . was the ignorance of a population which had been suffered, in the neighbourhood of palaces, theatres, temples, to grow up as rude and stupid as any tribe of tattooed cannibals in New Zealand, . . . as any drove of beasts in Smithfield Market."[68] Then naming half a dozen similar outrages against person and property committed by the malcontents of the Industrial Revolution, he came to the main argument for popular instruction:

> Could such things have been done in a country in which the mind of the labourer had been opened by education, in which he had been taught to find pleasure in the exercise of his intellect, taught to revere his Maker, taught to respect legitimate authority, and taught at the same time to seek the redress of real wrongs by peaceful and constitutional means?
>
> This then is my argument. It is the duty of Government to protect our persons and property from danger. The gross ignorance of the common people is a principal cause of danger to our persons and property. Therefore, it is the duty of the Government to take care that the common people shall not be grossly ignorant.[69]

The state, already remiss in its educational duties, had no choice but to resort to "the dread of the sword and the halter" in punishing those responsible for such breaches of public order, "since we had omitted to take the best way of keeping these people quiet."[70]

The Regeneration of the Arab

> *The regeneration of the Arab is being accomplished in more ways than one. Apart from the direct processes, of which the school and the prison are instruments, other influences, less direct but still powerful, are ceaselessly at work to mould his character. These influences, which may be summed up as the environment of Western society, spread along the track of the railroad and the telegraph over the country at large.*
>
> W. Basil Worsfold,
> *The Redemption of Egypt*, 1899[71]

Faith in the power of education to mold not only individual character, but the very fabric of society, had spread like Methodist revival during the latter half of the nineteenth century, and was brought actively to bear on the problems of rural and urban social control both domestically and in the far-flung regions of the Empire. As Foucault and Mitchell have shown, older forms of threat and punishment came to be considered not only cruel, but inefficient, and strategies based on discipline, organization, and moral intervention were tested as alternatives to brute force. In March of 1883, at the urging of Lord Dufferin, the Egyptian Khedive Tawfiq Pasha issued a decree to local notables and officers of his government abolishing the use of the *courbash*, a tough hippopotamus-hide whip, for the punishment of criminals, the extortion of confessions, or the collection of taxes in arrears. The abolition, dubbed by Cromer a "remarkable reform—if I may apply the word reform to what is really nothing less than a social and administrative revolution,"[72] was hailed as a triumph of humanitarian government even though the more immediate result was, in the words of the deputy-inspector of Alexandria, "that Mudirs [local Egyptian officials] and police officers are not now as much feared as they should be."[73] The vice-consul of Damietta reported to Cairo that

> the effect . . . is apparent in a steadily growing exhibition of a higher moral tone, and hopeful feeling, a feeling that they are being cared for, in a way they have hitherto been totally unaccustomed to; they are grateful . . . and

there is every reason to hope that by a careful continuance of the efforts being made in their behalf they will become a prosperous, contented, and loyal people.[74]

But the majority of local administrators were less sanguine. In general, provincial officials replied to Cromer's queries about the abolition by saying that, as a result, "insolence and offences have increased, especially among the lower classes"; that it helps "lead them to shirk duty, and thus further aid to embarrass the present regime of the Government, and bring about the present deadlock in the public finances"; that the effect of the change "has been to increase crime and weaken authority."[75] The British consul Spencer Carr wrote explaining the breakdown of authority and the uselessness of concurrent British reform of the prisons:

> The summary suppression of the courbash has had a very bad effect on the population, as by this measure the Sheikhs of villages have been deprived of most of their power and authority, and the fellahs [peasants], having no fear of the whip, and being improvident and lazy by nature, it is a very difficult matter, under the present regime, to compel them to do their duty, especially as the reorganization of the prisons has rendered them so comfortable that the fellah has no longer any fear of imprisonment, and makes no secret of saying that he is better treated in prison than at home, and the only privation he has to put up with is the temporary separation from his harem.[76]

This paradoxical increase in the crime rate, which continued to rise throughout the Occupation, went along with an increasing prosperity that Cromer was certain had filtered to the countryside. By the early years of the twentieth century, the problem of "brigandage" that had plagued cultivated regions of Egypt in the past had disappeared with the creation of an effective standing army. The main trouble in rural areas now was property crime and acts of vengeance: the burning of neighbor's crops or houses, the poisoning of cattle, attempted murder, or false accusations. Noting that Britons were more likely to associate crime with poverty and alcohol than with rising living standards, the consul general attributed the problem to envy and to vengeance for personal quarrels. Referring in 1905 to "the special economic and moral phase through which Egypt and the Egyptians are now passing," Cromer optimistically concluded that "improved education and the general spread of enlightenment . . . constitute the ultimate remedies" to the problem of rural crime.[77]

The expectation of an educational remedy for crime was not confined to Lord Cromer, who might be expected, like his fellow litterateur Macaulay, to attribute moral betterment to liberal study. When Horatio Herbert Kitchener, engineer, professional soldier, and war hero, took the consul generalcy from Sir Eldon Gorst in 1911, he complained bitterly of the police problems plaguing Asyut, the province with the highest crime rate in the country. Reporting that there were 297 murders or attempted murders in that province alone in 1911, Kitchener lamented,

> Human life appears to be of little account, and the most trifling incidents result in homicide. Only recently a man who expostulated with his neighbor for crossing the end of his garden was murdered the same afternoon for no other or better reason. Such crimes, arising from sudden quarrels, family feuds, or revenge, have little connection with public security, and it is difficult to cope with them. They can only be finally checked by the spread of education and civilised ideas.[78]

Again in 1912 he illustrated Asyut's problems by citing the case of a woman murdered "for refusing to give a glass of water, a man for taking a handful of flour." In Behera, Gharbia, and Girga, murders were committed for the stealing of single ears of corn, dates, an errant sheep eating a neighbor's clover. These offenses, incomprehensible to the European, "can only be finally eradicated by the spread of education and enlightenment."[79] Changes in the rural economy during the nineteenth century, including the extension of year-round commercial cultivation to much of the delta, necessitated the movement of agricultural workers from regions of Upper Egypt, where slack periods in the agricultural cycle still created available labor. While such workers had long been forced to perform corvée labor both locally and in faraway regions like the Suez canal, this system was declining due to pressure from delta landowners to retain the labor of their own peasants year-round and not let them work elsewhere. This meant that workers from the south were increasingly contract laborers induced with wages and lacking the sort of supervision that accompanied the corvée. Landowners, complaining that such itinerant workers tended to criminal pursuits, thus looked kindly on efforts to extend mechanisms of socialization that promised to domesticate and render workers susceptible to efficient administrative controls rather than clumsy physical ones.[80]

Moreover, the peasant's abandonment of false ideas and primitive customs would have an invigorating effect on the maintenance of public security as well as on the progress of the economy. Lord Curzon, viceroy of India from 1899 to 1905, linked ignorance and disorder in a 1901 speech in which he held that lack of knowledge was "the source of suspicion, superstition, outbreaks, crime — yes, and also of much of the agrarian discontent and suffering of the masses."[81] Not confining their optimism to a merely theoretical expectation of enlightenment through mass education, the British imported two practical new institutions to Egypt using instruction as a specific remedy for crime. The first was the Boys' Reformatory, founded in Alexandria in 1895 and moved to Giza three years later. Under the supervision of the British director of prisons, the reformatory was established to remove "the evils, attendant on a system in which juveniles are mixed up with adult prisoners."[82] John Scott, in a report to the consul general on the state of the reformatory, proposed that a strict age requirement be set for the inmates of the facility since experience had shown that "manhood with its qualities and defects arrives soon in southern climates, and permanent moral influences can only be obtained over boys of tender age."[83]

The reformatory's young inmates cultivated its garden, cleaned the buildings and were drilled daily in gymnastics, attending school in the morning to learn the elements of reading and writing. Workshops taught carpentry and other manual trades so the boys could "have an honest means of livelihood when they go back to the world." Some years after its founding, the good work of the reformatory "elicited the special commendation of a high British authority on educational matters,"[84] and a new, expanded reformatory was constructed in 1905.[85]

The other establishment for the direct educational amelioration of crime came after the First World War, when an "industrial farm school" was established in Khanka Province, built with surplus military supplies. Large enough for several dozen adolescent boys, the farm school was intended to house destitute urban children at risk of falling into lives of petty crime. Between November of 1918 and the November following, Sir Edmund Allenby noted, Cairo police had reported over nine hundred thefts by children between the ages of nine and fifteen, and estimated that "500 vagabond juveniles could be collected at any time off the Cairo streets." In explaining the need for the school, he wrote,

> The problem [of juvenile vagrancy] can only be solved by education and training in suitable schools . . . [where] the younger and more promising of the waifs and strays could be sent. Instruction would necessarily be of a very elementary character combined with the simplest of regimes under which cleanliness, decent living, the formation of good habits, and training for livelihood would be the chief aims. For girls, domestic work, with such

simple manual trades as straw plaiting and basket work, and for boys, such trades as tailoring, boot and shoe making, carpentry and weaving would be the chief subjects of instruction.[86]

Wild Fanatics and Impostors

But a second police concern was far more serious than the commission of petty crimes by children, or even jealous murders in Egypt's isolated villages. This was the question of political uprisings, often associated with religious zealotry. The Mahdist rebellion in the Sudan in 1881, and Colonel Ahmed 'Urabi's army revolt shortly afterward had sensitized the British to the ease with which Egyptians could be mobilized around a charismatic leader. A permanent solution to the possibility of revolt was clearly not to be found solely in an expensive increase of the British garrison, so foreign officials sought ways to immunize the masses against political or religious excitement. Writing to the earl of Granville in February 1883, Lord Dufferin noted that the villages of Egypt "have more than once been the birthplace of wild fanatics and impostors, who have passed themselves off upon the simple population as endowed with supernatural mission."[87] Consistent with Adam Smith's charge, ignorance increased susceptibility to political enthusiasms. A year later, the earl of Northbrook expressed similar feelings to Granville, adding that "Mahomedans who are instructed in the tenets of their religion have always looked upon [the Mahdi] as an impostor; any feeling in his favour was confined to the lower classes."[88] But even the landowning classes could not be trusted, in their natural state of ignorance, with the new representative institutions to be introduced to Egypt in place of the terror of the courbash and the scourge of arbitrary rule. Dufferin feared that a local body modeled on the House of Commons "would simply prove an uninstructed and unmanageable mob, with a very low level both of character and intelligence, incapable of discussing public business or of understanding finance, and to which it would be dangerous to accord anything but the most restricted privileges."[89] Even were such classes to benefit from some sort of higher education, India had taught the British that an unregulated native intelligentsia was a potential political liability, and that higher education could essentially act as a system for manufacturing indigenous leaders (always referred to in contemporary records as "demagogues") who would contest foreign influence.

By the mid-1890s officials were beginning to express unease that, "year by year, as higher education increases, the intellectual breach between the upper and lower classes of Egyptian society becomes wider."[90] The political danger inherent in such a gap, together with the hope that the spread of basic education would hasten the success of economic development projects, created pressure for a rational program of popular schooling, "so that the people may be rendered accessible to ideas other than those sanctioned by tradition."[91]

> The time seems now to have come for the introduction of practical measures which would aim at bringing the great mass of the people within the range of the influence of the Public Instruction Department. . . . In particular, the little private schools ("kuttabs") attached to almost all the mosques in Egypt, might, by means of the Grant-in-Aid system, be made instrumental in disseminating a sound education, however elementary, among the poorer classes.[92]

Noting the limited scope of the kuttabs and the lack of formal training and certification of their teachers, Cromer yet concluded that "it is more to the point to bear in mind that these little schools have proved their utility by their continuous survival in spite of the neglect, contempt, and other adverse circumstances to which they have for centuries been exposed."[93] The grant-in- aid system, used both in England and in India for decades, would not provide financial aid for each school that applied, but would bring inspected schools into competition with each other for available money, and thus, it was assumed, improve their standards with the incentive of possible future reward. Through this program, the country's multitude of isolated kuttabs would be changed into "an organization of cheap but efficient elementary schools, in which is given an essential but limited amount of religious instruction, together with a course of secular instruction designed merely to equip the pupil with sufficient knowledge to take care of his own interests in his own station of life."[94]

In April of 1895 the Department of Public Instruction began its experiment with the subvention of kuttabs, having forty-six of the schools transferred to its administration from the Ministry of Religious Endowments, and publishing, the following September, a set of regulations and a syllabus for study. Agreeing to open their schools to monthly inspection by the department, "fiqis" (*fuqaha'*, sing. *fiqhi*; literally "jurist/theologian," but used popularly to refer to a Qur'an reciter and teacher) became eligible to receive small grants based on enrollment, provided that they concentrated on reading, writing, and arithmetic, and that no foreign language instruction was attempted.[95] Inspectors were to be drawn, "to command the confidence of the native community, and to be in full sympathy with the teachers, . . . from the class who have received at least part of their education in the El-Azhar or some other mosque school."[96]

One of the more sensitive issues to confront the reformers of the kuttab was the question of what to do — or not to do — about the actual content of instruction. It was decided early on not to interfere with the primarily religious focus of the kuttab, the British assuming that to do so would "inflame public opinion." "It is hardly necessary to point out," Cromer wrote, "how much tact, prudence, and caution are called for in making any attempt to direct or encourage these indigenous schools. There must, of course, be an entire abstinence from interference with religious instruction."[97] Fortunately, along with the systematization of the scattered rural institutions came the mania for regulation and record-keeping so characteristic of the British, and passed by them to the professional classes of their foreign territories. Consuls general soon found that they could use regulations and statistics as rhetorical weapons against any who might claim that the extension of ministerial control to the kuttabs undermined their original mission.

There cannot, in fact, be a doubt that, far from the introduction of any process of deterioration, religious instruction has shared in the general improvement which has taken place in the schools under Government control. I may mention that, in order to qualify for the post of head-teacher in a Mohamedan "kuttab," a thorough knowledge of the Koran and of the principles of Islam is required.[98]

Three years later, in 1906, Cromer elaborated on the improvement, explaining that

a scheme of practical instruction in the principles and religious history of Islam has been introduced into these schools, and an endeavor has been made generally to improve and vitalize the religious instruction. . . . If we take as a test facility for repeating the Koran by heart — a point to which the Moslem inhabitants of this country attach great importance — the following figures speak for themselves. At the last annual inspection of the Kuttabs, no less than 4,531 of the pupils were able to recite the whole of the Koran from memory, 3,538 were able to recite more than three-quarters, 4,180 more than a half, and 6,212 more than a quarter. The remainder of the scholars, being of very tender years, were at the spelling stage, or were learning the earlier chapters of the Koran.[99]

Despite this happy state of affairs, there were those who criticized the continued predominance of religious instruction as a misdirection of effort for schools that were intended to draw the peasantry into modern — albeit still local — pursuits and practical states of mind. Less than a decade after the grant-in-aid program got under way, complaints were surfacing that the inspected kuttabs were failing in their new role as "useful village and district schools" to produce useful village and district citizens. In 1904, of the 124,486 pupils in inspected kuttabs, "81,000 had received no instruction in writing, 70,000 had not commenced to learn arithmetic, and 54,000 had not even begun to learn to read";[100] at the following year's inspection these figures stood at 94,000, 87,000, and 68,000, respectively, out of 145,694 students, slightly worse on the whole than the previous year.[101]

At the same time, there was unease about the school's response to changes in the economy. With indigenous manufactures rapidly declining and the demand for European-style wares increasing, it became clear that some of the previously agricultural population would have to be shifted to other productive pursuits. Products of the kuttab, however, seemed not to be interested. Writing in the context of a new movement to bring simple industrial education into the rural kuttabs through a system of "supervised apprenticeship" (an idea championed by a former missionary and long-time advisor to the Ministry of Education), the consul general explained that the current system of kuttab education was being abused to the detriment both of its clients and the wider society.

The influence of the "Kuttabs" has hitherto tended to divert the children of the poor from their natural avocations in the fields, or in the family workshops, and to embark them upon a career generally lapsing into mendicancy. The children flock to the "Kuttabs," not to receive instruction, which will fit them for their position in life, but to commit to memory the whole of the Koran, and thereby, as reputed "fikis," to escape from liability to military conscription. And, in Egypt, a "fiki," unless he be attached [as] a reader to a "Kuttab," and, except for casual employment in reciting the Koran at funerals and festivals, is virtually a beggar.[102]

Despite appreciable gains, Egyptians seemed not to be utilizing their new intellectual resource for the intended purpose, and their persistence in having habits and ideas the British wished them not to, earned them repeated criticism for "credulity." In 1909 Sir Eldon Gorst castigated the Cairene press for trying to "arouse the passions of the mass of the people, who are, and must remain for years to come, far too ignorant to appreciate the absurdities and the falseness of the diatribes which are read out to them daily in the villages."[103] Clearly, voluntary education would not suffice for the eradication of a dangerous political innocence. More intensive measures were necessary. But it was not until near the end of the First World War that the Egyptian minister of education, Adly Yeghen (a member of the old Turco-Circassian political elite), charged a committee of experts with studying the systematic universal extension of elementary schooling throughout the country. The commission was appointed at the end of May 1917, and consisted of six Egyptians, functionaries in various ministries, educators, and provincial officials; and five Englishmen employed in the Egyptian civil service. It was under the presidency of Isma'il Hassanein Pasha, the under secretary of state in the Ministry of Education.[104] In their preface outlining the need for universal elementary education, the authors quoted liberally from the works of contemporary reformers on the vital interest of new nations in the eradication of illiteracy and the spread of modern skills. But they also pointed out the political dangers inherent in allowing the continued ignorance of large populations, using examples from India, Russia, and America.

Inevitably, the commission relied heavily on Lord Cromer's experience in Egypt, as expressed in his memoir of the period, *Modern Egypt*. In discussing the political ramifications of educational policy, the committee selected a passage from Cromer that first referred approvingly to Macaulay's policy in India, and then explained,

> If [higher education] is to be carried on without danger to the State, the ignorance of the masses should be tempered *pari passu* with the intellectual advance of those who are destined to be their leaders. It is neither wise nor just that the people should be left intellectually defenceless in the presence of the hare-brained and empirical projects which the political charlatan, himself but half-educated, will not fail to pour into their credulous ears. In this early part of the twentieth century, there is no possible general remedy against the demagogue except that which consists in educating those who are his natural prey to such an extent that they may, at all events, have some chance of discerning the imposture which but too often lurks beneath his perfervid eloquence and political quackery.[105]

The commission, writing in 1919, added ominously that "the recent history of Russia supplies a tragic illustration of this danger in actual operation." The frequent identity of rural crime and political protest in Egypt was not recognized by the British administration.[106] But the connection between the "perfervid eloquence" of the demagogue and the mobilization of popular unrest certainly was. Paradoxically, their solution to the problem was not to quarantine the infectious enthusiasm of the "political quack," but rather to inoculate the populace against his harangues. Through education, the public could not only be convinced of the value of order and stability, but could, through the inculcation of new skills and habits of thought, be drawn into a new set of social relationships that would give them a vested interest in the maintenance of a new system of class relations.

Work: The Observation of Facts

Macaulay was not alone in his confidence in the power of education to pacify the laboring beasts of the Smithfield market, and children were not alone in benefiting from learning. In fact, Macaulay's speech came late in the movement to reconcile England's laboring population to the necessities of the new industrial order. Beginning in 1823 with the foundation of the London Mechanic's Institute, worker self-help societies and employer-sponsored literacy and technical training programs began to serve England's urban work force; by 1860, two hundred thousand students were attending such institutes in England, with similar developments in France. In addition to service as a moral prophylactic, the supporters of the worker education movement extolled education's contribution to the development of manual dexterity, observation, and other skills that would increase industrial productivity.

Such concrete skills and scientific methods of thought were the very opposite of the wild surges of intemperance and violence to which the working classes, lacking self-control as well as self-respect, were assumed to be subject. In the early 1860s, while the French minister of education Victor Duruy was busy trying to increase the enrollment in French worker training courses, the Académie des sciences morales et politiques asserted that "it is from instruction that we must ask the appeasement of the passions, of which ignorance has always been and remains the first source."[107] The discipline of study, observation of his surroundings, and meditation on his condition were to create in the worker a concern for the immediate, an appreciation for the proper management of resources and the natural consequences of improvidence. Contemporaries hoped education would not only reduce levels of drunkenness and crime, but "would bring the worker to respect property rights and to understand the inevitability of inequality in the world. Some [worker education] institutes offered courses in political economy in order to help workers revise their 'erroneous views' on the nature of capitalism."[108] The same benefits could accrue to residents in Britain's overseas possessions, but only after education broke down old social bonds and reconnected them in ways more conducive to a European outlook and the necessities of a presumably more rational political and economic system. In India, the directors of missionary schools wrote to their sponsors of the salutary effects of education in weakening traditional authority structures. As in England, some thought that the teaching of political economy might "contribute vitally to the undermining of 'the all comprehending framework of superstition in this land' by challenging received views on marriage, employment, and labour."[109]

Shortly before the First World War, Consul General Lord Kitchener derided Egyptian elementary education for still being excessively "bookish," and held that schools should have pragmatic aims, such as encouraging the spread of savings banks in villages and teaching careful fiscal habits to keep the peasant out of debt "without inducing him to leave the land."[110] The value of schooling lay in "the discipline which the character and the intellect undergo thereby." Hearkening back to the worker education movement in Europe, he championed "manual exercises [that] train the eye to accuracy in observation, the hand to skill in execution, and the mind to a sense of the importance of truthfulness in work. They cultivate habits of diligence, neatness, and attention to detail, and quicken the general intelligence."[111] In 1919 the Egyptian Commission on Elementary Education repeated that rural schools

> should be *modern and practical in their methods and aims*. Government would clearly not be justified in eventually imposing compulsory attendance unless the education provided in the schools was such as would make the children better able to earn their livelihood in practical directions, in which all his faculties will be awakened and developed and he will be made capable of *understanding and doing* as well as of *repeating* from memory.[112]

Again citing the lessons of British India, the report quoted Mr. Orange, a former director general of education in India, that popular schools should first aim at forming good citizens, then at imparting "useful knowledge, not forgetting while doing so to train the eye and the hand so that the children when they leave school, whether for the field or the workshop, will have begun to learn the value of accurate observation and to feel the joy of intelligent and exact work."[113] In thus encouraging instruction in manual skills, colonial education policy matched domestic policy. Merely by substituting an "external proletariat" of foreign subjects for the domestic working class, policymakers could transfer almost unchanged many of the techniques and philosophical foundations of European-style mass schooling from home to abroad and back again.[114] Observers even compared Egyptian schools favorably with their English counterparts when efforts had been made to match curriculum to local needs. Villiers Stuart, who had visited the country in 1883–84 as a member of Lord Dufferin's fact-finding mission, toured the country again in the 1890s, and saw the government primary schools at Esna and Zagazig, noting that the classrooms were

> surrounded with large coloured cartoons on technical subjects, illustrating various trades, such as bread-making, cooking, weaving, tailoring, hat-making, laundry-work, printing &c . . . some knowledge of these arts is more likely to be useful to them and to interest them than the stock subjects with which village children are crammed at home, such as the precise position of Kamschatka or the distance of the moon.[115]

Education in the "village schools," mostly kuttabs under inspection, and those few under the direct control of the Ministry of Education, now had a dual purpose: religious instruction, their original task, and a new one set for them by the new regime: "to equip the pupil with sufficient knowledge to take care of his own interests in his own station of life, as small land-owner, fellah, petty shop-keeper, handicraftsman, weaver, village headman, boatman, fisherman"; their curriculum could not be extended beyond these needs "without lifting the schools above the needs of the classes for whom they are primarily intended."[116] The notion that "sufficient knowledge" to carry out any of these pursuits was best attained through schools testifies to a sweeping change in what it meant to be an Egyptian. No longer were traditional means of socialization into village life considered to be sufficient preparation. In assuming a parental role, appropriating to itself the definition of competency to take care of one's own interests, the state could now promulgate specific curricula satisfying the requirements of any "station in life" as defined on the national level. In the new rural social order, the peasant, the small shopkeeper, and the *'umda* (mayor, or village headman) were viewed as equivalent in terms of the type of training they needed. Seen from Cairo, their differences were swamped by the rise of an indigenous class of technocrats and clerks with primary and secondary school certificates.

This practical outlook on popular instruction, adapted to the limited needs and capacities of "the lower orders," was reinforced late in the century by British historian William Lecky's two-volume *Democracy and Liberty*, which Cromer admired enough to quote both in his Annual Report for 1904, and later in *Modern Egypt*. "The great mistake in the education of the poor," Lecky wrote,

> has in general been that it has been too largely and too ambitiously literary. Primary education should . . . teach the poor to write well and to count well; but, for the rest, it should be much more technical and industrial than literary, and should be more concerned with the observation of facts than with any form of speculative reasoning or opinions. There is much evidence to support the conclusion that the kinds of popular education which have proved morally, as well as intellectually, the most beneficial have been those in which a very moderate amount of purely mental instruction has been combined with physical or industrial training.[117]

Lecky also drew the attention of the members of the postwar Egyptian Commission on Elementary Education, who cited a passage in which the author praised education for diverting individuals from vice and temptation, and for "cultivat[ing] the civic and industrial virtues."[118] An empirical orientation to the world would produce a laboring class whose interests were local, without any use for "speculative reasoning or opinions," whose passions were held in check and who exhibited such concern for thrift, temperance, and obedience as was required of useful members of society. The transformation of individual character went hand in hand with the transformation of the social order.

Creation of a well-functioning social machine in turn required the differentiation of parts: "Industrial conditions require to be adjusted to the new order of things," wrote the consul general in 1904, "and among the needs for this adjustment is the creation of a numerous and well-trained artisan class, possessing an education of at least the 'Kuttab' grade, and of a restricted but better educated and more highly qualified class, capable of acting as designers, foremen, and managers."[119] An interest in maintaining the Egyptian class system, or, in fact, remodeling it after the British, in which the lower orders had become literate (and thus better able to serve their purpose), was one of the vital functions of the new school system. By drawing the population into a new division of labor, they would be made dependent not only on the new material goods and new criteria for status differentiation that the system brought with it, but on the new system of schooling that helped create it. But even ancient occupations and stations in life could be perfected through educational refinement. The value of literacy, defined by its contribution to morality, efficiency, and order, lay not in its provision of an avenue to individual emancipation, but in its ability to reinforce a comfortable hierarchy. In this connection W. Basil Worsfold penned near the end of the nineteenth century one of the most moving paeans on record to the lofty purposes of British educational policy in its overseas empire. Marking an increased Nubian interest in the study of English after the British victory at Omdurman, Worsfold rhapsodized,

> The English language has become very popular in the primary schools of the towns, while within the last few years a commencement of a genuine system of national education has been made by the endeavor of the Education Ministry to utilize and regenerate the mosque schools — the Kuttabs — which form the sole resource of the small towns and villages. If the regeneration of the Kuttab brings with it the education of the hitherto neglected girls, a new era of moral and intellectual development will ensue, and one of the results of this development will be to provide a new and more reliable class of [domestic] servants.[120]

Women: An Educated and Enlightened Motherhood

Finally, having addressed the moral needs of the pupil, the ignorance of the criminal, the enthusiasm of the malcontent, and the diligence of the worker, the school was directed to a final group whose betterment represented perhaps the best hope for the reconstruction of the nation. In 1831–32, when the French expatriate Clot Bey established within his four-year-old School of Medicine a division for the training of midwives, he could find no females in Egypt willing to attend the institute. Fortunately, Egypt's social structure still allowed for the creative staffing of such experiments, and the problem was solved by the enrollment of "ten Abyssinian and Sudanese girls bought in the

Cairo slave market, together with two eunuchs sent by Muhammad Ali from his palace."[121] By the beginning of the twentieth century, the supporters of female education had, by their own estimation, made great strides. In 1905, for example, there were eight times more schools admitting girls, and six times more female students, than just five years before.[122] In order to encourage female participation in schools, government grants-in-aid (disbursed on the basis of enrollment) counted the attendance of one girl as equal to two boys.

Officials cited increasing demand by parents for facilities for the education of girls as one of the most surprising and heartening developments in the educational field, and strove to provide practical programs in "housewifery" or "domestic economy," hygiene and child care in addition to basic training in reading, writing, and arithmetic. But they saw the provision of female education as more than an issue of equal access to public facilities, or even an issue of public health (the combating of high infant mortality through basic health education). Predictably, Victorians were both fascinated and repelled by "oriental" systems of marriage and family life, particularly by polygamy and the seclusion of women. When discussing outreach to Muslim lands, missionaries often made the degradation of women through polygyny — rather than doctrinal questions — the central justification for Christian proselytization. "Time would fail me to enter into the whole subject of the marriage relationship in the Mohammedan races," declaimed the Reverend Robert Bruce at an 1888 London conference on Protestant missions,

> and of the evils which spring from the immense difference between the glorious state which our Lord introduced into Christianity when He raised woman to her proper state in society, and on the other hand, the opposite effect in Mohammedanism, caused by Mohammed when he degraded women even lower than she had ever been before.[123]

His colleague, the Reverend G. E. Post, M.D., of the Syrian Protestant College in Beirut, articulated later that day the theoretical basis for missionary concern with women:

> Women determine the social condition of any country and any race. No race has risen above the condition of its women, nor can it ever be so in the history of the world. The boy is father of the man, but the woman is mother of the boy, and she determines the whole social state, not only of her own generation, but of the generations that are to follow.[124]

The environment of the harem, "with its unpalatable gossip and frequent intrigue," was felt to be psychologically damaging to young boys raised in its midst, to predispose young girls to idleness and mental deterioration, and to be harmful to social life in general.[125] "The element in [the Egyptian boy's] education which is lacking is that imparted by an educated, pure, and dignified motherhood," who realizes "the important part she should play in her son's home education and moral training, from his infancy upwards."[126] The work of regenerating Egypt, therefore, required a regenerated Egyptian woman who could take advantage of a state-sponsored education "aim[ed] at preparing them for the duties of home-life."[127] This, in turn, called for an alteration of the family unit that would allow girls not only to attend school, but to stay in school, and to help filter new ideas and outlooks into the heart of the family. The challenge was to open up the family to the modern influences that were beginning to encompass the rest of the social order, to crack open the shell of secrecy and isolation past which reformers had not been able to see, and expose the family, the last remaining stronghold of native male authority, to the rule of law and progress. "It is not possible," wrote Cromer, near the end of his tenure in Egypt,

> neither perhaps is it desirable, that every feature of national character should undergo a complete transformation in a quarter of a century. In so rapid a process, the good is very liable to disappear with the bad. Nevertheless, . . . forces are now at work which have already modified, and must eventually still further modify, the Egyptian national character. . . . How far the movement now rapidly progressing in favour of female education will eventually modify the ideas, the character, and the position of the next generation of Egyptian women remains to be seen. Should any changes in their position take place, it is greatly to be hoped that they will be gradual. . . . In this case, hurry might produce a moral cataclysm. Nevertheless, it is . . . true that, until a gradual change is effected in the position of women in this country, the Egyptians, however much they may assimilate the outward forms, can never hope to imbibe the true spirit of European civilization in its best aspects.[128]

For missionaries, Leila Ahmed writes, the targeting of women with the Christian message would lay a trail of gunpowder into the heart of Islam and prepare the way for the conversion of future generations. For colonial administrators, this "Colonial feminism, or feminism as used against other cultures in the service of colonialism,"[129] complemented what might be called "colonial populism," their expression of concern for the fate of the peasantry whom they wished to liberate from the grip of landowners and local officials in order more efficiently to extract their labor for production directed toward a world market. But in either case, whether for the Christianization or the rationalization of Egyptians, an emphasis on educating women as potential mothers was a strategy that promised revolutionary results. It endures today, as a vision of a back door to cultural change, in economic and social development schemes of many types, and has been articulated by colonizers of Muslim populations well into the 1980s. "[I]n the tradition that has evolved [in Central Asia]," wrote Soviet Islamic specialist Sergei Poliakov in 1989,

> the woman is the chief shaper of the next generation. By depriving this educator of a public life, traditionalism also deprives her of new information; in fact, it deprives her of any information that is not controlled by the traditional institutions of the village. The subject of the major role women play in the material education of children has been overlooked by theory and practice alike, but it is precisely here that we may find the foundation of all our mistakes, failures, and powerlessness, in atheistic and other propaganda.[130]

Conclusion

At the beginning of this chapter I stated that Mitchell's Foucauldian analysis of Egyptian schools, focusing on the theoretical principles behind mass education and its disciplinary conventions, was inadequate to understand the school's ambiguous role in Egyptian society. While it is true both that increasing numbers of students were enrolled in public education projects during the latter nineteenth and early twentieth centuries, and that the patrons and planners of such projects hoped they would thereby become useful, productive, and contented citizens, it does not follow from this that the latter goal was necessarily achieved. Nor does it follow that no other, unanticipated results were achieved by the institution of mass schooling. As Mitchell himself recognized, even though the colonial order penetrated local discourse "through its textbooks, school teachers, universities, newspapers, novels and magazines," still

> this colonising process never fully succeeded, for there always remained regions of resistance and voices of rejection. The schools, universities and the press, moreover, like the military barracks, were always liable to become centres of some kind of revolt, turning the colonisers' methods of instruction and discipline into the means of organized opposition. (Hence the rise

after the First World War of disciplinary political movements opposed to European occupation, such as the Muslim Brotherhood in Egypt, whose leaders were almost invariably school teachers.)[131]

As another example, the role of Egyptian schools as cradles of nationalist sentiment and the consequent participation of students in nationwide anti-British strikes and demonstrations in March and October of 1919 gave officials pause and indicates some discrepancy between theory and practice. The dilemma of "disciplinary spread" from the point of view of political and cultural elites is, as we saw in the introduction, a serious problem, and highlights the inability of policymakers and educators to reconcile reality to their theories about it. If schools, universities, the press, and the military barracks act as centers of revolt, it is because the spread of their unique disciplinary practices across the whole of society is accompanied by the spread of the distinctly new techniques and potentials for revolt associated with them. A new system of power uniformly diffused, serves, among other things, to surround dominant classes with new sources of anxiety and threat. One way of tracing the historical genesis of the Jihad group that assassinated Egyptian president Anwar Sadat in 1981 leads back to Sadat's own encouragement of Islamic student organizations on Egyptian university campuses in the early 1970s, which he intended to wipe out the leftist organizations who supported the policies of his predecessor, Gamal ʿAbd al-Nasser.[132] Quickly losing control over the forces he had purposely unleashed, Sadat engaged throughout the decade in a series of repressions and rapprochements with Islamist and other opposition groups that resulted in the alienation of substantial portions of the country's intelligentsia and eventually in his death at the hands of members of his own military. Neither the barracks nor the school had done its job.

So society's elites as well as its working classes are caught up in the "self-damnation" (the image is Paul Willis's) of contradictory process of cultural and social reproduction. If the working classes help reproduce their own subordination, so cultural and political elites regularly make choices that threaten their own power in the very attempt to ensure its spread. By relying on techniques of power that are "slow, uninterrupted and without external manifestation,"[133] imperial and Egyptian elites began in the nineteenth century to relinquish the predictability of control they sought to gain, for as Raymond Williams has pointed out with respect to Europe, "There was no way to teach a man to read the Bible

. . . which did not also enable him to read the radical press"[134] —precisely the problem about which Eldon Gorst complained in 1909.

And yet we continue to face the problem of historical narratives that describe Egypt's passage into "modern" politics and culture (either of the modernization or the Foucauldian brand) as a glacial transformation: homogenous, all-encompassing, and ineluctable. Before continuing with our own narrative of educational change in Egypt, it is worthwhile to pause momentarily and examine this tendency, for it will tell us something important about how scholarship, in creating the objects of its study, often acts to reproduce the very intellectual categories it argues explicitly against. Christopher Herbert, in his recent book *Culture and Anomie*, has argued — with respect to Williams himself — that "the presumption that history is logically coherent and intelligible, and therefore subject to extensive operations of summary and synthesis without serious distortion," is mistaken. Instead, history (and its reflection in literature) "is bound to be an affair of paradoxes, dense textures of implication, logical disjunctions and circularities, ambiguities and illegibilities."[135] While understanding the complexities of history would seem to require not only recognition of this fact, but a conscientious attempt to address it, much historical writing — including some of the most theoretically informed — serves to reproduce standing metanarratives of development with very old historical roots.

With respect to Egypt, this is accomplished in part by downplaying the failures of disciplinary projects that can be used as central examples or tropes of wide-ranging social changes. Mitchell, for example, uses the minute disciplinary conventions of the nineteenth-century Lancaster school — developed in India and Britain to provide cheap instruction for the working classes — as the type specimen of the new Egyptian government school, despite scant evidence that the Lancaster model reached beyond a single model institution in Cairo and the writings of several Egyptian intellectuals and civil servants who had trained in the Lancaster method abroad. Despite the method's enthusiasts, proposals to revive and propagate the model failed.[136] The "model villages" established on rectilinear plans by the French in mid-century, attempting to use army methods in the village "to achieve the new order of the barracks," are also used as a metaphor for disciplinary encroachment, but in reality these soon broke down and left neither plans nor remains.[137] In fact, again and again the plans made by the new educated elites can be read as a history of spectacular failures rather than insidious successes. Egyptians studying abroad in Europe in the 1830s and hoping to school Egyptians in European philosophies of discipline and development had their proposals for school construction rejected,[138] and those who idealistically translated works on European educational philosophy later became nationalist leaders rejecting European domination.[139]

The developmental sequences read into Egyptian history by Mitchell (and into European history by Foucault), namely, that personal and physical power gives way to disciplinary power, are precisely the same as those read by nineteenth-century evolutionism and twentieth-century modernization theory (arbitrary power gives way to rational power), merely with a different moral evaluation. We need a way to reconcile the confident and commonsense writings and records left to us by history, with the anxious, ambiguous, and asymmetrical experiences those writings reflected and provoked within their lived context. Let me suggest — as a prelude to the textual analyses in the following chapters — that administrative memoirs and educational planning documents are neither descriptive nor strictly hortatory, but performative and hegemonic in Williams's sense, representing

> a saturation of the whole process of living . . . to such a depth that the pressures and limits of what can ultimately be seen as a specific economic, political, and cultural system seem to most of us the pressures and limits of simple experience and common sense. . . . [Hegemony] is a whole body of practices and expectations, over the whole of living: our senses and assignments of energy, our shaping perceptions of ourselves and our world. It is a lived system of meanings and values — constitutive and constituting — which as they are experienced as practices appear as reciprocally confirming.[140]

This hegemony, the cultural level through which Willis sees structural determinants being mediated, hides structural tensions and cultural contradictions both from subordinate and dominant classes. The articulate ideologies of educational theorists and colonial administrators are among the elite's tools of self-construction, tools they use to create for themselves consistent experiences of inconsistent social processes. But the creation and application of a plan, the attempt to transform reality into the facsimile of a specific text, is a complex process whose results do not simultaneously or efficiently serve all the interests of the dominant groups or classes in society. It is always historically contingent, problematic, and uncertain. Although colonial educational policies were in some ways relatively generic European blueprints for the imposition of social order, most policies were tailored by and for specific populations at specific times. In Egypt, popular schools were restricted to Arabic to prevent flight from the fields, and religion was retained as the primary focus of instruction in inspected kuttabs. In Morocco, on the other hand, French policy toward the education of Berber children made French the language of teaching and prohibited instruction in Arabic and in Islam to prevent alliance of the mountain tribes with the Arabic-speaking Muslims of the plains.[141] In the Arabian desert, education for bedouin children derides nomadic values and practices, stressing urban values and settled life-styles, but the results have not been the settlement of mobile populations, but the avoidance of too much schooling in favor of practical training in the military and a subsequent reinvestment in herding.[142] Each of these policies has had different and largely unforeseeable empirical effects. One of the interesting and significant questions to ask, then, is not about whether strategies of social control are implicit in educational systems (they always are), but how elites use such strategies as part of their self-definition with respect to specific subordinated populations, and how these latter populations appropriate educational systems for their own purposes.

During the course of the nineteenth century the Egyptian kuttab was made to take on new subjects (arithmetic, geography, etc.). It also continued to fulfill its original function, the transmission of religious culture, but in a different way, and with a different manner of articulation to the community and to the state. The development of new forms of teacher training and certification, the institution of "a scheme of practical instruction in the principles and religious history of Islam," the spread of testing in specific subjects and of inspection and accountability to a distant bureaucracy, all served to alter the social and spiritual role of Islamic instruction. The fiqhi's responsibility to the men who sent their sons to learn from him was first joined, and later replaced, by his responsibility to the Ministry of Education or to the provincial council.

Likewise, these bureaucracies assumed the responsibility to provide for the spiritual and intellectual well-being of individuals in the communities where they aided or administered schools. Thus not only the kuttabs themselves, but the social relationships (between parent and fiqhi) that had constituted them, were functionalized, appropriated by outside forces for the satisfaction of outside ends. In order to effect this and other important transformations in the social and mental life of the Egyptians, schools would in principle have to overcome what Europeans viewed as the cumulative intellectual degradation that education had allegedly suffered through the centuries at the hand of the "barren tradition" of Islam. It is this effort to which we now turn.

CHAPTER 3

The Progressive Policy of the Government

Egyptian education presents no compelling philosophy like Fascism or Communism to warrant the perpetuation of such a centralized machine for indoctrination. In Egypt, the educational wheels of indoctrination are all set up, but there is no national ideology to be indoctrinated. The wheels grind on for their own sake.

Russell Galt, *The Effects of Centralization on Education in Modern Egypt*, 1936[1]

The transformation of the Egyptian kuttab from a local circle for the inculcation of sacred text, into a local institution aimed at the cultivation of national political and social objectives, was a process spanning three or four generations after Muhammad ʿAli initiated his programs. But although the ideological transformation of the kuttab's mission was accomplished by the first decade of the twentieth century, the practical changes were just beginning. This chapter traces Egypt's response to the professionalization of teaching and educational administration during the twentieth century, insofar as the expansion of schooling as a social institution, with its accompanying theoretical elaboration, affected ideas about the nature and transmission of Islamic religious culture. In essence, the functionalization of Egypt's religious tradition meant that the ideas, symbols, and behaviors constituting "true" Islam came to be judged not by their adherence to contemporary popular or high traditions, but by their utility in performing social work, either in furthering programs of social reform or in fulfilling the police functions that Europeans attributed to education as such.

For the new Egyptian elites created by the schools, educational institutions eventually became centers of nationalist resistance to imperial goals, as they struggled both with the British and with the traditional Turco-Circassian elite of the Palace for control over the benefits of schooling as an engine of agricultural productivity, a tool of social control, and later as a basis for mass mobilization. Rural Egyptian notables and landowners, as well as urban commercial elites and intellectuals, often found ways to turn new imported institutions in their favor rather than succumb to the radical potential of political forms being imposed by the European powers. Throughout the first half of the twentieth century, for example, parliamentary elections were used successfully by rural notables to perpetuate their control over villages rather than engage in the democratic ideal of opening political participation to the mass of peasants.[2] In a very different vein, schoolteacher Hasan al-Banna began in 1928 to build the Muslim Brotherhood, a modern-style party organization using schools, youth groups, news media, national congresses, and social service provision to mobilize hundreds of thousands of active members around the anticolonial cause. It is not very surprising that the criticisms Europeans had leveled at the Islamic establishment in the nineteenth century — that it was "dry, dead, ritualistic, and irrelevant to the needs of living Muslims"[3] — were repeated in the twentieth century by the Muslim Brotherhood itself. The creation of an objectified and functionalized Islamic tradition served the political purposes of very different interest groups. Meanwhile, each side accused the other of "reactionary obscurantism," the British aiming the charge at the Brotherhood, whom it perceived as a cynically antimodern force allied with the Palace of King Fuʾad; the Brotherhood aiming the charge at al-Azhar, whose version of Islam they denounced as being "supported and maintained by the imperialists."[4] In terms of mass religious education, intellectuals of all political viewpoints began coming to the conclusion — particularly during the interwar years — that properly crafted and carefully targeted programs of "modern" Islamic instruction could be simultaneously socially stabilizing and economically progressive forces.

Reaction and Responsibility

Financial support for mass education was minimal through the Occupation — hence the strategy of partially subsidizing existing rural institutions instead of creating new ones. In 1905 a new movement for private funding of schools emerged in the provinces, a development viewed with some ambiguity from Cairo, which wanted above all to direct curricula in its favor. Voluntary societies funded by private subscriptions succeeded by the end of that year in completing over seven hundred new kuttabs, commencing construction on nearly two hundred, and repairing more than three hundred others.[5] As one local example, by 1907 in the northern delta province of Daqahliyya, £E 80,000 had been raised from wealthy landowners and local residents for the construction of 268 kuttabs. The mudir, Mustafa Maher Pasha, oversaw the reservation of over 300 *feddans* (a feddan is a little more than an acre) of land as *waqfs* (private, tax-exempt endowments for the support of pious institutions) to generate income in perpetuity for the maintenance of the new schools, enough to provide one-quarter to one-fifth of their annual operating expenses. Encouraged by a program of qualified government land-grants begun in 1905 for the construction of kuttabs, this private effort continued for half a decade in many provinces.[6] By 1909 over 1,200 feddans of agricultural land had been committed by private individuals for the support of local schools, bringing the expected annual revenue available for expenses to £E 9,000.[7]

The development of private interest in rural education both pleased and worried the national administration, which feared that overzealous local officials might use the collection of subscriptions as a "means of oppression," that "the movement may be dominated by those who are out of sympathy with the progressive policy of the Government, and that it may thus be used in the direction of reaction," and that locally funded projects might shut out non-Muslim students.[8] This last concern became especially prominent after legislative changes made the provincial councils responsible for funding elementary instruction. As of 1 January 1910, the new law gave provincial councils power to levy taxes to support public works, including a mandate to devote seventy percent of the educational tax receipts for "elementary vernacular instruction."[9] The new British agent heartily approved the change, which he predicted

> will not only have great educative value, but, being intrusted to bodies composed almost entirely of landowners and those engaged in the cultivation of the soil, will ensure the system of education in the rural districts being brought into harmony with the necessities of agriculture. A local Council, acquainted with local conditions, will be in a very advantageous position to devise for the children of the fellaheen a system of training which

will fortify their preference for agricultural pursuits, and will not tempt them to drift into the towns.[10]

The Religious Difficulty

But local councils would, unlike privately funded voluntary associations, be fully accountable to all citizens of the province, Muslim and non-Muslim, and would therefore be responsible for turning the kuttabs already administered, and any new ones built, into truly national elementary schools. When the grant-in-aid system was first established a dozen years earlier, the government had pledged not only to refrain from interference with religious instruction in the schools, but to ignore the confessional affiliation of schools applying for grants, making them available equally "to schools professing the Mahommedan, Coptic, Jewish, or other faith."[11] Now it faced a problem delicately labeled "the religious difficulty."

Most kuttabs inspected by the government had also received funds from the Ministry of Religious Endowments, which defined them as Muslim schools in which the principles of Islam could be taught. If Coptic children happened to attend, they were separated from the other children while Qur'an lessons were given. In 1902 it was estimated that only 17 of Egypt's 500 Coptic kuttabs were under inspection, largely, officials guessed, because most Coptic schools wished not to be bound by the restriction on teaching European languages as a prerequisite to financial support.[12] By 1909 there were still only 28 Coptic kuttabs under inspection.[13] With only one substantial religious minority population to consider, educational planning in Egypt was often easier than in Britain itself, or in other dependencies like Iraq.[14] Yet by 1910 tensions had grown high enough that a Coptic congress was called for 6 March in Asyut. After several days of discussion, the five hundred conferees issued a list of demands including nondiscrimination in government employment and grants, the provision of an alternate day of rest for Copts employed in the government, representation in all new representative institutions, and the "Right of Copts to take advantage of the educational facilities provided by the new Provincial Councils."[15] The unequal geographical distribution of Coptic communities meant that they would be contributing as little as 3 percent of the local tax receipts in some provinces, but over 30 percent in provinces like Asyut in Upper Egypt, making a uniform national policy difficult to achieve.[16]

In the end, most of the provincial councils decided that their primary schools would follow the system employed in government primary schools. They would be open to both Muslims and Christians, with specially trained Coptic teachers (or priests) giving Christian religious instruction at specified times if there were sufficient demand (this meant at least fifteen Christian pupils; it should be noted that religious instruction was mandatory for Muslim students, but optional for Copts). In order to train Coptic teachers in the delivery of religious instruction, Christian religion classes were formed for students of the Khedivial Training College in 1910, qualifying them to teach the subject in primary schools.[17] In the kuttabs, which would be open both to Muslim and Christian children, the Qur'an would be taught, and Christian children could be excused if they wished. If there were sufficient numerical support in neighboring communities, a Coptic kuttab could be established in which special religious instruction was delivered. Financial arrangements were being made in Asyut, Minya, Girgah, Qena, and Sohag for the sharing of tax revenues between Muslims and Copts. Although Copts had demanded that priests be allowed to tutor Christian children in the kuttabs while Muslim students learned the Qur'an, this was thought impracticable. "I fear," wrote Gorst,

> that the day has not yet arrived in Egypt, though I do not say that it never will, when the sheikh and the priest could safely be allowed to impart rival religious instruction to children of the lowest class simultaneously and in the restricted space of the Kuttab, which, in some cases, consists of not more than one or two rooms. Where the Coptic children are not sufficiently numerous to warrant the creation of a special Kuttab, they must be content, for the present, to receive their religious teaching at home.[18]

In 1919 the Elementary Education Commission reiterated this concern, noting that the provision of Coptic teachers for all of the needful kuttabs would be impossible, and that

> apart from this, whilst mutual tolerance and goodwill can be guaranteed in a few Government schools which are under strict control, regrettable incidents would inevitably occur under this dual arrangement in some of the scattered thousands of elementary schools, under loose control, staffed by teachers of a lower level of education.[19]

The government was beginning to face the contradictions inherent in its choice to retain and even expand religious instruction in new tax-supported schools. The strategy of encouraging religious instruction as a political anaesthetic was joined with the fear of popular unrest if it were removed from the curriculum. Too little religion and the ignorant masses were left without moral compass; too much and the students felt themselves fitted only for employment as itinerant Qur'an reciters. The Coptic/Muslim difference only exacerbated the problem, since it was the political danger perceived in simultaneous sacred instruction for the different communities — not the integration of the schools themselves — that prompted administrative concerns about "regrettable incidents." Even so, just as in Great Britain, where religious instruction in the form of Bible reading formed part of a growing nondenominational vision of moral instruction, so in Egypt leaders stressed the common morality of the nation. In a speech delivered in early October of 1908, future prime minister Sa'd Zaghlul, then minister of education, repeated the rationale behind the continued expansion of elementary education:

> The Government has found itself the means of developing general morality amongst the popular masses, in order to diminish the number of noxious and blameworthy acts due to the ignorance of true principles and of the exact rules of the religion; besides which it declares that the materials taught in the Kuttabs are to be none other than those notions indispensable to all men.[20]

"The Four R's"

The first paragraph of Article 1 of the Elementary Education Commission's 1919 Draft Law for the Better Provision of Elementary Education in Egypt set out the minimum curricular requirements of a projected program of mass education:

> The term *"Elementary School"* means a school in which suitable education is provided exclusively in Arabic for Egyptian children between the ages of six to eleven years in accordance with a syllabus prescribed or approved by the Ministry of Education. This syllabus shall include, at least, instruction in religion, reading, writing and arithmetic, and such other subjects as the Ministry of Education may determine.[21]

These subjects, "the four R's," were already the backbone of the Egyptian elementary school program for children between five and thirteen years of age, which the proposed Draft Law meant to extend and provide with public monies. Elementary schooling had been growing rapidly during the first two decades of the twentieth century. In 1905, for example, there were more than a hundred kuttabs administered directly by the Ministry of Education, with nearly seventy-five hundred pupils. Over twenty-five hundred schools and seventy-six thousand students were under inspection. By 1906 the number of inspected kuttabs had jumped 70 percent, and the number of students had more than doubled. Article 19 of the Egyptian Constitution of 1923 declared elementary education compulsory for all seven- to twelve-year-old children within two miles of an elementary school. And despite the vital role played by the Coptic community in the Egyptian nationalist movement, with its secular political ideology, the Constitution also formalized Islam as the religion of the Egyptian state, reinforcing its presence in the curriculum.[22] General subjects were added to the curriculum, as was physical education for boys, and "Home and Health Information" for girls (which took the place of half of their Qur'anic studies in the final three years of the elementary curriculum; see table 1).

The growth of the school population was slower through the First World War, but picked up explosively in the 1920s. The largest increases by far were in the kuttabs administered directly by the government, effecting a centralization of authority. In 1922, one hundred forty-five administered schools served over twenty-three thousand students, but by 1930, thirteen times as many kuttabs served eleven times as many students. The number of schools under the provincial councils declined nearly 30 percent during that period, and fewer than five hundred schools remained under inspection.[23]

In the more prestigious primary schools, whose graduates — unlike those of the elementary schools — could continue on to higher education, the program of study looked quite different. The four-year program was identical for boys and girls, stressing Arabic, foreign language, and arithmetic, relegating religion to a tiny corner of the program. For the elite children paying to attend primary schools, the imperative of class control was absent, and even religious instruction was to be "secular," forming a part of the cultural background of the cultivated individual, and nothing more. In a discussion of secularism in Egypt, Professor Ibrahim Salama of Dar al-'Ulum (originally a teacher-training college) described the new attitude in 1939:

If one means by secularization the scientific study of reality *as* reality, setting aside every a priori idea and every religious idea, the Egyptian system —

Table 1 *Relative Time Devoted to Subjects—Elementary Schools*

	1903	1933
Qur'an	31%	33%
Religion	11	7
Arabic	29	31
Arithmetic	14	19
Calligraphy	14	—
General	—	8
Physical Education	—	2

excepting al-Azhar, of course—can perhaps be regarded as secular. Religious education does figure in the programs of the State schools, it is true, but always in the form of moral precepts, no more no less. For the student in the current programs of the State primary schools, whether those of girls or boys, we are able to discover evidence of this sort of secularization. The goal of the Qur'anic recitation is before all else a linguistic goal. The Ministry of Public Instruction advises the masters to read without rocking, and in a very simple manner, paying attention to Arabic phonetics, whatever Qur'anic verses figure in the syllabus.[24]

As befitting a "modern" and middle-class habitus, the stigmatized rocking of kuttab children was eliminated, and in fact the Qur'an itself seems to have been disconnected almost completely from the idea of "religious" instruction, constituting instead a source of linguistic exercises.

But these middle-class primary school students, as important as they were for the construction of the modern state, were not the sole concern of the Ministry of Education. Reports and plans for educational reform throughout the 1930s still hinged upon the concept that "Egyptian prosperity depends in the last analysis upon the existence of a pre-eminently large class of industrious, contented and intelligent agricultural workers."[25] Although British civil servants continued to fill important positions in a number of Egyptian ministries, and the British Ministry of Education continued to provide consultants to the Egyptian government, another trend in educational planning and administration concerned the growth of new interest groups based in the schools and universities themselves. Professional educators influenced by the work of John Dewey and other popular school reformers moved strongly against the highly centralized and test-driven school organization developed by the French and the British to feed the ranks of the colonial government. Far from heralding a new era of decentralized local control of educational institutions, though, they in fact solidified the international linkages now growing between professional educators in the developed and developing worlds, continually transferring the latest pedagogical theories into an area that was still working to adjust itself to the idea of mass schooling.[26]

Three of these reformers, whose writings on the Egyptian school system were particularly influential in framing Egypt as a case study of the failures and successes of educational policy in modernizing countries, were Amir Boktor and Russell Galt, of the American University in Cairo, and Abu al-Futouh Ahmad Radwan, who taught at Ibrahim Pasha University (now the University of ʿAin Shams). All three studied at the Teachers' College at Columbia University, foreshadowing the growth of American influence in Egypt's development during the latter part of the century. Though they wrote in English, their academic standing gave their writings an air of disinterest — all three felt free to criticize colonial education policies — even though in many respects they perpetuated educational trends like "secularization" and the use of schooling as an instrument of social planning that were begun during the Occupation.

Continuing to characterize the content of the elementary curriculum as "exceedingly bookish and academic for a peasant people," educators of the 1930s repeated the call for new teaching methods and more attention to sound thinking, rather than test-driven memorization of government-issue subject matter textbooks. In the elementary school,

> the absence of games, play, activities, and physical education, the heart of the modern elementary school, is conspicuous. Even the printed outline reveals that almost the entire time of the child in the school is given to a bookish type of study, with from one-half to two-thirds of the program devoted to memorization of the Qurʾan, religious instruction, and the study of the classical Arabic language.[27]

The result, Galt wrote, was "an emphasis on the acquisition of irrelevant knowledge, formal learning, discipline by punishments, reverence for tradition, and the acceptance of authority."[28] These problems were not confined to the elementary schools, but spread in various degrees to the primary and higher schools in the "Europeanized" system as well. Mere literacy was no longer enough, particularly if restricted to "the sacredness of the printed word in the Ministry's books."[29] It was only by challenging its own traditions that Egypt could move beyond "[t]he invariable outcome of Oriental education [which] is a social order which possesses stability, but lacks progressiveness."[30] But even as they championed secular learning and criticized "outdated" worldviews, educators were unwilling to call for the elimination of religious study. Merely the method and goal of that study would change. The traditional study of the Qur'an, whose purpose had been to learn how to use the sacred word in appropriate contexts,[31] now became the study of Islam as a moral system, a study removed from its living context and placed on the same level as other secular categories of knowledge.

> Such subjects as hygiene, civics, ethics, and religion should be definitely planned to develop habits, build attitudes, and such a frame of mind as will bring home to the child the practical ways of living ethically, religiously, and so forth. This should not prevent the school from requiring advanced students to memorize certain sections of the Koran in connection with the study of Arabic literature. Owing to the mervellous [*sic*] beauty of the Koranic style, students of all religions should be offered this opportunity.[32]

This was much closer to the goal of religious study in the British school system, which mined divine writ for lessons (which can be evaluated rationally, and ignored if modified or contradicted by new evidence, as opposed to the *furud* of Islamic law, requirements or duties which are, in theory, eternal and compelling). This new manner of presenting religious subjects pleased professional educational theorists, who saw their adversary in the type of learning fostered by al-Azhar.[33] The future lay in the creation of a new secular Egypt in which agriculturalists would devote increasing amounts of time to the study of nature, farming, and physical fitness in elementary schools, while the elite would study science, literature, and history in the primary schools. Religious instruction would remain for both, but for different reasons.

Landowners and some Egyptian educators feared the advent of universal instruction in rural areas without a corresponding boost for higher education, claiming that it might mobilize "a formidable army of half-educated, third-educated and fourth-educated citizens who see things not in the way they ought to be seen."[34] But religious education seems partially to have escaped the stigma of misapplication to the rural masses. At least one large landowner wrote in an Egyptian newspaper that the *fellahin* (peasants), with their limited needs, were happier than other Egyptians, "and that the most urgent reform in the countryside was the diffusion of religious instruction,"[35] an echo of the Reverend Wilson's sentiments a century before. If technical education might tempt cultivators to leave the fields for more lucrative employment, an emphasis on more traditional forms of instruction might dissuade them from leaving the land, either through reinforcing older loyalties, or merely by depriving them of the skills necessary to acquire alternative occupations.

Even the violence of the Second World War only gave further impetus to the faith that inculcating "moral precepts" through the school would be the foundation of a postwar internationalism based on liberal democratic ideals. Not long after Rommel's defeat in the western desert, the Egyptian minister of education, His Excellency Neguib el-Hilali Pasha, wrote of the faith of "all free nations" that "intellectual development coupled with moral reinforcement are of greater import than material reconstruction . . . the education which strengthens faith and fortifies character is the most solid bulwark against the vicissitudes of life."[36] Arguing in favor of extending the period of compulsory schooling and instituting continuing education requirements for graduates, the Muslim Egyptian minister cited — on the authority of the archbishop of Canterbury himself — the vital importance of educating children in late adolescence. If the age of compulsory school attendance was not raised, el-Hilali feared, "they are apt to forget all or most of what they have learnt at school and are exposed to moral, mental and physical decadence."[37] By now entirely dependent on foreign models of schooling, el-Hilali even found himself incapable of justifying religious education in the Egyptian school without citing a British model:

> The British Government has declared in both Houses of Parliament that it is its intention to pay more care to religious education. The White Paper . . . acknowledges the importance of this sort of education in school life and claims for it a more prominent place in the syllabus, together with religious practices. It behooves our country to follow this example and to give to religious teaching and practice their due place in the school curriculum. The Ministry of Education on its part promises to bear this in mind in its intended educational reform.[38]

Moral education in the new Egypt would operate along several lines, at once "arous[ing] in . . . pupils an interest in the responsibilities of citizens towards their own country and the world at large,"[39] and, in rural areas, avoiding the alienation of children from the land. Schools here would "link education with agriculture and . . . rural industries," so that boys could "gain an enlightened insight into the defects and shortcomings of their homes and villages, and visualise the measures of reform to be introduced," while at the same time preparing them "for village communal life in a way that makes the work that awaits them in their surroundings appeal to them."[40] Even religious instruction "should be of a practical rather than of a theoretical nature," dealing with rural or industrial subjects in village and urban schools, respectively, and including "domestic studies" for girls.[41]

Religious education was conceived explicitly as just one more part of a comprehensive system of social planning operating through the school, rather than the mastery of a body of spiritual literature. "All present or proposed post-war reforms lay great stress on religious teaching," the minister explained:

> Spiritual education and moral uplift are essential factors in education, and many of the calamities that beset the world at present are due to lack of spiritual education. But religious teaching should not be confined to the memorisation of religious precepts; it should rather take a practical trend. A service should be regularly held in school with an Imam leading the boys in prayer. Sermons should be preached on simple subjects bearing on everyday life, within the comprehension of the young. The ulemas or students of religion should inculcate into the boys the habits of cleanliness and the elements of co-operation of which every Egyptian village is in great need. In the sphere of physical culture village games and sports should take a prominent place.[42]

By placing "spiritual education and moral uplift" on the same level as habits of cleanliness and cooperation-enhancing village games, the functionalization of Egypt's Islamic heritage was completed, so that what counted as real religion could now be defined by its social utility. Practices outside the sphere of planning thus became "superstition," targeted, like ophthalmia or bilharzia, for elimination through centralized programs of scientific modernization.

This ever-growing faith in the power of mass education came at the same time as a revolution in the theory of teaching methodology that was drawn from the writings of European and American educators and applied at first in two small Egyptian experimental primary schools beginning in 1932. Responding to criticisms of the bookishness of elementary education generally, theoretical education was to take a back seat to active participation in projects revolving around practical application of ideas and skills. This was not the same as technical training; in fact, specific marketable skills were not in question. Rather, children were to learn by investigating natural, material, and social phenomena in small groups. Studying the production of milk products, collecting butterflies (for which students constructed their own display boxes), beekeeping, firefighting, and printing were all included in the "project method," as were projects in which children played employees of the post office, acted out a historical episode dressed up as ancient Egyptians, or pretended to go on the pilgrimage to Mecca.[43] Advocates of this manner of instruction argued that the school, after all, was merely a "miniature society" in which children "inevitably soak up the values and moral criteria that prevail in their practical lives, whatever the ideas and principles offered them theoretically in lessons."[44]

> If we want to give the school a spiritual mission, we need to work towards establishing its life and its various interpersonal relations on a high plane. More than this, we need to provide for the student the opportunity to experience social life in accordance with the values we wish them to apply in their future lives. In order to prepare the student for a democratic spiritual life, he should practice the modes of this life in the school. Some educational philosophers — like the great American philosopher John Dewey — have gone on to say that the student should discover social and moral values for himself experimentally within the milieu of the school, because these values will not have the desired effect in the direction of his life unless they are the outcome of experience and personal experiment.[45]

The experimental method never caught on widely in Egypt because of the high level of teacher training and small class size it demanded, although aspects of its underlying philosophy became part of everyday educational planning and curriculum design. The project method, in making the study of Islam into an activity like chemistry and nature study, removed it further than ever from its textual roots in the name of making it practical, easily accessible, and fun. The methodology of practicing or modeling religious duties was to rationalize religious study and bring it into line with the secular subjects.

But secularism, "the scientific study of reality," and the cultivation of a modern mentality on a large scale proved to be more difficult to inculcate in Egypt than its new intellectual classes anticipated. Fees for the primary schools were eliminated entirely in 1949, effectively creating a unified school system at the primary level, with a single curriculum that could allow more and more Egyptians, even those not from the wealthiest and most Europeanized families, to enter higher stages of education. The changing class composition of the schools, in concert with the pervasive idea that Egypt was in the process of catching up with the developed world, meant that long after the Second World War, Egyptian educators would continue to complain that their countrymen still placed entirely too much emphasis on "antiquated traditions" in looking for the solution to social problems, rather than relying on "a frank examination of the consequences that follow from [their] various social practices."[46]

Abd al-Futouh Ahmad Radwan's work at the Teacher's College at Columbia University had made him impatient with "the mode of thinking of the average Egyptian [which] is far removed from that pattern which we call scientific." Belittling popular belief in the intercession of saints and the cult surrounding such shrines as Cairo's tomb of Imam al-Shafi'i, Radwan wrote that

> The conflict between the old and the new is quite apparent in those who engage in these superstitious practices. Many go to consult a modern trained doctor, but they also carry a charm in their pocket or on the aching spot in their bodies, and if they recover they do not know whether it was the doctor's prescription or the charm that brought about their recovery. . . . Some University students even visit the shrine of al-Husayn or Al-Sayida Zaynab before they undertake their examination in science. The new modes of thinking are gaining ground, but the strength of old beliefs persists and hinders the development of a scientific mentality.[47]

Schools were to be the primary weapons against "the problem of superstitions and harmful customs," such as "whether a Dhikr [a technique for drawing the individual into mystical contact with God] is a real religious experience, or whether a visit to a shrine really helps a person to recover from sickness, or whether growing a vine in one's home actually causes misfortune"; and they should not just "take a negative attitude toward such issues or be content with casual reference to their false or harmful nature, but should take an explicit attitude against them and try to uproot them altogether from the minds of the young."[48] In response to the experimental and progressive schools founded in the 1930s, Radwan called for a still more critical approach to the curriculum, asserting that merely encouraging active emulation of social patterns rather than theoretical study of them did not achieve the goal of helping children "to examine the social experiences behind these activities, so as to gain insights into social affairs." He criticized the Pilgrimage project in particular, for not having students interview a pilgrim

> in order to ask him what problems . . . he discusses with the Muslims from other lands when they meet in Mecca. Nor do they ask . . . why he gave the little saving he had to the rich steamship company instead of using it to buy a mechanical plow to improve his business. Nor are they led to see that an

action of this sort is not in line with the original principles of the tradition of pilgrimage according to which it is supposed to be reserved for those who can afford to undertake such a costly journey.[49]

Radwan's view of education as a key to social progress, in which "the curriculum of schools should reflect [the] needs of the nation in both a qualitative and a quantitative sense,"[50] and in which religious scholars are seen as useful primarily insofar as they can issue rulings consonant with national advancement, underlines the sense that Egyptian educators were coming to share that religious instruction in public schools should serve primarily national political and economic ends rather than purely personal, spiritual, or communal ones.

What proved frustrating to intellectuals and administrators was precisely the stubbornly personal and local nature of popular concerns. Villagers were far more interested in religious specialists acting as "religious literates, not . . . spiritual guides,"[51] to the chagrin both of professional educators and private organizations like the Muslim Brotherhood (which had never been very successful in rural recruiting). If peasants were resigned — within limits — to the appropriation of their labor and their surplus production, they more actively resisted the appropriation of their loyalty or attention to national political projects except insofar as these had direct local impact.[52] In meetings with visiting ʿulama from urban areas, rural Egyptians were primarily concerned with questions of

whether one lifts his hand up to his shoulder or up to his ears [during prayer], how one sits on after prostration, what one might say before and after prayers. Other questions that arose were queries about whether certain sayings or deeds were considered to be religiously approved or disapproved, how and to whom one would make a sacrifice oath, whether visiting saints' tombs is a good thing or not, and so forth.[53]

On the ground, in remote villages like Silwa in far southern Aswan Province, the changing educational landscape at the national level was marked physically by the simultaneous existence of kuttabs as well as an elementary and a primary school. Studied in the early 1950s by native son anthropologist Hamed Ammar, Silwa provided a concise portrait of the difficult process of adapting national pedagogical goals to local structures of expectation. The kuttab, which transmitted respect for the patriarchal village authority structure as well as the text of the Qurʾan, "fulfill[ed] the task demanded of it by the people in maintaining the standards of Islamic learning in which the memorizing of the Koran comes first and foremost."[54] The compulsory elementary school, on the other hand, stationed at the north end of the village along with the police station and post office, had been a failure since its founding in 1925, as it neither maintained a properly religious atmosphere nor provided for advancement into the civil service. Instead, along with reading and writing it taught arithmetic, drawing, singing, and "rhythmic movements," subjects either of little practical use to villagers or which were assumed to be transmitted in the course of daily life itself. As a result, literacy skills learned in the school were quickly lost by graduates, and both parents and children ridiculed the school and took pains to avoid compulsory attendance, until a free lunch program was implemented in the late 1940s.

The primary school, on the other hand — built just as Ammar left the field in 1951 — proved a huge success with its promise of wealth and prestige through possible government employment. Student comments on the school emphasized that "we shall become government officials when we pass our examinations," and "we like the new school, as we wear [European] suits, which are much nicer than the gallabiahs we used to wear in the elementary school. The former is better than the latter in its lessons, order, and cleanliness."[55] In fact, Ammar's presentation of the three schools fits them neatly into an evolutionary sequence that shows the village opening into a new national structure of incentive and prestige. The exotic and ambiguous elementary school, which did a poor job of preparing either religious literates who could serve local goals or potential bureaucrats who could serve national goals, occupied a space of transition. Unlike the alternately confident and jittery officials in Cairo, local parents knew their children did not need to attend school in order to fill their place in the rural social order. The economic rationality of a policy that sought to confine peasants to the fields seems partially to have given way to one that recognized the necessity of giving local communities an incentive for study in return for the promise of translocal loyalties.

The Nasser Years, 1952–1970

By the time Radwan and Ammar were entering the scene, on the eve of the 1952 revolution, religious instruction had been removed from the curriculum of the first two years of primary school, but in the remaining four, twenty lessons per week were reserved for religion. The revolution restored religious instruction to the first two years, although no textbooks were written for them until some time after 1958–59, the year that the program of study was revised and new religious textbooks were produced.[56] These books articulated an interpretation of Islamic history and doctrine for a society that was to be both religious and modern, both "integralist" and socialist.[57]

The postrevolutionary expansion of primary education was explosive, with the school population more than doubling in the decade after 1953. At the same time, the number of teachers enrolled in training institutes increased by barely half, and the number of school buildings by only 12 percent, leading to severe teacher shortages, a serious matter for a nation bent on developing its rural areas. Growth in the student population slowed somewhat during the 1960s, but school building projects still lagged behind, and the number of teachers being trained actually declined. Religious study in Nasser's primary schools altered the previous emphasis on manners like humility, time management, and good behavior, focusing instead on social values necessary to a popular reconstruction of society by the masses: sincerity, fulfilling obligations, forbearance, and the rights of the nation. Discussion of the value of *jihad*—personal struggle against temptation, injustice, or wrongdoing—was increased in line with the mobilization of this concept for ideological purposes against external enemies like the new state of Israel.[58] Teacher training manuals for students in teacher education institutes placed the study of religion on par with other types of education aimed at "spiritual development" (*al-namw al-ruhi*). Attempting a delicate balance between personal piety and mass mobilization, these manuals called for providing children with sound doctrine and the desire to perform religious rituals, while preparing them for working life in the local environment, instilling in the pupil "devotion to the milieu in which he lives, loving and having pride in it, and not looking down on it." Teachers were charged with instilling pride in the greater Arab nation and preparing the child for life in "a cooperative, democratic, socialist society."[59] These goals, as well as those of social, personal, intellectual, and physical development, formed part of the comprehensive goal of the elementary school, which the Supreme Council on Education had articulated in 1941, but which now took on a new political cast. Education was not merely for the amelioration of illiteracy, but the "enculturation of the children of the nation's masses" (*tathqif abna' al-sha'b*), "leading them to an appropriate national life."[60] Molding students into happy rural citizens, and not merely stationary and productive peasants, became an explicit justification for educational extension.

Because of the revolution's new emphasis on formally articulated political ideology as part of a program of mass mobilization, schools encouraged identification with the regime and its goals in the form of ritualized appreciations of the revolutionary program, much as has been the case in Turkey, with a "major stress on memorization of texts . . . and on ritual and unison repetition of slogans and formulae, especially the sayings [of the leader]."[61] Whereas in Turkey students recited the sayings of Ataturk, in Egypt students repeated phrases from Nasser's speeches and memorized portions of the National Charter. Village schools whose teachers or headmasters were active in the new village committees set up under the auspices of Nasser's mass political party, the Arab Socialist Union, were particularly active in using schools for political indoctrination. But regardless of the personal connections of teachers, schools up and down the Nile Valley rang daily with the shouted chant "Nasser! Nasser! Nasser!" along with the repetition of revolutionary slogans. By the mid-1960s the occupational choice expressed by rural primary school students like those in Silwa had become elaborated into specific categories: "military officer," "engineer," and "schoolteacher" replaced the bare "government official" in the imaginations of children making their way through the apparatus of class mobility.[62]

According to Rif'at Sayyid Ahmad, by the end of Nasser's rule, the curriculum consistently socialized its presentation of religion, highlighting the importance of the individual's cooperation in programs to raise the national standard of living, and instilling "the faith that reward and punishment are founded upon justice." The conscious invention of public ceremonies became an important part of the state's mass mobilization program, and schools began to capitalize on public events like the Prophet's Birthday, Unity Day, and Mother's Day to clothe nationalist values like unity, cooperation and brotherhood with the appearance of important religious principles.[63] The functionalization of traditional celebrations like the Prophet's Birthday was accompanied by the functionalization of local religious personnel. Egypt's revolutionary regime took a pragmatic approach to religion, pressing village *imams* (prayer leaders) into national service as heads of local committees and as ideological intermediaries who could find scriptural justification for policies like family planning, savings, and village economic development. On their own initiative, some local imams also worked to "modernize" (read "discourage and eliminate") local religious practices such as Sufism, which the regime itself had tolerated.[64]

Science and Faith: Sadat and After

Under Anwar Sadat's leadership (1970–81) the elementary student population continued to increase much as it had during the 1960s, and the Ministry of Education's school building program accelerated slightly to keep pace. But, emblematic of the new president's personal and political interest in strengthening al-Azhar and other governmental religious agencies (the Ministry of Religious Endowments and the Supreme Council for Islamic Affairs) as a counterweight to his predecessor's socialist institution-building, a far more impressive increase took place in another class of primary school, the al-Azhar primary institutes, whose enrollment jumped by 70 percent in the four years between 1976/77 and 1980/81. These institutes, staffed by Azhar graduates and feeding students into preparatory, secondary and university study at al-Azhar, rapidly became a fixture in poor urban and rural areas where the Ministry of Education could not keep up.

As part of Sadat's attempt to steer the nation from the Soviet into the American military and economic spheres, a renewed commitment to Islamic symbols became part of government policy. Scores of Islamic activists from the Muslim Brotherhood, imprisoned during the 1950s and 1960s, were released, and Islamic student organizations at universities were encouraged to vie for influence with leftist groups. The new Constitution, drafted at the order of the president in 1971, specifically mandated religious education in the schools, and specified that the Islamic shariʿa was to be a major source—later to become *the* major source—of legislation.[65] Sadat's motto "Science and Faith" came to symbolize the hope that Egypt could benefit from closer incorporation into the international market while at the same time retaining a unique cultural identity. And when that closer integration resulted in a disastrous multiplication of the country's foreign debt, and IMF-negotiated reductions in basic food subsidies led to nationwide food riots in January of 1977, enhanced religious education was one of the solutions the president called for to try to restore political stability. Speaking to a group of the nation's top religious leaders at a meeting he convened a little more than two weeks after the riots, Sadat told them that he wanted to talk about

> the inner structure of the individual. What we suffer from today is not the difficult economic situation, because this shall be solved. . . . You may ask now, what is the real trouble? It is hatred and bitterness. It is the inner structure of the Egyptian man that was corrupted through 20 years [of Nasserism]. . . . I called you today to discuss what we are going to do in order to protect our forthcoming generations from hatred, how are we going to build them up correctly and how are we to cure those who deviated?

Harkening back to another generation concerned with armies of malcontents "who see things not in the way they ought to be seen," Sadat proposed his remedy for the moral crisis that seemed to have seized the nation:

> At my meeting with the political leadership, I asked that religious knowledge should be a compulsory subject for a student to pass the academic year as of next year. Our brothers the Moslems and the Christians should be prepared for that with teachers and books written in a modern style. Let us face up to the age like every other country does. The old style is no good, not any more. We want a new style by which religion, values and faith would be part of our children's mentality from the start of their life. . . . Starting from the next academic year I want you to be ready with Moslem and Christian teachers capable of teaching religion in a new style by which we can protect our forthcoming generations and face up to the problems of today. . . . The most important matter is to restore faith, tolerance and love and to uproot the hatred that seems to still possess some souls.[66]

Sadat's curious allusion to a "new style" of instruction deserves some comment. Religious textbooks of the mid-1970s, for example, though slightly different in format from current ones, are nearly identical in style (see chapter 5), and as fully bound to the goal of nationalist character formation as ever. Sadat's comment appears to recognize that the hegemony of the government's functionalized religious instruction had been only partial, incapable of preventing violence in the streets. But such a conclusion, literally unthinkable to a modern leader habituated to think in terms of educational amelioration, could only be expressed as the implication that an obsolete "old style" of instruction still held sway, and that some elusive new style could be found that would meet the goals of social control. This case of sublimated rhetorical force is hardly unique. After a century of obsession with the issue, Egyptian educational planning documents still implore "curriculum change to emphasize critical, scientific thinking to replace rote learning and memorization,"[67] a call that echoes Milner in its assumption that old ways of thinking have kept Egypt back, and that new ways of thinking cannot by definition have taken hold as long as the country remains on the international periphery. If the power of positive thinking can rescue the country economically, an unspecified "new style" of religious instruction can yet be found to keep the populace quiet.

In fact, if we look at the relative class time devoted to religious study in curricula set near the end of Sadat's tenure by Law no. 139 of 1981, which was in force through the end of the decade, other subjects actually crowded out religious instruction.

As shown in table 1, the relative proportion of time assigned to religious studies for the lower classes in elementary schools remained stable between 1903 and 1933, rising only slightly from 31.4 percent to 33.3 percent. At the same time (1932), the curriculum of the primary school, intended for the children of the urban middle and upper classes, devoted slightly less than 6 percent of class time to religion (see table 2). In 1951–52, a unified primary curriculum assigned 8.5 percent of class time to religion, a figure that increased to 9.5 percent the following year.[68] The primary curriculum of 1963 assigned 10.6 percent of class time to the study of religion. Despite Sadat's apparent concern, Law no. 139 actually reduced the amount of time assigned for religious instruction by almost 30 percent relative to its position during the "twenty years of inner corruption" in Nasser's schools.

Religion in Postprimary Schools

Over the long run, the decline in the proportion of the week's classes devoted to religious study at the primary level has been compensated for both by an increase in the number of periods and by a gradual increase in the number of years of postprimary schooling during which religious instruction was mandated. Religion had been emphasized throughout the monarchy in the Institutes of Domestic Economy, and in normal schools for teachers in kuttabs (both male and female), emphasizing the special responsibility of future mothers and elementary teachers in the moral education of the nation,[69] but in 1930, only one class per week of religious instruction was required in the first two years of the secondary curriculum. The content of this curriculum

Table 2 *Relative Time Devoted to Subjects—Primary Schools*

	1932	1963	1981
Religion	6%	11%	8%
Arabic	30	30	25
Arithmetic	15	16	16
Science	5	8	6
Social Studies	5	7	4
Physical Education	5	8	7
Music	—	4	4
Technical/Practical	13	16	8
Foreign Language	20	—	22

shows clearly the functionalization of religious doctrine and strongly contrasts the ritual-centeredness of either Azhari instruction or of peasant concern. Instead, it foregrounds the psychological, behavioral, sociological, and historical implications of the Islamic tradition. In the first year of secondary school, students were to learn about:

> The influence of Islam on self-improvement (*tahdhib al-nafs*) and behavior; giving examples of the impress of the Islamic religion on the life of the Arabs [such as] their reunification, the refinement of their character and the extirpation of evil deeds that were spread among them.
>
> The Glorious Qur'an: how it descended, the revelation, its collection and recording; a concise summary of what it contains of cultural and personal status matters, with the citation of some verses.
>
> The student memorizes fifteen Qur'anic verses and ten Prophetic traditions on various topics, with an understanding of their meaning.

In the second year of secondary school, five more topics completed the formal contribution of state schools to the religious development of the Egyptian adolescent:

[Divine] Messengers and the reason for their mission; their necessary attributes; their famous miracles; Muhammad, may God bless and save him; announcement that he is the seal of the Prophets and the Messenger of God unto all people.

The rivalry of leadership between Mecca and Medina; the cultural background of the Hijra.

The Way of the Prophet in speech and practice, and its derivation from the

[true] religion; the establishment of Islamic jurisprudence; the four orthodox schools; the best-known divisions of Islam (Sunni and Shi'i).

Consultation in Islam; freedom and equality in Islam; the rights of women in Islam, derived from the Book and the way of the Prophet; the various well-known innovations in religion.

The student memorizes fifteen Qur'anic verses, and ten Prophetic traditions on various topics, with an understanding of their meaning.[70]

Having mastered elementary doctrine and *'ibada* (worship) in primary school, students at the secondary stage were to devote themselves to character formation, Islamic history, basic religious institutions, and the religious principles that underlay and justified the country's emerging liberal political organization. Particularly worth noting is the manner in which the Qur'an was treated for purposes of memorization. God's revelation was no longer to be taken to heart in its thirty traditional sections and their subdivisions, or even in chapters; rather, each individual verse was to be treated as an entity, and memorized because of its connection to a certain topic. The achievement of understanding the verse, once the subject of an entire science of interpretation in traditional Islamic education, was now implicit in the verse's very selection and use, a clear parallel to European practice. During the two decades preceding the revolution, the amount of time assigned to religious instruction in the post-primary curriculum rose slowly but steadily,[71] and the subject matter shifted toward "concern with religious associations, attention to the location of prayer and the doing of pious works, help for the poor, and other social/religious values that underline the connection between religion as a subject of study and the society in which the student lives."[72] The political influence of the Muslim Brotherhood, whose support for the revolution was critical early on, manifested itself in the religious curriculum as a growing emphasis on personal piety and social responsibility.[73]

And the curriculum kept changing as new political realities emerged, new university entrance requirements were promulgated, and the demographics of the school system changed. The content of lessons followed that of the elementary schools in supporting socialist values. As Olivier Carré quotes from the preface of the 1958 ninth grade religious studies textbook:

Religious instruction is one of the most powerful factors in the preparation of a virtuous youth, who believes in his Lord and in his country, even as he works for the benefit of his society on the bases of socialism, democracy, and cooperation, all things called for and affirmed by religion.[74]

Religious instruction ensured "the values of loyalty to the nation and to its goals, which correspond to the goals of religion and its struggle in opposition to imperialism."[75] It sought, as one part of a comprehensive system of public mobilization, to provide an ideological path leading from the filial values of the family unit to the nationalist and socialist values of the various mass organizations into which the Egyptian citizen would be ushered in his transition from the school and family to the workplace. The presence of religious instruction in preparatory and secondary schools beginning in the 1920s and 1930s indicates an important realization on the part of planners and politicians that the absolute distinction between the religious mentality of the Azharites and the modern mentality supposedly inculcated by the modern educationist was perhaps a false one; or at least that it was less important than the potential power of Islamic symbols to carry a number of different meanings, a feature too important to ignore in the age of the newspaper and the radio.

In the early years of the monarchy, too, Islamic culture took on a nationalist tint that it could not have possessed at the time when European-style education was introduced into the country a hundred years before. Its use in the higher schools at that time was at least in part a reaction against the Euro-centeredness of elite education during the later years of Cromer's agency, when "third and fourth-year Egyptian students were following a history and government syllabus that might have come from Eton or Harrow."[76] By the end of the 1960s the function of Islamic instruction had shifted as the nature of the schools and the demographic characteristics of the students changed. No longer merely for the wealthy, higher schools became the last venue of centrally supervised socialization for large numbers of literate young people about to enter the work force, begin their own families, and become a political force either useful or dangerous to the state.

As the Egyptian educational system continues to expand physically, its supporters grow ever more convinced of its moral impact, as it "rais[es] successive generations of children and youth according to firm fundamentals of science and faith, implant[s] spiritual and religious values, principles and ideals and creat[es] advanced abilities and talents."[77] The state's responsibility for the creation of individual values is paramount, since values and behavior are intimately linked to economic and social well-being. Egypt's Second Five-Year Plan for Socio-Economic Development described the relationship this way:

The individual is the main focus of any effort to build a society and the most important component of development. The state has devoted special attention to his spiritual and intellectual formation, taking care to place him on the right course to absorb the knowledge and technological achievements of the modern age. Education strengthens and increases the positive traits in an individual's personality and helps him discover and overcome any negative traits he may have. . . . The state works to integrate the functions of education by imbedding and developing religious values, responsible behavior, self-dignity and sense of individualism . . . promoting spiritual, behavioral and educational values in the young to provide a basis for future behavior, while implanting national values, loyalty and patriotism.[78]

In the following chapters the focus will shift from the historical transformation of religious instruction in the public school to the institutional context in which Islamic messages are constructed and delivered to the urban Egyptian child. Highlighting how the parental role of the state is expressed in various types of religious education programs, the next three chapters will show how religious instruction has become one of the strategic arenas in which political tensions and conflicts are fought out. Central to these conflicts is increased public discussion of the moral problems and prospects of Egyptian children (*awlad*) and youth (*shabab*), which have become, respectively, the primary symbols of the country's long-term aspirations, and of its current political and economic difficulties.

PART III

What matters is that lives do not serve as models; only stories do that. And it is a hard thing to make up stories to live by. We can only retell and live by the stories we have read or heard. We live our lives through texts. They may be read, or chanted, or experienced electronically, or come to us, like the murmerings of our mothers, telling us what conventions demand. Whatever their form or medium, these stories have formed us all; they are what we must use to make . . . new narratives.

Carolyn G. Heilbrun,
Writing a Woman's Life, 1988

The spiritual and cultural reservations that the Oriental peoples may have toward our technology will avail them not at all. The effects of technology do not occur at the level of opinions or concepts, but alter sense ratios or patterns of perception steadily and without resistance.

H. Marshall McLuhan,
The Medium Is the Message, 1975

CHAPTER 4

Learning about God

> *[Psychologically,] God is not the creation of the child alone. God is found in the family. Most of the time he is offered by the parents to the child; he is found in everyday conversation, art, architecture, and social events. He is presented as invisible but nonetheless real. Finally, most children are officially introduced to the "house of God," a place where God supposedly dwells one way or the other. That house is governed by rules very different from any others; the child is introduced to ritual, to the official behavior he is expected to exhibit there, and to other events in which the encounter with God is socially organized and prearranged.*
>
> Ana-Maria Rizzuto, *The Birth of the Living God*, 1979[1]

Education is not, of course, confined to the classroom. The whole manufactured environment that humans create and in which we live is both a record of our ultimate concerns and a silent instructor in constant attendance. Egypt's public environment is swamped with the signifiers of religion: on signs, billboards, murals, advertisements, radio and television programs, public events, the covers of books and magazines for sale on every streetcorner, and in the style of public dress and grooming.[2] The ubiquity of religious messages is one result of a decades-long struggle between the state and the forces of the Islamic "revival," whose more spectacular manifestations are splashed across the covers of international news magazines and scholarly journals alike under the heading of "fundamentalism," "fanaticism," and "extremism." The rise of political opposition movements has contributed to this deepening hegemony of Islamic discourse and been attributed variously to a primitive mentality, to cynical political manipulations, to the frustration of youth, to the disillusionment of the middle-aged, or to poverty, anti-Western hysteria and the rage bred by political impotence or persecution. But to allow the Islamic Trend (*al-tayyar al-islami*),[3] in Egypt or elsewhere, to be defined by its most violent or exotic manifestations, is to allow the geopolitical security concerns triggered by the 1979 Iranian Revolution and the 1992 Algerian coup to act as a conceptual filter for one's examination of the changing Egyptian religious landscape.

Doing so results in a serious misreading of reality. Sadat's 1981 assassination by the Jihad organization, a continuing series of attacks on government ministers, intellectuals and tourists in the capital, the recent guerrilla insurgency in Upper Egypt and its savage police response, have drawn an enormous amount of international attention. But these are not, arguably, either very typical events, or very important for understanding the Islamic Trend's social origins, manifestations, or long-range significance. Focusing solely on these events is as senseless as to construct a roadmap on which only freeway cloverleafs are drawn, unconnected and isolated from each other by wide blank spaces that mask the smaller but more important routes that bear the mundane commerce of everyday life. Given this, much of Euroamerican popular (and elite) perception of Islamic movements in the Middle East either confuses them for "Islam" itself, or denies that these movements could have arisen except for the operation of entirely pathological processes, as if the freeway cloverleaf were an anomalous knotted inflammation on a seamless plane rather than a regular intersection of rectilinear paths.

Egypt's Islamic Trend, far from being an essentially violent fringe political movement, is pervasive, persistent, and normal, an immense counterculture whose effects on individuals and society do not remain confined to the immediate adherents of specifically political movements and organizations.[4] Its most characteristic manifestations are not unpredictable outbreaks of sectarian violence, bombing conspiracies, or the angry denunciation of creative artists (whether Salman Rushdie or Neguib Mahfouz), but rather the manifold changes it has created in the way educated Egyptians practice, apprehend, and represent their religious heritage. Nevertheless, the Trend's signs are often striking, and even partially quantifiable. Between 1981 and 1987, for example, while the enrollment in arts and humanities faculties at Egyptian universities increased by a total of 8.2 percent overall, the number of students in the Faculty of Islamic Law at al-Azhar increased by 42 percent, and the enrollment at the Faculty of Theology increased by slightly more than 70 percent.[5] Between 1983 and 1986, the number of monthly public sector religious periodicals published in Egypt increased from four to five, but their circulation more than tripled, from 181,000 to 558,000.[6]

At the national universities, student attitudes reflect the extent to which religious questions have become living concerns for educated youth. Dr. Samia al-Khashab's 1988 survey of Cairo University students indicates that they perceive the official religious establishment to be derelict in its duties and ineffective in meeting the religious needs of young people, while being optimistic about the role of private sector religious organizations for fulfilling such needs. Over 80 percent of the 450 students she interviewed (randomly chosen from the university's several faculties) told her that they thought *higab* (modest dress in which the head and arms are covered) should be required of all Muslim women, and more than half (some estimates range as high as three-quarters) of Cairene women over the age of puberty actually dress this way.[7] More people are praying, more people are reading about Islam and listening to its preachers, more people are discovering consciously the salience of religious ideas and practices to their private and public lives, than did a generation ago.

If we are to make sense of these developments within the institutional context of Egyptian society, we cannot dismiss religious concerns as benighted survivals of earlier social stages, or merely "inflammations" symptomatic of social pathology and political strife.[8] Instead, we must see them as perennial questions that persist in an active manner, adapting and reproducing themselves within and between generations through increasingly complex interactions with institutions and communications media whose own advent was supposed to *reduce* rather than increase the influence of religious ideas in society. One of these institutions has been compulsory popular schooling. As we saw in the last chapter, the growth of the secular education system in Egypt has encouraged rather than discouraged attachment to Islamic culture, contrary to the expectations of educational theorists who encouraged schooling as a remedy to "traditional" mentalities. The Islamic content of mass schooling is just one aspect of the general process through which Islam and secularism have embraced one another. But it contributes to making that embrace a mutual choke hold that won't allow either to escape again unharmed. On the one hand, every one of the major political parties in the country has been scrambling for the support of the partisans of the religious awakening since it became apparent that catering to religious concerns delivers votes.[9] Once having committed themselves to Islamic rhetoric, it may be difficult for any of them to pull back from promoting an Islamic future for Egypt. On the other hand, the sacred tradition has also committed itself fully to the products and processes of secular life, a retreat from which might be even more threatening. The more firmly entrenched those ideas are in public space, the more difficult it is to dispose of them, and the more pervasive their influence. Islam makes full use of the communications revolution and the industrial economy to manifest itself in every conceivable medium, saturating the physical environment with messages, objects, structures, and signs whose power emerges from the "reciprocation of thought in worked matter, and of worked matter into thought."[10] Objects and images that become the foci of human interaction evoke enormous social energy, which feeds back into their continued production and elaboration.

In fact, the shape and the sensory content of the public environment is central to the question of how social reproduction is culturally mediated. The Islamic messages in Egyptian public space, including those within the walls of the school, are not merely manifestations or examples of the hegemony of Islamic discourse in Egypt—they are one of the historical and psychological sources of that hegemony. They have created for themselves a public need, which Marx recognized as one of the processes through which goods and their manufacture transform the world:

> Production . . . creates the consumer. Production not only supplies a material for the need, but it also supplies a need for the material. . . . The object of art—like every other product—creates a public which is sensitive to art and enjoys beauty. . . . Thus production produces consumption (1) by creating the material for it; (2) by determining the manner of consumption; and (3) by creating the products, initially posited by it as objects, in the form of a need felt by the consumer.[11]

More recent European sociology recognizes the same processes in family and institutional pedagogy, which "consecrat[e] religious or cultural goods of salvation as worthy of being pursued, and . . . produc[e] the need for these goods by the mere fact of imposing their consumption."[12] In other words, education that is aimed at implanting specific beliefs in the minds of the young, such as religious indoctrination in schools, not only creates a specific ideology, but creates the very need for one.[13]

On a practical level, education and technological innovation both widen the influence of public religious messages, expanding the range of individuals who can enter the ideological trade either as producers or consumers. As a result of this, Eickelman has suggested, a "great transformation" is taking place in the way that religious authority is distributed in the Muslim world, as

> socially recognized carriers of religious learning are no longer confined to those who have studied accepted texts in circumstances equivalent to those of the mosque-universities, with their bias toward favoring members of the elite. . . . The carriers of religious knowledge will increasingly be anyone who can claim a strong Islamic commitment, as is the case among many of the educated urban youth. Freed from mnemonic domination, religious knowledge can be delineated and interpreted in a more abstract and flexible fashion. A long apprenticeship under an established man of learning is no longer a necessary prerequisite to legitimizing one's own religious knowledge. Printed and mimeographed tracts and the clandestine dissemination of "lessons" on cassettes have begun to replace the mosque as the center for disseminating visions of Islam that challenge those offered by the state.[14]

Technological innovation helps make ideas that were formerly restricted to the literate directly available to the masses of the nonliterate as well (through audiotapes, television, radio, videotape), after being filtered through intermediaries who select, interpret, and comment upon the ideas that were previously the domain of the specialist. Participation in this mass-media culture is one of the nationalist rituals of the modern age, fulfilling both the communication functions and the group solidarity functions that anthropologists have attributed to ritual of other sorts (it was Hegel, Benedict Anderson informs us, who first identified newspaper reading as a substitute for morning prayers).[15] Particularly in the context of group- and party-sponsored media, the reading of a newspaper can act as a rite of communion as well as a public signal.

But despite the predictions of modernization theorists that the spread of media would hasten the development of a "modern" consciousness in the Middle East by "enlarg[ing] a person's view of the world ('opinion range') by increasing his capacity to imagine himself in new and strange situations ('empathy')),"[16] it is clear that media exposure can and does act as a powerful tool of propaganda as well, restricting or confirming as easily as broadening one's perspective. The growth of book publishing in the Arab world resulted in, among other things, at least five different editions of the infamous European anti-Semitic tract "The Protocols of the Elders of Zion" being available for sale on the streets of Cairo in 1989.[17] The medium is not the only message.

Postmodern Knowledge

Communications media and educational institutions of all types are interactive, not only in the sense that they act together in creating an environment that helps shape us as individuals, but in the sense that each incessantly feeds on the imagery and discourses of the others. As we will see, Egyptian mothers talk about didactic moral stories they have heard on the radio and passed on to their children. School textbooks portray eager parents guiding their youngsters' moral development with the aid of Qur'anic quotations. Television programs interview young children at work memorizing the Qur'an in afterschool programs. Religious scholars trained in the "traditional" atmosphere of al-Azhar issue *fatwas* (nonbinding legal opinions) on the use of prerecorded calls to prayer, through the venue of weekly newspaper advice columns.

New communications media and new technologies of intellectual production do not drive out old ones, but merely alter their use and significance, often bolstering older forms on which they depend (as computers depend on printed manuals to explain their function). Even in reinforcing and extending the role of written communication, electronic media also subtly alter the social significance of writing. Once the primary privileged technology of communication, because it requires specialized training for both the producer and the recipient, writing has been bypassed in terms of prestige and ease of control by broadcast (though not, significantly, audio- or videotaped) communication, because the latter requires large capital outlays and technical expertise, thus allowing relatively tight control on production. For the recipient, however, electronic media are far more democratic, obviating the special training needed for reading written or print communications. New media have not replaced old ones, but have merely "complicated everything endlessly."[18]

Two of these complications are of potential interest. The first is the phenomenon of "secondary orality," the use of oral communication fostered not by the absence of writing and print (as in societies without written languages), but by the advent of the electronically mediated voice.[19] As Brinkley Messick has shown in a series of works on the culture of writing in Yemen,[20] Islamic scholarship in the Middle East has historically been centered on the importance of authorial presence, meaning that the production of written documents (whether in scholarship or legal practice) has always been secondary to memory, recitation, and the reproduction of the authoritative presence of the human voice. Texts, considered unreliable and ambiguous without human interpreters or witnesses, were byproducts of legal and pedagogical practice rather than their focus. Teaching relied on the oral transmission from master to student of key texts and their commentaries. Writing was seen as an alienation of that relationship, and required living testimony for its validation. As the culture of print communications spread through the Middle East in the late nineteenth and early twentieth centuries, this unique relationship had largely been lost, as printed communication — through its status as the voice of the modern state — began to acquire its own unique authority. With the advent of radio, television, audio and video recording, and newer computer technologies, some of the dynamic of oral communication can be recaptured and "appear . . . to restore *presence*, which for the alternative advantages of record and durability writing systems had moved away from."[21] The political effectiveness of taped copies of Ayatollah Khomeini's sermons in immediately prerevolutionary Iran testifies to the power — both logistical and motivational — of technologies that can capture some of the features of oral communication missing in print.[22]

On the eve of the Second World War British colonial officials took new oral media seriously enough to use them consciously — like all governments since — as instruments of rule. In the early days of radio broadcasting in Egypt they quickly recognized the special nature of the new technology, so that in 1939 His Majesty's Ambassador wrote, in a confidential memorandum on the B.B.C.'s Arabic broadcasts, that

> I am . . . inclined to agree with the body of opinion which favours talks on Arab-Muslim history, literature and civilization generally. . . . The possibilities of educational broadcasts is . . . immense, but development of the programme on these lines should be cautious and tentative. . . . Owing to the struggle in the East between the new and the old, between the supporters of Western and Eastern cultures, the Egypto-Arab world is passing through phases of hesitation and complexity, and in this realm we must be cautious not to rush in where even Orientals fear to tread. For instance, it is not to Great Britain's interest to encourage the reactionary obscurantism of the Islamic movement in Egypt encouraged by the Palace and cynical Muslim clerics for obvious political reasons. This movement leads to increased xenophobia and has an adverse effect on Anglo-Egyptian cooperation. Too much pandering . . . to the Islamic theological and cultural past would be

as dangerous as entirely to ignore the aspects of Arab-Muslim history and civilization which appeal strongly even to the "westerners" in the Egypto-Arab world today. In other words, attention should be paid to these aspects of Arab civilization which have a universal appeal and are not in contradiction to the modern Eastern movement towards Western civilization.[23]

Some things have changed little in fifty years. Today, Egyptian film and television producers generally ignore religious issues in most dramatic production, segregating them — with the partial exception of Ramadan programming — into a ghetto of religious chat shows, songs, and televised sermons. But the pedagogical outlook remains much the same. Egypt's director of television film and serial production told Lila Abu-Lughod in 1990 that

Egypt is one of the developing nations and we as a country are very concerned with the cultural education of our people. . . . Our most important goal in relation to the citizens is to help individuals become cultured. We must educate them, teach them the basics of morality and religious duty. The individual needs direction. He needs information and we need to inculcate the spirit of patriotism, morality, religion, courage, and enterprise. We have found that the best means to reach the individual is through drama. It works like magic.[24]

Part of the magic of this broadcast drama is its portability. Like us, Egyptians carry with them the transistorized machines that relay it, taking their radios to the beach, fixing them in their cars, placing television sets in positions of honor in their homes, offering them like sweets to visiting guests. Like the scattered village kuttabs of the nineteenth century, the infrastructure is in place wherever there are people. Bedouins in the Sinai draw on Saudi radio programs for folklore, news, and for the epic tribal poems they no longer memorize themselves. The same is true of the western desert, where Abu-Lughod's hosts explained, "If you don't tell the stories you forget them. Now that there are radios, we don't tell stories anymore."[25] Instead, bedouins listen to taped and broadcast Qur'an recitations and Islamic lessons from Cairo or from Arabia, and are drawn — particularly the younger people, even over the opposition and the cynicism of their elders — to the "twin faces of modernity," secular urban life and the Islamic Trend.[26]

The second complication of the new media is the fact that communications are commodities, and thus enter into the asymmetrical dynamics of market relations, state licensing and control, and popular taste.[27]

In his outline of the character of "postmodern knowledge," Jean-François Lyotard announced that

> the relationship of the suppliers and users of knowledge to the knowledge they supply and use is now tending . . . to assume the form already taken by the relationship of commodity producers and consumers to the commodities they produce and consume — that is, the form of value. Knowledge is and will be produced in order to be sold, it is and will be consumed in order to be valorized in a new production: in both cases, the goal is exchange. Knowledge ceases to be an end in itself, it loses its "use-value."[28]

Though the notion of an altogether devalued and commoditized information is seductive, we are not yet at the point — particularly given our interest in the functionalization of religious knowledge in the Egyptian school — where knowledge has entirely lost its rhetorical and persuasive function, its use value. Politics is not yet wholly subsumed by the market. But Lyotard's suggestion does point toward one of the mechanisms responsible for the dilemma faced by Egypt's political and cultural elites. The operation of a market in cultural goods, information, and knowledge triggers multiple conflicts between it and the state (and the state's "official reproductive institutions" like the school). In capitalist or state capitalist societies, politically sanctioned institutions of cultural reproduction have an interest both in the reproduction of market relations and also in constraining the specific content of cultural products that might threaten established institutions or populations of culture producers.[29] In Egypt, the authority of the ʿulama, the "traditional" state-trained and subsidized religious scholars, is under threat by a new market-driven economy of religious commodities produced by private sector companies, secular intellectuals (psychologists, lawyers, physicians, and academics), and independent movements like the Muslim Brotherhood and the smaller Islamic groups, which are the political and military vanguard of the Islamic Trend. The state under Mubarak has responded to this new informational economy not by restraining it heavily, but by entering the fray with products carrying the invisible imprimatur of al-Azhar, the Ministry of Religious Endowments, the Supreme Council on Islamic Affairs, and subsidiary organizations.[30] Later we will examine some of the political repercussions of this strategy. But we will begin here at the beginning, by sketching the multiple social contexts in which parents and their growing children are treated to stories — verbal, written, or electronic — about Islam.

Religious education participates fully in the urban sprawl of the postmodern world, and thus one of its chief characteristics is its practical decenteredness. Socialization is a diffuse set of processes that has multiple sources, and whose outcomes are as various as the patterns of intersecting ripples in a pond, always moving and changing. This decenteredness is reflected here as a series of vignettes, each situated in a different social arena: the home, the school, the public agency, the holiday celebration, the pages of the newspaper. In presenting these vignettes, I wish less to claim that they are "typical" or representative than to show how they exemplify the rhetoric of moral instruction as developed by Egyptian educators over the last century. We will begin, as Egyptians do, with the family.

Just Like Getting Tall

About the time Egyptian Minister of Education Neguib el-Hilali Pasha was championing a new mode of moral instruction in Egyptian schools, Samia ʿAbd al-Rahman entered the first grade in a public school near her home in Alexandria. Graduating from high school in 1956, the year of the Suez crisis, she left Egypt for the first time to attend university in the United States, first at a large land-grant institution in Indiana, then moving east to take a master's degree at Boston University. Returning to Egypt, she began work as a journalist, then taught in one of the Gulf states for several years before coming back to Cairo to stay. She lives in a worn but comfortable apartment in Giza with her daughter, Nadia (fifteen in 1989), and writes on culture and the arts for various magazines.

Samia calls herself a "committed Muslim," and wears what is colloquially known as *higab,* modest dress, although she herself prefers to reserve that term for face-veiling, calling her dress *"al-zayy al-islami,"* Islamic dress. Like many of Egypt's journalists and intellectuals, she has spent time in prison, the last episode during Sadat's September 1981 roundup of suspected subversives. To this day, she bears gratitude toward the small militant group that assassinated Sadat on 6 October of that year, and still recounts to friends the dramatic story of how the joyous news reverberated down the concrete halls of the women's prison on that day. These days Samia struggles, like other middle-class Egyptians, with the difficult economic climate. She spends a lot of time on the phone with colleagues and editors, discussing meetings, conferences, story deadlines, payment. In the crowded sitting room of her fourth-story flat, she does her writing — by hand — and receives guests, to the sound of the buses rumbling down the street below. She will not shake hands with men but will converse, argue, query, and joke with them about topics as diverse as international politics, women's rights, and the Philips stereo system she just bought while at a conference in Denmark.

I asked Samia about how she herself experienced the history of the school in Egypt in the 1940s, a country still under British military occupation; a country less congested, quieter, but still in the process of making sense of its multiple identities as its foreign and domestic political elites, its indigenous bureaucracy and working classes, and its multinational commercial, technical, and professional establishments fought over the soul of the country. In the 1940s, the high point of the power of the Muslim Brotherhood as well as of the vision of a secular postwar internationalism, was there such a thing as "Islamic education" taught in the schools? "Yes and no," she replied.

You must understand that in my generation my country was trying to practice European education and European *tarbiya* [upbringing], thinking that this might be the better way to do it, what they called the modern way. There were some things then that were referred to as *frangi* or *afrangi* [foreign]. Like bathrooms, for example. In my house now I have two bathrooms, one *afrangi*, and one *baladi*, or local. And the *baladi* is really more sanitary, you know, because you clean off with water. Buildings that are built nowadays, though, only have *afrangi* bathrooms. But in my generation, if you did something according to the European way, it was called *"à la frangi,"* spelled the French way with the "à" and the "la" [i.e., rather than the Arabic *'ala*]. We would never wear very short dresses, of course, or anything without sleeves, but neither did we think of covering our faces or our hair; this was the time when women were taking off their *higab*, which really refers to the veil over the face, although they now call it *niqab*. In school we learned the Qur'an and Hadiths, and *adab*; that's what they called *tarbiya islamiyya* then. And also at that time, the teacher would tell us that we should cover our heads, but unfortunately nobody heeded her.

During my generation, Islamic education was something obvious. You did it because that was just the only way to raise children. I grew up in a house where I saw my parents fasting and praying, and I learned from that. My parents were raising me without having to say that it was Islamic education. Now, when I'm raising Nadia, I have to be sure that what I'm doing is Islamic. When I was a girl the only alternative was new, and was considered a shame, like wearing sleeveless dresses. My parents still talked about things being permitted [*halal*] and forbidden [*haram*]. We weren't allowed to have friendships between men and women. So when my brother's friends, my older brother's friends would come to the house, I would answer the door, because I was just a little girl, but then when we saw who it was I had to make sure that my older sisters had all gone to the back part of the house so they wouldn't be out with these boys. That was the only way.[31]

Her ambivalence about westernized Egyptian and authentic Islamic cultures was expressed in the most fundamental way, by referring to bodily function, disposition, and display. Gender segregation, clothing, hygiene, fasting and prostration are the outward and visible signs of a socially unobjectified Islam that was "the only way." On one level, her story distinguishes sharply between the public domain of the school ("my country was trying to practice European education and European *tarbiya*, thinking this might be the better way to do it") and the private domain of the home ("Islamic education was something obvious. You did it because it was the only way to raise children"). But on another level it invokes the Europeanization that has penetrated quite literally into the most intimate parts of the home. The ambiguity persists in that her own family's standards of dress were contradicted by her teacher, a public functionary who counseled modest dress despite her representing a "European *tarbiya*." Changes and conflicts penetrate the public and private spheres indiscriminately and inconsistently.

But clearly the practical assimilation of everyday adab precedes the doctrinal formulations of religion both in the daily activities of the family and in the mind of the child, whose first exposure to life as a Muslim is within the family. Samia's story illustrates in both empirical and in ideal terms the primary importance of parental practices, and the child's imitation, *taqlid*, in religious socialization. When I asked, she denied that her own daughter Nadia ever asked her specific questions about Islam, because it was such a natural part of the home environment: "This development in her was so natural, it was just like getting tall. Everything was so normal to her, that I never remember discussing anything with her in order to convince her to do something."[32]

Taqlid, Egyptians say, is the most important agent of religious education in the early years of childhood. Before the age of seven or so, they make little effort to teach children about religious duties or practices; children are portrayed as naturally taking on the habits of their parents.

And of course the children imitate, so that when they see the parents doing prayers, the child will put something over her head and join in naturally. And at the same time you'll be teaching the child right from wrong, and things that are allowed and things that are prohibited. Like sometimes in America you'll make a small pig, as a toy, for example, or have a little pig in a story. But here pigs are forbidden [*haram*], pigs are dirty, so to pigs you say *"ixxs!"* We say *fil* [elephant] instead. I remember once I was telling Nadia a story that I had heard on the radio when I was a child, about an elephant, a frog, and two pigeons. Now, the story goes that the elephant was very cruel, and was destroying the nest of the pigeons, and saying, Oh, I'm going to crush and destroy this nest and destroy you both! But the pigeons escaped, and along with the frog they planned to make revenge. The frog would distract the elephant, and then the two pigeons would come over and peck out both its eyes. But when I got to this part, Nadia screamed and said, *"la! la! fil halal! fil halal!"* [No, no! Elephants are OK!] So I had to change the end of the story so that the elephant apologized for destroying the pigeon's nest, and in the end the pigeons and the frog forgave him, and Nadia said to me, "*aywa, fil hilw*!" [Yeah, elephants are sweet]. We say *fil*, or we say *qutt* [cat], because *qutt* is all right, but *kalb* [dog], we never use *kalb* because it's *ixxs* like the pig. When the child sees a dog in the street, then, they shy away, because they know the dog is *haram*. So all these things, like knowing what's *haram* and what's *halal*, and imitating and prayer, these things are just like learning to walk, it's all learning matter-of-fact, like learning to walk.[33]

"I remember during Ramadan," another Egyptian writer recalls, "that I would try to fast, my sister and I, in imitation of the grownups, but the truth is that we couldn't hold out for long because we were so young at that time."[34] Children begin to practice fasting in earnest beginning at age nine or ten, usually for a few days at first, then adding more each year until the age of twelve. For children whose parents also fast on Mondays and Thursdays during the months of Sha'ban and Ragab, the two months before Ramadan, there is extra practice, but "whether children fast at all depends on whether their parents do; some children just never learn to do it."[35] One Egyptian communist told me that he was having to take care of his four children alone for the first time, during Ramadan 1409 (1989), since his wife was on the *'umra* in Saudi Arabia. He fretted that he was having to be extra careful around the kids now, since the oldest one, at age twelve, was fasting for the first time that year, and he didn't want the boy to know that his father didn't fast. "I think he knows anyway," he added, shaking his head.[36]

Theoretically, parental influence operates through two separate channels, *al-wiratha*, "heredity," and *al-tarbiya*, "upbringing." With respect to the former, educated Egyptians believe that the child's inborn nature as a moral being has two sources. The first is its status as a human created by God.

> Every child is born *'ala fitra*. There's a famous saying [*hadith*] of our Prophet—God's peace and blessings upon him—where he says that every child is born *'ala fitra*, with a certain nature, a certain essence, and that essence is Islam. Later, it's the parents that make it Jewish or Christian, or whatever. If the mother is well educated—Islamically, I mean, not in the university—then she's picking up the child and saying "In the name of God" [*bismillah*], and "thank God" [*subhan allah*], and when the child burps she'll say "praise be to God" [*al-hamdu li-llah*], and if it coughs, "I take refuge in God" [*a'uzu bi-llah*]. And so the first words that the child hears are about Allah, and Allah is one of the first words the child learns to pronounce, along with mama and baba. And actually, you know that the first words that are supposed to be pronounced into the child's ear after it's born is the first part of the call to prayer [*izan*]: "God is great, God is great, there is no God but God!" [*allahu akbar, allahu akbar, la ilaha illa-llah*!]—but very softly, not loud! ["Not through a loudspeaker?" I asked jokingly. "No, not through a loudspeaker!" she laughed].[37]

The second innate source of children's moral character is the unique moral character of the parents, at least part of which is transmitted hereditarily to children.[38] This theme is a favorite of religious writers who encourage young people to select their mates on the basis of personal morality, manners, and knowledge of Islamic duties. The advice, according to these writers, is derived not from the science of genetics, but from the traditionally attested behavior (*sunna*) of the Prophet, which has been corroborated only recently by modern research in biology and psychology. The most widely cited hadith to this effect is the saying of the Prophet, "Choose for your sperm, for blood will tell."[39]

> This selection that the Messenger of Islam (God's peace and blessings upon him) addressed, numbers among the greatest scientific truths and educational theories of the modern age . . . for the science of heredity demonstrates that the child takes on the qualities of his parents, moral, physical, and intellectual, from birth. . . . And when sound hereditary factors are combined in the child with superior upbringing, the child attains the summit of religion and morals, and is exemplary in strength and virtue, well-behaved and noble.[40]

In addition to inherited factors, character is influenced by all the social practices that fall under the heading "*tarbiya*." The word *tarbiya* is derived from the causative form of the Arabic root *rbw* (to make or let grow, to raise, rear, bring up, teach, instruct, or breed). *Tarbiya* differs from *ta'lim* because "*ta'lim* just means education, teaching people knowledge. But *tarbiya* includes upbringing, and raising people to have values and *adab. Ta'lim* is included within the meaning of *tarbiya*."[41] Once the child is born, mothers and fathers bear different types of responsibility toward it, based largely on the child's age. Karim Shafik, a young father in his early thirties, worked in the creative department of an Islamic publishing house near Samia. When I asked him if he used any of the material his company produced in raising his own children, he told me,

> My oldest child is only five years old. And I really believe in the division of the child's life into three stages. During the first seven years, the child needs to be free to explore, to look at things and try things without any restrictions. If I gave them things like this, they might be interested in them, and they might not be, but I wouldn't be able to force them on them. During the second seven years, though, that's the time when you start to teach the child right from wrong, and correct from incorrect, and to discipline them and start to get them to pray, and so on. It's really that during the first seven years, the child should be the child of his mother, and she should take care of him and develop an emotional attachment to him, and supervise him as he plays and explores. And that, of course, is why we use women to take care of children in the nursery schools. But during the second seven years the child needs to be the son of his father, and learn things from him in a structured and more serious way.[42]

This three-stage division of childhood derives from a saying of the Prophet, "Play with your son [for] seven [years], then discipline him [for] seven [years], then be his friend [for] seven [years], then give free rein to him."[43] The hadith is widely quoted in literature on Islamic childrearing, and is recognized by educated people who, even if they don't cite the hadith itself, describe their own childrearing practices in its light. According to educational pundits the age from birth to seven years is "the stage of the cultivation of faith in the human psyche,"[44] before the child is required to master and perform the *'ibadat* (acts of worship). The mother's role in tarbiya is vital since she is the primary caregiver for younger children; it is the father's duty later to teach the child the Qur'an and, at age seven, begin to require him or her to do the daily prayers; this derives from another hadith, "Go through the prayers with your children [at] seven [years], then impose it upon them [at] ten, and separate them in their beds," the latter referring to the segregation of male and female children before the onset of puberty.[45] "They should start [praying] by age seven," an elementary school teacher told me, exemplifying this hadith,

That's when the parents should really teach the children — both boys and girls — to pray, and then after they're ten, they should do the prayers on their own, and if they don't, the parent can make them, compel them to do the prayers. But my own children, when they see me doing the prayers, they imitate me, and learn to do the same motions, at a much earlier age than seven, when they're just little. It's the parents' job to be a good model for their children, because then the children will learn by seeing with their eyes and doing the same thing.[46]

School as the House of God

But as we have seen, parental responsibility for the moral education of children is not exclusive, and has in many particulars been assumed by the state. The parents' or community's contribution to socialization has long been recognized as incomplete, as affirmed by the colonial conception of the school as a place designed "to equip the pupil with sufficient knowledge to take care of his own interests in his own station of life." And since "the school-centered authority of the nation-state"[47] in Egypt revolves around a nucleus of ideas including that of Islamic legitimacy, the school becomes the first, and in some ways the primary, public institution "in which the encounter with God is socially organized and prearranged."

When I asked an elementary school teacher why schools teach Islam, when that should be the parent's responsibility, she immediately repeated the reasoning of earlier educational theorists who equated religious study with hygiene and civics:

It's a basic subject, like science or English or anything else. Of course it's the responsibility of the parents to teach the kids the most basic things about Islam, like how to pray, and this is right, and this is wrong, and to do this, and not to do that. But beyond that, the school teaches them about it, because not all parents, not all families, can do this, or know enough themselves about the religion.[48]

Apart from the rather general aim of teaching children right from wrong, educational planners in Egypt have more specific political goals for religious study in primary schools, because "the Primary stage is the basic framework for the formation of the personality and ideas of young people [*al-shabab*], and we need more than anything else to strengthen this framework through true religious education which fortifies them against surges of extremism [*al-tatarruf*] and epidemic intellectual trends."[49] As part of the continuing functionalization of the religious tradition, Islamic curricula from the primary level on up have been targeted, since the mid-1980s, at reducing young people's susceptibility to "political Islam," another shorthand term for the oppositional aspect of the Islamic Trend.

It is here that matters become more complicated, for although there is, in theory, something like a unified curriculum (or at least a single set of approved textbooks), the country had, in the late 1980s, five different kinds of primary schools. Apart from the schools of the foreign communities (where a few Egyptian children attend along with the children of German, British, French, and American expatriates), all satisfy the curriculum requirements of the Ministry of Education, and lead to the conferral of the primary certificate after the fifth or sixth grade.[50] Three types of schools are administered by government agencies: general primary schools are administered by the Ministry of Education, as are the relatively new "experimental language schools," which teach some subjects in Arabic and others (usually math and science) in a foreign language, generally English or French. Al-Azhar maintains its own system of primary, preparatory, and secondary schools, which feed students into al-Azhar University.[51] Experimental language schools enroll only a tiny number of Egyptian students: in 1986, fewer than twenty-four thousand at all educational levels from the primary through secondary grades. Significantly, the al-Azhar system has continued to expand more rapidly than the general primary system during President Husni Mubarak's tenure in office; the number of al-Azhar primary institutes increased by 85 percent, and the number of students by 125 percent, in the six years after Sadat's death.

Enrollment in primary education is extensive but not universal in Egypt. The Egyptian Fertility Survey, based on information collected between 1976 and 1979, indicated that 75 percent of Egyptian children (63 percent of girls and 88 percent of boys) of primary school age were actually enrolled in school. Between 1976 and 1986, the population between ages five and fourteen increased by almost a third, while the number of pupils enrolled in primary schools increased by nearly half due to an energetic program of school-building and promotion. Unfortunately, the rate of increase in the number of students has been nearly double the rate of increase in the number of schools and classrooms, leading to a steady increase in average class size and the institution of split shifts in schools around the country. The government has claimed, dubiously, that over 96 percent of eligible students are enrolled in primary school.[52] Most studies show wide disparities in enrollment between boys and girls, between urban and rural areas, and between Upper and Lower Egypt.

Finally, there are private schools. Unfortunately, statistics are not published regularly on Egypt's more than sixteen hundred private schools, which are under the nominal supervision of the Ministry of Education. Often criticized for their high costs and occasionally nontraditional curricula (some private schools offer subjects like horseback riding or Montessori-type programs),[53] private schools are popular with Egyptian families who can afford to pay for a higher quality of education than that available at most public schools. Property owners, businessmen, military officers, and government officials are particularly likely to enroll their children in private schools, and even minor public sector employees will make extra sacrifices to scrape together tuition money. Charging tuition ranging from a few hundred to a few thousand pounds per year, private primary schools in Egypt are often language schools, offering part of their curricula exclusively in foreign languages, like the government's experimental language schools. Some of them also offer costly training that public institutions cannot afford, like computer literacy courses from very early grades. Though private schools follow the Ministry of Education's curriculum, administer standard tests, and are regularly inspected by governorate-level educational bureaucrats, they are exempt from the public school's requirement that they hire only members of the teacher's union, that is, people with degrees in education. Many private school teachers are only secondary school graduates, or have university degrees from science, arts, or commerce faculties.

The Nasr Language School

The history of the school represents a routinization of institutional charisma. Historically, and from the perspective of social planners, the school is a unique tool for the achievement of social equilibrium, political progress, and prosperity. But from the perspective of its clients, it is either an important status granting institution or an unremarkable and sometimes unavoidable staple of the life cycle. Because local ministerial oversight and the worldwide culture of schooling both limit the range of variation, the reestablishment of a tradition of private schooling has done little structurally to differentiate the public from the private school, either in Egypt or anywhere else. The differences between public and private sector institutions in Egypt lie primarily in funding level, while the differences between individual institutions depend upon the background, energy, and commitment of owners, principals, and staff. Their gatekeeping function ensures that a single accepted model of education characterizes both public and private schools. But private schools have a marginal advantage over public in preparing students for success on state examinations and in private sector hiring. In an ironic twist stemming from the fiscal and logistical problems of extending state primary education universally, private sector efforts have gained back the prestige that state schools once enjoyed over unstandardized, unlicensed kuttabs.

The Nasr Language School in the eastern suburb of Masr al-Gadida occupies a three-story 1940s-vintage villa at the intersection of two quiet, tree-lined streets, across from a tiny bookstore and a Mercedes-Benz repair shop. In 1988–89, Nasr was owned by Mme. Hala Sharif, the tall, elegant, chain-smoking wife of a senior official in the Ministry of Defense. She had inherited the property from her father but had never lived there, so when, in the mid-1970s, her husband began traveling outside of Egypt as a military attaché, she rented the villa on a long-term lease to a man she assumed was planning to live there himself. After returning to Egypt in 1986, she found that the renter had turned the building into a private primary school, and when the lease expired she faced the choice of buying the school from him, or moving him out entirely and facing the expense of reconverting the villa into a residence. Though she had never run a school, she did have some business experience, and decided to make a go of it.

Like the owner of a private company, the principal of an Egyptian private school is its absolute master, answerable only to the inspectors who visit from the Ministry of Education to check the books and year-end grade sheets. The teachers at Nasr, without degrees in education, and thus not eligible to join the national Teachers Union, were employed entirely at her discretion, a fact that was to cause a great deal of trouble some months after my first visit. Two weeks before the 1989–90 school year was to start, Mme. Hala, tired of being a school principal and contemplating a move overseas, sold the school to a pious electrical engineer, who summarily fired all of the teachers because the school was an English language school and none of the teachers had degrees in English. Though still collecting their pay — the younger teachers made between £E 70 and £E 150 ($28 to $60) a month — until new teachers could be hired, the former staff were eligible for none of the social security benefits available through membership in the Teachers Union, and feared that they would be without any employment for the coming year. The new owner himself had no previous school administration experience but was intensely interested in education and had spent the previous few years studying the subject in his spare time.

The facility he bought worked well enough. While Mme. Hala owned the school, sun porches and bedrooms had been converted into classroom space. The sitting room was now the principal's office and the wide hallway at the foot of the staircase provided display space for children's artwork. A former walled garden now served as a dusty playground and assembly yard where children began the school day with a civic ritual imported a century ago by the British: physical education in the form of military drill.[54] Each morning the age- and size-graded ranks of children marched in place while saluting the flag and singing a shrill version of the national anthem, "My Country," followed by a pledge of allegiance and the rhythmic chanting of "Gum-huriyya — Masr al-Arabiyya! Gum-huriyya — Masr al-Arabiyya!" (A-rab Repub-lic of E — gypt!)

For most grades, religion was taught every other day, alternating with Arabic. Mme. Mona Hamdi taught the fifth, third, and second grade religion classes. In her mid-forties, she was one of the older Muslim teachers, and the only one who did not cover her hair, which she wore in a short permanent. Her small fifth grade class — thirteen girls and two boys — met in a tiny room built from a converted porch, with a green corrugated fiberglass roof. The space was separated from the large fourth grade class next door only by a row of rust-colored wooden shutters. There was room for ten low two-pupil desks arranged one behind the other on either side of an aisle only slightly more than a foot wide. Strips of wallpaper with drawings of wide-eyed children and posters made from newspaper clippings about the president shared the walls with Arabic translations of Disney comic books suspended by the crease over strings tacked into the plaster. Behind the teacher's desk a poster diagrammed the heart in red and blue magic marker; a section of wall between two sets of shutters bore a carefully hand-drawn map of Egypt in black, and some posters illustrating simple English sentences: "What is this for?" "It is for sugar."

I first visited Nasr in Ramadan 1409 (April 1989), and the students were already familiar with the material. Some of the children had memorized their entire books in preparation for year-end examinations. Teachers spent class time going back over material that had been learned, having children read aloud, either alone or in unison, correcting their pronunciation, asking questions and expounding upon points raised in the lesson. Mme. Mona talked to the children about Ramadan. She followed the outline of the book, but added points, freestyle, as they occurred to her: Ramadan is the month in which the Qur'an descended from heaven, but the Qur'an was written down only later, during the time of the Caliph 'Uthman, although the number of daily prayers had been fixed by the Prophet Muhammad after his journey through the seven heavens.

"Who has to fast during Ramadan?" she asked suddenly. Students shot their hands up and clamored to answer. For some of them, this was the first year during which they themselves were fasting. A girl rose and replied that the sick do not need to fast, nor do travelers. Mme. Mona nodded, adding rapidly that pregnant women and the insane do not fast either, and asking the class, "What are the pillars of Islam?" After another student replied, she had the entire class repeat them again in unison. "Who can tell me about the *zakat?*"Another girl stood and said that it is money paid by all Muslims for the support of the poor and the needy, the collectors of the alms themselves and for recent and potential converts to Islam, for the freeing of slaves, for aiding debtors and those who do good works for God and country, and for indigent travelers. Mme. Mona reminded students about the percentage due on different categories of property, and that the money was due before the celebration of the *'Id al-Fitr*, otherwise it is not considered *zakat*.

At the teacher's command, the class stood and read from the textbook Qur'anic sura 78, or "The good news," forty beautifully rhyming verses on the structure of creation, earth, hell, and heaven; the afterlife's reward for the faithful and the horrible fate of those who do not fear God but instead argue vainly against the notion of an eventual resurrection and judgment. After the reading Mme. Mona talked about *al-hisab* (the accounting or reckoning of deeds) and *al-jiza'* (God's recompense to humans based on their actions). Qur'an readings were performed without *tajwid* (rhythmic cantillation), consistent with the modern practice of "reading without the rocking, and in a very simple manner" (see p. 69). In the fourth grade class, two or three of the boys rocked slightly when reading the Qur'an, a skill acquired either at home or from extracurricular study at a mosque or kuttab.

During the next recitation, this one from the text itself, the students stood individually to read, the teacher stopping them every few words to explain a difficult vocabulary item, expound on the point being made, or recapitulate the text. Well-worn books had passages underlined and extra voweling marks added by the children themselves, although well over half the words were already at least partially voweled (written and printed Arabic consists of consonants only, with voweling diacritics above and below the letters customarily added only in Qur'anic and other texts where ambiguity cannot be allowed). Some students in the second grade class were using textbook editions from previous years, hand-me-downs from older brothers and sisters; this can make life difficult for the student who is told to turn to page 40 and read the story of Isma'il, only to find that in his copy the story begins on page 54. (Students are not alone in recycling books; the government does the same, removing the covers for reuse—the cover of my copy of the seventh grade religious studies textbook was the inside-out cover of a 1984 vocational crafts workbook—and sending the texts themselves off for use in the Sudan.)

During readings, Mme. Mona corrected mistakes in voweling only. Although education in Egypt is supposedly conducted in *fusha* (Modern Standard Arabic, the formal descendant of the Qur'an's classical Arabic), there are few Egyptians, even adults, who can consistently avoid colloquial pronunciation when reading aloud. Even when reciting the Qur'an, for example, consonants retain their colloquial pronunciations when there are equivalent words in local dialect, so *jism* (body) is *gism* and *dhanb* (sin) is *zanb*. With the letter *qaf* in words such as *Qur'an, qal* (he said), *iqra'* (recite) or *khalaqa* (he created), which are important and often repeated in the shorter suras that children learn early, pronunciation usually retains its classical value when the Qur'an is read or recited, but pronunciation is inconsistent otherwise, sometimes shifting to a glottal stop in reading from the textbook proper. Perhaps one student in ten uses the classical pronunciation most of the time when reading aloud. In general, girls are far more fluent readers than boys in the same class.

About halfway through the text, the squawk of a loudspeaker on a nearby building broke into the lesson with the noon call to prayer. The fifth grade classroom was generally quite noisy, both because of the large fourth grade class next door, muted only by the wooden shutters, and from the noise of the younger children from the kindergarten playing out in the yard on the other side. But the call to prayer disrupted work entirely, and the class sat quietly, waiting for it to end. Mme. Mona tapped her foot softly. One girl in the front row held her hands out close in front of her with palms upward just below the chin (as if cradling a small open book), in an attitude of prayer, but after a little while she looked about surreptitiously and, noticing that none of her classmates was doing likewise, put her hands back in her lap. The class endured the *idhan* with the same resigned patience of teachers and students waiting for the end to the principal's squawk-box announcements in an American homeroom. Mme. Mona made no attempt to encourage her students actually to heed the call to prayer, although all of them were old enough to be compelled. (She could not have led the prayers herself in any case, as, ironically, the male children in the room would have been entitled to that duty before her. At some schools, provision is made for daily prayer, with an interior courtyard doubling as a play yard—complete with basketball hoops—and as a *misalla*, an open place for prayer. One section of the inner wall might be lined with porcelain sinks and faucets for performing the ablution (*wudu'*), and used also by school custodians for water for mopping floors.)

The reading resumed shortly, and when it was done Mme. Mona instructed her class to turn to page 78 of their texts and read aloud the story of the prophet Joseph, which lasted until the end of the period. During this reading the teacher was getting tired. It was after noon during the first week of Ramadan, when people were still struggling to adjust to the new schedule. She took her seat after standing up for most of the class period, propping her left elbow on the scarred green desk and resting her cheek in the palm of her hand, looking bored. From this position she continued asking questions, instructing the readers when to switch, correcting pronunciation. By 12:15 the pupils were getting restless and impatient for the class to end. One of the girls at the desk in front of me kept checking the next page in the book to see when the story would be over.

Children in the lower grades were more boisterous, due in part to their age and to the larger size of the second, third, and fourth grade classes, and in part to the fact that some of the fifth-graders were tired from fasting for the first time. In Mme. Mona's second grade class, the children competed with each other for who could shout the Qur'an louder during collective readings, forcing a teacher from the adjoining room to come in and complain about the volume. Children jumped to their feet with their arms raised, yelling (in English), "Miss! Miss! Miss!" when she asked a question. The passing of notes earned one student a stern rebuke, "*'eeb!*" (shame!); another got his ear twisted for laughing, and a third prompted the exasperated Mme. Mona to scold, "*haza hissa-ddin!*" (This is a *religion* class!) In the meantime, she quizzed them on the relatives of the Prophet Muhammad and they read the story of Isma'il out loud.

Students are taught, in religion class as elsewhere, to memorize and to perform. As in American classrooms, the better students are keenly competitive when it comes to currying the teacher's favor and answering questions, and the poorer students try to avoid being chosen to read, recite, or answer. Ahmad, one of the brighter students in Mme. Fayza's large fourth grade class was particularly energetic; after he had shouted out the answers to three of the teacher's last four questions, she called on Hisham, the student sitting in the row behind him to answer the next one, about how many *rak'a*s (repetitions of the ritual cycle of body movement and recitation) occur in each of the five daily prayers. When Hisham hesitated and began stammering, Ahmad turned half-way around in his seat and crouched down with his face almost resting on Hisham's desk, whispering the answer insistently to his classmate ("the *fajr* has two, the *dhuhr* has four . . . ") and fidgeting in an effort to contain his frustration at not being able to continue displaying publicly his mastery of the material.

Islam Outside the Religion Class

The shape of the formal religion curriculum does not exhaust the religious content of the school day. Obviously the amount of religion to which students are exposed at school depends on the nature of the school and the personality of the teacher, who can encourage or discourage religious expression on the part of pupils. The first grade religion teacher at Nasr, for example, insisted that pupils begin all of their answers to questions with the *basmallah*, "In the Name of God, the Merciful, the Compassionate," a practice ignored by the other instructors (at some schools, pupils are taught to begin all written communication, even telephone messages, with the basmallah). On my second visit to Nasr, the arts and crafts teacher, Mme. Fatima, started talking to me about my studies, and we spent a little while talking about which mosques I had visited. Suddenly a dreamy look came across her face and she beckoned me to lean down toward her, whispering in my ear, "Sayyida Nefisa!" She closed her eyes and nodded. "When I'm not feeling well, I go to Sayyida Nefisa." Then she asked if I had been to the mosque of al-Rifa'i (a large, airy structure rebuilt near the beginning of this century, al-Rifa'i is the final resting place of the founder of an important Sufi order and, coincidentally, of the late King Faruq and his family, and Muhammad Reza Pahlavi, the last shah of Iran). When I said I had, she put her left hand to her breast and drew in a deep breath to indicate the emotional power of the place. A *muhaggaba* (a woman who wears modest Islamic dress) in her early fifties, Mme. Fatima's piety emerged in the activities of her pupils. Religious themes often suffuse her students' art projects, which hang on bulletin boards in the first-floor hallway: a watercolor painting of six or seven men praying in a mosque; several paintings prominently featuring mosques and minarets (by themselves or in the context of other Egyptian landmarks); paintings of the *'arusa al-mawlid*— a kind of sugar doll that has for centuries been distributed to Egyptian children at the time of the Prophet's birthday— posted outside the front door of the school; a tiny weaving spelling "Allah" in light blue yarn on a background of yellow, red, and green; a sheet of paper with pistachio-nut shells glued to it to spell "Allahu akbar" (God is great); and another spelling just "Allah," with shells individually wrapped in aluminum foil, surrounded by four leaf-shaped decorations from the same material. Posted high on the wall of the second grade classroom, an art-class poster depicted a sturdy tree with its five branches labeled for the *"qawa'id al-islam al-khamis"* (the five foundations of Islam).[55]

Islam does not respect disciplinary boundaries. It enters the curriculum in areas entirely removed from questions of language or history. In primary school science texts, sections dealing with the animal kingdom treat the close fit between animals and their surroundings implicitly as the result of design rather than evolution. The authors place science both in a religious context, where scientific activity reveals and fulfills God's design (since He gave senses and reason to human beings), and in a nationalistic context in which science, as a force for economic and political progress, helps elevate the status of its Arab practitioners. The introduction to the 1988–89 sixth grade text *Science*, for experimental language schools (written in English by Egyptians for the Ministry of Education) reads in part,

> We have also cared for a number of educational targets as to exel [*sic*]the role of the scientists in serving science and specifically the arab scientists. We also study how to take care of the organs of sensation and the nervous system, and how to keep the whole body healthy. Then we show that the progress, un [*sic*] man's life and in the discovery of the secrets of this universe, is a gift of God. This makes us praise and glorify the creator. Finally, the success of this programme in schools depends on the teacher's constructive role, and his sincere efforts to help this, and future generations, in their search for knowledge. May God grant success.

Other primary school materials, like reading books, have long contained Qur'anic verses and prophetic sayings. Under its current head, Husayn Kamal Baha'al-Din, the Ministry of Education has been seen as secularizing the curriculum by reviewing the religious content of general education textbooks. But such reviews are of long standing. In late March 1989, for example, press reports began to circulate that the Ministry of Education had ordered the omission of certain verses and traditions from reading books. The resulting outcry from some sectors of the religious and educational establishments, concerned that the connection between the Arabic language and its classical roots was being breached, forced Dr. Ahmad Fathy Surur, then minister of education,[56] to convene hastily a "High Islamic Commission" to consult on the inclusion of Islamic materials in reading texts at all levels. Led by Egypt's mufti, or chief religious official, Dr. Muhammad Sayyid Tantawi,[57] along with the former minister of religious endowments, the general counsel of the Arabic Language Academy, the director of the Office for the Preservation of the Glorious Qur'an at al-Azhar, and others, this commission was to aid "students at all levels with the acquisition of linguistic proficiency, and the deepening of values and morals and sound perspectives based on the choice of verses and traditions that help plant commendable values without being tied to doctrines and rituals."[58] After several weeks, the mufti and the minister of education appeared on television to explain and justify the proposal. The verses and traditions in question were merely to be moved to the religion books, explained the Mufti, leaving in the reading books only those "pointing to values shared by all religions, such as honesty, for example." In reaction, the Islamic press linked the proposed changes to the mufti's acknowledged efforts to combat extremism in the schools through curriculum changes, and speculated about the source and timing of the decision to remove some Islamic material from reading texts:

> We haven't heard that the doctrinal and ritual verses in the books under study — from the viewpoint of their safety — have led to grievous accidents or deaths or the spread of epidemics and diseases, or even factional strife. But it appears that [outside] agencies bent on interference [have chosen] this of all times to set this process in motion. It's obvious that these are the same agencies that fund and direct notions of educational procedure at the present time, and their domestic allies. A short time ago we heard a high official laud an American aid foundation which furnished the government in recent years with school buildings, opening a [new] school every day. This is the same foundation that funds elementary education programs and provides them with maps carrying the name of the Zionist Entity [Israel]. Perhaps they and other agencies have begun to disburse money for schoolbooks and curriculum preparation . . . having as a result that this foundation could specify conditions on the content of these books, and naturally these specifications wouldn't be Islamic.[59]

Continuing to criticize the government books, *al-Sha'b*, the organ of the Socialist Workers Party, and one of the major outlets for the ideas of the Muslim Brotherhood, printed a photograph of one of the illustrations in the second grade reading textbook, showing a male schoolteacher acting as the imam of his class during prayer. Standing in the second position of the first rak'a of prayer (in which the individual recites selections from the Qur'an, with head bowed and hands clasped at the waist), the imam and his class were depicted with their left hands covering their right, when in truth the right hands should be covering the left. The drawing thus inverted a gesture of prayer (probably the result of reversing one of the photographic negatives during the preparation of the books). Attributing the reversal to malice rather than mere incompetence, the paper charged that "the alleged curriculum development proclaimed by the Ministry of Education has turned into a mockery of legitimate doctrines and their violation; it's not development, but an organized plan to obliterate the Islamic nature of our society."[60]

Incidents like this one demonstrate the extent to which the public school system is identified by Egyptians — including the Islamic opposition — as the primary public force in the reinforcement and transmission of Islamic culture. It eclipses all other institutions, programs, and facilities, including the mosque, the home, radio and television broadcasting, and print in the importance attributed to it as a publicly directed Islamizing force. There are two reasons for this. First, it is the only institution in which the participation of all citizens is compelled by law. Although the literacy rate in Egypt is below 50 percent and enrollment is by no means universal — in 1979, 28 percent of males and 61 percent of females between twenty and twenty-four years of age had never been enrolled in school at all — the school still represents the most widely utilized public service in the country, consuming an enormous portion of the government's annual budget. Having a captive audience, the school represents an ideal laboratory for social engineering, particularly if the knowledge imparted to children is taken home to their families.[61] But it also represents, in itself, the nation and the idea of national social, economic, and technical progress. Although the Ministry of Education operates with some independence from — and with some influence over — the religious ministries and the official religious elite, it is charged with a religious function and by that token is open to criticism and to political influence by groups who feel the focus of its religious curricula is inappropriate. Few would have the ministry relinquish its role as a purveyor of Islam. Its influence and its influenceability are too valuable.

Second, schooling is invested with great personal emotion by parents and students. As one of the primary rationers of social status, schools are sorting machines that separate individuals into socially validated status categories based on the type of school certificate earned. For those lower in the social scale, schooling represents a genuine and highly valued means of upward mobility. Umm Samira, the cleaning woman who worked in my apartment, was terribly anxious and preoccupied on the final day of her daughter's preparatory school exams because the subject was the one that she was dreading most: science. She told me how much she wanted Samira to get good marks on the tests so that she could get into general secondary school, because with a high school diploma she could "do anything, work in a bank, or an office, " whereas with a *diblum* (preparatory certificate) only, the best she could hope for would be *"shughl basit bi-murattab basit"* (simple work for simple pay). If she passed the high school test after three years, her mother concluded, she could go on to university and become a doctor, a businessperson, or anything else: "That's the way up."[62] In the end, Samira's scores were not high enough to qualify her for general secondary school, and since her family was unable to afford a private tutor (widely assumed to be indispensable for success on examinations), it was unlikely that she would be able to pass the tests on a second try. Her score was good enough, however, to enroll her in one of the commercial institutes that would teach typing, business arithmetic, and supplementary skills that would qualify Samira to work, for example, as a shop-girl at a salary of £E 50/month (about $20).

The motivation to acquire education as a mark of status, even independent of actual financial rewards, invests subjects with a visceral importance they would not otherwise have. It leads to constant reexamination and criticism of curricula from all sides, since everyone has an interest in the operation of status-conferring institutions. On the one hand, the religion curriculum is touted by the government as a "basic subject" that must be mastered by all in an attempt to preserve, if not raise, the general moral level of society. On the other hand, it is chided from all positions on the political spectrum as being incomplete, intentionally corrupting, or vacuous. Wafa'i Isma'il, a recent American University in Cairo graduate whose family supports the Wafd, an opposition party associated historically with landowners and businessmen, dismissed the entire religion program in the schools as hollow.

> They [religion classes] didn't affect me at all. Not one bit. It's just another subject that you learn for the test and then forget afterward. Besides, nobody listens to anything the government says. The NDP [National Democratic Party] has to make everybody think that it's so big and powerful and has so much support, but really it's nothing. . . . The books they give you in school, they don't say anything. It's like, who sends the light in the morning? It's God. Really nothing.

When I asked him why, if nobody listens to what the government says, they spend so much time and effort saying it, he waved his hand and sneered, "Because, I mean, they're aiming at people who don't know anything."[63] This is, of course, precisely the point. Even for people who do "know something," the most useful communication is that whose source is forgotten, so that it becomes something one feels one has always known, something it is pointless, trite, and annoying to restate. Far from being unaffected by the religious curricula of the schools he attended, Wafa'i absorbed an enormous amount from them, but regards the information either as false, as self-evident, or as misdirected. "Learning," according to Bourdieu, "is an irreversible process . . . and the habitus acquired at school conditions the level of reception and degree of assimilation of the messages produced and diffused by the culture industry."[64] The information and mental habits developed during the school career render students influenceable at subsequent stages in their lives, able to recognize and participate in the official discourses of Islam.

Reviving the Kuttab

The government's responsibility for religious education does not end at the back cover of the twelfth-grade religious studies textbook. Among other things, the Ministry of Education is charged by the Constitution and by Law no. 139 of 1981 with the inculcation of religion in Egypt's youth. In a country where Islam is the religion of the state, and Arabic its official language, this means that some special attention must be devoted to the Qur'an, the source of both. Proclaiming that "religious education is a basic subject in all educational stages," and specifying the passing score in religion examinations, Law no. 139 requires the Ministry of Education to "organize periodic competitions for recital of the Holy Qur'an; and winners are to be given awards and incentives according to the system to be established by the Higher Council of Education."[65] Various schemes for encouraging Qur'an memorization and recitation outside the classroom have been proposed, including the notion of reviving kuttabs. But the Ministry of Education has not been eager to involve itself in the construction of new kuttabs, instead searching for other ways to encourage and facilitate Qur'an memorization. In September 1989, 'Atif 'Amir, an Islamic education expert at the ministry, submitted a proposal detailing a "new, evolved approach to the work of the kuttabs, which were widespread not so long ago, and had positive effects on the educational process."

The project would use existing Ministry of Education facilities, which are "the appropriate place for the study and memorization of the Glorious Qur'an." Recommending that Qur'an programs be run during summer vacation, with volunteer teachers and students receiving small monthly fees, 'Amir pointed out that "there exists within the Ministry the technical apparatus for the pursuit and supervision of the project in an advanced, scientific manner, since it is fully provided with the modern equipment and media for the inculcation of the Qur'an and its public recitation by audio-visual means."[66] In sharp contrast to the historical drive to secularize kuttabs because of the allegedly harmful cognitive effects of reliance on memorization, plans such as this seek to revive the subject matter while altering the venue or the methodology of inculcation. The use of modern technology to pursue a traditional goal would allow the ministry to cater to the desires of the pious while avoiding criticism that its teaching techniques are outmoded.[67] Other intellectuals ignore the methodology and focus instead on the psychological and social benefits of Qur'an memorization, linking it with the domains of personal success and international economics rather than technology. In a newspaper interview, Dr. Rushdie Fakkar, an Egyptian professor of psychology at Muhammad V University in Morocco, attributed his success at the Sorbonne to having learned the Qur'an as a child in the small village of Karnak in Upper Egypt, crediting the linguistic skills he learned in the kuttab with the subsequent ease with which he picked up European languages. "Egypt is in need of an educational revolution," he said, "and it's necessary that a system of kuttabs for the memorization of the Holy Qur'an returns to her, for our real crisis has to do with the poverty of education, and it must restore principles and substance to the child's mind in order [for the child] to become an Egyptian person able to compete in the twenty-first century."[68] Invoking competition, development, and the future, such language recalls the Egyptian Second Five-Year Plan's linkage of individual and social achievement (see p. 86). But it approaches the problem differently, implying that the state's interventions are powerless without the revival of an institution that is emphatically not one of the achievements of the modern age.

In fact, the establishment of pre-school and after-school kuttabs and youth organizations has been one of the primary strategies used by the Ministry of Religious Endowments to revive Qur'an study. During the official Ramadan speeches in 1989 that marked *Laylat al-Qadr*, the anniversary of the descent of the Qur'an to the Prophet Muhammad, President Mubarak announced at the al-Ahmadi mosque in Tanta that he was earmarking one million Egyptian pounds for Qur'an memorization and study, an activity which, according to Muhammad 'Ali Mahgub, the minister of religious endowments, "is the guardian of Youth against deviance and extremism" (*al-'asim li al-shabab min al-inhiraf wa al-tatarruf*).[69] This money was targeted for the construction of new kuttabs in Egypt's smaller villages and cities, beginning in the governorates of Qalyubiya, Daqahliya, and Minufiya, an effort to which the popular preacher Shaykh Muhammad Mutawalli Sha'rawi later pledged a million pounds.[70]

Clubs and Contests

Just a few days after the celebration in Tanta, Mahgub announced that he had authorized "a plan to revive and popularize kuttabs in every Egyptian Governorate," placing the project under the supervision of the ministry's counselor for Qur'anic affairs, who was already leading activities designed to strengthen Islamic culture among Egyptian children. As the president of the Muslim Family Association and the Little Muslim Club (*nadi al-muslim al-saghir*), the counselor, Mr. Marzuq Hilal, helped direct the religious education of the latter organization's six thousand members. Founded for "the Islamic preparation of the little Muslim from many angles, the cultural, the social, and the educational," the club published a monthly illustrated magazine, *The Little Muslim*, with articles on science, nature, history, geography, and literature as well as religious topics (proper Qur'an recitation; stories of the prophets; a column of *fatawa*, the judgments of a religious scholar responding to children's letters). It organized field trips to historic Islamic sites, and had an Islamic theater troupe that performed scenes from the life of Muhammad and from Islamic history. But the club's main activity was encouraging study of the Qur'an and hadith, "especially those which teach the child Islamic conduct"; it organized an annual Qur'an recitation competition, the prize total for which reached twenty-two thousand Egyptian pounds ($8,800) in 1988, and whose winners could compete in the annual competition sponsored by the Ministry of Religious Endowments during Ramadan, or the annual World Competition in Mecca.[71]

Created to draw attention to the virtues of soup mixes and candy, the lure of cash and the creeping thrill of competition and chance has made such contests (*musabqa* or *musab'a*) increasingly popular devices for attracting public attention and participation. Quite substantial prizes and sums of money can be involved. In late May 1989, for example, the Supreme Council for Population and Family Planning sponsored a contest on family planning information, which it advertised in the religious weekly *al-Liwa' al-islami* and other government newspapers. Ads invited readers to answer five simple questions—including one concerning the divine sanction for family planning—to qualify for cash prizes ranging from £E 15 to £E 1000 (up to $400, several times the monthly salary of most public sector employees).[72] In the Ministry of Religious Endowments's annual Qur'an competition, the 339 prizewinners were granted all-expenses-paid pilgrimages to Mecca for the *hajj* or 'umra pilgrimages, and cash prizes ranging from £E 200 to £E 1000, depending on how much of the Qur'an they had committed to memory.[73] Local and regional contests are held throughout the year on the occasion of national holidays. The previous February a seven-year-old Nubian boy had been honored by the governor of Aswan for his memorization of the entire Qur'an. His prize was the deed to an apartment worth £E 18,000, donated by the Construction Bank of Aswan.[74]

Social Service Agencies and Charitable Organizations

If these competitions treat the internalization of the Qur-'an as a rare feat of personal enrichment, an embellishment of manners and of personal refinement, other institutions treat it as part of the social safety net, to be provided along with pension checks and low-cost medical treatment. Public and semipublic social service agencies and private charitable organizations are proliferating in Egypt, which now has as many registered Private Voluntary Associations as all other Arab countries combined.[75] Some of Cairo's larger private mosques in well-to-do areas, such as Anas Ibn Malik and Mustafa Mahmud, both in Muhandisin, have large and well-established social service agencies administered and funded privately (some also receive grants from foreign governments, both Muslim and non-Muslim, for specific programs). These might include free medical clinics for the poor, equipped with expensive high-technology diagnostic and treatment devices, adult literacy training programs, Qur'an memorization and religious study groups, youth programs, kindergartens, and other social services such as counseling, charitable distribution, and so on. During clinic hours scores of people, many of whom have traveled for hours on buses, come to take advantage of the services provided. Organized religious study programs, which take place in the evenings, are offered at a number of levels.

Less impressive public social service centers are heavily utilized as well, offering the distribution of social security payments to the elderly and disabled, maternal and child welfare, care for the aged, vocational training and family planning. The number of such multiple-service "social care societies" increased by over a third in the early 1980s, to nearly three thousand. While the average multipurpose public center only provides two or three of the programs mentioned above, some offer all of them, and more than three-quarters offer "cultural, education and religious services," the category including Qur'an memorization. Almost

40 percent of the nearly six thousand single-purpose public centers specialize in cultural and religious outreach.[76]

Like other government buildings, public and ruling party–sponsored social service centers are coated inside and out with the signifiers of benevolent authority, heightening the irony of the statement such facilities make about the depth of the country's economic malaise and bureaucratic inertia. Huge images of the president in bold billboard colors compete with immense green handpainted signs advertising Qur-ʾan memorization, family planning, child care, vocational education, and sports programs for youth, sanctioned with the seal of their Ministry of Social Services registration numbers. Glossy presidential photographs usher clients past gray rooms full of sewing machines or ping-pong games popping in time to the car horns outside. At the ruling National Democratic Party-sponsored *Gamʿiyya al-Rahman li-riʿaya al-usra* (The Rahman Society for Family Care), near the Presidential Palace complex in downtown Cairo, the assistant director outlined the center's mission.

This is a lower middle-class and lower-class neighborhood, with a lot of children, and the parents often need help with the care and education of the kids, as well as being in need of some of our services themselves. So we have a nursery for children from 3–6 years of age; not so many during the summer—we've got thirty or forty here now—but during the year we may get 80 or 90 kids every day, in four different sessions. We try to teach them the alphabet, and the names of animals, and things like this, and also, for example, simple words in English, like the numbers, and animal names, just so they have a sense of sounds outside their own language. For the older children who are already in school, we have some other things to supplement their education, because often after several years in school they still can't read or write, because there are just too many children in each room and some of them get lost or ignored, and don't learn anything.

As for the workshop, there are lessons in sewing, and operation of some kinds of sewing machines, so that when they grow up and go to work in a factory, they'll know how to do this kind of thing. There's a family planning program, too, but the flow in and out of there isn't steady. Sometimes the people there will sit all day with nobody coming in, and then suddenly there will be five or six women coming in saying that they want to stop having children—they're twenty-five and already have four or five kids.

Now, the reason we have the Qurʾan memorization program, is because we want these people to know about both this world and the next [*ad-dinya wal-ʿakhir*], so we bring in responsible people from the universities to teach them about religion. If there are Christian kids, we find someone to teach them about Christianity, but most of the children are Muslim. In this program, the students are mostly very young: from four or so all the way up to, maybe, fifteen. It's very important, because the love of religion brings the whole world together.[77]

The society's Qur'an program in the mosque next door used one of the scores of earnest, emaciated student shaykhs that al-Azhar sends out each summer to teach at the city's social service agencies as part of the university's summer outreach campaign.[78] An hour before midday prayers the shaykh gathered his students in the mosque (built around 1910, the assistant director joked with me, it was "older than America") and distributed copies of the Qur'an from a small table next to the mosque's library. The library was actually a glass-domed bookcase full of dusty volumes on sunna and hadith leaning on the wall a few feet from the *mihrab* that marked the direction of Mecca. Each day the students memorized ten verses or a short chapter, reading from the Qur'an while the teacher recited the verses out loud several times. Responsible for committing the verses to memory at home that night, they were quizzed the following day, reciting the assigned section without looking at the text. As in traditional kuttabs, and very unlike their experience in school, children learned here the elements of tajwid, the proper cantillation of the text and other rituals surrounding *al-tilawa* (the public reading of the Qur'an). (Teaching these skills is also a goal of organizations like the Little Muslim Club, whose magazine occasionally publishes short articles on these topics.[79])

Models and Media

The term usually used in Arabic for learning to recite the word of God is *tahfidh al-Qur'an, tahfidh* being a verbal noun derived from the causative form of the verbal root meaning "to preserve, protect, guard, commit to memory." The phrase thus means "inculcation of the Qur'an" rather than "memorization." It is spoken and written of in the causative, so one does not generally memorize the Qur'an on one's own, one has it inculcated in one by others, as Muhammad had it inculcated in him by the angel Gabriel. In theory, the primary force behind this activity is the family, particularly the father, who has the traditional duty to teach his sons the Qur'an, or to send them to competent masters who can. The ideal that the family is the center of social and religious life is constantly invoked in the media, in political speeches, and at public events. During Ramadan 1409, for example, at the ceremonies marking the Ministry of Religious Endowments' annual Laylat al-Qadr[80] Qur'an recitation contest, a family of six from an eastern delta village was singled out for media attention because each one of them had memorized the entire Qur'an. Mahmud Mahdi, marveling at this unusual feat of family devotion, wrote in *al-Ahram* that

> this family began their journey with the Glorious Qur'an twelve years ago, as the father, 'Abd al-Ghaffar 'Abd al-Khaliq al-Zalbani (42 years old) told me. He added that after he memorized [*hafadha*] the Qur'an he undertook inculcating it in his wife [*qama bi-tahfidhihi li-zawjatihi*], then the two of them participated in inculcating it in their four children, two twin boys and two twin girls, all of whom are members of the Little Muslim Club, which they frequent every Friday, and to which belongs the credit for encouraging their children in the memorization [*hifdh*] of the Qur'an.[81]

In this media celebration of the family, the path of the sacred book runs initially along the family's internal lines of authority, from husband to wife and from husband and wife together to the children. But then the autonomy of the family is ruptured symbolically along generational lines by a state-sponsored organization claiming partial credit for the children's accomplishments. Even in the midst of showcasing the self-sufficiency of a model family, the protective envelope of the home is opened to admit the benevolence and support of public institutions. No family is an island, the story says.

And in fact, life is not divided between analytically discrete scenes or sources of religious socialization. Parents and relatives, the school, the mosque, the social service agency, the Ministry of Religious Endowments, programming on television and radio, government and private youth organizations, publications aimed at children; all of these shower religious language on the child like a cascade of boxes tumbling off the top shelf of an overcrowded closet. Once the door is open the avalanche is inescapable. Public representations of model families and model children whose accomplishments are to be admired and emulated by their peers are a central feature of the complex environment of textbook and media Islam. These models of everyday uprightness and piety update the stories of Islamic history by placing ordinary citizens in the role of model personalities. During my fieldwork, Channel Two on Egyptian television had a short weekly program in which young children memorizing the Qur'an were asked about why they love studying it, and given the opportunity to recite some of what they have learned. One of the parents of a student at the Nasr Language School, a military officer in his forties, told me a story about one of the children he had seen on this program, explaining that religious education comes

> in many forms. This past week I saw on television a little girl, only four years old, and she had memorized three parts [out of thirty] of the Qur'an. Three parts! But she was from a family that was a bit religious [*mutadayyina shwayya*], and she heard this all day, and listened to [cassette] tapes and the television, broadcasts of the Qur'an.[82]

Before her introduction either to the mosque or to the school as the official house of God, this little girl was introduced by her family to electronic mediations of the voice of God, and listening, was quite literally drawn into them to become a public image of the ideal child. What she would encounter upon entering school — as we will see in the next chapter — would be a further series of idealizations purveyed by textbooks: idealizations of herself, her family, and her nation.

CHAPTER 5

The Path of Clarification

All school culture is necessarily standardized and ritualized . . . by and for exercises of repetition and reconstitution which must be sufficiently stereotyped to be repeated ad infinitum under the direction of coaches . . . themselves as little irreplaceable as possible (e.g. manuals, summaries, synopses, religious or political breviaries and catechisms, glosses, commentaries, cribs, encyclopedias, corpuses, selections, past examination papers, model answers, compilations of dictums, apothegms, mnemonic verses, topics, etc.).

Pierre Bourdieu and Jean-Claude Passeron,
Reproduction in Education, Society, and Culture, 1977[1]

The Interpretation of Culture and the Culture of Interpretation

At the height of the Second World War, psychological anthropologist George Devereaux and his colleague Edwin Loeb, members of a generation of American scholars who found their civilization under the threat of an aggressive foreign military machine, wrote an article outlining the strategies a besieged culture might use to resist annihilation. One of these strategies, "antagonistic acculturation," they described as the process of adopting lower-order practices and institutions from foreign cultures for the purpose of resisting adoption of their higher-order goals; essentially, adopting new cultural tactics to resist the adoption of new values.[2] The authors criticized the earlier trend of diffusionist scholarship by emphasizing the purposive nature of what they termed "autoplastic culture change," and in an unusual literary conceit, they quoted from the Qur'an itself as the best possible summary of the human interest in setting boundaries: "And I shall not worship that which ye worship/Nor will ye worship that which I worship/Unto you your religion, and unto me my religion" (sura 109, al-Kafirun, 4–6).

The phrase "antagonistic acculturation" has not aged well, perhaps because of a vague semantic prejudice sparked by the alliterative terms, the latter recalling the stolid scientific neutralism of some colonial acculturation studies, and the former implying perhaps that indigenous resistance to "culture contact" was a matter of the stubborn native's impenetrable rejection of progressive change. But while the phrase has been all but forgotten by anthropologists, who now prefer the concept of resistance, the process it describes is a central feature of cultural flow in the colonial and post- or neocolonial world. As we saw in examining the development of European-style education in Egypt, this was the force behind the calculated military appropriation of schooling in the early nineteenth century. Since that time, the state's strategies for maintaining a Muslim identity while extending ideological influence over an increasingly urbanized and literate populace has included the transformation of Islamic institutions, beliefs, and values through altering the form and the context of their production and their inculcation. That context — the European-style school — works both through new principles of organizing interpersonal authority on a massive and centrally administered scale and through the use of new types of cultural production, particularly the imported form of the school textbook. This chapter addresses the specific mechanisms through which the textbook both furthers and expresses the functionalization of the Islamic tradition.

The process of altering cultural production to match, compete with, and fend off imported models, while simultaneously increasing its political usefulness, is obviously not confined to the Nile Valley. In his important book *The Calligraphic State*, Brinkley Messick has shown how Ottoman and Yemeni nationalist reformers of the nineteenth and twentieth centuries transformed the flexible and multivocal tradition of Islamic legal scholarship, the *shari'a*, into a closed, self- contained, and relatively rigid set of "modern" legal codes. Ottoman reformers in the second half of the nineteenth century had likened the shari'a to "an ocean without shores," vast, difficult to access because of the specialized training required, and inappropriate for the times.[3] Criticizing its "lack of order" relative to European-style legal codes, they were concerned with making the law "known," fixing it in structured form in numbered paragraphs, "making a portion of the shariʿa manageable and perusable," and issuing works that contained "only the least contested and least controversial opinions and composed in a manner which would be sufficiently clear so that anyone could study it easily and act in conformity with it."[4] At the same time that colonial translations of Muslim legal works were pulling together different versions to create authoritative Arabic texts, local elites as well as the colonial powers themselves endeavored to spread shariʿa consciousness to the hinterlands of Yemen, both because it was considered " 'tidier' and more predictable than custom" and because, according to contemporary sources, it "provides better political propaganda."[5] With more recent reorganizations of Yemeni political life, responsibility for the production of a corpus of "Islamic law" has been removed from the hands of the ʿulama and given over to public officials and parliaments.

The same sorts of processes have operated in Egypt through the production of both official textbooks and private sector childrens' literature. Textbooks are an offspring of print (as opposed to manuscript) culture, both because printing allows the creation of sufficient numbers of books to allow feasible mass instruction and also because of the uniformity of printed products. "With print," Walter Ong writes,

> for the first time, a teacher could stand before a class and say, "Everybody turn to page 48, fifth line from the top, third word from the left," and everybody could find the word. In a manuscript culture the students might all have had manuscripts, but you would have had to pronounce the word and wait for them to locate it because it would be in a different position on a different page in virtually every manuscript.[6]

As we have seen in the classroom itself, the text recycling that springs from practical economic pressures means this is not always so, but the infinite standardization of the textbook does have the universal effect of flattening controversy and rigidifying current understandings of open questions as indisputable fact.

Moreover, and most importantly, by propagating a synoptic vision of Islamic belief and practice, sanctioned either by the state or by groups of "experts" working in the private sector, mass education and its pedagogical materials effectively create a new Islamic tradition derived from, but not identical with, the historical tradition (just as Yemen's "Islamic" legal codes drew on the corpus of shariʿa scholarship, while the latter drew directly on the Qurʾan and sunna.) Furthermore, these materials automatically draw new populations into the field of cultural reproduction: not only the new elites of the Ministry of Education and the corporate boardroom, but, importantly, the students themselves, who are supposed to derive from their classroom training the ability to produce "correct" Muslim behavior. This installation of habitus, however, is complicated by the fact that it is an explicit, verbal inculcation that couches Muslim behavior in functionalist terms, terms that actively encourage students to draw connections between the world of life and the world of texts. Once the possibility of this sort of interpretation is opened, the construction of additional, or alternate, readings of Muslim practice is inevitable.

Encountering the Word

As one of their functions, elementary schools introduce students not only to the psychological and physical skills of reading and writing, but to the proper social and political use of official texts, and to the way in which texts are deployed by authorities, whether as books, assignments, examinations, instructions, or forms. Contemporary educators — inspired by the historical insistence that religious education further "moral" and not merely "ritual" ends — transform the sacred texts of the Islamic tradition into systematic, socially and politically useful products for mass socialization. The historical processes of functionalization we viewed earlier — in which personal and institutional relationships and then the social ends of the Islamic tradition itself were altered to underwrite changing understandings of the utility of religion — will be augmented here by a close examination of mass-produced texts themselves. With respect to the school textbook, functionalization is a process of reading and explicating the physiological, social, and political function of Muslim practices in such a way that these practices appear uniquely effective tools for the conduct of modern life.

The practices of memorization and recitation, question and response are taught from the very beginning of the school career, even before children have mastered the art of writing. As we have seen, children spend much class time reading their textbooks aloud, in unison or individually, as the teacher corrects mistakes of pronunciation and then breaks to expound on obscure points or to quiz students on past material. The task of reading aloud and memorization for repetition is a central feature of everyday student activity, motivated by the structure of official examinations and the desire of students and their families to obtain scores high enough to continue to higher grades and perhaps, eventually, to gain admission to the most prestigious faculties in university.

This is not to say that all pedagogical practices aim always at a single, consistent goal, or that these goals necessarily change predictably in response to political and social needs, independent of the structural constraints of educational institutions themselves.[7] The latter always exert pressures on curriculum design and teaching technique in order to satisfy internal aims as well as external ones. As an example, when Anwar Sadat called in 1977 for "teaching religion in a new style by which we can protect our forthcoming generations and face up to the problems of today," his intent was rhetorical, for a new style had already overtaken religious studies in Egyptian schools. Inculcating proper social behavior has been a prime pedagogical goal long before the mid-1970s. If anything, some textbooks have become less vivid and more traditional than they were. For example, in the sixth grade religious readers for both 1976 and 1981 we find sura 58, 6, from the Qur'an:

> Hast thou not seen that God knows whatsoever is in the heavens, and whatsoever is in the earth? Three men conspire not secretly together, but He is the fourth of them, neither five men, but He is the sixth of them, neither fewer than that, neither more, but He is with them, wherever they may be; then He shall tell them what they have done, on the Day of Resurrection. Surely God has knowledge of everything.[8]

But while the 1976 edition stresses this verse in isolation and asks the student to memorize it as a reminder of "God's Surveillance of what is Secret and what is Open," the 1981 edition includes the verse in the context of the rest of its sura. The earlier edition not only defines difficult vocabulary items but includes three and a half pages of *tafsir*, or "explanation," followed by a full page of review questions. In 1981 the sura is presented without tafsir at all, accompanying the text merely with lists of difficult vocabulary items and their definitions. The more recent book requires the student to memorize the entire sura, and is closer in spirit to older practices than is the earlier version, which picks a single verse and emphasizes the moral lesson to be drawn from it.

Similarly, both editions contain the following hadith, a saying of the Prophet Muhammad:

A person walks in the same path as his friend; so [a Muslim] pays attention whom he befriends.

The 1976 book placed the hadith within the context of a short story about the proper choice of friends and the relationships between parents, children, and the school:

Saʿid's father was delighted. He saw his son Saʿid advancing in his studies, and in his manners, and in his character, and in his behavior towards his playmates and teachers at school and his siblings at home. So his father said, "I am pleased with you, Saʿid, for you've gotten much better than you used to be."

Saʿid said, "Yes, my father."

"I notice that you changed your friends."

"Yes, I left Asʿad and ʿUthman and Ibrahim, because they didn't think about anything except playing, and weren't interested in their studies and didn't do their homework, and in thing after thing I became like them, and it seemed to me that I was lost, so I turned away from them and chose Ishraf and Hasan and Ismaʿil, and I've learned from their earnestness and good manners and good taste."

"Excellent choice."

"Yes, and the school gets the credit for it."

"How's that?"

"Father, I learned from it many things about friendship and friends. I learned that for each one of us there is treasure in friendship, because a friend talks to me and I to him, and I walk with him, and if I need anything I ask him for it, and if something hurt me, I complain to him about it. And He and I are like one person. I ask him things, and he asks me. I buy things for him, and he for me, and I know him by heart, and benefit from his knowledge and wisdom, and he benefits from me. And I learned that the person is changed by his friend. He is changed in his etiquette, and his behavior, and he takes on many of his characteristics; and I put this to the test myself, father. And I learned that one must proceed slowly in the choice of one's friends, and that their choice must be based on knowledge of their manners and habits, and not to take friends without checking them out."

Saʿid's father rejoiced, and his joy grew when he knew that [Saʿid] applied the lessons of religion to [his] life, and that he memorized the following saying [of the Prophet] about the choosing of friends: "He said, may God bless and save him, 'A person walks in the same path as his friend, so [a Muslim] pays attention whom he befriends.' "[9]

The 1981 edition, on the other hand, merely cites the hadith, defines the difficult vocabulary, and summarizes its meaning thus:

From this hadith you learn:

> That one is influenced by his friends, and copies their dispositions and character and perception, and follows in their paths.
>
> That it is a Muslim's duty to go slowly and think and check a person out before making him a friend.
>
> Among Islam's guidelines for choosing a friend: that he be well-mannered and clean-tongued, and careful of his appointments and his work and his religion, sincere in his friendship both in private and in public, and supportive in whatever way possible.[10]

Aside from eliminating the saccharin story format, the real change in the second version is the creation of an easy-to-memorize list of rules that can be repeated verbatim on an examination. In this case, logistical factors won out in the contest between embedding moral guidelines in a contemporary narrative that pictures their self-conscious application, or presenting them as objects of test-driven analysis and memorization. The same sorts of tensions continue to operate today.

Form and Content

The goals of contemporary religious education at the primary level are set out in the introduction to the first grade religion textbook, which reminds teachers that "religious education [*al-tarbiya al-diniyya*] is not material restricted to classrooms, but rather is a complete life curriculum, including the classroom milieu with all its activities and information and knowledge. It also includes the home environment, and society as a whole."[11]

The classroom portion of this curriculum has several distinct goals: the planting (*ghars*) of Islamic morals and values in the psyche of the child, along with a grasp of the five pillars of Islam; the development of faith in God; acquainting the child with the biography of the Prophet; memorization of some verses and suras of the Qur'an; and knowledge and practice of the process of ablution and prayer. The authors explain that religion is related to other school subjects "like the Arabic language or science," and that their selection of Qur'anic extracts "benefit[s] from the fact that the Qur'an can be understood at many levels." They highlight a variety of instructional methods like the use of pictures and drawings, which help impart the meaning of abstract concepts and make the process of learning more enjoyable and attractive, "increasing [the pupil's] desire to learn."[12] And finally, they draw attention to two developmental and social issues:

> The importance of satisfying the needs of the pupil in this grade level for freedom in expressing his abilities and his reliance on what he touches and sees and hears at this stage of his life, and [his] proper response to life situations at home and in school and in society. [And] the importance of the social environment in which the pupil lives, in such a way that religious education has a role in the advancement and development of this milieu [*tarqiyya tilka al-bi'a wa tanmiyyatiha*].[13]

These themes are carried through in texts for the higher grades, which provide pupils with "Islamic religious information appropriate to their ages, springing forth from the glorious Qur'an and the noble traditions of the Prophet."[14] These later books emphasize proper public recitation (*tilawa*) of Qur'anic extracts and urge teachers to have students memorize and explain designated passages, "extracti[ng] . . . the values and principles to which they point."[15] Finally, they direct that children be taught diligence in their work, compassion for others and good manners in public places, for adab is part of "an integrated view of Islamic education that presents the meaning of Qur'anic verses and Prophetic traditions . . . through life situations" familiar to the child.[16]

By the end of the fifth grade, the industrious Egyptian schoolchild will have read hundreds of pages about Islam in her textbooks, memorizing most of them for repetition on year-end examinations. Teachers and principals place a great deal of confidence in their students' ability to memorize, a fact I learned firsthand, with a great deal of embarrassment, at the Nasr School, when I asked if they had spare copies of the textbooks. Pulling all but the fifth grade book out of a storage cabinet, Mme. Hala told me they didn't seem to have an extra there, but she knew where to get one. Leaving the room, she returned with the book two minutes later. Unlike the others, this one was well-worn and covered inside with penciled notes. She had simply gone to the fifth grade room and asked who had finished memorizing their book already, choosing one student among the three that raised their hand. Horrified, I insisted that she return the book to the student, who would certainly need it to study. "No," she replied, pointing at her head, "she's already knows the whole thing." She refused to let me return it.

The religion textbooks contain five broad categories of content: Qur'an and hadith; *qawa'id al-islam* (the pillars of Islam); *usul al-din* (theology); *sira* (biographies of the prophets and famous Muslims); and adab (rules for behavior in public and private). These are crosscut by different media of presentation. Texts make use of direct quotations from the Qur'an and hadith; tafsir (consisting of definitions, explanations and clarifications of Qur'anic or traditional material in the voice of the text's authors); *durus* (sing. *dars*; or lessons, narrative presentations of material in the voice of the text's authors); *anashid* (sing. *nashid*; poems, songs, or recitations to be repeated aloud in unison); *munaqashat* (questions or topics for discussion); *tadribat* (activities such as matching exercises); *tamthilat* (short plays or dialogues for students to read or act out); and finally, pictures and drawings.

Most lessons use more than one format, combining pictures with narratives, discussion questions and anashid, for example. Pictures are meant to stimulate discussion or to be used as part of an exercise, but occasionally serve merely an illustrative function. Qur'an and hadith are both subject matter and media because each book contains, in addition to verses cited to illustrate the point of a lesson or ground it in scripture, a section of Qur'an to be memorized by the student for its own sake.

Table 3 shows the proportion of space devoted to each of the five subject categories in the primary-level religion textbooks used during the 1988–89 school year.[17] While the space allotted to basic theology and Prophetic biography rises and falls unpredictably throughout the years, the remaining categories show more definite trends. That devoted to Qur'an, hadith, and adab increases fourfold between the first and the fifth grades, while the volume taken up by the pillars of Islam declines by more than 60 percent. Including longer passages from the Qur'an is a function of the child's growing capacity for recitation and memory work, while moving from basic elements of faith and worship to the application of Muslim values to life reflects the growing importance of explicit moral training as children enter their second seven years of life and begin facing responsibility for proper behavior and the performance of religious duties.

The Transformation of Texts

Since political elites and professional educators alike see religious education as an important applied subject, textbook authors strive in various ways to emphasize Islam's place in the child's daily life.

Table 3 *Content of Primary School Religion Texts (Rounded to the nearest one percent)*

	Grade Level				
	1	2	3	4	5
Qur'an/Hadith	5	10	17	16	20
Qawa'id	42	30	20	13	16
Usul al-din	26	15	22	29	14
Sira	21	26	20	17	29
Adab	6	17	20	25	20

Even sacred history is made immediate by linking events of long ago and far away to the child's own familiar world. One of the earliest lessons in the Ministry of Education's first grade religion textbook is the story of the Prophet Muhammad's early life, and the names and kinship ties of the relatives who raised and cared for him. Introducing children to the Islamic tradition with the simple, accessible vocabulary of kinship terms, the text draws pupils into an immediate relationship with the Prophet, while drawing the family itself into the universe of discourse of the school. Before dealing in some detail with the way textbooks treat family and school as sources of moral authority, let us first examine how functionalization — which we have already examined with respect to institutional transformations — operates on a textual level.

In examining the form of Egyptian religious studies textbooks, functionalization appears as one of four textual processes, along with consolidation, grading, and reinterpretation, which help transform the larger written corpus of Islamic tradition (and local custom) into socially and politically useful forms for use in the public school.[18] Consolidation, like grading, is an editorial process stemming from the need to systematize and simplify the Islamic heritage for mass consumption. One of the more mundane differences between sacred revelation and classroom instruction is that the Qur'an is notoriously repetitive and meandering by contemporary pedagogical standards. Verses concerning a single subject, even a single person, are scattered throughout the twenty-two years of the Prophet's recorded mission, sometimes repeating information, sometimes adding new insights or taking different points of view. For example, in the Qur'an, the twenty-eight-verse chapter called Nuh (Noah) does not contain the most comprehensive account of the title character's life and works. The richer account is given in twenty-four verses in sura 11, Hud (25–49), although there is supplementary information scattered throughout thirteen other chapters as well, in blocks of between one and seventeen verses. The synoptic tale of Noah that the fourth-grader reads is an amalgamation and paraphrase of the Qur'anic revelation illustrated with pictures and a simplified vocabulary.

As important as textual organization is the temporal allocation of knowledge, the very essence of school hierarchy. Grading doles out age-appropriate wisdom at the same time that it reinforces lessons learned in earlier years and builds a foundation for the future. As an example, Egyptian first-graders greet Ramadan officially with a simple nashid:

> Come on, brothers, let's come on,
> Let's rejoice in Ramadan
> Month of fasting and of alms,
> In you, goodness and Qur'an
> Yours the honor, Ramadan[19]

Next, they find a list of Ramadan activities: the scheduling of meals, listening to the Qur'an, helping the poor and unfortunate. They are reminded that "you learn the fast with your father and your mother," and boys learn that "you go to the mosque with your father." An exercise and a color drawing of a neighborhood mosque round out the youngest student's lesson.[20] The following year, Ramadan becomes the subject of a dialogue between a father and his two children, Fatima and Ali, who have all gone to the market on the night of the first day of the sacred month. The children ask how and why Muslims fast, and learn that one must refrain from eating, but also from quarrelling, and they must increase the frequency of prayers. Their father (anonymous, like all textbook parents) explains that "God directed us to fast during Ramadan because it cleanses our minds and accustoms us to patience and compassion for the poor and unfortunate when we feel hunger like them. And so we may all be saved from God's punishment when we enter heaven."[21] He ends his lesson by quoting from the Qur'an, sura 2, al-Baqara,185: "Ramadan is the month/In which was sent down/the Qur'an, as a guide/To mankind, also clear (signs)/For guidance and judgement (Between right and wrong)./So every one of you who is present during the month should spend it fasting." In the third grade, Ramadan takes the form of a series of descriptive phrases. Again citing verse 185, the book tells pupils that fasting "benefits the body and makes it strong," and teaches them the customs and prescriptions that validate or invalidate the ritual. The lesson is completed, as always, by a block of exercises:

How does the fast benefit Muslims?

Recite the verse that indicates the fast is incumbent upon Muslims.

Put the following words into appropriate sentences:
Fasting Ramadan *suhur*

Complete: Among the traditions of the fast is the acceleration of the ___________ and the delay of the ___________, by which the faster ___________ his fast.[22]

The fourth grade text places Ramadan in the context of the Muslim ritual year, explaining in detail the conduct of the two Muslim feast days, *'Id al-Fitr*, commemorating the close of Ramadan, and *'Id al-Adha*, the Feast of Sacrifice during the month of Pilgrimage. The fifth grade book summarizes previous lessons and tells children who is required to fast. Reprising the theme of restraint, "because the fast is not simply a cessation of food and drink, but is indeed an act of worship that refines the character and brings the person to his lord through good works," the book reminds students to eat the *suhur* meal (in effect, being moderate even in the fast itself), and to increase almsgiving, prayer, and study of the Qur'an. Then the primary school's treatment of Ramadan ends as it began, with a nashid—this one longer and far more complex—celebrating the growth of faith through contemplating the natural and celestial signs of God's existence and participating in the Ramadan fast.

In the early grades, the meaning and significance of Ramadan is expressed with the formal joy of classroom song and through the ritual fast's place in the life of the family. With time, students begin to learn more about the ritual details of the fast, personal restrictions that are balanced immediately by their beneficial effects on self and others. Next, fast and feast find their place in the yearly ritual cycle of Islam, their importance matched only by the celebration of sacrifice during the season of pilgrimage. And finally, as the child reaches the age of personal participation, learning about Ramadan becomes learning about individual and social responsibilities.

In contrast to the editorial processes of consolidation and grading, reinterpretation and functionalization are authorial processes, shaping the meaning of Islamic history and practice by interpreting them in fresh ways. Although the Qur'an contains its own explicit messages about God's intentions, the social and political use of the Qur'an can require that it bear additional semantic loads. In textbooks, the derivation of additional moral or political lessons from the Qur'an or sunna is accomplished in part through the transformation of sacred text into durus, or "lessons." Retelling stories from the Qur'an in a straightforward narrative form allows textbook authors to make claims about reality in a way that insulates their own commentary from the sacred text itself. Their interpretations of the story are not tafsir in a strict sense, explanations that seek to illuminate the meaning of the Qur'anic verse in its context, but rather paraphrases and commentaries on the events and personalities that the verses describe.

Take, for example, the story of the prophet Joseph. The story of Joseph in the fifth grade textbook is a ten-page paraphrase of the 111-verse sura 12, Yusuf, in the Qur'an. Aside from shuttling introductory and concluding exhortations off into another section, the schoolbook version is a straightforward paraphrase of the Qur'anic story, with a simplified grammar and vocabulary. Because of his power as an interpreter of dreams and the favor he found with Pharaoh, Joseph was made minister of Egypt and saved the country from famine; even after being reunited with his father (Jacob/Israel) and brothers, he retained his mighty position in the country and instead of returning to Canaan invited his family to settle with him in Memphis. But at the end of the life story of Joseph in the Egyptian fifth grade book, the authors of the text have appended a short patriotic paragraph:

> And thus Egypt has always been, and still is, a refuge for the prophets and the illustrious and outstanding people from the Arab nation and the Islamic world, who have been delighted to experience it, always sure of its welcome, and living within its family as beloved brothers.[23]

While Joseph was not an Arab, he was a Muslim, both as a prophet of God in his own right and as the great-grandson of Abraham, builder of the *ka'ba* in Mecca (sura 12,101). With this brief paragraph the text's authors have effectively Islamized Egypt twenty-three centuries before Muhammad.[24]

While this reinterpretation constructs readings of history that legitimate the authority of policymakers, functionalization as a specific textual process harnesses divine intention to public policy itself, helping to bring religious instruction into the conscious service of independent social and political ends. To illustrate this process, we can look at the textbooks' use of science, technology, and medicine. On one level, the interdependence of Islam and science is stressed in order to avoid the pitfall of implying that secular knowledge is inseparable from secularism. On another level, though, the linkage is made to bless elements from the religious sphere with the elevated status of science's secular mystique. This interdependence of science and religion is a constant refrain in both public and private sector Islamic literature for all age levels, an important part of a technocratic approach to economic and social policy. It is handled in different ways for different purposes, depending on the nature of the audience, the medium, and the rhetorical goal of the author. But in general, there are three relatively well-defined techniques.

First, new technologies or techniques are used to help maintain the religious reference system. Using loudspeakers for the call to prayer, cassette tapes to record famous Qur'an reciters, or observatories to determine scientifically the exact times of dawn and dusk prayers are all pragmatic applications of science and technology to aid worship, education and da'wa (Islamic outreach activities). Second, new technologies are legitimized by Islamic principles. This practice supports new medical technologies such as *in vitro* fertilization, plastic surgery, and birth control programs, which potentially threaten the integrity or function of God's creation. When properly bounded within certain limits, such practices can protect or further divine interests by correcting accidental errors or by satisfying other legitimate goals of the individual, the family, or the community.[25]

Finally, Islamic concepts and practices are corroborated by modern science. Scientific research, particularly from foreign countries or international agencies, is cited to show that secularists are finally discovering those truths that Muslims have known all along. This process is not limited to government-issued textbooks, but is a general feature of the production of contemporary genres of Islamic literature. Some of the best examples of the use of medical knowledge to further faith, in fact, are from the private sector, as in the following report in the July 1989 issue of *Zamzam*, the children's supplement to *al-Mukhtar al-Islami* (The Islamic Digest), a monthly magazine associated with the Muslim Brotherhood. Presenting a picture of an EKG chart, the article begins,

> If you look carefully at this picture, you will see that it repeatedly draws a specific word; scrutinizing the letters of every word, you will see that every word is made of the letters A L L H, written in the Arabic language in *raq'a* script; indeed, it is the term of Majesty. . . . And this picture that you see was not drawn by a human hand, but by a machine, a medical instrument made by a man who didn't know Arabic. The machine was not intended to write this word or any other, but is used to show the beating of the heart (that is, its pulsations) and to turn it into a picture on paper. . . . Scientists

didn't know at first that this drawing resembled a word in Arabic, but finally the great discovery was made that every beat says, in this drawing that an EKG makes of every human heart, every beat says in the testimony of this electrical device, "Allah, Allah, Allah."[26]

God has literally written His name upon the hearts of His creation, an act revealed by the use of technology. This natural theology attempts systematically to read God's presence and characteristics from those of the natural world which He created, using the hidden rhythms of the body itself as a measurable record of His existence.[27]

The use of science or natural phenomena to reinforce faith finds its way into the official religious studies curriculum as it did in the science curriculum, by binding science and religion to national progress. In the fifth grade class discussed in the last chapter, the class reading that was interrupted by the noon call to prayer had come from the section of the text on "cleanliness:"

Cleanliness is next to Godliness [*al-nidhafa min al-iman*], and . . . distinguishes a Muslim person, because our Islamic religion . . . impels the Muslim to it, even making cleanliness of the body and clothing one of the basic rules of prayer. Cleanliness includes that of the body and the clothing, and of food and drink, and cleanliness of the home and school, and mosque, and street, and so on. And on top of that Islam makes us desirous of personal adornment and sweet fragrances and the choice of good clean clothes. God (may He be exalted) says in verse 31 of Sura *al-A'raf*, "Oh Children of Adam! Wear your adornment at every place of worship." And the Messenger, may God bless and save him, used to wear white scented garments on Fridays and the two feast days, and he loved sweet-smelling things. Cleanliness . . . is a token of advancement and civilization, strongly bound to the progress of peoples, for advanced peoples are cleaner in their attire than others, and in their food and drink, and their streets. Islam had preceded all advanced nations by ages — in its call for cleanliness — and it made "cleanliness next to Godliness" when the Messenger, may God bless and save him, says "God is pleasant [*tayyib*] and loves pleasant things." Perhaps the *wudu'* [ritual ablution before prayer] clarifies best the scope of Islam's interest in cleanliness, since it is part of prayer . . . and — there's no doubt — it cleans man's body, and the modern physician has established that the *wudu'* a number of times a day brings health and keeps away skin diseases, just as he has proved that the *istinshaq* [the inhalation of water through the nostrils during the *wudu'*] protects people from the various respiratory diseases, and just as in rinsing there is a cleaning of the teeth guaranteed to freshen the breath; this had been mentioned in the noble Hadith: "Not to burden my people, I ordered them to use the *siwak* [a short stick for cleaning the teeth] at every prayer." And that because in the use of the *siwak* or the toothbrush there are clear effects in the cleaning of the teeth and their whiteness, and in killing the germs that cling to them due to the food that is found between the teeth if they are not cleaned well, which has caused teeth to fall out, creating horrible breath. And among the manifestations of Islam's concern with cleanliness: that it calls on us to bathe for prayer on Fridays and on the two feast days. . . . And the modern physician agrees with Islam in this, for doctors call on us to bathe at least once a week, guarding the body's cleanliness and freeing it from diseases. . . . The conclusion is that whoever wants to maintain the teachings of his religion looks after cleanliness. And whoever wants people to love and respect him is neat and clean, for Islam is a religion of cleanliness, and therefore it's a religion of advancement and civilization.[28]

The passage is striking in its equation of the ritual purity of the wudu' with the physical purity of a secular bath, a hygienic practice within the domain of the physician rather than the theologian. The sacred requirement of ablution has been functionalized, implying that the *reason* for the prescription is its presumed effect on health and well-being, rather than to mark a separation between sacred and profane.[29] The passage then forges further linkages between cleanliness (e.g., of streets) and civilization, creating a hierarchy of peoples in which the Islamic community is historically the first, and placing the sunna of the Prophet in the domain of the urban planner and the public health official.[30]

The treatment of the wudu' throughout primary school texts consistently stresses its hygienic aspects. A note to the teacher in the first grade text, for example, advises her to demonstrate the ablutions to her pupils and watch them perform it, explaining "the benefits of the *wudu'* and the importance of its repetition to the maintenance of cleanliness, that this cleanliness induces health and vitality in the pupil, just as it produces pleasure in social intercourse with people, and not estrangement from them."[31] In the second grade, pupils learn that "the *wudu'* is cleanliness"; that it "protects you from illnesses" and "invigorates the body and protects it from diseases."[32] In the fourth grade pupils are introduced to the *istinja'*, the cleansing of the excretory regions of the body: "Islam . . . calls on us always to bathe twice, or at least once a week. . . . The person must purify himself of remaining traces of urine or feces, and clean their outlets, until there isn't an unpleasant smell, and one doesn't run the risk of diseases."[33] Praising soap and water, the lesson ends with a set of exercises including these two items:

7. Write the following statement in beautiful script: "The clean person washes his hands with soap and water when he emerges from the bathroom."

8. Your little brother exits the bathroom and hasn't washed his hands—what do you say to him?[34]

Presenting moral lessons in the context of activities or hypothetical situations is intended to raise them above the level of mere memorization, phrasing rules in terms that the child can not only remember, but remember to apply in everyday situations. Significantly, this specific equation of moral and hygienic behavior is of long standing in Egypt; both are considered applied subjects in which the real test is the conduct of life rather than performance on written examinations.[35]

Logically, if not psychologically, this functionalization is a two-step process. First, social functions (increased health, cleanliness, order) are attributed to Islamic practices. Then these functions are interpreted not only as effects, but as the primary intent of given practices, and therefore divinely sanctioned themselves. Moreover, as in the case of ablutions, additional terms can be added to the formula. In stressing cleanliness both as a contributor to individual health and a token of social progress (*'unwan al-ruqiy wa al-hadara*), the text closes the causal circle. Since advanced civilizations are noted for attention to cleanliness and the Islamic community is the first among peoples, then physical cleanliness must be the primary function of the ablution.

If reinterpretation is an anachronistic reading of historical events, functionalization is in part a recontextualized rendering of divine intention. These two methods help shape the content of classroom texts, while consolidation and grading affect their format. There is, finally, a fifth process at work in the composition and use of these texts. That is the process of ritualization, which does not figure in the transformation of scripture into lesson, but in the resacralization of the lesson itself. Structured recitation and memorization of the textbook in anticipation of examinations, periodic in-class quizzing, the regular appearance of activities and exercises for which determined responses are often expected, and the implied double audience (text for students, footnoted instructions for the instructor) build around the textbook a congregation engaged several times a week in its ritual appreciation. The textbook provides the liturgy for ritual dramatizations of the moral authority of the state.

Family and School as Sources of Moral Authority

This authority is clear in the textbook treatment of the family and the school as sources of moral knowledge.[36] The image of the family in the contemporary textbook is ambiguous, for although parents, siblings, and other relatives are portrayed as central foci of the child's own moral duties, they are hardly ever portrayed as sources of moral enlightenment. That place has been usurped by the public functionaries of the school itself. As we saw at the end of the last chapter, this symbolic confiscation of moral authority feeds back into the constant media representation of the ideal family, making the family the target of moral development rather than the source. For the textbook to be used as an authoritative source of knowledge, it must help to define its institutional context as authoritative. We have already seen that lessons have sometimes been altered in newer textbooks to move away from stories and plays, but this has not been the case universally. It is still an important pedagogical strategy not to set out moral precepts in isolation, but to nest them within an image of idealized life, whether within the family, on the streets, or elsewhere.

Not surprisingly, such images often include the school as one of the primary characters, as we saw in the story of Saʿid and his father earlier in this chapter. In these images the school is not only one of the arenas of the child's day-to-day life, it is portrayed as the source of the child's most elementary articulable moral knowledge, a knowledge that the child proudly carries back to his or her grateful family. In primary school textbooks it is also the sole representative of the state. The very first lesson on adab in the second grade book provides a fine illustration of this technique. In the story, ʿAbir returns from school to find that her mother is preparing food for her father and some of his friends, whom he is bringing home after work. ʿAbir volunteers her help with food preparation and cleaning the reception room, and volunteers her brother Muhammad to go to the store and pick up some things. When the evening is over, their father sits with them and commends their behavior, thanking them for cleaning, preparing, and for serving the guests.

> ʿAbir said, "This is my duty towards my mother and my father, and we learned in school today a great lesson about loving one's parents and cooperating with them, and we memorized [part of] the glorious Qurʾan and

a noble tradition [of the Prophet], and I want you to hear them, father, and you, mother. [God] said, may he be exalted, 'Serve God, and join not any partners with Him; and do good to parents' [sura 2, 36]. 'A man came to the Prophet, may God bless and save him, and said, O Messenger of God: what person is most deserving of perfect friendship? [The Prophet] said, Your mother. [The man] asked, Then who? [The Prophet] said, Your mother. [The man] asked, Then who? [The Prophet] said, Your mother. [The man] asked, Then who? [The Prophet] said, Your father.' "[37]

The story is followed by a drawing of 'Abir and Muhammad helping their parents with the guests, and a short nashid about loving one's parents: "What pleases God except what pleases [your] parents/What is the beauty of life but the affection of [your] parents/Love your parents to live in happiness/And [if you] offer [your] spirit as a sacrifice to them, you will find good reward."[38]

Given the importance invested in the child's duties toward the family, it might seem surprising that parents are only rarely depicted as founts of religious or moral counsel. Children are advised always to help and obey their parents even if they have differences of opinion with them, "because [your parents] both love you and wish only the best for you always, and never think of anything but your happiness."[39] But children are sometimes portrayed as the wiser parties in moral quandaries. A story in the third grade book tells of how 'Umar Ibn al-Khattab, the companion of the Prophet and second caliph of the Muslim community, was wandering the streets of Medina before dawn one day when he heard a conversation between a mother and daughter. The mother instructs the daughter to water down the milk the girl has just brought, so they can sell it for a greater profit. The girl reminds her mother that Islam has prohibited such a practice, and what would the Commander of the Faithful say? The woman replies that neither the Commander of the Faithful nor anyone else can see what they are doing, but the girl counters that God can see them, and that they must please him both in secret and in public.

Mother: Do what I tell you, sweetheart.

Daughter: Should I obey you and disobey God, dear mother? Certainly not.

Mother: If you don't mix the milk with water, we won't make any profit.

Daughter: If we please God, he will bless us with profit and expand our subsistence.

Mother: God bless you, daughter. You are better than I, and have just taught me a great lesson.[40]

ʿUmar is so pleased with the young girl that when he goes home to tell his sons the story, he asks which of them will marry her. His son ʿAsim volunteers, noting that "such a girl will make a virtuous wife." The reward for virtuous behavior is material and immediate, as in the example below of telling the truth about a low mark at school.

Aside from the story about Ramadan discussed above, the only sustained example in this series of books of parents serving as a source of moral instruction occurs in the fourth grade. The story is an interesting one in that it combines several of the themes we have been discussing, and reminds us of the real-life story at the end of the last chapter, of the young girl's electronically mediated knowledge of the Qurʾan. This story deals with Ahmad and his father.

Ahmad was used to turning on the [radio] broadcast of the Glorious Qurʾan every morning upon waking up. For he loved always to begin his day by listening to some verses of the book of God (may He be exalted), and his father encouraged him in this good habit. A lot of times, Ahmad asked his parents, when the family gathered together over breakfast, about the meaning of some Qurʾanic words and verses he had heard.[41]

This particular morning, Ahmad asks his father about verse 185 of the sura ʾAl ʿImran, "Every soul shall have a taste of death, and only on the Day of Judgment shall you be paid your full recompense." When will the Day of Judgment come, he asks, and what will happen then? His father explains what the Day of Judgment is, but says that only God knows when it will be. Ahmad, assiduously thanking his father for each answer, still doesn't understand the meaning of one of the terms his father has used, *"yawm al-baʿth,"* the Day of Resurrection, but his father doesn't have time to explain it before school, so promises Ahmad he will give him a book about it later that day.

After school Ahmad flips eagerly through the book and realizes that it contains all the information he needs about the resurrection and judgment. He agrees to his father's suggestion that he divide the book into sections, reading just one part each day for a week, so as not to interfere with his schoolwork. At the end of the week, he delightedly gathers excerpts to share with his classmates at school by publishing them in the class newsletter "so they would benefit from the good religious information he had."[42] This story brings together the father, the Qurʾan, radio broadcasts, religious publications, and the school newsletter as sources of religious instruction. The lesson ends by quoting Ahmad's excerpts on death, resurrection, and judgment, but its didactic purpose is not defined merely by their presentation. Like the newspaper story about the virtuous village family memorizing the Qur'an in the last chapter, this fable provides an idealized model of the Muslim family in which parents and children cooperate to strengthen family piety with the help of social institutions responsible for publishing books and broadcasting the Qur'an. This strength and motivation is then transferred to the public domain of the school, just as in the example of 'Abir and her brother, moral lessons from school were transferred to the home.[43]

In the fourth grade book the school reappears in the very next lesson about a schoolteacher teaching his students about proper Muslim forms of greeting after having them practice their ablutions in the school mosque,[44] and then again where a section on the names and occupations of the angels is framed by a story about the teacher leading his pupils together in the noon prayer:

> And the teacher had been used, from time to time, after doing the prayer, to give each one of them a book from the library of the prayer area, to read for a little while, then he directed a little talk and discussion about the topics they wanted to investigate and understand, and to answer their questions, and point them to those things that were right and beneficial in this world and the next.[45]

But the textbooks portray school not just as a place to discover ancient moral truths. School is, in proper Deweyan fashion, a miniature moral universe where looking after one's classroom and one's books, and remembering one's lessons, is one way in which the child serves God.[46] School is like life, with the year-end test differentiating justly between the diligent and negligent students just as God's just accounting on the Day of Judgment will differentiate between people who do good and those who do evil.[47] A section on telling the truth uses a school example to show the child that lying only hurts the liar, and that the rewards for good behavior are immediate and material as well as deferred and spiritual:

> For example, if you got a low score on one of your subjects, you have to tell your parents, without exaggerating or minimizing; and you know that truth will benefit you in this case, because when your father learns that your score is low in a subject, he'll help you until you're strong in it, and you

will excel among your classmates; truth makes you a winner, and lying a loser.[48]

This passage reveals an interesting idealization of parental behavior keyed to the middle-class home (where, to be sure, the parents are just as likely to hire the pupil's teacher to give after-school lessons, as to help the child themselves). Going to school is the child's job, just as the peasant, the truck driver, and the parent all have their employment, without which society, imagined as an organism very much like the human body in the differentiation and interdependence of its parts, could not function.[49] Islam is the charter for the function of modern society and requires attentiveness to work and mutual cooperation. Even the Prophet, one story shows, worked hard to accomplish group tasks, and refused to eschew manual labor or to be marked with special privilege.[50]

Supplements to Public Sector Instructional Media

There are a number of public and private sector publishing companies in Egypt that develop and market religious material for children. Stories about the lives of the prophets are particularly popular, as are manuals for adults on Islamic upbringing. During my stay in Cairo bookstalls carried, in addition to numerous general works on Islamic childrearing, at least four different manuals on prayer. One of these was for adults newly interested in fulfilling their Islamic obligations, one was for older children who could already read, and two were illustrated guides for parents and families on how to teach children to pray properly. Some companies are moving into a more upscale market as well, selling their products to private schools and through selected bookstores. The Safir Publishing Company was established in 1982 to do advertising and publicity (they placed advertising for, among other periodicals, the Muslim Brotherhood's monthly *al-I'tisam*). In 1986 they opened a new operation, the design and publication of Islamic instructional material for younger children.

These materials are designed by the Children's Culture Unit (*Wahda Thaqafa al-Tifl*) in the company's main office in Muhandisin, a modern and prestigious area in Giza that has been the beneficiary of much of the new wealth of Sadat's post-1974 Open Door policy, which substantially liberalized regulation of foreign investment in Egypt. The company has a well-planned and aggressive sales policy, with representatives in each Egyptian governorate marketing their material to local bookstores and private schools. They also sell their products in other countries, both Islamic and non-Islamic (in Britain and the United States, for example), taking advantage of national, regional, and international book fairs.

Karim Shafik, whom we met briefly in the last chapter, had helped found the Children's Culture Unit at Safir before moving on to another publisher. He explained to me that the company had perceived a need for books concentrating on the preschool level, because all of the available ones were too simple. The basic idea behind Safir products was to provide a supplement (*idafa*) or an aid (*masa'da*) for parents and for teachers in private schools, to give children a strong foundation in basic skills. The other goal of the company was to "Islamize the curricula," since the basis of all knowledge is religion (*haqiqat il-'ilm id-din*).

The company felt, he said, that books specifically about Islam should operate through *"bab al-idah,"* the path of clarification, attending to the child's nature and relying on *"tabsit mafahim al-islam,"* the simplification of Islamic concepts, by involving children in activities, like games. "I saw children playing some of the games of the kind you have had in America," Karim said, "and how they concentrated on them and learned from playing them. That was the beginning of games like Battles of the Prophet," one of the board games the company produced. When the government produces religious books, one member of Safir's staff complained, all they care about is *al-hukm* (authority, governmental control) and cost; and although Safir tries to produce economical materials, "it's not a charitable institution."[51]

The company's pedagogical strategy, according to Karim, was rooted in the idea that

> the child's capacity for memorization is much greater than his capacity for understanding. The memorization of the Qur'an can do a lot of things. It can improve pronunciation and diction, it can provide a basis for *adab*. But one thing that the memorization of the Qur'an cannot do, is to change your behavior or your comportment by itself. Because even if it's memorized, it's not understood, and the explanation of the meaning of the Qur'an requires a lot of work, and what modern methods do is to explain the context of the Qur'an in simple terms by breaking it down into principles and dwelling on those. So by the use both of memorization—and I myself have never

memorized the Qur'an — and modern methods, we can fulfil all the aims we seek.

For example, we see that in the United States there are all kinds of social problems stemming from sexual excess and perversions, which lead to things like the AIDS epidemic, and we want to avoid that kind of thing here, but how do you explain such things to a child? The answer is that you start out by building a strong foundation based on clear, basic principles. *Tarbiya* has to do with the sound upbringing of the child (*tanshi'a wa salihat it-tifl*), to make an individual who is useful to society. You can think of *da'wa* as the delivery of information (*tawsil al-mafahim*), whereas *tarbiya* is the formation of the human personality.[52]

Aside from acquiring specifically moral skills, the company expects children to benefit in other ways from using such products. In the introduction to one of their coloring book series, the editors explain that, since childhood is the time when the basic features of the human personality are set in place and the faculties of the child develop quickly, it is important to pay close attention to these processes. The use of these coloring books will "improve the capabilities of the child" through helping him develop nervous and muscular coordination, an appreciation of beauty, "a sense for the harmony of spaces and sizes and colors," and artistic ability. Furthermore, it "plants divine doctrine in the child's emotional life by tying together the whole universe with its Creator, who has command over everything he created." The job of the teacher or parent is to demonstrate to the child "God's abilities and his wisdom in the creation of the various creatures presented in [the] book." And finally, by coloring the pictures himself, the child learns self-confidence, and the importance of caring for his own property.[53]

These goals are pursued skillfully in a number of series of books and other materials. Unlike cheap public sector religious textbooks, Safir's materials are of the highest quality, using well-printed colored pictures on slick paper stock, clear line drawings, and calligraphy. In addition to board games, of which the company produces at least three, there are several series of coloring books, flash cards, paper models of Islamic monuments, illustrated stories, books on adab and on the principles of Islam, capsule summaries of famous Islamic books, and workbooks for different subjects, from religion to arithmetic and English. Safir also sells Islamic jigsaw puzzles and produces posters with Islamic themes, all printed in color on heavy card stock, and a line of Islamic greeting cards. Various outside consultants, including educators, psychologists, and religious scholars cooperate in the conception, design, and writing of the books and other materials.

By and large, the books are quite close thematically to the products of the Ministry of Education. Stories illustrate basic rules of faith and behavior: put your trust in God during times of adversity, keep the streets clean, obey your parents. Model social practices are described in stories of model — and not so model — children as well. In one story a young boy learns through a painful experience not to disobey his parents.[54] In another, a series of annotated cartoon panels shows us "A Day in the Life of a Muslim Child." Like the government, private sector publishers functionalize Islamic teachings and practices, reading divine intention from the shape of the social and natural worlds. Just as the government books teach that daily prayers "invigorate the body," and "accustom the Muslim to organization, and respect for appointed times,"[55] Safir produces materials like the illustrated story book *al-Sufuf al-Munadhdhama* (Orderly Lines), which emphasize that *"al-nidham min al-iman,"* orderliness proceeds from faith. The book's pictures and text compare alternate realities on facing pages. On one page, a clerk at a service window waits on patient men standing in a neat, quiet line, while on the facing page an employee in a different office serves a pushy, unruly, and ill-mannered crowd whose own behavior undermines his ability to attend to their requests. The first line proceeds in an orderly manner, each petitioner's papers being processed quickly and efficiently, while in the second scenario, men butt into the front of the line, fights break out, a wallet is stolen in the confusion of pushing and shouting. Soon the first employee has finished his work and can break for lunch, while no work at all has been completed in the second case.

In the final illustrations, the clerk in the first picture steps out of his office and begins to lecture to the assembly on the facing page. "If only you knew the lesson that we learned from prayer," he says. "During collective prayer we must straighten the rows, just as in all our lives, we must have order, order . . . " In the ensuing conversation he informs the crowd that God will not look favorably at prayer rows that are crooked, because Islam is a religion of order and discipline (*al-islam din al-nidham wa al-indibat*). Order saves time and ensures fairness, and the men of the crowd finally realize that God teaches us through everything, and that the straight rows of prayer teach us that order and discipline will help tranquility and satisfaction to prevail in all human endeavor.[56]

The proposition that "Islam is a religion of order and discipline," and that the straight rows of prayer are part of a divine pedagogy, contrasts sharply with the colonial perception of Muslim ritual behavior (whether prayer or the rhythmic rocking during kuttab study) as a primitive feature of a backward faith. It places Islamic rituals on a par with the disciplinary technologies of the school, as described by Foucault and Mitchell, borrowing a modern European conception of self and projecting it backward in time, so that the Muslim *umma* becomes, once again, the historical antecedent and type specimen of civilized community. One interpretation of this statement might take it seriously in a Bourdieuian sense, and posit that the straight lines of prayer are one manifestation of a pervasive but implicit habitus that causes Egyptians to experience spatial and kinesic regimentation as natural, simply by living it in their everyday lives.[57] The mental habits and the physical skills of prayer, taught implicitly at home and then explicitly in the religion class, and displayed publicly there in the form of recitation, response, and even on-demand display of proper prayer positions (rehearsed and mastered, at least in pantomime fashion, in the first grade), could be seen as part of the habitus.

But things are not as simple as this. While the practice of prayer might install the habitus of prayer, there is no reason to believe that this habitus becomes a generalized behavioral template, extended indefinitely to other realms of experience. The significant feature of this discourse of order and discipline is, instead, its framing of ritual behavior as a code that should be read rather than merely a habit that should be cultivated. In learning that "Islam is a religion of order and discipline," through the example of the straight lines of prayer, the child is prompted to interpret aspects of social reality as having meanings beyond those that they proclaim or manifest directly. I would argue that contemporary pedagogy implicitly instills this habit of interpretation, this tafsir of the phenomenal world, in effect democratizing the creation of political ideologies, even if this means merely bringing implicit assumptions into the realm of the spoken.[58]

Through the school, students learn to derive ideologies from the *observation* of social practices or natural phenomena. Egyptians do not carry the hexis of orderly prayer into other areas of their lives. It is context-bound, and only the symbolic elaboration that has come with the functionalization of the religious tradition allows the reading of a portable "order and discipline" into it.[59] In fact, as John Bowen has shown in the case of Indonesia, the Muslim prayer ritual "cannot be 'decoded' semantically because it is not designed according to a single symbolic or iconic code. In particular times and places Muslims have construed the *salat* as conveying iconic or semantic meanings, but as part of particular spiritual, social and political discourses."[60]

In any ritual there are a number of features that can be made to signify. In Bowen's Indonesian example, local communities, governments and Islamic reform movements make specific aspects of prayer (e.g., its formality and periodicity, its communicative functions, its public nature) express ideal models of society, political divisions, theological notions, and community structure. Muslims elsewhere sometimes interpret the straight rows of prayer as battle lines arrayed against the forces of evil.[61] The ritual is a rich source of alternative meanings that can be foregrounded and mobilized by specific groups. But underlying those specific mobilizations is the explicitness of the interpretive framework encouraged by an educational discourse centered on the abstraction of "principles" from the *turath*, the Islamic heritage.

Two things should be emphasized here with respect to the Egyptian case. The first is that the preoccupation with function is a general cognitive framework for the interpretation of social objects and events, an intellectual practice that is applied publicly both in strategic educational planning and in the mundane communication of subject matter in the classroom. Again, to take the example of ritual ablutions, educators use the connection between cleanliness and the Islamic tradition to encourage hygienic behavior, advising students that hygiene is the primary intent of the ritual. In learning this lesson, children learn both the explicit message that Islam looks after the individual's health and the implicit message that Islamic practices are to be examined for their latent functions and their social effect. In essence, the intertextual structure of "traditional" Islamic scholarship, which linked primary texts with written commentaries and glosses, has been broken. For in schoolbook discourse, sacred texts are linked with the observable world, both natural and social, as both their referent and their best proof. The ordinary educated Muslim need not master a complex body of legal or philosophical material in order to participate in functionalist discourse; the physician, the engineer, and the bureaucrat are equally well-equipped to bring their experiences of social, mechanical, and natural order into the discussion of God's nature.

Second, this functionalization occurs without the desacralization of the material, so that the process Durkheim described early in this century as one of the goals of the modern educational system is subverted.[62] Naturalistic and materialistic explanations coexist with supernatural ones, for Muslims perceive the two as noncontradictory. The "real" reasons for religious practices do not strip off their theological cloaks. Since God is concerned with the welfare of the Muslim community, the prescriptions of Islam are not only beneficial, but manifestly rational. What is left is to see how these utilitarian ideologies are consolidated and maintained in public culture after the child leaves the elementary school's moral assembly line.

CHAPTER 6

Growing Up: Four Stories

The youth of every nation are the secret of its strength, and the pillars of its rebirth, and the sign of its advancement; indeed, the believing youngster spends the period of his youth preparing himself for a noble life, and directs his energy toward useful works in building his future and raising his moral and intellectual level.

Ninth grade religious studies textbook, 1988–89[1]

The processes reviewed in the last chapter transform the Islamic tradition not merely by molding it into a novel format — one could just as easily spend class time memorizing condensed legal manuals — but specifically by folding the child's phenomenal experience of the everyday into his understanding of the sacred, coaxing illuminations of God's will from the humble intersection of personal habit and the image of public good. Coded by age grade and supervised by the mechanics of the examination, these books (as well as children's literature produced by the private sector) act as supplementary revelation and updated sunna in which archetypal modern characters mingle with the prophets of the Qur'an and the exemplary citizens of Medina depicted in hadiths. The textbooks' wise fictional parents and teachers are messengers who bridge the imperfections of reality and the perfection of the divine. In the same way, the discoveries of science display God's will in an EKG pattern as surely as do Qur'anic evocations of the movement of the stars. In using the phenomenal world — both natural and social — as a framework through which divine truth is to be understood and in which it is to be applied, these texts continually renew divinity's instantiations to match human experiences at particular times and places.

Functionalization, as a set of discursive and social practices that provides both for the interpretation and the application of these divine truths, constructs not so much a single reading of Islam, but a framework in which Islam is to be read. Diametrically opposed positions can be derived from the same assumptions or observations, and disagreements then acquire the spurious appearance of fundamental difference when in fact they reveal a common set of understandings. As an example, compare the following three passages:

1. The renaissance of Islamic society stands upon the faith of individuals, and on the effects of this faith on their behavior. . . . [The Muslim] balances the demands of religion and the world, and works for [this] world as he does for the next, is precise in his work, and increases production without delay or indifference, until he has achieved prosperity, advancement and economic development for society.[2]

2. Work is a fundamental in the life of the individual, because it provides him with what he needs, and maintains his dignity and sets up for him and his family a respectable level of living, just as it is a fundamental in the life of society, because the wealth of the *umma* is a result of the work of its individuals, and there is no way to increase production without work in various fields: agriculture, manufacturing, trade, construction, teaching, and other profitable areas.[3]

3. There is in the Mahomedan religion itself a great want of encouragement to art, science, or industry. It does not give honour to labour. The book and the sword are the only two objects which it presents as worthy of the ambition or the reverence of its votaries. The Imams, who sometimes preach with the Koran in one hand and a wooden scimitar in the other, are living emblems of the present state of the Mussulman world — for the sword is powerless, and the book speaks in vain. Agriculture has no praise in the Koran, nor has manufacture nor commerce: it is the book of the desert, addressed to the inhabitants of the wilderness. . . . The Koran was addressed to warriors — to the fighting men of the waste. The Mahometan cultivator seems to accept and resign himself to a recognised condition of humiliation and inferiority — for him there is little comfort in the holy book.[4]

Despite their surface differences, the first two passages are essentially identical to the last in their understanding of the nature of religion. (The shorter passages are drawn from the Egyptian government's 1988 eighth grade religious studies textbook; the third is from the report on Egypt and Cyprus that Bowring submitted to the British government a century and a half earlier.) The extent to which Bowring's superficially distinctive passage is an ethnocentric representation of difference, a libel against Islam, and an offensive stereotype of the "indolent Oriental" is beside the point. What is significant is its agreement with the first two excerpts in their construction of the social categories into which religion in general is thought to fit. In this case, religion as a system of belief and practice should have something to say about work. There is, of course, no a priori reason why religious systems should pay any attention at all to productive or commercial activity, whether encouraging or discouraging it (although Islamic law, specifically, does have a long tradition of concern for commerce). What statements of this type do is not merely construct specific content—whether Islam does or does not honor work—but construct Islam as a whole by defining its extension, by defining work as one of the things about which Islam has something to say.

This discourse of work, as well as those of personal respectability, intellectual humility, and social accountability, are important and recurrent themes. Having seen in the last two chapters how adults structure religious communication with youngsters, we can continue to explore these themes by entering the religious environment of the older Egyptian child struggling to create his own personality while parents, politicians, and educators continue to guide him along various paths to adulthood. The stories teachers and parents tell their children in the process of forming them into responsible family members and useful citizens are obviously only a part—and arguably a very small part—of the stories they hear, the stories they live, and the stories they make for themselves.

We have seen in Islamic theory that the child passes through three stages of social and spiritual development. But alongside this religious progression lie other sets of age labels. Like its American counterpart, the Egyptian periodization of aging is imprecise and context-dependent. In rural Egypt, as in Yemen and elsewhere, children are often referred to as *juhhal* (sing. *jahil*), meaning "ignorant." They are socially unformed beings in whom proper adab has to be cultivated.[5] Among middle-class urbanites, the word often used is *tifl* (pl. *atfal*), which means "baby," a word that can refer to young babies specifically, or to children in general anywhere from birth to age eighteen or so, as can *walad* (pl. *awlad*), which means "boy." Either term essentially refers to "kids." *Sibbi*, "child" or "youth," is sometimes used by teachers and psychologists for children between the ages of six and sixteen. Other terms are *murahiq*, "teenager" or "adolescent," a learned word that applies to the older end of the age range, and *tali'a*, which means, literally, "vanguard," and is usually used in the plural, *tala'i'*. Like *sibbi*, these last two terms are more commonly used in writing than in speech. Far more common is the social and age category *shabb* (pl. *shabab*), which begins between the ages of thirteen to sixteen or eighteen, and extends through the late twenties or early thirties. The shabab are essentially marriageable (or sexually mature) but unmarried young people. The word is used in much the same way as the English word *youth*, referring to a collective, almost as if it were an organized and independent social force. When pundits refer to the children or youth of the nation, they speak of *awladna* or *atfalna*, "our children," and *al-shabab*, "the youth," or *shababna*, "our youth." This primary contrast set directs our movement from looking at the religious discourse aimed at children toward looking at that aimed at youth.

There are four areas where state interests intersect with the life cycle of the shabab: sexual development and marriage; the awakening of political consciousness and the beginnings of economic activity; the development of attitudes toward official religious institutions; and the role of educational and public outreach programs in the moral guidance of youth as they cross the threshold to adulthood and find their place in the worlds of family and work irrevocably altered. The stories people tell about this transition coexist, merge, and contrast in various ways with the stories they find ready-made for them in the increasingly Islamicized public environment. As we continue to explore these stories told by the textbook, the newspaper, and the radio, the political implications of this "mediated" Islam will become clearer. What we will see is that a religious authority based on the creation and utilization of mass literacy destabilizes the relationship between traditional religious elites, secular professionals, and the public. In Egypt as elsewhere in the Muslim world, religious messages become increasingly hard to govern the more intensely they are deployed.

It's Not Haram, But They Might Not Understand It

Samia 'Abd al-Rahman's daughter, Nadia, was in the ninth grade when I first met her in 1989. She resembled Samia both in appearance and in dress, since she had been a muhaggaba since puberty. "Girls *biyithaggibu* [don *higab*] when they first get their period," Samia explained, naturalizing her daughter's experience despite the fact that most Egyptian women today have made that choice later in their lives. Just as in her younger days, when learning about Islam was just as natural as getting tall, Nadia had always remained a good girl, her mother said, who never had to be coaxed or prodded to do the right thing. "Except," she remembered,

> about six months ago, she said to me, I have friends who are boys, why don't I call them on the phone, or have them call me. At first I said, don't call them, and don't let them call you. It's not *haram*, but they might not understand it, and might think the wrong thing.
>
> And she said to me, well, you have male friends, and you talk to them on the phone, and they come over here and talk to you, why can't I do the same? I told her that it was because I had chosen these friends, and I trusted them, and that I am mature enough and experienced enough to know how to handle the situation if something isn't correct. She said to me, but in Islam, there's *halal* and *haram*, and if it's not the one, you shouldn't do it.
>
> We went on like that, and I said that if she called them, the family of the boy might not understand, and so on. She finally solved the problem herself, by saying, I will not speak to him anymore, and he will not speak to me, because I think I love him, but he's in love with another girl. Now, since she's a teenager, she's very anti-men. They're all dirty, she says, and they just don't deserve to be paid attention to. Now she makes my days black, because when *my* friends call, she says I shouldn't speak to them!
>
> I'm very frank in dealing with Nadia. I tell her things directly, and don't approach things by indirect ways. So I told her, it's *haram* to kiss boys or let them kiss you. And she said, Mama! How can you talk about things like this? But you know, at her age, boys and girls are always touching and pulling at each other, and slapping, and so on. She does shake hands with men. But on the schoolbus that she takes, she has seen some girls sitting in the laps of the boys, and was shocked by that.[6]

Nadia, turning against her mother the adolescent's universal sensitivity to discrepancies between theory and its application, was practicing with a rhetorical power aimed at asserting her own status as an arbiter of culture and custom.[7] Manipulating and experimenting with the discourse of absolutes, she claimed a position of superiority when her life circumstances changed and a plausible interpretation of Islamic gender segregation made a virtue of her necessity. Such disputes and negotiations over the nature of rules ("it's not *haram*, but . . . "), where rules apply ("she does shake hands with men") and—most importantly—

who can apply them ("now, when *my* friends call, she says I shouldn't speak to them!"), are as common between age grades as they are between political, ethnic, gender, or class rivals.

As in the home, schools deal with the potentials and problems of young teens by continuing to present them with models of proper behavior. Sex is approached gingerly in the religion curriculum for students like Nadia. It is confined, in the preparatory schoolbooks, to a single dialogue in which a teacher condemns youths' harassing comments to young women on the street.[8] Deeper consideration of sex and marriage is postponed until the final year of secondary school, when the issues of engagement, marriage, and the rearing of children enter the religion curriculum. In Cairo the average age of marriage for both men and women is rising steadily as it takes longer and longer each year for struggling families to save or borrow the money to finance a marriage. Marriage expenses include not only payments by the groom and the bride's accumulation of a suitable trousseau, but the celebration itself and the acquisition of an apartment in an artificially tight housing market. As Diane Singerman has shown, the investments families make in the marriage of their children are often the largest capital outlays of their lives. The prolonged period between physical maturity and marriage, together with family pressures that discourage the free association between young men and women, is stressful for everyone, particularly because families count on their reputations for upright behavior to attract suitable marriage partners for their children when the time comes.[9]

Since the reproduction of the family is at the center of everyday political and economic activities for most Egyptians, as well as being in theory the primary basis for a true Muslim society, schoolbooks depict marriage as one of God's principal intentions for humankind. Books advise young people to select their companions for religious and moral values rather than superficial qualities like looks or wealth.[10] While textbooks do not delineate the precise extent of parental responsibility in the choice of spouses for their children, they do advise that men and women at least be able to see each other before the engagement, even if the sunna restricts this viewing to the girl's face and hands, with conversation conducted in the presence of a *mahram* (a male relative of the woman not eligible to marry her).[11] In fact, although restrictions are hardly ever quite so draconian, the interactions of young people both before and after their engagements are closely monitored by relatives and constitute a frequent trigger for family quarrels, gossip, and public comment.[12]

Textbook discussions of family life cover the legal conditions of engagement and marriage, the legal rituals involved in their completion, and the respective rights of husband and wife. As in much of Islamic political writing, the rights of marriage partners are expressed as duties owed to them by other parties, in this case, their mates. Thus, the husband's rights include the expectation that his wife will obey him, manage the household, raise the children properly, and support the family emotionally. She bears the responsibility neither to leave nor to invite people into her husband's house without his permission (either general or specific), a custom of wrenching significance for women moving some distance from their extended families. The rights of the wife include her husband's payment of brideprice, and his financial support for her and her children, along with a suitable residence, sexual intimacy, sympathy, care and cooperation, all after the model of the Prophet's marriages. For young people who cannot marry for reasons of health, disposition, or finance, the Ministry of Education offers the Prophet's advice that fasting helps overcome carnal desires by strengthening control over the conscience and helping one transcend appetites that might otherwise lead to the sin of an unlawful "natural relationship" (*'alaqa tabi'iyya*).[13]

According to Egyptian pundits, the moral confusion responsible for premarital sexual activity, as well as social problems like street violence and drug use, can be traced to a variety of insidious influences. These include not only a staggeringly uneven economy where unemployment and inflationary pressures strangle family income in the face of continually rising expectations, but also the impact of globalized popular culture. Critiques of Egyptian cultural policy, which mandates the centralized monitoring and censorship of radio, film, television, and print production, and the regulation of imported films, videos, and music, cluster around three perspectives. While some critics decry the tendency to look abroad for popular culture when it could be produced more authentically at home, others target sex and violence in entertainment media either as psychologically harmful in general, or specifically as corruptions emanating from "the West."

Arguing on the basis of economic as much as cultural independence, some newspaper columnists have asked, Why do Egyptians not manufacture girls' dolls named 'Aisha to compete with Barbie? Why do Mickey Mouse and Tom and Jerry usurp the rightful place of *Kalila wa Dimna* (a popular pair of Arabic folktale characters)?[14] While Egypt is a prolific producer of soap operas,[15] most local products are outshone both in production quality and in popularity by American serials like

Dallas, *Knot's Landing*, and *Falcon Crest*. Heavily edited for Egyptian viewing, these shows nevertheless saturate the airwaves with images of the wealthy, the decadent, and the promiscuous (albeit wealthy, decadent and promiscuous extended families often living in joint households, which partially accounts for their fascination: it is the social world of the Egyptian family with both its economic resources and its values precisely reversed). These shows are a constant subject not only of friendly conversations, but of newspaper editorials and letters, like this one in *al-Ahram*, written by the superintendent of geography at a private secondary school in Alexandria:

> Great throngs of viewers have developed a powerful infatuation with [*Falcon Crest*], the proof of which is the increase in the length of commercials preceding it! It's certain that this series is nothing but a summons destructive and ruinous to every standard. For it deals, with great charm and detail, with how to murder one's brothers, and how to carry out wife-swapping with ease, and how to hatch every kind of vile and base plot! [It shows] how forbidden affections are open and public and acceptable to everybody, and practiced by everybody!! All this without any obstacle from religion or human nature or conscience.

After extolling the show's lavish production values, acting, photography, and the wardrobe of the stars, which is provided by "some of the trendiest fashion houses in the world," the author demands,

> Is this series a devastating cultural assault intended to infiltrate without awareness the subconscious of our youth and our daughters and our wives? Or is it a hidden appeal for the disintegration of values and the decay of society? And where is the supervision of all this? Of course I don't have official censorship in mind, for that has allowed its presentation . . . on the contrary, I contemplate supervision by the conscience of the nation [*damir al-'umma*] as represented by venerable men of religion and social scientists and the greatest intellectuals and writers and critics. . . . In general I call on all the viewers of this series to delve deeply into its contents and to perceive for themselves its danger and its aim: that it is, as I believe myself, deadly poison covered in the sweetest wrapping![16]

This sort of cultural critique, familiar to Americans in the conservative post-Reagan era, is an important reflection of a growing worldwide debate about the social, psychological and moral effects of market-based cultural production. Another columnist reminds the public that "We owe it to our children not to leave their enculturation to chance and dim-sightedness, and then to complain that among them are young addicts and deviants from our values."[17] Medical experts counsel the public that media images can disrupt the balance between good and evil within a person, potentially triggering outbursts of random violence, as demonstrated by a press report of a young Australian man who wounded two dozen people in Melbourne after a rampage induced by seeing the movie *Rambo*. According to Dr. Muhammad Sha'lan, professor of psychiatry at al-Azhar,

> Sometimes artistic works contradict what is within a certain person living in certain circumstances, and the two are thrown together and cause an explosion . . . this doesn't mean that the artistic works are responsible, but if the works gave admirable models in leading roles, this person would have imitated a good model rather than a bad model like Rambo; these days violence is getting the better of us; violence in art and violence in life. We used to watch "Cinderella," and now karate films are what we watch.[18]

Other mental health professionals concur. Dr. Sayyid Subhi, a professor of mental health and therapy at 'Ain Shams, and chair of the Psychology Department at the College of Education in Medina in Saudi Arabia, argues that the victory of self-centered values in modern society, a condition he refers to as "moral retardation" (*al-i'aqa al-khuluqiyya*; or "absence of conscience," *ghiyab al-damir*), results from noncommitment to religious morals. It manifests itself in, among other things, the spread of drug addiction among Egyptian youth.[19] This is not a discourse rejecting "the West," but a discourse questioning the nature of "modern society" as such. Often it contrasts a culture anchored in religious values with a culture that has lost its spiritual moorings, a culture become coarse, uncivil, and obsessed by cultural products organized around images of undomesticated (unmarried) sex and (nonmilitary and thus unpatriotic) violence.

The third critical response goes beyond encouraging cultural self-sufficiency or rejecting psychologically damaging entertainment, to foreground the specific cultural differences that distinguish an ideal Muslim society from the mores of Euroamerican society. Islamic critics, in particular, accuse the government of promulgating cultural and educational policies that are not only inconsistent, but positively harmful. While Islamic behavior is emphasized in religion textbooks and political speeches, it is obviously not a feature of Sylvester Stallone epics, nor, the critics say, is it even encouraged across the school curriculum. In a 1989 exposé in *al-Nur*, the weekly organ of Egypt's tiny Liberal Party, 'Adil al-Ansari castigated the Ministry of Education and the administration of al-Azhar's secondary institutes for allowing the use of history books that delete mention of the great Muslim victories against the Mongols and Crusaders, and, even worse, the use of English language texts that portray "unveiling and the mixing of the sexes." Al-Ansari reviewed several cases in which stories and dialogues present Egyptian and European women "unveiled and adorned"; parties and nights on the town in which men and women — both Egyptian and foreign — mix freely and stay out dancing "until three in the morning." There were pictures of women at hairstylists, or sitting on the ground with hair and knees exposed, and in one instance a mosque in an illustration was complimented for its archaeological rather than its religious significance.

In a final example al-Ansari invoked a story told in the second-year secondary English textbook, in which an English businessman is invited to the apartment of Ibrahim, an Egyptian. Before coming to visit, the Englishman stops to buy flowers for the lady of the house, with her husband's full knowledge: "And when he goes to the home [of his friend], Layla the Egyptian opens [the door] to him and she is unveiled, and she greets this foreign man freely and he gives her the roses and she thanks him and brings him food amidst broad smiles."[20] From the point of view of the religious activist, the breathless pornographic intent of these examples is clear. They are not merely descriptions of the interactions of English-speaking Egyptians and foreigners (some of the episodes take place abroad, in Lebanon and London, for example), but they are "a clear call to unveiling," dancing, movie-going, and the mixing of the sexes. Description is perceived as exhortation. Critiques like this are commonplace in the popular press, arguing against the moral laxity of the elites who administer communications and schooling. In this particular case, the article referred to the use of these textbooks in al-Azhar secondary institutes, hinting that even the official religious elites do not have the nation's moral health at heart.

The discursive strategy of such critiques, and of much mainstream reporting as well, is what historian Laurence Moore has called "moral sensationalism,"[21] a strategy widespread in the nineteenth-century United States, where the growing market for written material stimulated publishers to attract wide audiences, and simultaneously drew a sharp response from Christian religious denominations who condemned the salacious content apparently demanded by the masses. In response, writers for mass audiences portrayed themselves as religious messengers and developed a hybrid style in which they could pander to public prurience by recounting in graphic detail the worst kinds of personal and social outrages (drunkenness, gambling, fornication, rape, and murder), for the purposes of criticizing lapses in public morality and the coarsening of public discussion. In both the Christian and Muslim traditions, this strategy has been one of the prime mechanisms moving public religious discourse from concern with doctrine and legal minutiae to concern with abstract moral questions.[22] No longer is religious writing expected to be purely exegesis, legal interpretation, or instruction in ritual performance. Now it can comment on political events, gender roles, or sensational crimes, and still bear a useful moral message. The economic imperatives of mass-produced print force a two-way syncretism in which religious themes benefit from the selling power of suggestiveness, while bawdy or violent themes are partly legitimized by their attendant religious critique. The market in cultural goods steadily alters the corpus of "Islamic" literature by predisposing some kinds of communications rather than others. Related to this transformation of journalistic style is the role university professors, physicians, and mental health specialists play in publicly and authoritatively encouraging religious adherence as a remedy for social and moral disintegration. Whereas in the last chapter we encountered the functionalization of religious practices in the context of teaching religion, here we find it in the context of explaining social and psychological problems. The same rhetorical process that lent medical legitimation to the wudu' operates here as well: promotion of religion by disinterested secular professionals can be more compelling than the testimony of 'ulama.

People Use Religion, Too

Because the child is not forever isolated within the family unit, and because of the complexity of modern society with its wealth of opportunities for distraction and corruption, children are exposed to influences that the pious family and the devout instructor can neither approve nor anticipate. Sometimes family standards even conflict with the moral vision of the school, but most busy parents, as concerned as they might be, lack the time to monitor the specifics of their children's school experience, trusting that their own models of adab will suffice, and that personal and family moral commitments will transcend the specific political biases of the state curriculum. Samia 'Abd al-Rahman told me,

I've never read any of [Nadia's] textbooks, but I do try to correct misunderstandings that she gets from them. Like she might come to me and say, Mama, is it true that the Ottoman empire, or the Mamluk period was bad? I would correct these impressions, saying that the authors were biased in favor of nationalism or secularism, or so on. These two periods of our history are a target of those who want to attack Islam, but instead of attacking the religion of Islam, the rule of the *shari'a* and so on, they attack the Ottoman Empire for the mistakes that it made. But we defend it as a frame for Islamic government [*al-hukm al-islami*]. [Nadia] would hear things here, and she would read *In the Shadow of the Qur'an*,[23] and other things by Sayyid Qutb, and she was brought up with discussions of Islam and the Islamic Republic and its revolution, and so on.

She tried to teach Nadia to be a critical reader and to focus her thoughts on a career. In 1993 Nadia was studying English and journalism at Cairo University in order, her mother said, "to serve Islam through the medium of English, and through writing."

Samia herself came late to Islam, having been a socialist and Arab nationalist throughout her marriage to Nadia's father, and discovering only during the 1970s the spiritual significance of religion. On a January 1972 pilgrimage to Mecca she "*higab*ed" (the Egyptian word is *"ithaggab"*), and

felt that it was *khisara* [loss, waste, pity] to lose it, to take off the Islamic cover. During the Hajj there's something that works inside of you, developing you, making progress in your feelings, making you really aware of the real things in life. And so I decided that for God I should be more obedient. Nothing is worth disobeying Him. Before this I didn't realize that not wearing Islamic garb is disobedient.[24]

During the late 1970s as Iran struggled to find its way around the sterile Cold War choices of capitalism and communism, she discovered the political significance of Islam as well, joining many more prominent Egyptian leftist and secularist intellectuals who made this journey and accrued the label *"turathiyun judud"* (new adherents to the Islamic heritage), for their apparent "return" to an acknowledgment of the unique qualities of "Eastern" values as against "Western" cultural imperialism.[25] Personal journeys, while in many ways patterned systematically by the intersections of gender, class, and historical change, can be enormously unpredictable. With respect to religious commitment, both the bland universal truisms of formal instruction and the deeply personal images of the divine developed in the heart of the family can form a personal image of the sacred, which, "if it loses its meaning . . . can be set aside without being forgotten,"[26] and then regain its salience at another point in life. During periods in life when religious stories have no hold, their meanings are very different.

Muhammad Sulayman, like Samia, is a writer constantly struggling to maintain his standard of living despite holding a full-time job. An assistant editor for a small leftist publishing house in downtown Cairo, he published his first book — a slim black-and-purple volume of modernist poetry — at age thirty-six. Married, but with no children ("they need so much money to raise them. It's just too much to be responsible for"), he is from a town in the delta, where his father was one of the leaders of the local Muslim Brotherhood.

I grew up in a town in Minufiyya with 160,000 people, where the climate [*manakh*] was very religious. I used to pray [he holds his hands up beside his face and leans forward slightly to indicate prostration], and fast, and all that. Then when I was fifteen or so, my friends and I would go to the theater, and I started reading the work of a playwright named [Bertolt] Brecht, who was a socialist. And it was then that I learned that socialism was not just a book, a monolithic thing with only one idea to it, like there's a God and that's that. Socialism was wide [*wasi'*], and it talked about poverty and solutions for poverty and the causes of poverty. Poverty wasn't caused by God, but by people, and people use religion, too. Brecht was full of ideas; tough, difficult ideas.

I wanted to be a director, and I read all of Brecht's plays, and when I understood them I became a leftist. Before that — this was around 1972 or 1973, when I was twenty years old, I was very religious [*mutadayyin*], but then I just left it altogether. Now, my father taught us everything about religion. He made me memorize the Qur'an. And I've really benefitted from knowing the Qur'an, especially out in the streets.

I was embarrassed when my father found out about my socialism. He said it was forbidden (*muharram*), and as soon as he learned of it there was a big argument and he kicked me out of the house, just like that, because he was convinced I was an atheist. I saw him just once after that, when he came to visit me in prison in 1977. Just that one time, and then afterwards he died. I have one brother, but he's gone; moved to Canada. And one sister, who's 28 now. She used to be a socialist, but now she's a religious *muhaggaba*. She's married to a businessman with a lot of money, and is concentrated on her work and on raising her kids. She's an assistant professor at the college of engineering, and is also getting her Ph.D there. My sister, we talk on the phone about once a year, but otherwise have no contact. You know how it is, we have relations of love because we're brother and sister, but not relations of friendship. She had taken on *higab* during the time I was in prison, because she was living in the house of my father.

In prison I met all kinds of people, including the religious ones, but they all thought I was a heathen [*kafir*] so although we had lots of discussions of things all the time, in terms of personal relations things never went beyond greetings. It's the same with my religious friends from childhood. They don't like to talk to me, because there's a verse in the Qur'an [he recites the verse] that says you're not supposed to associate with the *kuffar*.[27]

Muhammad's depressing story of estrangement from family and friends illustrates the suspicion with which different portions of the religious and political spectra view each other both then and now, as well as the paranoid politics of Sadat's regime, which imprisoned at one time or another nearly every dissenting voice in the country. The year during which Muhammad was imprisoned, 1977, was the year in which Sadat issued his call for a renewal of religious education in response to the January food riots, a call that underscored the importance accorded to this activity as a foundation of social and political stability. In the religion curricula of preparatory and secondary schools, political and economic concerns play a substantial role. In particular, there is a sustained emphasis on the role Islamic values and conduct play in the solution of problems like those that drove Muhammad Sulayman to socialism: the causes and effects of poverty. More than one-third of the eleventh grade textbook, in fact, is devoted to the presentation of Islamic prescriptions on lawful and unlawful gain, interest, usury, business practices, and spending on righteous causes. (This is also where the excerpts on Islam and work, quoted at the beginning of the chapter, are to be found.)

Religious studies textbooks for the preparatory school (roughly an American junior high or middle school, grades seven through nine) and secondary school (equivalent to grades ten through twelve in high school) are far more consistent in a formal sense than those in the primary curriculum. Each section of text regularly consists of a selection of Qur'anic verses or a Prophetic saying, followed directly by definitions of difficult vocabulary, an exposition of the meaning and intent of the passage, and a set of questions for discussion. Gone are the hymns, pictures, and matching exercises of the earlier grades. In their place are logical and legal arguments, beginning with ontological and teleological proofs of God's existence and power, based on two carefully distinguished sorts of evidence: rational and traditional (*al-'aql wa al-naql*).[28]

Consistently emphasizing natural theology, books elaborate themes introduced in earlier grades, developing logical proofs from natural models of the necessity for the division of labor and the orderliness of society. So just as communities of ants, bees, and humans have leaders, the cosmos must have a supreme authority in God.[29] Expanding on the theme of authority and discipline, the requirement of prayer is adduced as traditional evidence for the necessity of order in society. Prayer is incumbent upon Muslims not only because God ordered it as a link between the divine and the created, but

> because in prayer there is rising and bowing and prostration, all actions that invigorate the body, and the Muslim devotes himself to work with zeal and energy, and increases production and spreads the good, and promotes [the progress of] the nation. . . . [P]rayer accustoms us to order, and the keeping of appointments, and the binding together of Muslims with cooperative ties and love and harmony. . . . [C]ollective prayer binds society with ties of brotherhood and equality, as it acquaints every Muslim with the condition of his brothers.[30]

Moral behavior is closely linked not only with public order, but with economic development. The Ramadan fast, the books explain, reduces friction between the rich and poor by letting the wealthy experience the hunger and privation of the needy, prompting generous alms. This produces serenity in the hearts of the poor so that "everybody applies themselves to their work, and production increases, society becomes happy, and its economy develops."[31] The fast also works indirectly by giving Muslims practice in willpower, helping to free them of "ugly habits like smoking, which takes its evil toll on the person's health, and then he can't do his work, and it reduces his productivity and reduces family income and causes the country's economy to slump."[32]

Although humans are responsible for cooperating with each other to build and reform society, the process is still guided by God, who can override human effort as he pleases. Children are taught that the fulfillment of their own desires is secondary to the good of the society of believers, which God's wisdom safeguards. In the eighth grade children read the story of Ahmad, who

> had wanted, after taking the General Secondary examination, to enroll in the College of Medicine, but his scores didn't enable him to realize his hope, and he enrolled in the War College. Emerging an officer, he had the honor of participating in the 10th of Ramadan War, whose heroes became eligible to be decorated because of their participation. He was most happy for this honor, as were his father and his family. *Ahmad had wanted, and his father had wanted, and his family had wanted, but God does what he wants, and it was to the greatest good what He decided and willed.*[33]

Elementary and preparatory schooling, a fictive teacher explains, provide technical education for every Egyptian so that he will have a vocation that will help him in "satisfying his needs and gratifying his desires." Love for Egypt and for Islam requires everyone to seek responsible employment, which will promote "the honor of the nation and its citizens,"[34] but those who avoid honest labor are "weeds that suck up their nutrients to destroy useful plants and living things."[35] A hadith of the Prophet condemning the destruction of shade trees in the desert is extended to all kinds of contemporary public facilities: means of transport such as buses and trains; means of communication such as telegraph, telephone, and mail offices; and public services such as schools, hospitals, libraries, museums, gardens and public restrooms. Students are warned against vandalizing or interfering with them, promising "those who would destroy them of a painful punishment on the Day of Resurrection."[36]

Such discussions of work show how far the functionalization of religion can go toward wholly transforming religion's symbolic import. In its simplest form, the connection between Islam and labor may be expressed in a phrase from one of Safir's coloring books: *"al-islam din al-'amal"* (Islam is a religion of work). More than the concrete notion that "Islam is a religion of cleanliness," or the abstract one that "Islam is a religion of order and discipline," the idea that "Islam is a religion of work" brings the whole weight of the religious heritage down behind a political program. It not only marks labor with divine intent, but marks the religious system with sociopolitical intent, and in so doing changes that system into something new. Function is a self-fulfilling prophecy, for once religion is perceived as useful in achieving given ends, it becomes used in prosecuting those ends (whether or not it does in fact achieve them), and that imputed functionality becomes in turn one of its empirical features.

I Had Some Friends There

Despite the relatively tight social controls Egyptian families impose on their children, many urban shabab, like the restless young *hittistes* ("wall-leaners") of Algeria,[37] find ample opportunity for social and ideological experimentation in Cairo's broad shopping avenues, its backstreet drug subculture, its movie houses, schoolyards, and mosques. The spreading demands of the school, the workshop, or the office require that many young people be away from their families for long periods each day, and for the millions of unemployed the negative freedom of time opens up all sorts of opportunities that worry parents, politicians, and intellectuals alike. The cultural experimentation of youth—sometimes fickle and transitory, sometimes life-changing—unites across as well as divides along class and geographical lines. Brecht finds his way to the provinces, and inspired provincial youth flock to university or employment in the capital. Bedouin boys grow Islamist beards and receive impossible teasing from relatives, while bedouin girls, inspired by their teachers, show off school-bred religious knowledge to their elders and yearn to wear the urbane Islamist veil, one of the symbols of sophisticated Nile Valley modernity.[38] On city buses bald civil servants hunch over tiny copies of the Qur'an while behind them smudged shabab in tattered galabiyyas squint and struggle with moving lips to read articles about official corruption in the Muslim Brotherhood's *al-Sha'b* newspaper; middle-class young women hidden behind face-veils and gloves ride the Cairo subway clutching popular manuals on Islamic gender roles, while lower-class women sit in mosque courtyards before weekly religious classes, debating the meaning of traditional rituals, amulets, and scriptural passages.[39]

While this seemingly collective intellectual experimentation with religion sometimes seems to be an ineluctable and unidirectional process, there are always gaps, reversals, and complications. Sometimes people outgrow intellectual inspirations; sometimes they are frightened away from them; and sometimes their penumbra persists in altered form. Almost like a mirror image of the leftist Muhammad Sulayman, Wafa'i Isma'il was in many ways a "typical" American University in Cairo graduate, whom I met through an American acquaintance he was dating. Handsome, bilingual, well-to-do, and worldly, he studied political science at AUC, and later worked for his father's small architectural consulting firm in Ma'adi, a wealthy bedroom community south of Cairo. Once he asked me about my own research, and when I mentioned that I had just visited the mosque of Anas Ibn Malik in Giza, he broke into a wide, embarrassed grin. Looking down at the glass of water he was holding, he chuckled,

Yeah, I used to go to Anas all the time. They have a lot of things going on there. I used to go there with my friends all the time to pray; there and a couple of little mosques, just tiny ones like the one you saw in [the documentary videotape] "The Sword of Islam". You wouldn't think looking at me now, but I used to be into these kinds of groups, with some friends.

Probably from the time I was sixteen until I was twenty I used to be really religious, praying, and having all these kinds of discussions and whatever. None of my family is religious at all, and my family was very concerned about me; my father used to send people to talk to me. But I used to get up every morning to go pray at the mosque; sometimes I had to go out the window, because my father was against it.

I don't know, it's kind of what one of my professors was saying, that when you don't believe in something, and then you go to a place like this, and there are people there so friendly and caring and concerned about you. And you're so smart, and your father is so stupid and everything, and he doesn't pray, and he drinks and whatever, and you start wondering about your real identity.

But you go to one of these places and they're telling you, oh, the world is really horrible, and you're like, yes, yes, and they say that people are robbing each other, and it's so terrible, and you're agreeing, and then at the end they ask you to join, and of course you say, "sure!". But I had some friends there, and we would have all kinds of discussions about *sunna*, and *qadar* [predestination], and this kind of stuff; this was all before Sadat [was killed]; then I stopped going. Three or four of my friends were arrested in September 1981, and then I knew some people arrested afterwards. But they soon got out.

Also I saw a lot of the stuff going on at the University, and I used to be involved a little in that, calling for the prayers and clearing the areas and stuff. I was in Commerce [at Cairo University] just for a semester before going to AUC. That was in 1982.[40]

This surprising revelation ("You wouldn't think looking at me now . . . ") helped make sense of one of his ruling interests in 1989: applying to graduate school at Cairo University and also in the United States, where he wanted to earn a degree in Middle East Studies with research on the politics of Islamist movements. An intellectualized response to his own former involvement, this desire was coupled with an alienation from Egyptian life that led him to question me persistently about why Americans came to live in his country, when all he wanted to do was go abroad.

Youngsters beginning more and more to move within the circle of their peers and to separate themselves from the enveloping bonds of the family experience a growing awareness of social injustices, political affairs, alternate viewpoints and role models, which subject them to conflicts both at home and elsewhere. The ideological success of small private sector Islamic groups among Egyptian youth depends partly on this disaffection and the consequent search for social and intellectual alternatives. These groups seem to have the tacit support of an enormous proportion of shabab, even those who never consider joining them. According to Samia Mustafa al-Khashab's 1988 survey, three-quarters of Cairo University students felt that the official religious establishment centered around the al-Azhar mosque was either partially or wholly ineffective in meeting the religious needs of Egyptian youth. Most of these felt that the institution needed to increase its activity in grappling with social problems,[41] and improve the performance of Islamic da'wa, or outreach.[42] Almost all students felt that mosques needed to become more active in society, holding meetings for the religious enlightenment of youth (87 percent), establishing schools for religious instruction (66 percent), creating classes to fight illiteracy (60 percent), and setting up popular clinics for those who came to prayer (58 percent).[43] Each of these activities is currently provided by high-profile private sector social service agencies, whom students suggest the government emulate.

Overwhelmingly, students taking part in the survey were hostile to Sufi orders, which are often perceived by the middle and upper classes as *sha'bi*: low class, popular, primitive, and fundamentally mistaken about the requirements of a true Islam. Although almost 85 percent of the students expressed ignorance of the goals of Sufism, they felt that Sufi orders were unnecessary (66 percent), and without positive roles in the solution of social problems (75 percent), in the political sphere (84 percent), or in spreading Islamic da'wa (60 percent).[44] All these sentiments are strongly encouraged by the rationalistic modernism of the Islamist groups (despite the fact that leaders of the movement like Hasan al-Banna—not to mention Iran's Khomeini—had Sufi roots themselves). By contrast, a large majority of these students knew some of the names and goals of the Islamist groups (*"Takfir wal-Hijra," al-Jihad*, etc.) that operated in Egypt during the 1970s and 1980s.[45] Almost three-quarters believed that these groups take the feelings and opinions of Egyptian youth into account, and thought that some or all of Egyptian youth are sympathetic to them. They did not think that these groups should be eliminated (82 percent), because they are trying to change society for the better, and because they have contributed to the Islamic Awakening (*al- sahwa al-islamiyya*).[46] These feelings may have changed somewhat over the past decade as the government has waged its ever more intensive propaganda campaign against the Islamists, changing its label for them from "extremists" to "terrorists" since the beginning of the violent 1992 insurgency based in southern Egypt.

But by the late 1980s the state was responding through its schools. The theme of the Islamic education curricula for shabab — students in preparatory and secondary schools — was "Islamic Society," and lessons clustered around "the three tightly interwoven themes of Faith, Morals, and Social Solidarity."[47] The competition between public and private sector religious organizations for status and authority in the eyes of Egypt's youth lent particular urgency to the government's religious education programs, particularly at the primary and preparatory levels, where, according to newspapers, the religious curricula were being adjusted to create study materials that "translate knowledge into practice" (*yatatarjamu al-ʿilm ila al-ʿamal*).[48] This holds true of the secondary curriculum as well, where, along with the principles of faith and social solidarity, textbooks and syllabi emphasized the role of legitimate authority in the government of Islamic society and the enforcement of Islamic conduct.

A ninth grade commentary on three verses in the Qurʾan's sura 3, ʾAl ʿImran (103–5), outlines the state's theory of religious authority. The verses remind the new Muslim community of the blessing of their unification and warn them against disputation and divisiveness, laying out the advantages of "security and fidelity and stability." If, according to the textbook, every person adheres to the sunna and "knows the limits of his responsibility," then society "will be a strong, solid, cohesive, loving, cooperative, active and productive one whose strength and solidity no artful plot can weaken or disturb, whose unity no malicious sedition can sunder."[49] The lesson goes on to say that the limits of individual responsibility for the enforcement of Islamic conduct are set by the Qurʾan itself: "Let there arise out of you/A band of people/Inviting to all that is good,/Enjoining what is right/And forbidding what is wrong:/They are the ones/To attain felicity" (sura 3, 104).

The word *umma*, translated in this verse by A. Yusuf ʿAli as "band," or "group," usually denotes an entire community, such as the community of believers. (A. J. Arberry, for example, interprets the verse this way: "Let there be one nation of you, calling to good/And bidding to honour, and forbidding dishonour;/Those are the prosperers.") The textbook writers, however, have chosen to interpret *umma* in the phrase *"wa l-takun minkum umma,"* to mean *"ʾayy taʾifa tadʿu ila al-khayr"* (any group or class that calls [people] to what is right).[50] Glossed like this, the verse calls for one group of people *within* society, rather than the society as a whole, to bear responsibility for enjoining good and forbidding evil. "Calling [people] to the good lies in the domain of the teachings of the Qur'an and *sunna*, and no one can engage in this *da'wa* except one who is an *'alim* of the book of God and the *sunna* of the Prophet. And the verse has conferred success upon this group, and their success is the success and righteousness of society."[51]

Some of the discussion questions at the end of this lesson are essentially ideological tests that prompt teachers to gauge student feelings about religious unity and the specialized role of the *da'iya* (the maker of da'wa, or Islamic outreach). Questions ask students if they would like to be da'iyas, and then enquire, "If your answer is yes, to what [objectives] would you call your classmates, the individuals in your family, and your neighbors?" Next the student confronts a hypothetical colleague whose ideas are not sanctioned by authoritative texts or persons:

3. You observed a classmate frequently repeating statements and concepts that you haven't heard from a teacher or read in a book. Do you:

   Attack him and call him names and hit him?

   Correct his mistaken understandings and convince him of what is right through calm discussion?

   Incite your classmates to argue and break off their friendship with him?

   Advise him and show him books from which he can derive true information?[52]

On the other side of the equation, the Ministry of Education has recently begun requesting in its teacher-education exams, an essay on "The role of the teacher in combating terrorism," the most recent gloss of the term *extremism*, which was used more commonly throughout the 1980s.[53] Such devices respond to the ideological competition of Islamist groups and the Muslim Brotherhood, whose lay members often harshly criticize state policy, both within and outside of the religious sphere. Most of the prominent and intellectually important Islamic activists in twentieth-century Egypt (and elsewhere) have been trained in fields other than Islamic studies. Hasan al-Banna, the founder of the Muslim Brotherhood, was a graduate of Dar al-'Ulum, in Arabic, and worked as a primary school teacher. Sayyid Qutb was trained as a literary critic and worked as a consultant to the Egyptian Ministry of Education. 'Abd al-Salam Faraj, the ideological leader of the group that assassinated Anwar Sadat, was an electrician. The prolific writer and religious philanthropist Mustafa Mahmud was originally a physician.[54] Their movements and the institutions they built were the result not of an appeal to traditional forms of religious authority and discourse, but of mobilizing charisma and modern forms of organization, communication, and recruitment. By restricting the range of moral authority to the circle of scholars trained by the religious faculties of al-Azhar, on the other hand, the state hopes to limit the appeal of such groups, although there are many competent ʿulama, like Muhammad al-Ghazali for the Muslim Brotherhood, and ʿUmar ʿAbd al-Rahman for the smaller Islamic radical groups, who can lend legitimacy to the opposition.

The state's third-party "calls to order" (to borrow a concept from Bourdieu's writings on class) with respect to interpretive authority suffuse public culture. The minister of religious endowments, in an interview published in the Ramadan 1409 issue of Egypt's official Sufi magazine, confirmed forcefully the need to leave religious matters to specialists, saying that Egypt's youth are basically good, but that they lack "direction and guidance." When asked about the difference between "religion" (*al-din*) and "religiousness" (*al-tadayyun*), the minister replied,

> Religiousness is open to everyone, to all young people—[it is] even expected of every man, woman, youngster and old person. As for religion—as it is understood as theology, applied ethics, and dogma—we need to leave these . . . to specialists in them, because . . . among them are men of distinction and scholars who studied them and specialized in them from childhood. . . . It's enough [for the shabab] to know the general principles in religious matters. . . . The shame of our youth is that they want to make judgements on everything, and as a result of this there has been killing in the name of religion and splintering in the name of religion and destruction in the name of religion and fear and alarm in the name of religion, all of which happened because they are ignorant of the essential nature of religion.[55]

The nation's youth have a right to be enlightened and instructed and corrected by people with knowledge about Islam,

> a religion of reason and order and gentleness and sympathy and tolerance . . . our youngsters need to know the essence and greatness of Islam, a religion of kindness, even to animals, even with enemies, and in war with the armies of the enemy. In summary, our youth need to know the truth of Islam and that the truth of the Islamic religion lives within the purview of the *ʿulama*. . . . Changing the abomination by the hand falls under the responsibility of the ruler and the [public] guardian, and on the rest of the people falls the responsibility of advice and guidance by the tongue, or to despise the abomination in the heart.[56]

As a way to help them winnow reliable from unreliable advice, advanced students receive guidelines for approaching the mass media through which so many ideological battles are fought:

> Modern science has extended the scope of the influence of the word, and people have begun to read them in newspapers and hear them in broadcasts and other means of communication on an immense scale. It is the duty of the Muslim to weigh his words, to measure his speech and not to aim at slander and calumny or insults, not to reveal a secret, and not to spread indecency and not to stir up animosity, but to speak noble words that please God and his Apostle.[57]

They are reminded that God ordered mankind, "But say not — for any false thing that your tongues may put forth — 'This is lawful, and this is forbidden,' so as to ascribe false things to God" (sura 16, al- Nahl, 116), and that He forbade "sins and trespasses against truth or reason; assigning/Of partners to God, for which/He hath given no authority;/ And saying things about God/Of which ye have no knowledge"(sura 7, al-ʾAʿraf, 33). Such practices are the primary source of distortion in corrupted religions,

> so no one should forbid anything for religious reasons to any servant of God, or require anything of him, except by a true text of God and his Apostle, and whoever assails that has set himself up as an equal [*sharik*] to God, and whoever follows him in it has made him his Lord, and God has renounced anyone who attributes any allowance or prohibition to his religion without proof.[58]

Truly obeying God necessitates not just hearkening to His instructions, but understanding who may be trusted to know what His instructions are, so "we should stay within our limits and leave independent judgement in religion to the knowledgeable scholars [*al-ʿulamaʾal-ʿarifin*], who bring together the motives and the means of independent judgement [*ijtihad*]."[59]

Likewise, the enforcement of Islamic conduct falls to specialists. Although Islam operates largely through cooperation and mutual advice (*nasiha*), between the government and the governed as well as between individuals, nasiha in religious matters is, according to the textbooks, a *fard kifaya* (a duty not incumbent upon all the individuals in the community, as long as some one person or group of persons attends to it), which applies to the ʿulama alone.[60] The government and the governed "cooperate together in obeying God and defending His book and tradition and Prophet," so that if someone refuses to obey God's law, there is a graduated series of appropriate responses. First, notifying the person that he is in error; second, admonishing him to behave correctly; third, reprimanding him for his misbehavior; and finally, if he still desists from proper conduct, forcible prevention. This last remedy, however, is also a fard kifaya, entrusted only to those whose job it is to enforce the rules of society (*al-qa'imin bil-'amr*).[61]

Islam's commitment to human rights, according to the texts, includes freedom of belief and opinion and requires a cordial attitude toward the members of other religious communities. Precisely because of its cautious apportionment of responsibility, Egypt's experience with the religion of the Seal of the Prophets has been a special one. This is how the Ministry of Education concludes its twelfth grade book:

> Islam was Egypt's choice, and the environment of Egypt — through its religious culture since the time of the monotheist Akhenaton — was prepared for Islam, and absorbed it all: doctrine and law, science, culture and conduct. Since then, Egypt's features have differed from other Islamic countries. Islam in Egypt is Islam without fanaticism, Islam without extremism, and it is remarkable that Islamic Egypt alone, through fourteen centuries, has never been linked with excess or extremism in its religious conduct. . . . Indeed, the Egyptian personality is moderate in its religiosity and behavior, middle-of-the-road in its thought and practice, neither excessive nor negligent, and from here were the riches of civilization.[62]

As with the work ethic, the sections on religious authority consist of statements that are neither empirical claims nor exhortations. Instead, they are performative utterances, "rituals of social magic" whose very statement alters the world, for they become true by establishing a normative background against which reality is to be judged by those setting the terms.[63] These are not abstract matters of theory, but practical matters that — as we will see in the next chapter — frame legal prosecutions, political purges, and police roundups. Despite progressive expectations to the contrary, the creation and dissemination of instructive truths by the school has not so much replaced the use of physical force, as it has provided new opportunities on which to use it.

This Wonderful Girl Who Wore the Higab

The closest most Egyptian youth come to an organized rite of spiritual passage is the series of examinations that punctuates their school careers and finally grants them their certificates. Their families, who press them to study and who scrape together money for tutoring; their teachers, who sometimes earn several times their salaries by doing that tutoring; the state, which outlaws that tutoring altogether as a conflict of interest; and private companies that produce condensed study guides and summaries for the tests, are all involved as players in the summertime ritual that takes its most intense form in *al-thanawiyya al-'amma*, the general secondary exams.

The short-term pressures of nationwide testing are powerful motivators for the principal actors in this drama. Ordinary Egyptians respect education and use schooling as a means of status enhancement (particularly for girls, who, it is believed, are more attractive marriage partners if they have a certificate and can not only bring in income from outside employment, but save money by tutoring their own children[64]). But in part because teaching is the lowest-paid professional occupation in the country — the salary of a public sector secondary school teacher in the late 1980s was about thirty-five dollars a month; that in the private sector about twice that, but still not a living wage — it often attracts idealists who want to make a difference in the lives of young people. Particularly at private religious schools, committed community members join teachers to volunteer for tutoring work, help with bookkeeping, coach sports, and perform other tasks out of a sense that Islam is calling them to work with young Muslims.

Layla al-Shamsi was the head of the Literature Department at a private Islamic language school in Masr al-Gidida, the "New Cairo" northeast of the city center. The area — founded just after the turn of the century as a planned community for expatriates and well-to-do locals — is a modern and expansive area where military installations, airports, government agencies and factories are mixed with private mosques, villas, shopping centers and apartment blocks. In contrast to Samia 'Abd al-Rahman's *zayy islami*, which consists of a long-sleeved dress and a designer scarf covering her hair and neck (called *tarha*), Layla wears *khimar*, which is one step more conservative. "I've been a *muhaggaba* for seven years now," she said.

Before that I was really a Muslim in name only. I was educated in a Christian school — the English missions school. I consider myself that I was a non-Muslim then. I was an airline hostess for Saudia airlines, and travelled all over the world; to Europe, and Asia. I've spent a lot of time in England, and I was an English major [in college]. I don't have a teaching degree, or an advanced degree in anything, but I'm very good with children. I love working with children.

I'm 33 now. But seven years ago, when I was around 25, I began wearing *higab*. I had met this girl, this wonderful girl who wore the *higab*, and she began to tell me about Islam, and about being a real Muslim. And for a while I kind of felt both ways. While I was working, I really used to admire Western ways, and was very impressed with the West and their way of doing things, and thought, like a lot of you do, that women who wear the *higab* are oppressed by men, or retarded, socially or mentally retarded somehow. It wasn't a decision I made, really, it's not like there was some sudden inspiration from Allah or anything; but God always puts someone in our life, sets this person in our path to guide us, and for me it was this wonderful girl.

I started reading the Qur'an, but at first I did it with a critical eye, like you might, understanding it but not believing everything it said, trying to keep some kind of critical distance. And at the same time I was living in my old way — oh, I used to fast during Ramadan, and that kind of thing, but really I was a Muslim in name only — but I would go out with friends, even when I didn't drink anything, I would go to discos with people, where there was alcohol around, and I would try to sit there and have a good time, but started thinking that this really is a bad thing to be doing. I started feeling guilt. And believe me, I had never felt guilty about this kind of thing before! But I slowly began reading more and more, and deciding that I was living the wrong way. It took about a year between the time I met this girl, and the time I put on *higab*.

By 1989, Layla had taught at the school for four years, and was beginning her fifth. Strongly devoted to her students and to the institution, she told me that "when you work at this school, you're working for Islam. I have a lot of work here — when you're working for Islam you don't just say, 'that's not my job'; you do a lot of different things for the good of the school."[65] In her previous teaching job, which was not at an Islamic school, she says that the students were "very naughty," but that here, they are well-behaved. "They've gone here, most of them, since they were in kindergarten, and they know that you should respect people, and be well-behaved. I really think that it's Islam that makes them so well-behaved. They know that for everything they do, they are accountable to God."[66] She was quite sensitive to her own accountability, and worked inside and outside of class to lead her students down a different path than the one she herself had been made to travel.

I'm not married. I am too busy working with the children, and trying to plan things at the school, and have no plans to get married, because I have my own ideas about marriage and Muslim men. I love working with our children here, and that's the important thing to me. A Muslim woman keeps her own name, and her own economic resources, and keeps her own personality, her own individuality. I think that it's very important to work with children here, not to increase the number of Muslims in the world, but to work with the Muslims that are here already, to extend *da'wa* to them and teach them how to be more than Muslims in name only. And I think it's very important to teach children about being Muslims so that they don't have to go through the kinds of things that we had to go through, not knowing about how to lead a good life. Because Islam isn't just the rituals; those are important, but Islam includes all aspects of life as well.[67]

I have small study groups, mostly with girls and women, but I've got one with some boys. Usually they say that men teachers should be teaching boys of this age, but since they were my pupils anyway. . . . But I picked these five boys out of one of my English classes to talk to them more about religious things, and about Islamic ways of life. Boys of this age are really very impressed by things they see in the movies or on television about the West, things they see in *Knot's Landing* and so on, and I try to teach them about the right alternatives. I really had no special criterion for choosing these five except I felt that they were closer to me, and we understood each other.[68]

On a visit to Egypt in 1993 I found these study groups had been discontinued because of Layla's marriage to an oil company executive who expected her to spend her time at home caring for their young son. When I tried to set up an interview appointment, she put me in touch with her husband, who, she assured me, could tell me anything I wanted to know. He explained that her new role is primarily to take care of the family and "to have things ready for me—whether it's food, or sex, or anything else." While she still performed some administrative work at the school, she was trying very hard to restrict her interactions with people outside her family, particularly men. "She really doesn't mix with men," her husband confided, "and it's not because of me, it's just the way she is." Marriage appears to have shifted Layla's sense of accountability quite radically. Beginning her adulthood as an airline stewardess, the stereotypical specimen of female liberation and (literally) jet-setting mobility, she entered on a journey of slow but steady introspection and circumscription of activity. Accountability to herself, expressed as a love for travel and experience and pleasure, was superseded by concern for living right, and for being a Muslim in more than name only. So her sense of accountability—the acknowledgment that one is responsible for providing for the rights of others—shifted first to her students, whose right to their heritage she worked to protect, and then to her husband and child. But this shift was a difficult and unexpected one. Even draped in her long khimar in 1989 she expressed no desire to marry, but instead contravened even her own convictions about gender segregation by reaching out to young men to serve as a model, a habit that made her marriage and seclusion appear all the more dramatic.

In a sense, accountability to God and to the Islamic heritage is expressed as a complex series of accountabilities to other human beings. Sometimes the balance between accounts is a delicate negotiation, as when different sets of auditors — family, peers, the state — are in conflict, as they were for Muhammad Sulayman, Wafa'i Isma'il, and Layla al-Shamsi. Layla lamented that parents send their children to her school "because they want their children to grow up as good Muslims," but sadly, some parents "only stress the interior aspects" of Islam and let their daughters, for example, take off the uniform higab after school.[69] Inner piety without the strength to display proper public behavior is a serious flaw, because although God can monitor inner intentions, God's community cannot. Therefore displays of responsible behavior are vital, and the accountability of young people to their families, to their schools, and to their nation is ceaselessly reiterated in the press. Although youth have been receiving increasingly bad press in recent years, as concerns about their moral degradation and political dangerousness are aired, they are regularly redeemed through annual celebration of their struggle through high school exit exams.

Following Foucault (not to mention the lower-grade textbook that compares God's Day of Judgment with the school examination), we can highlight the sense in which the school imposes "a principle of compulsory visibility"[70] upon its students not only through a forced display of signifying dress and daily discipline, but through "highly ritualized" examinations in which "are combined the ceremony of power and the form of the experiment, the deployment of force and the establishment of truth."[71] The examination, at the critical point of the final secondary exam, is not, however, a closed and secretive ritual. It is, in some ways, a highly public drama. Every summer newspapers publish analyses and debates about testing policy, and page after page of numerical listings detail the results that qualify for entrance into university. The religious press, for its part, uses the occasion to represent Islamic values as the key to academic accomplishment. Parents of students who excel in the general secondary exam extol the role of the family in the student's success. One father allocated 80 percent of his son's achievement to a supportive home environment and 20 percent to what he learned in school.[72] Pious students attribute high scores to higher powers. Sahar Ahmad Fikry, who scored eighth in the nation in the literature section, told a newspaper that she "performed the prayers, and read what she could of the Qur'an every day before beginning her studying and after finishing it . . . prayer was for her the only escape, to achieve rest and serenity and self-confidence, and gave her the opportunity to organize her time in relation to her studying."[73]

On 11 June 1989, on the second day of the general secondary examination, almost one-quarter of a million Egyptian students sat for one and a half hours to answer five questions about Islam, questions that would help determine whether or not they would be able to attend university, and which field they could enter. For the first time, "objective" (also known as "American style") questions were to be used on the examination. As with almost every decision taken by the government, this change was criticized in the opposition press. In the fortnight preceding the examinations, professors of education complained about the new style of question, which they conceded might be appropriate for the sciences or engineering, but which, when applied to religion, would not allow the student "the opportunity to express his views, . . . to reveal and explain his perspective, and if he had read any other sources or not."[74]

Reprising the educational discourse of a century before, pundits admitted that while the old method of essay testing might have contributed to "a culture of memory, . . . of accumulation and retrieval," the new method, although it would reveal the student's ability to apply scientific methods of thought to theoretical information in the curriculum, would not reveal his "interpretation of values and morals, and the connection of Qur'anic verses and Prophetic sayings to daily life."[75] (In the end, the only question on the religion section of 1989's general secondary examination that actually included an objective portion was a question about sex: specifically, about the Prophet's advice for cooling the ardor of young celibates.)

Although students didn't find the exam particularly difficult,[76] some of them criticized the religious studies curriculum as weak in general, complaining that the subject, often occupying the last class of the school day, was easily skipped or ignored, and that it would be better taught by "specialized 'ulama."[77] For the following academic year, the Ministry of Education, jointly with the Ministry of Religious Endowments, had planned to place "religious visitors" in schools to organize religious meetings and discussions with students.[78] Criticisms of al-Azhar and other official religious institutions for dereliction of duty toward the country's youth — evident in al-Khashab's survey results — have led to public pleas by officials all the way up to the Shaykh of al-Azhar University, that religious scholars listen carefully to the concerns of the young and enter with them into constructive dialogue, so as to avoid the inevitable consequence of defection to alternate sources of inspiration.

Persuasion Beyond the Classroom

One way to engage in this dialogue and to reach citizens no longer in school is through public meetings and forums arranged through youth centers, universities, and summer camps. In recent years officials of the Ministry of Religious Endowments, the Office of the Mufti and the Ministry of Youth Affairs and Sport have embarked each summer on an extensive spiritual chautauqua circuit referred to as "The Religious Awareness Caravan" (*qawafil al-taw'iyya al- diniyya*). While the locations change, the themes remain largely the same, continuing the discourse of work, responsibility, humility, and accountability introduced in the school curriculum. During the second week of July 1989, for example, senior officials kicked off a new summer program at a youth camp at Abu Qir in Alexandria, answering questions late into the night and trying to "enlighten young people to the dangers that threaten them, like intellectual extremism that wears the cloak of religion, and [drug] addiction that leads to ruin."[79] The Caravan planned to tour seven governorates in Lower Egypt and the Sinai. The minister of religious endowments announced that the purpose of the meetings was both to "alert youth to the dangers and temptations coming at us from without," and to correct mistaken religious ideas (*tashih al- mafahim al-diniyya al-khati'a*). Explaining to an audience in Alexandria that acts of worship are not required by law in Egypt, because its people are "steadfast and religious by nature," he summoned Egyptian youth to use the strength of religious conviction "for the sake of building and prosperity and increasing production."[80]

Convention of official meetings and forums — sometimes televised — with groups of young people, professionals, workers, and students is not restricted to the summer months. In late March 1989, religious experts met for three days with students at the University of Sohag, answering questions about higab, the application of Islamic law in Egypt, the perceived gap between al-Azhar and popular concerns, and other matters.[81] The minister of religious endowments announced a program of public meetings to begin during the month of Ramadan, in which religious scholars and officials could "answer the inquiries of citizens and simplify religious matters for them."[82] In April the minister met with students at the University of Minufiyya[83] and along with the mufti staged a week-long tour of the villages of Upper Egypt.[84] Later he counseled the youth of Damietta.[85] After the summer Caravan, public visits, meetings, and ceremonies continued as officials opened two mosques and answered the public's questions in the governorate of Behera.[86]

Aside from occasionally answering questions on the debt crisis or foreign affairs, officials return regularly to a set of common themes. The first theme is Islam's attitude toward work and production, with the mufti and the minister of religious endowments each warning audiences that "flight from the domains of work and production is a crime that the truth of Islam cannot forgive."[87] At the same time, a Committee for Religious Affairs chaired by Dr. ʿAbd al- Munʿim al-Nimr, a specialist in the religious and social problems of youth, announced the need for

> deepening religious understanding among children and young people, since these understandings exalt the value of work in all its forms, and this is what we need in the coming stage, to shake mistaken social concepts that are firmly established, like the constant desire for [guaranteed] work with university certificates, and the avoidance of gainful [vocational] employment; . . . if Islamic values were deeply held, every citizen would honor any work, regardless of its nature.[88]

Almost two years later, under a new plan by President Mubarak to organize "meetings with various portions of the shabab in every workplace and production unit in the governorates, to clarify the view of Islam on the nature of mankind and the call to increased production in conformity with the summons of the Islamic religion," the theme of work and production was maintained. "Egypt," according to the minister of religious endowments, "is now living in a period of economic construction that demands the close cooperation of the efforts of the *shabab*, who hold fast to the true principles of their religion in order to pass through this economic crisis, and provide them with an appropriate life far from the extremism that leads to deviant behavior."[89]

The second theme of the meetings is that of the dependence of Egyptian youth on the specialized knowledge of the ʿulama. At the end of August 1989, students at Alexandria University heard the minister of religious endowments, Muhammad Ali Mahgub, warning them away from "merchants of religion who try to achieve their political goals in the name of religion, even if they turn Egypt into seas of blood." Educated youth are to be makers of daʿwa only, not fuqahaʾ (jurists) as well; "Don't mix up these subjects or confuse these practices," Mahgub warned them. "And don't let the extremists slip into your ranks to achieve their political goals." Knowledge should be obtained from the knowledgeable (*yatalqa al-ʿilm min al-ʿulama*), and not to do so is "the cause of violence and terrorism and extremism." Firing a shot directly at the Muslim Brotherhood, the minister declared,

> There's a pretty slogan, "Islam is the Solution" [*al-islam huwa al-hall*, the campaign slogan of the Muslim Brotherhood]. I say in all frankness: Yes, Islam is the solution to all political, economic, and social problems. But it demands calm, reflective planning, and is far from application until we have calmly, rationally ascertained the means we desire.[90]

A week later in Mansura, he reiterated that "there are things in religion that are not suitable to the comprehension of the *shabab*, and they need to leave debate about them and judgements on them to specialized scholars so as not to divide the *umma* or [threaten] its unity."[91]

The third theme the public meetings share with the Ministry of Education's curricula is the rehearsal of Egypt's pacific heritage. Appeals are made "not to turn to the tools of violence and hatred, nor to the means of destruction and sabotage, and not to turn a stable and secure Egypt into a pit of struggle." "For all its long history," students in Alexandria were reminded, "Egypt has been a nation of tolerance and peace, and has never been a nation for extremist ideas, and the state and the *shabab* are one entity . . . the duty of the religious youth is to protect Islam's reputation and stay away from extremism; they should be religious in *daʿwa* only, and not in judging or commanding."[92]

Throughout the religious campaign the statistical idiom pioneered by Cromer's contemporaries fixed social reality for public consumption. Port Said was assured in early August 1989 that all of the pillars of Islam are observed in Egypt, and that "ninety-five percent of the *shariʿa* of God . . . has been applied" as well.[93] Fewer than three weeks later, Alexandrians had to content themselves with the thought that only "ninety percent of the Islamic *shariʿa* is applied in Egypt,"[94] although a month earlier they had been assured "that moderate ideas now represent more than eighty percent among the *shabab*, and that the problem of extremist thinking has almost disappeared from Egypt through constructive dialogue."[95] The Orwellian tint of such statistical formulations is striking, although in this case they do not mask a sinister truth, but merely clothe unverifiable pronouncements in the cloak of numerical certainty, a mode of discourse made possible only by the preparation afforded by the modern school. Even as estimates, the significance of such numbers lies not in their magnitude, but in the fact that the public is receptive to thinking about religious questions quantitatively, as if obedience to God were a variable that the state could measure and adjust like the production of electricity or the tonnage of fertilizer imported each year.

Conclusion

The ruling class is and will continue to be the class of decision makers. Even now it is no longer composed of the traditional political class, but of a composite layer of corporate leaders, high-level administrators, and the heads of the major professional, labor, political, and religious organizations.

Jean-François Lyotard,
The Postmodern Condition, 1979[96]

What becomes clear from the study of these themes is not only the tension between the country's youth and its official religious establishment, but a tension at the very heart of the state's effort to maintain the authority of that establishment. On the one hand, in order to be considered legitimate spokesmen of the Islamic tradition, the ʿulama must maintain a distinctive identity through a specialized program of training and socialization with a long history of its own. But on the other hand, in order to make use of this legitimacy they must rely on other professionals—journalists, scientists, secular academics, educators, and government officials—to help frame that tradition in socially useful terms. The dilemma of the professional religious class is that the thinner the tradition spreads itself over social, political, and economic problems—the more useful the tradition is—the more control over it they have to concede to others.

At the other end of the authority relationship stand the students, who are expected to learn to exclude themselves from the practice of ijtihad, independent reasoning about religious questions. In the words of Bourdieu and Passeron, schooling becomes, on this expectation, "the imposition of recognition of the dominant culture as legitimate culture and . . . of the illegitimacy of the cultures of the dominated groups or classes."[97] They go on to claim that

> one of the least noticed effects of compulsory schooling is that it succeeds in obtaining from the dominated classes a recognition of legitimate knowledge and know-how (e.g. in law, medicine, technology, entertainment or art), entailing the devaluation of the knowledge and know-how they effectively command . . . and so providing a market for material and especially symbolic products of which the means of production (not least, higher education) are virtually monopolized by the dominant classes (e.g. clinical diagnosis, legal advice, the culture industry, etc.).[98]

The curious feature of the Egyptian case is that the path to cultural legitimacy is not sequential to compulsory schooling, but parallel to it. Within the sphere of religious legitimacy, the holders of authority have an entirely different training from those who do not hold authority. The exclusivity of "higher" education is therefore irrelevant, and in fact the religious programs at al-Azhar tend to attract students from lower socioeconomic strata than many secular university programs. In order for compulsory schooling to relay knowledge of "legitimate" religious culture sufficient to attain its goal of social control, it must use pedagogical techniques that work to undermine the authority of the holders of religious legitimacy by marginalizing the means of cultural production that they possess. But at the same time, religion has been reformulated to apply broadly to areas of social planning that are outside the competence of the religious specialist. One of the results of mass religious instruction is thus to prepare students just enough to question the authority of the keepers of the Muslim tradition, and to question their own exclusion from its manipulation.

This dilemma is a special case of a distinction Raymond Williams has drawn between restricted cultural production, intended for other culture producers, and large-scale cultural production, intended for the general public.[99] It is a special case because traditionally trained religious scholars are charged both with the maintenance of their legitimate and legitimizing Islamic discourse, and also with the production — through very different means — of belief for the general public. The complicating factor is that groups and institutions that are more effective at the latter — schools and the market — can outcompete the traditional scholars and overwhelm their production, based in part on new organizations of knowledge production (the committee, the Children's Culture Unit, the interdisciplinary team of experts). This kind of knowledge-produced-for-exchange is what Lyotard labels "postmodern"; it is knowledge whose claim to attention is its social efficiency and the speed with which it is produced, rather than its place in a metanarrative of progress or salvation.[100] The state-subsidized intellectual production techniques of the ʿulama, protected from market forces, are made to represent a standard against which "innovation" is measured,[101] and is thus forced into an appearance of false uniformity and spurious completeness (it is "the Islam").

Rather than benefiting from its patronage of the ʿulama, the state has suffered from the public realization that there are, empirically, a number of alternatives available on the market, and that the state version hardly looks like the most disinterested. "One of the difficulties of orthodox defence against heretical transformations," according to Bourdieu, "is the fact that polemics imply a form of recognition; adversaries whom one would prefer to destroy by ignoring them cannot be combatted without consecrating them."[102] Claiming their own return to sacred sources, lay religious intellectuals combat the subsidized ʿulama by capitalizing on their access to market-oriented organizations and technologies and working to create a new and enlivened tradition of religious literature.[103]

PART IV

Utilitarian economists, skeletons of schoolmasters, Commissioners of Fact, genteel and used-up infidels, gabblers of many little dog's-eared creeds, the poor you will always have with you. Cultivate in them, while there is yet time, the utmost graces of the fancies and affections to adorn their lives so much in need of ornament; or, in the day of your triumph, when romance is utterly driven out of their souls, and they and a bare existence stand face to face, Reality will take a wolfish turn and make an end of you.

Charles Dickens, *Hard Times*, 1854

CHAPTER 7

State of Emergency

And in the state of emergency which is not the exception but the rule, every possibility is a fact.
Michael Taussig, *The Nervous System*, 1992[1]

The struggle for ideological authority on the part of the state and its religious establishment is part of a broader political conflict. Since Anwar Sadat's 1981 assassination Egypt has been ruled under an Emergency Law that allows for certain press restrictions, the banning of public political gatherings, and the detention without charge of people suspected of certain categories of crime, including subversion and political violence. Because the president was killed by members of an organization that preached that struggle against an unjust ruler is as important a part of Islam as prayer and fasting,[2] the state of emergency is generally associated with the government's fight against a range of Islamist opposition groups who vary widely in their size, their activities, and their strategies for changing Egyptian society. The Emergency Law, though, also shapes the political activities of liberal, leftist, feminist, human rights, and other groups as well. Repeated pleas to repeal them and return the country to a state of normality have been rejected on national security grounds, and some of the restrictions on the press have been tightened rather than relieved in the last several years.

The Islamic Trend, as I have labeled the wide range of cultural and social phenomena that include specifically political movements, is extremely complex. It ranges from the Islamization of the publishing industry and the increase in enrollment in Islamic studies programs, to the odious violence of terrorist organizations with scripture-based ideologies and the sophisticated legal maneuvering of Islamist lawyers within the court system. From the network of private businesses that are funded by and contribute to Islamic political and charitable activities to the quotidian spats and arguments that reveal just "how close religion is to the surface," in the words of Andrea Rugh,[3] the Trend has moved beyond the level of a "movement" to become one of the most important contexts in which everyday life is lived. Along with its ubiquitous symbol of the veil, many aspects of the Trend have been described and analyzed in exhaustive detail over the past two decades, so no effort will be made here to sketch its historical roots or intellectual development.[4] Instead I shall examine a few small examples of the way the public economy of information — the part of culture most firmly grounded in the apprehensions and expectations generated by schooling — shapes representations of the political uses of Islam. The examples are chosen for what they reveal of the public (in its three senses — governmental, popular, and open) image of Islamicized political activity and the creation of what sociologist Armando Salvatore has recently called "Islamic publicness."

Trainings

Shortly before 8:00 on Sunday morning, 18 July 1993, residents of the Zeinhom District of Cairo, a working-class neighborhood south and east of the mosque of Sayyida Zeinab, were awakened by the sound of gunfire. The street was beginning to come to life on the first day of the workweek. Students were walking to summer trade school workshops, glass merchants and street peddlers were opening their shops, the guard at a charitable kindergarten was unlocking its front gate. The traffic of office minibuses and trucks and taxis was beginning to thicken. A dark taxi stopped in front of the Zeinhom morgue and half a dozen nervous shabab got out, pairing off into three groups in the street. They were dressed in new blue jeans and T-shirts with cheap rubber "kootchie" sandals, and each wore a black cloth band around his forehead. Underneath these clothes they wore polyester athletic warmup suits, or "trainings." In their hands were automatic rifles and 9mm Helwan police-issue pistols with extra ammunition clips tucked in their pockets. Under their clothing at least two of them carried hand grenades, and one wore a dynamite belt.

According to one account they screamed "God is Great!" and cursed before opening fire on a police car pulling up in front of the morgue. Their shots hit the building, a number of cars and two bystanders leaving their homes for work. The confused and contradictory newspaper accounts that appeared the next day portray a bewildering set of subsequent events. Some eyewitnesses said the young men got back in their car and pursued the fleeing police car they had attacked. Others tell of them fleeing together on foot, chased by another patrol car, which exchanged fire with them and eventually wounded one of them before it was disabled. Some saw a Honda half-size pickup being used as a getaway car, others reported one of the young men loping down the street trying to convince bystanders he was a police officer in pursuit of terrorists, and that he needed to commandeer a taxi and give chase. During the course of their escape the young men continued to fire their weapons and threw or discarded at least four explosive devices, one toward the wall surrounding the kindergarten, and two at the Zeinhom Youth Center. These had not been armed, but one bomb exploded near the morgue, scattering fragments for fifty meters but fortunately injuring no one.

As the police entered the pursuit, so did the residents of the Zeinhom and Sayyida Zeinab neighborhoods. Drivers, painters, deliverymen, butchers, kiosk merchants, locksmiths, restaurant owners, private guards, mechanics, and auto-body repairmen followed the fleeing youth, armed with rocks, sticks, and butcher knives. One of the young fugitives, probably wounded by police fire, was hit by a passing car and fell behind a parked vehicle whence he shot at neighborhood residents surrounding him. When his gun jammed, the locals jumped on him and beat him nearly to death. When one of the other shabab ran out of ammunition he met a similar fate before he could reload. He was beaten unconscious with rocks and sticks, but when one of his colleagues wounded him in the process of firing on his captors, the crowd dragged the bleeding youth to safety behind the walls of the youth center so they could deliver him to the police.

Two of the young militants forced their way into a Fiat 128 taxicab and ordered the driver to head for a main highway that would whisk them behind Salah al-Din's twelfth-century Citadel and then northeastward out of the city. A butcher's meat delivery motorcycle and sidecar loaded with a dozen angry neighbors chased it for two and a half kilometers, until, a hundred meters before the onramp, the taxi crossed the path of a police patrol car. The taxi driver slowed the vehicle and rolled out of the door, yelling for help. When the patrol car stopped and the officers got out, the armed men turned their rifle fire from the escaping driver to the police captain and his sergeant, wounding both in the process of pumping thirty bullets into their vehicle. One of the young men escaped into the nearby Sayyida ʿAisha Cemetery on foot, and the other ran under the highway overpass, where he unhooked his belt and desperately tried to remove his jeans in order to escape, disguised in the training suit he wore underneath. But another patrol car had arrived by this time, and while one officer laid down cover fire, wounding the young man, another ran behind and killed him with two bullets in the back.

In the end, the moving firefight between the police and the young men — the latter used almost two hundred fifty rounds of ammunition during the chase — resulted in the wounding of at least four civilians, including a middle-aged woman out buying bread for her daughters, a local merchant, a bus driver, and an office worker. A seventeen-year-old secondary school student was killed by a bullet shattering his spine, and a handful of police and military personnel were wounded, including police captain Ahmad al-Baltagi, who died that afternoon in Qasr al-ʿAini Hospital of internal bleeding from the bullet that ruptured his left femoral artery. Of the two captured militants, one, Ragab ʿAbd al-Wakil, a thirty-one year old from Dayrut with a secondary school diploma in industrial sciences, died of his wounds after five hours in police custody. The other, twenty-one-year-old Mahmud Salah Fahmi, a secondary student from the village of al-Qawsiyya in Asyut Province, was immediately detained at the hospital and placed under interrogation by police detectives and security officials from the Office of the National Security Prosecutor. The young man shot to death under the Sayyida ʿAisha Bridge was more of a mystery figure. He was carrying forged papers identifying him as a twenty-five-year-old from Sohag, attending the University of Asyut. But — like the accounts of the chase — different stories on different pages of even the same newspaper gave inconsistent information about his identity. The three government newspapers reported his name variously as Muhammad ʿAtif Kamil, Muhammad ʿAtif Kamil ʿAli, Muhammad ʿAtif Sadiq, and Muhammad ʿAtif Kamil Mustafa. But the name that caused the most excitement was *al-Akhbar*'s page one identification of the young man as twenty-three-year-old Mustafa ʿAwni Kamil, the holder of a diploma in agricultural sciences and a fugitive wanted for the assassination of a state security official in Asyut (a front-page photo caption in *al-Ahram* concurred with that identification).

A search of the corpse turned up a bomb detonator, four hundred fifty Egyptian pounds, and a wad of newspaper articles about the hanging of five Islamists convicted in the case of fourteen men known as "The Returnees from Afghanistan," referring to Egyptian veterans of the anti-Soviet Muslim resistance forces of the 1980s. In January 1993 the group had launched a wave of attacks in Egypt, first against tourist buses at the Giza pyramids and then in front of the Egyptian Museum in Cairo's Tahrir Square. Later they placed a bomb under a police car, which killed a member of the Cairo bomb squad, and finally on 20 April they ambushed Dr. Safwa al-Sharif, Egypt's minister of information, as he returned to his home one afternoon, wounding him, his driver, and his bodyguard. Their nineteen-day trial — heard before a military rather than a civilian court, as has been the custom for recent cases of political violence — ended with a guilty verdict on 27 May. On 17 July, a day before the Zeinhom incident, the five were executed and their bodies were transferred from prison to the Zeinhom morgue for their families to retrieve.

Based on Mahmud Salah Fahmi's statements to security officials, the young men captured and killed at Zeinhom were members of the military wing of the Jihad organization based in the southern province of Asyut, and were staging a revenge attack on the police and the medical facility, wearing black headbands to signal their state of mourning for the executed "Returnees." They had arrived from Upper Egypt two days previously and surveyed the neighborhood at least three times before their attack, the last time on Saturday night, when they cruised through the area in a Honda pickup. The newspaper articles in the mysterious corpse's pocket had been part of an antiterrorism media blitz carried out in Cairo newspapers beginning the day before the execution. Full-page photo spreads of the blood-soaked bodies of victims, wounded and orphaned children, screaming mothers, and burning automobiles, had appeared under enormous headlines announcing "This Is Terrorism: Their Bullets Target Everyone!"[5] On the morning of the Zeinhom incident details of the Returnees' crimes, and of the conviction and sentencing, were accompanied by mugshots of the five newly executed men. The patriotic and religious rhetoric are impossible to separate:

In an application of God's Law and Revelation, punishment was carried out against five enemies of the people. They conspired in killing and sabotage.

They shed the blood of the innocent. They corrupted and spoiled the very earth that God has promised as a safe haven. They wanted to frighten and alarm society and the national economy by trying to strike at tourism. They allowed what God forbade, and the court applied to them the Divine Ordinance of God and the ruling of the law.[6]

This Is Not a Demonstration

By now, events and their descriptions were leapfrogging rapidly over one another. The attackers at Zeinhom, carrying newspaper stories on the execution of the five Afghan veterans, were themselves described the following day in stories blanketing the daily papers. Their clothing, the events of the chase, and praise for the heroism of their working-class captors were mixed with forensic details from the crime lab investigators: the number of bullets dug out of Captain al-Baltagi's patrol car; the chemical constituents of the unexploded bombs. Capping the stories like dim illuminated borders were photographs: the shot-out patrol car window; the taxi used as a getaway car; faces of neighbors and pursuers; the wailing relatives of the wounded and dead gathered at the hospital; a magnificent view of the Muhammad 'Ali mosque atop the Citadel, as a backdrop to the Sayyida 'Aisha overpass, below which the mysterious corpse is being examined by relaxed traffic officers and a plainclothes crime lab investigator. Inset are a police academy photograph of al-Baltagi, a photo of his wounded sergeant in the hospital, and a closeup of the blood-streaked face of Muhammad Salama al-Sayyid Muhammad, the student killed on his way to school.[7] Several photos show closeups of the dead militant displayed like a trophy of the security apparatus. In some he is covered with newspapers. In others they have been pulled away from his body to show his open eyes and mouth, his belt undone, his "trainings" pulled up to reveal the blood caked on his chest.

What the residents of Zeinhom had experienced on Sunday, the rest of Cairo learned from Monday's papers, simultaneously with the funerals of the two "martyrs," the term used to describe the victims killed in the attack. Just after noon prayers Captain al-Baltagi was given a state funeral ceremony at the Omar Makram mosque across the street from the Mugamma', the main government administrative building on Tahrir Square. The area was under heavy security provided both by the thin and weary conscripts of the Central Security forces, and by grave and muscular plainclothes security men gripping pistols and stubby machine guns. They kept pedestrians from getting too close to the street, and searched the bags of passersby. Listening attentively to walkie-talkies, they scanned the ground and surrounding buildings for threats to the safety of the dozen dignitaries attending the ceremony. These included the mufti in a blinding white robe and fez, the suited and sunglassed ministers of education and the interior, the first deputy foreign minister, the governor of Cairo, a general representing the president, and top officials of the Ministry of the Interior, which operates the national police, security, and prisons services. Much of the city was on alert during that week, and armored personnel carriers were parked — quite unusually — outside the national radio and television building on the Nile Corniche.

I happened to be in Cairo that week. Having come downtown on some errands at midday, I ran accidentally across the funeral and, not knowing at that point what was going on, I asked one of the plainclothesmen what the demonstration (*mudhahira*) was. "It's not a demonstration," he said curtly. "What is it?" "Someone died," he replied, turning his back to me and facing the crowd again. "Who?" "An officer." "The terrorists shot him?" "Yeah." Ranged along the sidewalk across the street from the mosque, children and young people carried banners: "Yes to Social Tranquility! No to Terrorism! No to Terrorism!" After prayers and speeches inside the mosque were completed, the police marching band struck up a funeral dirge from Chopin and led forty rows of police officers goose-stepping down the street, three abreast, followed by the somber walking dignitaries and then the body, draped in green cloth with gold Qur'anic verses, carried on the shoulders of marchers. Finally the children with their banners and tiny Egyptian flags followed. The procession of several hundred was led in patriotic chants by a man on top of a firetruck, and the whole cortege was guided down the street by a human barrier formed by the black-clad Central Security forces, who held hands along the sidewalk to separate marchers from the spectators. Journalists snapped pictures and television cameras rolled.

I assumed the procession would continue south and east toward the cemeteries on the eastern side of the city, but instead it stopped suddenly after a couple of blocks and the students with their banners, the dignitaries with their escorts, and the marchers themselves wandered back down the street toward Omar Makram. The mufti passed two feet behind me on his way to a waiting car, and the students headed for the bridge to take them back across the river to the Gezira Youth Center that had sent them there. The body of Ahmad al-Baltagi[8] itself was put on a truck and taken off to the family cemetery in the delta town of Mansura. The crowd of spectators, drawn from the busy workday pedestrian traffic in Tahrir and Qasr al-Dubara Squares, dissolved.

The next day the funeral itself and its accompanying *mudhahira sha'biyya* (popular demonstration) was splashed across the newspapers, with photos of the march and interviews with spectators, relatives, neighbors, and colleagues of the martyred captain, along with statements of his police superiors and Interior Ministry officials. Al-Baltagi, it turned out, was a heroic figure both personally and professionally. His mother's sister was quoted as saying that

> he was at the height of his youth, and he regularly prayed and fasted, read the Qur'an aloud and prayed the dawn prayer before going off to work. He had high morals and treated all people alike — he was humble and never arrogant — his only aspiration was to work and serve his country. His supervisors at work knew him for his good morals and achievement, and after he graduated from police academy he decided to marry his work!

A neighbor testified that "his heart was like a child; he didn't know malice or hatred," and then demanded rhetorically, "You tell me one religion or one people who are allowed to shed the blood of our youth and our children??!" Another affirmed that "his love of goodness was above all else, and he was a devoted son to his parents, postponing his own marriage after the death of his father five years ago, so as not to leave his mother after his older brother 'Umar went off to Saudi Arabia."[9] More to the point, the first deputy minister of the interior affirmed that al- Baltagi showed "the utmost courage and bravery; he sacrificed with his soul and never thought for a moment about his own life, but thought about Egypt as a country that had to be made safe, and even though he was far away from the weapons fire, he turned there in his car as soon as he heard the sound of bullets."[10] As for the neighbors who had pursued and caught the militants,

> they acted as one man in the utmost boldness and decency, undeterred by the bullets. What was seen [that day] among the sons of Egypt is not found in any other country in the world; what happened is not new to Egyptians, what is new is the anomalous and temporary negativism that has reared its head. . . . I say that one martyr or a thousand martyrs, we will never alter our will or our plans to confront those who forsake the law, no matter who they are![11]

The Sons of Egypt

Who the principals in this drama were was still somewhat unsettled, as the papers reported the day after the funeral that the mysterious corpse under the Sayyida ʿAisha Bridge was *not* Mustafa ʿAwni after all. While still officially unidentified, it was suspected to be Muhammad ʿAbd al-ʿAl, a student expelled from a military high school in Dayrut. Three others were still being sought in connection with the attack, all men in their twenties and thirties; two of them from Upper Egypt and all of them wanted on other charges. One of them, the fugitive Talʿat Muhammad Yasin Hamam, already carried a death sentence in the case of the Returnees, which had triggered Zeinhom.

The images at play in this print record of the incident and its aftermath are quite clear, however, in their sketch of the cracks in the social order and of the tensions surrounding changing patterns of power and wealth, education and migration in Egypt today. Research from around the Middle East on the armed manifestations of the Islamic Trend emphasize that it is a phenomenon of young people. Moreover, they are getting younger all the time. The average age of young Islamists arrested in police sweeps declined from twenty-seven in the 1970s to twenty-one by 1990; as in Pakistan and elsewhere, Islamist groups are recruiting more and more among high school students.[12] More specifically, the young men who bomb and shoot tourist buses, government ministers, and police tend also to be modern educated, with degrees and diplomas in technical subjects. In Egypt, many of them are from the largely agricultural regions of the south. Like the overwhelming majority of Egyptian youth, these would-be members of the overstaffed technical and administrative classes are disturbed by the moral degradation of society and by its scarcity of economic and political opportunity, and believe that a new social framework based on Islamic law is the best solution.[13]

This being so, the rhetoric of age, class, and regional origin suffuses coverage of the Zeinhom incident in complex ways. Youths strange to the neighborhood are reported lurking at night. The attack and subsequent pursuit pit these rootless students not only against the police, but against a neighborhood of working-class family men — butchers, mechanics, and bus drivers — that forcefully resists. And their resistance succeeds, despite the clean-cut militants' attempts at disguise: the jeans and T-shirts hiding warmup suits that hide the invisible spectres of white skullcaps, galabiyyas and beards of the newspaper cartoon's stereotyped Islamist fanatic. Even discarding the black headbands that mark their mourning, the militants cannot blend entirely into the crowd. When one of the armed men tries to convince skeptical neighbors that he is a plainclothes policeman, he is given away by the hand grenade tucked under his clothes. In his pocket is a telephone credit card for making international calls, unmasking an outside campaign of subversion. (For weeks afterward, young people around the city were subjected to popular scrutiny. In early August the owner of a kiosk in Tahrir Square reported to the police that two suspicious young men — one carrying a large leather valise — were hanging around a group of tourist buses. They were immediately arrested but the interrogation showed that the suitcase held nothing but clothes and that the men — one from Alexandria and the other from Holland — had simply been processing some papers at the Mugamma' administration building.[14])

The young Jihadists pose, moreover, a comprehensive threat. They target police but wound civilians as well; they attack symbols of state violence but end up killing their own (one of the casualties was a high school student, and eyewitnesses claim that one of the escaped militants tried to kill his captured colleague after failing to free him from the crowd). The shabab are consuming themselves alive. Furthermore, they disrupt — actually and symbolically — the connection between responsible adulthood and the innocence and dependency of childhood. Two of the wounded civilians, a driver and a housewife, were rushed to hospital without their children and pleaded with reporters for information about what had happened to them. The slain police captain was praised for his role as son and for having the pious and innocent heart of a child, without malice. Newspaper stories playing on the grief of his mother report a barber approaching her at the funeral and consoling her, "Don't cry, my mother — your son the hero isn't dead — for he's in the vastness of God and he will stay eternally in the hearts of all Egyptians. Don't cry, my mother, for all Egyptians are your sons!"[15] As if to underscore this sense of family, the minister of education announced that summer that the medical bills of the victims of terrorism, and the cost of their children's schooling — public or private, domestic or foreign — would be paid by the state.

The rhetorical power of the newspaper coverage of the Zeinhom attack and al-Baltagi's funeral lies in the creation of interlinked stories that mold its principal players into archetypes, and which manipulate the scale of kinship and national solidarity by representing collectives as individuals and individuals as selfless servants of the collective. The captain, married to his work, thinks of Egypt's security rather than himself, and sacrifices his life for the greater good. Meanwhile his neighbors in chasing down the Jihadists have acted as a single person in confronting the threat to their lives and the security of the nation. When the officer is slain by the enemies of the people, his mother becomes their mother in turn, as they march down the street calling for vengeance, shouting, "To the Paradise of the Everlasting, O martyr!" and "With our soul, with our blood, may we be a sacrifice for you, O Egypt!"[16] This is the heroism of the ordinary, in which the duty of each citizen is set in its place: officer, mechanic, student, son. But it is also "the Spirit of October," in the words of one of the Zeinhom residents (referring to the patriotic spirit of the 1973 war). Suddenly the pious textbooks have come alive, their models inscribed in another form, with photographs of real but everyday people substituting for generic line drawings of imagined moral models.

A Thousand Martyrs

Even before General ʿAbd al-Rahim al-Nahhas's funeral promise to "make war on the terrorists even if a thousand martyrs fall," state security forces had begun another roundup of suspected Islamist militants, arresting thirty on the day of the Zeinhom attack and thirteen more the day of the funeral. The afternoon of the attack a special force of state security agents flew to Asyut to carry out investigations and "tighten the noose around the criminals."[17] The governorates of Minya, Asyut, and Sohag, some three hundred kilometers south of the capital, have been at the center of the latest round of antigovernment Islamist military activity, which is usually dated from the summer of 1992. The towns and villages of the area—Asyut itself, Mallawi, Dayrut, al-Qawsiyya, and others, appear repeatedly as the birthplaces and residences of arrested militants from the Jihad and al-Gamaʿa (or al-Jamaʿa) al-Islamiyya (Islamic Group) organizations. The leaders of southern groups are commonly university students, while those based in Cairo and the delta tend to be military officers, engineers, doctors, and other professionals.[18]

Whatever the case, the state has given many residents of Upper Egypt—"Saʿidis"—ample rationalization for political discontent. The region is largely ignored by private and government investment (the northern coastal city of Alexandria reportedly received several times the government investment of the equally populous southern province of Minya in 1994),[19] so much of the attention regional cities get is from the security forces that occasionally sweep their residences — arresting a hundred suspected Islamists here, a few dozen there — and bulldoze the houses of suspect's families after taking family members, including children, hostage in lieu of their quarry. (The same tactic is used in other low-income areas as well, like Cairo's Imbaba neighborhood.) Police have prohibited farmers from using some of their land for planting, since escaping militants have hidden in sugarcane stands along the roads after attacks (the interior minister is currently appealing for night-vision and other high-tech transportation and communications equipment for security forces searching the country's mountains and dense agricultural fields for Islamist forces).[20] And in some areas like the lucrative tourist sites in Luxor further south, broad-based economic development is purposely stifled in favor of dependence on tourist revenue. Villagers are prohibited from setting up factories or workshops, and must build in mud brick to keep the area looking appropriately ancient, while international consulting firms advise the Ministry of Tourism on how to channel the flow of tourist cash to a small fraction of the populace.[21] Under such conditions attacks on Nile tourist boats might be less a response to xenophobia (although the behavior of many Western tourists is fundamentally shocking and inappropriate) than they are an attempt to drive the business away, simultaneously creating a public relations crisis and an economic crisis that some militants hope will bring the government down. Local Christians are popular class and ethnic scapegoats, and are often the target of violence as well.

Because of their experience dealing with Islamists locally, Cairo has regularly named its recent interior ministers — including former Asyut governor Hasan al-Alfi and his two immediate predecessors — from the south. But the conflict, as we saw above, is not regionally confined. In December 1992 the security forces staged one of their largest operations ever, dispatching between ten and twelve thousand troops to Cairo's poor Imbaba suburb and arresting six hundred suspected al-Gamaʿa al-islamiyya members in a three-week operation. Nine hundred were rounded up around the country in a single week in February 1994, and every week during the summer of 1993 newspapers carried reports of suspects falling into the hands of the authorities in the neighborhood of the capital as well as the south.[22] During the summer of 1995 relations between Egypt and the Islamist state of the Sudan hit new lows after Egyptian president Husni Mubarak accused his southern neighbor of complicity in the Gamaʿa al-Islamiyya's latest attempt to assassinate him while on a visit to Ethiopia on 26 June. Altogether, over the last three years over nine hundred people have died in battles between Islamist militants and Egyptian security forces. That number includes police officers, tourists, legislators, government ministers, officials, and intellectuals shot; Islamists shot in the street, in domestic raids, and in police custody, or hanged in prison after conviction; and hapless civilians caught in the crossfire.

This is a low-level insurgency, to be sure; nothing compared to recent carnage in Bosnia or Chechnya, Algeria or Iraq, Rwanda or Guatemala. Certainly not even terribly significant compared with Egypt's annual infant mortality rate, or the instant fatalities from 1994's oil fire on the Nile or the 1992 Cairo earthquake, both of which claimed hundreds of lives through various combinations of natural disaster and human error. Yet threats to life are always more spectacular and memorable when they are phrased in terms of threats to the social order, and the insurgency's fetishized body count is regularly exploited by the local and international press as an easy index of the conflict, focusing attention away from other issues. Other numerical indices of the insurgency are somewhat less often reported: the outlawed Egyptian Organization for Human Rights reports that ten thousand Egyptians are in jail as suspected "Islamic militants" (other reported numbers go as high as twenty thousand).[23] Most are held without charge under the 1981 Emergency Law, and many endure threats to their families and regular torture, including beatings, scalding showers, psychological pressure, and electric shock. Thirty-eight have been shot while in custody, and in police attacks, civilians — like the eight men killed by police at prayer time in an Aswan mosque in the summer of 1993 — are not necessarily spared.[24] In return for the state's increasing savagery, ordinary citizens in many areas have turned against the ruling party, and militant groups increase the frequency of their own attacks, executing police by the roadside, killing officers who try to keep them from posting political signs, robbing banks and jewelry stores, killing Christian businessmen and government imams, even firing on the police escorts ferrying high school examination questions from Asyut to surrounding towns (a small sample from the first seven months of 1995).

One Hundred Percent Under Control

Just a few months after al-Gama'a al-Islamiyya first began its attacks on the tourist industry in 1992, igniting its current war with the government, a senior security official said that they were obviously engaged in provocation, but "we will not be provoked. The problem is 100% under control."[25] Several cultural strategies for combatting the Islamic Trend continue to be applied in tandem with police and military activities (although one appears no more efficient than the other). A day after the Zeinhom incident, as security forces flown in the day before were once again scouring Asyut for Islamist militants, the minister of religious endowments was meeting with a different group of shabab in the same city. He told them President Mubarak was doing everything in his power to provide them with job opportunities and a good life, and that most of the youth of the region reject terrorism and intellectual extremism out of hand. The governor of Asyut, seated near the minister, added that from now on youth centers, sporting clubs, and schools in all cities and villages in the governorate would distribute free sports clothing and equipment, as well as cultural and religious books and magazines, to young people.[26] The minister had been traveling that week with colleagues from al-Azhar and the Ministry of Youth and Sport, in the yearly summer Religious Awareness Caravan. In Minya on the day of the Zeinhom attack he told the audience that only ministry-certified preachers can deliver sermons in mosques, and plugged a new book prepared by the ministry that — with the input of al-Azhar — discussed the reasons why some young people held "mistaken and corrupted" religious ideas. Five million copies of the book *Declaration to the People* were to be distributed through youth centers throughout the nation, to occupy the minds of youth while the promised free sporting equipment occupied their bodies.

This well-publicized strategy of moderation, reason, and public dialogue is tempered both by the frequency of reports of mass arrests of suspected militants and also by reportage on public reactions to the violence. Press coverage of Captain al-Baltagi's funeral had quoted bystanders — from lawyers to barbers — calling for trials within twenty-four hours for arrested terrorists, and their public execution. Egyptians who had worked in Saudi Arabia said that public executions there kept the crime rate low. Reiterating General al-Nahhas's equation of Egypt and her people, one observer of the funeral demanded "the broadcast of executions on television screens, so that all the people and the servants of terrorism will know that in Egypt the state is strong and fears for the people and takes care of them and will never abandon them, and that the people will never abandon its leaders."[27]

These calls for public execution communicate a real and widespread popular patriotism and a nearly universal Egyptian tough-on-crime attitude. But when set in the machinery of print they also speak as the voice of a political order declaring its own strength and announcing that any and all police action to deal with Islamist militancy is justifiable on the grounds of public assent. The state demonstrates its own restraint (largely for an external audience that perceives it as a "secular" entity rather than a Saudi-style Islamic government) by *not* holding public executions, despite the news that the funeral turned into "a shouting popular demonstration" calling for "execution in public squares [of] . . . the enemies of country and religion."[28] News coverage of the funeral summarized the extent of this sentiment in a statistical idiom as fluid as it was familiar. Like the identity of al-Baltagi's dead assassin, the reported size of the funeral crowd mutated rapidly in published reports. My own head count — perhaps six hundred people in the procession and an equal number of observers — was confirmed by a photo caption in *al-Wafd*, the liberal opposition daily ("hundreds"). But the accompanying article counted five thousand people from every governorate in the country, with a thousand schoolchildren carrying banners.[29] Another paper reported two hundred students; a third, seven hundred.[30] The crowd as a whole swelled to "thousands,"[31] and then to "tens of thousands,"[32] with wide-angle photographs turning narrow streets into broad plazas, and low camera angles exaggerating the mass of bodies whose depth was invisible and therefore potentially endless. What was in fact a moderate sized and highly orchestrated event blossomed on paper into a massive and spontaneous eruption of popular will.

The Drop of a Gun

But Zeinhom's sequel, as it turned out, was to be even better than the original, reading like the script of an action movie (*"wa huna bada'at al-tafasil al-muthira"* [and here the exciting details began . . .], teased *al-Ahram's* police-blotter coverage).[33] Two weeks after the funeral, the real Mustafa ʿAwni Zaki — first thought to have been killed beneath the Sayyida ʿAisha Bridge — was captured. He and a colleague, on their way to a meeting allegedly to plan another Cairo attack, got lost near a public park in the Amiriyya neighborhood on the northeast end of the city. They stopped to ask directions of Mahmud Ibrahim, a seventeen-year-old peddler, who became suspicious and tried to get rid of them when they pulled out a detailed street map of the neighborhood. But then a pistol unexpectedly dropped from the clothing of one of the fugitives onto the ground. The young peddler began shouting to the scores of people enjoying the park's cool evening weather, and suddenly a new neighborhood, primed by press coverage of terrorist incidents and alert to the power of Everyman, came alive with indignation as its blacksmiths, fruit vendors, and carpenters gave chase. The militants both ran, shooting into the crowd and wounding two people. They stopped a taxi and threatened the driver, but when he refused to let them in, the second militant shot him, and Mustafa ʿAwni jumped over the cab and rushed with his companion into a Suzuki pickup. The two quickly abandoned that vehicle, too, after ʿAwni shot and killed a civilian motorcyclist pursuing them. While his colleague escaped, he commandeered a bus, holding his gun to the driver's neck with an order to keep the doors closed. But the pursuing crowd grabbed onto the open window frames and began pulling themselves up, and when the gunman pointed his pistol at them the driver opened the door and men streamed onto the vehicle, grabbing ʿAwni and beating him badly. By the time he was handed to police and taken to the hospital his blood pressure had dropped so low he was put on intravenous fluids.

Celebratory newspaper photographs the day after showed ʿAwni dressed in jeans and a torn and bloody T-shirt with the word "SPORT" printed boldly across the front. He was blindfolded, his face smeared with blood. Another photograph displayed his impounded 9mm pistol and his forged identity papers. National security investigators fingered him as a leader of the Jihad's military wing and the "prime mover" behind the Zeinhom incident, wanted in addition for the deaths of eight police officers in Dayrut and a market sentry in a nearby village, and armed attacks on a tourist bus and the *Nile Elite* tourist steamer.[34] Six teams of security agents meanwhile combed the nearby ʿAin Shams and Matariyya neighborhoods for the escaped militant. They arrested dozens of people, including the man ʿAwni identified as his arms dealer.

The same day ʿAwni was captured, a mentally unstable religious bookseller — upset that sewer workers showed up in front of his apartment to fix a backup—opened fire on neighbors and was wounded by police after a standoff. His neighbors broke through the police line and rushed up the stairs to the balcony where he fell, carrying his body through the streets before the police managed to get it back.[35] He reportedly sold books and collected donations at a mosque where members of ʿAwni's organization had been meeting, and then used the proceeds to buy guns for the market in Asyut.[36] Mosques, both public and private, have long been targets of Interior Ministry raids, since they offer convenient meeting places, fundraising platforms, and venues for discussion, mobilization, and instruction. The previous week, half a dozen mosques and apartments in the central delta province of Gharbiyya were raided by security forces looking for "extremist elements who infiltrated Ministry of Waqfs mosques with the intention of spreading their ideas among shabab . . . by holding lessons" after the evening prayers.[37] Police recovered dozens of weapons, including starting pistols modified to fire live ammunition, and arrested over a hundred people from three different underground organizations and eight different provinces.

They Need to Get Rid of Some People

One measure of Egypt's current political dilemma is that, while the Interior Ministry and the state security prosecutor process arrestees through interrogation rooms, prisons, special courts, and the gallows, other parts of the legal system actively aid the partisans of the Islamist opposition. Egypt's Constitution declares that the Islamic shariʿa is the nation's main source of legislation. It should not be very surprising, then, when the courts issue rulings that appear to advance an Islamist cultural agenda. On 14 June 1995, an appeals court ruled that a controversial literary analysis of the Qurʾan written by Cairo University professor Nasr Abu Zayd, implicitly questioned the book's divine origins, and therefore made Abu Zayd an apostate who could not legally be married to a Muslim woman under Egyptian personal status law. The court—acting on a two-year-old suit brought by Islamist lawyers—ruled that Abu Zayd should be separated from his wife. But once it issued its ruling, in effect declaring Abu Zayd an apostate in the eyes of the Egyptian state, former Parliament member Shaykh Yusuf al-Badri called on the state not only to remove him from his wife, but to execute him. Conversion from Islam to other religions has been construed as illegal by the courts, and according to some Muslims, the penalty for apostasy should be death. This notion was made famous, of course, by Iranian Ayatollah Khomeini's 1989 opinion that Anglo-Pakistani author Salman Rushdie was liable to execution for his alleged insults to Islam in his novel *The Satanic Verses*, and later by the 1992 assassination of Egyptian writer Farag Foda. One team of human rights lawyers seeking to appeal the Abu Zayd ruling withdrew after a month when al-Badri and one of the lawyers who had brought the original suit threatened to have them declared apostates as well.[38] Abu Zayd's colleagues at Cairo University feel the intellectual chill, and have coined a new term for it: *cultural terrorism*. A meeting of faculty in July to organize a defense of Abu Zayd was broken up by the University Club president, and other faculty at the university have been told by their department chairs to alter sensitive parts of the curriculum to avoid criticism by Islamists.[39]

Two years before this, in April 1993, Abu Zayd had been denied promotion to full professor because ʿAbd al-Subur Shahin, a colleague in the Arabic Language and Literature Department, and a member of the university's academic review committee, objected to portions of his work. In interviews with reporters, Abu Zayd suggested that the conflict would have remained restricted to the university except that Shahin denounced him from a mosque pulpit on 2 April, and by the following Friday mosques "all over the country" were repeating his charges. In terms eerily reminiscent of Sir Eldon Gorst, Abu Zayd explained that

> such a situation could only have arisen within a context that involves the hammering home of a message by constant repetition before an illiterate audience, be that a real or cultural illiteracy. I would have liked to have been treated like the repentant terrorist who was given an opportunity to appear on television and talk to the nation. I would have liked to have been able to debate my views with whomever on television. But television has contrived to ignore my case. Yet, of course, the broadcast media open their doors wide to the discourse of all those who have declared me an apostate.[40]

By this he does not mean the same people whom the state so assiduously hunts down in Upper Egyptian sugarcane fields — these are usually denied even mention on television and radio — but rather "moderates" like the Muslim Brotherhood and conservative sympathizers within and without the state's own religious establishment. In other interviews he has pointed out that while the state has been depending on "moderate" Islamists for support in marginalizing militant groups, it is precisely these moderates, who prefer to work for change through the courts and the Parliament, who opposed his promotion and sought to end his marriage, both tactics aimed at intimidating intellectuals in ways more subtle than that chosen by writer Farag Foda's assassins in 1992. "Silencing is at the heart of my case," Abu Zayd told interviewers. "Expelling someone from the university is a way of silencing him. Taking someone away from his specialization is a way of silencing him. Killing someone is a way of silencing him. They need to get rid of some people."[41]

Too Many Secrets

Whether the "they" refers to the government specifically or to Islamists in general is as unclear in the context of the interview as it is in the context of the intellectual politics the state is trying so desperately to control. *Declaration to the People*, the book Muhammad ʿAli Mahgub was publicizing the week Mustafa ʿAwni and his colleagues opened fire in Zeinhom, is only one of the literary projects the public sector has undertaken to wean Egyptians of intellectual dependence on freelance Islamist writers. The government and the ruling party have for more than a decade provided the marketplace with Islamic literature such as the NDP's weekly tabloid *al-Liwaʾ al-Islami* (The Islamic Standard), *al-Muslim al-Saghir* (The Little Muslim), the children's monthly from the Ministry of Religious Endowments, and others.[42] Both these public sector productions emphasize the application of Islamic principles to daily life, and in an interesting reversal of standing broadcast policy—in which female television characters and newscasters are prohibited from covering their hair—such periodicals universally show women as muhaggabat in drawings and photographs. Each tries to outbid its private sector competitors with conservative cultural credentials while featuring the president and members of the religious establishment in the place of the private sector's glowing profiles of martyred Muslim Brotherhood leaders Hasan al-Banna and Sayyid Qutb. Throughout the mid-1980s, the circulation figures for private sector religious periodicals in Egypt were fifty times those of public sector production, but their numbers remained relatively stable while the circulation of public sector religious titles increased by more than 300 percent. This has been part of a concentrated effort to adopt the language and tactics of the Islamist movement so as better to compete with them on their own ground.

But this policy, although well-coordinated through the NDP and across several ministries, is not monolithic. In a very different tactical move, the public sector General Egyptian Book Organization (GEBO) began in 1993 a new series of reprints of classic Islamic modernist texts, called the *Muwajaha* (Confrontation) series. Each book bore on its back the strongly-worded declaration that

> The conspiracy of extremism and terror in Egypt has reached unprecedented proportions in the last year. . . . Egypt is now experiencing a human, cultural and civilizational tragedy and an economic and political catastrophe. Therefore, it has become necessary for Egyptian intellectuals and the institutions of civil society to rise and confront extremism and terror, to surround and contain them in preparation for their complete uprooting.[43]

The series contains classic works by Egyptian authors Taha Hussein, Qasim Amin, Shaykh Muhammad Abduh, and more recent intellectuals, all of whom have explored the meaning of Islam in the modern age. Soon after its first appearance the series was denounced by officials at al-Azhar and other Islamic institutions for reissuing volumes by Muslim scholars like ʿAli ʿAbd al-Raziq, who proposed in 1925 that Egypt should become a secular state like Turkey. When first published, the book was condemned by al-Azhar, and ʿAbd al-Raziq was denounced as unfit to hold public position.[44] Ironically, at the same time that the minister of religious endowments was plugging *Declaration to the People* during the summer 1993 Religious Awareness Caravan, Dr. ʿAbd al-Subur Marzuq, the general superintendent of the Supreme Council for Islamic Affairs, told a Caravan audience of Alexandria University students in mid-July that the "Confrontation" series was merely "the latest campaign of communism and secularism in their war against Islam and its enlightened thought. . . . This collection contains ludicrous and perverted books, and it [isn't] necessary to start printing them again, or having the state budget pay for them."[45] At that very same meeting, the minister announced that Dr. Marzuq and the mufti had been named to a three-man commission responsible for planning the process of development and composition for new religious studies books for public schools.[46] The third member of the commission was to be Shaykh Muhammad al-Ghazali.

Shaykh al-Ghazali — a popular conservative ʿalim and teacher who had written a weekly column for the Muslim Brotherhood's weekly outlet *al-Shaʿb* in the late 1980s, and gained international stature as a teacher and media personality in Algeria — was in the news for other reasons in the summer of 1993. In June he had been called as a witness for the defense at the trial of writer Farag Foda's assassins (several of whom were themselves Islamist lawyers). He testified that Muslims who object to the application of Islamic law are apostates, and that the killers of apostates are merely carrying out the punishment set in place by the shariʿa itself, which the Constitution purportedly takes as the main source of legislation.[47] Despite the rapprochement between the government and the Muslim Brothers, the embarrassed Shaykh of al-Azhar and the minister of religious endowments were forced to repeat publicly that only the ruler and his law enforcement officials could take upon themselves the responsibility to investigate and declare apostasy or to carry out the death sentence.[48] "Playing around in the political sphere is far from the holiness of religion," Mahgub told audiences during the days immediately before and after the Zeinhom attack; no one except the ruler is entitled to administer divine ordinances or to claim that homicide is religiously permissible. Nothing, he said, can excuse people setting themselves up as legislators and judges and executioners.[49] In July the state called ʿAtiyya Saqr, the head of the fatwa committee at al-Azhar, to testify at the Foda assassination trial in response to al-Ghazali and to the similar testimony of another expert witness, Dr. Mahmud Mazruʿa. But once the prosecution had rested its case, one of the defense attorneys dared the court to criminalize the defendants' own legal justification for killing apostates, lest it be forced to try the prominent scholars al-Ghazali and Mazruʿa as well. When the prosecutor entered into evidence volumes from the "Confrontation" book series, one of the defendants asked his lawyer to call witnesses to respond to them, as well as to enter into evidence volumes of Islamic jurisprudence.

Suddenly the case seemed to be less about a criminal prosecution than it was about the right to interpret and apply the principles of divine law in a society whose leaders proclaim that "our constitution is Islam."[50] The defense claimed that the trial was about the cultural effects of Foda's anti-Islamist writings, which represented "atheism's struggle to obliterate the knowledge of religion and to guide our children with principles that leave them with no connection to us."[51] That this is essentially the same charge Dr. Marzuq leveled at the General Egyptian Book Organization reveals the difficulty of disentangling the twisted strands of state cultural policy.

Similar ambiguities and contradictions are easy to find. In 1994, after allowing the Nasserist magazine *Ruz al-Yusuf* to publish excerpts from works censored by al-Azhar, President Mubarak announced at the annual Cairo Book Fair that he was releasing some controversial works that had been seized at the fair the previous year. "I am convinced," said *Ruz al-Yusuf*'s editor, "that this government's trend is secular."[52] But at its party convention two years previously the ruling NDP had reinforced its stand that Egypt is an Islamic state committed to the norms of Islam, and underlining support for comprehensive religious education in the schools.[53] Cultural policy is oddly split, along with the conscience of the nation. The same government that declares Islam the religion of the state produces public sector beer and wine (but then bans their sale in several southern provinces to quiet Islamist opposition). Like Saudi Arabia and Iran (and, for that matter, China), Egypt has recently moved to ban satellite dishes "to preserve and protect the values, morals and traditions of society," and in early July 1995 a court sentenced a movie theater owner to a short prison sentence for displaying a 1973 movie poster showing a woman's cleavage (this suit as well was brought by Yusuf al-Badri, among others). No one seems to be able accurately to identify, characterize, or predict the direction government policy will take with respect to the Islamization of public life.

What is clear is that civil society is increasingly a self-consciously Islamic space. In September 1992 the Egyptian Lawyers Syndicate—essentially a public sector union of legal professionals—was taken over by Islamist candidates in the elections for its executive committee. This followed Muslim Brotherhood victories in the board elections of the Cairo University Faculty Club (1990) and the Pharmacists (1990), Physicians (1988), and Engineers (1987) Syndicates.[54] Thousands of these professionals, along with accountants, teachers, social workers, students, and others, volunteer their time providing social, educational, and health services for the poor through private voluntary organizations operating in centers associated with private mosques. Increasingly common during the 1980s, this has been a response both to the impotence of the government to provide the volume and quality of services required by the country's growing population, and to a sense that the fortunate in the Muslim community should devote time and their income to alleviating the misery of the poor, the sick, and the needy.

The same increasingly applies to the business community as well. In 1989 Muslim Brotherhood candidates won several seats on the board of the Commerce Graduate's Association, and Islamic banks and investment companies have become part of the financial scene. Despite new regulations on such companies in the late 1980s, and the prosecution and subsequent collapse of some of them for fraudulent practices (e.g., the enormous Rayan company, which owned everything from financial services companies to restaurants and parking lots), networks of Islamist businesses are spreading with the aid of heavy capital investment from Egyptian professionals working abroad, as well as direct investment by foreign individuals, corporations, and governments. Safir Publishing Company, for example, recently began issuing a discount card good at participating businesses such as gift stores, doctor's offices, and others, testimony to the strength of private business networks.

Such formal networks are matched by an extraordinarily extensive system of informal economic networks and associations as well. Despite the fact that many educated people crave secure guaranteed jobs in the public sector, the wait for such employment is long and the pay low, so the majority of Cairenes who work in the public sector, as well as those who do not, have second and third jobs to make ends meet. Untaxed and unrecorded economic transactions from informal activities probably account for between a third and a half of the country's reported GNP, and the vast majority of remittances from abroad are through illegal channels. Diane Singerman suggests that there might be developing, in addition to the parallel economy, a "parallel polis" (a term coined by Czech dissident-turned-president Vaclav Havel) similar to that in 1980s Eastern Europe, an economic basis for an alternative to the state system of production, distribution, and political mobilization. With a stagnant formal economy, widespread corruption, and a sense of the ineffectiveness of repressive violence, elites in Egypt might well be losing faith in the legitimacy of the government and looking for other ways out of the political and economic crisis.[55] Even in lower-middle-class working neighborhoods, ordinary people who do not see themselves as belonging to an "Islamic movement" still believe in many of the elements of the Islamist platform, such as ending corruption and applying Islamic law. Political organizations or movements promising such changes have a potential for wide popular political support, as well as an immense potential economic base.

Perceiving the power of this alternative, the government has recently broadened its anti-Islamist political and police actions to include the Muslim Brotherhood, an organization with tens of thousands of members and perhaps a million supporters, which has for almost a generation enjoyed relatively little attention from security forces. Although it is an illegal organization, it has not been targeted like Jihad or al-Gamaʿa al-islamiyya, which make strategic use of violence, or even some human rights and women's associations, which have seen their assets liquidated under the laws regulating private voluntary organizations.[56] Instead, it has fielded candidates for the People's Assembly through legal political parties; published and distributed books, magazines, and newspapers through the monopoly public sector distribution companies; set up youth, educational, social service, and medical service programs; and in general forged a rapprochement with the government and a symbiotic relationship with many sectors of civil society since the 1970s.

But in January 1995, and increasingly after the 26 June assassination attempt on President Mubarak in Addis Ababa, the Ministry of the Interior turned its attention anew to the Muslim Brotherhood. On 17 July it arrested seventeen Brotherhood leaders in sixteen different provinces, seizing computers, books, documents, and videotapes purportedly showing the organization in contact with the Sudanese National Islamic Front, which Egypt publicly implicated in the assassination try. Dozens of other Brotherhood members had been detained without charges since the beginning of the year, and the July arrestees included four former members of Parliament, the head of the information department at al-Azhar, teachers, bankers, civil servants, and local officials. Eight more were taken into custody the following week, and a few days after that another two hundred Brotherhood members were arrested in security sweeps of Alexandria and Minufiyya, most of them at what the government claimed were Brotherhood military training camps. The Brotherhood itself reported that they were in fact summer youth camps established by the Ministry of Youth and Sports. The young men were arrested after having been observed practicing kung fu and karate, which has often been interpreted as terrorist training and resulted in arrests elsewhere in the country.[57]

At the time, the Muslim Brotherhood accused the NDP of using the Addis Ababa incident as an excuse for a crackdown in preparation for discrediting the organization before the scheduled People's Assembly elections in November. The prediction was apparently accurate, as arrests continued through the fall, including not only Islamists but leftist and other intellectuals as well. Journalists, including the editors of the liberal opposition daily *al-Wafd*, and the Brotherhood/Labor Party's *al-Sha'b*, have been alternately harassed, arrested, detained, and beaten. Three days before the 29 November voting, between one hundred forty (the government figure) and six hundred (the Brotherhood figure) Brotherhood members were arrested, and shortly before that, fifty-four were convicted in court and sentenced to prison for holding secret meetings and preparing antigovernment leaflets. The elections themselves, criticized by both local and foreign organizations for ballot-box stuffing and physical intimidation of voters, resulted in an overwhelming NDP victory. Some intellectuals are comparing recent waves of arrests and political repression with the paranoid atmosphere of the months leading up to Sadat's assassination in 1981.

At the same time that confidence in the government erodes, the Islamist opposition is seen as ever more ubiquitous and effective. "I don't trust the government," Layla al-Shamsi's husband told me in 1993,

> they keep too many secrets. And the only thing I read in the government papers, the only thing they're completely honest about, is the sports. For anything else, you've got to look at the opposition papers, which are really quite good, and about seventy-five percent true. Like the incident over on Salah Salem [street, referring to the Zeinhom incident]; do you remember that? They shot an officer, the fanatics did, because of the move of the terrorist trials from civil to military courts. That's what they *told* the officer before killing him. But did that appear in the government papers? Of course not. They hid the reason for the killing. The fanatics know more about the government and what it does than any of the rest of us; they pay attention. Like with [recently dismissed Defense Minister] Abu Ghazala: when photographs were produced in court showing him, I don't know, kissing the foot of some belly dancer. Where did they get those photos? Like I say, [the fanatics] know about everything that goes on.[58]

There Is No Terrorism in Egypt

And so it goes, week after week after week, month after month. The situation "100% under control" turns instead into a web of subterranean connections between bearded radicals and young men in jeans and t-shirts, between north and south, between central Cairo and its suburbs, between Egypt and the outside. (Iran, the papers quote from a German magazine, spent 186 million dollars to train terrorists around the world, including the Sudan, but at the same time, Shaykh 'Umar 'Abd al-Rahman, one of the leaders of the Gama'a al-Islamiyya, was a paid CIA informer.[59]) Money mediates the transformation of books into guns and vice versa (with Afghani heroin occasionally making a reported appearance in the equation as well).[60] Parks, youth centers, and kindergartens become arenas of violence, sporting equipment turns deadly, martial arts migrate from the movie screen to the summer camp, buses and taxis, delivery trucks and motorcycles facilitate the speedy exchange of gunfire. Even state-run mosques are infiltrated by unofficial voices. There seems no safe haven, no respite, and no way to decide whom or what to believe. In Egypt's fifteen-year-long state of emergency, every possibility becomes a fact.

The government's vacillating and ambiguous support for and reaction against the Islamic Trend in its many manifestations, along with fluctuating press restrictions, the harassment of journalists and intellectuals, mass arrests, unemployment and economic crisis, the sudden international realignment of the region following the Second Gulf War, the disappearance of the Soviet Union, and the surprising Palestinian-Israeli negotiations, make anything possible. "Now, the government and the religious groupings have a single set of interests," said the leftist journalist and poet Muhammad Sulayman in 1989, "which is to stay in power."

> America is on the side of the *mutadayyinin* [the religious ones] as well, because they perceive that they have more in common with them, and both will do anything to keep the communists out of power. Under Nasser, during that period, Egypt benefitted greatly from the Soviet Union. We got the High Dam, and there was no inflation, and things were going well. But Sadat kicked the Soviet Union out at the instigation of the CIA. They would do anything to keep out socialism.
>
> *Me:* You mean Egypt isn't a socialist country? What about the huge public sector?
>
> *Him:* (Laughing.) They're capitalist!
>
> *Me:* So what's the difference between the public and the private sector?
>
> *Him:* The private sector is succeeding! They have America on their side. Do you know that sixty percent of the private sector is under the control of the Muslim Brotherhood? I'm very angry with America. Very angry. The CIA is a party in Egypt. Not just a few here and there, but a party.[61]

Samia 'Abd al-Rahman swore to me that Egyptians, Sudanese, and Iranians had nothing whatsoever to do with the terrorist bombings that struck Cairo in 1993. She explained that they could not possibly have any interest in carrying out these atrocities, since it could only hurt the cause of Islam. Look instead for an Israeli connection, she said. The Israeli intelligence service Mossad must have been the culprit, as they have no respect at all for human life, and will do anything to hurt Muslims. Others apparently agreed with her. The leftist weekly *al-Ahali* reportedly told its readers in late June 1993 that

> rumors that 30 Israeli Uzi submachine guns were discovered in the possession of arrested militants and that a number of Israel's national carrier El Al and Alexandria-based Israeli Cultural Center employees have been arrested further fueled . . . conspiracy theories. And the former Israeli academic center chief also made a surprise visit to Cairo last week. Both stories were attributed to an unnamed Egyptian security official quoted in the London-based *al-Wasat*.[62]

The paper also reported that American national security agents had entered the country in May to give weapons and money to the Gamaʿa al-Islamiyya in retribution for Egypt's arrest of a missionary who had salted copies of the Qurʾan with Bible verses. (This is a particularly interesting hypothesis in that it allies Egyptian leftist thinking with that of Muslim Brother Sayyid Qutb, who viewed modern colonialism as a thinly disguised reprisal of the medieval Crusades to take back the Holy Land for Christianity. In 1989 a private sector Muslim periodical claimed that the Ministry of Religious Endowments had been working closely with the University of Chicago and the U.S. National Council of Churches, who had spent fifty million dollars over several years to meet with imams in Egypt and other Muslim countries "to steer [them] onto an unsound path."[63]) After an August 1993 attempt on the life of the interior minister near the American University in Cairo, students began reporting that a bomb had been planted on campus at the same time, but that it was being hushed up by officials. Rumors circulated throughout 1992 and 1993 that (unidentified) Islamists were throwing acid on the exposed legs of (unspecified) women on the street (the version I heard), or more generally "at" (unspecified) unveiled women on the subway (the version that made it to some international press reports).[64]

Rumor upon rumor upon rumor in dizzying sequence crowd the information economy. Interior Minister Hasan al-Alfi's predecessor, it was said, was fired for counseling dialogue with the Islamist militants. *His* predecessor, Zaki Badr, was reportedly fired for counseling their extermination. Al-Alfi himself avoided the question by telling journalists that he leaves the talking to Waqfs and al-Azhar, and that he has different procedures for dealing with troublemakers.[65] The Mubarak government encourages religiousness, he said, and despite its bloody suppression of the Islamist groups in Upper Egypt, his ministry does not make war on Islam because "we are all Muslims."[66] The Shaykh of al-Azhar publicly calls on religious scholars to listen without reservation to the concerns of young people and to respond to them as straightforwardly as possible, but the minister of religious endowments clarifies that there can be no dialogue with those who bear arms.[67] If the strategy for dealing with an Islamist threat to the ruling party is unclear, perhaps it is because the outline of the problem itself is in flux. The Shaykh of al-Azhar declared in the midst of the manhunt for Mustafa ʿAwni that "there is no terrorism in Egypt; what's happening is ordinary crime, and it needs to be approached with that understanding." The minister of religious endowments agreed, declaring that "there is no battle between the extremists and the state, and there is not going to be a battle ever; the real battle is against killers and terrorists, in the protection of religious people."[68]

Meanwhile, every publicized roundup of suspected Islamist militants, every story linking the Muslim Brotherhood with Sudan's NIF, every series of stories on the latest policeman killed by militants seems to be accompanied by the bright news of plans to establish new Islamic colleges and religion academies in the delta and Upper Egypt. Mosques are to become social and cultural centers, and soon every village in the country will boast a religious library and an institution for Qurʾan memorization. Five thousand private mosques are to be drawn under the supervision of the Ministry of Religious Endowments, and soon all state children's services establishments will include religious instruction.[69]

Just as nineteenth-century Englishmen believed that if workingmen were instructed in the elements of political economy, they would understand the forces acting on them and become content thereby, so Egyptians — and, I think, Muslims more generally — believe that Islam is a more a matter of logic and of knowledge than of faith. Ideas have an inherent power to compel. The extremist, on the one hand, and the pervert, on the other, are simply ignorant, or in the possession of mistaken ideas. "When we improve a youth with enlightened Islamic ideas," Dr. ʿAbd al-ʿAdhim al-Mutany told a newspaper,

> there cannot be an opportunity for any other ideas outside of them, or different from them, because the prophylactic mechanism [*jihaz manaʿi*] of the youth is strong and he can dismiss these ideas. If the youth's mind is empty of any Islamic culture then there is an atmosphere in which other ideas can proliferate. I think that extremism results from ignorance of religion. Its treatment is easy — directing [him] along the path of intellectual improvement with this culture and the correction of mistaken ideas.[70]

The more authentic Islamic culture there is in the public environment, the theory goes, the less likely it is that anyone can hold nonconformist ideas. But, as I hope I have been able to show, precisely the opposite is true: it is not the paucity of Islamic culture that accounts for the growth of the oppositional tendencies of the Islamic Trend, but rather its bounty. Each new attempt to correct mistaken ideas by furthering the penetration of Islamic discourse in public space creates an intensification of the conflict between parties seeking to control the discourse. In becoming hegemonic, Islam (like political economy, or evolutionary theory, or Marxism, or any of a half-dozen other comprehensive ideological systems) is forced by necessity not only to provoke limited counterlanguages, but to become itself the language in which cultural and political battles are fought by the vast majority of interested parties. That language, moreover, does not merely express social divisions, but by the logic of translation from its traditional technologies of reproduction to the technologies of the school (and, increasingly, the market), it creates new divisions, new complications and conflicts, new ambiguities. The economy of information, which is meant — like ritual — both to comfort and to induce directive anxiety in the population, instead produces an anxiety that is increasingly unfocused. Not knowing what is true, everything becomes true, every possibility becomes a fact. "There are so many contradictory messages these days, it's all a big confusion," an Egyptian friend told me. "Even the terrorists just don't know whom to hate anymore."[71]

CHAPTER 8

Broken Boundaries and the Politics of Fear

Why open the eyes of the people? They will only be more difficult to rule.

Sa'id Pasha, viceroy of Egypt, 1854–1863[1]

All transitions are dangerous; and the most dangerous is the transition from the restraint of the family circle to the non-restraint of the world.

Herbert Spencer, "Moral Education", 1858[2]

We will end where we began, with the drama of summer camps in Alexandria being stormed by the Egyptian state security forces. The raids are significant for more than just their illustration of the conflict between public and private sector religious interests, or because of their titillation value for journalists and academics covering the battles between governments and "Islamic fundamentalism" in the Middle East and elsewhere. Their central importance lies in their specific message to the Egyptian public: the implication that children are at risk from "extremism." This is a substantially new claim, representing a shift in emphasis from the reigning paradigm of recent years that attributes "Islamic extremism" to social and economic forces affecting young adults, the shabab. The fear that children can fall prey to unsanctioned religious ideas reflects a partial recognition of how deep are the cultural and institutional roots of the Islamic Trend. Recent news reports claim that groups like the Gama'a al-Islamiyya have moved beyond the indoctrination of children in private kindergartens, to use women and young people as couriers, messengers, arms buyers, lookouts, and bomb placers.[3] A pointed recognition of this change is seen in one of the first scenes in Egyptian actor ʿAdel Imam's popular 1994 anti-Islamist movie *The Terrorist*, which shows an outdoor school in an Upper Egyptian village, where the fanatic Shaykh Sayf (Sword) is delivering a harangue to twenty young boys and youth, telling them that watching television or reading the newspapers of the "infidel government" are innovations and transgressions that will lead to hell, that they should never greet or shake hands with Christians, or let their mothers or sisters go out of the house without their faces covered (advice reminiscent of that given to the boys in Alexandria). Art does imitate life, whether in the northern urban flat or the palm-roofed rural southern classroom. The current minister of education, Husayn Kamal Bahaʾ al-Din, worries publicly that Islamists have for years recruited "operatives within educational establishments to undertake to destroy the minds of students."[4] The recognition that normal processes of cultural transmission might be at play in the Islamization of public and political culture is important because it appears to move discussion of the Trend's social origins away from the notion of a class pathology onto more subtle ground.

Since the late 1970s the dominant explanation for the rise of militant Islamic groups, and for the general religious rebirth in Egypt, has been that the economic and political policies of Anwar Sadat's *infitah*, the Open Door policy initiated in 1974, have resulted in a widening disparity between the wealthy and the poor in Egypt, together with the downward mobility of educated middle classes no longer able to support lifestyles consistent with their background and aspirations. Inflation, the breakdown of public facilities and services in rapidly growing cities, the overcrowding of universities and schools, and the overburdened health-care, transportation, housing, and sanitation systems have, on this theory, contributed to a consciousness on the part of the people that the government is not doing its part to provide the nation with the necessities of life. All of this on the tail of the political and military humiliation of the 1967 war with Israel has precipitated a crisis of legitimacy and forced secularizing Egyptians to reconsider the course of the nation. There emerged a widespread dissatisfaction with the ruling establishment as well as with the entire series of Western political ideologies that have formed the basis for Egyptian government since the 1920s. The end result of this dissatisfaction has been a return to Islam, the traditional root of Arab and Muslim greatness. Following the anti-imperialist lead of Hasan al-Banna in the 1930s, Muslim intellectuals like Sayyid Qutb had by the mid-1960s provided an explanation for the ills of the nation: Egyptian society, not ruled by the dictates of the Islamic shariʿa, is not Muslim at all, but rather, jahili, in a state of moral ignorance comparable to that of pre-Islamic Arabia (a notion borrowed from the Pakistani activist Mawlana Abul-Aʿla Mawdudi). The only solution is to alter or overthrow the existing system and replace it with one based on the principles of Islam.

This is the way many Egyptian intellectuals and journalists explain the rise of activist Islam, and as a result this is the explanation most widespread among the nation's educated community who read such theories in the popular press, if not in scholarly journals and government reports, and deploy them in cocktail conversations, interviews, and public statements. I once mentioned to Muhammad Sulayman, who had found socialism through reading the plays of Bertolt Brecht, that I found it curious that there were two or three muhaggabat working in the office of his leftist publishing house.

"Oh, they're not religious," he replied.

"How so?" I asked, surprised that this most obvious mark of religiosity might not be religious after all.

"They wear the higab for economic reasons [*min bab iqtisadi*], not religious reasons [*mish bab at-tadayyun*]," he explained.

"Really?"

"Yes."

"Are you sure?"

"Yes."

Some secularist intellectuals, not content to let political economy bear the entire burden, link the Islamic revival not only with economic and social stresses, but with darker psychological and social pathologies such as prostitution and mental illness. A prominent Egyptian intellectual, Hani Sharif Mahmud, explained the prevalence of the higab this way:

Now, part of it [the return to the veil] is economic: you don't have to wear makeup, or go to the coiffure, which is expensive, and you don't have to change your dress so often. And there's also an element of feeling protected, of gaining a respectability that might be more important now than other things. You know, it's a well-known fact that even prostitutes dress in these things, because it makes it easier to escape from the police. Really! So much so, that when a girl from a traditional quarter suddenly puts on the veil, people will say, oh, so now she's going to a brothel! . . . The new Islamic Trend is not really genuine, most of it, because it's generated from frustrations. . . . This is why you have the Islamists so active in a situation [of high inflation and widespread corruption] like this, stressing honesty and so forth, it's because they want their piece of the pie, and politics has been discredited. The Islamic movement is just another kind of extremism, and it just takes different forms . . . [Islamists and Marxists] take old authors and read them and use them as the basis on which to argue for different things. Sometimes they're the same arguments in a Marxist or an Islamic debate, just using different authors and a different language. Extremism is the expression of frustrations from one sphere in the activities of another.[5]

Other Egyptian leftists, shocked to find their daughters donning the higab, send them for psychiatric treatment,[6] and explain the defection of secularist intellectuals to the Islamic Trend as the result of "personal crisis." In the movie *The Terrorist*, one of the characters, a worldly American University in Cairo student, explains to her family that extremists are "full of complexes, victims of repression," a fine collegiate Freudianism that seems to accord with the title character's frustrated projection of lechery onto unveiled women, and to his subsequent reactionary violence. Diagnoses linking religion with personal trauma or mental illness appeared again when Hani Sharif Mahmud told me there had never been any religious activity in his own house when he was raising his two sons. His father, a landowner, had not been religious. "As for myself," he said, "I was educated in a Lycée, a French secular school, and then received a Marxist education after that, so I learned very early the French tradition of 'libre pensée.' I was very influenced, like my sons have been, by Bertrand Russell, and so on." But then he paused and added quickly,

The only time there was anything religious with my sons was that for a time they were both having problems with manic depressive disorders, you know, and the one who had the manic stage, very suddenly took — this was at the time when his grandmother was dying — suddenly, without warning, became very religious, and took to reading from the Qur'an, just standing at the head of his grandmother's bed reading out of the Qur'an. But that was a very short time . . . a period of days, just days, then it was over.[7]

Religion and Social Class

These materialist explanations of the Islamic revival assume that beliefs and commitments are expressions either of psychopathology (William James's "medical materialism") or of structural contradictions and the historical materialist dialectic that coaxes cognitive frameworks from the struggles between social classes. Religion is a translation of social dislocation, political conflict, and psychological trauma. Eric Davis, for example, has argued in one of the most sophisticated and convincing analyses of the Islamic Trend,

> that ideology is a reflection of class interests in that Islamic radicals . . . come from a particular social class and . . . seek to acquire a greater share of society's material resources. Ideology can also be understood in terms of social strains as Islamic militants . . . seek refuge in Islam to soothe the alienation stemming from the status deprivation which they have experienced.[8]

Theoretically, this model relies both on the assumption that religion is a response to psychosocial stress, which it has the unique power to soothe, and that class background lends individuals certain cognitive predispositions more likely to be satisfied by one kind of ideological system than by another. The first idea derives of course from Marx, for whom religion was the spiritual aroma of an unjust social order, "an *expression* of real suffering and a *protest* against real suffering."[9] Real conflicts take imaginary form as religion, alienating human powers from the terrestrial to the cosmic plane. The second idea draws on Max Weber's subtle outline of the religious tendencies of the noble, peasant, bureaucratic, bourgeois, and intellectual classes in various world religions.[10] Davis writes, for example, that most members of radical groups "are recent immigrants to urban areas . . . [whose] occupations and educational backgrounds belie [*sic*] a traditional socialization in the countryside."[11] Furthermore, these radicals, "whose contacts with Western culture are minimal at best,"[12] use Islam as "a way of reasserting the corporate unity of Egyptian society which [they] perceived to exist from the vantage point of their early socialization in the countryside." Islamic ideology "does this using symbols which possess strong emotive power since they are the ones with which members of the lower middle class have been acquainted since early childhood and they evoke memories of a romanticized past in which life was integrated and devoid of conflict."[13] Clearly the urban/rural dichotomy is being used as a master symbol of transition from tradition to modernity, with tradition and religion clustered in the remote Egyptian village, while the city represents an alienated West.

The difficulty with such an argument is that there is little evidence that the sociological makeup of Islamic political groups is different from that of other activist political organizations. The social profiles of members of Islamist groups is very similar to members of socialist and communist organizations, and such groups working on Egyptian university campuses in the 1970s competed for the allegiance of — and drew their membership from — precisely the same kinds of students (just as did their Iranian counterparts, where the competition could take the form of literal tugs-of-war over new Iranian arrivals at U.S. universities).[14] There appears to be no good reason to assume that Liberal, Marxist, and Nasserist symbols, unlike Islamic ones, "are equally inadequate in performing a cognitive function for the lower middle classes."[15] In the case of Muhammad Sulayman, we have seen that socialist symbols can be extremely attractive to young mobile Egyptians, even those with extremely religious backgrounds. Wafaʾi Ismaʿil, on the other hand, was drawn to Islamic symbols precisely because of their broad appeal to youth of many backgrounds.

Other work linking migration with politicization in Egypt indicates that, "with the exception of Cairo and Alexandria [urban/rural contrasts] are *always* overstated."[16] The migration hypothesis does not do a very good job explaining the strength of Islamist groups in smaller cities like Asyut and Minya, along with the dozen other regional towns and villages where security forces have focused their attention. Furthermore, this model assumes that there is something like a unitary traditional socialization process and a "traditional consciousness,"[17] which are unique parts of the rural and not the urban environment. We should remember, though, that the Egyptian public school system gives both urban and rural children the opportunity for a "traditional" upbringing, presenting to growing citizens models of personal virtue, social cohesion, and political triumph that tie traditional Islamic symbols in a systematic way to the complexities of modern life. Although immense disparities remain, schooling can in fact flatten out some of the differences between the experiences of different social classes in a way that Weber — working with historical examples long predating mass schooling — could not foresee. In any case, if rural migration is part of the etiology of the Islamic Trend, it is precisely those individuals who have made use of that educational system — agronomists; university, commerce, and industrial arts students; lawyers and physicians, rather than farmers and day laborers — who are doing the migration. Their school background itself constitutes extensive contact with Western institutions, whose encounter might very well be shocking, not because of its contrast with rural life, but rather because of its internal contradictions.[18]

On another front, Davis's clear-eyed political economy perspective faults earlier approaches to the study of Islamic revival for their "emphasis on seeing change in the realm of ideas. This leads to a concentration on the thought of major Islamic thinkers and hence to an elitist bias."[19] But with the development of mass literacy — not to mention the secondary orality of electronically mediated Islamic cultural production — matters of philosophy can hardly be considered merely elitist without making the mistake of depriving non-elites of specifically cultural concerns. One of the manifestations of Egypt's growing interest in religion is an extraordinary proliferation of widely affordable religious literature. This includes the production of low-cost editions of classic Islamic thought and reference books, like the *Sahih* of Muslim, one of Sunni Islam's six major hadith collections. In the late 1980s this eight-volume work was being reissued by Dar al-Ghad al-ʿArabi, under the supervision of al-Azhar. Each volume had been divided into five sections of approximately 190 pages, and every month one section, printed on newsprint with cheap paper covers, was sold at popular newsstands around Cairo at a cost of between two and three Egyptian pounds. Purchasers were informed on the back cover of each section that, once they completed their collection, the publisher would bind them at a cost of two pounds (in 1989, about eighty cents) per volume. I saw similar products awaiting attention at independent book binderies as well. Making such works available cheaply, by obviating a large initial investment, broadens the audience for theological learning and debate among nonspecialists. This is not even to mention the hundreds of "new Islamic books" (the term coined by Yves Gonzales-Quijano) that flood street markets, bookstores, and the annual Cairo Book Fair. Covering topics ranging from Israeli conspiracies to dream interpretation to the world of the *jinn*, from adab manuals for men, women, and children to treatises on the afterlife and the lives of the prophets, these cheap volumes muster evidence from the Qurʾan, the hadiths, as well as politics, current events, history, and the sciences, to illuminate matters of popular concern. They are not necessarily — or even very often — the work of Azhari-trained religious scholars, but of physicians, professors, businessmen, activists, and professional writers.

Education and Authority

Such books, the market in intellectual goods of which they are a part, and the educational institutions that prepare people for their use are important elements of the cultural context in which ordinary educated Egyptians perceive their religious duties and fashion personal commitments. As a context, intellectual goods are important not merely in proportion to the number of people who actually consume them, but insofar as they provide a subject for talk and an opportunity for the crystallization of viewpoints within a public discourse whose boundaries are set by the kinds of products available on the market. Some time before the First World War, Weber warned specifically against focusing on cultural production as a causal agent:

> [A] religious renascence [cannot] be generated by the need of authors to compose books, or by the far more effective need of clever publishers to sell such books. No matter how much the appearance of a widespread religious interest might be simulated, no new religion has ever resulted from the needs of intellectuals or from their chatter. The whirligig of fashion will presently remove this subject of conversation and journalism, which fashion has made popular.[20]

But this confidence in the limited appeal of intellectual chatter made more sense in an era before radio and television broadcasts, before the political projects of decolonization and school-based nationalist mobilization, before the market-driven successes of Scientology, est, and the New Age in the West. It makes less sense now, particularly in the Egyptian context, where both the fact and its opposition increasingly participate in what Weber called "the struggle of priests against indifference . . . and against the danger that the zeal of the membership would stagnate,"[21] a struggle that reaches to the heart of both the school and the market. Since Islam is not a new religion but rather an elaborate set of contexts—political and economic, historical and institutional, intellectual, social and personal—in which new discourses are apprehended, evaluated, and employed, both "proletarian intellectualism" and "the need of literary, academic, [and] cafe-society intellectuals to include religious feelings . . . among their topics for discussion"[22] are in fact important sources and constituents of broad-based public religious interest and activity.[23]

The standard theory of social action, in which individuals and groups respond to social stress by taking refuge in religion, implies that, were the stress relieved, they would return to the *status quo ante*, rather like the mercury in a barometer responding to changes in atmospheric pressure (Davis and others, in fact, use terms like *pressurized* to describe the crisis of the petite bourgeoisie).[24] As part of the Egyptian government's own folk theory of the etiology of Islamism, this barometric metaphor results in an enormous volume of talk about job creation, family planning, housing construction, slum clearance, and recreational opportunities for bored and idle youth, in addition to police and educational strategies. If things get better, the theory runs, people will either accept official interpretations of Islamic law, abandoning their false and mistaken ideas, or they will cease to care about religion quite so much, relieved of the need to seek refuge in its symbols of comfort or of resistance.

But in thereby treating culture as a dependent variable, the barometric approach ignores the institutional frameworks and social processes through which culture is created and transmitted. Like other institutions, religious and educational ones fill not only a social need, but a social space. They take on a very real life of their own with interests, dynamics, and potentials that are only incompletely determined by the intersection of forces that brought them about. The development of educational facilities is a prime case in point. Popular schools were first established in Europe to foster basic skills and basic piety among the working classes. And while they still fulfill similar functions on a wider scale, they have now become traditional institutions whose presence is taken for granted. It is almost impossible, now, to think about childhood without thinking of the school. It is simply what children do, and at higher levels, as we have seen in Egypt, the school has come to play an indispensable role as a status-granting institution as well. Older marks of social status such as aristocratic standing or wealth become nearly irrelevant if not coupled with long-term schooling, and in fact to "be educated" is a prime constituent of status itself, regardless of the actual skills, dispositions, or material rewards it has fostered.

Important social movements like the crusade for popular schooling or the Islamic Trend do not leave either their participants or their observers unchanged, and never leave the social environment unchanged. They either succeed in transforming various aspects of social reality in which the next generation of actors must live, or merely strew it with the litter of bygone upheavals in the form of a literature that can be rediscovered later and reinterpreted in new contexts. The barometric theory of political action does not acknowledge that, after the mercury rises, a new equilibrium point is created such that relief of the initial pressure will not result in its return to its old starting point. History may repeat itself, but such repetition is not cyclical. Underlying the oscillation of the economy and the rise and fall of political movements is a cultural, social, and infrastructural background that is cumulative rather than substitutive. New generations of Egyptians confronting the choice between ideological allegiances will always perceive the choice differently, because of the specific historical point at which they enter the system. Therefore, the explanations that we offer for their choices must also change, taking into account the new conditions in which human beings live. This most basic conundrum of human life is of course the theoretical core of both sociology and anthropology: that, in Max Weber's words, society is "an immense cosmos into which the individual is born, and which presents itself to him . . . as an unalterable order of things in which he must live."[25] Or, in the more powerful imagery of Marx, "Men make their own history, but they do not make it just as they please; they do not make it under circumstances chosen by themselves, but under circumstances directly found, given and transmitted from the past. The tradition of all the dead generations weighs like a nightmare on the brain of the living."[26]

In Egypt, the religious environment of the 1920s or the 1950s was not the same as that of the 1970s, and neither is comparable to that of the 1990s. One of the reasons for this is that compulsory formal religious education reaches so many more people than it ever has before, and that Islamic publications, broadcasts, lectures, public meetings, and other institutions are becoming an inescapable part of public culture, generating their own controversies, reactions, and imitations. The spread of literacy together with the functionalization of the religious tradition has created a new Islam, one that is defined as a necessary instrument of public policy. The part the educational system plays in this creation lies not so much in any of the specific communications it makes about the locus of authority or the character of Islamic government — which can be and are ignored as propaganda — but in the creation of the need for religious information, the tendency to look toward religion for certain things, the creation of certain compartments in a conceptual order that can only be filled by something, regardless of its specific content, labeled "Islamic." Just as advertising in capitalist societies works not so much by building loyalty to particular products, but by reinforcing the advantages of consumption in general, so religious messages in public space largely exert general rather than specific effects.[27] This is why the state is finding it so difficult to control the movements it helped set in motion. Like its own Islamist opposition groups or Algeria's Islamic Salvation Front, it has participated in a relentless "establishment of Islamized spaces"[28] and created a need for which it cannot provide sole satisfaction.

Thus, while it true that at various historical moments, anticolonial sentiment, or rural-urban migration, or military humiliation, or the relative deprivation of the lower middle classes, have contributed to the rise of the Muslim Brotherhood (in the 1930s) and its derivative organizations (in the 1970s), viewing these same conditions as both necessary and sufficient for the formation of the contemporary Islamic Trend is unsatisfactory. For while motivations change from generation to generation, the common thread *linking* these generations — a long-term change in the social relations of Islamic cultural production — has to be considered central. As we have seen, the Islamization of Egyptian public culture is not just the effect of the Islamic Trend; it is one of its sources. This fact has an important practical implication. Given the continuity of a functionalized Islamic discourse in concert with the changing motivations of different generations for joining the Trend, no single political or economic strategy can disable it.

Habeas Corpus?

What distinguishes this new Islamic culture from that which Egyptians have experienced historically? Davis and many others have argued that "Islamic radicalism should not be understood in terms of the concept of revival or resurgence but rather as the *politicization* of Islam."[29] Indeed, one of the more popular glosses of the phenomenon in both the Middle East and the West is "Political Islam," a label that both identifies the Islamic Trend with conflicts about political power, and which tends to delegitimize it by implicitly contrasting it with something else ("Social Islam"? "Personal Islam"? "Spiritual Islam?" "Real, Genuine Islam"?). The difficulty with the label is that Islam — like Christianity — has always been available as a political discourse, and has been "politicized" for most of this century insofar as it has been appropriated for self-conscious use by institutions like the Ministry of Education for the purpose of furthering state goals, whether hygienic reform or social control. In fact, the Trend is partly a reaction against that politicization, or at least against the groups that claim exclusive, state-sanctioned authority to interpret Islamic scripture. It is, in Asad's terms, a new religious tradition.

In this sense, Islamic activist groups are similar to the Christian Protestant movements of sixteenth-century Europe.[30] The central feature of both movements is that they "transferred religious authority away from officially sanctioned individuals who interpret texts to ordinary citizens."[31] According to Ellis Goldberg,

> Both early Protestantism and the Islamist movement seek to force believers to confront directly the authority of the basic texts of revelation and to read them directly, rather than through the intervening medium of received authority. Both believe that Scripture is a transparent medium for anyone who cares to confront it.[32]

As the imprisoned leader of one Islamist group argued at his 1977 trial (on charges of kidnapping and murdering a former minister of religious endowments), the Qur'an was delivered, in its own words, in clear Arabic, and therefore anyone wishing to discover its meaning need only consult a good dictionary. One need not have been trained as a religious scholar for this, and thus, "In terms of power the issue of *ijtihad* [the authority to reach independent conclusions about religious questions] has to do . . . with the kind of education needed to make valid judgements on Islamic law."[33] The Islamic Trend results not from differential class responses to the penetration of capitalism, as a Marxist or Weberian analysis might hold, but from the building of a modern state and the consequent competition between alternative modes of socialization.[34]

Universal popular schooling simplifies, systematizes, and packages religious traditions as it does other aspects of the known world. The proclamations of the minister of religious endowments about what percentage of the shari'a is applied in Egypt, or what portion of the nation's youth hold "moderate" opinions are only comprehensible within the cognitive framework bestowed by a "modern" education, in which Islam is considered a tangible, measurable object, a durable good in circulation amongst the populace. What is happening, in effect, is that the 'ulama, as the nation's sole legitimate arbiters of religious judgment, are being forced by the state into a position both more powerful and more precarious than before. Their monopoly on access to sacred texts, once guaranteed by mass illiteracy, has been broken by the extension of education and the growth of publishing. While they were once the sole possessors of written knowledge, they are now referred to in a modern idiom as "specialists" in their field. Just as prestige based on exclusivity gives way to prestige based on authenticity, once formerly rare luxury commodities become widespread within a market, so religious specialists in Egypt are now having to find ways to convince the public that their versions of the truth are qualitatively superior to the look-alikes flooding public space.[35] While the 'ulama's knowledge of Islam is open to the qualified exercise of ijtihad, it expects the public to rely on the simplified, bounded, and established version learned in school, which is meant to remain stable until altered from above.

But instead of stability, what we have witnessed throughout the Muslim world in the twentieth century is the emergence of what Olivier Roy has dubbed "the new Islamist intellectual," and his audience, the broad "lumpenintelligentsia" of school graduates. Their books and pamphlets, cassettes and videos, represent a collage of information drawn from numerous disciplines — from biology to Prophetic biography — and united not by the transmitted tradition of a single disciplinary methodology, but by the notion that all knowledge is contained in the Qur'an. Freed from traditional processes of knowledge acquisition — apprenticeship to a man of learning — these new autodidact intellectuals stand outside of traditional authorizing institutions, instead authorizing themselves in the process of knowledge production and dissemination. A new field of knowledge is thereby generated in which "the corpus is no longer defined by a place and a specific process of acquisition: anything printed or even 'said' (cassettes) is the corpus."[36]

This genre of Islamic knowledge is neither as new nor as haphazard as Roy claims, since the very model for the integration of modern science with the Qur'an — the public school religion textbook — is such a long-established part of the educational experience. Even if the methodology behind its construction is not part of the socialization process in the religion classroom, the textbook's functionalization of the Islamic tradition stands as a model product that lay intellectuals can thereafter attempt to emulate. "Resolutely rationalist" in style, as Roy writes of Islamist productions, the official textbook and the Religious Awareness Caravan are both, just as much as the Islamist tract, instruments of mobilization in which "the corpus [of sacred literature] becomes a mere point of departure, even just a reference, ever susceptible to being transformed into rhetoric, proverbs, epigraphs, and interpolations — in short, into a reservoir of quotes."[37]

This combination of religion and modern education has proved dangerous to the religious establishment and the government that relies on it for legitimacy, because in the world of mass literacy, mass marketing, and mass (not to mention international) communication, the *exclusive* interpretive authority of local, state-based 'ulama has been permanently broken. Authority is now more a characteristic of products themselves (sermons, lessons, advice, books, magazines, cassette tapes, computer software) than productive processes (apprenticeship, certification, jurisprudential skill). Who the producer is — when that can be determined — is less important than the marketability of what he has to say.

This being the case, shutting off the specifically political threat posed by Islamists (whether through force or through reform) will not restore the power of state-subsidized religious intellectuals. Like government economists in Europe and the United States, agencies can use them to advise and justify policy decisions, but cannot force private specialists or the public at large to listen to or agree with them. In the real world, ordinary people use their own rules of thumb, practical understandings, political rhetoric, snippets of advice and learned principles skimmed from the radio, the newspaper, and that all-but-forgotten high school course to make sense of the world of religion, just as they do in the world of commerce. Attempts to enforce an orthodoxy shaped by the intersecting interests of legitimate culture producers and power elites have always been futile without the exercise of physical power through police raids, inquisitions and censorship, all of which undermine the goals of education's enlightened liberal utopia.[38]

The Realization of Distant Consequences

We are left, then, with one persistent question: Why does the Egyptian government persist in using educational tactics in its battle with the Islamic Trend, if education is one of the contributing factors to the climate of religious activism in the first place? It has been mentioned elsewhere that the government's consistent utilization of Islam for gathering mass political support "has been a crucial factor in sustaining and deepening the influence of Islam as the hard core of politics and most convenient terms of reference . . . [as well as in] the creation of a convenient climate for breeding Muslim fundamentalist movements."[39] So how is a renewed and enhanced emphasis on religious education supposed to dampen popular religious activism?

The answer lies in a set of ideas that form the core of the Egyptian elite's conception of itself, a conception born in the mid-nineteenth century and nurtured through the next hundred years in a form so stable that it has seldom been seriously examined. It is a conception that Egyptians share with elites — and ordinary citizens — in America, Europe, and elsewhere, which identifies the state of "being educated" not only with the standing of particular classes within particular societies, but with the standing of whole civilizations relative to one another. Catherine Lutz and Jane Collins, in their research on American perceptions of cultural Others, have shown that one of the primary explanations ordinary Americans give for the existence of cultural and economic difference around the world is one of schooling, such that "lack of education must also imply a less adequate form of society or culture."[40] The idea of education is deployed within an evolutionary narrative that associates it with wealth, with power, with worldliness, and, above all, with modernity, the fact of living in a present state contemporaneous with and similar to the most advanced nations.

The new Egyptian elite, which began to define itself during the late nineteenth century around the idea of education on the European model saw itself as "an elite of superior men"[41] who would jolt the country out of its second-class standing on the world stage. Their consciousness of themselves as a class was woven in part from a set of interlocking positivist dichotomies drawn from nineteenth-century social theory, of which tradition and modernity, ignorance and enlightenment, and religion and secularism, were central. Indeed, these pairs of evolutionary opposites have run like twin strands through research and public policy discussions in Egypt for more than a hundred years, acting like high-voltage cables that generation after generation have used to power their worldview. Enlightenment, secularism, and modernity form a tightly bundled conceptual package opposed to that of religion and its companions, superstition and blind adherence to tradition. In the era of postmodernity, though, with its purported incredulity toward metanarratives, such bundling is increasingly hard to maintain, and the twin ideological power lines are so brittle and frayed that the theoretical circuit they sustain has all but burned out. It is no longer possible in theory, any more than it ever has been in fact, to distinguish between well-marked poles of religious and secular endeavor. If we trace these two ideological strands to their point of origin and back again, we will find that the discourse of education as the road to progress, so central to the self-image of modernity, in fact relies on precisely the same foundations as the religious discourse of salvation. This being the case, then, the institution of schooling can no more face interrogation as a possible source of social discord than could church attendance be suspected as a source of moral failure.

Considering Herbert Spencer's deep suspicion of nineteenth-century national education projects reminded us of the contingency of historical developments, the sense in which institutional trajectories are never inevitable but remain open until finally pushed in one direction or another by changing intersections of power, interest, and circumstance. In the same way, a rereading of the works of mass education's early proponents helps us see how suspicions and fears of another sort were set aside, unresolved, in the face of seemingly more pressing needs, resulting in the image of education as a political panacea. The fear of peasant mobility, both geographical and social, that so concerned the British administration of Egypt, was founded on the perception of two complementary threats. First, a rural exodus inspired by faulty educational policies would threaten the economic stability of the entire country by depriving Egypt of its most valuable export commodity, cheap cotton that was produced by a large and predictable workforce.[42] And second, this exodus would result in a crowding of the cities with rural immigrants either lacking the skills to find urban employment or lacking job opportunities suitable to their educational level. The latter possibility was more immediately frightening than the former, since the effect of a large class of educated but unemployed malcontents posed a more practical short-term political threat to the occupying power. While some education was necessary in order to prevent specific social evils, it nonetheless had the potential to create an entire class of Egyptians who could neither find employment in the civil service nor initiate enterprises of their own. This dangerously "half-educated" and unemployed potential mob elicited a great deal of soul-searching by British intellectuals and imperial bureaucrats.

William Lecky, the popular political theorist who influenced Cromer's ideas on vocational training, had identified in England the same problem administrators faced in India and Egypt. Education, he wrote,

> produces desires which it cannot always sate, and it affects very considerably the disposition and relations of classes. One common result is the strong preference for town to country life. A marked and unhappy characteristic of the present age in England is the constant depletion of the country districts by the migration of multitudes of its old, healthy population to the debilitating, and often depraving, atmosphere of the great towns.[43]

Citing the "bitterly falsified" hopes and ambitions of such urban migrants whose sights had been set too high, Lecky detailed the political effects of the consequent "restlessness and discontent":

> Education nearly always promotes peaceful tastes and orderly habits in the

community, but in other respects its political value is often greatly overrated. The more dangerous forms of animosity and dissension are usually undiminished, and are often stimulated by [education's] influence. An immense proportion of those who have learnt to read, never read anything but a party newspaper—very probably a newspaper specially intended to inflame or to mislead them—and the half-educated mind is peculiarly open to political Utopias and fanaticisms. Very few such men can realise distant consequences, or even consequences which are distant but one remove from the primary or direct one.[44]

In Egypt, education had similarly "awakened ambitions which were formerly dormant," according to Cromer, such that "it can be no matter for surprise that the educated youth should begin to clamour for a greater share than heretofore in the government and administration of the country."[45] The danger of disaffection was treated by limiting the number of individuals who could receive access to higher primary education, to prevent the creation of "déclassés" who felt they were above engaging in manual trades.[46] If frustrated in their ambitions, such men posed a threat to stability. "[I]n my opinion," the director of the School of Medicine wrote to the consul general, exemplifying this fear, "it is hardly possible to set loose on the country a more dangerous element than the needy medical man."[47]

The Disturbed Surface of the Public Mind

And yet, as we have seen, this fear of overeducation coexisted with a matching fear of undereducation. The 1919 report of the Egyptian Elementary Educational Commission concluded with a number of inspiring quotations among which was a line from a 10 August 1918 article in the *Times* of London: "If education is allowed to wait, children do not wait for it: they grow up uneducated; and if we have learned one thing from the war, it is that the uneducated are a danger to the State."[48] It was this latter threat that was eventually to triumph, and to permanently foreclose the possibility of scaling back educational institutions. The question instead became, not whether to educate the masses, but how best to do so? The term *half-educated*, so often used to refer to those whose education resulted in political inconvenience, requires an image of what a complete and sufficient education should accomplish. The tension between the perceived danger and promise of schooling reveals deeper tensions both between the imperatives of economic development and those of social control, and between the intellectual categories in which Europeans, and later Egyptians, thought about the relationship between their societies. A traditional, superstitious society could be transformed into a modern, rational one, but such a transformation would take untold amounts of time. Expressing the long-term nature of such changes, Cromer resorted to the gradualist idiom of Spencer and Darwin when he wrote of the introduction of democratic processes into Egypt. By the careful cultivation of preexisting parliamentary principles, he wrote, "we may succeed in creating a vitalized and self-existent organism, instinct with evolutionary force."[49] And such change, as Anna Tsing points out with respect to the global narrative of development, "appears as a category which, by default, brings us toward what we know."[50]

The problem was that neither the British nor the Egyptians possessed a good model for what the transitional stages between tradition and modernity would look like. When they saw what was happening in fact, they found the results grotesque, upsetting, confounding of normal categories of thought, and counter to all predictions: it appeared that the little-educated refused to turn to manual labor even to escape poverty; while the much-educated were irrational fanatics. One writer expressed this confusion with respect to India (although it might just as well have been written of Egypt):

> The English in India . . . sow secular education broadcast among the most religious races in the world; and they invite all kinds of free criticism, by classes totally unaccustomed to such privileges, upon the acts of a bureaucratic government. The confusion of ideas that is sometimes generated by this confounding of heterogeneous elements, by the inexperience of the people and the candour of their rulers, is hard to describe; but very curious instances can be observed every day in the native newspapers, which reflect the disturbed surface of the public mind, without representing the deeper currents of native opinion and prepossessions. The press often appeals in the same breath to the primitive prejudices of Indian religion, and to the latest notions of European civilization.[51]

This profound anxiety and sense of danger stems from the confusion of categories that occurs whenever cultural boundaries are shattered and unlikely elements come to coexist.[52] Transitional states that fall between conceptual categories occasion a sense of dread, just as "people living in the interstices of the power structure [are] felt to be a threat to those with better defined status."[53] This is the real shortcoming of theoretical systems that contrast the initial and final states of societies moving from one to another ideal type: they cannot deal fruitfully with the transition itself, which is never entirely thorough, predictable, or bounded in time.

The passage quoted above, on the English in India, is from an 1884 article in the *Edinburgh Review*, by Sir Alfred Lyall, an Indian administrator who was friend and intellectual mentor to Egypt's Lord Cromer.[54] Both worked under the influence of their colleague Sir Henry Maine's trendsetting 1861 book *Ancient Law*, one of the first works to capitalize on Comte's comparative method as a means of tracing evolutionary sequences in society. For Maine, ancient societies as exemplified by contemporary India were collective, patriarchal despotisms in which the family was the basic unit of organization. Evolutionary change in Europe had long ago altered the very foundation of that society, so that "starting, as from one terminus of history, from a condition of society in which all the relations of Persons are summed up in the relations of Family, we seem to have steadily moved towards a phase of social order in which all these relations arise from the free agreement of Individuals."[55] For his part, Lyall believed that the British arrival in India would free that country from its "arrested development" and set it on a similar evolutionary course. This conservative position assumed that social change would be a gradual process of organic development, with the indigenous religious system an important part of the engine driving that evolution. (Lyall's predecessor, Sir William Jones, had composed devotional poetry to the Hindu gods promising that the British would undermine a "priest-ridden Hinduism,"[56] and Lyall himself believed that Hinduism might move up the evolutionary scale of religion from "naturalism" to "supernaturalism," in which religious concern turned inward and otherworldly. He feared, however, that higher education for Indians would lead to atheism among the Western-educated elite.[57]) In Egypt, Cromer cautioned his own Ministry of the Interior in 1895 that there was no ministry in which "the zeal of the earnest reformer is more to be deprecated. The habits and customs of an oriental people must not be trifled with lightly."[58] Religion and culture had to remain unmolested not only to avoid popular reaction, but to allow beliefs and institutions to take their own evolutionary course.

It is hard to overstate how different this view was from that of the other European philosophical camp, that of the Utilitarian radicals led by Jeremy Bentham and James Mill. For the Utilitarians, who deprecated both "customary" (e.g., indigenous Indian) law, and British Common Law as unsystematic and therefore barbarous, real social change could only take root with a revolutionary revision in legal practice, a revision that would not hesitate to trifle with the customs and habits of indigenous peoples. While common and customary legal practices exhibited a "superstitious respect for antiquity," according to Bentham, modern legislation and the creation of written codes could prompt immediate social change in a rationally anticipated direction.[59] "Give me the words of the Koran," Bentham boasted,

> give me the ideas that belong to them; I ask no more: out of them, and them alone, I undertake to produce you a code, which shall contain a hundred times the useful matter there is in that, without any of those absurdities, the existence of which, upon comparison with the ideas of utility we have at present, you cannot but acknowledge.[60]

Although the Bentham/Mill model of social change preceded that of the conservatives, it was not discarded with the development of evolutionary social theory by Maine, Spencer, and others. Its survival into the later part of the century contributed to a subtle duel at the heart of Victorian social theory. Along with competing theories of social change, competing theories of social structure and function stumbled over each other in the pages of learned periodicals and even cohabited uneasily within the pages of single monographs. One particularly prominent tension was that between a machine model of social organization, which seemed to imply the ability freely to engineer, tinker, and reconstruct, and the organic model of the evolutionists, later bequeathed to French and British functionalism, which appeared to favor caution and patience.

Cromer himself used the machine analogy with abandon in *Modern Egypt*, likening both society itself and the institutions of governance to mechanical devices (although in concert with his understanding of Egyptian society as an organism "instinct with evolutionary force," this should be enough to wean us of the idea that there is a necessary correspondence between models of structure and change, or that there is much consistency either in individual thought or in the intellectual field as a whole).[61] But while Mitchell sees a transformation of Egyptian social imagery in the 1890s, where "the body as a harmony of interacting parts has been replaced with the body as an apparatus," in fact the two models of social order and social transformation engaged in a desultory battle for European and Egyptian minds for most of the century. Not only was there no clear winner, but the normative image of either the social machine or the evolving social body is deeply ambiguous (viz., Durkheim's use of "mechanical" for primitive, and "organic" for advanced principles of social organization, a delightful jab at German Romantic scholars who privileged the authentic simplicity of village and field over the cold alienation of city and factory). Both the machine and the evolutionary metaphors for society had as many detractors as they had proponents. And to complicate matters still further, those detractors often recognized the applicability of social models only to denounce their effects.[62]

What is significant for our purposes is this: that politicians, administrators, and intellectuals concerned with the imperial interface between Europe and the East, regardless of the social model they favored, were able to convince themselves that the creation or re-creation of social order in the colonies was less for the purposes of control for its own sake than it was for the purpose of jolting the stalled and backward societies of India and Egypt out of their evolutionary torpor. Cromer's "vitalized and self-existent organism" would regulate *itself* with emergent structural properties once it was set in motion. Victorian understandings of the relationship between structure and evolution, then, need to be explored further, for they show us, finally, why the distinction between the religious and the secular is such a fragile one.

The British notion that Indians, Egyptians, and the English working classes were in need of an education consisting of restraint and discipline owes its power to cultural roots far deeper than the nascent labor requirements of the Industrial Revolution. In fact, as Christopher Herbert shows in his important book *Culture and Anomie*, the secular Victorian theory that "natural" human indiscipline necessitated specific disciplinary training grew initially from the religious climate of Christian evangelicalism and "the Wesleyan . . . story of human nature as a bundle of unruly drives needing to be severely repressed."[63] Sin, understood as a surrender to unlimited human desire, changed over the course of the nineteenth century into the secular social doctrine of "instinct," against which all civilization was thought to be a struggle.[64]

But how does civilization restrain us and keep us from acting on our inner nature? "From the point of departure of a text like *Ancient Law*," Herbert writes,

> a crucial move toward the ethnographic culture concept occurs . . . when the theory of social control comes to frame itself chiefly not in terms of external agencies of enforcement (patriarchs, sovereigns, laws) but of internalized, unconscious controls which one does not so much obey as simply

exhibit — a move rendering the concept of "control," like that of "freedom," philosophically ambiguous ever after.[65]

It is clear, then, that Mitchell's characterization of the historical change in Egypt as one "replacing a power concentrated in personal command, and always liable to diminish, with powers that were systematically and uniformly diffused"[66] is in fact little different in one sense from Maine's progression from status to contract, and in another sense, from the general movement in social theory itself from that which understood society as a system of external constraints to that which saw control operating through internal sanctions gained through socialization. As an advance over existing nineteenth-century theories of social dynamics, therefore, this approach, like Foucault's, is ultimately somewhat limited. Where we need to look instead is at the way the contradictions and ambiguities in these theories made education appear as the key to progress.

Accompanying the change in Europe's recipe for social control was an alteration in its evaluation of non-Western societies. In the early part of the nineteenth century, non-Western peoples were thought to suffer from an "anarchical and selfish restlessness"[67] stemming from a lack of behavioral controls that kept them from effectively structuring their wants and achieving social progress. But in mid- to late-century, this vision changes, and the European notion of "civilization" takes on an anomalous cast:

> for on the one hand, "civilization" is identified . . . in the conventional way with a system of fixed restraints upon human drives, and is identified almost in the same breath with fluidity and progressive, expansive movement as against the stultifying fixity of "savage" society. It was apparently in order to resolve the dilemma posed by this highly unstable configuration of ideas that nineteenth-century writers initiated a long campaign to refute the myth of unbridled primitive desire, and . . . to replace it with something like its very opposite. . . . What we see . . . is a broad reversal of assumptions in which "savage" society is transformed from a void of institutional control where desire is rampant to a spectacle of controls exerted systematically upon the smallest details of daily life [through taboo and tradition].[68]

Of course European understandings of the primitive were partly mirror images of their self-understanding.[69] Herbert traces the change itself to the economic depression of the 1870s and the growing subversion of Victorian ideals of discipline. As the notion of institutional discipline, policing, surveillance and control began to draw public criticism, it became a natural operation now to discover it in its most oppressive forms in primitive society, much as the previous generation of sensibility steeped in Evangelical thinking had constructed its own didactic image of primitives as figures of crazily uncontrolled passion. In contrast to the ethic of emancipated critical thought . . . tribal societies . . . were now disparagingly seen as "fettered," "bound," "chained down" by mindless conventionality. . . . Savages' exhorbitant devotion to custom and discipline . . . is precisely the reason for their (manifest) inferiority to progressive, developing European societies.[70]

Both of these stereotypes are prominent in writings about Egypt, which was considered implicitly primitive despite its objective status as a "high" civilization in its own right.[71] By the second quarter of the twentieth century, Egyptian educators came to believe that their country's political position was due to the chains of custom rather than to unbridled passion, but for the four decades between the British Occupation and Egypt's nominal independence in 1923, both theories coexisted in the worldview of foreign and indigenous elites. And this is precisely why, despite its recognized dangers, education was chosen as a tool of the state's expansion: because it promised simultaneously to constrain and control the irrational impulses of the populace that kept them from advancement, and also to free them of traditional social, behavioral, and intellectual constraints that kept them from advancement. In promising change, progress, and the amelioration of social problems from two opposite philosophical stances — promising all things simultaneously to all people — the school was immune to changes in the philosophy of public policy.

Schooling retains this aura in contemporary educational planning documents that speak of inculcating values representing "the Egyptian character, which has been forged in the country's history and traditions," and at the same time of developing "the skills that are required to produce a scientifically and technologically sound individual."[72] The school's ambiguous promises result in the bifurcation of its human product into a stabilizing repository of values, on the one hand, and a skilled engine of change and progress, on the other. In contemporary public policy discourse, the language of national security and the language of economic development, though they appear to be about different aspects of the world, in fact refer to the same thing. This highlights the fact that religious and secular political theories are of a piece, having grown together from the same roots and maintaining, with different vocabularies, the same unstable dialectics of moral responsibility and free will, of imperfection and progress. I would venture to disagree with Lecky, and suggest that the educated, far from being immune to "political Utopias and fanaticisms," in fact bear as their central sacred image the unborn utopia to be shaped by the school, anticipated always, in nearly millennial terms, as the New Jerusalem just beyond the horizon.

The Past in the Present

Fear of the "déclassés," and of other liminal states and individuals, is being revived in contemporary Egypt through the recapitulation of colonial population management theories in the current literature on Islamic resurgence. The image of Muslim militants as being "from [the] lower middle class of recent migrants to urban areas"[73] depicts the safe boundaries of the city being transgressed by invaders from another place and time.[74] Some Egyptian intellectuals suggest that the Islamic Trend, far from being the result of the frustration of a downwardly mobile middle class, is due instead to the growing power of upwardly mobile rural classes who take advantage of new educational opportunities by infiltrating various sectors of public culture, including the media, "allowing them to spread their habits of thought and patterns of behavior to the whole society."[75] Radicals are denounced as "the new Kharijites" or "the new Bedouin" engaged in the latest round of a centuries-old conflict between urban civilization and the forces of social fragmentation pressing in from the countryside.[76] Political, geographical, and moral boundaries blend into one another as the contrast between countryside and city is used to symbolize a threatening relationship with a past that might overcome the modernist narrative of progress.[77]

As in the summer camp raids in Alexandria, shabab are portrayed as threats to the normal order in which the family and the state share responsibility for moral instruction. Young men who have left the confines of their own families are exiled into the wasteland of drugs, unemployment, and extremism. The "déclassés" exist in a liminal state, bright and educated but unemployed, sexually mature but unmarried, raised in the country but living in the city. And increasingly, they not only represent threats to themselves and to the adult establishment, but threaten, through their participation in Islamist institution-building, to carry the country's children along with them. The solution is to provide Egyptian youth with internal restraints that will compensate for their rootlessness once they make the transition into "the non-restraint of the world." Just as the earl of Northbrook had claimed that "Mahomedans who are instructed in the tenets of their religion have always looked upon [the Mahdi] as an impostor," and that religious enthusiasm was a lower-class phenomenon, so secular Egyptian intellectuals prescribe education as a cure for radicalism. Egyptians need to be taught the difference between truth and error, including a knowledge of past sects and heresies.

> [It] is vital for the government to open widely the subject of the Shariʿa, to explain to the people the various forms it can take, i.e., which is Shiʿa, which is Wahhabi, Kharijite, etc. Because religious education has deteriorated and has been limited to teaching children enough of the Qurʾan to perform rituals, most people in the country are not really aware that there are such differences.[78]

Traditional modes of home and mosque-based socialization are stereotyped as ignorant and backward, contributing to "the spread of extremist thinking among young people, who are ill-equipped to resist brainwashing."[79] Cromer's desire to use education as a defense against "the hare-brained . . . projects . . . [of] the political charlatan, himself but half-educated," is felt by a new generation that perceives the ideological positions of Islamic radicals not merely as errors, but as ancient errors that have already been refuted. Egyptians who see the Islamic Trend as a return to the past, a regression to the oppressive theocracies of ancient times, find the solution in the quintessential modernizing force of education. True culture becomes, according to Charles Hirschkind, "the realization of state power in the individual," providing a shield against propaganda and generating enlightenment in the form of assent to moderate, modern opinions.[80] Ironically, as part of its slow reworking of religious life, the functionalization of Islam has provided a quasi back door to Sufism as an alternative notion of individual spiritual development. Assimilated to the imperative of social control, the modern ideal of spiritual growth replaces the Sufi's mystical communion with God, with Everyman's incorporation of statist ideology into his very being through the process of socialization.[81]

Religion as a Politically Constituted Defense Mechanism[82]

The overlapping series of dichotomies used to express the differences between tradition and modernity in Egypt — religion versus secular politics, memorization versus thought, rural versus urban, ignorance versus enlightenment — are primarily ideological rather than analytical devices. They are used by indigenous intellectuals and by outside analysts to imply that "tradition" (and therefore religion) is an imperfect realization of human potential. Remember how Hani Sharif Mahmud dismissed the Islamic Trend as "not genuine, most of it, because it's generated from frustrations."[83] Religious ideas and commitments have no independent cognitive force, no power and no attraction aside from the socioeconomic correlates that predispose particular groups to adopt them. The language of secular modernity cannot consider religious ideas, by themselves, compelling. Women adopt modest dress for economic reasons, for fashion considerations, or to escape the police. Even when ennobled as "resistance" rather than explained away as a symptom of pathology or poverty, practices like veiling are often denied religious import. Valerie Hoffman's and Arlene MacLeod's insightful analyses of recent religious change in Egypt agree that "only a very small percentage of these veiling women seem to be actually turning to religion in a genuine way,"[84] and that women themselves claimed they "were not more religious after wearing the hijab than they had been before wearing it. They had simply become better educated."[85] Resort to the language of "genuineness" is as significant here as it was when Victorians mistook the kuttab student's rocking as a sign of intellectual stultification and spiritual aridity. A century after William Robertson Smith, it would certainly be an odd anthropological interpretation of "religiousness" that required a transformation of inner state (how, after all, can we tell?) rather than public performance of a religiously meaningful action. The act of veiling, whatever its individual motivation and spiritual consequences, *is* a ritual act that contributes de facto to the Islamization of public space, altering the social and cultural universe in which subsequent perceptions arise and subsequent choices are made.

Similarly, government efforts at public education, such as the National Democratic Party's weekly *al-Liwa' al-islami* (The Islamic Standard) are dismissed by secularist Egyptians like Hani Sharif Mahmud as

> just a fake. I know the people who write it. It's more the Minister of the Interior speaking than it is the Minister of Religious Endowments. They're merely reacting to the stronger radical trends by taking the subject of religion, about which there's so much concern, and bending it around to come from their perspective. It's not a positive, genuine thing, just a reaction to outside forces.[86]

Coming from a self-described atheist, this ability to distinguish between "genuine" and "fake" religion is quite remarkable. To him, "genuine" religion is "religion that stays in the background, as it always has in Egypt." Genuine religion is that of the masses, a religion he was able to escape through an education that brought to light the true causes of religious behavior and allowed him, like Bertrand Russell, to formulate an alternative belief system. Only the insidious effects of personal trauma and mental illness could strip that system away and force the members of his family to resort to the primitive solaces of religion. This discourse is redolent with a dated evolutionism linking together the superstitions of savages and the working classes as representatives of primitive thought. As the higher mental functions of the cultivated individual fail, the residue reverts to religion, which lies just below the surface of the rational mind like a Comtean religious phase of history lies beneath the layer of modernity, always ready to erupt if the smooth surface of progress is subjected to sufficient stress. Religion, it seems, is the human default setting.

But when it becomes more than this and spreads rapidly through the whole of public space, it appears to stand as a fundamental threat, a metastasizing cancer requiring a diagnosis and a cure. Particularly when lay intellectuals begin to intrude on the territory of traditionally sanctioned religious elites, both those elites and the corps of secularist intellectuals become caught up in a cycle of reaction. Each tries to discredit the Islamist's abilities and intentions, the former by challenging his lack of training (he is uncertified and therefore incompetent), the latter by challenging his rationality (he is either an opportunist or mad). In either case, he is neutered because his religious thought is neither true religion nor true thought. He is not worth listening to.

Critiques of Islamism that frame it in this way as a defense mechanism for the maladjusted and the relatively deprived, rather than a "genuine" religious exercise, can function themselves as politically constituted defense mechanisms for those who offer them. These explanations comfort the powerful, the fortunate, and the wise that the Islamic Trend is an incoherent movement destined to failure if treated with the right combination of economic prosperity, political reform, and the fine-tuning of the apparatus of socialization (cf. the very title of Roy's *The Failure of Political Islam*). That this was precisely Cromer's prescription for treating the inconvenient political proclivities of the natives should give us pause and lead us to reflect on the continuity between his worldview and our own. If we treat Islamism as a pathology, the result of the faulty operation of modern institutions rather than of the potentials and contradictions inherent within them, we can continue to believe that our own personal, religious and political convictions are, by contrast, consistent, coherent, and grounded in truth and reason, rather than desperate practical refuges always on the verge of crisis and change. And in so doing we abandon the potential relevance of the Egyptian case for understanding the role of religion and politics in our own society, believing that the wolf knocking at the palace door in Cairo is hungrier than the wolf at our own. From a liberal American president's public assurance that "religion is too important to our history and heritage to keep it out of our schools,"[87] to the growing vehemence and violence of the debate over abortion, to the more acute eruptions of barbarism in our own midst (the fatal 1993 government siege of a religious commune in Waco, Texas; the 1995 terrorist bombing of a federal office building in Oklahoma City; and the rash of financial crimes committed by the suddenly discovered antigovernment "militia" and "patriot" movements), our own society is facing political questions comparable to those faced by Muslims around the world.[88] Such incidents raise fundamental questions about the limits of freedom, the rationality of political ideologies, the relevance of religion in public life, and the character of the state. How, we ask, are we to deal with people who do not believe what we want them to believe?

Just as average Americans are increasingly concerned with ideologically loaded issues like abortion and school prayer, the battle between genuine and spurious, or authentic and erroneous Islam, is being joined today by more and more Egyptians from different positions in society. But the internal debates that have been conducted in many forms since the time of the Prophet are now augmented by the rhetorical strategies and research results of the modern educational and scientific establishments. This augmentation does not make the debates any more or less genuinely "about" religion, nor do the social control aspects of the religion curricula in the public schools necessarily make that teaching any more or less authentically Islamic, at least from an anthropological perspective.

What this augmentation does do is create a special danger when we attempt to interpret the forms Islam takes in the modern (some would say postmodern) world, a special responsibility not to mistake secularism for rationality, or method for authenticity. What I have written about the teaching of Islam in the modern public school should not be read as an indictment of the Egyptian government for using that teaching for its own political purposes. Nor should it be read as agreement with them that their interpretations of Islamic legitimacy are the only ones possible. The opinions of Muslims who share the prejudices of the anthropologist should not override the opinions of those who do not. For the social scientist, especially the non-Muslim one, Islam *is* what Muslims *do* (which includes, of course, the characteristic human behaviors of speaking and writing). What we need to do increasingly is not only explore the *continuity* between rational and symbolic processes within the constantly changing institutional constellations of complex societies,[89] but interrogate the very categories of reason and religion themselves. Linking "fundamentalism" with regression or antimodernity not only misrepresents the lives of Muslims who experience such approaches to Islam as the pinnacle of civilization, but embraces an oddly skewed vision of history. "The rise of Islamic fundamentalism," in the words of Victoria Bernal, "is not a reaction against change, but change itself."[90] Moreover, it is part of a process of change without end.

Notes

Preface

1. Edward W. Lane, *Manners and Customs of the Modern Egyptians* (1860; rpt., J. W. Dent & Sons Ltd., 1963), p. 283.
2. Lane, *Manners and Customs*, p. 582.
3. Lane, *Manners and Customs*, p. 283.
4. House of Commons, "Correspondence Respecting Reorganization in Egypt," *Parliamentary Papers* (hereafter *Parl. Pap.*), 1883, vol. 83, p. 26.
5. "Correspondence," *Parl. Pap.*, 1883, p. 26.

Chapter 1. Creating an Object

1. *Al-Ahram*, 31 July 1993, p. 10.
2. *Al-Akhbar*, 31 August 1989, p. 1.
3. *Al-Akhbar*, 1 September 1989, p. 9.
4. *Al-Akhbar*, 1 September 1989, p. 9.
5. *Al-Ahram*, 31 August 1989, p. 10; *al-Jumhuriyya*, 31 August 1989, p. 3.
6. *Al-Wafd*, 2 September 1989, pp. 1–2.
7. Cassandra, "The Impending Crisis in Egypt," *Middle East Journal* 49, 1 (Winter 1995), pp. 9–27.
8. Richard Bulliet, *Islam: The View from the Edge* (New York: Columbia University Press, 1994), p. 4.
9. Talal Asad, "The Idea of an Anthropology of Islam," Occasional Paper Series, Georgetown University Center for Contemporary Arab Studies, March 1986, p. 14; see also Lila Abu-Lughod, "Zones of Theory in the Anthropology of the Arab World," *Annual Review of Anthropology* 18 (1989), pp. 267–306.
10. Asad, "Anthropology of Islam," p. 14.
11. L. Abu-Lughod, "Zones of Theory," p. 297.

12. Asad, "Anthropology of Islam," p. 15.

13. See, for example, John Bowen, "Elaborating Scriptures: Cain and Abel in Gayo Society," *Man*, n.s., 27, 3 (1992), pp. 495–516; and his *Muslims Through Discourse: Religion and Ritual in Gayo Society* (Princeton: Princeton University Press, 1993); Dale F. Eickelman, *Knowledge and Power in Morocco: The Education of a Twentieth-Century Notable* (Princeton: Princeton University Press, 1985), and his "Mass Higher Education and the Religious Imagination in Contemporary Arab Societies," *American Ethnologist* 19, 4 (1992), pp. 643–55; Michael M. J. Fischer and Mehdi Abedi, *Debating Muslims: Cultural Dialogues in Postmodernity and Tradition* (Madison: University of Wisconsin Press, 1990); Patricia Horvatich, "Ways of Knowing Islam," *American Ethnologist* 21, 4 (1994), pp. 811–26; Brinkley Messick, *The Calligraphic State: Textual Domination and History in a Muslim Society* (Berkeley: University of California Press, 1993).

14. For a recent review of the literature, see Gregory Starrett, "The Anthropology of Islam," in *Anthropology of Religion: A Handbook of Method and Theory*, ed. Stephen Glazier (Westport, Conn.: Greenwood, 1997), pp. 279–303.

15. The notion of "objectification" is borrowed ultimately from Bernard Cohn, by way of Dale Eickelman, "Identité nationale et discours religieux en Oman," in *Intellectuels et militants de l'Islam contemporain*, ed. Gilles Kepel and Yann Richard (Paris: Seuil, 1990), p. 121; see also his "Counting and Surveying an 'Inner' Omani Community: Hamra al-ʿAbriyin," in *Tribe and State: Essays in Honour of David Montgomery Hart*, ed. E. G. H. Joffe and C. R. Pennell (Wisbech, England: MENAS Press, 1991), pp. 253–77. See William E. Shepard, "Islam as a 'System' in the Later Writings of Sayyid Qutb," *Middle Eastern Studies* 25 (1989), pp. 31–50.

16. Eickelman, "Mass Higher Education," p. 650.

17. *Al-Ahram*, 17 February 1989, p. 13.

18. Messick, *The Calligraphic State*.

19. Dale Eickelman, "The Art of Memory: Islamic Education and Its Social Reproduction," *Comparative Studies in Society and History* 20 (1978), p. 485.

20. Eickelman, "The Art of Memory," p. 496. The work he is referring to is Durkheim's *The Evolution of Educational Thought*, trans. Peter Collins (London: Routledge & Kegan Paul, 1977).

21. Paul Willis, *Learning to Labour: How Working Class Kids Get Working Class Jobs* (Westmead, England: Saxon House, 1977), pp. 175–79.

22. Aside from efforts like Allan Peshkin's *God's Choice: The Total World of a Fundamentalist Christian School* (Chicago: University of Chicago Press, 1986), and Melinda B. Wagner's *God's Schools: Choice and Compromise in American Society* (New Brunswick, N.J.: Rutgers University Press, 1990), which are fine school ethnographies prompted by the political rise of the U.S. Christian Right in the 1980s, and the attendant expansion of Christian alternatives to the public schools. Unfortunately, both works are curiously distant from important theoretical debates in the educational literature.

23. This work will say little explicitly about gender, in part because of the substantial body of quality work already being done on gender and Islam. See, for example, Fadwa el-Guindi, "Veiling Infitah with Muslim Ethic: Egypt's Contemporary Islamic Movement," *Social Problems* 28 (1981), pp. 465–85; Arlene

Elowe Macleod, *Accommodating Protest: Working Women, the New Veiling, and Change in Cairo* (New York: Columbia University Press, 1991); Lila Abu-Lughod, *Writing Women's Worlds: Bedouin Stories* (Berkeley: University of California Press, 1993); Carol Delaney, *The Seed and the Soil: Gender and Cosmology in Turkish Village Society* (Berkeley: University of California Press, 1991); or any of the articles on women in Muslim societies in Valentine Moghadam, ed., *Identity Politics and Women: Cultural Reassertions and Feminisms in International Perspective* (Boulder, Colo.: Westview Press, 1994). For a more complete list of references, see L. Abu-Lughod, "Zones of Theory," and Starrett, "Anthropology of Islam."

24. I am referring, of course, to Eric Hobsbawm and Terence Ranger's *The Invention of Tradition* (Cambridge: Cambridge University Press, 1983), and more recent developments on the theme such as Don Handelman's *Models and Mirrors: Towards an Anthropology of Public Events* (Cambridge: Cambridge University Press, 1990).

25. Paul Willis, *Learning to Labour*, pp. 173–74.

26. Willis, *Learning to Labour*, p. 171.

27. Willis, *Learning to Labour*, p. 175.

28. Willis, *Learning to Labour*, p. 104.

29. Willis, *Learning to Labour*, p. 172.

30. Raymond Williams, *Marxism and Literature* (Oxford: Oxford University Press, 1977), p. 110.

31. This is the main theme of Timothy Mitchell's *Colonising Egypt* (Cambridge: Cambridge University Press, 1988).

32. Johannes Fabian, *Time and the Other: How Anthropology Makes Its Object* (New York: Columbia University Press, 1983).

33. Fabian, *Time and the Other*, p. 111.

34. Hisham Sharabi, "Islam and Modernization in the Arab World," in *Modernization of the Arab World*, ed. Jack H. Thompson and Robert D. Reischauer (Princeton: D. Van Nostrand Co., Inc., 1966), p. 26.

35. Sharabi, "Islam and Modernization," p. 29.

36. Sharabi, "Islam and Modernization," p. 31.

37. Durkheim's *Moral Education* stands, of course, as the best representative of this view.

38. Dale Eickelman's *Knowledge and Power in Morocco*; Roy Mottahedeh's *The Mantle of the Prophet* (New York: Pantheon, 1985); Michael M. J. Fischer's *Iran: From Religious Dispute to Revolution* (Cambridge: Harvard University Press, 1980); and Fischer and Abedi's *Debating Muslims*.

39. For traditional education in Morocco, see Eickelman, "The Art of Memory," pp. 485–516; Jennifer E. Spratt and Daniel A. Wagner, "The Making of a *Fqih*: The Transformation of Traditional Islamic Teachers in Modern Cultural Adaptation," in *The Cultural Transition: Human Experience and Social Transformation in the Third World and Japan*, ed. Merry I. White and Susan Pollak (London: Routledge and Kegan Paul, 1986), pp. 89–112; Daniel A. Wagner and Abdelhamid Lotfi, "Traditional Islamic Education in Morocco: Sociohistorical and Psychological Perspectives," *Comparative Education Review* 24 (1980), pp. 238–51; and their "Learning to Read by 'Rote,'" *International Journal of the So-*

ciology of Language, no. 42 (1983), pp. 111–21; Daniel A. Wagner and Jennifer E. Spratt, "Reading Acquisition in Morocco," in *Growth and Progress in Cross-Cultural Psychology*, ed. C. Kagitcibasi (Lisse: Swets & Zeitlinger B.V., 1987), pp. 346–55; and their "Cognitive Consequences of Contrasting Pedagogies: The Effects of Quranic Preschooling in Morocco," *Child Development* 58 (1987), pp. 1207–19. For the longer treatment, see Daniel Wagner, *Literacy, Culture, and Development: Becoming Literate in Morocco* (Cambridge: Cambridge University Press, 1993); and Jarmo Houtsonen, "Traditional Qur'anic Education in a Southern Moroccan Village," *International Journal of Middle East Studies* 26 (1994), pp. 489–500. For Java, see Sidney Jones, "Arabic Instruction and Literacy in Javanese Muslim Schools," *International Journal of the Sociology of Language*, no. 42 (1983), pp. 83–94; for Yemen, see Brinkley Messick, "Legal Documents and the Concept of 'Restricted Literacy' in a Traditional Society," *International Journal of the Sociology of Language*, no. 42 (1983), pp. 41–52; for Iran, see Brian V. Street, *Literacy in Theory and Practice* (Cambridge: Cambridge University Press, 1984).

40. Golnar Mehran, "Ideology and Education in the Islamic Republic of Iran," *Compare* 20 (1990), pp. 53–65; Bahram Mohsenpour, "Philosophy of Education in Postrevolutionary Iran," *Comparative Education Review* 32 (1988), pp. 76–86; and M. Mobin Shorish, "The Islamic Revolution and Education in Iran," *Comparative Education Review* 32 (1988), pp. 58–75.

41. Adeeb Khalid, "The Politics of Muslim Cultural Reform: Jadidism in Tsarist Central Asia," Ph.D. diss., Department of History, University of Wisconsin-Madison, 1993.

42. Olivier Carré, *Enseignement islamique et idéal socialiste* (Beirut: Dar el-Machreq Editeurs, 1974).

43. Sally Falk Moore, *Social Facts and Fabrications: Customary Law on Kilimanjaro, 1880–1980* (Cambridge: Cambridge University Press, 1986).

44. Javed Majeed, *Ungoverned Imaginings: James Mill's* The History of British India *and Orientalism* (Oxford: Clarendon Press, 1992), pp. 28, 36.

45. Dale Eickelman, *Moroccan Islam* (Austin: University of Texas Press, 1976), p. 21.

46. Hasan al-Alfi, quoted in *al-Ahram*, 26 July 1993, p. 10.

Chapter 2. Education and the Management of Populations

1. Quoted in Edwin G. West, "The Benthamites as Educational Engineers: The Reputation and the Record," *History of Political Economy* 24, 3 (1992), pp. 595–621.

2. Timothy Mitchell, *Colonising Egypt* (Cambridge: Cambridge University Press, 1988), p. 127).

3. Mitchell, *Colonising Egypt*, p. 64.

4. Mitchell, *Colonising Egypt*, pp. 102, 104.

5. Mitchell, *Colonising Egypt*, pp. 68, 74–75.

6. Mitchell, *Colonising Egypt*, p. 175.

7. Charles C. Adams, *Islam and Modernism in Egypt* (New York: Russell & Russell, 1968), p. 167.

8. Herbert Spencer, *Principles of Sociology*, 3rd ed., vol. 1 (New York: D. Appleton and Company, 1899), pp. 584–85. On the relationship between Social Darwinism and imperialism, see Bernard Semmel, *Imperialism and Social Reform* (Cambridge, Mass.: Harvard University Press, 1960), ch. 2.

9. Spencer, *Principles of Sociology*, p. 717.

10. Herbert Spencer, "National Education," in his *Social Statics* (1850; rpt., New York: D. Appleton & Co., 1892), pp. 156–87; and "State-Education," in his *Facts and Comments* (New York: D. Appleton & Co., 1902), pp. 82–93.

11. Spencer, "State-Education," p. 82.

12. Neil J. Smelser, *Social Paralysis and Social Change: British Working-Class Education in the Nineteenth Century* (Berkeley: University of California Press, 1991).

13. James Heyworth-Dunne, *An Introduction to the History of Education in Modern Egypt* (London: Luzac & Co., 1938), p. 153.

14. Yacoub Artin, quoted in Ibrahim Salama, *L'Enseignement islamique en Egypte: Son evolution, son influence sur les programmes modernes* (Cairo: Imprimerie Nationale, Boulaq, 1939), p. 207.

15. Heyworth-Dunne, *Introduction to the History of Education*, pp. 152–57.

16. For first-rate discussions of this system, see Mitchell, *Colonising Egypt*, and Messick, *The Calligraphic State*.

17. Heyworth-Dunne, *Introduction to the History of Education*, p. 157.

18. ʿAbd al-Karim, *Tarikh al-taʿlim fi ʿasr Muhammad ʿAli* (Cairo: Maktaba al-nahda al-Misriyya, 1938), pp. 176–80.

19. ʿAbd al-Karim, *Tarikh al-taʿlim*, pp. 180–81.

20. Heyworth-Dunne, *Introduction to the History of Education*, pp. 195–97, 210–17.

21. John Bowring, "Report on Egypt and Candia," *Parl. Pap.*, 1840, vol. 21, p. 121.

22. Heyworth-Dunne, *Introduction to the History of Education*, pp. 223–33.

23. Fritz Steppat, "National Education Projects in Egypt Before the British Occupation," in *Beginnings of Modernization in the Middle East: The Nineteenth Century*, ed. William R. Polk and Richard L. Chambers (Chicago: University of Chicago Press, 1968), pp. 289, 295.

24. Heyworth-Dunne, *Introduction to the History of Education*, p. 373.

25. Octave Sachot, "Rapport adresse a Son Excellence Monsieur Victor Duruy, Ministre de l'Instruction Publique, sur l'état des sciences, des lettres, et de l'instruction publique in Egypte dans la population indigène et dans la population Européenne" (Paris: n.p., 1868), p. 1. Translation mine.

26. And they operated with a foreign curriculum, as well. High school students learned little of local or Islamic history, instead studying "The Awakening of Learning in Europe," "The Expansion and Spread of the Western Nations," "The War of the Austrian Succession and the Seven Years War," etc. See Donald M. Ried, "Turn-of-the-Century Egyptian School Days," *Comparative Education Review* 27 (1983), pp. 374–93.

27. "Further Correspondence Respecting Reorganization in Egypt," *Parl. Pap.*, 1883, vol. 83, p. 88.

28. See Roger Owen, "The Influence of Lord Cromer's Indian Experience on British Policy in Egypt, 1883–1907," in *Middle Eastern Affairs*, ed. Albert Hourani (Oxford: Oxford University Press, 1965), pp. 109–39.

29. Bill Williamson, *Education and Social Change in Egypt and Turkey* (London: The Macmillan Press, 1987), p. 74.

30. Cromer, Annual Report, *Parl. Pap.*, 1905, vol. 137, p. 571.

31. Lord Macaulay, "On the Government of India," a speech delivered in the House of Commons on 10 July 1833. In *The Works of Lord Macaulay, Complete*, vol. 8, ed. Lady Trevelyan (London: Longman, Green, & Co. 1866), p. 141.

32. This policy was changed during the tenure of Saʿd Zaghlul—one of Egypt's most famous nationalist leaders—as minister of public instruction.

33. Cromer, Annual Report, *Parl. Pap.*, 1902, vol. 130, p. 744.

34. The switch to an emphasis on reading, writing, and arithmetic came at the behest of parents. As the Newcastle Commission reported in 1861,

> The general principle upon which almost every one who for the last half century has endeavoured to promote popular education has proceeded, has been that a large portion of the poorer classes of the population were in a condition injurious to their own interests, and dangerous and discreditable to the rest of the community; that it was the duty and the interest of the nation at large to raise them to a higher level, and that religious education was the most powerful instrument for the promotion of this object. The parents, on the other hand, cannot be expected to entertain the same view of the moral and social condition of their own class, or to have its general elevation in view. They act individually for the advantage of their respective children; and though they wish them to be imbued with religious principles, and taught to behave well, they perhaps attach a higher importance than the promoters and managers of schools to the specific knowledge which will be profitable to the child in life. It is of some importance in estimating the conduct of the parents to keep this difference of sentiment in view. (Quoted in David Vincent, *Literacy and Popular Culture: England, 1750–1914* [Cambridge: Cambridge University Press, 1989], p. 86)

35. Vincent, *Literacy and Popular Culture*, pp. 73–74.

36. Spencer, *Principles of Sociology*, vol. 3, p. 274. The image of the church and the school either as homologues or analogues has been often repeated, e.g., by Durkheim in *Moral Education*, p. 155; by more recent theorists like Pierre Bourdieu and Jean-Claude Passeron, *Reproduction in Education, Society, and Culture* (London: Sage, 1977), p. 64; and Eric Hobsbawm, "Mass-Producing Traditions: Europe, 1870- 1914," in *The Invention of Tradition*, ed. Eric Hobsbawm and Terence Ranger (Cambridge: Cambridge University Press, 1983), p. 271.

37. Vincent, *Literacy and Popular Culture*, p. 75.

38. Vincent, *Literacy and Popular Culture*, p. 76.

39. Quoted in Phillip McCann, "Popular Education, Socialization, and Social Control: Spitalfields, 1812–1824," in *Popular Education and Socialization in the Nineteenth Century*, ed. Phillip McCann (London: Methuen & Co. Ltd., 1977), p. 1.

40. Vincent, *Literacy and Popular Culture*, p. 76.

41. Lord Dufferin to the earl of Granville, "Further Correspondence Respecting Reorganization in Egypt," *Parl. Pap.*, 1883, vol. 83, p. 96.

42. Alfred Milner, *England in Egypt* (New York: Macmillan & Co., 1892), p. 390. The perception of Islam as fanaticism and bigotry was not, of course, confined to Egypt. In Aden, the next geographical stepping-stone on the way from England to India, plans were made in 1856 to start a school to train Arab boys for the civil service and "to attach our bigoted neighbors to us by the community of feelings and interests which must follow in the wake of a sound education." "If it were possible to give these boys a solid education in their language and ours," wrote the concerned British official,

> the influence for good they may exercise on the next generation is beyond calculation, by it we should instruct them in our system, and attach them by a link which would not be easily severed. Commerce would increase, we should hear no more of stoppage of the roads, and of the frequent paltry squabbles which having their origin in ignorance and bigotry, would cease with the spread of knowledge amongst the people. (Quoted in Z. H. Kour, *The History of Aden, 1839–72* [London: Frank Cass & Co., Ltd., 1981], p. 101)

43. Cromer often commented on the incomprehensibility of the Eastern mind.

> The ethnologist, the comparative philologist, and the sociologist would possibly be able to give explanations as regards many of the differences between the East and the West. As I am only a diplomatist and an administrator, whose proper study is also man, but from the point of view of governing him rather than from that of scientific research into how he comes to be what he is, I content myself with noting the fact that somehow or other the Oriental generally acts, speaks, and thinks in a manner exactly opposite to the European. (*Modern Egypt*, vol. 2 [New York: The Macmillan Co., 1908], p. 164)

44. The physical conditions of rural—and urban—popular schools in Egypt and in England were described by contemporaries in strikingly similar Dickensian detail. Compare, for example, Cromer in "Reports on the State of Egypt and the Progress of Administrative Reforms," *Parl. Pap.*, 1896, vol. 97, p. 1010; with Macaulay in his speech on "Education," delivered in the House of Commons on 19 April 1847. In *The Works of Lord Macaulay*, vol. 8, pp. 395–96.

45. James A. St. John, *Egypt and Nubia* (London: Chapman and Hall, 1845), pp. 31–32.

46. Viz., the educational theories of Jeremy Bentham, beloved of Foucauldian analysts. In *Panopticon*, Bentham effused of the possibilities of the Inspection-House as a school, in which "All play, all chattering—in short, all distraction of every kind, is effectually banished." *The Works of Jeremy Bentham*, vol. 4, ed. John Bowring (1838–43; rpt., New York: Russell & Russell, 1962), p. 63.

47. Amir Boktor, *School and Society in the Valley of the Nile* (Cairo: Elias' Modern Press, 1936), p. 130.

48. Bowring, "Report on Egypt and Candia," p. 136.

49. Florence Nightingale, *Letters from Egypt: A Journey on the Nile, 1849–50*, ed. Anthony Sattin (New York: Weidenfeld & Nicholson, 1987), p. 26.

50. W. Basil Worsfold, *The Redemption of Egypt* (London: George Allen, 1899), p. 54.

51. Sachot, "Rapport," p. 4. Translation by Anna Laura Jones.

52. Milner, *England in Egypt*, p. 366.

53. Emile Durkheim, *Elementary Forms of the Religious Life* (1912; rpt., New York: Free Press, 1965), p. 15.

54. R. R. Marett, *The Threshold of Religion* (London: n.p., 1914), p. xxxi.

55. Salama, *L'Enseignement islamique*, p. 300.

56. For a fuller discussion of European attitudes toward the Egyptian body, see Gregory Starrett, "The Hexis of Interpretation: Islam and the Body in the Egyptian Popular School," *American Ethnologist* 22, 4 (November 1995), pp. 953–69.

57. Mitchell, *Colonising Egypt*, p. 86.

58. Messick, *The Calligraphic State*, p. 17.

59. See Trygve R. Tholfsen, "Moral Education in the Victorian Sunday School," *History of Education Quarterly* 20 (1980), pp. 77–99; and Thomas W. Laqueur, *Religion and Respectability: Sunday Schools and Working Class Culture, 1780–1850* (New Haven: Yale University Press, 1976).

60. "I heartily rejoice that the life, the words, and works, and death of the Divine Saviour of the world should be read by children. But that is not the teaching of religion, unless the true meaning and the due intrinsic worth of all these things be taught. But this would perforce be doctrinal Christianity, prohibited by law." Cardinal Archbishop Henry Edward, "Is the Education Act of 1870 a Just Law?" *The Nineteenth Century* 12 (December 1882), p. 960.

61. William Edward Hartpole Lecky, *Democracy and Liberty*, vol. 2. (New York: Longmans, Green, & Co., 1896), p. 70.

62. Joseph Lancaster, *Improvements in Education as It Respects the Industrious Classes of the Community*, 3rd ed. (1805; rpt., Clifton, N.J.: Augustus M. Kelley Publishers, 1973), pp. 155–56.

63. H. Cunynghame, "The Present State of Education in Egypt," *Journal of the Royal Asiatic Society of Great Britain and Ireland*, n.s., 19 (1887), p. 232.

64. Bowring, "Report on Egypt and Candia," p. 137.

65. Milner, *England in Egypt*, p. 365.

66. Macaulay, "Education," p. 387.

67. The quote from Adam Smith, "The more [the inferior ranks of people] are instructed, the less liable they are to the delusions of enthusiasm and superstition, which, among ignorant nations, frequently occasion the most dreadful disorders," is from the first chapter of book 5 of *The Wealth of Nations* (New York: Random House, 1965), p. 740.

68. Macaulay, "Education," p. 388.

69. Macaulay, "Education," pp. 388–89.

70. Macaulay, "Education," p. 390.

71. W. Basil Worsfold, *The Redemption of Egypt* (London: George Allen, 1899), p. 143. Apropos the association of schools and prisons, Lord Dufferin had written to the earl of Granville in February of 1883 noting that "the consensus of foreign opinion in this country" supported a statement by an Egyptian leader, "that order in Egypt can only continue to exist under the combined discipline of a couple of foreign schoolmasters and the domestic 'courbash,' "a view with which, it should be acknowledged, he disagreed personally. "Further Correspondence Respecting Reorganization in Egypt," *Parl. Pap.*, 1883, vol. 83, p. 88.

72. Cromer, "Reports on the State of Egypt and the Progress of Administrative Reforms," *Parl. Pap.*, 1884–85, vol. 89, p. 15.

73. Cromer, "Reports," *Parl. Pap.*, 1884–85, p. 14.

74. Cromer, "Reports," *Parl. Pap.*, 1884–85, p. 13.

75. Cromer, "Reports," *Parl. Pap.*, 1884–85, p. 14.

76. Cromer, "Reports," *Parl. Pap.*, 1884–85, p. 13.

77. Cromer, Annual Report, *Parl. Pap.*, 1905, p. 1137.

78. Kitchener, Annual Report, *Parl. Pap.*, 1912, vol. 121, p. 31.

79. Kitchener, Annual Report, *Parl. Pap.*, 1913, vol. 81, p. 35.

80. See Nathan Brown, "Who Abolished Corvée Labour in Egypt and Why?" *Past and Present*, no. 144 (August 1994), pp. 116–37.

81. Quoted in Ministry of Education, Egypt, *Report of the Elementary Education Commission and Draft Law to Make Better Provision for the Extension of Elementary Education* (Cairo: Government Press, 1919), p. 7.

82. Cromer, Annual Report, *Parl. Pap.*, 1899, vol. 112, p. 961.

83. J. Scott's memorandum to Cromer, in "Report on the Finances, Administration, and Condition of Egypt and the Progress of Reforms," *Parl. Pap.*, 1897, vol. 102, p. 536. This idea has had great longevity. As recently as 1943, H. E. Neguib el-Hilali Pasha, the Egyptian minister of education, wrote,

> If we take into account the fact that compulsory education begins in England at the age of five and that bodily growth is quicker in Egypt owing to the climate, we see that it is only natural that the compulsory age [of schooling] should begin in this country one year earlier than it actually does, that is, at the end of the sixth year, and end at 13. (*Report on Educational Reform in Egypt* [Cairo: Government Press, Boulaq, 1943], p. 49)

84. Cromer, Annual Report, *Parl. Pap.*, 1903, vol. 87, p. 1014.

85. Cromer, Annual Report, *Parl. Pap.*, 1905, vol. 102, p. 1150.

86. Allenby, Annual Report, *Parl. Pap.*, 1921, vol. 42, p. 74. See Margaret May, "Innocence and Experience: The Evolution of the Concept of Juvenile Delinquency in the Mid-Nineteenth Century," *Victorian Studies* 18 (1973), pp. 7–30; for a contemporary view of the subject of reformatories, see Lord Norton's article, "Schools as Prisons and Prisons as Schools," *The Nineteenth Century* 21 (January 1887), pp. 110–18. Statistics were reported annually on the utilization of the Giza Reformatory, including the number of boys and girls confined there, and the disciplinary measures invoked. A typical example (from Gorst's Annual Report for the year 1910): "During the year 3,631 juveniles were whipped (2,589 in 1909). The number of juveniles on the 31st December at the reformatory was 715 (726 in 1909), 647 being boys and 68 girls. The daily average throughout the year being 764." *Parl. Pap.*, 1911, vol. 103, p. 41.

87. "Further Correspondence Respecting Reorganization in Egypt," *Parl. Pap.*, 1883, vol. 83, p. 89.

88. "Further Correspondence Respecting the Affairs of Egypt," *Parl. Pap.*, 1884–85, vol. 88, p. 230.

89. Lord Dufferin to the earl of Granville, "Further Correspondence Respecting Reorganization in Egypt," *Parl. Pap.*, 1883, vol. 88, p. 93. It is of course instructive to contrast this view with that of Egypt's own educated elite. On 8 October 1866 Nubar Pasha, a future prime minister of the Egyptian government

after the British Occupation, had written, "Our parliament is a school, by means of which the government, more advanced than the population, instructs and civilises the population." Quoted in Mitchell, *Colonising Egypt*, p. 75.

90. Cromer, "Reports on the State of Egypt and the Progress of Administrative Reforms," *Parl. Pap.*, 1896, vol. 97, p. 1010.

91. Cromer, Annual Report, *Parl. Pap.*, 1905, vol. 103, p. 1165.

92. Cromer, Annual Report, *Parl. Pap.*, 1905, pp. 1010–11.

93. Cromer, Annual Report, *Parl. Pap.*, 1905, pp. 1010–11.

94. Cromer, Annual Report, *Parl. Pap.*, 1905, p. 1166.

95. Cromer, Annual Report, *Parl. Pap.*, 1905, p. 1166; also Annual Report, *Parl. Pap.*, 1899, vol. 112, p. 1007.

96. Cromer, "Reports on the State of Egypt and the Progress of Administrative Reforms," *Parl. Pap.*, 1898, vol. 107, p. 665.

97. Cromer, "Reports on the State of Egypt and the Progress of Administrative Reforms," *Parl. Pap.*, 1896, vol. 97, p. 1011.

98. Cromer, Annual Report, *Parl. Pap.*, 1903, vol. 87, p. 1009.

99. Cromer, Annual Report, *Parl. Pap.*, 1906, vol. 138, pp. 569–70. The following year, "4,432 pupils were able to recite from memory the whole of the Koran, 3,833 more than three-quarters, 4,594 more than one-half, and 7,362 more than one-quarter, whilst 52,893 pupils had reached various stages in the first quarter of the sacred text." And this at a time when "the total number of children who had reached the age of 13 years was less than 3,000." Annual Report, *Parl. Pap.*, 1903, vol. 100, p. 714. Of the 46,762 students who attended 1913's annual inspection of kuttabs under the control of the Provincial Councils, "1,193 of the pupils were able to recite the whole of the Koran by heart, and 1,212 others at least one-half of the sacred text." Annual Report, *Parl. Pap.*, 1914, vol. 101, p. 44.

100. Cromer, Annual Report, *Parl. Pap.*, 1905, vol. 103, p. 1165.

101. Cromer, Annual Report, *Parl. Pap.*, 1906, vol. 137, p. 570.

102. Cromer, Annual Report, *Parl. Pap.*, 1906, p. 74.

103. Gorst, Annual Report, *Parl. Pap.*, 1909, vol. 105, p. 3. Gorst was extremely sensitive to the political expediency of education. In the same report, he notes that "it is . . . wise to avoid measures which run counter to the wishes or prejudices of the people until they have been educated up to them" (p. 28), but that the change cannot be rushed, despite those in the country who "believed that, by means of a rapid extension of public instruction, deficiencies which are the inheritance of centuries of ignorance can be made good in a comparatively short time" (p. 38).

104. Ministry of Education, *Report of the Elementary Education Commission*. The members of the commission were: His Excellency Ali Gamal el Din Pasha, mudir of Sharqiya; H. E. Mohammed Allam Pasha, mudir of Asyut; Mr. Patterson, director general of accounts, Ministry of Finance; Mr. Betts, director of the Municipalities and Local Commissions Department, Ministry of the Interior; Mr. McLean, chief engineer of the same department; Mr. Aldred Brown, controller of administrative service, and Mr. Robb, subcontroller of elementary education, both of the Ministry of Education; Mohammed Ali el Maghrabi Bey, the controller of elementary education in the ministry; Mohammed Aatef Bar-

akat Bey, the principal of the Cadis' College; Sheikh Mohammed Cherif Selim, principal of the Nasria Training College, and Hussein Kamel Bey, director of administrative service of the Ministry of the Interior. Adly Yeghen himself was a long-time enthusiast of British causes, having been elected in 1903 as president of the Society for the Prevention of Cruelty to Animals, an organization imported to Egypt in the 1890s. Cromer, Annual Report, *Parl. Pap.*, 1904, vol. 111, p. 250.

105. Cromer, *Modern Egypt*, vol. 2, pp. 534–35. Quoted in the commission's *Report* on p. 5.

106. Nathan Brown, *Peasant Politics in Modern Egypt* (New Haven: Yale University Press, 1990).

107. Quoted in Carter Jefferson, "Worker Education in England and France, 1800–1914," *Comparative Studies in Society and History* 4 (1964), p. 355.

108. Jefferson, "Worker Education," p. 346. Vincent provides another example from a British educational manifesto of 1839:

> The sole effectual means of preventing the tremendous evils with which the anarchical spirit of the manufacturing population threatens the country is, by giving the working people a good secular education, to enable them to understand the true causes which determine their physical condition and regulate the distribution of wealth among the several classes of society. (P. 83)

The notion that teaching political economy and social science to the masses was a remedy for labor unrest was current in the United States as late as the 1870s; see Richard Hofstadter, *Social Darwinism in American Thought* (Boston: Beacon Press, 1955), p. 47.

109. Andrew Porter, "Scottish Missions and Education in Nineteenth-Century India: The Changing Face of Trusteeship," *The Journal of Imperial and Commonwealth History* 16 (1988), p. 44.

110. Kitchener, Annual Report, *Parl. Pap.*, 1912, vol. 121, p. 3. For the same idea in Britain, see Agnes Lambert, "Thrift among the Children," *The Nineteenth Century* 19 (April 1886), p. 548.

111. Kitchener, Annual Report, *Parl. Pap.*, 1912, vol. 121, p. 4.

112. Ministry of Education, *Report of the Elementary Education Commission*, p. 26.

113. Ministry of Education, *Report of the Elementary Education Commission*, p. 26. Such training would complement the natural proclivities of the Egyptian student, who

> is deficient in inventive capacity, acts from impulse, is wayward and changeable in mind, and . . . is stunted as to his reasoning faculties, [although] . . . not without other compensating advantages. He has a vivid imagination, quick perception, and a power of intuitively sympathizing with others. He is therefore by nature more or less of an artist. (Cunynghame, "The Present State of Education in Egypt," p. 232)

114. On the interchangeability of the domestic worker and the colonial subject, and the consequent spread of "adapted education" projects throughout the empire, from Nigeria to New Zealand, see David Ruddell, "Class and Race: Neglected Determinants of Colonial 'Adapted Education' Policies," *Comparative Education* 18 (1982), pp. 293–303; and John M. Barrington, "Cultural Adaptation

and Maori Educational Policy: The African Connection," *Comparative Education Review* 20 (1976), pp. 1–10.

115. Villiers Stuart, "Reports . . . Respecting the Progress of Reorganization in Egypt since the British Occupation in 1882," *Parl. Pap.*, 1895, vol. 109, pp. 943, 961.

116. Cromer, Annual Report, *Parl. Pap.*, 1904, vol. 111, p. 267. Quoted also in Williamson, *Eduction and Social Change*, pp. 81–82.

117. Quoted in Cromer, Annual Report, *Parl. Pap.*, 1904, vol. 111, p. 267; also in *Modern Egypt*, vol. 2, p. 535n. Lecky, though little-known today, was at the time a major figure in the minds of educated Britons; he was, for example, one of the most frequently cited authorities in Darwin's discussion of ethics and society in *The Descent of Man*. Gertrude Himmelfarb, *Darwin and the Darwinian Revolution* (New York: Norton, 1962), p. 375.

118. Ministry of Education, *Report of the Elementary Education Commission*, p. 7.

119. Cromer, Annual Report, *Parl. Pap.*, 1904, vol. 111, p. 269.

120. Worsfold, *The Redemption of Egypt*, p. 195.

121. Heyworth-Dunne, *Introduction to the History of Education*, p. 132.

122. Cromer, Annual Report, *Parl. Pap.*, 1906, vol. 137, p. 570.

123. The Rev. James Johnston, F. S. S., ed., *Report of the Centenary Conference on the Protestant Missions of the World* (London: James Nisbet & Co., 1889), p. 19.

124. Johnston, *Report of the Centenary Conference*, p. 23.

125. Alfred Cunningham, *To-Day in Egypt* (London: Hurst & Blackett, 1912), p. 221.

126. Cunningham, *To-Day in Egypt*, pp. 221–22.

127. Kitchener, Annual Report, *Parl. Pap.*, 1914, vol. 101, p. 37.

128. Cromer, Annual Report, *Parl. Pap.*, 1905, vol. 103, pp. 1168–69.

129. Leila Ahmed, *Women and Gender in Islam* (New Haven: Yale University Press, 1992), p. 151.

130. Sergei P. Poliakov, *Everyday Islam: Religion and Tradition in Central Asia*, trans. Anthony Olcott (Armonk, N.Y.: M. E. Sharpe, 1992), pp. 66–67.

131. Mitchell, *Colonising Egypt*, p. 171.

132. Ahmad Abdalla, *The Student Movement and National Politics in Egypt, 1923–1973* (London: Al-Saqi Books, 1985).

133. Mitchell, *Colonising Egypt*, p. 79.

134. Raymond Williams, *The Sociology of Culture* (New York: Schocken Books, 1981), p. 110.

135. Christopher Herbert, *Culture and Anomie: Ethnographic Imagination in the Nineteenth Century* (Chicago: University of Chicago Press, 1991), p. 26.

136. Mitchell, *Colonising Egypt*, p. 74. For a detailed critique of Mitchell's portrayal of the model school's novelty and importance, see pp. 30–40 in my "Our Children and Our Youth: Religious Education and Political Authority in Mubarak's Egypt," Ph.D. diss., Department of Anthropology, Stanford University, 1991.

137. Mitchell asserts, rather oddly, that "there is no need to recount in detail

the way in which these practices failed, or the devastation they caused," *Colonising Egypt*, p. 42.

138. Mitchell, *Colonising Egypt*, p. 107.

139. Mitchell, *Colonising Egypt*, pp. 101–2.

140. Williams, *Marxism and Literature*, p. 110.

141. Wayne Shaefer, "The Responsibility of Berber School Policy for the Troubles of a Franco-Moroccan School," *The Maghreb Review* 14 (1989), p. 188.

142. William Lancaster, *The Rwala Bedouin Today* (Cambridge: Cambridge University Press, 1981), pp. 102–3.

Chapter 3. The Progressive Policy of the Government

1. Russell Galt, *The Effects of Centralization on Education in Modern Egypt* (Cairo: American University in Cairo, Department of Education, 1936), p. 121.

2. Brown, *Peasant Politics*.

3. Richard Mitchell, *The Society of the Muslim Brothers*. (London: Oxford University Press, 1969), p. 213.

4. R. Mitchell, *The Society of the Muslim Brothers*, p. 213.

5. Cromer, Annual Report, *Parl. Pap.*, 1906, vol. 137, p. 569.

6. Cromer, Annual Report, *Parl. Pap.*, 1907, vol. 100, pp. 714–15.

7. Gorst, Annual Report, *Parl. Pap.*, 1909, vol. 105, p. 42.

8. Cromer, Annual Report, *Parl. Pap.*, 1906, vol. 137, p. 569.

9. Gorst, Annual Report, *Parl. Pap.*, 1911, vol. 103, p. 36.

10. Gorst, Annual Report, *Parl. Pap.*, 1909, vol. 105, p. 39. Kitchener stressed the same fear of migration three years later:

> What seems most required for progress in this direction is to evolve the best type of rural school, adapted to the special practical needs of agricultural districts, and when this has been done we may confidently hope to see a considerable increase in the number of boys educated. It must not be forgotten that any hasty or unthought-out development of education in rural districts, unless it is carefully adapted to rural necessities, may imperil the agricultural interests on which the prosperity of the country so largely depends. A rural exodus in Egypt would be an economic and social disaster of considerable magnitude. (Annual Report, *Parl. Pap.*, 1912, vol. 121, p. 4)

11. Cromer, "Reports on the State of Egypt and the Progress of Administrative Reforms," *Parl. Pap.*, 1898, vol. 107, pp. 664–65.

12. Cromer, Annual Report, *Parl. Pap.*, 1903, vol. 87, p. 1009. The real problem arose in the primary system, in which the Qur'an was one of the required subjects, and yet Muslims formed less than 80 percent of the school population as a whole. Among the students who passed the primary certificate examination in 1903, there were 383 Muslims, 227 Copts, and 4 Jews. Annual Report, *Parl. Pap.*, 1904, vol. 111, p. 266. The primary curriculum was rewritten in 1907 and, in addition to the beginning of a conversion of all instruction to Arabic from English and French, religion was moved to the last school period so that Coptic students could leave. If there were more than 15 Coptic students in a school, they could be provided with a religion course by an unpaid visiting teacher, or, later, by a paid Coptic teacher. In 1908, 875 Coptic students attended religious

instruction by designated Coptic teachers (not priests) in fifteen of the government primary schools. Gorst, Annual Report, *Parl. Pap.*, 1909, vol. 105, p. 42.

13. Gorst, Annual Report, *Parl. Pap.*, 1910, vol. 112, p. 42.

14. In Britain, Dissenters and Non-Conformists as well as Roman Catholics were substantial opponents of many educational schemes proffered by adherents of the official Church of England; in Iraq after the First World War, British colonial authorities had to consider the complex and often contrasting interests of Sunnis and Shiʿites, Kurds, Jews, and various denominations of Christians, and how to deal with the looted remains of a small Europeanized educational system that heretofore had delivered instruction largely in Turkish. See Gertrude Bell, "Review of the Civil Administration of Mesopotamia," *Parl. Pap.*, 1920, vol. 51, pp. 10–13, 56–57, 103–7. The Commission on Elementary Education in Egypt noted that government schools were strictly secular, in Ministry of Education, *Report of the Elementary Education Commission*, p. 19.

15. Kitchener, Annual Report, *Parl. Pap.*, 1911, vol. 103, p. 7.

16. Kitchener, Annual Report, *Parl. Pap.*, 1911, pp. 37–38.

17. Kitchener, Annual Report, *Parl. Pap.*, 1911, p. 57.

18. Kitchener, Annual Report, *Parl. Pap.*, 1911, p. 38.

19. Ministry of Education, *Report of the Elementary Education Commission*, p. 20.

20. Quoted in Salama, *L'Enseignement islamique*, p. 303.

21. Ministry of Education, *Report of the Elementary Education Commission*, appendix, p. 41.

22. Egyptian Constitution of 1923, Article 149: "The Religion of the State is Islam. Arabic is the official language." In Nasser's 1964 Constitution, Article 5 reads, "Islam is the religion of the State and Arabic its official Language."

23. Boktor, *School and Society*, p. 122.

24. Salama, *L'Enseignement islamique*, p. 316.

25. F. O. Mann, *Report on Certain Aspects of Egyptian Education, Rendered to His Excellency, the Minister of Education at Cairo* (Cairo: Government Press, 1932).

26. For a good example, see Ismaʿil Mahmud al-Qabbani, *Siyasa al-taʿlim fi Misr* (Cairo: Lajnah al-taʾlif wa al-tarjama wa al-nashr, 1944).

27. Galt, *The Effects of Centralization*, p. 16.

28. Galt, *The Effects of Centralization*, p. 120.

29. Boktor, *School and Society*, p. 203.

30. Galt, *The Effects of Centralization*, p. 120.

31. Eickelman, "The Art of Memory."

32. Boktor, *School and Society*, p. 204.

33. Boktor, *School and Society*, p. 131.

34. From an article by "a prominent writer and educator" in *al- Ahram*, 8 March 1933, quoted in Boktor, *School and Society*, p. 154.

35. Quote from "a large landlord, perhaps the wealthiest in Egypt," in Charles Issawi, *Egypt: An Economic and Social Analysis* (London: Oxford University Press, 1947), p. 149.

36. Neguib el-Hilali, *Report on Educational Reform in Egypt* (Cairo: Government Press, Boulaq, 1943), pp. 1–2.

37. El-Hilali, *Report on Educational Reform*, pp. 42–43, 49.
38. El-Hilali, *Report on Educational Reform*, p. 69.
39. El-Hilali, *Report on Educational Reform*, p. 75.
40. El-Hilali, *Report on Educational Reform*, p. 50.
41. El-Hilali, *Report on Educational Reform*, p. 52.
42. El-Hilali, *Report on Educational Reform*, p. 52.
43. Al-Qabbani, *Siyasa al-ta'lim*, pp. 25–28.
44. Al-Qabbani, *Siyasa al-ta'lim*, p. 28. See also Durkheim, *Moral Education*, pp. 125, 148.
45. Al-Qabbani, *Siyasa al-ta'lim*, pp. 28–9.
46. Abu Al-Futouh Ahmad Radwan, *Old and New Forces in Egyptian Education* (New York: Bureau of Publications, Teachers College, Columbia University, 1951), p. 138.
47. Radwan, *Old and New Forces*, pp. 138–39.
48. Radwan, *Old and New Forces*, p. 159.
49. Radwan, *Old and New Forces*, pp. 128–29.
50. Radwan, *Old and New Forces*, p. 113.
51. A biographer of Hasan al-Banna, citing the latter's criticism of al-Azhar graduates; cited in R. Mitchell, *The Society of the Muslim Brothers*, p. 213.
52. Brown, *Peasant Politics*, pp. 42–43.
53. Hamed Ammar, *Growing Up in an Egyptian Village* (New York: Octagon Books), p. 78.
54. Ammar, *Growing Up*, p. 212.
55. Ammar, *Growing Up*, p. 220.
56. Carré, *Enseignement islamique*, pp. 8–9.
57. Carré, *Enseignement islamique*, p. 33.
58. Rif'at Sayyid Ahmad, *Al-Din wa al-dawla wa al-thawra* (Cairo: al-Dar al-sharqiyyah, 1989), pp. 269, 274.
59. Hasan al-Hariri, Muhammad Mustafa Zaydan, Alyas Barsum Matar, and Dr. Sayyid Khayr Allah, *Al-Madrasa al-ibtida'iyya* (Cairo: Maktaba al-nahda al-Misriyya, 1966), pp. 17–18.
60. Al-Hariri et al., *Al-Madrasa al-ibtida'iyya*, p. 3.
61. Richard Tapper and Nancy Tapper, "Religion, Education, and Continuity in a Provincial Town," in *Islam in Modern Turkey: Religion, Politics and Literature in a Secular State*, ed. Richard Tapper (London: I. B. Tauris & Co., 1991), p. 73.
62. James Mayfield, *Rural Politics in Nasser's Egypt: A Quest for Legitimacy* (Austin: University of Texas Press, 1971), pp. 152–53.
63. R. Ahmad, *Al-Din wa al-dawla*, p. 271; Hobsbawm, "Mass-Producing Traditions," p. 271.
64. Ilya Harik, *The Political Mobilization of Peasants* (Bloomington: Indiana University Press, 1974), pp. 180–83.
65. Article 19 states, "Al-Tarbiya al-diniyya madda asasiyya fi manahij al-ta'lim al-'amm" (Religious education is a basic subject in the general education curricula).
66. Anwar Sadat, "Meeting by President Mohamed Anwar el Sadat with the Moslem and Christian Religious Leaders, Cairo, February 8, 1977" (Cairo: Arab

Republic of Egypt, Ministry of Information, State Information Service), pp. 14–15.

67. Educational Planning Unit, Ministry of Education, Government of Egypt, "Reform of the Educational System of Egypt: A Sector Assessment," draft, USAID Development Information Center, 8 January 1990, p. 18.

68. R. Ahmad, *Al-Din wa al-dawla*, pp. 265–75.

69. Ahmad Hechmat Pacha, *Questions d'education et d'enseignement* (Cairo: 1914), pp. 148–265.

70. Wizara al-maʿarif al-ʿumumiyya, *Manhaj al-taʿlim al-thanawi lil-madaris al-banin wa al-banat* (Cairo: al-Mutabaʿa al- amiriyya, 1930), p. 1.

71. Boktor, *School and Society*, p. 126; Galt, *Effects of Centralization*, p. 127; R. Ahmad, *Al-Din wa al-dawla*, p. 269.

72. R. Ahmad, *Al-Din wa al-dawla*, p. 270.

73. Carré, *Enseignement islamique*, p. 6.

74. Quoted in Carre, *Enseignement islamique*, p. 72.

75. R. Ahmad, *Al-Din wa al-dawla*, p. 272.

76. Ried, "Turn-of-the-Century Egyptian School Days," p. 383.

77. Ronald G. Wolfe, trans., *Egypt's Second Five-Year Plan for Socio-Economic Development (1987/88–1991/2), with Plan for Year One (1987/88)* (Cairo: Professional Business Services Ltd.), p. 131.

78. Wolfe, trans., *Egypt's Second Five-Year Plan*, p. 142.

Chapter 4. Learning about God

1. Ana-Maria Rizzuto, M.D., *The Birth of the Living God: A Psychoanalytic Study* (Chicago: University of Chicago Press, 1979), p. 8.

2. See my "The Political Economy of Religious Commodities in Cairo," *American Anthropologist* 97, 1 (March 1995), pp. 51–68; and "Signposts along the Road: Monumental Public Writing in Egypt," *Anthropology Today* 11, 4 (1995), pp. 8–13.

3. This phenomenon is also referred to, by its participants, as *"al-sahwa al-islamiyya"* (the Islamic awakening), and by its critics as *"al-islam al-siyasi"* (political Islam), among other labels. I prefer "Islamic Trend" as a relatively neutral term that captures both the political sense of the recent "Islamism," which emphasizes political ideology, as well as the quiet but deepening spiritual engagement of large parts of the Egyptian population.

4. See Andrea Rugh, "Reshaping Personal Relations in Egypt," in *Fundamentalisms and Society*, vol. 2 of *The Fundamentalism Project*, ed. Martin Marty and R. Scott Appleby (Chicago: University of Chicago Press, 1993), pp. 151–80; also Gehad Auda, "The 'Normalization' of the Islamic Movement in Egypt from the 1970s to the Early 1990s," in *Accounting for Fundamentalisms*, vol. 4 of *The Fundamentalism Project*, ed. Marty and Appleby (1994), pp. 374–412.

5. Central Agency for Public Mobilization and Statistics (CAPMAS), *Statistical Yearbook, Arab Republic of Egypt, 1988* (Cairo: CAPMAS, 1988), pp. 174–78.

6. CAPMAS, *Al-Ihsaʾat al-thaqafiyya: Al-Idhaʿa wal-sahafa 1983* (Cairo:

CAPMAS, 1985), p. 28. I want to thank Sayyid Taha of CAPMAS for going out of his way to provide me with the unpublished information for 1986.

7. Samia Mustafa al-Khashab, *Al-Shabab wa al-tayyar al-islami fi al-mujtama' al-Misri al-mu'asir: Dirasa Ijtima'iyya midaniyya* (Cairo: Dar al-thaqafa al-'arabiyya, 1988).

8. Gilles Kepel, *Muslim Extremism in Egypt* (Berkeley: University of California Press, 1985), p. 22.

9. For example, in the 1984 elections to the Egyptian People's Assembly, candidates supported by the Muslim Brotherhood won seven seats in an alliance with the Wafd Party, an alliance that captured a total of 65 of the 455 places in the Assembly. In the 1987 elections, the Brotherhood broke its alliance with the Wafd and instead ran its candidates with two smaller parties, the Liberal and the Socialist Workers Parties; Brotherhood candidates captured 35 of the 60 seats won by that coalition. Saad Eddin Ibrahim, "Taqdim," in Nemat Guenena's *Tandhim al-jihad: Hal huwa al-badil al-islami fi Misr?* (Cairo: Dar al-huriyya, 1988), p. 16. Considering the fact that Egyptian elections are always fixed in favor of the ruling National Democratic Party, these results probably underestimate the strength of political sympathy for the Muslim Brotherhood and other representatives of the Islamic Trend.

10. Michael Taussig, *The Nervous System* (London: Routledge, 1992), p. 126.

11. Karl Marx, "The Grundrisse," in *The Marx-Engels Reader*, ed. Robert C. Tucker (New York: Norton, 1978), p. 230.

12. Bourdieu and Passeron, *Reproduction in Education*, p. 38.

13. Lambert Kelabora, "Assumptions Underlying Religious Instruction in Indonesia," *Comparative Education* 15 (1979), p. 333.

14. Eickelman, *Knowledge and Power in Morocco*, p. 168

15. Benedict Anderson, *Imagined Communities* (London: Verso, 1983), p. 39.

16. Daniel Lerner, *The Passing of Traditional Society* (New York: The Free Press, 1964), p. 96.

17. The "Protocols" are a famous series of anti-Semitic tracts with a tangled and horribly fascinating history; see Norman Cohn, *Warrant for Genocide* (Brown Judaic Studies 23) (Chico, Calif.: Scholar's Press, 1981).

18. Walter Ong, *Interfaces of the Word: Studies in the Evolution of Consciousness and Culture* (Ithaca: Cornell University Press, 1977), p. 90.

19. The concept is Walter Ong's, from his *Orality and Literacy: The Technologizing of the Word* (London: Methuen, 1982), p. 135.

20. In addition to Messick's *The Calligraphic State*, see his "Legal Documents and the Concept of 'Restricted Literacy' in a Traditional Society," *International Journal of the Sociology of Language*, no. 42 (1974), pp. 41–52; and "The Mufti, the Text and the World: Legal Interpretation in Yemen," *Man*, n.s., 21 (1986), pp. 102–19.

21. Williams, *Sociology of Culture*, p. 111.

22. Annabelle Sreberny-Mohammadi and Ali Mohammadi, *Small Media, Big Revolution: Communication, Culture, and the Iranian Revolution* (Minneapolis: University of Minnesota Press, 1994).

23. "Official reports on the Arabic broadcasts (Strictly Confidential)," item

7361, James Heyworth-Dunne Collection, Hoover Institution Archives, Stanford University.

24. Lila Abu-Lughod, "Finding a Place for Islam: Egyptian Television Serials and the National Interest," *Public Culture* 5 (1993), p. 500.

25. Lila Abu-Lughod, *Writing Women's Worlds* (Berkeley: University of California Press, 1993), p. 183.

26. L. Abu-Lughod, "Finding a Place for Islam," p. 495; "The Romance of Resistance: Tracing Transformations of Power through Bedouin Women," *American Ethnologist* 17, 1 (1990), p. 52; Smadar Lavie, *The Poetics of Military Occupation* (Berkeley: University of California Press, 1990), pp. 96, 169, 246, 295, 349, 350, 353.

27. Williams, *Sociology of Culture*, pp. 99- 100.

28. Jean-François Lyotard, *The Postmodern Condition: A Report on Knowledge* (Minneapolis: University of Minnesota Press, 1984), pp. 4–5.

29. Williams, *Sociology of Culture*, pp. 102–3.

30. None of these institutions has an imprimatur in the sense that the Roman Catholic Church does, but their reputation stands as legitimation for products issued under their supervision. However, academics who collect clandestinely produced Islamic material in Egypt tell me that the way to tell whether it is "hot," i.e., likely to get the author arrested, is to check the end pages for the registration number for Dar al-Kutub, the national library. If it's not registered, it's been judged by its producers too controversial to bring to the attention of the state.

31. Samia ʿAbd al-Rahman, interview, 26 July 1989, pp. 521–22.

32. Samia ʿAbd al-Rahman, interview, 26 July 1989, p. 525.

33. Samia ʿAbd al-Rahman, interview, 16 February 1990, pp. 282–83.

34. Amina al-Saʿid, *al-Wafd*, 7 April 1989, p. 6.

35. Umm Samira, interview, 27 April 1989, p. 363.

36. This conversation was particularly ironic as it took place in a bar on the last day of Ramadan, where he had had one of his Egyptian friends, a dual citizen with a Swiss passport, order an extra drink for him. Egyptians may not purchase alcohol during Ramadan, unless they can prove they're not Egyptian (p. 367).

37. Samia ʿAbd al-Rahman, interview, 16 February 1989, pp. 281–82. Based on this hadith, some American Muslim converts "refer to themselves as reverts, arguing that every child is born a Muslim." *New York Times*, 13 November 1990, p. A12.

38. Ahmad Rabiʿ al-Hamid Khalaq Allah, *Al-Fikar al-tarbawiy wa tatbiqatihi laday jamaʿat al-ikhwan al-muslimin* (Cairo: Maktaba Wahba, 1983), pp. 133–34.

39. "Takhiru li-nutfikum, faʾinna al-ʿaraq dassas," *al-Liwaʾ al-islami*, no. 357, 24 November 1988, p. 17; ʿAbdallah Nasih ʿAlwan, *Tarbiya al-awlad fi al-Islam* (Cairo: Dar al-Islam, 1985), pp. 42–43.

40. ʿAlwan, *Tarbiya al-awlad*, p. 43. The author adds that marriage with close relatives is not recommended; exogamy protects the child from "infectious diseases [and] hereditary ailments, widening the circle of family familiarity, and developing social ties." Citing two hadiths of the Prophet (for which, he notes, he is unable to find sources): "Don't marry a relative, or the child will be created scrawny," and "Marry outside, and don't debilitate," he reiterates the agreement

of modern scientific findings with the ancient wisdom of Islam: "The science of heredity has proven as well that marriage with relatives makes weak progeny . . . and that the children inherit blameworthy moral qualities and disapproved social habits. This truth was established by the Messenger of Islam (God's peace and blessings upon him), fourteen centuries ago, before science could say the same thing and bring his truths to light for those who can see it" (p. 44).

41. Samia ʿAbd al-Rahman, interview, 16 February 1989, p. 280.

42. Karim Shafik, interview, 9 August 1990, pp. 570–71.

43. Quoted in the editorial of *al-Liwaʾ al-islami*, no. 357, 24 November 1988; and by Dr. Ahmad Fuʾad al-Sharbini during a United Nations conference on the Rights of Children the previous week, in *al-Ahram*, 23 November 1988, p. 3.

44. Silwa Mashhur, in *al-Liwaʾ al-islami*, no. 357, 24 November 1990, p. 18.

45. *Al-Liwaʾ al-islami*, no. 357, 24 November 1988, pp. 1, 17.

46. Interview, 12 June 1989, p. 447.

47. This phrase is Timothy Mitchell's, *Colonising Egypt*, p. 132.

48. Interview, 12 June 1989, p. 447.

49. Mahmoud Mahdi, *al-Ahram*, 24 March 1989, p. 13.

50. During the academic year 1988–89, the sixth grade was abolished in a reorganization mandated by the Ministry of Education, resulting in the combination of the sixth and seventh grades. In 1995, this resulted in a doubling of the entering class at the already overcrowded Cairo University. The ministry is considering reversing its decision.

51. In August of 1989, the Shaykh of al-Azhar, Jad al-Haqq ʿAli Jad al-Haqq, agreed to submit to al-Azhar's High Council a Ministry of Education proposal that would bring the curriculum at al-Azhar primary institutes into line with the curricula of the Ministry of Education beginning the following academic year. The aim of the plan was the "raising [of] the practical educational level at al-Azhar and its adaptation to the spirit of the age, tying it to the solution of social problems." *Al-Jumhuriyya*, 26 August 1989, p. 6.

52. Wolfe, trans., *Egypt's Second Five-Year Plan*, p. 143; *Statistical Yearbook, 1977*, p. 146; *Statistical Yearbook, 1988*, p. 158; Susan H. Cochrane, Kalpana Mehra, and Ibrahim Taha Osheba, "The Educational Participation of Egyptian Children," World Bank Discussion Paper, December 1986.

53. The average Egyptian's image of proper education is very much tied to the "bookishness" derided by school reformers. Aisha Rafea, in an article on the Pyramids School in Giza, quotes a concerned mother:

> "I am determined to transfer my son to another school by the beginning of the new school year," said one mother who expressed great dissatisfaction with the fact that children are given no assignments at the Pyramids School, and are not taught the alphabet while children at their age at other schools start learning how to write at KG1 level. "Compared to his sister who is the same age but goes to the Ramses College, my son hardly knows how to write," she added, saying that in her opinion the year at the Pyramids School was a total waste of time. Yet she admitted that her son loves his school and his sister doesn't. The reason for that, she thinks, is that "his school is like a club while hers is a real place of education." ("The School of No Homework," *Cairo Today*, February 1989, pp. 46–47)

54. Cromer wrote in his Report for 1903 that

> the Egyptians, as a race, are somewhat inclined to sedentary pursuits, and until recent years the educational system confirmed, rather than corrected, this tendency. A few years ago, physical drill and English sports were introduced into the curriculum of the Government schools. The effect upon the physique and character of the pupils has been so manifestly beneficial that their advantages are now generally recognized, even in quarters where their introduction was at first opposed. (*Parl. Pap.*, 1904, vol. III, p. 267)

On the physical education movement in Europe, see J. S. Hurt, "Drill, Discipline and the Elementary School Ethos," in Phillip McCann, ed., *Popular Education and Socialization in the Nineteenth Century* (London: Methuen & Co. Ltd., 1977), pp. 167–92. In addition to tightening school discipline, the physical education movement was motivated by the fear of bodily degeneration associated with urbanization. For a contemporary view, see Lord Brabazon, "Decay of Bodily Strength in Towns," *The Nineteenth Century* 21 (1887), pp. 673–76. Aside from obvious humanitarian motivations, physical education, hygiene, and nutritional programs were called for in Egypt for political and economic reasons. Egypt's minister of education wrote in 1943 of assertions "that the rising generation is weaker in body, possesses less fortitude, and is more impatient with life than the preceding generation. Landowners bitterly complain of the indifferent health of agricultural labourers and their physical debility which has adversely affected their productiveness to a marked extent." El-Hilali, *Report on Educational Reform*, p. 48.

55. This poster was inspired by a similar picture on page 5 of the first grade religion textbook.

56. Dr. Surur later became—as of 1994—Speaker of Egypt's People's Assembly.

57. As of March 1996, Tantawi is the new Shaykh of al-Azhar, replacing the recently deceased Jad al-Haqq ʿAli Jad al-Haqq.

58. Labib al-Sabaʿi, *al-Ahram*, 31 March 1989, p. 13.

59. Dr. Muhammad Yahya, *al-Shaʿb*, 23 May 1989, p. 7. On the subject of maps bearing the name of Israel, Dr. Ahmad Fathy Surur, minister of education, promised the *Majlis al-shaʿb* on 14 May 1989 that "all maps not bearing the name of Palestine would be burned." *Al-Wafd*, 16 May 1989, p. 1.

60. *Al-Shaʿb*, 23 May 1989, p. 11.

61. Janet Abu-Lughod, "Rural Migration and Politics in Egypt," in *Rural Politics and Social Change in the Middle East*, ed. Richard Antoun and Ilya Harik (Bloomington: Indiana University Press, 1972), p. 326.

62. Umm Samira, interview, 2 June 1989, pp. 415–16.

63. Wafaʾi Ismaʿil, interview, 7 August 1989, p. 554

64. Bourdieu and Passeron, *Reproduction in Education*, p. 44.

65. Article 6 in *Qanun al-taʿlim raqam 139 lil-sana 1981* (Cairo: al-Hayʾa al-ʿamma li-shuʾun al-mutabiʿ al-amiriyya, 1986), p. 3.

66. *Al-Jumhuriyya*, 22 September 1989, p. 7.

67. Even given new techniques of inculcation, some Egyptian Christians argue that reliance on the Qurʾan as a text has a negative effect on the Egyptian educational system in general. A recent graduate of ʿAin Shams University told me, "The essays that people write [in school] are repetitive and unorganized, because the Qurʾan is that way, and people are taught, even if indirectly, to

mimic that style, held up as a model of the best there is. We have no multiple-choice tests here." Jihan al-Manar, interview, 17 October 1988, pp. 81–82.

68. Interview conducted by Hamid ʿIzz al-Din, *al-Akhbar*, 18 August 1989, p. 4.

69. *Al-Ahram*, 3 May 1989, p. 6.

70. *Al-Akhbar*, 16 June 1989, p. 1; *al-Ahram*, 13 August 1989, p. 8.

71. Mahmud Mahdi, *al-Ahram*, 12 May 1989, p. 13.

72. Sometimes the financial incentives are not quite as compelling; the magazine *al-Tasawwuf al-islami* (Islamic Sufism), for example, sponsored a contest in which individuals qualified for prizes by answering a few questions about Sufism; the prizes ranged from £E 50 ($20) for first prize to a year's subscription to the magazine, for those placing thirteenth to twentieth.

73. *Al-Ahram*, 3 May 1989, p. 6.

74. *Al-Ahram*, 10 February 1989, p. 11.

75. Denis Sullivan provides a comprehensive analysis of these institutions in *Private Voluntary Organizations in Egypt: Islamic Development, Private Initiative, and State Control* (Gainesville: University Press of Florida, 1994).

76. CAPMAS, *Statistical Yearbook, 1988*, pp. 135, 137.

77. Samir Shawqi, interview, 5 August 1989, p. 541.

78. *Al-Wafd*, 20 July 1989, p. 6.

79. *Al-Muslim al-saghir*, September 1988, p. 32.

80. Laylat al-Qadr (The night of power) is the anniversary of the date during Ramadan when Muhammad first began to receive revelations from God through the angel Gabriel.

81. *Al-Ahram*, 12 May 1989, p. 13.

82. Interview, 16 August 1989, p. 585.

Chapter 5. The Path of Clarification

1. Bourdieu and Passeron, *Reproduction in Education*, pp. 58–59.

2. George Devereaux and Edwin Loeb, "Antagonistic Acculturation," *American Sociological Review* 8, 2 (April 1943), pp. 133–47.

3. Messick, *The Calligraphic State*, p. 54.

4. Messick, *The Calligraphic State*, pp. 55–56.

5. Messick, *The Calligraphic State*, pp. 65–66.

6. Ong, *Interfaces of the Word*, p. 88.

7. See, especially, Willis, *Learning to Labour*, pp. 171–76; also Williams, *Sociology of Culture*, p. 188.

8. A. J. Arberry, *The Koran Interpreted*, vol. 2 (New York: Macmillan, 1955), p. 264.

9. Yusuf al-Hamadi and Muhammad Shahhat Wahdan, *Kitab al-tarbiya al-diniyya al-islamiyya*, lil-saff al-sadis al-ibtidaʾi (Cairo: al-Hayʾa al-ʿamma li-shuʾun al-mutabiʿ al-amiriyya, 1976), pp. 108–10.

10. Yusuf al-Hamadi, Muhammad Mukhtar Amin Mukram, and Dr. ʿAbd al-Maqsud Shalqami, *Tarbiya al-Muslim*, lil-saff al-sadis al-ibtidaʾi (Cairo: al-

Jihaz al-markazi lil-kutub al-jami'iyya wa al-madrasiyya wa al-wasa'il al-ta'limiyya, 1981), pp. 97–98.

11. First grade religious studies textbook, 1988–89, pp. v–vi.

12. Third grade religious studies textbook, 1988–89, p. 3.

13. First grade religious studies textbook, 1988–89, p. v.

14. Second grade religious studies textbook, 1988–89, p. 3.

15. Third grade religious studies textbook, 1988–89, p. 3.

16. Third and fourth grade religious studies textbook, 1988–89, p. 3.

17. Table 3 summarizes an analysis of the proportion of the textbooks devoted to specific topics. The analysis was made easier by the fact that the texts are divided into sections with particular, labeled themes. Because of the way the text was organized, each page could usually be treated as a unit for the purpose of coding; i.e., there was not usually more than one kind of material covered on a single page. Where this was not the case, and a page had more than one category of material on it, an even fraction (one-quarter, one-third, one-half, etc.), was usually sufficient to express the proportion of space devoted to particular topics. Where material of one type was included in a section of text of another type (e.g., a story about the Prophet Muhammad in a section on the pillars of Islam), it was not coded differently from the section in which it was included; the authors' categorization of material is treated as primary.

18. I should emphasize that these processes are derived from my own examination of the texts, and do not necessarily correspond to the conscious intentions or productive processes of their creators.

19. First grade religious studies textbook, 1988–89, p. 65.

20. Illustrating the Ramadan sections in the first, second, and fifth grade textbooks are what appear to be three different drawings of the same mosque, a medium-size structure set against the background of some multistory dwellings that could exist in any but the very smallest towns in the country.

21. Second grade religious studies textbook, 1988–89, p. 40.

22. Third grade religious studies textbook, 1988–89, p. 37.

23. Fifth grade religious studies textbook, 1988–89, p. 89. There is a matching question in the section of review questions following the story, "What is the role and status of Egypt in the Arab and Islamic world?" From an Islamic rather than a political perspective, this is an odd interpretation of the story of Joseph. A. Chris Eccel points out that he has "rarely seen the 'ulama' refer to ancient Egypt except as a symbol for paganism, as it is treated in the Kur'an." *Egypt, Islam, and Social Change: Al-Azhar in Conflict and Accommodation* (Berlin: Klaus Schwarz Verlag, 1984), p. 350.

24. This is an astounding feat, given that even the Pharaoh Akhenaton's monotheism was at that point still at least three hundred years in the future. Yusuf 'Ali's commentary on the Qur'an places the story of Joseph "somewhere between the 19th and the 17th century B.C." *The Holy Qur'an* (Brentwood, Md.: Amana Corporation, 1983), p. 406.

25. See, for example, discussions of plastic surgery (*al-Liwa' al-islami*, 1 December 1988, p. 5), or conversations with the mufti on family planning (*al-Ahram*, 7 February 1989, p. 8).

26. *Zamzam* (July 1989), p. 22. The discovery is credited to Dr. ʿAbd al-Nasir Ibrahim Muhammad Harara.

27. One will occasionally find photographs in Muslim periodicals of honeycombs in which the bees have blocked off cells to spell the divine name, or "Allah" inscribed by natural blight on the surface of a leaf. In the summer of 1993 I found a particularly good example of this convention on the wall of a Cairo juice bar. The proprietor had taped up a double-page spread from a private sector religious periodical purporting to be a photograph of a grove of trees, the trunks of which had naturally grown into the shape of Arabic letters spelling the *shahada*: "There is no God but God, and Muhammad is His Messenger." For similar understandings in Europe, see Michel Foucault, *The Order of Things: An Archaeology of the Human Sciences* (New York: Vintage, 1970), ch. 2.

28. Fifth grade religious studies textbook, 1988–89, pp. 73–75. "Al-nidafa min al-iman" is a common proverb in Egypt, appearing painted (ineffectually) on trash receptacles in some parts of Cairo. The *siwak* itself has become, in the rhetoric of the ʿulama, a symbol of Islamic alternatives to Western practices (e.g., *al-Liwa' al-islami*, 13 October 1988, p. 7).

29. See Mary Douglas, *Purity and Danger* (London: Routledge & Kegan Paul, 1966). "Even if some of Moses's dietary rules were hygienically beneficial," she wrote, "it is a pity to treat him as an enlightened public health administrator, rather than as a spiritual leader" (p. 29). Max Weber attributed such "reinterpretation of the ritualistic commandments of purity as hygienic prescriptions," to "modernization." *The Sociology of Religion* (Boston: Beacon, 1963), p. 93.

30. Concern with the health implications of ablution is relatively recent. A century ago, in his "Report on the Medical and Sanitary Administration of the Government of Egypt," H. R. Greene, surgeon major and under director of the Services Sanitaires d'Egypte wrote,

> Mosques in town and country are all provided with a basin for ablution, in which the water is seldom changed oftener than once in three months. Around this basin are placed a number of foul latrines communicating with a common drain, which, in most instances, runs into a tank or canal from where the drinking supply of the neighborhood is obtained. An examination of most of the principal mosque drains in Lower Egypt last year showed that 73 per cent. ended in the Nile or its branches and that 23 per cent. flowed into stagnant ponds of which the water was used for drinking purposes. In Egypt the Deity is invariably held to be the author of all disease, which should accordingly be submitted to with resignation; nor should any attempt be made by remedying defects to endeavor to controvert the will of the Almighty. (Enclosure in item no. 19 in "Egypt" no. 15 [1885], "Reports on the State of Egypt and the Progress of Administrative Reforms," *Parl. Pap.*, 1884–85, vol. 89, p. 78)

Sanitary reforms have been treated briefly in Mitchell's *Colonising Egypt*, pp. 64–68; and extensively in LaVerne Kuhnke's *Lives at Risk* (University of California Press, 1990).

31. First grade religious studies textbook, 1988–89, p. 44n.

32. Second grade religious studies textbook, 1988–89, p. 28.

33. Fourth grade religious studies textbook, 1988–89, p. 35.

34. Fourth grade religious studies textbook, 1988–89, p. 36.

35. F. O. Mann, who evaluated the Egyptian school system in 1929 at the request of the Egyptian Ministry of Education, complained that the

> process [of examination and cramming] is objectionable in itself but most of all when applied to such subjects as hygiene and morals. Not only is examination in these subjects apt to confuse the essential issue but it attempts to test what obviously cannot be tested by the simplicities of question and answer. The dirtiest little boy ever born might easily get full marks in a written examination in hygiene, and the most doubtful juvenile ever conceived the first place in morality by sheer capacity for the reproduction of platitudes, in the one case physiological, in the other, ethical. (*Report on Certain Aspects of Egyptian Education, Rendered to His Excellency, the Minister of Education at Cairo* [Cairo: Government Press, 1932], p. 21)

36. The choice of this topic should be obvious from the theme of the book, but should not be interpreted to mean that this theme is "dominant" in the texts in the sense of the proportion of space allotted to it, or that it is singled out for attention by the authors. The discussion here is representative of all instances in the texts in which either the family or the school is recommended or shown to be a source of moral advice to the child.

37. Second grade religious studies textbook, 1988–89, p. 73.

38. Second grade religious studies textbook, 1988–89, p. 75.

39. Fourth grade religious studies textbook, 1988–89, p. 54.

40. Third grade religious studies textbook, 1988–89, p. 24.

41. Fourth grade religious studies textbook, 1988–89, p. 13.

42. Fourth grade religious studies textbook, 1988–89, pp. 14–16.

43. The description of the trials and tribulations of ideal families was a central feature of the Victorian Sunday school textbook and the popular religious tract, a genre wonderfully parodied by Mark Twain in "The Story of the Bad Little Boy," *Complete Short Stories of Mark Twain*, ed. Charles Neider (New York: Bantam, 1957), pp. 6–9. In Egypt, the rhetorical technique of depicting the school as one of the primary sources of moral and religious lessons matches alterations in the behavior of educated rural families, in which mothers tend to encourage their children to spend their time studying or playing by themselves, isolated from the feared "bad influences" of neighborhood children. Neither exposed to their local age-mates nor expected to care for younger siblings, such children are raised to be more ego-oriented and less concerned with family loyalties. Schoolbook lessons become increasingly more important as sources of social knowledge because notions of neighborliness and of filial piety, as well as of appropriately differentiated sex roles, differ substantially in educated families from those of the surrounding communities. Judy H. Brink, "Changing Child Rearing Patterns in an Egyptian Village," paper presented at the Middle East Studies Association annual meeting, November 1990.

44. Second grade religious studies textbook, 1988–89, pp. 78–79.

45. Fourth grade religious studies textbook, 1988–89, p. 27.

46. Second grade religious studies textbook, 1988–89, p. 21.

47. Fourth grade religious studies textbook, 1988–89, pp. 20–21.

48. Fourth grade religious studies textbook, 1988–89, p. 20.

49. Third grade religious studies textbook, 1988–89, pp. 43–45; fourth grade religious studies textbook, 1988–89, pp. 75–76.

50. Third grade religious studies textbook, 1988–89, p. 46.

51. Karim Shafik, interview, 9 August 1989, p. 568.

52. Karim Shafik, interview, 9 August 1989, p. 569.

53. *Al-Muslim al-saghir fi 'alam al-talwin* (Cairo: Safir, n.d.), p. 1.

54. Muhammad 'Abd al-Latif and Dr. Yahya 'Abduh, *Al-Udhun al-kabira* (Cairo: Safir, n.d.).

55. Second grade religious studies textbook, 1988–89, p. 29.

56. 'Abd al-Tuwab Yusuf and Dr. Yahya 'Abduh, *Al-Sufuf al-munadhdhama* (Cairo: Safir, 1988), p. 14.

57. Pierre Bourdieu, *Outline of a Theory of Practice* (Cambridge: Cambridge University Press), pp. 87–94; see also Starrett, "The Hexis of Interpretation."

58. Bourdieu, *Outline*, pp. 167–69.

59. "Order," as Sami Zubaida reminds us in his review of Mitchell's *Colonising Egypt*, " . . . is not given in a particular situation, but *read* into that situation." "Exhibitions of Power," *Economy and Society* 19 (1990), p. 364.

60. John Bowen, "*Salat* in Indonesia: The Social Meanings of an Islamic Ritual," *Man*, n.s., 24 (1989), p. 615.

61. Fischer and Abedi, *Debating Muslims*, p. 291.

62. Emile Durkheim, *Moral Education* (New York: Free Press, 1961).

Chapter 6. Growing Up: Four Stories

1. Ninth grade religious studies textbook, 1988–89, p. 181.

2. Eighth grade religious studies textbook, 1987–88, p. 140.

3. Eighth grade religious studies textbook, 1987–88, pp. 198–99.

4. Bowring, "Report on Egypt and Candia," p. 5.

5. For the Yemeni understanding of maturation, see Messick, *The Calligraphic State*, pp. 77–84; for rural Egypt, see Ammar, *Growing Up in an Egyptian Village*, pp. 125–26.

6. Samia 'Abd al-Rahman, interview, 26 July 1989, pp. 521–26.

7. For an exemplary treatment of this theme, see Anna Tsing, *In the Realm of the Diamond Queen* (Princeton: Princeton University Press, 1993).

8. Eighth grade religious studies textbook, 1987–88, p. 166.

9. Diane Singerman, *Avenues of Participation: Family Politics and Networks in Urban Quarters of Cairo* (Princeton: Princeton University Press, 1995).

10. Twelfth grade religious studies textbook, 1989–90, pp. 44–45.

11. Ninth grade religious studies textbook, 1988–89, p. 97. An explanation of the *mahram* had been provided in the ninth grade in the context of the Pilgrimage.

12. Singerman, *Avenues of Participation*, pp. 85–94.

13. Twelfth grade religious studies textbook, 1989–90, pp. 51–55.

14. Dr. 'Abd al-Subur Shahin, *al-Akhbar*, 1 July 1989, p. 8.

15. L. Abu-Lughod, "Finding a Place for Islam."

16. Wadi' Thaluth Luqa, *al-Ahram*, 17 October 1988, p. 7. Significantly, the writer is a Copt, not a Muslim, indicating how widespread is the horror—and the attraction—of these shows.

17. *Al-Jumhuriyya*, 13 September 1989, p. 5.

18. *Al-Ahram*, 6 February 1989, p. 3.

19. *Al-Ahram*, 9 June 1989, p. 13.

20. *Al-Nur*, 12 September 1989, p. 3.

21. The term is from R. Laurence Moore's analysis of religious publishing in eighteenth- and nineteenth-century America in his *Selling God: American Religion in the Marketplace of Culture* (New York: Oxford University Press, 1994).

22. Moore, *Selling God*, p. 22.

23. This Qur'an commentary was banned in Egypt.

24. Samia 'Abd al-Rahman, interview, 24 July 1989, p. 522.

25. Alexander Flores, "Egypt: A New Secularism?" *Middle East Report*, no. 153 (July–August 1988), p. 27.

26. Rizzuto, *Birth of the Living God*, p. 202.

27. Muhammad Sulayman, interview, 7 August 1989, pp. 559–60.

28. Seventh grade religious studies textbook, 1986–87, p. 40.

29. Seventh grade religious studies textbook, 1986–87, pp. 40, 83, 87–88, 156.

30. Seventh grade religious studies textbook, 1986–87, p. 158.

31. Eighth grade religious studies textbook, 1987–88, p. 133.

32. Eighth grade religious studies textbook, 1987–88, p. 133.

33. Eighth grade religious studies textbook, 1987–88, p. 48.

34. Eighth grade religious studies textbook, 1987–88, p. 205.

35. Eighth grade religious studies textbook, 1987–88, p. 205.

36. Eighth grade religious studies textbook, 1987–88, p. 188. For a similar example from another "new nation," see Robert J. Foster, "Take Care of Public Telephones: Moral Education and Nation-State Formation in Papua New Guinea," *Public Culture* 4 (1992), pp. 31–45.

37. Meriem Verges, " 'I Am Living in a Foreign Country Here': A Conversation with an Algerian 'Hittiste,' "*Middle East Report*, no. 192 (January–February 1995), pp. 14–17.

38. L. Abu-Lughod, *Writing Women's Worlds*, pp. 236–37; "Finding a Place for Islam," p. 495.

39. Evelyn A. Early, *Baladi Women of Cairo: Playing with an Egg and a Stone* (Boulder, Colo.: Lynne Reinner Publishers, 1993), pp. 46, 118, 121–25.

40. Muhammad Sulayman, interview, 4 August 1989, 552–53.

41. Samia Mustafa al-Khashab, *Al-Shabab wa al-tayyar al-islami fi al-mujtama' al-Misri al-mu'asir: Dirasa ijtima'iyya midaniyya* (Cairo: Dar al-thaqafa al-'arabiyya, 1988), p. 77.

42. Al-Khashab, *Al-Shabab*, pp. 136–37.

43. Al-Khashab, *Al-Shabab*, p. 80.

44. Al-Khashab, *Al-Shabab*, pp. 104–5.

45. Al-Khashab, *Al-Shabab*, pp. 116–17. Interestingly, most of their knowledge of these groups came from specialized religious books and general-interest newspapers and magazines: 16.9 percent had gotten their information on Islamic groups from classmates who were members; 28.2 percent from religious meetings; 59.6 percent from specialized religious books; and 52 percent from the press (p. 123).

46. Al-Khashab, *Al-Shabab*, p. 118.

47. Ninth grade religious studies textbook, 1988–89, pp. 3–4.
48. *Al-Ahram*, 2 April 1991, p. 5.
49. Ninth grade religious studies textbook, 1988–89, p. 189.
50. Ninth grade religious studies textbook, 1988–89, p. 188.
51. Ninth grade religious studies textbook, 1988–89, p. 189.
52. Ninth grade religious studies textbook, 1988–89, p. 191.
53. *Al-Akhbar*, 27 July 1993, p. 7.
54. For a good review of the social origins of prominent Muslim political activists, see Valerie Hoffman, "Muslim Fundamentalists: Psychosocial Profiles," in *Fundamentalisms Comprehended*, vol. 5 of *The Fundamentalisms Project*, ed. Marty and Appleby (Chicago: University of Chicago Press, 1995), pp. 199–230.
55. *Al-Tasawwuf al-islami* 11, 4 (Ramadan 1409 [April 1989]), pp. 18–19.
56. *Al-Tasawwuf al-islami* 11, 4 (Ramadan 1409 [April 1989]), pp. 18–19.
57. Tenth grade religious studies textbook, 1986–87, p. 38.
58. Tenth grade religious studies textbook, 1986–87, p. 83.
59. Tenth grade religious studies textbook, 1986–87, p. 84.
60. Twelfth grade religious studies textbook, 1989–90, p. 78.
61. Twelfth grade religious studies textbook, 1989–90, p. 78.
62. Twelfth grade religious studies textbook, 1989–90, pp. 130–31.
63. Pierre Bourdieu, "Authorized Language: The Social Conditions of the Effectiveness of Ritual Discourse," in *Language and Symbolic Power* (Cambridge: Harvard University Press, 1991), pp. 109–11.
64. Singerman, *Avenues of Participation*, p. 164.
65. Layla al-Shamsi, interview, 24 September 1989, p. 656.
66. Layla al-Shamsi, interview, 24 September 1989, p. 658.
67. Layla al-Shamsi, interview, 9 August 1989, pp. 574–77.
68. Layla al-Shamsi, interview, 9 August 1989, pp. 574–77.
69. Layla al-Shamsi, interview, 24 September 1989, p. 655.
70. In a literal as well as a figurative sense, it turns out. In May 1996 the Egyptian Constitutional Court upheld a 1994 decree by the minister of education banning girls from wearing the face-covering *niqab* to school.
71. Foucault, *Discipline and Punish*, pp. 186, 184.
72. *Al-Nur*, 16 August 1989, p. 3.
73. *Al-Nur*, 16 August 1989, p. 3.
74. Dr. Fathi Yusuf Mubarak, Professor of Curriculum and Teaching Methodology at the College of Education, ʿAin Shams, quoted in *al-Ahali*, 23 May 1989, p. 10.
75. Dr. Hasan Shahata, assistant professor of education at the University of ʿAin Shams, quoted in *al-Ahali*, 23 May 1989, p. 10.
76. *Al-Akhbar*, 12 June 1989, p. 1.
77. *Al-Nur*, 16 August 1989, p. 3.
78. *Al-Ahram*, 5 August 1989, p. 8.
79. *Al-Wafd*, 10 July 1989, p. 2.
80. *Al-Ahram*, 10 July 1989, p. 8; 7 July 1989, p. 6.
81. *Al-Wafd*, 31 March 1989, p. 6.
82. *Al-Ahram*, 28 March 1989, p. 8.
83. *Al-Ahram*, 8 March 1989, p. 8.

84. *Al-Ahram*, 17 April 1989, p. 8.

85. *Al-Ahram*, 27 April 1989, p. 8.

86. *Al-Jumhuriyya*, 16 September 1989, p. 7.

87. *Al-Akhbar*, 31 July 1989, p. 6. "The Minister of Waqfs said that flight from the domains of work and production are destructive to society." *Al-Ahram*, 2 September 1989, p. 8.

88. *Al-Ahram*, 22 July 1989, p. 9.

89. *Al-Ahram*, 2 April 1991, p. 5.

90. *Al-Akhbar*, 25 August 1989, p. 3.

91. *Al-Ahram*, 2 September 1989, p. 8.

92. *Al-Ahram*, 25 August 1989, p. 8.

93. *Al-Ahram*, 5 August 1989, p. 8.

94. *Al-Akhbar*, 25 August 1989, p. 3.

95. *Al-Akhbar*, 21 July 1989, p. 6.

96. Lyotard, *The Postmodern Condition*, p. 14.

97. Bourdieu and Passeron, *Reproduction in Education*, p. 41.

98. Bourdieu and Passeron, *Reproduction in Education*, pp. 41–42.

99. Pierre Bourdieu, *The Field of Cultural Production: Essays in Art & Literature* (New York: Columbia University Press, 1993), p. 115.

100. Lyotard, *The Postmodern Condition*, pp. 52–53.

101. Williams, *Sociology of Culture*, pp. 106–7.

102. Bourdieu, *Field of Cultural Production*, p. 42.

103. Bourdieu, *Field of Cultural Production*, pp. 83–84.

Chapter 7. State of Emergency

1. Michael Taussig, *The Nervous System* (London: Routledge, 1992), p. 34.

2. Nemat Guenena, *Tandhim al-jihad: Hal Huwa al-badil al-islami fi Misr?* (Cairo: Dar al-hurriyya, 1988).

3. Andrea Rugh, "Reshaping Personal Relations in Egypt," p. 152.

4. For the classic description of the Muslim Brotherhood, see Richard Mitchell, *The Society of the Muslim Brothers* (Oxford: Oxford University Press, 1969); also Gilles Kepel, *Muslim Extremism in Egypt: The Prophet and Pharaoh* (Berkeley: University of California Press, 1986); Barbara Freyer Stowasser, *The Islamic Impulse* (Washington, D.C.: Center for Contemporary Arab Studies, 1987); Arlene Elowe McLeod, *Accommodating Protest*; Olivier Roy, *The Failure of Political Islam*; and volumes in Martin Marty and R. Scott Appleby's *The Fundamentalisms Project* series from University of Chicago Press.

5. *Al-Jumhuriyya*, 16 July 1993, pp. 1, 3; 18 July 1993, p. 5. *Al-Wafd*, 18 July 1993, p. 3.

6. *Al-Akhbar*, 18 July 1993, p. 3.

7. *Al-Ahram*, 19 July 1993, p. 1; *al-Akhbar*, 19 July 1993, p. 3.

8. Newspapers consistently referred to the bodies of the dead martyrs as "mortal remains," while the bodies of the dead or executed militants were referred to as "corpses" or "carcasses."

9. *Al-Ahram*, 20 July 1993, p. 7.

10. *Al-Jumhuriyya*, 20 August 1993, p. 5. Accounts of the incident the previous day made it clear that his encounter with the escaping militants was a matter of chance.

11. *Al-Jumhuriyya*, 20 July 1995, p. 5.

12. Cassandra, "The Impending Crisis in Egypt," p. 20; Olivier Roy, *The Failure of Political Islam*, pp. 86–87.

13. Hoffman, "Muslim Fundamentalists," p. 220.

14. *Al-Akhbar*, 4 August 1993, p. 1.

15. *Al-Akhbar*, 20 July 1993, p. 4.

16. *Al-Jumhuriyya*, 20 July 1993, p. 5.

17. *Al-Ahram*, 20 July 1993, p. 1.

18. Mamoun Fandy, "Egypt's Islamic Group: Regional Revenge?" *Middle East Journal* 48, 4 (1994), p. 609. Fandy claims that al-Jamaʿa al-Islamiyya is essentially a regional separatist organization resisting the extension of northern state power and privilege to the central and southern regions of the country. Their use of violence against police targets may be in part the result of a strongly developed regional tradition of blood vengeance. In an area where police and political authority often run along family lines, the killing of a police officer might be "merely" the result of vengeance between kinship groups. According to Reuters, for example, in July 1995 a police major general in Asyut was killed along with five others when police tried to intervene in an interfamily dispute. The fact that one of the families was led by an ex-army officer who had been dismissed for Islamist sympathies initially made the incident seem part of the battle between the government and the Islamists, an explanation that was quickly dropped.

19. Karim el-Gawhary, "Report from a War Zone: Gamaʿat vs. Government in Upper Egypt," *Middle East Report*, nos. 194–195 (May–June/July–August 1995), p. 51.

20. El-Gawhary, "Report from a War Zone," p. 51; *al-Ahram*, 20 May 1996, p. 18.

21. Timothy Mitchell, "Worlds Apart: An Egyptian Village and the International Tourism Industry," *Middle East Report*, no. 196 (September–October 1995), p. 9.

22. See *The Economist*, 19 December 1992, p. 41; 19 February 1994, p. 45.

23. *The Economist*, 4 February 1995, p. 15.

24. Ahmed Abdalla, "Egypt's Islamists and the State: From Complicity to Confrontation," *Middle East Report*, no. 183 (July–August 1993), p. 29.

25. An ex-general, ʿAbd al-Sattar Amin, who served as a military aide to the prime minister; quoted in *The Economist*, 31 October 1992, p. 42.

26. *Al-Ahram*, 20 July 1993, p. 10.

27. *Al-Ahram*, 20 July 1993, p. 7; *al-Akhbar*, 20 July 1993, p. 4.

28. *Al-Akhbar*, 20 July 1993, p. 4.

29. *Al-Wafd*, 20 July 1993, p. 1.

30. *Al-Ahram*, 20 July 1993, p. 7; *al-Akhbar*, 20 July 1993, p. 4.

31. *Al-Akhbar*, 20 July 1993, p. 4; *al-Jumhuriyya*, 20 July 1993, p. 5.

32. *Al-Akhbar*, 20 July 1993, p. 1.

33. *Al-Ahram*, 3 August 1993, p. 18.

34. *Al-Ahram*, 3 August 1993, p. 18.

35. *Al-Ahram*, 3 August 1993, p. 18.

36. *Al-Wafd*, 4 August 1993, p. 9.

37. *Al-Wafd*, 26 July 1993, p. 8.

38. Reuters, 18 July 1995.

39. Reuters, 17 July 1995.

40. Amira Howeidy, Mona al-Nahhas and Mona Anis, "The Persecution of Abu Zeid," *al-Ahram Weekly*, 22–28 June 1995; rpt., *World Press Review* 45 (October 1995).

41. Ayman Bakr and Elliot Colla, "Silencing Is at the Heart of My Case," interview with Nasr Hamid Abu Zayd, *Middle East Report*, no. 185 (November–December 1993), p. 29.

42. CAPMAS, *Al-Ihsa'at al-thaqafiyya: Al-idha'a wa al-sahafa* (Cairo: CAPMAS, 1983, 1988); see also *Al-Ihsa'at al-thaqafiyya: Al-Kutub wa al-maktabat* (Cairo: CAPMAS, 1987).

43. Quoted in Joel Beinin, "The Egyptian Regime and the Left: Between Islamism and Secularism," *Middle East Report*, no. 185 (November–December 1993), p. 25.

44. Albert Hourani, *Arabic Thought in the Liberal Age, 1798–1939* (Cambridge: Cambridge University Press, 1983), p. 189. Nasr Abu Zayd claims that the GEBO removed a section from another book in the series—by Farah Anton—that called for a secular state in Egypt as well. Bakr and Colla, "Silencing," p. 29.

45. *Al-Jumhuriyya*, 15 July 1993, p. 7.

46. *Al-Akhbar*, 15 July 1993.

47. U.S. Department of State, *Country Reports on Human Rights Practices for 1993* (Washington, D.C.: Government Printing Office, 1994), p. 1171.

48. *Al-Akhbar*, 9 July 1993, p. 1.

49. *Al-Jumhuriyya*, 15 July 1993, p. 7; *al-Wafd*, 19 July 1993, p. 2; *al-Akhbar*, 19 July 1993, p. 6.

50. Muhammad 'Ali Mahgub, minister of religious endowments, quoted in *al-Wafd*, 31 July 1993, p. 2.

51. *Al-Wafd*, 2 August 1993, p. 8.

52. Quoted in *The Economist*, 19 February 1994, p. 45.

53. Auda, "The 'Normalization' of the Islamic Movement," p. 394.

54. Scott Mattoon, "Egypt: Islam by Profession," *The Middle East*, no. 218 (December 1992). See also Auda, "The 'Normalization' of the Islamic Movement," p. 387.

55. Singerman, *Avenues of Participation*, pp. 149–50, 237, 243.

56. Denis Sullivan, *Private Voluntary Organizations*, p. 25.

57. Reuters, 18, 25, 29 July 1995. In August 1993 eight young men were arrested in Minya after having been observed receiving karate and kung fu lessons in the hills above the town. *Al-Ahram*, 5 August 1993, p. 1.

58. Interview, 24 July 1993, pp. 65–66.

59. *Al-Ahram*, 4 August 1993, p. 1; *al-Wafd*, 14 July 1993, p. 1.

60. *Ruz al-Yusuf*, 19 July 1993, p. 11.

61. Muhammad Sulayman, interview, 8 August 1989, pp. 561–62.

62. *Middle East Times—Egypt*, 29 June–5 July 1993, p. 1. For a review of

conspiracy theories, see Nabil Abdel-Fattah, "Cairo Bombings: The Plot Thickens," *al-Ahram Weekly*, 8–14 July 1993, p. 9.

63. *Liwa' al-Islam*, 3 August 1989, p. 49.

64. *The Economist*, 4 July 1992, p. 38.

65. *Al-Ahram*, 26 July 1993, p. 1.

66. Faruq 'Abd al-Majid, "The Police Guard the Application of the Law," *al-Ahram*, 26 July 1993, p. 10.

67. *Al-Akhbar*, 16 July 1993, p. 6; *al-Wafd*, 31 July 1993, p. 2.

68. Shaykh Jad al-Haq 'Ali Jad al-Haq, quoted in *al-Wafd*, 30 July 1993, p. 8; Muhammad 'Ali Mahgub, quoted in *al-Wafd*, 31 July 1993, p. 8.

69. *Al-Wafd*, 30 July 1993, p. 8; *al-Wafd*, 2 August 1993, p. 2; *al-Ahram*, 19 July 1993, p. 10.

70. *Al-Jumhuriyya*, 30 July 1993, p. 7.

71. *Al-Jumhuriyya*, 15 July 1993, p. 29.

Chapter 8. Broken Boundaries and the Politics of Fear

1. Quoted in James Williams, *Education in Egypt Before British Control* (Birmingham, n.p., 1939), p. 79.

2. Spencer, "Moral Education," pp. 112–13.

3. El-Gawhary, "Report from a War Zone," p. 50; *al-Ahram*, 26 July 1993, p. 7.

4. *Al-Ahram*, 31 July 1993, p. 10.

5. Hani Sharif Mahmud, interview, 18 April 1989, pp. 342–44.

6. Joel Beinin, personal communication, 1989.

7. Hani Sharif Mahmud, interview, 9 June 1989, pp. 339–40.

8. Eric Davis, "Ideology, Social Class, and Islamic Radicalism in Modern Egypt," in *From Nationalism to Revolutionary Islam*, ed. Said Amir Arjomand (London: The Macmillan Press, Ltd., 1984), pp. 139–40.

9. Karl Marx, in the introduction to his "Contribution to a Critique of Hegel's *Philosophy of Right*," in *The Marx-Engels Reader*, 2nd ed., ed. Robert C. Tucker (New York: Norton, 1978), p. 54.

10. The section on religion in *Economy and Society* is published in English as *The Sociology of Religion*, trans. Ephraim Fischoff (1922; rpt., Boston: Beacon, 1963). Curiously, Davis does not cite Weber.

11. Davis, "Ideology, Social Class, and Islamic Radicalism," p. 141.

12. Davis, "Ideology, Social Class, and Islamic Radicalism," p. 147.

13. Davis, "Ideology, Social Class, and Islamic Radicalism," p. 146.

14. Saad Eddin Ibrahim, "Anatomy of Egypt's Militant Islamic Groups: Methodological Note and Preliminary Findings," *International Journal of Middle East Studies* 12 (1980), pp. 423–53; Ahmad Abdalla, *The Student Movement*; Fischer and Abedi, *Debating Muslims*, p. 86.

15. Davis, "Ideology, Social Class, and Islamic Radicalism," p. 147.

16. Janet Abu-Lughod, "Rural Migration and Politics in Egypt," p. 324.

17. "The emphasis on a unitary, holistic Islam is very compatible with the overall world-view of the rural *petite-bourgeoisie*. It has been argued that there is

no contradiction between the fact that such a large percentage of Islamic militants have been educated in the natural sciences and still subscribe to radical interpretations of Islam. Since the natural sciences stress an absolute approach to knowledge (either something is right or it is wrong), it is erroneous to assume that a 'modern' education will necessarily erode a traditional consciousness which likewise emphasizes absolute categories of thought." Davis, "Ideology, Social Class, and Islamic Radicalism," p. 146. It is worth noting here that the Egyptian educational system has long been criticized for teaching *all* subjects as if there were an absolute quality to knowledge. The difference between the teaching of literature and of engineering is thus not necessarily very great. It is also worth noting that Hassan al-Banna, Sayyid Qutb, Samia 'Abd al-Rahman, and Layla al-Shamsi were all trained in literature rather than the sciences.

18. The weakness of class analysis in this case becomes manifest in the conceptual effort it takes to squeeze together the various occupations that Davis discusses into a single class category ("bourgeoisie," or, oxymoronically, "rural petite-bourgeoisie") that can experience socioeconomic pressures in a consistent way. Inferring the cognitive needs or social networks of ill-defined classes is a troublesome undertaking. Even when restricted to single occupations, theoretical statements about political susceptibility are always underdetermined. For example, Davis points to the large number of high school teachers involved in the Muslim Brotherhood in rural areas, interpreting their apparent overrepresentation as an indication of kinship relations between urban radicals and rural teachers, concluding with the non sequitur that "Secondary school teacher-training entails considerable religious education which is an indicator of the traditional origin of religious radicals." But there are simpler ways to explain the apparent abundance of teachers in these groups and movements. If data on the representation of teachers in Islamic movements is in fact correct, there are other reasonable explanations of their participation that have to do with personal and organizational strategies rather than with inferences from class background and kinship networks. The first is that Islamist organizations target teachers for recruitment because of their influence over children—and adults—in rural communities (in smaller communities, secondary school teachers are more likely than the general population to be literate and politically aware in the first place). The second is that individuals attracted to the Islamic Trend will tend to select high school teaching as a profession because of its positive social effects. As we saw in the last chapter, Layla al-Shamsi exemplifies this type of linkage, which is likely to be particularly strong in private schools. In the Islamic school where she taught, volunteers from the Islamic activist community played an active part in teaching and administration (one of the volunteers I met was a young man with an Islamic beard, a junior member of the Engineering faculty from Cairo University).

19. Davis, "Ideology, Social Class, and Islamic Radicalism," p. 136.

20. Max Weber, *The Sociology of Religion*, p. 137.

21. Weber, *Sociology of Religion*, p. 71.

22. Weber, *Sociology of Religion*, pp. 125, 137.

23. Engels reacted to early vulgarizations of Marxist theory by criticizing

the fatuous notion of the ideologists that because we deny an independent historical development to the various ideological spheres which play a part in history we also deny them any *effect upon history*. The basis of this is the common undialectical conception of cause and effect as rigidly opposite poles, the total disregarding of interaction. These gentlemen often almost deliberately forget that once a historic element has been brought into the world by other, ultimately economic causes, it reacts, can react on its environment and even on the causes that have given rise to it. (Friedrich Engels to Franz Mehring, 14 July 1893, in *The Marx-Engels Reader*, 2nd ed. Robert Tucker [New York: Norton, 1978], p. 767)

24. Davis, "Ideology, Social Class, and Islamic Radicalism," p. 143.

25. Max Weber, *The Protestant Ethic and the Spirit of Capitalism* (New York: Charles Scribner's Sons, 1958), p. 54.

26. Karl Marx, "The Eighteenth Brumaire of Louis Bonaparte," in *The Marx-Engels Reader*, p. 595.

27. Michael Schudson, *Advertising: The Uneasy Persuasion* (New York: Basic books, 1984).

28. Olivier Roy, *The Failure of Political Islam*, p. 79. See also Hannah Davis's interview with Rabia Bekkar, "Taking up Space in Tlemcen: The Islamist Occupation of Urban Algeria," *Middle East Report*, no. 179 (November–December 1992), pp. 11–15; and Kate Zebiri, "Islamic Revival in Algeria: An Overview," *The Muslim World* 83, 3–4 (July–October 1993), pp. 203–26.

29. Davis, "Ideology, Social Class, and Islamic Radicalism," p. 140.

30. Ellis Goldberg, "Smashing Idols and the State: The Protestant Ethic and Egyptian Sunni Radicalism," *Comparative Studies in Society and History* 31 (1991), pp. 3–35.

31. Goldberg, "Smashing Idols," p. 3.

32. Goldberg, "Smashing Idols," p. 4.

33. Goldberg, "Smashing Idols," p. 28; see also Gilles Kepel, *Muslim Extremism in Egypt*, p. 79.

34. Goldberg, "Smashing Idols," pp. 34–35.

35. Brian Spooner, "Weavers and Dealers: The Authenticity of an Oriental Carpet," in *The Social Life of Things: Commodities in Cultural Perspective*, ed. Arjun Appadurai (Cambridge: Cambridge University Press, 1986), pp. 195–235.

36. Roy, *Failure of Political Islam*, pp. 94–95.

37. Roy, *Failure of Political Islam*, p. 103.

38. See Carlos Ginsburg, *The Cheese and the Worms* (New York: Penguin, 1980).

39. Raouf Abbas Hamed, "Factors Behind the Political Islamic Movement in Egypt," paper delivered at the annual meeting of the Middle East Studies Association of North America, San Antonio, Texas, 24–26 November 1990, p. 10. Dr. Hamed also notes that the summer camps set up by the government to train young people in proper Islam have been prime recruiting grounds for Islamic radical groups.

40. Catherine Lutz and Jane Collins, *Reading National Geographic* (Chicago: University of Chicago Press, 1993), p. 233.

41. Mitchell, *Colonising Egypt*, p. 124.

42. "What seems to be most required for progress . . . is to evolve the best

type of rural school, adapted to the special practical needs of agricultural districts, and when this has been done we may confidently hope to see a considerable increase in the number of boys educated. It must not be forgotten that any hasty or unthought-out development of education in rural districts, unless it is carefully adapted to rural necessities, may imperil the agricultural interests on which the prosperity of the country so largely depends. A rural exodus in Egypt would be an economic and social disaster of considerable magnitude." Kitchener, Annual Report, *Parl. Pap.*, 1912, vol. 121, p. 4.

43. Lecky, *Democracy and Liberty*, vol. 1, p. 319. "It is by no means desirable," he wrote one page earlier, "that the flower of the working class, or their children, should learn to despise manual labour and the simple, inexpensive habits of their parents, in order to become very commonplace doctors, attorneys, clerks, or newspaper writers." Perhaps the flower of the working class were listening to the contemporary equivalent of Willie Nelson's sage advice, "Mamas, Don't Let Your Babies Grow Up to Be Cowboys," in which medicine and law are compared favorably to the simple, inexpensive habits of playing guitar and riding around in old pickup trucks.

44. Lecky, *Democracy and Liberty*, vol. 1, pp. 319–20.

45. Cromer, Annual Report, *Parl. Pap.*, 1907, vol. 100, p. 630.

46. Cromer, Annual Report, *Parl. Pap.*, 1903, vol. 87, p. 1011; Annual Report, *Parl. Pap.*, 1906, vol. 137, p. 566. Cf. Bowring,

> No sooner has a boy learned to read and to write, than he is unwilling to pursue any trade, whatever prospects it may offer of reputation, usefulness, or even wealth. The boy will rather be a scribe with small, than an artisan with large, emoluments. To obtain the name of effendi is an object of higher ambition than to lay the foundation even of opulence. This defect pervades the whole of Oriental society, and is an impassable barrier to the advance of the general prosperity. ("Report on Egypt and Candia," p. 137)

47. Cromer, Annual Report, *Parl. Pap.*, 1906, pp. 720–21.

48. Ministry of Education, *Report of the Elementary Education Commission*, p. 40.

49. "Further Correspondences Respecting Reorganization in Egypt," *Parl. Pap.*, 1883, vol. 83, p. 47.

50. Tsing, *In the Realm of the Diamond Queen*, p. 87.

51. "Government of the Indian Empire," *Edinburgh Review* 159 (January–April 1884), pp. 11–12.

52. "[I]deas about separating, purifying, demarcating . . . have as their main function to impose system on an inherently untidy experience. It is only by exaggerating the difference between within and without, above and below, male and female, with and against, that a semblance of order is created." Douglas, *Purity and Danger*, p. 4.

53. Douglas, *Purity and Danger*, pp. 96, 104.

54. Roger Owen, "Anthropology and Imperial Administration: Sir Alfred Lyall and the Official Use of Theories of Social Change Developed in India after 1857," in *Anthropology and the Colonial Encounter*, ed. Talal Asad (London: Ithaca Press), pp. 241–42.

55. Sir Henry Sumner Maine, *Ancient Law* (n.p.: Dorset Press, 1986 [1861]), p. 140.

56. Majeed, *Ungoverned Imaginings*, p. 23.

57. Owen, "Anthropology and Imperial Administration," p. 230.

58. Cromer, Annual Report, *Parl. Pap.*, 1895, vol. 109, p. 12. Quoted in Owen, "Anthropology and Imperial Administration," p. 242.

59. Majeed, *Ungoverned Imaginings*, p. 148.

60. Jeremy Bentham, "Of the Influence of Time and Place in Matters of Legislation," in *The Works of Jeremy Bentham*, ed John Bowring, p. 191. See Majeed, *Ungoverned Imaginings*, p. 183; for Ottoman understandings of legal reform during the Tanzimat period, see Messick, *The Calligraphic State*, p. 64.

61. Mitchell, *Colonising Egypt*, pp. 156–60.

62. One interesting, almost parenthetical, result of schooling's growing importance to the Egyptian economy was a new way of describing educated individuals that matched them to their function. After European training, the native was transformed metaphorically from an untamed beast into a handy tool, a commodity that could be traded on the open market. In the Annual Report of 1903 (*Parl. Pap.*, vol. 87, p. 1034), Cromer quoted Mr. Currie, the director general of education for the Sudan, on his "heartfelt pity" for the beleaguered local administrators who had to rely on Egyptian help:

> Their clerical staff is beyond description bad. Add to this the fact that it is proportionately expensive and absolutely unacclimatized, and I think the need for higher primary schools, as a matter of urgency, is made out. In a couple of years, even without the institution of any beginning of secondary education, these schools will turn out a product infinitely better than is often found here at present, and, it is important to remember, a product at once acclimatized and comparatively cheap.

Though the mechanical analogy was not restricted to official usage, neither was it universally praised. Florence Nightingale, writing to her mother after an 1850 visit to a convent school in Alexandria, recalled with distaste "the patent improved-man-making principle at home—the machine warranted to turn out children wholesale, like pins, with patent heads,—I did not wonder at the small success of our education." Nightingale, *Letters*, p. 204. As early as 1829 Thomas Carlyle characterized his times as The Mechanical Age, both because of the booming metallic din of factory machinery and because of "the deep, almost exclusive faith we have in Mechanism . . . in the Politics of this time. . . . We term it indeed, in ordinary language, the Machine of Society, and talk of it as the grand working wheel from which all private machines must derive, or to which they must adapt, their movements." "Signs of the Times," in his *Selected Writings*, ed. Alan Shelston (New York: Penguin, 1971), p. 70.

63. I owe this and part of the succeeding discussion to Christopher Herbert's *Culture and Anomie*.

64. Herbert, *Culture and Anomie*, pp. 36–8.

65. Herbert, *Culture and Anomie*, pp. 39–40.

66. Mitchell, *Colonising Egypt*, p. 175.

67. W. Cooke Taylor, ca. 1840, quoted in Herbert, *Culture and Anomie*, p. 62.

68. Herbert, *Culture and Anomie*, pp. 64–65.

69. In addition to Fabian's *Time and the Other*, see Adam Kuper, *The Invention of Primitive Society: Transformations of an Illusion* (London: Routledge, 1988).

70. Herbert, *Culture and Anomie*, pp. 65–66.

71. In 1988 an international conference in Cairo actually contained a discussion between Arab intellectuals about whether peasants did or did not have "culture," so such perspectives have hardly disappeared from the intellectual landscape.

72. Educational Planning Unit, Ministry of Education, Government of Egypt, "Reform of the Educational System of Egypt: A Sector Assessment," draft, USAID Development Information Center, 8 January 1990, pp. 14, 106. See also Dr. Ahmed Fathy Surour, *Towards Education Reform in Egypt: A Strategy for Reform and Examples of Implementation, 1987–1990* (Cairo: Al-Ahram Commercial Presses, 1991).

73. Hamed, "Factors Behind the Political Islamic Movement," p. 1.

74. Saadek Samaan, an Egyptian educator writing in the early years of the Nasser period, wrote that reactionaries like Hasan al-Banna "are advocating a strong theocracy modeled after that of the ninth-century society of Arabia," *Value Reconstruction and Egyptian Education* (New York: Bureau of Publications, Teacher's College, Columbia University, 1955), p. 19.

75. Galal Amin, "Migration, Inflation and Social Mobility: A Sociological Interpretation of Egypt's Current Economic and Political Crisis," in *Egypt Under Mubarak*, ed. Charles Tripp and Roger Owen (London: Routledge, 1989), p. 118.

76. ʿAbd Allah Imam, "Al-Khawarij al-judud!" *Ruz al-Yusuf*, 17 April 1989, pp. 30–33; Muhammad Saʿid al-ʿAshmawi, "Al-Siraʿ al-hadari fi al-Islam," *al-Azmina*, January–February 1989, pp. 18–27. Talal Asad has pointed out that this representation of Islamic society as composed of "protagonists engaged in a dramatic struggle" is widespread in the anthropology and historiography of Islam; "The Idea of an Anthropology of Islam." Center for Contemporary Arab Studies, Occasional Papers Series, Georgetown University, 1986, p. 8.

77. Even the unconscious motivations that scholars like Davis impute to modern-day radicals match quite precisely the idiom of recapturing the past that Raymond Williams has traced through British "pastoral" literature in *The Country and the City* (New York: Oxford University Press, 1973), pp. 290–304.

78. Amira el-Azhary Sonbol, "Egypt," in *The Politics of Islamic Revivalism*, ed. Shireen Hunter (Bloomington: Indiana University Press, 1988), p. 35. Her faulty perception of Islamic instruction in Egypt is due in part to misunderstanding the reason why different kinds of Islam are not discussed. For pedagogical purposes, there *is* only one kind of Islam.

79. An editorial in *al-Ahram*, quoted in Charles Hirschkind, "Culture and Counterterrorism: Notes on Contemporary Public Discourse in Egypt," paper presented at the 1993 meetings of the Middle East Studies Association, Research Triangle Park, North Carolina.

80. Charles Hirschkind, personal communication. For an outstanding survey of media depictions of education as a modernizing force, see Walter Armbrust, *Mass Culture and Modernism in Egypt* (Cambridge: Cambridge University Press, 1996). James P. Young has pointed out, after Jacques Ellul, that not only is education no prophylactic against propaganda, but it "makes propaganda possible, helps propaganda accomplish its ends, and is in many ways itself a form

of propaganda." "Intimate Allies in Migration: Education and Propaganda in a Philippine Village," *Comparative Education Review* 26 (1982), p. 218.

81. Olivier Roy sees the resurrection of the Sufi ideal of the *insan kamil*, or "ideal man," as a feature of Islamist thought, but in fact its resurrection can be traced to the work of modern educational elites generally; see his *Failure of Political Islam*, p. 101.

82. With apologies to Melford Spiro, on whose paper title, "Religious Systems as Culturally Constituted Defense Mechanisms" (in *Context and Meaning in Anthropology*, ed. Melford Spiro [New York: The Free Press, 1965], pp. 100–13), this phrase is modeled.

83. Hani Sharif Mahmud, interview, 18 April 1989, p. 342.

84. MacLeod, *Accommodating Protest*, p. 110.

85. Hoffman, "Muslim Fundamentalists: Psychosocial Profiles," p. 221.

86. Hani Sharif Mahmud, interview, 18 April 1989, p. 342.

87. John Aloysius Farrel, "Clinton Calls for Religion in Schools," *Boston Globe*, 13 July 1995, p. 1.

88. For a discussion of the sources of the American government's understanding of the category "religion," see James Tabor and Eugene Gallagher, *Why Waco? Cults and the Battle for Religious Freedom in America* (Berkeley: University of California Press, 1995).

89. Michael Herzfeld, *The Social Production of Indifference: Exploring the Symbolic Roots of Western Bureaucracy* (New York: Berg, 1992).

90. Victoria Bernal, "Gender, Culture, and Capitalism: Women and the Remaking of Islamic 'Tradition' in a Sudanese Village," *Comparative Studies in Society and History* 36 (1994), p. 42.

Bibliography

Religious Studies Textbooks in Arabic

The following religious studies textbooks were used during the 1988–89 and 1989–90 school years in Egypt. They are ordered here, and referred to in the notes, by grade level (e.g., "fourth grade religious studies textbook"). All are published in Cairo by the Central Agency for School and University Books and Instructional Materials (al-Jihaz al-markazi lil-kutub al-jamiʿiyya wa al-madrasiyya wa al-wasaʾil al-taʿlimiyya).

Yunis, Dr. Fathi ʿAli, et al. *Al-Tarbiya al-islamiyya*. Lil-saff al-awwal min al-taʿlim al-asasi [first grade religious studies textbook], 1988–89.
al-Naqa, Dr. Mahmud Kamil, et al. *Al-Tarbiya al-islamiyya*. Al-halqa al-awwal min al-taʿlim al-asasi, al-saff al-thani [second grade religious studies textbook], 1988–89.
Shahhat, Dr. ʿAbd Allah Mahmud, et al. *Al-Tarbiya al-islamiyya*. Al-halqa al-awwal min al-taʿlim al-asasi, al-saff al-thalith [third grade religious studies textbook], 1988–89.
Yunis, Dr. Fathi ʿAli, et al. *Al-Tarbiya al-islamiyya*. Al-halqa al-ibtidaʾiyya min al-taʿlim al-asasi, al-saff al-rabiʿ [fourth grade religious studies textbook], 1987.
———. *Al-Tarbiya al-islamiyya*. Al-halqa al-ibtidaʾiyya min al-taʿlim al-asasi, al-saff al-khamis [fifth grade religious studies textbook], 1987–88.
al-Dawwah, Mahmud al-Sayyid, et al. *Al-Tarbiya al-islamiyya*. Al-saff al-sabiʿ min al-halqa al-thaniya min al-taʿlim al-asasi [seventh grade religious studies textbook], 1986–87.
———. *Al-Tarbiya al-islamiyya*. Al-saff al-thamin min al-halqa al-thaniya min al-taʿlim al-asasi [eighth grade religious studies textbook], 1987–88.
ʿAlish, Muhammad Sayf al-Din, et al. *Al-Tarbiya al-islamiyya*. Al-saff al-tasiʿ

min al-halqa al-thaniya min al-ta'lim al-asasi [ninth grade religious studies textbook], 1988–89.
Shahata, Dr. 'Abd Allah Mahmud, et al. *Al-Tarbiya al-islamiyya*. Lil-saff al-awwal al-thanawi [tenth grade religious studies textbook], 1986–87.
Fawzi, Dr. Rif'at. *Al-Tarbiya al-islamiyya*. Lil-saff al-thani al-thanawi [eleventh grade religious studies textbook], 1986–87.
———. *Al-Tarbiya al-islamiyya*. Lil-saff al-thalith al-thanawi [twelfth grade religious studies textbook], 1989–90.

Other Works in Arabic

'Abd al-Karim, Ahmad 'Izzat. *Tarikh al-ta'lim fi 'asr Muhammad 'Ali*. Cairo: Maktaba al-nahda al-Misriyya, 1938.
'Abd al-Latif, Muhammad, and Dr. Yahya 'Abduh. *Al-'Udhun al-kabira*. Cairo: Safir, n.d.
Ahmad, Dr. Rif'at Sayyid. *Al-Din wa al-dawla wa al-thawra*. Cairo: al-Dar al-sharqiyya, 1989.
'Alwan, 'Abdallah Nasih. *Tarbiya al-awlad fi al-Islam*. Cairo: Dar al-Islam, 1985.
'Ashmawi, Muhammad Sa'id. "Al-Sira' al-hadari fi al-islam". *Al-Azmina*, January–February 1989, pp. 18–27.
Central Agency for Public Mobilization and Statistics (CAPMAS) [al-Jihaz al-markazi li-ta'bi'a al-'amma wa al-ihsa']. *Al-Ihsa'at al-thaqafiyya: Al-Idha'a wa al-sahafa*. Cairo: CAPMAS, 1983, 1985, 1987.
———. *Al-Ihsa'at al-thaqafiyya: Al-Kutub wa al-maktabat*. Cairo: CAPMAS, 1987.
Guenena, Nemat [Na'ma Allah Junayna]. *Tandhim al-jihad: Hal huwa al-badil al-islami fi Misr?* Cairo: Dar al-hurriyya, 1988.
al-Hamadi, Yusuf, Muhammad Mukhtar Amin Mukram, and Dr. 'Abd al-Maqsud Shalqami. *Tarbiya al-Muslim*. Lil-saff al-sadis al-ibtida'i. Cairo: al-Jihaz al-markazi lil-kutub al-jami'iyya wa al-madrasiyya wa al-wasa'il al-ta'limiyya, 1981.
al-Hamadi, Yusuf, and Muhammad Shahhat Wahdan. *Kitab al-tarbiya al-diniyya al-islamiyya*. Lil-saff al-sadis al-ibtida'i. Cairo: al-Hay'a al-'amma li-shu'un al-mutabi' al-amiriyya, 1976.
al-Hariri, Hasan, Muhammad Mustafa Zaydan, Alyas Barsum Matar, and Dr. Sayyid Khayr Allah. *Al-Madrasa al-ibtida'iyya*. Cairo: Maktaba al-nahda al-Misriyya, 1966.
Imam, 'Abd Allah. "Al-Khawarij al-judud!" *Ruz al-Yusuf*, 17 April 1989, pp. 30–33.
Khalaq Allah, Ahmad Rabi' al-Hamid. *Al-Fikar al-tarbawi wa tatbiqatihi laday jama'a al-ikhwan al-muslimin*. Cairo: Maktaba Wahba, 1983.
al-Khashab, Samia Mustafa. *Al-Shabab wa al-tayyar al-islami fi al-mujtama' al-Misri al-mu'asir: Dirasa ijtima'iyya midaniyya*. Cairo: Dar al-thaqafa al-'arabiyya, 1988.
Al-Muslim al-saghir fi 'alam al-talwin. Cairo: Safir, n.d.

al-Qabbani, Isma'il Mahmud. *Siyasa al-ta'lim fi Misr*. Cairo: Lajna al-ta'lif wa al-tarjama wa al-nashr, 1944.

Wahda thaqafa al-tifl, and Ahmad 'Abd al-'Aziz. *Kitab al-muslim al-saghir 2*. Cairo: Safir, 1987.

Wizara al-ma'arif al-'umumiyya. *Manhaj al-ta'lim al-thanawi lil-madaris al-banin wa al-banat*. Cairo: al-Mutaba'a al-'amiriyya, 1930.

Yusuf, 'Abd al-Tuwab, and Dr. Yahya 'Abduh. *Al-Sufuf al-munadhdhama*. Cairo: Safir, 1988.

Works in English and French

Abdalla, Ahmed. *The Student Movement and National Politics in Egypt, 1923–1973*. London: Al Saqi Books, 1985.

———. "Egypt's Islamists and the State: From Complicity to Confrontation". *Middle East Report*, no. 183 (July–August 1993), pp. 2–3.

Abu-Lughod, Janet. "Rural Migration and Politics in Egypt". In *Rural Politics and Social Change in the Middle East*, ed. Richard Antoun and Ilya Harik. Bloomington: Indiana University Press, 1972.

Abu-Lughod, Lila. "Zones of Theory in the Anthropology of the Arab World". *Annual Review of Anthropology*, no. 18 (1989), pp. 267–306.

———. "Finding a Place for Islam: Egyptian Television Serials and the National Interest". *Public Culture* 5 (1993), pp. 493–513.

———. *Writing Women's Worlds: Bedouin Stories*. Berkeley: University of California Press, 1993.

Adams, Charles C. *Islam and Modernism in Egypt*. New York: Russell & Russell, 1968.

Ahmed, Leila. *Women and Gender in Islam*. New Haven: Yale University Press, 1992.

'Ali, A. Yusuf. *The Holy Qur'an*. Brentwood, Md.: Amana Corporation, 1983.

Amin, Galal. "Migration, Inflation, and Social Mobility: A Sociological Interpretation of Egypt's Current Economic and Political Crisis". In *Egypt under Mubarak*, ed. Charles Tripp and Roger Owen, pp. 103–20. London: Routledge, 1989.

Ammar, Hamed. *Growing Up in an Egyptian Village*. London: Routledge & Kegan Paul, Ltd., 1954.

Anderson, Benedict. *Imagined Communities: Reflections on the Origin and Spread of Nationalism*. London: Verso, 1983.

Appadurai, Arjun. "Introduction: Commodities and the Politics of Value". In *The Social Life of Things: Commodities in Cultural Perspective*, ed. Arjun Appadurai, pp. 3–63. Cambridge: Cambridge University Press, 1986.

Arberry, A. J. *The Koran Interpreted*. New York: Macmillan, 1955.

Armbrust, Walter. *Mass Culture and Modernism in Egypt*. Cambridge: Cambridge University Press, 1996.

Asad, Talal. *The Idea of an Anthropology of Islam*. Center for Contemporary Arab Studies, Occasional Papers Series. Washington, D.C.: Georgetown University, 1986.

Auda, Gehad. "The "Normalization" of the Islamic Movement in Egypt from the 1970s to the Early 1990s". In *Accounting for Fundamentalisms*. Vol. 4 of *The Fundamentalism Project*, ed. Martin Marty and R. Scott Appleby, pp. 374–412. Chicago: University of Chicago Press, 1994.

Badran, Adnan, ed. *At the Crossroads: Education in the Middle East*. New York: Paragon House, 1989.

Bakr, Ayman, and Elliot Colla. "Silencing Is at the Heart of My Case". Interview with Nasr Hamid Abu Zayd. *Middle East Report*, no. 185 (November–December 1993), pp. 27–29.

Barrington, John M. "Cultural Adaptation and Maori Educational Policy: the African Connection". *Comparative Education Review* 20 (1976), pp. 1–10.

Beinin, Joel. "The Egyptian Regime and the Left: Between Islamism and Secularism". *Middle East Report*, no. 185 (November–December 1993), pp. 25–26.

Bentham, Jeremy. *The Works of Jeremy Bentham*. Ed. John Bowring. 1838–43. Rpt., New York: Russell & Russell, 1962.

Berger, Peter. "Some Second Thoughts on Substantive Versus Functional Definitions of Religion". *Journal for the Scientific Study of Religion* 13 (1974), pp. 125–33.

Bernal, Victoria. "Gender, Culture, and Capitalism: Women and the Remaking of Islamic "Tradition" in a Sudanese Village". *Comparative Studies in Society and History* 36 (1994), pp. 36–67.

Boktor, Amir. *School and Society in the Valley of the Nile*. Cairo: Elias' Modern Press, 1936.

———. *The Development and Expansion of Education in the U.A.R.* Cairo: American University in Cairo Press, 1963.

Bourdieu, Pierre. *Outline of a Theory of Practice*. Cambridge: Cambridge University Press, 1977.

———. "Authorized Language: The Social Conditions of the Effectiveness of Ritual Discourse". In *Language and Symbolic Power*. Cambridge, Mass.: Harvard University Press, 1991.

———. *The Field of Cultural Production: Essays in Art and Literature*. New York: Columbia University Press, 1993.

Bourdieu, Pierre, and Jean-Claude Passeron. *Reproduction in Education, Society, and Culture*. London: Sage, 1977.

Bowen, John. "*Salat* in Indonesia: The Social Meanings of an Islamic Ritual". *Man*, n.s., 24 (1989), pp. 600–619.

———. "Elaborating Scriptures: Cain and Abel in Gayo Society". *Man*, n.s., 27, 3 (1992), pp. 495–516.

———. *Muslims Through Discourse: Religion and Ritual in Gayo Society*. Princeton: Princeton University Press, 1993.

Bowring, John. "Report on Egypt and Candia". In House of Commons, *Parliamentary Papers*, 1840, vol. 21.

Brabazon, Lord. "Decay of Bodily Strength in Towns". *The Nineteenth Century* 21 (1887), pp. 673–76.

Brink, Judy H. "Changing Child Rearing Patterns in an Egyptian Village". Pa-

per presented at the annual meeting of the Middle East Studies Association of North America, San Antonio, Texas, 23–26 November 1990.
Brown, Nathan. *Peasant Politics in Modern Egypt*. New Haven: Yale University Press, 1990.
———. "Who Abolished Corvée Labor in Egypt and Why?" *Past and Present*, no. 144 (1994), pp. 116–37.
Bulliet, Richard. *Islam: The View from the Edge*. New York: Columbia University Press, 1994.
Carré, Olivier. *Enseignement islamique et idéal socialiste*. Beirut: Dar el-Machreq Editeurs, 1974.
Cassandra. "The Impending Crisis in Egypt". *Middle East Journal* 49 (1995), pp. 9–27.
Central Agency for Public Mobilization and Statistics [CAPMAS]. *Statistical Yearbook, Arab Republic of Egypt, 1988*. Cairo: CAPMAS, 1988.
Cochran, Judith. *Education in Egypt*. London: Croom Helm, 1986.
Cohn, Norman. *Warrant for Genocide*. Brown Judaic Studies 23. Chico, Calif.: Scholar's Press, 1981.
Cromer, Lord [Sir Evelyn Baring]. *Modern Egypt*. 2 vols. New York: The Macmillan Co., 1908.
———. *Ancient and Modern Imperialism*. London: John Murray, 1910.
Cunningham, Alfred. *To-Day in Egypt*. London: Hurst & Blackett, 1912.
Cunynghame, H. "The Present State of Education in Egypt". *Journal of the Royal Asiatic Society of Great Britain and Ireland*, n.s., 19 (1887), pp. 223–237.
Davis, Eric. "Ideology, Social Class, and Islamic Radicalism in Modern Egypt". In *From Nationalism to Revolutionary Islam*, ed. Said Amir Arjomand, pp. 134–57. London: The Macmillan Press, Ltd., 1984.
Delaney, Carol. *The Seed and the Soil: Gender and Cosmology in Turkish Village Society*. Berkeley: University of California Press, 1991.
Dickens, Charles. *Hard Times*. 1854. Rpt., New York: Bantam, 1981.
Dor, V. Edouard. *L'Instruction publique en Egypte*. Paris: A. Lacroix, Verboeckhoven et cie., Editeurs, 1872.
Douglas, Mary. *Purity and Danger*. London: Routledge & Kegan Paul, 1966.
Durkheim, Emile. *Education and Sociology*. Trans. Sherwood D. Fox. Glencoe, Ill.: The Free Press, 1956.
———. *The Evolution of Educational Thought*. Trans. Peter Collins. London: Routledge & Kegan Paul, 1977.
Early, Evelyn. *Baladi Women of Cairo: Playing with an Egg and a Stone*. Boulder, Colo.: Lynne Reiner Publishers, 1993.
Eccel, A. Chris. *Egypt, Islam, and Social Change: Al-Azhar in Conflict and Accommodation*. Berlin: Klaus Schwarz Verlag, 1984.
Educational Planning Unit, Ministry of Education, Government of Egypt. "Reform of the Educational System of Egypt: A Sector Assessment". Draft, USAID Development Information Center, Cairo, 8 January 1990.
Edward, Cardinal Archbishop Henry. "Is the Education Act of 1870 a Just Law?" *The Nineteenth Century* 12 (December 1882), pp. 958–68.
Eickelman, Dale. *Moroccan Islam: Tradition and Society in a Pilgrimage Center*. Austin: University of Texas Press, 1976.

———. "The Art of Memory: Islamic Education and Its Social Reproduction". *Comparative Studies in Society and History* 20 (1978), pp. 485–516.

———. *Knowledge and Power in Morocco*. Princeton: Princeton University Press, 1985.

———. "Identité nationale et discours religieux en Oman". In *Intellectuels et militants de l'Islam contemporain*, ed. Gilles Kepel and Yann Richard, pp. 103–28. Paris: Seuil, 1990.

———. "Counting and Surveying an "Inner" Omani Community: Hamra al-ʿAbriyin". In *Tribe and State: Essays in Honour of David Montgomery Hart*, ed. E. G. G. Joffe and C. R. Pennel, pp. 253–77. Wisbeck, England: MENAS Press, 1991.

———. "Mass Higher Education and the Religious Imagination in Contemporary Arab Societies". *American Ethnologist* 19 (1992), pp. 643–54.

Fabian, Johannes. *Time and the Other: How Anthropology Makes Its Object*. New York: Columbia University Press, 1983.

Faksh, Mahmud A. "The Consequences of the Introduction and Spread of Modern Education: Education and National Integration in Egypt". In *Modern Egypt: Studies in Politics and Society*, ed. Elie Kedourie and Sylvia G. Haim, pp. 42–55. London: Frank Cass & Co., Ltd., 1980.

Fandy, Mamoun. "Egypt's Islamic Group: Regional Revenge?" *Middle East Journal* 48 (1994), 607–625.

Fischer, Michael M. J. *Iran: From Religious Dispute to Revolution*. Cambridge, Mass.: Harvard University Press, 1980.

Fischer, Michael M. J., and Mehdi Abedi. *Debating Muslims: Cultural Dialogues in Postmodernity and Tradition*. Madison: University of Wisconsin Press, 1990.

Flores, Alexander. "Egypt: A New Secularism?" *Middle East Report*, no. 153 (July–August 1988), 27–29.

Foley, Douglas. *Learning Capitalist Culture: Deep in the Heart of Tejas*. Philadelphia: University of Pennsylvania Press, 1990.

Foster, Robert J. "Take Care of Public Telephones: Moral Education and Nation-State Formation in Papua New Guinea". *Public Culture* 4 (1992), pp. 31–45.

Foucault, Michel. *The Order of Things: An Archaeology of the Human Sciences*. New York: Vintage, 1970.

———. *Discipline and Punish*. Trans. Alan Sheridan. New York: Pantheon, 1977.

———. *Politics, Philosophy, Culture: Interviews and Other Writings, 1977–1984*. Ed. Lawrence D. Kritzman. New York: Routledge, 1988.

Gaffney, Patrick. *The Prophet's Pulpit: Islamic Preaching in Contemporary Egypt*. Berkeley: University of California Press, 1994.

Galt, Russell. *The Effects of Centralization on Education in Modern Egypt*. Cairo: American University in Cairo, Department of Education, 1936.

el-Gawhary, Karim. "Report from a War Zone: Gamaʿat vs. Government in Upper Egypt". *Middle East Report*, no. 194–95 (May–June/July–August 1995), pp. 49–51.

Geertz, Clifford. *Islam Observed: Religious Development in Morocco and Indonesia*. Chicago: University of Chicago Press, 1968.
Ginsburg, Carlos. *The Cheese and the Worms*. New York: Penguin, 1980.
Goldberg, Ellis. "Smashing Idols and the State: The Protestant Ethic and Egyptian Sunni Radicalism". *Comparative Studies in Society and History* 33 (1991), pp. 3–35.
Gonzalez-Quijano, Yves. *Les Gens du livre: Champ intellectuel et édition dans l'Egypte républicaine (1952–1993)*. Thèse de doctorat de l'Institut d'études politiques de Paris, Mention Science Politiques, 1994.
el-Guindi, Fadwa. "Veiling Infitah with Muslim Ethic: Egypt's Contemporary Islamic Movement". *Social Problems* 28 (1981), pp. 465–85.
Hamed, Raouf Abbas. "Factors Behind the Political Islamic Movement in Egypt". Paper presented at the annual meeting of the Middle East Studies Association of North America, San Antonio, Texas, 23–26 November 1990.
Handelman, Don. *Models and Mirrors: Towards an Anthropology of Public Events*. Cambridge: Cambridge University Press, 1990.
Hannerz, Ulf. *Cultural Complexity: Studies in the Social Organization of Meaning*. New York: Columbia University Press, 1992.
Harik, Ilya. *The Political Mobilization of Peasants*. Bloomington: Indiana University Press, 1974.
Hechmat, Ahmad Pacha. *Questions d'education et d'enseignement*. Cairo: n.p., 1914.
Heggoy, Alf Andrew. "Education in French Algeria: An Essay on Cultural Conflict". *Comparative Education Review* 17 (1973), pp. 180–97.
Heilbrun, Carolyn G. *Writing a Woman's Life*. New York: Ballantine, 1988.
Herbert, Christopher. *Culture and Anomie: Ethnographic Imagination in the Nineteenth Century*. Chicago: University of Chicago Press, 1991.
Herzfeld, Michael. *The Social Production of Indifference: Exploring the Symbolic Roots of Western Bureaucracy*. New York: Berg, 1992.
Heyworth-Dunne, James. *An Introduction to the History of Education in Modern Egypt*. London: Luzac & Co., 1938.
el-Hilali, Neguib. *Report on Educational Reform in Egypt*. Cairo: Government Press, Boulaq, 1943.
Himmelfarb, Gertrude. *Darwin and the Darwinian Revolution*. New York: Norton, 1962.
Hirschkind, Charles. "Culture and Counterterrorism: Notes on Contemporary Public Discourse in Egypt". Paper presented at the 1993 meeting of the Middle East Studies Association of North America, Research Triangle Park, North Carolina.
Hobsbawm, Eric. "Mass-Producing Traditions: Europe, 1870–1914". In *The Invention of Tradition*, ed. Eric Hobsbawm and Terence Ranger, pp. 263–307. Cambridge: Cambridge University Press, 1983.
Hoffman, Valerie. "Muslim Fundamentalists: Psychosocial Profiles". In *Fundamentalisms Comprehended*. Vol. 5 of *The Fundamentalism Project*, ed. Martin Marty and R. Scott Appleby, pp. 199–230. Chicago: University of Chicago Press, 1995.

Hofstadter, Richard. *Social Darwinism in American Thought*. Boston: Beacon Press, 1955.

Holland, Dorothy, and Margaret A. Eisenhart. *Educated in Romance: Women, Achievement, and College Culture*. Chicago: University of Chicago Press, 1990.

Horvatich, Patricia. "Ways of Knowing Islam". *American Ethnologist* 21, 4 (1994), pp. 811–826.

Hourani, Albert. *Arabic Thought in the Liberal Age, 1798–1939*. Cambridge: Cambridge University Press, 1983.

Houtsonen, Jarmo. "Traditional Qur'anic Education in a Southern Moroccan Village". *International Journal of Middle East Studies* 26 (1994), pp. 489–500.

Howeidy, Amira, Mona al-Nahhas, and Mona Anis. "The Persecution of Abu Zeid". *Al-Ahram Weekly*, 22–28 June 1995. Reprinted in *World Press Review*45 (October 1995).

Humes, Walter. "Evolution and Educational Theory in the Nineteenth Century". In *The Wider Domain of Evolutionary Thought*, ed. D. Oldroyd and I. Lanham, pp. 27–56. N.p.: D. Reidel Publishing Co., 1983.

Hurt, J. S. "Drill, Discipline, and the Elementary School Ethos". In *Popular Education and Socialization in the Nineteenth Century*, ed. Phillip McCann, pp. 167–92. London: Methuen & Co., Ltd., 1977.

Hyde, Georgie D. M.. *Education in Modern Egypt: Ideals and Realities*. London: Routledge & Kegan Paul, 1978.

Ibrahim, Saad Eddin. "Anatomy of Egypt's Militant Islamic Groups: Methodological Note and Preliminary Findings". *International Journal of Middle East Studies* 12 (1980), pp. 423–53.

Issawi, Charles. *Egypt: An Economic and Social Analysis*. London: Oxford University Press, 1947.

Jefferson, Carter. "Worker Education in England and France, 1800–1914". *Comparative Studies in Society and History* 4 (1964), pp. 345–66.

Johnston, Rev. James, F.S.S., ed. *Report of the Centenary Conference on the Protestant Missions of the World*. London: James Nisbet & Co., 1889.

Jones, Sidney. "Arabic Instruction and Literacy in Javanese Muslim Schools". *International Journal of the Sociology of Language*, no. 42 (1983), pp. 83–94.

Kabbaj, Mohammed Mostafa. "Traditional Child Socialization and the Incursion of Mass Communication in Morocco". *International Social Science Journal* 31 (1979), pp. 429–43.

Katz, Michael B. *The Irony of Early School Reform*. Cambridge, Mass.: Harvard University Press, 1968.

Kelabora, Lambert. "Assumptions Underlying Religious Instruction in Indonesia". *Comparative Education* 15 (1979), pp. 325–39.

Kepel, Gilles. *Muslim Extremism in Egypt*. Berkeley: University of California Press, 1985.

Khalid, Adeeb. "The Politics of Muslim Cultural Reform: Jadidism in Tsarist Central Asia". Ph.D. diss., Department of History, University of Wisconsin at Madison, 1993.

Kinsey, David C. "Efforts for Educational Synthesis under Colonial Rule: Egypt and Tunisia". *Comparative Education Review* 15 (1971), pp. 172–87.
Kour, Z. H. *The History of Aden, 1839–72*. London: Frank Cass & Co., Ltd., 1981.
Kuhnke, LaVerne. *Lives at Risk*. Berkeley: University of California Press, 1990.
Kuper, Adam. *The Invention of Primitive Society: Transformations of an Illusion*. London: Routledge, 1988.
Lambert, Agnes. "Thrift among the Children". *The Nineteenth Century* 19 (April 1886), pp. 539–60.
Lancaster, Joseph. *Improvements in Education as It Respects the Industrious Classes of the Community*. 3rd ed. 1805. Rpt., Clifton, N.J.: Augustus M. Kelley Publishers, 1973.
Lancaster, William. *The Rwala Bedouin Today*. Cambridge: Cambridge University Press, 1981.
Lane, Edward W. *Manners and Customs of the Modern Egyptians*. 1860. Rpt., London: J. M. Dent & Sons Ltd., 1963.
Laqueur, Thomas Walter. *Religion and Respectability: Sunday Schools and Working Class Culture, 1780–1850*. New Haven: Yale University Press, 1976.
Lavie, Smadar. *The Poetics of Military Occupation: Mzeini Allegories of Identity*. Berkeley: University of California Press, 1990.
Leathers, Charles G., and J. Patrick Raines. "Adam Smith on Competitive Religious Markets". *History of Political Economy* 24, 2 (1992), pp. 499–513.
Lecky, William. *Democracy and Liberty*. 2 vols. New York: Longmans, Green & Co., 1896.
Lerner, Daniel. *The Passing of Traditional Society*. New York: Free Press, 1964.
Lutz, Catherine, and Jane Collins. *Reading National Geographic*. Chicago: University of Chicago Press, 1993.
Lyall, Alfred. "Government of the Indian Empire". *Edinburgh Review* 159 (January–April 1884).
Lyotard, Jean-François. *The Postmodern Condition: A Report on Knowledge*. Trans. Geoff Bennington and Brian Massumi. Minneapolis: University of Minnesota Press, 1984 (1979).
———. *The Postmodern Explained: Correspondence 1982–1985*. Trans. Don Barry et al. Minneapolis: University of Minnesota Press, 1992.
Macaulay, Thomas Babington. *The Works of Lord Macaulay, Complete*. Ed. Lady Trevelyan. Vol. 8. London: Longman, Green, & Co., 1866.
MacLeod, Arlene Elowe. *Accommodating Protest: Working Women, the New Veiling, and Change in Cairo*. New York: Columbia University Press, 1991.
Mahfouz, Naguib. *Midaq Alley*. Washington, D.C.: Three Continents Press, 1989.
Maine, Sir Henry Sumner. *Ancient Law*. 1861. Rpt., n.p.: Dorset Press, 1986.
Majeed, Javed. *Ungoverned Imaginings: James Mill's* The History of British India *and Orientalism*. Oxford: Clarendon Press, 1992.
Mann, F. O. *Report on Certain Aspects of Egyptian Education, Rendered to His Excellency, the Minister of Education at Cairo*. Cairo: Government Press, 1932.
Marett, R. R. *The Threshold of Religion*. London: n.p., 1914.

Martin, Luther H., Huck Gutman, and Patrick H. Hutton, eds. *Technologies of the Self: A Seminar with Michel Foucault*. Amherst: University of Massachusetts Press, 1988.

Marx, Karl. "Contribution to a Critique of Hegel's *Philosophy of Right*. In *The Marx-Engels Reader*. Ed. Robert C. Tucker. New York: Norton, 1978.

———. "The Eighteenth Brumaire of Louis Bonaparte". In *The Marx-Engels Reader*, pp. 594–617.

———. "The Grundrisse". In *The Marx-Engels Reader, pp*. 221–93.

Massialas, Byron G., and Amir Ahmed Jarrar. *Education in the Arab World*. New York: Praeger, 1983.

Matthews, Roderic D., and Matta Akrawi. *Education in Arab Countries of the Near East*. Washington, D.C.: American Council on Education, 1949.

Mattoon, Scott. "Egypt: Islam by Profession". *The Middle East*, no. 218 (December 1992).

May, Margaret. "Innocence and Experience: The Evolution of the Concept of Juvenile Delinquency in the Mid-Nineteenth Century". *Victorian Studies* 18 (1973), pp. 7–30.

Mayfield, James. *Rural Politics in Nasser's Egypt: A Quest for Legitimacy*. Austin: University of Texas Press, 1971.

McCann, Phillip, ed. *Popular Education and Socialization in the Nineteenth Century*. London: Methuen & Co. Ltd., 1977.

McLuhan, H. Marshall. "The Medium Is the Message". In *Mass Media and Society*. 2nd ed. Ed. Alan Wells. Palo Alto, Calif.: Mayfield, 1975.

Mehran, Golnar. "Ideology and Education in the Islamic Republic of Iran". *Compare* 20 (1990), pp. 53–65.

Messick, Brinkley. "Legal Documents and the Concept of "Restricted Literacy" in a Traditional Society". *International Journal of the Sociology of Language*, no. 42 (1983), pp. 41–52.

———. *The Calligraphic State: Textual Domination and History in a Muslim Society*. Berkeley: University of California Press, 1993.

Milner, Alfred. *England in Egypt*. New York: Macmillan & Co., 1892.

Ministry of Education, Egypt. *Report of the Elementary Education Commission and Draft Law to Make Better Provision for the Extension of Elementary Education*. Cairo: Government Press, 1919.

Mitchell, Richard. *The Society of the Muslim Brothers*. London: Oxford University Press, 1969.

Mitchell, Timothy. *Colonising Egypt*. Cambridge: Cambridge University Press, 1988.

———. "The Invention and Reinvention of the Egyptian Peasant". *International Journal of Middle East Studies* 22 (1990), pp. 129–50.

———. "Worlds Apart: An Egyptian Village and the International Tourism Industry". *Middle East Report*, no. 196 (September–October 1995), pp. 8–11.

Moghadam, Valentine. *Identity Politics and Women: Cultural Reassertions and Feminisms in International Perspective*. Boulder, Colo.: Westview Press, 1994.

Mohsenpour, Bahram. "Philosophy of Education in Post-revolutionary Iran". *Comparative Education Review* 32 (1988), pp. 76–86.

Moore, R. Laurence. *Selling God: American Religion in the Marketplace of Culture*. New York: Oxford University Press, 1994.
Moore, Sally Falk. *Social Facts and Fabrications: Customary Law on Kilimanjaro, 1880–1980*. Cambridge: Cambridge University Press.
Morgan, Lewis Henry. *Ancient Society*. 1877. Rpt., Tucson: University of Arizona Press, 1985.
Mottahedeh, Roy. *The Mantle of the Prophet: Religion and Politics in Iran*. New York: Pantheon, 1985.
Nagata, Judith. "Islamic Revival and the Problem of Legitimacy among Rural Religious Elites in Malaysia". *Man*, n.s., 17 (1982), pp. 42–57.
Nightingale, Florence. *Letters from Egypt: A Journey on the Nile, 1849–50*. Ed. Anthony Sattin. New York: Weidenfeld & Nicholson, 1987.
Norton, Lord. "Schools as Prisons and Prisons as Schools". *The Nineteenth Century* 21 (January 1887), pp. 110–18.
Ong, Walter, S.J. *Interfaces of the Word: Studies in the Evolution of Consciousness and Culture*. Ithaca: Cornell University Press, 1977.
———. *Orality and Literacy: The Technologizing of the Word*. London: Methuen, 1982.
Owen, Roger. "The Influence of Lord Cromer's Indian Experience on British Policy in Egypt, 1883–1907". In *Middle Eastern Affairs*, ed. Albert Hourani, pp. 109–39. Oxford: Oxford University Press, 1965.
———. "Anthropology and Imperial Administration: Sir Alfred Lyall and the Official Use of Theories of Social Change Developed in India after 1857". In *Anthropology and the Colonial Encounter*, ed. Talal Asad, pp. 223–43. London: Ithaca Press, 1973.
Peshkin, Allan. *God's Choice: The Total World of a Fundamentalist Christian School*. Chicago: University of Chicago Press, 1986.
Poliakov, Sergei P. *Everyday Islam: Religion and Tradition in Rural Central Asia*. Trans. Anthony Olcott. Armonk, N.Y.: M. E. Sharpe, 1992.
Porter, Andrew. "Scottish Missions and Education in Nineteenth-Century India: The Changing Face of Trusteeship". *The Journal of Imperial and Commonwealth History* 16 (May 1988), pp. 35–57.
Radwan, Abu Al-Futouh Ahmad. *Old and New Forces in Egyptian Education: Proposals for the Reconstruction of the Program of Egyptian Education in the Light of Recent Trends*. New York: Bureau of Publications, Teachers College, Columbia University, 1951.
Reid, Donald M. "Turn-of-the-Century Egyptian School Days". *Comparative Education Review* 27 (1983), pp. 374–93.
Rizzuto, Ana-Maria, M.D. *The Birth of the Living God*. Chicago: University of Chicago Press, 1979.
Roy, Olivier. *The Failure of Political Islam*. Cambridge, Mass.: Harvard University Press, 1994.
Ruddell, David. "Class and Race: Neglected Determinants of Colonial "Adapted Education" Policies". *Comparative Education* 18 (1982), pp. 293–303.
Rugh, Andrea. "Reshaping Personal Relations in Egypt". In *Fundamentalisms*

and Society. Vol. 2 of *The Fundamentalism Project*, ed. Martin Marty and R. Scott Appleby, pp. 151–80. Chicago: University of Chicago Press.

Sachot, Octave. "Rapport adresse a Son Excellence Monsieur Victor Duruy, Ministre de l'Instruction Publique, sur l'état des sciences, des lettres, et de l'instruction publique en Egypte dans la population indigène et dans la population Européenne". Paris: n.p., 1868.

Sadat, Anwar. "Meeting by President Mohamed Anwar el-Sadat with the Moslem and Christian Religious Leaders, Cairo, February 8, 1977". Cairo: Arab Republic of Egypt, Ministry of Education, State Information Service, 1977.

Salama, Ibrahim. *L'Enseignement islamique en Egypte: Son Evolution, son influence sur les programmes modernes*. Cairo: Imprimerie Nationale, Boulaq, 1939.

Salvatore, Armando. "From Political Islam to Islamic Publicness". Unpublished manuscript, 1995.

Samaan, Saadek. *Value Reconstruction and Egyptian Education*. New York: Bureau of Publications, Teacher's College, Columbia University, 1955.

Saqib, Ghulam Nabi. *Modernization of Muslim Education in Egypt, Pakistan, and Turkey: A Comparative Study*. Lahore: Islamic Book Service, 1983.

Schaefer, Wayne. "The Responsibility of Berber School Policy for the Troubles of a Franco-Moroccan School". *The Maghreb Review* 14 (1989), pp. 187–95.

Schudson, Michael. *Advertising: The Uneasy Persuasion*. New York: Basic Books, 1984.

Semmel, Bernard. *Imperialism and Social Reform*. Cambridge, Mass.: Harvard University Press, 1960.

Shalaba, Ahmad. *History of Muslim Education*. Beirut: Dar al-Kashshaf, 1954.

Sharabi, Hisham. "Islam and Modernization in the Arab World". In *Modernization of the Arab World*, ed. Jack H. Thompson and Robert D. Reischauer, pp. 26–36. Princeton: D. Van Nostrand Co., Inc., 1966.

Sheperd, William E. "Islam as a "System" in the Later Writings of Sayyid Qutb". *Middle Eastern Studies* 25 (1989), pp. 31–50.

Shorish, M. Mobin. "The Islamic Revolution and Education in Iran". *Comparative Education Review* 32 (1988), pp. 58–75.

Singerman, Diane. *Avenues of Participation: Family Politics and Networks in Urban Quarters of Cairo*. Princeton: Princeton University Press, 1995.

Smelser, Neil. J. *Social Paralysis and Social Change: British Working-Class Education in the Nineteenth Century*. Berkeley: University of California Press, 1991.

Smith, Adam. *The Wealth of Nations*. New York: Random House, 1965.

Sonbol, Amira el-Azhary. "Egypt". In *The Politics of Islamic Revivalism*, ed. Shireen Hunter, pp. 23–38. Bloomington: Indiana University Press, 1988.

Spencer, Herbert. "National Education". In *Social Statics*. 1850. Rpt., New York: D. Appleton & Co., 1892.

———. *Principles of Sociology*. 3rd ed. 3 vols. New York: D. Appleton and Company, 1899.

———. "State-Education". In *Facts and Comments*. New York: D. Appleton & Co., 1902.

———. "Moral Education". In *Essays on Education*. New York: Dutton, 1911.

Spiro, Melford. "Religious Systems as Culturally Constituted Defense Mechanisms". In *Context and Meaning in Anthropology*, ed. Melford Spiro. New York: Free Press, 1965.

Spooner, Brian. "Weavers and Dealers: The Authenticity of an Oriental Carpet". In *The Social Life of Things: Commodities in Cultural Perspective*, ed. Arjun Appadurai, pp. 195–235. Cambridge: Cambridge University Press, 1986.

Spratt, Jennifer E., and Daniel A. Wagner. "The Making of a *Fqih:* The Transformation of Traditional Islamic Teachers in Modern Cultural Adaptation". In *The Cultural Transition: Human Experience and Social Transformation in the Third World and Japan*, ed. Merry I. White and Susan Pollak, pp. 89–112. London: Routledge and Kegan Paul, 1986.

Sreberny-Mohammadi, Annabelle, and Ali Mohammadi. *Small Media, Big Revolution: Communication, Culture, and the Iranian Revolution*. Minneapolis: University of Minnesota Press, 1994.

Starrett, Gregory. "Our Children and Our Youth: Religious Education and Political Authority in Mubarak's Egypt". Ph.D. diss., Department of Anthropology, Stanford University, 1991.

———. "The Hexis of Interpretation: Islam and the Body in the Egyptian Popular School". *American Ethnologist* 22 (1995), pp. 953–69.

———. "The Political Economy of Religious Commodities in Cairo". *American Anthropologist* 97, 1 (1995), pp. 51–68.

———. "Signposts along the Road: Monumental Public Writing in Egypt". *Anthropology Today* 11 (1995), pp. 8–13.

———. "The Margins of Print: Children's Religious Literature in Egypt". *Journal of the Royal Anthropological Institute* (incorporating *Man*), n.s., 2 (1996), pp. 117–39.

Steppat, Fritz. "National Education Projects in Egypt Before the British Occupation". In *Beginnings of Modernization in the Middle East: The Nineteenth Century*, ed. William R. Polk and Richard L. Chambers, pp. 281–97. Chicago: University of Chicago Press, 1968.

St. John, James A. *Egypt and Mohammed Ali*. 2 vols. London: Longman, Rees, Orme, Brown, Green, & Longman, 1834.

———. *Egypt and Nubia*. London: Chapman and Hall, 1845.

Stowasser, Barbara Freyer, ed. *The Islamic Impulse*. Washington, D.C.: Center for Contemporary Arab Studies, Georgetown University, 1987.

Street, Brian V. *Literacy in Theory and Practice*. Cambridge: Cambridge University Press, 1984.

Sullivan, Denis. *Private Voluntary Organizations in Egypt: Islamic Development, Private Initiative, and State Control*. Gainesville: University Press of Florida, 1994.

Surour, Dr. Ahmed Fathy. *Towards Education Reform in Egypt: A Strategy for Reform and Examples of Implementation, 1987–1990*. Cairo: Al-Ahram Commercial Presses, 1991.

Szyliowicz, Joseph S. *Education and Modernization in the Middle East*. Ithaca: Cornell University Press, 1973.

Tabor, James, and Eugene Gallagher. *Why Waco? Cults and the Battle for Religious Freedom in America*. Berkeley: University of California Press, 1995.

Tapper, Richard, and Nancy Tapper. "Religion, Education, and Continuity in a Provincial Town". In *Islam in Modern Turkey: Religion, Politics, and Literature in a Secular State*, ed. Richard Tapper. London: I. B. Tauris & Co., 1991.

Taussig, Michael. *The Nervous System*. London: Routledge, 1992.

Tholfsen, Trygve R. "Moral Education in the Victorian Sunday School". *History of Education Quarterly* 20 (1980), pp. 77–99.

Tibawi, A. L. *Islamic Education*. London: Luzac & Co., Ltd., 1972.

Trevelyan, Charles E. *On the Education of the People of India*. London: Longman, Orme, Brown, Green, & Longmans, 1838.

Tsing, Anna L. *In the Realm of the Diamond Queen*. Princeton: Princeton University Press, 1993.

Tucker, Judith. "Decline of the Family Economy in Mid-Nineteenth Century Egypt". *Arab Studies Quarterly* 1 (1981), pp. 245–71.

Twain, Mark. "The Story of the Bad Little Boy". In *Complete Short Stories of Mark Twain*. Ed. Charles Neider, pp. 6–9. New York: Bantam, 1957.

U.S. Department of State. *Country Reports on Human Rights Practices for 1993*. Washington, D.C.: Government Printing Office, 1994.

Verges, Meriem. ""I Am Living in a Foreign Country Here": A Conversation with an Algerian "Hittiste"". *Middle East Report*, no. 192 (January–February 1995), pp. 14–17.

Vincent, David. *Literacy and Popular Culture: England, 1750–1914*. Cambridge: Cambridge University Press, 1989.

Wagner, Daniel. *Literacy, Culture, and Development: Becoming Literate in Morocco*. Cambridge: Cambridge University Press, 1993.

Wagner, Daniel, and Abdelhamid Lotfi. "Traditional Islamic Education in Morocco: Sociohistorical and Psychological Perspectives". *Comparative Education Review* 24 (1980), pp. 238–51.

———. "Learning to Read by "Rote"". *International Journal of the Sociology of Language*, no. 42 (1983), pp. 111–21.

Wagner, Daniel, and Jennifer E. Spratt. "Cognitive Consequences of Contrasting Pedagogies: The Effects of Quranic Preschooling in Morocco". *Child Development* 58 (1987), pp. 1207–19.

———. "Reading Acquisition in Morocco". In *Growth and Progress in Cross-Cultural Psychology*, ed. C. Kagitcibasi, pp. 346–55. Lisse: Swets & Zeitlinger B.V., 1987.

Wagner, Melinda B. *God's Schools: Choice and Compromise in American Society*. New Brunswick, N.J.: Rutgers University Press, 1990.

Weber, Max. *The Protestant Ethic and the Spirit of Capitalism*. New York: Charles Scribner's Sons, 1958.

———. *The Sociology of Religion*. Trans. Ephraim Fischoff. 1922. Rpt., Boston: Beacon, 1963.

West, Edwin G. "The Benthamites as Educational Engineers: The Reputation and the Record". *History of Political Economy* 24, 3 (1992), pp. 595–621.

Williams, James. *Education in Egypt Before British Control*. Birmingham: n.p., 1939.
Williams, Raymond. *The Country and the City*. New York: Oxford University Press, 1973.
———. *Marxism and Literature*. Oxford: Oxford University Press, 1977.
———. *The Sociology of Culture*. New York: Schocken Books, 1981.
Williamson, Bill. *Education and Social Change in Egypt and Turkey*. London: The Macmillan Press, 1987.
Willis, Paul E. *Learning to Labour: How Working Class Kids Get Working Class Jobs*. Westmead, England: Saxon House, 1977.
Wolfe, Ronald G., trans. *Egypt's Second Five-Year Plan for Socio-Economic Development (1987/88–1991/92), with Plan for Year One (1987/88)*. Cairo: Professional Business Services, Ltd., 1986.
Worsfold, W. Basil. *The Redemption of Egypt*. London: George Allen, 1899.
Yates, William Holt, M.D. *The Modern History and Condition of Egypt*. 2 vols. London: Smith, Elder and Co., 1843.
Young, James P. "Intimate Allies in Migration: Education and Propaganda in a Philippine Village". *Comparative Education Review* 26 (1982), 218–34.
Zubaida, Sami. "Exhibitions of Power" (review of Timothy Mitchell's *Colonising Egypt*). *Economy and Society* 19 (1990), pp. 359–75.

Index

Designer:	Barbara Jellow
Compositor:	Impressions Book and Journal Services, Inc.
Text:	10/13 Galliard
Display:	Galliard
Printer and Binder:	BookCrafters, Inc.

John Donne

Bee Wise as serpents
but innocent as Doue.
LXXX.
SERMONS
PREACHED BY THAT LEAR
NED AND REVEREND DIVINE
IOHN DONNE. Dr IN DIVINITIE
LATE DEANE OF Ye CATHEDRALL
CHVRCH OF St PAVLES
LONDON.
M Merian Iun

John Donne

Man of Flesh and Spirit

David L. Edwards

CONTINUUM
London and New York

Continuum
The Tower Building
11 York Road
London SE1 7NX

370 Lexington Avenue
New York
NY 10017-6503

First published 2001

British Library Cataloguing-in-Publication Data
A catalogue record for this book is available from the British Library.

ISBN 0 8264 51551

Designed and typeset by Ben Cracknell Studios
Printed and bound in Great Britain by Biddles Ltd, Guildford and King's Lynn

Contents

Preface

I have tried to write a book which will interest and persuade a variety of readers because nowadays Donne's public is both large and varied. He is best known as a poet of love, never describing physical beauty in detail but brilliantly able to re-create a man's experience of love's emotions and realities. And he is much else – a poet of the spiritual journey who is so human that he is able to speak to others who find the journey uncomfortable, and in the last quarter of his life a great preacher who can soar into word-music or condense a mysterious area of theology into an epigram. But he is always a wit and although he sparkles he has aroused much disagreement about what he means. What lies behind the clever talk? Is he ever serious? If he is, what is he serious about? In my first chapter I face these questions, which even an enthusiast should not avoid.

When so many books have already been written about Donne, very probably I have no need to mention that his name is best pronounced 'Dun', but certainly I need to explain why I hope that my book will fill a gap. This is not a detailed study of a limited part of the subject, written for other specialists, but I have spent a lot of time reading Donne and much of the vast Donnean literature. After thinking, I have then attempted to make a credible portrait of the man in Chapters 2, 3 and 4. I have offered some fresh suggestions about what seems probable in the story of his life but most of the facts which can be known were assembled in R. C. Bald's solidly factual biography (1970) and I gladly acknowledge my debt to that standard work. I have included two chapters (5 and 6) indicating where I venture to disagree with books about him which seem to be excessively favourable or hostile, or exaggerated in some other way, and I have given references for my quotations from the books by John Carey and Paul Oliver of which I am especially critical, so that readers may check to see whether my criticisms are fair. A lot depends on the interpretation of Donne's work which is offered in the last section of the book, so there I have quoted extensively from the poems and the sermons. My longest chapters are about the relationships which I believe meant most to him – with his wife and his God. I hope I may be forgiven for entering into controversy with scholars who do not share this belief but to me there is nothing very odd in thinking that this very human man was very confused over a long period, very erotic, very much married, and in his latter years very devout.

I give references by volume and page to my quotations from the sermons in their modern edition. Their length (in ten volumes) is one reason why they have often been neglected as evidence about the character of the man, but when dealing with Dr Donne the preacher I may have an advantage over commentators who have concentrated on the poems to the exclusion of the sermons: I have myself been a preacher. I believe that this is the first book about Donne ever to have been written by a man who has preached often in London, as he did. Of course I am prejudiced in favour of giving a preacher a fair hearing, but this approach may be welcomed by readers as a change from the attitude taken in some attempts to get hold of Donne from a position entirely different from his. Any prejudice on my part does not amount to a claim that he was always admirable and my sympathy with Donne does not include a pretence that he always said what I agree with. If any reader is interested in my own opinions I have tried to present them in other books but here, I hope, Donne speaks for himself.

Since I have found my own time with Donne fascinating, my ambition is to reach readers who are not specialists. When rejecting some of the suggestions made by previous writers I always try to say, positively but not elaborately, how I see things (for what that is worth) and in its details I have tried to make the material accessible without difficulty. I have tried to make all my quotations from Donne immediately understandable by a silent reader and I have found that this policy has to involve changing some of the punctuation to modern usage, especially in the sermons. It seems that the rash of commas in the original printing was designed to help the reader to read the writing out aloud and I hope that no one in the twenty-first century is going to preach exactly what Donne said. Commas may, however, be especially useful in the poems since the metre can be half-hidden or deliberately broken, and here I have been more strictly conservative although I do not have the space or the expertise with which to discuss the metrical patterns. I have made other small changes in addition to details which have become standard in modern editions: 'then' becomes 'than' when appropriate and in order to avoid making Donne seem hysterical I have not kept the italics except when he is quoting a passage from the Bible.

I claim to have a precedent for such attempts to help a reader, because when Donne's poems, letters and sermons were printed after his death the editor or the typesetter often used his own judgement about details. For example, Donne wrote his letters with so many abbreviations that if they were to be printed for the public's attention they had to be virtually rewritten. But I have not modernized either the spelling or the capitalization, because I believe that the reader will want my quotations to be as authentic as is possible if the whole of this book is to be readable. A capital letter which to us seems to be oddly placed can be a trouble-free sign that a word is to be slightly stressed, and spelling which is strange to us can remind us that many things must remain mysterious in Donne and his age: the evidence is limited and so is our power to penetrate the past.

As was my happy experience when working on earlier books in my retirement from official duties, I am very thankful for the encouragement of my publisher, for the rich resources of the Cambridge University Library, for the secretarial skills of Khadidjah Mattar, for the eagle eye of Fiona McKenzie, and for the loving support of my wife Sybil.

David L. Edwards

Winchester
Easter 2000

Illustrations

Dates

1572	Born into Roman Catholic family in London
1584–89	Under tutors in Oxford and Cambridge
1589–91	Travels in France, Italy and Spain
1591–96	Studies law and writes poetry
1593	Death of brother Henry; becomes Anglican (?)
1596–97	Volunteer in naval expeditions
1597	Secretary to Sir Thomas Egerton
1601	*Metempsychosis* and marriage
1602–05	In Pyrford, unemployed
1603	Accession of James I
1605–06	Travels with Sir Walter Chute
1606–11	In Mitcham with London lodgings
1607	Refuses parish
1608	*Biathanatos* discusses suicide
1609	'Holy Sonnets'; near despair
1610	*Pseudo-Martyr* defends allegiance
1611	*Ignatius his Conclave* attacks Jesuits
1611–12	'Anniversaries' and travel with Drurys
1614	Last hopes of secular employment
1615	Ordination in Church of England
1616	Reader in Divinity, Lincoln's Inn

1617	Death of wife Anne
1619–20	Chaplain to Viscount Doncaster's embassy
1621	Dean of St Paul's
1623–24	Severe illness, writes *Devotions*
1624	Vicar of St Dunstan-in-the-West
1625	Accession of Charles I
1627	Depression returns, writes 'Nocturnall' (?)
1630–31	Last illness and *Death's Duell*
1631	Dies on 31 March
1633	First edition of poems
1635	Second edition
1640	First volume of sermons; Walton's *Life*

To Sybil

Love, all alike, no season knows, nor clyme,
Nor houres, dayes, moneths, which are the rags of time.

John Donne

PART ONE

Donne's Life

1 The questions

Oh, to vex me, contraryes meet in one
Holy Sonnets *XIX*

In much of his poetry John Donne is brilliant, with a voice which is very much his own. Here he is not really interested either in nature or in society; he does not celebrate either beauty or greatness; he is fascinated by his own emotions. About them he writes with what Coleridge called 'wonder-exciting vigour, intenseness and peculiarity of thought'. But a part of being so self-centred is that he needs to tell others how he feels and although he destroys much of what he writes, and has no wish to see even the best of his work in print, he shows or sends some of his poems to a small circle of friends or patrons. For many years some of the most important remained in private collections while other poems which he had not written were attributed to him, but the surviving and available poems, a mixture of the brilliant and the disappointing, were printed after his death, without any arrangement by date. Now they are accessible all over the English-speaking world, so that if we wish we can all be told what the poem says. And what is that?

Often we can feel close to him for although he is extraordinarily fluent and agile with words these words often express feelings which are no more noble than our own. And he is normal in that his feelings and thoughts are not in different compartments. What he wrote about a blushing girl has become famous:

> One whose cleare body was so pure, and thin,
>   Because it neede disguise no thought within.
> 'Twas but a through-light scarfe . . .
>   . . . her pure and eloquent blood
> Spoke in her cheekes, and so distincktly wrought
> That one might almost say, her body thought . . .

But for him the unity of body and thought was not confined to innocent young virgins. He is sexual, and poems which express deep and troubled thought can be given a climax which is explicitly sexual. In other poems he displays himself to us as a man being sexually active in bed or melancholic after rejection, wearing nothing except his body to enclose what he calls the 'naked thinking heart'. 'Full nakedness!' he writes. 'All joyes are due to thee.' So we meet him as an intellectual who is also a man of flesh and blood, passionate rather than calmly wise, up and down in his moods, knowing ecstasy and also knowing grim depression. He has a brain and it never stops working but it is what he calls a 'feeling braine'.

Thus a poem by Donne carries with it a ticket of admission to a world of feelings and thoughts which does not seem entirely strange to us: he is an individual using his own voice but across the centuries we can often recognize what he is talking about. Recently, however, the distance between us and a man who died in 1631 has seemed a deterrent to many readers, in one way at least. His union of feelings and thoughts can make him seem close but his union of sensuality with intense religion can make him seem as distant as a star whose light comes from a remote century. Here is a man who is thoroughly human, and energetically masculine, as well as being highly intelligent – yet he cannot stop talking about religion when he is supposed to be talking about sex, any more than he can stop talking about sex when we expect him to be pious. And he is as passionate about religion as he is, or has been, about his other enthusiasm.

Many readers have found it hard to imagine why or how the Donne of the erotic poetry became first a self-torturing penitent and then an ardent churchman. Should we accept – even if only for the time being, in order to understand – his own interpretation of his life, which was that it was a journey into the God taught by Christianity? Or should we find that explanation false, dishonest or repulsive? Should we study the 'holy sonnets', other 'divine' poems and the sermons, even if it is only in order to enjoy the eloquence or to see how a great poet could feel and think about religion? Or should we pay very little or no attention to him when he is on his knees or in the pulpit – as has often been the practice, even in scholarly books about Donne? Or should we do what he hoped hearers or readers would do, thinking for ourselves about the message he delivers? What are we to make of this man who is clearly not a saint or a mystic, not even a very good man – who is one of us – but who preaches with an urgency more to be expected when a man is inviting a woman into bed?

He preaches that we too stand on the brink of eternity, 'naked before God, without that apparell which he made for us, without all righteousness, and without that apparell which we made for ourselves; not a fig-leaf, not an excuse to cover us' (1:265). He told the doomed Charles I and his courtiers that when they had had the time of their lives they would be in eternity, where 'all the powerful Kings, and all the beautifull Queenes of this world, were but a bed of flowers, some gathered at six, some at seven, some at eight, all in one Morning' (7:138). And we can find ourselves moved by this strange preacher. He has not reached his position by a short or smooth path. Before ordination to the priesthood he has lived most of his life and it has been a life far from any monastery. He has experienced the passions of 'pride and lust' – his words – and much disappointment, much confusion, some acute shame and some despair. And he is emphatic that during his rebellious pilgrimage he has experienced God. That is what he communicates with all the power he can command. Joan Webber, whose *Contrary Music* was a useful book about his prose style in 1963, concluded that 'Donne, as a writer, was only good at one thing, though that one thing was very intense and valuable. He was good at communicating his own experience . . .' No earlier English poet or preacher had been so eloquently intimate before Donne drew on his own experience to speak about those basic and inexhaustible human interests which are indicated by the two three-letter words, sex and God.

So the poet Donne, and Donne the preacher, can seem to be sincere as he experiences and as he communicates. But is he? Are they? Since he was gradually rediscovered in the nineteenth century, and began to be studied as a major figure in the twentieth, confusion has been added to the subject of Donne. A flood of commentary and controversy seems to have drowned the common belief of his contemporaries that he was simply a very masculine lover of women or simply a very devout lover of God, talking about truths which he had found by experiencing them. In 1619, in a letter to a friend which has often been used as a key to his life, he himself contrasted the 'Jack Donne' of the earlier years, brilliant but unhappy, with the 'Dr Donne' who now preached. But how were the two connected? Indeed, what was the truth about either Donne? Or will this great self-exhibitionist always be an enigma if we look closely?

The riddle has been stated in a number of ways, some more historical, others more literary.

There can be questions about how Jack Donne actually behaved while a bachelor. Was he as promiscuous as his poetry suggests? Or did a little casual sex supply raw material for the manufacture of a lot of crafted poetry? Looking back in 1625, he told Sir Robert Ker that 'I did best when I had least truth for my subjects'. Did he then remember with pride his poetic performances as a ventriloquist, able to create many women and many male selves by his skill with voices? Or did he mean that he had done best when he had for his subjects not ideas but people, usually a woman and himself? The phrase which he used to Ker has often been quoted by commentators who have not considered its context. It came in a letter enclosing a poem written at Ker's request in honour of a dead friend of his whom the poet had met only casually. The poem was about the ideas of body and soul, sin and heaven, not about the friend (least of all about the rumour that he had been poisoned). Its grand subjects contained, he wrote, 'so much truth as defeats all Poetry'. So was Donne acknowledging that his best poetry had made things up – or was he reflecting that it had been 'best' when it had dealt with manageable subjects like a man and a woman, not with eternal mysteries (for him, the topic of sermons)? And what did he think had been his 'best' work? He did not say.

If he had many relationships with women in real life, did he always despise and exploit them with a 'masculine perswasive force' which could be cruel because entirely selfish? Or was he in reality as vulnerable and as easily hurt as they were? Or is it impossible to say, because most of the early poetry about unconfined sex was written in order to entertain other men with little or no foundation other than fantasy? Did his anxious courtship and sensational marriage inspire all, or any, of those poems of longing, ecstasy and delight? In 'The Canonization' he wrote some of his most famous words: 'We'll build in sonnets pretty roomes'. Did he refer to a real woman by the 'we' – or to the construction of an artefact by the 'build'? Did he seduce Anne More because he thought she was a rich girl, or did he throw away his career because he loved her with his whole heart? How did he behave after marriage – still as a 'libertine' lusting after many women when he wrote poems or when he prowled around in real life, or was he a family man now that he had settled down? What did he mean when he based his long poems called 'Anniversaries' on the idea that a girl's death had ruined the world? Or when he wrote in a shorter and more heartfelt poem that his wife's death had 'ruin'd mee'? Was he, after all, a bit of a feminist? In her study of *Feminine Engendered Faith* (1992) Maureen Sabine claimed that the Virgin Mary was very close to the centre of his religion and that the half-hidden theme of his 'Anniversaries' was a lament for the psychologically disastrous results of the Protestant destruction of the cult which had been vitally important for English Christians over a thousand years, devotion to Mary. Evidence to support that idea is lacking but Donne did write that he had been led to seek God by a woman, his wife Anne. No English poet before him had been so frank and vivid in the celebration of sexual freedom, but was he also, as has been suggested by Anthony Low, the first English poet who celebrated marriage as a delighted and glorious commitment, in a 'reinvention of love'?

How was it possible for him to combine in the 1590s the writing of frankly and brutally erotic 'elegies' with the writing of loftily censorious 'satyres' rebuking other people's vices? (In his time an 'elegie' was a poem written in elegiac couplets, imitating Latin authors such as Ovid, and was not necessarily serious. A 'satyre' was a harsh attack on vice, imitating other Latin authors such as Juvenal, and was not intended to be comic.) Was the erotic poetry itself a warning against vice, by showing that every sexual relationship outside marriage is bound to end in tears – so that Jack Donne was a preacher long before he entered a pulpit? Why were the 55 poems which were grouped together when printed as 'Songs and Sonets' so mixed both in poetic form and in emotional tone? (Any short poem could called a 'sonet', a word which means 'little sound', although Donne did write sonnets in the form which became standard, in fourteen lines each of ten syllables and with a rhyme in one of a few patterns.) Was the long poem about the transmission of evil in the history of fallen humanity

(*Metempsychosis*) written in bitter disillusionment – or in high spirits? Why was it abandoned? And why was much of the later poetry so polite about the good and the great? Was this deferential poet himself a good man, glad to praise the virtues he admired in others? Or was he writing for money? Or while being less corrupt than some others were in the time of the Tudors and Stuarts, did he need to flatter patrons like everyone else who had talent rather than wealth?

Was Dr Donne the preacher a hypocrite, or at least a poseur? Was he in the pulpit only because he had been so disappointed in his long search for a job in the royal court, in the civil service or in diplomacy? If this was not the only reason why he accepted the king's advice that he should become a preacher, the experience of many years of unemployment while a layman was certainly a factor in his decision: so how important was it? When he reached – or was dragged to – his pulpit, did he preach what the king commanded? Or did he become absorbed by his discovery of a power to deceive and bully the ignorant and the gullible, as he had deceived and bullied women in his youth? If he tried to communicate a sincerely believed religious message, what was it? Did he incline to the Catholicism of his parents or to the Calvinism of many of his fellow Protestants? Or was he one of the pioneers in the Anglican 'middle way' between those positions? Was he surprisingly liberal, tolerant and generously comprehensive? Or did he preach a religion which looked back to the Middle Ages and forward only to the fundamentalism which survives like a museum in the twenty-first century? Or was his religion tortured, almost as if he anticipated the *angst* of the twentieth century in the poems of guilt, doubt and near-despair which W. H. Auden persuaded Benjamin Britten to set to troubled music?

Did religion really mean as much to Donne as he said it did after the time of his marriage, and even more emphatically after his ordination? In his history of English poetry, *Lives of the Poets* (1998),

Michael Schmidt observed that Donne developed a 'talent for sermons' and was willing 'to give sermons on themes and occasions where political interests claimed the right to use him'. But we are told that he 'dealt too with diplomatic correspondence (a form of secular work more to his taste)'. This dismissive verdict on the preaching was delivered although many more than a million words of the sermons have survived. All of them are full of references to the Bible and the Fathers of the Church, and of religious emotion, whereas the whole of the correspondence which may be termed diplomatic (although it was almost certainly about church life and religious controversy in continental Europe) has disappeared. What is interesting is that Schmidt, who has an attractive enthusiasm for a wide variety of poets, feels under no obligation to acknowledge any integrity in Donne the preacher. Even the love poetry may, he thinks, have no 'actual subject', and to him it seems obvious that the actual subject of the sermons is not what Donne says it is.

Has the religion which he preached any right to be heard in our time? In a contribution to a book of essays in 1990 entitled *Soliciting Interpretation*, Professor Stanley Fish put the question sharply. He argued that 'the God Donne imagines' is remarkably like Donne, 'a jealous and overbearing master who brooks no rivals and will go to any lengths (even to the extent of depriving Donne of his wife) in order to secure his rights'. In the erotic poetry about men conquering women Fish saw 'sado-masochism elevated to a principle and glorified . . . in the name of a power that is (supposedly) divine' and in the religious poetry he saw only further self-glorification by the 'self-aggrandizing' poet. 'There is', Fish said, 'no reason to believe that the turn to God is anything but one more instance of feigned devotion' since in reality 'it is the poem's verbal felicity and nothing else that is doing either the assuring (which thus is no more than whistling in the dark) or the assuming' and 'he is no more assured of what he assumes than anyone else'. So Fish concluded that 'Donne is sick and his poetry is sick'.

When Donne preached, was his religion crumbling in his mind like the stonework of the Gothic cathedral around him? Certainly his mind could be changed by new ideas through books. It seems that as a young man he was excited by the poetry and philosophy of the Italian Renaissance. It can also be suggested that when he meditated in his religious poetry he used not direct experience or observation but 'emblem books' which reproduced images recommended for contemplation. We know that during his years as a preacher much of his theology was derived from books. Some were medieval and provided neatly arranged quotations from the Fathers of the Church in an even earlier period, and some were books by the Fathers themselves, but it can be suggested that this traditional faith was deeply troubled by what he learned from books of the sixteenth and seventeenth centuries about astronomy, for example. That was the 'new Philosophy' which 'cals all in doubt' according to his famous reference to the new science in his 'Anniversaries': the earth is no longer stable or central, it moves around the sun. Deep down, was his religion no longer stable and no longer central to life? Was he as full of doubt as are many of his modern or post-modern readers? Dante had thought that God's love moved the sun around the earth. If that was not true, did Donne suspect that God was not real?

Many other questions can be asked about John Donne. He wrote a poem imagining his name engraved on a window, a 'ragged bony name', and he saw that these bones lacked 'the Muscle, Sinew, and Veine' which could make them live. Coleridge was right about his fluency and power in self-expression but in the final analysis his poems, his letters and his sermons can all seem like that skeleton, so that we ask: here are the words, clever no doubt, but after all these fireworks where is the man?

Although Ben Jonson thought Donne 'the first poet in the World, in some things', he also believed that 'Done himself for not being understood would perish'. Another remark, that Donne deserved to be hanged for neglecting 'accent', showed that part of the complaint was about an apparent neglect of metre, which would puzzle readers who expected the conventions of poetry to be observed in a way easy to understand at first sight. But mainly Jonson complained about the difficulty of grasping the sense of many passages: when using his own 'plain' style he proved that he did not overestimate other people's intelligence. Clever wit could seem to be the chief feature of Donne's poetry, and it could be praised – but it could also seem too clever.

After Donne's death a tribute was paid by a minor poet who was a disciple, Thomas Carew:

> The Muses' garden with Pedantique weedes
> O'rspred, was purg'd by thee; The lazie seeds
> Of servile imitation throwne away;
> And fresh invention planted . . .
> Since to the awe of thy imperious wit
> Our stubborne language bends . . .
>
> *Here lies a King, that rul'd as hee thought fit*
> *The universall Monarchy of Wit . . .*

And there Carew left it. But he was a courtier of King Charles I and inevitably readers who do not want to be mere courtiers singing the praises of John Donne as the monarch of wit have exercised their own wits. In the modern age 'new' critics have pointed out that a poem by him can be as artificial as any garden and that it is often a waste of time to look for the earth beneath the flowers and the weeds, although it may be useful to search for sources in Latin, Italian, Spanish or other literature. The only productive approach, we are told, is to concentrate on the writing in its intricate density, on its strategic arrangement of images and feelings, and on its defiantly personal choice of grammar, syntax and metre, since the poet's life outside his mind at that moment is hidden from us. The poem should be enjoyed as what the poet has created, as his 'invention' – for it cannot be more than that.

That 'new' criticism advocated by T. S. Eliot for a time was vigorous in the middle of the twentieth century but – as tends to happen in intellectual history – its emphasis was to seem too narrow while not being entirely wrong. Later critics have insisted that while literature is indeed an artefact created by authors the reader still has a right to think about its substance as well as its form. That analysis has produced a biographical approach to Eliot's own poetry, reducing his status. And these critics (would 'newer' be the right term?) have often been very critical of the substance of Donne's work. They have maintained that the language of a poem constructs what may appear to be a timeless reality but what is in fact the product of the writer's own psychology, gender or position in society – and so we are encouraged to be suspicious. And of course we are advised to be even more suspicious when a poet becomes a preacher.

This most recent approach, which may be called deconstructive or post-structuralist or post-modern, and which owes much to the theories about 'culture' taught by thinkers such as Althusser, Foucault and Raymond Williams, has great advantages in that it invites a reading which is even closer than anything thought necessary when the study of 'great literature' was more deferential. Valuable issues have been raised by connecting a poet such as Donne with psychoanalysis (what emotional wounds suffered in the past were bleeding as he wrote?) or feminism (why did he treat women like that?) or sociology (what ideology was he defending, and with how much conviction?). There are, however, difficulties in this deconstructive criticism, because in its attempt to answer the questions it raises it can construct speculations which are not based very firmly on the evidence now available.

It is difficult enough to psychoanalyse the living but the problems are larger when the passions have been dead for a long time, leaving behind evidence which is no more than what Donne saw on the seashore at low tide – 'embroider'd works upon the sand'. Some critics write as if the waves had created solid and large sandcastles still available for them to examine. It is difficult enough to get to the bottom of relationships between living people but our curiosity may have to remain unsatisfied if we try to probe too deeply into the lives of the dead. For example, we now speak freely about someone's need to acknowledge a 'homosexual' nature – but no one called himself or herself a 'homosexual' before late in the nineteenth century and this was not merely a matter of not using the word: it was believed that everyone was by nature heterosexual but was capable of perversity. We now think that a 'suicide' should arouse compassion – but that word was not used within Donne's lifetime about an action which was treated as a deadly sin and a terrible crime. We now think that a woman should not allow herself to be exploited outside or inside marriage – but in Donne's time men and women were taught inequality from childhood. We now despise people who flatter dictators – but in that age courtiers were thought to be honouring monarchs anointed by God. And it is difficult enough to know what really motivates the living without trying to reach certainty about the real preoccupations of the dead. When Donne was marrying a woman or writing a religious poem or preaching a sermon he was also a man who was ambitious for money and power, but critics who have asserted that he was always driven by careerism make a suggestion which goes beyond what we can know about him or about what we normally expect from lovers or worshippers or intellectuals when at their own kinds of work. We cannot be certain that a book or article offering a sour interpretation of Donne's motives was written mainly because the author wanted promotion or reputation in the academic world; it therefore seems fair to give the benefit of the doubt to the commentators – and, at least in some instances, to Donne.

Because they have tended to treat his poems and sermons as elaborate codes which need to be deciphered if we are to be shown what Donne was really thinking, some recent critics have left the impression that reading him is hard work which is best left to those who are exceptionally clever and exceptionally suspicious.

When Andrew Mousley edited contemporary critical essays on *John Donne* (1999), he summed up the conclusions of his contributors: 'we might say that a typical Donne text is at once that densely populated place where diverse ideas, feelings and cultural references meet, clash, and interchange; and at the same time a distinctive verbal construct, driven by its own idiosyncratic logic'. And in his study of *John Donne, Coterie Poet* (1986) Arthur Marotti thought that even for the poet's first readers, who might have been expected to belong to his world of thought, the metaphors in his poems were 'multivalent, ambiguous, and fundamentally *resistant* to interpretation'. Agreeing with this verdict in the volume edited by Mousley, Richard Halpern has written of Donne's intention to generate 'a fog of obscurity'. But as he reflected on many years spent in the compilation of bibliographies of criticism of Donne, John Roberts issued a warning that critics could be more difficult to understand than Donne himself. 'In many cases', he wrote in the inaugural number of the *John Donne Journal* (1982), 'Donne has been so successfully returned to his niche in the seventeenth century that many readers are content to leave him there. In other instances, Donne has been explained in such complicated terms that even highly educated readers feel intimidated and put off.' Roberts regarded this as paradoxical, since 'his poems were intended to communicate his particularly brilliant sense of reality' – as were his sermons.

So uncertainties and difficulties piled up in the twentieth century's debate about Donne. Ought we now to say out loud that he was a wit who entertained his contemporaries but has very little to say to us? A case can be made for that dismissive conclusion. His poems are not only varied in mood: even a short poem can have an end which contradicts the beginning. We may hope to hear his real voice in his letters but these, too, are often literary exercises – especially his letters in verse, a sixth of all his surviving poems, where the compliments are often ridiculously extravagant. His religious poems seem to open his heart and his sermons seem to be the answers to his own religious questions, but when what he says is an echo of orthodoxy we may wonder whether he really means it. He always seems to be passionate, but how seriously should we take him as a feeler? He always seems to be arguing, but is he a serious thinker?

Was Rupert Brooke right to say that 'when passion shook him, and his being ached for utterance to relieve the stress, expression came through the intellect'? The reply can be made that Brooke was too enthusiastic because he was looking for an alternative to most of the poetry of his time, including his own poetry. Was T. S. Eliot right to say that 'a thought to Donne was an experience; it modified his sensibility'? Eliot himself became worried because that widely quoted and accepted phrase of his did not correspond to the reality of Donne, which included much that was not wholly real. He published a second opinion, which was that a thought could attract Donne because it could fit into a poem or sermon. The 'sensuous apprehension of thought' which had previously seemed to involve the whole self like the experience of smelling a rose now appeared to be a literary craftsman's more detached enjoyment of an idea, 'almost as if it were something he could touch or stroke'. What Eliot now found in Donne was not 'thinking' at all but 'a vast jumble of incoherent erudition on which he drew for purely poetic effects'. And A. E. Housman, who cultivated simplicity as a poet and felt that the beauty of nature was the only reliable consolation for the tragedy of life, more briefly dismissed Donne as 'intellectually frivolous'.

The concentration by some twentieth-century critics on the artificiality of Donne was a return to what had been said by earlier critics.

In 1693 John Dryden could anticipate the harsher condemnations of wit that were to come in the Age of Reason: 'if we are not so great wits as Donne, yet certainly we are better poets'. His complaint about an over-clever poet was that he 'perplexes the minds of the fair sex with nice speculations of philosophy, when he should engage their hearts, and entertain them with the softness of love'. He seems to have been under the impression that Donne wrote for a readership of genteel young ladies who wanted poets to offer flowery compliments and perhaps a few soft kisses – but Donne wrote about raw sex, either for the enjoyment of other lusty young bachelors or in celebration of his own promiscuity, courtship and marriage.

Dryden was on safer ground when he was the first to use the term 'metaphysical' about Donne's poetry. The Greek word *metaphysika* was originally used simply in order to group together the books which Aristotle wrote apart from those on physical subjects, but later it was applied to any philosophy which attempted to rise above physical reality into speculative abstract or over-subtle thought. Dryden complained that poets such as Donne were too fanciful and his criticism of this style was developed by others who thought that (like everyone else with a claim to be civilized) poets ought to be realistic and reasonable. In the eighteenth century an attack by David Hume, normally a calm and urbane philosopher, was more savage: as he saw Donne, the wit was 'totally suffocated and buried by the harshest and most uncouth expression that is any-where to be met with'.

A more famous rebuke was delivered by Samuel Johnson when in 1779 he gave 'some account' of 'a race of writers that may be termed the metaphysical poets'. 'Their thoughts', he declared, 'are often new, but seldom natural; they are not devious, but neither are they just.' In particular he objected to the frequency of a 'conceit', which he defined. 'The most heterogeneous ideas are yoked by violence together; nature and art are ransacked for illustrations, comparisons and allusions; their learning instructs, and their subtilty surprises; but the reader, . . . though he sometimes admires, is seldom pleased' – because the reader is not shown 'truth' by these ingeniously artificial 'conceits'. 'To shew their learning', said the great Dr Johnson, 'was their whole endeavour.' He was not entirely hostile to these 'metaphysical' poets: 'to write on their plan it was at least necessary to read and think'. But his verdict was that they 'fail to give delight by their desire of exciting admiration'. He complained that 'their courtship is devoid of fondness, and their lamentation of sorrow'. And this verdict has been thought to apply to Donne, although Johnson was writing mainly about Abraham Cowley, a later poet.

In 1713 Alexander Pope admired Donne but thought it necessary to translate him into 'correct' verse if a more polished age was to give him a hearing. In 1733 Donne's poetry could be called by Lewis Theobald a 'continued Heap of Riddles'. A century later the young Henry Alford made an attempt to persuade the public to buy and admire reprinted sermons by Donne, but the six volumes did not sell; down-to-earth Englishmen, if they noticed, were indignant to see that the preacher's arguments too often depended not on facts but on conceits. When tributes were paid to Donne in the nineteenth century, it was often as if nuggets of gold had been found in the bed of a remote river. Thomas Campbell included four pieces in his *Specimens* of English poetry in 1819, but he reproduced only two of them completely and he added this comment: 'His ruggedness and whim are almost proverbially known, yet there is a beauty of thought which at intervals arises from his chaotic imagination, like Venus smiling on the waters.' A *Cyclopaedia of English Literature* in 1844 acknowledged that 'there is much real poetry, and that of a high order' – but only 'amid much rubbish'. Robert Browning often praised Donne's poetry, particularly when it was conversational, but did not imitate it: he wanted to achieve something more lifelike. Anthologists might include isolated specimens of Donne's poetry, and in 1872 A. B. Grosart collected most of it in a new edition, but it was presented with apologies for its 'faults' and when editing the most influential of all the anthologies, his *Golden Treasury* of English poetry in 1861, Francis Palgrave thought it wisest to omit Donne altogether.

Yet the most eloquent of Donne's critics was Donne – and he would certainly have agreed that he was complicated and that his style in poetry or prose reflected this personal complexity. On his own testimony he should not be interpreted in any oversimple fashion and the acceptance of his own realistic self-assessment must be our starting point as we try to understand him as he really was: not praising or condemning, but understanding. There were different periods in his life, and within any period, perhaps within any day, there were different moods. He often watched himself, and he saw not a simple character but a whole little world, divided by a civil war:

> I am a little world made cunningly
> Of Elements, and an Angelike spright,
> But black sinne hath betraid to endless night
> My world's both parts, and (oh) both parts must die.

He hoped that the spirit in him linked him with God's angels. But he knew that the elements in his body, which the Creator had made cunningly, could drag body and soul down to endless night.

And he knew that his mind was a battlefield between the forces of light and the powers of 'lust and envie'. He could occupy the high moral ground but soon find himself rolling in the mud of sex or trying to climb in the world by flattery of the rich. He could pray and preach with a burning intensity but soon find his mind wandering. He could, he said, 'neglect God and his Angels for the noise of a Flie, for the ratling of a Coach, for the whining of a dore . . . A memory of yesterday's pleasures, a fear of tomorrow's dangers, a straw under my knee, a noise in mine eare, an any thing, a nothing, a fancy . . . troubles me in my prayer' (7:264–5). While in the pulpit he could be 'at home in my Library' asking whether some other commentator had not interpreted the Bible better – or he could be wondering 'what is likely you will say to one another, when I have done' (3:110).

The medical authorities of his age, repeating the second-century Galen, had taught him that a character or a mood was caused when a 'humour' overflowed. There were four of these humours in any human body: blood, phlegm, black and yellow bile. They made a person sanguine or phlegmatic, choleric or melancholy. But Donne found other humours in himself, one heating him with lust, another icing him with shame:

> Oh, to vex me, contraryes meet in one:
> Inconstancy unnaturally hath begott
> A constant habit; that when I would not
> I change in vowes, and in devotione.
> As humorous is my contritione
> As my prophane Love, and as soon forgott . . .

There was, he claimed, truth in his mind: once he wrote about his 'minde's white truth'. In this poem he declared

> Those are my best days, when I shake with feare.

But he was honest with himself and confessed that he had other days:

> As ridlingly distempered, cold and hott . . .
> I durst not view heaven yesterday; and to day
> In prayers and flattering speeches I court God:
> To morrow I quake with true feare of his rod.

That poem seems to have been written when Donne had been for some time a priest and a preacher and if this was the case we can see why there is an unusual intensity in its ashamed selfexamination: he is not the assured Christian whom the public sees. Even in his private 'devotione' or his penitential 'contritione' his piety comes and goes like a fever. And yet we should notice both his honesty and his humility: he does not admire himself when he prays and he dares not 'view heaven' like a tourist. He quakes with fear as he remembers that God is just, and he is at his 'best' when begging for mercy. In a letter he told a friend that short prayers are best 'for long prayers have more of the man, as ambition of eloquence and a complacencie in the work, and more of the Devil . . .'

Such was Donne as he saw himself when he thought he was standing and trembling in the presence of his Judge. If we want to discover the truth about such a man, we must not try to cover his personality by one small and neat label. Behind all the clever words, and behind the varying moods which the words express, there is a man whom we can meet and he is a living man with what belongs to humanity (including us): the complications, the limitations, the strengths. He is a man not of words only but also of flesh and spirit. Such a man is not simple – but perhaps he is understandable.

We can profitably begin the task of understanding the real, complex, not always admirable Donne by comparing him with a few of his contemporaries. At least the comparison will bring out what he was not. If we compare him with George Herbert, also a great poet and also a man who became an Anglican priest after many troubled years, we can see why Donne is never likely to be treated by the public as a saint, whatever may be claimed by some of his fans: he lacked simplicity, he lacked serenity, he was not sufficiently willing to forget himself in the love of God and neighbour, he was too like George Herbert's brother Edward. If we compare him with two other great poets of his generation, Jonson and Shakespeare, we can see how he was more limited in his interests and therefore why he is more restricted in his appeal: he was always so interested in himself, and often also so interested in God in relation to himself, that he was never content simply to write about other people with a care to describe their independent reality.

In their boyhoods both John Donne and George Herbert were greatly influenced by a widowed mother, but while Donne inherited great complications from the fervent Roman Catholicism of the family into which he was born, Herbert's mother was (as Donne declared eloquently when preaching at her memorial service) an Anglican saint. Both received a good education, but while Donne had to learn from tutors, Herbert went to a famous school and became a Fellow of Trinity College, Cambridge. Both men had ambitions for a profitable career in the service of the Crown and both were frustrated, but Herbert's financial worries were comparatively mild and his efforts to get a job comparatively relaxed. Both had the feelings of a young man and Herbert wrote that 'my stuffe is flesh, not brasse', but only Donne had reasons to feel any great guilt. (Herbert's confessions were that as a boy 'I had my way' amid 'milk and sweetnesses', that he sought and enjoyed 'academick praise' for his elegance as the university's official orator, and that he hoped to get a position with 'Honour' by 'the quick returns of courtesie and wit' in his contacts with the king and the court.) Both resisted ordination to the priesthood but Herbert found that his resistance, called by him 'fierce and wilde', could be silenced quite easily:

> Methought I heard one calling, 'Childe',
> And I reply'd, 'My Lord'.

The ways in which the two men married and were ordained were significantly different. Donne threw away a career because he loved a girl with passion. He became an unemployed father of a rapidly expanding family but refused the offer of an exceptionally good income as a parish priest, condemning himself to seven more years of anxious job-hunting, the jobs he wanted being rather grand. Herbert seems to have decided to become a husband and a priest at more or less the same time; he was then aged 36 and according to Izaak Walton proposed to the lady only three days after meeting her. He never became a father but he accepted the position of rector in a country parish, Fugglestone-cum-Bemerton; it had about four hundred inhabitants, almost all of them peasants. It was not a wilderness: it was near Salisbury Cathedral where he enjoyed Evensong twice a week and also near Wilton House, the seat of the Earls of Pembroke who belonged to a much richer branch of the Herbert family. But he wrote a little book about the duties of a parish priest as a 'mark to aim at' and seems to have found a genuine fulfilment as an obscure pastor; none of his sermons has survived but the happiest of his poems seem to date from this time. He died of tuberculosis in 1633, after two and a half years in the priesthood.

His little book in prose, called *A Priest to the Temple*, was not published until 1651, at a time when the Church of England had been overthrown, but in that situation the idealism about pastoral care and devoutly careful worship answered contempt for the Church and the book's influence continued for some three hundred years. And a small volume of his poems, *The Temple: Sacred Poems and Private Ejaculations,* became a book which many treasured when it had been published by the Cambridge University Press soon after his death in the year which also saw the first edition of Donne's poetry. Like Donne he was a poet brilliantly inventive technically and a frequent user of 'conceits' but unlike him he kept his cleverness and learning well under control, liked to use natural and homely images, disciplined his emotions by a glad submission to the Bible and the Church, and even when his subject was not heaven could express pure joy in his religion. Reaching a simplicity which Donne never achieved, he dedicated himself to 'Jesus my Master' with his 'utmost art' as a poet of a plainly holy love and as a courtier serving an invisible king in a tiny parish. And unlike Donne, when dying he entrusted his poems to a friend, with the hope that they would be published in order to edify.

Soon after his own ordination Donne sent George Herbert a Latin poem ending with best wishes for favour from the royal court. Later he became aware of the younger man's spirituality and they seem to have exchanged copies of their poems in English, although the only strong evidence for this is somewhat ridiculous. In 'To Mr Tilman' Donne complained that 'Gentry' refused to serve the Church

> As if their day were onely to be spent
> In dressing, Mistressing and complement. . .

This poem seems to have been sent to George Herbert – and to have been obliquely aimed at him while he hesitated about a descent in the class system through ordination, for in one of his own poems ('The Church Porch') Herbert included the advice that a young gentleman should not waste his time dressing up before paying visits and compliments to young ladies. Alternatively, Donne may have borrowed the line. However, it seems clear that he felt closer to George's elder brother Edward, with whom he exchanged whole poems in friendly competition.

Edward (who became Lord Herbert of Cherbury) was very much a man, outstandingly handsome, a tough and brave soldier, eager to fight duels with men who might be said to have insulted him and to make love to women who were known to admire him; he recorded his exploits in a boastful autobiography. He was also energetic in the field of religious controversy: while ambassador in Paris he wrote a book of philosophy and later he ventured into theology, with conclusions very different from his brother's since while thinking the existence of God obvious he regarded Christianity as no more than the best of the available religions, was not enthusiastic about Jesus, and cared little for priests. In a verse-letter of 1610 Donne assured Edward Herbert that although himself a writer not a soldier he admired a military man ('Actions are authors') and on the day of his ordination he wrote to him affectionately, trusting that their friendship was not over. Less solemnly he once wrote a short 'Essay of Valour' which teased the gallant soldier who easily impresses women. This macho, man-of-the-world side to Donne was a part of his complex character. It made him unlike George Herbert.

Ben Jonson was born in the same year as Donne and was in some ways like him in character. He was assertively masculine and never at a loss for words; he was very much a Londoner and for many years drank and talked with Donne; he looked to the court of James I for patronage; and he could write in a style so like his friend's that when a collection of his poems called *Underwood* was published in 1640 it included four which have also been attributed to Donne. But Jonson's writing was much more varied in subject and tone, and one reason was that as a professional writer (in a profession which had not existed before the 1590s) he had to apply his skill to any job which came his way. He could not afford to be always writing about himself. Nor could he afford to be too clever. It seems, however, that he had no wish to be. It was more in his nature to be comic or sad with a warm-hearted humanity, and to write poems which were simply beautiful or simply affectionate. He was as clever as Donne but not an intellectual.

Jonson's father was an Anglican clergyman who died before he was born, and his mother then married a man slightly lower in the class system: a bricklayer who had a cottage near the site which is now Trafalgar Square. With that home the boy was able to get an education locally – in Westminster School like George Herbert – but not a decent job. If he was to rise above his early years in his stepfather's trade and in the ranks of the army, he had to make money as an actor and as a writer of plays. What he wrote for a theatre had to please first the manager and then the audience, and in order to please it had to represent life as known to the audience, with attacks on the classes above. Before long, however, the highly talented young man saw a more profitable market for his words: scripts were needed for the 'masques' performed regularly in the royal court. What was most important in these entertainments celebrating the government's current policy was the dancing, in which the queen herself performed when more or less sober. The king watched and as the history of his reign demonstrated a good dancer could be rewarded far more handsomely than any script-writer. Jonson wrote what was needed and in 1616 included his scripts along with plays and poems in an edition of his *Workes*, in a year when the king's own literary works also appeared in a collected edition. That unprecedented volume was the height of a professional's career but it left the author still vulnerable. Even when under the patronage of King James his indiscretions could get him into trouble and under the stricter King Charles he was permanently out of favour, left to years of illness and renewed poverty.

Donne thought that his proper place would be among the courtiers who watched the masque. He was willing to criticize poems submitted to him by Jonson, and to write in praise of his friend's *Volpone*, but he had no intention of living in the ungentlemanly world which mere playwrights inhabited. Jonson, who was often drunk and often quarrelsome, once killed an actor and escaped a hanging only because he could translate some verses of the Latin Bible and so take advantage of the 'benefit of clergy' which remained as a strange survival from the privileges of the clergy in the Middle Ages. Whereas Donne wrote short poems about his experiences as a gentleman volunteering for naval expeditions during the war with Spain, Jonson wrote a long one about a voyage through an open sewer in the centre of London, the Fleet Ditch: it was an allegory of the life which he knew. He shared this low life with Christopher Marlowe, the first of the great playwrights but also not a real gentleman. A cobbler's son, Marlowe earned money by acting as a spy for the government but while drinking would say things which could get him into deep trouble as an 'atheist'. In the end he was killed in a tavern, during a fight which may have been arranged by the government. His most famous plays had been about the intoxications of power and knowledge but the reality was that playwrights knew that they could not hope for security. The custom was that the writer of a play was paid a single fee which was not large; most of the actors were paid a labourer's wage and the profits were kept by the small group of 'sharers' who also retained the manuscripts of the plays; Shakespeare's plays were not collected for publication until seven years after his death. In his second 'satyre' Donne mocked the dramatist who

> gives ideot actors meanes
> (Starving himself) to live by his labor'd sceanes . . .

And how does Donne look in comparison with Shakespeare?

As a shareholder in theatre business Shakespeare was more than a mere writer or actor, and that was the main reason why he was able to afford the best house in Stratford-on-Avon and recognition as a gentleman by the College of Heralds. He was also indebted to James I as his royal patron (as Donne and Jonson were and as George Herbert tried to be). And he was a genius who was interested in humanity – and who, as Harold Bloom has suggested, in a sense 'invented' it by the richness and depth of his understanding: into his plays he put men and women of every class and temperament, in every kind of situation, and he always allowed them to speak for themselves. But he never found his own life so interesting that he had to make a drama out of it. His sonnets are more self-revealing than anything else that he wrote, and they reveal a hard struggle for self-fulfilment not entirely unlike Donne's, but they were not reprinted in his lifetime and it has often been thought that this was because their author thought them too personal. Whether or not that was so, C. S. Lewis was surely right about the poetry of love: 'in Donne's most serious lyrics . . . we have a poetry which is almost exactly opposite to that of Shakespeare's *Sonnets.* In Shakespeare each experience of the lover becomes a window through which we look out on immense prospects – on nature, the seasons, life and death, time and eternity. In Donne . . . a particular man is mocking, flattering, browbeating, laughing at, or laughing with, or adoring, a particular woman.'

For Donne nature was to be kept in the background, philosophy was to be used and forgotten like a piece of furniture on the stage, and the most interesting bit of humanity in the comedy or tragedy was always himself. One climax in the drama of his life was his sensational marriage six years after the probable date of the first performance of *Romeo and Juliet.* Then came years of Hamlet-like indecision, even of Lear-like suffering which caused a Hamlet-like temptation to suicide, with the consolation of a romance somewhat like the world-losing love of Antony and Cleopatra. Then he moved on into a world of explicitly religious emotions and theological arguments into which Shakespeare never entered although many references in his plays show that he was familiar with the Bible and with the Book of Common Prayer. And as Donne preached many listened – with a response which encouraged him to go on preaching until he was very near death, and to preach after death in a highly unusual monument with a statue of himself as a shrouded corpse and a long inscription about his life, all carefully planned.

The monument to Shakespeare is on a wall of his parish church and there he is as silent as he had been during many a sermon. The bust depicts a happy, well-fed man holding a quill pen in order to show what he did before retirement. Beneath it are inscribed a Latin couplet and six lines of verse in English praising 'all that he hath writ' without mentioning anything specific and saying, with a breath-taking inadequacy, that his name 'doth deck this tomb' far more than the money spent on the monument. It is clear that William Shakespeare, the greatest man in English history and arguably also in the literature of the world, had left no instructions as to how his life and work were to be commemorated; family and friends have had to do their best. Here the only writing by him – or phrased as a message from him – is a request, in a tiny bit of very simple verse, that his bones should not be moved so that the grave can be reused.

Although Donne's own personality was such that other people were left almost entirely silent as he retold the drama of his life, it does not seem exaggerated to say that in a limited way he is fit to stand comparison with Shakespeare. In *The Donne Tradition* (1930) George Williamson wrote that 'of all the explorers of the soul who come with the seventeenth century, Donne, and not Milton, deserves to stand nearest to Shakespeare. . . Love poetry could never be quite the same after him, and religious verse that is poetry descends from him. His was one of the prodigious intellects which take all learning for their province, and one of those even rarer minds whose very thinking is poetical.' At least we can think of Donne standing not far from the greater man. There is no record that they met but they had friends in common including Ben Jonson. Sir Richard Baker, Donne's fellow student both in Oxford and in London, remembered that he had been well dressed and 'a great frequenter of Playes' when a young man-about-town. It seems very likely that he attended early performances of Shakespeare's plays right up to *Hamlet* in 1601. In 1600 a plan for a book was registered with the Stationers' Company, *Amours by J.D. with certain other sonnets by W.S.* So far as we know the project was abandoned but it would be very surprising if the two never got together. The surprise would come if the two men met and Donne never talked about himself. Perhaps the collaboration came to nothing because Shakespeare could not stand his fellow poet's egotism.

The platform on which Donne usually performed was London, and during a sermon about the life and death of a rich merchant who had 'acted great and various parts in it' he observed that 'this City is a great Theatre' (7:274). He was commemorating William Cockayne, about whom much could have been said had the preacher been discussing economics. One of Cockayne's schemes had wrecked an industry on which England had depended for centuries, the manufacture of cloth to be 'finished' and dyed abroad. In 1613 Cockayne secured from King James a monopoly for a company which would undertake all the final processes in London, but foreign merchants refused to buy its products and the result was the loss of the export market. The economic depression which followed – and which was one of the motives for emigration to America – was caused mainly by overpopulation in England and war in Europe, but Cockayne had played his part.

However, what fascinated Donne was not economics but personality. He therefore spoke about Cockayne the prominent man of business who had joined the dead and was now remembered for deeds which could commend him to the divine mercy: bringing up a family, being active in charity, saying prayers as his best investment. As a young poet Donne would no doubt have mocked and denounced a rich man who had done so much damage by a scheme to make himself even richer, but now that he was a preacher he thought it his duty to concentrate on the individual in relation to eternity. Did he therefore deserve to be condemned himself, as a stooge of the rich? That question will have to be faced. What is obvious is that as he lived his own life and approached his own death Donne would perform his part with a great sense of the drama of the individual living and dying before spectators – and even as a young poet who felt free to despise his seniors, he attacked their characters rather than their policies.

He did not wish to perform in the London of the theatres and of cruder entertainments on the south bank of the Thames. The stage of his life was a narrow strip on the north bank, about two miles long but never far from the road which ran from St Paul's Cathedral to royal Westminster. He was born in Bread Street, a short distance from the cathedral where he was to preach and be buried. He studied law in Lincoln's Inn which was down the road, down Fleet Street and the Strand, and began his career in York House which was a little further down. When his career collapsed his prison was in Fleet Street, near the chapel where he had been married in secret. When his career slowly revived he took lodgings in Fleet Street and was then housed more handsomely in nearby Drury Lane, before moving to the Deanery of the cathedral whose decaying medieval bulk was London's only building to be really tall.

If we can understand the plot of the drama of Donne's life, played out in the great theatre of London, that will not answer all the questions. We do not know all the facts and we ought not to suppose that all the words which Donne left behind in writing which has survived refer directly to his life. In a sermon (4:87) he reflected on the power of preaching and poetry to describe a world which, however, actually exists only in the responses of readers. 'How empty a thing is Rhetorique? (and yet Rhetorique will make absent and remote things present to your understanding). How weak a thing is Poetry? (and yet Poetry is a counterfeit Creation, and makes things that are not, as though they were).' So we must not expect to agree about the significance of the 'bracelet of bright haire' which his imagination placed on the arm of a skeleton. Nor must we expect all our more sensible questions to be answered by facts more solid than that bracelet. But if the known facts can be gathered and the probabilities assessed, and if much thought can be added, we may find that the plot of the drama of this complicated man's life emerges; we may be able to understand what can be understood. It is a large but limited ambition.

It seems good to make this attempt now because interest in Donne, including discussion in the academic world, has grown and grown in recent years, especially (but not solely) in the USA. 1995 saw the first two publications in an American project to reprint all his poetry in ten volumes, devotedly giving all the variations between the handwritten sources and the printed editions (with the assistance of computers). 160 of his sermons were written out by him and published after his death by his son John, to be re-edited in ten volumes in 1953–62 as a tribute from California to his enduring position in the history of preaching. No Englishman's private letters had previously been printed on the scale which was thought suitable for John Donne, in a collection published twenty years after his death – and not many writers of any nation or age have continued to arouse such personal interest that a larger and more accurate edition of some two hundred letters was being prepared in America some 350 years later. In 1982 the

John Donne Journal was founded as a medium for scholarly articles about his life and work; many conferences have been held; and many American scholars have published books providing an analysis in depth. And all this re-editing and re-thinking has come from a continent which Donne never saw, although he was keenly interested in the new colony in Virginia and was a contemporary of the Pilgrim Fathers who founded New England. How wrong T. S. Eliot was when he wrote in 1931 that 'Donne's poetry is a concern of the present and of the recent past rather than of the future'! And how wrong he was to predict that another revival would prove short-lived, saying that 'his sermons will disappear as quickly as they have appeared'! As the twenty-first century begins it seems clear that an interest in Donne has become a part of any serious interest in the heights of literature in English.

2 At the dore

I tune the Instrument here at the dore

'A Hymne to God my God'

He was born at an unknown date during the first half of 1572. His mother Elizabeth came from a family which was religious to the point of martyrdom and which was also literary: in so far as the talents of this poet and preacher were inherited, the genes responsible were, it seems, transmitted by his mother. His father was a prosperous ironmonger who in fast-expanding London ran a business attached to his home, making and selling kitchen utensils. John, the eldest son, was introduced to the power of death when this father died before the boy's fourth birthday, to be followed by one sister next year and two others in 1582. His mother quickly made a second marriage, to a leading London doctor, John Symingеs, and the family moved into a house which had a garden. His childhood seems to have been reasonably happy, with care about his education. When he thought he was near death in 1623, he was to remember that 'my parents would not give mee over to a Servant's correction'. When preaching he was to remark that 'a man can remember when he began to spell but not when he began to read perfectly, and when he began to joyne his letters but not when he began to write perfectly' (4:149).

It is frustrating that Donne, who could write well enough on many other subjects, left behind him very little evidence about the years before he became a student of law. However, his first biographer, Izaak Walton, recorded that having been well grounded while in London he was sent to other tutors in Oxford and Cambridge, and there seems to be no good reason to contradict this statement. It is known that in October 1584 he was admitted as a student in Hart Hall, Oxford, along with his brother Henry, who was a year younger. Their ages were young by the standards of that time, but not impossibly so. Boys were sent to school to learn 'grammar' when about seven years old and from that age young John would have had Latin beaten into him, either in a school or at home, before Oxford at the age of twelve.

In Oxford Henry Wotton became one of Donne's lifelong friends and he was probably the source of Walton's report that even before he entered Hart Hall the lad was already so well educated that he was compared with a scholar of the Italian Renaissance, Pico della Mirandola, 'of whom Story says, *That he was rather born, than made wise by study*'. He already had 'a good command both of the French and Latine Tongue' – and as Henry Wotton evidently found, he was also not slow to develop a gift for friendship. From an early age he had the knack of combining the solitary work of a reader and writer with active friendship, which he called his 'second religion': he knew that in fact no one is born wise – or becomes wise by meeting only books. Also, he needed an audience.

One of the attractions of Hart Hall was that it had no chapel from which absences could be noted by an authority on the lookout for dangerous 'Papists'. When registering for admission the two Donne boys stated their age as a year younger than was the truth and the explanation seems to be that the statutes of the university demanded that at or after the age of sixteen anyone wishing to proceed to a degree should take an oath accepting the supremacy of Queen Elizabeth over the State and 'in all spiritual or ecclesiastical things'. The boys had a firmly Roman Catholic mother who wanted their Oxford education to last a little longer than this Protestant law intended. In due course, when he was obviously of an age when his religion had to be declared, John

Donne was withdrawn from Oxford. Walton says that he went to Cambridge where he was a 'most laborious Student, often changing his studies but endeavouring to take no degree'.

Donne seems to have told him about Cambridge and it seems very likely that the build-up of knowledge and wit continued in the environment of the other university. Cambridge had no equivalent to Oxford's demand that the royal supremacy over the Church must be accepted by all students over sixteen but the colleges did not welcome Papists and Donne probably kept a low profile as an unregistered student, chosing his own tutors, books and lectures. But Walton was inaccurate in a comparatively minor matter. He says that Donne remained in Cambridge 'till his seventeenth year', which by his reckoning was 1590 (because he also made a slip by giving the year of birth as 1573 instead of 1572). The more probable dates are 1586 or 1587 for the move from Oxford to Cambridge and 1588 or 1589 for the start of foreign travel. Walton says that the travel began in 1597 and lasted for 'some years' but we know that at the turn of 1597–98 Donne began a job in London; so scholarly opinion is that the journey to see the world was undertaken immediately after the more academic education which could be provided by tutors in Oxford and Cambridge.

He had inherited from his father funds which could be used for education and travel and from his mother he must have gained a great sense of belonging to Catholic Europe; her own family's history included Catholic martyrs among whom Sir Thomas More was the most famous but not the last. What is certain is that Donne was deeply interested in Italy and Spain, knew their languages and read their books. It is also certain that by the age of eighteen, when he became a student of law, he had developed a self-confidence which would have been less likely had he remained a 'most laborious Student'.

Walton says that Donne often mentioned with a 'deploration' his disappointment that he had not been able to afford to proceed from Italy to 'the Holy Land, for viewing Jerusalem and the Sepulchre of our Saviour'; he had gone to Spain instead. There he would have had a problem which was not merely financial: England was at war with Spain until 1604 and narrowly escaped invasion by the Spanish Armada in 1588. But the difficulty would have vanished if he could present himself as one of the many refugees from Elizabethan Protestantism and it is highly probable that this is what he did in the year after the Armada. We know that in 1591 he could pose for a miniature portrait which depicted him as an eager Roman Catholic. The miniature has not survived but a clumsy engraving of it was used as the frontispiece to the 1635 edition of his poems. It is full of character. It has been suggested that the original picture was the work of a leading artist, Nicholas Hilliard (on the ground that Donne's poem on 'The Storme' includes a compliment to his skill), but it seems very unlikely that this fashionable painter would have risked losing the patronage of the queen and her court in order to glamorize an obscure but cocky young Papist.

It would not be surprising if the miniature was intended to please his mother. It would mark his return to London and her third marriage, to another staunch Roman Catholic (Richard Rainsford), before February 1591. The picture is of an eager youth who flaunts both his masculinity and his faith: his age is given as eighteen. His face, while not beautiful, begins to have power. His hair is long (this was the new fashion) although the moustache is not yet growing at the desired strength. His dark doublet (coat) is also fashionable, with padded shoulders, many buttons down the front and sleeves cut so as to show the shirt. Rather awkwardly he lifts a gentleman's short sword in order to get it into the picture. A coat of arms is also displayed, belonging to the ancient and rich Welsh family of Dwyn; this too may be a bit awkward, since he is a London ironmonger's son. But certainly it is a portrait of a swashbuckling crusader. His earring is a little cross, a sign that he is ready to fight any Protestant who objects to this 'Popish' symbol. The motto, presumably around the edge of the miniature, means 'Sooner dead than changed'. It is defiantly in Spanish although that language is being used only three years after the Protestant nation's great moment of danger from the Spanish Armada.

That portrait announces that a crusader is willing to join the Catholic martyrs in his mother's family, even if it means being branded as a friend of the hated and feared Spaniards. But does the young man actually mean that? Does he know that in the Spanish play these words were sung by a young woman who was going to transfer her affections to another lover? Had Donne lost his Catholic enthusiasm as well as his virginity while abroad? We cannot know – but another portrait, also by an unknown artist, shows that for him much had changed after a few years.

This portrait was painted in the pose of a man being martyred in the cause of the fashionable religion of love. He is no longer bareheaded. His black hat is very large, as was expected when a young gentleman wished to conceal from the world his disappointment in love, although in Donne's case the hat is lifted back so as to reveal his face, which seems not utterly tragic. His lips look sensual under a carefully tended moustache. An expensive, transparent shirt falls over an elaborate lace collar with a tie which is embroidered. One hand is fully visible, displaying fingers which seem long enough to caress a woman acceptably (and are too long to be accurate work by the painter), but the other hand is half-hidden in the darkness and covered by a fur glove. The Latin motto around the top of the picture means 'O Lady, lighten our darkness'. It has been suggested that this is a serious prayer addressed to the Virgin Mary, but the pose in this portrait is far from devotional and the words are a deliberate misquotation of a prayer to the 'Lord' transferred from the service of Compline in the medieval

Sarum Breviary to Evening Prayer in the Church of England's Book of Common Prayer.

In 1959 this portrait in the possession of the Marquis of Lothian was recognized as 'that Picture of myne which is taken in Shadowes' and which Donne bequeathed to his friend Sir Robert Ker, an ancestor of the marquis. It had been hanging in the Deanery of St Paul's and Donne felt it necessary to explain in his will that it was painted 'very many yeares before I was of this profession'. In his old age Thomas Morton, then Bishop of Durham, recalled seeing this portrait at an earlier stage in a 'chamber' of Lincoln's Inn occupied by a 'dear friend' of Donne's, almost certainly Christopher Brooke. It seems that on Brooke's death in 1628 this picture of a fashionably melancholic lover was moved to the Deanery. (The dean's wife would not have cared for it but she had been dead for eleven years.) It is interesting that Donne was not ashamed to display this relic of his unclerical past; out of that past, as out of shadows, the great preacher had come.

By the time this portrait was painted he had left behind any thought of being a Catholic crusader and martyr. Instead, what had endured from his time in Italy, and had grown during his time back in London, was his willingness to play a role which was fashionable in Italian Renaissance poetry, the role of the lover left to sulk in the dark by a coldly unattainable mistress. It was a role inherited from the medieval tradition of songs of 'courtly' love – which by convention was never consummated, one reason being that the mistress was usually married to someone else, someone with the power to punish. This was the role played famously by two poets, Boccaccio as he flirted with the noble Fiametta and Petrarch as he lamented snubs by Laura or her death. In England the 'Petrarchan' tradition in this style of poetry went back to Chaucer's adaptation of Boccaccio in *Troilus and Criseyde* but it was given a boost in the Elizabethan age when actual or would-be courtiers had to express a devotion to the Virgin Queen.

So the pose in this picture belongs to a convention – yet the sadness may also be heartfelt, giving us a glimpse of the first great love of Donne's life. The probability that this portrait hung in Christopher Brooke's chamber can be linked with the verse-letter 'To Mr C. B.'. There Donne laments that the 'Saint of his affection' who is his 'Sunne', 'thrice-fairer' than the sun which warms the world, has left London for a place which has already been reached by 'sterne winter'. The poet is in 'amorous paine' because he feels that the lady is being cold towards him and no expression of his own hot love seems able to touch her:

> Yet, love's hot fires, which martyr my sad minde,
> Doe send forth scalding sighes, which have the Art
> To melt all Ice, but that which walls her heart.

Presumably this letter was sent to Christopher Brooke because he was then near the lady and in a position to influence her in Donne's favour. It seems possible that she was Brooke's sister, now living in York where Brooke's father was a rich merchant – and also possible that the picture was sent to her and, when the affair ended, passed by her to her brother. If it was, the rejected Donne seems to have grown sentimental rather than angry, since his friendship with Christopher Brooke survived the display of the picture. Or did Donne give Brooke the picture in order to reinforce the plea in that verse-letter?

The verse-letter 'To Mr I. L.' (who cannot be identified) almost certainly refers to the same lady. She is worshipped as 'my Sun' and she has gone to 'your North parts', leaving Donne in a London where he experiences 'no Sommer' but 'pestilence' instead. In contrast, I. L. is 'in Paradise', enjoying not only the company of Donne's own beloved 'Sun' but also 'thy lov'd wife' and an estate rich in pasture and woods – and so the despairing Donne sends a plea similar to that made in 'To Mr C. B.': 'helpe thy friend to save'.

Another piece of evidence that Donne was influenced by this tradition of Petrarchan love, adoring the unattainable, is that he copied an Italian motto from Petrarch into many of the books which he owned: it announced that his role in life was contemplative, not active. But in the 1590s he could not be expected to confine himself to contemplation. He was bursting with energy and had to prepare to earn his living. Also, he did not intend to be entirely inactive in his relations with women.

He was admitted as a student of law in Lincoln's Inn in May 1592, on financial terms which show that he had already spent a year in a preparatory college, Thavies Inn. The four 'Inns of Court' in London were in this period the leading centre for higher education in England, since Oxford and Cambridge were still basically medieval in their syllabus for undergraduates and heavily theological in the interests of the resident graduates, and there was no other university in England. But the young men who went there (often after an Oxbridge spell without necessarily taking a degree) were a mixed lot. Probably most of them wanted to meet marriageable women although they were still on the young side for marriage, and probably most of them also dreamed of attracting attention in the court of Queen Elizabeth, partly because they were patriotic subjects of a woman who had become the centre of a national cult but mainly perhaps because they hoped for the wealth which could follow royal favour. But there was a mixture in the students' social origins. Some had been born into privilege. While in London they would acquire some knowledge of the law which would be useful when they were landowners and magistrates, but their main interest probably lay in their pleasures. These would include the development of social skills such as making love, making a disturbance and making or appreciating music and poetry. Other young men were, however, more genuine students because they knew that their more limited financial prospects meant that they must acquire the knowledge of the law and the eloquence in court which they would need if they were to make a success of being professional lawyers. In Lincoln's Inn there were about forty students of one kind or the other.

Donne did not completely belong to either set in this small community where about a hundred lawyers were also based. He did study law. In his fourth 'satyre' he included a nightmare when

> mee thought I saw
> One of our Giant Statutes ope his jaw
> To sucke me in . . .

but it would be in character for him to enjoy arguing about the law more than merely memorizing what a long law contained. The art of argument formed a great part of higher education in that age. In the universities the young were required to take part in disputations three times a week, as a test of what they had already learned in their studies of logic and rhetoric, and in the Inns of Court students spent much of their time either listening to the arguments of barristers in courts or holding their own 'moots' where they had to argue for or against a given plea. It was also hoped that they would talk about law at dinners which were compulsory. We know from what he wrote that the young Donne loved an argument. He wrote 'paradoxes' setting out unconventional opinions which he defended – as he claimed, in the expectation that someone else would defend common sense. (One of his paradoxes was 'that a Wise man is knowne by much Laughinge'.) In his love poems he was very prone to argue, although the woman concerned was very seldom allowed to reply.

Moreover, Donne seems to have learned from his enjoyment of arguments that it would strengthen his position if he did learn what the law said. While formally enrolled in Lincoln's Inn he seems to have postponed most of that labour, but when he was unemployed in the early 1600s he resumed his study of law – to such effect that Walton thought that he rapidly acquired 'such a perfection as was judged' to be comparable 'with many who had made that study the employment of their whole life'. No doubt Walton was exaggerating but we do know that as late as 1612 Donne consulted a senior friend (Thomas Morton) about an idea that he might resume his study and become a full-time ecclesiastical lawyer. He dropped the idea after discouragement but claimed in a letter that the study of the law remained his favourite 'entertainment'. In the 1620s he became a part-time ecclesiastical judge, sitting on commissions which decided cases known to modern researchers.

However, any serious interest in the laws lay in the future. In the 1590s he was more anxious to be a gentleman and spent money and time in being one, knowing that the course in the Inns of Court, which usually lasted for about seven years, did not involve either formal examinations or a tutorial system. In his first 'satyre' we are given a glimpse of his wide reading in his study, separated by a wooden partition from the 'chamber' which he shared with Christopher Brooke:

> Leave mee, and in this standing woodden chest,
> Consorted with these few bookes, let me lye
> In prison, and here be coffin'd, when I dye;
> Here are God's conduits, grave Divines . . .

together with more secular literature: the works of Aristotle 'the Philosopher' who was also 'Nature's Secretary', the writings of statesmen and the 'gathering Chronicles' of historians, together with 'Giddie fantastique Poëts of each land'. The Latin poets almost certainly included Horace, who was to some extent imitated in this 'satyre'. No law books were mentioned.

Donne was later to criticize himself for having neglected legal studies in his youth; he blamed his 'immoderate' desire for wider knowledge. But his contempt for lawyers could be fierce. In his second 'satyre' he dismissed 'men which chuse Law practise for meere gaine' as worse prostitutes than 'imbrothel'd strumpets'. He mocked them for being unable to woo a woman with any words except legal jargon. (He had a particular lawyer-poet in mind.) He denounced them for taking bribes and uttering lies which would enable them to accumulate estates while the 'old landlords' were left to decline and 'winds in our ruin'd Abbeys rore'.

The young Donne must have spent time writing about lawyers which he ought to have spent reading laws, but this was surely excusable, for in the 1590s it was fashionable for young poets to mock the corrupt older men who had got the jobs in the law courts and at the royal court – and Donne was ahead of the pack. He must have seen that he had it in him to be a poet equal or superior to any contemporary. The first volume of Spenser's *Faerie Queene* was published in 1590, and Sidney's *Astrophel and Stella* in 1591. Shakespeare's less fanciful *Venus and Adonis* and *The Rape of Lucrece* followed in 1593–94. Marlowe's *Hero and Leander*, even closer to Donne's own earthy eroticism, was not printed until 1598 but seems to have circulated quite widely before that. Although (like a courtier such as Sidney) Donne was not interested in being printed in his lifetime, it is highly probable that he thought he could write as least as well as any of his contemporaries, with a style of his own, rejecting the Spenser–Sidney belief that the purpose of poetry was to 'delight' by sweetness and to 'teach' by high morality. The temptation to quote his love poetry must be resisted for the time being but here it can be said that his originality entitled Donne to laugh in his second 'satyre' at second-rate poets. These, he said, 'digested' the work of the masters whom they imitated, but they produced as their own work only 'excrement'.

Bishops would have agreed with Donne's estimate of the work of one fellow poet in the Inns of Court, John Davies, although no doubt they would have avoided the reference to dung. Davies dedicated to his friend Richard Martin a poem called *Orchestra*, a celebration of the decorum in the dancing of that age, but in 1598 he was expelled from the legal profession because in a fit of rage he violently assaulted Martin. Next year Davies made another mistake: he arranged for his *Epigrams and Elegies* to be printed. They were excessively improper; the bishops were scandalized; the hangman was ordered to burn them publicly; and the censor was told to forbid the publication of any further pornography.

Ben Jonson, who unlike Davies was a major poet, told William Drummond that Donne had written 'all his best pieces' by the age of 25. Jonson could be imprecise about dates, and could not be sure of knowing everything which Donne had written, but having been born in the same year he had reason to be jealous of what his contemporary had achieved: in 1597 he was imprisoned for his share in the writing of a low comedy which the authorities had found offensive, and in 1598 he was so dispirited that he made a brief return to his first job, as a bricklayer. Next year he bounced back into writing plays – and he dedicated one of them to the Inns of Court, 'the Noblest Nurserie of Humanity and Liberty in this Kingdom'.

Clearly Donne found the freedom in Lincoln's Inn a 'Nurserie' for his growth as a poet (if not as a lawyer), but it was not a nursery isolated from the sorrows of the world. For much of his time there it was surrounded by a London being massacred by epidemics. A verse-letter 'To Mr T. W.' reported that in every street 'Infections follow, overtake and meete'. In its context that sounds as if this young man did not expect to meet his own death and another such letter 'To Mr E. G.' claimed that 'by staying in London' Donne was bored rather than distraught. The theatres and the streets had no life in them and the only amusements on offer were the unsubtle sport of the baiting of a tethered bear by dogs – plus such fun as could be provided by the course in law:

> Our Theatres are fill'd with emptines.
> As lancke and thin is every street and way
> As a woman deliver'd yesterday.
> Nothing whereat to laugh my spleen espyes
> But bearbaitings or Law exercise.

But in 1593 Donne's public face had to be brave because, as he told a closer friend, Rowland Woodward, in his personal life he experienced 'Griefe which did drowne me'. His sorrow tempted him to write bitterly 'satirique' poetry 'in skorne of all'. For his only brother died tragically.

In his first published book, the *Pseudo-Martyr* of 1610, Donne lets us see the family in his background. He then recalled how difficult it had been for him to 'blot out certaine impressions of the Romane religion' because in his early years a family which 'by nature had a power and superiority over my will', and later tutors who had impressed him 'by their learning and good life', had naturally enough made him think of himself as a Roman Catholic. In 1610 he was still willing to make public his pride in members of his family who had been courageous in their refusal to deny their faith. He was 'derived from such a stocke and race, as, I beleeve, no family (which is not of far longer extent and greater branches) hath endured and suffered more in their persons and fortunes, for obeying the Teachers of Romane Doctrine, than it hath done'. Indeed, 'I have been ever kept awake in a meditation of Martyrdome'.

In his unpublished book *Biathanatos* he called the martyred Thomas More, whose sister was his own mother's great-grandmother, 'a man of the most tender and delicate conscience that the world saw since St Augustine'. Like More, Donne's grandfather John Heywood had incurred the wrath of Henry VIII. He had been imprisoned in the Tower of London, told that he was to be dragged through the streets to execution as a traitor, and fastened to a wicker hurdle for this grim purpose, before being reprieved. Perhaps this had been a sick joke, for the victim was a comic entertainer well known for his witty sallies which in happier circumstances had entertained the royal court. When Elizabeth I made England officially Protestant, John Heywood fled abroad. Donne's great-uncle Thomas Heywood had been seriously executed; his uncle Ellis Heywood had been forced into exile; and another uncle, Jasper Heywood, had been the leader of the Jesuit mission to England and had very nearly joined his fellow Jesuits in a very painful death.

In Oxford Ellis and Jasper Heywood had been promising scholars before accepting a vocation as Catholic priests. In 1610 Donne remembered being present at 'a Consultation of Jesuits in the Tower' and almost certainly the occasion had been when his mother took him along with another Jesuit in order to visit the imprisoned Jasper and to discuss a petition to the Crown for toleration. The government felt too threatened to be tolerant: captured Catholics could be tortured severely, taken through the streets amid derision, hanged, cut down alive and butchered by the hangman, and in the reign of Elizabeth almost three hundred people suffered all or most of these cruelties. It seems that the reason why Jasper was allowed to go into exile rather than subjected to this fate was twofold: he had been less hotheaded than the Catholics who were actively planning to support a foreign invasion, and the savagery in the public executions of priests had aroused indignation abroad, causing Elizabeth's chief minister (Burghley) to write a defensive pamphlet about *The Execution of Justice in England.*

For John Donne the year 1593 started well. He was assured of his popularity with his fellow students when they elected him as Master of the Revels and he could look forward to receiving and spending the remainder of his father's legacy to him: in June he would be 21. But early in May came tragedy. His brother Henry, who was now in Thavies Inn preparing to join him in Lincoln's Inn, was loyal to their mother's strong faith. He showed this when a Catholic priest, William Harrington, visited him in his chamber. The young man confessed his sins, presumably in the knowledge that this had been made an act of treason under a law of 1571. Presumably after a tip-off by an informer, government agents arrested both men. As previously instructed, Harrington denied being a priest even under torture, but in his own pain Henry made the fatal admission. No doubt full of self-condemnation, he was imprisoned and soon died from the epidemic then raging in the sordid cells. Next February Harrington was executed publicly and barbarously: he struggled with the hangman before being disembowelled.

Whether or not John Donne had already drifted far away from his mother's strong faith while enjoying the pleasures of Italy, Spain or London, it seems probable that the shocks of these terrible deaths in 1593–4 clinched his decision not to be identified with his family's martyr-making legacy. He would no longer 'bind my conscience to any locall religion' (as he was to put it in 1610) if the religion of his inheritance meant being regarded, certainly penalized and possibly executed, as a traitor to his country.

The plague which had killed his brother gave Donne some free time during the second half of 1593, when the normal activities of Lincoln's Inn were suspended, and he seems to have plunged into theological study, purchasing and heavily marking the recently published long defence of Roman Catholicism by Cardinal Bellarmine. He could show a heavily marked copy to an Anglican clergyman who interrogated him. Later he could say that he had 'surveyed and digested the whole body of divinity controverted between ours and the Roman Church' before deciding that the Church of England was 'ours'. Meanwhile he conformed to the government's religion outwardly, his comments on Bellarmine seem to have satisfied his Anglican examiner, and the principle which governed his private thoughts was stated in his third 'satyre', a poem which no doubt he kept private: 'doubt wisely'.

His name disappears from the records of Lincoln's Inn at the end of 1594. He was a student there that autumn and was elected Steward of Christmas, but he paid a fine and declined that responsibility for the festivities. (It was the first Christmas to be celebrated in the traditional style since 1591; at last London had a brief freedom from plague.) More importantly, he had decided not to complete the long course required before admission to the legal profession. The only surviving trace of his life in 1595 is that in July he employed young Thomas Danby as a servant, but after eighteen months Danby vanished together with some of Donne's clothes. The probability is that Donne was living in lodgings near the Inn, spending his time as he wished and also spending his inheritance from his father, which had been increased by the share previously reserved for Henry. This was a period when he was free to write and to add to the experiences which directly or indirectly equipped him to write about sexual relationships.

What he wrote was not mere 'excrement' but its coarseness is shown up if we compare it with Shakespeare's light-hearted masterpiece, *A Midsummer Night's Dream*, which was certainly written about this time and may have been first performed at an aristocratic wedding in 1594. It is of course a celebration of marriage, full of joy as well as humour. There is a great contrast between this play and a poem which Donne seems to have written for performance during the students' revels at midsummer in 1595.

His 'Epithalamion made at Lincoln's Inn' was a 'marriage song' superficially like Shakespeare's play, and there seem to be mocking references to Spenser's lushly romantic *Epithalamium*, published in the first half of 1595. Unlike plays and poems which went down well at the court of Elizabeth (where it was the custom for courtiers to pretend that they were in love with the Virgin Queen), Donne's poem is crudely for men only. Unlike more formal plays and poems which invoked divine blessings on the happiness of lovers who married, this 'marriage song' gloats over the deflowering of a virgin who is not allowed to speak, partly because the words accompany a charade in which the part of the bride is taken by a man. This script appears to be designed to raise cheers from tipsy and hormone-infested young bachelors who recite the refrain

> *Today put on perfection and a woman's name.*

At first the girl is told that 'your solitary bed nourseth sadnesse' and is a grave for 'that warme balme-breathing thigh'. Then 'Daughters of London' (who, it is hoped, will be 'our Golden Mines' when they marry these young gentlemen) are invited to attend the marriage of a girl who is 'faire and rich'. After further remarks about her sexually available body, the bridegroom comes and she is sacrificed

> Like an appointed lambe, when tenderly
> The priest comes on his knees t'embowell her.

Thus Donne demonstrated that he was one of the lads, but he had still to prove to his little social world that he was a Protestant fit for employment by the Crown. This he did by becoming one of the gentlemen who volunteered for active service in naval expeditions in 1596–97, episodes in the long war between England and Spain. Sending a verse-letter to a friend, he said frankly that his motives were mixed, for he himself did not know

> Whether a rotten state, and hope of gaine,
> Or to disuse me from the queasie paine
> Of being belov'd, and loving, or the thirst
> Of honour, or faire death, out pusht me first . . .

By now he needed money and hoped to have a share in the prizes to be gained by looting Cadiz or capturing some of the fleet bringing to the Azores treasure from the mines controlled by the Spaniards in South America. But his fifth 'elegie' sounded heroic. It seems to have been addressed to a mistress, real or imaginary, before embarking on the voyage into Cadiz and danger. He hoped to find her still faithful when he returned 'weather-beaten' with 'Sun-beams tann'd', perhaps with hands torn by having to row with 'rude oares', perhaps with the 'blew staines' of gunpowder on his skin, perhaps with his whole body a 'sack of bones'. He may have genuinely hoped to impress a woman when he returned as a veteran of war, but he does not impress modern readers by the brutality of his short poem which gloats over the burning of the Spanish flagship, when some men 'leap'd forth' and were killed by the English guns and others who remained on board were drowned when the ship went down. The behaviour of the English troops when they briefly occupied Cadiz was also brutal; their vandalism was directed with a special zest against the images of Popery.

More impressive poems reported to Christopher Brooke two near-disasters during the second (futile) voyage, to the Azores. One was a storm when winds and waves roared, the sun was hidden by clouds and rain, and the sails were torn into rags looking like the strips of flesh on the corpse of 'one hang'd in chaines, a year ago'. Another was very different: the English fleet was becalmed, with the ocean as smooth as a mirror. Some of the sailors hung out clothes to dry and some dived into the hot sea, to find it a 'brimstone Bath' which made them 'parboyl'd wretches'. No one had the energy to clean the ship, so that 'feathers and dust' lay 'in one place . . . today and yesterday'. Donne thought about poetry during these experiences at sea and he described them in imagery to be expected not from a sailor but from a very urbane and very superior observer. His earliest letter to survive was written in Plymouth in 1597. It complains about the 'stinke of 150 land soldiers' and 'so very very bad weather' during the voyage which had landed him back in a port where prices were too high.

He had learned that he was not cut out to be a military hero. His poem 'Love's Warre' exhibited a total lack of patriotism (which may have been one reason why it was not printed before 1802) but was realistic about the field in which he might still hope to make conquests. He has no wish to serve in the wars in the Netherlands or in Ireland, or in any more naval expeditions:

> Long voyages are long consumptions,
> And ships are carts for executions.

He prefers the 'more glorious service' of love, not war:

> Here let mee warr; in these armes let mee lye;
> Here lett mee parlee, batter, bleede, and dye.
> Thy armes imprison me, and myne armes thee,
> Thy hart thy ransome is: take myne for mee . . .
> There men kill men, we'll make one by and by.

These expeditions had brought him more than an experience of war and a renewed appetite for peaceful pursuits in and out of bed. During the second voyage he made friends with a fellow volunteer who was the son of Sir Thomas Egerton, Lord Keeper of the Great Seal, Master of the Rolls and a Privy Councillor close to Queen Elizabeth whose messages he communicated to the House of Lords (before being made Lord Chancellor in 1603). Through this friendship a door was opened into the great world, for Donne was employed as one of the great man's secretaries. He was now at last an insider. In his second 'satyre' he said that both Papists and poets seemed to be 'poore, disarm'd, . . . not worth hate' and he had belonged to both categories. Now he had his foot on the ladder of promotion and Egerton made a specially suitable patron, partly because he was fond of poetry and poets and partly because he had himself been listed as a 'recusant' or non-conformist Papist as recently as the 1570s. So Donne was now an established civil servant and a letter which has survived from Sir William Cornwallis, in verse suggesting a visit to a theatre, was addressed 'to my ever to be respeckted friend Mr John Done'. He was especially excited to be involved in plans to reduce the corruption and delays in the law courts. In his fifth 'satyre', which he probably showed to a delighted employer, he added to a denunciation of the law courts contempt for the dishonesty both of their officers and of many of the plaintiffs. But whereas the Roman poet Juvenal had ended his satire attacking lawyers with a lament that nothing could be done, Donne expressed delight that Queen Elizabeth was now willing for the abuses to be brought to her attention, and that Egerton was the ideal reformer:

> Greatest and fairest Empresse, know you this?
> Alas, no more than Thames' calme head doth know
> Whose meades her armes drown, or whose corne o'rflow:
> You Sir, whose righteousnes she loves, whom I
> By having leave to serve am most richly
> For service paid, authoriz'd, now beginne
> To know and weed out this enormous sinne.

Like many others, he seems to have been full of genuine admiration for Egerton. He was to send a copy of his first published book to the great man with a letter saying that 'those poor sparks of Understandinge or Judgement which are in mee were derived and kindled from you'. That tribute does not seem to be an example of the artificial flattery of which he was capable; the poetry which he had already written was proof of his 'wit' or cleverness but his life so far had left room for the development of wisdom, and he had been lucky to be given the education provided by daily contact with a wise and honest senior who truly deserved to be 'respeckted'. But letters surviving from these busy days show that his mind was not wholly absorbed in reforms of the law courts. He found time to write a good deal of poetry. He also enjoyed gossip about the royal court, although in his fourth 'satyre' he expressed a lofty scorn for a courtier:

> Of triviall household trash he knowes; He knowes
> When the Queene frown'd, or smil'd, and he knowes what
> A subtle States-man may gather of that;
> He knowes who loves; whom; and who by poyson
> Hasts to an Office's reversion . . .

With the support of that 'subtle States-man', Egerton, he seemed to be hastening to wealth himself, and as a first instalment he accepted a grant by the queen of some land in Lincolnshire. His acceptance has been thought to be out of keeping with his morally severe denunciations of lawyers and courtiers who built up estates out of corruption, but actually he was given only the rent received from land which belonged to his grandfather John Heywood, then a 'Papist' in exile, and it is probable that he handed the money over (a practice which the government allowed). Anyway a grant of land would have been part of a system which rightly or wrongly seemed to be incurable. A poet could mock the courtiers (as both Donne and Ben Jonson did) but could look to the court for rewards: the mockery was a standard practice, but so was a poet's need to live.

For centuries the main function of a king had been to lead the nobility with an eye on the need to defend, and if possible expand, the realm. For such government as there was, he had been served by literate and numerate 'clerks' mostly supplied and rewarded by the Church. He had relied on the chief landowners being able to produce soldiers, and on the richer laity and clergy being willing to produce subsidies, to respond to an emergency. Now there seemed to be a continuous emergency, for in an age of inflation the Crown needed not soldiers in person but more and more money, yet Parliament was never willing to vote for adequate taxation. One answer seemed to be the sale of offices under the Crown. From the Church the Crown now needed not 'clerks' but yet more money, so that clergymen wishing to become bishops were expected to hand over money or at least to agree that estates which had financed their predecessors should now support laymen favoured or used by the Crown. Laymen appointed to positions in the royal court or the government were still paid only minimal salaries. They were expected to reimburse themselves either by receiving grants (of land or commercial privileges) from the Crown, or by welcoming bribes from individuals. The corruption could make the Crown's agents liable to being deserted by the Crown: thus King James was to abandon Francis Bacon, his extremely clever Lord Chancellor, when the House of Commons was determined on his fall. A similar fate was to overtake the Earl of Suffolk, who while Lord Treasurer and embezzler-in-chief had built himself a palace at Audley End. But discreet corruption did not cause too much scandal: thus Robert Cecil, now Earl of Salisbury, was to build himself two palaces while in charge of the administration and died at the height of respectability, having given one of these palaces to the king. Under this system, everything depended on access to the Crown's favour.

Everyone knew that the system was corrupt and the young Donne was only one of the many writers who said so, in private or more dangerously in public, but no one clearly saw any realistic alternative – and Donne was only one of the clever young men who were willing to join the system. At the time his conscience may have troubled him, and later on, when he looked back from a pulpit, it clearly did. 'We make Satyrs', he preached, 'and we looke that the world should call that wit, when God knows that this is great part self-guiltinesse and we do but reprehend things which we ourselves have done; we cry out upon the illnesse of the times and we make the times ill' (7:408). However, in October 1601 Donne seems to have had no difficulty about accepting an offer of a seat in Parliament: he was one of the two members 'elected' to represent a small borough in Northamptonshire which was controlled by the Lord of the Manor, Egerton's son John.

He felt close to the top of politics when the Earl of Essex, formerly his commander in the war ('Our Earle' in a poem), formerly also the queen's favourite, disobeyed her by leaving his command of the army in Ireland without her permission, burst into her bedroom unannounced, fell very sharply from favour, was confined to York House as Egerton's unwilling guest, was allowed back to his own house, staged a farcical mini-rebellion, and was executed. Donne does not seem to have been greatly moved by the fate of Essex, who with his fellow-commander and great rival Ralegh had once seemed to embody the ambition and glamour of Elizabethan England immediately after the defeat of the Armada. But now there was another age and Donne called it an 'age of rusty iron' in his fifth 'satyre'. At Christmas 1599 he wrote to his friend Henry Wotton that the impetuous earl and the new age could not reach an understanding. Essex was not 'mist' in the circle which now had power and 'he plods on to his end'. That was also to be true about Ralegh, who was to be imprisoned for thirteen years and executed for treason in the next reign.

As Essex met his end Egerton's secretary was not going to stick his neck out – whereas Wotton, who had been employed by Essex, got in a panic and fled abroad. What did concern Donne was the general atmosphere of depression and intrigue as Elizabeth decayed towards death without naming any successor and without appointing anyone who had the combination of efficiency with charisma needed to be virtually her deputy in her old age. Robert Cecil, the son of the Lord Burghley who had been her indispensable chief minister in many happier years, had taken over from his father and was to keep the administration going until 1612; he was a tirelessly industrious worker but also a man on the make financially and a hunch-backed dwarf. The 1590s were a time of epidemics and bad harvests; the towns were almost as full of disease as of people and in the countryside about half the population lived below the level of decent subsistence. It was a time of an expensive and inconclusive war with Spain. And it was a time when the joyless creed of Calvinism was accepted by the more active of the clergy in the Church of England. This was the 'age of rusty iron' which inspired Donne to begin a long poem about evil in the history of the world.

It has often been thought that this poem, which after 520 lines was never completed, was to have ended with an attack either on the queen or on Robert Cecil. (Sir Herbert Grierson went so far as to say that it was 'obvious' that Elizabeth was Donne's target, but on p. 152 I shall argue that an error introduced by an editor or printer accounts for one reference to the target being 'shee' not 'hee'.) This seems very unlikely, for an ambitious civil servant such as Donne would have been mad to risk writing such an insult even if he kept it from the printer – and what he wrote included an 'Epistle' to the reader. Ben Jonson told William Drummond that the poem was to have ended by attacking John Calvin and this seems much more likely. It was safe to insult the Reformer: he was a foreigner and (since 1564) he was dead. It would be understandable if Donne wanted to express forcibly his strong disapproval of Calvinist influence over the Church of England. He was still enough of a Catholic to refer contemptuously to 'arguing' as 'heritiques' game' and to 'Luther and Mahomet' as evil figures in the part of the poem which he did finish, and Calvin would have seemed even more deplorable: Donne must have hated the destruction of order and beauty in church life and the cruelty of the doctrine that the great majority of the human race had been predestined by God to hell. Presumably the evil soul could migrate to Calvin after Luther's death (in 1546) – or possibly Donne, who was never entirely logical, did not fully think out the consequences of making both of these contemporaries 'prisons of flesh' to this one soul.

Calvin would fit the sarcastic passage in the poem which promised that 'the crowne and last straine of my song' would concern the evil influence over England of

> the great soule which here amongst us now
> Doth dwell, and moves that hand and tongue and brow,
> Which, as the Moone the sea, moves us . . .

Although Elizabeth was no Calvinist she had appointed and supported an Archbishop of Canterbury, John Whitgift, who in 1595 had been the chief architect of nineteen doctrinal statements called the Lambeth Articles. These constituted an attempt to push the Church of England into the official adoption of an extreme form of Calvinism. Since the Thirty-nine Articles had been accepted in 1571 as the Church's doctrinal position, already there had been a move quite far in this direction. Article 17 had affirmed the belief that by predestination God had decided to deliver some people 'chosen in Christ' from the 'damnation' awaiting 'mankind' – and had made this decision 'before the foundations of the world were laid'. However, it had not been made clear whether this was God's general policy or the choice of specified individuals before they were born, to be saved or damned. The Lambeth Articles were not so reticent: their teaching was that God had made a very long list of those destined to the torments of hell and had made that list before he made the world. The only question left unsettled was whether such a God could accurately be called good.

Five years after the Lambeth Articles Donne may well have feared that the Church to which he was obliged to conform was being tied to this repulsively cruel doctrine. He probably did not know that the queen refused to be impressed by her archbishop's tough theology although she used him as a tough administrator. He no doubt expected the ageing Elizabeth to be succeeded on the throne of England by a king from Scotland, the most thoroughly Calvinist country in Europe, but he cannot have been sure that this next Supreme Governor of the Church of England would leave the somewhat ambiguous Thirty-nine Articles untouched and try to make Scotland more Anglican. Least of all can he have expected King James to become his own patron after his ordination as an Anglican priest. Around 1600 he may well have thought that the 'great soule' of Calvin was gaining power over the mind of England, as a climax in the history of evil. It would not be surprising if this prospect helped to make him feel as gloomy as any Calvinist.

His poem was called *Metempsychosis* (Greek for 'transmigration of the soul') and had 'The Progresse of the Soule' as its sub-title. The tone is cynical and the view of the world is bleak. It is possible to gain a different impression after a careful study of the poem; one scholar who edited it with a commentary, Walter Milgate, found in it the 'high spirits', 'the grotesque fun and the sardonic humour', of a merry wit who enjoyed writing a 'mock-epic'. But probably few readers have found the poem amusing. Donne was never lyrical about nature but here he was relentless in the description of nature as a vast battlefield. There is no supervision by a commander; *Metempsychosis* was the nearest that Donne came to atheism. Endlessly one creature kills another, before being killed. Details in this poem can vividly represent a creature, its birth, its skill and its fate, but the 'progresse' of the sub-title is lacking both in the sordid process itself and in the poet's account of it. There seems to be an anticipation of the gloomiest emotions about the discovery of evolution 'red in tooth and claw' by the Victorians. But Donne was not a Darwinian scientist; he was a poet who at least in some moods (when he was alone in the evening after work?) was depressed by the 'age of rusty iron' and worried about his own future in a world of ruthless rivalries between competitors and factions. In the poem he addressed questions about himself to 'Great Destiny'. Would the new century bring him 'steepe ambition' or 'sleepie povertie'? For the time being he had enough ambition and self-confidence to boast:

> For though through many streights, and lands I roame,
> I launch at Paradise and I saile towards home

– 'home' being presumably Paradise itself in the long run, but more immediately London, where he hoped for steep promotion. At any rate the poem was intended to reach port with 'anchors laid' in the Thames.

From his wide reading he had picked up a notion which he now used as his poem's central 'conceit': the idea of the transmigration of a single soul through plants, beasts and people. The soul making this journey was the soul of evil and it began in the apple which infected Eve and Adam. Then it travelled through a mandrake (a legendary plant which fascinated Donne), a sparrow, a swan, a fish, an oyster-catcher, a whale, an elephant, a mouse, a wolf, a dog, an ape, the 'silly' Siphatecia who is raped by the ape, and Themech, 'sister and wife to Caine'. Some unity is given to this drama without a plot by the frequent references to sexual intercourse. Promiscuity is not condemned in the passage about the cock sparrow, and the wolf is not rebuked for the rape of the dog, but when human beings are involved there is a flicker of morality. Thus when Adam takes the fatal apple from Eve it is said that

> Man all at once was there by woman slaine . . .

About Themech their daughter it is said that she made a suitable 'sister and wife' to their son Cain the first murderer, for

> she knew treachery,
> Rapine, deceit, and lust, and ills enow
> To be a woman.

The date when the poem was abandoned was given as 16 August 1601. It was dedicated, it seems sarcastically, to 'Infinity' and it ended with what seems to be a reference to his own very uneasy position. Donne reflected that since he was the first murderer Cain was 'cursed' – yet according to the Bible most of 'those arts whence our lives are blest', 'plowing, building, ruling and the rest', were invented by Cain or his descendants. So was Cain good or bad? The truth was complicated and it had to be left to public opinion, not a reliable judge, to decide the difference between good and evil:

> Ther's nothing simply good, nor ill alone,
> Of every quality comparison
> The onely measure is, and judge, opinion.

No doubt Donne grew tired as he contemplated the almost infinite number of years and poetic lines (rhyming) through which the soul of evil would have to travel as it moved from Eve's apple to whoever was intended as the poem's climax. Near the beginning of the poem he had expressed a fear that its completion would take him thirty years ('sixe lustres') and bring 'expense of braine and spirit', and as he wrote he may well have seen more clearly that the whole project had been a mistake. But almost certainly the end was so abrupt because the poet had been overwhelmed by an event: he had fallen deeply in love. And he was afraid that because the woman he loved came from a very wealthy family, he would be treated as a criminal, almost as another Cain.

In a sense the Anne who was his Eve killed him, because marrying her was to kill his career when 'opinion' judged that their marriage had been a crime against the structure of society. But in August 1601 he saw no point in trying to write the rest of *Metempsychosis*. He was revising his fashionably male cynicism about what it means 'to be a woman', at least in one instance. He was now determined to marry this glorious woman, whatever the opinion of society and whatever the cost to him.

3 Winter-seeming

So, lovers dreame a rich and long delight,
But get a winter-seeming summer's night.

'Love's Alchymie'

He had fallen in love with his employer's niece, Anne More. It was a romance wide open to condemnation, for she was his superior in the class system, and having spent all the capital left to him by his father he had no money with which to maintain her in the grand style to which she was accustomed. Moreover, it could be said that he had taken advantage of his employment in a position of trust in order to seduce an innocent girl – as he had (rumour said) treated other women in his history. He was almost thirty years old, some five years past what was then the average age for men getting married, and she was approximately half his age, having led a very privileged and sheltered life. He must have understood how society was likely to react. Yet it was a romance and it would be natural for him to hope that he was entering a 'rich and long delight'.

They were married in secret not long before Christmas 1601. He must have known the legal situation, which was that the Church had retained from the Middle Ages jurisdiction in matrimonial cases. The ecclesiastical courts were therefore able to decide that any marriage was valid if the partners had freely consented and had consummated their union, if the man was over fourteen years of age and the woman over twelve, and if a priest had officiated. But in this case it would be folly to rely on an exemption from the rules being granted after the event, for this marriage was highly irregular. The canon law of the Church of England, soon to be restated in the revised code of 1604, prohibited marriages of persons under the age of 21 without the consent of their parents and of all marriages without announcements ('banns') in the parish churches of both partners on three Sundays, and the insistence on 'the banns of all that are to be married together' was plain in the Book of Common Prayer. It was also contrary to the custom of the Church to marry during the solemn season before Christmas (Advent). But even more to the point was the fact that Donne had defied the conventions of the society to which the Church belonged. And what happened was what Donne must have feared. When told about the secret wedding about two months later, Anne's father exploded in anger. He refused to part with the large financial dowry which would normally have accompanied such a bride. Instead, he demanded that the marriage should be annulled. His influence was such that the bridegroom, the officiating priest and the rising lawyer who had acted as witness were all thrown into prison, and Egerton dismissed his scandalous secretary. (The details will be discussed on pp. 254–9 and 283.)

Donne was shattered. In 1599 he had boasted to a friend: 'I have alwayes been either so strong or so stubborne against any assault of fortune, that she hath rather pickt quarrells with my friends than with my self.' Now he needed all the friends he could get to sustain him with money or at least encouragement. After a time the Archbishop of Canterbury's court accepted his marriage, his father-in-law's rage diminished and in 1606 money was produced for the modest support of Anne and a frequently growing brood of children. Moreover, Donne found new patrons in wealthy friends who came to the rescue or aristocratic ladies who were interested in flattering or teasing poems. For ten years, however, he had no patron who could afford to be lavish and until his ordination as a priest at the start of 1615 he had no regular job.

This may seem strange because he was so able, but in the universities student numbers had been enlarged, mainly in order to train Protestant preachers or civil servants. England was now oversupplied with graduates who had no wish to preach but who did compete for the kind of job which Donne needed for the exercise of his talents and the upkeep of his family. Almost all such positions were in the gift of the Crown or of the leading courtiers, and it was not surprising that appointments went to men who had not scorned society's conventions. This was particularly true about any job for which a half-trained lawyer and secretary such as Donne might apply. And one of the many reasons which he could have given for not 'going into business' was that really profitable commerce depended on monopolies granted by the Crown to favourites. Industry above the level of the cottage (or Donne's father's manufacture of kitchen utensils) scarcely existed: Francis Bacon's *Advancement of Learning* was published in 1605 with its vision of a brave new world transformed by science-based technology, but Bacon himself remained a lawyer – and a corrupt one.

It may also seem strange that, given empty days and years, Donne did not dedicate himself to the development of his gifts as a poet by tackling a large subject and producing the masterpiece which *Metempsychosis* was not. We may think of Edmund Spenser's *Faerie Queene*, achieved in the 1590s, when that poet had far less leisure than the unemployed Donne, or of George Chapman's magnificent translation into English verse of Homer's *Iliad* and *Odyssey*, completed in 1615 after labour covering some twenty years during which small sums of money had to be earned by writing many second-rate plays. But here we are reminded of the limitations of Donne as a poet, recently demonstrated by the failure of the over-ambitious *Metempsychosis*. He was best in short bursts of inspiration and about his own feelings, and he always thought of the main work of his life as being other than writing such poetry. He therefore felt miserable when he had no job which would stretch him in the ordinary business of the world and he occupied his empty hours by writing books in prose – books which fell below the level of the short poems which he also wrote as expressions of his depressed confusion. In the future he was to be fulfilled as a preacher, with a style which combined prose and poetry in outbursts sustained for an hour and with subjects which called for the powerful statement of his own feelings and convictions yet challenged him to submerge (or at least to conceal) the ego in concentration on God. He was to say that his marriage had made him seek God as never before and that his consequent experience of adversity had brought him treasure. But meanwhile he was at a loss.

Donne had sworn to Anne's father, and no doubt also to Anne herself, that he would do his utmost to support her and any children, but as the months and years passed he had to admit that he had become an outsider. The arduous education, the legal training, the abandonment of Roman Catholicism, the expensive volunteering for the Protestant naval expeditions, the work as a civil servant close to the centre of power – all this had come to nothing. Great Destiny had handed him 'sleepie povertie' and being unemployed he had to accept the offer of accommodation which came from his wife's cousin, at Pyrford in Surrey.

In 1603 Elizabeth I died and James VI of Scotland became also James I of England, but so far as we know Donne felt too dispirited to mark the new beginning with a poem. In the excited first months of his reign James created more than nine hundred new knights who could hope for new prosperity, and these included a considerable number of Donne's friends. Among them was Henry Wotton, who was sent to Venice as the English ambassador, at a time when it was hoped that this republic would reject the papacy and ally itself with the Protestants without losing its fabulous wealth and glamour. Wotton's association with the very foolish

Earl of Essex might have done permanent damage to his career, but the Grand Duke of Tuscany had sent him from his exile in Florence to warn King James about a plot; now he could enjoy Venice as his reward.

Another person favoured by the new king was John Davies. He had been readmitted to Lincoln's Inn and to the legal profession less than a year before the dismissal of Donne by Egerton; the Lord Keeper had used his influence in support of Davies, who dedicated poems to him (and also to the old queen and the new king). Donne's fellow poet, who had hurried up to Scotland in order to greet James, was sent to Ireland as the government's chief lawyer; he arranged the transfer of lands to Protestants in Ulster, became Speaker of the parliament, built up a fortune and had a daughter who was to become a countess. He was to die when he had just been appointed Lord Chief Justice. Donne was to preach at that funeral – but the new reign brought no job to him.

The unemployed ex-secretary might have given way to bitter jealousy. Instead he sent Wotton an assurance of good will which congratulated him on the 'activity' to which he had been appointed by 'our good and great King's lov'd hand and fear'd name'. This generous poem ended:

> For mee (if there be such a thing as I)
>   Fortune (if there be such a thing as shee)
> Spies that I bear so well her tyranny
>   That she thinks nothing else so fit for me;
>
> But though she part us, to heare my oft prayers
>   For your increase, God is as neere me here;
> And to send you what I shall begge, his staires
>   In length and ease are alike every where.

When friends saw that Donne was unemployed, ordination in the Church of England was suggested, knowing that he was at heart the man who wrote that poem – and, moreover, that he had an interest in theology. A 'probleme' which exercised his wit was 'Why doe young laymen so much study divinity?' The question was a bit of a joke and the suggested answers were also attempts to be funny, but there was some serious material beneath the surface. Perhaps young laymen think that it is their duty to work at 'divinity' since the clergy are too preoccupied by their hunts for larger incomes ('tending busily Church preferment') to have time for serious theology? Perhaps these young men want to expose the arrogance of the professional preachers who claim to be able to penetrate 'God's secrets'? And perhaps arrogance motivates the young men too, so that what they produce is not really 'divinity' since it has little or nothing to do with God? In this period of enforced leisure Donne was an attentive student of theology, seeking the truth like a man climbing to the top of a mountain, not a man who could talk confidently about God. It is not surprising that he despised those who could: the professionals who (as he wrote privately in a letter) 'write for Religion without it', the enthusiasts who know more than humanity can know, the amateurs who rush in where angels keep their distance.

Another problem was that the lifestyle of the average parish priest held few attractions for a gentleman who was a Christian believer but not keen to be a martyr. Many vicarages resembled small farmhouses, with manual work on the 'glebe' needed to supplement the meagre 'tithes' received from parishioners. In the 1630s Archbishop Laud was to conclude after an investigation that half the clergy lived in real poverty and in the 1620s Donne was to describe how the clergy could look while he pleaded that they should be given more respect. He said that 'Ministers may have clouds in their understanding and knowledge (some may be less learned than others), and clouds in their elocution and utterance (some may have an unacceptable deliverance), and clouds in their aspect and countenance (some may have an unpleasing presence), and clouds in their respect and maintenance (some may be oppressed in their fortunes) . . .' (4:83).

It was an age when favoured clergymen were allowed to draw incomes from more than one parish without residence, on the assumption that no one parish would produce the money needed to maintain such an exceptional clergyman on terms of equality with the gentry – but to obtain this privilege a man needed the patronage of the great and at this time Donne was totally unable to imagine himself as the royal chaplain and court preacher that he was to become. One of the 'problemes' which he set himself, it seems in this period of his life, was 'Why are Courtiers sooner Atheists than men of other Conditions?' The answer which he reached was that 'a familiarity with greatnesse' breeds 'a contempt of all greatnesse'.

In his second 'satyre' he had attacked lawyers who 'lye in every thing': they are

> Like a King's favourite, yea like a King.

And in his fourth 'satyre' he had painted a lurid picture of the royal court – of the court as it had been under a decaying queen, but under the new king the vices of the courtiers became more open, because his servants could imitate a monarch who combined the mind of a genuine scholar with a lifestyle far more coarse than Elizabeth's. Donne had described the courtiers assembling for worship of the monarch: to him it had seemed a 'Masse in jest'. They gathered from riding, from playing handball or tennis, from eating or a visit to the brothels, and like 'Pirats' they were looking out for 'Ladies' whom they could 'board'. Donne had no intention of trying to preach to such a flock: 'Preachers which are Seas of Wits and Arts' might attempt to 'drowne the sinnes of this place' but 'for mee . . . it enough shall bee to wash the staines away'. Merely to be in such company during a visit was 'Purgatorie', even 'hell'. In secret and in Latin he drew up a mock catalogue for a courtier's library: each title in it was a shrewd blow. And in his third 'satyre' he had mocked the Church of England with its 'vile ambitious preachers' such as the royal chaplains.

The laws defending this Established Church were not only cruel (his brother had died because of them) but also new ('still new like fashions' because as recently as 1558, under Queen Mary, the laws had enforced Roman Catholicism). Indeed, they were an insult to God because as Supreme Governor of the Church the monarch had usurped a place which belonged to Christ alone. It seems clear that these had been his real feelings in the reign of Elizabeth (although as a rising civil servant presumably he had kept them to himself and a small circle of friends), and a contempt for the royal court and for the State Church must have been a factor in his mind in the early stages of the new reign.

A combination of factors including that contempt seems to lie behind his refusal of an invitation to move to the financial security offered by a rural parish near York which, because it was large and fertile, provided exceptionally good 'tithes' (a tenth of the produce or other income of the parishioners). This opportunity was offered in 1607 by Thomas Morton, who had enjoyed this income but, having no family, felt no need for it now that he had been appointed Dean of Gloucester. He agreed with the patron (the layman who had the right to appoint in the parish) that the position should be offered to Donne, who (it seems) had helped him to write *Apologia Catholica*, a defence of the Church of England against the papacy and the Jesuits. But Donne said no. One reason may well have been that the life of a parish priest in Yorkshire did not appeal, but Morton had not spent all his time in the parish; the government had encouraged him to be absent often in the course of his writing and speaking as an Anglican apologist. Donne seems to have been willing to provide Morton with material from Roman Catholic sources but not willing to share his Anglican commitment. So for one reason or another he declined the offer – and he could plead unworthiness without much fear of being contradicted. No one who had been sacked by the head of the legal profession for seducing a girl could be blamed for not quickly becoming a parish priest.

Instead he applied for jobs which depended on the king's favour or acquiescence but did not involve Anglican ordination. What they did involve was a longing to end his unemployment – an emotion which temporarily overcame the fact that these positions would have been almost as unsuitable as a rural parish in Yorkshire. Not all his applications can be known now, but the evidence is that this man who had written so scornfully about courtiers wanted to become one, in the household of Queen Anne; that this man who had been so proud of his outspoken independence wanted to join the English civil service in Ireland, where the army of occupation faced rebellion by the 'natives'; and that this man who had been so glad to get ashore after the storm in 1597 wanted to be secretary of the Virginia Company which was trying to plant England's first colony overseas. Less strangely, Donne believed that he was well qualified to follow Henry Wotton as the English ambassador in sophisticated Venice. After each revival of hope, however, he was rejected.

In 1606 he felt able to afford to rent a 'little thin house' in Mitcham and he also hired a small apartment in the centre of his beloved London: it was only an hour's ride away. He took that ride so often that he could boast that his horse knew the direction and he could relax, 'inverted into my self'. He belonged to two clubs which met each month in London taverns, and as he reminded George Gerrard 'that which makes it London is the meeting of friends'. The club meeting in the Mitre enabled him to make or maintain friendships with men of the kind that he had sat with him in the House of Commons but the friends who met in the Mermaid were more literary. Writers such as Jonson, Beaumont and Fletcher gathered for an evening of competition in drinking and wit. Beaumont's lines have often been repeated:

> What things have wee seene
> Done at the Mermaide? heard words that have keene
> Soe nimble and soe full of subtill flame
> As if every one from whom they came
> Had meant to putt his whole witt in a Jeast . . .

For Donne political gossip in the Mitre or jesting in the Mermaid made a precious change but for the most of the time letters had to compensate for absence from friends; 'letters', he claimed, 'mingle Soules'. In one he wrote about the emotions which could overcome him. When dejected by sadness he tried to 'kindle squibs' as if his friends were around him exchanging firecrackers of wit, but even when he had company and was 'transported with jollity' he would think of his misfortunes, his advancing years and his duties as a husband and father, and these thoughts would drag him down as if leads had been attached to his heels.

The house in Mitcham, where he spent most of his time, was needed for his family but he also used it for long periods of reading and writing. Within four years the literary fruit had appeared in the shape of two books stuffed with arguments and quotations. The reading was so intense that after his death papers were found in his Deanery which contained (in Izaak Walton's words) 'the resultance of 1400 Authors, most of them abridged and analyzed in his own hand' and many of these notes (now lost) must date from that time of enforced leisure in the cottage. He wrote to a friend that 'I shall die reading' and be buried in the cellar beneath the study, a 'vault' from which 'raw vapors' already arose. His letters included many such complaints about a house which was his 'hospital' or 'prison'. He once wrote that 'I am oprest with such a sadnes as I am glad of nothing but that I am oprest with it . . . By all this labor of my pen my mind is no more comforted than a condemned prisoner would be to see his chamber swypte & made cleane.' In another letter he moaned: 'When I must shipwrack, I would do it in a Sea, where mine impotencie might have some excuse; not in a sullen weedy lake, where I could not have so much as exercise for my swimming.' He complained of the 'barbarousnesse and insipid dulnes of the Country' and in a poem sent to Henry Wotton he viewed the pleasant greenery of England as a 'desert' where 'men become beasts'. The countryside in spring increased his depression: 'Every thing refreshes and I wither.' In his exile from London he felt 'rather a sicknesse and disease of the world than a part of it'. The contrast with poets who have delighted to paint rural scenes in words which reflect the loveliness, or with the succession of poet-mystics who have found God in nature, could not be greater. But as a reward for this self-inflicted course of intense study, he was able to claim that 'it will please me a little to have had a long funerall, and to have kept myself above ground without putrefaction'.

In a later year he seems to have been thinking about himself in the past, as well as about others who had made no solid contribution to the world, when he preached about the man 'who never comes to the knowledge and consideration, *why* he was sent into this life?' He warned such a man: 'Thou passest out of the world, as thy hand passes out of a basin of water, which may be somewhat the fowler for thy washing in it, but retaines no other impression of thy having been there' (4:149). He did not really believe what he had told Wotton, that his one ambition had become the achievement of contentment, of building 'thine own Palace' within the self as a snail is happy within a shell, of being as inconspicuous as fishes which 'glide, leaving no print where they passe'. In his rural exile he was a fish out of water.

One of the books which he wrote in Mitcham, in or around 1608, was about suicide. In substance as well as style it was too agitated to be clear but it did show that Donne was wrestling with a question: would God forgive him if he decided to end his life?

Eleven years later, when he was going abroad and thought that he might die there, he entrusted this book in manuscript to Sir Robert Ker with the instruction 'publish it not'. 'Reserve it for me if I live, and if I die, I only forbid it the Presse, and the Fire: publish it not, but yet burn it not; and between these, do what you will with it.' If Ker showed it to others, he was to point out that it was 'a Book written by Jack Donne', not by the Doctor of Divinity who had become a leading preacher. He knew that it would cause a scandal if printed in his lifetime because he had refused to conclude that under all circumstances suicide should be reckoned a sin and a crime. Indeed, in the preface he confessed that he had often had this 'sickeley inclination' himself, feeling that 'I have the keyes of my prison in mine own hand'. Writing to Henry Goodyer, he recalled that he had sometimes desired death even in the years of hope 'when I went with the tyde', but the temptation was stronger now. He wanted to 'do something' but 'that I cannot tell what, is no wonder. For to chuse is to do: but to be no part of any body, is to be nothing.' Actually, he could not 'chuse' to belong because no one wanted to employ him. When he talked himself out of despair, it was with the thought that people have within themselves 'a torch, a soul, lighter and warmer'. Changing the metaphor, he reflected that 'we are therefore our own umbrellas'. But his torch did not burn steadily and his umbrella leaked.

The book with the unappetising title *Biathanatos* ('violent death' in Greek) was one long muddle, showing that its author did not know what he really thought. A multitude of quotations displayed Donne's learning in the branch of theology then called 'moral divinity' but not all of the references given were accurate and none of them was integrated into a coherent and convincing argument. It has been suggested that this big book was intended as nothing more than a parody of the tortuous style of 'moral divinity' – although spending so much labour on an unobvious joke seems unlikely, even when an author is so unusual as Donne. It seems more likely that the book was what he called a poem (or collection of poems) which he sent 'To Mr T. W.': 'the strict Map of my misery'. But he saw no escape from this misery: he could not get a job and he could not think of an argument which would justify his suicide.

Although he condemned suicide 'onely or principally' intended 'to avoyd temporall troubles' he never discussed at any depth the problem which interested him personally, which was whether a severe mental depression ever made suicide excusable. Nor did he consider cases of severe mental illness. Nor did he think carefully about voluntary euthanasia during the agony of the terminal stage of a physical illness. Instead he wandered around possible situations in which 'self-homicide' could be followed by 'a charitable interpretation of theyr action' – and he drifted towards the conclusion that it should be forgiven when 'the glory of God is respected and advanced'.

He made the self-sacrifice of Christ the supreme example in this category but he damaged his case by arguing not only that Christ put himself into the hands of his enemies by going to Jerusalem but also that he freely decided when to die on the cross. He could quote Fathers of the Church who had drawn this conclusion from the belief that being sinless, indeed divine, Christ was naturally immortal as Adam and Eve had been before the Fall, but of course the gospels presented Christ's acceptance of his death as being very different from suicide and his agony on the cross as having its natural end, with no escape. Donne had to admit the consistent tradition of Christian condemnation of suicide, and did so without thinking out how what had been condemned differed from the crucifixion which had been the centre of sixteen hundred years of devotion. He could not deny that theologians of the stature of Augustine and Aquinas had denounced suicide whatever the circumstances; Augustine had taught that Christian women should not kill themselves even when the alternative was rape by a barbarian. Since the fourth century teachers of the Church had disagreed at length with the Roman approval of heroic suicides and (at least) since the sixth century Christian burial had been firmly denied to people who committed that sin. Nor could he deny that English law treated an attempt at suicide as a specially grave crime which had to be punished with a special severity, although he claimed that the reason was that so many of the English wanted to commit this crime. (Suicide remained a crime until 1961.) Nor could he deny the general agreement that the laws of Nature and of Reason encouraged self-preservation. All that he felt able to do was hunt around for strange circumstances in which 'self-homicide' might be justified. He entirely missed the fundamental distinction made in Christian thought between a truly heroic death and suicide, which has been that the martyred hero would have chosen to act rightly even if death had not followed. He also failed to anticipate what has become the modern Christian attitude, that a suicide when the balance of the mind has been disturbed by great distress may not have been intended for God's glory but can be expected to receive God's mercy.

He claimed that pelicans and bees kill themselves, but spoiled the effect of this appeal to nature by the generalization that 'most vertuous actions are against Nature'. He drew attention to the praise for courageous suicides by defeated politicians in Ancient Rome or by widows in India, but again spoiled the effect both by admitting that he was writing for Christians and by adding ludicrous stories of suicides for trivial reasons. He pointed out that Samson was praised in the Bible for causing the death of Israel's enemies although this also caused his own, but he made the mistake of taking seriously a story that Judas Iscariot was rescued from his own suicide before he 'grew to so enormous a bignesse . . . that he was not able to withdraw himselfe out of a Coche's way, but had his Gutts crushed out'. He declared that his aim was 'to encourage Men to a just contempt of this Life' but he supplied no convincing answer to the traditional argument that to kill oneself shows a contempt for God's gift of this life. He suggested that 'in some cases, when we were destitute of other meanes, we might be to our selves the stewards of God's benefits, and the Ministers of his Mercyfull Justice', but he 'abstayned purposefully from extending this discourse to particular Rules, or instances, both because I dare not professe my selfe a Master in so curious a syence, and because the Limits are obscure, and steepy, and slippery, and narrow, and every Error deadly'. So he opted out of being useful. But one good thing about this book was that it was never printed in its author's lifetime.

When sending *Biathanatos* to a friend, Donne could claim that he had already shown it to 'some particular friends in both universities'. Their comment had been that 'there was a false thread in it, not easily found', but the book seems worth some attention precisely because it is a tapestry of false arguments, suggesting that around 1608 Donne was near to intellectual, if not to physical, suicide. A real opportunity to guide opinion sensibly had been missed. Although accurate statistics are impossible because many suicides were not reported and many records have been lost, modern researchers have concluded that the religious confusion caused by the Reformation caused the numbers to rise steeply and that after these tragedies the Protestant state enforced punishments which had not often been inflicted in the Middle Ages. A more charitable attitude was not thought to be 'Christian' until the eighteenth or nineteenth century, when the advocacy came mainly from outside the Churches. Before that, the blunt title of the theological response to Donne by Thomas Philipot in 1674 was typical: *Self-homicide Murther.* And since Donne's muddle was the only presentation of an alternative view to take account of theology, *Biathanatos*, first printed in 1647, was reissued in 1700.

A book which was quickly published, *Pseudo-Martyr*, also demonstrated the confusion in Donne's mind but it had a limited success. The number of copies surviving suggests that there was quite a large edition, sold from a bookshop in the courtyard of St Paul's Cathedral in January 1610. In contrast with the lack of current discussion about suicide, this book was a timely contribution to a public debate. After the Gunpowder Plot of 1605 a new oath had been imposed on Roman Catholics, not explicitly demanding their acceptance of the Church of England but making it clear that they rejected the right of the pope to release them from their allegiance to the king. If as instructed by the pope they refused to take this oath, they faced very severe penalties. The king himself published a defence of the oath, with a second book which reprinted the pope's instructions in the belief that merely to read them was to know they were wrong. There were, however, replies from the Roman Catholic side, to which the Anglicans including the great Bishop Andrewes responded. Donne expressed private contempt for at least one of these Anglican efforts (by another bishop) and rushed to do better. He used his accumulated notes to provide quotations and footnotes as impressive as those which had adorned the book on suicide; indeed, he recycled some of that material. But readers appear to have been disappointed and there was no call for a second edition. The only reply which was published came after a delay, in 1613. In it Thomas Fitzherbert was contemptuous, advising Donne to confine himself to writing poems 'wherein he has some talent, and may play the foole without controle'.

Donne was his own sharpest critic but he put his points in a private letter where he confessed that 'I think truly there is a perplexity (as far as I see yet) and both sides may be in justice, and innocence'. On the one hand, 'our State cannot be safe without the Oath', for the Roman Church maintains that its 'Clergie-men' are 'no Subjects, and that all the rest may be none tomorrow'. On the other hand, the 'Supremacy' which the Roman Church claims 'were diminished, if it were limited'. As kings are 'the onely judges of their prerogative', it is also the case that 'Roman Bishops' claim to be enlightened by the Holy Spirit. So may not the bishops as well as the kings be 'good witnesses of their own supremacie?'

In this private reflection Donne discerned the reason why it was at that time futile to hope that arguments which might be set out in a book could solve the problem. The problem was indeed soluble: the king always wished to halt the persecution of his Roman Catholic subjects provided only that they were loyal patriots who obeyed him, and in order to win this prize the leader ('archpriest') of the Roman Catholic clergy since 1598, George Blackwell, recommended that the oath should be taken. But in England public opinion was such that even James had to keep persecution as part of the law throughout his reign, and in Rome the official position was such that Blackwell had to be sacked. Many years had to pass before the average Englishman was prepared to acknowledge that Roman Catholics were decent citizens and before the papacy was prepared to see heretical rulers being obeyed. In England a turning point was to come in 1778, when the Vatican did not veto an arrangement initiated by the Catholic gentry resulting in prayers at Mass for the royal Protestants of the Hanoverian dynasty.

Considerable numbers of Roman Catholics took the post-1605 oath but the arguments which prevailed with them were not theological: they were more related to patriotism and a wish for a life without fines, exclusions and executions. The government offered such conformists little other encouragement. The oath was drawn up during the hysterical aftermath of the Guy Fawkes plot to blow up king and Parliament, when the men convicted of plotting were executed with great barbarity but amid the crowd's cheers outside St Paul's Cathedral, very near Donne's birthplace (he was then abroad). It included words at which any Roman Catholic would blink: 'I do from my heart abhor, detest and abjure as impious and heretical this damnable doctrine and position, that princes which be excommunicated and deprived by the Pope may be deposed or murdered by their subjects or any other whatsoever. And I do believe, and in my conscience am resolved, that neither the Pope nor any person whatsoever hath power to absolve me of this oath or of any part whatsoever.' So the pope must be treated as a heretic and the individual Roman Catholic as someone who was likely not to mean what he or she said on oath. Donne's mother and her new husband were among the Catholics who accepted punishment rather than say that.

Paul V was a pope who did not hesitate to excommunicate the senate of Venice and to demand that the French should withdraw a claim that only God could depose a king. He was preoccupied by enforcing discipline in his own Church, by canonizing the heroes of the Counter-Reformation as saints, and by adding to the physical splendours of Rome. He did not mince his words in his replies to King James. The dispute was between two monarchies both of whom claimed a right given by God to govern the Church and to decide what was moral in politics. And since he was so reluctant to admit in public the existence of this central problem, Donne also failed to say precisely where the frontier between the two jurisdictions ought to be drawn. In chapter 3 he wandered off into an attack on Roman Catholic doctrines and in chapter 5 he derided Franciscans and Jesuits for blind obedience to their spiritual superiors. Elsewhere he extended his case against the papacy into details of medieval and later history, getting into an argument about whether or not the council of Carthage had forbidden the clergy to wear beards in 525. The table of contents promised a chapter on the history of England but in the printed book this did not appear. Also missing was a promised chapter about France.

Donne now assumed that the 'Law of Nature' gave King James an obvious right to demand this oath from his subjects: 'To obey the Prince . . . belongs to us as men.' Obviously he was on strong ground when believing that government is better than anarchy, but obedience in this particular matter raised questions. In his third 'satyre' he had written very differently: God had not given to kings 'blanck-charters to kill whom they hate'. And in his book on suicide he had recorded his private opinion that 'this terme, the Law of Nature, is so variously and unconstantly delivered, as I confesse I read it abundant tymes, before I understand it once'. Then his attitude had been that 'a private man is emperor of himself' because 'the obligation which our conscience casts upon us is of stronger hold . . . than the precept of any superior, whether law or person'. And now his appeal to the Law of Nature had to avoid awkward questions.

He did not say whether that 'law' justified Henry VIII in executing Thomas More – or Thomas More and Henry's daughter Mary in burning Protestants. Nor did he dwell on the fact that the Elizabethan government had tried to end the pope's remaining influence in England not by an appeal to the Law of Nature but by the severe punishment of Roman Catholics, including executions with exceptional cruelty and publicity. Nor did he discuss the relevance of this mysterious law to France, where Henri IV had converted from Protestantism to Catholicism without much religious conviction and was murdered by a Roman Catholic, fanatical and perhaps mad, in this year 1610. He scored debating points but did not win the intellectual victory, for the propaganda war remained in the deadlock where it had been left by Lord Burghley and Cardinal Allen in the 1580s. Elizabeth's first minister Burghley (who like Elizabeth herself had conformed to Roman Catholicism under Queen Mary) had maintained that the purpose of the Protestant government was solely to eliminate traitors, while Rome's chief spokesman William Allen had maintained that the purpose of the Catholic mission in England was solely to feed souls. Theirs, too, had been a dialogue of the deaf.

Pseudo-Martyr was a success with the king, who allowed it to be dedicated to him. Whether he considered it superior to his own contributions to the controversy may be doubted, but it seems that it finally convinced him that Donne would be valuable to the Church of England if he could be persuaded to become a preacher. When the suggestion was put, however, the author pleaded unworthiness and continued to hope for a political job. Izaak Walton was to claim that James had begged Donne to write the book. No doubt there had been some encouragement (permission had to be secured for a dedication to royalty), but the book says that its author hoped to 'ascend' into the king's presence by writing and that he had observed that James had set an example because 'your Majestie had vouchsafed to descend to conversation with your Subjects, by way of your Bookes'.

The third book which came out of the study of the cottage in Mitcham was not long and did not pretend to be serious. Published in 1611, it was a satire on the Jesuits, *Ignatius his Conclave*. Undeniably the Jesuits had laid themselves open to criticism. Their mission to England during and since 1580 had handed the government a victory in the war of propaganda, for the mission could be denounced as a sinister band of priests, trained abroad, who had entered the country in disguise and were recruiting for supporters for a plan to welcome a foreign army and to cause a civil war. Protestant patriots reacted in the way to be expected: for example, blaming the Gunpowder Plot of 1605 on the Jesuits, who had nothing whatever to do with it. The Jesuits all denied that they were traitors, and some of them took their own patriotic acceptance of the Protestant government to the very brink of heresy, but the schools where they were educating the sons of English Catholic families outside England were subsidized heavily by the Spanish government. And within England many Roman Catholics deeply resented the Jesuits' trouble-making interference. These missionaries were the pope's agents, pledged to total obedience to his wishes and responsible directly to him, not to any local bishop or other authority; and what they were told to spread was the official message from the pope in far-away Rome that whatever the dangers might be there must be no arrangement with the Protestant government if any compromise carried with it any recognition of the Church which the government supported. For the clergy who were not Jesuits, the independence of this new and élitist Society of Jesus could be disliked because it created a more-Catholic-than-thou Church within the Church, and the tension became semi-public when there was a dispute between Jesuits and other priests who were imprisoned together in Wisbech. For the laity who faced poverty and imprisonment if they defied the government, with the risk of execution, the Jesuits' own heroism as martyrs was an attitude easier to praise in theory than to imitate in practice.

Donne could have written a devastating book about those Jesuits such as Robert Persons who by dependence on Spain had brought division and danger to the Catholic community in England. Instead he wrote a knock-about comedy, about the arrival of Ignatius Loyola (the founder of the Society of Jesus) in hell, intent on claiming the throne from Satan: the dispute produced a riot, ending only when the Jesuits were invited to make a new hell on the moon. This farce did not even glance at the serious questions raised by the true stories of Loyola himself (whose vision sent missionaries to India, China, Japan and both of the Americas, and in Europe created a large network of schools and colleges) and of his self-sacrificial disciples (including Donne's own uncles). It took no account of the existence within the Society of moderates such as Donne's uncle Jasper Heywood, who even before his imprisonment and release seems to have accepted Elizabeth's political authority. It included no hint that like many other Protestants including some Puritans Donne regularly used methods of meditation taught by Jesuits and scholarly books written by them. (He translated a lovely little poem by a Belgian Jesuit, Angelin Gazet.) It invited cheap laughs against this centrepiece of the Catholic Reformation and even cheaper applause when Donne also sent to hell innovators such as Copernicus (who saw the sun in its true splendour at the centre of our system of planets) and Columbus (who saw American soil on the other side of the frightening ocean). And Robert Persons, who ought to have been the target, was left in his grave in peace.

Donne had thought the public unworthy of a sight of his poetry. Now in giving the public the low-level prose of *Ignatius his Conclave*, he was stooping – and he knew it. In a preface which he half-disguised as 'the Printer to the Reader', he admitted that it was strange for an author of his 'gravity . . . to descend to this kind of writing'. He had, he claimed, been unwilling 'to have this booke published' – which had not prevented him from translating the book from Latin into English. In 1969 a Jesuit, Timothy Healy, was to make the perfect riposte. He bestowed great care and sympathy on the Oxford University Press edition of this scurrilous attack on the Society of Jesus, and in his introduction he claimed that Donne's main objection was to innovations in religion: the Jesuits had been attacked less for being bad than for being new. He quoted one of the most conservative passages in the sermons: 'Old doctrines, old disciplines, old words and formes of speech in his service, God loves best' (2:305). It will be less charitable but more just if Donne's words introducing *Ignatius* are now quoted against him: 'This Booke must teach what humane infirmity is.'

He was to stoop further as his debts mounted. In 1611 a very rich and ambitious gentleman, Sir Robert Drury, provided cash, a job as his secretary during a long foreign holiday, and on their return to London accommodation for the family in a recently built 'bricke howse' in Drury Lane. Donne saw no alternative to having Drury as his patron; indeed, he did all he could to secure this income and housing, in a contact that seems to have begun because his sister lived near the big country house of the Drurys. But like him, Sir Robert was never offered the position in the service of the Crown which he wanted and one reason was that he, too, had a reputation for indiscretion. So Donne's alliance with this politically unfashionable patron was not an avenue to political employment or to a career in the Church. Knowing this, in 1613 he approached Robert Carr, Viscount Rochester and the king's current favourite, saying that he had no existing obligations 'towards any other person in this State'. The response was encouraging: Carr needed secretarial help and, as Donne put it frankly in another letter to him, 'bought' the applicant. (Carr was related to Sir Robert Ker, already mentioned as one of Donne's close friends, but in order to prevent confusion the English version of the Scottish surname is used here.)

He had to pay a price in return for the favours of these patrons and in each case the price was high, costing him his reputation then or later. First we can see what resulted from his relationship with Sir Robert and Lady Drury.

He had to earn their favour by writing three poems, two of them the long poems called 'Anniversaries', consoling them for the loss of their only child, Elizabeth, who had died when aged fourteen. Donne first sent them a 'Funerall Elegie':

> To scape th'infirmities which waite upon
>   Woman, shee went away before sh' was one . . .
> Shee did no more but die; if after her
>   Any shall live, which dare true good prefer,
> Every such person is her delegate.

The parents were consoled and with their encouragement (expressed financially) he wrote at greater length about their daughter's physical and spiritual perfections and about the mourning of the world, which now felt that after her death it faced nothing but decay. These themes were familiar in poems marking the deaths of persons of distinction and Donne had handled them in the past: he was to do so again in the future and some other poets were to admire (and borrow from) his performance when consoling the Drurys. But people for whose opinion Donne cared were critical because the person now being commemorated was an obscure girl, because he wrote more than a thousand lines of verse allegedly about the cosmic disaster of her death, and because many of his lines consisted of flattery which was gross even by the standards of courtly poetry in that age.

Ben Jonson in particular rebuked Donne. As a professional writer he was willing to turn his hand to this kind of job connected with a funeral but it was his practice to say something substantial about the deceased. Donne did not attempt to describe Elizabeth Drury, partly because as he confessed 'I never saw the Gentlewoman'. Instead he very quickly linked her death with a much wider theme: the need to despise the world and to seek the joy of heaven. Jonson bluntly told his friend that 'if it had been written of ye Virgin Mary it had been something' but since it ascribed to the girl a place in the universe usually reserved for Christ himself this exercise in flattery was 'full of Blasphemies'.

Donne wrote to a more sympathetic friend admitting that at least the printing of these poems had been a mistake: 'I confesse I wonder how I declined to do it, and do not pardon myself.' He defied anyone to find faults in the dead girl but 'I cannot be understood to have spoken just truths'. He told Jonson (according to Jonson) that he had 'described the idea of a Woman and not as she was'. Whatever may have been meant by that much discussed phrase, a clearer response was made to the criticism: it had been the poet's intention, declared in both 'Anniversaries', to write further poems in an annual series but the decision was made to write no more. And it seems fair to say that the whole project was a great opportunity missed. The first 'Anniversarie' had a theme familiar in Christian literature (or at least, familiar before the eighteenth century): contempt for the world. The second had another: the consolation offered by the hope of heaven. But it seems that at this stage of his life the deepest concern in Donne's own spirituality was his relationship with Christ; this was to be expressed in his famous poem inspired by Good Friday in 1613. In the 'Anniversaries' Christ was never mentioned. Donne's masterpiece might have been a long poem about humanity's relationship with Christ but this was never written. (The 'Anniversaries' will be discussed further on pp. 218–22.)

Of all the people with whom Donne was associated in his life, Robert Carr was perhaps the most stupid and certainly the most repulsive. But because the unsavoury favourite of the king had 'bought' him, Donne was told to write a poem celebrating Carr's wedding. He was very reluctant and slow to obey, which is not surprising.

Carr's homosexual relationship with the king was breaking down; swollen-headed because of the money which James had showered on him, he refused to sleep any more in the royal bedroom. He was in fact bisexual (like James) and he fell in love with an aristocratic lady, Frances Howard. Unfortunately the lady was already married, in a marriage contracted for political reasons when the couple were scarcely in their teens. The king, being anxious to retain the services of his favourite, did his best to have her marriage dissolved, on the basis of her plea that her husband had been made sexually impotent by witchcraft. (It was later found that she had helped by administering a drug to prevent his arousal.) The problem was referred to a committee. Awkwardly, the

Archbishop of Canterbury (Abbot) proved obstinate: he sided with the husband, the young Earl of Essex who had inherited neither virility nor glamour from his father. The earl seems to have been somewhat incoherent when discussing his sexuality with the assembled bishops but he did mumble a claim that he would be happy to consummate another marriage: his present inability arose because he was incompatible with his wife. (He had good reason: Frances had been notorious even in the morally relaxed court of King James.) The unworldly archbishop therefore believed that the solution was to mend the marriage, or at least to make sure that the couple parted as friends. But the king added more co-operative (or was it realistic?) bishops to the committee; in the end it voted 7–5 as he wished.

Those in favour included the saintly Bishop Lancelot Andrewes, who had a conscience at least as active as the archbishop's. The king had talked to him privately but it seems probable that the main argument which persuaded him was of a pastoral nature: he had baptized the earl as a baby, his eyes were open to the character of Frances Howard, and he concluded that there ought to be an end to a hell of a marriage. Later he was to be pastorally sensitive to Archbishop Abbot, who while hunting accidentally killed a man instead of a deer.

Abbot's defiance of the king's wishes was not the only problem. Sir Thomas Overbury was a very able man who did not under-estimate his abilities and he had been secretary to the incompetent Carr. Knowing many secrets, he objected to the plan for the new marriage. Consequently he was offered a post which would have got him out of the way (as ambassador to Russia) and when he refused was imprisoned in the Tower. Since he remained critical and might prove talkative, he was murdered in September 1613, enabling the union of the happy couple to be celebrated in December. Almost certainly his murder had been planned by Frances Howard, although it had been necessary to add further poison to supplement the tarts and jellies which she had sent to his prison in her role as Lady Bountiful. It has been suggested that she was not telling the truth when she later admitted her guilt, and undeniably she was capable of lying, but had she been innocent every motive of self–interest would have encouraged her to play the role of a maligned heroine.

In 1615 a young man who was dying in Brussels confessed that he had been the apothecary's apprentice who had been bribed by Frances Howard to supply poisons, although the final blow had been delivered by a doctor whose prescription, when inserted into Overbury as medicine, did the trick. The story reached the ears of the king, who to his credit allowed justice to take its course (more or less). It was also relevant that by now James had developed another relationship with a handsome young man, George Villiers, who had been introduced into the royal presence by an anti-Carr group because with slender legs he was a superb dancer – and also had a brain. A trial for conspiracy to murder was arranged. Although her husband protested his innocence, Frances Howard did not deny that she had been the most prominent of those who had plotted the murder. The couple escaped the death to which other conspirators were sentenced (this seems to have been the bargain made before she pleaded guilty), but they replaced Overbury in the Tower, to be released in 1622 and pardoned shortly before the king's death. By a curious coincidence the governor of the Tower when they were imprisoned was Donne's father-in-law. (The governor who had had custody of Overbury was one of the conspirators and one of those executed.)

There is no evidence that before 1615 Donne knew of the guilt of Frances Howard, and his friendship with Overbury (who was also a poet) is shown by the fact that he contributed to a volume published in the victim's honour after the murder. The conduct of Frances Howard was so outrageously evil that it seems probable that he did not think her capable of it until the dying apprentice had revealed the secret. But it also seems probable that he was uneasy about Carr's marriage: he obeyed his patron's demand for a poem but what he produced was feeble. It began with flattery of the 'zeale and love', the 'sweet peace', of the court which honoured the king and his favourite. It continued with an apology that at present the poet was 'dead and buried' and therefore unable to join the court's celebration of the wedding – and with a hint that he expected a welcome at court in the future. It ended with the tactless thought that it would now be a 'divorce' even to think of the couple apart, 'so much one are you two'.

There was an anticlimax, for soon Donne was complaining that he had not been adequately rewarded.

The spiritual humiliation of these years of dependence first on Drury and then on Carr was all the more pathetic because in this period Donne was beginning to move towards his future as a Christian preacher. While in France he said in a letter about current religious controversies: 'I look upon nothing so intensively as these things'. On the first Good Friday after his return to England in 1613 he had the spiritual experience which he recounted in one of the greatest of his short poems (see p. 240). When he approached Carr seeking his support in a new career, it was with the declared intention of making 'Divinitie' his 'Profession', after 'much debatement within me' but also after the 'Inspirations (as I hope) of the Spirit of God'. He added that he hoped that the prayers which he would offer for Carr's happiness would be more 'effectual with God' if offered by a priest.

However, the humiliating confusion continued. He asked Lord Hay to hand this letter to Carr and in his covering letter he complained that 'my poor studies' had 'hitherto profited me nothing'. It was his thought that in the Church 'a fortune may either be made, or at least better missed', than in a lay profession. This was not an unworldly thought and the immediate sequel in

Donne's life was to show, after Carr's encouraging response, that the prospect of a financially rewarding career as a layman could rapidly eclipse any idea of dedication to 'Divinitie'. In another letter of this period he admitted that 'no man attends Court fortunes with more impatience than I do'. He could make a private joke about politicians who 'find matter of state in any wrinkle in the King's socks' but that did not prevent him from looking in the same direction. The fact seems to be that his personality was now divided more than at any other time: he was both an aspiring Christian and a grasping careerist. This was what he had implied when on Good Friday 1613 he had prayed that the Saviour might apply his 'corrections' and 'Burne off my rusts and my deformity'. He seems to have known that his deepest problem was that while he was now ashamed of the 'lust and envie' of his earlier years, and had good reason to believe that this record made it impossible for him ever to climb into a pulpit, his life since then had shown him still deformed. As a Christian he had still not risen to a spiritual level which could make him a convincing priest and preacher, and as a poet he had betrayed the integrity which had been his greatest pride in the 1590s. In his second 'satyre' he had mocked poets who flattered the great:

> And they who write to Lords, rewards to get,
> Are they not like singers at doores for meat?

When preaching years later he was to observe that sycophants contributed to the corruption of 'men of high degree': 'When I over-magnifie them in their place, flatter them, humour them, ascribe more to them, expect more from them, rely more upon them, than I should, then they are a lie of my making' (6:306–7). But it seems that at this sad stage of his life he saw little clearly except that he had to 'over-magnifie' rich patrons because he and his family needed the 'meat'. One of Donne's anxieties in this period was caused by trouble with his eyes. When he was supposed to be celebrating Christmas 1613 he wrote to a friend that he was 'almost blind'. But an earlier letter of that year had referred to a lack of another kind of vision: 'except demonstrations (and perchance there are very few of them) I find nothing without perplexities'.

In the early months of 1614 his association with a man such as Robert Carr almost led Donne into an indiscretion which could have prevented his ordination at the beginning of the next year. He told Goodyer that he was 'under an inescapable necessity' to print 'my Poems'. Presumably Carr had ordered this and the point was that the collection was to be dedicated to him. Donne was doing his best to limit the damage which might be caused: the poems would be printed 'not so much for publique view, but at mine own cost, a few Copies' to be sent to 'persons of rank'. But he was still extremely reluctant. For one thing he found it undignified to be the 'Rhapsoder of mine own rags, and that cost me more deligence to seek them, than it did to make them. This made me ask to borrow that old book of yours' – a manuscript which included poems of which he had not kept a copy. In other words, even on this small-scale publication would be against his wishes, after enduring the ridicule after the publication of his poems for the Drurys. 'I shall suffer many interpretations', he predicted, although he claimed that he was now 'at an end of much considering of that'. He might try to persuade himself that the book would be a suitable farewell to the secular world 'before I take Orders' but he must have known that erotic poems would shock many if he went on to preach as a priest, and that the poems flattering patrons would now upset those to whom they had been addressed, for they had not known how others were being praised with a similar extravagance. In particular he was worried about the reactions of the Countess of Bedford. Fortunately the project seems to have been cancelled, for no copy of a printed book of this kind has ever been found; presumably Carr had changed his mind. The way was open for Donne to be ordained without that burden from the past.

As a preparation for this possible step, he either wrote or completed a book which was for him a task more congenial than the collection of his embarrassing poems for the printer. It was a book designed to sort out the ideas he had gained from his religious meditations and theological studies over the years, and to add to the stock. Like the book on suicide it was written as if it must be ready for the printer but was not published. However, it could be shown to anyone (such as a bishop) who doubted whether he was a fit person for the pulpit. We do not know that it was ever used for that purpose, but we do know that he repeated some of its contents, consciously or unconsciously, when he began to preach. We also know that like *Biathanatos* or *Pseudo-Martyr* the book is more or less unreadable because of its dull style. It was not published until 1652 when some copies could be sold on the strength of his name.

These *Essayes in Divinity* were given a superficial unity, if not much impact, by being meditations on the first verses of the first two books in the Bible, assisted by an attempt to learn Hebrew which, we gather, was not entirely successful. Any deeper unity emerges only when we ask what essentially were his religious positions at this time when his mind was still considerably confused, and we have to admit that these positions were obscured because he felt the need to put on paper many thoughts less mature and less important. With good reason he prayed that the divine Spirit might 'now produce new Creatures, thoughts, words and deeds' after the 'shaking away' of 'confusion, darknesse, and barrenesse'. And after self-examination he believed that human reasoning could not replace that divine Spirit as the giver of wisdom, since 'you are the Children of the

Lust and Excrements of your parents, they and theirs the Children of Adam, the child of durt, the child of Nothing'. (He wrote about 'you' as if addressing a congregation – but even now he was not ready for that.)

One position which he was to occupy firmly, and develop strongly, as a preacher was this: God the Father has created the world out of Nothing; without that miracle nothing in the world would exist; and ultimately, without it nothing in the world makes any sense. In these *Essayes* he reflected that a summons to that position of worship was the great message of the book called Genesis. He did not deny the existence of evil in the world – the reality which had made him adopt a position of near-atheism in *Metempsychosis* – but for him now that fact was dwarfed by the obvious existence of the Creator, and evil was blamed on the rebellion of Adam and Eve.

The other position towards which he moved in the *Essayes* was a deep response to the work of God the Son. In the book called Exodus Moses led out of Egypt, and through the wilderness, a people which was very mixed to begin with and which had to pass through many trials before it could reach the promised land. In much the same way Christ had led a large and mixed company of people out of the 'Egypt of sin' and on through a wilderness of continuing temptations, all the way to the promised land. Out of his meditation arose what a later generation would call Donne's ecumenical vision, which was extraordinary in the setting of his age – a time of theological hatred and of war in the name of religion, Catholic versus Protestant. 'I do zealously wish', he wrote in these *Essayes,* 'that the whole Catholicke Church were reduced to such Unity and agreement, in the form and profession Established in any one of these Churches (though ours were principally to be wished) which have not by any additions destroyed the foundation and possibility of salvation in Christ Jesus; That then the Church, discharged of disputations, and misapprehensions and this defensive warr, might contemplate Christ clearly and uniformely.'

To Donne this emphasis on the supremacy of Christ over the divisions of Churches and the sins of Christians was to be of absolutely vital significance. It enabled him to see that in order to have a powerful religion it was not necessary to accept either the Roman Catholic or the Calvinist system, each of which restricted salvation to those who accepted the creed taught by its own clergy. Many active Christians in that age believed that this intolerance was necessary, but Donne did not.

However, still he hesitated to admit that his future lay in a pulpit. For two months in the spring of 1614 he was a Member of Parliament, nominated to Taunton constituents by a judge. His name had almost certainly been put forward by the Earl of Somerset, as Robert Carr had become. He served on four committees of the House of Commons but it is not at all likely that he added his voice to the opposition to the royal government which had its focus in criticism of the king's Scottish favourites. He was not going to end up in the Tower of London, which was how his friends Sir Walter Chute and John Hoskyns were punished. This 'Addled Parliament' was distinguished in that it did not pass any legislation whatsoever; its main result was to convince the king that he need not summon another Parliament for seven years.

After proving his loyalty in the Commons Donne wrote to his patron, asking him to 'admit into your memorie' that fact that he was now 'a year older' than when he had last been turned down for a job in the service of the State. He was 'broken with some sicknesse' but as honest as ever. So he begged Carr either to 'bid me hope for this businesse in your Lordship's hand' or to let him 'abandon all' in that field and 'pursue my first purpose' – ordination. We do not know what 'this businesse' was but once again no job was offered.

Ten years later Donne was to say in his *Devotions* that the king was not to blame: 'when I asked a temporall office, he denied not, refused not that'. But at least James must have assented to the frequent refusals and he now had no reason to want Donne in a political job since the married Earl of Somerset was falling out of favour, being replaced by George Villiers, who was to be made Duke of Buckingham. Villiers was superior to Carr in charm, in intelligence and in morals, and in the future Donne was to be helped by him; it seems significant that Charles the future king, genuinely devout and strictly heterosexual, became his close friend and relied on him as much as did the infatuated James. But in the autumn of 1614 Donne at last saw what had been obvious for some time: he must make a direct approach to the king with a clear decision that if he was offered a suitable opportunity to serve the Church he would take it. Sensibly, he wanted an opportunity which would suit his very unusual personality and gifts; in 1614 as when he had declined Morton's suggestion in 1607, he could not imagine himself as a normal clergyman in a parish.

In November he went to see the king and told him that he was now ready to take the course which James wanted for him, ordination. It seems that up to this point the royal wish had not been accompanied by any guarantee of a fulfilling career in the Church, for had Donne already been given a firm promise from the Supreme Governor of the Church, he would not have needed to beg for the patronage of the king's favourite, as he had done in that crawling letter to Carr in the spring of 1613. But in the autumn of 1614 he reported that he had 'received from the King as good allowance and encouragement as I could desire'.

He was also assured of support from Archbishop Abbot, but a whole world was ending for him. Although he did not make public his grief when his son Francis died this November at the age of seven, at the request of the Countess of Bedford he wrote a longish poem in honour of her brother, who had died at the age of 22. In it he announced that 'in thy grave I doe interre my Muse'. Both the countess and Henry Goodyer, who had been prominent among his patrons, were now themselves in debt after much extravagance, but other friends seem to have enabled him to make a fresh start financially. The mood in which he was ordained seems to be shown in his prayer added to the *Essayes in Divinity*. 'Thou hast set up many candlesticks, and kindled many lamps in mee; but I have either blown them out, or carried them to guide me in forbidden ways. Thou hast given me a desire of knowledge, and some meanes to it, and some possession of it; and I have arm'd myself with thy weapons against thee. Yet, O God, have mercy upon me . . .'

He was ordained both as a deacon and as a priest by the Bishop of London on 23 January 1615. In his *Devotions* of 1624 he was to thank God that King James 'first of any man conceiv'd a hope that I might be of some use in thy Church'. Previously, he recalled, he had been 'sicke of a vertiginous giddines and irresolution', so that he had 'almost spent all my time in consulting how I might spend it'.

4 Thou hast done

And having done that, thou hast done,
I feare no more.
'A Hymne to God the Father'

Looking back, Donne was to say that God the Holy Spirit had been active all through his long period of 'irresolution', keeping his ears open to the call to preach even while he was trying to place his feet on the ladder of secular promotion. Not all the 'I' and 'we' passages in the sermons are unadorned autobiography, any more than the poems are a prosaic record of his earlier life, but one passage does seem to refer to what he now saw as his spiritual journey. He reflected that to be genuine a divine command to preach 'must be a light; not a calling taken out of the darkness of melancholy, or darkness of discontent, or darkness of want and poverty, or darkness of a retired life to avoid the mutual duties and offices of society: it must be a light, and a light that shines; it is not enough to have knowledge and learning; it must shine out, and appear in preaching; and it must shine in our hearts, in the private testimony of the Spirit there' (4:109).

Donne had very thoroughly known for himself the darkness of melancholy and discontent, poverty and loneliness, and it is extremely unlikely that he ended his 'irresolution' about the priesthood because he was driven by motives which were exclusively high-minded. Like many other people who have been ordained as 'ministers of religion' he wanted to earn his pay and to support his family. But the commentators who have concluded that he was a fraud as a preacher would appear to have delivered one hostile verdict too many, for the fact that Donne wanted a job does not exclude the possibility that he had a vocation, either to be a servant of God in the spirit of his religious poetry or (if we prefer a secular way of putting things) to reach the public by using the talents which had been rusted by an almost unendurable period of unemployment.

After his ordination he remained interested in money: at the end of each year he compared income with expenditure, as no doubt had been the habit of his father the ironmonger. But his character was such that he not only wrote down a thanksgiving to God when his income was sufficient or more than sufficient: he also became dedicated to his new work – and highly skilled within a strikingly short space of time, as if all his life he had been preparing for the pulpit. He had not been a priest for two years before he was expounding the Scriptures and his own reflections Sunday by Sunday to an audience of lawyers and students of law, shrewd men who were trained to examine, dissect and contradict other men's arguments. Then and later he prepared his sermons by hard study and prayer; he tackled difficult subjects; he took trouble to express his thoughts in words often of the quality which he had attained in his poetry; he was far more coherent than he had been in his books about suicide and the Oath; he memorized what he had to say and took an hour to say it; later he could confidently re-create his spoken words in a text for the printer; and one of his messages, very properly, was that behaviour mattered more than anything said. If a clergyman was interested mainly in his income it was not necessary to go to all that trouble. In Donne's case there is plenty of evidence that many of those who heard him found him convincing, although not necessarily in every word. Being believers they would interpret this as the work of the Holy Spirit in his heart and theirs, and it does not seem to be our duty to say that they were utterly deluded because he was in fact pretending all the time.

But Donne also believed that King James had been the Holy Spirit's instrument in encouraging him to be ordained – and this belief, too, can seem strange to modern readers. Whatever may be true about the activity of God and about the right of a king to govern a Church (subjects on which no wise historian would wish to pontificate), the role of this particular king will be suspect. We have already seen him mixed up in the sordid affairs of Frances Howard, the biggest scandal of his reign but not the only one. So how was he mixed up with Donne? In a short piece of attempted humour in prose, 'The Character of a Scot at the First Sight', a younger Donne had ridiculed the uncouthness of some of the Scots who had followed James to England. He may well have had the same early attitude to James himself.

This is not a biography of James but it must be said that this king was no fool in his religious policy which included the encouragement of Donne. He had no personal glamour or natural dignity. He exposed himself to gossip, ridicule and failure as a king by his pathetic infatuations with a series of handsome young men, at a time when in theory sodomy was punishable by death. Of course Donne knew this; the sixteenth of the 'problemes' which he put to himself and his friends privately, probably in the 1600s, was 'Why are Statesmen most Incredible?' and in his answer referred to those 'by whome the Prince provokes his lust, and by whom hee vents it'. In that age of contempt for any sign of homosexuality it was not easy to believe in James as a model to his subjects. Physically he was very clumsy, in an England where physical elegance was expected of the élite; emotionally he had been damaged by an extraordinarily tough time, 1566–1603, between his birth and his move to England; and financially he had two great problems. One was that in reaction to those years of humiliations and fights in Scotland he was hopelessly extravagant in expenditure on pleasures when he had a chance in England. (He told Parliament that his first three years as King of England 'were to me a Christmas' and the rest of his reign was not very different.) The other was that in a period of roaring inflation he did not put the public finances in order by insisting on professionalism in control and audit and by making a long-term agreement with Parliament. The Great Contract talked about in the Parliament of 1610 came to nothing. An efficient businessman, Lionel Cranfield, was appointed Lord Treasurer in 1621 but sacked three years later when he argued that the country could not afford the war which was then demanded by the king's all-powerful favourite, George Villiers, against the whole previous policy of virtual pacifism.

A vision of James in glory was, however, painted by Rubens on the ceiling of the Banqueting House in Whitehall and it was a vision of the heavenly reward to peacemakers. It was his pride to have ended for ever wars between England and Scotland: he invented the idea of 'Great Britain' although in 1608 he had to admit that it would have to consist of two kingdoms with different laws. He was also proud to have stopped the long war between England and Spain; and he did what little he could to prevent or end the Thirty Years' War in central Europe, putting his trust in a characteristic policy not of military intervention but of royal marriages, first with a Protestant ruler in Germany, then with a Catholic princess in Spain and then with a Catholic princess in France. Peace had been secured between England and Scotland because Scotland's king had by birth the best claim to the throne of England, and perhaps royalty could bring peace to Europe.

He also had a vision of religious peace. In practice he was much more tolerant towards Roman Catholics than the Puritans wanted, and much more tolerant towards Puritans than some of the bishops wanted. His wife was a Roman Catholic convert and his son, Prince Henry, was developing as a Protestant hero before his death from typhoid fever. Early in his reign in England he tried to persuade other monarchs to join him in convening a General Council of the Church in order to reconcile Catholics and Protestants all over

Christendom. Inevitably that plan failed because it depended on the pope being willing to renounce much of his existing authority. The shrewd Henri IV of France advised James to become a Roman Catholic for the sake of peace, as he had done himself ('Paris is worth a Mass') – and to stop writing books. It was Henri who called James the most learned fool in Christendom. So the dream of being another Constantine faded. (The emperor Constantine had begun his career in Britain, had restored peace to the Roman world as the first Christian emperor, and had presided over the Church's first General Council.) But James was not completely deterred: he encouraged Pierre du Moulin's plan to unite all Protestants – another plan which was abortive – and he supported the Church of England's first contacts with the Eastern Orthodox. And in 1611 the fulsome dedication of the 'Authorized' or 'King James' Version of the Bible did point to a reality: James carried weight as a theologian as well as a king, he had insisted that all existing English translations were defective, and he had ordered that the new version should have no controversial footnotes. This Bible was to prove his most influential achievement.

He valued bishops because they could be his agents in keeping the Church in a peace which included submission to him but did not include a tight discipline. In 1610 he persuaded the Calvinist Scots to accept bishops consecrated in England. But equally, in England as in Scotland he valued preachers who were also scholars and his patronage of Donne was part of this policy. So despite his defects about which a younger Donne had been scornful, his record as a maker of peace and as a patron of religion was such that it did not seem totally and obviously shameful to accept his patronage.

We do not know exactly what Donne had been promised as royal encouragement, but the new priest was given two honours almost immediately: he was appointed one of the 48 chaplains to the king and was awarded a doctorate by a reluctant university in

Cambridge at the king's command. A cipher was entrusted to him for use in secret correspondence about developments in religion and politics abroad, taking advantage of his knowledge of other languages. Being a royal chaplain entitled him to draw income from two parishes without residence in either of them, and it must have been a help when the lawyers of Lincoln's Inn needed a new Reader in Divinity to take charge of their chapel. By the end of 1616 Donne felt financially secure – and he was also delighted to have work to do.

He made no apology for needing to be alert within the world of work and money. On the contrary, he preached that 'God hath not removed man, not with-drawne man, from this Earth; he hath not given him the Aire to flie in, as to the Birds, nor Spheares to move in, as to the Sun and Moone; he hath left him upon the Earth, and not only to tread upon it as in contempt or in meere Dominion, but to walke upon it in the discharge of the duties of his calling; and so to be conversant upon the Earth is not a falling' (6:69). God, he declared, 'produced plants in Paradise that they might grow; God hath planted us in this world that we might grow; and he that does not endeavour that by all lawful meanes is inexcusable' (6:308). Preaching to the court of Charles I, he was to issue a warning that 'he that stands in a place, and does not the duty of that place, is but a statue in that place; and but a statue without an inscription; Posterity shall not know him, not read who he was' (8:178). And he was to preach this gospel of personal growth through work on many other occasions, saying robustly that 'wee are not sent into this world to Suffer, but to Doe' (3:329).

He did something as a diplomat, obeying the king's command to take a leading part in a mission which was essentially flawed because the king's own purpose was not down-to-earth.

The mission was announced as a bid to stop the war in central Europe between Catholics and Protestants, a war which was to become unstoppable (until 1648) in August 1619, when the Protestants in Bohemia rebelled against their Catholic king, Ferdinand, and replaced him by the Protestant ruler of the Palatinate of the Rhine, Frederick. King James was anxious to make peace, partly in order to be seen to act as a peacemaker but also because Frederick was his son-in-law. But his position was complicated: he hoped that the daughter of the king of Spain would soon become his daughter-in-law, and the king of Spain was allied with fellow Catholics who were involved in the Bohemian crisis. James had, it seems, no clear idea about how peace could be made: as so often, he put his trust in the idea that somehow talk would make the problem go away. In February 1619, as trouble brewed, it was announced that a large and expensive mission from 'Great Britain', led by Viscount Doncaster, would conduct a charm-offensive and Donne was soon telling Goodyer that he had 'commandment from the King' to be one of its leading members as its chaplain.

Little evidence survives of what exactly he did, but it seems probable that in addition to the narrower duties of a chaplain he was used to make contacts with the Protestants encountered as the many coaches transporting the embassy trundled across Europe. An experience which he mentioned in a later sermon was witnessing the devout Catholicism of Ferdinand, now Holy Roman Emperor, when the embassy was at last given an audience, in October. He recalled this sight: 'the greatest Christian Prince (in Style and Title) . . . at the sound of a Bell kneele downe in our presence and pray; and God forbid, he should be blamed for doing so' (9:325). But both Doncaster and Donne were far more impressed by the danger facing the Protestants than by the devotion shown by the Catholics, and Donne was specially glad to be able to preach before Frederick and his wife Elizabeth; he had written the happiest and best of his 'marriage songs' to celebrate their wedding in 1613. These were memorable experiences. The difficulty, however, was that neither Ferdinand nor Frederick had any intention of reaching a solution by compromise – and in the background King James had no intention of trying to impose a solution by sending an army. Doncaster's mission therefore had no bargaining power and essentially it was wasting everyone's time.

A further test of Donne's ability as a diplomat came in December 1619, when he was called upon to preach in The Hague when the embassy was on its way back home. With no results to show, the diplomats had to do what they could to reassure the disappointed and frightened Dutch Protestants. Donne preached from notes a sermon which must have been even longer than usual, for when he came to write it out he divided it into two (2:269–310). It is not known who was in the audience, but whether the sermon was heard by the Dutch or merely reported to them it was a masterpiece of tact without abandoning the Gospel.

Tact was needed because the Synod of Dort, defining Calvinist orthodoxy and therefore the official religion of the Dutch, had recently concluded its business and the consequences were being felt very sharply. Donne must have welcomed the synod's decision that God had not predestined particular individuals to hell 'from eternity' before the Fall of Adam had begun the story of human sin, but he would have been far less happy about another decision: that Christ's death had been intended to save from hell no one except those (few?) whom God chose to save as his 'elect' when they had come into existence. And still less could he be happy about the per-secution of the Arminians whose belief that Christ had died in order to save 'all' had been rejected: hundreds of clergy who preached what Donne himself believed were being deprived of their pulpits by the Calvinist equivalent of the Inquisition. One reason for this persecution was that Arminian theology was linked with a political movement, advocating a policy of peaceful and profitable commerce instead of war alongside the Protestants of central Europe – precisely the policy which Donne's own royal master favoured in practice. In the Netherlands the leader of the peace party was executed.

In his sermon Donne was neither undiplomatic nor unfaithful. He preached about the call of Jesus to fishermen in Galilee, a Scriptural text generally acceptable in a religious and seafaring nation. He pointed out that the apostles were not told to disobey the authorities – and that was a signal from a royal chaplain which would satisfy the party now in power in the Netherlands. He also pointed out that fishermen earned good rewards – and that was a signal from a citizen of London of sympathy with the party which wanted to trade and make money in peace. And he stressed that the fishermen were not told to fish in the murky waters of theological controversy – a clear signal from a man who in many ways always thought as a layman and who now agreed with those of the Dutch who had not been fascinated by the agenda of the Synod of Dort. But he was also positive as a preacher of the Gospel, using (with good precedent) a parable as a teaching instrument. He said that the fish caught by the apostolic fishermen ended up in the banquet where God was the host because of that host's invitation – a message which endorsed the emphasis of all the Calvinists on the priority of God's gracious mercy. But he added that the fish missing from the banquet were absent not because they had never been invited but because by their own decisions they had swum away. It had been within their God-given power to reach their proper destination.

By that last twist in the parable Donne hinted at his own belief. But by his tact he had avoided offence to the victors at the Synod of Dort and was presented with one of the gold medals which had been struck in proud commemoration of that event. This was to be his only big taste of diplomatic work and he must have realized that a pompous mission to spread good will in Europe had achieved nothing over five months except polite but hollow exchanges.

He was to have no further cause to envy his friend Henry Wotton, a consummate diplomat who became disillusioned with that profession. While ambassador in Venice Wotton had discovered that the Venetians preferred a compromise with the papacy to an alliance with faraway England. He also found that his royal master preferred sending ambassadors to paying them. In 1611 he had returned to England, only to find that he was out of favour: his financial petitions irritated, his more cynical witticisms became known and gave offence (but did he actually say that an ambassador is an honest man sent to lie abroad for the good of his country?), he was given a nickname which suggested that he had become Italian. Eventually he was again employed as a diplomat but again there were problems over salary and expenses. When rewarded by appointment as the ill-paid Provost of Eton College his debts remained (once he was arrested) and his energies did not: he spoke of writing a history of England, a biography of Luther, a memoir of Donne, but little got written. He was ordained as a deacon and hoped for a Deanery but only a pension was granted. In his will he left pictures to King Charles, for whom he had acted in the choice and collection of Italian art – together with one last reminder that the Crown owed him money.

Wotton had spiritual depth (his poetry showed that) and a large circle of friends and admirers, but his career was not the complete fulfilment of the confident hopes of the days when he and Donne had begun their friendship in Oxford. The one who had been unemployed while his friend was in Venice was the one who died without a complaint; he had become an 'ambassador for God' and as Sir Frank Kermode wrote in 1971 'there is no possible doubt that the sermon suited Donne's talents perfectly'. Whatever we may think about the truth of what Donne preached, we ought to agree that he believed it well enough to perform convincingly and that in so doing he at last fulfilled himself.

A fine miniature portrait of Donne has survived, dated 1616. The work of the well-known artist Isaac Oliver, it depicts the new royal chaplain who will also be available as a diplomat. His hair is neatly trimmed, his face is smooth, his starched ruff is immaculate. But four years pass and almost another man is shown in a portrait (by an unknown artist) which has remained in the Deanery of St Paul's Cathedral. The smartness has gone; there are bags under the eyes; the clothes are vague, with no ruff or collar. At the age of 49 here is a man well acquainted with grief, for in 1617 his wife had died; and familiar also with hard work, for his sermons and his other activities as a priest have needed the habit of constant self-discipline. But he stares straight at us; he knows where he stands and he knows what he must say. It seems excessive to claim that the difference between these two portraits has been caused by a conversion after ordination or bereavement, but certainly his religious message has been deepened. The darkness of Anne's death has compelled him to be more deeply attentive to 'a light that shines' and to be more urgent about what he could say to others in the dark.

All but one of the bishops appointed by James I to be his assistants in governing the Church of England had enough learning to be doctors of 'divinity' and most were energetic preachers – which was to be expected, since the king was himself an author and poet who could handle religious subjects and he liked to have bishops who would be a credit to their Supreme Governor. He made his courtiers attend many sermons (some by Donne), although he was, it seems, not often in the congregation himself. In many districts the clergy formed 'combinations' which delivered sermons to each other, and to a surprising number of the laity gathered in the church of the market town, and then discussed them over dinner. 'Godly' laymen appointed special 'lecturers' to preach regularly in churches which could be crowded for the occasion. The Puritans who formed the strongest spiritual movement in the Church of England thought that nothing was more important than Bible-based preaching and were indignant when parish priests were 'dumb'. The House of Commons petitioned for more sermons throughout the country when the king allowed it to meet, and corporately attended long sermons in St Margaret's church in Westminster.

By the end of the changeful sixteenth century the English people seem to have become in the main Protestant, chiefly perhaps because it seemed treasonable to be a Roman Catholic, but if the Protestantism was to be heartfelt, filling the emotional vacuum left by the disappearance of the great Church of the Middle Ages, it must be preached. Protestantism based itself on the Bible and 'the Bible only' but actually the Bible needed to be interpreted if its complexity was not to seem too confusing, and its message needed to be earthed in the realities of daily life if its moral standards were not to seem impossibly high. In the near future great attempts were to be made to use the power of the government to impose an Anglican system of worship as ordered by king and clergy, and then to impose a Puritan system of faith and godliness after a triumphant revolution, but in Donne's time the answer to the religious needs of the nation seemed to lie mainly in preaching which would arrest, inform and convince, and there was no great gulf between the 'Anglicans' (a term not yet used) and the 'Puritans' (a nickname used by scornful Elizabethans). A sign of this was that although Elizabeth had removed from Edmund Grindal the authority to function as Archbishop of Canterbury because he was not tough enough on the Puritans, James chose as his archbishop (1611–31) George Abbot, who had a strong sympathy with them. 'High' Church men stressed the sacraments of the Church more than did the Puritans, but what united these two movements was far larger than any division. All accepted the Church of England as the nation's Church, and the king as its Supreme Governor on earth; all accepted the Bible as the supreme and infallible revelation of

God; and all accepted preaching the Bible's message as the Church's main responsibility. Moreover, all agreed that preaching ought to be reasonable, not hysterical, and that scholars were needed. Preaching in 1624, Donne's friend Joseph Hall claimed that the scholars among the Church of England's clergy were *stupor mundi*, the wonder of the world. We should not exaggerate the theological unity of the Church which King James governed: one of the ablest of its theologians, William Ames, had to live in a Puritan nonconformist's exile from 1610. But the clergy were more united than they were to be in the next reign.

The message which united most of them was confidently authoritative, for the Church of England was not in the business of encouraging a do-it-yourself religion. (After the Gunpowder Plot executions of traitors were conducted with the usual barbarity outside St Paul's Cathedral and in 1612 two Protestants accused of gross heresy were burned, the last in English history to suffer this fate.) Any atheists, or people indifferent to religion, must be told firmly that nature proved the existence of God; Roman Catholics must be shown that the Bible proved that their Church had not been faithful to God's self-revelation, particularly in the matter of the royal supremacy; and individualists in religion must be appropriately rebuked. Unlike the poet Donne, Dr Donne the preacher repeatedly denounced 'singularity' and we find him saying that 'the generall opinion . . . is for the most part good evidence' (4:155). He believed that he had been authorized by Church and State to teach the people to walk in 'a way that the Fathers and the Church have walked before'; his mission was not to advertise 'a discovery made by our curiosity or our confidence' (7:267). Reason was, he was sure, on the side of Revelation although not necessarily a supporter of an individual's emotions. 'Let us therefore looke first to that which is best in us naturally, that is, Reason; For if we lose that . . . and strike into an incapable and barren stupidity, there is no footing, no subsistence for grace' from God (10:46). 'It is not true in any sense . . . that there is faith, where there is nothing but faith' (7:228–9). So Donne was one of those who trusted that 'the sincere preaching of the Gospel in our settled and well disciplined Church shall prevaile against those four pestilent opposites, Atheists and Papists and Sectaries and Carnal, indifferent men' (10:60).

Many sermons have survived from that period and scholars who have had the patience to work through considerable numbers of them assure us that most of the preachers were not major poets, deep thinkers or magnificent orators. For better or for worse, their material was often far simpler than what Donne felt he could offer in the royal court and in the cathedral and churches of London. He complained about some fellow preachers in his day who 'make the emergent affairs of the time their Text, and the humours of the hearers their Bible' (4:276), but it is clear that such a complaint would not be fair if made about most of the preachers, most of whom fell more or less into the category now called 'Puritan'. We know, from their great impact on England and New England in the years to come, that Puritan preachers were less nervous than Donne was when handling politics or 'emergent affairs'. But we also know that their main thrusts were severely biblical and austerely moral, and that when they had the opportunity they were going to do what they could to impose their beliefs and morals on people who, in Shakespeare's famous phrase, preferred 'cakes and ale'. A younger Donne had set himself a 'probleme': 'Why do Puritans make long sermons?' His answer had been 'It is their duty to Preach on till their Auditory awake'. But the Puritans had the last laugh – until they awakened a violent reaction.

A Puritan preacher whom Donne may have heard lecturing in Cambridge in the 1580s, William Perkins, had a wide influence before his death in 1602. His *Arte of Prophecying* was the manifesto of the 'plain' style, breaking away from the medieval tradition. That had been sharply divided into the academic and the popular, but whether the preacher had made his points by logical arguments based on Scripture and the Fathers of the Church, or by anecdotes, the message had always been essentially the same: believe the Bible, believe the Church, use the Church's sacraments. Now Perkins affirmed that 'to prophesie signifieth to teach the Word of God to the people of God by applying the same to the consciences for their edification'. Only thus could the art of preaching end in 'the science of living blessedly for ever'. 'Believe the Bible' was still the main point but it was the task of the preacher to state plainly the 'sense of Scripture' without reliance either on the Fathers or on anecdotes, and to apply Scripture to the conscience without much dependence on what could be done by the sacraments. Like Donne, Perkins preached without a script but with notes for reference in the pulpit; younger Puritans revived the popular medieval style of preaching from the heart, without notes; and with or without notes in the pulpit all were in earnest. A Puritan who succeeded Donne in the pulpit of Lincoln's Inn, John Preston, combined that pulpit with the headship of a Cambridge college and the duties of a royal chaplain, but he died, worn out by too much preaching, in 1628. Had he lived he might have been influential in reducing the tension which was to grow into a great rift between these 'plain' preachers and the monarchy.

It seems that in his lifetime Donne was himself attacked by some Puritans, not so much because of his theology as because of the complexity of his language. After his death one of his admirers, 'R. B.', wrote a poetic tribute which recalled that he had been 'humm'd against' because his 'fine words' made him a 'bad edifier' – and also because some fellow preachers 'envy'd' him while he was 'magnifi'd' by the congregations who welcomed the fact that he did not preach like his critics. It seems that many of those who gathered to hear Donne in the pulpit had a number of reasons to prefer his style. Without an entirely medieval insistence on the authority of the Church, Donne was impressive through his quotations from the teachers of the Church over many generations.

Without a naïve over-simplification of the authority of the Bible, he loved every word of it and relished the exploration of the significance of every word. Without being as simple as the Puritans were, his interpretation was a heartfelt reaction to what the Bible said. And without either ascending to airborne perfectionism or descending to earthy anecdotes, he applied the Bible's message to daily life.

By 1660 it could be seen that the rigour of Calvinist theology was discredited and that the enthusiastic crusade to purify the nation's morals by compulsion was over. Yet the 'plain style' of the Puritans survived – with a different message. What seemed to be needed now was a simple presentation of reasonable piety and everyday morality, in reaction against the wars which in the name of religion had done great damage both in England and in central Europe. The first master of this style was John Tillotson, the Archbishop of Canterbury who had been another of Donne's successors in the pulpit of Lincoln's Inn. Donne anticipated the tone of Tillotson's preaching when he remarked that 'rectified Reason is religion' (2:293). Despite the differences in his style from the simplicity advocated by Perkins, Preston and other Puritans, despite the humming against his love and use of language with a scholarly poet's sophistication, he at least told himself that he ought to be 'plain', helpfully pastoral and moral, a sinner speaking to sinners. And at least he was plainer than Lancelot Andrewes, approximately his equal as the leading non-Puritan preacher – and he gave a higher priority to preaching. After the death of Andrewes in 1626 he stood alone and no equal arose for many years after his own death. He was far from being the only preacher in the style which was to be called 'metaphysical' because full of 'conceits' but he and Andrewes were its acknowledged masters.

When he was in the pulpit Andrewes impressed, for his personality was unified and beautiful in its holiness and his learning seemed to be inexhaustible. King James appears to have felt awed in his presence and summoned him to preach at court on the greatest occasions, celebrating festivals of the Church's year with sermons which were feasts in themselves. But Andrewes had spent 34 years learning or teaching in Cambridge University and at heart he always remained the academic theologian who studied much and prayed much but, if he could, saved up speaking for lectures or sermons. The strangest of all the king's favourites, he was honoured by membership of the Privy Council but is reported to have said little during its deliberations. Although he became the bishop of a succession of dioceses including Winchester it seems that he could be content to spend only two months in the year in his diocese and only two hours of the day on doing business and receiving visitors (after his midday dinner). The preparation of the sermons which were later printed must have involved a great deal of work but he does not seem to have preached frequently. Certainly he did not share the Puritans' emphasis on preaching in the parishes: he thought that most of the clergy would talk nonsense if they preached too often. They would be wiser to read the Bible itself to their people and to concentrate on private prayer, public worship and pastoral care. He valued the sacraments very highly, as the principal means of God's grace to sinners. In his own chapel he maintained a dignity in ceremonial and ornament which was by the standards of his time High Church, and on his knees he wrote and used a book of private prayers which when printed was to be a treasure of Anglican spirituality; the handwritten copy was stained by his tears.

In contrast with Andrewes the sacramentalist, Donne could claim that 'to take away preaching were to disarm God' (4:195) and that a word preached was 'a portion of the bloud of thy Saviour' (3:364). He compared the sermon with a trumpet sounding various calls in a military camp: the alarm, the call to battle, the summons to a meeting, the order to retreat for 'a safe repairing of our souls' (2:169–70). His first sermon in St Paul's Cathedral was about the mission of St John the Baptist to be a 'witness to the Light' and more than once he returned to that text and, as he hoped, 'not to a light which is His, but a light which is He'. In his poem 'To Mr Tilman' he called the privilege of preaching a 'Coronation' and asked:

> Why doth the foolish world scorne that profession,
> Whose joyes passe speech? . . .
> What function is so noble, as to bee
> Embassadour to God and destinie?
> To open life, to give kingdomes to more
> Than kings give dignities; to keep heaven's doore?

But of course Donne was not always God's noble ambassador. We can find some unedifying evidence that he was human in some surviving documents which give us bits of the story of his relationship with his daughter Constance.

In 1617 his wife died (and much more will be said about Anne Donne in Chapter 9). After that bereavement which affected him far more deeply than has always been acknowledged Constance kept house for him: a situation which meant that men of her own age who might marry her did not appear in the Deanery and that her father was not very active in arranging a marriage. Eventually a husband did appear who was well-off but considerably older than Constance: he was Edward Alleyn, once a mere actor but now a theatre manager and large-scale dealer in properties. At the time Donne was pleased for her sake but the atmosphere soon soured. Alleyn asked Donne for a loan; Constance asked him for a horse and a promised diamond ring; her father refused the loan, sent the horse to Constance's brother in Oxford and kept the ring, perhaps feeling that Alleyn who had now secured a good housekeeper ought to be old and rich enough to manage his own financial affairs and buy his wife a horse and a ring. An indignant letter from Alleyn survives in a much-revised draft, saying that he had been shocked by the dean's behaviour and language. But he did not live long, Constance inherited a small fortune from him and married again, and during his long, last illness Donne was looked after in her home.

Having observed a man who had still not managed to become a saint, we can now make a brief study of this scholarly poet who did manage to become a preacher.

His mature style was dignified, learned and spiritually authoritative, but also self-involving for preacher and congregation alike. Donne had to make his own convictions clear and public, as he had not done when writing either poems using many voices or books which were tangled in language and argument. Now congregations knew that he was in earnest about the content of his message and about its urgency. 'To call upon the Congregation to heare what God hath done for my soule is a blessed preaching of my selfe' (9:279), but at last he felt no need to talk all the time about his own emotions: he had a message to deliver. The skills which he had developed in order to impress (or imagine?) a mistress (or a wife?) must now be redirected, for 'True Instruction is making love to the Congregation, and to every soule in it' (9:350). One cannot imagine either a Puritan or Bishop Andrewes saying that. But this self-involvement by the preacher must be matched by the listener. If a listener 'heares but the Logique, or the Rhetorique or the Ethique, or the poetry of the Sermon', he does not hear what matters most, for 'the Sermon of the Sermon he hears not' (7:512).

'A man', he warned, 'may thread Sermons by half dozens a day, and place his merit in the number, a man may have been all day in the perfume and incense of preaching' without really hearing a single sermon (6:149). By the same token, a man may preach eloquently without making any real impression. 'Twenty of our Sermons edifie not so much, as if the Congregation might see one man converted by us. Any one of you might out-preach us. That one man would leave his beloved sinne, that one man would restore ill-gotten goods, had made a better Sermon than ever I shall, and should gain more soules by his act than all our words (as they are ours) can doe' (2:275–6).

He insisted that 'a Sermon intends Exhortation principally and Edification, and a holy stirring of religious affections, and then matters Doctrine, and points of Divinity, occasionally, secondarily, as the words of the text may invite them' (8:95). A preacher must not offer 'a Pye of Plums without meat' or an 'Oration of Floweres and Figures, and Phrases without Strength' (7:329). 'It is not the depth, not the wit, not the eloquence of the Preacher that pierces us, but his nearnesse' (3:295). A preacher of the Gospel must be 'acceptable to God's people, and available for their Edification' by speaking 'plainly, sincerely, inelegantly, inartificially' (4:91).

Of course Dr Donne the preacher had Jack Donne the poet inside him and he could not stop being witty. One of his little jokes was that he had heard 'men preach against witty preaching, and doe it with as much wit as they have; and against learned preaching with as much learning as they could compasse' (10:148) – but some who heard that joke no doubt felt that Donne ought to have been laughing at himself (as perhaps he was). He had been called to preach the Gospel but he pointed out that when the holy apostles had been called to stop being fishermen, 'they did but leave their nets, they did not burne them' (2:285). All his surviving sermons, even those where he is obviously trying to be as simple and as pastoral as possible, are the work of a man who enjoyed displaying both his scholarship and his skill with words including both memorable epigrams and purple passages of prose-poetry. But Donne well understood what the best teachers of 'rhetoric' in the Renaissance recommended. This was not only 'elocution' with the Latin masters as models, whether Ciceronian (stately) or Senecan (pithy). The art of rhetoric included also 'invention' and 'disposition', finding the theme and arranging the material; and after that preparatory work, it involved 'memory' and 'pronunciation' as no less essential if the material assembled around the theme was to be retained in the mind and delivered without a script. And Donne showed that he did not shirk any of these professional labours.

He was not absolutely tied to London. His zeal diminished after preaching every Sunday during term to the friendly but limited congregation in the chapel of Lincoln's Inn, and in the early 1620s he hoped to be made Dean of Salisbury, or failing that Dean of Gloucester. In the event he was appointed to a Deanery within London but had he lived he might have accepted a bishopric in the early 1630s. (His name appeared in a small list of senior clergy being considered in this connection, before his last illness.) However, London was what he knew and in it he had audiences which he could not have found anywhere else: the royal court to which he preached regularly over fifteen years as a royal chaplain (and it seems that about 1,700 people, whether courtiers, clerks or servants, were to be found in Whitehall Palace); exceptionally intelligent and active people making a success of a business or a profession; people who might have less money but who were willing to spend it on going to a new play by Shakespeare; and clergy and others who became eager fans or critics of the leading preachers, often taking notes. In a sermon to the Lord Mayor and Aldermen of London which must have taken two and a half hours if it was preached as it was written out, Donne boasted that 'this City hath the ablest preaching Clergy of any City in Christendom' (4:113). He could say that a businessman who had failed to be charitable to the poor might be reminded on the Last Day that while on earth it had been his habit to hear two sermons on a Sunday and go to 'lectures' by preachers on weekdays (10:62). Congregations were so interested that Donne could complain about 'the murmurings and noises which you make when the Preacher concludeth any point'. Whether these noises expressed enthusiasm or disapproval, they were 'impertinent Interjections' which could 'swallow up one quarter of his houre' while the preacher still had much to say. And some of the noise could come from 'many who were not within the distance of hearing the Sermon' but remained standing in the cathedral and trying to hear it amid the noise (10:133).

Donne was fortunate in that he was able to develop his preaching in the encouraging atmosphere which surrounded him while he was 'Reader in Divinity' in Lincoln's Inn, 1616–21. His main task there was to prepare and deliver a lecture-like sermon for every Sunday during term. He must have preached at least two hundred such sermons although only about a tenth of that number survives.

With his past, the new role might have been difficult. The Benchers (senior lawyers) might have objected that they did not wish to entrust this prestigious pulpit to a man whose history was scandalous and whose ordination was recent, and they might have grumbled even if the nomination came from the king. The students might have been interested in him only as a man who in his own student days had written erotic and anti-Establishment poems which could now be passed from hand to hand. Many of the sermons which we can read from this period when Donne was back in that haunted scene refer with some passion to sin, its power, its persistence and its guilt. 'We labour to break hedges', he said, 'and to steale wood, and gather up a stick out of one sin and a stick out of another, and make a fagot to load us in this life and burne us in the next.' Changing the metaphor, he said that while drowning in a sea of sin a man can find himself held up 'by the chin' – yet God will withdraw that helping hand if the sinner so relies on it that he goes on sinning (2:124). However, it seems clear that the seniors grew to respect Donne: he, like them, had laboured to study his subject and had prepared carefully what he said in public; he, like them, could be charming in private; and he seemed sincere in his religion. For their part, the students saw that he was both sincere and human. He had known what it is to want money, to want a woman, to want a job, and he was not so hypocritical as to deny it – but he had also wanted God.

He was able to persuade Lincoln's Inn to do something after saying for years that the chapel needed to be rebuilt. His friend Christopher Brooke seems to have been in charge of the fund-raising and Donne was invited back to preach when the new chapel was consecrated in 1623. He then prayed: 'In these walles to them that love Profit and Gaine, manifest thy selfe as a Treasure and fill them so; To them that love Pleasure, manifest thy selfe as Marrow and Fatnesse, and fill them so; And to them that love Preferment, manifest thy selfe as a Kingdome, and fill them so' (4:363). He knew his congregation so well that he knew how to offer heaven in terms which lawyers would immediately understand: it is 'where all Clients shall retain but one Counsellor, our Advocate Christ Jesus, nor present him any other fee but his own blood, and yet every Client have a judgment on his side' (2:244). And he could tease them about their excuses for absence from the chapel: 'Beloved, it is not always colder upon Sunday than upon Satterday; nor any colder in the Chapell than in Westminster Hall' where judges and barristers went to work (4:377). He could even tease them about their sex lives: 'Chastity is not chastity in an old man, but a disability to be unchast' (2:244).

In 1621 he was installed as a Dean of St Paul's and that cathedral in whose shadow he had been born (almost literally) became the centre of his life until his death in 1631. In the year before his appointment King James had visited St Paul's in state, in order to launch an appeal for the necessary restoration of its medieval fabric. The response had been disappointing but the king must have known that although he had played a leading role in the building of the new chapel for Lincoln's Inn Donne would not be likely to put the very much larger cathedral's physical needs at the top of his agenda. Letters of petition or gratitude addressed very humbly to the king's current favourite, George Villiers Duke of Buckingham, are among the evidence which shows how anxious this 'poor worm' had been to get the job, once again crawling with a complaint about his 'narrow and penurious' finances. Having left no stone unturned in his efforts to secure his move to St Paul's, Donne had no intention of devoting his life to fund-raising and the repair of the cathedral's stonework. When some material already collected to begin the cathedral's restoration found its way to the Duke of Buckingham's mansion (this was York House, being repaired and extended) its movement suited the dean as well as the duke.

When Donne was dead the project to restore the physical appearance of the cathedral was relaunched. William Laud was then Bishop of London on his way to Canterbury and the scheme was the centre-piece of his strategy which was to bring back the dignity of the Church of England's churches. The 'high' (main) altar was made visibly holy and separate from the people. The little houses close to the walls of the cathedral were demolished. The outside pulpit from which preachers had delivered sermons which were more or less the equivalent of modern broadcasts was also pulled down, and preachers were told that they must submit their sermons to the bishop before reading them out. These special sermons were transferred to the nave, from which Laud excluded the noise and disorder of daily use by the public. If they wanted merely to gossip or do business, Londoners must use the large portico which Inigo Jones constructed in a Palladian (classical) style out of keeping with the main fabric, which was patched up but remained dirty. Some thirty years later, it was all wrecked by fire.

That lay in the future. Under his own patron, King James, Donne was free to concentrate on the construction of sermons.

He was not now under any obligation to preach every Sunday but Walton says that he usually did, 'if not oftener', apart from the time which he spent in his two country parishes each summer. When in London his life could be called a 'continued study' since he worked at meditation, reading and writing throughout many a week unless he had to attend to business, before taking Saturday off to relax with friends and refresh himself for Sunday's performance. A sermon made heavy demands on his memory of what he had planned to say as well as on his energy as an orator and the routine of long preparation for the pulpit cannot have been easy to maintain, but it helped that since student days he had been accustomed to rise at four in the morning. More work would be required in writing out and polishing a fuller version of the sermon, if this was required; again both memory and energy were needed, since only notes remained as the basis. Donne made versions which could be published of 80 of these sermons while taking refuge in Chelsea for five months during the plague of 1625. He mentioned in a letter that it normally took him eight hours to do this job. He did more work on old sermons during his long and last illness in the winter of 1630–31.

No manuscript written out by this painstaking preacher has survived but one has been discovered which, although the work of a professional copyist, included corrections in style and substance made in Donne's own handwriting. It seems clear that the text which was eventually printed differed considerably from what had been preached. However, the modern convention of writing that he 'said' this or that which reaches us in print would probably not have displeased Donne. He always regarded a sermon as essentially something to be spoken and included in his own written version some tricks of a preacher's trade, as when he moved the climax of a sermon to its beginning, in case he or anyone else died before the urgent message was finished (3:226). On another occasion he went on preaching when the sand in his hour-glass told him that his hour was up, saying that the eternal destiny of his hearers, who were the king and his courtiers, might depend on their allowing him a few more minutes (7:368).

He did not ignore the sacraments in his enthusiasm for sermons. 'Christ', he said, 'preached the Christian Doctrine long before he instituted the Sacraments', which are 'subsidiary things' – but he went on to compare the sacraments with the miracles of Christ, for both are 'visible signs of invisible grace' (10:69). We know from sermons preached at 'Christenings' that he could be eloquent about Baptism as a new birth, a regeneration. 'We know no ordinary means of sowing grace for a child but Baptisme; neither are we to doubt of the fulnesse of salvation in them that have received it' (9:105). Baptism 'washes away' the 'Originall sin' inherited from the sin of Adam and Eve – but alas, Baptism cannot halt the piling up of 'actuall and habitual sins' committed by the baptized and destroying the prospect of their salvation unless there is 'reconciliation to God' (9:272).

About the Eucharist, he told the congregation in the cathedral on Christmas Day 1626: 'Beloved, in the blessed, and glorious, and mysterious Sacrament of the Body and Blood of Christ Jesus, thou seest the Lord's Salvation and thy Salvation' (7:294). He accepted a High Church theology about that sacrament, one of the many survivals from his Roman Catholic upbringing. He taught firmly that 'the Communion Table is an Altar; and in the Sacrament there is a Sacrifice. Not onely a Sacrifice of Thanksgiving, common to all the Congregation, but a Sacrifice peculiar to the Priest, though for the People. There he offers up to God the Father (that is, to the remembrance, to the contemplation of God the Father) the whole body of the merits of Christ Jesus, and begges of him, that in contemplation of the Sacrifice so offered, of that Body of his merits, he would vouchsafe to return, and to apply those merits to that Congregation' (7:429). He believed that in principle 'it is no Church that hath no Priest' with 'a spiritual power received from them, who have the same power in themselves' – preferably by 'such a Succession and Ordination, we have had, from the hands of men such as were made Bishops' according to the canon law of the Roman Catholic Church. Reformed Churches were, however, entitled to dispensation from this law 'in cases of necessity' (9:128–30).

In keeping with the belief that the Communion was holy but 'subsidiary' – a means of 'sealing' the faith of the faithful, not of adding to their number – it was held in St Paul's infrequently, on the great festivals in the Church's calendar and otherwise only once a month. In contrast, the services of Mattins and Evensong were sung by the choir every weekday and included lessons from the Old and New Testaments, and two long sermons were preached every Sunday, with at least two additional sermons in the course of the week. Shortly before Donne's arrival the clergy had agreed that the laity should be admitted to seats near the pulpit – although the new dean complained that some laymen were still unwilling to take off their hats or kneel.

In the Middle Ages the cathedral would have been colourfully full of pictures in glass, statues in wood and stone, and other ornaments which were the 'Bible of the poor' who could not read. Donne collected pictures when he could afford them for enjoyment in his Deanery, but had little interest in seeing such images in a church. 'We should wonder to see a Mother in the midst of many sweet Children passing her time in making babies and puppets for her own delight. We should wonder to see a man, whose Chambers and galleries were full of curious master-peeces, thrust in a Village Fair to looke upon sixpenny pictures and three farthing prints' (9:80). Now English Protestants could be assured that they had direct access to the 'Image of God' in their own souls and to the 'Word of God' in the Scriptures – and if they needed further images and words, they needed sermons.

Three years after his arrival in St Paul's he was glad to accept an invitation from his admirer the Earl of Dorset to become also the vicar of the nearby church of St Dunstan-in-the-West, where the earl had the right of appointment. In the first of his sermons to that congregation he spoke at length about the relationship of pastor and parish as being like the marriage of husband and wife, and it seems clear that St Dunstan's was to some extent therapy for his continuing sense of loss after Anne's death and as his children left home. It brought him extra work and he did not need the extra money, which was not much, but it also brought him into pastoral and social relationships which were harder to form in the vast, gloomy, cold and decaying cathedral. His predecessor had been vicar for almost half a century but seems not to have been very active in this particular post among those which he held. In contrast, Donne preached there often, attended the committee meetings and dinners of the 'vestry', and had such personal relationships that the parishioners gave him a substantial present of wine each Christmas. After the middle of 1628 this involvement was reduced, but in 1630 Donne told a friend that he still intended to preach there 'as often as my condition of body will permit'. He gave or bequeathed money to the poor of this parish, as well as to the poor in the two rural parishes which were also his and where he spent time each summer.

In order to supplement his income he had been granted the rectory of Keyston in Huntingdonshire in 1616, soon followed by the rectory of Sevenoaks in Kent, but he had resigned from Keyston shortly before his installation as Dean of St Paul's and in 1622 he was instituted as rector of Blunham in Bedfordshire, keeping Sevenoaks. A rather wicked poem by C. H. Sisson tries to imagine what this outspoken preacher might say to the modern parishioners in Sevenoaks, but another question is what parishioners might say nowadays to a rector who spent almost all his time outside the parish.

Naturally, to modern eyes it is something of a scandal that Donne accepted income from these three parishes as well as from St Paul's. However, it was the custom (inherited from the Middle Ages) that clergymen who were specially studious, or specially favoured, should be encouraged by being allowed to be 'pluralists', and few consciences objected, provided that the regular services and the pastoral duties were in the hands of a curate for whom the absentee rector paid. The deeply respected Bishop Andrewes had refused to be a bishop on the financial terms offered by Queen Elizabeth but had seen nothing wrong in drawing a range of incomes while Dean of Westminster Abbey.

Although after ordination Donne was primarily a preacher, part of his message in the pulpit was the importance of conversation outside it. 'Men onely can speake', he pointed out; 'therefore speech is the Glue, the Cyment, the soul of Conversation, and of Religion too' (8:338). We cannot know much about this talk in private and not many personal letters can be used as evidence about this period, partly because he was much busier than in the years of unemployment, partly because in London he had more opportunities to talk with friends, and partly because the considerable quantity of correspondence found in his study after his death has not survived. Izaak Walton appears to have looked through these papers. They included notes about 'all businesses that past of any publick consequence, either in this, or any of our neighbour-nations': notes written 'either in Latine, or in the Language of that Nation'. But the papers also included 'Copies of divers Letters and cases of Conscience that had concerned his friends, with his observations and solutions of them' – copies which, if preserved, would have transformed the task of Walton's successors as biographers and commentators. They would have been compelled to take seriously the fact that those who knew Donne best consulted him about their troubles and their moral problems. However, we have some glimpses of the dean being friendly with colleagues and staff in the cathedral. When making his will he remembered many names. He performed his duty to be hospitable and preached that by his presence at parties Christ justified 'Feasting, somewhat more than was merely necessary for society and chearful conversation' (7:143).

These easy relationships were no doubt helped by an unwillingness to spend time on trying to reform the Church. He accepted the practices of appointing friends and relations to positions at the disposal of the senior clergy, and of leasing out the cathedral's estates to favoured laymen who paid rents far below the rate of inflation but also 'fines' which went to the senior clergy when a lease was renewed. Walton was told that the dean had a reputation for being honest (and he passed on an anecdote about how this strange dean had refused to profit from one suggestion about how his income could be increased) but this could not be said about everyone else. Donne seems to have thought that a blind eye had to be turned towards some situations if he was to be able to devote himself to what he regarded as his vocation, preaching.

In the winter of 1623–24 he had occasion to preach to himself, when he and the doctors who were summoned in a panic had good reason to believe that he might well be very near death. The illness seems to have been a 'relapsing' fever, which in those days was often fatal. Naturally Donne, who at the best of times was extremely interested in himself, felt and thought about his illness and about its possible end, and was both emotional and clever with an agitated intensity; and since he could not move from his bed to a pulpit, and was forbidden to read, naturally he kept a kind of diary. This diary seems to have been polished and completed when the crisis was over. It was published as *Devotions upon Emergent Occasions*, a little book which provides a large amount of the evidence about his psychology as he prayed: 'O Eternall and most gracious God, who considered in thy selfe art a circle, first and last and altogether; but considered in thy working upon us art a direct line and leadest us from our beginning, through all our wayes, to our end . . .'

The *Devotions* are certainly not a get-well card to himself: they are gloomy thoughts about sickness as typical of the human condition, resulting in 'Debatements with God' which combine a devout humility with a continuing insistence on argument. They begin with this response to a sudden illness: 'We study Health, and deliberate upon our meats, and drink, and Ayre, and exercises' but 'in a minute a Cannon batters all'. Donne expects a 'torment of sicknes' – earthquakes, lightning, thunders, eclipses, blazing stars and rivers of blood, all within his body – and tries to persuade himself that this, not God's 'musique', is what he needs. He is in his bed but that is no comfort: he remembers it was a 'bed of wantonesse' in past years. Strangely, 'the Physician' is sent for only on the fourth day of this crisis; less strangely in view of seventeenth-century medical expertise, Dr Fox is 'afraid'. So the king sends his own physician and the assembled doctors 'use Cordialls', they 'apply Pidgeons' (dead) to draw 'vapours' out of the feet, and they tell Donne to cheer up – advice which gets this indignant response: 'Did I drinke in Melancolly into myselfe? It is my thoughtfulnesse. Was I not made to thinke? It is my Study; doth not my Calling call for that?' The patient turns to thoughts about eternity ('Eternity had bin the same, as it is, though time never had beene') and about his sinful use of time ('I have sinned . . . in my ostentation and the mingling of a respect of my selfe, in preaching thy Word'). Already, on the fourth day of this illness, he has decided that if a man is a little world then 'selfe' is no bigger than the size of the land while 'misery' is as large as the oceans. But on the sixteenth day he hears the 'passing' bell which announces that a neighbour is approaching death, and the sound summons him to think about other people and about the positive use which God makes of the afflictions which everyone suffers. Donne recovers. He returns to the Scriptures more attentively and the use which he makes of his experience is to write up and publish these thoughts in order to help other people in their afflictions. But he never addresses the reader directly: he is preaching to himself.

By permission he dedicated the little book to Charles, Prince of Wales, for he did not underestimate the importance of an occasion when a Dean of St Paul's bared his heart. In his sermons a reference to 'I' is not always meant to be autobiographical, but here as Donne addresses himself or his Maker he exposes himself in self-pity and, ultimately, in self-sacrifice – with, as Sir Thomas Browne put it, 'Strange Fire'. His sickness has brought him closer to his God: 'how fully O my abundant God, how gently O my sweet and easy God, doest thou entangle me'!

The *Devotions* include a meditation which is as beautiful as anything in his sermons and which is a reminder of other features to be found also in them: a vision of human unity in life and death, a pride in the Catholic Church of Christ, a love of learning in an international fellowship. That was why, three centuries later, Ernest Hemingway could call his greatest novel *For Whom the Bell Tolls*: it was about the Spanish civil war as a warning that the whole of Europe was about to suffer in war. Donne wrote:

> The Church is Catholike, universall, so are all her Actions; All that she does, belongs to All. When she baptizes a child, that action concerns mee; for that child is thereby connected to that Head which is my Head too, and engrafted into that body, whereof I am a member. And when she buries a Man, that action concernes me; All mankinde is of one Author, and is one volume; when one Man dies, one Chapter is not torne out of the booke, but translated into a better language; and every Chapter must be so translated; God emploies several translators; some peeces are translated by Age, some by sicknesse, some by warre, some by justice; but God's hand is in every translation; and his hand shall bind up all our scattered leaves againe, for that Library where every booke shall lie open to one another . . .

> No Man is an Iland, intire of it selfe, every man is a peece of the Continent, a part of the maine; if a Clod be washed away by the Sea, Europe is the lesse, as well as if a Promonterie were, as well as if a Mannor of thy friend's, or of thine own were; Any Man's death diminishes me, because I am involved in Mankinde; And therefore never send to know for whom the bell tolls; It tolls for thee.

During the winter of 1630–31 Donne astonished his friends twice. That autumn he had gone to his daughter Constance's home in Essex; he wanted her to care for him during an illness which was almost certainly cancer. He took his mind off the pain and debility by writing out old sermons for which he had kept his notes, but he did not return to London to preach. Then, feeling that the end was near, he accepted the usual invitation to preach to the royal court in Whitehall Palace on the first Friday in Lent, which in 1631 fell on 25 February. When he returned to the Deanery his friends were so shocked by his appearance that they begged him to cancel the engagement, but he persevered and his farewell to the king and to the pulpit took the form of a passionate meditation on the inescapable destination of death, all human life being a progress to that and to the resurrection (described at less length).

> We celebrate our own funeralls with cryes, even at our birth . . . That which we call life is . . . our life spent in dying . . . Our youth is worse than our infancy and our age worse than our youth. Our youth is hungry and thirsty after those sinnes which our infancy knew not; And our age is sorry and angry that it cannot pursue those sinnes which our youth did. And besides, at the way, so many deaths, that is to say so many deadly calamities, accompany

> every condition, and every period of this life, as that death it selfe would bee an ease to them that suffer them.

He had handled this theme before, but the sermon which was published as *Death's Duell* was his own sermon for his funeral and like flowers on a coffin it clothed the suffering and total decay of death with the beauty of the English language in which he had become a master. Perhaps for the first time in his life, he read out a fully prepared script.

To him the unreliability of his memory would be a sign of senile weakness but the sermon was not totally morbid. 'The humble soule (and onely the humble soule is the religious soule) rests himselfe upon God's purposes and decrees; but then it is upon those purposes and decrees of God which he hath declared and manifested; not such as are conceived and imagined in our selves . . .' He reminded his hearers of what Christ had suffered in order to fulfil the purposes of the Father: 'a sadnes even in his soule to death, and an agony even to a bloody sweate in his body, and expostulations with God, and exclamations upon the crosse'. 'God doth not say, Live well and thou shalt dye well, that is an easie and a quiet death; But live well here and thou shalt live for ever.' 'Whether the gate of my prison be opened with an oyld key (by a gentle and preparing sicknes), or the gate be hewen downe by a violent death, or the gate be burnt downe by a raging and frantique feaver, a gate into heaven I shall have . . .' His trust was, he said, in 'God's care that the soule be safe, what agonies so ever the body suffers in the hour of death'. He ended on the same note as in the *Devotions* (discussed on pp. 172–4).

He was exhausted but obstinate: he attended a business meeting on the next day and dealt with the affairs of the cathedral until 21 March, although he had written out his long will on 13 December (on St Lucy's Day). One piece of business was to prepare his monument. Walton records that his doctor suggested this;

presumably he thought it a kind way of warning the dean that the end was near. Donne threw himself into the project, which is easier to understand if we remember that coffins were not yet fashionable. He had fires lit in his study, stripped naked, was clothed in a shroud as for burial, left his emaciated face visible, and had a sketch made. This astonishing portrait he then kept in the bedroom to which he retired, taking leave of his friends but concentrating on his prayers, in the end simply repeating the Lord's Prayer. He died on 31 March 1631, and those who were near him at the time reported that he died in peace, closing his own eyes as he composed himself for the experience of what he had so often imagined.

As had been intended, the sketch was used not only when *Death's Duell* was printed but also by the sculptor Nicholas Stone, who had made Anne's monument back in 1617. Donne's intention to be buried with her had been cancelled: now he belonged to his cathedral and to London. Thirty-five years later St Paul's was to be reduced to a ruin by the Great Fire but this monument survived and was placed in the crypt of Wren's cathedral. Late in the Victorian age it was brought upstairs, to the south choir aisle. In that position, however, the face of the statue is no longer turned to the east, as was the final point of the epitaph which Donne composed. What remains from his plan is that he is standing, not sleeping, and although the eyes are not yet open the expression on the face, no longer cancer-ridden, is one of delight at the approaching resurrection. But he is not dressed as a clergyman: in his shroud, he is simply a human being who needs resurrection. In his present position he confronts a Bishop of London in bronze, robed in all the pomp of the Established Church before 1914.

The Latin epitaph which he wrote as a miniature autobiography is now placed high above this strange statue, and at the time it was carved in quite small letters as a piece of prose, so that it is hard to read even if the Latin can be understood. But it is as interesting for its silences as much as for what it says. It stresses the labours of the scholar but ignores all the poetry. It recalls the ordination but does not mention anything from the earlier life except the education. It gives thanks for the influence of the Holy Spirit but hints that this might not have been decisive without King James. It remembers when he became Dean of St Paul's but gets the date slightly wrong; presumably he had been too ill to look it up. (But he did not make a mistake about the year in which he became a priest: according to the calendar then in use January 1615 was still within 1614.) It preaches that no earthly honour lasts for ever but over the grave it proclaims a Christian's one hope, 'his Jesus'. It makes it difficult to remember the sensuality and the cynicism of his early manhood, or the unemployment with the depressions and confusions which had brought temptations to despair, even to suicide.

JOHN DONNE

Doctor of Divinity,

after varied studies, pursued from early years
with perseverance and not without success,
entered into Holy Orders
under the influence and pressure of the Holy Spirit
and by the advice and exhortation of King James,
in the year of his Jesus 1614 and of his age 42.
Having been invested with the Deanery of this church
on 27 November 1621,
he was stripped of it by death on the last day of March 1631.
He lies here in the dust but beholds Him
whose name is Rising.

PART TWO

About Donne

5 Thou hast not done

When thou hast done, thou hast not done,
For I have more.
'A Hymne to God the Father'

The surviving evidence about the life of Donne is, as we have seen, quite substantial, and in much of it he seems to be exhibiting himself, right up to the days of the dying and the burial. But the literature of opinions about him is much larger and it proves that the evidence can be interpreted in very different ways, by biographers and commentators who vary from the over-awed to those who think themselves superior. All these interpretations cannot be equally correct; so it has to be said that not everyone who has written about Donne has done an equally good job.

In the twentieth century some scholars, mainly in the USA, offered a solution to the problem of the connection between Jack Donne and Dr Donne by claiming that even in the young poet the great preacher could already be heard, solemnly and impressively. Thus in the 1990s published work by commentators with academic credentials suggested that when the speaker in a poem by Donne was ordering a mistress to undress he was seeking a spiritual revelation; that when he said that he was fascinated by the 'centrique part' of a woman he meant that he wanted to find the centre of All; that when he composed a mock marriage song for the entertainment of other students he was celebrating the triumph of life over death; that when flirting wittily he was exercising skills in the branch of theology known as 'casuistry' because it pondered difficult cases in ethics; and that when he was trying to seduce a girl (in 'The Flea') his arguments are best interpreted as theology about the Eucharist. And in each case it proved possible to make such a surprising suggestion by interpreting some evidence in the poem with considerable ingenuity. But the difficulty is, of course, that the suggestion becomes extremely improbable for most of us when we reflect on what we know about Donne as a young man. A collection of essays on *John Donne's Religious Imagination* in 1995 included a number of such suggestions which were too religious, and therefore too imaginative, in comparison with the evidence.

In a different approach taken by less devoted commentators, the emphasis has been on a Donne who was more or less sick in mind. An American scholar, Stanley Fish, has already been mentioned (on pp. 10–11). In *John Donne, Undone* (1986) Thomas Docherty, a lecturer in Trinity College, Dublin, swept aside the work of other writers and the facts about which they had written. He suggested that since the facts are 'deliberately obscure and secretive' what helps most is 'an attempt to release Donne's texts into their full obscurity, so to speak: to make them *difficult*'. With this aim he released himself from any need to consider strictly 'what the text says' and to argue with earlier opinions about what it means. Unfortunately for him, the evidence which we have does not support his bold suggestions that Donne was intensely troubled by the discovery of the earth's true relationship with the sun and that his whole way of relating to things on the earth was transformed by the invention of the telescope. Nor does the evidence demonstrate that Donne's erotic poetry resulted from a long struggle against *female* promiscuity, or that 'the priestly hand of Donne converts sexual foreplay into the activity of blessing', or that the speaker of a poem can change sex during it. Nor does the evidence show that for Donne the male and female roles in sex and society became interchangeable, or that for him the moment of death could not be distinguished from the moment of the present.

Nor does it present us with a Donne who, 'striving towards God-head in an untrammelled ambition', equated himself with the Son of God or dressed himself in the form of the Mother of God in order to bring forth the Word of God. In fact the evidence is clearly against each and all of these suggestions.

The truth seems to be that Donne was neither a saint nor a madman. Yet it needs to be admitted that modern commentators who have suggested that he was either the one or the other have not been the first to exaggerate.

Donne's first biographer, Izaak Walton, was a fan. In a poem dated four days after the funeral he said it: 'he lov'd me . . . I am his Convert'. This became one of the tributes printed in the first edition of Donne's collected poems. Seven years later he paid a longer tribute in prose, inviting his readers to meet his hero.

> He was of Stature moderately tall, of a strait and equally-proportioned body, to which all his words and actions gave an inexpressible addition of Comeliness. The melancholy and pleasant humours were in him so contempered, that each gave advantage to the other, and made his Company one of the delights of Mankind. His fancy was unimitably high, equalled only by his great wit . . . His aspect was chearful and such as gave a silent testimony of a clear knowing soul and of a Conscience at peace with itself. His melting eye shewed that he had a soft heart, full of noble compassion . . . He was by nature highly passionate, but more apt to reluct at the excesses of it . . . He was earnest and unwearied in the search of knowledge . . .

Meeting Donne changed Walton's life. In the 1620s he was in his thirties and kept a shop in London. He attended the nearby church of St Dunstan-in-the-West and was impressed by the vicar – so impressed that he was delighted to be allowed to get to know him outside his pulpit, to enjoy the delight of his company and, although a social inferior, to be introduced to some in his circle of grand friends. After Donne's death one of these, Sir Henry Wotton, asked him to supply notes about Donne's life. David Novarr, who included the most thorough study of Walton's connection with Donne in his book on *The Making of Walton's Lives* (1958), argued persuasively that the connection cannot have been intimate; in particular, it is very unlikely that Donne told him the whole story of his life with him taking notes. Unfortunately Wotton died before this material supplied by a parishioner could be used in a memoir and the project seemed to die with him. But in 1639 Donne's son announced a plan to print some of his father's sermons, over which he had gained control. There was, it seems, some anxiety about their reception: the publication of some of the sermons of Bishop Andrewes in 1629 had gone well but Donne's own recently published poems had not been reassuring about his preparation for the pulpit. It was therefore agreed that Walton should introduce the book with a brief but edifying 'Life and Death' of Donne, concentrating on the exemplary death.

First printed in 1640, this memoir was expanded, and made still more dignified by small changes, in successive editions until 1675, and thereafter its popularity continued. The shopkeeper had been launched as a biographer. He was encouraged to produce 'Lives' of other Anglican churchmen: Wotton the model layman, Robert Sanderson the learned and holy bishop, and two priests who were to become about as famous as Donne himself, Richard Hooker and George Herbert. And amid the hard times for Anglicans under Cromwell in the 1650s he wrote the most loved of all his writings, his *Compleat Angler*. Having lived to see the monarchy and the Church of England reinstated, he concentrated on his memories, his friendships and his fishing. He was buried in Winchester

Cathedral more than half a century after the death of John Donne, who is now commemorated in the window above his grave.

His was a portrait of a saint at a time when the Church of England, already threatened by the troubles which were to destroy its Supreme Governor, Charles I, wanted to be assured that it could produce saints. Yet this was an Englishman's portrait of a very English saint, charmingly casual and homely in its presentation, with a subject which (as he treated it) made no great spiritual or intellectual demands. For about 250 years it was enjoyed while Donne's own works in prose, his sermons and even his poems were given less attention. It did not seem to matter that Walton had attempted only a few sentences about what Donne wrote; nor was the appeal of his 'Life' much reduced when between 1796 and 1825 Thomas Zouch made some corrections and additions. If defects were noticed, it could be thought that Walton had already made a sufficiently disarming apology: in view of his 'education and mean abilities' it was a wonder that he had written anything, but his 'artless Pensil' had produced a 'plain Picture'.

In fact his portrait was not nearly so artless as he pretended, for he knew what to stress or omit if this was to be an icon of an Anglican saint. There were many subtle touches, gathered in the final version. The first paragraph began the snobbery: 'the Reader may be pleased to know, that his Father was masculinely and lineally descended from a very antient family in Wales' and that 'he had his first breeding in his Father's house'. This claim that Donne was connected with the Dwyns seems more plausible than some modern scholars have allowed, for Donne used that family's crest on the ring with which he sealed letters and it reappeared on his monument in St Paul's. We have no record of anyone having mocked or disputed the claim, which was repeated by his son John. But it is also the case that no evidence has survived which proves that the father was so descended, or which shows Donne using such a family connection to his own advantage (although Sir David

Dun, for example, was a prominent lawyer and as the 'Dean of the Arches' the senior judge in the legal machinery of the Church, a man characterized succinctly by the Archbishop of Canterbury as 'corrupt'). Anyway, the family tree on the father's side mattered far less in Donne's life than did his link through his mother with Sir Thomas More and other Roman Catholic martyrs, on whom Walton would be less keen.

Another touch was to postpone the travel through Catholic Italy and Spain to the end of the 1590s, when Donne had demonstrated his manly patriotism by joining the two naval expeditions against the Spaniards. The 'Picture of him at the age of eighteen' which (as we have seen) was the portrait of an aggressively Roman Catholic crusader was also handled tactfully. It was postponed until after a description of the monument in the cathedral, and the motto around the picture was mistranslated so as to suggest that it was a prediction that the young man would be transformed into an Anglican dignitary:

> How much shall I be chang'd
> Before I am chang'd . . .

The tragic death of Donne's brother was not mentioned. Donne's early activity as a lover and poet was left in an almost equal obscurity, although Walton had to admit that something had taken place. He did this by recording that his hero had expressed great regret about 'some irregularities of my life' and about the writing of poems 'made only to exercise his sharp wit, and high fancy'. Some of these poems had been 'facetiously composed and carelessly scattered' although Donne had wisely destroyed others.

Donne's marriage was 'the remarkable error of his life' which he would 'occasionally condemn', as Walton finally decided to say, having written in the 1640 edition that the husband 'never seemed to justifie' marrying his wife. In the 1658 edition he took the opportunity to preach a pompous layman's sermon about love, as 'a passion! that carries us to commit errors with as much ease as whirlwinds remove feathers'. In defiance of the law courts he added his opinion that because this marriage was without the 'approbation' of 'friends', it was not even 'lawful'. Then he admitted that Anne had been 'curiously and plentifully educated' – presumably because her proud husband had said so – but he never gave her name. His reference to her father included several mistakes. He also got the date of her death wrong although it was recorded on her tomb in a church not far from where he was writing. The death did move him to write about 'that abundant affection which once was betwixt him and her, who had long been the delight of his eyes, and the Companion of his youth', but now the focus was on the survivor's grief and his problems as 'the careful father of seven children then living'. In the end, the most positive thing which Walton could bring himself to say about the marriage was that their 'mutual and cordial affections' meant that his hero's repentance for his error was not 'heavy'.

Although Walton printed extracts from some of Donne's letters in his middle period, the bitterness of this time was greatly reduced. The religious poetry was almost all dated to the years when he was a priest and, although not much of it was quoted, it was used to show an edifying Christian humility in this distinguished and popular priest. It was not used to show spiritual struggles before ordination; these were 'high, holy and harmonious composures'. Mitcham, which Donne called a prison when writing to his friends, became for Walton (almost as if he was selling a house in it) 'a place noted for good air, and choice company'. There his hero was so happy, reading and writing, that he would have been glad to remain 'during his life'. His lodgings in London were said to be rather grander than the reality: they were 'near to White-Hall' and this proximity to the royal palace would make high-level contacts convenient. He was 'often visited by many of the Nobility' and consulted by 'most Ambassadours of forraign Nations'. The king himself was 'much pleas'd when Mr Donne attended him' for 'deep discourses'. After one of these conversations *Pseudo-Martyr* was written 'within six weeks' as the king had urged. In the (wisely unpublished) book about suicide 'all the Laws violated by that Act were diligently surveyed and judiciously censured'. In Walton's pages Donne moves through the years of unemployment as if in control; in reality, he became a high-class beggar.

The time which Donne reluctantly spent in France because he needed the money from the Drurys who were tourists was presented by Walton as being participation in a 'glorious Embassie' to King Henri IV – who at the time was dead. And three anecdotes were told about this middle period which cannot be accurate. One was a vividly detailed ghost story about the anxious husband's vision during that trip with the Drurys in 1612; he saw his wife with a dead baby in her arms on the very day of the baby's death, shortly before a messenger brought the news from London. But we know that Donne was still ignorant about his family's tragedy two months after the event; so the 'Person of Honour' who told the tale must have got something wrong. Another story, also detailed, was of conversation in 1607 about the highly profitable parish which was offered to him. But this long story was sent to Walton by a bishop (Morton) then in his nineties, recalling an event some fifty years before. A third, shorter, anecdote was of Donne being summoned by 'the Earl of Somerset when at his greatest height of favour', and told to 'Stay in this Garden' while the earl fixed his appointment to fill a vacancy as one of the secretaries of the Privy Council. The king, however, persisted in his wish that Donne should be ordained. But there was no such vacancy on the council's staff at this time.

The theme of Walton's tribute to his vicar was that Donne was a second St Augustine, resembling the great Bishop of Hippo in a youth to be regretted ('he accounted the former part of his life to be lost'), in a conversion to be celebrated, and in 'learning and holiness' very seldom equalled. The change made by conversion and ordination seemed so obvious that when Donne was 'made Doctor in Divinity' by Cambridge University it was with 'exprest gladness' (in fact it was with great reluctance, but the king was obeyed). The impression had been made on Walton by his knowledge of this delightful saint as his parish priest. He cannot have known much about Donne's life as Reader in Divinity in Lincoln's Inn, for he mistakenly thought that his hero was given that post after his wife's death, as a consolation; he was vague about the activities as Dean of St Paul's and royal chaplain; he thought that Donne was vicar of St Dunstan's for longer than was true; he did not venture to analyse the theology preached; but he did remember the man speaking like an angel and becoming his friend. He was proud to have been among the friends with whom Donne wanted to talk during his last days (and he passed on the memory of the dean's refusal to drink all the milk ordered by the doctor). He knew that Donne's flesh had by now been reduced to dust but he ended his tribute by saying that he was sure that on the day of resurrection he would see the dust 'reanimated'. He himself breathed life into our thinking about Donne by his little book; it preserved facts and impressions which otherwise would have been lost, and it did so in style.

Some two hundred years later Augustus Jessopp resembled Walton in his devotion to this poet turned preacher. As a Cambridge undergraduate he became fascinated. In 1855 he edited the *Essayes in Divinity* for Victorian readers with elaborate notes. They remained uninterested, however, and when he published a short study of *John Donne, Sometime Dean of St Paul's* in a series on 'Leaders of Religion' 42 years later, he introduced it by confessing that 'I have never been able to feel much enthusiasm for Donne as a poet'. His verdict was that 'if we except some few exquisite passages . . . it is difficult to believe that these earlier poems were not loved for the poet's sake'. Some poems were not such as Donne himself 'would wish to be read and dwelt on by the pure and innocent'.

Jessopp's enthusiasm was reserved for the man who despite a lack of innocence was going to become a pure churchman. 'The wits and the courtiers, the nobility and the luminaries of the law courts' all, he thought, agreed in their admiration of the young Donne, and his own admiration was not shaken by the book about suicide: the idea that Donne was tempted to commit this sin 'must always appear incredible to any who have learned to know the man, and to appreciate the true nobility of his character'.

In the end Jessopp paid Donne a tribute more impressive than all this sentimentality. Research into Donne's life had been his hobby during many years as a country clergyman and the results were published in his substantial article in the *Dictionary of National Biography* (together with a tribute to Walton's less laborious work, which 'stands, and must remain for ever, the materpiece of English biography'), but he knew that he could not understand the erotic or spiritually disturbed poetry; so he withdrew from a plan to write a big biography jointly with Edmund Gosse. Sending him a copy of his own little book in 1897, he promised to follow this gift with all the material which his industry had produced over the years.

Gosse had fewer inhibitions and only two years passed before the two volumes of his *Life and Letters* were on sale. Until 1970 this was the standard biography but it depended on Jessopp's work and on the copying of manuscripts by a research assistant who was less reliable – and it was not only in details that Gosse's own contributions were defective. When he tackled the secular poetry, it was with a Victorian disapproval as firm as Jessopp's. He saw no alternative to treating the most striking of the poems as records of actual affairs with mistresses including at least one married woman (a 'great criminal liaison'). Donne, he reckoned, 'was above all things sincere', so that it had to be said that 'his writings, like his actions, were faulty, violent, a little morbid even, and abnormal'. And so Gosse was quick to denounce.

Various poems were condemned as 'most frankly sensual', 'with no evidence of soul' but with 'the symptoms of a malady of the mind'. Some were read as a series of outbursts of a passionate lover when rejected by a mistress – a bitterness which lasted until the exhausted writing of the 'Nocturnall'. The fourth 'elegie' was Donne's account of his behaviour while courting Anne: 'that it is a recital of facts I do not for a moment doubt' and the facts were, Gosse thought, greatly to Donne's discredit. Poems with more tenderness and beauty in them cannot have come from the developing love, since 'at this moment of his life his poetical talent seems to have almost entirely deserted him'. Donne's chief talent, it appears, was for behaving badly.

Gosse was convinced that 'penitence and a genuine sorrow for faults of instinct' took a long time to develop after the marriage. When Donne attempted poems on religious subjects, these amounted to no more than 'extremely ingenious exercises in metrical theology', corrupted by the influence of 'Spanish ingenuities'. When he began to write poems more deeply religious, 'nothing could be more odious' than the poem on Good Friday 1613; the 'Anniversaries' were 'positively preposterous' and 'it is difficult to understand how the desire to please and the intoxication of his ingenuity have so blinded Donne to the claims of self-respect'; the lament for Prince Henry was 'not animated by one touch of sincere emotion'. The prose was also condemned; even the *Essayes in Divinity* were an intellectual exercise where 'nothing is for edification'.

Although Donne was ordained in January 1615, and was chosen in October 1616 as Reader in Divinity by the Benchers (senior lawyers) in Lincoln's Inn many of whom were Puritans, Gosse was strangely sure that 'there is abundant evidence to show' that he did not experience a Christian conversion before the winter of 1617, after Anne's death in August. Even then the convert was still capable of gross flattery in order to secure his appointment as Dean of St Paul's, and his *Devotions* of 1624 were full of 'diseased vivacity' and 'painful ingenuity'. As a layman Gosse shied away from any close examination of the sermons, which might have modified some of these verdicts. It is therefore not surprising to read at the end of the *Life and Letters* that 'we are tempted to declare that of all great men he is the one of whom least is essentially known. Is not this, perhaps, the secret of his perennial fascination?' Readers were warned not to accept him solely as a 'prophet of the intricacies of fleshly feeling', or as a 'crafty courtier' or as a 'crystal-hearted saint', for 'he was none of these, or all of these, or more'.

But Donne's modern readers have had some reasons to be grateful for Gosse's two fat Victorian volumes. Although he himself owed much to Jessopp, the air in his book was free of incense. He was the first to print the letters which illuminate the drama of the marriage and the three poems in the Westmoreland manuscript which throw light on the religious development. Gosse corrected some of Walton's errors and did much (not all) of the editorial work which Donne's son ought to have done when publishing some of the correspondence.

Not before the twentieth century did scholars emerge who applied themselves to a thorough study of the texts of Donne's surviving writings and painstaking research into what remained of evidence about his life. The best editors of his poetry made possible an understanding of his personality at a level different from the hero-worship of Walton and Jessopp and from the Victorian morality of Sir Edmund Gosse. These came from Scotland (Sir Herbert Grierson, 1912), England (Dame Helen Gardner, 1952 and 1965) and the USA (Professor John Shawcross, 1967). And then Australia and the USA jointly produced a scholar, R. C. Bald, who gathered together research already done in England, added his own labours although he had no English base, and wrote a biography which when published in 1970 at last placed the study of Donne on a foundation of recorded facts.

Herbert Grierson's edition of the poems in 1912 was the most careful yet seen, but his achievement was to make the subsequent debate possible, not to prevent it. He included as authentically by Donne some poems which either he or later editors later found unconvincing and his text did not take into account all the manuscripts which later editors were to consult. And like Gosse he found it difficult to understand the personality behind the poems. In his introduction to a revised edition published in 1933 he still thought it was not possible to do much more than 'make explicit these contradictions'. He found it comparatively easy to contrast Donne's boyhood in the devout and strict atmosphere of the 'Catholic revival' with the young man's 'sensuality, naturalism and cynicism', and he saw the break as occurring during his time in Italy and Spain when 'the blood was flowing passionately in his veins', producing 'an intense susceptibility to the fascination of sex'. But Grierson found it harder to connect the 'manifold contradictions' of the later years, when ambition for a career was combined with the plan to end *Metempsychosis* with an all-out attack on his queen and poems and letters with a high moral tone were combined with 'excesses of flattery' to Donne's patrons including 'protestations of devotion to James's abominable favourites'. These 'ambitious compliances' were for Grierson much harder to forgive than the passions of early manhood.

If Donne's middle period remained a puzzle to Grierson, so did the period after ordination. He found it easy to praise the religious poems (ascribed to this period) which recaptured the strong passions of the love poetry, and also to admire the sermons where 'the talk is poetry'. But he thought that the poems showed that the heart of the preacher was 'never at rest'. In particular he found evidence of continuing unease in the sonnet which begins 'Show me, deare Christ, thy Spouse'. He interpreted this poem as meaning that Donne was still not at all sure that he had been shown that the Church of England truly was a part of the Bride of Christ.

Helen Gardner made important advances on Grierson's edition. She did more work on the manuscripts and thought with more determination about the poems as evidence on the personality. She was subtle and wise about the idea that what Donne wrote was straightforward autobiography: to her it was clearly not that, yet poems can be used with discretion as evidence about the life, somewhat as the work of an artist can be used to build up a portrait of the painter. 'The truths of Donne's love poetry', she wrote, 'are truths of the imagination, which freely transmutes personal experience.' Thus she agreed with Grierson that this poetry reflects the influence of Italy and Spain, although for her the influence came mainly through books, not through the passionate pulsating of Donne's young blood when under the even hotter Mediterranean sun. She also agreed in principle that the poetry can be used to show a transition from promiscuity to married 'union', although unlike Grierson she was careful not to say that particular poems must be about the marriage. And she made a breakthrough in the understanding of the religious poetry.

Gardner examined it more closely and gave reasons for her conclusion that most of it was written before, not after, ordination: it was troubled, but these were not the secret doubts of a preacher. And she convincingly explained why the religious poetry differs from the erotic in being not the celebration of a conquest but a struggle to surrender. 'The Divine Poems', she wrote, are 'records of struggles to appropriate a truth which has been revealed.' Donne did not invent the Christianity; he inherited it from the Bible and the Fathers of the Church and from more recent teachers both Catholic and Protestant, but he made this heritage his own in a style of his own. The sonnet to which Grierson had drawn particular attention was one of the few poems dated by Gardner after the ordination, but she did not find it to be either disturbed or disturbing. On the contrary, she thought that it demonstrated that Donne had become a convinced Anglican. He looked round at other Churches and gave thanks for the Church of England, in itself both Catholic and Protestant. The poem 'could hardly have been written by anyone but an Anglican'. (It will be discussed on pp. 242–3.)

In 1967 John Shawcross published what he rightly claimed was the first 'complete annotated edition' of Donne's poetry. He was highly critical of Gardner's work on the text, basing his own attempt to come 'close to what Donne intended' on three times the number of manuscripts and including a long list of his disagreements. (In a volume published in 1995 to honour Shawcross, Ted-Larry Pebworth said that he would not give his own list since 'the shortcomings in Gardner's approach and practice are too numerous'.) He also thought that Gardner's cautious proposal that some of the poems were influenced by the marriage was 'most unconvincing' and his own position was that 'dating is and must be very tentative'. However, in order to 'elicit new discussion' he supplied a 'Chronological Schedule' suggesting dates for many of the poems including one for the 'Elegies' (1593–96) and another for the 'Songs and Sonets' (1593–1601?). Later discussion of this chronology has sometimes been critical, as he no doubt expected, but his work on the manuscripts was one of the inspirations behind the launch in 1995 of the *Variorum Edition* comparing printed and handwritten texts after study by many scholars aided by computers. Until this project is completed, the Shawcross edition is almost always cited by Americans writing about Donne.

In 1984 another American professor, C. A. Patrides, published another annotated edition of the poems. He differed from Shawcross in relying on the printed editions of the 1630s except 'where they are self-evidently inadequate' and in refusing to 'theorize on dates of composition'. But this apparent dismissal of manuscripts and dates did not prevent him from listing the most important disagreements between printed and handwritten sources. He also discussed dates, although without constructing another new chronology. So far from ignoring other scholars, he supplied a long bibliography of their contributions. This attention to detail explains why his edition, so far from being an unresearched attack on Shawcross, took nine years to prepare. After widespread use, his work was updated by Robin Hamilton in 1994. One generalization which Patrides commended to readers willing to be as careful as he was affirmed that 'Donne's skill is of the highest technical expertness in English poetry', contradicting the impression which the middle-aged Donne often tried to convey: that his poems had been tossed off in an idle and probably foolish hour.

It is surely understandable that there have been these differences of expert opinion about the text of Donne's poems. However, very seldom, if ever, does any difficult decision which is significant for a biography depend on a decision between textual variants. One interesting decision seems easy if one relies on common sense: when the 'Epistle' introducing *Metempsychosis* was first printed in 1633, the 'soule' that was in 'that apple which Eve ate' was called 'she' because it was the custom to treat every soul as feminine. But there was a reference to this soul of evil ending up in 'hee, whose life you shall finde in the end of this booke'. Two years later the printer changed that final 'hee' to 'shee' and the change, which was probably careless, has been quoted in support of the suggestion that the poem was to have ended with a massive insult to Queen Elizabeth as the embodiment of evil. But the reason why it seems probable that the printer made a mistake in 1635 is that it is very improbable that Donne made the mistake of treason.

John Donne: A Life by R. C. Bald (1970) has never been equalled as a biography based on research. It was almost entirely the work of an Australian scholar (for much of his career a professor in the

University of Chicago) and on his death it was completed by another, Wesley Milgate. Its claims about its six hundred pages, full of facts old or new, were just: 'In the scholarly enthusiasm for Donne of the last fifty years a good many fresh details have come to light and have been published here and there in the learned periodicals; these must be incorporated in any complete account. Other facts appear here for the first time, and it is hoped that the archival resources of the Anglo-Saxon world will have relatively little still to yield.' It may have been uncharacteristically naughty for Bald to hope that other researchers would be disappointed but the next thirty years did not produce much information both new and important. At present it seems unlikely that the work will ever need to be done again. It included some treatment of what Donne wrote and preached, and as was to be expected Bald was always sensible, but the space allocated to literary criticism was smaller than that devoted to historical facts. The result is that we close this invaluable book having learned more about Donne's activities than about his feelings.

Recently the centre of Donnean studies has shifted decisively to North America. An Englishman may be allowed to make in this connection some points which to him seem obvious. Here is a text which although remote in geography springs from English roots, as does much else in North American life. It is in a language which, although now unfamiliar in the form used by Donne, is not totally foreign, and there is a special interest in the fact that he used this language as the great English migration to New England was beginning. And here is a text which is full of human interest; as Professor Shawcross noted, in the twentieth century as in the seventeenth 'readers' interest lay in the wittiness of Jack Donne's love themes'. But to these points may be added two suggestions which are perhaps less obvious.

When viewed from across the Atlantic, the island which is partially occupied by the English appears to belong to Europe; and when work has been needed to investigate the sources behind Donne's poetry and prose, most of the hard work has been done by North American academics who have not been content to confine their researches to English sources. These scholars have greatly refined the meaning of the labels traditionally attached to Donne, 'Renaissance', 'metaphysical' and 'original'. Especially in his preaching, Donne was a mixture of the medieval and the modern, and it has been shown in detail how that was true of the whole of the Renaissance, although the fusion in Donne was his own. Especially in his poetry, Donne used 'conceits' which made surprising connections between things apparently very dissimilar, and a knowledge of the European literature of his time has been used to show how extensive was this 'metaphysical wit' although the electrifying power in Donne's hands came from his brain. And in religion Donne was vigorously original, not by being 'singular' (a word which he more or less equated with 'arrogant' or 'ignorant') but by drawing on a vast heritage both Catholic and Protestant, both ancient and modern – and making it his own living faith, a European faith.

North American scholars have also been well-equipped and motivated to study Donne's religion, in a time when in Europe, including Britain for this purpose, the surrounding society has become if not more secular then certainly far less church-related. Many North American academics have a respect for traditional Christianity as small as any European's but in general the contrast between North American and European attitudes has been striking. Religion has boomed in the USA, and to a lesser extent in Canada, and inevitably it has influenced the academic world. It is not surprising that there have been some suggestions which to a European seem to arise from an unreasonable belief that even when writing erotic poetry the young Donne was being moral and even theological. Nor is it surprising that an attempt has been made to overthrow the usual account of his early formation.

Dennis Flynn's *John Donne and the Ancient Catholic Nobility* (1995) was one of a series of studies in which this respected scholar explored the influence of the Roman Catholic heritage. The question is not whether there was a large influence; clearly there was. But it has to be asked whether Flynn was right in his suggestions about the way in which the young man had experienced this influence.

He suggested that John Donne was withdrawn from Oxford after only one term because his family feared that even at the age of thirteen he might be required to take an oath accepting the Church of England. Flynn then argued that he was the 'Mr John Donnes' whose name appears near the bottom of the list of 'noble men knightes and Esquires and Gentlemene giving their Attendance one the Righte Honorable the Earle of Derby' who was sent on a specially grand mission to Paris in order to invest the French king with the insignia of the Order of the Garter: the earl was classified by Flynn as a member of the ancient Catholic nobility. The name of 'Mr John Downes' also appears among the 'Gentlemen Waiters' in a list of the earl's 'Householde Servants' in 1587. Flynn also suggested that John Donne was present in the Spanish army at the siege of Antwerp in the spring of 1585, since in 1652 epigrams said to have been originally written in Latin by him, but now translated by Jasper Mayne, were published along with material since agreed to be authentically Donnean, and some of these English verses seem to refer to that siege.

That is an interesting reconstruction of Donne's life between the two dates which are certain: his two enrolments, in Hart Hall, Oxford, in 1584 and in Lincoln's Inn in 1592 after a preparatory year in Thavies Inn. However, Flynn's theory is open to a number of objections.

While it is plainly true that in the early 1580s the Elizabethan government was in a panic about the possibility of an invasion by French Catholics in order to place Mary Queen of Scots on the throne, it is unlikely that this reaction was much of a threat to John Donne while he was well below the age at which Oxford University would demand his acceptance of the Church of England if he was to proceed to a degree. If this lad had been required to swear his loyalty to Queen and Church, probably he would have done so in company with many others whose real faith was Roman Catholic, and without disagreement with his stepfather, the London doctor who also kept out of trouble with the authorities. If as a Catholic he was in real danger in Oxford, it seems very unlikely that he would have been taken into the service of the Earl of Derby, who like most of the aristocracy was no Protestant but who at this time was in the government's good books, to the extent that he represented it in an embassy designed to put an end to the threat from France.

Had the young Donne been included in this delicate mission to Paris it seems improbable that he would have been taken to join the siege of Antwerp. If a mature Donne did write Latin poetry about that siege, the poetry did not depend very obviously on the experiences of a boy of thirteen on his first trip abroad: its English version is in the voice of a soldier familiar with war and also a sophisticated wit. But did Donne actually write such a poem? Jasper Mayne, who claimed to be its translator, was a clergyman fairly well known as a poet, dramatist and practical joker; in his will he left a legacy to a servant – a red herring. Most scholars have been very sceptical.

However, the strongest argument against Flynn's claim that the famous John Donne was in domestic service from 1584 to 1587 is that we know that only five years later he was flourishing as an extraordinarily clever and accomplished poet, as a man-about-town who had money to spend among friends of high social status, and as a rising star who rapidly acquired enough legal knowledge and ease in society to be suitable as a member of the small staff of Egerton, a man widely admired and trusted as a leading judge and a minister frequently consulted and used by the queen in confidential matters (for example, in dealing with the Earl of Essex). And many modern scholars think that at this stage Donne was already familiar both with the Latin classics and with the poetry of the Italian Renaissance, while being so confident of his own powers that he was ready to stand alone in the style of his poetry and to walk away from the opportunity to become a lawyer. A 'gentleman waiter' in an earl's household may well have had opportunities to develop skills in addition to those expected in his domestic duties, but there needs to be stronger evidence than any which is provided by Professor Flynn against Izaak Walton's report that Donne was well educated in Oxford and Cambridge, and kept up friendships begun in those years as a student. In particular Walton stressed that Donne and Wotton became friends in Oxford: 'the friendship . . . was generously elemented: And it was begun in their Youth, and in a University, and there maintained by correspondent Inclinations and Studies, so it lasted till Age and Death forced a Separation'. Walton made mistakes, but this does not appear to have been one of them: he was recording what these two men, both heroes to him, had told him about their shared youth.

6 Deare honestie

If our Soules have stain'd their first white, yet wee
May cloth them with faith and deare honestie . . .

'To Mr Rowland Woodward'

In this chapter I shall discuss two recent books by English scholars which claim to present an honest account of Donne, in particular of his religion. My objection is not to honesty: it is to unfairness.

Professor John Carey's book on *John Donne: Life, Mind and Art*, first published in 1981, has been widely used. It incorporates many of the researches assembled in Professor Bald's biography but is shorter and more lively, and it offers a fuller treatment of Donne's psychology as seen in his writings. Another reason for the welcome given to the book is that it is, on the whole, hostile to Donne: an approach which can be thought to make for realism and also for readability, exposing without any cover-up a Great Poet who is compulsory in courses on English Literature. However, I hope to demonstrate that while making many true observations Carey does not relate himself sufficiently to the evidence. In particular he despises Donne's religion so emphatically that he avoids the trouble involved in trying to understand it.

He is convinced that 'every theological issue hinges ultimately on imagination' (p. 158) and his central aim in his book is to demonstrate that 'Donne's opinions upon such furiously controverted issues as original sin, election, resurrection and the state of the soul after death, were generated by recognizably the same imagination as the poems about love and women' (p. xiv). Such theological opinions were, it is argued, not vitally important to the preacher, a cool customer who as a young man 'doesn't even seem to feel sexually excited' (p. x). What did excite Donne is, Carey thinks, shown in words which are repeated in the titles of the chapters in the first half of his book: 'apostasy' and 'ambition'. The book begins by telling the reader to remember that Donne was a Catholic who 'betrayed his Faith'. It continues by claiming that 'he chose hell' because he abandoned Catholicism while knowing that it 'must be right'. 'No church would ever be the same to him again', we are told (p. 16); indeed, he 'relinquished his religion' (p. 199), being motivated by ambition.

These are strange words to use about a man who gave many years of his life to his labours as a preacher in the Church of England, 1615–31. He certainly was ambitious – with such talents and industry, who would not be? – but it seems unfair to say that ambition was the emotion which dominated his life. Before being ordained he had spent almost as many years without a regular job and with a large family, and he had refused to draw an income from the Church of England although offers were made. He had lost his first job, when he had seemed well placed for a distinguished and profitable career, because he had secretly married, being sexually excited. Carey thinks that he married a girl believing that her rich father, when told, would produce a blessing and a large sum of money, but this suggestion does not stand up to examination (as I shall try to show on pp. 254–9).

Certainly he was an 'apostate' in the sense that he ceased to be a Roman Catholic, but it seems wrong to say that he 'chose hell'. What he chose was conformity to the Church of England and for many years this seems to have amounted to no more than occasional attendance at Anglican services and a willingness to swear an oath that he did not accept the deposition of Elizabeth I and James I by the pope. However, in the reigns of Elizabeth and James this was the practice of most of the English who in their hearts remained faithful to the 'old religion' and hoped for its restoration. Many Roman Catholic priests, including some who accepted martyrdom for themselves, tolerated this degree of conformity to the government and its Church, and they did not refuse Communion to those who saw no alternative to it. In particular they allowed it in cases where influence on society would have been lost by total honesty: thus some aristocrats who would have welcomed a restoration of the old Church but who were large landowners conformed, as did some courtiers and men in government. Moreover, English people who were really Roman Catholic in religion could think themselves entitled to add 'mental reservations' to any answers which they made in self-defence against their persecutors. This practice was not condemned by the papacy before 1679. So if Donne chose to conform superficially to the Church of England it is unlikely that he felt that he was going to hell. But the question remains: in his heart, did he feel ashamed?

In his third 'satyre', probably written in the 1590s, he asks himself with 'feare' whether 'thy father's spirit' will 'heare thee damn'd' –

> Thee, whom hee taught so easie wayes, and neare,
> To follow . . .

And he tells himself to 'aske thy father' which is the true religion. He does not explain clearly what he means: was he referring to his natural father the prosperous ironmonger who died when he was not yet aged four, or to his stepfather the prosperous doctor who (as Professor Flynn has shown) was 'easie' rather than enthusiastic in his old-style Catholicism? He does not refer to his mother who was the religious enthusiast and martyr in the family, in the new style of the Catholic Reformation. What he does say is that his father should ask his grandfather, for 'truth' is 'a little elder' than any falsehood in religion – and what matters is not the decision whether 'to adore or scorne an image'. Truth, he says, is what matters. It lived in Rome 'a thousand yeares agoe' but has now disappeared from that city apart from some 'ragges' of it. He announces that he will not now take instruction from image-adoring Pope Gregory, any more than he will obey King Philip of Spain or any of the image-breaking Protestant authorities. Instead,

> To stand inquiring right, is not to stray;
> To sleepe, or run wrong, is: on a huge hill,
> Cragg'd and steep, Truth stands, and hee that will
> Reach her, about must, and about must goe . . .

The comment by Helen Gardner is discerning. 'The poem shows that if Donne rejected the Roman obedience, he had derived from his upbringing an unquestioning acceptance of the claim of religion. The argument rests on two assumptions: that the search for "true Religion" is the primary duty of a moral being, and that truth exists and can be known.' For Donne this search was to be different from the 'easie wayes' which would have been 'neare' an Englishman who without any fuss had fitted into the society which had functioned around the medieval Church. The medieval civilization and its 'old religion' having ended, the search was now to be through great uncertainty, as if a traveller were to climb a mountain in a mist – but it was to be a pilgrimage upwards towards Truth, not a journey downward to eternal damnation.

The eighth of Donne's 'Holy Sonnets' was written while he was still trying to find his way up that mountain, guided by 'my minde's white truth'. His heart was still full of 'griefe', but at least he thought he knew this:

> If faithfull soules be alike glorifi'd
> As Angels, then my father's soul doth see,
> And adds this even to full felicitie,
> That valiantly I hel's wide mouth o'rstride . . .

And already in his third 'satyre' he showed that he was in earnest about religion. He must 'not laugh, nor weepe' about this subject. In other poems he has celebrated or attacked a long line of human mistresses, but to be serious 'Is not our Mistresse fair Religion'? Is not the thought of 'heaven's joyes' the only cure for earthly lusts? And does not the search for 'true religion' call for 'great courage', more than does either war or the exploration of the world? What matters supremely in this heartfelt third 'satyre' is the prospect of 'the last day' when some souls will 'perish'. They are doomed if they have trusted not in God himself but in mortals who have wrongly claimed 'Power from God'. Evidently Donne has rejected the power claimed by the papacy, but he also rejects both 'sullen' Calvinism and the 'vile ambitious' preachers of the new Church of England under royal supremacy. He condemns equally both the arrogant Puritans who 'abhorre all, because all cannot be good' and the Erastians who think that because all the faiths are of 'one kinde' the ruler is entitled to choose which faith will be made compulsory as the religion of the people. As he sees it, the road to Truth is not crowded.

There is, however, no evidence to support Carey's idea that 'the love poems are a veil for religious perturbations', where he 'rids himself of disloyalty by transferring it to women' (p. 24). It seems more likely that in real life women of the kind glimpsed in the poems of the 1590s, whether girlfriends, married women or prostitutes, would see no reason to be loyal for life to a young man whose financial prospects were uncertain, and whose favourite subject was his own cleverness. Not knowing that they had been in contact with one of the greatest poets in the English language, his women either got bored and dumped him, or else forgot him after taking his money. It also seems likely that Donne had not begun these relationships because he was feeling exceptionally religious.

It was an age when most educated people were interested in religious controversies which asked what was the truth about the God in whose existence almost everyone believed. These disputes were about eternity and about who would spend it in heaven, purgatory or hell. Meanwhile, before death, religious questions were morally, socially and politically important – and they could bring death, imprisonment, exile or poverty. It is not at all surprising that Donne was seriously interested. Nor is it surprising to find him telling us that from early years he thought seriously about suicide: he was as sensitive as any young person who has ever dreamed of that escape from a troublesome life. But like most young people Donne decided to go on living and to try to enjoy himself in the process. His poems show that he became fond of using 'dye' as slang for an orgasm and 'rise' as slang for a man's sexual arousal. And he could be happy to make a flippant use of other religious language.

In 'Change' the speaker says that 'much, much I feare thee'. But this is not the fear of God. He is worried that he will lose a mistress who has in the past proved her 'faith' by her 'good workes' in sex. He fears that her 'apostasie' will consist of a willingness to 'fall back' – and her Fall will consist of lying down to have sex with another man. But then the speaker reflects that another man is entitled to 'catch the same bird' if he can: 'these things bee' and 'change' (not religion) is the nursery 'of musicke, joy, life, and eternity'.

When Donne was looking for startling images to use in erotic poetry he could fall back on memories of Catholicism. In 'The Funerall' a rejected lover is 'Love's martyr'. In 'The Canonization' he imagines lovers who make each other's body a 'hermitage' and are then 'canoniz'd' like the Church's saints. In 'The Relique' he pictures two skeletons of lovers being venerated as the relics of saints, so that

All women shall adore us, and some men . . .

What these pious fools will not know is that when alive the two did not have sex, that in reality their restraint was the 'miracles wee did'. They will be adored as 'a Mary Magdalen' (believed to be an ex-prostitute) and, in his case, as 'a something else' – which may refer with a wink to the speculation that Jesus had a sexual relationship with that Mary.

'The Bracelet' is an early poem, as Carey agrees, and being immature it goes on too long. It concerns a very expensive 'seaven fold chaine' of gold which the speaker has somehow 'lost' and which needs to be replaced at 'the bitter cost' of twelve gold coins called 'angels': these must now be melted down. The word 'angels' sets him off on a lengthy pun which can be met in other Elizabethan poetry but is not to be expected from a poem from a man deeply perturbed by the prospect of hell. He pictures these angels being 'burnt and tyed in chains' by the command of his mistress, a 'dread judge'. He tells her that he accepts her demand for a new chain, but he uses the Lord's Prayer and the image of the Virgin Mary on the first Good Friday with a striking lack of religious sensitivity:

Thy will be done;
Yet with such anguish, as her onely sonne
The Mother in the hungry grave doth lay,
Unto the fire these Martyrs I betray.

In Donne's sixth 'elegie' there are references to Protestants who reject the pope's religious authority, to recusants who reject the queen's authority in obedience to the pope, and to sinners who are excommunicated. But the references are all really about the double prospect that his present lover will reject him and that he will get over it:

I shall
As nations do from Rome, from thy love fall.
My hate shall outgrow thine, and utterly,
I will renounce thy dalliance; and when I
Am the Recusant, in that absolute state,
What hurts it mee to be excommunicate?

Carey is able to underplay Donne's youthful delight in enjoying, or imagining, promiscuity because he thinks it probable that all the 'Songs and Sonets' where this is a frequent theme were written considerably later than the poet's traumatic 'apostasy' and later than his marriage. In his critical edition of the major works published in 1990 page 88 is reached before any of the 'Songs and Sonets' is printed, and we are told that there is no evidence for dating any of them before 1602. But there is strong evidence, for in the 1600s Donne was married to a wife for whom he had sacrificed his career and they produced children, about as often as was physically possible. Did he have a series of adulterous relationships, or a lot of vivid dreams about them? If so, why did he send poems celebrating serial adultery to his men friends, along with solemn thoughts about morality and religion? Carey himself believes that after his marriage Donne's fidelity to Anne was absolute: 'when he had her, he wanted no other woman' (p. 59). That seems to be true although it cannot be proved, and the only dating of the 'Songs and Sonets' which is consistent with Donne's fidelity after marriage is that those of them which celebrate promiscuity were written before he was married. If that is the case, it follows that the flippant use of religious language shows a young man who was not much troubled by the fear of hell.

It is also clear that he never regarded himself as an 'apostate' from the Catholic Faith. As much that he wrote proves, for him the central issue was not whether the Faith was true. It was one of jurisdiction: who had the supreme power, the pope or the national sovereign?

Once he had rejected the authority of the pope over the English monarchy, other rejections of Roman Catholicism followed but it seems clear that for him (as for many others in England from Henry VIII onwards) the decisive question was about papal jurisdiction: the popes had abused their authority by adding objectionable doctrines and practices to the Faith as defined by the Bible and the early Christian centuries. In his ironic but light-hearted poem 'The Will' he left legacies to people who 'had too much' already: so 'my faith I give to Roman Catholiques'. And the developments which he now attacked were not only doctrinal. During the 1620s he devoted two sermons preached in Whitehall Palace to a defence of the English Reformation (10:140–77). He took as his text the denunciation by the prophet Ezekiel of the bad shepherds who had made the Lord's own flock eat and drink 'that which yee have fouled with your feet'. He interpreted this text as a criticism of pastors who had muddied the waters of religion, motivated by 'covetousness and love of money' (10:172).

His attack was on legends, superstitions and complicated ceremonies all of which were designed to strengthen the power of the clergy over the minds of the people when the emphasis ought to have been on what the Bible said about simple prayer and good behaviour. While his preaching showed that he valued the practice of confessing sins to a priest (e.g. 9:310), he protested against making this compulsory. He denounced the wealth which the senior clergy and the monks had derived from this system and concentrated his heaviest fire on the Vatican, where popes surrounded themselves with splendour as they tried to control not only the clergy and laity but also the kings of the earth. And almost four hundred years after these protests, many Roman Catholics are known to agree very largely with Donne's line that such medieval developments are no part of permanent and essential Catholicism.

Certainly he never cut himself off from Roman Catholics as individuals, despite his growing disagreement with much of what was taught in their Church. The best – but not the only – example is his attitude to his mother. After being widowed for a second time, she married Richard Rainsford and went into exile with him in 1595 in order that they might both be free to practise their ardent Catholicism. After their return to England eleven years later he was twice imprisoned, in 1611 and 1613. Then she was widowed again, but her son gave her a home in his Deanery. (She died two months before him.) Earlier Donne had assured her that as the only one of her children 'left now', he would make up for the fact that her first husband's legacy to her had melted away over the years and would 'provide for your relief, as for my own wife and children'.

And certainly Donne never cut himself off from the Catholic spiritual tradition. It would be truer to use about him the nickname of people who tried to be both old and new in their religion, 'Church Papists'. Modern scholars have shown how his poems reveal a continuing use of Catholic forms of devotion, for example the form of reciting the rosary made popular by the Dominicans and used by Donne in 'La Corona' in 1607 (see pp. 224–6). It is also a fact that twenty years later he observed with great feeling the midwinter festival of St Lucy, which was not in the Anglican calendar (see pp. 272–5). As Professor Martz has demonstrated, he also made intensive use of the Jesuit method of meditation. In his prose works he cited a vast array of Catholic writers. His farewell gift to the senior lawyers of Lincoln's Inn, many of whom were stout Puritans, was a recently reprinted Latin Bible in six volumes with a commentary dating from the fourteenth century. This included many references to the Fathers of the Church, as did the books of a Jesuit contemporary of Donne's, Cornelius à Lapide, often consulted as he prepared sermons. The biblical quotations in these sermons show that he instinctively quoted first the Latin

Bible in the pre-1592 Vulgate version – and often quoted from memory, sometimes making a small slip. The last word in the epitaph which he wrote for his own grave, referring to Christ as *Oriens* ('Rising' in the east), is from the Vulgate Bible, which mistranslated Zechariah 6:12.

Writing to the Duke of Buckingham in 1623, Donne did not criticize the highly unpopular mission which that minister was undertaking as the companion of Prince Charles in his attempt to arrange marriage with the Catholic daughter of the King of Spain. Instead, he told the duke that in his own library Spanish authors were represented better than those of any other nation. He reflected that 'their autors in Divinity, though they do not show us the best way to heaven, yet thinke they doe. And so, though they say not true, yet they do not ly, because they speak their Conscience.'

In a poem congratulating Prince Charles on this plan, he called the Roman Catholic, Lutheran and Calvinist versions of Christianity 'beames' coming from the single 'sunne'. On another occasion he wrote that the Roman and English Churches were 'sister teats of his graces, yet both diseased and infected'. In one sermon he exhorted his hearers to 'love those universall and fundamentall doctrines which in all Christian ages, and in all Christian Churches, have been agreed by all to be necessary to salvation; and then thou art a true Catholique' (2:280). In another he said that if God asked him what his religion was, 'shall I not be able to say, It is that which thy word and thy Catholique Church hath imprinted in me?' (7:61). A little later he told Sir Robert Ker that 'my Tenets are always for the Religion I was born in, and the peace of the State, and the rectifying of the Conscience'. Presumably he had not forgotten that he had been born as a Roman Catholic, but now as an Anglican dean he claimed that he had never changed his religion. He expected his friend to know what he meant. In his *Essayes in Divinity* he declared that 'through all my thanksgivings to God I ever humbly acknowledge as one of his greatest Mercies to me that he gave me my Pasture in this Park and my milk from the breasts of this Church' – by which he meant, of course, the Church of his family and early years. But he wrote that book as a test of his fitness to become an Anglican preacher and what he preached in that capacity was what he had come to believe: that 'in another Church the Additonall things exceed the Fundamentall . . . and the Traditions of Men, the Commandments of God' (5:295). As a Roman Catholic boy he had imbibed the fundamental commandments and as an Anglican adult he was prepared to teach them.

He may have startled some of his hearers when he preached from an Anglican pulpit: 'I am a Papist, that is, I will fast and pray as much as any Papist and enable my selfe for the service of my God, as seriously, as sedulously, as laboriously as an Papist' (9:166). Admittedly he went on to say 'I am a Puritan, that is, I will endeavour to be pure as my Father in heaven is pure, as far as any Puritan' – but he had made his point in a time of English hysteria against Popery. Donne had to defend himself 'when we acknowledge the Church of Rome to be truly a Church'. He did it by calling that Church a 'Pest-house', where people with infectious diseases ought to be isolated – but 'the Pest-house is a house' (9:344).

Thus Catholic elements could be retained, both while Donne regarded himself as a 'Christian' without any other label and later when he became an Anglican priest and preacher. Carey reckons that 'restless desire for work and worldly success' (p. 46) explains why he joined 'the Anglican propaganda machine' (p. 37). There is some truth in these severe words, for Donne did write some less than reasonable propaganda against the teachings and behaviour of popes and Jesuits, and his motives in writing these books, and later in being ordained, included a desire to escape from long-term unemployment. But when he had been ordained, his eloquence about what he had found in the Church of England was so passionate that there appears to be no need to dismiss it as insincere.

He now identified the ultimate Truth with the living Christ and out of his experience he answered the question 'Where are we likeliest to find him?' His answer was that everyone must undertake the search personally, for 'thou must not so think him in heaven, as that thou canst not have immediate accesse to him without intercession of others'. There was no need to look for Christ 'beyond the Sea' – either in Rome where 'the Church is but an Antiquaries' Cabinet, full of rags and fragments of antiquity', or in Geneva where the Church of the Calvinists is 'so new a built house with bare walls, that it is yet unfurnished of such Ceremonies as should make it comly and reverend'. No, Christ is accessible to everyone who seeks, for 'Christ is at home with thee, he is at home within thee, and there is the nearest way to find him' (1:246).

In a later sermon he said that 'the aire is not so full of Moats, of Atomes, as the Church is full of Mercies; and as we can suck in no part of aire, but we take in these Moats, these Atomes; so here in the Congregation we cannot suck in a word from the preacher, we cannot speak, we cannot sigh a prayer to God, but that that whole breath and aire is made of mercy' (6:170–1).

Donne also seems to have been speaking out of experience – this time, of his years when he had been a churchless Christian – when he contrasted this discovery of mercy with the confusion and distress which could spoil private prayers. 'I locke my doore to my selfe, and I throw my selfe downe in the presence of my God, I devest my selfe of all worldly thoughts, and I bend all my powers and faculties upon God, as I think, and suddenly I find my selfe scattered, melted, fallen into vaine thoughts, into no thoughts; I am upon my knees, and I talke, and think nothing; I deprehend my selfe in it, and I goe about to mend it. I gather new forces, new purposes to try againe, and I doe the same thing againe. I beleeve in the Holy Ghost, but do not finde him, if I seeke him onely in private prayer; But when I go to meet him in Church, when I seeke him where he hath promised to bee found . . . I have . . . incorruption in the midst of my dunghill, spirit in the midst of my flesh, heaven upon earth' (5:249–50).

When preaching about the need for a better chapel in Lincoln's Inn he admitted that many saints of the Old Testament had found God outside a temple: Job on a dunghill, Hezekiah in a bed, Jeremiah in a dungeon, Jonah in a whale, Daniel in a den of lions, others in a fiery furnace. But he maintained that God could be found most easily in a church, which in his case was now Anglican (2:213–18). Preaching in St Paul's Cathedral one Whit Sunday he looked back: 'Of those who do professe Christ Jesus, some grovell still in the superstitions they were fallen into, and some are raised, by God's grace, out of them; and I am one of these . . . We are in the favour, and care of God; We, our Nation, we, our Church; There I am at home.' And so he gave thanks for 'what God hath done for me, and my soule; There is the Ego, the particular, the individual, I' (5:70–1). He now saw no great gap between the Church of England and God: indeed, 'nearer to him, and to the institutions of his Christ, can no Church, no not of the Reformation, be said to have come closer than ours does' (7:409). But he never ceased to feel that he was a Catholic, for he saw no great gap between the Church of England and the essentials of the Catholic Faith as held in the Church of his baptism and boyhood.

Carey tells us that 'to be moralistic about Donne would be foolish (p. 81) and that 'belittling him as a human being' is not his aim (p. 85). However he finds it 'hard to suppress a shudder' when Donne remarks in the pulpit that 'he that travails weary, and late towards a great City, is glad when he comes to a place of execution, because he knows that is neer the town' (p. 81). But the preacher uses this shudder-making idea in order to assure his congregation that someone dying is near a resurrection into glory, 'but one stop to thy Jerusalem' (2:266).

Carey does shudder (on p. 48) when he reads in Donne's *Devotions upon Emergent Occasions* the much-quoted words 'any man's death diminishes *me . . . never send to know* for whom the bell tolls, it tolls for thee' (the ironic italics are Carey's). But here Donne is not thinking only of himself, nor is he being so lazy that he sends someone to ask instead of satisfying his curiosity himself. In the *Devotions* the context is clear. Donne is confined to bed with a fever which may end in his death; he is troubled by the noise of bell-ringing which invades his bedroom from the nearby parish church of St Gregory, and he complains; then he hears the 'passing bell' tolling in order to call neighbours to prayer for someone who is dying. Donne does pray, now and after the death, and he meditates at considerable length on the solemn facts that this person is not only a neighbour but also a fellow member of the Church which is the Body of Christ, and that another soul is now going to judgement by Christ. In a later sermon he asks: 'is there any man, that in his chamber hears a bell toll for another man, and does not kneel down to pray for that dying man?' (8:174).

Unsurprisingly, Carey reckons that in Donne 'there is no thought about the man for whom the bell might be tolling', for 'the tone and the advice are entirely self-regarding' (p. 48) – and to be sure, Donne is as usual fascinated to observe his own reactions. Previously he has grumbled about the noise from the church ('that steeple which never ceases'), as it invades the room where he is a 'Prisoner' in a 'sicke bed' feeling very sorry for himself. He cannot sleep 'and oh, if I be entering now into Eternitie, where there shall be no distinction of houres, why is it al my businesse now to tell Clocks?' But the bell which invites him to pray for a fellow Christian who actually is 'entering now into Eternitie' is heard as a new sound. It is received as an invitation to escape from the prison created by his self-centredness.

His earlier concentration on his own woes is not amazing. He has felt that 'a sicke bed is a grave' and has complained that 'we doe not onely die, but die upon a Rack, die by a torment of sicknesse'. Being anxious to make his own diagnosis, he has 'cut up mine Anatomy, dissected my selfe' and in his anxiety he has watched the equally puzzled 'Phisician with the same diligence as hee the disease'. Then he has watched himself getting weaker even when his own doctor has called in colleagues to consult about the emergency. He has felt that if 'before hee had a beeing' he could have expected 'this miserie' he would not have chosen to be born, and he has moaned that even if a man 'tastes happinesse' he 'drinkes misery'. He has been forbidden to read and has often been left alone, complaining that 'the greatest misery of sicknes is solitude' and that 'Solitude is a torment which is not threatened in hell it selfe'. He has told himself that other people may be worse off: the paupers who cannot afford a doctor so that 'the first that takes knowledge is the Sexten that buries them', and the destitute who die not in a bed but on 'the flint of the street'. But until he hears this church bell, he is not fully moved by that vision of people who deserve pity even more than he does. It is only now that he is carried away by a flood of emotion. Because his own death may be very near he must make 'my recourse to my God' and if he survives he will be very fortunate. This bell is what teaches him to feel sharply that others may be 'farre more miserable, and farre more worthy to be less miserable than I'.

While we are on this point we may note that Carey is not alone in being unfair to the Donne of the *Devotions*.

When he usefully included many extracts in the Penguin edition of *John Donne: Selected Prose* (1987), Neil Rhodes called these meditations 'predominantly secular' because 'they do not resemble anything in the Christian meditative tradition, either Catholic or Protestant', adding that the 'expostulations' which are 'anguished' protests to God have a 'hectoring quality'. And to be sure, the style in which Donne meditates and prays is uniquely his own. But the position in which he finds himself is not unique. Believing that he may be about to die, he turns to God without formality about his faith and without pretence about his despair. He is not being secular. Roughly the same mixture of disturbed emotions may be found in the psalms of the Bible, and what is said in the gospels about Christ in Gethsemane and on the cross is not altogether different. As a Christian in distress Donne claims the right to make his protest with these precedents to 'my God, my God'. He knows that he must speak to God as a sinner who is 'the dust and the ashes of the Temple of the Holy Ghost' but he can ask 'what Marble is so precious?' because 'I am my best part, I am my soule'. This soul is 'the breath of God' in him and so 'I may breathe back these pious expostulations to my God'. That is not a man who is 'predominantly secular' or, when he prays, 'hectoring'. He belongs to a long tradition of prayer to God *de profundis*: 'Out of the deep . . .'. The self-pity in the *Devotions* is characteristic of humanity, and the self-exhibition involved in the publishing of these intimate thoughts is characteristic of Donne, but what he reveals in this strange little book is a double exposure. The tolling of a bell exposes him to a fellow Christian who is dying – and his fear that he too is about to die exposes him to 'my God' like a swimmer who is stripped on the edge of the cold sea.

Carey is obviously right to condemn as 'callousness' Donne's warning that family or friends ought not to shorten the suffering of people being hanged by tugging at their legs, on the ground that the law has 'appointed a painfull death to deterre others' and should not be 'defrauded'. Our indignation against the cold heart of this moralist is increased when we know that some of the people being choked to death by the hangman within reach of those who loved them were already so miserable that they had attempted to commit suicide and, when they had failed in that attempt, had made themselves criminals who had earned the death penalty and the confiscation of their goods under the law of that age. They were now being executed before burial in unconsecrated ground although they might have welcomed a fresh chance to rebuild their lives and support their families. But the passage which is quoted comes not from a sermon but from *Biathanatos*, where the thoroughly confused Donne is taking to this extreme the platitude that suicide ought to be discouraged although he expresses a bold sympathy with people tempted by this 'sickely inclination' and, also bravely, confesses that he himself has been so tempted. It is unfair to claim that this error of judgement was not only serious but also typical of 'Donne's relative immunity to the suffering of others' which is to be found 'throughout his work, in poetry and prose' (p. 192).

Carey is shocked when he hears Donne 'rhapsodizing' about the 'inexpressible comfort' which the passengers on Noah's ark 'must have felt when they saw everyone else drown' (p. 81). But we find that here the preacher is not gloating over the fate of sinners. He is trying to reduce their numbers and is talking about 'the joy in his safety' which 'a Christian is to take, even in this, that God hath taken him into his Church' (5:106). Certainly Donne accepted the belief that in the end humankind will be divided into the saved and the damned, but what is far more unusual in his sermons is his persistence in hoping for the best as he ponders the destiny of the majority of his fellow humans. Carey is far less charitable towards Donne, who is left to drown in a sea of false accusations.

Carey is also shocked to find Donne expressing a 'violent dislike' for beggars and 'denouncing the destitute' (pp. 81–2). And certainly in his early years Donne could be heartless about beggars, as in this disgusting epigram:

> I am unable, yonder beggar cries,
> To stand or move; if hee say true, he *lies*.

And even when his heart had been softened by life's knocks he could say something foolish about men who refused to work, as in this sermon: 'It will scarcely admit doubt, but that the incorrigible vagabond is farther from all the wayes of goodnesse than the corruptest rich man' (6:304). 'Thinkest thou to eat bread', he once asked a workshy beggar (who, however, was not in the congregation to hear him), 'and not sweat?' (1:207). He once warned the man who refuses to work that 'he kills himself' (1:209), for 'he that undertakes no course, no vocation, is no part, no member, no limbe of the body of this world' (4:160). He was specially indignant that in London 'street-beggary has become a calling, for Parents bring up their children to it, nay they doe almost take prentises to it, some expert beggars teach others about what they shall say, how shall they looke, how they shall lie, how they shall cry'. These were the beggars 'whom our lawes call Incorrigible' and whom Donne called 'vermin' because they 'devoure that which belongs to them who are truly poore' (6:304).

But about the neglect of 'them who are truly poore', Donne could be alarmingly eloquent. In an early sermon he said bluntly: 'The poore are He, He is the poore. And so he that oppreseth the poore, reproaches God' (1:287). He told the lawyers of Lincoln's Inn: 'Thou seest a needy person, and thou turnest away thine eye; but it is the Prince of Darknesse that casts this mist upon thee; Thou stoppest thy nose at his sores, but they are thine owne incompassionate bowels that stinke within thee' (3:137). He told a congregation in St Paul's Cathedral: 'He that makes himselfe insensible to the cries and curses of the poor here in this world doth but prepare himselfe for the howlings, and gnashings of the teeth, in the world to come' (8:280). 'Rich and poor are Images, Pictures of God', he explained; 'but (as Clement of Alexandria says wittily and strongly) the poor is *Nuda Imago*, a naked picture without any drapery, any clothes about it. And it is a much harder thing, and there is much more art showed in making a naked picture, than in all the rich attire that can be put upon it. And howsoever the rich man, that is invested in Power and Greatnesse, be made a better picture of God, of God considered in himself who is all Greatnesse, all Power, yet of God considered in Christ (which is the contemplation that concerns us most), the poor man is the better picture.' This is because the poor man 'most resembles Christ who liv'd in continual poverty' (8:285). And Bald's biography shows that Donne was not a hypocrite when he preached about the Christian's obligation to give to the poor, for in his own charitable giving he was generous and systematic.

Carey tells us that Donne was a hypocrite when he preached about the Christian's humble hope of heaven: he 'does speak of heavenly harmony and the joy of reunion with the dead, but these are sideshows compared with his personal advancement' (p. 212). In 1990 Carey wrote an introduction to a new edition of Donne's major works, ending with an allegation that Donne believed that in heaven he would not lose 'his style, or his aspiration, or his wish to attract and deceive spectators'. 'So Donne thinks', says Carey. 'Or says he thinks.'

The evidence produced for this astonishingly harsh conclusion is a quotation from a sermon, where Donne hopes that 'I shall be so like God, as the Devil himself shall not know me from God'. But the quotation is not completed by Carey. What Donne actually hopes for is that in heaven he will be like God himself, free of any temptation to sin. He says: 'the Devil himselfe shall not know me from God, so far as to find any more place to fasten a tentation upon me, than upon God'. Donne hopes to be in the kingdom of heaven and to find that Satan will not be able 'to conceive any more hope of my falling from that Kingdome, than of God's being driven out of it'. He hopes to be 'as immortal as God' not because he will be divine but because he will receive immortality as the gift of God, as 'the Sunne by shining upon the Moone makes the

Moone a Planet, a Star'. He hopes that 'those beames of Glory which shall issue from my God' will 'fall upon me, shall make me . . . an Angell of Light, a Star of Glory, a something that I cannot name now, not imagine now, nor tomorrow, nor next yeare'. But without God's mercy he is 'a clod of earth, and worse, a dark Soule, a Spirit of darknesse' (9:89).

We are told by Carey that Donne found 'in God, and in his own position as God's spokesman, a final and fully adequate expression of his power lust . . . for he had found something far more corrosive than satire with which to attack mankind, namely Christianity . . . Terror afforded him a histrionic triumph' (pp. 108, 110, 120). In later chapters I shall quote some passages in the sermons which to me, as well as to Carey, would seem to be bullying. But it is right that we should listen to Donne explaining what he thought was his duty. 'The Preacher makes a holy noise in the conscience of the Congregation, and when hee hath awakened them by stirring the nest, hee casts some claps of thunder, some intimidations, in denouncing the judgements of God, and he flings open the gates of Heaven, that they may heare, and look up, and see a man sent from God, with power to infuse his feare into them.' But Donne's motive in 'denouncing' (we should say 'announcing') judgements was, he said, that his hearers should find God's mercy. He continued: 'The Preacher doth so infuse the feare of God into his Auditory, that they shall feare nothing but God, and then they shall feare God, but so as he is God; and God is Mercy; God is Love. Then he shews them Heaven, and God in Heaven, sanctifying all their crosses in this World, inanimating all their worldly blessings, rayning downe his blood into their emptinesse, and his balme into their wounds, making their bed in all their sicknesse . . .' (8:43–4).

As Donne reflected on his experience as a pastor, he said that he had found seven 'dejected' people to one who was over-confident. He added that when he had given some comfort to someone depressed, 'that man hath given me a Sacrament . . . I go away

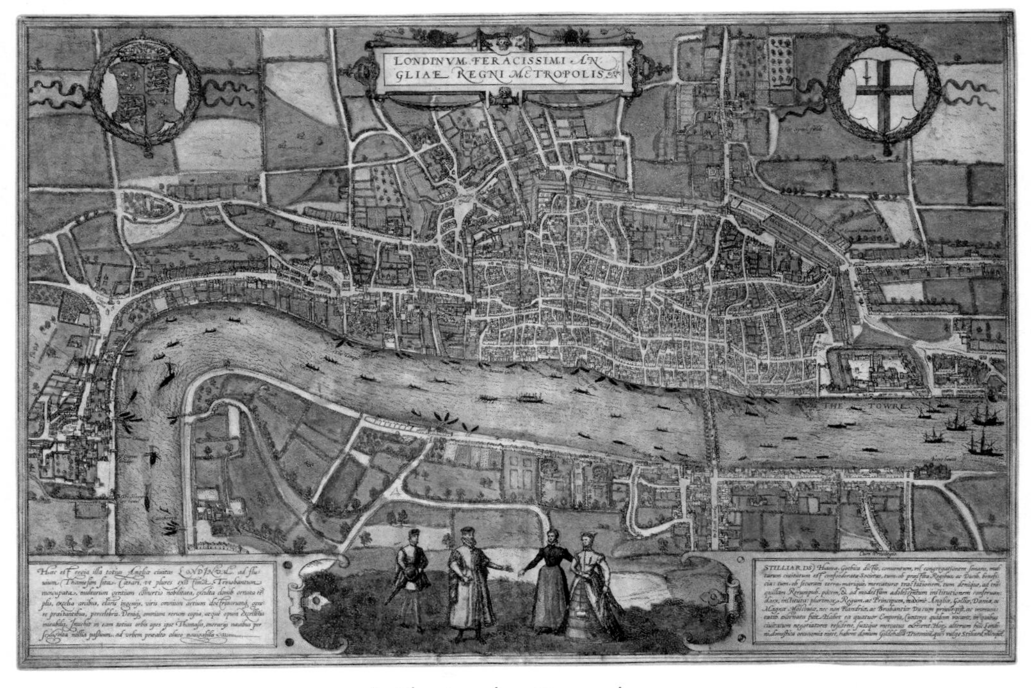

1. The London Donne knew

2. Donne in 1591

3. Donne in 1616

4. Donne in 1620

153

Sr

I send yow back by this bearer
the letter wch I borrowed of yow. If yow wyll
now to ease my imprisonmt spare me some of
the French negotiations, yow shall have them
as faythfully kept and as redely returnd as
these. And when I ame worth yor commandinge
I ame wholy yors. From my prison in my
chamber. 20 Febru. 1601

Yor honest assured frend

J. Donne

5. Donne asks for a book while under arrest

6° Julij 1602

Receiued the Day and yeare abouewritten of the
right ho: Sr Thomas Egerton knight L: keeper of
the great Seale of England, my ho: L: and Master
by the hands of hys seruant Mr John Panton the
sum of one hundred pounds of lawfull Money
of England: wch sayd hundred pounds was giuen by
the right ho: the Lady Egerton late wyfe to the
sayd L: keeper, to her Neece, Anne the Daughter
of Sr George More, now my wyfe, and ys now for
her receiued by me

J: Donne

6. Donne's receipt for a legacy authorized by Egerton

7. Preaching at Paul's Cross in Donne's time

8. An engraving of Donne in his shroud used as a frontispiece for *Death's Duell*, 1632

9. Donne's effigy

comforted in my selfe, that Christ Jesus hath made me an instrument of the dispensation of his mercy' (8:249). His advice to one and all was: 'never consider the judgment of God for sin alone, but in the company of the mercies of Christ' (8:207). And forty years after Donne's death Richard Gibson wrote to Samuel Pepys, remembering one of the great dean's sermons. What had stuck in his mind was that 'ye Goodnes of God was not so much seene in our Creation as Redemption, nor soe much that wee are his, as that nothing can take us out of his hands'.

We are also told by Carey that although he dared not criticize the 'impossibilities that Christianity required him to believe' (p. 157) because of his position in the Church, yet 'we can be sure that Donne's scepticism lasted throughout his life' (p. 222). He assures us that 'it was precisely the impossibility of having true ideas about God which agitated Donne in his religious writing, and it is this above all which accounts for the sense of strain and confusion in the sermons when we compare them with the great love poems' (pp. 239–40). Is that so? The sermons can be felt to be too dogmatic when we compare them with many modern sermons, but when they do admit that no ideas or images referring to God can be completely accurate they do no more than repeat what has often been taught by the Scriptures and by the mystics and theologians: that the essence of God is beyond human sight, understanding or expression. That is the theme of the 'apophatic' theology in the tradition of Eastern Orthodoxy, and of the *via negativa* in the theology and spirituality of Western Catholicism.

It can be suggested that the 'new Philosophy' had thrown educated people including Donne into scepticism about the fundamental claims of Christianity but there is no evidence that this was the case. A thorough denial of the existence of God (atheism) seems to have been very rare and although disbelief in actions by God after the creation (Deism) was beginning to grow it does not appear to have been numerically significant in Donne's lifetime. As we shall see, he preached eloquently against these ideas. Here we may note that the most spectacular feat in the new 'natural philosophy' or science was the bold theory of Copernicus that the earth moves around the sun (published in 1543). This contradicted the Old Testament but Donne seems to have shared the general belief of educated Englishmen in his time that it did not destroy belief in the Creator and the Saviour: England was not responsible for the foolish persecution of Galileo, who proved the theory right, by the authorities of the Church in Italy.

Donne was of course interested. He mentioned to the Countess of Bedford that

> As new Philosophy arrests the Sunne,
>   And bids the passive earth about it runne,
> So wee have dull'd our minde, it hath no ends . . .

And in his 'First Anniversarie' he mentioned that

> . . . new Philosophy cals all in doubt,
> The Element of fire is quite put out;
> The Sun is lost, and th'earth, and no man's wit
> Can well direct him, where to look for it.

But Donne could write or preach without bothering with the 'new Philosophy', when the old idea that the sun runs around the sky seemed more suitable for a poem or a sermon. As Carey notes (on p. 271), in 'The Sunne Rising' even before his invitation to the sun to circle around the lovers' bed he rebukes it for moving in such a way that it disturbs their sex-exhausted sleep:

> Busie old foole, unruly Sunne, . . .
> Must to thy motions lovers' seasons run?

Probably more than twenty years later, on Christmas Day in 1624, he compared the Church's expansion across the Atlantic with the sun's daily journey round the earth. The sun, he reminded the congregation, moves 'circularly'. Similarly, 'this Church . . . moves . . . circularly; It began in the East, it came to us, and is passing now, shining out now, in the farthest West' (6:173). In his *Devotions* there was a rare touch of flippancy: when he feels giddy he remembers that he is on a planet which is not stable. But on Easter Day in 1627 he told the congregation that 'the standing still of the Sun for Joshua's use' in the Old Testament was a miracle, but a greater miracle was the fact that 'so vast and immense a body as the Sun should run so many miles in a minute' (7:374). And in *Ignatius his Conclave* Donne sent Copernicus to join the Jesuits in hell, as another troublesome innovator – but put into the mouth of Ignatius a greeting which showed a lack of profound interest, with the cool words that the new theory 'may well be right'.

So was Donne permanently sceptical about Christianity despite his eloquence in the pulpit? As we shall see when we look at his sermons in Chapter 10, he was aware of some questions which may be called modern and his answers could suggest that a particular part of the Bible or of the Church's tradition needs to be treated in a way which begins to be modern. But Carey cannot produce a shred of evidence to support his accusation of basic hypocrisy, for every word that has survived is consistent with what can be expected reasonably: Donne was neither a fundamentalist nor an unbeliever. Whereas in his earlier years he could express politically conformist loyalties in public while being in private quite cynical about the regime, neither before ordination nor after it did he ever leave on record any question about the truth of what he regarded as the essentials of Christianity. His private letters were as full of piety as were his sermons: they confessed to depression but never to unbelief. Like a considerable number of other seventeenth-century Englishmen who put their thoughts on paper, quite often he found difficulty – even agony – in relating Christianity to himself and to the world around him, but like almost all of them he attributed that to his sin or his blindness, not to the falsehood of his religion; or to God being infinite, not to God being unreal. Carey's suggestion that Donne was at heart a sceptic arises from twentieth-century secular feelings, not from seventeenth-century facts. We may prefer the verdict given by another great poet, W. B. Yeats, who wrote in 1912 to Sir Herbert Grierson, congratulating him on his edition of Donne's poetry: 'the more precise and learned the thought the greater the beauty, the passion; the intricacy and subtleties of his imagination are the length and depth of the furrow made by his passion'. Yeats thought that 'his pedantry and his obscenity . . . make me more certain that one who is but a man like us all has seen God'.

What kind of God did Donne worship?

Carey notes that Donne 'quotes St Augustine approvingly: "Never propose to thy self such a God, as thou wert not bound to imitate"' (p. 226), but it seems that he thinks that Donne decided to imitate an extremely cruel God. His God is 'the most hideous that Christianity had yet evolved', a 'Calvinist monster in the sky who creates large numbers of men for the express purpose of torturing them for all eternity' (p. 225). What makes Donne's religion even worse in Carey's eyes is that (as he thinks) he came to believe that God had arbitrarily decided to create him with a destination in heaven: he quotes the preacher as saying 'God did elect mee, before he did actually create mee' (8:282). But Carey's interpretation of the position which Donne reached is demonstrably a misinterpretation.

Like many other sensitive Christians, Donne became full of wonder that such a sinner as he was could be loved by the all-holy God and he could draw no conclusion other than the belief that God had freely chosen to love or 'elect' him as he had freely chosen to 'elect' everyone except those who persistently rebelled against his good purpose for them. (This was the version of predestination which appealed to the greatest modern theologian in the Calvinist or 'Reformed' tradition, Karl Barth.) But Donne knew that for many years he had resisted the call of God and had been left free to do so. He also knew, from experience both as a convert and as a pastor, that any man 'can answer the inspiration of God, when his grace comes, and exhibit acceptable service to him, and co-operate with him' (1:271–2), for 'even naturall man may, out of the use of that free will, come to Church, heare the Word preached, and believe it to be true' (3:36). Therefore he insisted that there is freedom on both sides: God is free to say yes, the sinner is free to say no. As he put it in an age when men could be recruited for an army or navy by force: 'Christ beats his Drum, but he does not Press men; Christ is served by Voluntaries' (5:156).

To put it in more theological terms, Donne believed in 'election', the choice by God of whom to 'save' among sinners, but had no sympathy with the belief that before anyone was created God had already decided exactly who was to be a 'reprobate', perpetually incapable of hearing and obeying him. Donne was very far from teaching that God 'hated some of his creatures so virulently as to damn them even before they have come into being' (Carey, p. 277). He stated what he did believe by quoting St Augustine: 'There is no predestination in God, but to good.' 'Our destruction', he added, 'is from our owne sinne, and the Devill that infuses it; not from God, or from any ill purpose in him that enforces us' (5:53–4).

He maintained that 'he is our God; and God is love; and therefore to conceive a cruell God, a God that hated us, even to damnation, before we were . . . or to conceive a God so cruell, as that at our death, or in our way, he will afford us no assurance that hee is ours and we are his . . . this is not to professe God to be terrible in his works; For . . . God hath never done, or said anything to induce so terrible an opinion of him' (8:125). To say that God could 'peremptorily hate' anyone who was not guilty 'as a manifold sinner, and as an obdurate sinner' – to say that God could 'mean to make him, that he might damne him' – is 'to impute to God, a sowrer and worse affected nature, than falls to any man . . . Doth any man beget a sonne therefore, that he might dis-inherit him? Doth God hate any man therefore, because he will hate him?' (9:390). His teaching was unambiguous: 'God does not Reward or Condemn out of his decrees but out of our actions' (7:17).

We have already glanced at the Synod of Dort which defined Calvinist orthodoxy (on pp. 105–6). It is clear that Donne's own beliefs were those which the synod condemned as Arminian heresy. But even the victorious orthodox did not dare to say at Dort that God condemns the innocent. They taught that 'God has decreed to leave certain people in the common misery into which they have plunged themselves by their own fault'. Nowadays almost everyone would agree that this formula left God guilty of almost the greatest cruelty imaginable, but it is different from the further step of saying that God is the 'Calvinist monster in the sky' who has no mercy on faultless people, the divine sadist who creates people because he knows for sure that they will spend eternity in his torture chamber. And in his sermon in The Hague in 1619 Donne showed some of his impatience with this whole fierce debate. He did not deny that people are sinners; he was one. But he believed that God wishes to save sinners; that, too, had been his experience, which he wanted to share. People, he said, were weary of hearing from pulpits nothing but talk of 'Election and Reprobation, and whom, and when, and how, and why God hath chosen, or cast away'. It was enough 'to know enough for the salvation of your soules; If you will search farther into God's eternall Decrees and unrevealed Councels, you should not cast your nets into that Sea, for you are not fishers there' (2:279). On another occasion he was even more homely: 'I enquire not what God did in his bed-chamber' (2:323). When back in England he was unabashed in claiming that the synod had shown the same restraint: ignoring its discussions of predestination, he simply reported that 'in the last forraine Synod which our divines assisted, with what blessed sobriety they delivered their sentence: That all men are truly and in earnest called to eternall life by God's Minister' (7:127). When making his will he bequeathed to Henry King his gold medal commemorating the synod – and accompanied it by two portraits of Roman Catholic theologians which he had displayed more prominently in the Deanery.

In an exceptionally public and controversial sermon preached at St Paul's Cross in 1629, he mocked 'the over-pure despisers of others; Men that will abridge and contract the large mercies of God in Christ, and elude and frustrate, in a great part, the generall promises of God. Men that are loth that God should speak out so loud as to say, *He would have all men saved*, And loth that Christ should spread his armes, or shed his blood in such a compasse as might fall upon all. Men that think no sinne can hurt them, because they are elect, and that every sin makes every other man a Reprobate. But with the Lord there is . . . plentifull redemption, and *an overflowing cup of mercy*' (9:119).

The faith which Donne proclaimed was thus a faith that God's will is that all can be saved, and that Christ has died for the benefit of all, declaring the divine love for all, but that sinners can resist God's will, even to the end. Those who are being saved by God are those who respond both by faith and by life to the gracious goodness of God, for 'as his mercy is new every morning, so his grace is renewed in me every minute, . . . the eye of God is upon me, though I winke at his light, and watches over me, though I sleep' (8:368). There can be no human goodness without this grace of God inspiring it, but it is also true that 'Grace could not worke upon man to Salvation, if man had not a faculty of will to worke upon . . . God saves no man without, or against, his will' (5:317). Everything does not depend on God's 'election' of his favourites without regard to behaviour. Donne recalled how Christ had replied to the rich young man who asked how he could enter eternal life among the saved: he had told him first to obey the commandments about behaviour and then to get rid of his wealth. He had not told him 'you must look into the eternal decree of Election first, and see whether that stand for you or no' (6:229).

A result of this vision of God as good was a sharp decline in the estimate of the population of hell. While many Christians were eager to send most people, including many fellow Christians, to hell, Donne maintained that because he is Love 'God hath made all mankinde of one blood and all Christians of one calling' (1:122) and he could go so far as to say that 'whosoever lives according to rectified Reason, which is the Law of nature, he is a Christian' (4:119). 'There are an infinite number of Stars, more than we can distinguish', Donne said, 'and so by God's grace, there may be an infinite number of soules saved, more than those of whose salvation we discern the ways and meanes' (6:161).

He claimed that this generous belief could be found in the teaching of the Fathers of the Church in the days when the Church was surrounded by a pagan world. 'Those blessed Fathers of tender bowells' saw God's mercy extending to 'the Pagans that had no knowledge of Christ in any established Church'. 'Partly', he explained, 'they goe upon that rule, which goes through so many of the Fathers, . . . That to that man who does so much as he can, by the light of nature, God never denies grace; and then, say they, why should not these good men be saved? . . . I know God can be as mercifull as those tender Fathers present him to be; and I would be as charitable as they are; and therefore, humbly imbracing that manifestation of his Son which he hath afforded me, I leave God to his unsearchable waies of working upon others, without further inquisition' (4:78–9).

In 1990 a second edition of Carey's *John Donne: Life, Mind and Art* was published, without revision but with the addition of an 'afterword' which was a highly critical examination of two books of 1986, Thomas Docherty's *John Donne, Undone* and Arthur Marotti's *John Donne, Coterie Poet.* He complained that Docherty's 'reading practice is guided largely by ingenuity and whim' rather than by 'historical criteria' and that much of Marotti's study of possible influences on the poetry by the limited readership expected for it is 'undeniably sited in a wilderness of unsatisfactory conjecture'. I do not have the space in which to discuss these criticisms, which are far less justified about Marotti than about Docherty. But I have to ask whether Carey is in a position to make them.

In his study of *Donne's Religious Writing* (1997) Paul Oliver tells us that 'John Carey's work on Donne was the initial stimulus to my own'. The sub-title of his book is 'A Discourse of Feigned Devotion', which seems to promise a demonstration that everything Donne said or wrote about religion was 'feigned'. As we have seen, he was a tough self-critic, but in sermons already quoted (pp. 20, 170) Donne explained clearly enough what he meant by 'feigned devotion': he suffered – as who does not? – from wandering thoughts while trying to pray.

Oliver has found some good points in Donne's prose. He admires the letters, where the voice is 'frank, humble, pliant, frequently self-mocking (or something very close to it)' (p. 239). He even admires the 'very different' voice of Donne the preacher – sometimes. In the sermons he praises their 'creation and sustained utilization of an extraordinarily forceful style whose main features are a capacity for surprise which guarantees attention, a rich sense of humour and irony, a propensity for vivid, often homely imagery and a tendency to apparent self-exposure' (p. 265). But he has no respect for the message of the sermons or for the personality to which the religious writing gives 'apparent self-exposure'.

The emphasis in his onslaught is on the preacher's hypocrisy. He rejects 'the assumption that the writing puts us in direct contact with Donne's own beliefs and piety' (p. 6). Before his ordination the preacher has been 'the professional propagandist who is capable of writing on either side in a given dispute and decides to work for the higher bidder' (p. 18). Now his sermons 'present this specially constructed self in a highly ostentatious manner' (p. 239), making of him 'something of a hypocrite' (p. 213). The preacher has written religious poems, but these showed 'a complete lack of interest in religious doctrines' (p. 58), since religion was to him 'merely a rich source of exploitable religious raw material' (p. 193). Prayers expressed as poems were 'melodramatic posturing' (p. 115) with 'no concern for morality' (p. 118). Petitions to the Trinity were 'a brusque demand' (p. 124), 'harshly imperative' (p. 226) and 'emotional blackmail' (p. 216). When Donne asks God the Father to 'find both Adams met in me' (the first Adam the Sinner and the second Adam the Saviour), it is claimed that he 'splits the Trinity' (p. 220). When his wife has died and he turns to God in a new intensity of prayer, it is claimed that he has 'lost much of his sense of purpose' (p. 45).

When making these crude attacks on Donne's sermons and prayers, Oliver appears to ignore the fact that phrases which he dislikes had already been used by innumerable Christians. And when assessing Donne's position in the religious life of his age he exposes himself to criticisms – not about his own sincerity, nor about his own beliefs and values, but about a repeated failure to understand the theology and spirituality of that age which has now vanished. For example, he is under the impression that Calvin taught that 'good works and the view of the sacraments as channels of grace' are 'abominable' (p. 188) – teaching which would have astonished those who in Calvin's Geneva lived under a famously strict code of moral discipline and knew how fervently congregations addressed by Calvin's spoken or written words were exhorted to take both Baptism and Holy Communion with the utmost seriousness. It is demonstrably and grossly untrue to say that the 'Anti-Calvinist model' is unique in that it alone 'leaves room for personal striving and prayer' (p. 232).

A writer such as John Carey or Paul Oliver is very ready to accuse Donne of a lack of honesty when he preaches or prays. But what should we say about a writer who claims to be expounding Donne's religious thought, when he gives almost no sign that he understands it? Certainly Donne ought to be criticized. As we have seen (and will see again in the next chapter), he attacked himself in an agony of penitence. But he invested his life in his belief that he was not being thoroughly dishonest when he held to God throughout all his moods, or when he was a priest and preacher in the Church of England. In a verse-letter he gracefully told Rowland Woodward that he was not willing to send him copies of his early poems, called by him 'love-song weeds' and 'Satyrique thornes'. His position now was 'there is no Vertue' except the virtue to be found in the practice of 'Religion'. In all honesty he admitted that 'our Soules have stain'd their first white' but he told his friend that this was not the end of the matter.

> Seeke wee then our selves in our selves; for as
> Men force the Sunne with much more force to passe,
> By gathering his beames with a christall glasse,
>
> So wee, If wee into our selves will turne,
> Blowing our sparkes of vertue, may outburne
> The straw, which doth about our hearts sojourne.

But we need to see at greater length what Donne says when he speaks up for himself. He says much in his poetry about sex which would shock Walton and Gosse – and he says much in his poetry and sermons about God which would displease Carey and Oliver. But he is also a poet about married love, which he regards as an education in love for God.

PART THREE

Donne Speaks

7 Let my body raigne

Till then, Love, let my body raigne, and let
Mee travell, sojourne, snatch, plot, have, forget . . .

'Love's Usury'

When no longer young and no longer arrogant Donne referred to his poetry dismissively and he appears to have been sincere in this attitude which astonishes us. Indeed, it seems that he destroyed many poems. When sending a poem to Magdalen Herbert he said that it had barely escaped being burned

With all those sonnes whom my braine did create

but he told the paper that it would have been wiser if it had remained

hid with mee, till thou returne
To rags againe, which is thy native state.

More than once he called his poems 'rags' (paper was then made from compacted cloth) and his verse-letters to friends and patrons could be 'salads and onions' (not meat). When Henry Wotton asked to see what had not been burned, Donne begged him not to allow anyone to copy the poems. 'To my satyres', he wrote, 'there belongs some feare and to some elegies . . . perhaps shame.' When Henry Goodyer advised him to approach the rich Countess of Huntingdon with a poem in her honour, he hesitated because he now wished to be thought of as pursuing 'a graver course than of a Poet, into which (that I may also keep my dignity) I would not seem to relapse. The Spanish proverb informes me that he is a fool which cannot mak one Sonnet, and is mad which makes two.' In the end he settled for being a clergyman – and in that capacity preached that 'if we be over-vehemently affected or transported with Poetry' it is a sin (4:143). He gave Ben Jonson the impression that having become a preacher 'he seeketh to destroy all his poems' and certainly he announced that he had buried his poetic Muse.

Only one poem in his handwriting has been discovered by modern researchers and it is not an important one. In 1614 Donne had to go to the trouble of asking friends to send him copies of his own poems, now needed for the (aborted) project to print a collection, and what he gathered then may have been the manuscript deposited with Ker when he went abroad on his diplomatic mission five years later. It may have been used in the preparation of the first printed edition but that is not certain and it can be argued that some of the surviving manuscripts reflect what the author wrote more reliably than the printed text does. It is surprising that Donne, who originally must have taken great trouble to write the poems, did not make more careful arrangements for their survival and publication, but the fact is that he did not. They were not mentioned in his long will, although he specified which of his friends were to receive which of the paintings in his possession. In contrast, contemporaries who were careful to collect and revise their poetry for publication included not only George Herbert and Ben Jonson but also lesser figures such as Samuel Daniel and Michael Drayton.

It does not seem to have troubled Donne that he died without putting his poems into any logical or chronological order, although during his painful last illness he wrote out sermons with a view to publication and during his last days the priest who ministered to him was himself a poet, Henry King, who was entrusted with the sermons but apparently not with the poems. It has been suggested that he planned for the poems to be left in disorder because he wanted them to be judged as literature and not as the records of his life, and perhaps also because he regarded them as literature about the very varied emotions which are stirred up by 'love', but so far as we know he never said so and a simple lack of attention seems a more probable explanation. It is unlikely that he would have welcomed what happened.

The first edition, put together by the bookseller John Marriot, included poems which were in fact by other men. It was introduced by the boring *Metempsychosis* and it was not a complete collection. The next edition tidied the poems up a bit and added 28 more, and it has been suggested that Izaak Walton was responsible for the improvement, but if he performed this service to his hero's memory (he certainly wrote the poem under the frontispiece) it is surprising that the first poem was now the most flippant, 'The Flea'. The lack of a clear order showing Donne's development as a man and as a poet may have been one of the reasons why within half a century of his death his life was known only through Walton's memoir – and Walton had expressed nothing but regret about the secular poetry while causing bewilderment by dating the religious poems, many of which were highly disturbed, as having been written in the period when Donne was in public an orthodox and fervent preacher. It was easy, and not totally unreasonable, to draw the conclusion that the poetry which Donne had left behind so casually was little more than a display of pointless wit when secular and of a shocking uncertainty when religious. Readers were not encouraged: there were seven editions of his poetry in 1633–69, when people still alive could remember the world which had been his background, but between 1669 and 1779 there was only one, published as a curiosity in 1719 and (as we have seen) regarded as a 'Heap of Riddles' in the Age of Reason.

It is now impossible to establish the precise order in which the poems were written. It is not even possible to be certain in every case about the periods in which they originated. However, by now the work of many scholars can be used if we want to make an effort to clear up the confusion to a certain extent. It seems reasonable to believe that the poems which advocated sexual promiscuity were written before his marriage, that the poems which reflected a great confusion and unhappiness in his feelings about religion were written before his ordination, and that the poems which sound as if they were inspired by a marriage were not written by a bachelor or an adulterer. That is what we should expect and evidence stronger than any which is known would be needed to prove that our natural expectation is wrong. Also, a few of the poems can be dated more precisely.

In her introduction to her edition of Donne's *Divine Poems* in 1952 Helen Gardner stressed that the development of a religious teacher out of the young poet is very surprising. 'In his early poetry', she wrote, 'there is nothing to suggest a latent spirituality. He is by nature arrogant, egotistical, and irreverent. His mind is naturally sceptical and curious, holding little sacred. In his love poetry he is only rarely tender and never humble . . . In his almost total blindness to the beauty of the natural world he reveals a lack of that receptivity, that capacity for disinterested joy which is one of the marks of a spiritual man . . . But . . . in spite of his temperament Donne was genuinely religious, if by a religious person we understand a person to whom the idea of God not only is self-evident, but brings with it a sense of absolute obligation.' It was out of this sense of obligation to God that the development came, but even in his religious poetry Donne is, Gardner thought, a 'religious person' largely in the sense which is true of most 'religious' people: 'for all his genius as a poet, his intellectual vivacity and his passionate and complex temperament, his religious experience seems . . . to have been largely a matter of faith and moral effort'.

However, it seems possible to say something more than Gardner did both about Donne's love poetry and about his religion. When introducing the love poetry in her 1965 edition she applauded 'the rapture of fulfilment and of the bliss of union in love', going beyond her earlier emphasis that he was 'only rarely tender'. She also pointed out that 'in his love poetry he is not concerned with what he ought or ought not to feel, but with the expression of feeling itself. Passion is there its own justification, and so is disgust, or hatred or grief.' But she added that 'gratitude for love bestowed, the sense of unworthiness in the face of the overwhelming worth of the beloved, self-forgetting worship of her as she is: these notes Donne does not strike' – and there she seems too cautious. She appears to underestimate the contrast between the poems about promiscuity which record 'disgust, or hatred or grief', and the poems, also passionate, about the 'bliss of union in love'. Some experience must have caused this contrast and it seems very unlikely that it was experience confined to the writing or reading of literature. If an actual union in love which lasted was the basic cause, we know of no one apart from his wife who could have transformed Donne in that way. It therefore seems sensible to ask whether there is any evidence that she did.

In Chapter 9 I shall produce evidence from the sermons to show what Donne thought and taught about marriage, but here I appeal to the evidence in the poems. As Alan Sinfield noted in *Literature in Protestant England* (1983), 'Donne's poems of reciprocated, fulfilling and enduring sexual love are generally his most popular and they are without precedent'. In his study of *The Reinvention of Love* (1993) Anthony Low demonstrated that in the literature of the seventeenth century there was a new, modern, emphasis on marriage as a richly emotional relationship which flourished in a private world, often in tension with the world outside – and he put John and Anne Donne at the centre of this profoundly important development. As books more in the sociological mode have reminded us, these changes in literature should be weighed alongside the probability that many marriages of which no literary evidence survives did not change: there had been marriages based on love before the revolution in literature and there would be marriages based on less romantic factors after it. But within the world of literature there was indeed a revolution and within that revolution Donne was indeed, as Low said, 'a chief actor and influence'. Many years before Low, Sir Herbert Grierson thought that one must believe that the poems 'in which ardour is combined with elevation and delicacy of feeling were addressed to Anne More before and after their marriage'. Subsequent discussion has made it clear that he ought not to have claimed that all such poems 'must have been addressed to Anne', for some may have been merely influenced by her and others may have been influenced by earlier relationships which softened and matured Donne in preparation for marriage. But the key point is that, whether or not a particular poem was addressed to Anne, it is not stupid to ask whether his marriage was decisive in the 'reinvention' of the poet and therefore of 'love' in English literature.

It is true that Donne had an arduous spiritual journey, amid confusion and depression: his prose shows that, and conclusive evidence is provided by his religious poems to be considered in the next chapter. It is also true that he never expressed the mystical assurance and identification with Christ which are recorded about some of the saints (Francis of Assisi, for example). Gardner was surely right about his need for 'faith and moral effort'. However, there seems to be more of an overlap than she allowed between some of the religious poems and the sermons (where some passages seem close to what Francis felt about Christ). The poet and the preacher were not different men: instead, some of the poems as well as all of the sermons testify that Donne came to believe in the depths of his personality that he had not been merely seeking what Gardner called 'the meditation's deliberate stimulation of the emotions'. That makes is sound as if he believed that he did all the work. He had been praying that God would act to reveal his love by his power. He had been genuinely and unwillingly disturbed, filled with anxiety and fear, brought face to face with death, made to picture himself being ultimately rejected by God as well as by employers on earth. He had been to hell and back – and by the end of that crisis, he believed that he had not always been talking to himself: in his spiritual journey as in his search for sexual fulfilment, love had been given to him and the seeker had been found.

Although they have done excellent work in this field, some scholars have been unconvincing when they have attempted to overturn Gardner's verdict that in the early poetry of Donne there is nothing to suggest even 'latent spirituality'.

In *John Donne, Conservative Revolutionary* (1967), Nancy Andreasen argued that he was advocating a conservative moral position even in the poems about sexual relationships outside marriage. She suggested that when he appears to be celebrating or lamenting his fortunes or misfortunes as a sexual predator in fact he is already a kind of preacher, exposing the 'wrong use of the things of the world; the lovers, overly committed to goods which are transient by nature, bring misery on themselves because the joys of transient goods are transient joys; the lovers sin by making the things of the world an end rather than a means, and they punish themselves by choosing to love something which cannot fulfil their inordinate love'. In *Doubting Conscience* (1975) Dwight Cathcart wrote in a similar vein about the arguments with girlfriends which occupy a great deal of the erotic poetry: 'Donne's speaker, wanting to be in harmony with order but stymied because that order is unclear and not reflected in the special situation, needs a particular instrument to clarify the law which he feels governs his actions and to apply that law to his particular case. That instrument is casuistry' (philosophy about ethics, in that period usually based on theology). And in *Kinde Pity and Brave Scorn* (1982) M. Thomas Hester argued that any scorn in Donne's 'satyres' was due to the earnestness with which the young 'religious devotee' advocated a 'process of active Christian reform'.

But these are, it seems, the charitable verdicts of Christian scholars who have been too kind to the future preacher, and it is far more likely that the truth about the young Donne is less abnormal. If he combined a high moral tone when attacking the vices of women, courtiers and lawyers with a private life which was a combination of hot sexuality with cold ambition, he was not unique. And he would not be the only young man who while attacking other people's faults did not display a truly Christian spirit. The opening lines of his third 'satyre' used by Professor Hester in the title of his generous book may be understood less charitably if we feel less generous. They may be interpreted as a display of self-satisfied and patronizing contempt for those whom he is about to denounce:

> Kinde pitty chokes my spleene; brave scorn forbids
> Those teares to issue which swell my eye-lids . . .

Donne told a friend that the bitterness with which he poured 'skorne' on his seniors during and after 1593 was due in part to his grief that his brother had been the victim of laws which these seniors administered (we saw this on p. 46), but the mixture of scorn for older men with love for young women is not uncommon in young men, for the 1590s were not the last time in the history of the world when demonstrations of sincere idealism about the need for a new generation to strive for justice and peace in public life have been combined with a more indulgent attitude to youth's own sexual needs, resulting in a motto such as 'make love not war'. And the mixture is not incompatible with some uneasy self-questioning or self-criticism, as honesty breaks through. Donne's first 'satyre' seems to be an example of this. It has been interpreted as the acceptance of the duty of a Christian scholar to benefit others by being an evangelist or pastor in the wicked world (to be sure, the phrase 'lost sheep' occurs). It has also been understood as a debate between the body ('thou' or 'he') and the soul ('I'). But it seems more likely that this 'satyre' resulted from the introspection of a young man who is intelligent enough to see that emotionally he is two men.

A 'fondling motley humourist' (a foolish, changeable clown) comes to a scholar's study and suggests that he could have fun away from his books and his ideals. The scholar hesitates. He fears that if he comes on an expedition his companion will find him less attractive than someone 'more spruce' such as a soldier or a courtier, a magistrate clothed in velvet or a rich man handsome in silk and gold – or, alternatively, will prefer the company of a 'plumpe muddy whore or prostitute boy'. But after a brief conference 'with God and with the Muses' the scholar falls to the temptation: 'come, let's go'. In the street they do indeed come across more than one 'fine, silken, painted foole', and his red-blooded companion does indeed spot 'his Love in a windowe' – only to find that when he enters the brothel the place is overcrowded, a fight follows, and he is 'turn'd out of dore'. So the tempting companion returns to the boring scholar, 'hanging the head'. The last line of the poem reveals that the scholar's study is also the tempter's home. This is where the tempter 'must keepe his bed', waiting for the next time when the passions of youth may overcome ideals learned from books. Both of these men are Donne.

That first 'satyre' reminds us that Donne was a dramatist able to re-create street life, including low life, knowing something about it. Although his poems may not record his actual experiences they can show us what were the realities if a student in London in the 1590s felt that he needed a sexual relationship. He might have to visit a brothel and face dangers not only from venereal disease ('the Poxe') but also from other infections ('the Plague'). The alternative was to attempt to strike up a relationship with a woman who did not need to be paid – but who, if she was married, might have a furious husband and who, if single, might get bored.

Donne had at least one 'Sun' to brighten his life temporarily (as we saw on pp. 39–40), but whoever this sun was, she set. Perhaps she broke off their relationship because she sensed what was his normal attitude to women in this period. It was expressed in one of the witty 'paradoxes' which he wrote out for the entertainment of other young men, pretending to argue against a general opinion. The paradox which he advanced was that 'it is possible to find some vertue in some women' and his argument was that they overthrow valiant men and are patient when themselves overthrown. And despite the talk of some critics about the obscurity of his 'riddles', Donne could be very explicit about what he meant by women being overthrown. In *Metempsychosis* he gave this account of the reaction of the girl to the amorous ape:

> First she was silly and knew not what he ment . . .
> Succeeds an itchie warmth, that melts her quite;
> She knew not first, now cares not what he doth . . .

It would not be surprising if having been overthrown in this manner by an ape-like student, a woman were to recover her balance and escape as rapidly as possible. Then Donne would have to console himself by the kind of sour grapes which he set out in his paradox called 'A Defence of Women's Inconstancy':

'Women are like Flyes which feed amongst us at our Table, or Fleas sucking our verie blood, who leave not our most retired places free from their familiaritie.' A similar attitude was taken in another short piece of prose written somewhat later but also believed to be witty: women do not have souls any more than do apes, goats, foxes or serpents whose natures are similar to theirs and if men 'have given woemen soules' it is 'onely to make them capable of damnation'.

Usually the male speaker in the poems of the 1590s celebrates the release of his sexual urges in promiscuity. In 'Communitie' he begins as if he is in training to preach: 'Good wee must love, and must hate ill.' However, there are, he says, things which are neither good nor bad but simply natural, and among them is the law of 'wise Nature' that 'all may use' women. Women are themselves neither good nor evil,

> But they are ours as fruits are ours . . .
> Chang'd loves are but chang'd sorts of meat,
> And when he hath the kernell eate,
> Who doth not fling away the shell?

And in 'The Indifferent' (which means 'The Impartial') the speaker claims that he can love and discard not only blondes and brunettes but also the rich and the poor, the loners and the joiners, the country girls and the streetwise, the trusting and the sceptical, the sad and the happy:

> I can love her, and her, and you and you,
> I can love any, so she be not true.

So he practises promiscuity and preaches it:

Let mee, and doe you, twenty know.
Rob mee, but binde me not, and let me goe.

Several poems express this enthusiasm about the blessing bestowed by 'wise Nature' on promiscuity. In the seventeenth 'elegie' the speaker celebrates the bounty with which Nature pours out her gifts on one and all. In gratitude he announces that he will not confine his love to a dark lady – or to a blonde:

Let no man tell me such a one is faire,
And worthy all alone my love to share . . .
I love her well, and would, if need were, dye
To do her service. But followes it that I
Must serve her onely, when I may have choice?
The law is hard, and shall not have my voice.
The last I saw in all extreames is faire,
And holds me in the Sun-beames of her haire; . . .
Another's brown, I like her not the worse,
Her tongue is soft and takes me with discourse . . .
How happy were our Syres in ancient times
Who held plurality of loves no crime!

And in 'Confined Love' the speaker makes the witty suggestion that the law that a woman must 'know' only one man was invented – and the inventor was a man who was too 'false or weake' to enjoy what Nature has provided. 'Sunne, Moone, or Starres' are not forbidden to smile on all; birds and beasts are not rebuked when they choose new lovers; ships are built to 'seeke new lands'; and a man knows that to spread oneself is not only natural, it is good:

Good is not good, unlesse
A thousand it possesse . . .

In 'Love's Deitie' the speaker recalls that it is the work of Cupid to fit 'actives to passives' and to unite two hearts by one 'even flame', of course keeping the woman passive – but now this woman loves someone else and he is hurt. His first thought is that Cupid's law that two hearts must be united in love and loyalty must be forgotten now that she has left him. He must remember the good old days, before Cupid got to work, when everyone was free and 'lov'd most' without any law about the need for loyal love. So

> I long to talke with some old lover's ghost,
> Who died before the god of Love was borne . . .

But he is still irritated by the fact that she, not he, made the decision to leave. Then on second thoughts he sees that even now people have freedom – and that includes women. If his ex-mistress were to pretend to love him, that would be 'falsehood'. So she must be free of him – and he must be free of her. And in 'Love's Diet' the speaker rejoices that he need not waste many tears because a mere woman has 'burnt my letters'. There are plenty of women left and the sport of sex is like starting up birds for hawks to chase:

> I spring a mistresse, sweare, write, sigh and weepe:
> And the game kill'd, or lost, goe talke, and sleepe.

Casualness when an affair ends is possible because 'love' is simply sex, as 'Love's Progress' declares. Men can claim that in their wives they admire virtue, beauty or money, but if 'we'

> Make love to woman; virtue is not she:
> As beauty is not, nor wealth . . .

Only 'one thing' in a woman matters to a man and it is 'the Centrique part'. To find it, a man should not begin with the hair, or with the feet although the feet are 'the first part that comes to bed'. A man should go straight for the centre, which is compared with an open purse. The message of 'The Prohibition' is that sex is not really about love, any more than it is about hate; it is about a man's need of the 'one thing'.

In 'Woman's Constancy' the speaker works through possible arguments which a woman will use when she has left him after loving him 'one whole day'. They are all bad arguments, he knows, and she uses them only in order to 'justifie' herself when she has already 'purpos'd change'. He could 'dispute and conquer' – but he will not bother to argue, partly because she is a 'lunatique' and partly because 'by to morrow I may thinke so too'. (Here the light-hearted bachelor is not yet the father of the Donnes' first daughter, named Constance.)

In other poems he is also very far from being the husband who through marriage has learned both loyalty and sensitivity. In 'The Curse' he exclaims at the start:

> Who ever guesses, thinks, or dreames he knows
> Who is my mistris, wither by this curse . . .

But at the end he shows that he is not worried that scandal may harm a woman's reputation. Let his curse, he says,

> Fall on that man; For if it be a shee
> Nature beforehand hath out-cursed mee.

And in 'The Triple Foole' he again treats women as raw material for his lusts and his poems. Clearly he does not intend his apology

> For loving, and for saying so
> In whining Poëtry

to be taken seriously, for he explains that for him – which is what matters – writing poetry can 'allay' the 'paines' of love. His only complaint is that when he has written a poem 'some man' can make a song of it, 'his art and voice to show'. Then the poet's pain can come back, which is irritating.

In some other poems he does seem to acknowledge that parting with a woman may bring 'anguish' to her, but that is still treated as a bit of a joke. It is the theme of 'The Message' but this poem is not totally heart-broken, for it is a song which was set to music, like the song which laments that finding a woman who is both 'true and faire' would be like catching 'a falling starre'. It is also the theme of 'The Apparition' but this poem is not totally about a man's defeat. A mistress has become the speaker's 'Murdresse' by scorning him, but he enjoys himself as he expects to return as a ghost. He will find her in bed with her new partner. She will pinch the new man when she wakes up in the middle of the night, needing comfort, but he is already 'tyr'd' of her and will pretend to sleep while he thinks 'thou calls't for more'. As a neglected wretch now bathed in a cold sweat, she will 'lye a veryer ghost than I'. And the speaker adds to his gloating pleasure by refusing to divulge what he will then say or do.

A man, he reckons, should not worry too much about the partings and other disappointments which occur in a life of promiscuity, but it is illuminating to notice what at this stage Donne thinks will worry a man. In 'Love's Alchymie' he looks back over his career as a lover, when 'I have lov'd, and got, and told', and finds 'Oh, 'tis imposture all'. Lovers dream of getting 'a rich and long delight' in a 'summer's night' – and find that the night is like winter, for an evening of love grows cold and then the darkness is long. There is nothing substantial or lasting in sex; it is a mere 'Buble's shadow'. For men, the lesson is 'hope not for minde in women' – and hope not for lasting physical satisfaction either, for when 'possest' at the end of the excitement women feel like dead flesh, like 'Mummy', a powder made by grinding Egyptian mummies in order to make a medicine which was in this period recommended by some doctors. In 'Farewell to Love' the speaker regrets that after intercourse comes

> A kinde of sorrowing dulnesse to the minde.

But then he sees why Nature has made a man 'eager' only 'for a minute': sex is exhausting and shortens life, so the eagerness is not meant to satisfy for long, yet sex is necessary in order to beget children, so the eagerness must return. Sex is Nature's game too.

Twice the young Donne adopted the voice of a woman in order to write a poem about sex and each time he suggested that women are really interested only in the 'one thing' which all men possess. In 'Breake of Day' (a song) he imagined a mistress complaining that her man thinks it necessary to go to work just because the sun has risen. Surely, all we need is love? Love 'brought us hether', so why 'Must businesse thee from hence remove?' In 'Sapho to Philaenis' he wrote what has been welcomed as 'the first female homosexual love poem in English', as if he was a precursor of Katherine Philips in the celebration of 'female friendship'. But in his poem the relationship between the women is not, and never has been, unalterably lesbian. The weeping Sappho remembers her absent female lover, and their love 'brest to brest or thighs to thighs', but she weeps because Philaenis has abandoned her in favour of 'some soft boy' or 'harsh rough man'. At an earlier stage she had herself been dropped by a male lover, here called Phao. In the end she manages to express best wishes for a heterosexual future:

> So may thy mighty, amazing beauty move
> Envy in all women and in all men love.

This poem which appears to be liberal about homosexuality has more aptly been called (by Ronald Corthell) a 'heterosexual male fantasy' since in the end it repeats a familiar message to women: every woman needs a man, they are made to fit together. It is a bold poem: it depicts Sappho touching her body in front of a mirror while thinking about her female lover and it took courage to do this in an age when the possibility of a lesbian relationship was unmentionable in polite society. (Even Ovid, normally very relaxed in all matters to do with sex, wrote his poem about Sappho's grief when her male lover deserted her.) But all Donne's references to homosexual relationships between men are hostile and there is no good reason to think that he made an exception for such relationships between women. The explanation of this poem seems to need to take account of the almost certain fact that it was written for the amusement and encouragement of randy young men, to remind them that it takes a man to satisfy a woman.

The most famous of the poems about sex could not be published before 1669 (during the merry Restoration over which Charles II presided) because it is so explicitly lustful, being then entitled 'To his Mistress Going to Bed'. She is imagined as a wealthy woman and (presumably) as someone else's wife: she wears a 'glittering' girdle, a star-spangled 'breast plate', a chiming watch and a coronet. Or at least she wears all this until instructed by the speaker to strip. The most relevant part of him is already 'standing' but he becomes further excited as her gown comes off. Theological terms are now used with a touch of blasphemy: women are 'mystick books' when their bodies are 'reveal'd' and like the Saviour they have merits which can be 'imputed' as 'grace' to men who are sinners. Geography is also used with a touch of humour which partly conceals the brutality of the comparison between colonization and the conquest of a woman's body:

> Licence my roaving hands, and let them go
> Before, behind, between, above, below.
> O my America! my new-found-land,
> My kingdome, safeliest with one man man'd . . .

But there is no ambiguity about what is going to happen:

> Full nakedness! All joyes are due to thee . . .

And we are told where he locates this woman's self: 'as to a Midwife shew thy self'.

'Full nakedness' is what we are invited to praise in other 'elegies'. One tells a mistress not to worry about her husband's jealousy when in reality she would be delighted to see him dead. The second recommends a friend to marry Flavia, a woman who is exceptionally 'foule': because of her age and looks, she will have no alternative to being faithful. The third proclaims that 'women are made for men, not him, not mee' and a jilted lover must take the consequences of that law of nature. The fourth denounces the protective family of a mistress. The father threatens to deprive her of the money which is the 'food of our love'; the mother suspects that she is pregnant as the fruit of that love; the little brothers are bribed to tell tales of what is going on in 'our chamber'. Now the speaker is really fed up; he has taught his silk clothes to stay silent as he makes his way to 'our chamber' but he has been betrayed by his loud perfume. The seventh 'elegie' attacks a woman to whom he has taught the whole art of love including the 'Alphabet of flowers': now she is making love to another (her husband?). The eighth is a merciless portrait of someone else's mistress. The tenth announces that a dream is better than any real mistress, since 'all our joyes' are 'fantasticall'. And other 'elegies' which may or may not be by Donne have the same character.

Clearly not all these celebrations of promiscuity can be autobiographical. He seems to have been guarding himself against all his poems being read as such when he said in a much later sermon that he had written some poems in order to impress young men who 'thought it wit to make Sonnets of their own sins'. In real life he 'had no means to doe some sins, whereby I might be equal to my fellow', but he would 'say I had done that which I never did'. What had been genuine, he claimed, had been 'the pride I had to write feelingly about it' (2:107–8). But even if many or all of the details were imagined in order to titillate his fellow students, it still says a lot about the young Donne that he could imagine so vividly a life so promiscuous and so contemptuous. We have before us evidence of what he thought would impress men who impressed him, even if it was not what he often practised – and of what tempted him, even if he stuck to his books for most of the time.

The erotic poems of the 1590s were no doubt influenced by Donne's reading of Ovid, the Roman poet who was highly fashionable among the sophisticated English of the Elizabethan Renaissance, but Donne added to this influence something which made his own celebration of love distinctively his own. There was in his poetry a disquiet, a dramatic intensity, an anxious tenseness, a brutality, not to be found in the other Elizabethan Ovidians – or in Ovid himself. And Donne could write poetry in a tradition which was similar to the Ovidian fashion only in that it, too, was imported from Italy. He could write in the 'Petrarchan' style begun by Boccaccio, Petrarch and their followers in the Italian Renaissance. This was poetry about love-without-physical-sex. There could be drama in it but it was the drama of frustrated suffering – and there could be anxiety, the anxiety of being perpetually unable either to get, or to forget, the woman who was desired. But about this Petrarchan tradition there was also an air of unreality and when Donne wrote poems in this tradition the unreality became their most striking feature. These are the places at which the attacks on 'conceits' without foundations in facts ought to have been directed.

A good example is 'Twicknam Garden', so named after one of the residences of Lucy, the sparkling young Countess of Bedford; she took it over in 1607. It is most unlikely that Donne, who was then unemployed, was in a sexual relationship with a countess who was one of the richest, most fashionable and most influential women in England and the queen's closest friend. But Donne adopts the Petrarchan stance in order to flatter and tease her:

> Blasted with sighs, and surrounded with teares,
> Hither I come to seek the spring . . .

The speaker now wishes, however, that it was still winter, so that the budding trees might not 'laugh' at his misery. He would like to remain in the garden like 'a stone fountain weeping', so that lovers could 'take my teares' and by a test see that in comparison with his sorrow the tears of the lady who says good-bye are 'false' because she does not really love him, surprising as this is. 'None is true but shee'; the countess persists in being faithful to her husband, to whom she had been married at the age of thirteen and to whom she was to remain faithful when he had been paralysed by a fall from a horse; so 'her truth kills me'.

Another example of Petrarchan flirtation which seems artificial may also have been written for the enjoyment of the unattainable Countess of Bedford. 'The Blossome' is placed in a garden and again the time is spring. During a visit for 'sixe or seaven dayes' the speaker has watched the birth and growth of a blossom which now 'dost laugh and triumph on this bough' – but tonight there will be a frost and tomorrow this blossom will lie fallen on the ground. The speaker now addresses his heart: it, too, must fall from the 'forbidden tree' in the Garden of Eden, the tree of 'knowledge' which is slang for sex, since the lady of the garden will not respond sexually. To this the heart replies that its charm will prove irresistible if the speaker removes his body from the scene. So it is allowed to stay behind for 'twenty dayes', without the body. But it is warned:

> A naked thinking heart, that makes no show,
> Is to a woman but a kinde of Ghost.

Meanwhile the speaker is off to London, where he will become 'more fat by being with men' and then, rejoined by the heart, will give himself to a 'friend' who will be 'as glad to have my body as my minde'. Here is another poem of flirtation which ends with a reaffirmation of marriage for the lady and for the visiting poet, in different marriages – and both poems may well have been written as thank-you letters at the end of visits to the countess in Twickenham.

It does not seem merely sentimental if we guess that the reference to growing fatter 'by being with men' points to the eating, drinking and men's talk in one of the clubs to which Donne belonged in London, before he went back to Mitcham to offer heart, mind and body to his long-suffering wife. But Anne would have reason to be suspicious or jealous of her husband's connection with this rich and glamorous Lucy, specially when the countess condescended to be a godmother of the Donnes' second daughter, to attend the baptism in Mitcham when the baby was named Lucy, and to visit their cottage. Donne had cosy suppers with this patroness in London while his wife was left at home with their children. He told her in a letter that 'my best depth of understanding is to be governed by you' and promised to write poems only for her, explaining to a friend that she 'only hath power to cast the fetters of verse upon my free meditations'. She asked for copies of his poems and in return showed him some of her own. There was mutual admiration.

One of his new poems was addressed to her with a flattery which would have amounted to blasphemy had it been meant – or taken – literally:

> Reason is our Soule's left hand, Faith her right,
> By these wee reach divinity, that's you . . .
> But soone the reasons why you are loved by all
> Grow infinite, and so passe reason's reach . . .

The poem went on to praise her 'birth and beauty', her 'learning and religion'. She was 'God's masterpeece' and

> The first good Angell, since the world's frame stood,
> That ever did in woman's shape appeare.

Another poem flattering the Countess of Bedford to the point of obvious unreality began 'You have refin'd me' but Donne was not too refined: he reused some of these ideas in his poem flattering the Countess of Huntingdon. He found that his anxiety was justified, for the first countess who had bestowed her favour on him was indeed mightily offended. She was not going to compete with other ladies for the attention of a poet; poets were meant to compete for her favour (and cash). She was even more put out when Donne wrote – and actually printed – long poems in fulsome praise of an obscure girl, Elizabeth Drury. While still in France with the Drurys the chastened poet began a verse-letter of apology and a draft survives, uncompleted. He wrote to Goodyer that 'I have been heretofore too immodest towards her, and I suffer this purgatory for it'. After a reconciliation she promised to settle all his debts. In the end she did not, pleading that she now had her own financial problems but also letting it be known that she did not think that the poet who had called her God's masterpiece would make an ideal priest. She fell ill and became both the patient and the convert of a doctor who was also a Puritan – and who definitely disapproved of Donne. A relationship which had once been overheated cooled permanently, no doubt to Anne's relief.

Not much heat was left to warm the heart of the Countess of Huntingdon, but Donne did his best. He began by teasing her:

> Man to God's image, Eve to man's was made.

But he continued by acclaiming her as a miraculous 'new starre' in the sky: 'that's heavenly things, that's you'. And he cleverly pretended he was not exaggerating:

> If you can thinke these flatteries they are,
> For then your judgement is below my praise.

Even less heat could be produced in honour of the Countess of Salisbury. His poem to her in August 1614 compared her with a summer's day:

> Faire, great and good, since seeing you we see
> What Heaven can doe, and what any Earth can be.

But this time the poet was not really in the Petrarchan mood. For reasons already set out in Chapter 3, Donne felt that he was lying 'in a dark Cave, yea in a Grave'.

A less fraught relationship developed with the widowed Magdalen Herbert, the calm and thoroughly good mother of Donne's friends Sir Edward and the poet George, and a poem somewhat like 'Twicknam Garden' seems to have resulted from a visit to Montgomery Castle in Wales, the Herberts' family seat.

The castle stood on Primrose Hill and the 1635 edition of the poems added a sub-title to 'The Primrose', saying that this location was why this poem was so named. In it the speaker declared that on this hill 'I walke to finde a true Love', but he has found that the lady must be 'more than woman' because 'shee would get above all thought of sexe' and would 'thinke to move my heart to study her, and not to love'. If this meeting was with Magdalen Herbert, it was part of a close friendship which continued when she married again. When she died Donne preached a passionate sermon about her life (7:61–93) which ended by saying that following her example could make anyone a saint.

Izaak Walton, who heard that sermon and saw him weep, linked Donne's poem 'The Autumnall' with Magdalen Herbert. There seems to be no way to prove that he was wrong, but if he was right the poem must have been a piece of teasing, not a serious description of reality. If this poem seriously referred to her, and was shown to her, it is a wonder that the friendship grew, for here is a struggle to find compliments for the beauty of an 'Autumnall face' complete with 'wrinkles', before old age brings a winter face with a 'slacke' skin, a 'worne out' mouth and missing teeth. The most that he can offer is the thought that her wrinkles are 'Love's graves' because as a 'trench' or 'tombe' each wrinkle records a past which has been spent loving – with this hope for the future:

> Since such love's motion natural is, may still
>   My love descend and journey down the hill,
> Not panting after growing beauties, so
>   I shall ebbe out with them who home-ward goe.

That offer to accompany the woman downhill all the way does not sound as if it was made to one with a husband already at her side, and if it was made to Magdalen Herbert before her second marriage (in 1608) it was made before she was aged 42. At that age she married a rich man who was twenty years younger and famously handsome (John Aubrey, who was his friend, says that people would go out in the street in order to admire); so it seems probable that she had not lost her looks or her charm. Almost twenty years later Donne could still praise her 'comeliness' as he preached about her life. He admitted that 'melancholy' had afflicted her in her declining years but he preached the hope that her beauty would be restored in her resurrection: 'That body at last shall have her last expectation satisfied, and dwell bodily with that Righteousnesse, in these new Heavens and new Earth, for ever, and ever, and ever, and infinite and super-infinite evers' (8:92). It seems very unlikely that such a woman would have received 'The Autumnall' as 'an exquisite compliment', which was Grierson's guess.

In 'The Undertaking' the speaker gives the advice to keep Platonic 'love' well hidden because no one will believe that in real life a man and a woman who are close friends can 'forget the Hee and Shee' and love only the 'loveliness within'. And in 'The Relique' he imagines the interpretation which will be put on the bones of friends who say about themselves that they knew 'no difference of sexe': people will dismiss the idea of a sexless partnership and the bones will be venerated as the relics of lovers. And it seems that Donne's own emotions could not be stirred deeply unless the difference between 'Hee and Shee' had in it the possibility of physical expression. Without that, what he writes about women sounds unreal.

The same atmosphere of unreality is found in verse-letters to men. Donne was a pioneer in using this medium which became fashionable suddenly in the 1590s. He tells Samuel Brooke 'I am harsh' – but he is not, for he flatters extravagantly. Thomas Woodward is told that he has produced 'wit and Art' better than anything 'before or after': Donne admits that he has helped his friend to be a poet, but 'I am thy Creator, thou my Saviour'. Samuel Brooke is praised for the 'bright sparkes' of his own poetry and Donne apologizes that there is 'noe fuell' in the poems which he sends. This tone is found in the tributes of homage and love paid to each other by many men of this period but its adoption by the arrogant Donne is notable.

The poems of mourning are also extravagant. Two were written at the request of the Countess of Bedford, to honour cousins of hers who had died in her home in Twickenham. Lady Marckham could be flattered like the countess herself:

> She sinn'd, but just enough to let us see
> That God's word must be true, *All sinners be.*

About Cecilia Boulstred he wrote that she had been 'proofe 'gainst sins of youth' although in an honest poem (which to his horror had been shown to her) Ben Jonson had called the living woman the resident prostitute in the royal court. After the death of Henry, Prince of Wales, in November 1612, Donne's sense of the nation's loss was probably genuine, but in the tribute which he added to those coming from other poets he wrote so obscurely that Jonson claimed that the lament had been composed solely in order 'to match Sir Ed: Herbert in obscurenesse'.

His two 'Anniversaries' were also a lament and also disregarded common sense; Edmund Gosse thought them 'preposterous'. Many readers have found them very obscure because of the difficulty of answering the question: what did Donne mean when he told Jonson that they had been written about 'the idea of a Woman' and not specifically about the life of young Elizabeth Drury? It has been suggested that he had Queen Elizabeth I in mind, partly because near the beginning of the 'First Anniversarie' he referred to the custom of a royal 'progress' through the houses of the nobility and richer gentry in a region of the countryside before returning to a palace well before winter:

> When that Queene ended here her progresse time,
> And as t'her standing house, to heaven did clymbe . . .

But that is the only comparison made between the two Elizabeths and it seems very improbable that Donne's motive was to write a long lament for the real queen so long after her death (as it is improbable that he had planned to attack her in *Metempsychosis* while she was alive). Equally far-fetched is the proposal that he was lamenting the suppression of the cult of the Virgin Mary, although the cult of England's Protestant queen had been more or less the official substitute for that Catholic devotion. Had Donne so wished, he could have crushed Jonson's criticism by saying that he had indeed paid a tribute to Mary, but instead he said repeatedly in his poem 'Shee's dead' – which no devotee would have said about the Blessed Virgin. And if he intended the 'Shee' to refer to the *anima mundi* ('soul of the world') in pagan thought, or to the Wisdom within the creation in the Old Testament (also feminine), or to the *logos* or divine Word within all that exists in the New Testament, he left no clear indication. It seems that we must accept what he did say: that he wrote about a woman. And we must accept that her name was Elizabeth Drury, because that was why her parents rewarded Donne for honouring her.

However, we must also accept that Donne did not mean to write about her 'as she was', as if he had been writing a school report about the girl's progress or lack of it. As he explained to a friend, 'when I had received so very good testimony of her worthinesse . . . it became me to say, not what I was sure was just truth, but the best that I could conceive'. It seems that he wrote about the Image of God in a woman's immortal soul. He had done so before. When flattering a great lady such as the Countess of Bedford he had claimed that he stopped short of idolatry, for he was praising 'that Deitie which dwells in you', in 'your vertuous Soule'. Similarly, when he called the Countess of Huntingdon a star or 'heavenly things', he could claim that his intention was 'God in you to praise'. Now he could not classify Elizabeth Drury as a great lady but he could celebrate her as a pure virgin – and did so, not only in the

'Anniversaries' but also in the epitaph for this 'Paradise without a serpent' which he composed for her tomb. And he could praise her as a model soul, as an unblemished Image of God, as

> Shee that was best, and first originall
> Of all fair copies . . .

Her death could then be used as a peg on which to hang a wide-ranging religious meditation.

Of course he exaggerated her merits, as he exaggerated the world's grief, decay and matching death. He told the world that it would have found it easier to spare 'the Sunne, or Man' than to lose her, for

> Her name defin'd thee, gave thee forme and frame.

He wrote that 'a fainte weake love of virtue and of good' remaining in the world was only 'her Ghost' walking in the 'twi-light'. He wrote that no health was left, lives were short, sizes were small. In the new society

> 'Tis all in pieces, all cohaerence gone . . .
> Prince, Subject, Father, Sonne, are things forgot . . .

He wrote that the world had no more beauty of proportion or colour, that the sky now dropped not rain but meteors – and he wrote much other nonsense. In her study of the impact of the new science Marjorie Hope Nicolson claimed that the 'Anniversaries' were 'an "epitome" of the intellectual universe in which Donne lived', of 'what the Elizabethans had made of the world and the universe' – but as other scholars have demonstrated, the Elizabethan world-picture could be pessimistic or optimistic according to one's mood. The compliment paid by Joseph Hall at the time was more accurate: what Donne created, he wrote, was a 'world of wit'. The poet himself denied that the 'Anniversaries' were intended to describe the world and the universe in the light of new knowledge. He asked

> What hope have we to know our selves, when wee
> Know not the least things, which for our own use bee?
> We see in Authors, to stiffe to recant,
> A hundred controversies of an Ant

– and he had no intention of wasting time on a close observation of ants. Nor did he propose to discuss questions about 'why grasse is greene' or 'why our blood is red' or 'what Caesar did' or what 'Cicero said'. Such 'matters of fact' were to him 'unconcerning'.

Donne was in debt and very depressed at this time. The world which the poem said had been devastated by Elizabeth Drury's death was, it seems, his own mental world, darkened by the problems in his own life – although no doubt he was also sensitive to the grief of the girl's parents. But as he had done before, in his depression he kept his wit. He also kept the faith which he had expressed in his 'Holy Sonnets' (to be discussed very shortly), that the cure for the sorrows of life is death. It is illuminating to compare the 'Anniversaries' with *Metempsychosis*. They are united by a sub-title: in 1601 the long poem was sub-titled 'The Progresse of the Soule' and in 1611 Donne put at the head of his second 'Anniversarie' the words 'Of the Progresse of the Soule'. They are also united by a depressed atmosphere: in 1601 the 'age of rusty iron' made a poet who was close to the fighting between individuals and factions think of the world as a battlefield without morality, while in 1611 the disappointment of his hopes made him view the world as a desert without life. But the intervening ten years have strengthened his beliefs that the 'soule' belongs to one individual person (he had long ago abandoned the 'conceit' that the soul of evil could transmigrate through many creatures) and that the person's only ultimate hope must lie in heaven. In that limited but supremely important sense, the soul can make 'progress'.

In the 'Second Anniversarie' he began with the most tasteless of all his 'conceits': the world is now like the head of a criminal who has just been beheaded. But he continued in a style which seems to be a sign of a far greater seriousness, for he moved to the 'essentiall joy' of heaven and this theme inspired snatches of poetry as fine as anything he ever wrote, for example:

> Thinke then, My soule, that death is but a Groome,
> Which brings a Taper to the outward roome,
> Whence thou spiest first a little glimmering light,
> And after brings it nearer to thy sight . . .

What seems to have happened at a deep level in Donne's personality is that he had been cut down. In the 'pride and lust' of his early manhood he had used women promiscuously, as objects which could briefly satisfy his strong sexuality. He had despised them, as in his moral-seeming arrogance he had despised men who for the time being ranked above him in society. Then the 'idea of a Woman' had taken flesh before his eyes, in the person of Anne More whom he married in a great act of self-sacrifice – to be followed by a miserable period in which he paid the price. Now he had to flatter courtiers, or great ladies, or the rich parents of a dead girl, in order to earn money to keep his own head above water and for the support of his family. He had been humbled and a part of the humiliation had been having to adopt what he had previously despised as the feminine position, at the receiving end. It was relevant that when he thought of his soul – the essential Donne – he thought of it in the manner of his age, as feminine. And so he learned to accept as an undeserved gift the salvation which does not seem to be available from any other source. At any rate, that is what his 'Divine Poems' said he was learning, step by step, and to them we now turn.

8 Batter my heart

Batter my heart, three person'd God: for you
As yet but knocke, breathe, shine,
and seeke to mend . . .
Holy Sonnets *XIV*

Donne's poem called 'The Crosse' was probably written when he was about 35. It is not a meditation on the Passion of Christ but it reuses ancient and medieval suggestions that cross-like images are widespread and, with this heritage, it is a defence of the Church of England's retention of the ceremony of 'signing with the cross' in Baptism. To Puritans the ceremony seemed unbiblical and Popish but to Donne it was a reminder that crosses are seen everywhere in daily life and particularly in the life of a Christian. He wrote

Swimme, and at every stroake thou art thy Crosse . . .

A bird in flight, or a mast with arms for the sails, also makes a cross. But more importantly, a Christian must find 'joy in crosses': 'the eye needs crossing', so does the heart and so does 'concupiscence of witt', the lust to be clever with words.

He seems to have yielded to that last temptation even while writing that poem, which was bookish: many books were available helping devotion to the cross of Christ and some offered pictures of the crosses to be met in daily life. His seven sonnets called 'La Corona' (because they are woven together somewhat like a crown) are of much the same character although they suggest a real effort to make the traditional images more relevant to him personally.

The effort was being urged in this period by many Catholic writers on spirituality and some Anglican Protestants such as Joseph Hall, who wrote on *The Arte of Divine Meditation* in 1607. (Hall supplied verses to commend the 'Anniversaries': he, too, owed much to the Drurys, and he ended up as Bishop of Norwich.) These seven sonnets seem to be the 'Hymns' sent with a verse-letter to Magdalen Herbert in 1607.

The first is a prayer of preparation. Donne's mood is 'low devout melancholie', but the closure is more hopeful than strict Calvinists would allow, for he asks

> that heart and voice be lifted high,
> *Salvation to all that will is nigh.*

A rejection of strict Calvinism is seen in the remaining sonnets, which adapt the Catholic tradition of 'saying the rosary', reciting a series of prayers in honour of the Blessed Virgin. Some adaptation is necessary because the centre must now be the Saviour, not his sorrowful or joyful mother, but the devotion expressed is more Catholic than Protestant. It is said of the Virgin that in her womb Christ 'can take no sinne' and an old form of praise is quoted:

> Thy Maker's maker, and thy Father's mother,
> Thou hast light in darke; and shutst in little roome,
> *Immensity cloystered in thy deare wombe.*

More striking still in this meditation on the Annunciation to Mary is Donne's reuse of three lines from *Metempsychosis.* There these lines had been a passing mention of the crucifixion, in the course of a reference to the story ('as devout and sharpe men may fittly guesse') that the cross stood on the very place where the forbidden tree had stood in the garden of Eden. Now the lines became a far more reverent contemplation of what had entered the Virgin's womb:

> That All which alwayes is All every where,
> Which cannot sin, and yet all sinnes must beare,
> Which cannot die, yet cannot chuse but die . . .

In accordance with the tradition of the rosary the poem then moves from the Nativity to the Crucifixion, stopping only to consider the visit to the Jerusalem temple in Christ's boyhood. It moves devoutly and these meditations employ praises which had been voiced by the devout in earlier generations: in the temple the Word which had been silent in infancy 'speakes wonders', on the cross evil men 'prescribe a Fate' to the Lord 'whose creature Fate is'. But when the poet finally addresses the crucified Christ directly, at the end of the fifth sonnet, it is with words which sound conventional rather than intense, and the remaining two sonnets maintain the same tone. The impression is left that Donne is doing his best to imagine salvation, but as yet it does not mean everything to him, so that his poetry – always essentially about his own feelings – remains frigid.

In 1608 the feast of the Annunciation (Lady Day) fell on the same day as Good Friday and this coincidence in the calendar inspired Donne to write a poem about his soul in contemplation of the Christ who is conceived in the womb and killed on the cross:

> Shee sees him nothing twice at once, who is all;
> Shee sees a Cedar plant it selfe, and fall,
> Her Maker put to making, and the head
> Of life, at once, not yet alive, yet dead . . .

But on this Good Friday did Christ mean 'all' to Donne? It seems from this poem that he was more preoccupied with thinking up 'conceits' which would rhyme. Yet poems which appear to have been written during the next twelve months are of a very different character, following a long period of depression and an illness which seems to have been neuritis.

Helen Gardner gained wide acceptance for her theory that early in 1609 Donne sent six sonnets about the 'Last Things' (death and its sequels) to Richard Sackville, who had just inherited the earldom of Dorset. Some facts appeared to support this theory. Six sonnets with this character have been included among the 'Divine Poems' in the printed editions, which have also included a verse-letter addressed 'To E. of D. with six holy Sonnets'. Also, this earl was the patron who appointed Donne as vicar of St Dunstan's in 1624, shortly before his own death. And three of the sonnets about death seem to have been written before the middle of 1609, for they express views which are contradicted by what Donne wrote after that date. However, there are problems about this suggestion.

One is that the verse-letter 'To E. of D.' pays tribute to the 'fatherly yet lusty Ryme' of the person addressed, and it is said that his poetry is related to Donne's own 'drossie Rymes' as a father is related to his son. This is puzzling because in 1609 Richard Sackville was seventeen years younger than Donne and although his grandfather was a good poet if the young man wrote poems none has survived. Another problem is that since the poems sent were about the fear of death and hell – although they were called 'songs' – they would have been a very strange present to send as the 'fruits' of his own poems to a young man who had just inherited a fortune and was resolved to spend it to the limit and beyond. John Aubrey mentioned in his *Brief Lives* that this earl 'lived in the greatest grandeur of any nobleman of his time in England'. However, having no son he left his estates to his brother heavily encumbered with debts. It therefore seems probable that Donne can be spared the charge that he bared his soul with thoughts about God, sin and hell in the hope of receiving some of the money which an immature aristocrat was about to spend on luxury with gusto.

Were the 'six holy Sonnets' sent to another patron? It seems probable that they were and a suggestion has been made, based on the fact that in the important Westmoreland manuscript which was copied out by Rowland Woodward, and in the first printed collection of the poetry, this verse-letter which submits the sonnets to a patron was included among other verse-letters which date from a period before 1609. To add slightly to the confusion, here in the title 'E. of D.' becomes 'L. of D.'.

In 1988 Dennis Flynn therefore proposed that the verse-letter was sent to the Earl of Derby ten years or so before 1609, but he still maintained that the poems enclosed were about the Last Things. This proposal was connected with Flynn's theory that the Earl of Derby was the member of the Catholic nobility who had acted as Donne's employer and patron. However, here fresh problems arise. These poems are not Catholic in doctrine about the Last Things and they are joined to other sonnets which find no solution for their religious anxiety in the Catholic reliance on the sacraments. And if Donne was so seriously troubled about his sins when confronting death in the early 1600s, it is indeed curious that he also wrote *Metempsychosis.* The only safe conclusion seems to be that we simply do not know who 'E. of D.' or 'L. of D.' was. 'E. of D.' was probably part of a title added many years after the writing of the poem. 'L. of D.' would imply a less formal reference to the same man; for example, the Earl of Dorset could be called 'My Lord of Dorset'.

If a reader is intrigued by this little puzzle, it may be worth mentioning my own guess about the identity of 'E. of D'. Henry Danvers was a brother of the John who married Magdalen Herbert in 1608. He was a soldier who at that time was one of the commanders in Ireland but he was to be given more agreeable positions by two kings, and was to be created Earl of Danby in

1622. Like the other earls who have been nominated as E. of D. he is not known to have written poetry, but if Donne did flatter his efforts in that hobby as 'fatherly' and 'lusty' it would not have been very extraordinary: the two men were of almost the same age and although in his hotblooded youth Henry Danvers had killed an enemy in the course of a family feud he had been pardoned and seems to have developed a character which was compatible with a feeling for poetry and poets. He may have been influenced by his years as a page in attendance on a soldier-poet, Sir Philip Sidney.

Years later he formed a close relationship with George Herbert. Walton wrote that he 'lov'd Mr Herbert so very much' that he had him to stay in his 'noble House' in Wiltshire so that he might regain health. While enjoying the sensitive hospitality the patient did indeed recover, so 'improv'd to a good degree of strength and chearfulness' that he resolved to marry a neighbour's daughter and to become a parish priest. In the same spirit Henry Danvers was a benefactor of Oxford University, paying for the creation of its beautiful Botanic Garden in the year when he was made an earl. John Aubrey, who was not sentimental, praised him as a man 'of a magnificent and munificent spirit'. It would therefore not be surprising if in 1609, when he was sick at heart as well as physically ill, Donne thought that having recently dedicated some of his religious poems to Magdalen Herbert he would send others to her brother-in-law.

John Carey has (perhaps wisely) dismissed this little debate about whether 'E. of D.' was the earl of Dorset, of Derby or of Danby. In his edition of Donne's poetry (1990, p. xxviii) he suggested that the Holy Sonnets may 'belong to Donne's relationship with the Countess of Bedford' and may be essentially a lament about the poet's social and financial humiliation although this basically secular concern is clothed in religious language in order to take account of 'the Countess's Calvinism'. But no solid argument was added to this theory. Equally questionable is the theory of Arthur

Marotti that these poems 'encoded' Donne's dissatisfaction with unemployment and illness. However, in his earlier book on Donne Carey offered an interpretation which was more probable. Then he found in the Holy Sonnets a 'need for God', a fear of damnation', a 'fear that he belongs to the devil', a 'writhing in the trap' because the Protestant insistence on an emotional faith which he could not feel was for Donne 'a recipe for anguish' (pp. 35–43). That emphasis on the genuinely religious content of these poems – of course not excluding the influence of the experiences of unemployment and illness – does much more justice to what Donne wrote.

Carey's earlier emphasis on the poet's genuine 'anguish' also illuminates the fact that Donne turned to the formal structure of the fourteen-line rhyming sonnet in order to express painfully real religious emotions. The sonnet had been used in English love poetry since Sir Thomas Wyatt and Henry Howard, Earl of Surrey, had imitated and developed Petrarch's *Canzoniere*; both men had died in the 1540s. Shakespeare had of course written sonnets of a wider character, and Henry Lok published *Sundry Christian Passions Contained in Two Hundred Sonnets* while Donne was writing about other passions in the 1590s, but Donne was the first major English poet to use the sonnet for a definitely religious purpose, to be followed by Milton among others. In 'La Corona' the formality had contributed to the impression of some shallowness in the emotions but now the passion was obviously profound and it seems that Donne kept it within the sonnet's structure not merely in order to please a patron but mainly so as to keep in order this torrent of religious emotion. Sonnets had been used like the banks of a river in order to control feelings about women which might be very strong; Petrarch had made such poems when he could not get near Laura. Donne made them now when he could not get near God.

In these 'Holy Sonnets' God is addressed by a man who is extremely anxious because he has not yet been given any sign that he is one of the 'elect' predestined to salvation. According to Calvinism, the God who was merciful to the 'elect' also gave them the assurance that they had been chosen, together with the power to 'persevere' and (it was often added) health, happiness and prosperity as encouragement. Donne felt no such power in him and enjoyed no such blessings in his life of unemployment and sickness. He was genuinely interested in religion, as his previous poetry had shown, but his rejection both of his Catholic heritage and of an Anglican parish had shown he had found no institution in which his spirituality could find a home and flourish. Since he had been taught – by Roman Catholics and Anglicans alike – that God is active, he now begged God to act decisively, to clear up the mess which was Donne, to give him faith and peace, to show him the way ahead. These were deeply sincere emotions and, to give them shape, he worked them out in a series of sixteen sonnets.

In various sonnets, surely we hear from a heart:

> Except thou rise and for thine owne worke fight,
> Oh I shall soone despaire, when I doe see
> That thou lov'st mankind well, yet wilt not chuse mee . . .
>
> Oh my blacke Soule! now thou art summoned
> By sicknesse, death's herald and champion . . .
> Or wash thee in Christ's blood, which hath this might
> That being red, it dyes red soules to white.
>
> This is my playe's last scene, here heavens appoint
> My pilgrimage's last mile; and my race
> Idly, yet quickly runne, hath this last pace,
> My span's last inch, my minute's latest point . . .

Teach me how to repent; for that's as good
As if thou hadst seal'd my pardon, with thy blood . . .

And mercy being easie, and glorious
To God, in his sterne wrath why threatens hee?
But who am I, that dare dispute with thee?

In these sonnets Donne entered a new depth in his relationship with Christ. He could say to Christ's enemies

Buffet and scoffe, scourge and crucifie mee

but he felt that he was one of the enemies: 'I crucifie him daily'. He could see the 'strange love' of the Eternal being incarnate in the crucified when

God cloth'd himselfe in vile man's flesh, that so
He might be weake enough to suffer woe

but he knew that his vision of that love was intermittent:

I runne to death, and death meets me as fast,
And all my pleasures are like yesterday,
I dare not move my dimme eyes any way,
Despaire behind, and death before doth cast
Such terrour, and my febled flesh doth waste
By sinne in it, which it t'wards hell doth weigh;
Onely thou art above, and when towards thee
By thy leave I can looke, I rise againe
But our old subtle foe so tempteth me,
That not one houre my selfe I can sustaine . . .

So he prays that 'Thy Grace may wing me' to the security for which he longs; that his 'iron heart' may be drawn by the magnet of 'Grace'.

In one sonnet he tried to persuade himself that death is not terrible: presumably that is what he tried to believe when contemplating suicide. He claimed that death is only 'rest and sleepe' and that 'our best men' show that they prefer it by dying young. Alternatively, anything can make us die – Fate, chance, kings, desperate men, poison, war, sickness – so why not accept it calmly? But in this same year he wrote other poems which took a more realistic view – St Paul's view of death as 'the last enemy':

> Th' earth's face is but thy Table; there are set
> Plants, cattell, men, dishes for Death to eate.
> In a rude hunger now hee millions drawes
> Into his bloody, or plaguy, or sterv'd jawes.

> Man is the World, and death th' Ocean,
> To which God gives the lower parts of man.
> This Sea invirons all, and though as yet
> God hath set markes, and bounds, 'twixt us and it,
> Yet it doth rore, and gnaw . . .

Thus he lamented the deaths of Cecilia Boulstred and Lady Marckham.

In two sonnets he expressed his emotions in a way which has shocked many readers and commentators. Their complaint has been that in addition to any excess of emotion about Christ he spoils the poem by a reference to sex which seems wholly inappropriate if the devout emotion is genuine; to John Carey this is 'hideous piffle' (p. 33). But for Donne himself, religion at its most intense is best described by comparing it with the other experience which has meant most to him: rightly or wrongly he thinks that the sex in the poem does not wreck, it illuminates. So he writes:

> Marke in my heart, O Soule, where thou dost dwell,
> The picture of Christ crucified, and tell
> Whether that countenance can thee affright.
> Teares in his eyes quench the amasing light,
> Blood fills his frownes, which from his pierc'd head fell,
> And can that tongue adjudge thee unto hell,
> Which pray'd forgivenesse . . . ?

And then, at this moment which to any sensitive believing Christian must be the most sacred of all moments, he remembers saying 'to all my profane mistresses' that beauty in a face is a sure sign of pity in a heart. How extraordinary! How inexcusable! Yet something can be said for Donne, even in this situation. He had praised pretty faces and soft hearts in order to persuade girl-friends not to send him away disappointed – and however oddly, that memory helps him to see that the 'beauteous forme' of the dying Christ shows a 'pity' which means that he is not being told to go to hell. The poem begins with the question: 'What if this present were the world's last night?' It gives the answer: you must be serious. And however strange or repulsive this may seem, Donne is being serious when at the foot of the cross he recalls the intensity of sexual experience. If tonight were to be the end of the world, it is likely that this last night would find this man (at this stage of his life) thinking about two subjects with a supremely important connection between them: God and sex. And if we are still shocked, it may help us to forgive Donne's error of taste if we remember that even poets who are usually praised for their impeccable taste can lapse when they use 'conceits' which make their impact precisely by being unexpected. Thus George Herbert can lapse into a suggestion that Christ on the cross teaches the music which the poet loves:

> His stretched sinews taught all strings what key
> Is best to celebrate this most high day.

And he can get worse:

> Christ left His grave-clothes, that we might, when grief
> Draws tears or bloud, not want an handkerchief.

In the most powerful and famous of these 'Holy Sonnets' sex is again introduced into a solemn meditation, for the poem ends with this extraordinary prayer to the Holy Trinity:

> Take mee to you, imprison mee, for I
> Except you enthrall mee, never shall be free,
> Nor ever chast, except you ravish mee.

And, not surprisingly, commentators whose belief is that Donne is not really talking to the real God have not been slow to offer suggestions about the fantasy in which he is indulging. Perhaps he is imagining himself as a woman who fantasizes that she is being raped? Or perhaps he is still aware that he is a man and he is imagining the homosexual pleasure of sodomy? Or perhaps he is a sado-masochist, begging for the delight of being made to suffer pain? To Edmund Gosse 'nothing could be more odious' than this closure to the poem.

However, an interpretation which is not quite so sensational is possible if we remember that in company with most of his contemporaries Donne believes not only in the ultimate reality but also in the utter holiness of God. Long before any critic can rebuke him he sees how dangerous it is going to be to end the poem with the image of his soul – his soul which by convention is spoken of as being feminine – being ravished by God. At the start of the poem he says that his 'heart' must be the target of God's attention and that God is 'three person'd' – Father, Son and Holy Spirit, not a man. He goes on to say that so far his experience of God has been too feeble. The God he has known has been too like a tinker asked to mend some old kitchen utensil: as yet, God has not been known by him to do more than 'knocke, breathe, shine and seek to mend'. He prays that God will now use his almighty force less gently. He must 'brake, blowe, burn and make me new'. His heart and soul need this drastic treatment because he can compare himself to a town which tries to admit its proper lord into its gates, 'but Oh, to no end', since at present it is under the control of a usurper and the ruler who was appointed by the lord has proved 'weake or untrue'. In yet other words, he is married to God's 'enemie' and God must act to secure his divorce. Reason, which is intended to be God's 'viceroy' ruling over his evil passions, is unable to exert the power required.

What he means by this succession of images is that he feels that he is the prisoner of Satan – but he can say to God 'dearely I love you' and he longs to be able to 'rise and stand' when he is 'free'. And by 'free' he does not mean free to enjoy a form of sex which is condemned by the Christian tradition's understanding of the Law of God. He means being free to be 'chast' – free to be cleansed thoroughly from his sexual behaviour in the past and from any lingering thoughts which are unclean, free to be chaste within a Christian marriage (he does not ask to be celibate).

In 1608 and 1609 Donne went through a spiritual crisis, almost a mental breakdown, which in some moods later he tried to forget, and the depth of this crisis would have been unknown to the world had these poems not survived for publication. Without them, we should have known only that he grumbled about depression in the countryside and wrote a muddled and unprintable book half-defending suicide.

After this time of mental suffering Donne seems to have known a period of calm, for the Holy Sonnets include one where the soul is asked to 'digest' in 'wholesome meditation' the fact that God 'hath deign'd to chuse thee by adoption' as one of his sons, destined to the glory of heaven. And another sonnet gives thanks to God for 'thy all-healing grace' and for the command which in the end requires only 'love'.

Donne's experience of sickness was not over, but it seems that when confined to his bed once again in the winter of 1609–10 he composed a 'Litanie' of prayers and sent copies to a few of his closest friends. A letter to Henry Goodyer in which he says that 'since my imprisonment in my bed' he has 'made a meditation in verse, which I will call a Litany' is not dated. Helen Gardner thought it possible that Donne wrote it before all or most of the 'Holy Sonnets', partly because another letter to Goodyer which includes some phrases echoed in the Litany is known to have been written in September 1608. But it seems best to attach more importance to the tone of the Litany, which suggests a recovery of balance after the highly disturbed sonnets of 1608–09. Donne may then have repeated phrases used in an earlier letter.

In these prayers we meet a poet who surprises us not by being sexual but by being sensible. He begins by saying, as in the Holy Sonnets, that he has 'growne ruinous', adding that he is still tempted to suicide:

> My heart is by dejection, clay
> And by selfe-murder, red . . .

And he prays for the known cure:

> O be thou nail'd unto my heart,
> And crucified againe . . .

But he now feels able to add other prayers to the petition in the sixth of the Holy Sonnets, which was 'Impute me righteous' (because I am a sinner, my only hope is that I may be reckoned to be righteous by being mercifully considered by God as Christlike). Some of the new prayers echo, while silently reforming, his Roman Catholic past. Others are influenced by the Anglican spirit, which instinctively prefers the 'middle way' as a compromise between more dramatic positions at the extremities.

He uses Catholic prayers although he makes a Protestant alteration: here, he does not pray to anyone except God. He thanks God for the Virgin Mary:

> For that faire blessed Mother-maid,
> Whose flesh redeem'd us; That she-Cherubin,
> Which unlock'd Paradise, and made
> One claime for innocence . . .

He even thanks God for 'her prayers'. When ordained as an Anglican, he was going to renounce this remnant of Popery, preaching that 'the Virgin Mary had not the same interest in our salvation as Eve had in our destruction; nothing that she did entered into that treasure, that ransom that redeemed us' (1:200).

He thanks God for the angels, for the patriarchs of Israel ('those great Grandfathers of thy Church'), for 'thy Eagle-sighted Prophets', for the apostles, for the martyrs, for the confessors, for the virgins, for the 'doctors' who taught the Church on earth, for the whole of 'that Church in triumph' in heaven. And he adds appropriate prayers about himself. When considering the prophets he prays to be delivered from 'excesse in Poëtiquenesse' and when praising the apostles he asks that his own 'comment' on Scripture will not merely 'make thy word mine'. When admiring the martyrs he remembers that his own escape from the fates of martyred members of his family must not mean the end of heroism for him, for in more complicated situations

> Oh, to some
> Not to be Martyrs, is a martyrdome.

And when admiring past teachers of the Church, he remembers that they may have 'misdone or mis-said' when they were not faithful to 'thy Scriptures': so, 'Lord let us . . . call them stars, but not the Sunne'.

Donne's own psychological needs come out even more clearly when he asks to be given the wisdom to avoid the many pitfalls of daily life – which for him must often mean not rushing to extremes. Thus he prays to be made neither 'anxious' nor 'secure' and to be prevented from thinking either that 'all happinesse' lies in 'great courts' or that no happiness is there. He must seek God with all his might but must not think that 'this earth is only for our prison fram'd'. He must trust in the blood of Christ but also attend to the welfare of his own soul. He must be spiritual but also perform 'our mutuall duties'. He must avoid both 'Vanitie' and excessive 'humilitie'; he must resemble the Christ who calmly accepts both 'Povertie' and 'kings' gifts'. And he must learn to reject his own most pressing temptations: to wish to die 'ere this world doe bid us goe' and to 'seeme religious only to vent wit'. Instead of his present 'Pietie' which depends on moods, he asks that he may 'change to evennesse', hearing the 'musique of thy promises'.

It seems, however, that his prayer for the peace of 'evennesse' was never granted – and could not be, granted that he had the perpetually uneasy temperament which made him what he was.

The poem which grew out of his meditation while on horseback on Good Friday in 1613 showed that he still had a troubled relationship with the Christ whom he now regarded as his Saviour. He was 'riding westward', to the family home of the Herberts in Wales, as he often rode on 'pleasure or businesse'. Yet he was far from relaxed, since on Good Friday 'my Soule's forme bends towards the East', towards Jerusalem with 'Christ on this Crosse'. He felt 'almost glad' that

I do not see
That spectacle of too much weight for mee

for he had no natural wish 'to see God dye'. Yet he did know that 'thou look'st towards mee' and so he prayed:

O Saviour, as thou hang'st upon the tree;
I turne my backe to thee, but to receive
Corrections, till thy mercies bid thee leave.
O thinke me worth thine anger, punish mee,
Burne off my rusts, and my deformity,
Restore thine Image, so much, by thy grace,
That thou may'st know mee, and I'll turne my face.

In 1619 he was asked to embark on another journey, this time across the English Channel. He greatly exaggerated its dangers but it gave him the stimulus for his 'Hymne to Christ'.

In what torne ship soever I embarke,
That ship shall be my embleme of thy Arke;
What sea soever swallow mee, that flood
Shall be to mee an embleme of thy bloode;
Though thou with clouds of anger do disguise
Thy face; yet through that maske I know those eyes,

Which, though they turne away sometimes,
They never will despise.

He was still troubled; he would not be Donne if he had not been. He was still being witty; it was his way of expressing himself. In reality his ship for the brief crossing to France was going to be safe enough to carry the leadership of the most expensive diplomatic mission ever financed in seventeenth-century England, but here is some evidence that his main response to the image of Christ had developed between 1613 and 1619. He had turned and now could say 'I know those eyes'.

He was still troubled in the two poems which were written as companions to his *Devotions* in prose after his grave illness in 1623. One was his 'Hymne to God my God, in my sicknesse'. It bore all the marks of his practice of meditation using the method taught by St Ignatius Loyola, with four stages: the soul must be prepared, the scene must be imagined, an analysis of its meaning must be thought out, prayer must be made for divine assistance in living out that meaning. After a time when 'I tune the Instrument here at the dore', Donne pictures his body, lying 'flat on this bed' under the eyes of the worried physicians. He compares this with a 'mapp' unrolled under the eyes of 'Cosmographers'. He sees on this one map both West and East and to him the West, where the sun sets, means Death. He imagines the 'Pacifique Sea' far in the West and reflects that the 'streights' through which that ocean is entered are symbols of the dire straits in which he finds himself as he suffers. But as he contemplates the prospect of a painful death, his imagination fastens on a new symbol. Reviving the legend which he mentioned in *Metempsychosis*, he sees that at the centre of the world is 'Adam's tree' which became 'Christ's Crosse' and he prays:

As the first Adam's sweat surrounds my face,
May the last Adam's blood my soule embrace.

Finally he preaches 'my Sermon to mine owne' (himself), with the lesson that 'the Lord throws down' in order to 'raise'. From the ocean of Death he may be raised to Resurrection, as 'Easterne riches' may be found by sailing into the Pacific.

His 'Hymne to God the Father' is much simpler: of its 144 words, 132 are of only one syllable and four are 'forgive'. It was set to music at Donne's request and sung as an actual hymn. But its simplicity includes the admission of 'feare'. He still fears that his sins are so great that he cannot be forgiven and therefore, when he dies, he must perish. He is still witty, but the wit is now restrained: there is only the old pun about God's 'sonne' or the 'sunne' shining into his darkness, added to the pun about 'done' and possibly a pun about 'more'.

And even when he is one of the leading spokesmen of the Church of England he is still capable of writing a poem so unconventional that it must be kept almost entirely secret, surviving in a single copy. He prays about the Church:

> Show me, deare Christ, thy Spouse, so bright and clear.

Is it the Catholic Church, 'richly painted' like a prostitute? Is it the Protestant Church, in a torn dress as it 'laments and mournes in Germany and here' because the Thirty Years' War is going against the Protestant cause? The Roman Catholic Church claims to be infallible – 'and errs'. But what about the equally false Protestant claim that the Catholicism of the Middle Ages was a sleep of a thousand years? And then, in the intensity of his concern about the condition of Christ's Church, comes another tasteless reference to sex. Must Anglicans 'travaile' in order to 'seeke' the Bride of Christ like the 'adventuring knights' of the old tales of chivalry – 'and then make Love'? Or is the Church of England where Donne is now at home, God's 'mild Dove', able to satisfy 'myne amorous soule'? Is it wrong that this Church is so imperfect and untidy because it wants to include the whole English people, Catholic or Protestant? Or is this Bride of Christ 'most trew, and pleasing to thee'

> When she is embrac'd and open to most men?

This comparison between the Bride of Christ and a wife who is encouraged by her husband to be sexually promiscuous is of course startling. That, surely, is what Donne meant it to be – but his motive was not to end a poem with a bang by reverting to the 'libertine' advocacy of promiscuity which is on record in the erotic poetry of the 1590s. He now wanted to say that he knew that the idea of the true Church being tolerant and comprehensive would startle most of the most earnest Christians in that age of the Thirty Years' War. Even in the Church of England uniformity was the official ideal. But he had come to think that being 'open to most men' was indeed the will of Christ for his Church.

How had Donne's religion developed to this maturity? He himself said that he owed more to his faithful wife than to anyone else. Sex had battered his young manhood but through his marriage as well as his conscience God had, he believed, battered his middle age.

9 Admyring her

Here the admyring her my mind did whett
To seek thee God
Holy Sonnets *XVII*

The development of the feminist movement, including related studies, has encouraged research, thinking and writing about Anne More and her marriage with John Donne. Previously it had been generally assumed that very little could be said about her with any confidence. She seemed to have lived and died in the shadows into which almost all the women in history have been banished (including Anne Shakespeare). Even now we cannot know as much as we want. In 1996 M. Thomas Hester edited essays which constituted the first book ever written about Anne, with the title *John Donne's 'Desire of More'*. But when Donne said in a sermon of 1627 that 'God hath implanted in every natural man . . . an endlesse and Undeterminable desire of more, than this life can minister to him' (8:75), did he mean to refer to his wife's surname before their marriage? It seems unlikely. However, I want to argue that something substantial can be known about Anne Donne because of what John Donne wrote.

In *John Donne's Articulations of the Feminine* (1998) H. L. Meakin observed that after all attempts 'Donne scholars are no closer to resolving the question of Donne and women' and added: 'This study seeks to celebrate rather than lament this phenomenon, because it is through the fissures created when Donne's representations of the feminine collide with one another that possibilities emerge for rescuing both the feminine and masculine from essentialism and the false universal.' But I am one of those many readers to whom the evidence suggests, more simply, that Donne was essentially heterosexual. It was an age when differences between the genders were somewhat different from what modern readers expect, as students of Shakespeare have often noted: not only did boys play the women's roles in the theatres but gentlemen expressed devotion to each other and made patronizing or misogynist remarks about women expecting these to be treated as normal or funny. But Donne's position is clear in his epigram:

> Thou call'st me effeminat, for I love women's joyes,
> I call not thee manly, though thou follow boyes.

He went through a development which, if not universal, is common in any age: he was fascinated by women although failing to respect or understand them, then he loved and married one. The most obvious facts about Anne are that John Donne loved her when she was barely an adult, loved her so much that he was prepared to sacrifice his career in order to marry her, loved her through years of unemployment, poverty and illness when she was pregnant for most of the time, and loved her when heartbroken by her death.

However, to modern eyes the glory of this love must be damaged by other facts which cannot be denied. As we have seen, some of Donne's early poems express with a rare eloquence a rare intensity of contempt for women and for the institution of marriage. Perhaps it was a reaction against a dominant mother which became a reaction against that mother's strict religion, or perhaps it was simply the reaction to women of an immature young man. Anyway, it was not a good starting point for a poet of married love. As we shall see, some of Donne's sermons repeat traditionally patriarchal ideas about the inherited status of women, and about their unclean bodily functions including childbirth, in attitudes which are nowadays seen as thoroughly diseased. That was not what is now hoped for from a teacher of married love. And above all other scandals is the terrible fact that Anne died of 'fever' after the delivery of a stillborn child when she was not yet 34 years old. Her body was worn out by the sexual appetite of her husband, who seems to have been feeling proud as he counted up her twelve pregnancies which went to their full term, on the monument over her grave. It is estimated that in this period of English history approximately one birth in every hundred was the direct cause of the mother's death and that statistic becomes all the more dreadful when one knows that many women experienced childbirth as often as Anne did. Her own mother had died in childbirth.

Donne was himself disgusted. He blamed men and women alike. He was ashamed of himself, as we have often seen, but a sermon gave the men of Lincoln's Inn a glimpse of Jezebel, one of the wicked queens of the Old Testament: 'she paints, she curls, she sings, she gazes, and is gazed upon' (2:57). In the same chapel, in 1618, he urged the congregation to wash their beds with tears if they were married, repenting because 'in that bed thy children were conceived in sinne' and 'thou hast made that bed which God gave thee for rest, and for the reparation of thy weary body, to be as thy dwelling and delight, and the bed of idleness and stupidity' – and of 'voluptuousnesse and licentiousnesse' (2:223). In company with countless preachers Donne fully acknowledged the power of sex and did not underestimate its ability to imprison people in evil. He once said that 'it is a lesse miracle to raise a man from a sick bed, than to hold a man from a wanton bed, a licentious bed; lesse to overcome and quench his fever, than to quench his lust. Joseph that refused his mistris was a greater miracle than Lazarus raised from the dead' (4:152). And he could continue in this vein even when the people enjoying sex were married parents. On his last Easter Day in St Paul's he made an approving reference to the married Luther's belief that 'God pardons some levities and half-wantonesses in married folkes' (9:199), but he still thought that such behaviour needed to be forgiven.

In 1618, when he was still trying hard to overcome his memories of enjoying sex within marriage, he preached fiercely at the 'churching' or purification of Lady Doncaster after giving birth to a son who had died. He claimed that for the 'greatest persons', who presumably ought to know better, 'there is more dung, more uncleannesse, more sinne, in the conception and birth of their children' than would be the case for 'meaner and poorer parents', who presumably might be excused because ignorant. A newborn infant was described as a 'barrell of dung' (5:171–2). The mother of this dead baby was only nineteen years old and must have been depressed, yet Donne could talk about 'the Curse that lyes upon women for the transgression of the first woman, which is a painfull and dangerous child-birth' (5:198). Eve had sinned and had lured Adam into sin: therefore every conception of a human being was unclean and every birth of a baby was a potentially fatal ordeal for the mother, because all inherited the original sin of humanity's first parents and deserved punishment. That seemed to be the will of God, revealed in Holy Scripture. Nowadays it must seem strange that the grieving parents were not offended, but within a year Donne was to be the chaplain accompanying a long and delicate mission led by Viscount Doncaster, who was always to be a close friend. Probably they accepted the sermon as something to be expected from a clergyman; perhaps they forgave Donne because they understood why in his bereavement he had become so harsh towards what is natural and so insensitive to their own grief.

Married sex might have been enjoyed and conception avoided by the practice of *coitus interruptus* or by the use of the primitive contraceptives then available in towns (plus a bit of luck), but it was believed that both were contrary to the laws of Nature and God. Donne preached about the story in the Old Testament that Onan was ordered to 'go in to his brother's widow' and beget a child: he went in but 'conceived such an unwillingnesse' to enable the woman to conceive that 'he came to that detestable act, for which God slew him' (5:116). The teaching of St Augustine was repeated: 'Marriage with a contract against children, or a practice against children, is not a marriage, but a solemn, an avowed, a dayly Adultery' (6:270).

Presumably Anne did not dare to contradict anything taught with such august authority and accepted by all, or almost all, of her contemporaries. But it is some consolation to know that the preacher who was her husband and ardent lover, and whose insistence on sex eventually killed her, could also stress the more humane side of the Bible and the Church's tradition.

In a sermon of 1617 he said that when 'the love of woman . . . is rightly placed upon one woman, it is dignified by the Apostle with the highest comparison, *Husbands love your wives as Christ loved his Church.* And God himself forbad not that this love should be great enough to change natural affection (for this, *a man shall leave his Father*), yea to change nature itself, *the two shall be one.*' 'The true nature of a good love,' he declared, 'is a constant union'. It is not fixing the eye on riches or honour; it is not even fascination with beauty. That would be like keeping the eye fixed on a piece of paper which is floating down the river into the sea. True love is 'not onely a contentment, an acquiescence, a satisfaction, a delight in this pureness of love; but love is a holy impatience in being without it . . . and it is a holy fervor and vehemency in the pursuit of it, and a preferring it before any other thing that can be compared to it; That's love' (1:198–200). We may hope that Anne was listening when her husband said this, for she was to die five months later – but that seems unlikely.

Donne could be very positive about marriage. He observed that the Bible is full of celebrations of its joys: 'God is Love, and the Holy Ghost is amorous in his metaphors; everie where his Scriptures abound with the notions of Love, of Spouse, and

Husband and Marriadge Songs, and Marriadge Supper, and Marriadge-Bedde' (7:87). And even his acceptance of doctrines which modern Christians tend to find offensive – doctrines about the subordination of Eve to Adam and about their infectious sinfulness – could be softened as he reflected on his experience of marriage. 'By being a husband', he said, 'I become subject to that sex which is naturally subject to Man, though this subjection be no more in this place, than to love that one woman' (5:117). In the same sermon he accepted that story that Eve was the first to eat the forbidden apple. More than once in his poetry he used this story which blamed the Fall on a woman to supply the 'conceit' that a woman then killed mankind – but he could add that women go on killing, for when enjoying sex a man 'dies'. In a bad mood he could say this about the role of sex in the Fall: 'Man was borne to love, he was made in the love of God; but then man falls in love, when he growes in love with the creature, he falls in love' (6:69–70). But that was not the last word to be spoken by Donne on this subject and on another occasion he liked the suggestion that Adam followed Eve's example in order to demonstrate his love for her, 'lest by refusing to eate, when she had done so, he should deject her into a desperate sense of her sinne' (5:114–15).

'God', he said, 'did not place Adam in a Monastery on one side, and Eve in a Nunnery on the other, and so a River between them' (3:242). On the contrary, although 'Adam was asleep when Eve was made' he 'knew Eve upon the very first sight to be bone of his bone and flesh of his flesh' (8:99). Adam was attracted to her because 'the law of God bindes men in generall . . . to Marriage'. This is mainly because children are needed. 'Man is borne into the world that others might be borne from him' (8:100–1). But Adam was also attracted because Eve had been made to be more than a breeding machine – and Adam knew that in her creation he had been smitten in order to be helped. Eve 'was not taken out of the foot, to be troden upon, nor out of the head, to be an overseer of him; but out of his side, where she weakens him enough, and therefore should do all she can, to be a Helper' (2:346).

The duty of all husbands now began for Adam: he must 'take her to his heart, and fill his heart with her, let her dwell there, and dwell there alone' (3:244). In a word, he must love her – and love 'is so noble, so soveraign an affection, as that it is due to very few things, and very few things worthy of it . . . Love delivers over him that loves into the possession of that that he loves; . . . it changes him that loves, into the very nature of that that he loves, and he is nothing else' (1:184–5).

Donne did not ignore the importance of intelligence in wives. On the one hand, a wife's essential virtues are not 'wit, learning, eloquence, musick, memory, cunning, and such': they are 'chastity, sobriety, taciturnity, verity and such' (2:346). On the other hand, this 'love between man and woman' may 'confess a satiety' unless she does sometimes talk with him – and talk intelligently. 'If a woman think to hold a man long, she provides herself some other capacity, some other title, than merely as she is a woman: Her wit, her conversation, must continue this love; and she must be a wife, a helper; else, merely as a woman, this love must necessarily have intermissions' (1:199). So he was aware that no honeymoon lasts for ever. 'As in all other states and conditions of life, there will arise some encumberances; betwixt all maried persons there will arise some unkindnesses, some mis-interpretations; or some quick interpretations may sometimes sprinkle a little sournesse, and spread a little, a thin, a dilute and washy cloud upon them' (8:97). A marriage, he said, may be 'shaked sometimes by domestique occasions, by Matrimoniall encumberances, by perversenesse of servants, by impertinences of Children, by private whisperings, and calumnies of Strangers' (8:108). And he believed that intelligent talk could drive away that kind of cloud.

Being a man of his time, he was sure that in marriage the man must be the master, having been given more strength by the

Creator; as in his poem 'The Canonization', marriage must be between 'the Eagle and the Dove'. In marriage the husband is like the head while the wife is like the hands; he is like the legs and she is like a staff so that 'he moves the better for her assistance' (3:247). But Donne was also sure that 'God hath given no master such imperiousnesse, no husband such superiority, no father such a soverainty, but that there lies a burden on them, to consider with a compassionate sensiblenesse the grievances that oppresse the other part which is coupled to them. For if the servant, the wife, the sonne be oppressed, worne out, annihilated, there is no such thing left as a Master, or a husband, or a father . . . The wife is to submit herselfe; and so is the husband too: They have a burden both' (5:114).

In these sermons we seem to be given glimpses of the Donnes' domestic life. A letter to Henry Goodyer in 1608 includes another suggestion that this masterful man would accept domestic responsibilities. An eagle, he wrote, 'should not spend a whole day upon a tree staring in contemplation of the majestie and glory of the Sun' while in the nest eaglets waited for food. And in his *Essayes in Divinity*, he gave thanks that Anne and the children had sometimes interrupted his thoughts when they were far from glorious. He was grateful that 'thou hast delivered me, O God, . . . from the monstrous and unnaturall Egypt of painfull and wearisome idleness, by the necessities of domestick and familiar cares and duties'.

Donne knew from his own experience that 'the heates and lusts of youth overflow all' but 'Behold a miracle, such a young Man limiting his affections in a wife'! 'As long as a Man's affections are scattered, there is nothing but accursed barrennesse; but when God says, and is heard and obeyed in it, . . . let all thy affections be settled upon one wife, then the earth and the waters become fruitfull, then God gives us a type and figure of the eternity of the joyes of heaven, in the succession and propagation of children . . . And since thou art bound to love her because she is thy wife, it must be as long as she is so . . . Husbands therefore are to love wives as the Mothers of their Children, as the comforters of their lives; but . . . to avoid fornication, that's not the subject of our love.' He explained that last point by saying that loving a wife is not the same as sex with 'a Mistresse'. Husbands must 'expresse your loves' not only sexually but also in 'a gentle behaviour towards them, and in a carefull providence of Conveniences for them' (5:116–20). So marriage is 'sanctified'. The divine love expressed in Christ's love for the Church must be 'a patterne of Men's loves to their wives here' and will be 'a meanes to bring Man and wife and child to the Kingdome of heaven' (5:129). Indeed, Donne claimed that the Christian ideal of marriage and family life could make a home a 'type' – a promise, a first instalment – of heaven itself. One Whit Sunday he told a congregation that 'the holy Ghost shall accompany you home to your own houses, and make your domestique peace there a type of your union with God in heaven; and make your eating and drinking there a type of the abundance and fulnesse of heaven; and make every daye's rising to you there a type of your joyfull Resurrection to heaven; and every night's rest a type of your eternall Sabbath; and your very dreames prayers and meditations and sacrifices to Almighty God' (5:57–8).

His attitude to his home-making wife seems therefore to have fitted into the more general attitude to women which he expressed in the course of his last Easter sermon. He was clear that women have souls: 'No author of gravity, of piety, of conversation in the Scriptures could admit that doubt, whether women were created in the Image of God, that is, in possession of a reasonable and an immortall soul.' But he went further, saying that 'the faculties and abilities of the soul appeare best in affaires of State, and in Ecclesiastical affaires'. In politics, 'our age hath given us such a Queen, as scarce any former King hath equalled . . . And then in matters of Religion, women have evermore had a great hand, though sometimes on the left, as well as on the right hand.' Women have 'been great instruments for the advancing of true Religion' – although also in the advancement of heresies (10:90).

He warned husbands 'not to call the sociableness of women prostitution' (6:239), but he was more ambiguous in his public reactions when women made themselves attractive by more than their charming conversation. He approved of slimming: 'the lesse flesh we carry, the liker we are to angels' (7:106). But was makeup really respectable? As a younger man he had argued (in a 'paradox') that the woman should be encouraged who shows her 'great love to thee' by taking pains 'to seem lovely to thee' – so 'women ought to paint'. As a preacher in a good mood he could say that 'if they that beautifie themselves meane no harme in it, therefore there should be no harm in it'. The Bible mentioned that during a famine in Israel a poor woman had one jar of oil left – no doubt, oil for cooking. Perhaps not very seriously, Donne interpreted and condoned the contents as 'oyle for unction, aromaticall oyle to make her looke better' (5:302–3). But in other moods he was not so approving. Perhaps it should be left to God on the day of resurrection 'to glorifie our bodies with such additions' (6:269)? He quoted the severe Tertullian: 'there's prostitution in drawing the eye to the skin'. And he complained: 'Our women expose their nakedness professedly, and paint it, to cast bird-lime for the passenger's eye. Beloved, good dyet makes the best Complexion . . .' (3:104). And at least once while preaching, he said that he was simply undecided. 'Scarce can you imagine a vainer thing than the looking-glasses of women' – but the preacher saw two circumstances which might excuse a lady's vanity in front of a mirror: a man looking at her as she looked at herself might be more vain, and secondly, Moses had decreed that mirrors were useful as showing women 'the spots of dirt which they had taken by the way' (8:224).

No communication between husband and wife was included when their son John edited extracts from grander correspondence: these were, as the title boasted, *Letters to Severall Persons of Honour*. But it seems almost certain that letters were written. The two were parted for more than a year and a half when they were engaged to marry in 1600–01; parted for about a year while John was abroad in 1605–06 (and their son George was born during this period); and parted again for ten months in 1611–12 (and during his absence Anne had to bury a stillborn child). If Donne got some letters to her during these absences despite the great difficulties in communicating, they were lost. We have no picture of Anne, no writing by her, no signature. But some letters mentioning her do survive.

One was written to her father asking for his consent to their secret marriage. It has been claimed that he never expected the father to be angry (John Carey, p. 57, says this), but this seems impossible. Donne was not such a fool as to ignore the risks he was running in disobedience both to the Church's law and to social conventions (as I summarized the situation on pp. 62–4). It cannot have been easy to persuade Christopher Brooke, who had shared a chamber with Donne in Lincoln's Inn, to be the witness who 'gave away' the bride in her father's place, and his brother Samuel had to be persuaded to be the officiating priest in this furtive ceremony. Neither was without intelligence, respectability or ambition: Christopher was to be a successful lawyer, often a Member of Parliament, and Samuel ended up as Master of Trinity College, Cambridge. These properly ambitious men must have known that they were liable to imprisonment if the enraged father, who had influence in high places, demanded this – as happened. When preaching at a wedding in 1621, Donne was to remind his hearers that 'as marriage is a Civill Contract, it must be done so in publick, as that it may have the testimony of men . . . In a marriage without testimony of men they cannot claim any benefit by the Law' (3:243).

The question about the validity of his own marriage was not answered in his favour until 27 April, almost five months after the event. Such risks would not have been run had it been thought possible that Sir George More would lay on a splendid public wedding, followed by a reception in Anne's home in Loseley in Surrey (where some fifty servants were kept) and by the transfer to the congratulated husband of a dowry which would have solved his financial problems even before his career continued in a smooth progress to profitable heights.

As it was, Donne clearly had enough sense to be fearful about the father's reaction. In his fear he made the situation worse by waiting until 2 February before he owned up to a marriage 'a few weeks before Christmas'; and he made the admission not face-to-face as man-to-man but in a confused letter which the Earl of Northumberland (whom we shall meet again on p. 334) had to be persuaded to convey, in the hope that as a neighbour and friend he could act as mediator. When he wrote Donne knew that Sir George already knew – and was furious. In part of the letter he did not expect contradiction: 'I know this letter shall find you full of passion' and 'I knew that to have given any intimation of yt would have been to impossibilitate the whole matter', resulting in 'our hindrance and torment'.

He had to admit that he had been deceiving Sir George for some time before the marriage. He had found 'meanes' to see Anne 'twice or thrice' while she had been back in London accompanying her father during the Parliament which had begun on 27 October, and on one of those occasions they had promised each other to marry. Donne's defence was that they had 'adventurd equally' knowing 'the obligacions which lay upon us' once they had made this 'promise and contract' – a defence which was unlikely to silence Sir George, since it amounted to saying that the two had been equal in deceiving him but did not admit that Donne, who as the man had made the proposal, was more responsible than the young

Anne. The nervous husband expressed the hope that 'my endevors and industrie, if it please you to prosper them, may soone make me somewhat worthyer of her'. But this apparently manly ambition to earn more implied the admission that he needed Sir George's blessing if his career was to continue at all. All that he could offer was the argument that since the marriage was 'irremediably donne' (did he make a pun, even in this situation?) the logical result was for the father to accept it and subsidize it, if only in the interests of his daughter and of any future grandchildren. This was the strongest of Donne's arguments and after a cooling-off period it was to persuade Sir George to accept the *fait accompli*, but the letter could have put the matter more tactfully.

Nine days later he wrote again to Sir George, more humbly. He now declared that 'all my endevors and the whole course of my lyfe shall be bent to make myselfe worthy of yor favor and her love, whose peace of conscience and quiett I know must be much wounded and violenced if your displeasure sever us'. This was of course a reference to Anne's insistence on defying her irate father although she had to remain in his house, a tearful prisoner. But still Donne could offer no assurance that he could make his way in the world without Sir George's support. He could deny a charge that he still loved a 'corrupt religion' but not the fact that he had been educated by people who did love it. He could claim that stories that he had 'deceivd some gentlewomen' were 'vanished and smoaked away' but he could not deny that he had this reputation which in later years he was to admit was accurate, there being no smoke without a fire. He could say that rumour had 'at least' doubled his debts, but he had to admit that he was in debt.

Writing to Goodyer on 23 February, he had been hopeful that Sir George's 'good nature and her Sorrow will worke something' and that he would be welcomed back to his job when Sir George had softened: 'you know my meanes and therefore my hopes'. But when he made his appeal to his former employer on 1 March, his 'meanes' did not include any careful consideration of Egerton's own feelings about his ex-secretary's clandestine liaison with his innocent young niece.

Donne concentrated on the consequences for himself if he was not reinstated in his job. The 'sweetnes and security of a freedome and independency' which he had enjoyed as a student had ended because he had worked through his father's legacy; he had no savings because as one of Egerton's secretaries he had been 'not dishonest nor gredy'; and now it would be 'a madness' to think that anyone else would give him a suitable job, because 'every great man' to whom he might apply would think that he had been 'flung away' by Egerton for some 'great fault'. He saw 'no way before me' if Egerton did not take him back – and it seems probable that even before his marriage he had realized that unemployment was at least a risk, for like the Brooke brothers he was not an innocent babe in the woods of reality.

His letters both to Sir George and to Sir Thomas read like the cries of a man who had a nightmare before waking up to find real life no better. He begged Sir Thomas to allow him back into his presence. 'Affliction, misery, and destruction are not there; and everywher else where I ame, they are.' But Egerton was not to be persuaded. He had dismissed Donne when urged to do so by Sir George and did not now wish to show weakness by cancelling his decision because Sir George had somewhat relented – but there was another factor in the situation: despite his abilities and charm which had earned him his employer's satisfaction, the ex-secretary had become unwelcome in circles which demanded the maintenance of dignity within the acceptance of society as it was. Donne had caused a scandal even while the anti-Establishment cynicism of his poetry remained hidden from view.

All these documents were used in R. C. Bald's biography in 1970 but later, in 1986, in a collection of articles with the title *The Eagle and the Dove*, an American scholar, Iona Bell, put forward another letter as belonging to this crisis and as being one of three surviving 'love letters' to Anne. It had been found among papers once belonging to Donne's friend Sir Henry Wotton and had been printed in 1924, but it had not then been thought to be what Bell now claimed. It is certainly unlike the polished *Letters to Severall Persons of Honour*. It begins abruptly, without giving the name of the person being addressed, and it is ungrammatical, presumably because written in agitation and haste. It expresses 'wonder and grief' that Lord Latimer had spread a story that the writer had 'dishonored yo' and that this story had been taken by 'yr father' as 'good fuell of anger against mr davis & me to'. The exact meaning of the letter is not clear but it may well have been scribbled by a panic-stricken Donne in love. The greatest puzzle about it is why it was kept in the first place, and then sent to Wotton. If Anne kept it as a kind of love letter, why was it not destroyed? If it was sent to Wotton because he was planning to write a biography of Donne, who sent it? It reads like a mere draft of a letter, but it is not in Donne's handwriting; so why was a scribe told to make this copy and what happened to the original? The same unanswerable questions can be asked about the other two documents claimed by Iona Bell to be 'love letters'.

But more eloquent than any of these letters is the refusal of both John and Anne to agree that their marriage was invalid. When John saw the full cost of being married he could have withdrawn his petition to have the wedding ceremony declared legal – and when Anne experienced her father's full fury during months when she was at his mercy in their home she might have ended the relationship which had caused so much trouble, and might have consoled herself with the prospect of a 'good' marriage in the class of the alliances into which her sisters entered without any controversy or ill effects. The persistence with which both John and Anne wanted their marriage to be recognized by the archbishop's court seems to have made the decisive impression on the ecclesiastical judges although they were under strong pressure from her father to deny the legality (and there would have been precedents if a bribe had been offered). And sooner or later the whole of Anne's family accepted the marriage, supported Anne and made friends with her legally wedded husband.

More coherent letters to other correspondents sometimes give us glimpses of the lovers' married life. One letter records the husband's great anxiety about the wife's 'anguish' during the birth of their son Francis. That night in January 1607 was 'the saddest night's passage that I ever had' and John had thought about ending his own life if Anne died: 'I should hardly have abstained from recompensing for her company in this world, with accompanying her out of it.'

A happier scene surrounded the composition of a letter to Henry Goodyer 'from the fire side of my Parler and in the noise of three gamesome children'. He was sitting 'by the side of her whom, because I have transplanted into a wretched fortune, I must labour to disguise that from her by all such honest devices as giving her my company and discourse'. The reply to Goodyer had to be short because 'I steal from her all the time which I give this Letter'. The letter has been interpreted by John Carey as showing that Donne regarded conversation with the 'virtually uneducated' Anne as 'scarcely more than a benign duty' (p. 60), while in her short study of *John Donne* (1994) Stevie Davis found it 'difficult to believe' that he accepted more than 'a duty of allegiance'. She thought she could detect an 'aghast quality in his experience of the aftermath of marriage . . . Poverty, dependency, boredom, illness, and claustrophobia in the company of a growing family of children bred melancholy and aggravation.' But the surviving evidence does not demonstrate either that Anne's head was empty or that her husband's heart had grown cold. On the contrary, the letter just quoted shows that they treated one another with sensitivity: Donne felt that 'I melt into a melancholy as I write' but he must hide it because 'I sit by one too tender towards these impressions' and he must not cause 'sad apprehensions'.

We know that in some rich families daughters could receive an education from tutors although only boys were sent to the grammar schools and universities, and we also know that Anne had been sent to be polished in the sophisticated household of a lawyer-statesman in London. If she could hold an intelligent conversation with men there when scarcely into her teens, years later she was surely capable of interesting Donne with her mind. As we have noted, he seems to have told Izaak Walton that she had been 'curiously and plentifully educated', 'curiously' then meaning 'unusually'. If – a big 'if' – the letter about Lord Latimer does refer to Donne's relationship with Anne, it expresses dismay that Sir George should find 'any defect' in her when he had been an instrument in 'ye building of so fayre a pallace as yo are and so furnishing it as his care hath done'. In other words, having seen to her education he ought not to have been surprised when she fell for a brilliant scholar such as Donne instead of marrying a man who merely possessed land. And that letter ends with a kiss to the woman's 'fayre, learned hand'.

When lamenting his own unemployment to Sir Robert Ker whose life was happily busy, Donne wrote that 'I stand like a tree which once a year beares, though no fruit, this mast of Children', 'mast' meaning acorns or other droppings fed to pigs. But that bitter remark need not be taken as proof that he was permanently angry with his wife and children for existing and with himself for being connected with them. On the contrary, he was inviting his busy friend to act as godfather to the latest baby and was assuring him that the request would not be repeated every year. When he called himself a 'tree' he may have been making a between-men joke about the tall and fertile member of his body; in a poem about a mistress ('Nature's lay

Ideot') the phrase had been 'I planted life's tree in thee'. And the comparison of his children to acorns may have been an affectionate look at their potential for growth.

It is natural to suspect that Donne was cold-hearted if he wrote all or any of the very tender 'valedictions' preserved among his poems – and then went abroad leaving his wife to cope alone with the last months of pregnancy. Helen Gardner, for example, thought it 'impossible' that the poems could have been addressed to Anne in such circumstances. But whether or not they were, the evidence does not seem to support a very severe condemnation of Donne. Both of the journeys abroad which he undertook after his marriage, in 1605–06 and in 1611–12, were essentially business trips, when he seems to have acted as companion, translator and secretary to rich patrons who presumably paid for his services and expenses and who might be expected to continue to reward him in the future. And on both occasions he left Anne and the children in the care of a sister who had her own household and no financial worries.

In February 1605 a licence was granted to Sir Walter Chute to travel abroad with Donne, two servants and four horses, for three years. It was an opportunity for Donne to escape gracefully from his stay with Sir Francis Wolley at Pyrford in Surrey. It was embarrassing that this cousin kept a mistress by whom he had a daughter while his own wife remained childless. The Donnes already had two children and must have hoped for a place of their own. The most attractive way to recover financial independence was for him to be taken back into the service of the government and a free trip abroad seemed an opportunity to acquire a further qualification. The travellers spent time both in Paris and (almost certainly) in Venice, where Donne's newly knighted friend Wotton was the ambassador. They may also have visited Spain (now at peace with Britain) where Donne could have deepened his knowledge of the language and the literature. In the event he was back in England by the beginning of April 1606 and although no job was forthcoming the house in Mitcham could be afforded.

In July 1611 another licence to travel abroad was issued, also for three years. It allowed Sir Robert Drury to take his family and a coach with twelve horses. Walton says that Anne protested so strongly against the idea that Donne should accompany the Drurys that he decided not to go, only to change his decision with Anne's reluctant consent, when his patron insisted. The offer made must have seemed irresistible, for on the strength of it the Donnes ended their tenancy of the house at Mitcham although a gloomy farewell letter to Goodyer shows that they were heavily in debt. Then Drury was delayed by business affairs and it was November before the Channel was crossed; a pack of hounds and some hawks were taken along with the very worried Donne.

On 7 February he wrote to Anne's brother Sir Robert enclosing a letter to her which has not survived and begging for news of her condition: 'this silence doth somewhat more affect me than I had thought anything of this world could have done'. On 14 April he complained to Goodyer that 'I have received no syllable, either from herself, nor from any other, how my wife hath passed her danger'. He did not then know that on 24 January a stillborn son had been buried with a note in the parish register that the mother was the 'best of women'. However, his employer did not allow him to return to England until September. It seems reasonable to conclude that communications between rural England and France were not easy but that Donne felt it necessary to work for his patron because he so badly needed the money for himself and his family, while Anne took the children to stay with her sister on the Isle of Wight.

One reason why Donne had missed his wife is hinted at in a letter he wrote to Wotton in 1612: 'You (I think) and I are much of one sect in the Philosophy of love; which though it be directed upon the minde, doth inhere in the body, and find prety entertainment there.' (The 'piety' of the printed version needs correction into 'prety'.) Nine months after his return home, he was given another son – and Francis had been born nine months after an earlier return, in 1606. Anne recovered from the birth of Nicholas (who was to die very soon) by taking a holiday away from their new home in London and in a moment of freedom from domestic cares Donne joked to Goodyer that 'I have now two of the best happinesses which could befall me; which are, to be a widower and my wife alive'. It is not inconceivable that Anne was also happy, to have a break from his moods and his sexual needs. But his good humour did not last. In February 1614 he was reporting that Anne had had a miscarriage and 'fallen into an indisposition, which would afflict her much, but that the sicknesse of her children stupefies her'. A month later he was writing that 'my wife hath now confessed her self to be extremely sick; she hath held out thus long to assist me, but is now overturn'd & here we be in two beds, or graves'. His depression made him tell Goodyer bitterly that 'if God should ease us with burialls' among the sick children he did not know how he would be able to pay for their funerals. To us it is of course surprising that Izaak Walton printed that outburst, presumably thinking that it showed only how sadly his hero 'did bemoan himself', but it was an age when people believed that God controlled the deaths of innocent children, took care of them in eternity and relieved the suffering of those who had watched them die. In such an age this would not be an extreme example of Donne's insensitivity. In fact his daughter Mary died. He recovered: as he wrote, 'I have paid death one of my Children for my Ransome'. Again we may be shocked, although we need not jump to the conclusion that the cost of this 'Ransome' seemed cheap to an entirely selfish Donne.

We need to understand why he felt that he had to apologize to Goodyer for including such a 'homely' fact as 'the death of one of my Children' in a letter. Goodyer, a Warwickshire squire to whom he wrote every week partly because of his correspondent's financial generosity, would have been expecting an elegant letter of philosophy presented as literature. He might have been embarrassed when he was sent instead domestic news of illness and tragedy. And even parents were not meant to display too much grief after a child's death, because children died so often. Donne knew Goodyer well enough to write to him now that 'I loved it well' but the 'it' may have been his polite bow to that social convention which was meant to be merciful. How he reacted in private we do not know. Ben Jonson wrote poems about his children but if Donne did they have not survived. Yet we shall shortly see that he knew how to grieve and we do know that his children's deaths gave him causes to do so. Of his four sons who survived birth, Nicholas died in infancy and Francis did not live to be eight. Of his six daughters who survived birth, Lucy did not live to be nineteen and Mary did not live to be four.

He could grow so depressed during his years of unemployment, financial anxiety and solitary (and perhaps pointless) study that he could moan to his men friends that his marriage had ruined him. In 1608, writing to Lord Hay (the future Viscount Doncaster), he lamented 'that intemperate and hastie act of mine' which had been 'the worst part of my historie' but the one best remembered by potential employers. Amid his gloom in 1612 he told Goodyer 'I must confess, I died ten years ago'. But two years later he was reminding Sir Robert More (her brother) that he and Anne 'had not one another at so cheap a rate, as that we should ever be wearye of one another'. In that letter he was worrying about Anne being lonely without him; he was lonely himself although he had his books. And pregnancies continued to suggest how their reunited love was enacted. Back in 1602 he had assured her father that 'my love is directed unchangeably' upon 'her whom I tender more than my fortunes or my lyfe', and fifteen years later the keeping of their marriage vows was reflected in the epitaph which he composed for Anne's monument in their London parish church, St Clement Danes, which was later rebuilt with the loss of the monument although written copies of his words had been made.

He listed some of her distinguished ancestors and the copy of his draft which was kept in their family's seat, Loseley Park, shows that this final act of reconciliation was very acceptable. He publicly recorded his wish to be buried in the same grave (although when he had become Dean of St Paul's he was to think that his body belonged there). He did not explicitly mention Christ as the Saviour, but he may well have implied much when recording that she had died at the traditional age of the Saviour's death. Nor did he explicitly mention the Christian hope of resurrection, but there was probably that significance in his mind when he gave the date of her death, for 15 August was the date of the Catholic Church's celebration of the Assumption of the Blessed Virgin Mary into heaven.

This epitaph praised Anne as

A woman most special, most beloved,
a spouse most dear, most chaste,
a mother most dutifull, most indulgent,
having completed fifteen years in marriage
seven days after giving birth for the twelfth time,
with seven surviving children,
she was carried off by a ravishing fever.
Commanding this stone to speak
because grief made him as speechless as an infant,
a husband most wretched, once dear to the dear,
pledges his own ashes to hers
in a new marriage (if God bless it) together here.
She withdrew
in her 33rd year, in the 1617th year of Jesus,
on August 15.

What did he say in poetry about her?

Izaak Walton told his readers that after her death Donne 'betook himself to a most retired and solitary life', and then preached a heart-broken sermon in the church where she was buried: it was on the text 'I am the man that hath seen affliction'. No such sermon has survived and the one that was printed with this text would not support Walton's description, but since he had no wish to exaggerate the importance of Anne (whom he had never met), it seems reasonable to accept his account. What we know for certain is that Donne wrote some deeply felt poems about her death. One said that marriage to her had been his religious education:

> Since she whom I lov'd hath payed her last debt
> To Nature, and to hers, and my good is dead,
> And her Soule early into heaven ravished,
> Wholly in heavenly things my mind is sett.
> Here the admyring her my mind did whett
> To seeke thee God: so streames do show their head . . .

Commentaries on it have shown that the significance of this poem can be debated and it has even been suggested that he thought that her death had been 'good' for him because he wanted to get rid of her – or more subtly, that he accepted that being dead she could no longer do 'good' to herself or to him. It is much more likely, however, that what he meant was that it was 'good' for her to be in heaven and for him to have to concentrate on loving God. Walton says that he now told his children that he would never marry again – a considerable sacrifice, and not only because he would miss the sex, the love and all that he meant by a wife being a 'help'. His household including six younger children now had to be run by his daughter Constance, in 1617 only fourteen years old, and the domestic problems were increased when he soon became Dean of St Paul's. But it seems that he had made his decision partly out of loyalty to Anne and partly because her death intensified his conviction that his only ultimate good, beyond death, was God. What he meant by that is shown in a prayer at the end of a sermon which he preached four months after losing her: 'O glorious Beauty, infinitely reverend, infinitely fresh and young, we come late to thy love, if we consider the past daies of our lives, but early if thou be pleased to reckon with us from the houre of the shining of thy grace upon us' (1:250).

He was adapting what St Augustine had said about what he had sought and found when sexual activity had been put into the past. He was doing, or trying to do, what other great poets had had to do before him – Dante when he saw beyond Beatrice to 'the Love', Petrarch when he had to turn from Laura to God, and among the Elizabethans what Sidney and Spenser had also found necessary. He was taking, or trying to take, the advice which he had given to his distressed mother when Anne was still alive: God's purpose was 'to keep your Soul in continuall exercise, and longing and assurance of comming immediately to him' and 'to remove out of your heart all such love of this world's happinesse, as might put Him out of possession of it. He will have you entirelie.' And he was achieving, or trying to achieve, what he had urged after Elizabeth Drury's death:

> Up, up my drowsie soule, where thy new eare
> Shall in the Angels' songs no discord heare . . .
> And what essentiall joy canst thou expect
> Here upon earth? . . .
> Onely in Heaven joie's strength is never spent . . .

It is difficult for commentators who think that any idea of joy's strength in heaven is an illusion to appreciate why Donne developed his poem about 'she whom I lov'd' into a meditation about his own relationship with God, but the matter is seen differently if it is understood that Donne actually believed that if he handled this supreme relationship aright he would join Anne in heaven. It was in this belief that he continued the poem as a prayer. She had persuaded him to drink from a river which came from God, with the result that 'I have found thee, and thou my thirst hast fed'. But there had been a further result: his thirst for God had become 'a holy thirsty dropsy' – an unrestrainable thirst. He told himself that it was mad for him to 'begg more Love' from Anne More or from God, when he could already say to God 'thou dost wooe my soule'. God had Anne's soul in his keeping and offered to share with this mourner's soul the whole of his own eternal reality and glory; it was as if God longed to marry both souls. And God was entitled to 'thy tender jealousy' if Donne gave his love instead to 'things divine' such as mere 'Saints and Angels' or if he shut God out of his life in favour of 'the World, Fleshe, yea Devill' – the 'fleshe' including carnal thoughts about Anne.

Another poem about Anne's death is called 'The Dissolution' and ends with her maiden name. It begins 'Shee is dead' and recalls that they were 'made of one another' so that 'my body then doth hers involve'. Since her body is dead he finds that memories of marriage only increase

> My fire of Passion, sighs of ayre,
> Water of teares, and earthly sad despaire . . .
> And I might live long wretched so . . .

Yet he is also 'amaz'd that I can speake' of a life beyond the death of her body, a life where he can join her:

> And so my soule more earnestly releas'd,
> Will outstrip hers; As bullets flowen before
> A latter bullet may o'rtake, the pouder being more.

And the significance of that last word may be an example of a general rule which Donne propounded in the pulpit: 'in all Metricall compositions . . . the force of the whole piece, frame of the Poem is a beating out of gold, but the last clause is the impression of the stamp, and that is it that makes it currant' (6:41).

However, it was not easy for him to forget the passion, the sighs and tears, the despair and ecstasy, of his love for Anne More. In 1613 he had written the best of his marriage songs, celebrating the wedding on St Valentine's Day of the king's only daughter (Elizabeth) with one of the Protestants' strongest hopes (Frederick, Elector Palatine). Its tone was very different from his juvenile effort contributed to the students' revels in Lincoln's Inn, but it was no less physical as it pictured a union of man and wife where she was no longer the moon reflecting the masculine sun and sex was no longer the payment of a 'debt' which the married pay reluctantly.

> He comes and passes through Spheare after Spheare,
> First her sheetes, then her Armes, then any where.
>
> Here lies a shee Sunne, and a he Moone here,
>   She gives the best light to his Spheare,
>   Or each is both, and all, and so
> They to one another nothing owe,
>   And yet they doe, but are
> So just and rich in that coyne which they pay,
> That neither would, nor needs forbeare nor stay;
> Neither desires to be spar'd, nor to spare,
>   They quickly pay their debt, and then
> Take no acquittances, but pay again:
> They pay, they give, they lend, and so let fall
> No such occasion to be liberall . . .

It was not easy for the Donne who had written that poem to sacrifice marriage and to bury his memories of its earthly joys. In 1619 he wrote a 'Hymne to Christ' in which he once again told himself that he must move on – to the love which God offered and to death. He was so depressed that he expected his death to occur in the near future, completing his sacrifice.

> I sacrifice this Iland unto thee,
> And all whom I lov'd there, and who lov'd mee . . .
> As the tree's sap doth seeke the roote below
> In winter, in my winter now I goe
> Where none but thee, th' Eternall root
> Of true love I may know.

And so he prayed for help to forget, after two years:

> Thou lov'st not, till from loving more, thou free
> My soule . . .

But does Christ really want him to forget Anne More?

> O, if thou car'st not whom I love
> Alas, thou lov'st not mee.

At this time he wrote in a letter: 'I leave a scattered flock of wretched children, and I carry an infirm and valetudinary body, and I goe into the mouth of such adversaries, as I cannot blame for hating me, the Jesuites, and yet I goe . . .' He felt that he had to go, because the king had ordered it and also because he depended on the king's support for his own future if he lived. It was not the letter of a man who found it easy to sacrifice his 'I-land' (puns had become a habit) or his family or his memories. But it was also not the letter of the man described by John Carey, who argues that Anne's death brought to a head the 'obsession' still caused by 'the early crisis of his apostasy from Rome', so that 'he found it impossible to believe that he was loved enough, even by God' (p. 45). On the contrary, Donne attacked himself for loving humans too much, when the 'Eternall root of true Love' is God.

In the end he did manage to pray that all the loves of his past, good or bad, might be married not to him but to Christ:

> Seale then this bill of my Divorce to All,
> On whom those fainter beames of love did fall;
> Marry those loves, which in youth scattered be
> On Fame, Wit, Hopes (false mistresses) to thee.

And so far from packing for a holiday he looked forward to death:

> Churches are best for Prayer, that have least light:
> To see God onely, I goe out of sight:
> And to scape stormy dayes, I chuse
> An Everlasting night.

Naturally that negative mood faded as the intensity of his bereavement grew less. In a sermon on Easter Day 1622 he spoke positively about what he called 'the first Resurrection': 'Let that be, The shutting of thine eyes from looking upon things in things, upon beauty in that face that misleads thee, or upon honour in that place that possesses thee; And let the opening of thine eyes be, to look upon God in every object, to represent to thyself the beauty of his holiness, and the honour of his service in every action' (4:76). The spring sunshine was perhaps warming his mind as he said that, and as he added: 'Man is but a vapour; but a glorious and blessed vapour, when he is attracted and caught up by this Sun, the Son of Man, the Son of God'

(4:82–3). Two years later he consoled a widow by assuring her that God's purpose is to reunite husband and wife: 'that piece which he takes to himselfe is presently cast in a mould, and in an instant made fit for his use . . . That piece which he leaves behinde in the world by the death of a part thereof growes fitter and fitter for him by the good use of his corrections, and the intire conformity to his will. Nothing so disproportions us, nor makes us so uncapable of being reunited to those whom we loved here, as murmuring . . . We are not bound to think that souls departed have devested all affections towards them whom they left here; but we are bound to think that for all their loves they would not be here again.'

But, especially when he was out of the pulpit and alone, the cold and the dark could return.

His 'Nocturnall upon S. Lucie's Day' is weeping in the dark. It refers to the night offices of the Roman Catholic Church during what was popularly regarded as the longest night of the year, 'the yeare's midnight', before the commemoration of St Lucy on 13 December. An intimate self-disclosure of which few copies seem to have been made, it clearly mourns someone who is dead and has been loved:

> Study me then, you who shall lovers bee
> At the next world, that is, at the next Spring:
> For I am every dead thing,
> In whom love wrought new Alchimie.

The experience of loving Anne has produced for him not the *elixir vitae* which would be a 'cordial' or magic medicine curing all diseases, as was the dream of the experimenting alchemist in that age, but something which is the essence of Nothing,

A quintessence even from nothingnesse,
From dull privations, and leane emptinesse
He ruin'd mee, and I am re-begot
Of absence, darknesse, death; things which are not.

He mourns his loss of a woman who has shared many sorrows with him:

Oft a flood
Have we two wept, and so
Drowned the whole world, us two, oft did we grow
To be two Chaosses, when we did show
Care to ought else; and often absences
Withdrew our soules, and made us carcasses.

'By her death (which word wrongs her)' he has become 'None'. There seems to be no one except Anne about whom such words could have been written – and written after her death. However, some scholars have taken literally Donne's announcement that he was abandoning poetry in 1614 and have done their best to find a date before that. Because of its reference to 'Lucy' in its title Herbert Grierson suggested in 1912 that the 'Nocturnall' was written in 1612, when Lucy, Countess of Bedford, was severely ill – but she was Donne's aristocratic patron, not his partner in sorrows and in sex, and Grierson had the wisdom to say that this was a 'hazardous suggestion' about a poem which remained 'enigmatical'. With less wisdom Arthur Marotti suggested that the woman being mourned was not the Countess of Bedford but a 'transcendent female' of the poet's imagination, so that Donne probably composed the 'Nocturnall' about the same time as the 'Anniversaries' – to which the reply must be that the artificiality of the lament for Elizabeth Drury in the 'Anniversaries' is totally different from the heartbreak in the 'Nocturnall'. Other scholars, recognizing that it must be about his wife, have connected the poem with one or other of the times when he was afraid that Anne was going to die. But in the poem he has been reduced to despair by 'her death', unambiguously.

So was the poem written soon after her death?

It may have been but if so, there is a problem about why St Lucy's Day in particular should have released such a flood of grief and despair. Another problem – which does not seem to have been taken into account – is that on the day after St Lucy's Day in 1617 Donne delivered a sermon before Queen Anne and her courtiers (1:236–51) which sounds like a declaration of faith by a man who is trying to replace worldly loves which were tainted by sin – is trying, and not entirely failing. It claims that the soul 'that hath been transported upon any particular worldly pleasure, when it is intirely turn'd upon God and the contemplation of his all-sufficiency and abundance, doth find in God a fit subject, and just occasion, to exercise the same affection piously and religiously, which had before so sinfully transported and possest it . . . So will a voluptuous man who is turned to God find plenty and deliciousness enough in him to feed his soul . . . Solomon, whose disposition was amorous and excessive in the love of women, when he turn'd to God, he departed not utterly from his old phrase and language, but . . . conveyes all his loving approaches to God, and all God's gracious answers to his amorous soul, into songs . . .' And Donne goes on to quote St Augustine's disgust with his memories of 'sensual love' in comparison with love for God: women had led to 'nothing but to be scourg'd with burning iron rods, rods of jealousie, of suspicion and of quarrels'.

Such references to King Solomon and St Augustine may well have been coded hints to Queen Anne that she could find in a passionate religion a substitute for the disappointment in her sexual relationship with King James, but it does not seem likely that Donne could have preached that sermon if two nights previously he had been so profoundly grief-stricken that his poem could say that by his own wife's death he had been reduced to the 'quintessence' of 'nothingnesse' without a glimpse of God. And in November 1617 a sermon had already reflected some confidence that he was not defeated in the struggle to think positively about Anne's death. He had then claimed that 'this death, this dissolution, this change, is a new creation; this Divorce is a new Marriage; this very Parting of the soul is an Infusion of a Soul and a Transmigration thereof out of my bosome into the bosome of Abraham' (1:231–2). No doubt his moods varied, and no doubt his sermons did not tell the whole story about his private feelings, but this evidence suggests that as winter began in 1617 he had made a recovery from the early intensity of his natural grief after her death. He was now preaching to himself that sex must be over, that Anne must be in heaven, and that he could look forward to joining her there. And through any remaining tears he was trying to see the eternal God.

It seems certain that the 'Nocturnall', which was an outburst of uncontrolled and totally desolating grief not mentioning God, was written about Anne – and it seems probable that it was written ten years after her death. My suggestion is that when Donne thought about Anne as St Lucy's Day began in 1627 his continuing sense of what he had lost when she had died was intensified by mourning after other deaths and by depression over other events which had brought sadness to himself, his family and his country – and then the river of grief burst its banks. If we are looking for a St Lucy's Day whose long, black eve would have revived memories of the damage which he had received in 1617, 13 December 1627 is it.

In January his daughter Lucy had died: she had barely reached the age of eighteen. In May her godmother Lucy, Countess of Bedford, had been buried after a long decline in health and glamour: Donne was no longer close to her but death made the distance greater. Magdalen, Lady Danvers, had joined her in death, and on

1 July he had preached about her the most personal of all his surviving sermons. Walton remembered his tears in the pulpit.

In other ways also, it had been a miserable year. One incident must have suggested to Donne that although he could still preach with power he was becoming yesterday's man. He had been asked to preach in defence of the marriage of the new king with Henrietta Maria, who was unpopular as being both French and Catholic. Cautiously, he had admitted that 'very religious kings may have had wives that may have retained some tincture, some impressions, of error, which they may have sucked in their infancy, from another Church' (7:409). It was a guarded admission of a possible defect in the new queen, but not guarded enough for King Charles, who sent for a copy of the sermon through his favourite bishop, William Laud. Donne sensed danger and begged his friends at court to use their influence. The king, 'who hath let his eye fall upon some of my Poems', ought to see that the 'study and deligence' bestowed on them was less than the care which Donne had taken over this and every sermon, in this case care to support the king – but would Charles see? Donne grew so anxious that he had to apologize in a letter to Robert Ker, a friend at court: he had knocked on Ker's front door, had grown too nervous, and had run away before the door could be opened. Eventually Laud examined the sermon and found nothing in it which was clearly intended to be disloyal; Donne apologized for 'certain slips' (as Laud recorded in his diary); and the king forgave him. But Donne was warned: he could not rely on the steady support which King James had given him.

In 1627 it was difficult to remember that recently James had dreamed of securing peace by a royal marriage, first with Spain and (when that failed) then with France: Britain was now at war with the combined forces of Spain and France. Donne was patriotic in the pulpit but his private correspondence showed intense concern at the collapse of the peacemaking policy, to add to the disaster of the Protestant defeats in Germany. And his soldier son George had been lucky to return to England after the disaster of the expedition led by the Duke of Buckingham to the Isle de Ré in the autumn of 1626, from which half the English force did not return. George did not stay in England for long: he was soon sent to command a small garrison in the Caribbean and was taken to Spain as a prisoner: his father never saw him again. Buckingham was to be assassinated by a naval officer with a grievance in 1628.

It was probably in the Lent of 1627 that Donne said in the pulpit that 'if there were any other way to be saved and to get to Heaven, than by being born to this life, I would not wish to have come into this world' (7:359). At Easter 1627 he preached about the resurrection of the dead but did not conceal his own grief after his unmarried daughter's death. 'If I had fixt a Son in Court, or married a daughter into a plentifull Fortune, I were satisfied for that son and that daughter. Shall I not be so, when the King of Heaven hath taken that son to himselfe, and married himselfe to that daughter, for ever? . . . This is the faith that sustaines me, when I lose by the death of others or when I suffer by living in misery my selfe, That the dead, and we, are now all in one Church, and at the resurrection shall be all in one Quire' (7:384).

In May he preached about the 'tendernesse' of God, saying that 'many of us are Fathers' and should 'learne' from that. On Whit Sunday he preached about the 'comfort' (strengthening) given by the Holy Spirit. But he ended that sermon: 'Onely consider that Comfort presumes Sadnesse . . . In great buildings the Turrets are high in the Aire; but the Foundations are deep in the earth. The Comforts of the Holy Ghost work so, as that only that soule is exalted, which was dejected' (7:451).

In November he preached at the wedding of the grand-daughter of Sir Thomas Egerton, whose patronage had meant so much, to the eldest son of Lord Herbert of Cherbury, who as Sir Edward Herbert had been a close friend of his. Briefly noting that the purposes of marriage were well known and that the happy couple had good examples in their parents, he concentrated on the fact that after death there would be no marriage in heaven. The most that he thought possible was recognition without the restoration of the old union. 'In the Resurrection there shall be no Marriage, because it conduces to no end; but if it conduces to God's glory and to my happinesse (as it may piously be believed that it does) to know them there whom I knew here, I shall know them' (8:100).

Soon he was preaching in St Paul's on the text 'Say unto God, how terrible art thou in thy works!' He took the opportunity to mention that 'it is not the king that commands but the power of God in the king' (8:115), but also to stress that, like the king, God is to be feared. 'Not only a feare of God must, but a terror of God may, fall upon the Best', as when 'a horror of great darkness fell upon Abraham . . . I cannot look upon God in what line I will, nor take hold of God, by what handle I will; Hee is a terrible God, I take him so; and then I cannot discontinue, I cannot break off this terriblenesse, and say, Hee hath been terrible to that man, and that is the end of his terror; it reaches not to me. Why not to me? In me there is no merit, nor shadow of merit' (8:123–4).

Donne did not forget to add that 'this Terriblenesse' is 'Majestic not Tyrannical' but his sermon reached its climax in a vision of God's power: 'It must be power . . . his power extended, exalted . . . his power magnified, his power multiplied upon us.' And on Christmas Day 1627 Donne did not proclaim God's love, or preach with any other seasonal message. Instead he was eloquent about the difficulties of God's spokesmen and the evils of the world to which they must speak, offering only the hope that God 'will not be angry with us for ever' (8:156). A month later he was preaching about St Paul's warning to the elders of the Church in Ephesus that they would 'see my face no more'. He sounded as if he was about to disappear also: 'When you come to heare us here, heare us with such affection as if you heard us upon our death-beds' (8:171).

The depression expressed in such sermons is compatible with the suggestion that he wrote the 'Nocturnall' in December 1627. But the depression lifted. Preaching on the national Fast Day in April 1628 he told the king and the courtiers not to be permanently depressed. 'They must have teares first', he said, 'first thou must come to this weeping, or else God cannot come to this wiping' (8:201). A little later he preached to the court about the martyrdom of St Stephen. He might have been grim after this ominous start: 'He that will dye with Christ upon Good-Friday, must hear his own bell toll all Lent . . . We begin to hear Christ's bell toll now, and is not our bell in the chime? We must be in his grave before we come to his resurrection, and we must be in his death-bed before we come to his grave: we must do as he did, fast and pray . . .' But his sermon was not depressed. It offered 'two general considerations: first, that every man is bound to do something before he dye; and then to that man who hath done these things which the duties of his calling bind him to, death is but a sleep' (8:174–5). That sermon ended with some glorious words about heaven (quoted on p. 350).

The Easter sermon for 1628 promised the 'light of glory' in comparison with which 'the light of honour is but a glow-worm; and majesty itself but a twilight'. God 'crownes all other joyes and glories' but 'this very crown is crowned', for '*we shall be made partakers of the Divine nature*; Immortal as the Father, righteous as the Son, and full of all comfort as the Holy Ghost' (8:232, 236).

Other poems have been thought to refer to Anne More, particularly since they include the word 'more' or reach a climax with it. One is the 'Hymne to God the Father' where twice the confession of sins ends with 'I have more' and in most of the manuscripts the poem ends with 'I have no more'. This can suggest that Donne thought that his spiritual troubles would be over when he had finally escaped from his relationship with Anne More. But it seems highly unlikely that he did think this: his other poems testify against it, although as we have seen they are eloquent about the need to love God even more than her. We know that this poem was set to music as a hymn, and Izaak Walton said that it was often sung in St Paul's Cathedral in Donne's presence – which makes it unlikely that its climax was intended to be a shocking attack on his dead wife. It is probable that the poem ended with 'I feare no more' in the printed versions from 1633 onwards in order to avoid this misunderstanding.

The 'Valediction of my name, in the window' is by far the most light-hearted of the four surviving 'Valedictions'. It does not sound like a farewell to a wife but conceivably may come from the days of courtship. It may imagine Anne More seeing her own face in a window where he has carved his name with a diamond:

> 'Tis more, that it shews thee to thee
> And cleare reflects thee to thine eye.

And it may tease her by saying that one day while they are separated she may look out of that window and see another lover advancing through the garden. If so, his name 'scratch'd' in the glass will still be there to rebuke any temptation:

> So since this name was cut
> When love and griefe their exaltation had,
> No doore 'gainst this name's influence shut,
> As much more loving, as more sad,
> 'Twill make thee; and thou shoulst, till I returne,
> Since I die daily, daily mourne.

But there is at least one snag in any attempt to link this poem with Donne's courtship of Anne. It is very unlikely that he would have dared to carve his name in a window, either in York House where she lived while in London or in her palatial home in the country. If the poem was inspired by Anne, it was an imaginative exercise.

This difficulty raises again a bigger question: is it sensible to connect any poem with Donne's courtship or marriage?

In her introduction to her edition of the 'Songs and Sonets' Helen Gardner argued that Donne's love poems 'are too far from the reality of what we know of for us to speak of them as written to Ann More or even about her'. She divided the 'Songs and Sonets' which ever since 1633 had been printed as a jumble into two 'sets', before and after 1602, but she stressed that 'it is not the mark of the second set . . . that they all handle the theme of love as union': instead, 'their distinction lies in their more subtle and complex conception of form and style'. Her emphasis on reading rather than loving was so firm, so securely academic, that she believed that Donne was attracted by 'authors whose speculations had already fascinated him by a theory of love radically different from the naturalistic view' – and she 'would add' (no more) that he was also influenced 'by his own experience' when he 'lost the world for love'. She thought that he resumed 'considerable literary activity' in 1607, more than five years after his marriage, and she suggested that when he celebrated the faithful union of lovers the poet 'turned to his own uses his reading in the Neoplatonists'. This was in keeping with her basic attitude to the poems, which was that 'each expresses its mood with that lack of hesitation, or equivocation, that purity of tone, that gives sincerity to a work of art and makes it appear veracious, or imaginatively coherent'. But surely we can agree that every poem is a 'work of art' without supposing that 'reading in the Neoplatonists' is sufficient to account by itself for passionate poetry about love. Echoes suggest that Donne was influenced by Serafino's poetry and Ficino's philosophy, but common sense suggests that he was more decisively influenced by his relationship with Anne. He was more bookish than most men have been, but he allowed himself to be controlled by only one book – the Bible. In a letter which seems to have been written around 1600 he said that 'to know how to live by the booke is a pedantry, and to do it is a bondage'. In later life he could not claim, as he did in this letter, that 'I am no great voyager in other men's works: no swallower or devourer of volumes nor pursuant of authors' – but even when he became a learned scholar he did not rely on 'other men's works' to tell him 'how to live'.

Gardner gave no good reasons for her belief that 'the empty period in Donne's literary career is from 1599 to 1607'. There are, on the contrary, strong grounds for thinking it probable that having worked on *Metempsychosis* until August 1601 Donne wrote poetry inspired by two situations which he had never experienced before and which changed the course of his life: courting a young woman whom he desperately wanted to marry despite the obvious difficulties, and being married in defiance of society's code of conduct and at the cost of his career. It is interesting that Arthur Marotti, whose *John Donne, Coterie Poet* (1986) was the most extensive exploration yet made of probable or possible intentions to write for a restricted 'coterie' of fellow students or male friends, accepted that Donne wrote also for Anne's enjoyment, although he reckoned that an earlier scholar, J. B. Leishman, went too far in believing that twenty poems should be listed in this category. Marotti argued that knowing what were the conventional attitudes in Donne's 'coterie' of ambitious and often promiscuous men, and knowing also that Donne continued to long for a career, helps us to see the serious courage of the poet's love for his wife, whom he married 'for love'. 'Romantic without being soft-headed', 'intellectually and emotionally complex', these poems connected with Anne are in Marotti's verdict 'Donne at his best'.

Donne met Anne More while she was staying in London as the guest of Lady Egerton: her mother had died and she was being shown this kindness partly because Lady Egerton had a son by a previous marriage, Francis Wolley, who after her husband's death was brought up by the Mores in their great home in Surrey. The lovers seem to have developed quite a deep relationship before Lady Egerton died in January 1600, after which Anne was taken back into her own family's home. She did not return to London before October 1601. It does not seem stupid to believe that poetry was used by Donne to keep their love alive during this physical separation lasting almost two years. Presumably it was impossible for them to meet and Donne had to rely on smuggled letters if these could be arranged. He could scarcely have hoped to please her by sharing with her the completely unromantic *Metempsychosis* but if he could write it would be natural for him to use his rare ability as a poet. When they could not communicate at all, it would be equally natural for him to pour his anxiety into a poem. And when he had succeeded in marrying her, the failure of his career must have helped to concentrate his thoughts on her. It therefore seems allowable to consider some possibilities that he wrote to or about her.

In 'Love's Exchange' the speaker has fallen in love – without naming Anne, but in an experience which actually overwhelmed John Donne in his relationship with Anne. Love, he says, makes a man weak and blind; it is childish; when others knew about it, it results in embarrassment, in a 'tender shame'; it tortures, kills and cuts up a man – and he is glad, for he has seen

> This face, which whereso'er it comes
> Can call vowe'd men from cloisters, dead from tombes,
> And melt both Poles at once, and store
> Deserts with cities . . .

In 'The Broken Heart' love is a developing disease and the speaker asks

> Who will beleeve me, if I sweare
> That I have had the plague a yeare?

Indeed the beloved has been a surgeon, cutting out his heart:

> If 'twere not so, what did become
>   Of my heart, when I first saw thee?
> I brought a heart into the roome,
>   But from that roome, I carried none with mee . . .

She cannot have kept his heart, otherwise she would have shown 'more pitty unto me', but he has discovered some remnants of it in himself, so

> My ragges of heart can like, wish, and adore
> But after one such love, can love no more

– and she had better mend his heart by proving that she loves him.

'Lovers' Infinitesse' may be another example of teasing Anne More during their courtship. The speaker says that he has run out of sighs, tears and promises after their engagement:

> And all my treasure, which should purchase thee,
> Sighs, teares, and oathes, and letters I have spent,
> Yet no more can be due to mee,
> Than at the bargaine made was meant . . .

But his love had continued to grow:

Hee that hath all can have no more,
And since my love doth every day admit
New growth, thou shouldst have new rewards in store . . .

In 'The Anniversarie' the speaker refers to the passing of a year since the two 'first saw' each other, but he may well mean 'really saw', as lovers. And he refers to 'kings' including his beloved, but this does not mean that the poem cannot have been written in the reign of Elizabeth I.

The Sun it selfe, which makes times, as they passe,
Is elder by a yeare, now, than it was
When thou and I first one another saw . . .

The lovers are not (yet) entitled to the single tomb of the married:

Two graves must hide thine and my coarse,
If one might, death were no divorce . . .

But they are not bored with each other:

All other things, to their destruction draw,
  Only our love hath no decay;
This no to morrow hath, nor yesterday . . .

They feel that they are 'Prince enough in one another', that

Here on earth, we are Kings, and none but wee
Can be such Kings, nor of such subjects bee;
Who is so safe as wee? where none can doe
Treason to us, except one of us two.

They have no need to fear such treason, so

Let us love nobly, and live, and add againe
Yeares and yeares unto yeares, till we attaine
To write threescore, this is the second of our raigne.

'Aire and Angels' is a sophisticated poem about which critics have disagreed. Helen Gardner disarmingly confessed that 'it has had many unsuccessful readers, of whom I am one'. It is not a poem which a sensible poet would address to a girl of Anne's age. But it makes fairly simple sense if we spot a familiar topic, lust, beneath the sophistication. (Therefore no sensible poet would have addressed it to the Countess of Bedford, despite a modern commentator's suggestion.) It seems possible that it originated in Donne's turbulent emotions as he asked himself whether his relationship with Anne would ever become physical – and as he tried to keep his balance by his old trick: write a witty poem.

It begins by saying that this woman looked like an angel, like a 'lovely glorious nothing' or a 'shapeless flame', when he first saw her. But love must 'take a body' and be fixed on 'thy lip, eye, and brow',

For not in nothing, nor in things
Extreme, and scatt'ring bright, can love inhere . . .

However, even when a relationship of love becomes physical the woman can still be angelic because angels have 'face and wings of aire'. These pieces of equipment are not so pure as the angels' souls but they are necessary if there is to be any contact with embodied humanity. In much the same way, 'women's love' must be physical if it is to be 'my love's spheare' – which seems to mean: if it can be like the sun circling round the earth in the old Ptolemaic and medieval picture of the sky. This argument seems to refer to the teaching (of St Thomas Aquinas, for example) that angels have strange bodies of air, and in a sermon at a wedding Donne was to explain more solemnly that angels 'are Creatures, that have not so much of a Body as flesh is, as froth is, as a vapour is, as a sigh is, and yet with a touch they shall moulder a rocke into lesse Atomes, than the sand that it stands upon' (8:126). But then the speaker lowers the level of argument by claiming that his own love is so superior that it is always like 'Angells' puritie' – when it is evidently nothing of the kind. He has begun by saying that the woman cannot remain purely angelic if he is to love her fully; now he ends by saying that a man can be earthy and yet remain pure. He is being Donne, very witty and very masculine, alluding to the man-made tradition that it is the woman who most wants the sex.

A redeeming feature in Donne's character is the honesty which surfaces. 'Love's Growth' was perhaps a further meditation about Anne and the 'love which cures all sorrow with more'. The man now confesses that he is longing to embrace the woman:

> I scarce beleeve my love to be so pure
> As I had thought it was . . .
> Love's not so pure, and abstract, as they use
> To say, which have no Mistresse but their Muse,
> But as all else, being elemented too,
> Love sometimes would contemplate, sometimes do.

The same theme runs through 'The Extasie', a poem which C. S. Lewis once found 'singularly unpleasant' because it argues that the flesh is inferior to the spirit, yet can be used well – precisely the Christian attitude to the spiritual side to human nature, as Joan Bennett reminded Lewis in her reply. (This was before Lewis was 'surprised by joy' and married.) 'The Extasie' begins with a picture of the lovers gazing at each other 'all day', their 'eye-beames' united as if by 'one double string' and their hands 'firmely cimented' by the sweat of excitement. And we may be excited by this teasing overture: the bank on which they lie is 'pregnant' because 'like a pillow on a bed' and perspiration accompanies the 'propagation' of images in their eyes. But they only contemplate; they do not 'do'. 'Wee said nothing, all the day', and 'it was not sexe'. (Donne is listed in the Oxford English Dictionary as being the first writer to use the late medieval word 'sex' as referring to 'the sum of those differences in the structure and function of the reproductive organs on the ground of which beings are distinguished as male and female'.) But the speaker is hoping for action which 'interanimates two soules' and can control 'defects of loneliness' in a 'dialogue of one'. If that action is open to the procreation of children when 'our blood labours to beget Spirits', it will be 'that subtile knot, which makes us man' – but if there is no such action, 'a great Prince in prison lies'. Previously the poets' comparison to a prince in prison had referred to the imprisonment of the soul in the body until released into eternity by death, but now release is to come by the action which can create a new generation on earth. The speaker's down-to-bed message is clear enough:

> Love's mysteries in soules do grow,
>   But yet the body is his booke . . .

If that is the message, it seems that Helen Gardner was wrong to think that the proposal made in the poem is 'the perfectly modest one that the lovers' souls, having enjoyed the rare privilege of union outside the body, should now resume possession of their separate bodies and reanimate these virtual corpses'. She thought that this teaching that physical contact is best avoided supplies 'the key to Donne's greatest love poetry' and was put into the poet's mind not by what the body teaches but by a study of Leone Ebreo's book *Dialoghi d'Amore*. We may ask whether Donne, a very physical poet, would not have laughed when he had overcome his astonishment at reading such a bookish suggestion. A more realistic comment was made by

A. J. Smith, who saw in 'The Extasie' 'people who are in the act of making a momentous self-discovery intelligible to themselves' – the discovery that the deepest reality about sexual love is that the joy of union is consummated, not automatically produced, by physical sex. The lovers' commitment to each other is spiritual and sexual intercourse is a sign, almost a sacrament of it, in accordance with what Donne said in his Easter sermon of 1623: 'All that the soule does, it does in, and with, and by the body' (4:358).

A poem which in 1650 was given a strange title, 'A Lecture upon the Shadow', is a rather simpler expression of a courting lover's impatience and John Shawcross believed that a connection with Anne was 'unavoidable'. The speaker has been on a walk with his girl 'these three houres' and when 'the Sunne is just above our head' he lectures her about the implications of the fact that they no longer have separate shadows. In the past

> Disguises did, and shadowes, flow,
> From us and our cares; but, now 'tis not so.

But danger lies ahead! Earlier in their walk together their shadows separate in order to 'blinde others' since their love has had to be kept secret. But he warns that if they walk on in this secrecy, still avoiding the publicity of marriage, new shadows will form and will blind their own eyes, for the lovers will begin to keep secrets from each other. They may think that they are merely continuing their walk into the afternoon,

> But oh, love's day is short, if love decay.

> Love is a growing, or full constant light;
> And his first minute, after noone, is night.

However, if the married walk through life they cannot always be together physically. Just as it seems likely that Donne used his power as a poet when courting Anne, so it seems probable that he did so as emotions arose when they parted for a long period. Some commentators have stressed that this cannot be proved, which is of course the case. But an appeal may be made to common sense. There are three poems called 'Valedictions' which are different from every other poem which Donne wrote: they are consistently personal and tender; they offer comfort to the sadness of someone else, and are not about his own emotions; and they are about partings before long absences. Only a few such absences occurred in his life. Three were when he went to Italy and Spain as a tourist and when he went on expeditions against the Spaniards, and we know that the emotions in these poems were not his emotions then. His other long absences came after his marriage and common sense asks: from whom could he have parted with such tenderness, if not from his wife? And if the answer should be that all the poems arose from an unusually vivid imagination, common sense asks another question: how could he so well imagine feeling like that, if in all his life he had never actually felt the pain of good-bye? And if he actually felt it only once, directly inspiring only one poem, that would be an interesting connection with his wife.

The 'Valediction to his Booke' may refer to a book which once existed and which collected their love-letters written when they were parted in 1600–01:

> Study our manuscripts, those Myriades
> Of letters, which have past twixt thee and mee,
> Thence write our Annals, and in them will be
> To all whom love's subliming fire invades,
> Rule and example found . . .

And certainly this poem suggests that Donne would have had no objection in principle to an attempt to see whether any of his writing is about his own courtship and marriage; he would not have dismissed the possibility with the scorn which we find in some of the twentieth-century commentators. The poem suggests that love letters can instruct 'Divines' (theologians) about love as a reality which is not entirely spiritual:

> Love this grace to us affords,
> To make, to keep, to use, to be these his Records . . .
> Here Love's Divines (since all Divinity
> Is love or wonder) may find all they seeke . . .
> For though minde be the heaven, where love doth sit
> Beauty a convenient type may be to figure it.

Yet part of the 'wonder' of this love which is physical, not heavenly, is that it need not die when the lovers are separated physically, for

> How great love is, presence best tryall makes,
> But absence tryes how long this love will bee . . .

The 'Valediction Forbidding Mourning' may also have been a good-bye to Anne; Walton thought that it was, in 1611. Helen Gardner thought this impossible: a wife would not be expected to keep her grief at her husband's departure private or to be involved in 'the romantic conception of passionate love as the *summum bonum*'. These objections, however, do not necessarily apply either to all marriages or to the relationship between the highly emotional John and the usually pregnant Anne. At least, the poem is about the parting of two people, real or imagined, who have been physically very close, who have achieved a spiritual union also, and who must now be content that for a while their relationship will be spiritual. Other lovers, it says, may indulge in 'teare-floods' and 'sigh-tempests' when they part – and there is a hint that the woman is now doing precisely that.

> But we by a love, so much refin'd,
>   That our selves know not what it is,
> Inter-assured of the mind,
>   Care lesse, eyes, lips, hands to misse.
>
> Our two soules, therefore, which are one,
>   Though I must goe, endure not yet
> A breach, but an expansion,
>   Like gold to ayery thinnesse beate.

This suggestion that the union of souls need not be destroyed by a geographical separation seems fairly simple and common, but there has been much critical discussion about the rest of the poem, which compares the parted lovers to two legs of a compass. Donne was not the first poet to use this 'conceit' in order to talk about a separation which is also a continuing union, but it has often been objected that in a poem which is beautifully tender the cold artificiality of the compass is out of place. This objection deserves some thought.

As used by Donne, this image does not minimize the difficulty caused by the separation. Just as gold beaten until it is as thin as air (as 'gold leaf' used in decoration) is not the same as the gold ring which symbolizes the full union of marriage, so the legs of a compass are definitely parted when only one leg is making a circle. Indeed, the comparison with the compass is introduced by the admission that the lovers' souls, about which it has just been said that they 'are one', in fact 'are two'. But the point now made is that the 'fixt foot' (the woman who stays behind) remains 'fixt' in the sense of being constant, but 'doth move' in the sense of turning in sympathy as the other moves (so the woman can follow her man's movements in her mind). Even when 'the other far doth rome' the 'fixt foot' moves towards the other and 'leanes and hearkens after it', until the circle (with detours) is completed when the other 'comes home'. Then the 'fixt foot' is delighted and 'growes erect'. Somewhat as beaten gold leaf remains gold and is not entirely different from the metal which can be melted into a coin or a bracelet, the two legs of the compass are not completely out of touch and can be completely united again. In brief, the speaker very gently begs the woman (Anne?) to stop crying and to think about how she must be loyal and hopeful when they are parted, until her 'firmnes' enables him to 'end where I begunne' – with her.

The mood is the same in a song which seems to have been written to accompany an existing tune (and which Walton also associated with their parting in 1611):

> Sweetest love, I do not goe,
> For wearinesse of thee,
> Nor in hope the world can show
> A fitter Love for mee . . .

Here, too, the beloved is begged not to weep:

> When thou sigh'st, thou sigh'st not winde,
> But sigh'st my soule away,
> When thou weep'st, unkindly kinde,
> My life's blood doth decay . . .
>
> But thinke that wee
> Are but turn'd aside to sleepe;
> They who one another keepe
> Alive, ne'r parted bee.

In the 'Valediction of Weeping' the word 'more' may well be a clue to the identity of the lover to whom this farewell is addressed. In response to her tears which are 'emblemes of more' he has to 'powre forth' his own tears. But still having his wit, he is afraid that if they both go on crying like this the water may 'overflow this world' in a Flood of biblical size even before he embarks on his risky voyage:

> O more than Moone,
> Draw not up seas to drowne me in thy sphere,
> Weepe me not dead in thine armes, but forbeare
> To teach the sea, what it may do too soone . . .

And he begs the lady not to create a great 'winde' by her sighs, pointing out that 'thou and I sigh one another's breath': the one who 'sighes most' is 'cruellest' without meaning to be.

Since 'A Feaver' combines teasing with an intimate tenderness, it may well have been addressed to Anne, who was often ill. (It was clearly not addressed to the Countess of Bedford.) The beginning would be offensive if the speaker were not tolerated and loved by the recipient:

> Oh doe not die, for I shall hate
> All women so, when thou art gone,
> That thee I shall not celebrate,
> When I remember, thou wast one.

But by its end the poem has become an outburst of uncomplicated, sexual love:

> These burning fits but meteors bee,
> Whose matter in thee is soon spent.
> Thy beauty, and all parts, which are thee,
> Are unchangeable firmament . . .

For I had rather owner bee
 Of thee one houre, than all else ever.

Three poems which are much happier almost certainly record the ecstasy of the early days and nights of their married love, when they first fully owned each other. One of these, 'The Canonization', seems to date from the reign of a king not a queen, for it mentions 'his stamped face' on coins. It is addressed to friends who regard the speaker's absorption in love as an error, and begins dramatically

For Godsake hold your tongue, and let me love . . .

and asks 'who's injur'd by my love?' The world's business has not been interrupted as the lovers 'dye and rise' (familiar slang for sexual intercourse) 'at our own coste'. And the poet assures friends that this love is inspiring poetry which will be their memorial:

We'll build in sonnets pretty roomes;
As well a well wrought urne becomes
The greatest ashes, as half-acre tombes . . .

So there is irony in the fact that the reference to a 'well wrought urne' as a monument which 'becomes' (suits) 'the greatest ashes' was used as the title of the book which in 1947 was a manifesto of the 'new criticism'. *The Well-Wrought Urn* by Cleanth Brooks argued that the attempts of earlier critics to find autobiography behind poetry were futile. Yet Donne himself said that like an urn holding the ashes of an aristocrat so 'sonnets' can be rooms holding the spirits of lovers who once 'did the whole world's soule contract' into their love which would be a 'patterne' to future lovers.

'The Sunne Rising' also seems to date from after their marriage, since it seems later than the accession to the throne in 1603 of King James. His enthusiasm for hunting is, it appears, mentioned:

Goe tell the Court-huntsmen, that the King will ride.

The sun is rebuked for calling on the lovers to get out of a bed which contains 'both the Indias of spice and Myne' (both the spices of the East and the gold of the West) plus all the kings of the earth, 'all here in one bed'. The speaker exults:

She is all States, and all Princes, I.
Nothing else is.
Princes do but play us, compar'd to this,
All honor's mimique; All wealth alchimie . . .

And the end of the poem transcends the traditional *aubade*, where the dawn is merely resented as an intrusion on love. Now the lovers' bed is the centre of the universe and 'if her eyes have not blinded thine' the sun is instructed to circle round the room and to warm 'us' with its beams:

Shine here to us, and thou art every where;
This bed thy center is, these walls, thy sphere.

But if the sun should be unable to do its duty that will not matter, for it has already been reminded that deep love is a foretaste of eternity:

Love, all alike, no season knows, nor clyme,
Nor houres, dayes, moneths, which are the rags of time.

'The Good-morrow' is a poem with the same mood of joy as sunshine pours into the bedroom after a night of love. This love is different from the fumblings of adolescents as they explore bodies and emotions.

> I wonder by my troth, what thou, and I
> Did, till we lov'd? were we not weaned till then?
> But sucked on countrey pleasures, childishly? . . .
> 'Twas so; But this, all pleasures fancies bee
> If ever any beauty I did see,
> Which I desir'd, and got, t'was but a dreame of thee.
>
> And now good morrow to our waking soules,
> Which watch not one another out of feare;
> For love, all love of other sights controules,
> And makes one little roome, an everywhere.

The love-intoxicated speaker dismisses the 'new worlds' being opened up by 'sea-discoverers' and the new stars now shown on maps of the night sky. What matters as 'true plain hearts' come to rest is 'let us possesse one world, each hath one, and is one', for eternity is here:

> If our two loves be one, or, thou and I
> Love so alike, that none can slacken, none can die.

Thus a number of Donne's love poems may be connected with Anne: nothing in them makes this impossible and we do not know of any other woman who could arouse in the poet feelings so deep, so tender and so wise. It seems sensible to think it highly probable that Donne wrote poetry about his love for his wife, for it would be extraordinary if he did not. But it would be wrong to claim certainty about the background to any particular poem. In 1982 a scholar, Patricia Pinka, could publish *The Dialogue of One* as a detailed study of the 'seven types of lover' on view in the 'Songs and Sonets' without ever mentioning Donne's wife. 'More' need not always be a pun on her surname before marriage; valedictions have been written by many poets as literary exercises; many poets have imagined situations not belonging to their own lives; many men have had lovers in short or long relationships who were not their wives. Only one conclusion is, it seems, undeniable: marriage with Anne contributed decisively to the deepening and purification of Jack Donne. He said so himself: admiration for her when she was his physical partner made him seek God and after her death intense grief deepened both his emotions and his prayers. Also, his sermons celebrated married love as 'union' in addition to their less attractive echoes of the traditional subordination of the wife to the husband. The contrast with his attitudes as a young poet makes this transformation by marriage little less than a new birth psychologically. And since these were facts, we should not be surprised to find it probable that he could still find himself in an agony of bereavement ten years after Anne's death.

Why, then, did he in the end decide to be buried in the cathedral where he had preached instead of in her grave as he had intended in 1617? And why did he take no steps to make sure that the poetry of their love was kept in the text which he had written, and in an intelligible order? It was, I suggest, because he had been captured by a vocation which he believed to come from God, and thus he felt that he was under the pressure of a love even greater than their married love.

10 The Trumpet

Thou art the Proclamation; and I ame
The Trumpet, at whose voice the people came.

'The Second Anniversarie'

Donne's sermons may have been neglected as evidence about what he really was but they have often been praised as one of the glories of English literature, as eloquence not unworthy of a major poet. They combine grandeur and intimacy, tenderness and drama, reminding us that this was the age of the Authorized (or King James) Version of the Bible and also the age of Shakespeare. Attention was drawn to his many-splendoured eloquence by Coleridge in the nineteenth century but more effectively by the publication of *Donne's Sermons: Selected Passages*, first in 1919 and later in many reprints. However, the editor, Logan Pearsall Smith, felt that a rather nervous introduction was necessary since the sermons had 'received no very adequate attention'. He recognized that it was not only their 'great number and length which daunts the reader; there is much in the writing itself which is difficult and distasteful to the modern mind'. The editor signalled to the reader, however, that he was himself 'secular minded' and that his purpose was not 'theological, didactic or even historical': it was to make known a great writer of enjoyable prose.

He had to rely on the texts printed during the seventeenth century: on the six sermons published during Donne's lifetime, on the seven which the Cambridge University Press brought out in 1631–34, and on the three folio volumes which were edited by Donne's son. One problem was carelessness in editor or printer.

When Donne began writing out a collection of his sermons in 1625, he told a correspondent that he hoped that publication would bring benefit to his son John, then aged 21. But the son's ordination was delayed and during his last illness Donne entrusted his sermons and other papers to the more reliable care of Henry King, his closest friend among his colleagues in the cathedral, without mentioning them in his will. However, King became too busy to complete the work still needed and in the end the unsatisfactory son did have the honour of arranging the publication.

In a fit of rage one day in 1634 John Donne junior struck a boy who subsequently died and although he was acquitted of manslaughter he thought it wise to leave Oxford for further study in Italy. On his return to England in 1637 he got hold of his father's papers by some action which left Henry King aggrieved; he did some work on them while drawing incomes from a number of rural parishes; and in 1640 a handsome volume was published containing 80 sermons. During the civil war and the Cromwellian regime he lived in London and edited (more or less) more of his father's works: a volume of 50 sermons in 1646, the book on suicide in the same year, a new edition of the poems in 1650, followed by the letters and a collection of short pieces. He made a mess of the letters, not arranging them in any sort of order and often not saying correctly to whom they were addressed. He rushed out 500 copies of some more sermons in 1660, taking advantage of the restoration of the Church of England along with Charles II (who accepted the dedication), and on the title page claimed that the contents were 26 sermons instead of the actual 23. He died in 1663, the last of John Donne's sons to survive; his brother George had had various adventures as a soldier but had died in 1639 while on a voyage to Virginia.

John Donne junior has usually been treated as a son who remained prodigal. Anthony Wood wrote about him as 'an atheistical buffoon, a banterer, and a person of over free thoughts'. A parishioner (called by him 'a pitifull ignorant Baker') rebuked him publicly as 'an idle man' who 'never preached' – as we know from a letter in which he defended himself as having been busy with his father's sermons. However, his will, made in 1662, was impressive: one earl was named as his executor, another witnessed his signature. He returned the cabinet which had contained his father's papers to King and his intention was that King (now Bishop of Chichester) should be sent all the summaries of books. He also intended that Walton should receive all the other papers. But in a letter written in November 1664, which Walton printed with King's agreement, King expressed dignified regret that the papers had disappeared: 'how these were got out of my hands . . . is not now seasonable to complain' and the unexplained fact was that they had now been finally 'lost both to me and to your self'. They had also been lost to posterity.

Logan Pearsall Smith confessed that the volumes edited by John Donne junior 'stood for years on my bookshelves' before 'it occurred to me that it might be interesting to read them' – and eighteen years passed before the publication of the extracts which he edited. In 1839 a young clergyman, Henry Alford, had published an edition of many of the sermons with some censorship, and also modernized spelling, in the hope of interesting Victorian readers, but his work had attracted few readers and no praise from scholars; his publisher had told him to abandon his hopes of editing more Donnean material (although he went on to become Dean of Canterbury). A text taking account of the printed versions and of many of the manuscripts, with a useful commentary, became available only in 1953–62, when the University of California Press undertook the publication of 160 sermons. In the triumphant introduction to the final volume there was a cool glance at anthologies: 'In the selection of purple passages the morbid and the rhetorical will always have too large a place. It is only by reading four or five sermons that we can realize Donne's sense of form, the carefully thought out scheme by which he arranged his material, his common sense, his shrewdness, his psychological insight, and his real religious fervour.' This major feat was achieved by an English scholar, Evelyn Simpson, with the collaboration of George Potter until his early death.

Their labours eased the path of a number of other good scholars who since then have published studies of the sermons considered either as theology or as literature. But the problem has remained that if many potential readers are to find it easily digestible the material has to be chopped up. On what principle should this be done? It seems best to concentrate on the message of the preacher, for this is what Donne wanted to deliver. But this does not exclude the enjoyment of his unique eloquence, for that is what he offered his congregations with all the work and skill required.

Unlike his poems, his sermons seldom begin with a phrase which arrests attention. Instead the introduction often includes a *divisio*, a division of the text taken from the Bible into small sections each of which will be expounded. Questions about translation from the Hebrew or the Greek may be mentioned but there is no immediate translation of the biblical words into everyday speech about everyday events. It seems to be taken for granted that the congregation will be as fascinated by the Bible as the preacher is, and eager to hear how he is going to handle this precious material.

After this introduction it is assumed that Christians of the seventeenth century will be impressed, edified and even delighted by a sermon which piles quotations from the Bible on top of one another, supporting them with many references to the Fathers of the Church who had interpreted Scripture but had been dead for more than a thousand years. It seems probable that this scholarly apparatus was enlarged when he wrote out sermons for the printer, but equally probable that he took not a few quotations with him into the pulpit. And modern Christians can scarcely believe that their predecessors enjoyed it all. Even in the Victorian age, when preachers were still heard patiently in England, one of Donne's successors as Dean of St Paul's, Henry Milman, wondered how a large congregation could have been attracted to 'these interminable disquisitions, to us teeming with laboured obscurity, false and misplaced wit, fatiguing antitheses'.

What Dean Milman said in the pulpit has been entirely forgotten. Whether he was right in his verdict on Donne should be decided after some study of what Donne actually said.

He had to find his own voice as a preacher and we are not surprised to be told by Izaak Walton that it took a little time: what is astonishing is how little was needed. Accompanied by a friend, this middle-aged apprentice would visit churches which would allow him to experiment in the pulpit. Not all the experiments worked, it seems. A sermon survives from a visit to the parish church in Greenwich and Donne must have been proud of it, for years later he wrote it out with a view to publication. He did what he could for an audience which cannot have been highly cultured, and made references to commerce; and one hopes that the references to Latin and Hebrew were added later. But it is unlikely that he bridged the intellectual space between that pulpit and that congregation. Indeed, it is so unlikely that it has been suggested that he was preaching to the court of Queen Anne, whose palace at Greenwich was being reconstructed at that time – but nothing in the sermon itself suggests this. Essentially he was still talking to himself and warning himself against covetousness, which he often attacked as the sin of men no longer young.

The contrast between that early effort and the mature style, which was emotionally as well as intellectually strong, can be seen at its extreme in one of the best known of his sermons, preached to the Virginia Company before a feast in November 1622 (4:264–82).

The young English colony was extremely insecure as Donne spoke. The boundless hopes of 1606 – voiced, for example, in Michael Drayton's 'To the Virginian Voyage' – had been dashed and the sponsoring company was now deeply divided between those who still believed that Virginia might be the Paradise of a new life in a new world and those who impatiently waited for a return on the investment. Many of the settlers had recently been massacred by the 'Indians' and those who survived found it difficult to earn a living before tobacco was exported after being grown by slave labour. In England, the venture had attracted supporters who were suspected by the government and two and a half years after this sermon the Virginia Company was to be dissolved. But that afternoon, almost four hundred people gathered in the church to hear this preacher as he raised morale.

He did not do this by urging a war of vengeance against the 'Indians': instead, 'preach to them Practically' by 'your Justice and (as far as may consist with your security) your Civilitie'. Nor did he advocate emigration by people who found England unsatisfactory. Nor did he recommend Virginia as a good investment. 'Those whom liberty drawes to goe', he declared, 'or present profit draws to adventure, are not yet in the right way.' Nor did he think that the main motive ought to be politics, whether conservative or radical: 'if you seeke to establish a temporall Kingdome there, you are not rectified'. His glowing vision was of a religious mission to the new world, taking the Gospel of the kingdom of God across the Atlantic as the children of Israel had once taken themselves across the Red Sea. For once, Donne did not treat the West as the area of sunset. On the contrary, if the Virginia Company dedicates itself to the conversion of the 'Indians' that will be a part of the building of a new part of Christendom in the new world. 'You shall have made this Iland which is as but the Suburb of the old world a Bridge, a Gallery, to the new; to join all to that world which shall never grow old, to the Kingdome of heaven.'

The obvious danger of the emotionalism of this style was that the rhetoric could lapse into irrationality. Sometimes he lapsed in order to raise the tone above everyday reality (but did Donne the preacher remember that he had once applied for the down-to-earth job of being secretary to the Virginia Company?) and sometimes in order to make the flesh creep. A notorious example is when he used a plague to warn his congregation that they must reckon with death – as if that was not already causing them enough grief. 'Have you not left a dead son at home, . . . whom you should have beaten with a rod, to deliver his soul from hell, and have not?' He imagined 'men whose lust carried them into the jaws of infection in lewd houses, and seeking one sore perished with another; men whose rapine and covetousnesse broke into houses, and seeking the wardrobes of others stole their own death'. And he imagined the dust which was all that remained of the bodies of the dead blowing around the church: 'Every puff of wind within these walls may blow the father into the son's eyes, or the wife into her husband's, or his into hers, or both into their children's, or their children's into both' (6:362, 389). This was said to people who had just buried those whom they loved.

But these performances were not what he said on the average Sunday and so far as we know he remained on good terms with the anxious supporters of the Virginia Company, who arranged for the sermon to be printed, and with the congregation of St Dunstan's, who remained astonishingly loyal. The explanation seems to be that when he preached people liked the preacher even while they did not like – or perhaps did not choose to hear? – what he said. (One secret about the art of preaching is that a congregation is often more interested in the messenger than in the message.) It seems that what mattered most on those occasions was that Donne showed that he was moved to eloquence by what was moving his hearers to fears or tears; he really cared about Virginia, he was really upset by the deaths in the plague, what he actually said might be silly or deeply offensive but his 'nearnesse' pierced.

Izaak Walton often heard him preach, and remembered him: 'A Preacher in earnest; weeping sometimes for his Auditory, sometimes with them, always preaching to himself, like an Angel from a cloud, but in none; carrying some, a S. Paul was, to Heaven in holy raptures, and inticing others by a sacred Art and Courtship to amend their lives; here picturing a vice so as to make it ugly to those that practised it; and vertue so as to make it beloved even by those that lov'd it not; and all this with a most particular grace and an unexpressible addition of comeliness.' That memory does something to compensate for a truth in Donne's letter when he sent a copy of a sermon requested by the Countess of Montgomery: 'I know what dead carkasses things written are, in respect of things spoken.'

His sermons have the disadvantage and the advantage of being based on the belief that from cover to cover the Bible had been dictated to 'secretaries of the Holy Ghost'. The disadvantage is obvious to most modern people, and it is intellectual: his understanding of how the literature called *ta biblia* ('the books') was compiled could not be modern. For example, he believed that Moses had been the secretary to whom God dictated the first part of Holy Scripture. Consequently, Moses knew more than any scientist of whom Donne was aware and 'to depart from the literall sense . . . in the book of Genesis is dangerous, because if we do so there, we have no history of the Creation of the world in any other place to stick to' (6:62). He does not seem to have doubted that Genesis was reliable: he reminded the court of Charles I that in 'our age' people had sailed round the world but he still believed that God had taken only six days to create 'that earth and that heaven' (9:47).

In Donne's view a king of Israel could also be a king of literature, for David wrote all the psalms and Solomon all the 'wisdom' literature traditionally connected with him. That made David a 'better Poet' than Virgil (4:140). Solomon was 'wiser than Adam, than Moses, than the Prophets, than the Apostles' – and Donne added to that list which he drew from medieval sources. Since the Virgin Mary was not a marvel 'of natural and civil knowledge' she, too, was less wise than Solomon (3:48).

The advantage in this essentially medieval attitude to the Bible was that it inspired great care in the preacher's study, meditation and exposition, with close attention to both Testaments. Of the 160 of Donne's sermons which have survived, almost exactly half began with a text taken from the Old Testament and almost as many were based on a psalm as on a gospel. The preacher felt that he was standing in line with the Fathers of the Church as he preached from the divinely dictated Bible, and he was sure of his authority to do so. He quoted St Augustine of Hippo some seven hundred times in his surviving sermons, and one quotation was this: 'that which the Scripture says, God sayes, for the Scripture is his word; and that which the Church says, the Scriptures say, for she is their word, they speak in her; they authorize her and she explicates them' (6:282). But this following of the Fathers was not slavish, for as the Fathers had admitted, and as this preacher was not afraid to demonstrate, they could make mistakes: 'Let us follow the Fathers as Guides, not as Lords over our understandings' (9:161). As Donne put it, 'to that Heaven which belongs to the Catholique Church I shall never come except I go by the way of the Catholique Church . . . To beleeve according to ancient beliefs, to pray according to ancient formes, to preach according to former meditations' (7:61). But he was also a Protestant for whom the Catholic Church could never be superior to what the Bible said and should never be dogmatic where the Bible was silent. And he was a scholar who appealed to reason and to facts as seen by educated people in his time, holding that 'faith without a root, without reason, is no faith, but an opinion' (5:102). St Paul's Cathedral had been dedicated in honour of one of the giants of the Bible, built during the Middle Ages when the power of the Catholic Church rose above the little city, and taken over by the Protestant National Church in the early modern age – and when Donne preached in it, his sermons suited that formidable background.

One consequence was that he did not present the Jesus of the gospels as being human and attractive, the homeless friend of the poor and of women, of those excluded from respectable society and of those who were hungry for spiritual food not on offer from official religion. Inevitably he accepted what was thought by scholars in his own time: that Matthew's was the earliest of the gospels, written for Jews, and that Mark's was a 'just and intire history of our blessed Saviour' written for 'the Western Church' and based on 'Peter's Dictates'. John 'handleth his Divinity and his Sermons' while Luke merely 'cut off excesse and superfluity' (5:239–40). Earlier he had more sensibly thought that John's gospel was the last to be written (3:348). But his dismissal of Luke as an abbreviator shows how much he missed.

On Christmas Day in 1625 he told the congregation: 'He had a heavenly birth by which he was the eternall Son of God, and without that he had not been a person to redeem thee; He had a humane birth by which he was the Son of Mary, and without which he would not have been sensible in himself of thine infirmities and necessities; but this day (if thou wilt) he hath a spiritual birth in thy soul, without which both his divine and his humane births are utterly unprofitable to thee, and thou art no better than if there had never been Son of God in heaven, nor Son of Mary on earth' (6:335). This passage makes it appear that Donne believed that even in the congregation of St Paul's Cathedral, a quarter of the way through the seventeenth Christian century, there were people who needed a 'spiritual birth' and it may be thought that he would have been a more effective evangelist had he drawn more attention to the Jesus of Luke's gospel.

But Luke's account of Paul's conversion in the Acts of the Apostles did mean a great deal to this Dean of St Paul's who had himself been converted – although less dramatically – and he seized opportunities to preach about it. And the accounts of the crucifixion in all four gospels meant everything to him. 'I know nothing, if I know not Christ crucified' (5:276). He rejected the Calvinist's idea of God's 'irresistible' grace, because he remembered for how long he had resisted it himself, but now he accepted with his whole heart the teaching of Calvin and many others, Catholic and Protestant, about the cross as the supreme suffering and sacrifice. The devout emotion which he had tried to stir up and to increase in the poems written before ordination now flooded out. He told people: 'The Son of Man . . . hath himself formerly felt all our infirmities, and hath had as sad a soule at the approach of death, as bitter a Cup in the forme of Death, as heavy a feare of God's forsaking him in the agony of death, as we can have . . . The sins of all men, and all women, and all children, the sins of all Nations, all the East and West, all the North and South, the sins of all times and ages . . . were at once upon Christ' (6:275).

To him this was more that a 'theory of the atonement'. It mattered supremely that 'Christ doth suffer in our sufferings' (6:221); that after Christ's substitution of himself for us on the cross, 'Christ is the sinner and not I' (6:239); that 'no man hath any work of righteousness of his own, as can save him; for howsoever it be made his, by that Application or Imputation, yet the righteousness that saves him, is the very righteousness of Christ' (7:158–9). 'If I could dye a thousand times for Christ this were nothing, if Christ had not died for me before' (2:302). 'Preaching must be a continuall application of all that Christ Jesus said and did, and suffered, to thee' (7:232).

And how great were the gains when the Bible was read closely and lovingly by a major poet! One reason why he loved the psalms was that he knew what work went into a poem which 'requires diligence in the making and then when it is made can have nothing, no syllable taken from it, nor added to it' (2:50). He believed that in the Bible the poet's work was done by the Holy Spirit. 'The Holy Ghost in penning the Scriptures', he said, 'delights himself, not only with a propriety, but with a delicacy, and harmony, and melody of language and height of Metaphors, and other figures, which may work greater impressions upon the Readers, and not with barbarous, or triviall, or market, or homely language . . .' (6:55). Again: 'The Holy Ghost is an eloquent Author, a vehement and an abundant Author, but yet not luxuriant; he is far from a penurious, but as far from a superfluous style too' (5:287).

He did his best to repay the Bible in its own coin by using images which were either substantial metaphors provoking thought or else little pictures which could be flashed to keep a congregation awake. In the first category came more than one elaborate meditation on what the sea meant to Christians. London was then a very busy port, and England was then the base for the exploration of the oceans, so that many of his contemporaries were fascinated by maps and globes, but the impression made on Donne by his voyages in the 1590s still seems to fill his own imagination with salt air. 'A Sea is subject to stormes and tempests . . . And then, it is never the shallower for the calmnesse . . . It is as bottomlesse to any line which we can sound into it, and endlesse to any discovery which we can make of it' (2:306). Christians could be exhorted to embark bravely on voyages to heaven, choosing a sound ship with the safety given by the ballast in the hold but the speed given by the sails up aloft. They would face many dangers including the possibility that an innocent-looking fisherman might turn out to be a pirate (3:54), but the preacher could promise a rich profit on the cargo after a happy landing. He could use nautical terms accurately: 'we can ride out a storm at anchor; we can beat out a storm at sea, with boarding to and again; . . . though we be put to take in our sayls, and to take down our masts, yet we can hull it out' (3:184–5). And he could compare the mysterious vastness of eternity with the ocean: 'Give God sea-roome, give him his latitude' (8:318).

In his *Devotions* and in his 'Hymne to God my God' Donne also meditated elaborately on the spiritual lessons to be learned from sickness, and the scene when doctors probed the secrets of his body reminded him of a need which he had urged when preaching: 'Let every one of us dissect and cut up himself' (1:273). His sermons included many shorter references to medical knowledge and physical sufferings – topics of special interest to his fellow Londoners, as well as to him, since their city was overcrowded, insanitary and at the mercy of epidemics. A doctor's stepson and the patient of many other doctors, Donne was not nervous when pointing to parts of the human body. 'We know . . . the capacity of . . . the stomach of man, how much it can hold; . . . and we know the receipt of all receptacles of blood . . . ; and so we doe of all the other conduits and cisterns of the body . . . When I looke into the larders, and cellars, and vaults, into the vessels of our body for drink, for blood, for urine, they are pottles and gallons; when I look into the furnaces of our spirits, the ventricles of the heart and the braine, they are not thimbles' (3:236). He could even preach about the penis, that 'sewar of all sinne', reflecting that Abraham was wise to have himself circumcised when 99 years old (6:190–3). But all this frank acceptance of human physicality was connected with his acceptance of the Bible, which of course says a great deal about flesh.

He was unambiguous about the supremacy of the Bible. 'All knowledge is ignorance except it conduce to the knowledge of the Scriptures, and all the Scriptures lead us to Christ' (4:124). So the Scriptures must be supreme over the Church and over all human life. 'The Scriptures are God's Voyce; the Church is his Eccho' (6:223). And the Scriptures can teach things not known to 'Reason': 'though Reason cannot apprehend that a Virgin should have a Son, or that God should be made Man and dye', yet 'when our Reason hath carried us so far as to accept these Scriptures for the Word of God, then these particular Articles, a Virgin's Son and a mortall God, will follow evidently enough' (9:355). 'The Scripture is our Judge, and God proceeds with us according to those promises and Judgments, which he hath laid down in the Scripture.' There is even a sense in which 'the Scripture is a Judge by which God himself will be tryed' (8:281–2) – meaning that God does not hold himself free to act in contradiction of the holy love which he has revealed in Scripture. But the main point about the Bible is that the Christian must use it for life. There is little to be gained when a Christian is proudly able 'to ruffle the Bible and upon any word to turn to the Chapter and to the verse'. Truly to 'search the Scriptures', Donne said, 'is to finde all the histories to be examples to me, all the prophecies to induce the Saviour for me, all the Gospel to apply Christ Jesu to me' (3:367). A Christian ought to use the Bible 'as thou wouldest search at a wardrobe, not to make an Inventory of it, but to finde in it something fit for thy wearing' (3:367).

What matters most about the psalms is their power to speak about the deep things of God as people recite them and meditate on them, in generation after generation. More than once he claimed that if the rest of the Bible were to be lost the psalms would still enable the Christian faith to be known and spread. That was an obvious exaggeration but he was strict to maintain the custom of St Paul's Cathedral 'that the whole booke of Psalmes should every day, day by day, bee rehearsed by us who make the Body of this Church in the eares of Almighty God' (6:293). He recited the five psalms allocated to him daily and showed in his preaching that he had absorbed them with a special care, but the whole psalter fed his soul and was on hand as food for the congregation. One of his sermons was based on a text from one of the psalms (63:7) which were his daily ration: 'Because thou hast been my helpe, therefore in the shadow of thy wings will I rejoyce.' 'As the spirit and soule of the whole booke of Psalmes is contracted into this psalme, so is the spirit and soule of this whole psalme contracted into this verse' (7:52).

This love of the psalms may well have been the main reason why he began to study Hebrew seriously amid all the problems of his life in 1613. In contrast, the extent of his knowledge of Greek is questionable and it seems that he never thought it necessary to fill this gap left by his education. As we have already noted, Latin had been no problem to him since boyhood: his instinct was to quote the Bible first in Latin – or at least, this is suggested by the sermons which he prepared for future publication.

Donne was perfectly clear that the high authority of the sermon derived mainly from this authority of the Bible, not from the preacher's own holiness. 'I doubt not of mine own salvation; and in whom can I have so much occasion of doubt, as in my self? When I come to heaven shall I be able to say to any there, Lord! how got you hither? Was any man less likely to come thither than I?' (8:371). 'Whatsoever any Preacher can say of sinne, all the way, all that belongs to me, for no man hath ever done any sin which I should not have done if God had left me to my selfe' (5:41). His frequent identification of himself as a sinner was what made acceptable his equally frequent denunciations of 'all the wantonnesses of your youth, all the Ambitions of the middle years, all the covetous desires of your age' (5:182). And it was now his ambition, or at least his prayer, that how he lived might not contradict how he preached.

'Every minister of God', he told his parishioners in London, must have 'the courage of a Lion, the labourisness of an Oxe, the perspicuity and cleare sight of an Eagle, and the humanity, the discourse, the reason, the affability, the applicableness of a Man.' And he meditated in detail on the challenges offered by the traditional symbols of the four gospel-writers in the New

Testament. Lion-like courage must be 'proof against Persecution (which is a great) and against Preferment (which is a greater temptation); that neither Feares nor Hopes shake his constancy'. The ox-like minister will 'preach for the saving of soules, and not for the sharpening of wits'. Like an eagle who can look directly at the sun the minister must 'dare to looke upon other men's sins' although 'he is guilty of the same himself' – but must not look 'through other men's spectacles'. And being human, the minister requires 'a gentle, a supple, an appliable disposition, a reasoning, a perswasive disposition' (8:41–2).

A preacher who had to struggle to live up to those ideals also had to speak to sinners who would refuse to hear his message because they were in church in order to impress. 'The worldly man will hear thee', he told himself, 'yet though it be but to beget an opinion of holiness in others' – so that the preacher's task was to 'put thorns and brambles into his conscience'. 'The fashionall man . . . will hear' but only because he will go to church if he knows that 'great men' already go there, perhaps out of curiosity (2:174). It was not the job of the preacher to put 'pillows under great men's elbows' (2:105). On the contrary, prophet-like preachers have been commanded by God to 'see and discern the highest sins of the highest persons, in the highest places; they are not onely to look down towards the streets, and lanes, and alleys, and cellars, and reprehend the abuses and excesses of persons of lower quality there; all their service lies not below staires' with the servants. Preachers are ordered to 'look into the chamber, and reprehend the wantonesses and licentiousnesse of both sexes there'; they are to go 'unto the house top' and attack the 'ambitious machinations and practises' needed to climb up there; and they are to climb themselves, into a 'watchtower' where they must denounce sins 'done so much more immediately towards God, as they are done upon colour and pretence of Religion' (2:164–5).

If any sinner dared to reply by claiming to be guilty of no more than small sins, Donne could point out that 'as men that rob houses thrust in a child at the window, and he opens greater doores for them, so lesser sins make way for greater' (9:302). 'As a spider builds always where he knows there is most access and haunt of flies, so the Devil that hath cast these light cobwebs into thy heart, knows that that heart is made of vanities and levities' – so that 'lascivious glances' become adultery, 'covetous wishes' can lead to theft, and angry words can end up in murder (1:195).

Whether sins are full-grown or ominously pregnant, Donne claimed that the sinner ought to be glad that inside every church was a stone, namely Christ the Judge and Saviour – not a bed of flowers, not a pillow of feathers, not a river 'to disport, and refresh, and strengthen himself in his sinne', but a stone to stop him falling into hell (2:190). And in the Church 'the Ordinance of preaching batters the soule, and by that breach the Spirit enters; His Ministers are an Earth-quake and shake an earthly soule; They are the sonnes of thunder and scatter a cloudy conscience; They are the fall of waters and carry with them whole Congregations' (7:396). That vision of the preacher's momentous task explains why he thought it legitimate for a preacher to batter, shake, alarm and move sinners by shock tactics, and it may help us to forgive the rhetoric. And his preaching was not all melodramatic. He could preach as practical pastor. Having experienced them, he could speak about night thoughts when the Devil tempted and God seemed distant or hostile, but he recommended a defence – a 'shaking hands with God' at bedtime, 'and when thou shakest hands with God, let those hands be clean' (9:217). And he could preach with love. 'Who but myselfe can conceive the sweetnesse of that salutation, when the Spirit of God sayes to me in a morning, Go forth today and preach, and preach consolation, preach peace, preach mercy?' (7:133).

It can come as a shock to modern readers when they see that the preacher's commission to denounce the sins of the 'highest persons' was believed to stop short of the king. Like many other preachers who praised the princes governing as well as reigning in that age, Donne taught that 'Obedience to lawfull Autoritie is always an Essentiall part of Religion' (6:258). In particular is obedience due to a king. 'All forms of Government have one and the same Soul, that is Soveraignty . . . and this Soveraignty is in them all from one and the same Root, from the Lord of Lords, from God himself, for all Power is of God: But yet this form of a Monarchy, of a Kingdome, is a more lively and a more masculin Organ and Instrument of this Soul of Soveraigntie than the other forms are' since 'God himselfe, in his Unity, is the Modell, He is the Type of Monarchy' (4:240–1). Accordingly he endorsed the common description of kings as 'Lieutenants and Images of God', 'of whom God hath said, *Ye are Gods*' (4:334, quoting as many others did Psalm 82:6). This preacher who had once poured scorn on royal courts could now even bring himself to say that 'a Religious King is the Image of God, and a Religious Court is a Copy of the Communion of Saints' (8:336). And this royal chaplain made his loyalty clear in practical terms, for example in a sermon to lawyers. He maintained that the king 'is accountable to God only, and neither to any great Officer at home, not to the whole body of the people there, nor to any neighbour Prince or State abroad' (4:137).

In another sermon he put the Crown at the apex of a class structure which was like a pyramid. He claimed that despite his rough appearance and his diet of locusts and wild honey John the Baptist was 'of a good family and extraction', indeed was of the 'nobility', with 'his father a Priest, and his mother also descended from Aaron'. It had to be admitted that John's mother was not a virgin like the mother of his cousin Jesus, but 'to be born of a Virgin is but a degree more than to be borne of a barren woman'. The Baptist received a good education and enjoyed a good reputation: he was full of 'knowledge' and was 'reputed an honest man' (4:146–7). His dress and diet were not of the high quality to be expected of a member of a high class, but Donne's point was that this only showed how remarkable the Baptist was: 'for a Sonne of such Parents, an onely Sonne, a Sonne so miraculously afforded to them, to passe on with that apparell and that diet is certainly remarkable, and an evidence of an extraordinary austerity, and an argument of extraordinary sanctity' (4:154).

He knew perfectly well that the Baptist denounced his own king as a sinner and tyrant, but he had no intention of preaching about the unconventional sex life of King James or the consequent alcoholism of his queen. Nor did he directly attack the favourites of the happily married King Charles. He excused himself with the argument that Christian monarchs were responsible to God – as both James and Charles admitted – and would be judged by him, and that meanwhile God had not instructed either popes or preachers to take his reserved place (2:303). But this royal chaplain now exposed himself to the question he had asked in his 'Second Anniversarie':

> Shalt thou not finde a spongy slack Divine
> Drink and sucke in th' Instructions of Great men,
> And for the word of God, vent them agen?

The contempt which Donne the layman had felt for flattering preachers is bound to be shared when modern people accustomed to democracy listen to Donne the preacher. However, it needs to be remembered that when Donne preached that kings were 'such Images of God as have eares and can hear; and have hands and can strike' (9:59), no one in his congregation would have been disgusted. He belonged to an England where it was commonly agreed that monarchy was the only realistic alternative to anarchy and in that period Puritan preachers were among those who agreed. James was personally unpopular after 1619 – he seemed to be unpatriotic as he tried to be the ally of Spain and unwise as he relied on ministers who were corrupt or incompetent or both – but complaints were not rebellion. Within a dozen years of Donne's death the atmosphere had changed and King Charles was on his way to the executioner's scaffold erected outside the Banqueting House in the palace of Whitehall, but only a few years later order was to be restored very firmly by Oliver Cromwell, who was a king in all but name. After another short period, Charles II (a worse king than either his father or his grandfather) was to be restored the throne of his ancestors amid popular rejoicing. His brother James had to become a Roman Catholic without discretion in order to lose that throne. And two of the three monarchs in whose reigns Donne lived were people who knew how to survive exceptional dangers by the exercise of exceptional skills. Elizabeth, once addressed by Donne as 'Greatest and fairest Empresse', ruled men by dazzling them and the less glamorous James, once called by him 'the learnedst king that any age hath produced' (10:161), ruled them by being indispensable. Both survived a number of plots to assassinate them and it was truly said about them both that a nation survived because its monarch did.

Donne's first sermon which invited publicity and criticism by being preached in the open air at Paul's Cross came in 1617, remarkably soon after his ordination (1:183–221). It was 'exceedingly well liked generally' according to the critical and gossipy John Chamberlain who was there. This was because 'he did Quene Elizabeth great right' and said even more to honour King James, whose accession to the throne was being celebrated – and did all this in the context of a plea for peaceable Christian living which could not be regarded as at all controversial.

If such a sermon is now thought to be an example of the blind preaching to the blind, we should remember that Donne once said that 'Princes are God's Trumpet, and the Church is God's Organ, but Christ Jesus is his voyce' (6:217). So far from being a complete Cavalier, he had much in common with the Puritans who were to give such trouble to the Stuart dynasty. He shared their enthusiasm for preaching based on the Bible. He shared their insistence on at least the struggle for holiness ('sanctification') after the personal acceptance of Christ as the Saviour who shared his righteousness so that sinners might be treated as righteous ('justification'). 'God', he says, 'requires the heart, the whole man, all the faculties of that man, for onely that is intire, and indivisible, is immovable' (9:196). He shared their Protestant patriotism. He could still denounce the cruelty of the full Calvinist system in theology, but he now used Calvin as a biblical scholar and called him 'a very great man' (5:65). He could laugh at the Puritan who 'imagines a Church that shall be defective in nothing' and sometimes imagines himself 'to be that Church' (9:168–9), and he could warn Puritans who thought that crossing the Atlantic was necessary in order to be pure: 'we shall not need any re-Reformation, or super-Reformation, as swimming Brains must needs cross the Seas for' (4:107) – but he knew that most Puritans in his time had no wish to leave England or the Church of England.

He belonged to the sizeable group in the Church under James I which was in important ways Puritan without being fully Calvinist. That was why the senior lawyers of Lincoln's Inn were willing to have him as their preacher; many of them were Puritans, Donne's predecessor and successor in the office were both definite Puritans, and a chaplain who assisted Donne but attacked Puritans too personally was sacked. It is also significant that Donne maintained close friendships with Lincoln's Inn lawyers who had opposed the king during the 1614 Parliament, of which he himself had been a member. When invited to preach before Queen Anne and her courtiers in 1617, without mentioning the well-known fact that Her Majesty was a Roman Catholic he produced eloquence in praise of the Protestant Church of England of which any Puritan would have been proud. And when he delivered the first sermon which Charles I heard as king (6:241–61), he spoke in a style to which no Puritan could object, for he spoke of a kingdom where king and subjects, Church and State, were united in maintaining laws which should not offend any reasonable Christian's conscience. Maybe it was a dream – but it was an ideal which, if it had consistently inspired the king's policies, could have saved the country from civil war.

We should not dismiss Donne as a mere courtier and snob. One great test came in September 1622. King James had recently issued 'Directions to Preachers' forbidding any clergyman who was not a bishop or a dean from discussing in the pulpit the main theological controversy of the day – and no preacher was to 'meddle with matters of state and the differences between Prince and people'. Emotions were running high because the people were agitated about the disasters which seemed to be overwhelming the Protestants in central Europe while the king seemed more interested in an alliance with Catholic Spain to be cemented by a marriage between his son and heir and the king of Spain's daughter. Rumours spread that King James was going to become a Roman Catholic like his wife and that 'Papists' were going to be tolerated (secretly James I agreed that such toleration could follow such a marriage, and it was to happen under James II, causing a revolution). Puritan and some other preachers were loud in affirming their Protestantism and their patriotism, calling for war, not alliance, with 'Papists'. Some private correspondence of Donne's has survived which shows that he fully shared the general anxiety, and he wrote the very anxious poem 'Show me deare Christ' although this was not made public before 1899.

He was instructed to explain and defend the king's 'Directions' in a sermon at Paul's Cross, outside the cathedral of which he had recently been made dean. A large, excited and distinguished congregation assembled to hear him perform; most had to listen standing, for over two hours. What they heard pleased the king, who told the Earl of Carlisle to assure the preacher that the sermon was 'a piece of such perfection, as could admit neither addition nor diminution'. By royal command it was printed, as the first of Donne's sermons to receive that degree of fame, and the pamphlet was dedicated by permission to the king's first minister, the Duke of Buckingham. Yet a layman in the congregation, John Chamberlain, told a friend that the preacher had given 'no great satisfaction, or as some say spake as yf himself were not so well satisfied'.

In fact Donne had performed with high skill. On the one hand, he had no wish to criticize his royal master's plan to banish theological controversy from pulpits in the parishes. A pastorally minded preacher in a parish had more than enough to do if he preached 'the Gospell, onely the Gospell, and all the Gospell' (5:261). He snubbed the ignorant impertinence of lay or clerical commentators on current affairs: 'Pretend not thou who art but a private man, to be an Overseer of the Publick' (4:137). And the royal supremacy over the Church of England, now being invoked in order to control pulpits, did not trouble Donne at this stage: he thought it right that the king should have 'the same autoritie in causes Ecclesiastical that the godly Kings of Judah, and the Christian Emperors in the primitive Church, had' (4:199). And this authority should be extensive: 'The rituall and ceremoniall, the outward worship of God, the places, the times, the manner of meetings, are in the disposition of Christian Princes, and by the favours of those Churches which are in their government' (10:221).

On the other hand, like the Puritans whom the king was trying to muzzle Donne did not think that 'Catechizing' would be enough for the average congregation. The 'Directions to Preachers' ordered that this exercise should take place every Sunday afternoon although they allowed a sermon in the morning, and in the next reign the emphasis of bishops such as William Laud was to be on catechizing rather than preaching. One reason for this preference was that this substitute for a sermon, being intended mainly for the instruction of children, was based on the catechism of questions and answers printed in the Book of Common Prayer. The clergymen were expected to add only reinforcements of the Prayer Book's answers – and what was taught was in part this: 'My duty towards my neighbour is . . . To honour and obey the King, and all that are put in authority under him: To submit myself to all my governors, teachers, spiritual pastors and masters: To order myself lowly and reverently to all my betters: . . . To keep my hands from picking and stealing . . . To do my duty in that state of life, in which it shall please God to call me.' Donne would not have disagreed with any of that but he wanted, and offered, a preacher's appeal to the mind and the heart of an adult, pointing to the Bible rather than to any lesser authority.

He therefore based this tricky sermon in 1622 on an obscure text in the Old Testament: 'the stars in their courses fought against Sisera'. He interpreted this text as meaning that preachers, being 'Starrs', would always fight against error. He offered no detailed defence of the new directions, merely arguing that the king had reaffirmed the Church of England's traditional position, which surely all of its clergy would also wish to endorse. While avoiding all criticism of the monarch he was unenthusiastic in public and in a private letter to a friend he said that his hope was that his hearers had 'received comfortable assurance of His Majestie's constancy in Religion', which meant the rejection of 'the superstition of Rome'. In the event the 'Directions to Preachers' were ineffective since, led by Archbishop Abbot, the bishops were not willing to enforce censorship on their clergy and James lost interest in seeking it. Also the plan for a Spanish alliance came to nothing. Within two years Puritan preachers were in the pulpit which Donne had occupied, expounding the controversial Calvinist theology which had been forbidden. Nor did Puritan preachers avoid political controversy.

On 5 November that year Donne preached on another occasion when political tensions came to a head. He could not preach at Paul's Cross because of the rain, but to those who took refuge inside the cathedral he expounded a celebration of the deliverance of the king from 'the Powder Treason'. He combined this with discreet admissions that the king was being criticized on a number of grounds: he signalled his loyalty to his royal master but also a feeling that the critics needed to be reassured. 'Many times a Prince departs from the exact rule of his duty' he admitted, before adding that this need not be 'out of his own indisposition to truth, and clearnesse', but could a tactic designed to 'countermine underminers' as when rival tunnels were dug in the siege of a city. With the same cunning a Prince could be 'crafty and perchance false' with neighbours – a clear hint that Donne thought that James was being both secretive and devious in his negotiation with Catholic Spain, but had a strategy in mind. 'When Princes pretermit in some things the present benefit of their Subjects, and confer favours on others . . . you may think the King an ill King' – a hint that Donne understood the resentment of the English against favourites chosen by James partly because they came from Scotland. Another criticism mentioned was against a king who 'exercises his Prerogative without just cause' – the charge laid against James by the opposition in Parliament. And Donne even dared to mention a complaint against 'that King that gives himselfe to intemperate hunting' – a frequent complaint against James, who was said to neglect the business of the kingdom because he was out hunting. Accusations against kings might have some substance in them, so that they should be referred to the judgement of God; meanwhile those who have 'that great honour and that great charge' of having access to a king have a duty to warn him of dangers, for instead of killing kings 'we must endevour to preserve their persons' (4:249–50). King James sent for a copy of the sermon and, no doubt by his decision, it was not given the wider publicity of print. Donne had risked losing his support permanently.

Another test of his integrity came in April 1625 when he preached to the courtiers assembled 'at Denmark House, some few days before the body of King James was removed from thence, to his burial'. Of course it had to be a sermon in mourning and the preacher's grief was, no doubt, genuine, for he owed much to this patron. He ended: 'let none of us goe so farre from him or from one another, in any of our wayes, but that all we that have served him may meet once a day, the first time we see the Sunne, in the eares of Almighty God, with humble and hearty prayer that he will be pleased to hasten that day in which it shall be an addition even to the joy of that place, as perfect as it is and as infinite as it is, to see that face again, and to see those eyes open there, which we have seen closed here' (6:291). And of course the king was praised, eloquently. But this sermon was not only a courtier's tribute to the 'anoynted of the Lord', the 'breath of our nostrils' (4:250). It was also eloquent in a silence, for while praising James as a man who had been powerful and wise, and in these ways Godlike, Donne did not praise him as a man who had been good. And he did emphasize that James was now a man who was 'dead': the word came five times in the sentence which was the climax of the tribute. His alarming eloquence about corpses did not falter even now, with one – and such a one – near him and the royal household gathered round. And in the printed sermon only two pages are occupied by references to James, while nine and a half deploy the same eloquence in celebration of the one deathless king, Christ as proclaimed by Bible and Church. One wonders how many other royal chaplains would have kept this sense of proportion in that situation, in the seventeenth century or in any other age, with the conviction that 'so are all men, one kind of dust' (6:228).

Finally we may notice that during the constitutional crisis of 1629, when the House of Commons was accusing King Charles of breaking the law and destroying the liberty of England, Donne was summoned to preach before the king – and spoke about the necessary combination of law and liberty. It was the same vision as in 1620, when he had preached to the court of the wiser King James about the unity of 'Prince and people' in 'Peace, Plenty, and Health' (3:90). But in March 1629 Charles dismissed Parliament and began his personal rule, also aiming at 'Peace, Plenty, and Health' but believing that he knew what was best for his subjects without needing the advice of the House of Commons. At the time protests were on a small scale (five ships, the famous 'first fleet', sailed in April taking Puritans to Massachusetts). However, the day would come when the king needed the taxes which only the Commons could authorize. Summoned to vote for taxation, in the end the Commons voted for a civil war.

In 1625 Donne wrote out many of his sermons while taking refuge from the plague in the house of Sir John Danvers, who had married Magdalen Herbert. In 1649 Danvers was to be one of the 'regicides' who signed the condemnation of Charles I to death.

We have seen that in politics Donne was a royalist who refused to be tied down to the unquestioning royalism which was to be called Cavalier. When preaching his approach was essentially the same: he was a conservative who refused to be tied down to the kind of orthodoxy which was to be called fundamentalism. He felt the power of the old images – of the Holy Trinity as three co-operating persons, of eternal life as the resurrection of the flesh, of eternal death as the torments of hell, of sinfulness as the poison which began to flow when Eve ate the apple, and so forth. But he also knew that these traditional images needed interpretation to some of those who heard him in that early modern age.

'Almost every meanes between God and man suffers some adulterings and disguises: But Prayer is best' (5:232). That was for him the key to many problems in theology and its communication. Human religion has to be imperfect – but there can be prayer, and intelligent prayer, to the God who is real, as a key to open a huge door which will resist merely human battering.

It should not be assumed that because he accepted and repeated the standard imagery when expounding the doctrine of the Trinity Donne was naïve when thinking about God. There could be other imagery. 'God', he said, 'is not onely a multiplied Elephant, millions of Elephants multiplied into one, but a multiplied World, a multiplied All, All that can be conceived by us, infinite many times over' (10:35). And no imagery could fully express the reality: 'We can expresse God himselfe in no clearer termes, nor in termes expressing more dignity, than in saying we cannot expresse him' (8:105). Donne was no philosopher, yet by meditating on the self-revelation of God to Moses in the story of the burning bush ('I am'), he reached a philosophical conclusion: 'Jehovah is a name that denotes Essence, Beeing: Beeing is the name of God, and of God onely; for . . . the name of the Creator is *I am* but of every creature rather I am not, I am nothing' (8:145).

'The Trinity is the most mysterious part of our religion, and the hardest to be comprehended . . . But these mysteries are not to be chawed by reason, but swallowed by faith' (5:46–7). Why should they be swallowed? Donne's basic answer was that because of a combination of God's own self-revelation with human experience a Christian can 'apprehend not onely that I am in the care of a great and a powerful God, but that there is a Father that made me, a Sonne that redeemed me, a holy Ghost that applies this good purpose of the Father and Sonne upon me, to me' (9:52).

He taught that the mystery of the Trinity is illuminated by the experience of existing instead of being the alternative,

'Nothing'; and of being saved by Christ instead of the alternative, hell; and of reading the inspired Scriptures and finding that an inspired response arises in the mind and the heart. Often he stressed the power of the Father, the wisdom of the Son and the goodness of the Holy Spirit (as in 5:88) although in his final sermon while keeping 'power' he spoke chiefly of 'mercy' and 'comfort' (10:231). This belief in the threefold God found in Christian experience fitted in well with his frequently expressed conviction that the human desire for community and love is rooted in the being of God, in whose image human nature has been created. And even in the individual he found the work of the threefold Creator: 'finde impressions of the Trinity in the three faculties of thine own soule, thy Reason, thy Will and thy Memory' (as in 3:359). Elsewhere he put memory before will. But he took all this, as he took so much else, from St Augustine and certainly he did not believe in three gods. On the contrary, like St Augustine he usually referred to 'God' in the singular. 'These notions that we have of God, as a Father, as a Son, as a Holy Ghost . . . are so many handles by which we may take hold of God, and so many breasts by which we may suck such a knowledge of God, as that by it we may grow up into him' (3:263).

He often used the picture of God as the Circle, beginning and ending in simple perfection. So he began his praise of 'the translation of the Psalmes by Sir Philip Sydney, and the Countess of Pembroke his Sister', with this invocation:

> Eternall God, (for whom who ever dare
> Seeke new expressions, doe the Circle square,
> And thrust into strait corners of poore wit
> Thee, who art cornerlesse and infinite)
> I would but blesse thy Name, not name thee now . . .

It seems that one reason why he welcomed that translation was that it preserved the sense of wonder in the psalms while a version often used in churches at that time, the metrical version of 1562, was doggerel (but the Sidney translation, not printed until 1823, was never used). And although his imagination delighted in the spectacle of the resurrection of the body by God's supermiracle, here too he was not completely naïve in his thinking about a part of the Church's tradition.

In the eighteenth meditation of his *Devotions*, he thinks that 'every body is sure' that someone who has just died had a soul, and of course he agrees. But 'if I will aske mere Philosophers, what the soule is, I shall finde amongst them some that will tell me it is nothing but the harmony . . . of the elements in the body, which produces all those faculties, which we ascribe to the soule . . . If I will ask . . . Philosophicall Divines how the soule, being a separate substance, enters into Man, I shall finde some that will tell me, that it is by . . . procreation from parents . . . ; and I shall finde some that will tell mee that it is by immediate infusion from God . . . If I will aske not a few men but almost whole bodies, whole Churches, what becomes of the soules of the righteous at the departing thereof from the body, I shall bee told by some, They attend . . . a purification in a place of torment; By some, that they attend . . . in a place of rest, . . . of expectation; By some that they passe to an immediate possession of the presence of God.' And so the experts differ. 'But yet I have . . . mine owne Charity; I aske that; and that tels me, He is gone to everlasting rest, and joy, and glory.' And charity combined with faith bids him pray for more than that, since the 'Saints in heaven lacke yet . . . the consummation of their happinesse' – and so he prays for the soul's 'joyful reunion to that body which it hath left'.

As we saw in connection with his love poetry, he preached that 'all that the soule does it does in, and with, and by the body' (4:358). Accordingly he believed that since this was the case before death the resurrection of the dead could not be fully glorious if it did not include the body. But he did face some questions which are likely to arise if it is believed that bodies will literally 'live again'. 'Where be all the splinters of that Bone which a shot hath shivered and shattered in the Ayre? Where be all the Atoms of that flesh which a corrasive hath eat away, or a Consumption hath breath'd, and exhal'd away from our arms and other Limbs? In what wrinkle, in what furrow, in what bowel of the earth, ly all the graines of the ashes of a body burnt a thousand years since? In what corner, in what ventricle of the sea, lies all the jelly of a Body drowned in the generall flood?' He did not shrink from asking how there could be a reunion 'between that arm that was lost in Europe, and that legge that was lost in Afrique or Asia, scores of yeers between'. Nor did he shirk questions about bodies deformed by disease, when 'a Dropsie hath extended me to an enormous corpulency, and unweildenesse' or when 'a Consumption hath attenuated one to a feeble macilency and leannesse'. Nor did he escape from such problems by believing (as many Christians including St Paul have done) that the 'body' of the resurrection will be a new, spiritual body, so that what is really believed in is the resurrection of the personality. He insisted: 'I shall have my old eies, and eares, and tongue, and knees, and receive such glory in my body my selfe as that, in that body, so glorifyed by God, I also shall glorify him' (8:98).

Those last words give the clue about Donne's motive in imagining so exuberantly that final world of stupendous miracles. He believed that all three persons of the Trinity had been involved in the creation of human bodies and would not rest content until what had been created was brought to perfection. 'In those infinite millions of millions of generations, in which the holy, blessed and glorious Trinity enjoyed themselves one another, and no more, they thought not their glory so perfect, but that it might receive an addition from creatures; and therefore they made a world, a materiall world, a corporeall world, they would have bodies' (4:47). Donne often quoted Genesis 1:26: '*Let us make man*, that consultation of the whole Trinity in making man, is exercised even upon this lower part of man, the dignifying of his body.' So he was not surprised that 'very many of the Fathers' had taught that 'the soule of man comes not to the presence of God, but remaines in some out-places until the Resurrection of the body' (6:266). He thought that the human body was the 'Master-piece' of the physical creation (4:294) and expected the work to be completed triumphantly on the day of resurrection. 'All dies, and all dries, and moulders into dust, and that dust is blowen into the River and that puddled water tumbled into the sea, and that ebbs and flows in infinite revolutions, and still, still God knowes . . . in what part of the world every graine of every man's dust lies; and . . . he whispers, he hisses, he beckons for the bodies of his Saints, and in the twinckling of an eye, that body that was scattered over all the elements, is sate down at the right hand of God, in a glorious resurrection' (8:98).

Here Donne the preacher put into spoken rhetoric what Donne the poet had imagined almost twenty years before:

> At the round earth's imagin'd corners, blow
> Your trumpets, Angells, and arise, arise
> From death, you numberlesse infinities
> Of soules, and to your scattered bodies goe,
> All whom the flood did, and fire shall o'erthrow,
> All whom warre, dearth, age, agues, tyrannies,
> Despaire, law, chance, hath slaine . . .

Thus Donne enjoyed imagining the physical resurrection of the body, but he admitted that it would be incredible were it not part of the Apostles' Creed, which he believed had been composed by

Christ's apostles (4:62). 'There are so many evidences of the immortality of the soule, even to a naturall man's reason, that it required not an Article of the Creed, to fix this notion of the Immortality of the soule. But the Resurrection of the Body is discernible by no other Right, but that of Faith, nor could it be fixed by any lesse assurance than by an Article of the Creed' (7:98). And he could be cautious about detailed predictions of heaven, even while he accepted the Church's creed. 'Of these new heavens, and this new earth', he once said, 'we must say at last, that we can say nothing.' This was because eternity is 'where every thing is every minute in the highest exaltation, as good as it can be, yet super-exalted, infinitely multiplied, by every minute's addition; every minute infinitely better than it was before' (8:82).

Like many others in the history of Christian beliefs about life after death, Donne used various comparisons with life before death and was not able to fit them together into a smoothly logical system. At the time of the tenth of his 'Holy Sonnets' he concentrated on the comparison with sleep as he addressed Death:

> From rest and sleepe, which but thy pictures bee,
> Much pleasure, then from thee, much more must flow . . .
> One short sleepe past, wee wake eternally,
> And death shall be no more, death, thou shalt die.

He did not then discuss what we should enjoy when 'wee wake eternally' – but then, he did not mention God in that poem. In a sermon some fifteen years later he used another image, which did not involve any contrast between sleeping and waking. He said that 'true joy in this world shall flow into the joy of Heaven as a River flows into the Sea; That joy shall not be put out by death and a new joy kindled for me in Heaven'. He expected that 'my soule, as soon as it is out of my body, is in Heaven and does not stay for the possession of Heaven . . . but without the thousandth part of a minute's stop as soon as it issues is in a glorious light, which is Heaven'. He summed up: 'that soule that goes to Heaven meets Heaven here' (7:70–1). But he saw, it seems, that it was not altogether logical to say that immediately after death the soul 'meets Heaven' if we must also say that the resurrection of the body is needed for the fullness of joy. In another sermon he sounded as if he had seen this problem, saying defensively and illogically that 'though those Joyes of heaven, which we shall possesse immediately after our death, be infinite, yet even to these infinite Joyes, the Resurrection gives an addition, and enlarges even that which was infinite' (5:212).

Of course it was a mosaic or muddle of images, but at different times – probably without any clear development in systematic thought – Donne let his imagination work on different parts in the rich tradition which he accepted: rest in sleep, the soul's immortality, physical resurrection. His essential belief was, it seems, that everything depends on God – that 'whom God loves, he loves to the end: and not onely to their own end, to their death, but to his end, and his end is that he might love them still . . . The Sun is not weary with sixe thousand yeares' shining; God cannot be weary of doing good' (6:173–4).

Donne the preacher was always eloquent about the inevitability of death. In an early sermon he was already ridiculously gloomy: 'It is but our mistaking, when we call any thing Health . . . Before we can craule, we runne to meet death' (2:80). He was fascinated by deathbeds, including his own. But for him the deathbed's drama need not end in darkness. 'The sun is setting to thee, and that for ever; thy houses and furnitures, thy gardens and orchards, thy titles and offices, are departing from thee; a cloud of faintnesse is come over thine eyes, and a cloud of sorrow over all theirs.' And yet! – 'when his hand that loves thee best hangs tremblingly over thee to close thine eyes . . . behold then a new light, thy Saviour's hand shall open thine eyes, and in his light thou shalt see light' (2:267). In death a human being dies like an animal, yet for humanity death is the fulfilment of the lifelong feeling that something better must lie ahead: 'Creatures of an inferiour nature are possest with the present, Man is a future creature. In a holy and usefull sense wee may say that God is a future God; to man especially he is so; Man's consideration of God is specially for the future' (8:75).

That belief that the good God is trustworthy in life and death is a simple belief, but it can be clothed in rhetoric as splendid as any passage that Donne ever achieved. 'God hath made no decree to distinguish the seasons of his mercies: In paradise the fruits were ripe the first minute, and in heaven it is always Autumne, his mercies are ever in their maturity . . . If some King of the earth have so large an extent of Dominion in North and South as that he hath day and night together in his Dominions' – preaching in London on Christmas Day 1624, Donne did not like to refer directly to the king of Spain – 'much more hath God mercy and judgement together: He brought light out of darknesse, not out of a lesser light; he can bring thy Summer out of Winter, though thou have no Spring; though in the Wayes of fortune, or understanding, or conscience, thou hast been benighted till now, wintred and frozen, clouded and eclypsed, damped and benummed, smothered and stupefied till now, now God comes to thee, not as the dawning of the day, not as in the bud of spring, but as the Sun at noon to illustrate all shadowes, as the sheaves in harvest to fill all penuries; all occasions invite his mercies and all times are his seasons' (6:172).

As we have seen, Donne has sometimes been condemned as a hellfire preacher who terrified his ignorant congregation, and a part of the truth is that he did indeed use the traditional images of everlasting torment. No preacher of that age could think of depopulating hell and no poet with Donne's imagination could fail to be fascinated by hell's horrors – 'the intensenesse of that fire, the ayre of that brimstone, the anguish of that worm, the discord of that howling, and gnashing of teeth' (4:86). It is also true that he could be frightening about the possibility of a quick removal from sin on earth to hell in eternity. 'God is the Lord of Hosts', he warned, 'and he can proceed by Martial Law: he can hang thee on the next tree; he can choak thee with a crum, with a drop, at a voluptuous feast; he can sink down the Stage and the player . . . in to the mouth of hell; he can surprise thee even in the act of sinning' (1:176–7). Donne could conjure up a picture of the sinner who 'thought death his end; It ends his seventy yeares, but it begins his seventy millions of generations of torments, even in his body, and he never thought of that' (6:277).

However, when his preaching is taken as a whole what stands out in this connection is his insistence that the traditional images of hell signify most importantly exile from the joy of life in God's heaven, and the traditional doctrine about hell is meant chiefly as a warning given in order to alert and change sinners. Moreover, his only surviving sermon to be entirely about hell was preached (probably in 1622) not to people who could easily be terrified out of their wits because their wits were few, but 'to the Earle of Carlile, and his Company at Sion'. While ranking only as Viscount Doncaster, the Earl of Carlisle had been the head of the lavish diplomatic mission to which Donne had been chaplain, and while merely Lord Hay he had acquired the reputation of being among the courtiers of James I both one of the most sophisticated (he had spent time in France and had a polished courtesy) and one of the most extravagant (he had invented the 'ante-supper', a large display of cold food which guests admired, only to find that it was removed in favour of an even larger meal of hot food). Sion House was one of the houses owned by the Earl of Northumberland, the 'Wizard Earl' so called because he had passed the time by conducting scientific experiments while imprisoned for sixteen years in the Tower of London. Back in 1602 he had carried to Sir George More

Donne's fateful letter announcing his marriage. And we can be sure that the 'Company' included guests who could hold their own in conversation with these two earls.

To that distinguished gathering which had probably assembled in church in a mood of relaxed happiness, Donne said: 'When we have given to those words by which hell is expressed in the Scriptures the heaviest significations, . . . when all is done, the hell of hels, the torment of torments is the everlasting absence of God, and the everlasting impossibility of returning to his presence . . . To fall out of the hands of the living God is a horror beyond our expression, beyond our imagination . . . That that God should loose and frustrate all his owne purposes and practises upon me, and leave me, and cast me away as though I had cost him nothing, that this God at last should let this soule go away as a smoake, as a vapour, as a bubble, and that then this soule cannot be a smoake, nor a vapour, nor a bubble, but must lie in darknesse as long as the Lord of light is light it selfe, and never a sparke of that light reach to my soule; What Tophet is not Paradise, what Brimstone is not Amber, what gnashing is not a comfort, what gnawing of the worme is not a tickling, what torment is not a marriage bed to this damnation, to be secluded eternally, eternally, eternally, from the sight of God?' (5:265–7).

Speaking to a more mixed congregation in St Paul's Cathedral on Easter Day 1622, Donne quoted St John Chrysostom to the effect that 'Hell is not a monument of God's cruelty, but of his mercy. If we were not told of hell, we should all fall into hell; and so there is mercy in hell . . . We are bound to praise God as much for driving Adam out of Paradise, as for placing him there, And to give him thanks as well for hell as for Heaven. For whether he cauterise or foment, whether he draw blood, or apply Cordialls, he is the same Physitian, and seekes but one end (our spirituall health) by his divers ways' (4:82). Rightly or wrongly, Donne was one of the preachers who have believed that when the aim is the conversion of sinners a vivid picture of hell complete with all the traditional horrors can be more effective than a less alarming exhortation to see warnings around them now – to 'see your dishonesty in your accounts, looke upon your ward-robes and know your excesses, looke upon your children's faces and know your fornications' (4:150). But it does not follow that he thought that all the images of hell must be taken literally. In his 'Hymne to God the Father' he expressed his own fear of what might become of him after his death: this mature fear was that 'I shall perish', not go to hell.

Repeatedly Donne treated himself and all who listened to him as sinners. He had been converted and he preached in order to convert others. 'I came to a feeling in my selfe, what my sinfull condition was', he recalled. 'This is our quickning in our regeneration and second birth; and till this come a sinner lies as the Chaos in the beginning of the Creation' (9:299). Without question he accepted and expounded the account of the origins of this human condition given by Bible and Church as understood by all Christians in his time. 'We were all wrapped up in the first Adam, all Mankind', he preached in 1618, 'so that we inherit death from him, whether we will or no; before any consent of ours be actually given to any Sin we are the children of wrath and death.' 'Miserable men!' he exclaimed in that sermon delivered as a chaplain to the royal court. 'A Toad is a bag of Poyson, and a Spider is a blister of Poyson, and yet a Toad and a Spider cannot poyson themselves; Man hath a dram of poyson, originall-Sin, in an invisible corner, we know not where, and he cannot choose but poyson himself and all his actions with it' (1:293).

Such words may be dismissed as rhetoric not likely to trouble a courtier or anyone else. But when preaching in St Paul's Cathedral Donne was capable of being more specific about sins in his congregation than any modern preacher would dare to be in such a pulpit. 'Consider that when thou preparest any uncleane action, in any sinfull nakednesse, God is not onely present with thee in the roome then, but then tels thee, that at the day of Judgement thou must stand in his presence and in the presence of the whole World, not onely naked, but in that foule, and sinfull, and uncleane action, which thou commitedst then.' And the sins denounced were not only those of the flesh. 'You rob and spoile, and eat his people as bread, and then come hither, and so make God your Receiver and his house a den of Thieves . . . Let thy Master be thy god, or thy Mistresse thy god, or thy chests be thy god . . . The Lord is terrible above all gods' (7:318).

Thus Donne could bring down to the level of his audiences, and of himself, what to him was the fact that the sin of Adam and Eve lived on. He did believe that they had sinned, as a fact of history, and that since every man was 'in Adam' 'the will of every man concurred to that sin' (2:106), but in another sermon which was more mature and pastoral he showed awareness of the objection that God would be unjust to punish later generations merely because their first ancestors had sinned. 'Adam sinned, and I suffer; I forfeited before I had any Possession or could claim any Interest; I had a Punishment before I had a being. And God was displeased with me before I was I; I was built up scarce 50 years ago in my Mother's womb, and I was cast down almost 6,000 years ago in Adam's loynes; I was borne in the last Age of the world, and dyed in the first. How and how justly do we cry out against a Man that hath sold a Towne, or sold an Army. And Adam sold the World' (7:78). But he thought he was able to answer anyone who would 'cry out' against God, for he insisted that 'Originall sin' was not merely an event in the remote past. Adam and Eve had sinned – but so had every human being, both by being mysteriously present 'in Adam' and by being sinful in his or her own life. That, Donne thought, entitled him to deny that God's punishments are unjust.

In his time the question which dominated religious controversy was how to deal with this ingrained sinfulness. He felt obliged to attack both the Roman Catholic and the Calvinist positions as he understood them. He rejected as 'superstition' a form of Catholicism which now seems to be a parody or corruption of what Catholics really believe. He attacked the belief that admission to heaven could be earned by practices including fresh sacrifices of Christ by priests in the Mass, acts of penitence as prescribed by them and good deeds done as instructed by them with no great emphasis on inspiration by God. And he attacked the teaching that the clergy could draw on a 'treasury of merit' – merit earned by Christ's sufferings which were greater than was strictly necessary and by the good deeds of the saints – in order to secure the early release of sinners from the pains of purgatory after death. Donne also rejected what now seems to be a malicious parody of Protestantism: the belief that admission to heaven was restricted to the few who had been predestined by God for its delights, who had been unable to resist the 'grace' bestowed by God on the elect, but whose sole contribution was the faith that they were indeed among the few who, without any merit of their own, had been saved out of the 'damned mass' of humanity because Christ's unrepeatable sacrifice to the Father had been for their exclusive benefit. He denounced both positions and history has applauded his attacks, for crudities which may (or may not) have been taught and believed by Catholics or Calvinists in the sixteenth or seventeenth century have become incredible to most of their heirs. And, more tragically, history has also vindicated Donne's conviction that there is strong evil in the human heart.

So what is the heart of this preacher's message to people who live and think almost four hundred years after his death? Some writers who have been enthusiastic about his sermons appear to have believed that the message as he expressed it should be repeated in more or less the same form, although they have granted that good sermons may take less than an hour. But it seems more realistic to admit that in countries where it is conceivable that the language of England in his time may still be understood a greater difficulty exists: the age of science, and of science-based technology producing a comparatively affluent materialism, with a technology-based educational system, has meant that for many people the problem is not how to be reconciled to God; it is how to know that God is real.

In his middle period John Donne wrestled with God in the sense of being deeply unsure whether God loved him enough to 'save' him among the 'elect'. But in his preaching years he had far more assurance. 'The Holy Ghost bears witness', he now said, 'that is, he pleads, he produces that eternall Decree for my Election. And upon such Evidence shall I give sentence against my selfe?' (5:67). And he stated some of the evidence on which he now relied, together with the many Christians who surrounded him: 'I am of the number of thine elect, because I love the beauty of thy house, because I captivate mine understanding to thine Ordinances, because I subdue my will to obey thine, because I find thy Son Christ Jesus made mine in the preaching of thy Word, and my selfe made his in the administration of his Sacraments' (8:311). Of course that was not a complete statement of the evidence which had made him convinced, for he could have spoken about his own transformed life, given direction, usefulness and joy despite the dark nights. It was not that he had ever felt himself completely outside the Christian tradition. After a Roman Catholic boyhood had come the years when he had been a young man heated by lust. But he had kept going on the spiritual journey, he had become full of depression and self-accusation, as a pilgrim he had made progress, and eventually he had found his way into the most influential pulpits in the country.

He did not then say that he had come to believe in God, for he had never disbelieved. Even in *Metempsychosis* he had spoken of 'Great Destiny' and 'Infinity' and in other poems he had simply referred to 'God'. He lived in an age when 'atheist' was a term of abuse and a charge which, if pressed, could get anyone into serious trouble, for civilization was thought to depend on acceptance of moral laws decreed by the divine Law-giver. Usually, however, to call someone an 'atheist' seems to have meant no more than that someone was regarded as unorthodox in religion or morality: it did not necessarily mean that someone was so mad as not to believe in any kind of God. Donne thought that even a 'pratique Atheist' who had lived without a thought of God would be able to claim 'at the last day' that 'he was no speculative Atheist, he never thought in his heart that there was no God' (3:87). So he could use the term 'atheist' very imprecisely, about a non-Christian believer in God or about a Christian who was a heretic or a 'melancholique' (3:312).

In an age when modern science was in its infancy, it seemed obvious to almost everyone, even to the few Deists who were sceptical about the miracles in the Bible, that the order, the beauty and the usefulness of the world belonged to one vast miracle, the miracle of divine creation. Donne could claim that 'there is nothing that God hath established in the constant source of nature, and which therefore is done every day, but would seeme a Miracle and exercise our admiration, if it were done but once' (2:175). 'To make a King of a Beggar is not so much as to make a worm out of nothing' (4:86). 'The world is the Theatre that represents God, and every where every man may, nay must, see him' (8:224).

He quoted St Augustine: 'Nothing is Essentially good, but God' and yet 'this Essential goodness of God is so diffuse, so spreading, as there is nothing in the world, that doth not participate of that goodnesse' (6:231). Surely everyone must see the truth of both halves of that proposition: God is good, the world is good? Is not this the lesson taught clearly on every page of 'the whole booke of Creatures' (3:264)? The humble 'Marrigold opens to the Sunne, though it have no tongue to say so; the Atheist does see God though he have not grace to confesse it' (4:170). 'To beleeve in God, one great, one universall, one infinite power, does but distinguish us from beasts; For there are no men that do not acknowledge such a Power' (8:59). 'Ridling, perplexed, labyrinthicall soule! Thou couldst not say that thou beleevest not in God, if there were no God' (8:332).

When he reminded himself that there were, or might be, some such people as genuine atheists, he still found it easy to prove the reality and the rule of the Creator to 'the reason of Man'. It seemed obvious that 'this World, a frame of so much harmony, so much concinnitie and convenience, and such a correspondence and subordination in the parts thereof, must necessarily have had a workeman, for nothing can make it selfe'. It seemed equally obvious to him that 'no such workeman would deliver over a frame and worke of so much Majestie to be governed by Fortune, casually, but would still retain the Administration thereof in his owne hands' (3:358).

He went on to say that this divine workman and boss would expect 'a worship and service to him, for doing so', and would reveal 'what kind of worship and service shall be acceptable to him' – and reveal this in writing. He admitted that it could not be proved ('as that one and two are three') that the Scriptures of the Christians are 'of God' but he claimed that anyone comparing this Bible with other scriptures would reach that verdict. And he claimed that while the 'faint and dimme knowledge of God' provided by nature might be compared with 'one small coale' amid 'cold ashes'. 'If thou wilt take the paines to kneele downe, and blow that coale with thy devout Prayers, and light thee a little candle' of Bible study, that would persuade anyone to 'creep humbly into low and poor places' and 'finde thy Saviour in a Manger'. He was preaching his first Christmas sermon in St Paul's.

Because he had never entered into the mind of an atheist, he produced arguments which would not convince anyone in that position, in his own age or ours. Obviously in our own time many would say that much in the universe seems to be disorderly, or has an order which we cannot understand; that its origin is not to be compared glibly with the making of an object by a human craftsman; that its evolutionary history does not easily suggest its Maker's close control of every event; and that no one can be so unprejudiced as to be able to judge all the scriptures of the world impartially before pronouncing the verdict that the Bible is the Word of God. But Donne could bully the atheist, who to him seemed merely a fool.

Regretable sermons by Donne the hell-fire preacher have already been quoted. Here is another rant: 'Bee as confident as thou can in company; for company is the Atheist's Sanctuary' – but at the day of Judgement, 'when I may see thee upon thy knees, upon thy face, begging of the hills that they would falle down and cover thee from the fierce wrath of God', Donne will ask the victim, 'Is there a God now?' When the atheist is dying and must already 'feele Hell', Donne will already have asked that question by the deathbed. Even 'six houres' after the sermon, at 'midnight . . . wake then; and then in the darke and alone, Heare God aske thee then, remember that I asked thee now, Is there a God? and if thou darest, say No' (8:332–3). However, there were probably not many atheists in the cathedral to respond to this sermon after Evensong one dark and cold afternoon in January 1629; so perhaps no great harm was done.

To many modern people it seems unreasonable to believe that God is both good and powerful, since so much suffering lies within human experience. The question was not raised so sharply or so publicly in the early modern period but Donne was aware of it, partly because his own life had not been a bed of roses. He said about suffering that 'he praises not God, he prays not to God, he worships him not, whatsover he does, if he have not considered it, debated it, concluded it . . .' (1:278). He was no sentimentalist either, but he reached the point in his spiritual journey where he saw God for the most part not as the remote Creator, or as the terrifying Judge on the throne, but as the supreme Lover, coming to him in his own experience including the experience of suffering. He thought that he had to believe that all 'affliction' is either sent or permitted by God, but he also believed that 'that which we call the anger of God, the wrath of God, the fury of God, is the goodnesse of God' (6:238). He held that 'God inflicts no calamity, no cloud, no eclipse, without light, to see ease in it, if the patient will look upon that which God hath done to him in other cases, or to that which God hath done to others at other times' (6:214). In another sermon the point was put more vividly: 'As he that flings a ball to the ground or to a wall intends in that action, that that ball should return back, so even now, when God does throw me down, it is the way he hath chosen to returne me to himselfe' (3:193).

Donne's view of the world included an emphasis on many features which seemed to make atheism unreasonable. But the centre of the true world-view had become for him the crucifixion and resurrection of Christ, for to him that proclamation of the divine love amid great 'affliction' was what demonstrated that God not only exists but also loves and rules. He granted that the resurrection of Christ was, like the resurrection of Christians, 'a mystery, out of the compasse of reason', but he added that 'we beleeve it immediately, intirely, chearfully, undisputably, because we see it expressly delivered by the Holy Ghost' (7:100–1). In this light, the light of God's supreme miracle, Donne held that 'God cannot by any Miracle so worke upon himselfe as to make himselfe not himselfe, unmercifull or unjust' (2:309). 'Let the Devill make me so far desperate as to conceive a time when there was no mercy, and he hath made me so far as an Atheist as to conceive a time when there was no God' (6:170). He liked the speculation that the 'word' by which God made the creation was a song (4:180) and in his ears the song was renewed by Christ's victory. This conviction that the ultimate triumph of the merciful God is assured was what made Donne eloquent about the joy of Christian faith and life, for by temperament he was not an optimist.

'Religion is no sullen thing', he declared, 'it is not a melancholy, there is no such sociable thing as the love of Christ Jesus and Christ is at home with thee, he is at home within thee, and that is the neerest way to find him' (2:246). 'The Church', he said, 'is not a grave: it is a fold, it is an Arke, it is a net, it is a city, it is a kingdome . . . It is a garden worthy of your walking in it' (6:152). And in some moods Donne could look through the church door and see the whole world as a delightful garden, an Easter garden. 'See God in every thing, and then thou needst not take off thine eye from Beauty, from Riches, from Honour, from any thing' (8:69). 'God', he could promise, 'shall give thee the sweetnesse of this world, honour and ease, and plenty' – all the honey which is 'the dew of the flowres'. But he also knew that honey is 'the vomit of the Bee' – and bees can sting (3:233). He could not claim that the whole world is a garden.

He told a congregation in St Paul's: 'Be reconciled to God, and you can have . . . the Innocency of Paradise. Go home, and if you finde an over-burden of children, negligence in servants, crosses in your tradings, narrownesse, penury in your estate, yet this penurious and this encumbered house shall be your Paradise. Go forth into the country, and if you find unseasonablenesse in the weather, rots in your sheep, murrains in your cattell, worms in your corn, backwardnesse in your rents, oppression in your Landlord, yet this field of thorns and brambles shall be your Paradise.

Lock thy selfe up in thy selfe, in thine own bosome, and though thou finde every roome covered with the soot of former sins . . . yet this prison, this rack, this hell in thine own conscience shall be thy Paradise' (10:139).

He once preached in St Dunstan's on the text 'Rejoyce evermore' and he had plenty to say which perhaps we do not expect to hear from him. 'Man passes not from the miseries of this life to the joyes of heaven but by joy in this life too; for he that feeles no joy here shall finde none hereafter . . . Rejoyce in your prosperitie, and Rejoyce in your adversitie too . . . Beasts who are carnall men, who determine all their desires in the sensuall parts, come no farther than to a delight: but men who are truly men, and carry them to the intellectual part, they, and onely they, come to Joy . . . The best evidence that a Man is at peace, and in favour with God, is that he can rejoyce.' And human joy in work well done despite the difficulties is a share in God's joy. 'It is . . . the Essence of God to doe good; and when he does that, he is said to rejoyce . . . To have something to doe, to doe it, and then to Rejoyce in having done it, to embrace a calling, to performe the Duties of that calling, to joy and rest in the peacefull testimony of having done so; this is Christianly done, Christ did it; Angelically done, Angels doe it; Godly done, God does it' (10:214–16).

But he was left with the problem of evil, in particular of suffering, and he knew that it was not enough to say cheerily that what we see as misfortune is really 'the goodnesse of God', so that even then we should 'rejoyce'. His sermon about joy was a companion to another, preached to the royal court in Lent 1623, 'in another place . . . when we handled these two words, *Jesus wept*'. That sermon, too, has survived (4:324–44) and it is more in the style we have come to expect of the adult Donne. 'Jesus was troubled and he groaned; and vehemently, and often, his affections were stirred' – in particular, by grief after death. The text about Christ at the tomb of Lazarus brought back Donne's own mourning: 'Here in this world we who stay lack those who are gone out of it: we know that they shall never come to us; and when we shall go to them, whether we shall know them or no, we dispute.' But he also meditated on Christ's weeping over Jerusalem and the world. He pictured the Saviour sharing compassionately in humanity's sorrow ('every man is but a spunge, and but a spunge filled with teares') but also weeping divinely over humanity's sins.

These sermons about joy and sorrow must have been separated from each other by at least a year but their co-existence is one reminder that this preacher always carried in his own heart the 'spunge' to hold tears. He could call affliction 'our daily bread'. He could say that 'man is more miserable than any other creatures, and good men more miserable than other men', so that 'all our life is a continuall burden, yet we must not groane; A continual squeasing, yet we must not pant; and as in tendernesse of our childhood we suffer and yet are wipt if we cry, so are we complained of if we complaine' (7:54–5).

He took no interest in the attempts of philosophers to persuade people that they ought not to complain. He dismissed the 'stupidity' of allegedly wise men who advise those who suffer 'that no pain should make them say that they were in pain' (2:53). He knew suffering himself, from the inside, and said so. He was well acquainted with grief. But he also thought that he now knew why and how to endure.

In the course of an early sermon he claimed that 'no man hath suffered more than himselfe needed' (2:300) and of course that can sound repulsively complacent. But he was speaking about a solution to the problem of evil which is not intellectual but is something given, strangely and uncomfortably, within a Christian's experience of union with the suffering of Christ, even of union with the suffering of God. 'Every man hath afflictions, but every man hath not crosses. Onely those afflictions are crosses, *whereby the world is crucified to us, and we to the world* . . . As Elisha in raysing the Shunamite's dead child put his mouth upon the child's mouth, his eyes and his hands upon the hands and eyes of the child; so when my crosses have carried me upp to my Saviour's Crosse, I put my hands into his hands and hang upon his nailes, I put mine eyes upon his, and wash off all my former unchast looks and receive . . . a new life into my dead teares, from his teares. I put my mouth upon his mouth, and it is I that say *My God, my God, why hast thou forsaken me?* and it is I that recover againe and say *Into thy hands, O Lord, I commend my spirit*' (2:300). And 'God affords thee this manifestation of his Crosse, in the participation of those crosses and calamities that he suffered here' (8:319). The God who asks us to suffer has his own cross.

And the Donne who taught that suffering must always be a part of a Christian's life had himself suffered. 'Affliction', he said, 'is my Physick; that purges, that cleanses me' (6:237). 'I had rather God frowned upon mee, than not look upon mee; and I had rather God persued mee, than left me to myself' (7:85). Once again he quoted Augustine: 'I feele the hand of a father upon me when thou strokest mee, and when thou strikest me I feele the hand of a father too' (8:320). 'Affliction', he told himself, 'is a treasure and scarce any man hath enough of it. No man hath enough of it that is not matured and ripened by it, and made fit for God by that affliction.' That was a lesson re-learned from his illness in 1623, as he recorded in his *Devotions.* He at least understood a saint's view of affliction: 'It is not that I rejoyce, though I be afflicted, but I rejoyce because I am afflicted' (3:341).

Here he was not being insanely morbid and we should remember that the preacher was also a man who knew the pleasures of the flesh, both the pleasures of hot youth and the cooler pleasures of middle age with enough money: he did not seek suffering. He preached that 'since I am bound to take up my crosse, there must be a crosse that is mine to take up; that is a crosse prepared for me by God, and laid in my way . . . and I must not go out of my way to seeke a cross, for so it is not mine, nor laid for my taking up' (2:301). But he knew that suffering must come and taught that during it God must still be trusted and praised. 'God', he said in a sermon where he seems to have been speaking out of darkness, 'will have low voyces, as well as high; God will be glorified *De profundis* as well as *In excelsis*; God will have his tribute of praise out of our adversity, as well as out of prosperity . . . Even in the depth of any spiritual night, in the shadow of death, in the midnight of afflictions and tribulations, God brings light out of darknesse and gives his Saints occasion of glorifying him, not only in the dark (though it be dark) but from the dark (because it is dark) . . . This is a way unconceivable by any, unexpressible to any, but those that have felt that manner of God's proceeding in themselves, That be the night what night it will . . . they see God better in the dark' (8:53).

So Donne came to believe both that death is the deepest darkness and that God's love shines through it. It is both the supreme affliction and the supreme cause to 'rejoyce'.

He never took death lightly. When he heard someone say 'I care not though I were dead, it were but a candle blown out, and there were an end of it all', he saw Satan at work, and he prayed that 'where the Devil imprints that imagination God will imprint . . . a loathness to die, and fearful apprehension of his transmigration' (8:188). So far as we know he never finally believed that when he died he would be 'but a candle blown out' but his 'Holy Sonnets' show that he had a 'fearful apprehension' about his death and his 'Hymne to God the Father', written some fourteen years later when he was an established preacher, confessed frankly that he still had this 'sinne of feare': even if he escaped the torments of hell he might 'perish' utterly. In his 'Nocturnall' he poured out his grief for his wife, saying that he felt dead: 'I am None', knowing only 'absence, darknesse, death; things which are not'. But amid these fears and griefs, only human in their nature but rare in his ability to communicate passion, the faith prevailed that because to die is to meet God the main emotion should not be fear. 'I shall not live till I see God', he said; 'and when I have seen him I shall never dye' (3:751). When he preached about Magdalen Herbert he said that 'in the new Testament death is a promise . . . We get not Heaven but by death, now' (8:91). Life's journey towards death might, or might not, be pleasant but 'wherever we are, is the suburb of the great City' (3:288).

He had come to think of himself and his hearers as 'way-faring men; This life is but the high-way, and thou canst not build thy hopes here; Nay, to be buried in the high-way is no good marke; and therefore bury not thy selfe, thy labours, thy affections, upon this world' (3:287). Even the greatest men on earth, memorialized in elaborate tombs with flattering inscriptions ('half-acre tombes' was his phrase in 'The Canonization'), had bodies which were not much different from logs in a fireplace. 'The ashes of an Oak in the Chimney are no Epitaph of that Oak, to tell me how high or how large that was; It tells me not what flocks it sheltered while it stood or what men it hurt when it fell. The dust of great persons in the grave is speechless, it says nothing, it distinguishes nothing . . .' (4:53).

On Easter Day 1619 Donne preached to the House of Lords before they received the Holy Communion together. Death was in all their minds, not only because of the season in the Church's year but also because the queen had died a few weeks previously and the king was dangerously ill. Donne told their Lordships that they were 'Prisoners all', all condemned to die; 'and then all our life is but a going out to the place of Execution, to death. Now was there ever any man seen to sleep in the Cart between New-gate and Tyborne? Between the Prison and the place of Execution, does any man sleep?' (2:197).

But it was also his message that light could be seen even in the supreme darkness of death. He had other moods but after those dark nights he returned to his faith. Then he could compare death with the coronation of Charles I: 'The Resurrection being the Coronation of man, his Death and lying down in the grave is his enthroning, his sitting downe in that chayre where he is to receive the Crowne' (6:277). And he could compare the sight of earth from that chair with what an adult sees when watching children's games: when the saints 'look down and see Kings fighting for Crownes', earth's struggles look like 'boyes at stool-ball' (5:75). He promised Charles I and his courtiers that one day they would enter the court of the King of Heaven. It would be like the palace where he was speaking but far more importantly it would be unlike, for now this man of flesh – this poet and preacher who over so many years had taken such trouble to find appropriate words – could produce no image rooted in the earth. In heaven the righteous (not merely the predestined few or the doctrinally orthodox) 'shall awake . . . And into that gate they shall enter, and in that house they shall dwell, where there shall be no Cloud nor Sun, no darknesse nor dazzling but one equall light, no noyse nor silence but one equall musick, no fears nor hopes but one equall possession, no foes nor friends but one equall communion and Identity, no ends nor beginnings but one equall eternity' (8:191).

Further reading

I have used *John Donne: The Complete English Poems*, edited by C. A. Patrides and updated by Robin Hamilton with 1,034 items in its bibliography (J. M. Dent, 1994) and *The Complete Poetry of John Donne*, edited by John T. Shawcross (Doubleday, 1967; New York University Press and University of London Press, 1968). The publication of *The Variorum Edition of the Poetry of John Donne* in ten volumes comparing printed editions with manuscripts began in 1995 (Indiana University Press). Editions with modernized spelling include *John Donne: The Complete English Poems*, edited by A. J. Smith and updated by John Tobin (Penguin Books, 1996) and *John Donne* in the 'Oxford Authors' series, edited by John Carey (Oxford University Press, 1990). Important earlier editions from Oxford University Press were Herbert Grierson's *The Poems of John Donne* (2 volumes, 1912 and 1933), Helen Gardner's *John Donne: The Elegies and the Songs and Sonnets* (1965) and *John Donne: The Divine Poems* (2nd edn, 1978), and Walter Milgate, *John Donne: The Satires, Epigrams and Verse Letters* (1967).

The Sermons of John Donne were edited by George Potter and Evelyn Simpson in ten volumes (University of California Press, 1953–62). Editions of his prose include Helen Peters, *Paradoxes and Problems* (Oxford University Press, 1980), Ernest Sullivan, *Biathanatos* (University of Delaware Press, 1985), Anthony Rapsa, *Pseudo-Martyr* (1993) and *Devotions upon Emergent Occasions*

(1975, both McGill-Queen's University Press), Timothy Healy, *Ignatius His Conclave* (Oxford University Press, 1969), Evelyn Simpson, *Essayes in Divinity* (Oxford University Press, 1952), and *Selected Prose*, edited by H. Gardner and T. Healy (Oxford University Press, 1967) and by Neil Rhodes (Penguin Books, 1987). M. Thomas Hester edited *Letters to Several Persons of Honour* (Scholars' Facsimiles and Reprints, 1976) and has a more comprehensive edition of John Donne's surviving letters in preparation. Evelyn Simpson, *A Study of the Prose Works of John Donne* (3rd edn, Oxford University Press, 1962), is still useful. So is the *Bibliography of Dr John Donne* compiled by Sir Geoffrey Keynes (4th edn, Oxford University Press, 1973).

The standard biography is R. C. Bald, *John Donne: A Life* (2nd edn, Oxford University Press, 1986),. Thomas Docherty, *John Donne, Undone* (Methuen, 1986) is more open to criticism. George Parfit, *John Donne: A Literary Life* (Macmillan, 1989), is shorter, as is the study of *John Donne* by Stevie Davies (Northcote House, 1994). John Carey, *John Donne: Life, Mind and Art* (2nd edn, Faber and Faber, 1990), is discussed in my Chapter 6, as is P. M. Oliver, *Donne's Religious Writing* (Longman, 1997). Derek Palmer, *John Donne and His World* (Thames and Hudson, 1975), includes many illustrations. Presentations of his life with an emphasis on the religion include Frederick Rowe, *I Launch at Paradise* (Epworth Press, 1964), Edward Le Comte, *Grace to a Witty Sinner* (Victor Gollancz, 1965), and Richard Hughes, *The Progress of the Soul* (Bodley Head, London, and William Morrow, New York, 1968). And we should not forget Augustus Jessopp, *John Donne, Sometime Dean of St Paul's* (Methuen, 1897), and Edmund Gosse, *The Life and Letters of John Donne* (2 vols, Heinemann, 1899).

North American scholars have excelled in Donnean studies. A good introduction is Frank Warnke's *John Donne* (G. K. Hall, 1976). Books include N. J. C. Andreason, *John Donne, Conservative Revolutionary* (Princeton University Press, 1967),

James Baumlin, *John Donne and the Rhetorics of Renaissance Discourse* (University of Missouri Press, 1991), Meg Lota Brown, *Donne and the Politics of Conscience in Early Modern England* (Brill, Leiden 1995), Ronald Carthell, *Ideology and Desire in Renaissance Poetry: The Subject of Donne* (Wayne State University Press, 1997), Dwight Cathcart, *Doubting Conscience: Donne and the Poetry of Moral Argument* (University of Michigan Press, 1975), Gale Carrithers, *Donne at Sermons* (State University of New York Press, 1972), John Chamberlain, *Increase and Multiply: Arts-of-Discourse Procedure in the Preaching of John Donne* (University of North Carolina Press, 1976), Charles Coffin, *Donne and the New Philosophy* (Columbia University Press, 1937), Horton Davies, *Like Angels from a Cloud: The English Metaphysical Preachers 1588–1645* (Huntington Library, 1986), Heather Dubrow, *A Happier Eden: The Politics of Marriage and the Stuart Epithalamion* and *Echoes of Desire* on English Petrarchism (Cornell University Press, 1990 and 1995), Dennis Flynn, *John Donne and the Ancient Catholic Nobility* (Indiana University Press, 1995), Donald Guss, *John Donne, Petrarchist* (Wayne State University Press, 1995), William Halewood, *The Poetry of Grace* (Yale University Press, 1970), M. Thomas Hester, *Kinde Pity and Brave Scorne: John Donne's Satyres* (Duke University Press, 1982), Deborah Larson, *John Donne and Twentieth-Century Criticism* (Farleigh Dickinson University Press, 1989), Barbara Lewalski, *Donne's Anniversaries and the Poetry of Praise* (Princeton University Press, 1973) and *Protestant Poetics and the Seventeenth-Century Religious Lyric* (Princeton University Press, 1979), Arthur Marotti, *John Donne, Coterie Poet* (University of Wisconsin Press, 1986), Louis Martz, *The Poetry of Meditation* (2nd edn, Yale University Press, 1962) and *The Wit of Love* (University of Notre Dame Press, 1969), Earl Miner, *The Metaphysical Mode from Donne to Cowley* (Princeton University Press, 1969), Janet Mueller, *Donne's Prebend Sermons* (Harvard University Press, 1971), William Mueller, *John Donne:*

Preacher (Princeton University Press, 1962), Marjorie Hope Nicholson's study of the impact of science in *The Breaking of the Circle* (Columbia University Press, 1960), David Novarr, *The Making of Walton's Lives* (Cornell University Press, 1958), and *The Disinterested Muse: Donne's Texts and Contexts* (Cornell University Press, 1980), T. Anthony Perry, *Erotic Spirituality* (University of Alabama Press, 1981), Patricia Pinka, *The Dialogue of One: The Songs and Sonnets of John Donne* (University of Alabama Press, 1982), Winfried Schleiner, *The Imagery of John Donne's Sermons* (Brown University Press, 1970), Robert Shaw, *The Call of God: The Theme of Vocation in the Poetry of Donne and Herbert* (Cowley Publications, 1981), Terry Sherwood, *Fulfilling the Circle: A Study of John Donne's Thought* (University of Toronto Press, 1984), Deborah Shuger, *Habits of Thought in the English Renaissance* (University of California Press, 1990), Alan Sinfield, *Literature in Protestant England 1560–1660* (Princeton University Press, 1983), Camille Slights, *The Casuistical Tradition in Shakespeare, Donne, Herbert and Milton* (Princeton University Press, 1981), Judah Stampfer, *John Donne and the Metaphysical Gesture* (Funk and Wagnall, 1970), P. G. Stanwood and H. R. Asals, *John Donne and the Theology of Language* (University of Missouri Press, 1986), Arnold Stein, *John Donne's Lyrics* (University of Minnesota Press, 1993), Edward Tayler, *John Donne's Idea of a Woman: Structure and Meaning in The Anniversaries* (Columbia University Press, 1991), Rosamund Tuve, *Elizabethan and Metaphysical Imagery* (University of Chicago Press, 1947), Leonard Unger, *Donne's Poetry and Modern Criticism* (Henry Regnery, 1950), and Joan Webber, *Contrary Music: The Prose Style of John Donne* (University of Wisconsin Press, 1963).

The English Department of the North Carolina State University began to publish the *John Donne Journal* in 1982. Collections of articles include *Just So Much Honor*, edited by Peter Fiore (Pennsylvania State University Press, 1972), *Soliciting*

Interpretation, edited by Elizabeth Harvey and Katharine Maus (Chicago University Press, 1990), *Critical Essays on John Donne*, edited by Arthur Marotti (G. K. Hall, 1994), and *John Donne's Religious Imagination*, edited by Raymond-Jean Frontain and Frances Malpezzi (University of Central Arkansas Press, 1995). Claude Summers and Ted-Larry Pebworth edited *The Eagle and the Dove*, *Bright Shootes of Everlastingnesse* and *The Muses' Commonweal* for the University of Missouri Press in 1986, 1987 and 1988, respectively. M. Thomas Hester edited essays on possible references to Anne Donne as *John Donne's 'Desire of More'* (University of Delaware Press, 1996). Other studies are noted by John Roberts, *John Donne: An Annotated Bibliography of Modern Criticism, 1912–67* and *1968–78* (2 vols, University of Missouri Press, 1982): his scope is international. He edited *Essential Articles for the Study of John Donne's Poetry* (Archon Books, 1975) and *New Perspectives in the Seventeenth-Century Religious Lyrics* (University of Missouri Press, 1994). Paul Stellin studied *John Donne and Calvinist Views of Grace* (Free University Press, Amsterdam, 1983) and Donne in the Netherlands in *So Doth, So Is Religion* (University of Missouri Press, 1998).

But British scholarship has not been completely dwarfed. A. J. Smith edited *John Donne: The Critical Heritage* going up to c. 1900 (Routledge, 1975) and Andrew Mousley more recent criticism of *John Donne* (Macmillan, 1999). Julian Lovelock edited criticism of *Donne: Songs and Sonets,* going to c. 1950 and including the dialogue between C. S. Lewis and Joan Bennett (Macmillan, 1973). Earlier studies included Joan Bennett, *Five Metaphysical Poets* (3rd edn, Cambridge University Press, 1964), Frank Kermode, *Shakespeare, Spenser, Donne* (Routledge, 1971), J. B. Leishman, *The Monarch of Wit* (5th edn, Hutchinson, 1962), A. C. Partridge, *John Donne: Language and Style* (Deutsch, 1978), Murray Roston, *The Soul of Wit* (Oxford University Press, 1974), Wilbur Sanders, *John Donne's Poetry* (Cambridge University Press,

1971), A. J. Smith, *The Metaphysics of Love* (Cambridge University Press, 1985), and William Zunder, *The Poetry of John Donne* (Harvester Press, 1982). Feminist studies have included Maureen Sabine, *Feminine Engendered Faith* (Macmillan, 1992), and H. L. Meakin, *John Donne's Articulations of the Feminine* (Oxford University Press, 1998).

David Norbrook studied *Poetry and Politics in the English Renaissance* (Routledge, 1984) and Lawrence Manley *Literature and Politics in Early Modern London* (Cambridge University Press, 1995). The literary background was also illuminated by *The Cambridge Companion to English Poetry, Donne to Marvell*, edited by Thomas Corns (Cambridge University Press, 1993), and new essays on *Renaissance Poetry* were edited by Cristina Malcolmson (Longman, 1998). Jonathan Post surveyed *English Lyric Poetry: The Seventeenth Century* (Routledge, 1999). The ecclesiastical background was researched in recent studies such as Patrick Collinson, *The Religion of Protestants in England 1559–1625* (Oxford University Press, 1982), Julian Davies, *The Caroline Captivity of the Church* (Oxford University Press, 1992), K. T. Kendall, *Calvin and English Calvinism to 1649* (Oxford University Press, 1979), Anthony Milton, *Catholic and Reformed* (Cambridge University Press, 1995), Nicholas Tyacke, *Anti-Calvinists: The Rise of English Arminianism c.1590–1640* (2nd edn, Oxford University Press, 1990), and Peter White, *Predestination, Policy and Polemic* (Cambridge University Press, 1992). Kenneth Fincham edited essays on *The Early Stuart Church* (Macmillan, 1993) and examined the bishops in *Prelate as Pastor* (Oxford University Press, 1990). For Donne's Roman Catholic background studies include Adrian Morey, *The Catholic Subjects of Elizabeth I* (Allen and Unwin, 1978), Peter Holmes, *Resistance and Compromise: The Political Thought of the Elizabethan Catholics* (Cambridge University Press, 1982), and John Bossy, *The English Catholic Community 1570–1850* (Darton, Longman and Todd, 1975). Good biographies include *Ben Jonson* by David Riggs (Harvard University Press, 1989) and *George Herbert* by Amy Charles (Cornell University Press, 1977). Nicholas Lossky gave a good account of *Lancelot Andrewes the Preacher* (Oxford University Press, 1991).

Other studies include Bettie Doebler, *The Quickening Seed: Death in the Sermons of John Donne* (University of Salzburg Press, 1974), Itrat Husain, *The Dogmatic and Mystical Theology of John Donne* (SPCK, 1938), Millar MacLure, *The Paul's Cross Sermons 1534–1632* (University of Toronto Press, 1958), and W. Fraser Mitchell, *English Pulpit Oratory from Andrewes to Tillotson* (SPCK, 1932). Donne was included in Michael Schmidt's *Lives of the Poets* (Phoenix, 1998) and in L. William Countryman's study of the Anglican spiritual tradition as it has been expressed in *The Poetic Imagination* (Darton, Longman and Todd, 1999).

John Guy edited essays on *The Reign of Elizabeth I: Court and Culture in the Last Decade* (Cambridge University Press, 1995). Linda Peck did the same for *The Mental World of the Jacobean Court* (Cambridge University Press, 1991) and made her own study of *Court Patronage and Corruption in Early Stuart England* (Unwin Hyman, 1990). Roger Lockyear summed up recent studies of *James VI and I* (Longman, 1998), and Maurice Lee called him *Great Britain's Solomon* (University of Illinois Press, 1990). James's use of preachers was studied by Lori Anne Ferrell, *Government by Polemics* (Stanford University Press, 1998), and his visionary ecumenism by W. B. Patterson, *James VI and I and the Reunion of Christendom* (Cambridge University Press, 1997). Jonathan Goldberg explored *James I and the Politics of Literature* (2nd edn, Stanford University Press, 1989) and, with a different emphasis, Curtis Perry studied *The Making of Jacobean Culture* (Cambridge University Press, 1997). Recent social studies have included Michael MacDonald and T. R. Murphy, *Sleepless Souls: Suicide in Early Modern England* (1990), David Cressy, *Birth, Marriage and Death in Tudor and Stuart England* (1997), and Sara Mendelson and Patricia Crawford, *Women in Early Modern England* (1998; all Oxford University Press). Anthony Low celebrated the new intimacy of marriage in poetry as *The Reinvention of Love* (Cambridge University Press, 1993).

Index of Writings

Donne's Poetry

Donne's Prose

General Index

IHUMW 821
.309
D71E

TRAVELLING *the World* *with* MS… …IN A *Wheelchair*

McGowan, Linda, 1948-, author
Travelling the world with MS... : in a wheelchair / Linda McGowan.

ISBN 978-1-77141-064-9 (pbk.)

1. McGowan, Linda, 1948- --Health. 2. McGowan, Linda, 1948- --Travel. 3. Voyages and travels. 4. Multiple sclerosis--Patients--Canada--Biography. 5. Travelers--Canada--Biography. I. Title.

RC377.M375 2014 362.196'8340092 C2014-904804-1

TRAVELLING *the World with* MS... ...IN A *Wheelchair*

Linda McGowan

First Published in Canada 2014 by Influence Publishing

Book Cover Design: Marla Thompson
Typeset: Greg Salisbury
Portrait Photographer: L.A. Miele

DISCLAIMER: This book has been created to inform individuals with an interest in taking back control of their own health issues. It is not intended in any way to replace other professional health care or mental health advice, but to support it. Readers of this publication agree that neither Linda McGowan nor her publisher will be held responsible or liable for damages that may be alleged or resulting, directly or indirectly, from their use of this publication. All external links are provided as a resources only and are not guaranteed to remain active for any length of time. Neither the publisher nor the author can be held accountable for the information provided by, or actions resulting from accessing these resources.

For my sons, Patrick and Tim,
who always say, "Just go for it, Mom!"

In memory of my father, H. A. Carter,
who believed in me,

and

My grandchildren who will follow their dreams
and help create a world without barriers.

Testimonials

"Linda McGowan is one of the most well-travelled people I know. The fact that she uses a wheelchair makes her journeys even more remarkable. Her adventurous spirit has led her to be very resourceful and her experiences can be an inspiration and guide for other aspiring travellers."

Sam Sullivan, Former Mayor of Vancouver, Current MLA Vancouver-False Creek

"Linda McGowan's story teaches us to live each day to the fullest. The book is powerful, entertaining and it delivers a bold message. Definitely a 'must-read'!"

Adrianne Boothroyd, Executive Director, Lower Mainland Chapter, MS Society of Canada

"I am in awe of Linda's power and am proud to say that I was with her as we trekked through Nepal and the Himalayas. I am sure others will be inspired and take hope after reading her story."

Eoin White, Founder, Sherpa Encounters.com

"Linda embodies the true spirit of adventure, and does it with a fiercely independent mindset; where others might see barriers, she sees surmountable challenges. I have always admired her brave choices for travel experiences, many of which would seem too daunting for most able-bodied people!"

Shannon Gibney, Recreation Therapist and Programmer

"Linda is the epitome of CARPE DIEM, the Latin phrase which translated means 'to seize the day.' No moss grows on her! Her story awes, inspires and motivates!"

Cindy Hayto, Physiotherapist and Occupational Therapist

Acknowledgements

There are many who have contributed to the creation of this book. I thank you all from the bottom of my heart.

Firstly, thanks to my best friend, Bill Nicholson, who was willing to take a chance on travelling with a woman in a wheelchair.

My partner Doug Elliott made me meals, kept my mug full of hot coffee, and had his sleep interrupted whenever I straggled away from the computer at 2 a.m. We shared laughter and tears throughout the writing of this book.

Thank you to my brother, Glen, who also travels; and Connie Carter who shared happiness with my father and shares a close friendship with me.

Thanks to Julie Salisbury, the founder of Influence Publishing, and her team for their encouragement and guidance; and Mary Rosenblum for the hours she spent editing my book. We shared laughter over the differences between Canadian and American spelling.

Patricia Woods from the Neil Squire Society taught me to use Dragon NaturallySpeaking, a speech recognition software program that allows me to put pen to paper.

Thank you to Robin Appleton and Chelsea Sweeney, whose hands type faster than my speech recognition dictation program. Without their feedback the book would not be what it is today.

Thanks also to Judy Johnson who participated in the preliminary edits of this work.

I greatly appreciate the generous support of the Canada Council for the Arts and thank them for believing in my project.

Thank you to my travel companions, Barb Harris and Lourdes da Silva, who trekked in Nepal while I was carried. Much thanks also to my cousin Elizabeth Hart, who can push a wheelchair and pull two bags at the same time, and Victoria Toth who, bitten by the same travel bug, is willing to go anywhere.

I would especially like to thank my friend, Leona Missal, who believed in me from day one; Barb Harris and Lou da Silva who spent hours in cold water pools helping to maximize my mobility; and Barb Harris, Victoria Toth, Melani Adsley, Mellisa Kibsey and L.A. Miele who trekked with me to the Canada Games Pool to ward away stiffness.

Thank you also to the women, Home Support Workers, who have assisted me with daily activities throughout my journey with MS.

Finally, I thank the people of the world who welcomed me into their countries and shared their homes and families with me.

Contents

Chapter 1

At the Beginning

How it Started

"No pessimist ever discovered the secret of the stars, or sailed to an uncharted land, or opened a new doorway for the human spirit."
Helen Keller

Vulnerability accompanies me with every step and every action throughout life. Sometimes, my 1983 diagnosis of Multiple Sclerosis fills me with discouragement; however, it is not insurmountable.

I am determined not to be a woman who, upon nearing the autumn of life, declares in a state of boiling panic on my eightieth birthday, "Oh dear! It is almost over. I now wish that I had picked more daisies and danced more dances and worn purple more often." As I am well on the downhill journey, more commonly referred to as the second half of life, I try to live each day as if it is my last. Live like there is no tomorrow and love extravagantly.

When I moved into my apartment on the Fraser River, I promised myself that I would always have flowers in some form or another. To this day, I have maintained that commitment to myself—fresh flowers, hanging baskets in the spring and summer; Christmas cacti blooming in December; flowering potted plants; colourful dried flowers to brighten the grey days of Vancouver winter rain. I have lots of everyday apparel but I make a habit of including some "fun-to-wear" clothing in my wardrobe. I will continue to dance more dances, pick more daisies, and wear purple on a daily basis for as long as my energy and health allow.

I once had a friend say to me, "Nobody cares if you are not an expert ballroom dancer. Just get up and dance anyway! Just go for it." As I go for it, I smile, for what you think of me is none of my business.

I can hear your response already. There is not enough time in every day, or enough energy in my body's system to always be "doing something." How true! Living every day as if it is my last may be as complicated as travelling to the other side of the world to trek in the Himalayas; or, it may be as simple as spending a Saturday evening at home with a good book and peaceful music seeping into the depths of my soul. I may be thinking, reflecting, pondering, considering, planning, remembering. It is all good.

My growing years were tumultuous. My father's employment carried us across Canada from city to city, from province to province, from coast to coast. What an education! My brother and I, in our growing years, did not appreciate what we were gaining from the deluge of life experience. We now look upon things differently.

My mother was mostly unhappy at being far away from her family. She would leave to visit her family for two weeks and return three months later. My father was a self-managed alcoholic. He kept his drinking close to home. At the time of his death in 2008, to all of our benefits, he had been sober for thirty-eight years. I attended nine schools in twelve years and high school in a different province every year. I am always envious of friends who still maintain contact with childhood acquaintances and school chums. I don't know anyone from my elementary or high school years. Out of necessity, I was very much a loner. In order to survive continuous and constant change, I learned incredible independence.

Today, that independence is my biggest advantage. It is also my biggest disadvantage. For many years, I believed that if I couldn't do it alone, I was not going to do it. If I worked hard enough and long enough at anything, I would accomplish my goals. I am now older and wiser. I realize that no matter how hard I choose to work towards a desired goal, there are some things I will never be able to achieve.

I will never again walk a mile.

I both credit and blame my father for my tendency to be a workaholic, an unshakeable work ethic, and my implausible desire to explore each opportunity that presents itself. My dad had a stable, somewhat stern, philosophy of life: There was only one way to do things—the right way. He told me that if it is not hard work, it is probably not worth doing. His words echo in my ears as I tackle each challenge, round each corner, and surge through life.

During my early adult life, running had become a part of my routine. For many years, fifteen to be exact, I ran three or four miles (six kilometres in today's terms), three or four times a week. I came to the believable conclusion that my complex female body system, made up of physical, psychological, social, and spiritual components, could never run any greater distance. The first three miles were always agonizingly painful, unbelievably slow. I reviewed over and over the nagging question, "Why am I doing this?" Thus the belief that I could never run any further became embedded in my mind and body.

One Saturday morning the spring sunshine, tiny budding leaves on the trees, flowers in the process of emerging from their winter hibernation to unfurl bright petals, and the smell of newly cut grass, motivated me. With encouragement from my husband David, I headed for Burnaby Lake to attempt the bark mulch trail around the sparkling water's edge. It was 8 miles from my home to my home once more. It was to be a revealing journey.

Pussy willows were peeking their fuzzy heads from dark, rough bark cocoons. Water lilies were opening their yellow arms to greet the sunshine. Frogs were ribbiting in delight, gripping the edge of pale green lily pads with their webbed feet. Ducklings skittered across the water's surface, frolicking with their siblings, much to the chagrin of their moms who definitely had a more serious purpose in mind. Like most parents, the mother ducks were aiming to teach organization, discipline, safety, and consideration for fellow ducks. On this beautiful spring day, the young ducks wanted no part of it. My energy system entered a new learning cycle. As my feet began to move rhythmically along the shoreline, the rising level of endorphins in my brain led to an escalating state of euphoria that let me carry my body with ease. That run around the lake shook my previous belief that I could never run more than three or four miles. On a sunny day in early February, euphoria carried me eight miles without a hitch.

I could do it! I would do it! I began my training twelve weeks before the first Sunday in May, the day of the 1983 Vancouver Marathon. Between working full-time, attending night school to put the letters MBA after my name; chauffeuring my two boys to competitive swimming practices, soccer games, and school events, walking the dog—not to mention the housework, gardening, cooking, and laundry—I managed to squeeze in a daily run.

Evening fitness classes that emphasized stretching, flexibility, and concentration on my goal, changed my running schedule from fourteen miles a week to fifty miles weekly and more. My mind and body slipped into a rhythm. It became as simple as blinking my eyes. I was going to run the marathon and I was going to do it successfully. In the 1970s and early 1980s, you had to cross the finish line in four hours or less if your efforts were to be recorded as a completed marathon. More importantly, four hours and two seconds would mean no t-shirt! Who in their right mind would run 26.2 miles and not get a t-shirt? Not me! For those of you who only know distance in the metric system, 26.2 miles is 42 kilometres). Once a week I incorporated a long run starting with five miles and building to a 20-mile run two weeks before the marathon. If I could run 20, I would run 26.2.

I crossed the finish line in 3 hours and 23 minutes.

A very few months later, I sensed some mild numbness in my right forearm. Could it be ulna nerve palsy from leaning on my elbow late into the morning hours while working, studying, pondering very select, specific words that would lead to a high-quality paper that was due in two weeks? My doctor thought so. It never occurred to me that it was anything more. Over the next several months, I developed one other symptom: Lhermitte's sign. That is, when I flexed my neck, an electric shock travelled down my spine. On my first visit to a neurologist many months later, I described these two annoyances to him. Without even examining me, he put pen to paper and drew a sketch of the spinal cord to show me demyelization of some of the nerves. I was a Home Care nurse working in community health. I had worked for many years with individuals with multiple sclerosis in varying stages of disability. I easily identified the reason for his artwork. It was MS—Multiple Sclerosis!

"That's what you have," he said.

Ninety seconds had passed from entering the doctor's office to diagnosis. I stared at him in amazement and shock. I left the office, walked blindly to my car and made my way home. I did not notice the sun that warmed my shoulders. On this day, the thrill of driving my white on white, special edition convertible Volkswagen Rabbit was lost on me. How could this be? It could not be! I had run a marathon less than six months ago. I was still running. I had clicked off five miles before waking my sons, Patrick and Timothy, at 7:00 a.m. this very morning. I had done a full day's work, ten hours, without stopping for a coffee break or lunch to ensure that I would finish in time to make my way through snail-paced traffic to a 5:30 p.m. doctor's appointment. Before reaching the doctor's office, I had slipped into a produce store to purchase a variety of fruit and vegetables so I could throw together one of those "anything goes" salads when I reached home. The MS diagnosis could not be.

But it was.

Words from My Past

"Embrace change. True success can be defined by your ability to adapt to changing circumstances."
Connie Sky

In 1966, I graduated from high school with my senior matriculation. The movement from province to province in my high school years gave me the full benefit of completing the equivalent of a first university year at the age of seventeen. There it was in 1966 in Winnipeg, Manitoba, in black-and-white, for all to see, page 15 of the 1966 Westwood Collegiate yearbook: "Linda Carter: Ambition: To travel. Probable destination: Paddling around the world in a canoe."

Maybe, way back then, at the age of seventeen, I had a premonition. I wanted to see the world, feel the world, experience the world as we know it and as we don't know it; to sense the rush of the new and different. I wanted to see the sun rise and set over the horizon in the northern hemisphere, southern hemisphere, the Far East and the mid-West. Well I am not paddling a canoe but there is a reasonable comparison since the same shoulder and bicep muscles that I used to paddle a canoe in my younger years now propel a wheelchair.

By the late 1980s, I was beginning to feel buried alive by

overwhelming circumstances —marital separation, financial burdens, the happiness of my children, work, school, disability. Everything was coming all at once. Was I driving the wrong way on a one-way street?

Walking and balance were becoming more difficult. The time was coming when walking might be a part of my past life. I lived alone in a basement suite. On one of Vancouver's rainy winter weekends, I stayed at home, not answering the telephone, not turning on a radio or television. I spent my time sipping hot tea and thinking. By ten o'clock Sunday evening, I had come to terms with the fact that I only had two choices. One was to sit at home, moan, groan, and complain that life was not fair. The second option was to take the skills and strengths that I had and do the best that I could with them.

I chose the latter.

From childhood, I had dreamed of walking on the Great Wall of China. On Monday morning, I made a telephone call to book a round trip airline ticket to Beijing, China. By Friday of that same week, I had purchased my first wheelchair. And so it began. *Feel the fear and do it anyway.* Susan Jeffers said that. Not such a bad philosophy as long as you have calculated the risks versus the benefits, taken the reasonable precautions, made level-headed preparations, and become excited by the adrenaline rush.

What would happen when I ventured forth? Flexibility, innovation, a tendency to craziness—and some intrinsic fortitude—emerged as the essential ingredients I needed. Accessibility, as we know it in Canada and the United States, is defined differently, if at all, in many other parts of the world. Now when I plan a trip, many people will comment innocently, "It must be accessible if you are going there." In many cases, the places I visit are not even remotely manageable in the ordinary sense of "accessible".

Accessibility is directly related to attitude. At one point in my travels, at the top of a Himalayan mountain, the CEO of a disability foundation in the US asked me, "Where are you finding the accessibility here in Bhutan?"

I answered him quickly and confidently, "I am not finding it, I am creating it." When it is not obvious, and I do require some level of user-friendliness, I must find a way to create that needed ease of access! By doing so, it spreads understanding to others.

I have always believed that those with a disability have a responsibility to educate themselves, and communities everywhere. I cannot just sit back and wait for it to happen. I have to *make* it happen.

I now invite you to share with me the incredible experiences that I have encountered both near and far. You will not agree, nor do I always agree, with some of the practices that I have witnessed. In fact, it is not ours to judge. It is my goal to be fully present in different cultures and observe diverse ways of life, accepting people for who they are. Some moments will be exciting, others frightening, many frustrating, overwhelming, rewarding, tiring, or exhilarating. As you leaf through the pages that describe travels and adventures, some of you will be excited to discover that many things that seem totally impossible can actually come to pass. Others will look at my escapades with a jaded eye, thinking, "She has to be crazy—there is no way I would even attempt many of those things." If I can encourage or motivate even one person—able-bodied or with a disability—to venture forth to explore our wonderful universe, I will have accomplished my goal.

The First of Many

"There are no short cuts to any place worth going."
Beverly Sills

It had to start somewhere and it did in 1989!

Upon arriving at the Vancouver airport, I checked my luggage including the new blue Quickie 3 wheelchair. I boarded the airplane trying not to think about the insanity of my decision to travel alone to the other side of the world. I did not realize at the time that my future would hold many, many hours of air travel. Anticipation and excitement filled every cell of my body on that cool drizzly March morning. Even today, before I embark on a trip, people will ask, "Are you excited?" My standard answer is, "No, not yet. But when I get on that plane, an electrical spark will fill my entire being with expectancy and eagerness."

As the aerodynamics lifted the big bird off the runway, a deep thrill penetrated my gut. I have spent many hours in flight watching cloud formations, sipping red wine, reading, dozing, snacking, chatting with seatmates or quietly withdrawing into myself. It is all good.

When I first disembarked at the Beijing airport, I noticed flimsy wobbling walls made of thin plywood, poor lighting, no washrooms, no snack bar, no opportunity to purchase bottled water, no money exchange, and the entrances and exits were guarded by uniformed officials holding machine guns. There was a large cordoned-off area in the middle of the floor that contained bags, bundles, suitcases, cardboard boxes and one shiny, new, royal blue wheelchair. Line-ups began. I was directed to present a passport, display an immigration landing card, identify where I would be staying while in Beijing, and point out my luggage. With a different coloured stamp of approval on the back of my hand from the sentry at the head of each line, I was finally cleared to head for the bus.

The hotel was a three-storey concrete building located at the end of an unpaved roadway. In the pleasant and traditionally decorated lobby, all arriving guests were treated to a cup of tea while room keys were sorted out and assigned. "It is going to be fine," I kept repeating to myself. That little pocket of moxie buried in the base of my core would have to emerge. It was one thing to be a woman travelling alone. It was quite another to be a woman in a wheelchair travelling alone.

In the late 1980s, Chinese culture did not embrace independence in women. When visiting in foreign lands, knowledge of the local culture is one of the greatest advantages you can have. It will reduce or eliminate surprises. The reference section of the library at home had provided information about this wonderful land, so I was aware that it was not the norm for people with disabilities to be visible and active in public. It was also uncommon for women to be out on their own in the community. These abnormalities paled in comparison to the differences created by my Caucasian appearance—pale skin and long hair that was not the usual black in colour. My clothing was different, not the long white baggy pants and shirts worn by the locals—although, out of consideration for the accepted dress code, I avoided shorts and tank tops.

In 1989, a communist government ruled China. Beijing streets were narrow, uneven and rough. Few were paved. Walkers were vigilant to avoid stones and potholes. For me, on wheels, some of these obstacles were insurmountable. Local people, mostly grammas and grandpas, readily came to my aid. There were three hundred and fifty privately-owned vehicles in the city, a few trucks delivering large goods, some army vehicles such as trucks and tanks. The roads were crowded with people and millions and millions of bicycles. One could see a mother, father; a child, on a single bicycle pulling a trailer behind piled with food or building materials. In the early morning, I would often wheel to the end of the road to expand my knowledge and sense of the community structure. I was able to get a feel for family life where hard-working people rose before night was over, completed a series of Tai Chi exercises, packed up their child and necessary food, belongings, and tools for the day and headed to a worksite; not as a father or employee but as a family group. Each member would contribute in some manner to the earning of the day's wages that would feed and house the family for at least today. The elderly are respected and honoured. Their long years of work were unselfishly invested in their only child. Now the roles reverse. Young people honour, cherish, and care for the old.

Residences were in concrete apartment buildings, each suite with a small balcony and a window. The closeness of the verandas clearly demonstrated that the housing units were tiny. Laundry was strung over the railings to dry in the warm sun. There was not a blade of grass in sight. In the yards and in front of the buildings, the terrain was composed of dust, dry dirt, or food plants such as cabbage, spinach, and carrots. No arable land was wasted on decadence such as grass and flowers. If food could be grown in the tiniest of corners, it was.

The first Asian trip included a few essentials. One was to walk on the Great Wall of China. On Friday morning, I boarded a bus with my cane and unsteady gait, slipping thankfully into the front seat. The driver placed my chair underneath the bus in the luggage compartment. I found myself in the midst of a loud public discussion. I did not understand one word of Chinese nor did my fellow passengers comprehend one syllable of English. It became apparent that seats were pre-assigned. Out of necessity, I had occupied the seat closest to the front of the bus, causing the commotion. I had taken someone else's pre-purchased space. When 3 people noticed my cane and my inability to move easily, the public controversy was resolved. Amidst smiles, the nodding of many heads and pats on my knee, we headed off to the Great Wall.

Linda on the Great Wall of China

Why had I brought a chair to China? By alternating activity with rest, I could, using a cane, manage to walk short distances. I knew that if I had to walk any distance to get to the Wall, by the time I got to its base, I would not be able to fulfill my lifelong dream of experiencing this wonder of the world. I was definitely accurate in my guesstimate. The distance from the bus to the Great Wall was close to 3/4 mile. Some enthusiastically helpful students pushed me to the staircase that led to the pedestrian access where I secured the wheelchair with the bike lock that I had brought with me. I mounted the eight stairs by lifting my right leg with one hand on to the first step. My left leg followed suit. Grasping the handrail, I slowly ascended the stairs to my dream destination. With my cane in hand, I walked slowly, holding onto the side of the wall, for the entire length of the visitor pedestrian way. The thrill of accomplishment warmed me through and through. It was the first experience of many that would amaze me in years to come.

On Saturday morning, with patience and help from other passengers, I boarded a bus heading to Tiananmen Square. On that bright sunny morning, families—a mom, dad, and one child—flocked to the park areas of the square. The one-child policy in China makes that one offspring incredibly valuable. My bag was brimming with Canadian flag stickpins for the parents and brightly coloured animal and flower stickers for the children. After several tentative approaches, the parents realized that I was not a threat to their country or to their children. I found new friends and could exchange smiles with both parents and child. Many offered to share the family meal. Young children delighted in short rides on my lap in the wheelchair. The parents were thrilled with the Canadian flag pins, the children shrieked with joy at the funny animal stickers that I pulled from my bag. I wandered through the square for hours, unaware of the underlying current of political unrest. I chatted with university students who could communicate minimally in English and I accepted their generous invitation to an evening dinner at the University. Little did I realize that these students were, in fact, searching for information about the North American democratic government system!

When I arrived at the designated university address, I found the windows darkened by black curtains and the lighting inside was minimal. Silence dominated the room. Verbal exchanges were whispered. I was welcomed and treated royally. I shared the evening meal and chatted easily about life in Canada. At the end of the evening (there was a curfew at 8:30 p.m.) three young students accompanied me back to my hotel, ensuring my safe return from the university. One week later, the world was shocked by the massacre of students in Tiananmen Square. I had newly found friends. I was shattered to imagine that they may have been part of the Tiananmen massacre. In retrospect, I realize that I too could have been one of the victims!

In China, one day was the same as the rest in terms of shopping and commercial activities. One Sunday morning, a visit to a department store was in order. After a 20-minute bus ride, I found myself in the most congested market area one could imagine. Walking on two legs required finesse; moving through the crowd in a wheelchair was a feat of skill and determination.

In 1989, there were two currencies in China—friendship money and Chinese money. I could purchase goods from vendors who were permitted to accept only Chinese money and I could also shop in Friendship Stores. The Chinese people, on the other hand, were not permitted to enter or to purchase from Friendship Stores. I tucked away receipts representing both kinds of transactions.

At the entrance to the multipurpose department store, I connected with a thin, elderly, grey-haired, and bearded gentleman. His excitement was equal to mine. He was taking an

English conversation course at the local seniors' community centre and was delighted to find someone with whom to practice his English speaking skills. I was grateful to find someone who could understand even a few words of my native tongue. Between the usual charades and one-word phrases, we managed to share a cup of tea, and find *cloisonné* enamel beads for me to take home. At the end of the day we embraced in farewell.

I visited the Imperial Palace, the King's Residence, the Forbidden City. Yes, there were stairs, narrow doorways, large cobblestones on the pathways, but the local people and other tourists gave of their time, energy, and encouragement. I saw as much and more than I could expect.

I ate at small restaurants offering "real" Chinese food, not chow mein, chop suey, and egg rolls, but stir-fried garlic stems and meat of questionable sources. I was not brave enough to try any of the meats. It could have been dog, snake, rat or anything.

Rice, the staple food for the native population, became my standard fare.

NO aisle chair available!

Hong Kong

I was going to "shop until I dropped" but I did not expect the expression to turn out to be literal.

On arrival at the hotel, I quickly emptied the bag that hung on the back of my chair to make space available for my anticipated purchases. I grabbed a tote bag and went back out onto the street to begin a marathon shopping spree. Chaos reigned. Vendors, traffic, hagglers, and tourists, combined to create a unique symphony of noise. There were people and things everywhere. So many items of all sorts to choose from! Somewhat confused by the overwhelming display of clothes, jewellery, electronics, and "antiques", a system of organized priorities was clearly the only way to survive financially!

My sons had given me a list of all the cool things that teenagers think that they would like to have, but cannot afford to buy. "Mom, we don't expect you to bring anything home but just in case the price is really good and you have time..." The list included Vuarnet sunglasses, Sony Walkman speakers, scientific calculators, deep sea diving watches and any other electronic gadgets that were out of reach, price-wise in Canada, but perhaps within the budget here in Hong Kong.

The streets of Hong Kong offered a bewildering array of electronics stores where every technological gizmo was available along with cameras, jewellery, Gucci handbags, and all types of luxury items. I shopped from early morning to late in the afternoon. This was not a straightforward task of entering a store, selecting the desired product, paying the identified price, and leaving with the cherished merchandise in a paper sack. I visited many shops, chatted with many vendors, spoke with fellow travellers and local residents. It all helped to establish my comfort with quality of a product and awareness of reasonable cost. I compared prices. I moved along the street, surprised at the expansive array of products—colour, size, features and, of course, the variation in price. My limited knowledge of the electronic products that I was trying to buy for my sons did not help matters. However I did capitalize on the information sources around me. Over a cup of tea and a bowl of noodles, my mind raced, then rested. My decisions were finalized.

In the afternoon, I retraced my steps as best I could and, confident at last, made the purchases. I was proud of my selections and the bag on the back of my wheelchair was overflowing.

I eagerly began to wheel back towards the hotel. As I crossed the main street, an uphill grade of 45 degrees did not deter my enthusiasm—until the excessive weight in the bag on the back of my chair combined with the uphill incline, rocked my world. My chair tipped backwards (as my mother would have said, "ass over teakettle") in the middle of the main street. I lay on my back with feet in the air like an overturned turtle with its legs waving. Many cars passed by, missing me by inches, not seeming to notice this unusual obstruction in the middle of the road. But there were many pedestrians and some drivers who quickly came to the rescue, righted the chair, lifted me back onto the seat, recovered my parcels, then ushered me safely to the side of the road and up to the entrance to my hotel. Was I injured? Physically, no! My pride took the major beating but it was all in fun and yes, it was worth it when "mother world traveller" returned to Vancouver with the coveted electronics.

Jumbo, the floating restaurant in the middle of the Hong Kong harbour, could only be reached by boat, a Chinese junk. This huge, multi-level restaurant appeared like a forested island in the middle of the sea. Many levels were planted with trees, plants, and even a natural aviary amongst the tropical plants. There were toucans, cranes, vultures, eagles, and tiny canaries, all housed in gilded cages. The decor included large Chinese lanterns, a musical background provided by a harpist and Chinese gong, with bells playing softly in the background. Large oblong and round tables hosted Lazy Susans where a startling variety of local Chinese dishes rotated clockwise in front of each diner. The intricate dishes included stir fried vegetables, garlic stems decorated with colourful flora, Peking duck, Moo Shu pork with hoi sin sauce, lychee nuts, almond blanc mange. Beverages flowed copiously—beer in quart bottles, sickly sweet lemon soda, and of course, Chinese tea. Our stomachs overly filled, we boarded the Chinese junk and headed back through the dark waters to the bustling streets of Hong Kong where commercialism continues on a 24-hour basis.

My father was a classy clotheshorse. He highly recommended that while in Hong Kong, I make an appointment to visit with his favourite tailor, Patrick Wong. In the morning, I wheeled up and down the streets until I located the address that was neatly printed on a small piece of paper in my pocketbook. Upon introducing myself as Mr. Carter's daughter, I was treated like a piece of gold. The workers in the shop could not do enough for me. Bolts of cloth of every colour imaginable, in a multitude of textures, were ceremoniously presented to me. In a very short time, I selected a tiny houndstooth plaid in shades of dusty blue. It was ideal for the design of the fully lined, pleated waistband, cuffed trousers and matching skirt that was recommended by the tailor. A thigh-length dusty blue, soft, ultra suede jacket was the crowning touch for this stylish outfit. My height, width, depth and limb length were measured meticulously. I was sent off with a guarantee that my clothing would be ready by three o'clock on the next day. When I returned to the shop on the following afternoon, it was ready and perfect. No fitting or alteration required.

This being my first extended international trip, my packing experience was minimal. I admit I was green as grass. I had taken with me pale pink corduroys that did not see eye-to-eye with the dust and dirt of Mainland China. Laundries were available but communication and unscheduled times were at a minimum so I ventured to the Hong Kong market in search of clean casual clothes for the next leg of the trip. I purchased a pair of navy blue trousers—a colour more compatible with travel, for the enormous price of two dollars. An additional dollar bought me a long sleeved sloppy pink overshirt that guaranteed at least one clean outfit for the last segment of my journey.

Thailand

When I arrived in Bangkok in the early evening hours, I quickly learned to hold my breath in prayer. The streets of downtown Bangkok hosted ten lanes of traffic seeming to travel in no identified direction. There were no stop signs, no traffic signals, no streetlights. In the dark, cars scooted down the street and around the corner in non-existent lanes. Headlights, like the use of horns in North America, were only meant to alert fellow drivers and pedestrians of a car's imposing presence. Road rage, as we call it, was the norm—drivers shouting at one another, pedestrians flagging down and yelling for taxis, bus drivers shaking their fists—organized chaos.

Accommodation, on the opposite riverbank was "easily reached" by poling down the canal in a longboat. I caught a bus from the downtown core. Ascending the steps was a slow process. I could sense the driver's impatience through his placid veneer. The bus pulled up to the edge of the riverbank where bus passengers were ushered into long skinny boats. My wheelchair was folded and with assistance from the boatmen, I transferred onto a seat. We floated slowly down the waterway to the hotel that would be my home for the next six days.

Going out in the dark evening hours was not an option because the only available transportation was by longboat, sliding through gloomy oily, alligator-infested waters.

That's all right. It had been a long day. It was oppressively hot and humid. On the hotel grounds, tables were laden with characteristic Thai hors d'oeuvres—satay, spring rolls, and rice. Ice carvings depicting dolphins, swordfish, and whales, adorned the tables. A large, welcoming pool seemed inviting until I realized that the temperature was about that of a hot tub. After dinner, the ice carvings were removed from the tables and placed in the pool in an attempt to cool the water to a pleasant temperature. Swimming, or at least cooling off in the water, was only possible late at night and in the early morning hours before the rising sun once again produced scorching temperatures. This was in March. Can you imagine what it would be like in the summer months?

The next day, a shopping spree was in order. I joined a group of ladies and we all climbed into a longboat and headed into town where we were delighted to find stores offering "essential" outfits to buy in Bangkok—shorts, long pants, shirts made by name brands such as—Nike, Gap, Colors of Benetton. The tiny Thai sales lady profoundly assured me that, "One size fits all." For most of us, that was true. A larger Canadian woman shook her head. "Maybe you think one size fits all but realistically, one size fits *almost all*," she declared emphatically. There was no question that the "one size fits all" clothing, comparable to a North American size 10, was not going to accommodate a woman who clearly wore a Canadian size 18-20.

Unisex shorts in every colour imaginable were priced at four dollars. I had shorts for everyone—my friends, my children, myself. For years to come, Patrick, Tim and I mixed and matched the unisex cotton shorts that could easily be dressed up or down to go anywhere in the summertime.

Later in the evening, the night market provided more shopping opportunities where anything you wanted could be purchased for a price. Bargaining skill was a necessity. On the crowded streets, side by side stalls battled for space, stacked with shirts, shorts, pants, watches, CDs, VHS tapes, jewellery, socks, sandals, shoes, ties—and whatever else might meet your fancy. Vendors shouted and beckoned each shopper, competing with one another to offer the best price, the best quality and the best variety the street had to offer. In fact, one table was very similar to another but the name of the game was to explore each one, comparing quality, assortment, and price. You could get a massage on the sidewalk. Food was prepared on street corners. Tarot card readers would tell your fortune. Life lines on your palm were interpreted. At 4:00 a.m., large trunks were pulled out from under the stalls and goods were packed away until the night market opened again at 10:00 p.m. the next evening.

The next day in Bangkok, I rode an elephant and, with hesitation, agreed to have a large boa constrictor draped around my shoulders and neck. Am I afraid of snakes? Of course I am, but there was no way I was going to give my children an opportunity to call their mother "a wimp." Holy men in the temples beckoned to bring us into their sanctuaries. The incense and candles filled the spaces with soft light and fragrance. I boarded a small, flat boat to venture onto the canal where the Saturday morning floating market invited locals and tourists alike to purchase wood carvings, vegetables and fruit, jewellery, religious statues, bamboo mats, sun hats, and much more. A few hours in the floating market made me appreciate the purity of Canadian water. Small floating homes crowded the shores and waters of the canal. Children played and swam in the waterways, a mum washed clothing, a grandmother dipped breakfast dishes, a grandfather showered; another man relieved himself over the edge of his raft as a woman drew drinking water from the same common waterway. I decided to stick to bottled water while I was visiting here.

In the evening, I joined a group of new-found friends to visit breathtaking pagodas topped with gold spires, decorated with jewels and intricate designs. Our cultural tour was followed by a meal—a tongue-burning variety of Thai delicacies. This was accompanied by the talented dancing of tiny women dressed in heavily embossed robes. The weight of their dress was in sharp contrast to the delicacy of their bodies but it didn't interfere with their movement and skill. Every moment of the entire evening was steeped in local culture.

I boarded the bus the following morning, leaving Bangkok behind. I headed to Pattaya Beach, located 165 km southeast of Bangkok for a few days of respite before heading back to Canada. The fishing village of Pattaya now shares its popular beach with locals and tourists alike who frequent this vacation town.

My first visit to Asia in 1989 was a test of my self-esteem, an opportunity to emphasize my independence and to prove to myself that I could continue to pursue my goal of travelling the world. I went to Southeast Asia on my own.

Why China? In retrospect, I can see that there might have been easier choices but the destination was less important than the planting of the seed for future travel. As it turned out, the whole experience was amazing.

Chapter 2

Africa

Ancient Wonders

Egypt. I am so very glad that in 1991, I visited this remarkable area of the world. I experienced awe-inspiring fascination alternating with overwhelming challenges.

Cairo, the capital of Egypt, the largest metropolis in Africa, with a population of eight million, was then one of the most densely populated cities in the world. The contrast between ancient and cosmopolitan was remarkable. There seemed to be more people than available space. Sidewalks were intensely crowded and there were few breaks between moving vehicles on the roadways. I looked at a map to gain a sense of the geography. Where was I? Where to go? How to get there? There is a ring road around Cairo and, as with the hub on a wheel, the roads branch out like spokes to connect Cairo with other cities and villages. The ring road surrounding the city has exits that lead travellers to outer Cairo districts.

Cairo traffic is dense and overcrowded, however vehicles moved at a relatively fluid pace. Drivers were aggressive but there was no evidence of road rage. They were courteous at intersections, took turns proceeding, while police directed traffic at congested areas. The city had no wheelchair accessibility. I saw only one ramp during my stay in Egypt. It was at the airport where luggage carriers pushed and pulled heavily-laden carts to and from the airport terminal.

I wanted to see some of the historical and popular tourist sites within the city. Tackling the narrow, crowded sidewalks was not a reasonable consideration. Seeking an alternative, I scanned the small informal lobby of the hotel. I spoke with the reception desk clerk and followed his advice. Wandering out the door into the crowd, I found my option. On the sidewalk, there were two young men sitting on very low stools, shining shoes for businessmen hustling by. Their Arabic sign read, "Shoe Shining; Errands; Will Arrange Transportation; Housecleaning; Ask for Anything You Need."

I asked. One of the shoe shiners had a brother who was willing and available to push my chair and be my sidewalk tour guide. He arrived at the hotel at eight o'clock on the following morning and we set off to see the sights. Buildings were old and new, the old being the most interesting and remarkable. The Islamic architecture began its domination of the city a thousand years ago and continues now, in the 21st century. The observers of Islamic architecture sense and feel the presence of the Creator as they enter structures and observe from within. The Cairo Tower, completed in 1961, standing at 187 metres, has an observation platform accessed by elevator, providing a panoramic view and a great picture-taking opportunity. We wandered the grounds of Azhar University, the second oldest degree-granting institution in the world. Cairo has a large economic investment in the motion picture industry, music schools, and film production companies. Cairo Opera House, part of the Egyptian National Cultural Centre, opened October 10, 1988; seventeen years after the Royal Opera House had been destroyed by fire. The National Cultural Centre, a prominent feature for locals and visitors alike, holds performances of ballet, art, symphony, opera and contemporary music. If I was not finding much wheelchair accessibility in the modern parts of the city, I was definitely not going to find it in the old city, but it was an area that I had to see. Old Cairo contains sections built thousands of years ago, as well as current day vendors, food wagons, and children at play on the street. Appreciation for my local guide and his skills flooded my heart as our day drew to a close.

A morning bus ride to visit the ancient wonders of the world—the pyramids and Sphinx—was frequently ambushed by people on the side of the road who jumped in front of the bus in wild suicidal attempts to stop it, thus providing entrepreneurs an opportunity to make a sale. What kind of business, you ask? Polished ebony female heads with Arabic facial features were adorned with large gold rings in the ears and nose. The male ebony figurines had tightly curled wigs representative of ancient times. Even a crack in the bus door was interpreted as an invitation to enter the bus, to show and sell. When entry to the bus was denied, the local handicrafts were shoved through an open window. There was shouting and haranguing—anything to get a sale. The vendors did not easily take no for an answer. The accepted policy was that an item that entered the bus, no matter how, was considered sold. Some of my fellow travellers packed these black ebony wares into their bags that night. Anything to end the persistent pestering!

The Sphinx at Gaza, based on Greek mythology, is a world-famous statue of a lioness with a human head. Upon arrival, I was surprised to note that there was no typical North American marketing—no turnstiles, no asphalt pathway, no directional signage! There was just deep, soft sand. Flaming torches on either side of the Sphinx lit the early morning sky. Multiple huge pyramids rose above the sand in the distance. It was hard to believe that these well-preserved artifacts are four to five thousand years old. How were these enormous structures built without mechanization? How many lives were lost lifting and transporting the huge stones, and from where? Without question, the pyramids are a monument to the ancient cultures that built them. There was no rock in sight, only sand as far as the eye could see.

Pyramid and Sphinx

King Tutankhamun's tomb was open to the public on this particular day. How would I get there? It is challenging enough to wheel on a firm path. It seemed impossible to wheel through the sand but, as always, there was a way to make it work. As we got off the bus, a young boy, perhaps nine years old, riding a mottled, shaggy camel approached our group with enthusiasm. "A camel ride, a camel ride!" he called lustily. He was the answer to my problem. Of course, I wanted a camel ride. The animal would provide my transportation to King Tut's tomb. I left my chair in the midst of the Sahara desert. The kneeling camel, in his crouched position, was still an overwhelming six feet high. With the assistance of a few desert vagabonds, I found myself situated between the humps and on my way to the open pyramid.

Upon arrival at the coveted destination, the young lad held out his thin brown hand, demanding four dollars for the camel ride. When I did not respond to the demand for payment, he quickly revised his request to two dollars, which I was prepared to pay. I was about to enter the dark tomb when it occurred to me that yes, I had to get back to my chair, which by this time, was a half mile of soft sand away. I bargained with the boy.

"I am not going to pay you four dollars," I said. "If you wait for me and return me to my chair, I will pay you ten dollars." He shot me a crooked smile indicating agreement. I enthusiastically entered the pyramid.

In 1991, I could still walk a little bit using a cane in my left hand. The railing on the right side ensured my stability. The cavern was narrow. I wedged into the constricted space—difficult for some, a definite advantage for me, since the walls gave me added support. I explored the pyramid's dark halls and caverns. The small rooms were filled with jewels, silks, mummies, gold statues, and ancient Egyptian pottery. Periodically, during my explorations, my thoughts turned to my camel transportation. Would he wait for me? Yes, he did. The whole journey was experienced in reverse. The camel was brought to his knees and two Egyptian desert shepherds assisted me to settle between the humps. The young lad shouted commands to his animal as the camel lumbered across the sands, returning me to my chair. The sight of a wheelchair is not always inviting but in this situation, it was more than rewarding. I handed the young lad fifteen dollars and wheeled my way across the solid sandy path, back to the bus.

Next, there were caves to visit near the Sphinx. Their walls were extensively decorated with hieroglyphics and ancient names carved in stone—primitive sketches of village life and animals. Rock and stone, sand and dust made up the landscape. The area was peppered with large carved stones and columns, and remnants of ancient buildings. There was not a blade of grass, the twig of a tree, or a trickle of water. All in all, it was an inspiring, incredibly hot, exhausting, and humbling day at the pyramids.

When it was time to leave Cairo, the boats at the dock waited for our departure. Once again, challenges had to be overcome. The pathway down to the boats was composed of dust, sand, and dirt. There was no way to reach the boat except to slide on my bum. Try to keep your only clean pair of shorts clean while performing this feat!

At the dock that jutted into the river, the boats waited. They were lined up abreast of one another, side by side, away from the dock. In order to reach our assigned boat, which was three out from the dock, others walked across the decks and the planks in between the tied-up boats, lugging their baggage along. I crawled. Upon reaching the desired vessel, I gratefully accepted assistance from an Egyptian crewmember to climb back onto my chair. My bag was placed nearby. As we pulled away from the dock, I marvelled that I was sailing down the mighty Nile River. The shore was lined with tropical foliage. Birds screeched from the trees. Monkeys swung along vines. Children playing near the shoreline heralded the presence of a village.

Each culture around the globe has unique features. In Egypt, the moment-by-moment clamour of the people filled me with uncertainty. I needed to understand it better. It was so different from the often quiet, Caucasian way. It seemed as if everyone was yelling at everyone else—the men at each other; the husbands at their wives; the mothers at the children; the children at the donkeys. The tiniest of children carried a small stick to prod the creatures, encouraging their progress with taps on their grey furry backs, down to the edge of the Nile. Their cargo of clay pots were filled with the country's most valuable resource:

brown Nile river water. The donkeys slowly slipped and slid up the muddy bank, back to the village where the filled earthen jugs were emptied into a small concrete well. There seemed to be little obvious gratification for the children or the animals, but drinking water is one of the most valuable possessions that any living thing can possess. The residents of the village and their animals living in this very dry dusty region now had water to drink.

Sleeping accommodation on the "cruise ship," which was more like a large wooden tugboat, was a row of sleeping bags on the upper deck, exposed to the elements—heat, dust, mosquitoes, and the loud jungle cries of birds and animals. Food was eaten with spoons from clay bowls on our laps. Lettuce, washed in the questionable water, resulted in the expected outcome for foreigners. Reports state that 98% of North Americans get sick when they visit Egypt. Our group was no exception. Twenty-seven boat passengers, mostly from Canada, found themselves experiencing the dreaded phenomena. Two small washrooms at the end of the deck became the most popular destination of the day. As people moaned, groaned, and complained, an Egyptian crewmember, with little command of the English language, circulated through the group offering "medicine" to all who would accept. The remedy offered was a white, chalk-like "horse pill." They were so large it was doubtful that anyone could swallow this dry powdery antidote. At times like this, an experienced traveller quickly realizes the value of the local ethnic remedies. The Egyptian sailor who lives here has had numerous encounters with visitors and has much experience with the illness and how to deal with it.

"I am going to try these pills," I announced.

An acquaintance from Canada looked at me in alarm. "You're a nurse. You don't even know what you're taking. How can you possibly put something into your body that is unknown to you?

This is so different from the advice you give others." Right then, I felt as if I was going to die, and I hoped it happened quickly. In an attempt to avoid my fateful demise, I swallowed two of the large, chalky pills with considerable difficulty. My fellow passengers looked at me with amazement, expecting an instant miraculous recovery—or instant death!

"It's not like a light switch," I said.

I crawled into my sleeping bag, still feeling unsettled. I arose the next morning a little bit slower, a little bit weaker, but able to shower and dress and sit on the deck with my coffee. The others around me, meanwhile, continued their moaning and groaning parade to the washroom.

As we drifted down the Nile River, a heavy jungle dew moistened everything. This was a prime example of water—water everywhere and not a drop to drink! Jungle inhabitants, I am sure, harvest this water in vessels made from leaves and bamboo. The water is used for drinking and food preparation. We got off the boat, guided by an African warrior dressed in a loincloth. Bones, teeth, and beads hung on heavy strands around his neck. A headdress of horns, perhaps from a rhinoceros, graced his head. He guided us down a narrow jungle path. My wheelchair was entangled at times by the vines and ferns, which impeded progress. The warrior patiently cut me loose from the foliage, easing my frustration at being trapped. At the village, we found grass and bamboo huts, babies strapped to the front or back of their mum—depending on their activity for the moment—gardening, cooking, or weaving. A village square boasted small piles of harvested vegetables placed there to share with others whose harvests were less abundant.

Camouflaged alligators were bathing in the sun along the river's shoreline. They were initially hard to spot but eventually I could find them in the most remote spots. Less friendly river crocodiles could be seen slinking alongside the boat, opening their large mouths to capture a water duck. The crew was reluctant to put fishing lines into the water when in crocodile infested areas. Crocs do not discriminate between the fish on the hook, the rod, the lines, or, with a mighty pull, the fisherman holding the rod.

Sitting on the deck, we drifted along peacefully, observing our surroundings. It was too hot for much activity, but we could look forward to the upcoming coolness of our destination—Kenya. Three days in the heat and two overnights rewarded us with an arrival in cool air, bright sunshine, abundant green foliage, colourful flowers, and the chanting and singing of the local Kenyan people.

I've Died and Gone to Heaven

In Kenya, bright sunshine and cool breezes, not unlike springtime weather at home in Vancouver, replaced the oppressive heat and dust of Egypt. Yes, it was hot but not overwhelmingly so. The green foliage and a whisper of the occasional gentle breeze offered my body moments of respite and peace. Fields and orchards were thick with trees heavily laden with fruit and row upon row of vegetables. The sellers at roadside stands offered cool, freshly squeezed fruit juice: passionfruit, guava, mango. I indulged in meals of fresh produce and drank the local water without hesitation. At night, coolness lulled me into restful slumber.

This is what I imagined heaven to be!

Three days in Nairobi included trips to historic and natural history museums, sampling African food, local music, chanting, dance, and costumes. There were adorable tiny black babies tucked into a sling on their mother's hip, beautiful elderly faces—wrinkles revealing a long life of well-developed knowledge, patience, and coping skills. I explored the narrow streets and watched children at play. I bargained with the local street merchants for wooden salad servers hand-carved with elephants and giraffes on the handles. I learned about the history and present-day economic and political situations in Kenya. I introduced myself at the local hospital where I was welcomed to visit with patients and nurses on their break. The staff was excited to share their new equipment and nursing care based on teaching and information received from the World Health Organization and visiting Red Cross staff.

On Tuesday morning at 6:00 a.m., a black Land Rover arrived to ferry myself and other Canadian visitors from the outskirts of the city into the depths of the interior plains, the Masai Mara. It was a half-day rough and rapid ride through dense tropical foliage. En route, the six passengers, including me, searched every corner of the countryside looking for the much-anticipated animal life.

Star Crossed.

"Stop, stop!" we shouted in unanimous excitement. "There are giraffes and zebras in the field."

"It's okay, ma'am, it's okay," the black driver drawled, "You will see lots of them."

As we progressed along the roadway, we passed field after field, home to scores of zebras and giraffes. Suddenly a light bulb turned on! I realized that the folks in Kenya drive by these exotic plains animals in the same way that we in North America drive by pastures with horses and cows. For those who live in Kenya, it is an everyday happening. For us, it was the realization of a dream.

Upon our arrival at the Mount Kenya lodge—I use the word lodge loosely—the Swahili natives welcomed us. Tall, lanky Africans, dressed in thin red wrap-around tunics and holding tall wooden spears, welcomed us into the camp. We were served lunch in a covered, open-air marquee not unlike those that, as a young girl, I had encountered at Girl Guide camp. There were many diners; those of us who had arrived today by jeep, other travellers who had been at the camp for a few days, some native scouts and drivers, and of course, the resident baboons. They hung in groups from the rafters. There were large dads, medium-sized moms, behaviour-challenged youths, and tiny babies clinging to the back of a parent. When the table servers turned their backs, the monkeys shimmied down the supporting bamboo poles, stuck out a hand to grab a bun out of the basket on the table and quickly climbed back up the pole before the water pistol shots could strike them. At the top of the pillars, they laughed aloud while munching on their stolen treasures. Scolding from the humans below had no impact. This was their jungle, their home, their right to search for food, their right to harvest and benefit from all that they found.

Luxurious accommodations were assigned to each of us; canvas tents with an ensuite out back, a couple of low-to-the-floor camping cots, a small cracked mirror hung on a pole, and woven wicker baskets for clothing storage. After a brief settling in, the safari began.

For the eager and keen, a three-hour safari trip was available twice each day. I cannot imagine why anyone would come to Central Africa and not capitalize on every opportunity available to view the unique big game that is limited to this part of the world. Transportation in small topless Nissan vans meant I could stand precariously and hang on to the edge of the roof, stick my head out the opening to have an amazing view of all there was to see. I did see it all, or almost all. My encounter with animals included vast numbers of giraffes, zebras, warthogs, vultures, gazelles, and other types of antelope. Twice each day I and other visitors climbed into the vans. Morning and evening were the mostly likely times to see animals foraging for food, feeding their young, hunting for the next meal, resting in the sun, mating with lovers, arguing with enemies, soothing their wounds, or triumphing their success in battle.

As days went by, the list of animals that I had seen increased in size and variety. Hyenas, even the laughing kind, are vicious. Next to the lion, they are the predator that most deer-like creatures on the plains dread. On one occasion, we saw three male lions up close; one with blood dripping down his ripped face and nose, while another lay back nonchalantly. A third walked about with what looked like a freshly brushed mane, gloating over his victory. Five lionesses lounged in the shade. The victorious male had won that age-old possession: the rights to a female. The sheepish, bloodied face belonged to the obvious loser. On an old dead tree, a mother cheetah cleansed her two babes with a long swiping tongue. Hippopotami, the most dangerous creature of all, were numerous in the hippo pool. Yes, they looked just like those plastic toys that used to catch marbles when my children played "Hungry Hippos". The jungle foliage was thick with ferns and draping vines, large leafed ground cover and acacia trees. Acacia trees have large and pointed two-inch long spikes.

There are no swimming pools on the plains but there was a mud-lined swimming hole and, if you need to swim, you need to swim! Parking my chair at the edge, I slipped into the pool, gliding through the murky stagnant water until I was cool and refreshed (at least temperature-wise). My relaxation quickly disappeared when I emerged from the water to discover that an acacia needle had pierced one of the small pneumatic tires on the front of my wheelchair. A flat tire in Africa! Not to worry, I always carried extra tubes and tools with me. In my early years of travelling, I did not always have a bicycle pump. The air pump at the camp where I was staying turned out to be out of commission. What to do?

"I will take you to another camp." One of those big black capable Land Rover drivers, who spoke only a spattering of English, lifted me into his jeep, then tossed the chair in behind. We started to drive over plains, through rivers, up hills, down valleys, around trees. There were no roads to guide the way, of course. The sun descended and darkness fell, exaggerating every shadow. The jeep's two small headlight beams provided minimal illumination until the moonlight sneaked over the horizon.

After forty minutes of driving through the inky blackness, a few anxious thoughts drifted across my mind. Who was this local man I was driving with? Where was he taking me? How was he finding his way? Why were there no lights in sight? How would we find our way back? Did he recognize that my only need at the moment was to get a tire fixed? Where were we going?

At last, we crested a hill. In the distance, a settlement was visible in the valley below. As we pulled into the village, I saw a courtyard surrounded by grass mud huts. The total population of the village emerged, communicating loudly and rapidly amongst each other, in deep guttural conversation. The driver picked me up and placed me on a tall stool in a long thatched roof building, clearly the village workshop. This was one of those times when sign language is the most valuable form of communication. Between seven of us, the tire was removed, the punctured tube discarded, a new tube inserted, and the rubber tire put back on the rim. The air pump inflated my precious tire.

I started to put my dead tube into the pocket on the back of my chair, but the villagers exclaimed loudly. "No, no, don't throw away," they said. "Can we have?"

Of course, they could have it. Patching a wheelchair tire tube is not the most sensible thing to do when you are far away from home. The price of a new tube, eight dollars, is not out of the realm of reasonableness. It was not going to break my budget. The labour charge for my tire repair, three dollars, was today's greatest bargain. Over protests, I left a twenty-dollar bill on the worktable and we were ready to embark on our journey through the darkness back to home base.

Entertained and welcomed by the members of the tribe who worked at the lodge, I was so very interested in their tales of the geography, geology, flora, and fauna indigenous to the area. Likewise, the local people were all ears and had question after question after question about Canada, North America, my wheelchair, and airplane travel. It was difficult for some of the tribe members to comprehend that in Canada, we do not have giraffes, lions, zebras, but there is an abundance of cows, horses, and chickens. Late in the afternoon, the tall, lanky door attendant, dressed in a bright red sleeveless tunic, approached me. "Come to our village tonight," he said shyly.

The invitation was also extended to Georgina, another Canadian woman who was staying at the lodge. Curiosity and eagerness easily overcame apprehension.

"Yes, I would love to come to your village," I told him.

We left on foot in the early evening, with me on wheels, crossing grasslands to the village where a group of thatched roof huts surrounded the central courtyard. We were ushered into the home of the chief and quickly offered a beverage. The offer inspired concern and apprehension. The tribes of the Masai are honoured to share the Royal drink: animal blood.

My thoughts began to churn—I would have to be polite. I

didn't think I could stomach even a swallow of animal blood. The chief's son knelt on the floor to pull a covered wooden box out from under the bed. From the box, he removed a green glass bottle of 7Up. "We keep a special drink for all of our visitors. Would you like some?"

An instant smile spread over both our faces! The chief and his family drank from an animal skin pouch. I did not ask, nor was I ready to hear, what the contents of that pouch were. Georgina and I sipped from the bottle of 7Up, eager to please but also relieved at how easy it was to please!

Before leaving Vancouver, I was advised that if I wanted to see elephants, I might see them in the Masai, but I would certainly see them in Amboseli. I did see one large bull elephant on the plains of the Masai. I had booked a second safari to Amboseli National Park, located in the south of Kenya and spanning the Kenya-Tanzania border.

I, along with other solo Canadian tourists, arrived by Land Rover then settled into our "hotel": a tent. We quickly chose our van seats. Would we see elephants? As we rounded the second corner on the narrow, rugged park road, a herd of elephants—no less than four hundred—appeared before our eyes. They ranged in size from tiny through medium to large and enormous. I always thought that baby elephants, who hold their mom by the tail, was a trick taught by Barnum & Bailey's circus trainers. But that is not the case. As the wild herd of elephants lumbered across the plain, tiny baby elephants securely clutched their moms' tails; just as we moms hold our child's hand as we cross a road.

Although the elephants were the highlight of Amboseli, I had the continued privilege of viewing giraffes, zebras, lions, and other species. The one animal that I did not see was a rhinoceros. I would wait twelve years before I had this privilege—in the jungle of Nepal in 2003.

I moved on with the group from Canada to a more contemporary lodge. The accommodation was a series of self-contained cottages located in a bird sanctuary. Birds, small and large, freely invited themselves through an open door to check out the sitting room or bedroom in the cabins. My roommate, a woman from Germany, had an amazing fear of these harmless creatures. It was too hot to leave the door closed so I often sat on the porch in the evening reading my book and standing guard against the much-feared wildlife. Unlike my roommate, I found it amusing to wake in the morning to the nudge from a goose pecking at the quilt covering my feet. From the yard outside, we had a clear view of Mount Kenya, which was most prominent in the early morning. Following my several weeks of tenting and roughing it, any accommodation with a real washroom, running water, a handheld shower nozzle that could suffice for a wheel-in shower, a quilt on the bed, mosquito net over the bed frame, and fresh water to drink, was a welcome respite.

Reluctantly, it finally came time to move on. An overnight flight from Nairobi arrived in Amsterdam allowing us time to visit the early-morning tulip auction where thousands of budding tulips, sold to the highest bidder, were boxed and loaded onto awaiting airplanes for delivery to cities around the world. Later in the morning, we took a canal cruise in Amsterdam, then a walk along the shore where windmills and wooden shoes are at home. There was time to purchase Edam and Gouda cheeses before a second flight from Amsterdam carried me to Edmonton, then onward to Vancouver, bringing a successful close to my African adventure.

Chapter 3

My Trusty Rainbow

The pewter early morning light seeped around the edges of the bedroom blinds, urging my body to rouse itself. My mind quickly reviewed, from beginning to end, my "things to be done list," reminding me of the chores that had not been accomplished during my 80-hour workweek. These chores now cheerfully beckoned me to include them in the Saturday marathon of activity.

It was a swim day!

For most of my adult life, exercise had become as routine as brushing my teeth. It was just something I did without much thought. I ran three or four miles, three or four times a week. The only constant element in life is change, yet it took me awhile to recognize that it was time for a change. On one dark March evening, I acknowledged that it was not longer possible to throw a baggy old t-shirt over my head, pull on a pair of running shorts, slip my blistered feet into well used Brooks Chariots and ease into the morning rain to rhythmically stride along the sidewalks and through the trails in the park.

Running had become part of my past life.

I could no longer run, so I began to swim. Swimming soon eased into my routine and going to a pool became as regular as eating and sleeping. If the calendar book in my mind has today marked as a swim day, I find a way to get it done. When I was first living on my own in a basement suite, the community pool was the only option. It took a while to develop a manageable routine. Here we go—put on the bathing suit at home, pull on sweats, lift the wheelchair into the car, drive to the pool, get the chair out, squash my belongings into a locker, toss the shower necessities into the bag on the back of my chair, slip into the pool and execute thirty minutes of non-stop exercise. This half hour of aerobic practice required two to three hours to complete.

When I was running, the first three miles never got any easier. Likewise, the first ten lengths of the pool never get any easier. Even today, I am willing and eager to abort the swim during the first ten minutes. It always feels like I cannot go any further. I am sure that my life will end if I keep going. It takes a determined effort to continue. Despite what seems like overwhelming obstacles and ever-rising hurdles, there is a way to make it work. My silent prayer is always, *Please allow me to maintain enough body movement to exercise in some way*. It is a cherished gift!

So, as I said earlier, this particular Saturday was a swim day. When I dressed, I pulled a bathing suit on under my jeans. This ensures that some time, before I crawl into bed at night, I will have had a swim. Never mind the challenge of going to the washroom during the day. I have learned the means of doing this. Just pull the swimsuit aside allowing the same freedom that can be achieved by pulling panties down. Things work without taking the whole bathing suit off!

There was no time to swim and shower before tackling the chore list. I was heading to the library, to the produce store, to get the car washed, fill the gas tank, grab a few groceries, drop off the dry cleaning, pick up my watch at the jewellery store, deposit my pay cheque in the ATM and withdraw some cash, buy ingredients for the fruit/cheese tray that I was to bring to the potluck dinner tomorrow, find a liquor store to pick up a bottle of wine ... I was in a hurry to get started. The swim and shower would have to be squeezed in between the errands and meeting a friend for dinner at seven o'clock in the evening. The jangling of the telephone interrupted my forward focus.

Should I answer? Most parents will relate to my response. When you have children, one never knows if the phone call will be one of joy, need or pain. "Mom, I got 89% on my science exam." "Mom, can I borrow twenty dollars?" "Mom, today I hate you." "Mom, today I love you more than ever before." I answered the phone.

"Mom, Dad went to Costco this morning and bought these cool bags. He has fifteen of them and wants to know if you would like to buy one?" The price was enormous, fourteen dollars. I did not have time to listen to the chit-chat that followed. The description was flamboyant as Patrick expanded on the details—the size, colours, practicality and usefulness. Of course, he was hell-bent on convincing me that a multi-coloured Costco bag was an essential part of my continued life and happiness. For fourteen dollars. "Of course I will take one." I placed the receiver back into its cradle and wheeled out the door. I had no idea what I was committing myself to, but I suspected that it was a good buy and probably more practical than one could ever imagine. Besides, fourteen dollars would not exactly deplete my life savings. David, Patrick, and Timothy's father is one of the most skilled shoppers I have ever encountered. Like a dog searching out a bone or a squirrel routing for a hidden acorn, David could smell a bargain from two miles away. Store staff was never prepared for the skill and astuteness that they encountered when David crossed the threshold of their enterprise. The majority of men start their Christmas shopping on the weekend before Christmas and with any luck, they will exit from a multipurpose drugstore at six o'clock on Christmas Eve clutching their precious purchases. David is by far the exception. His Christmas shopping begins on December 26 and is finished at 6:00 p.m., December 24. A list is never needed. He can spot a good bargain three miles away, always knows your colour preference, size, what shape everyone is, and "need" is not even a consideration. It was with these thoughts that I tackled my errands.

On Sunday afternoon, my buzzer rang and an enthusiastic redhead appeared at my door with the precious bag. It was to become my trusty rainbow companion for the next fifteen years. It definitely was multi-coloured—hot pink, lime green, sunshine yellow, florescent metallic blue. It fit easily on my lap and did not extend over the wheels of my chair. It had a small zippered pouch resting upon a larger zippered pouch on one side. Zippers at both ends, when unzipped, allowed two six-inch hot pink extensions. When I left on a trip, both ends of the bag were securely closed. As I made purchases in foreign lands, the ends were unzipped to create more space. The additional six inches on either end of the bag, extended over the top of my wheels but what did it matter? By the time the expansion was needed, I was heading home.

How to pack? What to pack?

I developed an "always in the bag" routine. Whether I am away for five days, five weeks, or five months, I carry the same component of clothing—two pairs of shorts, one pair of long pants, three t-shirts, a bathing suit (cap and goggles) and a nightshirt. My colour combination is royal blue and red. All of the t-shirts can be worn with any of the bottoms. One shirt and a pair of shorts are not placed in the bag because, of course, I have to wear something on the airplane and increasing the number of articles is not an option. Female undergarments? I wear a sports bra on leaving home. If it becomes wet after laundry or is lost in the shuffle, I go bra-less. A small, tiny gold angel is pinned to my bra strap. It was a gift from Patrick before one of my first trips.

"Mom, keep her with you, close to your heart," he told me earnestly. "She will protect you and ensure your safety."

I always take three pairs of panties (my raggiest, sans elastic).

Colour is not important. With three pairs, I can have a clean pair in the bag, a pair on my bod and a pair that I have just washed, hanging on the doorknob. This always gives me more space on my return trip home as I only bring home the pair that I am wearing. I wear a pair of runners with ankle length socks. If travelling to a warm climate, a pair of sandals is tucked into a corner.

I start packing two to three weeks before a trip. Why start so early? When getting around in a wheelchair, there is more involved to packing than throwing in a few articles of clothing. My bag is always more than half-full before even a t-shirt is slipped in. In the bottom, I carry a small bicycle pump, wheelchair parts—tire tubes, allen keys, brake extension, brake cover, Vaseline, WD-40—and on it goes. Countries with lots of bicycles and bike shops present less challenge than those where motorized vehicles are the normal mode of transportation. A wheelchair tire is the same as a 24 3/8″ bicycle tire. Tires can be replaced at any bicycle shop except for the fact that, bike tires are black, wheelchair tires are grey. Some specialty bike shops in Vancouver carry wheelchair tires.

An MS bladder offers challenges of its own. I have amazing bladder control for someone with MS but that doesn't negate the fact that a spasm may cause leakage, so a small panty liner to protect against embarrassing moments is a good idea. A Ziploc bag containing small and medium-sized panty liners, waterless wash, wet wipes and a towel are next slipped into the bag. If going to countries where there may be long stretches between food and water, a box of granola bars and packages of fruit leather are packed into the corners.

I am a nurse! My body has had some sense of nursing since I was five years old. A small nylon pouch with prophylactic medication is always included in my bag. I don't think I have ever needed a dose of Imodium, I have never taken a Gravol tablet, Band-Aids are seldom used, I have not had a bladder infection for fifteen years, infected wounds rarely occur, but I am equipped with medication to deal with all of these situations. At some time we all can use cold medication. I do find that other travellers are not often so well prepared and they appreciate my medications in foreign and distant lands.

So where am I now? I have the bag two-thirds full and I am now ready to put in some clothing with the aim of leaving room for additions of "just throw it in" things that come up along the way. My bag will get less full as the days progress. I carry small bottles (hotel-sized) of shampoo, conditioner and moisturizer. As these toiletries are used, the discarded bottles generate a little more space.

The many colours of my rainbow bag made it easy to spot as it tumbles down the baggage chute in airports, as it is hoisted onto and off trains and buses. When it was stacked with hundreds of other pieces of luggage, mostly black and navy blue, I can always find my trusty rainbow readily.

My trusty rainbow bag has accompanied me to China, Australia, Africa, South America, Europe, and Asia. It survived the heat of Tahiti, cold overnight trains in India, the torrential rain of monsoons, the snow in the Falkland Islands, the jungle on the Caribbean side of Central America, the rain forests of Costa Rica, coast to coast in Canada and the United States.

After many years, the zippers pulled away from the nylon seams and corners, worn spots appeared on the bottom and on the edges, and more attention was required to maintain its balance as I wheeled with the bag on my lap. I was going to lose my close associate and friend, but Tim came to the rescue. Both my children had Costco bags. Tim had used his to store soccer gear and it was in almost perfect condition. A young man was certainly not going to take a hot pink, fluorescent blue nylon bag to the soccer field. It worked for both of us. He could have my old, almost worn out bag to store his extra soccer boots in the basement locker. I could have a nearly new famous Costco bag to continue on my travels.

All good things come to an end. By the time I returned from Vietnam in November 2005, my second Costco bag was in a terminal state. I could no longer use duct tape to hold together the splitting edges, there were no longer rings in which to insert the zap straps that doubled as security, socks were peaking out of the holes at the ends. All in all, it was time to face facts. Where could I find another multipurpose, easy to pack, easy to unpack, easy to carry, easy to identify, travel bag? A trip to Walmart produced a satchel that would address many of these issues—my new bag is narrow enough to carry on my lap, it has closure zippers as strong as iron. There are zippers at both ends (although the expansion is only three inches rather than six), it is easy to pack, easy to unpack. The only downfall is that it is a medium blue colour—not so bad when three quarters of my wardrobe is blue. When it comes down the chute at the airport, however, I have to look closely to identify my new travel companion.

Chapter 4

Under the Union Jack

Jolly Old England

It always amazes me that such a small island spreads its tentacles throughout the world to include in its Commonwealth such far away lands as Australia, India, Canada, Hong Kong, and parts of Africa. Now, more than fifty states are members of the British Commonwealth.

In 1979, on one of those whirlwind trips to see the highlights of Europe—you know the kind, "It's Tuesday, we must be in Belgium" —I captured the essence of a North American's visit to London. I rode on a double-decker bus, watched the changing of the guard at Buckingham Palace, walked on London Bridge, saw the crown jewels, was impressed and horrified by the images in Madame Tussaud's Wax Museum, and felt saddened by the history at the Tower of London. I got a good feel for London but did not have the opportunity to explore any other corners of this ancient world power.

In 1992, I had the urge to feel it, touch it, experience it. I did my research, then purchased a Brit Rail flex pass that allowed eight days of travel in sixteen days. The trains in Britain, although not modern and accessible, offer portable ramps and a large space in which to park a wheelchair. Of course, there was always that frequent British offer of help. I collected brochure after brochure describing bed and breakfast accommodations. I reviewed the atlas, three guidebooks and a book of British customs. I decided that it was time to explore every available corner of the British

Isles. Patrick stopped to visit one Wednesday evening, to find me pouring over maps and British traveller information. He had lots of questions and I could sense some degree of concern in his demeanor. The following day, at work, I received a telephone call from his father.

"Lin, Patrick is really worried about you. He came home last night and said, 'Dad, Mum's either lost her mind or she just found it, and I'm not sure which.'"

I laughed. "It's okay, David," I told him, smiling. "Tell him I've found it."

Accessibility in Britain in the early nineties was nothing to write home about. The boys were hesitant about this trip, because although I had been on my own on my fledgling international trips to the Orient and Africa, the airfare, accommodation, and movement from country to country had all been pre-booked and pre-planned. This time, all I had was a clean pair of blue jeans and a *Lonely Planet* tucked into the back of my wheelchair. I was otherwise accompanied only by brazenness. My children's realistic concerns centred around, "Mum, what happens if you get there and it's not accessible and you can't go anywhere? What will you do?"

At that time, the boys were not yet comfortable with my new found laissez-faire attitude. I knew that I wouldn't be able to do everything that other people did and that was okay. In England, if I can't go anywhere, I would find a nice bed and breakfast close to the water, a bookstore where I could unearth a good book, and I'd content myself with reading for two or three weeks. Of course, this didn't happen. I explored more of British soil than I ever thought possible. Before leaving home, I suspected that hills would be a challenge and that my energy might run out. So, on the back of my wheelchair was a small, neatly printed card with a decal of the Canadian flag. The card read, "Any push is greatly appreciated, THANK YOU." That card yielded two benefits: I conserved my energy and it opened the door to many lasting friendships.

Airfares are often reduced between October 1 and April 30, so I frequently travel near my birthday, October 5. The policy of Canadian Airlines was to seat people with disabilities in business class if space was available. It saved staff the long trip with an aisle chair to the rear of the aircraft. So, when I left for London on October 4, business class was where I sat, enjoying the decadence of white wine, warmed cashew nuts, smoked salmon, and gourmet meals, while those in economy class suffered through reheated TV dinner style meals.

On arrival at Gatwick airport, on October 5—Happy Birthday Lin—the flight attendants embraced me, offering to share accommodations in their hotel room. In the evening, we took the train to downtown London, dined at a pub (the only affordable place to eat) and found tickets to "Starlight Express," an Andrew Lloyd Webber musical where roller skaters zoom across walkways in the rafters of the theatre. After two days of exploration with my new-found friends, they boarded a plane to work their way home and I continued on my own journey.

In the university town of Cambridge, northeast of London, a green and cream open-top double-decker bus offered a tour. The tour bus guide enlightened his audience about ancient history and present day happenings of this historical city and the colleges. The On-Off Bus ticket, valid all day, encouraged me to climb on the bus (albeit slowly); disembark halfway through the tour to facilitate a visit to the colleges; join an organized walking tour and spend time browsing through the shops. I could rejoin the bus when I was ready. Alternatively, I could have stayed on the one-hour tour. However, the driver and other passengers were more than willing to help me exit and re-board. I used this luxury only once; I am always conscious of the "nuisance factor" of my immobility.

My Canadian flag stickpin provided unexpected benefits. Two students who were majoring in North American geography reached out in order to learn from my Canadian heritage. Fair deal! They treated me to lunch, a tour of the university, visits to popular university hangouts in town, an hour listening to the university band practice, and a quick soccer game, all while I proofread the rough drafts of their papers that described the geographical, political, and cultural aspects of Canada. The students escorted me to the train station. They hugged and kissed me and sent me safely on my way.

Before leaving Canada, I had explored the possibility of buying a ticket to "Miss Saigon" — but eighty Pounds? I think not! After 3:00 p.m., the London ticket office sells unsold theatre seats for that particular day, for ten Pounds. The Cambridge bus stopped across from the ticket office, where I picked up a last-minute seat for that ten Pounds. Mobilizing by wheelchair lends some restrictions to sitting in a multi-level ancient theatre with narrow doorways, constricted aisles, and steep balconies. But, for every disadvantage there always is an advantage! The acoustics were wonderful. To my delight, the seat that I had purchased was on the aisle, five rows back from the stage, giving me a panoramic view of the action and of the real life helicopter that landed in the jungle of Vietnam.

One hundred tracks lead in and out of Victoria Station carrying passengers in every direction. With my small bag perched on my lap, I traversed multiple level crossings and tracks, to find the engine that would pull me northwards through Britain.

At 5:08 a.m., the train was off to Doncaster, located in South Yorkshire, offering easy access to the central and more northerly parts of England. In Doncaster, the crossroads of the UK railway system connect London with Edinburgh. This city, because of its location, attracts an abundance of visitors who are en route to Scotland.

The hostess of a tiny bed & breakfast, very close to the station, welcomed me. This family offered a small basement suite that had been adapted for their youngest son, a paraplegic, who was now away at university. A hot cup of tea, homemade scones, a wheel-in shower and a bed whose height was level with my wheelchair, left me wanting nothing more.

At the train station, at 8:00 a.m. the following morning, the conductor shouted, "All aboard!" as he beckoned me to approach the steps where a portable ramp had been slipped into place. Most of the time I am on the receiving end of assistance but on this day, it was not the case. I shared a compartment with a single dad who was travelling with his two young children. Jenna and Richard had multiple questions for me, "Why can't you walk? How did you get from Canada to England? Can your wheelchair fit on the airplane? Did you bring it from Canada or did you buy a new one in Britain? Do you have children? Where are you going? Where have you been? Do you know how to play Go Fish? Would you like to play? We are going to get something to eat from the snack car. We will bring you something. What would you like?"

I gave the children the shillings from my pouch and trusted their selection of munchies for their dad, themselves, and myself. It didn't matter what we had to eat. What mattered was the valuable interaction that was happening among the four of us. The children were endearing. I played Fish and Old Maid for hours. We tried to replicate animals with our fingers. We laughed at the colts frolicking in the fields. Family secrets were exchanged while the clacking train sped towards Scotland. At the end of the four-hour train ride, Dad scooped up their belongings as he prodded reluctant children to prepare for their disembarkation at the next station. He thanked me profusely for providing an opportunity for his children to participate in an experience that demonstrated to them that people with a disability are contributing and functioning members of the world. Those of us who have a disability are blessed with the ongoing responsibility to educate. This is sometimes accomplished in the most non-obvious manner.

Thank you Jenna and Richard.

Heather on the Moors

Was I really in Scotland? Aberdeen was my first descent from the train. My inability to walk makes every train exit a bit of a dance.

So much is unique about this country—tartan and kilts, heather and moors, rain and wind, bagpipes and haggis, Scotch whisky. Did you know that kilt-wearing men wear nothing underneath their tartan attire? On occasion, workmen dressed in native costume were working high up on a ladder. No, I did not make a point of wheeling under the ladder. Interesting that males in Scotland wear full traditional dress while females wear only an arisaidh over modern clothes. The traditional 14th century arisaidh, a tartan wool scarf, hand pleated and belted around the waist, is elegant and practical. Extra fabric is pinned at the breast and worn as a hood to keep head and shoulders warm and dry. Children going to and from school played kick the can, boys snaffled the girls' backpacks, tossing them from one to another, and teased the little ones. The games and antics of schoolchildren are common throughout the world. The difference in Scotland, is that the children often wear traditional dress including tartan trousers, velvet waistcoats, and tartan dresses. The sound of bagpipes crooning and whining were frequently heard on the hillsides, in train stations, and outside local pubs. Oh yes, I knew where I was!"

Consulting my notes, I found my home away from home—literally. A young woman, residing alone, accepted only select female visitors into her home. One bed and breakfast room was occupied intermittently by a businessman who travelled from London for meetings in Aberdeen. John, an old family friend, had been staying here for years.

"The other room," Marion, my welcoming hostess, said, "is only available to young women who are travelling alone. It is also manageable for those with a disability."

In my mind, I questioned the adjective "young," but accepted that the accommodation was ideal for me. Marion said that she left for work early in the morning.

"John Chester is reliable and will help you with anything you need. I will set out breakfast on the table. Please come and go as you please."

Upon arising, I found John making our coffee using a glass espresso press. On the table, freshly squeezed orange juice, muesli, and a note that announced, "Warm biscuits are in the oven" welcomed the start of my day.

My immediate objective was to locate the tourist information centre. There, a cheerful, and knowledgeable lady painted me an inviting picture of the area. The brochures displayed stunning scenery, a picturesque harbour, frolicking dolphins, fairy tale castles, whiskey distilleries, tranquil hideaways, and centuries of Scottish culture. I visited a distillery where I observed the preparation of Scotch whiskey. I found a quiet spot in a park to read for a few hours. Later, I followed the advice of the young woman at the tourist office. I had thought that the Castle Trail would be too long and too difficult for me to navigate on my own but she disagreed. "You are such a wee thing," she told me enthusiastically (Who was she trying to kid?). A park ranger took a group along the trail each afternoon. It would be no problem, she assured me. He was always accompanied by two or three young 'uns.

Aberdeen is the richest area of Scottish castle tradition. On

Castle Trail (which is clearly signposted), I stepped back in time as I viewed thirteen spectacular specimens of world-famous Scottish castle architecture: structures cornered by stone turrets, fairy tale magic, majestic royal splendour. Ruins recorded the history of the country. Yes, the woman at the tourist bureau was correct. This "wee lass" was indeed expertly escorted along the Castle Trail by two young bonny lads. When making my way back to the B&B, my appreciation of my "push" sign on the back of my chair led to an encounter with a young travelling salesman by the name of Hunter, who peddled electronics to dealers in the small towns of northern Scotland. Later, I joined Hunter and his wife at the local pub where we had a pint of Guinness and a bowl of thick vegetable potage. Hunter enthusiastically offered me the opportunity to accompany him the following morning as he drove between small towns to visit the television and stereo stores in each village. Later that evening, while sharing a cup of tea with Marion, my B&B hostess, I discovered that she was a very good friend of Hunter and his wife. She recommended I accept Hunter's offer.

"You will see so much more of Scotland than is ever possible on BritRail."

Boxes of televisions, spools of wire, electrical cords, coloured advertising brochures, and other paraphernalia were my seating companions. We covered many kilometres as I observed heather-covered moors, green hillsides of thistle, flocks of grey and white woolly sheep and Black Angus cattle. In the small towns, I absorbed a feeling for the commerce, the residential housing, the markets, and the friendly, chatty, welcoming people. Morning sales calls completed, it was time for lunch. We entered an elegant dining room filled with a high-pitched noise—not a result of conversation but generated by clatter of bone china and the clinking of "real" silver cutlery. The doorman, with thick curly, auburn locks and a bushy, deep red beard, dressed in a lime-green tartan suit, was equally warm in his welcome and farewell. My brother, who is an avid golfer, was green with envy when I returned to Canada and told him that I had been treated to lunch at the world renowned Saint Andrews Golf Club.

After leaving Aberdeen and en route to Inverness, the train rolled into a small town, requiring me to change tracks. I discovered that my next train was two tracks over. The only way to reach the new track was to climb 32 stairs, go over the walkway, and descend the stairs on the other side. On this 32-stair ascent, every smidgeon of patience and every ounce of ingenuity that I possessed was called into play. My fellow passengers, two young women toting infants and diaper bags, could not help. Down the track and around the corner, came a handcar to the rescue, its handle being pumped up and down by a large young man. When he saw my predicament, he stopped his handcar and entered the station to find a companion. He returned with another young man. They lifted me up the stairs and over the walkway, sitting me on a bench at the bottom of the staircase on the far side. They returned with my chair and my bag. When somebody refers to a blessing in disguise, a friend of mine asks, "Why are they always in disguise?" In this case, there was no disguise. The blessing was in full view: the two willing young men right in front of me.

In Inverness, I consulted my notes again for possible accommodations. At the foot of each listing, tiny icons suggest the amenities available at each bed and breakfast: hot water showers, full English breakfast versus continental, telephone, and kitchen time for preparation of an evening meal. The universal blue and white wheelchair symbol indicated that the accommodation was appropriate for people with disabilities. When I approached the chosen home, I noted one step from the sidewalk to the front door. Steps and wheelchairs are never compatible!

Not a problem, unless I make it a problem! There had to be a way. I couldn't face any more pushing about today.

I wheeled over the grass to circumvent the step and was able to reach the brass doorknocker. In the early 1990s, I could still wall-walk for a short distance and mount stairs by holding onto a railing with one hand and manually lifting one foot at a time up the stairs. Delicacy and grace were not part of this little two-step but it did permit me some vertical movement. Mrs. Mackenzie, the lady of the house, showed me to my room—twenty-seven steep steps up from the main floor, a slow process to say the least. After I had reached the top of the staircase in classic Cirque du Soleil style, Mrs. Mackenzie, in all her innocence, asked, "Dear, would you like your chair brought up the stairs?"

I cannot navigate one forward step on the level. Of course I wanted my round, chrome-spoked legs. Unless my teal blue companion joined me, I would just stretch out beside Scruffy, the square-faced wire-haired terrier, who was comfortably curled up on the threadbare, oval burgundy carpet at the top of the stairway. No insult to Scruffy, but sliding between cool sheets was my preference tonight!

Spare me! But my father's words echoed in my mind. "At times like this, it is best to hold your tongue and open your heart and mind. Just count to ten before you speak." The cheeky response was on the tip of my tongue but hold it, I did.

"Yes please, that would be wonderful. I apologize for being such a nuisance but I only selected your home because the brochure indicates that your residence is appropriate for folks with a disability."

"Yes dear, it is," she assured me. "Your chair fits through the door. If the doorways are wide enough to admit a wheelchair, in Scotland we can advertise that the B&B is appropriate for people with a disability."

I have said it before and I will say it again—the definition of accessibility differs widely among communities, cities, countries, cultures, and people! It is always best to not show surprise when your expectations radically differ from reality.

In the morning, the breakfast room required another five-stair descent from the main floor to a dining area. Give thanks for small mercies! Mrs. Mackenzie served me a full English breakfast—back bacon, fried tomatoes, baked beans, eggs, fried bread, sausages, and tea— commonly known as a "fry-up." My expenditure of energy to gain a night's rest and to acquire the first food of the day had given me a fine appetite. The crusty white roll and strawberry jam served by most B&Bs could never have satisfied my appetite.

The Isle of Skye was my next target. This largest and most northern island in the Inner Hebrides presents a series of peninsulas that radiate from the centre. It is truly a land of contrast compared to the mainland. Over 30% of the residents on Skye speak Gaelic. Industry is primarily fishing, as it was done years ago. Rain falls over 85% of the time, with a rainfall record of ten millimetres in one minute! I boarded the ferry in the pouring rain and was thankful for a waterproof Gore-Tex jacket and water repellent pants. Wheeling at a snail's pace through the downpour, I climbed the steep road from the ferry dock then down into the town of Armadale. I overtook a young American couple and their two small children, which was quite amazing as my speed seldom allows me to catch up with anyone!

"We expected it to rain but not the monsoon style of today," the bedraggled mother lamented. "The children are having difficulty walking these wet roads."

"I'll carry," I negotiated. "And you push."

The three-year-old, who had been loudly objecting to the walk, settled happily on my lap while his dad pushed my wheelchair along the beach walkway. Sloshing through deep puddles, we made acquaintance with the narrow, charming streets of the small island town. Within two hours, drenched to the skin, we were overjoyed to discover the covered veranda of an old hotel on the shoreline. We welcomed the overhang that protected us from the rain, along with the hot tea and freshly baked scones placed before us.

Rain on the Isle of Skye.

Why do I subject myself to such conditions? Because it is not worth travelling to diverse parts of the world unless I am willing to experience the diverse aspects of geography, weather, customs, and culture. After warming up, we all agreed we had been keen to come to Skye but it was now time to leave. Homeward bound, the ferry carried us back through the waves.

Edinburgh, the capital of Scotland since 1433, is located in the east near the North Sea. Its rugged setting, peppered with Medieval and Georgian architecture, includes unique stone tenements that have earned Edinburgh the reputation as one of the most picturesque cities in Europe. The old town and new streets are now a UNESCO world heritage site and the buildings blend in a complimentary fashion.

Arts festivals abound in Edinburgh. As fortune would have it, I was present during the Edinburgh Fringe Festival, the largest performing arts festival in the world. I attended three short theatrical performances that left me laughing and examining my inner core; leading me to dream of days to come.

Edinburgh is the second most visited tourist destination in the United Kingdom, next to London. I was privileged to cross paths with a delightful woman who was studying at the university. She took it upon herself to proudly display some of the popular features of her home city and later that afternoon, treated me to a Wimpy's burger. In Edinburgh, I visited the castle and watched the changing of the guard, drank a Guinness, ate lamb stew in a pub, and thoroughly enjoyed the amiable society of this northern urban settlement.

Yet another BritRail train carried me to Glasgow, the largest city in Scotland, located in the west on the River Clyde. Glasgow is known worldwide for its shipbuilding, engineering, and as a financial centre. In the 18th century, the city became one of Europe's main transatlantic trade centres with the Americas. The Great Irish Famine of the 1840s brought large numbers of Irish-Scots and Irish Catholic immigrants to the city. At one point during this period, only New York City had a larger population of Irish Catholics than Glasgow. Many of the streets are named after 18th and 19th century tobacco lords, whose great wealth impelled the city as a world leader. Glasgow was chosen as the host city of the 2014 Commonwealth Games.

On a quiet street in Glasgow, I met up with Becky, a young Canadian woman who was attending a conference that focused on young children with developmental disabilities. At the end of her four-day conference, she had the use of the organization's

Honda Civic. Becky was heading to Ireland to explore and welcomed a fellow Canadian to share the Irish experience.

Leprechauns and Shamrocks

May the road rise up to meet you.
May the wind always be at your back.
May the sun shine warm upon your face,
and rains fall soft upon your fields.
And until we meet again,
May God hold you in the palm of His hand.
Author unknown

For many years throughout Ireland, violence and bitter conflict raged between the Nationalists (Roman Catholics), who wanted Northern Ireland to be united with the Republic of Ireland and the Unionists (Protestants), who wanted it to remain as part of the United Kingdom. Protestants consider themselves British; Catholics see themselves as Irish. There are some who see themselves as both British and Irish. The signing of the Belfast Agreement, known as the Good Friday Agreement, in May 1998, led the groups to declare that their war was over. The settlement focused on human rights, the decommissioning of arms, and the release of political prisoners.

Becky and I ferried from Stranraer (Troon) to Larne, a well-travelled ferry passage from Scotland to the outskirts of Belfast. The salt spray from the waves coated our hair, making it stiff —no hairspray needed today—and the brine splashed over the deck. Gale force winds heightened our awareness of our surroundings.

After arriving on land, we drove along the Giant's Causeway where steep, sheer cliffs descend to the ocean below. Thousands of columns, created by rapidly cooling lava, are a result of repeated ancient volcanic eruptions. This natural wonder was declared a World Heritage Site in 1986. The steep cliffs and stunning rock formations were strikingly beautiful in the early morning sunlight. Their impressive beauty carried on into the afternoon. The splendour of the rock formations escalated as the daylight diminished and increased as dusk enveloped our surroundings.

A small B&B, the Smugglers Inn, lay at the end of the causeway. On either side of the front entrance stood a gilded birdcage containing two lovebirds on one side and two blue budgies on the other. With her appealling Irish accent, the hostess welcomed us with warm embraces, rewarding my extra effort, which is always required when entering or exiting a car. Others just "hop" out of a car; I arrange my chair in precise placement and unceremoniously, and with hovering assistance, transfer over.

We were given thick, hot chowder to fill our empty stomachs. After the evening meal, we sat around the table to be entertained by legends and tales that recounted, in detail, both ancient and recent tumultuous events in this conflict-torn country. We were enlightened by Irish proverbs such as, "A handful of skill is worth a bagful of gold." "An old broom knows the dirty corners best." "A turkey never voted for an early Christmas."

We arose in the early morning to the scent and sounds of percolating coffee (I hadn't seen a coffee percolator in Canada for many years). There were fresh soda bread biscuits hot from the oven, and gooseberry jelly made from the fruit of the prickly bushes outside the back door. We were sent on our way with full stomachs, warm thoughts, and an invitation to come back soon and often.

Throughout the day, we travelled along small roadways, visiting quaint, charming villages that were struggling with the challenge of recuperation from the demise of trade and industry following the religious troubles that had devastated the country. I wondered if Ireland could ever recover economically. Concrete crumbled at the edges of buildings. Flattened churches and houses gave testimony to local bombing activities. "Paved" streets were anything but paved. Road repair was minimal or nonexistent. In restaurants, menus were offered on dog-eared, photocopied pages. No two chairs matched. But the people, despite their trials and tribulations, were cheerful and welcoming and appeared on the surface, to be happy.

Frequent lookouts along the causeway offered views of many stone formations. Some resembled amphitheatres, leading my imagination to be entertained by Irish music, a puppet show, or ethnic plays presented to cheering crowds of local people.

Before we tackled Carrick, Becky drove the small Honda down to a tiny village where we purchased Irish soda bread and cheese for a picnic in the meadow. The Carrick-A-Rede Rope Bridge, an astonishing manmade conveyance between the coast and the island of Carrick, allows locals and tourists alike to cross over the rocky waters below. The bridge has been traced back to the 1700s when it consisted of a single rope and wide wooden slats. In the 20th century, improvements to the bridge include a rope on either side, minimally reducing anxiety for those crossing. The bridge spans a yawning chasm and the terrifying eighty-foot deep gap can only be crossed via this swinging bridge—not for acrophobics or wheelchair users; the bridge is too narrow for even the narrowest of mobility devices.

The Carrick-A-Rede Rope Bridge was created by fishermen who didn't want to climb up and down the cliffs. They desired easier access to the island so that they could check the nets, in the hopes of yielding a harvest of migrating salmon to feed their families' hungry mouths over the winter.

Atlantic Irish salmon fishing is a thing of the past, but the bridge remains today as an attraction to visitors who have difficulty imagining the construction of such a bridge made without the use of modern technology, and who are challenged to match the courage of fishermen of old. The gaps between the ropes seems wide, necessitating firm control of young children.

For those who are patient enough to wait for ideal conditions, the coast of Scotland is clearly visible from the island. Along the island's edge, large caves once supplied shelter for boat builders and a place of safety during North Atlantic winter storms.

Carrick is more than the anchor for an intimidating bridge; it is also an island of outstanding natural beauty. Diverse birdlife includes fulmars, kittiwakes, guillemots, and razorbills (the ability to say these words alone is a challenge in itself). There is a breath-taking uninterrupted view across to Rathlin Island and Scotland.

The little white cottage on the side of the island, which seemed quite out of place, was another curiosity. It was surrounded by a very prim white picket fence covered with wild sweet peas; there were untended but healthy fruits and vegetables such as rhubarb and asparagus, as well as a yard full of fruit trees. It didn't seem to belong in this remote location. Like lonely, secluded lighthouses, this small cottage was home to the inlet keeper and guardian of the island.

Near the bridge in the town of Carrick, near the bridge, we found a small, quaint bed and breakfast. The host opened his heart and his arms, ladled out bowls of Irish stew that warded off the chill of the evening air, and poured Guinness beer. We chatted, played cards, and retired early, knowing that our wonderful short visit to Ireland would end the next day.

Part of going to Ireland is, of course, to visit and kiss the Blarney Stone. Its location on the south west coast in Cork, however, forced me to leave this romantic gesture for another venture. The green hills, rolling meadows, and flocks of sheep bade us farewell as the ferry rocked through the waves, heading back to Larne and Glasgow. Becky retraced her steps to Scotland to return the borrowed car.

I slowly pushed my way to the train station to board a train heading to the Lake District on the west side of England.

English Country Gardens

The vibrant loveliness of British gardens was revealed to me as the train rumbled along the tracks through the Lake District. I found myself in a small town where I located accommodation at a lodge managed by the Episcopal Church. I inched my way up a steep hill. My efforts were rewarded—I was welcomed by a wonderful character of a house, perched on the side of the hill. Flowers surrounded the outside and garnished every corner within. People, mostly seniors, came to this respite for a few days, a weekend, a week. For me, it was a sanctuary. Every incline was ramped. Open spaciousness inside made wheeling easy. There was a wheel-in shower and warm and friendly folks. My four-day stay here included delicious meals, card games, prayers, laughter, the exchange of stories, and visits with neighbourhood children.

After a breakfast of the usual white crusty roll and strawberry jam, I joined two elderly gentlemen for a delightful morning excursion—visiting the local cathedral, tiny parks with exquisite flower gardens, and the commercial area of the small village. Walking into a wonderful bookstore, I was able to pick up another cherished companion to fill the hours on the train.

After these few days of restoration, it was time to move on. I wandered (via rail, of course) over to Liverpool, just to feel the heritage of the long-haired quartet that was so much a part of my teenage years. Growing up in the 1960s and 1970s, the Beatles were simply part of life, much to the chagrin of many parents. The opportunity to view the hometown of the Beatles was not to be missed. It was just as pictures had represented it. Liverpool is located on the east side of the Mersey River. By the mid 19th century, 40% of the world's trade passed through Liverpool's docks, contributing to Liverpool's rise as a major city. The popularity of the Beatles, and the other groups from the Mersey beat era, plays a major factor in Liverpool's status as a tourist destination. Tourism forms a significant part of the city's modern economy today.

It would never do to travel through this small historical island without including Wales. Along the northwest coast of Wales, the train passed through hundreds of tiny villages on its way to Swansea. Small stone houses, cottages by the sea, rock walls covered with ivy, flowering shrubs, and carts pulled by donkeys, led me back in time. From Cardiff, across the water from Bristol, I spotted a sign that indicated the approach of Penzance, Lands End. I decided to leave the train and spend a few days in the area, which was only familiar to me from high school geography books.

Leaving the train station, I wheeled along the cobblestone path that hugged the shoreline. Wind from the Atlantic and the crashing waves were exhilarating. I breathed deeply and huddled on the shore, gripping my jacket tightly around my shoulders and firmly clutching a cardboard cup of coffee that served to warm my hands and my innards. Along the rocky shoreline, a small cozy home offered a bed for the night, a fire in the hearth, a hot bowl of chowder. Friendly conversation carried us into the wee hours of the morning.

It was time to head back to the big city. I travelled along the coast, visiting Plymouth, Southampton, Portsmouth, and New Haven then continued on to London. I had two days in the city so had time for one more theatre ticket to see *Buddy*, the story of Buddy Holly, a shopping excursion to Harrods, where I purchased nothing but smiled broadly as I interacted with the residents of a heaping display of hundreds of Paddington bears. I sampled handouts of British toffee. I viewed unusual and intriguing British fashion. I wheeled one more time past the gates of Buckingham Palace to give my respects to the royal family and for one last time, saw the changing of the guard.

Mom, the Celebrity

Before leaving Canada, my teenage boys had adamantly instructed, "Mum, you don't need to bring us anything but if you want a suggestion, you know that the original Hard Rock Cafe is in London. A shirt from there would be *sweet*."

On my last full day in London, in the early morn, I trained it from Gatwick where I once again was invited to share a hotel room with the same flight attendants who had welcomed me on my arrival in London three weeks earlier. They would now guide me home.

Like a dog after a bone, I was determined to get those shirts. At Victoria Station, I commenced my task with the energy of a mom who wanted to delight her kids. Before this thoroughly remarkable trip to Britain ended, I was going to get those cherished tees from the Hard Rock Cafe. It was slow going in a manual wheelchair but I had all day. I consulted my map and pestered hundreds of pedestrians with, "Where is the Hard Rock Cafe?" I diligently followed the various directions.

I wheeled, rested, sipped from my water bottle, admired the flowers in window boxes, window shopped and remained positive, yet wondered if I was ever going to make it. One young woman, bless her heart, was willing to take the time to give me very clear instructions.

"When you arrive at Hyde Park Corner," she said with a smile, "A roundabout with eight lanes of traffic will announce that you are there."

Yes, when I reached Hyde Park Corner, the traffic was there. An executive, whistling a tune, swinging his briefcase, and toting an umbrella over his forearm, pointed enthusiastically across those eight lanes of traffic, "There it is. It is just over there."

"How does a pedestrian cross this freeway of cars racing along in circles," I asked, horrified.

He merely shrugged as if it was a minor issue. "Follow the arrows," he said and strode on.

That seemed to make sense since there were no pedestrian crosswalks. Following the arrows, I found to my dismay, that the only way to cross this incredible urban rush was to descend the staircase, walk under the roadway and climb the stairs on the other side—difficult for some, possible for most, not even a remote consideration for me.

It only took a few moments to consider my options. I flagged down a small black cab. The driver leaned out his window with a smile. "Where do you want to go?" he asked in a thick British accent.

"Over there." I pointed to the bright red neon sign that beckoned to me. I felt a little bit crazy but the cabbie did not hesitate to leap from the driver's seat to assist me into the car, place my wheelchair in the boot, drive around the circle, and deposit me in front of the door of the Hard Rock Cafe. Have you ever considered spending twelve dollars to cross the road? I was so excited to reach my destination that the cost was not even relevant. I would have spent a hundred.

In the shop, I selected the desired t-shirts for the boys and included one for myself. Hunger pangs registered in my brain. I suddenly realized that I had not eaten since yesterday, so a bowl of hot chili and a beer were in the cards. After my indulgence, the waitress offered me the menu as a souvenir. With my hunger satisfied, I was bolstered enough to tackle the return to Victoria Station. The adrenaline rush that had been generated by the accomplishment of my desired task vanished when I wheeled out of the café to see darkness creeping around the edges of the buildings. I could make it here in daylight. Could I make it back in the dark? Upon seeing my confusion, an elderly woman, probably in her late 80s, approached me and offered her assistance.

"I am going in the direction of Victoria Station, dear. Why don't you come along with me? We will just have to cross Green Park."

My wheelchair pace and her walking speed suited each other so we set off side by side.

Green Park is one of the Royal parks of London. It covers fifty-three acres between Hyde Park and St James Park. In conjunction with Kensington Gardens and Buckingham Palace, the parks form an almost unbroken stretch of open land that extends from Victoria Station to Notting Hill. Green Park consists entirely of densely treed forest and wooded meadows. How scary is this—elderly woman tottering along with her cane, and me, creeping forward in a manual wheelchair, with darkness rapidly approaching. We needed to cross the park diagonally in order to reach civilization on the other side of the woods! I envisioned an attacker behind every tree.

"Don't worry, dear," she said, "It's okay. I do this all the time."

I didn't voice it, but I was thinking, I believe you, but thousands wouldn't.

I had nothing to lose and everything to lose. I did have to get back to the hotel at Gatwick in preparation for a 7:00 a.m. flight back to Canada. After forty minutes of trekking along pathways, peeking cautiously around bushes and trees, chatting cheerfully with my gramma companion, we did make it safely through the park. I thanked her, we hugged, and parted. She turned the corner, heading home to her flat and I wheeled further along the streets to Victoria Station. I was going to make it. I was blessed with another spurt of energy that partially grew from the satisfaction of completing my goal for the day, and partially from my apprehension at traversing the woods at night. In the morning, I shuttled it to Gatwick Airport, checked my rainbow bag, and occupied my business class seat for the next ten hours. When I finally arrived in Vancouver and opened my bag to reveal the precious purchase of Hard Rock Café shirts, I was a celebrity. When I showed the boys the menu, they exclaimed in unison, "You didn't eat there, Mum!"

"Of course I did. Eat your heart out!" I told them smugly.

Chapter 5

Friendship to Last a Lifetime

It was time to pursue the dreams that were snoozing in a niche in the back of my mind. They periodically emerged as whiffs of desire. My high school graduation yearbook reads, "Ambition: To travel." That statement nagged at me. I had to find a way to infiltrate the more remote, less accessible corners of the globe.

There are two daily newspapers in the City of Vancouver: the *Vancouver Sun* and the *Province*. They are great for local news. The free community papers such as the *News Leader*, the *Record Now*, and *Vancouver Courier* are published a few times each week. To find information about what was going on in the world, I read *The Globe and Mail*—a national daily paper. This first essential publication offers financial data that either confirmed that I was losing my shirt on the stock market, or that my retirement safety net was not quite as precarious as it had been yesterday. Sometimes the financial facts assured me that I could pay for another trip!

The coloured graphic front page of what I consider the second essential publication, the *Georgia Straight*, presents explicit artistic, sometimes sarcastic but always realistic, with vivid pictures encouraging the exploration of every page. This weekly paper is valuable for people of all ages and lifestyles who live in the metropolitan area of Vancouver. It reports on entertainment, education, services, city happenings and political issues, and, it is free of charge. The rag enlightens about theatre, music, clubs, restaurants, conventions, trade shows, lectures and educational events. Articles and editorials present opinions and facts from both sides of the table. Writers have no fear of stepping on toes. They "say it like it is," giving everyone the freedom to accept or reject the opinions and theories presented. This treasure oozes valuable bits of information. It appears each Thursday at small convenience stores, funky restaurants, Skytrain stations, public markets and paper boxes on street corners.

In the spring of 1983, reading deep into the pages of the *Georgia Straight*, I noticed that Wander Lust, a travel store in bohemian Kitsilano, was hosting an evening to meet fellow single travellers. What a cool idea! Most of us would prefer to travel with a compatible, joy-seeking partner. As we entered the small crowded store on that rainy Tuesday evening, we all eagerly, or tentatively, attached a sticker to our torsos, with our next intended destination written on it. Folks with similar destinations gathered in the same corner to share laughter, ideas, plans, telephone numbers, and addresses (e-mail was not yet part of our daily lives). Bill and I met for the first time with Australia and New Zealand plastered on our shirts. Although Bill did not drink coffee, we made a commitment to meet for "coffee" during the next week. The seeds for a golden friendship that has spanned many countries, many miles, and many years, were planted. It did not take long for the seeds to germinate, sprout, grow and flourish.

I felt comfortable with Bill from day one. My children were justifiably concerned about their mom leaving for a seven-week trip to the other side of the world with someone she had only known for a few months. Patrick and Timothy have come to love respect and cherish forever the friendship that Bill and I share. We left for Fiji, Australia, and New Zealand in August 1993, returning to Vancouver on October 5.

A strong mutual respect for each other developed. We shared rooms, activities, meals, quiet and crazy times, wine and market food on a picnic, beer and hot dogs at a sports event, cribbage and Scrabble, reading time, salmon barbeques, ethnic food, music concerts and late nights at festivals. We have wandered through markets, spent quiet hours in a library, sat on benches to people-watch, laughed and dozed in the sunshine. A Coke and Diet Coke have always been our trusty lunchtime companions. We have stayed in rundown hostels, on decadent cruise ships, in hotels that challenged our innovation and flexibility to make the room manageable when accessibility was lacking. My fear of mice complemented Bill's fear of spiders. We have traversed countries, deserts, rain forests, canyons, waterways, and continents on foot and on trains, ferry boats, and luxurious cruise ships. We have even gotten around by tourist bus, chicken bus, rented car, and taxi.

In cities where the terrain is very steep, Bill pushes for a bit but then I advise him to disappear! I wheel a little, struggle a lot, and then graciously accept an offer of help from strangers for a block or two. That help would not be given if Bill were walking beside the chair. At the beginning of a long trip, we ration energy and resources so they will not run out before the scheduled plane trip home. I wheel some more, accept another offer of help for a push up the grade for a few minutes. Slowly but surely, we make it to the top. At the summit of the hill, Bill and I eventually reconnect. Some of these hills are long and incredibly vertical!

When we are looking for accommodation, heading to a bus station, a ferry, or an airport, we carry all our worldly goods. Our practice of "I carry, you push," gets the job done and benefits both of us.

Perusing the fascinating goods in a duty-free shop, I always select a bottle of Bacardi rum. I have never had a drink of this alcoholic beverage but I consider it my "computer insurance." I do not have the computer expertise that Bill is blessed with so when I run into technical difficulties or am a victim of just plain ignorance, I call for help. I get the advice, "Push that button. Try this icon on the control panel. Plug and unplug, start and restart." Sometimes it comes to, "Uninstall and reinstall a program." When there is still no success, Bill asks his standard question, "Do you have rum and coke?" When my answer is affirmative, the reply is always, "I will be there in twenty minutes." Thus the bottle of Bacardi.

At times, my enthusiasm and energy level can exhaust those around me. I can be fairly demanding. I want activity and excitement in every day, at every crossroad and at every new location. Bill's unfailing sense of direction and his skill in negotiating street signs in various languages, a map, or the pages of a *Lonely Planet* guidebook are invaluable gifts. I know that at first, Bill looked at me with questioning eyes but as time went on—and as air, nautical, and land miles passed under us—we learned to honour and respect each other's limits and to push each other beyond our normal boundaries.

My jaw drops in amazement as I reflect on the adventures that we have shared. They include Australia, New Zealand, Fiji, Greece and Turkey, Vegas and the Grand Canyon, coast-to-coast Canada, a drive over the Alaska Highway returning southward on the Marine highway down the west coast to Seattle; and cruises traversing the Pacific Ocean from Vancouver to China, from Buenos Aeries to Chile with a stop at Volunteer Point in the Falklands to see seven hundred pairs of emperor penguins. We have shared time in Provence, France, and enjoyed the sunshine on the Cook Islands and in Mexico.

Bill and I continue to add to that treasure chest of memories and build on our well-rooted friendship. We share dinners, sunshine, walks in the rain, and ice cream cones. We consult with each other on books, financial investments, world news, wine, family gossip, politics, and economy. We have some favourite hangouts in Vancouver for annual birthday dinners or no special occasion dinners. When we cook at his place or mine, our standard dinners are salad and salmon—smoked or barbecued.

We have been blessed with an abundance of pleasurable hours and days. A wealth of memories will bring a smile to our faces and provide warm fuzzies in coming years as we sit in our rockers and think back on our world travels.

This friendship is a gift in my heart for all time.

We are both still travelling.

Chapter 6

South Pacific

Fiji

The end of summer 1993 found me packing my rainbow bag once more.

This was my first totally unplanned, "by the seat of my pants" trip. I was embarking on a two-month excursion with Bill, someone I had only recently met. Number Two son, Tim, loaded my chair, my bag, and me into his Ford Festiva. His tiny car reminded me of a can of tomato soup because the cranberry color and small size most resembled a Campbell's label: *Mmm-Mmm-Good.* A boom box replaced the back seat with door-to-door speakers that blasted out throbbing music. Throughout Tim's high school days, I always knew when he was nearing home. I could hear the music reverberating from blocks away. On this trip to the airport, my wheelchair lay on end behind the driver's seat. My bag was propped precariously on my lap. No matter how squashed I was, having my 18-year-old son willing to get up early on a Saturday morning to drive his ancient mom to the airport was a special benefit to be appreciated.

My sons, of course, had some concern about their mother taking off to another continent, another hemisphere, with someone she barely knew. In later years, they developed fondness and respect for my travel companion. Patrick, on hearing that I am planning another trip with Bill, always says, "Mom, I'm so glad that you are going with Bill. I know you will be safe and that you will both have an awesome time."

As the boys grew older, they began to develop their own

wings. They go on excursions now that range from one day to four months. As they leave, my parting words are always, "Travel safe. Travel fun!"

On that sunny August morn I was subjected to an interrogation that included, "Do you have everything? Where are your tickets? Keep your money in a safe place. Always carry your passport securely. Be sure to write to let us know how you are doing." And finally the words, "Travel safe. Travel fun!"

The blue parking permit, bearing the international wheelchair symbol, is often worth more than its weight in gold. Tim parked close to the airport entrance in the 45-minute handicap parking zone to unload the gear, come to the check-in counter with me, place my bag onto the scale, give me more cautionary advice, and offer final encouragement before making an exit. Anza Travel, the "Down Under" travel agency, had offered a deal too good to refuse. For one reasonable price, the ticket covered three months and three countries. Bill and I boarded the plane for a twelve-hour flight. As the plane soared over the water, leaving Vancouver, I felt sure that this was the right thing to be doing.

The way the wind blows.

It was an uneventful flight—as most of them are. The hours drifted by with wine to drink, food to eat, a book to entertain, pillows and blankets to comfort, and music to soothe. When we arrived in Fiji, sandy beaches curved around the shoreline as far as the eye could see. Palm trees swayed in the gentle breeze and fluorescent blue water glistened in the heat. The radical contrast to Vancouver's wet cool winter was a welcome sensation.

Anxious to get into the beckoning outdoors, we straight-lined it to collect our luggage. Suitcases, backpacks, boxes of every size and description, tumbled down onto the carousel. Bill's blue bag appeared over the rise and around the corner. I can always see my bright bag coming around the bend. Like an old friend, it is comfortingly familiar.

We removed Bill's bag from the moving carousel and lingered for mine. We waited. We waited patiently. Then, we waited impatiently. The area emptied quickly as people collected their luggage, but no rainbow bag appeared. I could not believe that this could happen at the beginning of a two-month trip. I had packed with such attention to detail—wheelchair parts which I hoped not to need on the bottom; jeans and a sweatshirt, that I hoped not to wear in the middle; shorts, tanks, bathing suit and nightshirt on top for summer relationships with the beach. But, where was it?

We reported, explained, described, and recorded every detail for the sympathetic clerk whose kindness went a long way to make me feel better, but did nothing for my hopes of recovering my bag. With seventy-five dollars of emergency compensation from the airline, we proceeded to the dock. The Blue Lagoon was scheduled to set sail to wind its way around the Fiji islands for seven days. I could not go on a boat for a week with no clothes, no cosmetics, no nothing!

I used my stipend wisely. In the hotel shop near the launching point, I purchased the only size 8 bathing suit to be found.

Fortunately, it was a tolerable floral blue. Like the true Libra I am, you will seldom find me wearing brown, yellow, or green. The essentials, a bottle of shampoo and some sunscreen in a hotel-labeled laundry bag, became my toiletries for the trip. I wheeled up the gangplank. The boat slipped its moorings and moved away from the dock.

The "cruise ship"—slightly more than a wooden tugboat, but definitely not a luxurious floating hotel—had two decks with a narrow twisting staircase between the two levels. Access to the toilet was a direct leap from my chair in the hallway. The "dining room," outdoor dining on the upper deck, was more my style than formal with tablecloths and silver. The buffet table, long and narrow, was perpetually laden with exotic tropical fruits, and at mealtime, *fruits de la mer* accompanied the already extravagant display. Bill and I shared this delightful bounty with new-found friends from countries all over the world. The complement of passengers on the ship was more representative of New Zealand, Australia, Brazil, and the US. But Germany, Russia, and France also had a presence.

I arose in the morning anticipating that when I called Anza Travel they would inform me that my bag had been recovered and would be returned to me in short order. Not so! For the next four days, I was dressed in my "travel uniform" of navy blue shorts, navy blue Harrods of London t-shirt, socks, and runners. These items were laundered nightly and hung on the deck to dry. In the morning, I had clean clothes. So be it! A bathing suit during the day was covered with my only t-shirt for mealtimes and with the addition of shorts to dress for dinner. After four days, a small powerboat eased along the side of the "cruise ship." My multicolored bag was slung onto the deck, confirming my belief that what is lost will one day be found!

Later in the day, after docking near a small village, we sat on the sand at a beach hut enjoying Fijian music and song along with a revitalizing dinner and a bottle of wine. The gentle crashing of waves later on encouraged our bodies into restful sleep.

Our first day of leisure was just that. Engulfed in tropical beauty, we lounged, read, dozed, and planted seeds of friendship with the locals and fellow passengers. I feel that travel from one hemisphere to another, north to south, and thousands of kilometers from east to west, gives one permission to have a day at ease before embarking on activity and more exploration.

After a decadent dinner, as we sipped cappuccino, the wind started to blow insistently across the deck. Crewmembers began to tie down the awnings outside the open-air windows. People closed doors and sealed the window shutters in an effort to keep out the huge raindrops that pounded against the walls of the ship.

As the evening wore on, the wind picked up strength and by 10:00 p.m., the swollen sea tossed the vessel back and forth, up and down. The storm escalated to full-blown hurricane status. Discretion is the better part of velour. I declined a beer so that I would remain clear-headed. Retiring to bed seemed the most sensible thing to do. I descended the staircase on my bum, bumping down the flight of stairs one-step at a time. A member of the crew followed closely with my wheelchair. The deck was only a metre wide so the room was wall-to-wall bed, the door barely missing the coverlet as it swung open. I transferred from my chair in the hallway onto the bed, sliding across the bed and into the washroom. I prayed that there would be enough stability to complete my evening routine before another forty-foot wave tilted the boat. After brushing my teeth, washing my face and using the washroom, I eased back onto the bed and gratefully tucked in under the quilt.

The wild wind was unrelenting. There was no space for my chair in the cabin so to prevent it from going overboard, two crewmembers secured it to a pole on the deck. The partying overhead continued. Music, singing, the clattering of bamboo sticks, toe tapping, laughter, the beating of bongo drums and dancing echoed through the ceiling. I had been in bed for an hour when Bill staggered through the door—not only because he had put away a few frothy ones, but because his only option was to grip the walls and rock from side to side as the ship rose and fell through the waves. We were just beginning to have our evening chat when Bill was reminded of the beer that he so confidently had consumed. He aimed for the toilet bowl—being sick is not easy at the best of times. Cleanup done, Bill gratefully crawled across the floor and into bed. We both urged the minimal contents of our stomachs to remain at rest for the night. Sleep was long in coming and lasted only briefly as clanging bells, creaking boards, and the sound of stretching sails combined with the howling winds.

As the morn dawned, the water's surface had transformed to glasslike smoothness. That peaceful feeling crept into us, the calm after the storm. This is why people come to sail the Fiji islands—sparkling azure water, palm trees swaying in the gentle breeze, clean, clear air, gulls lounging on the updrafts and the sweet, warm South Pacific sun. A full day to lounge on the sun-drenched deck with a book was a most welcome antidote to yesterday's storm.

I was here to see Fiji. The opportunity to interact with the Fijian people in their villages was next on my agenda. Our floating bathtub approached a long, narrow, lushly forested land mass. Was there a dock? Of course not!

The ship's rowboat (a.k.a cruise ship tender) was used for my fellow passengers in groups of two to get from the ship to shore. It could also take me to shore, but the space in a rowboat does not accommodate a passenger, a wheelchair, and the rower. The most natural alternative sprang to mind.

"I will swim to shore," I announced. "My chair can go in the boat."

The locals looked at me with disbelief. This turned to wide-eyed concern when it became clear that I was serious. This was the only option. Moses, a huge Fijian whose thighs were larger than my waist, slipped one arm around my midriff, flipped my legs into the air and lowered me over the side rail and into the bathwater warm sea. Stretching and swimming through the buoyant salt water is much preferable to perching on a wooden seat in a rowboat. My hands felt the soft sand as I reached the shore where my trusty companion, my chair, was already waiting on the beach. Moses effortlessly picked me up and settled me into my chariot. Laboriously pulling the chair tipped on the two large back wheels backwards through the sand is the only way to move across a beach. At the end of the soft sand, firm grasslands were a welcome relief. Anticipating the arrival of visitors, island residents had set up an outdoor market displaying jewellery, dishes, and knickknacks made from shells and raw materials native to the land.

They welcomed us with enthusiasm and not only because we were going to buy their wares but also from a natural, childlike curiosity. They wanted to know about everything— Canada, Caucasian life, my inability to walk, my "circular legs" —whatever was new, different, and unfamiliar. I readily accepted an invitation into a thatched roofed hut to meet Grandma, who was babysitting the small children. I sampled homemade cornbread, listened to the young children playing lutes and instruments made of palm wood, watched the mothers cook over the open fire. Can you believe that they actually cook over an open fire in this heat? We live on cool salad and watermelon at home in warm and summer temperatures.

Near lunchtime, my fellow passengers returned by rowboat, two by two, to the ship's deck for lunch. I opted to stay on the island. My skin, well endowed with melanin, could safely absorb an additional dose of ultraviolet rays while my spirit and soul could meditate in the amazing, mind-freeing atmosphere. I drifted into bliss. Moses, larger than life, approached in the tiny rowboat.

"I have brought you things. I have brought you gifts!"

Moses' handiwork, a bowler hat made of woven palm fronds, was placed on my head. "You must wear a hat," he told me in a worried tone. I never do, of course, but in order to demonstrate my appreciation and to show how touched I was by his thoughtfulness, the hat stayed on my head. Moses delicately pulled a red-checkered bundle out from under the bench. It was my lunch! As he carefully unwrapped it for me, it became obvious that the size of this lunch was more appropriate to his appetite than mine. This banquet would feed three people, for three days.

On the following day, we visited another island where a naturalist explained the flora, fauna, and ecological development of the region. We surveyed the land animals, endured long-winged, long-legged, flying and crawling insects. "They are your friends, you know," he chided as they crawled and stung, and we investigated the creatures living along the water's edge. A dexterous local youth climbed a nearby palm. We quenched our thirst with coconut water and dined on the fresh meat from inside the shell.

We had a final day to snorkel and swim—a clear evening sky where moonlight illuminated the water's surface, and galaxies of stars sparkled in the night sky. We awoke early, sharing the dawn with dolphins that frolicked around our vessel. We laughed, we slept, we ate, we played crib, and recharged our personal batteries in preparation for the next leg of our journey.

As all good things must end, so did the Fiji cruise. On our last day, Bill and I found ourselves docking on the coast, bussing it to the airport in Suva, and boarding a flight to Australia. Endings are also beginnings.

This was the beginning of four weeks in Australia.

G'day Mate

In the early spring months before I departed to the South Pacific, I began to investigate accessibility in Australia. The Disability Information Network Australia, or DINA, a group of organizations that provide service to people with disabilities, directed me to a wealth of information about Australian recreation and sport for people with disabilities. They covered essential topics such as accommodations and transportation, including a rudimentary introduction to wheelchair travel in their country. I have learned to take such distributed information with a grain of salt. I expect that it may not be quite as advertised—sometimes it's a pleasant surprise, at other times more of a challenge than anticipated. I depend a great deal on flexibility, ingenuity, adaptability, stubbornness, and determination.

Australia is a very large country. If you fly to Australia with a round trip air ticket, you will only be able see a small part of the country—where the plane lands and where it takes off again—usually Sydney and Melbourne. Purchasing an air pass facilitated air travel across the huge expanse of Australia—four flights between the city centres of our choice.

Bill and I boarded the plane in Fiji and flew to Melbourne. At the luggage carousel, bags, bundles, boxes and packs tumbled down. I waited patiently for my trusty rainbow bag, but to no avail. It was again missing. The door to the luggage slide closed. I found myself at the "Luggage Lost" counter reciting my tale of woe once more.

Since experience is life's best teacher, I had tucked a swimsuit, toothbrush, sunscreen and shampoo into the bag on the back of my wheelchair. I looked down at my "travel uniform"—navy blue shorts, navy t-shirt, white runners. It would become my daily attire once more, until the airline finally found and returned my trusty rainbow.

Melbourne, the capital of the State of Victoria, is Australia's business and financial centre. The city is located in the southeast corner of Australia on the shores of the Yarra River. Walkways along the river's edge invite exploration. Pathways called us into residential areas and led us through many botanical gardens and parks with unique trees, flowers, and duck breeding ponds. Melbourne's city farmers market provided most meals. We walked along both sides of the river, explored the architectural, cultural, and historic buildings of the city. Melbourne has the world's first and only travelling tramcar restaurant: a converted 1927 train that travels on the original tracks through the scenic streets while diners sip champagne and enjoy Australian cuisine. One-way glass windows have been installed so that diners can enjoy the passing scenery without curious stares from bystanders.

The Penguin Parade in Phillip Island National Park, a reserve designed to promote and protect "Little Penguins" (fairy penguins) is located one hundred and forty kilometres southeast of Melbourne. The park and its unique residents is not a sight to be missed. The sunset waddle of ten-inch fairy penguins lures millions of visitors. Against the backdrop of the sun's fading rays, thousands of tiny, rare, flightless birds march across the beach, seeking the safety of their breeding burrows.

We boarded the bus in the early afternoon with the intention of heading for the ocean shores to intercept the thousands of mini-penguins who would emerge from the waves in the early evening to nestle for the night in their sand caves on the shore. En route to Phillip Island, exclamations of amazement stopped the bus.

Our progress had been delayed by the appearance of three koalas high in a eucalyptus tree. Of course we all had to disembark from the bus to view them—even me, with my awkward one-step process. A tiny grey furry babe clung to his mother's back. A large koala feasted on leaves, long grass protruding from his lips. This was most definitely an unexpected bonus. Further, along the roadway we stopped at a koala reserve to hold, hug, touch, and snuggle these amazing marsupials. Not providing my children with an opportunity to call their mom "chicken," I even held a small alligator. Its mouth was not taped. With adequate instruction I emerged unscathed and have the pictures to prove my bravery.

Linda and alligator baby

Barbeques had been set up along the beach. We enjoyed soldier's bread, tropical fruit, and various meats. After seeing kangaroos with tiny Joey's peeking out from their pouches hopping nonchalantly along the road, my decision was made. No! I will not eat any kangaroo meat! I will stick with vegetables, thank you! As dusk descended, we chose our positions with an expansive view of the water's edge to wait for the flock of tiny penguins that would come running out of the ocean. And run they did! In groups, families, singly, in pairs, loved ones and enemies; they ran out of the water in search of security and overnight protection. It was just as the brochure had described.

Early the next morning, our first flight within Australia took us from Melbourne to Alice Springs.

Uluru and Tasmania

In Grade 5 geography class we learned about a large island continent deep in the South Pacific. Ayers Rock dominates the desert interior. Dreamtime represents the essence of life for the Aboriginal people of Australia. In dreams, ancestors, gods and living mortals come together to learn about their heritage and customs. Dreamtime is the core of the sacred sites in Australia, including Uluru.

Today, Kata Tjuta National Park possesses two unique structures, the result of an immense bed of sedimentary rock created by erosion and windblown sand. Kata Tjuta, Mount Olga (545m) and Uluru (348m), known to us in childhood as Ayers Rock, extends several kilometres into the earth. The sacred ground is leased to the commonwealth of Australia from the aboriginal owners. To a large degree, the mythology of the site is not disclosed to outsiders. Every moment spent on this hallowed land left me feeling deeply honoured and humble. Cultural and religious significance accompanied each moment during our visit to the park. Fascinating plants and animals and the spectacular geological events are inspirational. This unique part of Australia portrays two cultures—aboriginal groups and modern day thinkers working side by side to preserve the land.

Photographs, videos and displays at the park's Visitors Centre offered an information about Ayers Rock, the Olgas, local history, geology, plant and animal life, and aboriginal culture. It all inspired a resolute desire in me to see the sun rise and set over the sacred rock. At 4:30 a.m., our small rental car intruded on the dawn. As the sun eased over the edge of the horizon, the spectacular grey formation transformed into luminous radiance and red brilliance. As the glowing sunrise flooded the landscape, visible heat waves rose from the sand.

A 9 km wheel around Ayers Rock.

A limited number of visitors are permitted to climb the rock each day. Bill joined the energetic few and soon became a tiny moving speck on the face of the sandstone mass. I embarked upon a nine-kilometre wheel around the circumference along a firm pathway composed of small pebbles and solid sand.

Resolve motivated me to graciously decline offers of a push from other tourists. If I was going to achieve my goal of spiritual connection with this awe-inspiring monument, I must do it myself. I wheeled several metres, stopped for a rest then wheeled some more. I repeated this pattern as dawn merged into morning, morning into mid-day, mid-day into afternoon. The warm rays on my arms and legs soothed my soul and moved me forward. Desert sun is a double-edged sword—a glowing deep tan comes with physical fatigue, dehydration accompanies a super dose of vitamin D, but the emotional benefit is more significant to us Canadians with our long dark winters. I was exhilarated! I was spent!

Following Bill's climb and my hike, we reconnected and strolled back to the Visitor's Centre. We joined with the other tourists to listen to "Indigeny," an aboriginal group playing the didgeridoo, and bongo drum, as they chanted and sang. It gave us relaxation, exposure to Australian sound, and a few moments to veg.

On our route back to town we stopped at the Outback Barbeque in the town square, situated behind the tavern. This could definitely meet our immediate needs for relaxation, homemade Australian brew, with a selection of Australian meat and fish.

Bill, was the brave one. "Of course I'm going to try barbequed kangaroo!" he said enthusiastically.

"Can you do this after seeing those small joeys in their mother's pouches leaping across the sand?" I asked, incredulous. He could, but I could not. I settled for a salad and a sampling of unique Australian fruits and vegetables.

We needed a nap to replenish our energy for our evening and late night activities.

On the return to Uluru in the late afternoon, the beauty of the desert flowers was beyond imagination. We explored drawings on thousand-year-old cave walls, and visited the water holes in the dark, deep depths—so quiet and spiritual. We soaked up the coveted sunset. It equalled the extravagant magnificence of the early morning spectacle. As the sun began its final decline to the horizon, red light shimmered over the rock's surface and seeped across the sand. A thin veil of mist rose from the land's surface as the sun slipped into its nightly boudoir.

The night sky show, an Uluru experience, proved our grade school instructors' teachings to be correct. Central Australia has some of the world's clearest skies and offers an amazing display of stars—the highlight being the Southern Cross, and Alpha and Beta Cantus, the double stars. There is no Big Dipper or Little Dipper but the Southern Cross led our eyes to other identifiable stars and constellations. Seen with the naked eye it was amazing. Through the telescope, it was even more amazing. Saturn's rings looked more perfect than the images in picture books. We explored the night universe through the telescopes and with our human vision. The guides and local astronomers shared aboriginal legends of the constellations and explained the patterns of movement in the sky. Transfixed by the celestial display as we were, time flew. At 3:00 a.m., we stretched out on the hillside and closed our eyes.

After a very short sleep, we headed to Alice Springs. Roaming the streets earned us an invitation to an outback ranch. A cowboy flipped me into the back of his pickup truck and I found myself in the real outback amidst three thousand head of livestock. Six border collies herded sheep. Clotheslines were draped pole to pole with sheets and cowboy jeans blowing in the breeze. Chickens scratched in the yard. Grandma loudly rang the triangle calling all to the abundant feast that they call lunch. We had it all: biscuits with gravy, buttermilk, hard-boiled eggs, slabs of beef, fresh garden vegetables, with bread pudding and sugar pie for dessert. Large aluminum coffee pots swung over the outdoor fire pits, pouring out steaming black brew.

Loaded into the back of the truck, Bill and I were driven to our lodge in Alice Springs. The road was barely a road. After jostling and bouncing for over an hour, the stillness of our beds was more welcome than usual. We arose early to throw all of our belongings into our bags, in preparation for the morning flight to Tasmania, a small island, southeast off the mainland.

Hobart, the capital of the State of Tasmania, was crowded with government buildings, historical sites, and architectural surprises. We searched out a market to buy picnic ingredients and a small bottle of red wine. Leaving the wheelchair behind, carrying the lunch tucked into the backpack, we crawled across the rocks to settle in a secret cove under the Tasmanian Arch. At this point, water sloshes through a small round opening carved into the rock by ocean waves. We ate, sipped, dozed, and read. A dreamy respite from city scenes!

In the Tasmanian Arch State Reserve Park, amazing natural creations surrounded us. The Eaglehawk Neck, a narrow strip of land, formed the guard station when convicts were shipped from Britain to Australia to serve prison sentences. Sentries constantly patrolled the isthmus. Large dogs chained along the edges of the sheer cliff deterred convicts contemplating escape. For those who did manage to flee, all succumbed to cold water on the lengthy swim that they had hoped would lead to freedom.

Like a whale swimming by at high tide, the Tasman Blowhole spurts water ten to twelve metres into the air. A world-renowned artist, the ocean, sculpted the Devils Kitchen, a distinctive display of unusual rock formations.

Mount Field National Park boasts an accessible walk around the famous Russell Falls. I had to follow the pathway. Mist was welcome on a warm day. Three tiers of water cascaded down the mountainside. The falls, a recognized tourist attraction for over 100 years, are surrounded by a diverse array of flourishing vegetation ranging from tall swamp gum trees and massive tree ferns at the base, to rainforests on the hillside.

"I want to climb to the top," Bill declared. "If you wheel to the middle of the bridge, I will take some photographs that will capture the depth and deepness."

Game for anything, I confidently wheeled to the centre of the narrow wood plank bridge that stretched over a 100-metre deep crevice. I scanned the forested hillside following Bill's progress. My gaze was then drawn to the tumultuous raging river below. Was I nervous? No! I was excited! Bill, when he saw the risk from above, returned and met me on the bridge to wheel me to safety. I was oblivious to how close I had come to going over the edge. On our return to Vancouver, the film showed the wheels of my chair resting only six inches from the edge of the sloping suspension bridge without rails. Gutsy, yes! Foolish, even more so! If I were a cat, at least one of my nine lives would have been forfeit on this occasion.

Bridge over river in the South Pacific.

A 40-minute drive along the Lake Dobson Road led through towering forests up to the high country of snow patches, mountain top meadows, and glacial lakes. In fields close to the sky, a blaze of colourful flowers announced spring and trumpeted approaching summer. Back in Hobart we enjoyed a snacky dinner of finger foods—a taste of this and a taste of that—and a glass of wine at a quaint café by the rocky shore before retiring to town for the night.

After three days in Tasmania, on we flew to Cairns on the adventurous east coast.

From the Sky to My Thigh

Cairns (pronounced "Cans"), on the northeast coast of Australia, offers a marathon of activity. The airport is nestled between mountains and coastal mangroves. Cairns is the portal to both the World Heritage Great Barrier Reef and tropical rainforests.

The only significant street, with the shoreline on the east side, had a wide range of sleeping accommodations ranging from large one-room dorms with sleeping space on the floor for forty people snuggled together, to cots, to more luxurious Best Western hotels. The tourist bureau of Queensland divides accessible accommodation into three categories. There is "fully wheelchair accessible" establishments having one or more units with full wheelchair access and purpose-built facilities. Then comes "wheelchair accessible with assistance"—which have one or more units that are accessible to wheelchair users but it is recommended that an AB (able bodied) person come along for the ride. Finally, "wheelchair users without assistance" means just that. I can get my chair through the door and cannot expect anything more.

Some people say I am courageous, others describe it as crazy, but we opted for wheelchair accessible without assistance and this is what we found: a small room in a hostel. It was compact; so small in fact, that I transferred from my chair in the hallway to the bottom bunk, leaving the wheelchair in the hallway. "But someone might steal it," Bill protested. I didn't think so. Most people would not choose to mobilize as I do.

Bill climbed up the end of the iron bed frame onto the narrow bunk, realizing very quickly that the ceiling fan would decapitate him if he raised his head more than a few inches above the mattress. The ceiling fan did not really keep the room cool. Economy always makes the trials tolerable. We carry our own sleep sheets so renting a sheet for $1 was not necessary. The cost of the room was four dollars for two people. What do you need the room for anyway? Only to sleep for a few hours each night. Washrooms and showers were down the hall. There was more to do than could ever fit into our available time anyway.

Next morning we began our exploration by train. The golden era of luxury train travel has returned. The Kuranda Scenic Railway offers magnificent postcard views from every window. We ogled the views aboard historical carriages as the track weaved through lush rain forests, past deep gorges, rugged mountains, and spectacular waterfalls. The railway was built more than a hundred years ago in response to the demands of desperate miners along the Wild River where boggy roads prevented the delivery of food and supplies. The settlers along the coast joined in with loud and angry voices, demanding that a railway be built. Men swinging picks and shovels carved a pathway through the rocky terrain. Their sweat and labour created thirty-four kilometres of track that winds its way through fifteen handmade tunnels to the Botanical Gardens a.k.a. Kuranda Station. This engineering feat of monumental magnitude tested the ambition and fortitude of the hundreds who were engaged in its construction. Today, it stands as a memorial to many who lost their lives building it. Many bird, reptile, and animal displays, toad racing, slithery snake and crocodile antics, and frolicking cockatoo birds entertained us for hours at these gardens.

The Great Barrier Reef, a world heritage site was visible from our room. The world's largest coral reef houses an incredibly complex chain of life where thousands of species of plants and animals depend upon each other for food and survival. We boarded the Quicksilver, a motorized sailing vessel that carried us to the edge of Australia's continental shelf where an underwater wonderland, a dazzling kaleidoscope of colour and brilliance awaited us. Fitted with a snorkel and mask, I slid into the welcoming, warm water. Enthralled with the tiny brilliant tropical fish, small octopi, colourful coral, and intricately shaped shells resting on the ledge, I experienced firsthand the underwater beauty and magic of the reef by snorkeling for hours in the clear blue, tepid water. Slow movement through water often soothes MS spasm and stiffness. I was enjoying this benefit. After two hours, a crewmember tapped me on the shoulder to let me know that lunch was ready. I shook my head. Lunch can be had at anytime. The enchanting waters commanded my complete attention. I was collecting a lifetime of memories from this living natural wonder.

The salt water and life belt granted me enough buoyancy to enjoy three continuous, effortless hours in the water but eventually I had to leave my heavenly surroundings. The crew signaled "All Aboard." When strong hands lifted me onto the deck, I was greeted with a small miracle. I felt strong and steady. My leg muscles persuaded me to stand behind my chair. I slowly and carefully walked over to the shower where I rinsed off the brine and slipped a long shirt over my swimsuit. I finally sat down on a deck chair to eat and rest. This respite from immobility was short-lived but it will always remain as one of the highlights of my trip to the Great Barrier Reef.

On the shelf in my mind, this unexpected blessing is prominent and is labelled Australia.

The following day, it was time to sit back, relax and absorb this kind of venture. We boarded a small oceangoing vessel that could slip into small nooks and crannies. For most of the day, the brightest sunshine reflected off the water as we explored the eastern central coastline of Australia. Although we slapped on sun cream at regular intervals, lots of moisturizing lotion and soothing aloe vera would certainly be required tonight.

The mountains east of Cairns entice all visitors, but the excursions offered did not appear compatible with wheelchair users. Does that matter to me?

The suggestions included jeep trips over 4-wheel drive roads to the meadows, hikes on foot through the mountain trails, or air ballooning over the mountains, descending to the meadow below. I can hike in the mountains at home using a TrailRider, I can ascend with one of my sons in a 4-wheel drive vehicle. But could I air balloon? No! The decision was effortless.

The long-haired, lightly-bearded young man threw his arms up in an attempt to get his point across. "I have never taken anyone up in a balloon who can't walk, who uses a wheelchair!"

I wondered why not? Was there a valid reason or was it because nobody had ever asked?

"This must be your lucky day. Just think you will be the first person in the world to have had this special honour and you can spread the word. "I took a Canadian who walks on wheels, up in my air balloon."

It is often a challenge to convince others that yes, I can, and yes, I will. Joseph was at the door early in the morning to load us into the back of his pick-up truck. Some things are worth losing sleep over. Getting up at 4:00 a.m. to take a balloon ride over tablelands west of Cairns is definitely one of them. The ride into the Blue Mountains began over desert sand and ended at the foot of the mountains. In the early morning, the rock was delicately tinged with faint blue light.

The truck parked in a sandy pit. Our balloon waited. The crew lifted me into the basket. I was squeezed between a solid wooden box and the inner wall. I perched my bum on the edge of a stool and gripped the rim of the basket in anticipation of this world-class trip. The tight space squeezed my body, permitting little movement. No need for balance!

The heat and steam from the fired burner lifted the vibrantly coloured balloon from the sand high into the air. The noise, heat, and wind from the firebox could not be ignored but it had to be buried. I left apprehension behind. The balloon climbed into the air. There are times in my life when my disability is completely out of sight/out of mind. This was one of those times. My wheelchair rested all by itself in the mist below. We looked down on kangaroos in their early morning romp; plantations of coffee beans, vanilla beans, tobacco, mango, orchards, and termite mounds.

The two-hour ride in the sky that removed us from the modern world must have been similar to the experience that Dorothy had when she left Kansas to arrive in the Land of Oz. When it was time to land, the pilot put the fire out. Cool morning air surrounded us. The basket made a gentle landing with the deflated balloon coming to rest in the field beside us.

The venture was followed by a champagne brunch in the grassland—chicken, salad, cheese, fresh homemade bread, and local fruit. My first and only air balloon ride has a special place in my memory.

I am reminded daily of this phenomenal experience by the vivid, multicolored tattoo of a sun peaking around a brilliant air balloon on my right thigh.

Sydney

Every region in Australia exhibits a unique beauty. Some would say that we "saved the best for last." This point is certainly arguable. The journey from Cairns to Sydney marked our last intercity flight on this large, South Pacific island continent.

Sidney and Vancouver are often compared. Their similarities are unquestionable, however each has its own individuality. Both cities rest on an ocean shore but on different oceans. Both display a stunning harbour. Both facilitate and encourage outdoor life—patio eateries by the water, parks filled with trees and spectacular floral gardens, sailboats, yachts, deep sea fishing. Vancouver is nestled at the base of mountains. Both cities offer busy ports that support business activity. Sydney's harbour is more inviting to human traffic and has a design that enhances rather than mars the beauty.

Where to stay? The first attribute on the list should be "location, location, location," followed by amenities and price. As I look back over my years of travel and review in my mind where I have laid my head, the YWCA in Sydney, Australia quickly rises to the top of the list. From the harbour, at the top of a steep hill, a welcoming sign met our tired eyes. Inside, a cheerful front desk clerk greeted us. Complimentary coffee and fruit juice quenched our thirst. A spacious elevator delivered Bill and me to the second floor. There we opened the door to a bright, cheerful, airy room with two beds, a sitting area with big fluffy cushions on soft overstuffed chairs, luggage racks, drawers, and closets that insisted on more tidiness and organization then was our habit. The open window afforded a stunning view of the city, the harbour, and the Opera House. Down the hall in the ladies washroom, I found accessibility personified—a wheel-in shower, lowered counters open at the front, taps, soap dishes, and paper towels within easy reach, grab bars on the wall, non-slip floor surfaces. Hooks near the shower were out of range of the shower nozzle. When you only have three t-shirts you don't need to get the only clean one wet! On the main floor, we found an inviting cafeteria, racks of brochures offering a visit to this and that, and a book exchange—a gem for all travellers—where we could take one and leave one.

It is often our habit to roam the streets soon after arrival to get our bearings in a new location. Or, I should say, so that Bill can get familiar with the geography of the city. I have never been skilled at either map reading or navigating. When wandering we stumble upon new and different sites, surprises, and entertaining spots that we would never have found by reading brochures. We happen upon out-of-the-way parks, bands at practice, sporting events, markets, restaurants, historical sites and residential areas. On this particular night, we found ourselves in front of the Sydney Hard Rock Café where tasty food was generously served along with awesome music, memorabilia, and memory t-shirts.

Time to tour on the water's surface! In 2003, Jorn Utzon the Danish architect who designed the Sydney Opera House, received the Pritzker Prize, one of the world's premier architectural prizes, often referred to as the Nobel Prize of architecture. This prize is awarded to a living architect who contributes to humanity and the environment by using talent, vision, and commitment in his/her buildings. The citation described the opera house as "...one of the great iconic buildings of the 20th century, an image of great beauty that has become known throughout the world—a symbol for not only a city, but a whole country and continent." UNESCO, the United Nations Educational, Scientific, and Cultural Organization, granted the Opera House the designation of a World Heritage Site in 2007. Situated on a peninsula, surrounded on three sides by water, it serves more than opera. Theatre and ballet, symphony and mime, choir and contemporary jazz are performed here too. What better way to sense the music than to get closer to the activity. On a tour of the interior, the costumes and props in the basement enchanted us. We admired armor and masks, delicate tutus and flowing crinoline gowns, formal tuxedos and can-can feathers, wigs and hats, ballet slippers and boots. We heard the symphony at practice, saw artistic displays, and watched ballerinas during their daily stretch at the bar. I could, just as Jennifer Beals advises in *Flashdance*, close my eyes and see the music.

An early rise sent us exploring the circular Quay where we purchased a 3-day Sydney Discovery Tour Pass. In three days, we would see more of Sydney than most Aussies see in a lifetime. The ferries offered three daily cruises to tour the splendour, history and fun of this paradise of waterways. The excursions included commentary by a well-informed guide who conveyed copious information in an entertaining style. The morning river cruise carried us through the magnificent harbour. Meandering past Sharks Island—with no sharks in sight—our small seagoing vessel ventured westward, up the Parramatta River beyond the high arch of the Gladsville Bridge. On the riverbank, a graceful otter slid off the bank and into the water. Shorebirds hopped along singly and in groups. Bulrushes and water shore plants camouflaged the residents of the river community. The shrill of songbirds and the quiet lapping of water on the shoreline interrupted the morning stillness. We slid quietly by geese and their goslings, and mother ducks with their ducklings. The drift homeward, sliding by the Opera House, the Royal Botanical

Gardens, and multiple islands, once again integrated the city into our lives.

The harbour cruise presented a close-up view of the Opera House, the Royal Botanical Gardens, and harbour islands including Fort Denison, the 18th century convict residence. We explored the tranquil Lane Cove River, beautiful bays, viewed picturesque suburbs with elegant older homes, and waterfront play lands. We caught a close-up view of Darling Harbour where throngs of visitors and residents alike people-watch, listen to street music and stare at mimes, sip on cappuccino, read, and enjoy, enjoy, enjoy!

As the afternoon approached my body recommended rest, and I decided, as I often do, to override it. I will find a resting place later. We left the ferry and carried on.

As the sun rose high in the sky, we hurried to the world-renowned Manly Beach to munch on fish and chips, absorb warm rays, engage with children at play, and watch surfers challenging themselves against relentless waves. An hour of reading, a doze in the sun, and some food and drink recharged our batteries, making us ready for the evening Harbour Lights cruise.

Lights sparkled on the water's surface as the magical after-dark cruise made a circuit of the main harbour, sailing eastward as far as Double Bay and then turning west to Goat Island. A rainbow of colour and lapping water against the vessel's edge induced relaxation as we absorbed the sights along the harbour's edge; the Opera House, Harbour Bridge and a kaleidoscope of reflections on the rippling surface. The darkness displayed the city at new angles, and made us appreciate once more the architecture, horticulture, and geography. The respite gifted by this evening water excursion was somewhat tainted by the steep uphill walk back to the Y where our comfortable beds waited.

The Sydney Tramway was a quick, easy, and economical

way to travel between Sydney's oldest and newest attractions. The Tramway, juxtaposed between old and new, displayed the charm and colour of a bygone era.

Had we seen it all? Not quite! The Darling Harbour includes street entertainment—musicians, singers, mime, jugglers, stilt walkers, clowns—as well as shops, playgrounds, seating areas, stone chessboards under cover, benches, bike trails, trees and flowers. Multi-cultural and multi-generational visitors added to the ambiance.

I am sure you know those times when impulsiveness strikes and the feeling of *I see it, I want one.*

Ken Done is an Australian artist best known for his simple, brightly coloured images of Australian animals and landmarks. The Done (pronounced "doan") Art and Design brand includes swimwear, clothing, accessories, kids wear, and house wares. The word on the street is, "You can hang a Done on your wall or a Done on yourself." Smiling grey Koalas, rendered in broad brushstrokes of pink, blue, green, and khaki, suffused the shirt with colour and I wanted it. I searched every retail shop and found nothing in my size. A very helpful young woman directed me to the Done factory, miles away of course, but the laborious, steep uphill trek proved to be rewarding. I found a short-sleeve t-shirt, my size, in my chosen design. Now I had seen and truly "Done" it.

More Sheep than People

New Zealand is more like Canada than any country I have ever visited. People are down to earth and respectful of each other, their environment, and all living things. New Zealand geography is similar to that of western Canada—ocean shorelines, snow-capped mountains, evergreen forests, alpine meadows, and ice fields.

Our evening arrival in Christchurch on the South Island was

stunning. Lights on the roof and walls of the cathedral, the historical, and government buildings filled the sky with colour. We wandered the streets, which were devoid of cars and people, absorbing the beauty and mesmerized by the mellow warmth.

Cravings during pregnancy are considered normal. I was definitely not pregnant but I longed for the taste of banana. That yearning was only satisfied after three long hours of checking every small convenience store still open on the streets of Christchurch. Yum!

In the morning we boarded the TranzAlpine scenic train, journeying to Greymouth on the west coast. An open-air viewing carriage brought us close to the startling scenery. The four-and-a-half hour journey started from Christchurch—New Zealand's largest city on the South Island—and traversed westward for 224 kilometres through sixteen tunnels and five viaducts, the highest viaduct being the "Staircase" standing at seventy-three metres above the valley floor. While traversing across the South Island, we encountered numerous examples of New Zealand's varying geography. From the large viewing windows, we observed fields of the Canterbury Plains and fertile farmland, spectacular gorges, and river valleys of the Waimakariri River, snow-capped mountains, rocky peaks, and heavily treed hillsides. The train climbed into the Southern Alps then descended through lush beech rain forest to the west coast town of Greymouth—the entry point to view the always-popular glaciers.

Renting a car after our train trip allowed us to explore more than just the touristy areas. We wanted to see life off the beaten path.

Arrival in September brought us into the fantastic spring lambing season. Green fields were obscured by woolly, white masses. I spent countless hours fascinated by the antics of the new lambs as they frolicked and played. In the middle of a stroll across the meadow, they would take a three-foot leap into the air for no apparent reason. The sporadic jumps of the tiny creatures were reminiscent of popcorn kernels exploding over the heat of a campfire.

The Agrodome in Rotorua on the North Island delights and enlightens thousands of visitors each year. We saw nineteen breeds of champion ram stock, watched sheep being sheared and sheep dogs at work. I tried to milk a cow with questionable success and then wheeled through the farmyard nursery, enthralled as always by the young animals. We rode in a 4-wheel drive vehicle through the rolling pastures to see the many different varieties of livestock.

Throughout New Zealand, we sought accommodations that were unplanned and varied. We stayed in hostels—the first being a village of cabins with few occupants. Our own little house had enough beds to sleep eight, a pot-bellied cooking stove that warmed the cool interior and sufficed for dinner preparation. We had it all to ourselves. Sitting in rocking chairs on the porch in the evening, sipping wine, Bill and I heard the whistle of a distant train, breeze rustling the leaves, the chirping of mother birds tucking their chicks in for the night, choirs of frogs and crickets—pure peace and contentment.

Pub stays—sleeping rooms above local watering holes—offered economical opportunities to become part of the local revelry, hear folklore, listen to lively music, sing-along with vocalists, and try out ethnic food like bangers and mash. Those were not for me. After a few brews, we climbed up the narrow, steep staircase to our room. The climb was definitely one step at a time, and me on my bum. I remembered my Dad's words, "If it's not hard work, it's not worth doing." Climbing the stairs was hard work but the evening made the effort all worthwhile.

We stayed in a small log lodge deep in the forest, a fire lookout on the mountain, and on return to Auckland, a hotel. Fancy that!

We stayed in a campsite—no tent this time. A small canvas sided trailer furnished with two cots and plywood between serving as the bedside table could be rented for the night. We had our own sleep sheets. Quilts were provided. Shower and washroom facilities were more than adequate. I gathered the articles that I would need for my morning boudoir: shampoo, conditioner, soap, questionably clean clothes, hairbrush, and toothbrush. I wheeled to the common women's shower facilities only to realize that after opening the door that there was a 14-inch step down into the shower room. I couldn't navigate it in a manual chair so I quickly recruited a young man walking by.

"Could you please give me a hand to get into the shower room? It's pretty easy. Just tip my wheelchair back on the two big wheels and hold on tightly while I wheel on down the step."

"But there are women in there having their shower."

"Yes I know, but just think ..." I smiled up at him. "You have been dreaming of such an opportunity for years and I am giving you the chance to see fourteen naked women standing before you in the shower."

There were a few shrieks when the door opened. The cries were quickly followed by laughter as the young man assisted me down the step, and agreed to return in forty-five minutes to give me assistance to get back up.

To my delight, a family welcomed us for a farm stay. Members of the family proudly explained their animal and agricultural lifestyle, each expanding on his or her role in the system. A lush vegetable garden overflowed with produce—some species known to us, others native and unique. We plucked kiwi fruit from a vine, pulled carrots and cut Swiss chard to be steamed for dinner, picked raspberries from a prickly bush, and dug onions and potatoes from the ground as our ancestors have done since the beginning of time. We contributed to dinner preparation "from the ground up."

I passed the afternoon with the children, feeding baby black lambs from a bottle. The mothers didn't have enough milk. When we entered the farmhouse at dinnertime, delectable scents made us drool and pushed our appetites to the max. The meal consisted of fresh garden vegetables, homemade bread, and *lamb*! I only ate bread and vegetables. The memory of those bright eyes and snuggling woolly bodies that I had held in my arms reduced my appetite considerably. The children, raised on the farm, were better adapted than I to the transition of cute and snugly to meat on one's plate.

Snuggle Time.

Narrow roadways on the south island, less modern than one would expect, took me back to childhood days in eastern Quebec. At the entrance to the bridge, two coloured traffic lights, red and green, advised drivers when it was safe to cross. The yellow diamond-shaped signs in British Columbia warn us of deer crossing. In New Zealand, these signs show a three-member family group of penguins. We were on the lookout for penguins crossing the road and were rewarded by two small black and white fellows who waddled from one ditch to the other. We stopped to watch with fascination and photograph this unique event.

On the west coast of New Zealand's South Island the 12-kilometre long Franz Joseph glacier and the rapidly receding Fox glacier lie in the Westland National Park. Now part of a World Heritage Site, these glaciers descend through lush green temperate rain forest, from the Southern Alps to less than three hundred metres above sea level. The air close to the glacier was very cool. Out came multiple layers of clothing to ward against the evening chill. We found a very small sleeping lodge at the glacier station. In our clothes and under heavy quilts we slept comfortably, arising early to warm sunshine. Fifty people would be an exaggerated guesstimate of the station's population.

The Top House Museum, built in 1880, was home to hundreds of cattle and goats; Brent, the donkey, Thory, a four-day-old kid, bottle-fed as his Mom had died during delivery, and Salt, the guinea pig. A fireplace was used to cook a wonderful meal of roast lamb, vegetables, and homemade bread toasted over the coals. Bed warmers filled with hot water made the sheets toasty. Local folklore says that the fire in the fireplace has not been extinguished for five and a half years. The Top House, in the Nelson Lake District, was a stopover for sheepherders and cattle drivers moving livestock from one side of the island to the other and in need of a place for men and beasts to rest over night. We stayed there likewise in a small guest cabin. The silence on the mountain lulled us into restful sleep.

On the South Island is the world-renowned Milford Sound, a fjord that empties into the Tasman Sea. Milford Sound is one of the wettest locations in the world, however every disadvantage is balanced by a bonus. The mammoth rainfall generates trickling, flowing, and thunderous waterfalls that cascade down the rocky cliffs. The best way to see the landscape and benefit from the unique ecosystem is to board a tour boat, small enough to sneak into the narrow crevices along the shoreline.

On 320 of the 365 days in a year, fog and drizzle are expected. On the day that we explored Milford Sound, the sun rose above the water into a bright blue clear sky. Even the smallest cumulous cloud had taken a day off. The rain jackets and sweatshirts remained at the bottom of the pack while we absorbed the natural warmth of a rare sunny day.

The naturalist in the park nature house explained the ecosystem, the climate, the natural history, in preparation for what we would encounter. "You may see penguins, sea lions, dolphins, birds including cheeky parrots, white herons, kiwi, shorebirds, and other native species of New Zealand birdlife."

During the next eight hours, we delighted in seeing penguins—large and small—waddling along the shoreline in their natural tuxedo wardrobes, swimming through the water, playing and frolicking in the streams. Sea lions basked on the rocky cliffs. Dolphins swam across the surface and leaped into the air, both in the distance and almost within petting reach of the boat. Red, green, and blue parrots argued and cackled; tiny birds skittered along the shoreline. Tree branches revealed families of unique birdlife. White herons tried to catch fish, a squiggling reward clenched in their beaks when they succeeded. We had experienced all that was possible in this jewel of the South Island. At times like this, I ponder how I was chosen to witness such wonders. Back to the shore, nestled in the tiny car, we scanned the map and headed north.

We travelled along the curvy highway, a hilly, narrow beautiful seaside coastal road that delivered us to the ferry dock for a three-hour sail to the North Island. More like a cruise ship than a ferry, it offered a movie theatre, arcade, dining room, children's playground, video games, small lounges, massage beds, and outdoor sitting areas, some glassed in to protect from the wind. This lean towards modern was a distinct contrast to the natural ecology that we had explored on the South Island. It took only a few hours to drive from the ferry dock northward along the coast. The North Island, the smaller of the two, is home to Auckland, the largest metropolis in New Zealand, and the home of one third of the country's population. The 2009 Mercer Quality-Of-Living Survey ranked Auckland fourth in the world.

A seawall protects the entire shoreline of the city. Bill and I spent one full day walking in the sunshine, stopping for ice cream, taking an hour to read, watching anglers, freighters in the harbour, pleasure boats leaning their sails into the breeze.

I often reflect on the pleasurable moments I experienced in New Zealand—geography, landscape, harbour, and waves. It was my birthday. Bill presented me with a gift of strawberry perfume from the Body Shop. It would become one of my favourites over the coming years.

Before securing the cab that took us to dinner, we packed our belongings haphazardly into the bags knowing that an early rise was required. The 12-hour nonstop flight from Auckland to Los Angeles would depart at 8:00 a.m. taking us toward home again.

Chapter 7

Gain a Little Lose a Little

Thanks to cheaper airfares, I often spend my birthday travelling. How many people in the world have crossed the International Date Line on their birthday? Perhaps there are many. I am suggesting that there are few that have had the unique experience of crossing the dateline, on their birthday, in both directions. I am one of them!

In October 1993, I celebrated my special day in Auckland, New Zealand, on my trip there with Bill. On our last night in Auckland, Bill and I had been invited to the home of friends to experience true and authentic Chinese cuisine. We had made the acquaintance of George and Kara during the Blue Lagoon cruise that had carried us through the waters around the Fiji Islands. Our knowledgeable New Zealand cabdriver provided a running commentary about the history, botanical beauty, commercial activity, and neighbourhood strengths and weaknesses, as we wove our way into this exclusive and quiet residential area of Auckland. Ornamental Japanese trees, bonsai, lilies, delicate ironwork and unique cobblestone paving were discretely displayed amongst the foliage. The cab stopped in front of a gated property. The number posted on the fence was with the same as that scribbled on the corner of our map of Fiji. We traversed a small bridge that forded a deep pond, home to large goldfish, carp, and lily pads. As Bill's hand rose to the brass knocker, the door swung widely open and George welcomed us in A very small man, dressed in loosely fitting white cotton trousers and a white cotton oversized shirt, his dark, thin, long braid from the hairline on his neck down his back, to his waist reminded me of Hop Singh, the Cartwright family cook on the TV series, Bonanza.

Kara's beauty and stature combined with her gentle dialect made her the most gracious hostess. She knelt on a finely woven silk oriental carpet in a quilted hand-embroidered and tailored, pleated kimono. Kara and George treated us to a first class, homemade, eleven-course Chinese meal accompanied by warm Saki served in tiny hand painted pottery cups. In my honour, a beautifully decorated almond butter birthday cake covered in yellow icing flowers and candles, followed the main course. It was October 4 in New Zealand.

We arose early the following morning. At the airport, entering security, the questions, passport examinations, and the departure form were all familiar routines for both Bill and myself. As I presented my departure form to the customs officer, he looked at me impatiently. "This box is supposed to be your birthday, not today's date!"

"But, it is my birthday!" I told him. That made him smile, at least.

At the gate I was informed that transfer to the aisle chair would not be necessary. This could only mean one thing. Our assigned seats had again been upgraded to business class. What a bonus on such a long flight. I had no complaints. I quickly glided, in my own chair, into the front of the cabin and transferred to the first available seat. I was immediately presented with a small bottle of champagne to once again honour the day that I came into the world.

The long hours of flying were filled with reading, watching a couple of movies, beverage service, and meals. During this long passage of time, the plane crossed the International Date Line. When I arrived in Vancouver, it was the night of October 4. When I awoke on Tuesday morning, it was my birthday all over again! I had a gourmet dinner with my children—a birthday cake, more candles and with yet another wish, with parcels wrapped exquisitely in brightly coloured paper with ribbons and bows. "But Mom, you can't have two birthdays because if you do, you will have to be two years older," my sons protested. Kids!

In 2003, I crossed the Pacific Ocean on the Norwegian Wind, travelling from Vancouver, with numerous stops en route to Beijing China. On many cruise ships there is one exclusive restaurant that is mostly frequented by passengers to acknowledge and celebrate very special occasions. On board the Norwegian Wind, a private bistro held small intimate tables for parties ranging from two to eight people. It was certainly decadent dining—caviar, hot appetizers, salad, entrée, dessert, lime sherbet to cleanse your palate between each course, a different wine with each course, pre-dinner drinks and liqueurs served with coffee.

On October 4, I was invited to dine in the small, quaint formal dining room. The whole experience was one of self-indulgence with the multi-course meal culminating in the presentation of Black Forest cake (with real whipping cream of course) topped with lit candles. I made a wish, cut the cake, and passed pieces to the other patrons. All had a wonderful evening. I returned to my cabin with many happy birthday wishes; only in this case, I had no birthday. Dinner was served and my birthday was celebrated on October 4. When I awoke the following morning, it was October 6; overnight, we had crossed the International Date Line. I would not experience October 5 in 2003.

On my return home I informed Patrick—before he could produce his words of wisdom—that I did not have a birthday in 2003. Therefore, on my return in early November, I was not any older than I had been when I left Vancouver in late September.

"Mom, you did that on purpose," he told me.

Chapter 8

Greece and Turkey

The Greek Mainland

Can one really embark upon a trip to the other side of the world without any structured planning? My father could never understand how I could throw a minute amount of clothing into a bag, close the door of my apartment, and head to the airport with a *Lonely Planet* guidebook in the bottom of the bag hanging on the back of my wheelchair.

This is how Bill and I began our trip to Greece.

As is often the case, we arrived on October 5, my birthday. It was 5:00 p.m. on Friday evening in Athens. I have a priceless photograph of Bill in the Athens airport leaning against the wall at the payphone with a copy of the *Lonely Planet* in his hand, attempting to find accommodation in this city of three million people. Our criteria were that it was near enough to the must see sights, supported some degree of wheelchair accessibility (Ha! Good luck), and offered some sense of economy although maintaining the budget is never possible in urban areas. At least we were trying. After eighteen attempts, we found one! Throw the bags and chair into a taxi, drive through "rush hour" where mayhem rules the road, and arrive at our haven. It always seems like an oasis when Canada is twenty-two hours in the past and the unknown is in the future.

Getting to the room on the fourth floor was another challenge. My wheelchair fit into the elevator, tiny it was, only by removing the foot rests, lifting off the bag on the back, and squiggling inch-by-inch, kitty corner, into the minuscule cubicle. The hotel attendant pushed the button to close the gated door. As the elevator began to creak between floors, I was submerged in darkness. Bill ran up the stairs so that he could assist me when the elevator groaned and creaked to a standstill. The room was great—but only after removing two chairs, adjusting the beds so that I could see the Parthenon from a supine position, stacking our duffle bags on top of the one small table positioned between the two beds, and holding our breath and sucking in our stomachs as we moved from the bedroom to bathroom and back. There are some advantages to having a small room: there is nowhere to fall except onto a bed. Having to adjust furniture forces a little stretching and exercise and gave us a variety of desirable views. At night, the lights of the Acropolis and Parthenon gave life to the sky. These ancient structures serve as the sentinels of this city.

It never ceases to amaze me that one day I am at work in Burnaby, the next I am on the other side of the world. After long, tedious, uneventful flights and freshening up, I dug into my first Greek salad in the *pláka*, a historic neighbourhood of Athens and an area of culinary delight. In the oldest section of Athens, the streets are closed to automobile traffic. In the shadow of the Acropolis, the pláka forms a village within the city. Street vendors vied for attention. Performers of mime, freestyle music, and dance spread freely into the square, which was frequented by grandmas rocking infants, children scampering about while parents fruitlessly chased after them, and lovers in committed embrace. Horns honked and drivers shouted. Pedestrians laughed and sang.

The incredibly congested roadways and the uneven, narrow sidewalks made it impossible to navigate along the pedestrian track, a narrow lane adjacent to the sidewalk. Manholes located at frequent intervals, three or four to each block, supplied hiding spots for garbage cans. This refuse storage method reduces community clutter and somewhat reduced the sweaty, steamy odour of decaying rubbish. Some of the covers were dislodged, however, and others absent, allowing scents of last night's dinner to seep into the hot, humid air. My age-old fear of mice, and especially rats, arose each time I saw a resident lift a manhole cover. Do rodents live down there? Of course they do. Would they come running out? Despite my insane terror of mice, I tentatively took a quick look to see if any long-tailed, whiskered creatures called these sidewalk refuges home! With the assistance of a passerby, I tipped my wheelchair backwards, sliding onto a street that was packed with vehicles. I now could manoeuvre cautiously along the roadway, the map directing us to unknown places: the Acropolis, the Parthenon, open-air markets.

I seldom have the desire to spend time in large cities however one cannot go to Greece without spending a few days in Athens, to view the Parthenon, the Acropolis, the ancient stadiums, and residences ranging from mansions to hovels. No matter how extremely urban Athens becomes, a sudden unexpected discovery of the magnificent sights cannot help but fill you with wonder. One morning we departed on a detailed, self-created walking tour, exploring "things," and interacting with the local people and other travellers.

On that first morning, I was enthralled with the Ankara Museum. It displayed the architecture of Ancient Greece, which had been produced by the Greek-speaking people whose culture flourished on the Greek mainland, the Aegean Islands, and colonies in Asia Minor from 900 BC until the 1st century AD. The earliest remaining architectural works date from 600 BC.

I spent the afternoon at the National Greek Museum—it is inspiring to think about the artifacts that were striking components of life 2,500 to 3,000 years ago. In the museum, a large Egyptian display brought back vivid memories of my trip to Egypt in 1991.

Exploring fields of ruins transported me back to ancient times. In the evening, while sipping Greek wine, Bill and I reviewed our day, ensuring that we had included all of the essentials: the Acropolis, the Parthenon, the Parliament Buildings, and the National Gardens, where I found respite from the noise and traffic. We spent four days roaming the streets of Athens, climbing the hills, taking in as many sites as possible, with joyful delight. Was I really here?

Linda overlooking Delphi.

Most days ended with souvlaki and a Greek salad. I ate the local food and drank local wine. "When in Rome do as the Romans do," so when in Greece, drink Retsina wine as the Greeks do. An historical anecdote describes the evolution of this wine that many compare to turpentine. During the Roman invasion of Greece, Roman soldiers confiscated the cherished contents of the wine cellars. To deter the thirsty conquerors, the angered citizens began to put pine resin in their stores of wine. The Greek population became so accustomed to the bitter flavour that resin has remained an ingredient of Retsina until today.

The Greek Islands are where you find paradise, according to North American travellers, but in order to enlarge our horizons before leaving the mainland, a trip to Delphi was not to be missed.

Located three hours by bus north of Athens, Delphi expanded my education about life in ancient Greece. Sitting on the top of a cliff overlooking the Mediterranean was the site where ancient culture was born. According to myth, the Greek god Zeus released two eagles, one from the east, the other from the west. When the eagles met, Zeus marked the centre of the earth at that spot. The Delphi Oracle was located here. According to Greek mythology, the Delphi Oracle, known as the naval of the world, marks the beginning of all time.

For the past three thousand years, eagles have played a significant role in defining nationalism for many countries and empires. Some of these empires include the Ptolemaic rulers of Egypt, the Persian, and the Roman Empires. In the modern world, for many countries, eagles appear on crests, coats of arms, and flags. Although the eagle symbolizes great strength, leadership and new perspectives, the eagle was also the founding symbol of the swastika. Northwest of Vancouver in Brackendale, is the wintering home of thousands of Bald Eagles. This area is known as the "Eagle Run." In the month of January, I have wheeled along the dike next to the Cheakamus River to watch them. In First Nations culture, the eagle rules the sky, and therefore eagle feathers are incorporated into their chieftains' regalia to symbolize power.

I was intrigued by the little town at Delphi where a thousand people still live near the sanctuary. The economy, then and now, is based on the sale of knives for sacrifices of boats, goats, and bulls, and of religious objects. The first excavation at this archaeological site began in 1838, and was completed in 1935. Another famous site, the sanctuary of Apollo with the treasuries, temples, and government enclosures, lies on the south flank of Mount Parnassus. Festivals celebrate Apollo's victory over the serpent, Python. Nearby is the stadium, as remarkable today as it was three thousand years ago. Here is where the Python games, the precursor of the Olympic games of today, took place every four years.

Delphi is a headquarters for international meetings, architectural archaeological cultural symposiums. The congress of ancient drama programs, an all day affair, includes three tragedies followed by a comedy play. A day in Delphi provides a unique opportunity to get to know a Greece that is rarely seen by tourists. The facilities, both old traditional and contemporary in style, stand for both the Greece of today and the greatness of yesterday. They continued to amaze and stimulate my imagination.

At the end of the day's excursion, as we disembarked from the bus, dark clouds loomed and thunder showers soaked us to the skin. Temperatures continued to be humidly hot. The presence of the warm air and the beauty of this historical day comforted me from the inside out. Days that are over-filled with so much to see leave no time to eat. Fruit from the street vendors did it.

On our departure morning at the ferry dock, we saw a large and varied population of resident felines. I learned to accept that cats would be my constant companions. In Greece, the streets are filled with cats. At night, I could hear their romantic serenades to one another, the fighting of those that could not get along with their peers, and the cry of kittens searching for their mom. None of the cats seemed to have an owner. Perhaps they just owned themselves.

I am allergic to cats so my personal familiarity with felines is minimal. My knowledge is based on Felix, Sylvester, and

Garfield. The musical *Cats,* based on T.S. Eliot's collection *Old Possum's Book of Practical Cats*, introduced me to Mr. Mistoffelees. He is the original conjuring cat who deceives you into believing that he is only hunting for mice when, in fact, he is capable of performing feats of magic. He finds himself in deep trouble as a result of his mischief. He climbs onto the mantle, knocks over a cherished Ming vase from China and when his owners return, he is lying quietly before the fire looking and acting as innocent as he could possibly be. Calico cats, the magical cats, beautiful and charming, dance the night away. The St. James Street cat is a regular visitor to many gentlemen's clubs. Because he constantly lunches at clubs, he is remarkably fat. The St. James Street cat has a luxurious black coat with intricate white markings on his paws. Bustopher Jones, well known to people in the St. James area, is greeted by name as he walks down the street.

I interacted with more different kinds of cats than I could ever have imagined. Cats on the streets resembled Bustopher Jones, walking with their head held high, and a stance that indicated, "I'm not really a cat!" Some were magical, others mischievous, still others elderly and sublime. Could some of these Greek felines have participated in such a world famous musical review?

So be it. I became accustomed to sharing my wheelchair with a variety of these gentle four-legged creatures who were sometimes on my lap, sometimes lying on the chair when I wasn't in it, or sometimes sleeping in the bag on the back of my chair with their small furry heads peeking out.

I found cats not only in Athens, but on every Greek island, starting with the island of Mykonos.

Mykonos

The Cycladic Islands, a group of fifty-six islands of varying size, are scattered throughout the azure waters of the Aegean Sea.

The formation of the islands is attributed to a series of geological changes: earthquakes, volcanic eruptions and movement of the Earth's crust. Countless little churches, windmills, and narrow alleyways set against a storm-washed landscape, combine to grant unique charm to the islands. Despite the commonality of architectural and ecological characteristics, each island has retained its own particular style.

Perching on the tops of the waves, the Greek inter-island ferry was fully occupied by people, pets, and cargo. It eased its way over the sparkling blue water toward Mykonos, the most populous and most popular Greek island. Throughout the five-hour ferry trip, I continually scanned the horizon for dolphins but without any luck. As the island came into view, the spectacular sights that met my eyes were remarkably consistent with the videos, calendars, guidebook photos, and Internet visuals that I had seen before leaving home. Sun reflected on shining metal arms that spun in time with the breezes, as windmills quietly collected the wind's power from their white stone pillar bases. They produced electricity and pumped fresh water from the streams and springs to the populous areas. We heeded the warnings of fellow travellers who had told us that there would be hordes of hotel and lodge owners lined up at the ferry dock, in competition with each other for our business. We embarked with no confirmed accommodation.

"No stairs," I insisted when we arrived. The Greek businessmen offering rooms all wore the same hat perched sideways on their heads, a white sweater with horizontal navy blue stripes, jodhpurs, and calf-high black boots. One delightful man totally convinced me that there were "only two stairs." Upon arrival at his heralded guesthouse, we discovered two *flights* of stairs. So, back to the dock. Back to the drawing board, so to speak.

Those stairs that had forced us to look elsewhere worked to our advantage. We settled on a small, white marble, blue-roofed hotel that was situated beside the taverna where *Shirley Valentine* had been filmed. I felt privileged to be staying so very close to her experience, or at least the filming of it.

The landscape of Mykonos was made up of large mountains similar to those on most of the Cyclades, giving way to small rocky hills that sloped down toward beautiful beaches. The capital, Chora, had a colourful harbour where little fishing boats nestled happily side-by-side with luxury yachts. Most villages were built on a hillside, in amphitheatre style. The town of Mykonos was spread over a flat area yet projected an image of unusual cohesion. The brilliant white cubic houses with blue tiled domed roofs were built close together and seemingly on top of one another up the slopes. The churches were charming. Local merchants displayed folk items, art, and ethnic goods. Their stalls were clustered in narrow whitewashed alleyways. Grey-green rocks covered with prickly pear cacti and wildflowers generated a rural atmosphere in a semi-urban setting. It was an active, cosmopolitan locale by day and night, but we also found some quiet corners for those times when silence and peace were desirable.

Staying two kilometres outside the town of Mykonos, Bill and I found our own private haven in a little cottage near the beach. Awakening early the first morning, the wide open shutters invited us to share all the outside had to offer. Propped up on a pillow, I watched the turquoise sea, tiny fishing boats, and the sun rising over the horizon through the glassless window. It was Thanksgiving in Canada that day.

I had so much to be thankful for.

The water was a short distance away. The pleasantly warm sun blended with coolness as the sun occasionally sneaked behind a cloud. As I slipped under the water's surface, the first mouthful of water surprised me. I had not realized the water was so intensely salty. The salinity in the water provided natural buoyancy. Under and around me, tiny fish scurried in singles, pairs, and schools. My daily swim and the warm salt water brought me unbelievable benefits.

After each daily swim, sand clinging to the tires on my chair would mar the beautiful flawless flooring. Bill used a broom to swish the sand off the wheels of my chair before I entered. On our second day, while Bill was fulfilling this self-appointed chore, a feeling of all-encompassing wellness inspired me and, with a hand on the wall, I wall-walked into the room, up three stairs, showered, dressed, and returned to the patio. I had not walked this kind of distance for two years.

Bill took one startled look at me and said, "People at home will never believe this."

My regained mobility allowed me to walk short distances intermittently. My ability to walk was amazing, and often followed a daily swim in the Aegean Sea. Bill's mind was blown away. It was delightful to experience this emerging mobility and reduction of spasm. I could now walk short distances. With the support of a railing, I could use my free hand to lift my leg onto the next step and hoist my second leg up to follow. Travel to this region of the world removed stress, improved function, and I was not about to argue with the results. Freedom! On my return home, I visited the neurologist at the MS clinic in Vancouver to ask about this unbelievable temporary mobility.

"If I were you, I would move to Greece," he joked.

I look forward to sharing religious celebrations of the local people wherever I travel. On Sunday morning, while attending church in a white marble, blue domed, traditional building, we found ourselves in the midst of a Greek Orthodox service celebrating the Eucharist. My minimal wardrobe did not include a long skirt so a large striped towel wrapped around my waist over my shorts served the purpose of providing proper church service attire. Bill sat in a pew and I wheeled up beside him.

We were feeling quite comfortable until we realized that seating was gender segregated! Women sat on one side of the aisle, men on the other. One of us, namely me, had to move. I quietly slipped across the aisle and parked close to the women's side of the congregation.

Unlike North America where a wafer is placed onto your folded hands, in this church the representation of the body of Christ was distributed by young girls in delicate, white lacy dresses. They carried large baskets filled with chunks of fragrant, warm, homemade Greek bread. A Canadian woman sitting in a wheelchair fascinated the children. The little girls were obviously concerned about the lady. Was she sick? Was she hungry? Did she need help? Did she need more blessing? By the time I left the church, I had enough bread on my lap to feed us for a week. To this day, I am not sure if they thought I was hungry or if I needed extra blessings to restore mobility in my lower limbs.

The wine, representing the blood of Christ, Retsina, was also doled out to me in large quantities. After consuming the generous allotment of wine, I wondered if it would be possible to wheel my chair in a straight line. It seemed to me that some of my fellow celebrants became rather envious of the abundant blessings dispensed upon me.

We explored the island on foot/wheels and by bus. We relished the historical architecture, the fishing villages, the shops and stalls that sold produce and clothing. Before returning to our home base each night, we purchased a half litre of Retsina, small cucumbers, tomatoes, a purple onion, feta cheese and a green pepper for our evening feast. After dinner, we played cards, read, rehashed our day's explorations and tucked into bed as the moon was rising over the dark, glistening, navy blue water.

One night, with the shutters open, I was beginning to drift

into dreamland when an uninvited visitor jumped through the window and landed on Bill's bed. Our shrieks of surprise and fear dissolved into laughter as we realized it was a cat, seeking a warm cozy place to sleep for the night.

Most women have at least one shopping indulgence. For some it is shoes or handbags. For others, it is clothing. For still others, it is makeup and for others, perfume. For me, it is bathing suits. I constantly have one that I am using and one extra—but somehow I can always use more. If you swim on a regular basis and are committed to maintaining some degree of exercise schedule, an extra suit is always necessary. One of the little open market stalls sold great swimsuits. Being in a chair, I have more difficulty than most trying on new clothes and this— combined with the total lack of a private change room or even a tree to hide behind—presented a dilemma. The sales lady had an inventive idea. Her solution was unlike what one is used to in Canada. "Take the four swimsuits," she told me cheerfully. I was to go home and try them on, then return on the following day to bring back the suits I had not chosen. She asked for no money, no identification or place of residence. She simply trusted that I would be true to my word. The plain navy blue Speedo I chose carried me through many kilometres of water. Each time I wore it, cherished memories of Mykonos accompanied me as I swam. A friend pointed out later that the vendor could have stopped me at the ferry dock!

After five days of beauty, relaxation, and the remarkable physical wellness that I had achieved on Mykonos, after five days, it was time to move on.

Chora offered a beautiful harbour with narrow streets, cobblestone walkways, and exquisite tiny churches. A full day of sun included reading page after page of a book I had been hoarding for my next vacation as well as warming my body on the beach, cooling it in the sea then baking once more. Writing postcards on a daily basis provided me with a great reason to sit by the waterfront and have a cappuccino. I wrote my cards and mailed them before returning to our retreat on the south side of the island.

We took the bus to town planning to reserve a spot for the following day on the next ferry to Santorini. A large hand-painted red sign hung at the dock: "All ferries cancelled due to aggressive winds." It looked as if we would be here for a while. Daily, we took a cab to the ferry dock and sat patiently for one or two hours in the hopes that the boat would sail. The dock master's answer to our questions about service was a shrug and, "Nobody knows." If it did sail, and there was available space on board, we'd have to be at the dock ready to go when the announcement was made. We might have only five minutes' notice. There was an advantage to the continuing storm. Retsina wine was complementary at all restaurants. We waited out the storm by swimming, eating Greek salad and swordfish souvlaki, and sitting on the beach outside of town.

Frustration is never a reasonable use of time and energy. I found that I just enjoy the day and when tomorrow comes, another delightful day will blossom before me. Music and dancing, good food, wine, and laughter continued to ease the nuisance of being "trapped" on Mykonos.

Santorini

After five days of stormy weather on Mykonos, the locals offered all kinds of helpful solutions: "There is boat at noon." "There will be one at 2:30," (which did come but carried on to Athens without stopping). "If you say a rosary three times and look to the sky in the east, a ferry will come at four o'clock." Spare me! After waiting all day at the dock, we finally did get onto a ferry at 5:30 p.m., heading to the port of Athinios on Santorini.

Hundreds of people had been stranded on Mykonos by wind and rough seas for up to a week. The small ferry was packed with people—infants, nursing mothers, children clinging fearfully to any solid adult leg that they could clutch, fishermen, elderly grandmothers and grandpas, tourists, and travellers, all trying to get where they needed to go. There were not enough seats (and I am sure not enough lifejackets) by the time the undersized wooden ferry boat creaked out of the harbour through the misty fog and diminishing daylight. In the small cabin of the little vessel people stood, sat on luggage, on the floor, and on each other.

It was a rocky ride from start to finish. Some people were drinking, others eating, groups played cards and made merry. Within an hour of departure, a hundred or more travellers leaned over the railing. Many more were inside gripping plastic bags. Getting into a washroom was not even a remote possibility. I simply remained immobile, blocked my ears, closed my eyes, and prayed!

I had not eaten for twenty-four hours and I had had very little to drink all day; only small sips of bottled water. This saved me from a crisis I did not want even to imagine. There were so many people, huge suitcases, boxes, bags, packs, narrow doors, ledges and stairs between me and the rail. The only choice open to me was to stay in my chair, maintain a steady stance, focus on my feet and continue to look and feel green. An experience like this makes me think that I am very glad that my will is current, yet I don't want to leave this world today.

Ten years before, I could not have cared less. I was trapped in an unhappy marriage. I desperately wanted things to be happily ever after, just like in the storybooks, but unfortunately life was not like that. I was working long hours, fulfilling my compulsion to be a workaholic. I was studying for yet another university degree on a part-time basis. I was taxiing my children to the soccer field, hockey rink, and to competitive swimming practices. I was trying to be super mom. You must remember those times when nothing was acceptable unless it was homemade. I made my own everything: granola, peanut butter, cookies, mustard, yogurt, and mayonnaise. Everything was made from scratch and in quantity. I didn't make one lasagna—it was better to make four—one for dinner, three in the freezer. Making two or three pies was just a waste of time. I always made a dozen at a time. During harvest season, my husband and children would religiously peel fruit that I transformed into one hundred and four quarts of preserves (two bottles each week), and, of course, not using any sugar. In retrospect, it has certainly benefited children. Today they maintain healthy diets, have no tooth decay, get regular exercise, and live balanced lives that include work, play, rest, love, and relaxation. I should have practised what I preached. My incredible volume of accomplishments gave me a very full existence but it robbed me of a reasonable, balanced perspective on life. But now, in 1994, my life was different—so much better. It included travel, quiet evenings, music, books, laughter, exercise, work, and play.

As the ferry struggled into the dock on the shore of Santorini, I was ever so grateful to be alive. Near death experiences such as a storm on the water, a motor vehicle accident, a severe case of the flu or pneumonia, always reinforce my thankfulness for this great life.

It reminds me that we all must live each day as if it is our last, because it might be!

Each Greek Island offers exceptional charm, unique to itself. Santorini is part of a mountainous volcanic group, the highest point being 564 metres above sea level. Only one island in this group is inhabited. The majority of the population lives in a few small towns and villages on the island of Thera (Santorini). Over 3,600 years ago, the eruption of Santorini was one of the largest volcanic explosions in ten thousand years. Seven cubic miles of magna flowed out of the volcanic cone, creating a series of complex overlapping shields. The lava flows that made the shield are exposed in the cliffs below the town Fira, the capital of Santorini. Rough inconsistent volcanic terrain is not designed to accommodate wheelchairs, or perhaps wheelchairs are not intended to be wandering on steep, rocky Greek pathways. But, once again, "there is a way."

We examined the accommodation options and found that the most appealing guesthouses were high on the hill overlooking the cliffs. People were hospitable, the rooms spotlessly clean, water hot, with crisp white sheets and thick Turkish towels. Quite a difference from what we had experienced in Athens. Forced to take withdrawal from the world, I could sit in the sun on the balcony overlooking the courtyard. This was great respite on the first day, considering our arrival time had been 1:30 a.m. after a near-death stormy sail across the water followed by a five-kilometre bus ride up the narrow winding hill. There would be no beach access on this Island.

Having had a generous dose of sun and sand on Mykonos, we looked forward to a new kind of adventure.

I awoke to church bells ringing and sun shining over the water. I wanted to go and see the donkeys and determine how I could get on one. Bill and I followed the precipice alongside the town of Fira. We found the beginning of the path that wound down the crag to a deep pond, created by the formation of steep cone-shaped cliffs. Many visitors were eager to descend for a close-up view of the magmatic rock formations that had been formed by those ancient volcanoes. The usual means of transportation down the cliff path was by foot. The steep ascent was made possible, for all but the fittest, by riding a small donkey that appeared to have personal knowledge of each stone, rock, and crevice in the pathway.

Riding a donkey in Greece.

"Do you really want to go down there?"

This question was directed to me by other tourists and travellers. They could not believe that an individual mobilizing in a wheelchair would, in fact, want to explore the same regions that they did.

"Of course I do!" I said enthusiastically. It did not cross my mind that there was any other response.

I am well aware—both at home and when I am travelling in foreign lands—that desire is not always consistent with the ability to make it work. However, in this case, I was determined to find a way to get down the cliff side. An active small business offered donkey service to all who were reluctant to walk uphill. The owner of several donkeys was ever-present, from early morning until dusk and travellers who had walked down, now rode back up the steep trail.

I looked closely at the small asses who eagerly munched on grass or bushes along the path. A few had feedbags attached to their bridles. The owner of the donkey collection, a small, elderly Greek man, was dressed in the classic short khaki pants (we call them capris or jodhpurs), a navy-blue baggy sweater with a tam perched sideways over his black, greying hair. I often wonder when I see those grey hairs and wrinkles at the corners of peoples' eyes, about the hard times in life that contributed to these features. It may simply be age but I am certain that somewhere in the past, they have known financial stress, children (who are stresses in themselves), illness, joy, and pain. He smiled gently. My knowledge of Greek and his knowledge of English matched—I knew no Greek, he knew no English. With hugs, sign language, smiles, and laughter, it was mutually understood that, *Yes, I want to go down the cliff side. Yes, I will need to come back up. No, I cannot walk. Yes, the wheelchair is too wide.* It actually was two inches narrower than a standard chair but too wide to use on the pathway, not to mention that my control on the steepness would lead to my certain demise. I would ride a donkey down the cliff. According to the young boy who was assisting with the care of the animals, nobody had ever done this before, but I would, and I would return by the same means.

I was on the road again. Half a dozen grey donkeys, well brushed, long-eared, with a black cross on their backs, reminded of the days in Jerusalem. These frail looking specimens stood solemnly along the edge of the cliff. They all looked friendly but were they all equally surefooted and knowledgeable? "This one looks friendly enough, gentle and eager to please," a friendly fellow traveller commented.

I had tucked a few carrots into my pocket for this very moment. Pulling out one of these produced an imagined smile on Donkey's furry face. His dreamy, sad eyes beckoned me to his side. With a little help from my recently acquired friends,

I found myself sitting on an old brown burlap blanket on the back of Donkey. He knew exactly where he was going and without further adieu, he began carefully placing one foot in front of another, heading down the steep cliff side. His steps were quiet, interrupted only by the chirping of birds and the occasional rock slipping over the edge of the precipice. To say the pathway was steep is an understatement. Donkey's hoofed feet gingerly selected placement along the narrow trail.

There are times in my life when memories of Sunday school return vividly. Without question, this was one of those times. Prayer seemed to be the only option that I had to quiet my jangled nerves as Donkey headed down the narrow pathway. Others on the sandy walkway hugged the side of the cliff as my surefooted friend barrelled recklessly towards the deep pool of black water below. My focus returned to the beautiful sunshine, the rising volcanic mountain terrain, the sight of the other blended blues and deep purples of the water below. I tried to centre myself on the beauty and ignore the immediate presence of potential disaster. Foliage displayed lime green, Kelly green, British Racing green and every other shade of green imaginable. Leaves on some bushes were tiny, hugely shiny, rubbery, and tropical.

When we reached the water's edge, dismounting from Donkey's back was not an option. However, I had a great aerial view from my four-foot high perch with a panoramic perspective of all there was to see. Other travellers and tourists were picnicking on Greek bread, cheese, and vegetables. For me, a Diet Coke was always like manna from heaven, and today, as on many others, it was adequate hydration in the mid-day.

There was a fresh water trough for the donkeys to quench their thirst and they drank deeply. Half a dozen patient grey donkeys were waiting to carry weary walkers up the long steep hill toward their hotel rooms on the heights. My return trip was like that of the others. The donkeys plodded slowly up the hill. This time, there was no need for apprehension or prayer. My safety was in the hands, or more realistically, on the back of this trusty animal who worked day in and day out, carrying their human cargo up the cliff side.

A small boat tour through the channels and weaving between the volcanic islands, offered continuous views of spectacular solid rock formations. The wee villages, tucked into rock crevices were a strong statement of resistance to change. The beauty and quaintness of the homes and community were in total opposition to the designs of the modern day world. Here, people hung onto the old and familiar. The words of Joni Mitchell travelled through my mind: "They paved paradise and put up a parking lot."

Our "bateau" eased in and out of narrow fjords close to the shore. We entered luminous caves where glistening stalactites hung like icicles from the roof and stalagmites emerged from the dark waters on the floor of the cave, fireflies lit the darkened room. My generic gutsiness was squelched by the hordes of bats flying high in the cave, dipping and diving in and around our open-air boat.

When I was a little girl, my grandmother told me to wear a hat when going into the barn at night because the bats would get themselves tangled in my long hair. I was not prepared to take the chance that her warning was just an old wives tale. As a child, the threat of bats in my hair was probably Nana's guarantee that I keep my hat on as the evening air cooled. I quickly tied my long hair back and tucked my blue dotted cotton bandanna around it.

After lunch, the small tour boat dropped us along the southwestern shore. We wandered along the coastline, seeking a village that hadn't changed much in the last two hundred years. The small population of the settlement lived in natural fibre huts, cooked over open fires, and wove baskets that were used for everything—storing food, clothing, carrying babies, tipped upside down to serve as tables and chairs. Seashells were also multi-purpose—dishes, cups, jewellery, decoration. Reaching the village was an obstacle course for those on feet. For someone using a wheelchair it seemed impossible but my friend Bill and two other willing travellers lifted me and my chair over ancient stone walls, waded in the sea when the beach disappeared, pushed through thick jungle foliage, across rocky and sandy beaches until we reached the village. The local grandmas invited us to share their midday meal of cucumber-like vegetables, tomatoes, whole garlic cloves, and fresh warm bread from the stone oven perched over the open fire. We were privileged and honoured by the generosity of the villagers. In exchange, we purchased their unique handicrafts. Late in the afternoon, the thought of returning to the boat over the same intimidating pathway was overwhelming.

"It's okay guys," I told them. "I will swim."

Swimming is sometimes the easiest form of transportation. I will get my exercise; the guys will have a much easier time walking back to the boat. It would be quicker and I would have the reward of sitting on the deck, and drying off in the sunshine.

"Do you have a swimsuit?" Bill asked.

I did not, so I discarded my t-shirt and shorts slipping into the water in my bra and panties. "Just remember that when I reach the ladder at the boat, I will need a hand up and please have my clothes ready. Don't forget to warn the crew that I am coming so they don't leave without me."

Pacing myself, I swam steadily, knowing that the walkers would reach the boat before I did. As I stroked through the warm water, from time to time I noticed tiny colourful fish swimming alongside me. Their friendly presence encouraged me along the way. When the rusty hull came into view I searched for the ladder. I reached up for the first rung and lifted myself hand over hand, calling out, "I'm here!"

Two crew members leaned over the side and pulled me on board. Bill was standing at the ready with my shirt.

On return from our exploration of the volcanic islands and their surrounding waters, the bus slowly climbed the steep terrain and pulled onto a narrow gravel shoulder. We entered a small taverna on the edge of the cliff with a balcony—and our table—precariously overhanging the water. The setting offered a sunset that exhibited every colour of the rainbow.

After several active and adventurous days on Santorini, a three-hour ferry trip beckoned.

Naxos

When the ferry landed at Naxos in the early morning, I watched the unloading of boats from the edge of the small wooden dock. Box after box of silver fish were making their way to market and the dinner table! Some time in town was required to take care of pressing necessities—telephone my children, repairs to Bill's pack, and find a battery for my watch. I know there is no place for a watch on a vacation except that ferries and buses run by the clock.

Naxos, the largest and most fertile of the Cycladic islands, lies in the middle of the Aegean Sea. Meadows give way to endless stretches of sandy beach. Stony crags plunge into the sea in stark contrast to abundant agricultural valleys.

A local bus and a cheerful, keen-to-educate, bus driver became our expert tour guide. Naxos City, similar to Chora on Mykonos, is built in circular style on the side of a hill. Narrow streets and old stone houses touched my soul, making a lasting impression. As is common on the Greek Islands, flower boxes overrun with posies competed for brilliance with the hand-painted shutters on each window. Apolona, a beautiful seaside village, displayed an ancient marble quarry dating back to the 6th century BC. The countryside was pastoral. Shepherds were herding sheep; mothers with their young children headed to market; others headed home with their purchases wrapped in printed cloth bundles. Evening presented another seafood indulgence. Calamari is a hard habit to break but the amazing swordfish souvlaki was stiff competition. Retsina, sipped from a goblet in a Greek taverna or while sitting at the edge of the lapping waves, in no way resembles turpentine. Maybe it is the atmosphere. Maybe it's psychological but a cold glass of Retsina on the shore of a Greek island holds a wonderful appeal. Dessert complimented our salads. Fresh pineapple dripping with sweet juice was as tasty as that I have eaten on the island of Hawaii. Every day in Greece was summer—a hot, sunny beach and a swim in the sea. The evening produced clear skies, sometimes a slice of moon, and lots of stars.

Our humble abode, from my perspective, was absolute decadence: a small hotel where I could wheel out the door, cross a small road, traverse twenty feet of firm sand, and slip into the water for a swim.

The Hotel Sitar was adequately comfortable. A shower in the morning was a cool and crisp experience. Likewise, a shower in the evening was a cool and crisp experience when solar-heated water had been all used up by other travellers. After experimenting with different times of the day, I found that showering late in the afternoon before dinner generated the warmest water.

Paros

October 21, 1994 found us on the ferry between the islands of Naxos and Paros. The villa on Paros continued my wellness journey. It offered sun, warm wind, easy access to the water, quiet, and ambience that encouraged introspective thinking. White, fluffy cumulus clouds decorated the blue sky. They beckoned me to lie back and examine their formations just as I had as a child, when we lounged about for hours trying to pick out animal outlines in the cloud formations. For a moment, leaning back and looking up, this could well be childhood all over again.

That evening, I lay in bed with the shutters open, listening to the ebb and flow of the sea. The rhythmic sound of the moving waves on the shore lulled me to sleep. The stars and comets lit the sky and the reflection of the moon shone across the water.

We took the bus to the north end of the island. There we found a true "fishing village," Nerissa, with lots of locals mending nets, playing chess on the dock, and "shooting the breeze" with one another. There were no formal restaurants; only village homes where the women opened their doors, offering selections of cheese, tidbits of fish, baking, and cappuccino, served on the porch or by the water. The church was exquisite. Not only was the cannery a source of employment for many but it also doubled as a schoolroom for children; and as a cottage industry where women did weaving and as a community gathering site for all.

On our return from Nerissa, we met with thunder, lightning and torrential rains that covered the streets with four inches of water. There were no drains! We mounted a hill to our guest-house. Bill waded through water, pushing the wheelchair, avoiding boxes, bundles of soggy newspaper, and garbage cans that floated down the street in the torrents of water. Drenched, with water dripping from our hair, cool and wet, we were only thankful to reach our tiny, dry room.

"Do you want to go out for dinner?" Bill asked as we towelled off. I thought not. Dinner in the evening was down the drain—so

I thought. But Bill pulled on his soggy jacket and ventured out into the storm, returning in twenty minutes with donairs and two cold beers. A donair, also called a gyro or gyros, is a Greek wrap containing roasted meat sliced off a vertical spit, tomato, onion, and tzatziki sauce.

We awoke in the morning to the sounds of church bells tolling rhythmically, waves lapping on the shoreline, and warm, beautiful sunshine. We decided to visit another local place of worship. We went to the Greek Orthodox Church where we were met with generous servings of large chunks of hot homemade bread at Eucharist—enough for several breakfasts. It was a heart-warming, spiritual experience from beginning to end—incense, candles, chanting, all beautiful and most interesting, followed by greeting hugs, a walk along the beach and cappuccinos on a bench in the harbour.

Samos

Our final choice of Greek Islands was Samos as it is the only island where water transportation directly to Turkey is possible.

The ferries from Paros to Samos are night boats, leaving at 10:00 p.m. and sailing into the darkness and arriving in the morning hours in the heat of the sun on the shores of Samos. After a few hours in a coffee shop there and sharing travel stories with some folks from New Zealand, we boarded a bus to a small fishing village. Fourteen kilometres out of town, this quaint settlement boasted a lighthouse that overlooked the dark waters, illuminating the way for small boats leaving and returning home. Fishing shacks lined the shore, tiny boats bobbed on the water, and children played at the water's edge. Grandma, sitting on a log, rocked back and forth. After visiting the small ancient Greek church, I quietly observed fishermen lovingly mending their nets and watched others clearing their decks of the residue of today's catch. They hung nets and sang. Some worked in silence. Some smoked a pipe while others chewed on a wad of dried seaweed.

At the end of the day we needed to go back to our hotel. The night bus would not pull out of town until 10:00 p.m. so we waited, we watched the arrival of charcoal storm clouds, beams of sunshine that produced rainbows, thunder, lightning, and rain that made Vancouver winter rain seem like a myth. I boarded the bus, soaking wet, but the satisfaction of having been embraced in the arms of the ancient community warmed me through and through. Instead of calm before the storm, there was calm after the storm—humid heat and still air. Sometimes the breeze made me think of putting on a sweatshirt. At other times, every tiny wisp of air movement was welcome beneath the burning Mediterranean sun.

There was no need for us to take a Mediterranean cruise when ferries carry passengers across the Mediterranean waters between islands. The guesthouse in Pythagrion was perched on the edge of a small hill. From the porch, I discovered a beautiful view of the harbour. The hosts, an elderly Greek couple, welcomed Bill and me warmly, offering Greek coffee and biscuits when we arrived. The family's grandma frequently checked on me to see if there was anything that she could do to make my stay more comfortable. Each morning there was a timid knock on the bedroom door and she delivered a small tray with hot espresso coffee and warm biscuits. She enveloped me with warmth, truly from the heart. I felt her special gentle care and affection. A Canadian woman travelling on wheels is quite unusual, particularly to the natives of the smaller Greek Islands.

One morning I had washed some t-shirts and panties, pinning them with wooden pegs to the low line that stretched across the veranda. We departed in search of a day of adventure. In mid-afternoon, when it started to rain, I thought of my fresh laundry becoming wetter and wetter; to my surprise, when I returned to the guesthouse, the clothing and towels were neatly folded on a stool outside the bedroom door.

While in Greece, I consumed more hot homemade bread in five weeks than I had eaten in the last five years. I ate Greek salad and to-die-for fish. I never refused a second, third, fourth, fifth chunk of hot bread, and drank Retsina copiously. Through it all, I lost nine pounds. True to Wallis Simpson, Duchess of Windsor, "A woman can't be too rich or too thin."

Pythagrion is the town where travellers surrender their passports. It is always an uneasy feeling to be far away from home, on foreign soil, and without a Canadian passport. Canadian passports are one of the most coveted in the world and at that time, known as one of the easiest to copy. This is no longer true. In order to obtain a visa to Turkey, we were required to deposit our passports in the Turkish government office on the island of Samos for forty-eight hours. Reluctantly, I forfeited the precious document to the uniformed official. No receipt was offered in return.

Bill and I had two uneasy nights before we could expect the return of the passports. We wanted to go to Turkey! Why waste time worrying? We explored the town and chatted with the local people. The hospitable, kind-hearted folks were ready and willing to form lasting friendships with the Canadian visitors. We explored museums and archaeological sites, Roman Baths, ancient ruins from early Greek civilization, folklore, music, dance, and dress.

Some invitations are hard to turn down. As I sipped cappuccino in a cafe, some local nurses questioned me about the wheelchair: how I was travelling; what kind of reception I was receiving in their country; how did I make it work? Once a nurse, always a nurse! The opportunity to visit a medical clinic, as I had done in Kenya, gave me the chance to see how medical care is provided in Greece.

Despite my apprehension about leaving our documents in a foreign office, it turned out to be an uneventful experience. On the third day at 11:00 a.m., Bill and I entered the Turkish consulate office to receive our passports and visas. Upon presentation of $20 USD, along with two pieces of identification, our passports were returned with the desired Turkish visa.

We were off again.

Turkey

A beautiful, peaceful, and uneventful ferry trip from Samos to Kusadasi brought us to the pier in the early evening. We shared the fatigue, satisfaction and camaraderie of the fishermen who slipped their boats into assigned spaces. For these dedicated fishers, another day that had begun in the dark was at last completed in the early hours of the evening. Ropes were carefully coiled on the deck of the sloops, ready for the following morning. Other lines remained in heaps waiting to be washed, untangled, and put away for the night.

While Bill proceeded to explore accommodation options, I waited on the wharf to watch as fishing boats and their crews returned with the catch of the day. Dinnertime! Along the length of the wooden dock, small charcoal grills awaited the fresh catch from the nets. By the time Bill returned from securing a bed for the night, I had accepted a dinner invitation. We indulged in delicious, freshly grilled fish—species unknown. Accordions, lifted from the bilge of the boats, sent lively and melancholy notes into the night air. The captains and crew quietly droned melancholy stories followed by lively ditties, all in a language foreign to our ears. Late into the dark hours, before the workers and the guests began to make their way home, stars sprinkled the night sky and the moon rose above the horizon.

Fatigue sent us home. We had lucked into a very small, cozy

hotel. The expansive view of town and the harbour made the greater expenditure (this time $12 USD per person) all worthwhile. There were other benefits—hot water, and an elevator for entrance by wheelchair. Turkish music in the background was included even though it wasn't requested. I drifted off to sleep to the sound of local melodies and the clicking of the zils on the belly dancers' fingers. I awoke on Friday, the Moslem Sabbath, to the call for prayer. "Ohm, Ohm." Each morning, the standard "to-die-for" Turkish breakfast was served on the patio: two slices of garden fresh tomato, two slices of cucumber, olives, feta cheese, hot homemade bread and apple tea. Short of cash? An ATM spilled out Turkish money. Our local wealth was difficult to keep track of. Ten dollars bought us 260,000 lira. The result was lots and lots of bills. A 500,000 lira bill was equivalent to $20 USD. With a fistful of money, I felt like a millionaire!

This country presented different and new experiences everywhere we looked. With demitasse cups of Turkish coffee in hand, we lounged in a park while people watching and planning our day. The minibus inching along the roadway was full of homemakers who had been to the market. The women carried huge bundles of produce. It seemed that they had purchased enough food to last several months. Either large families or small families with large appetites were waiting for them at home. In fact, most people in Asia and Europe shop on a daily basis feeling that anything more than three days old is not fresh enough to put on their dining table. As the women descended the bus steps, they carried heavy-laden baskets on their heads with seeming ease and perfect balance.

My initial impression of Turkey was that it is one big bazaar. This is not a negative or critical comment as the specialized products—Turkish carpets, leather bags, leather jackets, knockoff designer clothing, spices, hand-painted plates, apple tea—are beautifully crafted. If your budget allows, they are all worth taking home. Salespeople, vendors, hawkers, manipulators, beckoned us into their shops and stalls along the streets. Wheelchair accessibility was never a concern in Turkey. Ramps are mandatory for the movement of large trailers that carry Turkish and Persian carpets. Not willing to take no for an answer, the vendors continually shouted, "What you want? We have it! Not to worry! Come in and join us for apple tea. The best of coffee is waiting here. We have magic carpets. They fly!"

I heard the sales pitch repeatedly. After forty-nine repetitions, I came to realize that the "magic flying carpets" referred to the willingness of the vendors—on the presentation of your Visa card—to fly your carpets home to Canada, or anywhere in the world for that matter.

Apple tea was the consistent enticement offered by the merchants. It was always hot, naturally sweet, and a welcome distraction from hunger. I drank apple tea many times daily in Turkey and almost daily for two years after my return home until I used up my supply of Asian dried apples.

Ephesus, an ancient city on the south west coast of Turkey, is the best-preserved Greek archaeology site in the world; it is 2,000 to 4,000 years old. Only approximately 15% of this ancient city with a BC population of 250,000 has been excavated. The churches, library, treasury, coliseum and theatre reveal the enormous size of the city structures.

When we arrived at the site, it looked like a large insurmountable mountain of stone walls, marble buildings, rocks and hills. Manageable in a wheelchair? Not a chance! As is often the case, I knew there had to be a way to explore this world heritage site. I spotted a farmer driving his horse and cart along the narrow dirt roadway. The wagon, pulled by one large grey mare, was beginning to head up the hill. I called to the farmer and waved to gain his attention. In spite of his lack of English and my lack of Turkish or Greek, I managed to negotiate a ride to the top of the hill for Bill, my wheelchair, and me. Travelling downhill through rock, ancient ruins, grass and trees seemed more logical than the impossible task of trying to go up. The Turkish farmer was more than delighted to facilitate my appreciation of this fascinating and expansive display of history and nature.

Curious onlookers waved enthusiastically. They nodded and gestured encouragement. The passing local people seemed thrilled at my enthusiasm to explore their country's past. At the top of the steep, rough terrain, we climbed down from the cart. In the midst of the ruins, grapevines trailed over irregular stone walls. Beautiful flowers and intricate foliage filled me with fascination. We set off down the hill, equipped with a camera, a guidebook, a Coke and Diet Coke, and novels to read while resting on a rock. The contents of our pack did us well for the day. In the sunshine, we perched on flat rocks to read about the structures before us. We photographed them all. When it was time for a break, we rested in a quiet corner and took a few moments to read, drink some water, and sip our colas. Bill and I had developed a habit over the years. Our day excursions always included some reading time, a guidebook, and our sodas.

It would never do to visit this part of the world without exploring the Bosporus by boat. This strait forms the boundary between Europe and Asia, linking the Black Sea with the Sea of Marmara. Asia stood on the eastern shore, its white stucco architecture capped by red tile roofs. Young people in modern dress skipped along the sidewalks. Europe on the western shore was made up of older buildings with elaborate palaces, narrow streets, and residents shuffling along in black shawls and grey skirts. The ferry made several stops at fishing villages, with elaborate mosques, fish markets, and lovely farms clinging to the hillside.

Bill went off for a few days of independent travel to Gallipoli and the World War I battle site across the Dardanelles. Heading in the other direction, I decided to explore a small Turkish village on the outskirts of the city of Antakya. I took a small van through the mountains at sunset and along the coastline with beautiful views of tiny seaside villages. The city finally emerged in the distance, backed by hillsides. I arrived in the small town at a crossroads and had to flag down another bus to take me to the rural settlement. As I entered the town, I saw horses, donkeys, poultry, and vendors with carpetbags full of lemons, produce, and more, all along the street. I found myself a wonderful small hotel with hot water, a toilet, breakfast, towels, and yes, Turkish coffee served at 6:00 a.m. I spent my days exploring the town, visiting the market. I was learning from the locals, who took delight in inviting this strange Canadian woman to take part in the family meal in their homes. I got to play with the children, listen to their music and share their stories and folklore.

Following my reconnection with Bill, we secured seats on a small van heading north on the coast. We found a small local guesthouse adjacent to the henhouse and farmhouse, located outside a little village. I brushed my teeth and washed my face at the hand pump under a tree in the yard. After another long day, I gratefully tumbled onto my small cot and an immediate acquaintance with the Sandman. When daylight broke through the lace-curtained window, an ear shattering moan and cry penetrated my early-morning drowsiness. What in the world could it be?

"I think it's a cow," Bill said.

"If it's a cow," I replied with a touch of sarcasm, "It's a very sick cow."

I pulled on a pair of shorts on under the ankle length t-shirt that served as a nightshirt and slipped out the door to investigate. I encountered the most amazing sight—a mother camel was carefully grooming her newborn infant with her long slurping tongue. Camels, from my limited past experience, are very tall but the little guy that had entered the world on that November morning, stood perhaps only three feet tall at the top of the little bump on his back. The mother was most intent on her task. The baby whimpered contentedly under the gentle bath from the sandpaper-like tongue. In spite of the language barrier, I was able to learn, from the farmer, that the mother was four years old and the gestational period for a camel is twelve to fourteen months.

We embarked on another minibus ride—this time to Izmir. Five miles north of Izmir, a city of 1.5 million people, trucks, buses, and cars whizzed by pack animals who trotted along in the slow right lane, carrying their goods to market. One poor little donkey, smaller than the rest, was carrying the largest of the loads.

Pamukkale, meaning "cotton castle" in Turkish, is a world heritage site in southwestern Turkey, where hotels and roads are absent. Hot springs emerge from the limestone deposits leaving terraces of sparkling white carbonate minerals. The temperate climate enables locals and tourists to enjoy soaking in the natural pools any time of the year. For thousands of years, people have bathed in the mineral springs. In order to preserve the limestone deposits, no shoes, food, or beverages other than water are permitted. Motor vehicles are banned from the area.

Bill and I climbed 160 m (525ft) to the summit and walked over eight kilometres from end to end. Bill, of course, got a much more vigorous workout—he was pushing the wheelchair while I sat. At the top, he enjoyed the much-deserved rest. We lounged, delighting in the spectacular view. Bill dangled his feet and legs in a warm pool to sooth his fatigue and prevent any soreness in his muscles. While we read a few chapters in our books and nibbled on snacks from the backpack, time was passing more quickly then we realized. As the sun began to slip below the horizon, we commenced our trek downhill. When we rounded a corner, the pathway had disappeared in the dusk. How were we going to get down? Water flow is directed by gravity. We knew that our destination lay below us so we followed a steady stream heading downhill. Overhead branches hid the moon's light. Bill tramped along the muddy creek bed through the darkness finding that the deep stream soaked his feet to above ankle height. I wheeled cautiously through the rocky creek, soaking my feet as well. After two hours of persistent trekking, we began to doubt the GPS of our minds. Were we going in the right direction? Would we spend the night in this tropical jungle? If we made it to the foot of the hill, would we be too late to catch a bus back to our hotel? In situations like this, it is always best to be positive. We managed to laugh, sang, and told jokes, burying any sense of apprehension. When we got too tired, we stopped for a rest.

Rounding a corner after three and a half hours, we saw lights in the distance—a roadway, headlights, the dimmed illumination of a window in a house. We emerged from the forest just in time to see the last minibus of the evening waiting patiently at the bus stop. At this point, it did not matter whether the driver was just having his break, waiting for us, or taking an extra few minutes to catch his breath. We gratefully settled into the bus and when we reached the guesthouse, beer never tasted so good!

After a good night's sleep we moved along, arriving in Dikili on the north coast once again after dark. Daylight fades early—about 5:00 p.m. In the sub-tropics, and unlike North America, there is little change in daylight hours between seasons. Day and night are almost equal all year round. We found a clean, cute little hotel that charged the huge price of four dollars per night. Dikili is a small coastal summer resort where we nested for a few days of quiet. I swam in the sea, much to the amazement of the locals who stood on the shore wrapped in their quilted jackets wondering how anyone could put on a bathing suit and get into the Black Sea. The salt water was easily 10°C warmer than it ever gets at home. For me it was pleasant and refreshing. The area, like most of Greece and Turkey, was rich with history and charm. We ate and slept. The Turkish diet was similar to that of Greece – vegetables, seafood, no butter, lots of hot fresh bread and, of course, wine. The diet of the Mediterranean people is low in saturated fat if you do not consume lamb. I hadn't eaten lamb since my time in New Zealand where I bottle-fed the baby lambs. I cannot eat my friends! There is no saturated fat in anything else. Fresh salty air, daily exercise, and reduced stress heightens well-being. As a trip winds down, it is always soul-nourishing to take a few days to step back and reflect on all that has been gained; the culture that has been shared; the warmth of the people and the overall satisfaction of the last several weeks. I will carry it with me for the rest of my life.

Once again, it was time to turn towards home but not without one more great encounter.

Istanbul early in November! I entered this amazingly beautiful city that generated a marathon of activity. After the relaxing, warm days at the beach and in the country, a city of 10 million is a shock to the system. We were, as always, up early for breakfast, and visited the Topkapi Palace and the Grand Bazaar. Dinner in the market included rack of lamb if you wanted it, seafood, and exotic belly dancing entertainment.

In the morning, the beautiful marble dome of the Blue Mosque rose high against a clear bright sky. There were fifty to one hundred stairs leading up to the entrance. I sat at the foot of the stairs in fascination and wonder, but only briefly. Two enthusiastic local Turkish gentlemen bounded down the stairs, quickly picked up me and my chair and, before I could catch my breath, they carried me to the entrance of the mosque. There were racks for shoes and warm water baths where visitors could wash their feet before entering this sacred religious temple. How was this going to work for a wheelchair? I could not wash my wheels to remove the dust and dirt from the city streets. The locals, however, were prepared to facilitate my visit. Two young men collected me and carried me into the mosque, propping me securely on a bench where I could observe the exquisite beauty of the stained-glass windows, tile ceiling, walls and the intricate marble mosaics. The young men returned in thirty minutes to once again lift me from the bench and back to my chair, which was resting safely at the door. For them, it seemed to be no problem. They easily carried me back down to the street. The words of my son echoed in my mind. "Mom, what will you do if you get there and it is inaccessible? You won't be able to see things."

Today there had been no barrier to accessibility. I have learned to believe in, and I have experienced time and time again, the innate strength and compassion of the human spirit. Visiting the Blue Mosque was another beautiful demonstration.

I spent a whole day at the Egyptian spice market, wandering through the covered market with its 4,000 stalls. I purchased cherished spices to fill my spice jars at home and those of my family and friends.

Exploring the side streets near the market, I was delighted to find incredibly beautiful handcrafted ceramic plates for an unbelievably reasonable price. The dilemma of what to bring back for female family members was immediately solved. I purchased four beautiful plates. The lady working in the shop wrapped them in layer upon layer of newsprint. I carefully carried these plates on my lap as we wheeled down the steep hillside. Cable car tracks on the roadway were surrounded by potholes, deep crevices and uneven cobblestones. As my speed picked up, Bill and I laughed and chattered on our way back to the hotel. Then, disaster struck! The front wheel of my chair caught in a pothole, stopping the chair but not stopping me. I flew out of my chair onto the road and my precious plates crashed to the ground, breaking into thousands of pieces. Luckily I wasn't hurt and through the kindness of Turkish bystanders was quickly returned to my chair. I was committed to bringing some of these beautiful plates home. We retraced our steps so that I could repurchase my treasures. The lady in the shop was very surprised to see us back so quickly. We retraced our path downhill very slowly and carefully and those coveted plates arrived back in Canada unscathed.

It was our last day and we wanted to keep it simple. An early morning flight does not often connect with public transportation so you must be willing to spend the night in the airport. It would work.

Why pay for a hotel room when it was only to go to bed late and arise at 4:00 a.m. to make a timely trek to the airport for a 7:00 a.m. flight? There are lots of ways to deal with this dilemma. We will go to the market for those last-minute irresistible bargains; we will go out for dinner to an ethnic Turkish restaurant, relishing our last opportunity to eat local food and sip Turkish wine, returning to the airport in a semiconscious state, so the ensuing hours will have smooth passage. Don't get me wrong. We were alert, awake, and excited to absorb every last moment. Duffle bags stacked on my lap, (you know the drill; "I carry—you push") we began to roam the aisles of the then full city market, scrutinizing the local crafts to ensure that we hadn't missed one of those "must have" items, and of course, I found it. Nike running suits for my friend's son and my own boys. Hence, another bag was added to the pile on my lap.

The cooking scents wafting from the food stalls inspired us to investigate restaurants down the side streets where we found just what we were looking for, our last meal of Turkish ethnic cuisine. We went for a wonderful Turkish dinner then grabbed an evening cab to the airport. We had learned that taxis before midnight are half the price of those hired at 12:01! It would be a long trip home—15½ hours in the air plus five hours in the Frankfurt airport—before we reached Canada. Closer to the midnight hour we hailed a cab to our "hotel," the Istanbul airport.

In some countries, systems are different. Before we even entered the airport, all of our bags, placed on conveyors, entered the airport without human companionship. We stood in the long single line for forty minutes before we reached the entrance, only to find bags, boxes, and bundles, strewn haphazardly across the floor inside. It seemed that possession was nine tenths of the law, or in this case, 100% of the law. Diligently searching we found our bags and some bundles, but not the plastic bags containing the running suits that I had just bought at the market. Hopefully, they are in the hands of some child who needs them more than the Canadian boys for whom they were intended.

Six weeks in Greece and Turkey provided added rest, less stress, and more free time than I had ever experienced in my life. As I was preparing to leave this Mediterranean paradise, I searched for a way to hold on to that stress-free feeling for a few more hours. I could not imagine being back at work but all good things come to an end.

Reality would arrive soon enough.

Chapter 9

Costa Rica

"You are not really going to go to Costa Rica by yourself, are you?"

My dad was always alarmed by my solitary escapades. With a *Lonely Planet* guidebook in hand and a substantial dose of determination, I'd booked a plane ticket for a three-week stay in Costa Rica. On the day of departure, I called my father and left a cheeky message on his answering machine, "Gone to Costa Rica. I'll call you in three weeks."

Three of us departed from Vancouver; Lynn, a wheel-walking buddy with Tamara, (Lynn's friend and helper), and me.

San Jose is the capital of and largest city in Costa Rica. It is located in the central valley and is the transportation hub of this Central American nation. The young Latin American capital city was born in 1738. At 1,161 metres above sea level, the climate is consistent throughout the year, averaging 23°C. The tropical rainforest showers the city with 1,800 mm of annual rainfall, the majority falling between May and November. The city's steep topography necessitated sidewalks twenty-four inches above street level with deep drainage gutters running alongside. Curb cuts? Why, no! Tamara, who accompanied Lynn on this trip, was a strong and willing pusher. How could I negotiate this terrain that was testing even for those on feet and impossible for those of us who walk on wheels? The answer was passionately playing hacky-sac on the street. For what he regarded as a generous offering of pesos, a young man was keen to push my wheelchair and introduce me to the unique features of his hometown. In third world countries hunger is common, so regular rest stops at bakeries and corner stores for snacks were an important component of the day's agenda. We visited national buildings, La Sabana Metropolitan Park, Avenida Central—a pedestrian thoroughfare that led us through the business and cultural areas of the city—the national theatre, and the breathtaking cathedral. National coffee and Spanish foods were featured in the open-air street cafes. Our small hotel room with wall-to-wall beds relegated our two wheelchairs to the hallway. Large cities always provide me with enlightenment and education but my goal was to move to the countryside as quickly as possible.

The Caribbean and the Pacific sides of this narrow country are as different as night and day. Two days in San Jose certainly satisfied our appetite for city life. It was time to seek rural alternatives. We travelled down a swampy river in a non-motorized boat that resembled a cross between a Kon Tiki raft and a dugout canoe. Heavy, oppressive humidity weighed the air. We, who rarely sweat, found ourselves dripping with perspiration. The tropical foliage canopied the slough. Alligators swam close at the boat's sides. Shrieking monkeys swung from the trees above. Vibrant, exotic birds attracted our attention with their chattering conversations. In the past, the closest I had ever come to a toucan was on a box of Kellogg's Fruit Loops. In the jungle we saw many of these amazing birds. Parakeets and multi-coloured birds of all types shrilled in the dense foliage.

Upon arrival at the "resort," we found thatched roofed huts with bamboo walls and soft, mossy floors. The cots were made of bamboo; the mattresses, both soft and prickly, were stuffed with bamboo fronds. Light was available from the evening stars and half a moon as well as from the small flashlights we carried in the bottom of our packs. We retired early, knowing that at 4:30 a.m. the wakeup call would rouse us from our beds to venture to the beach shore where millions of tiny turtles had hatched and were hiding out under large rocks. As he lifted the rocks, the park naturalist revealed the minute babies and described their life cycle—where they came from, how they got to their present residence, when and where they would go. Our coastal education was followed by breakfast at the local pub where the special of the day was minuscule turtle eggs. I think not! The local people dug in with gusto. I thought about the babies on the beach and settled for a strong cup of Costa Rican coffee.

After three days of jungle exploration, our desire to see it all led us to our next excursion. We entered the rainforest where open seating cable cars, including one that was even wheelchair accessible, ascended through the dense plant life. We were given hooded, plastic capes, which we donned over Gortex jackets, although neither garment provided much protection from the dampness. Forty-seven percent of Costa Rica's land is covered by rainforest, which is shrinking in size annually. The government conscientiously preserves biodiversity by delegating a large percentage of the country as protected national parks and private reserves. Globally, we all gain from these efforts.

Lynn and Tamara carried on to the central part of Costa Rica where they stayed with friends for two weeks. Now was time for my solo adventure. I waited at the bus station with my bag on my lap until the local bus (a retired American school bus) skidded across the gravel to a halt. The driver and conductor looked at me with puzzlement. That's not a surprise because in many countries, the locals have never met someone in a wheelchair, so they don't know what a wheelchair is, let alone knowing how to get me on the bus. A combination of laughter and sign language provided the tools to make it work. I headed to Fortuna. When I got off the bus a dedicated, local, American tour guide approached visitors. He offered assistance on locating accommodation, arranging tours up the volcano, and suggested local eateries. He started at the beginning of the line of disembarking travellers, handing out brochures, scribbling addresses and giving directions. When he reached the back of the line queue, he directed me to stay put until he had taken care of those standing ahead of me. When he returned he said, "You will come with me to my house. I am making a matrimony bed, which I have not had time to complete. My wife will be so excited to know I am bringing someone home to stay in the guest room. It will mean I have to finish our wedding bed before we can sleep tonight."

I was reluctant to be a nuisance, but his enthusiastic encouragement convinced me to accept the hospitality that included Costa Rican cuisine including ceviche (spicy, raw shellfish with fresh lime) and Costa Rican rice laced with liquid salsa and lots of vegetables. Tropical fruit—papayas, mangoes, bananas and pineapples—grew abundantly in yards and gardens, and along the side of the road. You could reach for a refreshing snack at any time. My culinary tastes and cooking skills were stimulated my Costa Rican hostess.

Gary worked as a visitors' guide to Volcano Arenal. While I had planned to visit the mountain, I had not anticipated a one-to-one, knowledgeable, personal guide. Nor had I imagined that on this particular night, the active volcano would display her glory. Glowing molten lava flowed, and red and yellow flames lit up the sky. The cool evening air was warmed by the mountain's activity. I was awestruck by this display—yet another gift from the universe.

Before leaving Vancouver, I was told about a moderately accessible resort at Playa Hermosa on the west coast, where long sandy beaches were caressed by both gentle trickles and thundering waves. After descending from the bus stairs—gravity certainly helps when heading downhill—I inched my way along a narrow pathway that divided the thick fern foliage. At the end of the shady trail, I found myself in a sunny oasis where laughter and music filled the air. There was an open dining area adjacent to the kitchen. Small cabins stretched into the jungle. I was immediately welcomed with a hug and a gentle kiss on each cheek.

An Italian family embraced each of the lone travellers who chose this friendly, peaceful setting with love and affection and "Momma Mia," could Dad ever cook: fresh pasta and gourmet Italian sauces, bread, salads, and killer tiramisu. My attempts to refuse large helpings were unsuccessful, thank goodness! The decadent delights were irresistible.

I was led to my small, one room cabin. A small bathroom in the corner of the room housed a mini-tub which I, of course, could not think of entering independently. The tub perched precariously on four claw feet. Plastic chairs were nowhere to be seen. When I spoke with the owner about my need for something to sit upon in the tub, he disappeared and soon returned with a jovial smile and a small, dark blue, rickety wooden table that fit neatly into the bathtub.

Presto! I would be able to transfer onto the table, shower, wash my hair, and emerge a new woman—maybe! I know that's a bit of a stretch. It wobbled a little. That table and I had a few heated discussions as it tipped and creaked. Would I end up on the floor or slip into the tub? Together, the little blue table and I, through persistence and most unattractive aerobatics on my part, managed to avoid both of these dreaded, helpless situations.

While sitting on my little wooden patio, sipping espresso coffee, Marc, the young French traveller from next door approached, "Tu aime nager?"

"Je parle seulement un peu de francais. Chez moi, je nage chaque deux jours."

Marc pushed my wheelchair to the water's edge and I slipped into the clear blue brine. He guided me over the huge waves to the calm glassy surface beyond. "Vingt minutes!"

Sure enough, he reappeared in twenty minutes to assist my return to the chair. This routine repeated itself daily for three days. On the fourth morning, when I ventured into the early morning mist, there was a note on my door, "Bon vacance!" I didn't know his full name or address so I never had a chance to thoroughly thank this young man for his insight and kindness.

My mother had a friend whose daughter lived near San Jose. Wendy and I connected through e-mail and arranged to meet at my hotel. I spent a day with Wendy and her three delightful children, visiting ox-carts in Sarchi. Sarchi is the famous home of gaily decorated, wooden carretas, or oxcarts, the internationally recognized symbol of Costa Rica. These handmade, intricately painted wagons dating back to the end of the 19th century, are adorned with detailed artwork. They range in size from very small to very large. This beautiful and practical means of transportation inspires local pride and visitor fascination.

The skilled artisans and their elaborate, complex work charmed me. The children were delighted to share the specialness of their country with the Canadian visitor. They took their role of assisting my mobility quite seriously.

On our return to San Jose, I accompanied Wendy and her children to their home for dinner. The large grounds surrounding their residence were gated and guarded. The amount of crime in the city requires that the children be accompanied to and from school and that they play within their own estate or be escorted to a friend's estate by the family chauffeur. At the end of the evening, Jamie, the butler of the house, arranged for a known, trustworthy taxi driver to deliver me to the Hampton Inn where I was staying. The huge, solar heated pool, invited me each time I wheeled by. My morning flight home required a 7:30 a.m. arrival at the airport. It is always advantageous to swim before I am confined in a plane for twelve hours but the pool didn't open until 6:00 a.m. I had become acquainted with the grounds keeper and he understood my need to get in the water. He agreed to open the gate at 5:00 a.m. so that I could enjoy a long, leisurely stretch and swim before tossing my wet swimsuit and other last-minute items into my bag and heading to the airport.

When I rolled through the door of my apartment the next day close to midnight, I had one late telephone call to make.

"Hi Dad, I'm home."

Carreta, a tradition - brightly painted oxcart.

Chapter 10

Mexico

Mexico, covering almost two million square kilometres, has an estimated population of over one hundred and thirteen million. It is the world's most populous Spanish-speaking country. This newly industrialized nation has one of the world's largest economies.

The temperate and tropical zones of Mexico lie within the Tropic of Cancer. The allure of sunshine every day to warm every cell in the body draws Canadians and Americans who live in snow or cold rain six to eight months of the year. On the beaches here it is hot. In contrast, up in the mountains, it is cool—ranging to downright cold.

Until 1996, my Mexican experience consisted of a walk across the border south of San Diego into Tijuana where the day's activities included attending a bullfight with my children. The boys were so keen, shouting, "Olé Olé," and waving red tea towels in the back of the camper van. Their enthusiasm was immediately dampened when a spear from the toreador caused explosive spurts of blood to fountain from the bull's neck.

"Let's go Mom," they begged, tugging at our arms. "Let's go Dad."

We rapidly exited the stadium. We had come to the bullfight by cab for the price of $8 but as expected, the cabbies know that the bullring in the middle of the desert is twenty kilometres from town. We were a captive audience.

"I will give you a deal." The first cabbie in line smiled brightly. "Only thirty-two dollars back to town."

I was too stubborn to accept this ridiculous price so with a redhead holding onto each hand, we began to walk. I did realize that walking twenty kilometres in 40° C weather was not going to be possible and that my determination might not achieve the desired goal but in this case, it did. We had only walked for five minutes when a taxi van pulled up behind and the driver said, "Okay, I will take you back to town for twelve dollars." I readily accepted this 50% mark-up and, needless to say, this was my only experience of a bullfight.

Bill had been to several small traditional towns in Mexico. When the cool rainy November days arrived on the west coast of British Columbia, two weeks of sunny respite in Mexico drew him. *The Lonely Planet of Mexico* and Bill's expertise formed the base for our planning of this 24-day trip. We flew to Los Angeles, on to Mexico City where rainy, windy weather (surely it hadn't accompanied us) dictated an extra long stay in this huge, highly populated, expansive airport. Mexico City Airport is a city unto itself. Finally we were able to complete the trip to Oaxaca.

Located in the foothills of the Sierra Madre, Oaxaca de Juárez, or simply Oaxaca, is the capital and largest city of the Mexican state of the same name. This is a popular retreat for hikers, bird watchers, and joggers seeking respite from busy urban settings.

In Oaxaca, daytime sunshine warms the air, but after five o'clock, mountain coolness descends. Our hotel had a pool. The unheated small, deep concrete square of water was squeezed into the centre of the hotel with tall brick walls on all four sides.

I always make it clear to my travel companions that if I do get into the water, they are not to let me emerge until I have had a good twenty-minute workout. The pool water in this Mexican mountainous town was chilly. That is an understatement. It was freezing. Not one ray of sunshine ever made it past the brick walls to warm the water. Getting into a swimsuit and going to the pool's edge means I won't give up on the swim.

Shower water was solar heated so once out of the pool I was able to have the momentary comfort of a warm shower. Hair dryers never make the cut because of their weight and space. Casual is the most important part of packing. I always felt great and energized following the swim, shower, and shampoo. The feeling continued during our evening dinner at an outdoor café. I was wearing shorts and a t-shirt; my hair was soaking wet. On this occasion, I'm not sure that my enhanced mobility following my chilly dip was worth the price of the weeklong head cold that followed.

Everybody lives out of doors in comfortable warm sunshine. The cool mountainous evening air is not a deterrent to this life choice. Restaurants lack walls. Tapas and wine are the favorite fare. Outdoor markets are crowded during the day, more crowded at dusk, and jam packed into the early morning hours.

Our days were spent visiting historical sites, including Templo de Santo Domingo de Guzman, one of the most beautiful churches in the world. It is lavishly embellished with gold. Monte Alban, an archaeological Zapote site near Oaxaca, was built 2,500 years ago, before the arrival of Europeans in Mexico. It remains sacred even after being abandoned.

Teatro Macedonio de Alcala, the theatre and opera house built in 1903, has wonderful balconies and amazing acoustics. During our visit to this theatre, a small operetta group of singers were rehearsing for their upcoming performance. We experienced first-hand this impressive auditory sensation.

The Zocalo plaza, the centre of social activity in Oaxaca, is surrounded by stores. It is also home to an 18th century cathedral, Basilica de la Soledad. Another old church contained a remarkable museum of religious art, with displays ranging from pre-historic religious art, to modern day exhibits. After this extensive cultural exposure, we were ready for music, markets, beer, and local food.

Benito Juarez Market (Mercado de Benito Juarez) presented everything imaginable. The market offered food, crafts, elegant and vintage junk, gold, costume jewellery, golf clubs, toys, panties, shirts, and shoes. We bargained with vendors, haggling and laughing to achieve mutually appealing prices that were rewarding for both parties. Their culture and boisterous enthusiasm made the experience a fun, enchanting, and entertaining competition.

The tourist bus was advertised as air conditioned, fast, and more comfortable, so we purchased tickets from Oaxaca to Puerto Escondido. What fools we were. North Americans often think that better will be better but in this case; we should have referred to previous travel experiences. The trip on the tourist bus took eleven hours with frequent stops for rest breaks, visits to souvenir shops, a mid-morning snack, a restaurant for lunch, and afternoon tea time, dividing the journey into tiny time-consuming segments. It was easy to perceive that the roadside vendors and the bus drivers all benefitted financially from each other's actions.

Puerto Escondido, meaning hidden cove, is a small village in the municipality of San Pedro. This town attracts an eclectic collection of visitors (mostly surfers), backpackers, and Mexican families. Bill and I, being comfortable in a range of settings from formal decadent cruises to backpacker lodges, found this town to be delightful for a two week stay in the sunshine and on the beach.

Puerto Escondido, the "Mexican Pipeline," is one of the top ten surfing meccas in the world. The coastline offers surfing conditions for beginners and professionals alike. The beaches are home to an international surfing contest in mid November. As fate would have it, we were in the town during this event.

Two days before the 1996 world championship the beaches were already lined with banners and posters, air balloons and vendors, Sol beer umbrellas, and coolers filled with icy bottles. There were children and grandmas; moms and dads; teens and babies, but mostly surfers dressed in brilliantly coloured and patterned board shorts. They critically scrutinized the waves, preparing for a successful ride during the preliminaries to ensure that they qualified to move forward to the semi-finals at the end of the week, then to the finals on the last of this 10-day competition.

Bill and I arrived by cab amidst all these preparations. We found a delightful little Mexican hotel that promised to meet all of our needs. The comfortable room had a veranda and a large window that overlooked the beach and the enormous Pacific Ocean waves. As always, a good book is a necessary friendly companion but our resources for reading material were dwindling. There was a library on the upper floor and no elevator. But with the willing help of the bar staff, my chair and I were readily carried up the stairs. There were books for all—hardcover and paperback, moderate print, and minute print, drama and romance, recipes and travel. They were published in Spanish, French, German, Portuguese, Chinese and, of course, English. No one would be deprived of the chance to read a good book.

Next door to the hotel there was a place to eat. Happy hour there commenced at 4:00 p.m.—two great Mexican beers for the price of $1.20 CDN. We each ordered two; Bill having three, me drinking one. The local chef had two grills made from cut-in-half oil drums and perched on a metal stand. He enthusiastically encouraged those passing by to sample his gourmet cooking abilities. Not knowing what kind of meat was sizzling on the grill, I decided that vegetarian quesadillas would serve as a hot meal and reduce the risk of eating snake or dog. Bill, not sharing my skepticism, ordered the daily meat. We became close friends with this gentleman and returned many evenings to eat our nightly meal. On some occasions he had fresh fish on the grill and I ventured that far. At other times, when there was nothing there but meat, he would nod at me and ask, "Quesadilla, Seniorita? Quesadilla, Lady?" I would nod and thank him.

There were numerous quaint restaurants down the beach. We visited many of them to enjoy a variety of fresh fish but we were always drawn back to the neighbourhood chef with his open oil drums.

West from the town was a large lagoon area, popular for fishing and bird-watching. It was also a popular breeding ground for mosquitoes. Bill and mosquitoes have a close but undesirable relationship; the application of bug repellant, socks that covered his ankles and frequent swatting were futile attempts to reduce the number of bites. Each morning, new itchy welts popped up beside the ones that had been planted there the day before. I always think that I must not taste very good because the mosquitoes certainly were not attracted to me.

We returned to Oaxaca for two days before boarding a plane back to Vancouver. This time we were wiser. We took the local bus and benefited from a trip that was three hours shorter with fewer stops—only a couple at local snack stands which sold authentic ethnic food. Our bus companions included many families with children, ducks, and even a small pig.

Back in Oaxaca, street vendors closed in around us with dedicated persistence. No, I do not want a basket purse. But after ten days of repeatedly denying the same young man his offer of a basket purse, which I had no need of or no intention of using, I caved and purchased said basket. I did truck it back to Vancouver and immediately mailed it to my mother who lived in Quebec. She was delighted.

I did purchase a variety of brightly coloured Paper Mache vegetables and fruit that annually emerge from the storage closet at harvest time and take up residence in a basket or wooden bowl on my dining table. In late November they are once again tucked away until the season turns from summer to fall again.

Oaxaca is well known for its white rubbery cheese. In December I open the doors of my home to friends, family, acquaintances, and strangers, to share the warm fuzzies of the holiday season. My habit is always to prepare food that is native to the countries that I have most recently visited.

So in December 1996, my all-day brunch featured tortillas and Oaxacan cheese.

Chapter 11

Guatemala

"Why Guatemala?" he asked.

"Because I have enough frequent flyer points for two round trip airfares and I have never been there before."

My dad rolled his eyes with exasperation. "I should know better than to ask."

Guatemala beckoned. But I knew I could not go alone. My friend Lourdes (Lou) was up to the task.

I will consider any trip if it is reasonably economical and the destination is new to me. Additionally, if the weather is warmer and sunnier than I am currently experiencing in Vancouver, it adds even more weight to the "let's take this trip" side of the scale. So we chose Guatemala.

Two round trip airfares came by email many weeks prior to our scheduled departure of Monday, November 5, 2007. Wait! How crazy is this? If those seats are available to leave on Saturday, Lou will not miss any additional work time and our trip could be extended by two days. The airline didn't see it that way. A daily phone call to American Airlines continued to net a negative response to my change request. The flight we needed was full. On November 2, however, two seats became vacant. Hooray! We were leaving on Saturday, November 3. By departing on Saturday, transportation to the airport became easier and much more fun. Leaving on a Monday morning meant a cab was the only option. On Saturday, friends could be coerced into taking the world travellers to the airport.

Seated in business class, I would have my choice of a hot

cheese omelette, sausages, croissants, yogurt, juice, coffee, and whatever else I might desire. In the 21st century, real food in economy class is virtually non-existent on domestic flights and minimal on international flights. Sitting in business or first class offers the only deluxe nourishment.

When we arrived in Guatemala City at 9:00 p.m., I knew from experience that finding accommodation after dark, in a city of six million people, in a non-English speaking country (my Spanish is minimal) might be a considerable challenge. The airline had offered an option of a first night's hotel along with our plane ticket. The assigned hotel, the Biltmore Express, was also the name of a hotel located in a sketchy area of Vancouver so I was initially a bit concerned. Leaving the airport, we located the hotel minivan. A very large driver operated the shuttle service. He cheerfully and easily picked me up and plunked me down on the seat. At the Biltmore Express, we were met by pleasant surroundings and an attentive staff at the front desk. They communicated fluently in English and Spanish. Our room was well adapted for persons with a disability. Lou and I easily shared the immense king-sized bed with eight pillows. A huge eiderdown comforter exuded welcome. The room had a kitchenette, a small refrigerator filled with snacks and beverages, a microwave, flat screen TV, and most beneficial of all, a shower that I could use. On arising in the early morn, we were treated to breakfast at the hotel, then secured a taxi to the city of Antigua, the first leg of our trip. Antigua is where travellers go to arrange other travels and excursions in Guatemala.

Once in Antigua, the first order of the day was to secure accommodation for one night. Visiting the tourist office, we spoke with one woman who was visiting from Finland. She had the same goal and adamantly advised us, "Do not go to the Yellow House. It is just too primitive!"

Lou and I had already selected the Yellow House as our first choice from the descriptions in the guidebook. As was commonly our habit, I guarded the luggage while Lou explored the guesthouse to check for safe, clean beds. Comfort is desirable but not always achievable. The Yellow House, from our perspective, was delightful. We were shown a room with three beds, a tall shelf which could be used for clothing or toiletries, and a table with a lamp between two beds. A window at one end of the room was covered with basic curtains. Instead of a view of the outdoors it offered a view of the interior hallway. A large backpack leaned against one of the beds. The innkeeper advised us that the backpack was owned by a gentleman and looked at us with hesitation. "That's ok," Lou and I said in unison. We had both been in dorm rooms in the past and were comfortable with the protocol. We slept in shorts and t-shirts. Rather than being concerned about a strange man in the other bed, we looked forward to learning more about a fellow traveller and the country of his residence. Our roommate turned out to be a nice fellow form Sweden.

The washroom was located across the hall but the doorway would not admit my wheelchair. My usual process of transferring to a plastic chair, Lou pulling the plastic chair into the washroom, transferring to the toilet, and then doing everything in reverse, made the washroom usable for me. Once again I would have to create my own accessibility.

At the end of the hallway, a large common area overflowed with tropical plants, bamboo chairs, ledges to sit upon, tables, and an open sunroof. Fellow travellers met here to share the highlights, trials, and tribulations of the day. This is where we would learn where to go, where not to go, how to get there, how not to get there, what to pay, what not to pay. In the early evening, we left our hotel to explore and satisfy our growing hunger pangs. For the enormous price of three Canadian dollars, we were treated to chicken, rice, salad, hot or cold lemonade, fresh fruit, homemade bread, and churned unsalted butter.

The capital of Guatemala, Antigua, was founded in 1543 by the Spanish. Cobblestone streets are composed of six- to twelve-inch round stones cemented in place. Wheelchair accessibility? Non-existent! The sidewalks were narrow, wide, smooth, or bumpy. At many corners, a small, blue square universal wheelchair symbol was painted on the sidewalk. There were no curb cuts so I could never figure out what they were trying to indicate and there were no other clues. Despite the mobility challenges, we were able to explore the Arco de Santa Catalina, an archway built in the 17th century between a convent and the school to allow private passage for cloistered nuns. At one time, all roads in Guatemala led from the Palicio National de la Cultura, the palace of the president of the state, an architectural monument built in the 1500s. I was content to be left at the Cathedral de Santiago to explore the statues, stained glass windows, candles, and to absorb the scents of various types of incense while Lou investigated the back alleys to become familiar with the community and to find a quaint eating-place for our next meal.

We found a Guatemalan eatery and enjoyed foods similar to that of Mexico, Guatemala's neighbor to the north. Throughout our stay we would take pleasure in Central American cuisine. The starting point of all meals was rice, supplemented by beans, corn, cheeses, and tortillas. The tortilla, a thin, flat corn cake, is a Guatemalan staple. It can be as cheap as five cents on the street. To spruce up the basic corn tortilla and beans, guacamole, spiced mango, and lime were frequent accompaniments.

At the Yellow House, we made the acquaintance of Daniel and Eva, two travellers from Germany. Eva had been staying at the lake, Lego de Atitlan, for the past eight weeks. She came to Antigua to expand her horizons but found the cost of hotels and food in the city was double. The higher prices did not work for her travel budget so after one night in Antigua, she returned to the lake. On our third day in Antigua, Daniel, Lou and I headed to the lake deciding that the most economical and fun way to travel would be on a chicken bus (all portable animals are welcome). Chicken buses are crowded—not only with people but often with chickens, ducks, pigs, and goats.

Public buses in Central America are often discarded school buses from America. Some still display the bright yellow colour and black "School Bus" lettering. Others were painted to fit into the modern world. Fluorescent stripes swirled down the side of one bus. Vivid red flames rose from the wheel well to the base of the windows of another. Other vehicles displayed brightly coloured flowers, environmental scenes of mountains and volcanoes, or blue oceans with multi-coloured tropical fish.

There are no bus stops, only a conductor leaning from the steps and barking out the bus's destination as the vehicle whips around the corners of the city streets. If one's Spanish is adequate and your hearing is good, you can identify the destination and shout out your desire for the bus to stop. Stops are generally a lengthy thirty seconds. Daniel's fluency in Spanish was a godsend. He told the conductor of our need for the bus to stop long enough for me to be lifted onto the bus and to throw the packs and chair up onto the roof. Roads are narrow and winding. Buses travel at breakneck speed. Fortunately, the bus driver recognized the value of my wheelchair. He tied it to the luggage rack with a few small pieces of rope to make sure that it would not fly off as the bus mounted hills, descended valleys and rounded corners. The bus was full and became fuller. People appeared out of nowhere. Sometimes there was a village or a visible farmhouse, other times a pathway, and still other times, not even a disturbance in the blowing grain. Our bus came to an abrupt stop at the summit of a hill. We looked with questioning faces at the driver who indicated that it was time for us to exit. We found ourselves standing on the edge of the road with our packs. A few other bus passengers were in the same predicament—no town, no village. A lone gas pump stood in a gravel patch on the side of the road next to a few tables manned by farmers selling fresh produce. Daniel's Spanish once again became our most valuable asset.

"It's okay," he said, "another bus will be along shortly. It is taking the route leading to the lake."

Fifteen minutes later, another speeding, rickety bus squealed to a halt. We loaded our belongings onto the roof and our bodies into a seat.

People are reluctant to give up their seats near the front of the bus but because I cannot walk, some very kindly souls vacated their spot in the front seat. At the first stop, a tiny elderly lady mounted the stairs of the bus carrying a large basket filled with vegetables. She placed the basket in the aisle but clearly did not want to lose sight of her most precious possession. There were two of us already seated on the front seat but we pressed closer and the tiny lady was able to squeeze in beside us. She lovingly touched my knees and whispered in broken English, "Good Good" and "Thank." I nodded my appreciation of her gratitude and we became immediate friends.

Over the next ten kilometres, children in school uniforms scampered onto the bus. It was the end of the school day and they were heading home. The bus careened over a hill and rounded the corner, squealing to a stop at a filling station where we were again directed to depart and to wait for the next chicken bus. While we waited, a minimum of fifteen buses passed by, their conductors shouting destinations that held no resemblance to "Lago de Atitlan." Finally it came! A conductor was shouting, "To the lake, Atitlan, Atitlan, to the lake."

Three chicken buses later, as the sun settled in the sky, we arrived at the dock where a boat with a full complement of passengers waited to take us to San Pedro. How to get to the boat? I saw stairs, gravel, and a wooden dock with wide spaces between the boards. It became manageable with the help of Daniel and the boatman who manoeuvered the chair and our packs down the steep wood ramp.

As the wind picked up, small white caps broke the water's surface.

"I don't like water," exclaimed Daniel, "but I am going to San Pedro."

His fear of water generated some decided greenness around his gills. I produced a few spoonfuls of yogurt, a Gravol tablet, and lots of reassurance and encouragement. These seemed to settle his nerves, albeit minimally.

It was a small wooden, partially covered boat. Backless benches stretched from side to side. A sign stated that the capacity was twelve. My last count was seventeen with a few more coming. Keyhole lifejackets lined the ceiling. There were twelve of them. One could only hope that if anything went wrong, that the route taken would be close to shore and that some of us could swim.

We arrived safely in San Pedro in the dark. The accommodation that Eva had recommended was full so we secured the first available room, recognizing that this would only be our choice for the first eight hours. The washroom facilities were unusable—a blocked toilet gave permission for the overwhelming smell of sewage to seep into the bedroom. The warm humid air was motionless with no fan—NO FUN! As is always the case, we survived our one night. In the morning, I guarded the luggage while Lou investigated other options for a clean, safe bed. She returned after twenty minutes with cheerful excitement and the news that she had found something that was ramped!

Could this be possible in a third world country in Central America? Yes, in fact, the hotel/hostel was ramped but the ramps consisted of two narrow cement trails spanning six feet of grass. In order to move up and down the hill, I had one wheel on the grass and one on the concrete. The three stairs at the bottom were uneven in height and width. However, the room had spacious diamond shaped windows on two sides—one overlooking the lake, the other overlooking a daunting active volcano. The room was large enough for two beds, our luggage—consisting of one backpack and a small nylon bag—table, chair, and a corner writing desk. The washroom across the hall had a level entry. After some spatial assessment, we decided I could shower, brush teeth, wash, and manage daily personal care with little issue as long as I faced in one direction and moved minimally.

Breakfast was at a hostel owned and operated by three Israeli men. The first meal of the day usually includes tortillas and beans supplemented by eggs and plantain, and of course a range of tropical fruit—bananas, papaya, mangoes, and avocado. At this hostel we were delighted to find that the typical fare was complimented by baked eggplant stuffed with mozzarella cheese and spices. It was a welcome way to start the day. Arising in the very early morning necessitates the inclusion of a large mug of world famous, piping hot Guatemalan coffee. It is strong enough for a spoon to stand mid-cup, unattended.

We explored the town—a series of Spanish-language schools, one gravel roadway along the hillside, an elementary school, and small bistros overlooking the lake. A level, grassy area halfway between the guesthouse and the lake was a great place to hang out, read, and absorb the beauty and peacefulness around us.

Lago de Atitlan is situated in a basin surrounded by steep volcanic hills and the many villages around the lake are accessible only by water travel. Lago de Atitlan spans eighteen kilometres from north to south, eight kilometers from east to west. The lake depth exceeds three hundred metres. Warm sun and blue water made the lake inviting, but the locals suggested the possibility of parasites and pollution. I decided to swim elsewhere.

The tiny communities around the lake offered relaxation, sunshine, a blend of traditional Central American culture, and were meeting places for world travellers, young and old. The steep hillsides, composed of volcanic ash, were endowed with hiking trails used by shepherds and their flocks, and green fields dotted with alpine flowers. The atmosphere was enhanced by sunrises and sunsets over the mountaintops, and thunderheads that brought rain and lightning.

Our next stop was Flores. We negotiated the price of a shuttle flight from San Pedro to Guatemala City airport. In this country, it is customary to negotiate for everything. The thirty-minute flight was definitely more attractive than the eleven and a half-hour bus ride. We arrived in Flores on a Friday evening, finding only a few available accommodations. Despite the large price tag, we took the first room that met our needs for the night, deciding that on Saturday morning we would search the streets for more economical sleeping quarters. Our usual practice prevailed. I sat on the street corner with the luggage while Lou investigated. She quickly returned with a triumphant, "I have it!"

A small family hotel with a clean and comfortable spacious room, washroom, and shower facilities that were more than manageable, would be our home for the next four days. For the length of our stay, the owner of the house willingly assisted us to navigate the three stairs at the entrance.

Our primary goal on the first day was to make arrangements for a trip to Tikal. Once again, I had to convince vendors that: Yes, I could manage the trip in a wheelchair; Yes, I could cope with the jungle; and no, I was not so fragile that I would dissolve on the rough ride over the 4-wheel drive road. The Sunrise Tour picked us up at the hotel at 3:30 a.m. and we arrived at the UNESCO World Heritage Site, Tikal, at 5:30 to see the sun rise over the volcanic hills. Lou and the group trekked four kilometres through the jungle to the temple. I travelled this distance in a 4-wheel drive vehicle. The driver deposited me at the base of the temple. As he left me alone, I assured him that the dark and the jungle noises were not a concern for me. It was still pitch black, damp and cool. Howler monkeys swung noisily through the branches of the ancient trees. Their loud, guttural calls echoed throughout the jungle. As I sat waiting and anticipating the arrival of my travel companions, two small spider monkeys, black with white tails, scurried by brushing my feet. The rustling behind me was the sound of two armadillos shuffling along the jungle floor, their armoured backs shifting back and forth with each step.

After ninety minutes, the walking group emerged from the thick foliage. They split into two, one English-speaking, one Spanish, to explore together this inspirational setting. Lou went with the English-speaking group. I joined the Spanish group because there were three muscular men who eagerly included me and my wheeled transportation. The guide spoke mostly in Spanish but it was spattered with enough English that I learned some of the history and the spectacular facts about Tikal. My three newly found friends were not content to leave me behind while they investigated narrow jungle pathways, small caverns disguised by rock formations, etched hieroglyphics, and the amazing flora and fauna. I accompanied them every step of the way. After several hours of exploration, we all met in the central square, a large grassy field where towering pyramids rose above the green jungle canopy, to catch the rising sun.

Tikal's Mayan construction is 3,500 years old. The central compound of the park is surrounded by ancient ruins. The melodic conversations of the tropical birds brought life to the structures of yesteryear. A large yellow-orange toucan, his enormous beak nodding, greeted us from the lower frond of a bamboo. The park is a photographer's paradise—Mayan sites, jungle ecology, exotic animals and birds. Arriving in the parking lot by late in the afternoon, we left this Shangri-La, returning by minibus to the rustic streets of Flores.

As the trip was coming to an end, a minimal amount of shopping on the streets of Flores was on the schedule. We found a small café tucked in a corner with tall bamboo chairs, glass tables, a simple eight-item menu and powerful Guatemalan coffee served in pottery mugs. The placemats and napkins were of brightly coloured woven cloth. As we sipped coffee and savoured this Central American cuisine, European classical music surrounded us. We emerged from this peaceful setting to embark upon a three-hour shopping experience. Every vendor displayed the same wares. It was simply a matter of bargaining for the best available price. There was little to buy. We settled on rain sticks for children at home, a small carved mask, miniature Mayan statues, souvenir gifts for friends. Our final night, before our return to the big city, found us packing and unpacking, squishing items into corners, discarding tattered and worn panties and t-shirts, reorganizing our bags over and over again to ensure that all items fit.

The final day in Flores brought rain. Of course, the checkout at the hotel was noon and our flight from Flores to Guatemala City was not until 6:00 p.m. Our plans to play cards in the sun by the lake, read, or doze, were quickly drowned by huge raindrops. What else was there to do? Eat! So we found an outdoor covered café and indulged in a leisurely late lunch/early dinner, then taxied to the airport. On our arrival in Guatemala City, the Biltmore's trusty Spanish bus driver effortlessly flung the wheelchair and our luggage into the shuttle, then gently deposited me on a seat.

We were looking forward to relaxing in our comfortable room of two weeks ago, but our reservation had been given away to members of a large conference group.

"It is okay, Madam. We will upgrade you to the Westin," the smiling manager told me.

We entered the Westin, an adjoining hotel, via the service elevator. The decadent lobby was framed by gilded pillars and mirrors, and there were deep soft lounge chairs, velvet swag window coverings and other finery that far outshone the condition of the room we were supposed to be staying in.

"We will send the maintenance man to remove the bathroom door. It will be fine for you," the smiling receptionist told me.

I was doubtful.

"Perhaps it would be best if we looked at the room before the maintenance man goes through any unnecessary work."

We followed the manger to the room, where Lou and I looked skeptically at each other. No amount of maintenance work would make the bathroom door wide enough to admit my wheelchair. It just would NOT.

"But we are full." The manager spread his hands. "There are no other rooms available."

I was not easily deterred. The reservation for the handicapped room had been made two weeks in advance. We returned to the Biltmore Express through the service tunnel and elevator. We were met by the pleasant, friendly staff and the homey atmosphere that, for us, far outweighed the superficial elegance of the supposed upgrade at the Westin. To our delight, the well-adapted room was now available. Its previous occupants had been escorted to an adjacent room. After a warm shower, shampoo, and hot cup of tea, we settled into the large king-sized bed under a substantial eight-inch thick duck down duvet. We ate a satisfying breakfast at the hotel and, at the airport, we checked our bags, leaving enough time to explore and to purchase duty free perfume and liquor.

I put on my one pair of long pants knowing that November weather in Vancouver would be a stark contrast to the "shorts and t-shirt" weather of Guatemala.

Chapter 12

South America

1997: Patrick's Adventure

"Have You Lost Your Mind?"

Could I instill in my sons the thrill I feel when the captain announces, "Fasten your seatbelts"? Would Patrick and Timothy feel the adrenaline rush as the engine roared? Would they feel the buzz in their stomachs as the soaring bird lifted off the runway? I always told my boys that when they graduated from university (with two degrees each), that their graduation gift from their mother would consist of round trip airfare anywhere in the world, to the destination of their choice. My desire was an attempt to facilitate their growth and encourage them to spread their wings.

Patrick completed law school at UBC in April, 1997. South America was his chosen reward. We had both been bitten by the travel bug and, by 1997, both Patrick and I had travelled to new lands, encountered fascinating and intriguing cultures. We had travel experiences that would intimidate some, but to quote my son, "Mom, it's gotta be fun!" We chatted about his forthcoming trip, examining guidebooks, reviewing immunization needs and comparing equipment and resources that he might need for four months in a foreign, non-English-speaking land.

Somehow—don't ask me how—we decided that it would be really cool if Mum accompanied Patrick for the first several weeks of his trip. We discussed and selected the juiciest destination offerings from the banquet table of the northernmost countries of South America. We agreed that while Mum was present, I would pay for the trip and when I returned to Canada, Patrick would be left with a return air ticket and his own ingenuity. When left on his own in the presence of excitement and an education in real life, it may be tempting to continue down new paths. My hope was that the provided ticket home would entice Patrick to return to Vancouver to complete his education but I would be content to support whatever course he chose. For me, this venture was, another once-in-a-lifetime opportunity. I would travel to a new continent and I would do so with my firstborn son.

In preparation for the trip, I attended a level 1 Spanish evening class at the local secondary school. I combed the shelves of the library for books and resources. My search was rewarded by discovering conversational tapes, "Learn Spanish in Your Car." For the next three months, on the way to work, on the way home, on the way to the pool, to the grocery store, sitting in dead stop traffic – wherever I drove – I listened to Spanish in the car. By the time I arrived in Peru, I could quite comfortably ask, "Where is the train station? What time does the bus come? We would like a room for the night. Do you have hot water for showers?"

The bonus was that I could read a menu. Don't ask how my Spanish is today because three months after returning home to a 100% English speaking environment, Spanish became a little sketchy. However, I can still order two beers please, "Dos cervezas por favor."

We decided to share five weeks of foreign travel. As the day of departure approached, some mornings when I awoke at 5:00 a.m. I would think, "This will be great." On other mornings, I would awake to, "Have you lost your mind?" Yes, my son had been home for Christmas and perhaps had stayed, on some occasions, at my apartment for a night or two, but he had had minimal exposure to a mother who mobilized in a wheelchair. At that time, I could wall-walk a little, shower while sitting on a chair, dress, get in and out of bed, and manage independently in washrooms. All of these tasks required an inordinate amount of time, not to mention energy and risk.

I had no need to worry. We spent five weeks enjoying wonder and laughter. In those days together, we developed patience, understanding, and warmer comfort with one another than we had ever known before.

Patrick's father delivered us to the Vancouver airport on the morning of April 15; American Airlines would carry as to Dallas, Miami, and then to Lima, Peru. In previous years I could always look forward to a meal on the airplane. In 1997, the trend towards airline economy was raising its head. In Miami, we were passed a paper bag that contained a bran muffin and a banana whose level of ripeness, in my kitchen, would relegate it to banana bread.

Visiting a foreign land is always accompanied by the risk of gastroenteritis. Before landing in Lima, Patrick became ill, very ill indeed. On arrival on the tarmac, we found a small walled flower garden outside the terminal where I left Patrick with his head hanging over the edge of the wall, "woofing his cookies" around the roots of the foliage.

Large cities (more than eight million people) offer little attraction for either of us, so our choice was to avoid the downtown cosmopolitan streets of Lima, and make an immediate transfer from the Lima airport to Cuzco, without visiting the urban capital of Peru. While Patrick nursed his very sick body, I wheeled through the airport, sneaking into each corner and negotiating with black market sellers to purchase two plane tickets to Cuzco.

With the tickets in my hand, I went back to the silent garden to share my success with Patrick. "Just stay where you are," I told him. "See if you can get stabilized by 6:00 a.m. It is another 85-minute flight to Cuzco." "I'll try," he said, sounding miserable. "But I can't promise."

I took his pack and my bag to check-in at the airline counter where the authorized tickets, in Patrick's and my name, waited. I struggled for optimism. I hoped Patrick would be able to board that plane at 6:00 a.m. It so reminded me of twenty years ago when my young boys became ill with a cold, flu, chicken pox, or measles. I was reliving that helpless feeling of "I just want to make him well."

He was able to make the flight. At the Cuzco airport, we found a taxi driver who could help. Between his slight English and my minimal Spanish, we were able to find a hotel room with an attached bathroom and minimal stairs. It was located close to city sights so that when Patrick was better, we could resume the role of active travellers. We also wanted reasonable access to the Inca ruins. We purchased bottled water and hibernated for forty-eight hours in our hotel. Patrick recovered from jet lag and his gastritis. I used the time to investigate guidebooks and brochures, scribble some postcards to send home, and finish a novel that was supposed to last for two weeks.

Two days later, Patrick was better. We hiked (Patrick hiked, I got pushed) into the mountains where the Inca ruins revealed how people lived thousands of years ago. These sites are now protected, but until 1951 they were open to the removal of precious ancient artifacts. Many beautiful stone cathedrals and heritage buildings in Cuzco were constructed with rock pillaged from the ruins.

It was hot! We carried multiple bottles of water in Patrick's daypack and in the back of my chair, knowing that drinking lots of fluid is essential to prevent altitude sickness and dehydration. After consuming several litres of water the need to use the washroom predictably struck.

"But Mom, you can't pee in the ruins," Patrick protested when I told him my intent. "This setting is sacred."

"Sacred or not, my bladder will not accommodate one more sip of water or one more bump on the rocky path," I told him firmly. I slid behind a large ancient ruin while Patrick stood sentry duty, ensuring my privacy. Relieved and feeling four pounds lighter, I returned to the trekking route. Patrick was quite disgusted with his mother. But it was not just his mom. Everyone's bladder capacity overflows at about two litres. Within a few hours, as the temperature rose and Patrick continued to exert himself on the Inca trail, consuming vast quantities of water. He gave me a sheepish look. "Mom, I have to go behind a rock," he said.

Altitude sickness manifests differently for different people, for different reasons, at different elevations. We departed from Cuzco (3,400 metres) and climbed steadily upwards to an altitude of more than of 4,000 metres. Altitude sickness manifests itself first as water retention, or edema, that may begin in the feet and ankles. At this point, it is not a big deal. You just don't have the attractive slim ankles that you might have at home. As edema becomes more generalized in the body, it affects the lungs as pulmonary edema, causing shortness of breath. The tiniest of headaches warns of cerebral edema which is water on the brain. When this occurs, it is time to start down with due haste. Medication like Diamox (a diuretic) is carried by most mountain hikers and is used either as a preventive measure or when symptoms occur.

Travellers learn that the locals know best and their advice should be heeded. On the trail, we encountered a Peruvian alpine shepherd whose English was adequate enough to introduce us to the plant "moonya," which he advocated as a guaranteed prevention of altitude sickness. "Just sniff the moonya," he told us.

We listened closely and learned the characteristics of the moonya plant. Each day while hiking along the Inca trail, into the mountains and at Machu Picchu, we searched out the moonya plant and diligently sniffed the leaves. The trusty shepherd also suggested drinking coca tea, a stimulant herbal tea native to the Andes Mountains. Unfortunately, coca tea is the source of the drug cocaine. I don't tolerate it well but Patrick indulged throughout the day, whenever coca tea was offered by the dwellers of the alpine huts. Who knows whether it was psychological optimism, the moonya, the coca tea, or just a fact of life, but neither of us experienced even minor altitude sickness. We explored the Inca ruins above Cuzco for two or three days then decided that it was time to investigate the local area before venturing on to Machu Picchu. In Cuzco, the regional capital of Peru, we visited the cathedrals, the natural history museum, and the university.

We wandered into the Peruvian market. My decision to not eat meat in third world countries where refrigeration is rare was reinforced by the tables of raw meat sitting out in the heat, covered with flies. There was no way! A large plate of aros blanca, or white rice, more than satisfied my appetite. Surprisingly, the vegetarian pizza in Peru had a thin crust and was more than delicious. As we wandered the stalls in the market I looked back to see Patrick clutching the side of his pants pocket and heard him say through clenched teeth, "I don't think you want to be there."

A local man had his hand deep into Patrick's pocket, his wrist now clasped tightly in my son's hand. Fear and concern spread over the man's face as he observed police officials wandering the aisles attempting to keep pickpockets and shoplifters in control. As always, our passports and financial resources were tucked into a money belt or neck safe but we kept ten dollars of local currency handy so that we could make a purchase in the market and keep our personal resources hidden. Local pickpockets are also aware of this common travellers habit; ten dollars is better than nothing.

"Just drop what you have, and away you go," Patrick instructed. And that is exactly what happened. The pickpocket discreetly disappeared into the crowd.

The streets of Cuzco and the market paths were lined with beggars who energetically implored me to give them money. This caused me some degree of puzzlement.

"Patrick," I said, "Why are they begging from me? I'm sitting in a wheelchair and obviously my abilities are restricted. You, a young man, are tripping along in a sprightly manner. They are ignoring you."

"Mum, it is obvious to them that someone who owns a wheelchair like yours and who has the resources to travel to South America, is not poverty stricken." Patrick smirked. "They think that your experience with disability will generate empathy for their situation."

Machu Picchu is a pre-Columbian Inca site located 2,400 metres above sea level. Situated on a mountain ridge, it is often referred to as "The Lost City of the Incas." Built around the year 1450, abandoned a hundred years later at the time of the Spanish conquest of the Inca Empire, it was forgotten for centuries. The site came to worldwide attention in 1911. Machu Picchu was declared a Peruvian Historical Sanctuary in 1981 and a UNESCO World Heritage Site in 1983. The city was built in the classical Inca style with polished dry-stone walls. The most popular buildings are the Intihuatana, the Temple of the Sun, and the Room of the Three Windows, located in the Sacred District of Machu Picchu.

There were two options—take a tourist bus for a one-day excursion or take the local train to the closest town on the Urubamba River, Aguas Calientes. For the adventure traveller, a local train is the only choice.

Before leaving Vancouver, we had decided that we would each pack two books that our travel partner would also be interested in reading. Therefore, four books each should be plenty for a five-week trip in South America. This was not the case! The train, scheduled to depart at 7:00 a.m., in actuality, pulled into the station at 9:15 a.m. We soon learned that train schedules, written with chalk on a blackboard in the station, are seldom accurate. Leaving the station, while waiting for a train, is not an option. It might arrive at any moment. The train pauses at the station for one to three minutes and if you miss today's train, it might be tomorrow or the next day before you have the opportunity to travel again.

Fortunately, both Patrick and I are avid readers so as we waited for transportation, we always had our books. Along the South American route we found several English book exchanges where we could, for a very small cost, exchange two of our books for two fresh ones. Hence, in my five weeks in South America, I devoured nine books.

The train ride along the river presented glorious scenery, incredible beauty, and the eye opening characteristics of local communities. Towns were small, perhaps three or four dwellings with their doors very close to the tracks. Toddlers played on the rail ties, and were scooped up by their moms when the train whistle sounded. The houses were made of old wood, scraps of corrugated metal, with dirt floors, and no windows. Smoke rose through holes in the roof. A chimney? Of course not! Animals lived both outdoors and in, keeping close company with the family. In the cold night air, body heat of the animals helped reduce the need for wood fuel.

At every village, the train slowed. Residents leaped from a platform that varied from one metre below the tracks to two metres above. They sold everything. Hunger was never a concern for railway passengers. The town folk sold slabs of barbecued pork, cobs of corn, grilled sweet potatoes, unidentifiable garden greens, and of course, coca tea. The local inhabitants would leap on at one village and depart at the next, making their way home along the railroad tracks with their precious earnings, perhaps six Peruvian neuvo sol (3 neuvo sol were equivalent to $1 USD).

In the late evening, we arrived at Aguas Calientes where the train screeched to a halt for the three-minute stop. The stone platform was four feet above us, leaving a narrow space between the railway car and the edge of the platform. When the train car door opened, Patrick shouted to a man above, "Please catch!"

He flung my wheelchair up onto the concrete platform. The chair was quickly followed by myself and the backpack. Then the man, lying on his stomach, reached a hand down to offer Patrick a grip and a pull. Safely on the platform, we watched as the train whistled and disappeared along the steep riverbank into the night.

We found accommodation right on the train platform. The small, weathered wooden structure advertised, "Welcome, Guests." The only guestroom available for rent suited our needs perfectly. Two single beds were separated by enough space to allow a wheelchair. A bathroom outside housed only a toilet. Washing facilities were available in the concrete laundry tub off the patio. The proprietors knocked on our door to offer delicious thick vegetable lamb soup that filled our empty stomachs.

On the following morning, we explored by walking a half-mile along the bank above the tracks looking for a level place to cross into the town. A large wooden cathedral overpowered the small, rustic residential dwellings. Commercial enterprises included small outdoor vegetable kiosks, a medical clinic and what looked like a blacksmith or tool making shop. Children were hurrying to school in immaculately clean white shirts and navy blue pants and tunics.

We boarded a bus to Machu Picchu where we found a long line of locals and tourists climbing two to three hundred metres of steep, uneven, rocky steps. Patrick's patience seemed unending as he pulled my chair backwards up the jagged stairs. After thirty minutes, a young Australian man jumped out of the crowd shouting, "I can't believe nobody has offered to help."

He accompanied Patrick and I to the entrance gate where we were able to mobilize along uneven gravel pathways. The very old stone structures oozed ancient history and fascinated us at every turn. I could see Patrick's eyes roaming the volcanic mountain at the base of the ancient city and sensed his desire to climb that peak.

"But Mom, I can't leave you alone," he protested when I told him to go climb it.

"Of course you can," I told him. "Just go Patrick. Just go. Leave me in a quiet, spiritual spot with a litre of water and a good book. I will be just fine."

So, off he went, rewarding himself with the hike and rewarding me with several hours of peaceful introspection. There was too much to absorb in a one-day visit so we returned again and again over the next three days.

For our trip back to Cuzco, we boarded the train closer to the town, where the climb was only one metre above the tracks instead of two. The local people jumped in to help. There were no empty seats on the train. Patrick stretched out on the floor leaning against the backpack and I dozed upright in my wheelchair.

Determined to experience all the possible highlights in Peru, we decided that a trip to the jungle was mandatory. We booked bus transportation for the following morning, and arrived at the depot at 6:00 a.m. It was a dirt field.

There was little space on the bus. Patrick's pack was placed between my knees with water, snacks, and the *Lonely Planet of South America*. Our novels to read in slow and slack times were tucked around our hips. The bus alternated between crawling at a snail's pace and speeding along like a bat out of hell. The roadway was a narrow, steep, uneven gravel thoroughfare between the trees. We laughed, chatted, dozed, and waited impatiently to reach the final destination—anticipating a jungle campsite, night sounds of the deep tropical forest, seeing monkeys and rain forest wildlife. The image in our minds was far from reality that we encountered. After eleven hours of travel, our vehicle came to a dead stop, overlooking a river that had washed out the road.

There was an hour of consulting and considering before a decision was reached. We could go no further. We would not see a jungle camp today. The only option was to turn around and head back to Cuzco. Oh well! A day, and a night, on the bus provided lots of scenery and saved us the cost of one night's hotel accommodation!

Were we game to try it again? Yes of course! The next day we selected a different jungle route. After four hours of riding we arrived at camp. We spent an afternoon exploring. Patrick went deep into the jungle with other adventure travellers. One of the camp residents enthusiastically propelled me, and my wheelchair, along jungle trails. I saw monkeys and snakes; heard macaws; and was amazed by the gargantuan foliage surrounding me. In the evening we sat outside eating rice with delicious tuberous and leafy vegetables. We listened to drum music and melodies played on wood pipes before retiring to our tent under the jungle canopy for the night. We returned safely to Cuzco the following day before midnight. It was all worth it.

Quito, Ecuador was our next destination. From here we could arrange a trip to the Galapagos Islands. We needed Ecuadorian cash so we wandered the streets of Quito to finally find an ATM in a tall, gold, shiny building. We then began to comb the avenues, finding travel companies that offered trips to the Galapagos Islands in varied and all measures of circumstance. Would we stay on a boat? Travel by boat between islands and sleep on land? Would we go for a day? A week? A month? Would we find something that could accommodate me in a chair and yet satisfy our need to see what the Galapagos had to offer? After several hours of investigation, we decided on a boat between islands and sleeping in cottages on land at night.

Could we book a trip using Visa? Of course not! The sum total of our travellers' cheques did not meet the price. Once again, we wandered the streets searching for that ATM we had previously used.

"I think it's down here. It was a gold building," I announced. "There is a park with a fountain nearby."

"The damned ATM must be close. That sign looks familiar," Patrick exclaimed. "The travel agent closes at seven o'clock. We have to find it."

Three hours later we finally found the machine and withdrew the maximum allowed cash.

Because Patrick had used the traveller's cheques that were supposed to cover his travelling expenses for the next several months, I reassured him that on my return to Vancouver, I would deposit an equivalent amount into his account so that he could access funds through bank machines for the remainder of his stay.

We travelled by boat between the islands, stopping periodically for an hour, an afternoon, a day, a night. At our first island stop, we were fascinated by the uninhibited wildlife and their fearlessness around humans. After lunch, I was waiting outside. An owl perched on a wood rail fence at arm's length from me, and looked into my eyes without fear. "Whooo are you?" it seemed to be saying.

One evening, we landed on an island where Patrick had to

pull my chair through two hundred metres of deep, soft sand to reach the lodge. I could see the exhaustion seeping from his pores. But, true to form, when we finally arrived at our cabin, he simply said, "I'm going for a swim." After a half hour dip in the warm ocean water he returned, showered, and emerged with a grin on his face. "Now it's time for dinner," he said cheerfully.

The following day, our boat eased onto the shore of a small tropical island. It was hot, the jungle terrain was dense and the path narrow. I encouraged Patrick to go with the group, climbing the narrow trail into the tropical forest. I would be comfortable sitting on the beach to absorb the sights and sounds of the terrain and the wildlife around me. Off he went. Within ten minutes, he came bounding back down the pathway.

"Mum, Mum, you have to come! You have to see this."

Iguana Friendly?

I looked skeptically at the steep narrow path but Patrick assured me that it would not be a problem. After a few close encounters with the foliage, with me ending up on the ground, and lots of laughs, we rounded a corner. The sight of thousands and thousands of pink flamingos appeared before my eyes. Yes, he was right! I had to see this.

On our return to the beach, as we waited for the boat to slide onto the sand, we slipped into the water for a cooling dip. The animals simply have no fear. A small seal eased through the water, bumped its nose on Patrick's mask and looked deeply into his eyes, inquisitive about this strange, red-headed visitor. We saw sea iguanas climbing on the rocks, land iguanas perched on the branch of a tree, more seals, sea lions, birds, and reptiles. They all oozed curiosity and bravado.

Tortoise 150 years old.

We arrived early in the evening on the main island of the Galapagos. Huge and ancient tortoises roamed freely in the fields around the town. Words are inadequate to describe these incredible giants. Their shells were often 1.5 metres across, their weight, 300 kg or more. As night fell, the temperature remained well above 38° Celsius. We had a light dinner and returned to our guesthouse where we slipped onto our soft, low to the ground, beds. Would I be able to get out of this in the morning? I didn't think so! Although a ceiling fan moved the air minimally, it was welcome as it cooled the air slightly.

Suddenly the fan came to a dead stop. "Patrick," I said, "The fan has stopped moving."

"I know, Mum." He spoke from the darkness. "Did you not see the sign on the door? There is no electricity between midnight and 5:00 a.m. so if you are hot now, just wait to see how you feel in three or four hours."

Next morning it was 42°C at 7:00 a.m. and getting hotter. We explored the trails along the shore of the island, continually fascinated by the wildlife that had no fear. Overall, it was a very satisfying five days in the World Heritage protected site, where mammals and man alike share mutual respect.

We returned to Quito. Independence is important to everyone but there are times when help from a friend is essential. At the guesthouse where we were staying, the entrance to the shower was eighteen inches, if you are being generous. Showering was not a possibility for me! Sponge baths, like those used years ago, are as valuable today as they were back then. As for my hair, I used the old stand-bys—baby powder as dry shampoo, pony tails and pig tails, wash the surface with a wet facecloth—but after several days, the make-do solutions had run their course.

"Patrick, it`s about the hair."

"No problem Mom."

He slipped out the door and returned fifteen minutes later with a crumpled paper cup. With our chamois draped around my neck, I leaned sideways over the tiny sink and the shampooing proceeded. Within a few minutes, I had clean, conditioned, towel dried (with a sweatshirt) hair. I was ready to go again.

To my delight, Patrick proposed that we celebrate Mother's Day a little belatedly but nevertheless a special treat. The day was warm and sunny. I was pampered and honoured. We ate brunch under a tree in beautiful gardens and plotted our next destination. We aimed to explore the market town of Chilcabamba. How to get there? Well, of course, by the local bus!

We waited on the side of the road early in the morning as buses streamed by. A conductor stood on the foot on the stairs, leaning out the door of the bus, shouting, "To the market, to the market!" We waved a bus down and were gratified by the patience and assistance offered by the conductor and fellow bus passengers. They threw my chair and the backpack onto the roof. Someone vacated the first seat on the bus, making Patrick's lifting distance much shorter.

The courtyard at the hostel in Chilcabamamba was overhung with jungle foliage filled with brightly coloured and loudly spoken birds. There were hammocks strung from palm trees where those on a more limited budget could rent a sleeping space for the night.

The animal market is a highlight of this town so at 4:00 a.m. we arose and headed down the long dirt trail to the market where local farmers brought their beasts to buy or sell. Family members of all ages led cows, pigs, geese, goats, and sheep, along the roadway. Chickens and homing pigeons in cages were carried on the backs of women, children, men, or on horses. We found ourselves amidst farm animals of all sizes and shapes. The pigs, larger than I had ever seen, stood as high as my hips. They brushed their runny snouts along my pant legs. Goats, who had obviously had too little breakfast, attempted to munch the rubber tires on my wheelchair or take a bite out of my pants. The auctioneer, standing on a tree stump, shouted out the escalating prices. Some went home pleased with their purchase and sales, others went home dissatisfied. After five hours, we all went home. I am not much of a breakfast eater, but in this case, after only three hours of sleep the night before, a breakfast of aros blanca and tropical fruit was a most welcome meal.

We went to the large and extensive craft market where anything could be purchased. Vendors sold hand-embroidered shirts, alpaca wool sweaters, grey and black sweatpants, hand-woven blankets, wicker baskets, natural fibre tapestries, food, and flowers. It would be easy to get carried away in this kind of setting. Beautiful alpaca wool sweaters sold for four dollars. I asked myself how often, in the temperate west coast climate, I would wear a sweater that provided warmth to 30°C below zero? One sweater was enough.

After several days in this market town, we returned to Quito to find warm summer like weather. Our last two days together included short explorations to villages between Quito and Columbia.

Time to go! For a flight leaving at 7:00 a.m., I must be at the airport at 5:00 a.m. There was no bus service from the border of Colombia and Ecuador during the dark hours. Staying at the airport was an option, if I arrived before midnight.

Patrick lifted me onto the bus, squeezed some local money into my hand and kissed me goodbye. The bus pulled onto the narrow curvy road hugging the mountainside to avoid a plunge to the river two hundred feet below steep rocky cliffs. The last few hours in a country always fill me with an urgency to see everything along the way in case I miss something spectacular. The ride passed with glimpses of tiny villages, stunning quartz and marble mansions, and children playing dangerously close to the road. Unsuccessful attempts to doze were peppered by peeks at my watch.

I was starting my 42-hour journey home to Canada while Patrick carried on to investigate more of South America. In their growing years, I used to tell the boys that when they grew up, there were only two things that I wanted them to acquire; one was roots, the other was wings. The last several weeks together had reinforced the existence of Patrick's roots. The next three months would provide Patrick an opportunity to spread his wings.

My memories of our journey are of a young man who was

realistic about his ability and that my capability and was not easily thwarted. We share memories of a challenging, amazing, meaningful trip together.

Chapter 13

French Polynesia—Tahiti

After his first trip to Tahiti, my friend Carl would not consider any other destination in the world. It is the laid-back manner of the people's "just let it be man," their down-to-earth acceptance of the moment; their forthcoming embracement of visitors; the restful climate; heat and burning sunshine always accompanied by a cooling trade wind; the food; and the immediate removal from North American stressful lifestyle, that made it irresistible.

"Do you want to go?" he asked me one evening as we were having dinner together.

I've said it before and I'll say it again. If it's somewhere I have never been before and the cost is reasonable, of course I want to go."

Not to mention, Carl and I are old friends from university days in Montreal. We are now both parents of two boys, and after no contact for twenty years, we discovered that we lived three blocks apart at New Westminster Quay.

Philip, an employee of Carl's, graciously drove through a cold, blinding rainstorm, to take Carl, his mother, and myself, to the SeaTac airport south of Seattle. There, we connected with our international flight to paradise. A brief stop in Honolulu introduced our heat-deprived bodies to sunbeams. North American flights land at 1:00 a.m. in Papeete, the capital of Tahiti. Flights to local islands only take place in daylight hours. I learned to play Bridge on the top of a backpack. When the play became too serious for my unconcerned manner, we reverted to Crib and Crazy Eights. I read, wandered through the flower market, and listened to the Tahitian music that oozed through the walls of the thatched huts. People here do not sleep at night; they take siestas in the overwhelming heat of the mid-day sun and are then prepared to party into the night. At 6:00 a.m., the pilot of a small six-seater prop plane beckoned us to join him. Boarding the plane was not the most ladylike activity. However, I am wise enough not to wear miniskirts or halter tops when I know that I may be lifted, pulled, twisted into a pretzel shape and pushed through a small compartment window.

After thirty-six hours on airplanes and twelve hours of airport stopovers, we arrived in Moorea. This extended travel time compromised my well-being. I was more stiff and immobile than I wanted to be. What was the best way to deal with it? Swim! A Princess cruise ship was anchored in the harbour. The water was tranquil, clear, and inviting. I donned a swimsuit, slipped into the water and swam across the harbour and around the cruise ship. On my return to the shore, fifty minutes later, I was met by my travel companion, Carl.

"Do you know how deep that water is? Forty metres! Do you know how long you were out there?" He was clearly upset and angry. "If you run into problems there is nothing I can do to help you!"

In my mind, running into problems is never a consideration, much to the consternation of my friends and loved ones. I am comfortable and confident of my ability in the water. However, over the years, I have realized that things can and do happen to the most competent of swimmers. To maintain peace between Carl and I for the next three weeks, my swimming consisted of laps back and forth, twelve feet out from shore. Looking always for the positive and advantageous aspects in my circumstances, I chose to admire the large variety of coloured tropical fish that swam in groups beneath me.

For three weeks my level of activity included sitting and

watching; watching and sitting; swimming and reading; reading and swimming; snorkeling, eating Tahitian hot dogs and drinking decadent rum punch. On the island, the colour of the mountains changed as the sun rose to its overhead position. I could gaze at the palm fronds moving slightly with each breath of breeze; I watched the colour of the water alter from turquoise, to teal, to royal, to navy, to azure. This was all I could cope with in one day!

In the early morning, before the heat increased and traffic began on the circle island road, we circumnavigated the island, picking papaya and grapefruit from the trees. We raided bushes in the ditch for lemons and limes and scavenged a pineapple or two that had innocently landed outside the farmer's fence. We rescued coconuts that had tumbled in the night.

The size of the bathroom in our hut was about the size of the computer room at home. Even though there was no tub, the magnitude of the room and a drain that led to the jungle floor eliminated shower floods. Dense sultry air filled the room. The outside wall of the shower was only one metre high and there was no roof overhead. Loving jungle plants served as the ceiling and cascading tropical foliage, the shower curtain. The roof over the shower was so impenetrable that rain never entered. The room, open to the air, admitted warmth, the scent of flowers, but also hungry geckos! Thank goodness for geckos! They are lizard-like friends who eat spiders, mosquitoes and other unwelcome flesh-munching creatures. While I sipped a glass of wine, enjoying the oppressive air and having my shower, the geckos ensured that I was not an appetizer for hungry bugs.

Following days of sunshine, we lived through six or seven days of monsoon rain. The water came down in sheets—thirty-one inches of rain in one week making the winter rains on the west coast look like a mere drizzle. Dressed only in shorts with water to our knees and over the axle of the large wheel on my chair, we continued our daily activities undeterred. On Sunday mornings, we walked the three miles to church through the oppressive, humid heat. I tied my long crinkle skirt in a knot around my waist and wore a tank top until the church came into sight. Then I donned a shirt, untied my skirt, and resumed ladylike decency.

In the small wooden church, Polynesian music filled the space. Children and dogs walked and played in the aisles. The people were gentle and kind. As usual, a lady in a wheelchair is a novelty. The Tahitian people opened their hearts to me while little children competed for rides on my lap. Grannies generously offered me extra servings of Eucharist bread and wine. I have seen much of the world but nowhere have I seen so many flowers, florescent tropical fish, and beautiful smiling children. I didn't have to so much as make a cup of coffee or pour a glass of water. Our gourmet diet consisted of rice, fresh fruit, leafy greens, and Pierre Marcel wine—rich red French wine.

My second trip to Tahiti was Robinson Crusoe style. Carl and I spent two weeks on a motu, a deserted tropical island, off the shores of Bora Bora. Just to offer perspective on how remote this destination was, when we arrived on Bora Bora, "Le truck" picked us up to transport us to the secluded shore on the opposite side of the island. "Le truck" is literally just that: a dump truck chassis with wooden benches around the perimeter, the centre crowded with the wheelchair, backpacks, toolboxes, baskets of food, children and their toys. People waving and shouting, "Bus bus!" along the roadside dictated frequent stops for local workmen, farmers, school children, mothers going to market, and the odd North American traveller, who hopped on and off. At the end of our bus ride, a small marketplace invited a grocery-shopping spree to purchase fresh vegetables, seven baguettes, rice, dried peas, and three bottles of Pierre Marcel wine (sold in 2 litre plastic bottles the way pop is bottled sold at home). What we didn't take we wouldn't have. The population of our remote haven was four; the island caretaker and his wife, travelling companion Carl and myself. Fresh fruit—papaya, mango, limes, and kiwi, could be picked from the island trees.

Our lodging was a two-level, thatched-roofed house that reminded me of the southern plantations from the movie *Gone with the Wind*. On the porch, soft cushions on cane and bamboo chairs invited comfortable lounging. Coconut-laden palms surrounded the veranda. Rolling fields of tall, waving grass led down to the turquoise blue water's edge. It did not take long for the heat of the day to beckon me to the shore's edge for a cooling dip. The sandy, shallow lagoon looked inviting but its appeal was quickly tarnished by the presence of large sea slugs all over the sandy bottom. For those who can walk, it is quite easy to step over the slugs until you reach the deeper, azure water. The only way for me to reach this point was to traverse three hundred metres on my hands with my legs floating behind, placing my hands between the slugs to avoid a squishy encounter.

Do I need to swim? Yes, of course, I do. I will do whatever is required to make that happen. Two or three times a day, while staying on the motu, I was privileged with face-to-face views of the sea slugs, their eyes peering at me and tentacles waving. The water was always warm and luxurious. Like obstetric amnesia, I never seemed to remember that I would have to negotiate the sea slugs again on the way back to shore.

There is a time to go and a time to come home. At the end of these South Pacific excursions, I always felt like someone had put heaven on earth and sent me there. Tom Peters talks about "the pursuit of wow"—my pursuit ended here. Paradise found!

Chapter 14

World's Greatest Shortcut – Panama Canal

In May 2004, my friend Lillian and I flew to Miami, and boarded a train at the Miami airport that carried us north to Jupiter, near West Palm Beach, where my daughter-in-law's parents reside. For the first time in this rail system's history, the computer crashed, delaying our train by three hours. The station was packed with people awaiting the train's arrival. Did this computer not know that dinner was on the table, that swim practice starts at 6:30 p.m., that Mary needs to be at a fitness class and that the babysitter will be here by 8:00 p.m.?!

Jill's dad had been patiently waiting for three hours for the arrival of us two dishevelled Canadian women. The Scott home, situated on the riverbank, offered uninterrupted diversions—paddlers, kayakers, alligators, manatees, children at play and grandpas with their fishing poles. The goings-on could not be considered commotion. They carried on amidst warm sunshine, the peaceful sounds of birds, the enticing smell of barbeques, along with laughter and music. We submerged ourselves in pure decadence over the next three days. We picked papaya and mango from the trees for breakfast. We swam in a large, solar heated pool covered by a thin, invisible mesh that deterred the bug population. We participated in a yoga class with our hostess. We explored the Saturday garage sales for riches—one man's junk is another man's treasure—rested and read. We were spoiled rotten.

When our stay was over, we once again boarded the train that dropped us in the Miami airport where we connected with a shuttle bus that took us to our floating home for the next 32 days: the Norwegian Wind. The Norwegian Wind hosts 1,750 guests each week and maintains a crew of six hundred.

Central America has been populated for thousands of years. Theories suggest that there may have been contact between the Americas and parts of Africa. Historically, Central America has served as both a physical and cultural bridge connecting the two continents of North and South America. Central America's ecosystem hosts a vast array of landscapes. It provides a plethora of wildlife and foliage due to its wide variety of altitudes and temperatures. Ferocious heat, sweltering humidity, and monsoon rains make this land lush; a green haven for banana plantations. Costa Rica was the first South American country to grow bananas. They export an average of eleven million bunches a year. Active volcanoes blend into peaceful, rolling green valleys.

The Panama Canal is over three hundred meters long and thirty meters wide. The idea to build a canal across the Isthmus was initiated in 1524 by King George V of Spain. In 1904, almost four hundred years after the initial idea for a canal, construction officially began. Ten years after construction commenced, the first ship sailed through. The canal was dominated by the U.S. until December 31, 1999, when Panama received ownership.

When cruising, days spent at sea are as valuable as those spent in port. There are more activities on a cruise ship than you could possibly do. The newsletter left outside the cabin door each night—I always refer to it as a storybook—needs to be thoroughly combed so that the activities of the following day can be planned. On board activities range from exercise—walks around the deck, fitness classes, spa, yoga—to cooking demonstrations by the chef, computer classes, win it or lose it in the casino, tax and duty free shopping, bingo, music, and evening shows. Daily lectures by university professors, historians, and naturalists, offer education about the geographical area, weather, culture, economic development, topography, and the ship's ports.

Food is available at any hour. Patrick often asked me if he could have ice cream at 3:00 a.m., so yes, in fact he could, by calling room service. Although we all eat differently than we would at home—and definitely more than we would at home—if you maintain your usual eating habits, weight will not become an issue. My preference is to eat in the dining room where a menu selection is offered by elegant service executed by waiters dressed in tux and tails, with white towels draped over their forearms. Buffet service is always available, but I find that a buffet offers too many things to try. Why would I serve myself when I can have another do it? Corn chips and salsa are served in Margarita bars; there are barbeques on the deck, accompanied by salsa steel band Caribbean music; hot appetizers and sushi on the observation deck accompanied by a glass of wine. Throughout the evening, in the casino, cheese and crackers, smoked salmon, fresh fruit, and vegetables appear in every corner.

Days in port present new opportunities. Known as the Switzerland of South America, Costa Rica developed a strong peace policy. Residents live comfortably without the need for the military. Costa Rica means, "Rich Coast," so named by Christopher Columbus. The lucrative Central American coffee business began in Costa Rica.

Excursions to shore are often restricted to the Abs, the able bodied. But in my usual determined manner, I approached the manager at the shore excursion desk to inquire about adventure opportunities for people who are unable to walk.

"What do you want to do?" the shore excursion manager asked, a bit warily.

"Swim with the dolphins or go whitewater rafting."

The manager, Brad, advised me that he would investigate possibilities and get back to me.

To my surprise, as I was getting ready for dinner, the phone rang. "Swimming with dolphins is not possible because there are stairs to navigate," he told me. "Be at the walkway at 8:00 a.m. You are going whitewater rafting."

The Central American Adventurers were keen and excited to have me along. They lifted me into the raft. I perched on the bottom because balancing on the inflated edge was a little too precarious for even my level of bravery. Whitewater rapids and swiftly flowing waters were pretty frightening. This was a Class II-III river. We skimmed over the surface, the water rose high above our heads as the river twisted between its banks, deluging us. I found myself sitting in six inches of cold water, looking like I just walked out of the shower. One of my boating companions exclaimed, "That's a Kodak moment if I ever saw one!"

Dry shirts were handed out to all and our dripping clothing was loaded into plastic garbage bags. After three more hours of rafting, we were soaked once again, making it necessary to buy the t-shirt. Is that coercion or isn't it?

An intriguing day of passage through the canal enlightened us all. The ship entered locks and then rose four to nine metres to the next level. We moved along slowly, lining up behind other large and small ships in preparation for entry into the next lock. The passage from one side of the canal to the other took an entire day. On exit from the canal, we sailed up the west coast of Mexico

For centuries the coastal oasis of Acapulco has welcomed archaeologists and visitors alike. The famous cliff divers plunge from the cliffs deep into the ocean. These fearless men dive 136 feet into the crashing Pacific below, landing in a 9½ foot-deep inlet. This has been one of Mexico's famous attractions since the 1940s. Lillian and I watched in awe.

Manzanillo, a busy rail and sea port, boasts narrow streets, and open air markets that display endless pottery. We visited citrus orchards where lemons weighed branches to the ground. Mariachi bands filled the roadways and street vendors entertained everyone.

The lure of gold and silver brought many pioneers to the settlement of Puerto Vallarta. Now, tiny cottages line the shores of the beaches. Mansions, owned by the rich and famous, are perched on the hills above.

Cabo San Lucas, Lands End, is located where the Pacific Ocean meets the Gulf of California, also called the Sea of Cortez. It is surrounded by a spectacular series of rock formations, dominated by a natural arch from which many small fishing boats can be seen. Sea birds and sea lions relax on the rocky cliffs. From the new dock at Cabo San Lucas, we ferried across to explore Puerto Vallarta on the mainland.

This trip was actually a combination of two cruises. One took us from Miami to Los Angeles and the second took us from Los Angeles to Vancouver. In L.A., many families and children boarded, changing the balance from a senior and adult group to fun and frolicking youth.

In San Francisco, we ascended the steep hills by cable car (one is actually wheelchair accessible), and visited Fisherman's Wharf. In Seattle, we took in the Space Needle and explored the Pike Street Market. Cruising into Victoria, definitely back in Canada now, we encountered the reserved British atmosphere of British Columbia's capital city. Home again, home again, jiggety-jig. We were compelled to rise at 5:00 a.m. to witness a spectacular sailing beneath the Lion's Gate Bridge, complete with majestic views of snow-capped mountains.

We disembarked at Canada Place, in downtown Vancouver.

Chapter 15

Nepal

"Draped along the greatest heights of the Himalaya, the Kingdom of Nepal is a land of eternal fascination, a place where the ice cold of the high Himalaya meets the heat of the steamy Indian plains. It is a land of ancient history, colorful cultures and people, superb scenery and some of the best trekking on earth."

Lonely Planet, Nepal 2001, page 11 (Reproduced with permission from Nepal 5, Hugh Finlay © 2001 Lonely Planet.)

Was it only a dream? After fifteen years of travel I was beginning to realize that there was always a way to convert my dreams into reality. Patrick and Jill, my future daughter-in-law, had trekked extensively in Nepal in 2001. When I quietly verbalized my thoughts to Patrick, they were met with the usual enthusiastic response, "Of course you can go! It will just take some innovative planning."

One of the university students who managed the hiking program for people with disabilities in Vancouver in the summer of 2002 had visited Nepal and talked enthusiastically about her experiences and her trek on the Annapurna circuit. We exchanged telephone numbers. On one dark rainy Friday evening in the winter, my anticipation began to percolate. I reached for the telephone and tentatively dialed Shauna's number. Doesn't it mostly turn out better than you anticipate? Well, almost always! Over the next thirty minutes, Shauna provided me with some insight and advice on various treks, what clothing to take, porters and guides, food and water, weather and equipment. She referred me to First Environment, the trekking company that she had used. It was to become the solid resource for my trekking experience in Nepal. Most importantly, Shauna showered me with enthusiasm and encouragement to pursue my dream.

I benefit by having a son that has travelled to many unusual places in the world. He always has a *Lonely Planet* guidebook, perhaps some other guidebooks, brochures, and certainly some knowledge to share about places to go, things to do, and sometimes people to see. My true friend Barb ecstatically agreed to accompany me.

How will I get from Kathmandu to Pokhara? I'm sure that they are not very familiar with wheelchairs and in particular how to get me on a bus. I don't speak Nepalese but I'm not bad at sign language. "It won't matter how it works," I told Patrick with a laugh. "Just get me on the bus."

"Mom," he told me, "You just make sure that you have some 50 and 100 rupee bills—about $1-$2 CDN—handy in your pocket. You pull a few of those out and offer to pay someone to get you and your chair on and off the bus. The sight of those bills will bring offers from three or four guys." And of course he was right!

A Visa card that earns frequent flyer points with each expenditure generated enough air travel credit for one round trip airplane ticket to Nepal. The other would be purchased. Our trek to Annapurna base camp was arranged through First Environment. We planned two rest and preparation days in Kathmandu before embarking on our trek. The Kathmandu Guest House has the reputation of being the favoured spot for travellers to rest their heads. The bonuses include shared experiences, laughter, tears, jokes, equipment bartering, information about where to go for the best deals, where to eat, what to eat, when to go and when to stay. This is all part of finding a popular place to stay—whether it be a hotel, guesthouse, hostel, back-packer lodge, sleeping room over a pub, a B&B, a farm stay, campsite, bench in a train station, or a blanket on a beach. I have slept in them all.

I sent e-mails requesting information regarding "accessibility," availability, and reservations. No response drifted across the wireless waves to my computer screen. During a Nepal orientation session with my son, Patrick decided to follow up with a telephone call to the Kathmandu Guest House. Here we go! Following extensive interaction with telephone information operators, both Canadian and Nepalese, I could hear Patrick speaking one word at a time, slowly and distinctly, in hopes of communicating some understanding, both ways.

"Yes, a chair. Yes a wheelchair. No doesn't walk. No not alone. Yes another lady. No stairs. Do you have an elevator? Do you have a lift?"

It sounds quite simple but after forty-five minutes, I left the room to put a cup of tea into the microwave, recognizing that this was not going to be a quick call. The questions were repeated, repeatedly! Patrick was scribbling madly on an envelope that he had rescued from the recycle bag so that after the call, between the two of us, we could hopefully decipher some of the information given to him more in Nepali than in English. After my tea mug was emptied for the second time, my Number One redhead son emerged from the computer room shaking his head and laughing.

"Good luck, Mom! They do not have an elevator because the gentleman on the phone advised me that there is 'no vader, just 'phants—elephants."

From the few English words, we were able to determine that there was a room with two beds that would require negotiation of "some stairs." How many stairs would be determined on our arrival.

Barb was a massage therapy student who had been working with me for two and a half years. Her board exams would be written in September of 2003. After the exams, she definitely deserved a holiday. I say that lightly because travelling with a person with a disability to parts of the world where accessibility is unheard of, could hardly be classified as a "holiday." But she was willing to go!

Two days after receiving the great news that she had passed her final exams, we boarded the plane.

A 14-hour flight carried us from Vancouver to Calcutta, India where for me, getting off the airplane, was not possible. A ramp or aisle chair was non-existent. The customs official boarded the plane to check my passport and identification. While other passengers were on the ground, I had time to take care of bladder issues. There are no accessible washrooms on an airplane and often no aisle chair to allow me to reach a washroom.

A tall uniformed man, a steward from first-class approached my seat, leaned over, and whispered, "I will carry you by piggyback." This is exactly what he did. The aisles are narrow and the washroom is minute, so transferring into the washroom fully-clothed, then jiggling out of your clothing is the only option. The door was not closable so staff was prepared to hold up a blanket to provide privacy. As the gentleman held up a blanket, Barb insisted that we have a female volunteer. A female flight attendant appeared immediately. With that task accomplished and other passengers back on board, we tackled another meal of delightful Asian food, watched yet another movie and attempted to catch forty winks. The hours droned by. As the sun rose over the horizon, golden rays danced along snow capped mountain ridges. The plane banked sharply and began its descent into a narrow corridor cradled between rocky cliffs.

Nepal is a continuous series of the most spectacular mountains in the world. The numerous trails and treks could keep one walking for a lifetime. Which one to choose? When I consulted with First Environment, their initial e-mail response was positive and encouraging. "Do you weigh more than two hundred pounds?" Of course I don't. With my chair, all my belongings, and myself, I still did not total two hundred pounds! Therefore, it was accepted that I could travel to Nepal and a porter would carry me in a basket on his back up the mountain. We were given a choice of three different treks. After consultation with Patrick, who had trekked extensively in Nepal, the decision was made to climb to Annapurna base camp. This 14-day trek would include a travel day by bus in each direction and twelve days on the mountain.

We arose early on Thursday morning, stuffed all our worldly goods that had travelled across the globe with us into Barb's pack, coerced assistance to mount the stairs in the guesthouse from a fellow traveller, and waited at the door for Sujan and the porters to arrive. In the early morning hours there were many travellers in the front hallway—some sleeping on packs, some chatting, some arriving with fatigue etched on their faces and some hugging goodbyes with promises to e-mail and one day meet again. The day was bright, the morning cool, dew moistened the leaves, birds chattered with one another as we waited for our travel companions to arrive. Public transportation is non-existent. Walking is the name of the game in cities, on mountains, across rivers. Sujan, Yo, Holm, and Rona arrived and the walking began as we headed towards the bus station.

Early-morning street activity surrounded us—children playing, shopkeepers unlocking their gates, businesses opening their offices, mothers at the market stalls purchasing the family's daily food. Laundry was stretched over balcony railing. Sheets and shirts adorned the roofs of cars, and panties and jeans were hung along fences and over tree boughs. We arrived at the bus station. It consisted of a vacant lot with an uneven dusty gravel surface, spotted with small mud puddles in which small children and toddlers played happily as they awaited the beckoning call from their moms.

Numerous government buses were identifiable by their blue and white décor. They were parked at various angles in order to avoid sinking a tire into a puddle or pothole. Drivers leaned against the bumpers catching twenty winks or three more drags on their one-inch long cigarette butts. Vendors with steaming trays balanced on their shoulders hawked freshly baked buns that, according to the enthusiastic sellers, should be tasted by all. For those of us who do not connect with food until the early afternoon or evening, the most appealing offer of food at 7:00 a.m. is never appetizing. Barb's eating habits are more usual. She eats three meals a day, with light snacks between. Nutritionists say that we all should eat breakfast, the most important meal of the day, but there is a discrepancy between the expert advice and my body's needs. I cannot eat breakfast. Needless to say, Barb entered into a close relationship with a warm, steaming, sweetened bread bun and enjoyed every morsel.

We were directed to a dilapidated transit vehicle. It resembled the cartoon character "Bobby the Bus" with large uneven tires, the chassis leaning at a precarious angle, and a smile painted between the two headlights. The bus had a cardboard sign taped over the windshield: "Pokhara." The luggage compartment was open but Sujan hesitated. He looked with question at the bus, mounted the stairs and spoke with the driver. On his descent of the stairs we were directed to get on a different bus that was not more modern but definitely not as occupied as the first. Two young boys volunteered to lift me onto the bus. They folded my chair in preparation for storage in the luggage compartment, which was now jam pecked with boxes, suitcases, backpacks displaying flags of various countries, farming tools, and bundles of belongings wrapped in blankets and tied with twine. There was no room for my chair so it was tied with rope on the roof, keeping close company with three small white goats who were chained to rings there. As goats generally feel that anything within their reach constitutes a meal, I had some concern about my tires being within munching range of the little white hairy folks. The driver demonstrated his awareness of the risks by placing two wooden boxes between my chair and the goats. We sat on the bus, watching passengers enter and occupy their assigned seats. There were young folk and old, male and female, some in farm clothes; others in what looked like their night attire. Small cages held chickens and ducks. A travelling farmer held a small piglet in his arms. One person got on the bus with two cages covered with towels. He sat in the seat behind us. What did this mean? Barb and I looked at each other as we recognized the gentle cooing of the pigeons that were to be fellow passengers for the next sixty-five kilometres.

This sixty-five-kilometre bus ride that stretched before us would take ten hours. We vacillated between fascination and boredom. The bus slowly inched its way through traffic, and out of the city limits. There were no traffic lights, no stop signs—no semblance of order in the traffic pattern. It was impossible to determine if the streets were one way, two ways, or multiple ways as the flow of traffic included trucks, buses, cars, rickshaws, bicycles, children, pedestrians, and cows. The urban atmosphere of Kathmandu gradually dissolved into gentle countryside, sheer rising mountains, deep valleys, and rice fields clinging to the mountainside. Goats and sheep, accompanied by shepherds, wandered along the roadside. The highway was narrow, barely wide enough for one vehicle. Our initial apprehension when trucks and buses passed one another on steep hairpin turns changed to blasé acceptance as the minutes and hours passed.

Vehicles travelled at breakneck speed, creating a continuous adrenaline rush. The Prithvi highway between Kathmandu and Pokera parallels the Trisuli River then follows the Mugling where it meets the equally large Marsyangdi Khola, which flows southeast.

Two hours after our departure, the bus stopped for a breakfast break. Barb wandered into the sheltered stand at the side of the road, returning with a newspaper, and a grease-soaked bundle of pakora, which was to become the staple of bus trip meals. Pakora consists of bite-size vegetables coated in spicy batter and deep-fried. The vegetables are slightly cooked, with a crisp brown exterior. They were often served with spicy dipping sauce. We would come to love this staple of our diet; get tired of pakora; despise it; then love it again!

We set off once more with the unrealistic anticipation that our trip would last only a few more hours. Oh how wrong we were! Around the next corner the bus abruptly stopped. The door opened and before we knew what was happening, four members of the local Army in camouflage uniforms, and with machine guns tucked under their arms, mounted the stairs of the bus, sharply directing the local Nepalese citizens to get out of the bus. The rest of us were ordered to produce passports, identify our country of birth, our country of residence, where we were going, why we were going, and for how long we would be in Nepal.

All local citizens, our guide and porters, began to walk up the hill in the blistering sun. The bus slowly inched up the grade for two kilometres until it reached the end gate of the Army check point and the bus then waited for the pedestrians. They slowly climbed the stairs of the bus, took out their warm bottles of water and drank wearily. Off we went again. This experience was repeated eleven times, about every five to eight kilometres. At each gate, a member of the armed forces mounted the stairs of the bus, closely scrutinized passports then nodded approval to his commanding officer. The driver and the remaining passengers on the bus were then approved to continue up the roadway.

We had been so focused upon the upcoming trek that our concern for safety was minimized. It was rekindled when we passed two buses in the ditch, a third belching smoke as tiny flames licked the edges of the engine compartment, a fourth at the base of the cliff in the river. Forty people had lost their lives yesterday in this bus mishap. Turning back was never a consideration. When your goal is to see the world, you need to appreciate the local culture and circumstances even if they are grossly different from the comforts at home in Canada.

The heat became oppressive. Air conditioning was definitely a North American luxury. The newspaper wrappings that we had collected from breakfast, snacks, and lunch could be turned into fans. Our meals now included vegetarian samosas. We had purchased bottled water before embarking, but the age-old problem for someone who cannot climb on and off the bus continues to exist. If you drink, the need arises to locate and use a washroom so it is better to remain thirsty and dehydrated until your feet and wheels touch the ground.

Finally, we arrived in Pokhara. We dismounted from the bus and began to ease along the dirt road towards a white building that resembled a large house or hotel. Several small children played in the yard, tiny white goats munched the grass along each side of the path and waist-high marigolds bordered the walkway. With the willing assistance of two young boys and my wheel chair tipped backwards, I was able to mount the seven stairs. We were ushered into a small bedroom with an adjoining bathroom. It was obvious that the owner's boudoir had been assigned to Barb and myself so that we were able to have a bed and bathroom on the ground floor. The bed sheets were clean. We were to learn that this is an element to be thankful for. Boxer shorts, socks, pantyhose and ladies undergarments lay strewn around the room, hung on the doorknobs, and piled on the dresser. Would it matter? Of course not! We had a clean comfortable bed in which to sleep, a place to store our pack and worldly possessions, running water, and a shower. This was luxury accommodation in comparison to what we would encounter over the next two weeks.

The dining room hosted a door laid over sawhorses as a table. The staple diet of dal bhaat (curried lentils and rice) was the daily fare. The liquid dal is served in a soup mug and poured over steaming white rice that covers the plate. We would later learn that for a jazzier meal, curried vegetables—cauliflower, potatoes, onions—are added to the dal bhaat, now called tarakari.

Following dinner, Yo, the porter who would carry me along the mountain pathways and up the steep terrain, was given money by Sujan our guide to buy a new pair of shoes. Currently his footwear consisted of a pair of rubber thongs: flip-flops. The porters departed with enthusiastic chatter and keen anticipation of their shopping trip. Yo and his companions returned an hour later with his prize purchase tucked under his arm. With a mile-wide grin, Yo proudly opened the newspaper-wrapped package to share his new purchase with us. It was another pair of rubber thongs—flip-flops—only this time they were red, not black. Sujan shrugged his shoulders. Yo had been trekking on the mountains barefoot all his life and only in recent years had upgraded to flip-flops. We couldn't change his way of life.

The second prize possession of the porters was a cone-shaped basket that was to become my daily residence for the next two weeks. I viewed it a little sceptically but it is my philosophy that it is necessary to put your faith and trust in those who have done this before. Time would tell!

Linda's custom transportation.

In the wee hours of the morning, as birds began to chirp, we began our daily routine: stretching, getting up, washing, and dressing. We readjusted the contents of our pack realizing that, as is often the case, we had brought too much. Before leaving Canada we had been told that the Nepalese did not approve of women in shorts, tank tops, or pants. To respect the cultural beliefs of the country, I had made a rapid shopping trip to Value Village to purchase two long skirts. Three days in Nepal had convinced me that skirts were not at all necessary. Shorts and t-shirts were quite acceptable for visiting foreigners who had come to experience the mountain highs and valley lows of the Himalayas. We repacked our belongings, ending with a bag full of unnecessary items to leave behind.

The trek began from Phedi (meaning "foot of the hill"), with a mile long, easy, uphill grade through a meadow where cows grazed in the morning sunshine. Long damp grass tickled our bare legs as Barb walked and I wheeled through the field. At the end of the pathway, we found a small, flat roofed, white washed residence next to an unpainted wood animal shelter. Our excess trekking gear would stay with the cats, mice, and heaven only knows what else, while we made our way up the mountain path. The cone-shaped basket was about twenty inches in diameter. Two cuts had been made about sixteen inches apart, slicing downwards ten inches. The piece of wicker between the two cuts was tipped into the basket to make a seat. I was assisted into this contraption and the trek began.

To my dismay, and of the porter who was carrying me I'm sure, we soon found that the basket was small and the seat tipped in such a way that when Yo was walking uphill, I was gradually sliding toward the ground. I tried to minimize my apprehension on the steep mountain hillsides but my thoughts were uncontrollably focused on one word. *Help*! There was no way that I would survive this customized chariot for the next two weeks. It was just not going to work and fortunately, I was not the only one who recognized that a revision was required. At the first village, after thirty minutes of trekking uphill, with me sliding farther, farther, and farther, we reached a small cluster of bamboo huts. Another basket was purchased from the local villagers and a new carrying arrangement was designed. This basket was a little larger and deeper. When the cuts were made in the rim, the seat was tipped downwards into the base of the basket meaning that my bum was down and my knees were up over the edge. I was quite at home in this new makeshift cocoon. It was comfort personified!

There is a common expression in Nepal—"jam jam"—meaning "We are ready—let's go." After the new wicker transportation invention was completed, the porters were anxious and ready to begin the trip. But before we could leave, the women of the village poured out of their huts. There were young and old: mothers with babies on their backs and on their hips and elderly with grey hair. They may have had no teeth but they definitely had an opinion. The women quickly began a barrage of verbal directions aimed at the porters. I had no idea what they were saying but they were obviously very determined to have their opinions heard and acted upon. We were not going anywhere in a hurry!

Barb positioned herself on a flat rock and munched leisurely on a hard green apple that one of the village children had presented to her. Why not take advantage of this unexpected break?

One of the women crouched and inched her way slowly and carefully through a narrow doorway that led into the donkey hut. She emerged moments later with a large bundle of fresh straw, carefully placing it into the bottom of the basket. The prickly straw was covered with a piece of cardboard that had been torn from a storage box that held miscellaneous bits of string, nails, and tools. Three of the women circled the basket pressing and patting the straw down carefully. I was then directed to get into the basket. The women moved around my new home, tucking straw over the rough edges, around my arms, under my legs and behind my back. They then asked Sujan, our guide, who was fluent in Napali and English, if I had an extra shirt or a piece of cloth. As carrying weight was limited, I had only brought two t-shirts with me: the one I was wearing and the other was squeezed into a corner of the pack. Without dismantling all of our morning's hard work of packing, I managed to pull the extra t-shirt from the pack. This created great delight and another continuous barrage of chatter. The women tucked the shirt around my legs covering the rawness at the front of the basket. They then circled the basket, inspecting their handiwork, and when they were satisfied that I was safe and comfortable, they turned to the porters and said, "Now, Jam Jam."

This experience brought me closer to these women who reside on the opposite side of the world. They spoke no English and I knew nothing of their spoken language, however our ability to communicate was strong and meaningful. It reinforced for me the realization that women are, without question, the nurturers of the world.

We were now on our way.

The first day on the mountain presented a 1,200-metre climb. The switchbacks were narrow and abrupt with stairs at the steep grades. These were made from logs wedged into the mountainside, dirt that had been shovelled or moulded into the shape of steps; rocks stacked one upon the other, odds and ends of wood. Whatever the composition, the stairs made the climb more manageable for all. This natural architecture, stairs fashioned from by-products of the land, was the only semblance of urban construction was visible in this natural Shangri-La. I was thankful for the beauty and peace. It warmed the cockles of my heart to know that the people were closely in tune with their environment. The country is beautiful and the Nepalese people are going to keep it that way!

There was a lot to see—nothing to see except the beauty of a well-preserved environment! Enormous Rhododendron trees promised to burst into colorful bloom in the spring. The smell of fresh pine filled the air and the layered pine needles on the ground made for a cushioned pathway. After several hours of green, two hotels or teahouses came into view. They were low buildings, walls made of concrete blocks and roofs of flat-black tarpaper weighted down by rocks. The whitewashing of their exterior ensured that those travelling on the mountain would see them well in advance of reaching their doorsteps. We would eat and sleep in similar buildings along the way.

We reached the courtyard. The marigold plants surrounding it were three or four feet in height, weighed down by an abundance of yellow orange blooms. Their pungent odour reminded me why I had not chosen to include them as bedding plants in my own garden. At the lunch break there was no need for me to get out of the basket so it was placed on the ground with my back propped against the picnic table. Time to eat! We were presented with the menu of the day. It had a little variety and provided a number of choices for lunch. We soon came to realize that the menus of the guesthouses and restaurants differed only by a pen stroke or their title. Vegetable noodle soup was to become my mainstay for lunch. Vegetable noodle soup in Nepal consists of chicken broth with a generous portion of thin noodles and a very few vegetables—one grate of carrot, a thread of celery and a smidge of onion. The menu often included pizza. The crust resembled Indian Naan bread covered with a thin wiping of tomato sauce. This provided the base for a few mushrooms, sometimes a slice of fresh tomato, sometimes a few slices of onion. Dahl bhatt, the mainstay of the Nepalese diet, was always available. The porters eat this in enormous quantities, plates mounded with rice (three or four cups) and covered with the thick curried lentils. Following lunch, a cook from the kitchen would come with his rice pot and dahl pot to offer seconds. Another equally large portion was always accepted by the guys. The distances that they walked and the weight that they carried obviously required the calories. They were all strong but slim. Carrying weight was a fact of life for them. On luxury nights, curried vegetables would be added to the daily fare. Curried vegetables, served in small portions, consisted largely of onions, and potatoes. On occasion, it included a floweret of cauliflower or a round of carrot.

After lunch we carried on, knowing that today's goal was to cover twelve kilometres, climbing three thousand metres. This was not as much of a challenge for me as it was for Barb. I was nestled in my basket. She was straining her muscles, breathing deeply. Some may think that I was lacking exercise and this is true, compared to the swimming or wheeling that I do on a regular basis at home. But I discovered that balancing myself as Yo jostled me over the uneven terrain, getting in and out of the basket, using washroom facilities, and getting in and out of bed provided me with my needed daily exercise. Although not aerobic, it offered a chance for strength, balance and flexibility.

The warmth of the sun diminished as the fireball in the sky crept its way towards the horizon. A teahouse, a white speck in the distant green, beckoned us along. We arrived in daylight to find, thankfully, that there were rooms available. There would be times along this trail when we would encounter a "No Vacancy" situation. We will think back to old times when these same words were spoken to Mary and Joseph. We, like Mary and Joseph, would have to journey on to find a place where we could rest our heads for the night.

We arrived at the first guesthouse, quickly rummaged through the pack to find the necessities: towel, soap, shampoo, and clean warm clothing. It may have been warm during the day—shorts and t-shirts were the accepted attire—but as dusk approached the air chilled. After a barely lukewarm shower and freshening up we shivered into long pants, socks, and sweatshirts. Entering the rustic dining room, we found rows of picnic tables and benches. With a push and a shove, one of the rows was widened to allow me to manoeuvre my chair to our selected table. A glass containing spoons and a stack of Melmac plates were placed on each table. The guests were trekkers who had travelled to Nepal from all corners of the world. We heard English, German, French, and Asian spoken as words of enthusiasm bubbled over one another. The guides and travellers were appreciative at the end of each trekking day to have dahl bhatt spooned generously onto the plates.

At this first guesthouse, we acquired knowledge of the trekking community culture. Sujan, our guide, would most often join us at the table for dinner. Other trekkers and their guides did likewise. The porters usually ate in the kitchen. We would learn that they were embarrassed to eat in the dining room because they did not use western cutlery. They ate with our God-given utensils: bare hands. As we became comfortable with one another, though, the porters finally joined us at mealtime. Second helpings, third helpings, four or five if you wanted, were always available. The beverage of choice was bottled water. Bottled water would not be available at higher elevations. The use of iodine to sanitize the mountain water would become routine.

There are many ways to cleanse non-potable water: filters, screening, tablets from the mountain equipment stores, boiling, and the good old-fashioned bottle of iodine. Before leaving Vancouver, Patrick had directed me to not bother with all of those modern equipment.

"Just buy some iodine!" he said.

I went to the health food store and bought a small brown bottle, equipped with a dropper, of potable iodine. Patrick gave me a lecture.

"Mom, you don't have to pay ten dollars at the health food store, just go to the drug store and buy a small bottle of iodine like you would use on a cut. It will be less than half the price. It does the trick. You just have to tolerate the taste of iodine in your water."

As much as I appreciated his determination to be financially astute, spending ten dollars to avoid the strong taste of iodine with each swallow was worth it to me.

After dinner, the tables were washed clean and the playing cards appeared. Nepalese Rummy was easy to learn. It had the same basic characteristics of any rummy game. The wild card changed with each hand so the challenge was to remember which card number was wild. We cajoled and encouraged one another through two hours of rummy. Then, flashlights in hand, Barb and I headed to the community washroom which we had used earlier in the daylight. We were now in tune with the bumpity-bump entrance, the unattached toilet seat, the 14-inch high toilet, the drips from the old wood ceiling supports. The convenience of washroom facilities was related inversely to the beauty of the mountains. As we climbed higher, scenic magnificence increased as washroom and shower facilities deteriorated. The increasing cold at night motivated us to move quickly.

When we had finished our nightly routine, the porters were waiting outside the door to guide us through the darkness and to assist me to enter our sleeping room: two single beds each consisting of a 6 x 8 sheet of plywood on a wooden frame, the mattresses, three quarters of an inch of vinyl-covered foam. Stretched between the two wooden beds was a narrow piece of wood. Through the shadows of the room, we were handed two candles and three matches. After fumbling in the darkness, we were finally able to light a candle. We tipped it on its side so that the wax dripped onto the strip of plywood. Now the candle could be stood precariously on its base, providing us with a dim light.

The room was chilly to say the least. The window was open to the mountain air. There was no glass in the frame. The wooden slats of the shutters perhaps were meant to close out the cold night air but the three-inch gaps between the slats thwarted any window closure. We could see an amazing array of bright stars in the dark sky and a small piece of moon easing its way between a break in the mountain peaks.

Barb donned her grandfather's large, thick Irish knit wool sweater, sweatpants, a toque and thick socks. This was to be her evening, go to bed, get up in the morning and daily uniform for the remainder of the trek. These items remained in the pack from midmorning to late afternoon but came out again as the sun dipped below the horizon. Barb had brought her own down sleeping bag from Canada, which was inserted into the large fluffy down sleeping bag provided by First Environmental trekking company. My heat sensitive MS shrieked at the thought of doubling up on down sleeping bags. I removed my pants and socks. My late afternoon, early morning, night time uniform consisted of a favourite blue-grey thermal underwear shirt that I had inherited as a result of one of those wash day mistakes. A newly married friend had put her husband's entire wardrobe of work clothes into a very warm Laundromat dryer. The shrunken thermal underwear top was his loss, my gain. I slept in my underclothes without adding the sweater, socks and toque.

With Barb's help, I squiggled into the down sleeping bag, pulled it up around my shoulders, over my head, and dropped into a deep sleep.

The Trek in Progress

"It is a rough road that leads to the heights of greatness."
Lucius Annaeus

Chirping birds and a *tap tap tap* on the door awakened us.

Could it be possible? We had actually slept through the cold night. In the warm snuggle of down sleeping bags we had survived to meet the morning sunrise. Even though I don't eat breakfast; if anything was going to tempt me it would have been the scent of fresh, warm Butanese bread baked in fire heated stone ovens, the yeast raised pretzel-shaped loaves coated with a shiny sugar glaze and carried from the kitchen on trays. Trekkers in various stages of preparation were brushing teeth, iodinating water, pulling on socks and boots, or yawning—all obviously anticipating the day's events before us. Coffee and hot bread were accepted by some. As we passed through small villages, the women were hard at work, sweeping the dirt floors of their huts, opening the shutters to admit fresh air and light. Children were perched upon rocks sipping hot milk and munching on the warm breakfast bread. The children were ready for school, wearing navy blue skirts, navy blue pants, and sparkling white, long sleeved shirts. The laundry from yesterday had been washed in the mountain creek and spread over rocks to dry. Bleach, Javex as we know it, had been replaced by nature's supply of bleach—ultraviolet light from the sun.

Mothers accompanied their children to the schoolroom, which in some cases, was two or three kilometres away. The wee ones, too young yet for school, scampered along, hiding behind bushes, picking up baby goats, laughing and playing while their mothers urged them to hurry, as all mothers do everywhere. This same long trek was repeated mid-afternoon when mothers once again hiked the mountain paths to the school to escort the children home. We saw students doing homework with slates and chalk as well as pen and paper. Boulders and rocks served as desks. Homework is a staple of childhood education throughout the world. The night's homework was tucked into a backpack for the teacher's perusal in the morning.

The porters were scheduled for a two-hour lunch break each day and they consumed the standard fare of dahl-bhaatt in enormous quantities. As much as I liked dahl-bhaat, I was conscious of the fact that Yo, a small but very strong Nepalese Sherpa was carrying me so I tried to stick to no breakfast, noodle soup for lunch, and dahl-bhaat with curried vegetables for dinner. Beverages included coffee in the morning, Coca Cola, lime soda (fresh lime squeezed into soda water), a very occasional well aged, strong bottle of wine, bottled water at lower elevations, and self filtered iodinized water as we climbed.

At the lunch break, if I had no need to use the restroom facilities, I stayed in my basket, propped against a picnic table or a tree. Visitors were frequent, both enthusiastic and timid. The young children came to examine the wheelchair. When I offered a ride, some would eagerly try it out, others would run away frightened until their playmates convinced them that, boy, this was fun! I sometimes had a wee babe dropped into my arms by a mother or a sibling—free babysitting for a couple of hours. On one occasion, a young boy came around the shed with two tiny goats in his arms that he was sure the Canadian "basket trekker" would love to hold. Yes, in fact, they were fun to hold, but I had to convince the child that their permanent residence with me in the basket was not an option.

On our second or third day, outside the guesthouse we found warm tubs of soapy water: "Lucy's Laundromat." We all took advantage of the opportunity to wash some clothes. In the dining room of the guest house there was a warm fire in a tall kerosene heater. Lines were strung around the heater, draped with every form of freshly washed clothing: t-shirts, underwear, bikini panties, thongs, socks, bras and shorts. Throughout the evening, the dry ones were removed and the dampest moved closest to the fire so that in the morning we could all enjoy clean clothing.

In Nepal, showers are available at all the guesthouses, although, many people would consider them mere "dribbles." At most guesthouses, solar heated water drizzles from a tiny pipe emerging from the wall in a wooden shed that is perched on the side of a hill. At the end of each day's trek, it is always a mad rush to make it to the shower quickly as the heated water supply is limited. On days when sunshine is at a premium, warm water is also at a premium so competition for those few trickles of this coveted resource is intense. One evening, at higher elevation (43,000 metres), Barb and I arrived at the shed anticipating the welcome experience of a tepid shower and clean clothes. I sat naked, shivering on my chair. Barb stood waiting her turn attired in matching designer bra and panties. Her lingerie always matches! As the water began to drip, we heard a thunderous, explosive roar that, had our dress been different, would have found us both flying out the shed door and down the mountain. We looked at each other with helpless alarm that quickly accelerated to panic. Was the mountain collapsing? Was it an earthquake? Was the shed crumbling?

The fear transformed to hilarious laughter as a gentle-looking, furry, grey donkey peeked around the corner. If I am not mistaken, there was a sly grin on his lips. The noise we had heard was simply his boisterous greeting. In close quarters, his gentle hello was a startling experience for Barb and me.

An attractive grey-haired woman was sitting on a patio outside a guesthouse. She was dressed in brilliant blue. There was an equally handsome man wearing a warm grey coat and a Tilley hat. These two Canadian teachers had spent twenty-five years teaching in Hong Kong and were taking their last Asian trek before returning home to Toronto where they would retire and be close to their children and grandchildren. As Yo rounded the corner with me perched on his back, they rose from their chairs. "We saw the chair come an hour ago and we could not believe that someone who cannot walk is actually trying to climb this mountain," the man exclaimed. "We had to wait to see who it was." We chatted on the patio, exchanging travel stories and information about the current conditions in Canada.

"Thank you so much for being here and giving us an inspirational tale to tell our grandchildren," she said as we took our leave.

One day our trek followed the river's edge and led to a natural pool of hot springs. Who needs a bathtub? Yes, of course we went in. It was early enough in the day that wet clothes could dry in the sun on the bushes during the lunch break. The hot silky smooth water soothed and massaged our aching muscles. Most places we'd pay big bucks to use a Jacuzzi or hot springs but here on the mountain it was a free gift.

As we climbed the mountain, daytime temperatures could reach 20-30°C, although the nights were cold. As the sun rose high in the sky, the fierce heat shone upon us. All of our extra clothing was stripped down to shorts and t-shirts—down to comfort. Streams rushed down the mountain, happily gurgling. As the sun set in the evening, cold penetrated our bones and we quickly reclaimed the clothing discarded earlier in the morning. Those friendly little creeks, in many cases, were frozen by morning. At higher elevations, as the evening temperatures became increasingly cold, the more sophisticated guesthouses offered heat to the trekkers. Was it free? Of course not. A small kerosene heater was placed under a picnic table. The table was covered with a blanket that draped to the floor. If I paid for heat, twenty-five cents at the first guesthouse, I could wheel up to the table, put the blanket over my knees and welcome the heat as it seeped into my body. I could have stayed there all night, but no, the twenty-five cents provided one hour of heat. Even if I was willing to pay for more, the number of trekkers wanting this special self-indulgence dictated the length of time that each person could enjoy warmth. As we climbed higher up on the mountain heat was available on a nightly basis at the guesthouses. But of course, as the elevation increased, so did the price. The cost of the service grew by twenty-five cents a day and at the top of base camp, we were paying $1.25 for one hour of warmth. But perhaps it was the best $1.25 I had ever spent in my life. One last long day of a totally vertical climb rewarded us with the sight of the sign: "Welcome to Annapurna Base Camp." We arrived very late in the afternoon and even with the anticipation of solar heated water, we made a unanimous decision that on this particular day, showering was not necessary. The thermometer already read 6oC. The shower nozzle trickled icy water in a dirt-floored outdoor shed.

We retired early to bed in anticipation of an early departure down the mountain in the morning. Packed up and ready to go at 6:00 a.m., breakfast eaters munched their Buthanese bread as we started to descend the mountain trails. It was a long day and as always, arrival at a guesthouse included fatigue, hunger and the need to freshen up and put on warm clothes. We were always ready for our evening meal and prepared for Nepalese rummy after dinner. Barb and I, after ten days, decided that a change was in order so we taught the porters to play Crazy Eights. They were delighted with this new card game and all quickly acquired a natural expertise. The morning after leaving base camp, we realized that luck had been with us. We looked back to see base camp, the top of the mountain, and the trail that we had traversed yesterday, covered in snow.

Along the pathway, the children on their way home from school gathered in a meadow to serenade trekkers from around the world. Of course, it was not simply from a desire to entertain the guests in their country. It was partly from the desire to supplement their income. In the guesthouses, a small behind-the-counter store offered snacks and candy to travellers. Like all children around the world who know the location of the candy store, the Nepalese children are no different. Rupees earned from their vocal talents could always be used for the purchase of sweets.

It would be wonderful to be on these mountains in the springtime. In Vancouver, there are beautiful blooming rhododendron bushes in the spring. In Nepal, the rhododendron trees are just that—huge trees that in spring must offer an astonishing huge array of colourful blossoms. In December, many of our homes are decorated with poinsettias in pots. Adjacent to the mountain paths, poinsettia bushes, four feet high and in full bloom, displayed a riot of crimson and snow white blossoms. Did your mother ever tell you that mountain air and sunshine would help you to grow healthy and strong? It must be the same for flowers because none of them were tiny. Marigolds and sweet peas adorned the fences surrounding the village. The fences were four to six feet high and so were the flowers! Small patches of vegetables grew in the yards of every residence. Huge green fields sloping along the mountainsides produced vegetables for local consumption and for export to neighbouring India.

Abundant sunshine could be counted on to be a part of every day. Precipitation and cloud cover, although uncommon, developed rapidly to produce unbelievable monsoon-type rains. The transition from warm and dry to saturation could occur in ten minutes. There was never a warning nor enough time to don Gortex jackets before the deluge. On our final day, we were offered shelter from the rainstorm in a warm, dry, farmhouse kitchen where Chai and muffins were spread before us.

The walk down the mountain seemed easy—was it really?

Or was it because the climbing portion of the journey was now over? After a seven-hour hike down the mountain, we arrived at the foot of the hill. We connected with the pathway through the meadows, walking another two kilometres back to civilization in Pokara.

At the conclusion of a trek, I always have an internal feeling of letdown, accompanied by the satisfaction that a dream of mine has been realized.

Chitwan

Some would call it brave; others would say we were crazy.

The porters arrived in the early dawn at the guesthouse to accompany us to the bus station. We needed these trusty Napalese caretakers to direct us to the right vehicle, share a few more laughs and stories, and deliver farewell hugs that represented the warm bonds that we had formed by sharing three weeks on the mountain. In the grey beginning of the day, groups of people streamed down the streets heading towards the vacant dirt lot where the buses waited. Tiny cups of steaming chai tea promised to give a kick-start to those whose bodies still wished to be under the sheets.

Open doors beckoned. After considerable deliberation between the porters and drivers, we were directed to an old school bus which was cheerfully brush painted with random red, yellow, and blue stripes. I was lifted onto the front seat and we began to settle when it was decided that we were on the wrong bus.

After two more transfers, reminding me of Goldilocks and the Three Bears, the third bus was deemed the correct one. Backpacks, boxes, bundles and bags were squeezed into the luggage compartment under the bus. Larger items, along with my chair, were slung up on the roof and secured with tatty, worn, tied together, bits of rope. After much ado, every seat finally filled, (sometimes more than filled), three or four people squished into a seat designed for two. Straining against the weight of its load, the bus rocked from side to side as it negotiated a path through mud and around other vehicles. It honked to shoo children who played in puddles, mothers who shouted at the little ones as father took the last drag on his cigarette, and a Grandma who balanced a basket of produce. We finally drove over the rickety planks that covered the deep, water-filled ditch and turned onto the roadway.

The winding road dipped into valleys, crossed riverbeds, and climbed to the summit of mountains, revealing incredible views of snow-capped peaks, dense, lush, green forests, cultivated fields, and rice paddies. Six hours later, the search for manageable accommodation once again became necessary. At our first choice of hotels, we were met with people leaving, complaining and warning us, "Don't stay here." We had been attracted by the enthusiastic recommendation of the locals but the reality did not match their description.

Our next selection, "Jungle Bungalows," was a series of many small, self-contained huts. Our humble abode contained a bedroom with two beds, a private bath, a balcony (only three stairs up) where we could sit and watch the local elephants have their morning bath in the river in front of the security patrolled, fenced property. In the evening, the groundskeeper lit a lantern and placed a mosquito-deterring coil on the veranda. A variety of international restaurants— cooking sheds on the beach, stools and rickety tables stuck in the soft sand—served a delightful variety of local vegetarian and fish dishes. Have you ever tried to wheel across a beach through six-inches of soft sand? The cooks and waiters were quick to respond to our mobility challenge. I'm not sure if it was their innate kindness or their desire for a paying customer that motivated the enthusiastic assistance that carried me quickly over the sand. I like to think that is was a combination of both. We received this red carpet treatment each evening. The return to the jungle bungalow property was not easy – is it ever? We had to climb a three foot muddy slope to the grassy yard, but the rustling of the tropical foliage announced our arrival to the night watchman who immediately responded by pulling the chair backwards up through the mud and continued to help out until we were safely returned to the porch of our cottage. He disappeared around the building's edge afterward, and always returned with two warm cups of herb tea.

In the morning we watched the elephants enjoy their bath from the river's edge. The elephant keepers scrubbed their backs, behind their ears and under their necks, with long wiry brushes as the elephants crooned with pleasure.

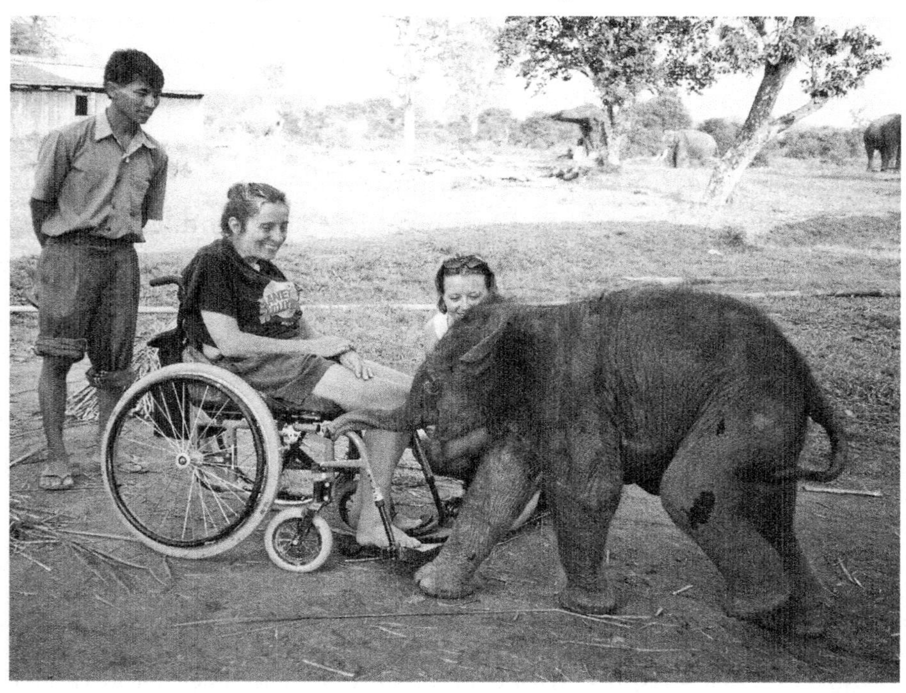

Chitwan Elephant Breeding Centre.

One of the must-do events in Chitwan is to ride an elephant into the jungle in search of tropical birds, Bengal tigers, and single-horn black rhinos. Heading down the back road we were stopped at an Army checkpoint where our identification and passports were examined. We were questioned once more, but again passed the scrutiny of the camouflage suited and heavily armed military. The roadway continued to narrow until we reached a small merchant shed where the owner agreed to keep my wheelchair during our elephant adventure. The guide lifted me up thirty-two stairs onto a small platform, level with the elephant's back. We each straddled a corner of the wooden frame perched on the elephant's back—four corners meant for four people but we were only two. We travelled half a mile to collect our other two travel companions. From the top floor balcony of their hotel, they slid into the other two corners and our seating arrangements were complete. The elephant driver, a young black-skinned man, perched on the crown of Dumbo's head, guided our lady mammoth. We journeyed into the deep tropical foliage, ducking vines, hearing the high-pitched screeching of monkeys as they swung from branch to branch by their tails. Birds called to one another, and the vibration from the elephant's footsteps encouraged the snakes to slither into the ferns. Riotous tropical flowers, unimaginable in their abundance, overwhelmed us.

When I was on safari in Africa, I encountered a multitude of large and small plains animals. The one that I had missed seeing was the rhinoceros. Our elephant driver was determined that we would find a black rhino. Our quest took us deeper into the jungle. Suddenly, we were surprised by a large, aggressive male elephant (complete with long ivory tusks) as he emerged from the foliage. In order to avoid confrontation, our driver urged our gentle giant deeper and deeper into the forest. This far into the bush, a mist gave the wooded area a magical spirit.

The driver's determination to find a rhino was eventually realized. We rounded a corner and were confronted with a large black single-horned rhino with a young calf by her side. We took delight in watching and photographing the animals.

Bengal tigers are native to parts of Asia and India and they live in the jungles of Nepal.

As we started our journey back to the village, we were content with wonders we had seen. Then we rounded a corner and caught sight of the orange stripes of a tiger as he fled from his fresh kill into the depths of the bushes. It was now definitely time to move along. As we headed home, the rewards of the day diminished the pain of sitting on the wooden frame.

Thanks to the unexpected interruptions, our four-hour scheduled elephant ride had turned into nearly eight and a half hours. Darkness was falling. The jungle's inviting daylight was becoming more ominous as night took over day.

When we emerged from the jungle, the laneway had been blocked off by Army personnel, equipped with machine guns, who directed us around the village towards the town of Chitwan. How would we deal with this one? My wheelchair was being babysat in a market shed on the other side of the military roadblock. They refused to let us go down that road.

With some persuasion from the elephant driver, the army captain agreed to allow him to go and retrieve my chair. Every positive is accompanied by a negative. Yes, we now had the chair, but we didn't have the staircase and platform we needed to get me off the elephant. A very large, tall haystack provided the solution. The driver guided the elephant in the pitch-black darkness close to the haystack. I leaned to the side, fell off my perch onto the hay pile, and slid down the side; then, with assistance, got into my waiting chair.

I hoped that those snack bars on the beach offered wine with their standard rice and curried vegetables.

The elephant breeding centre, one of three in the world, is accessed by a dugout canoe ride down the Narayani river. At the breeding centre, large young male elephants are tethered to prevent night-time expeditions into the jungle in search of females outside the breeding program.

"We want only the best elephant babies," the proud supervisor told us.

Large male elephants with their thick, curved ivory tusks were impressive. Pregnant females boasted huge abdomens which are almost as wide as the elephant was tall. Newly delivered moms stroked and caressed their newborns while older babies eagerly nursed. The parents were busy teaching their young ones how to eat hay and to lie down and roll over to scratch their backs and then get up again. They trumpeted in pleasure at their children's accomplishments, and impatience with youth's inattention.

Two irresistible tiny Dumbos invited our attention. The worker at the centre encouraged us to exchange close greetings with the female baby.

"Don't go near that one," he said when we looked at the other. "He is a boy. Boy elephants are bad."

"How can that be?" I asked, perplexed. "He is so small and cute."

Barb and I wandered over to the young lad only to become immediately aware of the truth of the elephant keeper's words. The young elephant wrapped his trunk around the foot pedal of my chair and lifted. How incredible. He was so tiny yet he was able to lift the castor wheels of my chair two feet into the air. While I remained in my chair, the prospect of having a close encounter with the ground and being squashed by those cute little feet that supported a solid 150 pounds was less than appealing.

Our trusty worker came running to my rescue. Through our

laughter, we heard the words of the worker, "I told you. Boy elephants are bad."

Further exploration led us to the park's visitor's centre which provided information on the natural history, geography, geology, meteorology and flora and fauna native to the Royal Chitwan National Park. In the evening, we wandered down the narrow, bumpy alleyway into town to locate the second hand bookstore for some English reading material to nourish our minds during stop times on the long return bus ride to Kathmandu in the morning.

Chapter 16

La Fin Du Monde

Bill and I were embarking on another adventure together. We boarded a flight from Vancouver to the delightful city of Buenos Aires, the capital of Argentina. After a few days of exploration here, we embarked upon a ship that would take us down the east coast of South America and around Cape Horn.

Reflecting on the sudden appearance of wheelchair accessibility in various destinations, it dawned on me that I could expect some degree of accessibility in any city that has been host to the modern day Olympics. Buenos Aries is no exception. Some buses were wheelchair accessible and telephone booths with the international wheelchair symbol posted on the side offered TTY (Talk to You: telephones for the hearing impaired,). I found lower tables for writing, large easy-to-read numbers on the telephone and a usable dialing system for those with compromised fine motor skills. Public washrooms had a stall to accommodate wheelchair users, elevator buttons and restaurant menus included Braille. Curb cuts on each corner made street crossings easy, stores were ramped, and the sales staff was aware of the need for width between display racks. Restaurants with stairs most often had ramped back door entrances; people of all ages and abilities were welcomed everywhere.

La Boca, an enchanting area of the city rich with European flavour, displayed unique architecture. Colour personified! Houses boasted fluorescent blue, fire engine red, sunshine yellow, eye-blinding lime green siding, shutters and doors. The non-symmetrical designs were fascinating. Houses ranged from single level cottages to residences with six or more multi-shaped, randomly arranged levels. The geometry included every mathematical angle, except of course, the standard 90° right angle. The community evidenced spontaneity, love of life, and a sense of "we'll do anything for fun."

The open air markets along the street offered crafts, original art, small sculptures ranging from paper clip configurations to carved soapstone; homemade wine and garden vegetables. Musicians playing the accordion, balalaika, castanets and drums serenaded our stroll through the market. They were joined by vocals ranging from operatic arias and Sunday morning hymns to children's nursery rhymes, and folk songs. Vendors promoted their wares by shouting, hawking, singing, dancing, and laughing. It was difficult to ignore their welcoming antics. They made me want to buy.

In Uruguay, Bill and I were fascinated by the many different styles of the houses of worship. Church bells sang out—sometimes in unison, sometimes in harmony, sometimes in conflict. Regardless of the degree of coordination or discord, it was music to our ears. Members of the elder generation, sitting on park benches, reached out to hug me and bless me. Little girls adorned me with fresh flowers while young lads challenged me to races. We wandered the quiet streets, capturing images in our minds and on Kodak film. The digital camera was not yet in common use. It always takes me a while to decide that a new product is a "must-have" article in my backpack. One of the best photographs I have ever taken was shot here on a deserted downtown street. The scene reminded me of the song *Sunday Morning Coming Down* by Kris Kristofferson from 1969, describing the quiet after a full-bodied Saturday night party. I captured an elegant 16th century stone building reflected in the mirrored glass walls of a modern day high rise. I ignored the negativity of those around me who insisted that it wouldn't turn out, but in fact I now treasure that perfect image.

On the dock in Paraguay, we hired a local driver to escort us throughout the countryside. We viewed large flocks of ostrich in the wild—adults, some chicks, some eggs—then roamed through the trails of a national park which led us to a silent sanctuary where 24-inch Magellanic penguins waddled along before us on the narrow pathway. They showed no sign of fear. These small black-and-white tuxedo-dressed birds built homes by nosing shallow burrows into the soft ground. Their heads peeked out to investigate the noise made by our approaching footsteps. We watched a young fox trying to satisfy his hunger by attempting to capture a small penguin. On the beach, we saw hundreds of enormous elephant seals. Despite their humongous size, they gently caressed one another in play as they argued, wrestled, and dozed side-by-side in the sun.

Magellanic penguin

Emperor penguins are those big guys (forty-eight inches) that I remember viewing in the Stanley Park Zoo when I was a young teenager. They strut around in their black-tie formality with yellow streaks sweeping across their cheeks. With erect posture and heads held high, they give the impression of elite high society living. One of my hopes and dreams has always been to one day meet these fellows in their natural habitat. Was even this possible? One rainy winter evening in Vancouver, I challenged Google late into the night and into the early morning hours, to find a way to make it work. My extensive computer search revealed four companies on the Falklands that offered penguin excursions. I diligently e-mailed each of these companies, explaining my desire, disability, and determination to have a close interaction with the protected species of King Penguins. My outlook was so positive and my anticipation so elevated that it was impossible to accept the discouraging answers I received.

"I regret that we are unable to take you because transportation is in a four-wheel drive jeep and it will not accommodate a wheelchair. As you know, wheelchairs do not fold up!" (Mine certainly does!)

"Thank you for your inquiry but we are unable to accommodate persons with a disability as the road, or lack of road, is muddy and steep. This experience is for the adventurous and able bodied. Only they can tolerate such conditions." (Ha, little do they know!)

"It is great that you are planning to come to the Falkland Islands and would like to visit the penguin reserve off Antarctica. We welcome our elderly visitors. Are you bringing your own nurses? There is a visitors' centre that shows film documentaries and has taxidermy samples of the species. I'm sure you will find it quite informative." (Maybe so. but that wasn't what I wanted!)

How could I convince these folks in faraway lands that yes, I have a disability, and yes, it slows me down, but no, it definitely does not stop me from pursuing my goals and adventures in life. My frustration bordered on helplessness but giving up is so foreign to me. There must be a way, I decided! But I did not have to dwell on it for long.

When I opened my work e-mail several days later, I had a bold message titled, "Penguins" in my in-box. With a meeting scheduled in ten minutes, I only had time to scan the contents.

"Sorry to take so long to get back to you. I have been away in Britain."

Work commitments faded next to my urgency to read on and respond.

Tony wrote enthusiastically, *"I have taken my mother-in-law to Volunteer Point, a private penguin colony in the Falklands, on a number of occasions. She uses a wheelchair. The message from you indicates to me that you possess the necessary adventurous elements to take such a trip."*

I was ecstatic. It is going to be possible. I will see the penguins.

My children's encouragement and support of my wild excursions is always a great blessing. At the beginning of this trip, on the way to the Vancouver airport, I said to Patrick, "It may be very expensive to go and see those penguins."

"Mom, the whole reason you are taking this trip is to see the big penguins so don't you dare come home until you've seen them. I don't care what it costs."

Shore excursions on cruise ships are costly and most often offer "touristy" type highlights. This is not usually my style. I really wanted to see the large King penguins in their natural habitat. Early morning disembarkation from a cruise ship is first available to those who have arranged their outings through the ship's shore services. I explained to the shore excursion director that I had made my own arrangements.

"I am going to Volunteer Point."

Upon hearing that I had organized a trip to see the penguins off the coast of Antarctica, there was no hesitation on the part of the cruise ship staff. In order to make this happen, the shore excursion director scheduled an unprecedented early disembarkation.

Tony collected us from the cruise ship at 7:00 a.m. Visits to Volunteer Point are restricted to four people per day so Bill and I offered the opportunity to another young couple who joined us for the most adventurous, unusual and rewarding experience of my life.

We travelled for two and a half hours by four-wheel drive—the first hour on a gravel road, the next hour and a half on no road at all—across rivers, over fallen trees, up hills, down valleys, until we reached the launching point. We then bounced across the wave tops in a black rubber zodiac. Leaping dolphins escorted us to the east coast of East Falkland Island. Gusting wind and rough water conditions offered significant challenge in landing the zodiac. With willing assistance from Tony and Bill, my chair made it across the rocks, over the beach, and up the hill to the private home of seven hundred pairs of Emperor (King) penguins. It is the largest population of these birds outside of the centre ice region of Antarctica.

Tony had obtained special permission for me to enter the sanctuary because viewing from outside the fence offered limited access to the penguins. Bill pushed me onto the expansive grassy slope, and in the distance we could see groups of black and white sentinels. Tony's instructions were clear and not to be reckoned with, "Just sit where you are and the penguins will come to you."

He was right. One large mama approached my chair and placed her beak gently on my hip. If it had not been an invasion of their personal space, I could have reached out and put my arm around the neck of one of the beautiful creatures to give it a friendly hug.

Colony of emperor penguins

Penguins stood in groups, perhaps fifty in a circle, surrounded by odd-shaped rocks. The birds themselves had pushed the rocks into these configurations. Some of the standing adults were fat, others skinny. The mothers and fathers equally shared in the parenting and daycare roles. Under the white feathers at the front of their tuxedos, babies and eggs are kept warm and nurtured. The thin parents had been on childcare duty for ten to fourteen days. During that entire time, they had not eaten. The chubbier penguins, mums and/or dads, had just returned from two weeks of continuous feasting off the shores of Antarctica. The native fish and sea life of this area is very specific to the needs of our elegant friends.

When the well-fed parent returned, it was time for the roles to reverse. The mum and dad make close rubbery-footed contact, the white feathers are lifted, and the babysitting parent tips to transfer the egg or the young penguin onto the feet of the waiting caregiver. If the egg slips to the ground during this transfer, it is left unattended. The embryo inside will never see the light of day. The babies, who have some degree of mobility, can crawl back onto their parent's feet. Skinny parents slip into the water to swim seven hundred miles to engage in a twelve to fourteen day feast while the other parent assumes the 24-hour role of fostering love and the chick's growth. The younger penguins played games outside the comfort circles with a mom or dad always standing guard against predators.

At the edge of the beach, Gentoo penguins, (only about 30 inches tall) with a white stripe across their heads that resembled a 19th century bonnet, ran along the shoreline with their bright orange feet flashing in the sun. They dropped to their stomachs, using their small wings to windmill themselves along. Magellanic penguins climbed the dunes then slid down toward the water on their tummies. Fun was had by all. The whole scene was comparable to a carnival where children play, parents watch, and infants are babysat in an atmosphere of organized chaos.

Another black rubber zodiac transported us along the Falklands shore where we were able to observe more Emperor penguins, walrus seals, and elephant sea lions. Self-arranged on-shore excursions are definitely more educational, more rewarding, and more affordable than those provided by many cruise lines.

On our return to the ship, we learned that those who had participated in the ship's excursion to the Penguin Park had seen only two Emperor penguins. Patrick would be proud of his mum, who had been privileged with the sight of seven hundred pairs. My father, who had taken a similar cruise, told me before I left home that the Falkland Islands had nothing to offer. For me, this was one of the highlights of my travel career.

The four-wheel drive return trip over the island retraced our early morning excursion. While in Stanley, the capital of the

Falklands, I tried to take pictures of the exotic wooden cathedral but my camera had stopped working! I had taken two complete rolls of film of the penguins. My camera chose to die only after I had secured these precious shots

Our cruise would end in Valparaiso, Chile, but this trip was not yet over. In Chile, we found an adventurer who was willing to take us into the forests and behind the scenes of the ski resorts in the Andes. We participated in a wine tour where grapes hung in dense clusters from the vines. They were harvested then squashed—no longer by feet but by electrically powered mallets. Juice was strained, poured into vats to age then bottled and buried in a cool underground wine cellar until party time. Of course, there were abundant samples. I poured more wine down my gullet than I had consumed over the last two years in that one afternoon. At least by mobilizing in a wheelchair, I did not have to worry about staggering and falling—although my directional steering weaved a bit!

We ventured to the southernmost tip of South America to a small town called La Fin du Monde. The population of 4,000 lives in wintery conditions for ten months of the year. At home in Canada, what I dread most about winter is the shortened daylight hours—it's dark at 3:30 p.m. and dawn does not appear until 8:00 a.m. How would I manage with twenty-two hours of darkness and two hours of dusk for ten months of the year? As much as I was enthralled with this region, the dark seemed oppressive. Thanks but no thanks!

Sometimes accessibility appears where you least expect to find it. We had perused the pages of *The Lonely Planet* to find a small hotel that seemed the one most likely to be manageable by those of us who walk on wheels. In fact, the delightful room was spacious. A small sitting room offered satellite TV, piped in classic rock music and in the bathroom, the luxury of a wheel-in shower. Perhaps La Fin du Monde is not always the "end" of the world!"

Chapter 17

Dominican Republic

Puerto Plata

As I sought a vacation beyond the ordinary, the Dominican Republic quickly rose to the top of the list. November precipitation on the west coast always motivates me to seek a drier environment where one of the benefits is an overdose of vitamin D. In 2004, the receptionist at Motion Physiotherapy (where I attended an hour of endurance stretching weekly) advised me that she had spent a week at an all-inclusive tropical resort in Puerto Plata. She enthusiastically expanded on the benefits, highly recommending its accessibility. On her suggestion, I booked the trip. Upon arrival, I was delighted to see her accurate assessment become my reality.

All the hotel accommodations were on the ground floor. The enormous, irregularly-shaped pool housed a swim-up bar, islands of tropical flora, warm semi-salt water, palm trees and umbrellas offering shade when needed. The pool had a gradual beach entry. What a bonus! After removing the cushion from the wheelchair, I could wheel into the pool until I reached enough depth to slide out of my chair to take a leisurely swim around the circumference.

The hotel room bathroom was large enough to use easily but small enough to limit falling space. The wall between counters and crowned mouldings offered reachable "hang-ons." The bathtub was too high to consider a transfer onto a chair for showering but showers outside by the pool fit the bill. Stairs were few. The flat terrain negated the need for ramps and I greatly appreciated the willingness of the local people to give a hand or a push when needed. During these interactions, I learned from the locals. They shared intimacies about their families, their living conditions, their lifestyle, their music, and the benefits and hang-ups of their country.

Two weeks with nothing to do presents little appeal for many people. For those of us who live life as if we're running a marathon, fourteen days of deciding how to do nothing is absolute decadence. Days consisted of reading in the sunshine until my body became heated enough for a leisurely swim in the pool. Three laps around the pool in each direction netted one kilometre of gentle aerobic exercise.

On some evenings, local craftsmen set up tables on the grounds of the resort and in the hotel lobby, encouraging visitors to buy their wares: cigars, jewellery, rum, wood carvings, paintings, shell craft, masks and bowls, men's laid-back, breezy shirts, women's long elegant mesh fabric dresses, marijuana pipes. A walk to the local market in bright burning sunshine was necessary to determine if the prices from the vendors at the hotel were competitive. At the market, all visitors buy coffee that surpasses anything that North American coffee shops have to offer.

Caribbean music was everywhere— in the dining room, the shops, in the whistle of the workers as they trimmed palm trees and cut grass, in the steps of the waiters and the agricultural workers in the fields. Rhythm and clapping seeped into every cell of my body as the cheerful tempo accompanied every activity, every moment. Dance featured colourful costumes, the beat of bongo drums and gracefully natural movements of the locals. Fatigue was never an issue. The very young, the very old, and all in between, danced the night away. Tourists made valiant attempts to join in but Caucasian folk "just don't have it."

Part of the appeal of an all-inclusive resort is the feature restaurants: Italian, seafood grill, Cajun, and of course, the buffet. I can easily turn down breakfast foods but the local garden produce— yucca, yams, green beans sautéed in garlic, curried cauliflower, cilantro, pumpkin, plantain as well as mango, pineapple, and papaya—made morning cuisine impossible to resist. At poolside, a sous-chef barbecued throughout the day; fish, pork, shellfish, and of course, for non-experimental North Americans, hamburgers and hotdogs.

Water sports included snorkelling, kayaking, windsurfing, and sailing on small catamarans. We played poolside chess with 2-foot high Styrofoam pieces. Lying by the poolside and dozing always appeals to me on sunny days. Board games and reading occupied us vacationers when it rained.

Day trips outside the resort were many. Although it was difficult to leave the sunshine and the pool, two excursions excited me. Yes, I want to swim with dolphins and yes, I want to venture outside of the resort area on a jungle safari.

Dolphins symbolize freedom, joy, grace, and serenity. They are warm-blooded mammals closely related to whales and porpoises. Unlike fish who lay eggs, dolphins give live birth to one calf at a time. They gather in small groups called pods. Their appeal to North Americans began with the TV show *Flipper*, recognized in our culture as the aquatic *Lassie*. This was another "dream come true". I was going to swim with the dolphins. Filled with eager anticipation, I eased down into the water, looking forward to genuine physical contact with these wonderful creatures. There were ten in the group, consisting of adults and youth, and two babies.

To my surprise, their soft, sleek skin is really not soft and sleek. It is thick and rubbery, protecting them from the elements in salt-water oceans, and, it aids in reducing heat loss. The affection that we see in photographs became a reality when a smiling grey fellow snuggled up to me in the water. Their streamlined body shape allows them to slip quickly through the waves. They are friendly creatures—some more than others. One young male was intent on cuddling with me, cheek-to-cheek. When I hugged him, he chortled. He was laughing out loud, enjoying the personal attention. There were few vacationers waiting, so my stay in the water lengthened to almost two hours.

The jungle safari vehicle was a flat-bed fitted with wooden benches on a truck chassis. The driver, blessed with upper body strength and enthusiasm, easily picked me up in one hand and flipped me into the bed of the truck. Committed to safety, he assisted my entry to and exit from the truck and made sure I was included in all the group activities. To navigate the jungle, the truck sported four-foot high, deep tread tires. Comfort was not a priority. The hard bumpy ride—climbing and descending slippery hillsides; climbing over logs through creeks and riverbeds—was rewarded with close up views of colourful toucans, white-tailed monkeys swinging from vines, and dense jungle flora adorned with huge vibrant flowers. On the floor of the jungle, armadillos swayed from side to side as they lumbered along. Huge hard-shelled beetle-like creatures crept out from under damp logs. Tiny slithery snakes appeared suddenly, disappearing just as quickly. The sounds of the rainforest assaulted our ears and piqued our curiosity. What kinds of birds, animals, and insects were generating this endless conversation? The air was heavy with heat and humidity. The scent of broad-leaved tropical foliage filled our noses. Dismounting from the truck, we examined hieroglyphics at the narrow entrance to stone caves. We rehydrated with bottled water, snacked on berries and nuts, and rested momentarily before climbing back on the jungle vehicle. The long hot day finished with appealing crushed ice pina coladas at poolside.

Rain is not exclusive to the west coast of North America.

Rain in the Dominican Republic was warm, inviting bare foot walking through puddles. It rained continuously for forty-eight hours. Heated raindrops cascaded over one's head and down one's back.

Evening entertainment focused on dance, board games, music, appetizers and bargaining with local vendors who continuously repeated, "You must have. You will not be happy without this monkey pot bowl. You must take back some specially made Dominican jewellery and cigars. There are none like them anywhere else in the world." Vivid paintings on rolled canvas exploded with colour. It is easy to be carried away with the local attractions. What looks great on this tropical Caribbean island may not generate the same enthusiasm in the dark rainy atmosphere of Vancouver.

Punta Cana

In May 2008 on the west coast, the absence of spring was so very evident. The weather in Vancouver was atypically cool and wet. How to deal with this? The usual solution is to seek the sun. After a few hours at the computer, and scanning the travel section of the local paper, the decision materialized—two weeks on a tropical Caribbean island. My partner Doug had been working without a break for more than two years so after three days of reflection, he and I boarded a plane for a spring escape.

The all-inclusive resort offered a trapeze, climbing wall, three swimming pools, feature restaurants, a seafood grill and a buffet, thus providing a different dining experience for each night of the week. Evening entertainment followed dinner—music, dance, a ventriloquist, mime, acrobatics, a magician. Dancing and partying carried on into the wee hours of the morning. Late-night snacks, board games, poolside and table shuffleboard, were there for those who desired more sedate activity. The casino was a last resort option.

Retiring to our room, we fell exhausted into the luxurious nine pillow, eight-inch deep duvet-covered king size bed. In this enormous bed, we felt like we were sleeping in different countries. What a contrast to the double bed at home that my partner Doug and I share, where competition for a few more inches takes on a variety of personalities. Sometimes, a squeeze for an extra inch is friendly, sometimes increasingly aggressive. "Let's snuggle I'm cold." "It's too hot to be close so move over to your own side of the bed." "I'm right on the edge." At this point, one of us sometimes gives up and moves to the couch. One night while lounging in bed in Punta Cana, we turned on the television, tuning in to a program that highlighted Dominican life, culture, people, children, economy, flora and fauna, sports, games and activities of this region. I was stunned to discover that they have chicken fights in Punta Cana. In Canadian culture, it is considered a form of animal abuse.

Activities like chicken fights, calf roping, greyhound dog races, old style jail-like zoos with cages and concrete animal housing are discouraged and in some cases outright illegal. However, in the Dominican Republic, various sorts of open gambling and planned chicken confrontations ("cockfights") are considered common entertainment.

"I want to go." It's not that I believe in the practice of cockfights (or any other questionable animal activity), but part of travelling to other countries is learning the differences, which are sometimes agreeable to me and sometimes offensive. If I am to fully absorb the diversity and exceptional qualities of other cultures, I want to explore every opportunity that is available.

The Dominican staff working at the resort were obviously coached not to promote controversial activities such as off property gambling. Much to Doug's chagrin, I asked every local resident that I encountered about how, why, where, when, I could see chicken fights. I wanted to learn about life here.

One morning as we were walking the grounds, I encountered some big strong men lifting boxes outside the warehouse where supplies for the resort were delivered. Bingo!

"Just walk outside the resort and talk to one of the cab drivers. They will help you out," a friendly worker said.

True to his word, I found a cab driver who spoke perfect English. For a negotiated price, he agreed to pick us up Saturday at noon to take us to the chicken fight ring. On arrival we were surprised to see a tiny, white, octagonal "coliseum," which was much smaller than expected. In the open-air lobby, men of all ages leaned over white plastic tables, some sitting on chairs, some on boxes, some standing. Energetic gambling games were in full swing. I don't know what the games were. They included domino-like tiles, playing cards, shouting and cursing, and pesos flying. The taxi driver went inside to seek permission for "the Canadians" to observe the afternoon activities. It was no problem for Doug to be admitted, but I was the only female in the house. It is unusual to find a woman in situations like this, particularly if she is Caucasian and in a wheelchair.

Plastic tube chairs sat side by side on wooden risers. The action would soon begin in the ring—only twelve feet in diameter. The level of your seating was directly related to the price of your entry ticket. The serious gamblers were seated in the bottom row close to the ring. These folks bet perhaps the equivalent of $3,000 (CAD) on each match. There were no stairs to aid ascension to our seats mid-way up the risers. Doug carried me up the steep bleachers, leaving the wheelchair at the bottom.

Betting occurred in two ways. Either through the master of ceremonies who charged 5% of the winnings or, by a tap on your neighbour's shoulder to establish a private bet. This was the more common practice because no one was willing to part with any portion of the winnings to the master of ceremonies.

The first confrontation was about to begin. The chicken handler appeared from behind a curtain accompanied by two young boys holding black cloth bags. The feathered rivals emerged from the bags. Another man held a female chicken. He aggravated the competitors by shaking the feathered lady right in their faces. When the two cocks were sufficiently agitated, they were dropped onto the ground. Wagering began. Jose, our taxi driver, negotiated with a fellow spectator.

"I will bet five pesos ($15) on the 'blue chicken'." Each cock had an identifying coloured band around his leg.

The fight was under way. It quickly became obvious that the 'blue chicken' was the superior competitor. The man seated beside me suddenly arose from his seat and shouted to Jose in Spanish. I had no idea what he was saying but Jose told me that the bet was off. My wagering neighbour had decided that the chances of his contender winning were diminishing. I had never heard of such a thing. In Canada, when a bet is made and hands shaken, the wager is firm and secure to the end. However this was not the case in the Dominican Republic.

The next fight began. Once again the "blue chicken" was the favoured feathered friend of the day because no one would agree to a dollar for dollar wager. This time, those betting five pesos on the blue cock would only receive four pesos if he was victorious, and should the bird lose, they would pay ten pesos to the winning party. No way. Fair is fair! If I bet five pesos, I expect to lose five pesos, but I also expect to line my pocket with five pesos if my selected chicken wins. This was not the way it worked here!

The third battle was about to begin. The noise level escalated as the gambling grew more frenzied. This was serious business! It certainly is if one's rent, grocery money, children's clothing allowance is dependent upon winning or losing.

The challengers fight for fifteen minutes. If there is not a winner after this time, the duel is considered a tie. In this case, the supremacy of the blue chicken was inarguable until the final 20 seconds. The white chicken was lying on the ground, weakly flapping his wings. Suddenly he was endowed with a burst of unexpected energy. He leapt three feet into the air from his supine position, landing squarely on the other rooster's comb, knocking the blue chicken to his knees. The blue chicken was down for the count!

Forty-four competitions were scheduled for the day. Contests would continue until midnight. Our contract with the taxi driver included transportation to and from the ring with two hours of interpretation and explanation. Enough was enough! Time to go.

On the following morning we were not unhappy when we arose to find clouds and drizzle. Who wants to leave a tropical paradise in the sunshine anticipating that rain would await us in Vancouver? The stopover in Calgary, scheduled to be one hour, stretched out to six and a half. I thought winter ended in March. Not so in 2008. A snowstorm in Calgary had closed the airport. We impatiently waited to learn the outcome of our long layover. We read, dozed, perused duty free shops. Hunger overcame willpower. Doug wandered off returning with two burgers. When we finally got on the plane, our selected seats were occupied. We were moved to business class. Of course it happened that salmon salad and wine were offered when our stomachs were already full. Life often delivers bonuses when we cannot take advantage of them. Unfortunately the airline had saved "The Best Till Last." (Vanessa Williams)

On the wall in my sitting room is a large vibrant oil painting that I purchased in the Dominican Republic. When I look at it, memories return. Although I don't have any natural rhythm, I find myself swaying from side to side as I remember the feeling of the music.

Chapter 18

India

Do You Want to Go?

In October of 2004, the wheels started to turn. Louise, one of my trusty home support workers who had worked with me for four years, always had her finger on the pulse of the Vancouver community. She also visits another client, Michelle, to assist her, with her home management. On one of these visits, Michelle asked Lou, "Do you know anyone who would be interested in going to India with me?"

"Of course I do," Lou told her enthusiastically. "Lin will go anywhere in the world if the weather at the point of destination is warmer and sunnier than at home, if the price is right, and if it is somewhere that she has not visited in the past."

I do not often take the time to read the newspaper or listen to an evening newscast. On Friday and Saturday mornings, throughout my fifteen-minute stretching routine (which may extend to thirty or forty-five minutes depending on the juiciness of current events), I catch up on the recent happenings that have been presented in the local newspaper, on the Canadian news, or worldwide news on the international television newscast. During my fifteen minutes of sometimes comfortable, sometimes painful, sometimes just plain annoying stretching, I will feel as if I have been transported to the Middle East as I view the war zone, and next minute, to the sidewalk in London, England to watch Queen Elizabeth II drive by in her motorcade. I will see the overabundant crop drooping from the branches of olive trees in the Tucson sun. I will know who won last night's hockey game; who has been shot by whom and where; when the rain will stop (does it ever in Vancouver?); who is on strike; who is sleeping with whom and who is the father of the newest baby in Hollywood. I will inevitably benefit from a great stretch and gain knowledge of the most recent news and current events that (shame on me) have not earned a place on the top of my priority list.

On that significant Saturday morning when Louise burst into my apartment with her usual, not-to-be-squelched enthusiasm, she emphatically directed me to lie flat in preparation for stretching. "Would you like to go to India? If you would like to, call Michelle."

The question came out of the blue as she manipulated my legs into pretzel position, which was the groundwork for my getting out of bed to tackle the excitement of yet another new day. My answer to questions about travel never wavers. My response is always keenly affirmative. The opportunity to visit yet another part of the world—to interact with persons of a culture I have yet to experience and the chance to explore a new corner of the map that I could now include in my growing collection of countries visited—is never turned down. It was as simple as that. A six-week trip halfway around the world to visit a country that is as different from Canada as night is from day came into being. One short phrase, yet again, gave birth to a once in a lifetime experience.

"Yes, of course I want to go."

When I spoke with Michelle, she said she was thinking of going to India maybe next year or in two years.

"No! Of course not!" I exclaimed. "If we're going to go to India, we want to go now!"

"Are you serious?" Michelle seemed so surprised. I was ready to place the Visa card on the table, giving little thought as to how two women in wheelchairs would maneuver and mobilize around a country where wheelchairs and people with disabilities are unknown or at least unseen.

The fact that I had never met Michelle and had no idea how compatible we were on Canadian soil, much less in India, did not enter into the decision. On that fateful day at the end of October, during a telephone conversation, Michelle and I agreed to meet and readily entered into a contract that would mean six-weeks of an amazing, incredible, unprecedented life experience.

Wheels were set in motion. Some may think that this is a play on words but it is not meant to be. We immediately engaged the gears in our hearts and minds. Investigation into weather conditions, high tourist season, reasonable costs, non-existent accessibility, must-see places, must-not go to places, food, water, and customs provided us with the information we needed to make our decision. We would go in January of 2005, leaving ten weeks to plan a trip to the other side of the world.

I was so enthusiastic. When I ran the idea past Patrick, his immediate response was, "Of course you should go. There is no reason why not."

As always, the enthusiasm and encouragement that I receive from my sons spurs me to greater and greater heights. The detailed planning began with borrowing the *Lonely Planet of India* from the library followed by many hours spent scanning the pages and ending in confusion. I didn't know where to go, how to interact, or what to do in an enormous, fascinating country that was surely filled with new, uncertain experiences.

Where to find airline tickets? I contacted each travel agent known to me. Jill, (now my daughter-in-law), attended a women's networking group. She referred me to a woman who was a member of the group. Initially Jill was trying to fulfill her obligation to make referrals, when possible, to other new entrepreneurial women who were in the process of developing their own space in the business world. Marta became our close partner in arranging transportation to and from India.

On investigation, we found that open-jaw tickets, at a reasonable price, were possible. Open-jaw means flying into one city and returning from another, thus eliminating back travel. We would fly into Delhi and return from Calcutta at the end of our stay. Now was the time to get our act together and plan for the excursion that would take us to a new world halfway around the globe.

Patrick had been to India a few years earlier, on the first flight that departed from Vancouver following the suicide flights into the twin towers in New York City on September 11, 2001. This never-to-be-forgotten historic event left thousands of people dead. Many firefighters and police officers in the line of duty were victims in this tragedy, leaving fatherless children and single mothers to sustain their families and rebuild their lives. Some occasions burrow into our memories. Where were you when you heard about the assassinations of John Fitzgerald Kennedy? Martin Luther King? Bobbie Kennedy? Where were you when you heard about the death of Walt Disney, the explosion of the space shuttle that carried the first civilian (a schoolteacher) to travel to the moon, the release of Mandela from his 25-year imprisonment in South Africa, and the bombing of the twin towers in New York City? When such events occur, we always remember the circumstances surrounding the announcement of such happenings. I will always remember that Patrick flew to India immediately following 9/11.

Jill, a Naturopathic Doctor, had chosen Bombay (now Mumbai), India as the location for her medical residency. Following her practicum, Patrick and Jill connected in Mumbai. They put aside their careers and studies for one year in order to pursue the inquiring urges in their hearts and to experience once in a lifetime opportunities—trekking in Nepal, travelling through India, Asia, Eastern Europe, and Tunisia. They absented themselves from the contemporary activities of North America for twelve months. They ended their one-year sabbatical with a five-month 4,000 kilometre trek through the coastal mountain range on the west coast of North America. The Pacific Crest Trail carried them from the Mexican American border to Manning Park, British Columbia, Canada. They walked twenty to twenty-five miles per day through the mountains. People often say that my determination and willingness to feel the fear and do it anyway, is amazing. I think it pales in comparison to the challenges that my children enthusiastically embrace. Their support is always "Go for it Mum. You can do it." Often these words echo in my head as I pursue my goal to travel the world.

Patrick and Jill arrived at my home one evening, with the *Lonely Planet of India* in hand and an adequate dose of guidance and suggestions as to where we could go, should go, must go. They provided Michelle and I with a suggested outline for our travel route, visiting as many parts of the country as possible, keeping travel duplication to a minimum. With their trusty outline and guesstimated prices scribbled on a few pieces of foolscap, and tucked into the guidebook, we were now ready to tackle a country on the other side of the world.

Where would we find someone who could accompany us to India? Should we confront the problem directly on our arrival, assuming the risk of finding assistance when we entered into a country where language and customs do not include women with disabilities needing personal care? It would mean eating, sharing train and bus seats, intimacies such as dressing and undressing, showering, and sleeping in the same room with total strangers. This is not foreign to those of us who live in North America and have a disability. Modesty ceases to be important when one needs assistance with showering, dressing, and personal care. Michelle lives in Surrey, an area where there is a large population of Indo-Canadians and new residents of Canada whose roots and background are founded in India or Pakistan. One of Michelle's neighbours has a sister, a retired nurse, who lives in Punjab. Margaret made contact with this sister across the wires, across continents, across oceans. Harriet, better known as Harry, lived in Chandigarh, the capital of Punjab.

Margaret, her husband, Michelle and I met together at my home to discuss what the needs of two Canadian women with disabilities would be, what assistance Harry could offer, terms of the employment offer, and compensation. Family ties are culturally strong. It was definitely in the best interest of Harriet's family that she be well compensated financially. If Harry had adequate funds to provide for her daily needs for the next several years, financial assistance from her relatives in Canada would not be required. Yes, Harry would meet us in the Delhi airport and accompany us through the mysteries and wonders of India.

How crazy is this? Two women who cannot walk, who speak only English and who reside on the opposite side of the globe from their destination are meeting on Monday afternoon. On January 23, 2005, Michelle and I connected at the entrance to the Vancouver airport. Michelle's husband Mark, accompanied by her sister Paula who viewed our plans to go to India with doubt, deposited us at the departure counter. Despite their skepticism, we felt sound in body and mind. We cheerfully hugged and kissed the well-wishers who were reluctantly sending us off to New Delhi.

On January 23 at 5:00 p.m., we boarded the flight that would carry us from Vancouver to Los Angeles. A brief stop followed by two more flights took us to Singapore. Before leaving home, I created an "India List" from the e-mail contacts on my computer. My habit is to send the same message to all, with my apologies that everyone gets the same information. Finding wheelchair accessible Internet sites is not easy on foreign soil. When compiling a list, I include my children, my friend Bill, Cathy, a colleague at work, Laurie and Doug, and my father. Knowing that my father might be unable to read my mail as he also is often travelling, I include my brother and my uncle in hopes that they will have telephone contact with Dad and tell him that I am indeed alive and well.

A short stopover in Singapore provided time to use a washroom then meander our way to the next gate using the free Internet access on our way. Free Internet is becoming a common perk in international airports. The first note that I sent simply said, "In Singapore airport, so far so good!" When replying to e-mails, I try to address each individual that has sent me a message, answer his or her questions, comment on their inquiries and follow with a general message about my travels. In the interest of conservation of time, energy, and money, the same message is forwarded to everyone on the "India List."

We boarded a Singapore Airlines flight that stopped in Osaka, Japan and progressed on to India. In-flight time ranged from six to hours. Nothing to worry about—not being able to use the washroom for long periods of time, not getting off the plane in stopover cities, and having difficulty with mobility and sleep are not even considerations when one decides to travel between continents. I kept my mind on the goal of exotic India.

"It will be no problem for you to recognize Harry. She looks just like me," Margaret had said. It sounded so simple. As the plane began its descent into the Delhi airport, Margaret's words, "She looks just like me," echoed in my mind. Harry might be a spitting image of Margaret but so also were the other four thousand or more women who were milling about the Delhi airport on the night of our arrival. I felt overwhelmed as I scanned the thousands of Indian women who thronged the arrival lounge.

They all had long, thick, shiny black hair. They were beautifully dressed in vibrantly coloured and elegantly draped saris. They were talking a mile a minute in tongues that were totally incomprehensible to Michelle and myself. What were we to do? They all looked the same!

Thousands of people spread out in every direction. It reminded me of ants leaving the anthill in search of their daily food. People emerged from every corner, going to and fro with determination and direction.

We inched forward, squeezing between the throngs of people clustered in groups of two to two hundred, towards the baggage carousel. Suddenly two strong, thin, brown arms embraced me from behind. My heart began a rapid acrobatic flip—racing, stopping and racing again. Was the stranger clutching my body a threat to my person? I have yet to be taken advantage of (except financially of course) on any of my foreign journeys. Was this going to be my first experience with harassment or assault? The gripping arms disappeared as quickly as they had arrived. I never did figure out who that had been. We continued to ease through the crowd toward the heaps of luggage where, we hoped, we would find my trusty rainbow bag and Michelle's standard black travel case.

Through the surge of arriving travellers and enthusiastic greetings, I heard, "This is Harry! I am Harry! I have come to show you India!"

A pretty, older Indian woman, not any larger than a twig, introduced herself as Harriet, but immediately said, "Call me Harry." She embraced me in a warm bear hug. "You must be Linda!" Harry still had her tiny arms around my chest. She had found us. Do you not think it would have been easier for her to spot two Caucasian women in wheelchairs rather than two Caucasian women trying to spot a small clone of her sister Margaret?

Harry became an equal partner in our travel group, contributing to and benefiting from the entire experience. It was both our challenge and objective to mesh as a trio that would live and travel together for six weeks.

Each one of us offered various highlights, strengths, and skills to the group. In the coming weeks, Harry would explain customs, purchase train tickets, translate menus, and order the most interesting food that Indian cuisine had to offer. She led us to the best bargains in the market, steered us away from merchants who were trying to rip off unknowing North American shoppers, shouted at taxi drivers and impatiently explained our mode of mobility when others did not move out of the way quickly enough. In exchange, Harry travelled (all-expenses-paid) thousands of kilometres, visiting small villages, mountaintops, and dense urban areas, sites of breathtaking beauty and those of unbelievable shocking poverty, religious rivers and temples, places of bedlam and of peace. Together we laughed, argued, became impatient and frustrated. Harry was fluent in Hindi and communicated adequately in English. Our requirements remained unchanged. What Michelle and I had expected and what Harry was willing to participate in certainly varied on a daily basis but somehow, despite occasional aggravation and disagreement, cooperation and friendship prevailed. Michelle and I enthusiastically embraced new adventures and we were able to introduce Harriet to many aspects of her own country that she had previously never experienced. We visited places in India that Harry had never dreamed of seeing. Indelible lasting, lifelong memories became a cherished gift for each of us .

Outside the Delhi airport, we secured a taxi to take us to the hotel that Patrick and I had carefully selected from the description in the guidebook. We had e-mailed the establishment and I had in hand a confirmation that assured me that the hotel was manageable for persons using wheelchairs and yes, a room was available with three beds. This night, we were to learn a lesson in custom that would follow us throughout our visit to India.

Linda with holy men at temple

Taxi drivers have their own agenda. Whatever, wherever we suggested, the cab driver would find forty-nine reasons why it was an inappropriate place for us to stay. It took some time but we eventually realized that hotel owners and taxi drivers are in cahoots. The cab driver that takes visitors to a hotel gets a cut of the hotel charges. Likewise, a hotel that favours a particular taxi, receives a portion of the money paid to that cab driver by the visitors staying in the hotel.

Delhi, the capital of India and the third largest city in the world, has a population of 13.8 million covering over 1,483 square kilometres. It is overwhelming to North American visitors. There was no way that we could know where to go without the assistance of a local. We secured a cab at the airport but learned that our selected hotel was "No good, no good" and that the cabbie said it had a large courtyard covered with gravel. Moving through the grounds in a wheelchair would be impossible. Rooms were small, there was no vacancy, it was too far away, it would be noisy, and it was unsafe for women. We will never know if any of these conditions were true because there was no way that we were going to be taken to our desired destination. Harry was familiar with the YWCA in Delhi so this is where we went. Fortunately, a room with three beds and a private washroom was available at the YWCA. Later that night, Michelle and I shared our skepticism as we lay in our beds. Was Harry also conspiring with the hotels and taxi drivers? When looking back at our trip, we realized that the room at the YWCA in Delhi was the most expensive room we stayed in. Learning is a lifelong endeavour!

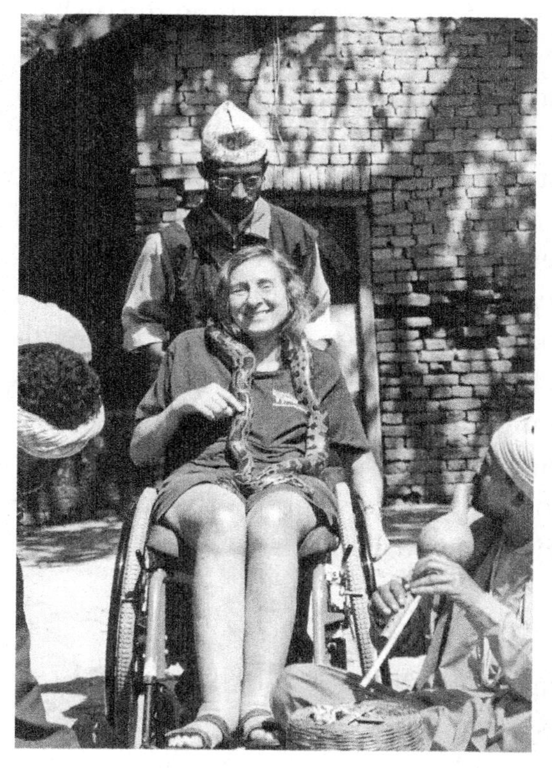

Charming the Snake.

This enormous country is more diverse than anywhere else in the world. Ancient traditions and beliefs walk hand in hand with modern transportation, computer literacy, and business development. The depths of gripping poverty and decadent wealth are found side by side.

Examples of spectacular architecture included the Taj Mahal, one of the Seven Wonders of the World. It stands majestically in the sparkling sun. Just down the road, along the railway tracks, one can find plastic tenting, dirt floors, and cookstoves created from old oil drums. Young children laugh and sing at they sit in the mud, playing with rocks and styrofoam cups as their only toys. Others cry out to their moms for love, attention, and something to eat. The mothers are washing clothes in deep grey water which also has to be used for baking, washing the dishes, and cooking meals.

Attire includes beautiful silk saris, brightly coloured gowns that trail over intricately beaded sandals. Bangles adorn women's arms from wrist to elbow; their waist-length, shining black hair is twisted into rolls at the nape of their necks. Beads and flowers are woven between the strands of their thick locks. Men in business attire wear black suits, white shirts and shoes that shine. Down the block are old men, young women with babies strapped on their backs and holding the hands of toddlers, elderly grandmas, and children scampering through the streets—all of them wearing clothing that looks as if it may not survive one more washing, one more sleep on the street, one more cold night, or one more hot summer day.

Overnight Trains

Why a train? The best way to see India is not at 30,000 feet. It is on the Indian railway system. No visit to this large complex country would be complete without the experience of travelling on Indian trains and negotiating busy Indian railway stations. Train travel is safe, cheap, and—in air-conditioned coaches—comfortable. Of course, this is not the route a true traveller will choose. Travel with the locals!

We chose non-air conditioned sleeper class for those prepared to take the rough with the smooth. By using overnight train travel, long distances could be covered more efficiently than by flying or travelling by bus. There are distinct advantages to overnight travel. In a large country such as India, many hours are consumed by moving between regions. In order to conserve daylight hours for more intriguing adventures and to avoid long hot daytime bus rides, we took as many overnight trains as was possible. During the dark hours, we ate, read, chatted, dozed, slept, and then ate again. The daylight hours at the end of the day and at the beginning of the morning provided views of the local landscape, agricultural fields, rivers and hillsides. Two hours of these observations is plenty; twelve hours too much. The dark hours break the monotony. The other advantage is that if you are going by train anyway you might as well do so during the night and save the cost of accommodation.

Throngs of people always milled about the train station forming large and larger groups—eating, drinking, smoking. The concrete walls and floors of most stations did not exude warmth, nor were they welcoming.

Lack of personal space had become the norm to me. Jostling crowds no longer overwhelmed me. Rubbing shoulders, hips and various other body parts with strangers while waiting in line was just part of maintaining one's place in the queue. In every train stations there were two lines: one clearly designated for Indian residents, the other for tourists. The tourist line was nearly at a standstill and weaved erratically out the door and down the block. It moved inch by inch. The Indian line, on the other hand, shuffled along at what, comparatively, seemed like breakneck speed. I observed that some persons in the tourist line were advancing with surprising swiftness. How was this accomplished? Ah ha! Money talks. Money discretely changed hands and presto, tickets were produced.

Harry grumbled and complained. She was hungry, and angry

with her fellow compatriots who pushed and shoved. She was impatient with those who pulled and tugged at my wheelchair and at me. The ticket clerk took so long to do what Harry was sure could be accomplished in a few seconds if he worked steadily, instead of sipping on chai tea and chatting with friends and relatives that he had probably seen only a few hours earlier. This frustrated her. Some sacred cows simply would not move out of the way. In the scheme of things, I considered the advantages. Harry was with us, therefore, we earned the right to stand in the "Indian" line. We arrived at stations early enough that we could book sleeping accommodation in the coveted and needed lower bunks.

I allowed one of my standby supporting thoughts to rumble through my mind: *If I keep my eye on the goal, I will never see the obstacles.* The choice to avoid the havoc of the train station and delay our departure by another day was never a consideration. It was time to move on. At times like this, I counted our blessings. Harry stood in the "locals" line and presto—she could soon exit, wiggling her small body through the crowds of people, with train tickets clutched tightly in her hand for seating in a second-class coach with two lower bunks and one at mid-level. We would be on our way again. It took one tenth of the time that would have been required for Michelle or me to hold a place in the tourist line, if, in fact, a wheelchair could even negotiate through the crowds.

On night trains, Chai was served in tiny pottery cups, the crumbling kind, at a huge cost of three rupees (six cents). I am always a little wary and cautious about the food in countries where refrigeration is suspect. As well, clothing that has been sitting on the platform in a big bushel basket with heaven only knows what (or who) else, is not exactly a "to die for" item. We reserved our shopping for the local markets where it would be possible to examine the wares before us, do some comparative quality and price shopping, and become involved in some vigorous bargaining.

In the early morning hours, as daylight seeped between the cracks of the metal window blinds, we roused ourselves, eagerly waiting for the "Chai man." The vendor of coveted Indian tea, chai, swayed back and forth down the aisle calling aloud, "Chai-chai, chai-chai." It was a signal to come to life again, gather together our belongings, open the blinds to look upon the sights that rolled past before our tired eyes. Any sense of fatigue was quickly dissipated by the array of wonders outside—grassy fields, grazing animals, children at play, tidy and untidy farmyards. There were elegant marble mosques, dilapidated hovels, herds of sheep and goats, and rice paddies—some dry, some flooded and buried beneath lakes of water. When you are travelling at night, you imagine snoozing most of the journey away and arriving rested at your destination.

Think again! The reality is that, on average, one achieves one to three hours of fitful sleep in an uncomfortable doze and arrives at the appointed place feeling like a zombie. Notice the dark circles under the eyes of those dismounting from an overnight journey. However, our daylight hours were precious. We needed to see the sights in this remarkable land. After brushing our teeth, scanning the *Lonely Planet* to assess the essential highlights around the corner at the next stop, the mounting anticipation in my chest and mind made me feel totally refreshed and ready for the adventures to come.

When my boys were growing up, I remember one early winter Saturday morning watching them struggle into the kitchen.

"Mom, I am so tired," one of them moaned. "I got home late last night so I don't think that I can go to work today. Will you call in sick for me so I can rest up for the party tonight?"

From the other side of the kitchen I heard, "Mom! Mom, please lend me $10 because I spent more money than I planned to spend last night. I need money for bus fare to get to work or maybe I should stay home too?"

I approached the breakfast table and quietly explained, "As you go through life there will be times when you decide to party all night or take part in new adventures and inevitably you will miss out on all or much of your sleep. There will be other times when you pull out your wallet and readily give up your wages and wealth. You need to do these things and sometimes you will enjoy, sometimes benefit, and sometimes lose on your decisions but decisions they are nonetheless. When it comes time to lose that sleep or spend that money, think about the value of that experience in advance. If you think it is worthwhile, go for it enthusiastically. On some you will win, others you will lose but all will provide one more opportunity to be part of life or learn from life's adventures. Neither one of you can stay home from your jobs today," I told them. "I will lend you ten dollars. The operative word being 'lend'. "

Here, right now, it was well worth the expenditure of my hard-earned cash to come to India. It was worth the lack of sleep on overnight trains to experience every possible opportunity. Most often, on arrival in a station, Indian coolies—train porters—arrived at the door of the coach wearing red silk jackets, shouting to attract the attention of those who wanted help and were willing to pay for it. The coolies pushed and shoved each other in competition for first place, announcing that they were prepared and available to negotiate a price. Throughout this trip, we spent more money on tips for assistance to manage the limitations created by our disabilities than anything else! Harry was not much help negotiating price in these situations because she, of course, had a soft spot for her fellow compatriots, was not used to bargaining and, thought we should pay the first requested price for everything. It took only a few days to realize that it was reasonable for us to pay 50% of the first demanded price. The recipient would be more than satisfied.

All aboard! What did we find inside the coach? Our tickets were assigned to the first compartment. If they were not, we negotiated to have them changed. A sleeping compartment consisted of three bunks on either side of a small space—wide enough only for knees when sitting, and completely exposed to other travellers without privacy. This allowed a six-inch space between our legs when one sat on one bunk, another on the other side.

The bunks were narrow, perhaps twenty inches in width; the covering vinyl with one inch of firm padding. In Jaipur, we had the fortunate experience of occupying a compartment with a vacancy! One man sat snugly beside Harry, and Michelle and I occupied the opposite seat. The top bunks were empty when we entered the train but they immediately became occupied by wheelchairs held in place by bungee cords. Our bags were placed on the floor between our legs, and provided a reasonably flat surface on which we could play cards.

Available space on upper bunks for wheelchair storage was not always available. On some trains, during the six and a half week trip, our experience ranged from six bunks occupied by three people—Michelle, Harriet and myself—to six bunks occupied by eight people with strange guys wedging together in the upper beds! When there was nowhere to store chairs or bags, they were placed on the ground, wedged between the two lower bunks; not a lot of leg room but if I took an unplanned turn in the night off that narrow bunk, I was comforted by the fact that rather than have a close conversation with the floor, I would land on the spokes of my chair with some padded bags around the edges. When this happened, I could always push myself back onto the bunk and try to capture forty winks in the remaining dark hours.

Some nights were quiet. Others were noisy. Young musicians strummed on out-of-tune guitars and blew on wooden flutes in raucous rehearsal, entertaining their captive audience—or so they thought.

Are there washrooms on the train? Of course! Wheelchair accessible? Of course NOT! Michelle could wall-walk, so in most situations she shuffled down the aisle holding on to the seatbacks as she moved along. The trick was to negotiate between the shifting cars because, yes of course, the restroom was always in the next car. I'm sure that many of you have travelled by train and are aware of what that jiggling platform between two cars is like; pre-assessment, balance, and prayer were required for this trip down the aisle every four hours. Michelle concentrated on every step and prayed for safe passage. During her absence, which might be five minutes to fifty-five minutes, her safe return was the only thought in my mind.

Now how did I manage? I cannot walk. Train rides ranged from eight hours to eighteen, so somehow I had to make it work. A female urinal, a pricey $6 investment, is not too much unlike a male urinal. That is, it's a bottle that will serve the purpose in a pinch. The female version has a wide lip at the top to direct liquid in the right direction.

The bonus of mine was a screw-on lid so I could carry it to a disposal station without making a mess. Disposable vinyl gloves, a small bottle of liquid detergent and waterless hand sanitizer are the accompanying essentials. So now we have a bed to sleep in and a washroom to use. What about dinner? Before getting on the train Harriet always bought what at first were novelty type snacks—samosas, pakoras, raisin-filled buns, and small oranges. Later, these tended to get monotonous.

Overnight trains offer good transportation—we could not ask for anything better, so with eager anticipation we boarded the trains. With equally eager anticipation, we exited from the long, cold, rocky rides looking forward to new adventures.

Rajasthan, Clothing and Camels

Before leaving Canada, Patrick passed along some valuable advice that would come to haunt us, "Mom, if you want to buy space on a train for Wednesday, you had better start early on Monday morning."

When it was time to move on from Delhi, we were relegated to bus transportation. If we wanted to depart on Friday, we sure did have to start on Tuesday to get a cherished sitting room on a railcar. The availability of space on the train is inversely related to the population of India— a lot of people live there and are going to and fro. If you snooze, you lose, so Friday afternoon found us facing a twelve-hour bus ride from Delhi to Jaipur, our next desired destination; but before leaving Dehli we were able to get train tickets for the trip from Jaipur to Jailsamer.

Our trusty taxi driver, Nelu, arrived and en route to the bus station, we stopped for silver bangles, at such a bargain! These bracelets could not be passed up. After only a few electrifying days in this entrepreneurial country, it is easy to get swept up in the shopping mode, acquiring unusual and appealing items to take home. Eventually one realizes that there is a network of buying and selling and everyone involved gets a piece of the action along the way. The locals know where to go and how to shop. Even if the driver gets a cut, it should not matter to us, as prices are better than one would find for a similar article in North America. With our small treasures tucked away, we boarded the bus for Jaipur, the Pink City, nicknamed as such because pink is the colour of the buildings in the old part of the city. Along the roadway to the capital of Rajasthan, Land of the Kings, the journey offered views of magical cities, desert, ancient battlefields, breathtaking palaces, dry grasslands, and green hillsides.

On arrival at the Jaipur bus station, we connected with a

delightful young man, Chico, who passionately advertised the benefits and attractions of his city. Using expressive body language, he promised to show us all that there was to see. Chico scraped his living from his occupation as a capable, charming, and eager driver of a small, bouncy motorized rickshaw. Three women, two wheelchairs and our odd collection of luggage did not deter him.

When others make negative comments about the youth of the world, I think of enterprising young men like Chico, whose enthusiasm and willingness to assist never wavered. He works seven days a week, saving to buy his own tuk tuk at a cost of 20,000 R ($400 CDN), equal to what many of us take home in one week. Chico has been saving for three years and thinks he has about two-thirds of his rickshaw price tucked away in a box. He currently rents the little yellow motorized vehicle for 1,000 R ($20 CDN) per month. He lives at home, supporting his mom and younger siblings. Chico welcomed us into his family, lovingly introducing his mom, sisters, brothers, and many friends. He was to become our constant companion for the five days that we spent in Jaipur.

We tried to cram as much as we could into each day. Rather than take time out to visit restaurants, we discovered "The Hutch" takeout. Chico stopped the tuk tuk, Harry ran to the window and bagged great Indian fast food that we munched as we moved along. While in Jaipur, the textile capital of India, we explored the intricate city centre, the tourist highlights, the back alleys, and residential areas of the local people. For most of the destinations, we needed two rickshaws: one for Harriet and the wheelchairs, one for Michelle and me. Chico would arrive with his brother early in the morning and give us an overview of the options for the day, expanding on the positives and negatives of each.

The two rocking little yellow rickshaws revved their engines and sprinted off to begin another adventure; to the market, to view historical sites and take pleasure in hearing others recount anecdotes of the past, or to experience local culture by infiltrating the residential areas of the city. We visited the textile vendors who brought their merchandise, roll after roll of silk and blends, for our perusal. As an enticement to select their wares, they served samosas, chai tea and, on occasion, wine. We were measured in sitting position. Tape measures, stretching and waving of arms, pinching, prodding, and ingenuity all contributed to the size of the finished product. If a particular vendor did not have the colour or pattern combination that we wanted, Chico would aim the rickshaw down yet another narrow alley to unearth a merchant who might have more compatible products. Our clothing was delivered to the hotel in the wee hours of the morning. We had not intended to shop until the last week of our trip—it would have to be carried. Nevertheless, what female could resist the wonderful textiles, made-to-measure silk pants for twelve dollars, intricate cushion covers, elaborate colour combinations, and coordinated pants and tops. I think we are as normal as women come—or maybe not. What two women, both mobilizing in wheelchairs, would embark upon a trip to India without a second thought? Now what to do with all of this stuff? Not to worry! The acquisition of another five-dollar tote bag solved the problem.

Five days in Jaipur could only be described as exhausting, exhilarating, and fun. On our departure evening, Chico and his brother arrived in the dusty back lane of the hotel bouncing along in their motorized rickshaws. They lifted and positioned Michelle and myself into one of the vehicles, stacking bags on our laps and around our legs. In the other tuk tuk, they placed our two wheelchairs, our trusty companion Harriet—who at this point wasn't quite sure whether to be overwhelmed by confusion and frustration, or joy and delight—and the remaining luggage, bundles and bags. The drivers drove the rickshaws onto the train station platform ignoring the signs that prohibited such action. They knew, and we knew, that two Canadian, English-speaking women could get away with it. Why? These foreign ladies would be hard-pressed on their own to locate the correct train and secure assistance to board! At these times of need, Harry vanished. Although this was part of the reason we had hired Harry, when push came to shove, she was always preoccupied with filling her bag with favourite snacks for the trip. We complained bitterly about her lack of assistance at times, but we were also more than willing to accept the munchies on the long, overnight journeys.

The train was scheduled to depart at 10:00 p.m. so in classic North American style, we arrived at the station with plenty of time to spare. With calm patience, we waited. Michelle and I sat in our chairs reviewing the highlights of the day, eagerly anticipating what was yet to come. Harriet perched herself upon a nylon travel bag. Chico and his brother met some friends and exchanged news of the day and the week

As we waited there was a lot to look at. We needed to become familiar with these sights and situations as train stations would become a major part of our travel agenda. Small children were lying on the floor, tucked snugly into quilts. Mothers attempted in vain to squelch the curiosity and interest of their wee ones hoping that a quick nap would help them settle, so that the twelve to fourteen-hour nighttime ride would be manageable for all. Vendors peddling their wares cried aloud in a variety of dialects: green grapes, apples, small quilts, lumpy pillows, playing cards, and books. Sacred cows wandered along putting their heads into garbage bins. The cows stepped over children, luggage, boxes, bundles, and crates of produce and somehow, the hooves never trod on those obstacles in the pathway. As tempting as the green grapes looked, the questions of if and how they had been washed and where they had been sitting all day, deterred us from purchase.

What was that creature that just skittered across in front of my feet? Could it be a mouse? You can imagine my semi-hysterical response when one of the rickshaw drivers tranquilly drawled, "Oh no, it is not a mouse. It is a 'chaua'."

A chaua is a healthy Indian rat. I swallowed the scream that rose in my throat. No, there was not one black, long-tailed rodent, there were many scurrying around on the platform. They threatened to run over my feet, up my leg and onto my shoulder. When I examine the situation sensibly, the rats were probably more afraid of me than I was of them, although that is impossible to imagine. I sat in my chair trying to control my nearly uncontrollable fear. When I am camping or hiking at home, I would rather encounter a bear than a mouse. How crazy is that? I can calmly watch a toad, spider, snake, or other creature cross my path. Bugs are easily brushed away. Large dogs are not intimidating but a tiny mouse is my total undoing! Now I know that makes no sense at all but that is the way it is!

Chico tried to calm me by saying, "Not to worry, they are also waiting to get on the train. When the coach pulls into the station, the chauas will jump onboard to keep you company."

How reassuring! I was trying to believe that could not happen but in fact, Patrick and Jill told me, after my return home of course, that when travelling in India they did see a rat run down the aisle of a train they were riding on. I try to spend my time and energy worrying about things that I can change. In this case, I closed it out of my mind and prayed. This would be the first of seven such overnight excursions so finding a way to cope with my fright of my platform companions, was essential.

At 11:25 p.m. the train pulled into the station. The doors opened, the steps dropped and the conductor shouted to all waiting passengers. In our vague understanding of Hindi, we assumed he was saying, "All aboard." Chico and his brother lifted us into the coach.

On our first overnight train ride, we recognized that India is not always hot—in fact the rail coaches could be bloody freezing throughout the night even when we wore every possible article of clothing within our reach. It seemed that vendors did not sell blankets or shawls to ward away the chill evening air. On our very first overnight train, we huddled, and shivered the night away.

Our first overnight train from Jaipur to Jaisalmer took over twenty hours. With lots of help from the red satin-coated station porters, we exited the station. The streets of Jaisalmer were chock-full of camels, more camels, and even more camels. At the train station, hotel proprietors bartered for business. With the hotel's jeep loaded, we found our way to a haven in the desert, recommended in the "budget bed" pages of the *Lonely Planet*. The proprietor was most accommodating but the facility was less then wheelchair friendly—multi-level with one or two stairs up then down between rooms and sections of the hotel, narrow doorways, Indian toilets—the usual hole in the ground. In this case, the room was so narrow that a wheelchair wheel could slide into the hole if we so much as sneezed. Well, this accommodation would not work.

"Let's move on and check out the next on our list."

After a few tries, we did find a manageable bed and bath. The long, cold hours on the train the night before moved us to tackle the uphill wheel to the local market with the intention of finding some source of portable heat that we could carry with us on the next overnight train. Options included fuzzy but too heavy blankets, gaudy heavy jackets (obviously not tailored by Christian Dior), a man's naked warm body, or a sweater. What would it be? The decision finally made, we bargained for shawls.

Throughout the market expedition, a long-haired camel driver stalked us trying to convince us that he, and only he, could meet all of the needs for these Canadian women on a camel safari. We tried gently to decline his convincing offer and agreed that we would consider his trip equally with the other options that were before us. As we read the guidebook recommendations, we decided that his camel safari options were varied, appealing, and worth keeping high on our list of priorities.

Retiring to our hotel room, we spread out coloured brochures, little scraps of paper with notes scribbled on them, and our guidebooks on the bed. We pulled from the depths of our memories the important features that had been described to us by the camel safari vendors. After much deliberation, the trip presented by the very first hotel operator offered the most appeal. Back in the cab, we returned to our first stop to book a three-day camel safari that would carry us over the sands. It was sure to be another once in a lifetime adventure.

At 6:00 a.m. we met at the appointed rendezvous spot and were loaded into a van that afforded no space for anyone who had eaten too much breakfast. The dusty road alternated between ancient times and modern day—old world elegance of palaces closely followed sandy, non-producing farms. Residences, questionably livable by North American standards, were conscientiously tended and lovingly cared for by proud owners. These gave way to nomadic villages, small groups of undernourished cattle, laughing children on their way to school, mothers weaving beautiful tapestry, and fathers herding camels.

We exited the van. One large camel pulled our next means of transportation, the camel cart, a two-wheeled wood wagon driven by a farmer. It was a rough and bumpy ride but hey, we were embarking on another escapade.

The safari leader, Meherdim, had two wives and an adolescent son who did not know his own age, and was accompanied by Padham, the albino camel jockey. Padham wore clothing as white as the color of his skin, contrasting sharply with the other camel drivers' bright clothes and dark skin. The camel blankets were multi-coloured, and, if clean, they would have been vivid.

We set off into the desert. Michelle and I were propped in the camel cart with Harry. Our chairs were lashed to the hump of a camel. Six camels were tied to the rear of the cart. Harry, facing forward, sat at the back of the wagon. The lead tethered camel loved Harriet. He would lean over her head, extend a two-foot long, slurpy tongue dangerously near her face and moan like Chewbacca from Star Wars, generating shrieks of alarm.

Camel Safari.

Lunch in the desert was a tepid, watery curried cauliflower garnished with grains of sand. It was served on a tin plate and, of course, our only option was nature's eating utensil. Which hand do you use for eating?

Our fellow safari travellers, a Korean man and his two daughters, had come to India anticipating tourist facilities more consistent with their previous travel experiences. Disappointed with conditions on the safari they griped about the meal, the windswept sand, the smell of the camels, the lack of cold water, the absence of tents and on it went. Meherdim's son backtracked to town and gathered some tents in an attempt to keep peace amongst the group members, to no avail. Michelle and I opted to camp on many layers of quilts, most of which had doubled as camel saddle blankets. We slept under the stars huddled together for warmth. There are rewards for sleeping on the sand—the beauty of the sunset and the remarkable sunrise at 5:00 a.m. The photograph I took lying on my back as the sun peeked over the horizon is the most beautiful of all the photos I took in India.

Our Korean friend continued to complain about everything and threatened loudly that he was going to tell his friends in Korea not to go to Jaisalmar or on a camel safari. Big deal! To our benefit, his sojourn was only hours. He and his daughters returned to town, leaving Michelle and I with the camels and the camel drivers to venture further into the desert.

After lunch on the second day, everyone disappeared to who knows where leaving Michelle and I in the shade of a one stick straggly tree. If they did not return, no one would know where we were; a common situation throughout this trip. The vultures would pick our bones clean. Old cowboy movies came to mind. Fortunately or unfortunately, depending on where on the food chain you sit, there was a shortage of vultures. During our wait, we did spot one vulture— sending our imaginations on a wild ride. Eventually Padham returned with the camels, with Harry riding one bare back. Harry's fear of camels was trumped by the prospect of a long walk on hot sand. The cart was used only for transportation between the van and the beginning of the desert sands. For the remaining hours of the trip, Michelle and I rode on camels. It may look like an easy ride but the rocking and swaying is incompatible with the lack of balance caused by MS. Padham and another member of the camel crew took it upon themselves to double ride with us. The unpleasantness of having an unshowered saddle-companion in close proximity was preferable to falling off a camel! Our two wheelchairs were strapped to another camel. Our photographs show a wheelchair-encumbered camel. Friends ask, "Where are you?" until Michelle and I appear in the next photos.

On the second night, Michelle and I once again took to the quilts. Harry lay in the back of the cart with her head wrapped in a shawl. The men curled up together on the sand to keep warm.

I noticed that some of the camels had their feet tied together.

"It's okay" Padham said, "They are the young men. If they are not hobbled, they will go off in the night to look for ladies. In the morning, we will have no transportation to return us to civilization. The female camels, not unlike human females, are not attracted to old guys so the grampa camels' feet are not tied."

As we dozed contentedly on our hard sandy bed, I did not notice any spiders or large insects but on return to Vancouver, Jill, my daughter-in-law exclaimed, "Weren't you afraid of the spiders? When my mom and I were there, creepy crawlies were all over the sand."

Ignorance is the ultimate blessing.

From the desert to the station—we departed Jaisalmer on yet again another train that carried us to the city where we would see the most famous landmark in India.

Agra

The Taj Mahal, one of the Seven Wonders of the World, is in Agra. Our arrival in the city was delayed by a fatal accident on the tracks. The railway crossings are not gated; train arrivals are not announced by either lights or sounds. Lethal accidents on the tracks happen often.

Our accommodation was in the "Lorries," a stunning old brick hotel built in 1886 with three hundred rooms, marble floors and staircases, bathtubs standing on curved feet, and mammoth chandeliers hung from high-beamed ceilings. Despite the cold, the grey concrete walls of the hotel invited us in. The chilly decor was at the same time cool yet warming and welcome. Proprietor Jonathan, an elderly Indian man dressed elegantly in a tweed jacket, a leather cap, and sporting an intricately carved wooden cane, spoke with a posh English accent. The only piece missing was the monocle. The British had employed him during their occupation of India. To our delight this talented historian, whose in-depth and first-hand knowledge of the British ruleera, supplemented the historical facts with real life stories throughout our stay.

A kitchen fire in 1947 eliminated the banquet hall and multicourse meals of yesteryear. It had been thirty-six hours since our last meal. This left only four choices: go out by taxi for food, snack on the crumbled granola bars in the bottom of our packs, stay hungry, or keep an eagle eye out for someone who was heading toward town and who could bring back some snacks. As time marched on we realized that other occupants of the hotel had gone to town to party for the evening and would not be back until the wee hours; there was no one to ask about grabbing some snacks for us.

No restaurant in the public house! As late evening darkness approached, we became increasingly hungry. There was nowhere to eat within reasonable distance, and hiring a taxi van in the evening that would accommodate wheelchairs was next to impossible. Lively activities in town were more profitable for the taxi drivers than a long drive out to the hotel. To our delight, the hotel owner recognized our predicament and stepped up to the plate. A short time later, a tuk tuk came speeding up the gravel driveway. A young boy, our host's nephew, sprang out of the little vehicle carrying a box filled with authentic Indian food that had been cooked at his home, and delivered to us at his uncle's request.

Early in the morning, we ventured forth to visit two Taj Mahals, the symbol of everlasting love. One, a mini replica of the Real McCoy, is located on the riverbank. The larger one sits one hundred metres back from the water's edge to escape any risk of flood. Both the large and small were constructed as monuments to a mother's devotion. Half the size of the identically proportioned full-size Taj Mahal, the miniature is an exact copy. Both were named World Heritage sites in 1983.

Linda in front of Taj Mahal

Between these two world famous structures is a parking lot crowded with thousands of bicycles, rickshaws, sacred cows, children at play, families cooking over open fires, tired old men sleeping in the grass, tourist busses and, today, two women in wheelchairs moving across the dirt. Those with the disability of MS often have minimal warning when a bladder wants attention. Michelle wanted Harriet to hold up a blanket lending privacy to nature's call. All was going well until a band, with vigour and enthusiasm, marched by playing sprightly national music. Harriet could not resist a peek at the shiny instruments and exuberant musicians. As she turned to look, the blanket providing Michelle's protection from the hundreds of onlookers ceased to fulfill its function. Michelle's preference was not to perform a "Full Monty" in the parking lot, but so be it! Mission accomplished, we moved on to more exciting activities.

At the entrance to the "real" Taj Mahal, double standards existed, as we were finding to be typical of India. The price of entry was 500 rupees ($10) for visitors, and 20 rupees ($.40) for Indian nationals. Is this an attempt to minimize the number of visitors to this sacred site? Is it a tax relief for locals? Is it a revenue-generating action? Whatever the reason, it was not going to keep us from visiting this incredible monument. The long steep staircase was only manageable because of an extended 70-degree sloped ramp and a healthy dose of personal determination.

"You go first," Michelle said, clearly hesitant. "If you make it, I will follow."

"Oh Michelle, not again." My friend was not quite as willing to take on this type of experience as I was.

"If I don't arrive safely at the bottom, just make sure you tell my boys that I love them."

Travelling down such a steep ramp in a forward direction is equivalent to taking your life in your own hands so I decided to travel backwards, but not alone. With sign language requests for assistance I found three adolescents who braced the chair to prevent its rapid acceleration down the ramp. With a deep breath and a feeling of relief, I reached the bottom.

The walls of the Taj Mahal consist of intricate marble mosaics, each colourful tile design distinct from the next. We wheeled along the walkway close to the walls, examining the beauty and diversity of every section. The alignment of each segment of marble was perfect. Hand painted mosaic tiles showed no evidence of their age. Bright, sophisticated colour on the unblemished surface of the outer walls showed no weather damage or erosion. The spires and domes on the roof reached perfectly straight, into the cloudless sky. I was mesmerized and content to sit basking in the sunshine for hours, looking at the intricately constructed temple, and watching people. Some exuded amazement and were enthralled; others revealed a bored and blasé attitude.

Outside the gate, hawkers sold miniatures of the Taj Mahal, booklets, pens, glass animal heads, t-shirts, prayer cards, maps, and tours. The last thing we needed was one more article to carry back to Canada. We avoided all until a tiny, timid little girl stopped us in our tracks. Nasha was selling glass pens. Her shy irresistible smile compelled Michelle to dig into her bag for some rupees. We boarded the taxi, proud owners of glass pens that displayed tacky images of the Taj,—just a few small items to tuck into a corner of a pack. The most valuable acquisition was the memory of the smile that had illuminated the big brown eyes of the tiny sales girl.

Bright lights and lanterns lit up the night sky, revealing the acres of land behind the hotel where coloured Big Top tents were being erected. For what? A circus? A carnival? Cirque du Soleil? No; to facilitate the exchange of nuptials of an arranged marriage. In full Indian tradition, eight hundred guests were expected. We changed rooms in the hotel three times to accommodate the arrival of new groups of people checking into the hotel to attend the wedding. The nearby wedding activities were a cultural education—cooking tents, musicians, hundreds of tables and chairs, dressing rooms, washrooms, and sleeping tents. The guests would not sleep at the wedding site but the staff guarded the marriage ceremony grounds and prepared for the festivities. Elegant gowns were carefully carried over the mud and grass to hang in wait for the bride and her bridal party. Hairdressers, makeup artists, and henna specialists awaited the women. Shoeshine boys, valets, and hair designers would meet every need of the groom and his entourage.

As the evening activity dwindled, we returned to our boudoir to find invitations slipped under the door. What an honour! We possessed very limited wardrobes: trekking pants, t-shirts, one sweatshirt and an Indian shawl. This boudoir did not seem compatible with the elegance that we observed across the backfield. But, ah ha! Our newly acquired outfits from Jaipur! Are the pants long enough to hide our trekking sandals? No makeup or sparkles for our hair! Bangles we had purchased at the market would suffice. Okay, let's try it with as much elegance as a trekker can muster. We graciously accepted the invitation to the pre-wedding lunch. We were charitably welcomed into the lunch tent where long narrow tables laden with ethnic delights awaited the arrival of invited guests. There were toasts to the bridal party, to the parents, grandparents, to uncles and aunts, brothers and sisters, friends, and strangers. Following prayers, the multi-course indulgence began. I was full after the first three dishes were served. Refusal to try each delicacy would be an unacceptable rejection of hospitality so we ate a bit more, then even more, and more after that. At the end of four hours, chai tea was served to all and we slowly made our way across the muddy fields back to the hotel. We could fudge our appearance for the lunch but our awkward lack of style would be blatantly inappropriate for the wedding ceremony. Honoured that we had touched the essence of this gathering, we offered our regrets to the bride's parents and made a discreet exit to the train station, via cab, in the early misty hours of the morning.

Arriving at the old station in Delhi, we headed to the "save luggage" room to store our belongings so that we wouldn't have to carry our worldly possessions to Shimla. The regulations required that luggage be locked. My trusty rainbow bag is a simple nylon zippered carryall that has never seen such a device. Could I buy a lock in the station? Vendors sold samosas, toys, children's games, green grapes, and chai tea—but definitely not locks. It was time once again to become inventive. A small zap strap connecting to the zipper pull and the carrying strap might suffice. I turned my bag over to the station attendant and was rewarded with a thin paper claim tag. I think it is called "pulling the wool over the stationmaster's eyes." A zap strap is definitely not a lock! If someone wanted to steal the t-shirts and panties that I was planning to leave behind anyway, they probably need them more than I did.

The train to Shimla left from the new train station in Delhi. Of course, the locomotive from Agra had deposited us at the old station. The exit from the old station to the taxi stand was on the opposite side from our arrival tracks. A speeding driver might get us to our next train, which was departing in forty-two minutes. Could we traverse this building, overrun with people, cows, pull carts, the ever-present vendors, in a brief few minutes? Of course not! A series of uneven up and down staircases, varying in widths from half a metre to two metres, created an impossible obstacle course for our chairs.

The coolies accompanied us to an alternate route. Then again, sometimes the cure is worse than the disease.

The "elevator," a rickety device resembling a dumbwaiter,

hung on worn, frayed ropes as it lowered us down a dark damp shaft into the narrow tunnel beneath the tracks. At the bottom of the shaft, dirt walls closed us in. The wet, earthen floor was covered in places by pressed board or cardboard in an attempt to protect feet from the mud and puddles. The only lighting was a flickering flashlight transferring back and forth from the coolie's hand to my lap.

I prayed for courage and safe passage. To my amusement, Michelle—who usually says, "You go first"—could not wait to see my safe arrival before committing herself, for once. The coolies pushed us as cold drips from the ceiling landed on our heads. The sound of chuas scampering underfoot was disconcerting to say the least. After twenty minutes that felt like five hours, we wheeled onto a flat wooden platform. Another dumbwaiter carried us up the shaft to safety. The coolie hailed a cab. The taxi driver, perhaps trained at the Indianapolis 500, got us to the new station in the nick of time.

From Delhi, three of us rode together to Kalka where we parted ways. Harriet was going home to Punjab for a few days. Michelle and I would grab the baby train to Shimla.

The Little Engine That Could

"Patrick, you didn't tell me about the enormous hills," I accused, when I was back, safe and sound, from our trip.

"But Mom, if I had told you, you might not have gone. It was the highlight of my trip."

He was right. It was also one of the highlights of mine. In Vancouver and especially in New Westminster where I live, there are some substantial hills. Shimla makes New Westminster look flat. Definitely not welcoming to wheelchair travel.

Harriet was still in Chandigarh (the capital of Punjab) for a few days to take care of family business. Michelle and I climbed up the mountain through pine, rhododendron and oak forests, to the Shangri-La of India. We planned our three-day trip to Shimla, a British colonial hill station set in the mountains at 2,200 metres of altitude. Shimla, north of Delhi, is one of the most popular tourist destinations in India. During British rule, hill stations high in the mountains were established to provide relief from the intense heat of spring, summer, and fall. The British escaped into the hills to give their bodies and minds a break from the congestion of humanity, and the heat.

Of course we could do it. Back to the rails once more—two trains from Delhi to Kalca where we connected with the "baby train," a narrow gauge toy train built in 1903. It wound upward in a tortuous switchback ascent, zigzagging over rickety bridges and through one hundred and three tunnels. The track climbed through alpine meadows, forested slopes, rock enclosed passageways, leading to incredible beauty and peace.

We knew it had tourist magnetism but neither Michelle nor I realized that Shimla, like Niagara Falls in Canada, is the honeymoon highlight of middle and northern India. There we were, amongst the elite, in our cargo trekking pants and old sweatshirts. Do you ever feel like a fifth wheel? Young people dressed in their post-wedding finery surrounded us. The handsome young couples looked positively towards their future, staring deeply into each other's eyes, quite oblivious to the natural surroundings outside the train.

For three and a half hours of bumps and jostling, we twisted our way up the mountain. Twenty-two hours and three trains later, we arrived at the tiny Shimla train station. Disembarking onto the wooden platform, we were confronted by mountains, more mountains, and on looking around, yet again more mountains.

"Well we're here for three days, so we have to find a way to make it work."

I squelched internal panic at the sight of the steep mountainous terrain. A man clad in a shepherd's robe that was tied around his middle with a coarse rope, emerged from the shadows wielding a gnarled pine walking stick. The appearance of a guardian angel? I think so!

"You need help, I will call friend," he said. He immediately left to return shortly with a short but muscular buddy.

Monsoong, a single and attractive hermit, was more than keen to practise his English and to offer guidance and assistance to the two Canadian women who had perhaps bitten off more than they could chew. The two guys pushed our chairs up the mountain to what, as they said, was the most accessible hotel—with forty-nine stairs at the front door. In fact, it *was* probably the most manageable guesthouse in town. We accepted, after a kilometre of steep climbing, that the climb to the front door was more gradual than to many others. It was now getting dark and cold. At the top of the stairs, the large patio promised a warm, comfortable, vitamin D-absorbing place to sit, if and when the sun came out.

Grey solid concrete walls, no insulation, some windows with glass, some with shutters only, did nothing to provide warmth. The solid structure of the hotel with no heat was a very chilly proposition. Since we had not eaten for hours, and food service was only available fourteen stairs up or nine stairs down, the owner arrived at the door with welcome curried vegetables and rice. It was terrible food but after twelve hours of fasting, it was food! We spread a towel over a round, rickety coffee table and ate with gusto and appreciation.

The room was large, the beds looked inviting but every advantage is accompanied by a disadvantage. My chair did not fit through the bathroom door so I engaged in my old routine of a towel on the floor, wiggling way forward in my chair, and voiding into a little plastic jug.

Through the evening, rain thundered down, beating loudly on the walls. Hail crackled against the shutters. At home, on long cold evenings, music and television are available. Here, electronic entertainment was non-existent. The most attractive option was to get into a bed that offered warmth. The hard mattresses were covered with canvas-like sheets. The duvets, and I use the word loosely, were solid heavy quilts that warded off the cold night air but the weight of the bedcovers (at least thirty pounds) allowed absolutely no movement beneath them. Still, we needed every ounce of the stuffing for warmth. We laid our heads on firm narrow pillows, not unlike those that I had knelt upon in church as a little girl.

Monsoong—we called him Mongoose—and his friend were keen to return for the evening to entertain us (or maybe to be entertained). When they rapped on the door at 8:00 p.m., we were already in bed. By morning, the skies had cleared, offering the promise of a better day. We sat in the sunshine on the outer deck sipping cappuccino and absorbing the much-needed warmth of those rays. When Monsoong and his companion arrived, we embarked on our introduction to the mountain paradise.

Heading up to the clean and quiet village (unusual for this part of the world), we found calm within the sanctuary of the old church. Horse drawn carts, laden with edibles and cottage industry wares on their way to the weekly Saturday market, intrigued us. Farther up the hillside simians roamed everywhere. The monkey temple had fewer worshippers than monkeys—of every size and description. They were everywhere and felt that they were entitled to be everywhere. Their bold friendliness was cute until I felt a heavy, furry trespasser on my back.

We hiked even higher, to the Indian Institute of Advanced Study, the residence of the British Viceroy, Lord Dufferin. At the fork in the road, Monsoong and I chose the sunny side.

Michelle and her assistant took the other. Thick woods formed the edges of the path. I was interested and enthralled with the historical information recorded on the signage. Michelle later told me that left alone with her unknown companion, she was more concerned about being lost, raped, or robbed in the forest. We connected at the top, picnicking at an oasis, a small alpine clearing amidst the trees, absorbing the view of the surrounding hills as our eyes travelled over the peaks and down the mountainside.

As evening approached, it was time to head home, down the very steep winding road. Now for the descent. Wheelchair gloves (biking gloves with leather palms) and a grip on the rims are the only available brakes to slow a chair, resulting in chafed fingers and worn skin. Michelle and her partner proceeded at a more then reasonable pace. Mongoose, on the other hand, slalomed down the roadway with me protesting all the way. The inevitable happened. My chair and I somersaulted face first into the rocks. Blood went everywhere and I ended up with a cut nose and two black eyes. The bleeding nose was quickly resolved. Two raccoon eyes adorned me for the next ten days. Ah, there are advantages to everything, even facial injury. Mongoose felt so badly that both men refused to accept our previously agreed-upon fees for the day. We returned to the hotel, where they parked Michelle and I in the sunshine to enjoy tea and Indian sweets. Mongoose's next offer was to provide me with an airline ticket to visit India once again, next summer. Under her breath, I heard Michelle mumble, "It must be love."

Dinner on the patio was followed by another cold, dark night. By 8:00 p.m., Michelle and I were once more cocooned in our beds, under the heavy quilts. A loud knock on the door announced the arrival of Mongoose and his friend, still trying to make up for the disaster of the late afternoon. They offered us dinner and beer. To their amazement, we were not willing to get out of bed even if a five-course gourmet dinner at a five-star hotel had been their recompense.

In the morning, our trusty companions arrived at the hotel, ordered puris with curried vegetables following which we embarked upon new explorations through the woods to visit historical buildings and monuments to English heroes. Late in the day, Mongoose and his friend accompanied us to the train station, arguing forcibly with the conductor to ensure that we were comfortably seated near the pot-bellied stove, the only available heat in the increasingly cold evening.

If we thought the train trip was steep going up, the baby train storming down the mountain was exhilarating and frightening. In Canada, particularly on the west coast, people value Super Natural British Columbia. In India, there is little regard for the unblemished beauty of their country. On the train, dinner was served airline style. After the meal, the locals threw empty water bottles, newspapers, tin foil wrapping, disposable eating utensils, and dishes out the windows! How could this be? When I travel, I encounter many circumstances that differ from those in Canada but in India, the blatant disrespect and destruction of their natural surroundings was always, for me, a source of discomfort.

At Kalka, we were required once again to change trains before beginning another eight-hour descent into New Delhi. Some say that English is the universal language but I have had experiences, and this was one of those times, when I might as well have been speaking Greek, in some country other than Greece. All we wanted was a women's washroom but no one on the platform was able to comprehend our request or to offer assistance. At last, we connected with a young man in the concession stand whose minimal comprehension of the English language was perhaps equal to our understanding of Hindi. His directions led us to the ladies' lounge. It was an enclosed

2x3 metre room—really just a tiled shower stall. It also served as a washroom. Western toilets are non-existent in many parts of the world and this was definitely the case here. So, amidst laughter, adaptation, and acceptance, we made it work.

Michelle uses mild sleep medication. As we settled on the wood sleep bench in the rocking sleeping car, I assured her, "Not to worry. I will be awake in the early morning hours and I will wake you when the chai man comes through."

Of course, this was the one overnight train when the chai man decided to have a day off. I was awake and eagerly awaiting his arrival in the morning, but it was not to be. Our first awareness of our arrival in Delhi was the locomotive screeching into the station. People disembarked in hordes, others boarded the train in equally large numbers. The stop was scheduled for three minutes so an open window was our only choice to offload wheelchair foot pedals, cushions, bundles and bags. Our worldly possessions flew willy-nilly onto the platform. Newcomers squeezed onto our laps guaranteeing themselves a seat for the next leg of the trip. We shouted out the window for help from coolies, the red-coated porters who would lift us, and our chairs, off the train. We made it off the train just as it began to chug along to its next destination.

Sitting amidst our cluster of belongings, we could only sigh with relief as we watched the departing train disappear around the corner.

The Holy Ganges

Varanasi, located on the bank of the Ganges River, is one of the holiest places in India. Bathing in the waters of the Ganges washes away all sins, instilling blessings upon you and your family. Hundreds of Hindu pilgrims come each year for this purpose. Our trusty guidebook directed us to a hotel removed from the urban bedlam and promising peaceful quiet in a garden setting with the advantage of easy access to the highlights of the city.

The largest yellow chrysanthemums I could ever have imagined surrounded an enclosed courtyard. There was the usual blistering hot sun. Some patches of shade made for pleasant relaxation as we enjoyed a few moments to read, sip on lime soda, reflect on the places visited in the last several weeks, and anticipate places yet to come.

Festivals abound in India at all times of the year and in every nook and cranny of the country. Varanasi is no exception. We found ourselves in the midst of two religious festivals, one Hindu, one Muslim. We questioned those around us to gain some understanding of the meaning and significance of the celebrations. One festival emphasized robustness and competition, the other beauty and peace.

Negotiating the city streets is always an adrenalin rush as the little tuk tuks skitter along avoiding pedestrian, animal, and vehicle traffic that comes simultaneously from all directions. As we drove down the main city thoroughfare, the rickshaws came to an abrupt standstill. In the midst of the chaotic traffic, we found ourselves squeezed tightly around a boxing ring. A crowd of viewers included the elderly, tiny tots, groups of boisterous men, school children on their way home from the classroom and, of course, animals—sacred cows, dogs, cats, an occasional camel or elephant. The throng of spectators cheered on the participants while bookies gathered money and recorded the wagers on scraps of paper.

Honking and shouting rose from all directions. Some drivers objected to the traffic congestion around the sports event. Others enthusiastically waved and encouraged their favorite participant. No objection from us! The rickshaw slowed, providing us the opportunity to see the afternoon's activity first-hand.

Our city tour continued. The hillside along the western bank of the Ganges River is lined with Ghats—temples that serve multiple purposes for family groups and seniors—bathing, praying, sharing food and drink, healing, education. More than one hundred Ghats can be visited at any time of the day but the magical sunrise is most popular.

We arose at 3:30 a.m. to begin the morning routine of stretching, washing, dressing, and getting comfortably seated in our wheelchairs. The sun begins its ascent over the Holy Ganges at 5:00 a.m. We would be there! On the slope leading down to the river, one hundred and ten tiny, large, deep, shallow, long, short, even, uneven, rocky, smooth, concrete steps stood between the water's edge and us. Innovation was required once more. I scanned my surroundings and spotted a few young men who appeared to be strong enough and willing enough to approach. Four young men, university students, lounging on the stairs and sipping chai from plastic cups, became my prey of the day. I explained our situation and emphasized our desire to be in a boat on the river at sunrise. I then spotted two very little boys who had a strong desire to earn some rupees so we hired them to carry the wheelchair bags and to provide singing and entertainment on the way down.

"Are you crazy?" Michelle exclaimed. "Aren't you afraid?"

"Michelle, I can't be afraid," I told her. "It is the only time in my life that I will have the opportunity to be on the Holy Ganges at sunrise. I need to find a way to get there with a reasonable degree of safety for us and for those who agree to help us. If you are afraid, there is no shame in viewing the river from above."

She laughed and said, "I want to go. I will watch you and if you get there safely, I will come along!"

The descent began. There are bound to be some surprises along the way when communication in English is sketchy, familiarity with wheelchairs is non-existent, and there is a complete unknown of what lies ahead. This morning, adjustments had to be minimal, made rapidly and most definitely without the helpers losing their grasp of the wheelchair.

Success was achieved. We made it.

I vetoed Michelle's idea of leaving our chairs on the dock and sitting on the wet floor of the boat. With brakes applied, our chairs were placed on the small flat, wooden deck. We drifted along watching the soul-stirring sunrise, encountering vendors selling brass vials of holy water from the river, jewellery, Coke, drinking water, religious photographs, and prayer cards. Passing the crematorium, we noticed stairs zigzagging up the hill behind. Each step was decorated with an elegantly dressed and flower-adorned body, awaiting their final journey.

Following the morning cruise on these sacred waters that oozed blessings, we relaxed on the dock in the sunshine, absorbing the specialness of this unique place. A large, black-robed, long-haired, bearded man approached and introduced himself as Buba. He explained that he was the assistant to the region's legendary guru. Buba was adamant that this guru could heal us and do away with our chairs!

Have I heard this before? The wheelchair attracts offers of religion, medication, teas, plants, and animals that will for sure have me rising from the wheelchair and walking on the surface of the water. I think not. However, anything is worth a try so we opened our ears and our hearts to this warm, endearing man. We agreed to meet him the following afternoon at an address that would turn out to be a small sinister room, down a very narrow lane. On Tuesday after lunch, we prepared to meet the guru who promised to shed unquestioningly positive light on our futures. The trusty rickshaw driver, Sanju, arrived at the hotel with one tuk tuk for Michelle and me. We opted to leave the wheelchairs behind with the assurance from the driver that he would lift us into the prayer room. Off we went down the road at breakneck speed, around corners and through the lanes with a narrow margin of space between the side of the rickshaw and the concrete walls. Turning a corner, we came face to face with a large black cow. Of course, cows have the right-of-way so we began a slow backup in the alley, passing young heroin addicts, old men sleeping in doorways, naked toddlers at play, allowing the cow to move freely down the alley. After three attempts, we did arrive at a small murky doorway. Buba awaited us. Sanju, our driver, with help from another young man, lifted us individually through the narrow doorway into a small dark and dingy room which contained two rickety, cracked, plastic chairs. As Michelle moved in her chair, two mice scampered down the back of her seat and along the muddy dirt floor. If I had been sceptical before, doubt now oozed from every one of my pores.

"Have faith!" laughed Michelle, "It will be the best twelve dollars you've ever spent."

Nothing in India costs twelve dollars. You can get a room for the night and food for a day for twelve dollars. I was beginning to think this was a royal rip off.

Bubba, with a clipboard and pen in hand, entered the small shadowy cavern and perched his large robust body on a small spindly barrel. His questions were short and numerous. They aimed at providing a detailed profile of who we are, where we come from, where we're going, where we want to go, who provides support in our lives, the challenges and trials that we encounter, our strengths and weaknesses. He asked about our children, family, jobs, finances, homes, and weather in Vancouver. I was surprised that he did not ask about the colour of my panties!

"If he asks for my SIN, I'm out of here," Michelle hissed in my ear.

After detailed note taking, Buba made his exit and shortly

reappeared with the guru who had scrutinized the questionnaire and was prepared with the answer to our woes. Our responses to the inquiries had been analyzed and now our future would be laid before us.

Michelle first. "You will walk again. When you go home, you will have the continued challenges of your sons who are not yet mature enough to offer the support that you require and deserve, but your independence and determination will carry you through. Attend physiotherapy and spend time each day in exercise and activity. Improvement will not be immediate but it will come."

The guru then approached my chair looking directly into my eyes. His head hung low in an attempt to camouflage his solemn expression.

"There is no hope for you."

Michelle struggled to contain her laughter.

The guru continued. "You will never walk again, but not to worry. You will have enough support in your life. You will manage just fine. You will take part in many different aspects of life and your physical restrictions will not stand in your way. Support, determination, a positive attitude, and the assistance that you need will abound."

I looked at Michelle skeptically. How could I believe that help to shore me up would suddenly come out of the woodwork? My sons are supportive but they are young people who should be leading their own lives. One lives four hundred kilometres away, works full time as a teacher, coaches skiing in the winter on weekends and works on a fishing boat in the summer. The other, a criminal lawyer, is so busy in practice that at times he cannot remember if he had a cup of coffee that morning. I live alone in a high-rise apartment building and after twelve years, I do not know more than ten people there by name. Urban lifestyle is like that. People have busy lives and when they get home at night, they go into their apartment and seek calm and shelter in their own surroundings. I am no different. After working eight to ten hours, I come home, discard my work clothes in favour of a nightshirt, throw together a salad, watch the news on TV, then head for the computer to continue the day's work, draft some letters, write a few memos and begin to formulate thoughts and plans for the next workday. My thoughts brought me back to square one. Where was this hidden support?

We left the guru wanting to believe his words but wondering if our doubts weren't better founded than his predictions.

Stay tuned and as the chapters unfold you can come to your own conclusions. Was the guru to be believed?

That evening on return to our hotel, Michelle and I decided that a massage would provide physical and psychological benefits. We showered, washed our hair, donned clean nightshirts (in the form of long t-shirts) and headed for the massage parlour. It sounds easy. It was not easy but manageable with the help of some bystanders who guided our chairs down the slope, over the eight-inch curb, through the narrow doorway and up two stairs into a small dimly lit room where a large woman enthusiastically welcomed her next two customers. With the help of the two massage therapists, we were each positioned supine on hard wood massage tables. We didn't realize that the massage would be a hot oil massage. The heated liquid ran over our breasts, glided through the foothills and skin mounds of our stomachs and down our legs. With an enthusiastic lift and flip, I found myself face down on the table with hot paddles tapping rhythmically on my back. The beating of my torso and limbs continued non-stop for ninety minutes. Hot oil is an understatement for the temperature of the liquid that was used for this robust attack. I am the heat sensitive MS person, personified! To finish, the massage therapist placed her hands into the bucket of hot oil and then deep into my clean hair, kneading vigorously. So much for the shower and shampoo that preceded our massage appointment. With the assistance of bystanders, we returned, weak and beaten, to our room, trying desperately to subdue the laughter that threatened to burst from our souls. Once again, we shampooed our hair in a vain attempt to remove the grease that permeated our scalps. The remainder of the rationed one bucket of warm water, and all of our shampoo did not make a dint in that task.

Harry had had a cute haircut at the hotel the day before. In the morning Michelle and I wheeled to the hairdresser in hopes of clean hair. Leaning sideways over a small basin, the "hairdresser" was able to give us semi-clean hair after numerous shampoos. Many hairdressers are obsessed by scissors and this one was no exception. The poster on the wall displayed photos of over twenty women, all with the same haircut. Obviously, the stylist only knew one haircut. We met Harriet for lunch—we three now mirrored the women in the poster.

Our last evening in Varanasi led us once again to the Ganges to drift along and experience the sacred atmosphere of the holy waters at sunset. The river was adorned with colour and light, and floating candles and flowers for the Hindu festival (similar to Diwali, the festival of light). Chants of "Om" echoed throughout the dark night. Adventure awaited us. The peace and beauty penetrated our souls as we drifted along the river.

Well, we had made it down the stairs. Now we had to get back up. We needed to find help amongst the people lurking in the shadows. Once again, some willing young men lifted us backwards up the long staircase where our trusty rickshaw driver awaited. Michelle felt that Sanju was her re-incarcerated brother—probably because he treated her as a loving sister.

On return to our hotel, we stuffed our bags in preparation for the late night train departure that would take us to Calcutta.

Kolkata and the Beach

We bid farewell to the Holy Ganges and the peaceful, sanctified men at the celebration of light. Tiny beautiful flowers continued to float in the shadows on the water. Silence was broken by low chanting voices that penetrated the deep night. We were leaving for Kolkata, formerly known as Calcutta. At the station two hours in advance of the scheduled train time, Sanju and the coolies agreed on a price. Sanju then instructed us not to part with any money until we, and all our worldly belongings, were onboard. This time we had to negotiate our chairs over dusty, rocky pathways and numerous tracks to get to the correct platform; dodging shunting trains along the way, avoiding cows grazing between the iron rails with not a care in the world, and children at play on the railway ties. The activity of the day continued non-stop. The coolies deposited us on the platform assuring Michelle and I that they would return to provide loading assistance when the train pulled in. One of our hard-earned lessons in this country was that those frequently heard promises are only kept if you have not yet exchanged any money. Pay in advance and lose. Pay at the conclusion of service and enjoy full benefits.

The multitude of assertive beggars in this station was greater than we had encountered before. Michelle gave two rupees to one old man who was missing several fingers (quite obviously from leprosy). He dropped the coins through the spokes of her wheelchair then persisted in seeking his money under and around the wheels, emerging successfully with a broad smile and two coins in his hand. We boarded the train, paid the coolies, and during a long and tedious trip, the only thing that maintained our sanity was knowing this was the last of our seven overnight trains.

On arrival in Howrah station—the busiest, second oldest, and one of the largest railway complexes in India—we encountered real life examples of the intimidating stories we had heard about the crowds and confusion. Undeterred, we gathered our bundles and bags and ploughed our way through the hordes of humanity.

Our intention was to see Kolkata. Nevertheless, it was now time for a break from the constant stimulation of the streets of India. Everything comes with some degree of haggle and hassle. We exited the train station to immediately locate a cab that ferried us through the early morning traffic congestion to the nondescript bus station where we boarded a bus for the next eight-hour leg of our journey to the beach at Digha, the Brighton of the East. We squeezed onto the crowded bus. After a few more stops, the bus was jam packed with people standing, sitting on laps, perching on bundles. Along the coast, it was refreshing to see palm trees sway in the wind, sandy beaches, white-capped waves, and children digging in the sand. It seemed so quiet and peaceful, contrasted with the intensity of urban India.

When we arrived in the small coastal beach village, we hired a rickshaw cab and, of course, the driver was adamant that he knew the perfect accommodation for our needs. I wonder why! At the first hotel stop, Harriet cheerfully went in to look, taking a wheelchair with her to guarantee that the bathroom door would accommodate its width. She emerged all smiles saying, "It is fine, it is fine." Michelle, with her customary sarcasm, looked at me with doubting eyes. How right she was! Later when the chair would not go through the bathroom door, we found that Harriet had folded the chair to make her assessment. Of course, it is different when the chair is open and someone is sitting in it! Back to the cab! Our eventual success ensured that we would spend the night in a bed, not lying in the sand on the beach. A large billiard room in the hotel, occupied by numerous healthy young men, guaranteed that Michelle and I (and our chairs) would have assistance to negotiate the five stairs at the entrance.

We spent three days exploring the shops and food stands along the beachfront. Basking in the warmth of the sun, I read, while Michelle people watched. We enjoyed the incredibly delicious dosa, the south Indian food. When the tide was out, cows roamed on the beach and surrounded us, leaving us trapped on the beach to do nothing but look intently out to sea. But hey, it IS the Indian Ocean!

The hotel food bill for three days would be sixteen hundred rupees—far too expensive for this part of the world—so we ventured next door where one hundred and twenty rupees (less than $3) would provide a gourmet meal for three. After a couple of days, we decided to explore some of the small villages along the coast. No motorized tuk tuks here! As is customary in this region, our transportation was by bicycle rickshaw. We were challenged by the narrow wooden seats along three sides of the box that balanced on the back of the fender of the bicycle. Michelle clutched the narrow bench near the taillight reflector and hung on for dear life. My non-existent balance made this seating arrangement impossible. Vicious bumps along the beach terrain forced me to sit on the floor of the wooden box. I gripped my wheelchair for steadiness as we bounced and bumped along.

Leaving Digha a day early, we obtained a visa to visit Sunderbans Wildlife Sanctuary, home of the Indian Bengal tigers. I thought back to my previous experiences with tigers—the San Diego zoo, the Toronto zoo, Sigmund and Roy in Vegas, and one wild one leaping into the bushes in the jungle of Chitwan National Park in Nepal. The Bengal tigers were difficult to spot but we did see two yellow-striped bodies slinking through the jungle foliage. A few mumbles of tiger greeting were audible.

After visiting the tigers, we occupied reserved seats on the bus that would return us to Kolkata. The bus dropped us at the side of a busy road. It was dark, minimizing the chances of flagging down a cab. If the traffic in Delhi was horrendous, it was more terrifying in Kolkata. Where to stay in Kolkata? Of course, in order to experience the real Kolkata, we chose the old part of town. Using the guidebook, we found the perfect place in the Chowringhee area, close to the Bull Market and Mother Theresa's Mission. Some people would say that it was dingy but for me it was the most real. I knew I was staying in an authentic Indian hotel when, after exploring for the afternoon, we found that our room had been given away to another traveller despite having been paid for. Why not collect twice for the same room if you can get away with it? The other traveller was sent on his way.

Calcutta's name changed to Kolkata in 2001. In that same year, street names also changed so now pertinent directional information is offered through landmarks. We reached Dominique Lapierre, the City of Joy, on a Sunday morning, just in time for the church service in the chapel which houses Mother Theresa's tomb. Members of her religious order, The Divine Light, were dressed in pale and medium blue habits. They greeted all visitors with love, joy, and peace. One "mini" nun, not any taller than I am (when sitting in my wheelchair), took it upon herself to welcome, protect, and care for me before, during, and after the service. She tucked a blanket around my knees, pressed a Mother Theresa medal into my hand, tucked snacks into the bag on my wheelchair, and placed paper photos of Mother Theresa along with prayers on my lap. I felt truly blessed.

At Mother Theresa's orphanage on Sunday afternoon, the laughter of happy children echoed through the garden. How different from the tiny waifs we had seen on the streets. Throughout her seventy-eight years, Mother Theresa had embraced them all.

Back in our tiny hotel room, somewhat inconsistent with the holiness of the day, Harriet bought snacks and a litre of beer for dinner. We wandered the dark alleys in the evening chatting with the street people, being entertained by the young children, and continually thanking the karma that had promoted our birth in Canada.

The following morning, we arose early. Along the streets of old Calcutta, there are hand water pumps over drains where the men of the city strip down to wash then don the same clothes again. Behind the buildings, women participated in the same activities. A tiny pottery cup of chai tea for three cents and a day-old bun offered free from the racks at the back door of the bakery provide the finishing touch.

A trip to India would be incomplete without a visit to the Bull Market, the largest in India. Construction and renovations are always ongoing. In various areas throughout the market workers dug with pick and shovel in large holes the size of houses. The men stood waist deep in water and mud, with frightening chauas hovering close by. Our last shopping experience included red and yellow chili powder, masala, and silver chains to hold our Mother Teresa medals. Shopping expedition complete, it was time to think about going home.

It was now time for Michelle and I to reflect on our trip. We were appreciative of Harry's presence but there were "moments"! It seemed to be difficult for Harry to remember that she was working for us as a helper. She always hesitated when someone asked if she was our servant. Then she would say, "No, I am taking them through India." Why anyone would think that she was our tour guide was beyond our understanding. Harriet's limited travel experience had included the Punjab and Delhi.

I would never have considered Harriet a servant. I have never heard this term used in Canada to refer to a helper. Harry was a helper and a friend, although at time she tried to direct our activity and sometimes disagreed with our decisions. However, she was eventually ready to comply with our destination choices. Of course, Michelle and I were paying for the trip. When we laughed, she would join in the humour. By the end of our seven weeks in India, she had seen more of India than most Indian people ever do. We paid her at the same rate that we pay for similar assistance in Canada. It placed her in the higher echelons of earned income for 2005 and several years following.

It might have been cold on the trains and in the mountains but as we were now in the month of March and, moving southward, it was quite hot. It was time to bid farewell to India. We were out of our room by noon. What to do for six hours? The heat, along with the balancing of bags and bundles on our laps, made a decision easy. Harriet's train to Punjab was leaving at 3:00 p.m. We needed to be at the airport by 6:00 p.m., so it only made sense to say our goodbyes at the train station and continue on.

We could bask in air-conditioned comfort at the airport, sipping on a diet Coke. No way! Nothing is quite as simple as it appears. The wheelchair accessible washroom was less than wheelchair accessible. Our determination to freshen up and change clothes before heading home, required transfer to a metal chair. We coerced a passerby to pull the chairs over the step and into the washroom where we suppressed gales of laughter as we sponge bathed and changed clothes in the small room where cold water trickled drip by drip from a leaking pipe onto the floor. The lighting flickered from florescent brightness to the dark of night. The toilet seat was not fastened to the toilet bowl, making transfers somewhat precarious. We would be clean and fresh before boarding the plane for our trip home!

Twenty-two hours after takeoff, we arrived in San Francisco. Once again, we visited the washroom to freshen up and reorganize, in preparation for the last leg home.

On Monday morning when Barb arrived to assist me with showering and unpacking, she was dressed in grungy jeans. "I did not shower or change before coming this morning because I knew what I was going to face," she explained. Every article in one bag needed washing. My hair begged for a triple shampoo to remove layers of dust. My feet required a long soak to clean off the accumulation of grime from ten days of hot weather, and bare feet in sandals.

A few days to overcome the jet lag and I will be ready to think about going off again!

Chapter 19

Vietnam

This chapter is dedicated in memory of Debra Lynn Lyons, 1956-2008, our trusty companion who was always full of vim and vigour on this adventure. She passed away at too young an age. I am so thankful that we shared these special days in Vietnam together.

A Start in the North

Anticipation, an important part of travel, intensifies as I read about a destination before leaving home. Patrick, my well-travelled son, always supports my uncontrollable urge to visit similar exciting lands. The *Lonely Planet,* considered by some the bible for seat of the pants adventure, is on Patrick's library shelf just waiting for his mom to borrow. His resources, both notes and memory, describe local culinary specialties and direct me to wonderful restaurants, historical sites, cultural festivals, touristy and not so touristy places to stop over.

Patrick and his wife, Jill, ventured to India, Nepal, and Vietnam over the past few years so I was able to inherit their guidebook—tattered pages with scribbled notations, stars, encouragement, realistic assessments and more personalized detail than is available in the book itself. As I turned the pages of the *Lonely Planet Vietnam,* I found matter-of-fact briefings about geography; descriptions of safe clean hotels; transportation: taxi, train, luxury coach and chicken buses, boats, and rickshaw; where to eat; and museums to visit. The pages review basics such as climate, customs, money, history, markets and much more. When I began to read about Vietnam, I felt a twinge of anticipation. The butterflies and excitement were exhilarating as our airplane left the runway in the fall of 2005. I was joined by Michelle, who travelled India with me, and her massage therapist friend, Debra.

I was able to purchase open-jaw tickets so that we wouldn't have to backtrack to our arrival city. Around every corner, down every road, is something new. Our open-jaw started in Hanoi, the northern tip of the north island of Vietnam. We would leave from Ho Chi Minh City, formerly Saigon, in the south.

The spacious room in our hotel overlooked the streets of Hanoi. It had three single beds, a large and accessible walk-through bathroom with a shower nozzle protruding from the wall over the drain in the middle of the uneven tile of the bathroom floor, creating a perfect wheel-in shower. To the delight of us three, away from home, adventurous women, there was an up-to-date PC with a Windows 2000 operating system and Internet in the room. We stayed in Hanoi for five nights and on return to our hotel room each evening, we drew straws to determine who got to access e-mails first.

Ten years ago, communication from the other side of the world was mostly a one-way affair—postcards and letters home, the occasional very expensive telephone call that was often ill-timed on my part. Although time zones are quite straightforward, daylight saving time, the International Date Line, personal schedules at home and abroad all contribute to the inaccurate timing of telephone calls home. Now e-mails are the norm. They facilitate two-way communication—I send some messages; I get answers back. Internet cafés are available in most countries. However they do present challenges. There is often a queue. Some keyboards are labeled with a foreign alphabet. Directions may not be in English. Sometimes the letters are worn away from heavy use. There may be a time limit for computer use because unlike North America, there is not a computer in every home. Logging onto my Canadian Yahoo account can be immediate or, in far-away places, reception may move at a snail's pace. The login process can consume much of my allotted time. At home, I use a voice recognition program. My typing is slow at best. Having a computer and Internet in our hotel room was a definite bonus. We diplomatically allotted thirty minutes of computer use each before beginning the rotation again so that everyone had the opportunity to read mail and compose messages to send home to family, friends, and the men in our lives!

Our first day in Hanoi started with a rickshaw tour around the city that blended into an investigation of unique and varied tourist and local destinations. Wandering the narrow streets, sharing a table with local residents and following their food choices without knowing what would be served, admiring and appreciating the cultural dress, language, and habits made for a good beginning. Women bearing yokes that supported baskets filled with fruit and vegetables hanging from either end lined the sidewalk. The Asian people, small in stature, moved gracefully under their heavy burdens. Bamboo poles of various lengths and diameters, without any regard for symmetry, formed the scaffolding at construction sites. Despite the asymmetrical ladders and cockeyed platforms, the workers scampered spryly from place to place, completing their tasks with ease. Tiny children were ported in slings on the hip or back of their moms. Toddlers tagged along holding on to Mother's skirt. Children old enough to help were engaged in family and community tasks. They swept sidewalks and streets with branch brooms, loaded and unloaded small trucks, cared for siblings when Mom was busy selling her products or otherwise engaged in business. Young adolescents seamlessly merged into adulthood. Most of the parents of young children would still be considered children themselves in North America.

Surprisingly, this city of almost four million people contains many lakes of varying size scattered through the urban landscape. Hoam Kiem Lake Cohen—surrounded by green parks, botanical gardens, duck ponds, play, and picnic areas—was located in the centre of the city. Not surprisingly, locals were absent from the lake. They were working. Leisure and play in the park was left mostly to visitors.

During one of our walks in the park, we connected with an American couple who were using the same guidebook. Joining Beth and James for the day, we visited a restaurant established to assist disadvantaged, abandoned street children. The kids ran the entire operation with minimal supervision; the older youth helping the younger children; everyone working together as a team. The sale of t-shirts, aprons, and carved serving utensils complimented their entrepreneurial operation. Many adults in the world are quick to criticize the youth of today but this lunchtime experience could not help but warm all of our hearts. These young people were amazing.

Vietnamese lady selling fruit

As we entered the Ba Dinh Square, a long line of people waited patiently. Ho Chi Minh, a highly visible political figure in this country, led the Viet Minh independence movement from 1941 onward, establishing the communist-governed Democratic

Republic of Vietnam. Following his death on September 2, 1969, it has become a ritual to display his embalmed body for nine months of the year at Ho Chi Minh mausoleum in Hanoi. Inside the mausoleum, security guards in snow-white uniforms stand five paces apart along the hallway to ensure safety and respect for this leader. The majority of the Vietnamese population makes an annual pilgrimage to pay respect to Ho Chi Minh. His embalmed body is transported to Russia for three months each year to undergo maintenance.

After a long day of exploration in this fascinating country and city, we picked up some Pho soup at the local restaurant and returned to the hotel to enjoy a quiet girls' evening—or so we thought. The elevator admitted only one chair at a time. It was my turn to go first, with Deb. Michelle, in second place, waited in the lobby for the elevator's return. After entering our hot, oven-like room, Deb and I quickly discarded our t-shirts and hung cool damp towels around our necks. Coffee mugs always suffice for bowls when one is in a hotel room. Wooden stir sticks do for spoons. We poured the soup into the mugs. Deb and I were taking turns checking e-mails on the computer, when we heard cries of, "Help, help!" coming from the elevator.

"I need help, I'm stuck!" Michelle's wail came to us faintly. "The door won't open!"

Deb frantically pulled a t-shirt over her head.

I dashed after Deb. Pushing the call button and the alarm bell failed to produce any assistance. I reassured Michelle that we would get her out, not knowing if this was even possible. Deb called the front desk. I tried to recruit a cleaning lady in the hallway who spoke no English. A businessman staying down the hall came out of his room to investigate the commotion. He was shocked by the appearance of women in varying degrees of undress. Unlike Deb, I hadn't bothered to put my shirt on, but he did listen to our tale of woe and agreed to help. Somehow, with investigative wisdom, he found a maintenance man with a toolbox who finally released the elevator door. A frantic Michelle wheeled out. The Pho soup was now cold but it still satisfied our hunger. Through gales of laughter, Deb exclaimed, "If you are ever in trouble, call Linda because she will come no matter what - dressed or not."

Named by the prisoners of war who were interred there, "The Hanoi Hilton" is an old prison building ironically situated adjacent to the modern Hilton Hotel where the wealthy of the world stay today in luxurious decadence. I found it an inconceivably harsh contrast. The premises, no longer used as a prison, are open to the public. Visiting the dark, dismal spaces inside was not exactly a pleasant activity for a sunny afternoon but I am a traveller who wants to understand the past, present, and future of the lands I visit. All involved in the Vietnam War experienced atrocities that belong in the past, hopefully never to be repeated.

Attending the water puppets performance is a must-do in Hanoi. This form of theatre originated a thousand years ago. The Vietnamese rice farmers spent much of their time in flooded rice paddies. They established the art of entertaining with water puppets. The surface of the water was used as a stage to entertain their children and fellow villagers. The original puppets were made from fig tree wood, which is water resistant. Ponds, lakes, and flooded paddy fields provided the stage. Today, the water puppet theatre in Hanoi attracts visitors from all over the world.

We arrived at the theatre, and as is often the case in Southeast Asia, there was no elevator. The people, however, were very keen to share the unique puppet theatre experience with us. At once, three young men appeared from nowhere to lift us up the steep staircase. Seated on a slightly elevated platform we didn't miss a beat. The puppets danced to music—flutes, bamboo xylophones, single string instruments that produced the exotic sounds of Vietnam—that flowed from behind a screen. The figures replicated animals and villagers performing activities of daily living. The marionettes sometimes displayed mythical creatures such as dragons and unicorns. We were fascinated as we watched farmers tend rice fields, children scamper to school, shepherds watch over flocks of goats, and ducklings splashing on the water's surface. Fire breathing dragons burst through the bubbling surface. Mothers cooked over open fire and grandparents cared for the babies of the family. It seemed so real: a perfect miniature replica of life in a Vietnamese village.

The waist deep tank of cloudy water protects the secrets used to create the unique performance. The brightly coloured puppets are glossy with special paint to make them water resistant and are repainted every three to six months. Puppeteers train for three years. Most of them stand in waist high water behind bamboo screens. To our amazement, at the end of the performance, three men wearing scuba equipment emerged from beneath the water's surface. They had obviously been responsible for the elements of the show that involved creatures emerging from the deep regions of the pond.

Exploring by Boat

Halong Bay, the Bay of the Descending Dragon, lies seventy kilometres east of Hanoi. Declared a World Heritage site in 1994, Halong Bay is home to three thousand limestone islands that rise magnificently from the water. In the tropically wet climate, most are covered with dense jungle vegetation. Several islands conceal huge caves. Many offer residence to monkeys, land and sea iguanas, bantam chickens, antelope and/or brilliantly coloured birds. Most support floating fishing villages where the age-old tradition continues of harvesting food for local consumption and for export. Floating on the water's surface in a junk, a type of sailboat, is another one-of-a-kind experience. A guide picked us up from our hotel in the early morning for a 3½-hour drive to Halong City where we boarded our junk, then cruised close to the islands' shores.

For most folks, climbing the narrow steps from the dock to the sleeping cabin deck is a mildly challenging task. For Michelle and I, going up the ladder was only possible with the willing help of the crew members whose amazing strength was disguised by their small build. Our tiny cabin was furnished with two low, narrow cots for Michelle and me, with an upper bunk for Deb. The wheelchairs stayed in the hallway. Not being able to walk does not have to be a deterrent. When confines are small, it is not unheard of to transfer from the wheelchair in the hall to a bunk close to the open cabin door, roll across it and move from the bed to the bathroom. Sometimes a mighty leap is necessary to span the two-foot space between the bunk and the toilet. Of course, when this has been performed successfully, the return trip also has to be effectively executed. This is probably the time to say that when the space between transfer points is too great to traverse, the old standby that I have used time and time again is to transfer from the wheelchair to a small table or chair, have someone pull it into the bathroom, shift onto the toilet, and do the same in reverse. It requires an inordinate amount of energy.

Ready for breakfast and the day's activities, Michele slowly climbed the stairs. I mounted the stairs one at a time on my bum. On the upper deck, we could move about freely. It was comfortably but sparsely furnished with wide-open passages from the inside to the outer deck. We found ourselves amidst enthusiastic travellers who were eager to experience every possibility and keen to include Michelle and me in their explorations.

We investigated natural caves, submerged ourselves in hot springs, swam in the warm Gulf of Tonkin, and sampled an endless array of fresh seafood. There were many boats in the bay; some junks, some obviously occupied by tourists. Others were vessels where the locals lived and worked. Children dove off the sides in play. Grandma hung laundry over the railings. Grandpa, who was assigned the task of acquiring the evening meal, kept a close eye on his fishing pole.

At the end of the day, we sat on deck sipping Vietnamese tea and exchanging travel stories with other folk. As darkness fell, the evening chill was welcome. The brilliant stars rivaled moonlight. Fireflies danced along the water's surface. The gentle rocking of the boat led us peacefully into slumber.

The following day we continued to enjoy the unique landscapes. On Monkey Island, hundreds of cheeky, furry fellows engaged assertively with visitors. One had to be cautious about nibbling on a granola bar because it would disappear quickly into the hands of one of these primates.

Two young women from France provided evening entertainment. They introduced us to a fun and easy to learn domino-like game with a fancy French name. On my return to Vancouver, I searched far and wide, and finally found this game in a seven-storey entertainment store in Gastown. Deluxe Tri-Ominos has provided many hours of fun and always brings back memories of the evening spent on the deck of the junk in Halong Bay.

When it was time to leave Hanoi there were two options: bus and plane. The bus meant a long, crowded local trip with no air conditioning in sultry 40-degree temperatures. Tickets would be available to the locals first and if space was remaining, only then to visitors. The number of passengers always exceeded the seat availability. The alternative? Encounters with other travellers who willingly shared their bus experiences, gave us our solution. We selected the second transportation option—flying in a small eight-seat prop plane from the Hanoi airport to Hue. Boarding from the tarmac via a steep narrow staircase was impossible for passengers using a wheelchair so the solution was to load us onto the dumb waiter where meals, beverages, and equipment were raised into the plane. Of course riding on the dumbwaiter in a wheelchair was not possible. My bum was propped on a cardboard box. I clung tightly to the railing and was slowly raised into the galley where I was then lifted onto a seat. Michelle's customary, "I'll watch you go first. If you make it safely, I will follow," hadn't changed. I was sipping a cool drink of pineapple juice when her cheery face appeared at the door. Three hours of boarding, flying, and deplaning was far superior to the long hot bus ride from Hanoi to Hue (the original capital of Vietnam before the country divided into North and South). We stayed in Hue for one night before securing transportation by minivan and moving on to Danang. After breakfast, our trip down the coast road and over the Hai Van pass was spectacular. We chose Non Nuoc Beach, internationally known as Danang's China Beach, as our home base because of its beauty and nearness to the sea.

Let's Move South

On the white sands of China Beach, a subtle onshore breeze from the azure sea soothed my soul as I watched delightful dolphins and seabirds frolic on the waves. It was a very welcome respite following a long travel day. As the afternoon wore on, we wandered down the beach pathway to chat with fishermen, examine their catch, and observe locals using metal detectors to search for coins and jewellery in the sand. When evening approached, we searched out a local food stand to buy a dinner of spring rolls, Pho soup, steamed noodles, and dragon fruit.

Deb, a motorcycle enthusiast, was keen to explore the rural areas by bike. She connected with a local rider who, for a fee, took her on an investigative exploration of the local countryside.

Michelle and I absorbed every possible sunbeam, bargained for funky designer sunglasses, took part in a beach volleyball game as scorekeepers—marking an X after each goal—chatted with babies and their moms, and watched young children at play. On her return to the hotel, Deb enthusiastically told us that she had arranged with Juan to pick us up the following morning to take us to the Vinh Moc tunnels.

In the morning, Juan arrived, driving an old Toyota van—with no air conditioning in 34°C weather. We travelled over unpaved roads to the site where hundreds of people had burrowed into the hillside during the war. Over a mile of multilevel tunnels with ingenious exit points inland and along the coast, had formed an extensive underground community.

The tunnels are a firm confirmation of human tenacity. About seventy feet below the surface, there were kitchens with cook fires elaborately vented into a hole in the soil above. A facade of trees and foliage camouflaged the smoke to ensure that the presence of the village was not detected. Dining areas, bedrooms, and entertainment quarters (I use these terms loosely), all roughed out earthen caverns where all activities of daily living took place, were connected by narrow passages. There were schoolrooms where dirt walls served as blackboards. Many people lived in these makeshift villages for up to six years. A field hospital and conference room emphasized the reason for the tunnels. We slowly moved through the dimly lit caverns, Deb advancing further as the passages became smaller. Four hours of exploration in the hot, clammy and claustrophobic atmosphere gave us a minute sample of what it had been like for the residents of these tunnels.

When we exited the tunnels, we encountered Jonathon, a firefighter from the United States who connected with us for a ride back to town. On our return to the hotel, Juan enthusiastically agreed to come back the next morning to again take us exploring.

In the morning, Juan's brother Mi (pronounced "my") arrived bearing a note, "I was called to work so I am unable to take you today. I have sent my brother who is willing to help you with whatever travel you wish to do in our country. Mi has a wife and a son. He often travels with visitors who are visiting in our country and is available for the next two weeks."

What a blessing! We negotiated with Mi. He was willing to accompany us for the next twelve days, from Danang's China Beach in the north to Ho Chi Min City in the south. Mi took us under his wing and was committed to show us every nook and cranny of Vietnam.

The beautiful coastline between Hue and Nah Trang was beyond description. Accompanied by our new-found friend, Jonathan, we explored the mountains around Danang. There were extensive views of agricultural farmlands where vegetables were planted in rows and at random around the rice paddies. Water buffalo pulled plows through the flooded fields where the staple of life grew abundantly. Children herded tiny flocks of goats; young boys led the family cow, with bursting udder, home for milking; Grandma scattered grain for the chickens. The trees were green, the fields greener.

After two days at China Beach, it was time to head south. Our shared living arrangements fell into place with ease. Instinct and the *Lonely Planet* guided us. Mi took us to places that were inaccessible by bus or train but were definitely reachable by van with a keen and willing driver. Initially, Mi removed himself at mealtime but with a little coaxing, he was open to being a natural part of our group. When it was time to seek accommodation for the night, the guidebook and suggestions from fellow travelers led to possible overnight lodging and Deb would go in to check it out. If she determined it would not be manageable for the three of us, two in chairs, Mi cheerfully nodded, and we moved on. He patiently waited while Deb jumped from the van to scrutinize two, sometimes three, sometimes four possible sleep sites. We always found one and after a quick freshening up, we set out for an evening of fun. Dinner at a local eating spot—sometimes in a restaurant, sometimes from a stand on the street—continued our culinary education. Every so often we would seek out an Internet café, the local market, traditional street musicians, or just people watch and wander.

In Hoi An, we were met with one day of monsoon rain that would have had us wheeling through eighteen inches of water. Enthusiastic Debra decided that she would explore the local town anyway. She donned a plastic cape, discarded her footwear and excitedly waved her way out the door. Her excursion lasted about seven seconds. She returned looking as if she had swum a river in her clothes. Water dripped from her chin and earlobes, and puddled at her feet. She did, however, share her brief adventures with those of us less courageous. For me rain is seldom a deterrent to outdoor activity. In this case, it was not rain; it was an absolute deluge. With limited changes of clothing and no place to dry out, it seemed reasonable to spend time with fellow travelers under cover. There was a large covered social room open to the outside. With many others who represented countries around the world, we shared culture, searched in the back corners of our minds for jokes that hadn't emerged for years, played cards, and learned to play Sudoku. Most importantly, we gained information that is always a valuable component of the group experience when a hodgepodge of travellers gather. Bored or confused by the chatting, Mi went off to visit friends for the day.

Overnight, the wind cleared the atmosphere, replacing the rain with sunshine, blue sky, and white fluffy cumulus clouds. A wild day in the market along the river's edge was ahead of us. We hired a "pusher" for one wheelchair, an essential asset. The young man willingly guided us everywhere we wanted to go, as we explored and roamed each alley and lane, discovering the busy local market. This amazing market sold almost everything—sandals, lanterns, children's dolls, sets of spice, tea, pottery, and clothes. Michelle and I were lured to the area where shoes were made on site. The shoes are round-toed flats with one strap over the instep attached with Velcro. Women in wheelchairs avoid slip-on shoes because they slip off as easily as they slip on. The Velcro strap attachment is one way to keep shoes on the feet. From a large array of material samples, we selected colour and pattern for our new shoes. With a pencil in hand, a tiny lady traced our left feet onto a piece of paper and directed us to return in three hours to collect the final product. As we wandered through the market, Michelle repeatedly joked, "I bet that when we go back, we get two left shoes." Despite her doubts, the final product that we collected included a left and a right. One pair was the wrong color. Others didn't have non-slip soles. The shoes came home with us anyway, accompanied by an enduring story to tell.

Before I left for Vietnam, I was advised by others to buy silk clothing. It is amazing to find that made-to-measure clothing—dresses, pants, and shirts—can be produced in a few hours. Competition was fierce as we combed the streets, searching for bargains. Vendors launched from their shops shouting wildly persuasive words to convince shoppers that they had the best variety of design and colour, the best tailors, reliable return policies, rapid production, affordable prices, and convenient pick up or hotel delivery. Not knowing who to believe, we chose a "Silk Garments in Minutes" shop. When in foreign countries, it is easy to get caught up in the convincing, coercing enthusiasm, and we were no exception. Taking accurate measurements when one sits in a wheelchair is a challenging process but, when you think about it, the garment is going to be worn when sitting in a chair so it so hopefully the tape measure and sewing machine will mesh. I have a dress and Capri pants that generate compliments from people every time I wear them. At the same time, I have a matching silk shirt and tank top that have great hanger appeal but are yet to be worn. They will probably end up in the "give away box."

Taking a Little Bit Home

En route to Qui Nhon, a picturesque coastal fishing village, we passed mile after mile of rice paddies. Once again, the advantage of having our own transportation was clear. It was difficult to find transportation because it was unusual for local buses and trains to travel to the My Lai massacre site. This was the location of the disastrous offense on the morning of March 16, 1968. It is said that the four-hour event unalterably devastated the world, damaging the Vietnam people physically, and the American people spiritually.

The My Lai massacre is one of the greatest war tragedies of all time. Hundreds of lives were lost in that small village, and the emotional stability of countless US soldiers was destroyed along with them. While the world struggled to understand why and how this could happen, the American soldiers involved were asking themselves the same questions. It remains a mystery that may never be answered.

In 2005, the village residents were welcoming and eager to show their current achievements: abundant vegetable gardens, enthusiastic and chatty schoolchildren, daycare provided by grandmothers while parents worked in the rice fields.

The Qui Hoa leper colony is a vibrant and active community established by a religious order of Catholic nuns. The model village and botanical garden-like grounds, located at Queen's Beach on the ocean shore, boasted a stimulating quality of life, and a healthy physical and sociological environment for residents and visitors. Everyone participates to their level of ability in all aspects of town life. Young children played freely in the park as adults watched close by. The schoolteacher invited us into the classroom where, just like other schoolrooms around the world, children sang, wrote in their scribblers, drew pictures, and were fascinated with two Caucasian women who, rather than walking, wheeled into the room. At recess, a pick-up soccer game on the school grounds included every child from age from five to fifteen. After school we walked along the waterfront with mothers and their children while older kids rambled through the field singing, laughing, and playing with their dogs.

Leprosy attacks and invades the cooler areas of the body—hands, feet, eyes, and skin. It is only mildly contagious and 95% of the world's population has a natural immunity to this disease. Despite what seems like infrequent occurrence, the Leprosy Mission International reports an excess of a thousand new cases daily. In the 20th century, multi-drug therapy can cure it. In the village, there was evidence that grandmas and grandpas had not experienced the advantage of modern medicine that the young adults and children have today. People sometimes have a preconceived idea that a leper colony is a terrible place to be. Here, we were welcomed by the residents of a beautiful little village situated under palm trees on the eastern coastline. We were delighted to be included in the noon hour meal and attend an afternoon church service. In the early evening, we returned to the van and headed off to new adventures.

In the beach town of Nah Trang, Michelle and I toured the market, the Buddhist monastery, and the Catholic community church while Deb explored via pedicab. A planned adventure by boat along the waterfront was cancelled by six-foot swells. One young man was delighted to find other people using wheelchairs. He was a paraplegic whose skill at hand painting t-shirts generated a substantial income. Deciding which shirt to buy was a challenge as we examined the uniquely beautiful patterns. There we were, three women trying to decide what colour, size, and design to take to the guys at home. The Asian population tends to be smaller than North Americans. To improve the accuracy of our size guesstimates we tried on shirts ourselves. Then I asked a man who was walking nearby, obviously another traveller, to give us his expert opinion about size, colour, and design. Our willingness to purchase a beer for our model definitely convinced him that this was the job for him tonight.

Some people with disabilities in North America complain about transportation, services, mobility devices, housing, and community access. But then, some people will complain about anything. A trip to other countries where inclusion is less of a priority quickly highlights how lucky we are in Canada to have fellow compatriots who welcome people with disabilities into the mainstream community and into a workplace, without question.

As we neared the end of our trip, we veered off the main track into the mountains where cooler air was a welcome relief from the intense heat in the lowlands. Along the highway, shepherds led tiny kids that leapt and scampered along the pathways. Meanwhile, the parent goats and the shepherd tried to settle the young ones. A grey-haired woman herded hundreds of sheep along the shoulder of the road. There were endless lush green hillsides, rice paddies tended by water buffalo and workers up to their knees in water.

On the edge of the roadside, vendors offered an endless variety of local culinary delights. We tried to follow the international eating guidelines that say, "If you can't peel it or boil it, don't eat or drink it." It is difficult to follow this advice when the stands offered copious varieties of fruit and vegetables, grouped in endless combinations, deep-fried and stewed. Every size, shape and colour of the rainbow, juicy legumes just waited for someone to buy and sample. We succumbed to temptation. However, some of the very best would have to wait until our return to Canada where our digestive systems are more receptive to the water and domestic bacteria.

Upon arrival at the southernmost tip of Vietnam, Deb checked out hotel after hotel. Mi, consistent with his gentle, accepting style, was still smiling, and willingly moved on when the first, second and third hotel was not suitable. We spent a few nights in Ho Chi Minh City exploring back alleys, street markets, temples, and parks during the day. People who don't enjoy crowds will benefit from letting that aversion go and wading knee-deep into the hustle and bustle of this exciting cosmopolitan city. A *laissez-faire* attitude is necessary for a full experience of the exhilaration, the feel, the stimulation, and the character of the metropolitan area, which in fact is reflective of the character of Vietnam itself. After twelve hours on the road, most people would want to pack it in for the night but this vibrant metropolis motivated us to go out into the streets crowded with people, where the sidewalk vendors offered samplings of the spicy, unique local fare. Dragon fruit, similar in taste to kiwi, looks scary on the outside, but its white flesh dotted with tiny black seeds is a thirst quenching delight. Vendors sold crafts, contemporary books (at a fraction of the cost in bookstores at home), and silk clothing for tiny children. It is here that I found silk sleep sheets for hiking. Most of us carry a single bed sheet sewn across the bottom and one third of the way up the side to avoid the cost of sheet rental at hostels. No longer! I now have a bright purple silk sleep sack to slide into my sleeping bag or to use on a cot at a backpackers lodge where community blankets are the norm. I found a double to bring home to Patrick and Jill. Stylishly groomed women with tiny enviable figures, men in business suits walking intently to their office, shared the sidewalk with traditionally-dressed women bearing yokes laden with wares for sale, babies on their hip, toddlers tugging their skirts. The war museum held photographs, airplanes and tanks, heart-wrenching descriptions of the early 60s. One wall displayed pictures drawn by children in school—their interpretation of the war years. From the mouths of babes. Most depicted a love of the environment and a desire for world peace. Wandering back to our guesthouse in the early morning hours, we caught a few winks before another day of exploration.

It is always near the end of a journey that I am filled with a fierce determination to see it all!

On our last night, we found an Internet café that was only usable after climbing seven stairs and negotiating our wheelchairs between the narrow desks and machines. My last message home was, "Great trip! See you in two days."

The night market was a frenzy of activity. Despite the fact that I give away my old, worn t-shirts and throw away my old panties at the end of a trip, there is always too much stuff. Packing for going home is never as easy or organized as it was when we started out. Before heading home, you just have to squish it in. Purchases made along the way, gifts from local folks, some dirty laundry, and brochures made it necessary to buy another bag for the return, and we did just that at the night market. Mi wanted to take gifts home to his family. He solicited the advice of his three Canadian charges as to what he should bring home to his wife and child. We found a silk tea cozy and a selection of unique Vietnamese tea that was proudly wrapped in pink tissue. Next was a wooden tube filled with beans that would give visual and auditory stimulation to his young baby son. The items were tucked away in the van. Late in the evening, Mi started the three-day trip of twenty-two driving hours per day back to North Vietnam.

Early the next morning, we secured a taxi to the airport where we began our 22-hour flight and airport trip back to Canada.

Chapter 20

Grandma Lives at the Airport

Katy's kindergarten class was discussing their grandparents. When Katy was asked where her grandma lives, she replied, "My grandma lives at the airport." The teacher questioned the accuracy of Katy's statement and the children were sent home with the assignment to discuss with their parents, the residence location of the grandparents. On return to school the following morning, Katy boldly announced that, "My grandma does live at the airport. When we want to see her, we just go get her. Then, when we're done having her visit, we take her back to the airport."

No, I don't live at the airport but it would not surprise me if my grandchildren have that impression. I have had some noteworthy airport experiences. I have eaten, slept, showered, gambled, dreamed, made new friends, argued, tried to balance a cheque book that wouldn't balance, e-mailed, telephoned, waited patiently—and sometimes impatiently.

Three Hours in Advance?

I can never figure out why I should be at the airport three hours in advance for an international flight. It only provides me with time to read, spend money, drink Starbucks coffee, and think about the bed that I could have stayed in for an extra hour because I won't see another one for three days! Arriving too early is a definite drawback. The continual recording that seeps through the ceiling speakers—"Do not leave luggage unattended. Any baggage found unattended will be removed by airport security" — is annoyingly repetitive. Investigating duty-free giveaways, using the washroom, walking up and down for exercise, grabbing a coffee; all is done with luggage in-tow until the airline check-in counter is open. Staff should arrive three hours in advance of the flight but seldom do. The only other option is to sit and guard the stuff until it can be checked-in. A jaunt through duty-free is essential if I want a squirt of perfume as liquids cannot be placed in carry-on luggage. Reviewing liquor prices allows me to decide on the most economical spot to buy duty-free on the way home.

Internet

In 2005, the world became inundated with technology communication that changed faster than I can blink an eye. Memorable postcards with details of every day scrunched into a small space, so that the recipient can absorb my feelings of wonder, are passé. Letters and telephone calls now take a back seat to e-mails. When one small bag has to store everything needed for a trip, a laptop is one of those items that doesn't make the cut.

In January 2005, as I wheeled through the Singapore airport, my eyes lit upon a small blue sign: "Free Internet." There they were, six computers available to anyone who had the patience to reach the front of the line and access your international e-mail account. The chairs were like barstools, the seat far above my head and the desktop definitely on stilts. A fellow passenger pointed out that one computer had a very long cord with also a very long waiting line. As it was the only option for us, Michelle went to search for snacks while I waited in the line, finally reaching the communication oasis. Sliding the keyboard onto my lap was barely possible. It actually hung suspended by the cord while determination conquered inconvenience. I was only just able to hunt and peck a brief message to my

"India list." It generated some attention because a week later I received a response from Cathy, a friend from work, who sent a note saying, "I know you are in Singapore airport but where are you going?" Where else but on to more airports!

Customs

Customs always welcomes me home. Carrying a pen in my passport case allows me to complete custom forms on the aircraft. Travelling with a wheelchair means multiple transfers on and off the plane—wheelchair to aisle chair to seat at the beginning; at the end of a flight—seat to aisle chair to wheelchair. Preboarding and waiting for the aisle chair at the end of the flight means I am always first on and last off. A twelve-hour flight becomes fourteen hours. With these disadvantages, there is an advantage. On exit, I am usually directed into the VIP/crew line to negotiate through customs where I wheel by my weary travel companions who are waiting in the long line-ups. They still get out of the airport faster than I do. The accessible route is always the longest; many elevators up and down, crowds around the baggage carousel where front-row admission is for the larger and more pushy individuals. Baggage carts are at a premium, my bag is often the last to come down the chute and at the end of the long flight, my wheeling speed is dead slow. Because I travel with one small bag on my lap (which is never as organized coming home as it was going), there is little space for purchases. I seldom come close to my purchase allowance so customs officials usually take a look at my declaration and wave me through.

Currency

In March 1999 Bill and I embarked on four weeks of sunny decadence in Provence, France. When travelling to foreign lands, the most economical way to access foreign currency is to slip your Canadian bankcard into an ATM and withdraw funds directly from your Canadian account. Bill and I both have accounts at a British Columbia credit union where a Member Services card is common. Bill stepped up to the plate at the airport and withdrew 2,000 French francs ($500 CDN) from the bank machine. I followed suit but to my horror, the bank machine swallowed my card.

A push of the emergency buzzer brought a bank clerk to the front counter. He was noticeably annoyed by the interruption of his coffee break. With my limited French, I tried to explain the crisis in a calm manner that differed radically from the panic in my gut.

The young man disappeared behind the façade of the ATM and quickly returned with my bankcard in hand, but with no intention of returning it to me. "Vous devrez le recuperer de votre propre banque," which of course is in Vancouver, Canada. This is the first day of a 30-day trip and my ability to access cash was essential. "Cette carte ne fonctionne pas en France." However, Bill's identical card had just generated hard cash. Frustration and raised voices were clearly not going to solve the problem. "Un directeur s'il vous plait," I requested as politely as I could.

A more pleasant senior staff member appeared. After an hour of explanations, signing waivers, committing myself to honesty, and denying highway robbery, my card was once again in my possession. I wheeled to the ATM and withdrew 2,000 Francs. The front counter clerk shouted, "Cette carte ne fonctionne pas en France." I triumphantly wheeled by him clutching my French francs. The need to arise at 5:00 a.m. made our decision in Portugal. The overnight accommodation in the Lisbon airport was less appealing than many others—moulded, hard plastic chairs, closely grouped together in a heavily trafficked area—but the convenience and price were attractive. With the right attitude, this becomes an opportunity. We found ourselves sitting in the midst of hundreds of parents and their offspring awaiting the return of their 10-year-old children, now blessed by the Pope, from Rome. I'm sure many hours of parent participation and fundraising had taken place over the previous year to ensure that these children would meet and be touched by the Pope. The culmination of their six day trip was in front of us—a band, balloons, posters, singing, tired, crying siblings, grandmothers weeping tears of happy relief—combined to create a joyous welcome home for the kids. It was however, less compatible with sleep-seeking, fatigued travellers.

Fatigue is always accompanied by hunger and feeling cold. To escape the frenzy, Doug, my travel companion on this trip, left on an intense search for interesting food. Is airport food ever interesting? Portuguese noodles in a plastic bowl and a slurpee satisfied hunger but did nothing to ward off the chill. I can never sleep in these situations, but the long-haired blue jean clad traveller on the chair next to me had no trouble snoring through the festivities and eventually leaned on my shoulder, ultimately dropping his head onto my lap. If I had been in need of male companionship, this might have been a potential opportunity.

Stopovers

Frankfurt is not my favourite stopover. Ten years ago this airport had long, low tables with three inches of upholstered foam on top. I'm sure they had not been designed as such, but Bill and I wasted no time in taking advantage of these makeshift beds in a dark, quiet corner. More recently, Frankfurt, like many other airports, has adopted "moulded" hard plastic chairs. Arriving passengers deplane in the middle of the tarmac. For those of us who walk on wheels, a forklift is wheeled up to the door of the plane. Travellers with disabilities were herded into a "refuge area" where unyielding frauleins directed the show and refused to allow our exit. They, like many others in the world, equate a wheelchair with lack of mental ability. Was I going to be relegated to this small lounge for three hours between planes? Some grammas dozed in their chairs, a young American who walked on crutches cursed and shouted, trying to gain release, children argued over the small cans of coke and packages of crackers that were offered. My persuasive skills finally allowed me to escape. I needed to find a bank machine and wanted to search out duty free bargains. There was no way those stern ladies were going to keep me boxed up for three hours. I was permitted forty-five minutes of freedom. When it was time to re-board, a friendly, uniformed official appeared at the door, clicked his heels together, and directed us to the departure gate.

Overbooking

It is well known to frequent travellers that airlines overbook flights. If your schedule is flexible, you can take advantage of the announcement at boarding time that a seat is needed. The benefit of delaying your departure by an hour or two is a credit in hand that can be applied to another trip. My return from my Tahiti trip with Carl, in February 2002, was at the end of the North American schools' spring break so the Los Angeles airport was overflowing with children and families returning home from trips to Disneyland. The announcement came. Anyone willing to give up their seat on this flight will be given a $300 credit from American Airlines. I looked at my friend Carl and there was no hesitation on either of our parts. It was only a two-hour wait. We got passes to the VIP executive lounge (where food and wine flow freely) along with the $300 credit to be used within one year. Patrick was impatiently waiting in

Vancouver for his mom's arrival home so he could bid farewell before embarking on his five-month Pacific Crest hike. It is important for moms to connect with their grown babies between adventurous wanderings. Two hours later we returned to the assigned departure gate only to hear again the announcement, "Five seats are needed on this plane. Is there anyone willing to give up your space? You will be rewarded with a $300 voucher on American Airlines." Carl and I looked at each other and our hands rose quickly into the air. This time there was no flight to Vancouver in two hours. With the $300 credit came vouchers for a taxi to a hotel, dinner, the overnight stay, and return to the airport in the morning to catch the first flight to Vancouver. A call to Patrick reassured me that he would wait for his missing mom, so he could see me before leaving on his own wanderings.

Wheelchairs

It always amazes me that my wheelchair arrives in one piece. In 1996, I travelled from Papetti, Tahiti to Los Angeles, to Seattle. We touched down in Seattle where a friend of Carl's was waiting for us. To my surprise (I guess it shouldn't be astonishing), there was no wheelchair. I was travelling with the only chair that I owned but, in fact, I had a new one on order because after eight years, replacement parts were hard to get and adjustments were becoming next to impossible. I was loaded into a golf cart and toured around the Seattle airport examining every wheelchair that we encountered to see whether or not it was in fact my personal property. No such luck. I was beginning to think that I was going to achieve another reward. If they could not locate my old chair, the airlines would be responsible for funding a replacement—hence my new $5,000 chair. The airline staff person asked, "How much is your chair worth—$400-$500?"

Get real! A new chair costs a minimum of $5,000. When they

heard this, the airline staff were reluctant to let me to leave Seattle without permitting them a thorough search for my missing chair. I was leant an airport wheelchair (a dinosaur of a chair I may add) to allow me to move semi-independently. The airline put us all up in a hotel—three different rooms, paid for our taxi and dinner, and breakfast the following morning as well—while they investigated my missing blue friend. It was found in Spokane, Washington. Apparently, a passenger who disembarked in Seattle and was en route to Spokane, saw my chair at the gate of the plane, thought it was an airport chair and, being short of time, decided to use it to make fast tracks to her Seattle to Spokane flight. The gate tag on the chair always identifies that it should be the last item loaded and the first unloaded so that it awaits my arrival at my destination. It was loaded into the baggage compartment in Seattle, unloaded in Spokane, and remained unclaimed in the Spokane airport. During the night, the airline staff determined that the abandoned chair in Spokane matched the description of my missing wheels.

I was new to the travel game in 1989, so arrival at the Vancouver airport to board a flight to Beijing increased my heart rate. At the counter, the adrenaline supply was further boosted when the airline clerk informed me that, "There is only one piece of luggage allowed on this flight."

"I only have one bag," I told her.

"Your wheelchair is considered extra luggage. The cost will be fifty-two dollars."

I glanced over my shoulder. "Are you going to charge the man behind me for his legs?" Now, my responses are not always rapidly fired but I was thankful for my quick retort. Needless to say, my fifty-two dollars remained in my pocket.

Wheelchairs made of aircraft aluminum have hollow frames so concealment of powdered products (i.e. illicit drugs) is not unheard of—particularly with a number of Vietnam War veterans and drug using tourists, returning to their home country from leisure in Mexico, the Caribbean and Central America. On two occasions, my chair was intently scrutinized with varied results. The Cuban airport officials requested that I transfer to a waiting room seat so that they could take my chair away and check it thoroughly. Obviously, they did a thorough investigation, because when it was returned, bless their hearts, they had tried to put it back together but with less than acceptable results. The khaki uniformed gentleman was very apologetic and was more than willing to accept my guidance regarding the proper assembly. I was less successful in Mexico City where the disassembly of my chair did not generate apologies nor was the airport staff concerned about returning it to me in a functional state. The disassembled pieces were placed in front of me, and I was left to coerce a fellow travellers to assist me with the reconstruction. Obviously, they could not find any contraband.

Airport Security

Airport security escalated following 9/11. I cannot wheel through the metal detector as my passage will certainly set off every alarm. I am always directed to go around the outside where I will be subjected to a "pat down" by a female security officer. They are always considerate—"Do you have any pain? Is there anywhere that I should not touch you?" they ask. Not that it would matter, they are going to touch everywhere anyway. "Can you take your shoes off?"

My response is always the same, "If you want them off you will have to take them off and put them back on again."

Most of the time, they let it go, but I have been asked, "How did you get them on this morning, how will you get them off tonight? Do you have anything in your shoes that shouldn't be there?"

Do you think if I was carrying a bomb I would tell you so? The bag on the back of my chair, my passport case, and my sweatshirt are placed on the conveyor belt and move through the x-ray machine. On my return from Calcutta, I was delayed by the security officials. The plane was held up for forty-five minutes while I repeatedly told them, "I am not carrying a knife. It is a brake extension for my wheelchair."

They were too afraid to look. They were sure that I had some explosive device attached to the "lethal knife" that I was carrying in the bag at the back of my wheelchair. Finally, pressure from Singapore airlines to the get plane off the ground motivated them to search the bag. What did they find? Of course, a non-threatening six-inch long piece of plastic that serves as a brake extension for my wheelchair. I don't think they know the expression "egg on my face," but this is a classic example.

The Vancouver airport is always a welcome destination for me, as my trips here in the last twenty years are always when I am getting on a plane or getting off. In 1997, I had to go to the airport to meet Patrick on his return from South America. What a rip-off. My only reason to go to the airport was to meet my son. I hope I don't have to make that trip for such a lame purpose again.

I always want to be coming or going.

Chapter 21

Follow Your Dreams

"Love the life you live. Live the life you love."
Bob Marley

In 1991 my dream to live in New Westminster at the Quay came to fruition. The New Westminster Quay is a coveted residential area located twenty-three kilometers east of downtown Vancouver, between the sea and the railway tracks. On the Vancouver side of the Fraser River, there are many low rise and high rise condominiums that accommodate seniors, families, yuppies, ordinary folk, and me. For those of you who are familiar with the geography of Vancouver, you will know that living and working on different sides of a bridge can create huge expenditures of commuting time when weather, accidents, stalled cars, and traffic, become part of your trip to and from work.

I camped out in a luxurious basement suite biding my time until just the right condo became available. I was only willing to settle for a view of the Fraser River—peek-a-boo or more; a mortgage, although barely manageable; and adequate space for myself and the boys should they choose to come for a day, a weekend, a week, a month, a year, or forever. My first two attempts at purchasing a home—offers on two different low-rise condos—were regrettably unsuccessful. In retrospect, however, someone must have been keeping a close eye on me. The third suite that I found and purchased (after successfully negotiating with the seller) was a larger, concrete construction and it has a swimming pool in the building which I use on a regular basis.

A walkway along the river's edge features buskers, local residents fishing, children riding bikes, an assortment of dogs, large and small, grandmas and grandpas sitting on benches sipping their coffee, people reading a favorite book in the sunshine. Life in the Quay is never lonely. Active entertainment from the water is guaranteed. Tugboats pulling barges and log booms, seals, jet skiers, pleasure and working boats guarantee entertainment from the water. The amazing horticultural department of the City of New Westminster pays serious attention to the flowers, trees, and hanging baskets along the boardwalk that forms a seawall between the seals, fish, the river and the human occupied condos. At the end of the boardwalk there is a community market. The market has many benefits. It is a vibrant place to hang out; meet friends, old and new; listen to live music, from jazz to folk; buy food, from bran muffins to eggplant stuffed with provolone cheese, or Jalapeño peppers stuffed with feta. The market features flowers, fresh baked goods, produce, organic tea, and little stalls selling a variety of hot food, sandwiches, bagels, coffee and ice cream. As well, there is a neighbourhood pub and a beer and wine shop.

I had been travelling for many years and each time I returned from one of these once-in-a-lifetime experiences, I remember saying to my sons, "This will be my last. I don't know how many more adventure trips I can orchestrate." Each journey requires physical, emotional, and financial resources.

Patrick's response is consistently, "Of course you can. Of course you will."

Tim's unfailing comeback is always, "Mum, you won't buy broccoli unless it is on sale, but if a good trip comes along, your Visa card comes flipping out rather quickly."

It was a classic spring day in Vancouver. The sun was shining in the early May sky. Temperatures suggested t-shirt attire in sunny patches, a long sleeved cotton over-shirt when shade, light breezes, or a stroll by the water's edge were part of the walk home. When I stopped at the market to pick up some fresh salad ingredients, I was drawn to a young man with gold loop earrings hanging from his ears. He wore a red plaid shirt, a bandana that covered his shoulder-length hair and a pair of jean overalls. He chanted quietly, gazing distantly into the universe. The sign to his left, printed in jagged, coloured letters, proclaimed that a tarot card reading was essential to "get an accurate picture of the future." Positive predictions were not guaranteed but a realistic overview of the future was assured. Charlie, the tarot card reader, shuffled and dealt, reshuffled and re-dealt, shuffled and dealt again until finally he laid out ten cards, face down. He turned the cards over one at a time before he began to speak in a quiet, serious and sensuous voice. He had asked no questions and I had provided no information.

"You have two sons. You have a compassionate occupation and career. Your job provides you with happiness and sadness. Although your aggressive athletic times have drifted away, (obviously! I was sitting in a wheelchair!), you continue to pursue exercise and health whenever the opportunity presents itself. You have taken many wonderful trips to many places in the world, meeting new friends and sharing new cultures. The cards tell me that you have five or more astounding trips ahead."

This guesstimate has been surpassed. Ten years later I am still making once-in-a-lifetime excursions throughout the world. After the next five major trips, I realized that fortunately the tarot card prediction was an underestimate. Since that prophecy by the cards, I have travelled to Guatemala, Bhutan, Mexico, Portugal, the Dominican Republic, the Middle East, Brazil, Russia, Finland, Estonia, Denmark—to name only a few. I have more to come. Although I love to travel, I also love to come home, where I relish the beauty of my native land.

The pages of this manuscript contain descriptions of significant personal experiences in my journeying life, up to and including the middle of 2008. In the fall of 2008, I climbed to Kala Pattar, 18,500 feet up on Mount Everest with the dedicated assistance of my friends Lou da Silva, Eoin White (a retired Burnaby firefighter who has guided many Canadians to Mount Everest Base Camp), Kala Pattar, and Natalie Chan, an occupational therapist. The groups guided by Eoin have not before included anyone with a disability.

I am continuing to write and look forward to sharing my travels with you in the future.

Since meeting with Multiple Sclerosis in 1983, I have learned much about myself, about humanity, about the world, about my abilities, and most significantly, about disability and what it feels like to face it every morning upon awakening. I go nowhere without a wheelchair. It sits at the side of the bed and accompanies me every moment of every day.

Disability, I hope, is foreign to you but with or without a disability I invite you, the reader, those around me, everyone around the world, to come and walk a mile in my moccasins. Please join me on future adventures. You may have found snippets of pain and sadness; loss and frustration; loneliness and aloneness; fear and apprehension; insecurity and lack of self-esteem in the pages of this manuscript. More importantly you will have found an over abundance of joy and laughter, love and life, courage and strength, support and friendship, craziness and gutsiness.

I invite you to join me.

Till we meet again, my friends.

Author Biography

Born in Montreal in 1948, Linda McGowan (nee Carter) grew up in several Canadian provinces before graduating from the Montreal General Hospital School of Nursing. Holding a Bachelor of Science in Nursing (BScN) from the University of British Columbia and a Masters of Business Administration (MBA) from City University, Linda has worked in community health for over 40 years. For many years, she was a runner, completing her last marathon several months before being diagnosed with Multiple Sclerosis (MS).

Since 1989, Linda has travelled in a wheelchair to more than 110 countries, touching every continent. Her travels were brought to light in the 2008 fall issue of *Canadian Living*. She was also featured in the award-winning TV documentary, *Access Challenge* (2001), a film that introduced wilderness hiking to people with disabilities and was awarded the American Humanitarian Award. Prior to her trek to 18,500 feet on Mount Everest in 2008, Linda participated in numerous media appearances on local television and radio stations.

An active writer, Linda has been published in *Abilities* magazine and contributes to newsletters such as the MS Society's *Shared Voices*, the Burnaby Health Department's *Healthvine*, and MVT Canadian Bus Inc.'s *In the Loop*. In 2008, she was awarded a grant from the Canadian Council of the Arts for her writing and a chapter of her book was short-listed in the Non-Fiction

Writing Contest at the Surrey International Writers Conference (2012).

Today, Linda is an Ambassador with the MS Society, an Accessibility Advocate and the Consumer Advocacy Manager for MVT Canadian Bus Inc., the custom transit operator in Metro Vancouver. She is a sought after speaker; passionate about motivating others to embrace their dreams. She has two sons, four grandchildren, and three step-grandsons.

More About Linda McGowan

Linda McGowan, an accessibility advocate who mobilizes in a wheelchair, facilitates detailed, heart-warming, and fun presentations and workshops to seniors, people with disabilities, and students. As a speaker, she includes inspiring stories and insights from her travels and encounters with people throughout the world. Drawing upon her wide range of experience in community health, and her travels around the globe, she emphasizes practical and resourceful problem-solving to create personalized accessibility solutions.

Linda's writing:

MS Canada, Spring-Summer 2014
Shared Voices, Lower Mainland, BC Yukon Division, MS Society, 1995-present
In the Loop, MVT Canadian Bus Inc, Newsletter, 2009-present
Surrey International Writers Conference, shortlisted non-fiction writing contest, Oct 2012
Canadian Council for the Arts, Grant, 2008
Canadian Living, Fall 2008
Abilities Magazine, Spring 2007

To learn more about Linda McGowan visit:
www.LindaMcGowan.ca

Contact Linda:
www.facebook.com/LindaMcGowan604
www.twitter.com/LindaGMcGowan

If you want to get on the path to be a published author by Influence Publishing please go to www.InfluencePublishing.com

More information on our other titles and how to submit your own proposal can be found at www.InfluencePublishing.com